MAKE THE MOST OF
YOUR STUDY TIME

BY ACCESSING EVERYTHING
YOU NEED TO SUCCEED

Make the grade by accessing the following study tools on the CourseMate site:

- INTERACTIVE EBOOK—Read, search, highlight, and take notes
- INTERACTIVE QUIZZING—Prepare for tests with reviews, interactive quizzes, and a test exam
- BONUS CONTENT—2011 Census data, framed by a discussion of the politics of the Census, adds currency and relevance that can spark lively discussion
- MULTIMEDIA—Watch short video clips that bring sociological concepts to life and challenge you to think critically about topical issues
- FLASHCARDS—Test your understanding of key terms with interactive and printable flashcards
- GAMES—Test your knowledge of key concepts using crossword puzzles and concentration games

To access **COURSEMATE** for **New Society, Seventh Edition,** always return to **www.nelsonbrain.com** and enter your email address and password to log in.

STUDY THE WAY THAT FITS YOU BEST

NEWSOCIETY

NEW SOCIETY

Robert J. Brym
University of Toronto

SEVENTH EDITION

NELSON EDUCATION

NELSON EDUCATION

New Society, Seventh Edition
by Robert J. Brym

Vice President, Editorial Higher Education:
Anne Williams

Acquisitions Editor:
Maya Castle

Marketing Manager:
Terry Fedorkiw

Developmental Editor:
Toni Chahley

Photo Researcher and Permissions Coordinator:
Carrie McGregor

Content Production Manager:
Jennifer Hare

Copy Editor:
Dawn Hunter

Proofreader:
Linda Szostak

Indexer:
Jin Tan

Production Coordinator:
Ferial Suleman

Design Director:
Ken Phipps

Managing Designer:
Franca Amore

Interior Design:
Sharon Lucas

Cover Design:
Sharon Lucas

Cover Image:
©Ted Soqui/Corbis

Compositor:
MPS Limited

Printer:
RR Donnelley

Printed and bound in the United States
1 2 3 4 16 15 14 13

For more information contact Nelson Education Ltd., 1120 Birchmount Road, Toronto, Ontario, M1K 5G4. Or you can visit our Internet site at http://www.nelson.com

Library and Archives Canada Cataloguing in Publication Data

Brym, Robert J., 1951-
New society / Robert J. Brym.—7th ed.

Includes bibliographical references and index.
ISBN 978-0-17-666220-2

1. Sociology—Textbooks.
I. Title.

HM586.B79 2013 301
C2012-905999-4

PKG ISBN-13: 978-0-17-666220-2
PKG ISBN-10: 0-17-666220-0

For my students. — RB

BRIEF CONTENTS

*Available online only at www.newsociety7e.nelson.com.

CONTENTS

PART 3 INEQUALITY

*Available online only at www.newsociety7e.nelson.com.

ABOUT THE AUTHORS

ABOUT THE GENERAL EDITOR AND CONTRIBUTOR

ROBERT J. BRYM

Robert Brym was born in Saint John, New Brunswick, and is Professor and Associate Chair (Undergraduate) of the Department of Sociology at the University of Toronto and a Fellow of the Royal Society of Canada. He has published widely on politics and social movements in Canada, Russia, and the Middle East. His most recent books are *Sociology: Your Compass for a New World*, 4th Can. Ed. (2012) and *SOC+* (2011), both published by Nelson. He has served as editor of several scholarly journals and won numerous awards for his teaching and scholarly work, including the Northrop Frye Award, the President's Teaching Award of the University of Toronto, and the Outstanding Contribution Award of the Canadian Sociology Association. He recently completed a funded project on state and collective violence in the Israeli-Palestinian conflict, the results of which were published in *Social Forces*, the *British Journal of Sociology*, and elsewhere. He is currently conducting funded research on the democracy movement in the Middle East and North Africa. You can visit his website at http://projects.chass.utoronto.ca/brym/.

ABOUT THE CONTRIBUTORS

S. HARRIS ALI

S. Harris Ali is a sociologist in the Faculty of Environmental Studies at York University, Toronto. His research interests include natural and technological disasters, environmental management, and the relationship of the environment to human health. He has written articles on a wide range of topics, including infectious disease outbreaks (*E. coli*, tuberculosis, SARS, H1N1), the political economy of disasters (a plastics recycling fire in Hamilton, Ontario, mining disasters in Nova Scotia, and heat waves in Toronto), and the environmental management of solid waste. His most recent research analyzes controversy over the proposed Northern Gateway and Keystone XL pipelines designed to carry oil from the Alberta tar sands to British Columbia and the U.S. Gulf Coast.

REGINALD W. BIBBY

Reginald W. Bibby is one of Canada's leading experts on religious and social trends. He holds the Board of Governors Research Chair in Sociology at the University of Lethbridge. For more than three decades, he has been monitoring Canadian social trends through his Project Canada national surveys of adults and teenagers. Dr. Bibby has presented his findings in academic settings around the world. He also has taken his work well beyond the academic community through innumerable public appearances, extensive media exposure, and 13 best-selling books. They include *Fragmented Gods* (Toronto: Irwin, 1987), *Beyond the Gods & Back* (Lethbridge, AB: Project Canada Books, 2011), *Mosaic Madness* (Toronto: Stoddart, 1990), *The Boomer Factor* (Toronto: ECW Press, 2006), and *The Emerging Millennials* (Lethbridge, AB: Project Canada Books, 2009). In recognition of his contribution to the nation, in 2006 the Governor General appointed him an Officer of the Order of Canada.

MONICA BOYD

Trained as a demographer and sociologist, Dr. Boyd has written numerous articles, books, and monographs on the changing family, gender inequality, international migration (with focuses on policy, on immigrant integration, and on immigrant women), and ethnic stratification. Her current research focuses on immigrant offspring, including the 1.5 and second generations, immigrant language skills and labour market integration, the migration of high-skilled labour, and immigrant reaccreditation difficulties, with research currently funded by the Social Sciences and Humanities Research Council of Canada. In addition to her numerous contributions in advisory and consultant capacities to nongovernmental organizations, Canadian government departments, the United Nations, and the Organisation for Economic Co-operation and Development, she has served as the president of the Canadian Sociological Association and the Canadian Population Society.

MICHAEL BURAWOY

Michael Burawoy teaches sociology at the University of California, Berkeley. He is President of the International Sociological Association and former President of the American Sociological Association. He has authored more than 125 scholarly articles and authored or co-authored 10 books, including *Manufacturing Consent* (Chicago: University of Chicago Press, 1982), a classic study of change in the capitalist labour process, and *Global Ethnography* (Berkeley, CA: University of California Press, 2000), a pioneering work on ethnographic sociological research in the postmodern world.

NEENA L. CHAPPELL

Neena L. Chappell, F.R.S.C., Canada Research Chair in social gerontology, has been conducting research in the area of aging for more than 30 years. Throughout her career, she has sought to demonstrate the value and relevance of sociological thought and research for applied issues in aging. She believes rigorous university-based social science research has a critical role to play in the non-university community. Her interests include caregiving, health, and social policy in Canada and cross-nationally. She has established two university research centres on aging, one at the University of Manitoba and the other at the University of Victoria, where she continues to conduct research. She has published more than three hundred academic articles and reports. She is currently President of the Canadian Association on Gerontology and President of Academy II (social sciences) of the Royal Society of Canada.

SANDRA COLAVECCHIA

Sandra Colavecchia received her Ph.D. from the University of Toronto and is now an Assistant Professor in the Department of Sociology at McMaster University, where she teaches introductory sociology and sociology of families. Her teaching interests include teaching technologies, active learning, and academic skill development. Her research interests are in sociology of families and family policy. As the first member of her family to attend university, she is committed to making postsecondary education more accessible to students from all backgrounds. Professor Colavecchia is highly reflective and critical about her teaching goals and practices and is committed to the ongoing improvement of her teaching and her courses. Sociology is not just a job for her. It is a lens through which she understands her life and the world around her. She strives to share her excitement about sociology with her students.

SCOTT DAVIES

Scott Davies is Professor of Sociology and Ontario Research Chair in Educational Achievement and At-Risk Students at McMaster University. He has studied social movements and organizational variety in education and is currently examining determinants and correlates of student achievement and the emergence of academic inequalities from preschool to postsecondary levels. He has won awards from the American Education Research Association and the Canadian Education Research Association, and has been an associate editor and editorial board member of several journals. With Neil Guppy, he is currently working on the third edition of *The Schooled Society*.

JOSH GREENBERG

Josh Greenberg is an Associate Professor in Communication Studies in the Department of Sociology and Anthropology at Carleton University. His research interests include public relations, journalism studies, media and social movements, social media, and qualitative methods. His work on these and related topics has appeared in numerous journals and books. He is the co-editor of *Communication in Question: Competing Perspectives on Controversial Issues in Communication Studies*, 2nd ed. (Toronto: Nelson, 2013).

NEIL GUPPY

Neil Guppy is Professor and Head of Sociology at the University of British Columbia. He is a graduate of Queen's University (B.A./B.P.H.E.) and the University of Waterloo (M.Sc./Ph.D., 1981). He has published several books, including *Education in Canada* (Ottawa: Statistics Canada, 1998, with Scott Davies), *The Schooled Society*, 2nd ed. (Toronto: Oxford University Press, 2010, with Scott Davies), and *Successful Surveys*, 4th ed. (Toronto: Thomson Nelson, 2008, with George Gray). Recently, he has published work in the *American Sociological Review* and *International Migration Review* on public opinion and immigration. At UBC, he has received both a University Killam Teaching Prize and a University Killam Research Prize.

JOHN HANNIGAN

John Hannigan is Professor of Sociology at the University of Toronto at Scarborough, where he teaches courses in urban sociology, collective behaviour, and environment and society. He attended the University of Western Ontario and Ohio State University, where he received his Ph.D. in 1976. While at Ohio State, he was a Research Associate at the Disaster Research Center. He is the author of two books: *Environmental Sociology* (1995, 2006) and *Fantasy City: Pleasure and Profit in the Postmodern City* (1998), both published by Routledge. *Fantasy City* was nominated for the 1999/2000 Canadian Sociology and Anthropology Association (CSAA) John Porter Award. *Environmental Sociology* has been translated into Portuguese, Japanese, Chinese, and Korean. Dr. Hannigan is a frequent contributor to media discussions of culture and urban development, having appeared on National Public Radio (United States), in *The Independent* (Britain), and in the *Globe & Mail* (Canada). He has served in a number of administrative posts including Graduate Director and Associate Chair in the Department of Sociology (1999–2002) and Interim Chair, Department of Social Sciences (2003), University of Toronto at Scarborough; and Secretary, CSAA (2000–03). He is presently working on a new book on the global character of disasters and complex emergencies.

JOSÉE JOHNSTON

Josée Johnston is Associate Professor of Sociology at the University of Toronto. Her major interest is the sociological study of food, which is a lens for investigating questions relating to culture, politics, gender, and the environment. She co-authored (with Shyon Baumann) *Foodies: Democracy and Distinction in the Gourmet Foodscape* (New York: Routledge, 2010), and has published articles in the *American Journal of Sociology*, *Theory and Society*, *Signs: Journal of Women in Culture and Society*, and *Gender and Society*. Her research has been supported by the Social Sciences and Humanities Research Council and the Canadian Institute for Health Research. In 2009 she was awarded the Province of Ontario's five-year Early Researcher Award. Professor Johnston teaches courses on the sociology of food and globalization with an emphasis on inequality, social justice, and sustainability.

GRAHAM KNIGHT

Graham Knight is Professor Emeritus at McMaster University in Hamilton where he taught courses on media sociology and sociological theory since receiving his Ph.D. in sociology from Carleton University. His current research interests lie in media and social movement framing of sweatshop labour practices and, most recently, climate change. His research has appeared in *Journalism Studies*, the *European Journal of Communication*, *Communication and Critical/Cultural Studies*, and *Social Movement Studies*, as well as in scholarly books.

HARVEY KRAHN

Harvey Krahn is Professor and Chair of Sociology at the University of Alberta. His research interests include social inequality, the sociology of work, the sociology of education, immigration, environmental sociology, and political sociology. He typically uses quantitative research methods but has also participated in studies employing qualitative and historical methods. His largest research project involves interviewing a sample of four hundred individuals seven times over 25 years to learn more about school-work transitions and how social inequality is reproduced across generations. He is one of three co-authors of a textbook on the sociology of work (*Work, Industry, and Canadian Society*, 6th ed. Toronto: Nelson, 2011) and has published research findings in a wide range of scholarly journals.

RHONDA L. LENTON

Rhonda Lenton is Vice-President Academic and Provost at York University. Before taking over this role in 2009–10, she was the Dean of the Atkinson Faculty of Liberal and Professional Studies at York. In addition to providing leadership in the areas of institutional change management and academic resource planning, she has administrative oversight for quality assurance at York and is currently involved in a Higher Education Quality Council of Ontario (HEQCO) Tuning Project about student learning outcomes in the social sciences sector. Her areas of teaching and research expertise include research methods and data analysis, gender, and family violence. She has published peer-reviewed book chapters and articles in an array of academic journals, and she is currently conducting a survey on marital conflict in Canada. She is also the team lead on a HEQCO project researching the impact of community-based and community-service learning on student learning, as well as opportunities for faculty development.

JOHN LIE

John Lie was born in South Korea, grew up in Japan and Hawaii, and received his A.B., A.M., and Ph.D. degrees from Harvard University. His main interests are in social theory and political economy. Currently he is the C.K. Cho Professor of Sociology at the University of California, Berkeley, where he previously served as the Dean of International and Area Studies. His recent publications include *Zainichi (Koreans in Japan)* (Berkeley, CA: University of California Press, 2008) and *Modern Peoplehood: On Race, Racism, Nationalism, Ethnicity, and Identity*, paperback ed. (Berkeley, CA: University of California Press, 2011).

DOROTHY PAWLUCH

Dorothy Pawluch is Associate Professor of Sociology at McMaster University. Her research interests lie in deviance and social problems, as well as in the sociology of health. Her *The New Pediatrics: A Profession in Transition* (New Jersey: Transaction Publishers, 2009) examines the expansion of pediatrics into behavioural problems and the role that this expansion played in the medicalization of childhood deviance. As a member of the McMaster HIV/AIDS Research Group, she has studied the experiences of people living with HIV/AIDS. She is also interested in the social constructionist perspective on social problems and has co-authored (with Steve Woolgar) a critique of that perspective. Her most recent publication explores the use of the Stockholm syndrome label in social problems debates.

MARGARET J. PENNING

Dr. Penning is interested in the sociology of health and healthcare, as well as aging. In particular, she is interested in examining self, informal, and formal care in relation to issues of chronic illness and disability in middle and later life, the impact of structural inequalities on health and healthcare, and healthcare restructuring and reform in the Canadian context. She is a principal investigator of a program of research focusing on transitions and trajectories in late-life care. She is the Social Science Theme Leader for the Canadian Longitudinal Study on Aging, a 20-year longitudinal study of 50 000 middle-aged and older Canadians funded by the Canadian Institutes of Health Research. She also serves as the editor-in-chief of the *Canadian Journal on Aging*.

LANCE ROBERTS

Lance W. Roberts was born in Calgary, Alberta, grew up in Edmonton, and received his Ph.D. from the University of Alberta. He is a Fellow of St. John's College and Professor of Sociology at the University of Manitoba, where he teaches introductory sociology, as well as research methods and statistics. In the last decade, he has received several teaching awards, including the 2011 Faculty of Arts Excellence in Teaching Award. His current research interests cover the comparative charting of social change, educational concerns, and mental health issues. In addition to publishing in research journals, he recently co-authored *Sociology: Your Compass for a New World*, 4th Can. Ed. (Toronto: Nelson, 2012), as well as *The Methods Coach* (2009) and *The Statistics Coach* (2010), both published by Oxford University Press, which aim to help students master fundamental research techniques. He enjoys teaching introductory sociology and is currently developing a variety of tools to enlarge his students' sociological imaginations.

VIC SATZEWICH

Vic Satzewich is Professor of Sociology at McMaster University. He has published many books and articles on various aspects of immigration, racism, and ethnic relations in Canada. His most recent books include *Racism in Canada* (Toronto: Oxford University Press, 2011); *"Race" and Ethnicity in Canada: A Critical Introduction* (Toronto: Oxford University Press, 2010); *Transnational Identities and Practices in Canada* (Vancouver: University of British Columbia Press, 2006); and *The Ukrainian Diaspora* (New York: Routledge, 2002). In 2005, he received the Outstanding Contribution Award of the Canadian Sociology Association.

WILLIAM SHAFFIR

William Shaffir received his Ph.D. from McGill University. He is a Professor in the Department of Sociology at McMaster University. He is the author of books and articles on Hassidic Jews, professional socialization, and field research methods. He has published on a Depression-era ethnic riot in Toronto, the dynamics of becoming religious and of leaving religious life, and the sustained efforts of Hassidic Jews to preserve their traditional lifestyle while addressing the challenges of modernity. He has also studied how politicians cope with electoral defeat, the immigration of Canadian Jews to Israel, and students in an elite undergraduate program. His most recent work examines the social organization of police work, particularly among recent immigrants and racialized minorities.

JULIAN TANNER

Julian Tanner is a Professor of Sociology at the University of Toronto. His interest in the sociology of crime and deviance, particularly youth crime and youth culture, derives from his school days in England—as both a student in an all-boys boarding school and, later on, as a secondary-school teacher. In addition to undergraduate and graduate courses in crime and deviance, he has taught and researched in the areas of school to work transitions (high-school dropouts, the effects of part-time jobs, and so on), the sociology of work (the industrial and political attitudes and behaviours of male manual workers, gender and the professions), young people, and popular music. Most recently, he has studied patterns of crime and victimization among young people in Toronto and youth gang activity.

SANDY WELSH

Sandy Welsh is Professor of Sociology and Special Advisor to the Dean, Faculty of Arts and Science, at the University of Toronto. She studies work and occupations, gender, the sociology of law, and social policy. Her primary research is centred on workplace harassment. Her research has appeared in *Gender and Society*, *Social Problems*, *Annual Review of Sociology*, *Sociology of Health and Illness*, and *Social Science and Medicine*. With Tracey Adams, she co-authored *The Organization and Experience of Work* (Toronto: Nelson, 2008). She has received funding from the Natural Sciences and Engineering Research Council of Canada, Canadian Institutes of Health Research, Status of Women Canada, and other foundations. Dr. Welsh provides expert testimony on sexual harassment for the Ontario and Canadian Human Rights Commissions and in other legal forums. She is a recipient of the University of Toronto Faculty of Arts and Sciences Outstanding Teaching Award.

ANTHONY WINSON

Anthony Winson's research and publications have focused on agriculture, food, and rural development issues related to Canada and the developing world. He is the author of *Coffee and Democracy in Modern Costa Rica* (London: Macmillan, 1989), *The Intimate Commodity: Food and the Development of the Agro-Industrial Complex in Canada* (Toronto: Garamond, 1993), and *Contingent Work, Disrupted Lives: Labour and Community in the New Rural Economy* (University of Toronto, 2002, with Belinda Leach). *Contingent Work* won the 2003 John Porter book prize of the Canadian Sociology and Anthropology Association. He has recently co-edited (with M. Koc and J. Sumner) *Critical Perspectives in Food Studies* (Toronto: Oxford University Press, 2012), and he is presently completing a book on the degradation of food and the struggle for healthful eating.

PREFACE

The job of figuring out what to do with our lives and how to act in the world is more difficult than ever. Sociology helps by analyzing the pressing social issues of the day, showing how those issues affect all of us, and setting out options for dealing with them. Moreover, as you will learn in the following pages, sociology views social issues from a unique disciplinary perspective. All in all, it is a controversial and exciting business. Social problems are typically complex. The options for action often involve different benefits and disadvantages for different groups. Sociologists usually see things differently from other social and natural scientists. Not surprisingly, therefore, sociology, like any vibrant academic discipline, involves a lot of heated debate.

Unfortunately, most introductory sociology textbooks don't give much of a feel for the excitement of the discipline. They usually resemble encyclopedias full of definitions and presumably undeniable facts. They make sociological knowledge resemble the tablets some people say were brought down by Moses from Mount Sinai: abstract principles carved in stone, eternal truths that most people agree with but that tell us little about the way life is actually lived.

In preparing this book, I tried to overcome this deficiency in two ways. First, when I recruited authors to write chapters, I asked them to focus on social issues that are likely to be of real, everyday concern to Canadian undergraduates. Second, I asked the authors to highlight the controversies in the field, not the clichés. There is no sense keeping secret what any good scientist knows: advances in knowledge usually result from intellectual conflict, not consensus.

WHAT'S NEW IN THE SEVENTH EDITION

With the helpful feedback of reviewers and a dedicated team of contributors, the seventh edition has been thoroughly revised with updated research results, 2011 census data, and illustrations. Beyond this comprehensive update, the chapters have undergone the following enhancements:

- **Chapter 1, Introduction to Sociology**, includes a new discussion on lesbian, gay, bisexual and youth suicide, along with revised figures on suicide rates by country and by age and sex.
- **Chapter 2, Culture** contains new material on language and cultural diversity, including a new box exploring how technological change shortens young people's attention span. We have also included new material on hip hop, including the politics of hip hop in North Africa.
- **Chapter 3, Socialization** has been enhanced to include new material on ethnic variations in socialization, Freud, and the impact of Internet-based media and cellphones on socialization.
- **Chapter 4, Gender and Sexuality** includes more material on feminist approaches to gender and sexuality and new material on sexual diversity and queer theory.
- **Chapter 5, Communication and Mass Media** contains a new discussion of Internet-based social media and an analysis of gender differences in media use.
- **Chapter 6, Social Stratification**, contains includes a new discussion of poverty, immigrant Canadians and unemployment, housing, and young adults, in addition to a discussion of the Occupy Wall Street movement in the section on material inequality.
- **Chapter 7, Gender Inequality: Economic and Political Aspects**, contains new material on the percentage of Federal Political Representatives who are women; coverage of Slutwalks; and a revised figure that reflects the ratio of women's to men's earnings in Canada.
- **Chapter 8, Race and Ethnic Relations**, has been enhanced with new material on the gap in weekly earnings between Canadian-born visible minorities and white workers.
- **Chapter 9, Development and Underdevelopment**, contains revised material on the role of the Maritime Provinces in Canada's industrial development and a new discussion of the Occupy Wall Street movement.
- **Chapter 10, Families** is an entirely new chapter, written by Sandra Colavecchia of McMaster University.
- **Chapter 11, Work and Occupations** has streamlined coverage of management theories and includes new material on the blurred line between work and leisure as a result of the use of smart phones.
- **Chapter 13, Religion**, has been enhanced with a new table that reflects service attendance, personal practices, and the importance of religion and spirituality by social change correlates among Canadian adults.
- **Chapter 14, Deviance and Crime** includes new material on noncriminal forms of deviance, cybercrime, and surveillance.
- **Chapter 15, Population and Urbanization**, contains a new table reflecting the proportion of Foreign-Born and Visible Minority Populations by Census Metropolitan Area, 2006 and 2031, in addition to a new discussion of a recent *Toronto Lifestory*, "The New Suburbanites."
- **Chapter 16, Sociology and the Environment** is an entirely new chapter, written by S. Harris Ali of York University.
- **Chapter 17, Health and Aging** has updated information on life expectancy in Canada and around the world, and a new box on why we haven't won the war on cancer.
- **Chapter 18, Politics and Social Movements** includes an engaging discussion of liberal Islam and the Arab Spring, and a new box called "Will the Revolution be Twittered?".
- **Chapter 19, Globalization**, includes new material on social movements in Tunisia and Egypt; a new figure reflecting foreign direct investment and announced mergers and acquisitions; a new figure showing corporate tax rates worldwide; and new data on the footprint of the U.S. military worldwide.
- **Chapter 20, Research Methods** has been enhanced with new material on research ethics, the strengths and weaknesses of Internet surveys, and feminist research methods. This chapter also includes a new discussion of the controversy over the Canadian long-form census.
- **Online Chapter 21, Networks, Groups, Bureaucracies, and Societies**, includes a new figure that reflects the correlation of social

distance with increased obedience to authority, and numerous new illustrations.

- **Epilogue.** The seventh edition also boasts a new Epilogue, entitled "The Future of Global Sociology," written by Michael Burawoy, President of the International Sociology Association, author of the renowned *Manufacturing Consent: Changes in the Labour Process Under Monopoly Capitalism*, and avid proponent of public sociology.

Students and instructors will also enjoy our new design, enhanced to increase visual appeal, with new part openers and chapter openers and the inclusion of new photos in every chapter.

ORGANIZATION OF THE TEXT

Chapter 1, Introduction to Sociology, sets the tone for the rest of the book and stands alone in **Part 1.** Instead of sermonizing on the question "What is sociology?" as most other textbooks do, I ask, in effect, "Why sociology?"—that is, why does an undergraduate in this particular time and place need to know what sociology has to offer? My chief aim in Chapter 1 is to show how sociological thinking can clarify and perhaps help to resolve the real-life social issues that confront all of us here and now.

The remainder of the book is divided into five parts. **Part 2** could be subtitled "Becoming Human." In **Chapter 2,** Culture, I make a case for the view that ours is an increasingly fragmented and globalized postmodern culture that increases our freedom to fashion identities that suit our individual tastes. I also show that, paradoxically, our increased cultural freedom develops within definite limits beyond which it is more and more difficult to move. In **Chapter 3,** Socialization, William Shaffir and Dorothy Pawluch thoroughly discuss the interactive mechanisms through which we learn beliefs, symbols, values, and self-identities throughout the life cycle and in various institutions. Rhonda L. Lenton then devotes **Chapter 4,** Gender and Sexuality to an in-depth analysis of what might seem to be the most intimate and biologically determined aspects of our identity—our gender and sexuality—and demonstrates that, in fact, they have deep roots in culture and society. In **Chapter 5,** Communication and Mass Media, Josh Greenberg and Graham Knight analyze the impact of one of the most pervasive and influential social institutions today. In sum, the analyses of Part 2 will give the reader a solid appreciation of how we become part of society and how society becomes part of us through the transmission of culture between generations.

Part 3 is about how people become and remain unequal. Harvey Krahn shows in **Chapter 6,** Social Stratification that despite recent assertions of the demise of social classes, stratification persists and continues to structure our life-chances in profound ways. Indeed, inequality is increasing in many societies, including Canada. In **Chapter 7,** Gender Inequality: Economic and Political Aspects, Monica Boyd convincingly demonstrates that gender is an equally important basis of social inequality, both in the economic and in the political sphere. Vic Satzewich devotes **Chapter 8,** Race and Ethnic Relations to highlighting the deficiencies of biological and purely cultural approaches to understanding the bases of ethnic and racial inequality. Finally, in **Chapter 9,** Development and Underdevelopment, Anthony Winson incisively criticizes modernization and other theories of economic underdevelopment and global inequality, offering a compelling argument for the analytical benefits of a modified dependency approach to the problem. The reader will complete Part 3 with a firm understanding of how people are highly differentiated and differentially rewarded, depending on their social location.

Part 4 shifts the reader's attention to some of society's fundamental institutions. Sandra Collavechia's **Chapter 10,** Families examines how and why families and intimate relationships have undergone change and diversification, particularly in the past several decades, and suggests where they may be headed. Sandy Welsh devotes **Chapter 11,** Work and Occupations to tracing the development and future shape of work. In **Chapter 12,** Education, Scott Davies dissects our educational system, demonstrating that, paradoxically, it is as much a cause of the persistence of inequality as it is an avenue for upward mobility. In **Chapter 13,** Religion, Reginald Bibby assesses the social origins, consequences, and future of religion, relying heavily on his own fundamentally important survey research to argue his case for the persistence of religion in Canadian society and the growing polarization of Canadians into religious and secular camps.

Change and Conflict are the subjects of **Part 5.** Here the reader is introduced to the main forces of turbulence in our society. In **Chapter 14,** Deviance and Crime, Julian Tanner elegantly analyzes one form of social conflict: deviant and criminal behaviour. He undermines several common misconceptions in the process. John Hannigan's analysis in **Chapter 15,** Population and Urbanization, is a novel and revealing look at how human populations have developed in cities from preindustrial to postmodern times. S. Harris Ali devotes **Chapter 16,** Sociology and the Environment to one of the most pressing issues of the day—the environment. He analyzes the rise of environmental awareness and its effects on the relationship among industry, the state, and the public; the process by which environmental issues are socially constructed; how the distribution of power in society affects strategies to manage and govern the environment; and the uneven distribution of environmental risks in society. In **Chapter 17,** Health and Aging, Neena Chappell and Margaret Penning expertly discuss the aging of the Canadian population and attendant health issues. In **Chapter 18,** Politics and Social Movements, I survey the evolution of politics and social movements, showing how various forms of conflict emerge, change our lives, and become institutionalized. Finally, Globalization is the subject and title of **Chapter 19,** by Josée Johnston. She shows that culturally, politically, and economically, the world is becoming a single place and its inhabitants are developing a global consciousness. This does not imply that we are becoming one big happy family. To the contrary, conflict has persisted and even intensified in the early twenty-first century.

In **Part 6, Chapter 20,** Research Methods concisely outlines how sociologists work. Neil Guppy's clarity, research experience, and balanced approach add much-needed lustre to a subject that first-year students often find dull. Guppy leaves the reader with the firm sense that, for all the intellectual liveliness and controversy displayed in this book, sociology can be and is disciplined by the judicious use of logic and evidence.

The book concludes with an **Epilogue,** The Future of Sociology, by Michael Burawoy, President of the International Sociological Association. With stunning historical sweep, he argues that three waves of marketization have transformed the dominant thrust of sociology since the nineteenth century. According to Burawoy, the latest neoliberal wave of marketization is causing many members of the discipline to become public sociologists, refusing collaboration with the market and the state, and instead engaging directly with communities, institutions, and social movements to defend society against rampant marketization.

As a bonus feature, Lance Roberts, John Lie, and I prepared **Online Chapter 21,** Networks, Groups, Bureaucracies, and Societies. It draws the connection between microlevel interactions, mesolevel organisation, and macrolevel social forces and institutions. We recommend that the chapter be assigned after Chapter 3, Socialization. This chapter is available at www.newsociety7e.nelson.com.

FEATURES OF THIS TEXT

While the content and organization of this text have been carefully rendered, you will also find updated visual and pedagogical features in *New Society*, Seventh Edition.

NEW PART AND CHAPTER OPENERS

A fresh new look for part and chapter openers uses vivid colours and arresting photos to engage students with sociological concepts.

Additionally, a point-form chapter overview—"*In this chapter you will learn that ...*"—prepares students to think critically and to absorb the material.

CHAPTER 10

FAMILIES

Sandra Colaveccchia
MCMASTER UNIVERSITY

IN THIS CHAPTER YOU WILL LEARN THAT

- Our definitions of family and marriage are embedded in social policies that influence personal decisions about intimate relationships.
- Functionalism, conflict theory, symbolic interactionism, and feminism view families through different lenses. Each provides a unique perspective on the relationship between families and the larger society, and on how individuals experience family life.
- Family forms vary historically and across societies, as do ideas about ideal marital relationships and parent-child relationships. Sociologists therefore argue that families are socially constructed: social contexts influence seemingly personal decisions about intimate relationships.
- Industrialization changed family life and redefined men's and women's roles. Increasingly, women—especially middle- and upper-class women—came to be identified with the private sphere of the family, and men came to be identified with the public sphere of politics and work for wages.
- Families, and intimate relationships in general, have undergone dramatic change in the past several decades. Family structures are more diverse. Divorce, cohabitation, lone-parent families, delayed home-leaving, same-sex families, transnational families, and one-person households are more common. Myriad social, economic, political, and ideological factors have shaped these trends.
- Compared with family policy in Western Europe, Canadian family policy does not provide sufficient support, particularly for working parents in need of high-quality child care.

BOXES

Key subjects are explored further by using boxes that break up the content of each chapter. Many of these discuss real-life examples drawn from current newspapers, journals, and academic papers, while others expand on a concept recently introduced. The effect is to provide visual interest and help readers to connect what they're learning to the outside world.

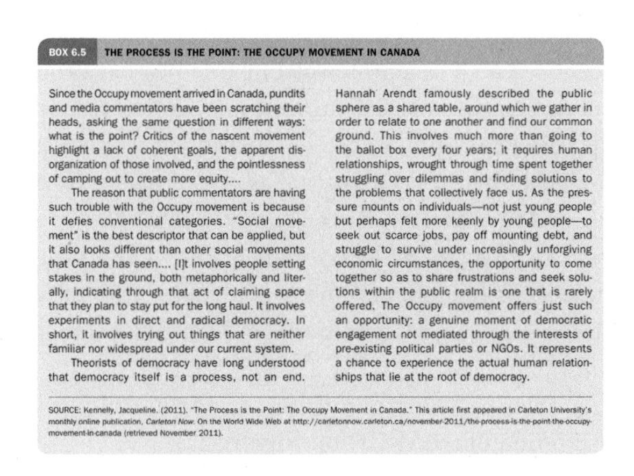
BOX 6.5 THE PROCESS IS THE POINT: THE OCCUPY MOVEMENT IN CANADA

Since the Occupy movement arrived in Canada, pundits and media commentators have been scratching their heads, asking the same question in different ways: what is the point? Critics of the nascent movement highlight a lack of coherent goals, the apparent disorganization of those involved, and the pointlessness of camping out to create more equity....

The reason that public commentators are having such trouble with the Occupy movement is because it defies conventional categories. "Social movement" is the best descriptor that can be applied, but it also looks different than other social movements that Canada has seen.... [I]t involves people setting stakes in the ground, both metaphorically and literally, indicating through that act of claiming space that they plan to stay put for the long haul. It involves experiments in direct and radical democracy. In short, it involves trying out things that are neither familiar nor widespread under our current system.

Theorists of democracy have long understood that democracy itself is a process, not an end. Hannah Arendt famously described the public sphere as a shared table, around which we gather in order to relate to one another and find our common ground. This involves much more than going to the ballot box every four years; it requires human relationships, wrought through time spent together struggling over dilemmas and finding solutions to the problems that collectively face us. As the pressure mounts on individuals—not just young people but perhaps felt more keenly by young people—to seek out scarce jobs, pay off mounting debt, and struggle to survive under increasingly unforgiving economic circumstances, the opportunity to come together so as to share frustrations and seek solutions within the public realm is one that is rarely offered. The Occupy movement offers just such an opportunity: a genuine moment of democratic engagement not mediated through the interests of pre-existing political parties or NGOs. It represents a chance to experience the actual human relationships that lie at the root of democracy.

SOURCE: Kennelly, Jacqueline. (2011). "The Process is the Point: The Occupy Movement in Canada." This article first appeared in Carleton University's monthly online publication, *Carleton Now*. On the World Wide Web at http://carletonnow.carleton.ca/november-2011/the-process-is-the-point-the-occupy-movement-in-canada (retrieved November 2011).

The Seventh Edition contains new boxes on topics that include how technological change shortens your attention span (Box 2.2), raising a genderless child (3.1), self-injuring as learned behaviour (3.5), the Occupy Movement in Canada (6.5), love and cohabitation (10.1), and many more engaging and relevant topics.

FIGURES AND TABLES

Current census data and other up-to-date research is easily compared when presented in one of 45 tables and 85 figures integrated throughout the book to enhance student learning—39 of these figures are completely new, and *New Society*, Seventh Edition, also includes four new maps.

FIGURE 4.3 THE DISTRIBUTION OF MALE AND FEMALE AGGRESSIVENESS

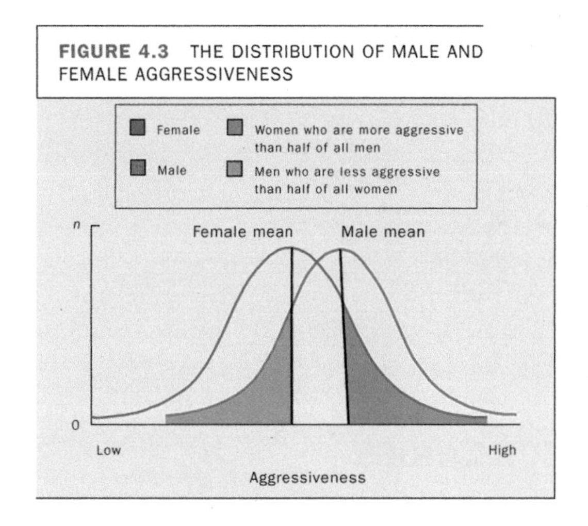

TABLE 4.1 SUMMARY OF BIOLOGICAL SEX DIFFERENCES DURING TYPICAL FETAL DEVELOPMENT

VARIABLE	FEMALE	MALE
Chromosomal pattern	XX	XY
Gonadal	Ovaries	Testes
Hormonal	More estrogens than androgens	More androgens than estrogens + MIH
Sex organs	Uterus, fallopian tubes, vagina, clitoris, labia	Epididymis, vas deferens, seminal vesicles, prostate, penis, scrotum

SOURCE: Adapted from *Gender in Canada* by E. D. Nelson and Barrie W. Robinson, 1999, p. 48, Pearson Education. Reprinted with permission by Pearson Education Canada Inc.

END-OF-CHAPTER RESOURCES

Each chapter concludes with a set of end-of-chapter resources to help students review and apply their knowledge. A **Summary** of numbered key points helps students to see the "bigger picture"—to interact with concepts, not just facts—while a set of **Questions to Consider** encourages readers to think critically about the material and to apply what they have learned against their own values, ideas, and experiences. A **Glossary** of key terms, definitions, and page references is also included, alongside a list of **Suggested Reading** that encourages students to research independently.

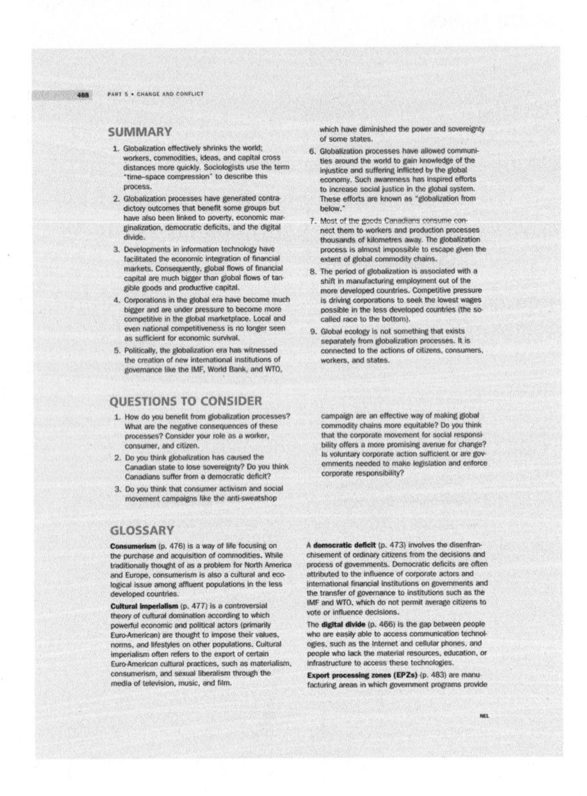
488 PART 5 • CHANGE AND CONFLICT

SUMMARY

1. Globalization effectively shrinks the world; workers, commodities, ideas, and capital cross distances more quickly. Sociologists use the term "time–space compression" to describe this process.
2. Globalization processes have generated contradictory outcomes that benefit some groups but have also been linked to poverty, economic marginalization, democratic deficits, and the digital divide.
3. Developments in information technology have facilitated the economic integration of financial markets. Consequently, global flows of financial capital are much bigger than global flows of tangible goods and productive capital.
4. Corporations in the global era have become much bigger and are under pressure to become more competitive in the global marketplace. Local and even national competitiveness is no longer seen as sufficient for economic survival.
5. Politically, the globalization era has witnessed the creation of new international institutions of governance like the IMF, World Bank, and WTO, which have diminished the power and sovereignty of some states.
6. Globalization processes have allowed communities around the world to gain knowledge of the injustice and suffering inflicted by the global economy. Such awareness has inspired efforts to increase social justice in the global system. These efforts are known as "globalization from below."
7. Most of the goods Canadians consume connect them to workers and production processes thousands of kilometres away. The globalization process is almost impossible to escape given the extent of global commodity chains.
8. The period of globalization is associated with a shift in manufacturing employment out of the more developed countries. Competitive pressure is driving corporations to seek the lowest wages possible in the less developed countries (the so-called race to the bottom).
9. Global ecology is not something that exists separately from globalization processes. It is connected to the actions of citizens, consumers, workers, and states.

QUESTIONS TO CONSIDER

1. How do you benefit from globalization processes? What are the negative consequences of these processes? Consider your role as a worker, consumer, and citizen.
2. Do you think globalization has caused the Canadian state to lose sovereignty? Do you think Canadians suffer from a democratic deficit?
3. Do you think that consumer activism and social movement campaigns like the anti-sweatshop campaign are an effective way of making global commodity chains more equitable? Do you think that the corporate movement for social responsibility offers a more promising avenue for change? Is voluntary corporate action sufficient or are governments needed to make legislation and enforce corporate responsibility?

GLOSSARY

Consumerism (p. 476) is a way of life focusing on the purchase and acquisition of commodities. While traditionally thought of as a problem for North America and Europe, consumerism is also a cultural and ecological issue among affluent populations in the less developed countries.

Cultural imperialism (p. 477) is a controversial theory of cultural domination according to which powerful economic and political actors (primarily Euro-American) are thought to impose their values, norms, and lifestyles on other populations. Cultural imperialism often refers to the export of certain Euro-American cultural practices, such as materialism, consumerism, and sexual liberalism through the media of television, music, and film.

A **democratic deficit** (p. 473) involves the disenfranchisement of ordinary citizens from the decisions and process of governments. Democratic deficits are often attributed to the influence of corporate actors and international financial institutions on governments and the transfer of governance to institutions such as the IMF and WTO, which do not permit average citizens to vote or influence decisions.

The **digital divide** (p. 466) is the gap between people who are easily able to access communication technologies, such as the Internet and cellular phones, and people who lack the material resources, education, or infrastructure to access these technologies.

Export processing zones (EPZs) (p. 483) are manufacturing areas in which government programs provide

NEL

ANCILLARIES

INSTRUCTOR ANCILLARIES

The **Nelson Education Teaching Advantage (NETA)** program delivers research-based instructor resources that promote student engagement and higher-order thinking to enable the success of Canadian students and educators.

Instructors today face many challenges. Resources are limited, time is scarce, and a new kind of student has emerged: one who is juggling school with work, has gaps in his or her basic knowledge, and is immersed in technology in a way that has led to a completely new style of learning. In response, Nelson Education has gathered a group of dedicated instructors to advise us on the creation of richer and more flexible ancillaries that respond to the needs of today's teaching environments.

In consultation with the editorial advisory board, Nelson Education has completely rethought the structure, approaches, and formats of our key textbook ancillaries. We have also increased our investment in editorial support for our ancillary authors. The result is the Nelson Education Teaching Advantage and its key components: *NETA Engagement*, *NETA Assessment*, and *NETA Presentation*. Each component includes one or more ancillaries prepared according to our best practices and a document explaining the theory behind the practices.

NETA Engagement presents materials that help instructors deliver engaging content and activities to their classes. Instead of Instructor's Manuals that regurgitate chapter outlines and key terms from the text, NETA Enriched Instructor's Manuals (EIMs) provide genuine assistance to teachers. The EIMs answer questions like *What should students learn?*, *Why should students care?*, and *What are some common student misconceptions and stumbling blocks?* EIMs not only identify the topics that cause students the most difficulty, but also describe techniques and resources to help students master these concepts. Dr. Roger Fisher's *Instructor's Guide to Classroom Engagement (IGCE)* accompanies every Enriched Instructor's Manual. (Information about the NETA Enriched Instructor's Manual prepared for *New Society*, Seventh Edition is included in the description of the *Instructor's Resource CD* (IRCD) on page xxvii.)

NETA Assessment relates to testing materials: not just Nelson's Test Banks and Computerized Test Banks but also in-text self-tests, Study Guides and web quizzes, and homework programs like CNOW. Under *NETA Assessment*, Nelson's authors create multiple-choice questions that reflect research-based best practices for constructing effective questions and testing not just recall but also higher-order thinking. Our guidelines were developed by David DiBattista, a 3M National Teaching Fellow whose recent research as a professor of psychology at Brock University has focused on multiple-choice testing. All Test Bank authors receive training at workshops conducted by Prof. DiBattista, as do the copy editors assigned to each Test Bank. A copy of *Multiple Choice Tests: Getting Beyond Remembering*, Prof. DiBattista's guide to writing effective tests, is included with every Nelson Test Bank/Computerized Test Bank package. (Information about the NETA Test Bank prepared for *New Society*, Seventh Edition, is included in the description of the IRCD on page xxvii.)

NETA Presentation has been developed to help instructors make the best use of PowerPoint® in their classrooms. With a clean and uncluttered design developed by Maureen Stone of StoneSoup Consulting, NETA Presentation features slides with improved readability, more multimedia and graphic materials, activities to use in class, and tips for instructors on the Notes page. A copy of *NETA Guidelines for Classroom Presentations* by Maureen Stone is included with each set of PowerPoint slides. (Information about the NETA PowerPoint® prepared for *New Society*, Seventh Edition, is included in the description of the IRCD below.)

IRCD

Key instructor ancillaries are provided on the *Instructor's Resource CD* (ISBN: 0176660704), giving instructors the ultimate tool for customizing lectures and presentations. (Downloadable web versions are also available at www.newsociety7e.nelson.com). The IRCD includes the following:

- **NETA Engagement:** The Enriched Instructor's Manual was written by Elizabeth Bishop. It is organized according to the textbook chapters and addresses eight key educational concerns, such as typical stumbling blocks student face and how to address them. Other features include video suggestions, Internet resources, and active learning exercises.
- **NETA Assessment:** The Test Bank was written by Tara Fidler of King's University College at The University of Western Ontario. It includes over 2100 multiple-choice questions written according to NETA guidelines for effective construction and development of higher-order questions. Also included are over 300 true/false questions, 160 short answer questions, and 160 essay questions. Test Bank files are provided in Word format for easy editing and in PDF format for convenient printing, whatever your system.

  The Computerized Test Bank by ExamView® includes all the questions from the Test Bank. The easy-to-use ExamView software is compatible with Microsoft Windows and Mac OS. Create tests by selecting questions from the question bank, modifying these questions as desired, and adding new questions that you write yourself. You can administer quizzes online and export tests to WebCT, Blackboard, and other formats.
- **NETA Presentation:** Microsoft PowerPoint lecture slides for every chapter have been created by Jaime Nikolaou of the University of Toronto. There is an average of 35 slides per chapter, many featuring key figures, tables, and photographs from *New Society*, Seventh Edition. NETA principles of clear design and engaging content have been incorporated throughout.
- **Image Library:** This resource consists of digital copies of figures, short tables, and photographs used in the book. Instructors may use these jpegs to create their own PowerPoint presentations.
- **DayOne:** DayOne—Prof InClass is a PowerPoint presentation that you can customize to orient students to the class and their text at the beginning of the course.

CourseMate CourseMate

Nelson Education's Sociology CourseMate brings course concepts to life with interactive learning and exam preparation tools that integrate with the printed textbook. Students activate their knowledge through quizzes, games, and flashcards, among many other tools.

CourseMate provides immediate feedback that enables students to connect results to the work they have just produced, increasing their learning efficiency. It encourages contact between students and faculty: You can select to monitor your students' level of engagement with CourseMate, correlating their efforts to their outcomes. You can even use CourseMate's quizzes to practise "Just in Time" teaching by tracking results in the Engagement Tracker and customizing your lesson plans to address their learning needs.

Watch student comprehension and engagement soar as your class engages with CourseMate. Ask your Nelson representative for a demo today.

DVD Resources

Enhance your classroom experience with the exciting and relevant videos of ***Think Outside the Book: The Nelson Sociology DVD Collection*** prepared to accompany New Society. Designed to enrich and support chapter concepts, this set of seven 30-minute video segments was created by Robert Brym to stimulate discussion of topics raised in sociology. Produced in conjunction with Face to Face Media (Vancouver), the Jesuit Communication Project (Toronto), and the National Film Board of Canada, the selections have been edited to optimize their impact in the classroom. Many of the selections are taken from films that have won national and international awards.

STUDENT ANCILLARIES

The more you study, the better the results. Make the most of your study time by accessing everything you need to succeed in one place. The Sociology CourseMate includes:

- An interactive eBook with highlighting, note taking, and an interactive glossary
- Interactive learning tools, including:
  - Quizzes
  - Flashcards
  - Videos
  - Applying Sociology to Your Life
- Sociology in the Media

... and more!

The following readers can be purchased at NelsonBrain.com in ebook or print-copy format:

- ***Sociology as a Life or Death Issue***, Second Canadian Edition (0176503560), was written by Robert J. Brym. In a series of beautifully written essays on hip-hop culture, the social bases of cancer, and the plight of hurricane victims in the Caribbean region and on the coast of the Gulf of Mexico, Robert Brym introduces sociology by analyzing the social causes of death. In doing so, he reveals the powerful social forces that help to determine who lives and who dies, and demonstrates the promise of a well-informed sociological understanding of the world. This brief and inexpensive volume is an eye-opener, an inspiration, and a guide for students of sociology and for anyone with an inquiring mind and who hopes for a better world for future generations.
- ***Controversies in Canadian Sociology***, First Edition (0176104682), by Reza Nakhaie, includes a range of classic and contemporary readings and employs the point-counterpoint method to challenge students to evaluate arguments on their merits, and to develop their critical imaginations.
- ***Society in Question***, Seventh Edition (0176509984), by Robert J. Brym, provides balanced coverage of the approaches and methods in current sociology as well as unique and surprising perspectives on many major sociological topics. All readings have been chosen for their ability to speak directly to contemporary Canadian students about how sociology can enable them to make sense of their lives in a rapidly changing world.
- ***Images of Society: Readings That Inspire and Inform Society***, Third Edition (0176514163), by Jerry P. White and Michael Carroll, is an exciting collection of readings designed for use within introductory sociology classes. The readings range from classic works within sociology to pieces illustrating recent sociological principles. Academic and journalistic readings have been selected by the authors to convey the distinctive way sociologists think. All readings are excerpts from longer pieces and are introduced with short prologues written by the editors.
- ***InfoTrac® College Edition***. Ignite discussions or augment your lectures with the latest developments in sociology and societal change. Create your own course reader by selecting articles or by using the search keywords provided at the end of each chapter. *InfoTrac® College Edition* (available with this text) gives you and your students four months of free access to an easy-to-use online database of reliable, full-length articles (not abstracts) from hundreds of top academic journals and popular sources. Among the journals available 24 hours a day, seven days a week are the *Canadian Review of Sociology and Anthropology*, the *Canadian Journal of Sociology*, *Canadian Ethnic Studies*, *Public Policy*, the *American Journal of Sociology*, *Social Forces*, *Social Research*, and *Sociology*. Contact your Nelson representative for more information. *InfoTrac® College Edition* is available only to North American college and university students. Journals are subject to change.

CUSTOM PUBLISHING OPTIONS

It's your course, why compromise? Nelson Education is making it easier than ever to customize this sociology textbook to create a highly personalized and convenient course resource for your students. Learn how Custom Publishing with Nelson Education can help you teach your course, your way, by visiting www.nelsoncustom.com.

FOSTERING CONVERSATIONS ABOUT TEACHING SOCIOLOGY IN CANADA

We invite you to join *Fostering Conversations about Teaching Sociology in Canada*, a virtual community site built by sociology educators for sociology educators. A dynamic, continually evolving blog that houses dozens of self-reflexive pieces about various aspects of teaching—including student engagement, assessment, course preparation, and teaching with technology—*Fostering Conversations* is an educator's toolkit and a virtual home for sharing teaching ideas, practices, and complexities. Housing contributions by educators from across the country, including universities and colleges, large and small, *Fostering Conversations* provides a framework for cross-institutional conversations about the craft of teaching in the twenty-first century. Join the conversation today! Visit **http://community.cengage.com/Site/fosteringconversations/.**

ACKNOWLEDGMENTS

The seventh edition of *New Society* still bears the imprint of Heather McWhinney, Dan Brooks, Megan Mueller, Semareh Al-Hillal, Brad Lambertus, Camille Isaacs, and Laura Macleod. They shepherded the book through its first editions, helping to make *New Society* distinctive and highly successful.

For the past year, I have been privileged to work closely with publishing professionals of the highest calibre, all of whom contributed heavily to the successful completion of the seventh edition. In particular, Maya Castle worked diligently and with good humour on this complex project, always mindful of the need to balance the diverse needs of instructors, students, and authors. Toni Chahley's energetic and meticulous approach to the project was evident from beginning to end. Visually and linguistically, this book owes much to her exemplary skill as a developmental editor. I would also like to thank Carrie MacGregor (photo researcher), Jennifer Hare (content production manager), Terry Fedorkiw (marketing manager), Dawn Hunter (copy editor), Linda Szostak (proofreader), and Megan Noels (permissions coordinator).

New Society could not have become what it is without the authors of each chapter. They are among the very best sociologists in Canada. I believe that, although concentrating on the exposition of their own subfields, they have conveyed to the novice a real sense of the excitement and promise of sociology. I am deeply indebted to them, as scores of thousands of introductory sociology students and their instructors inevitably have been and will be.

Finally, I would like to thank the following reviewers, whose insightful comments helped shape this edition:

Sonia Bookman, University of Manitoba
Jan Clarke, Algoma University
Linda Cohen, Memorial University of Newfoundland
Claudio Colaguori, York University
Stephen Dumas, University of Calgary
Tamy Superle, Carleton University
Eric Tompkins, College of New Caledonia

I would also like to thank the following reviewers, who provided feedback on the sixth edition:

Guy Letts, Georgian College
Lorna Doerkson, University of Saskatchewan
Peter Landstreet, York University
Kate Krug, Cape Breton University
Morgan Holmes, Wilfrid Laurier University

R.J.B.
Toronto

ABOUT THE COVER IMAGE:

As young people mature, they often discover that harsh realities thwart their rosy outlook. Prospects for upward mobility, control by authorities, and environmental degradation have intensified in recent decades, while racism and sexism are still pervasive. By startling us, Banksey's murals help us to appreciate these harsh realities, just as *New Society* helps us to analyze their causes, consequences, and possible solutions.

LETTER TO INSTRUCTORS

Dear Instructor,

CourseMate, Nelson Education's online engagement and assessment platform, is built with you and your students in mind.

CourseMate is designed to support your wonderful efforts to create an interactive, engaging online course, whether it accounts for 5 percent or 100 percent of your students' course experience. The digital assets found in this platform were selected for their pedagogical utility. Each digital asset contributes to the creation of an enriching online learning experience that respects diverse learning preferences and supports better student outcomes.

Our development of this learning tool has been guided by Arthur Chickering and Zelda Gamson's seminal work, "Seven Principles of Good Practice In Undergraduate Education" (*AAHE Bulletin*, 1987), and the follow-up work by Chickering and Stephen C. Ehrmann, "Implementing the Seven Principles: Technology as Lever"(*AAHE Bulletin*, 1996). Our attention to these principles ensures CourseMate appropriately reflects the core goals of contact, collaboration, multimodal learning, time on task, prompt feedback, active learning, and high expectations.

You can use CourseMate in several ways, including the following:

- ***To help students prepare for class:*** Instructors can assign pre-test questions before class. Students receive immediate feedback to the pre-test, including ebook excerpts covering the concepts they have yet to master. To confirm whether students have completed their pre-class assignment, instructors consult the Engagement Tracker for immediate insight into each student's time on task and achievement. Engagement Tracker helps instructors identify at-risk students early so they can intervene as needed.
- ***To engage students:*** Students can watch the video clips for each chapter and answer critical thinking questions. They practise comprehension by adding notes to the embedded eBook and highlighting important passages, as well as by using interactive flashcards and answering quiz questions.
- ***To help students develop their critical thinking skills:*** Students can challenge their higher-order thinking skills with the critical thinking questions that conclude almost all of the digital assets—including *Applying Sociology to My Life boxes, Focus on Social Policy boxes, Video Clips, Sociology in the Media boxes* and *Internet Activities*. Their responses are captured within the Engagement Tracker.
- ***To assess students:*** Instructors can attach grades to student responses to the pre-test, post-test, and critical thinking questions. Instructors might also choose to load the text's Test Bank to their learning management system (LMS).
- ***To create an online learning community:*** Instructors can ask students to watch a video clip or read one of the boxed assets (such as the *Sociology in the Media boxes*). Rather than have each student respond to the culminating critical thinking question, some instructors post the critical thinking question to the discussion board on their LMS. Yet others assign the question for in-class discussion or a small group response via email.

However you choose to incorporate CourseMate into your course, we sincerely hope it supports the construction of an online community of engaged learners.

Should you wish to contact me, please feel free to do so by emailing Maya.Castle@nelson.com.

Warmest wishes,

Maya Castle
Acquisitions Editor
Nelson Education
Canada's Learning Advantage

SOURCE: © Lárus Sigurðarson.

PART 1

INTRODUCTION

CHAPTER 1

INTRODUCTION TO SOCIOLOGY

Robert J. Brym
UNIVERSITY OF TORONTO

SOURCE: © Lárus Sigurðarson.

IN THIS CHAPTER YOU WILL LEARN THAT

- The causes of human behaviour lie partly in the patterns of social relations that surround and penetrate people.
- Sociologists examine the connection between personal troubles and social relations.
- Sociological research is often motivated by the desire to improve the social world. At the same time, sociologists adopt scientific methods to test their ideas.
- Sociology originated at the time of the Industrial Revolution. The founders of sociology diagnosed the massive social transformations of their day. They also suggested ways of overcoming the social problems created by the Industrial Revolution.
- Today's Postindustrial Revolution similarly challenges us. The chief value of sociology is that it can help clarify the scope, direction, and significance of social change. Sociology can also suggest ways of managing change.

INTRODUCTION

WHY I DECIDED NOT TO STUDY SOCIOLOGY

When I started university at the age of 18, I was bewildered by the wide variety of courses I could choose from. Having now taught sociology for more than 30 years, and having met thousands of undergraduates, I am quite sure most students today feel as I did then.

One source of confusion for me was uncertainty about why I was in university in the first place. Like you, I knew higher education could improve my chance of finding good work. But, like most students, I also had a sense that higher education is supposed to provide something more than just the training necessary to embark on a career that is interesting and pays well. Several high-school teachers and guidance counsellors had told me that university was also supposed to "broaden my horizons" and teach me to "think critically." I wasn't entirely sure what they meant, but they made it sound interesting enough to make me want to know more. Thus, I decided in my first year to take mainly "practical" courses that might prepare me for a law degree (economics, political science, and psychology). I also enrolled in a couple of other courses to indulge my "intellectual" side (philosophy, drama).

One thing I knew for sure: I didn't want to study sociology. Sociology, I came to believe, was thin soup with uncertain ingredients. When I asked a second-year student what sociology is, he told me it deals mainly with why people are unequal—why some are rich and others poor, some powerful and others weak. Coming as I did from a poor immigrant family in the Maritimes, an economically depressed region, it appeared that sociology could teach me something about my own life. But it also seemed a lot like what I imagined economics and political science to be about. What, then, was unique about sociology? My growing sense that sociology had nothing special to offer was confirmed when another second-year student told me that sociologists try to describe the ideal society and figure out how to make the world a better place. That description appealed to my youthful sense of the world's injustice. However, it also sounded a lot like philosophy. A third-year student explained that sociology analyzes how and why people assume different roles in their lives. She made sociology appear similar to drama. Finally, one student reported that in her sociology class, she was learning why people commit suicide, homicide, and other deviant acts. That seemed like abnormal psychology to me. I concluded that sociology had no distinct flavour all its own. Accordingly, I decided to forgo it for tastier courses.

A CHANGE OF MIND

Despite the opinion I'd formed, I found myself taking no fewer than four sociology courses a year after starting university. That revolution in my life was due partly to the pull of an extraordinary professor I happened to meet just before I began my second year. He set me thinking in an altogether new way about what I could and should do with my life. He exploded some of my deepest beliefs. He started me thinking sociologically.

Specifically, he first put Yorick's dilemma to me. Yorick is a character—sort of—in *Hamlet*. Toward the end of the play, Hamlet finds two gravediggers at work. They unearth the remains of the former court jester, Yorick, who used to amuse Hamlet and carry him around on his back when Hamlet was a child. Holding high his old friend's skull, Hamlet reflects on what we must all come to. Even the remains of Alexander the Great, he says, turn to dust.

This incident implies Yorick's dilemma and, indeed, the dilemma of all thinking people. Life is finite. If we want to make the most of it, we must figure out how best to live. That is no easy task. It requires study, reflection, and the selection of values and goals. Ideally, higher education is supposed to supply students with just that opportunity. Finally, I was beginning to understand what I could expect from university apart from job training.

The professor I met also convinced me that sociology in particular could open up a new and superior way of comprehending my world. Specifically, he said it could clarify my place in society, how I might best manoeuvre through it, and even, perhaps, how I might contribute to improving it, however modestly. Before beginning my study of sociology, I had

Life is finite, and if we want to make the most of it, we must figure out how best to live. Sociology offers a useful perspective for understanding our current predicament and seeing possible ways of dealing with it.

SOURCE: M.C. Escher's "Relativity" www.mcescher.com.

always taken for granted that things happen in the world—and to me—because physical and emotional forces cause them. Famine, I thought, is caused by drought, war by territorial greed, economic success by hard work, marriage by love, suicide by bottomless depression, rape by depraved lust. But now, this professor repeatedly threw evidence in my face that contradicted my easy formulas. If drought causes famine, why have so many famines occurred in perfectly normal weather conditions or involved some groups hoarding or destroying food so others would starve? If hard work causes prosperity, why are so many hard workers poor? If love causes marriage, why are so many families the site of violence against women and children? And so the questions multiplied.

As if it were not enough that the professor's sociological evidence upset many of my assumptions about the way the world worked, he also challenged me to understand sociology's unique way of explaining social life. He defined **sociology** as the systematic study of human behaviour in social context. He explained that *social* causes are distinct from physical and emotional causes. Understanding social causes can help clarify otherwise inexplicable features of famine, marriage, and so on. In public school, my teachers had taught me that people are free to do what they want with their lives. However, my new professor taught me that the organization of the social world opens some opportunities and closes others, thus constraining our freedom and helping to make us what we are. By examining the operation of these powerful social forces, he said, sociology can help us to know ourselves, our capabilities and limitations. I was hooked. And so, of course, I hope you will be, too.

THE GOALS OF THIS CHAPTER

In this chapter I aim to achieve three goals. First, I illustrate the power of sociology to dispel foggy assumptions and help us see the operation of the social world more clearly. To that end, I examine a phenomenon that at first glance appears to be solely the outcome of breakdowns in individual functioning: suicide. You will see that, in fact, *social relations* among people powerfully influence suicide rates. This exercise introduces you to what is unique about the sociological perspective.

Second, I show that, from its origins, sociological research has been motivated by a desire to improve the social world. Thus, sociology is not just a dry, academic exercise but a means of charting a better course for society. At the same time, however, sociologists adopt scientific methods to test their ideas, thus increasing the validity of the results. I illustrate these points by briefly analyzing the work of the founders of the discipline.

Third, I suggest that sociology can help you come to grips with your century, just as it helped the founders of sociology deal with theirs. Today we are witnessing massive and disorienting social changes. Entire countries are breaking up. Women are demanding equality with men in all spheres of life. New religions are emerging and old ones reviving. People's wants are increasingly governed by the mass media. Computers are radically altering the way people work and entertain themselves. There are proportionately fewer good jobs to go around. Environmental ruin threatens us all. As was the case a hundred years ago, sociologists today try to understand social phenomena and suggest credible ways of improving their societies. By promising to make sociology relevant to you, this chapter should be viewed as an open invitation to participate in sociology's challenge.

But first things first. Before showing how sociology can help us comprehend and better our world, let us briefly examine the problem of suicide. That will help to illustrate how the sociological perspective can clarify and sometimes overturn commonsense beliefs.

THE SOCIOLOGICAL PERSPECTIVE

By analyzing suicide sociologically, you can put to a tough test my claim that sociology gives you a unique, surprising, and enlightening perspective on social events. After all, suicide appears to be the supremely antisocial and nonsocial act. It is condemned by nearly everyone in society. It is typically committed in private, far from the public's intrusive glare. It is rare. In recent years, there have been about 13 suicides annually for every 100 000 people in Canada (Statistics Canada, 2004). Canada's suicide rate places us fortieth among the 105 countries that publish suicide statistics; see Figure 1.1. And when you think about why people commit such an act, you are likely to focus on their individual states of mind rather than on the state of society. In other words, what usually interests us are the aspects of specific individuals' lives that caused them to become depressed or angry enough to do something as awful as killing themselves. We usually do not think about the patterns

FIGURE 1.1 SUICIDE RATE BY COUNTRY, CIRCA 2011

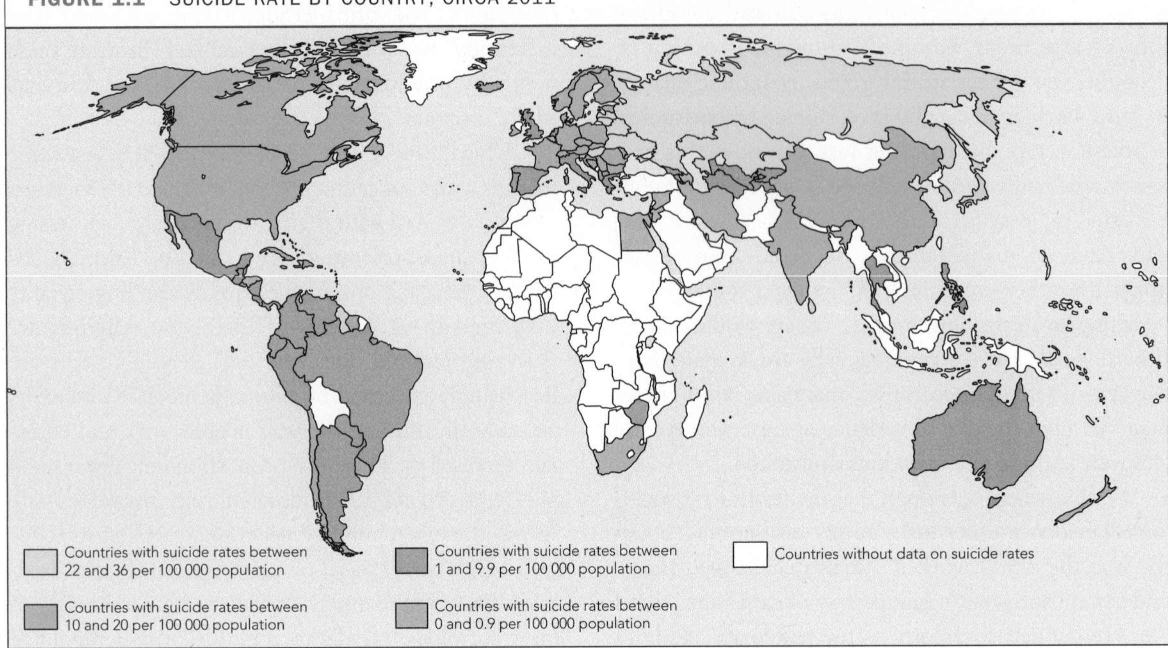

SOURCE: World Health Organization, 2011, "Suicide rates per 100,000 by country, year and sex (Table): Most recent year available; as of 2011." On the World Wide Web at http://www.who.int/mental_health/prevention/suicide_rates/en/ (retrieved 20 December 2011).

of social relations that might encourage such actions in general. If sociology can reveal the hidden social causes of such an apparently antisocial and nonsocial phenomenon, there must be something to it!

THE SOCIOLOGICAL EXPLANATION OF SUICIDE

At the end of the nineteenth century, French sociologist Émile Durkheim (1951 [1897]), one of the pioneers of the discipline, demonstrated that suicide is more than just an individual act of desperation resulting from psychological disorder, as was commonly believed at the time. Suicide rates, he showed, are strongly influenced by social forces.

Durkheim made his case by examining the association between rates of suicide and rates of psychological disorder for different groups. The idea that psychological disorder causes suicide is supported, he reasoned, only if suicide rates tend to be high where rates of psychological disorder are high, and low where rates of psychological disorder are low. However, his analysis of European government statistics, hospital records, and other sources revealed nothing of the kind. He discovered there were slightly more women than men in insane asylums. Yet there were four male suicides for every female suicide. Jews had the highest rate of psychological disorder among the major religious groups in France. However, they also had the lowest suicide rate. Psychological disorders occurred most frequently when a person reached maturity. Suicide rates, though, increased steadily with age.

Clearly, suicide rates and rates of psychological disorder did not vary proportionately. What then accounts for variations in suicide rates? Durkheim argued that suicide rates vary because of differences in the degree of **social solidarity** in different groups. According to Durkheim, the more a group's members share beliefs and values, and the more frequently and intensely they interact, the more social solidarity a group exhibits. In turn, the more social solidarity a group exhibits, the more firmly anchored individuals are to the social world, and the less likely they are to take their own lives if adversity strikes. In other words, Durkheim expected groups with a high degree of solidarity to have lower suicide rates than groups with a low degree of solidarity did—at least up to a certain point (see Figure 1.2).

To support his argument, Durkheim showed that married adults are half as likely as unmarried adults are to commit suicide. That is because marriage usually creates social ties and a sort of moral cement that bind the individual to society. Similarly, he argued that women are less likely to commit suicide than

FIGURE 1.2 DURKHEIM'S THEORY OF SUICIDE

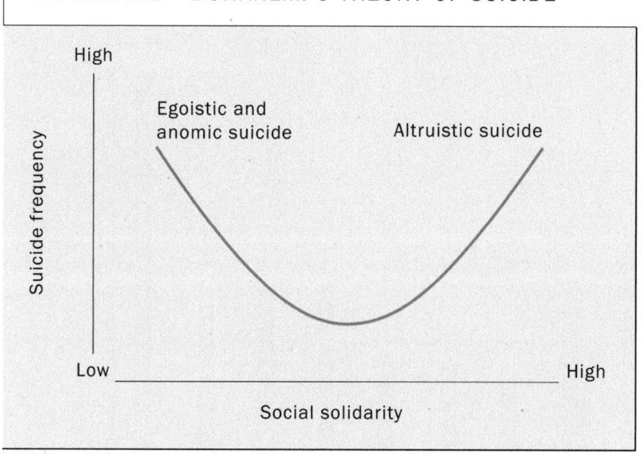

Durkheim argued that as the level of social solidarity increases, the suicide rate declines. Then, beyond a certain point, it starts to rise. Hence the U-shaped curve in this graph. Durkheim called suicides that occur in high-solidarity settings altruistic. Altruism means devotion to the interests of others. **Altruistic suicide** occurs when norms tightly govern behaviour so that individual actions are often in the group's interest. For example, when soldiers knowingly give up their lives to protect members of their unit, they commit altruistic suicide out of a deep sense of comradeship. In contrast, suicide that occurs in low-solidarity settings is egoistic or anomic, said Durkheim. **Egoistic suicide** results from a lack of integration of the individual into society because of weak social ties to others. *Anomie* means "without order." **Anomic suicide** occurs when norms governing behaviour are vaguely defined. For example, in Durkheim's view, when people live in a society that lacks a widely shared code of morality, the rate of anomic suicide is likely to be high.

men are. Why? Women are generally more involved in the intimate social relations of family life. Jews, Durkheim wrote, are less likely to commit suicide than Christians are. The reason? Centuries of persecution have turned them into a group that is more defensive and tightly knit. And seniors are more prone than the young and the middle-aged are to take their own lives in the face of misfortune. That is because they are most likely to live alone, to have lost a spouse, and to lack a job and a wide network of friends. In general, Durkheim wrote, "suicide varies with the degree of integration of the social groups of which the individual forms a part" (Durkheim, 1951 [1897]: 209). Note that his generalization tells us nothing about why any particular *individual* may take his or her life. That is a question for psychology. But it does tell us that a person's likelihood of committing suicide decreases with the degree to which he or she is anchored in society. And it says something surprising and uniquely sociological about how and why the suicide rate varies from group to group.

SUICIDE IN CANADA TODAY

Durkheim's theory is not just a historical curiosity. It sheds light on the factors that account for variations in suicide rates here and now. Consider Figure 1.3, which shows suicide rates by age and sex in Canada for 2008. Comparing rates for men and women, we immediately see that, as in Durkheim's France, men are much more likely than women are to commit suicide (3.6 times more likely, to be precise). However, looking at differences between age groups, we see a striking difference between Durkheim's France and contemporary Canada. When Durkheim wrote, youth suicide was extremely rare and suicide among working-age people was uncommon. In Canada today, suicide among people between the ages of 10 and 64 is much more common, having increased substantially since the 1960s. Suicide rates do *not* increase steadily with age in Canada today. True, the suicide rate is highest among people over the age of 89. However, it is higher for people between the ages of 40 and 59 than it is for people between the ages of 60 and 89. Moreover, the rate of suicide for people between the ages of 15 and 24, practically zero in Durkheim's France, stands at about 10 per 100 000 in Canada today.

Although the rate of suicide among young people was negligible in Durkheim's France, his theory of social solidarity helps us to understand why it has risen for this age cohort in Canada over the past half century. In brief, shared moral principles and strong social ties have eroded since the early 1960s for Canada's youth. Consider the following facts:

- Church, synagogue, mosque, and temple attendance is down, particularly for young people. Thus, more than half of Canadians attended religious services weekly in the 1960s. Today the figure is less than one-third, and it is only one-sixth for people born after 1960.
- Unemployment is up, again especially for youth. Thus, the unemployment rate was around 3 percent for most of the 1960s. It rose steadily to around 10 percent for most of the 1990s and stood at 7.4 percent in November 2011. Moreover, for Canadians between the ages of 15 and 24, the unemployment rate is about twice as high as it is for older Canadians (14.1 percent in November 2011; Statistics Canada, 2011b).
- The rate of divorce has increased sixfold since the early 1960s. Out-of-marriage births are also much more common than they used to be. As a result,

FIGURE 1.3 SUICIDE BY AGE AND SEX, CANADA, 2008

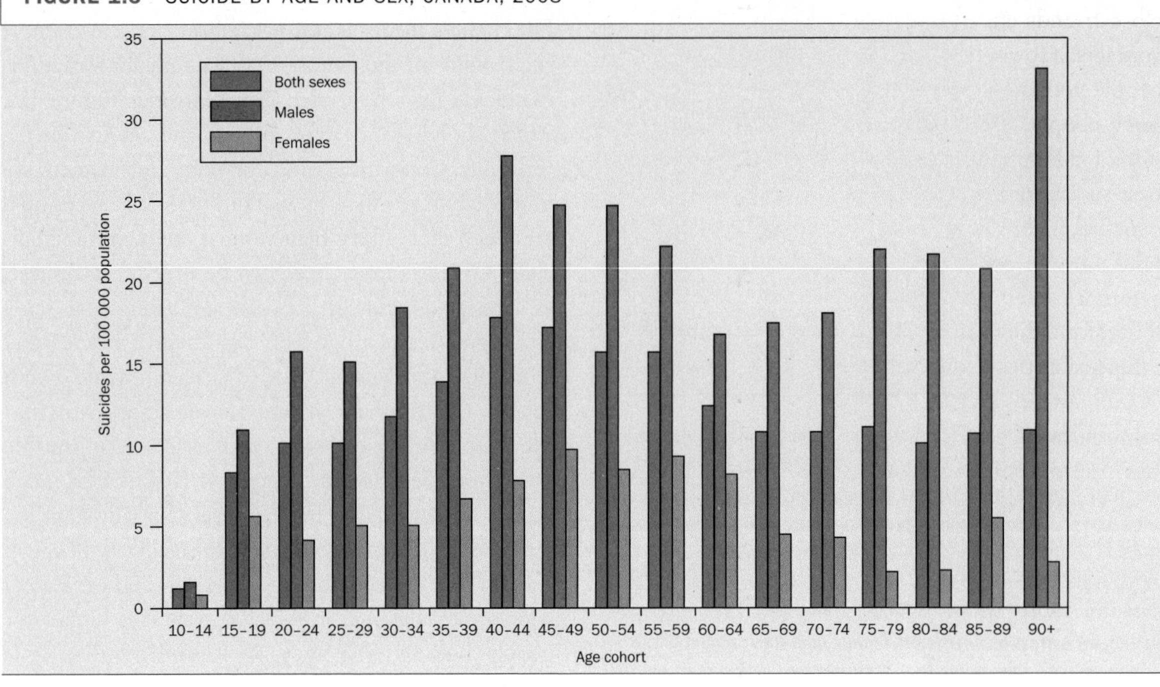

SOURCE: Statistics Canada (2011a).

children are more often brought up in single-parent families than in the past. This fact suggests that they enjoy less frequent and intimate social interaction with parents and less adult supervision.

- Since the 1960s, an increasingly large proportion of lesbians, gays, bisexuals, and transsexuals have come "out of the closet." Most Canadians accept the lifestyles of sexual minorities, but in many Canadian schools lesbians, gays, bisexuals, and transsexuals are prone to being bullied, terrorized, and socially excluded. Consequently, an alarmingly high proportion of youth suicides are committed by members of sexual minorities (Carole, 2011).

In sum, the figures cited above suggest that the level of social solidarity is now lower than it was just a few decades ago for young people. Less firmly rooted in society, and less likely to share moral standards, young people in Canada today are more likely than they were half a century ago to take their own lives if they find themselves in the midst of a personal crisis.

FROM PERSONAL TROUBLES TO SOCIAL STRUCTURES

You have known for a long time that you live in a society. Yet until now, you may not have fully appreciated that society also lives in you. That is, patterns of social relations affect your innermost thoughts and feelings, influence your actions, and thus help shape who you are. As we have seen, one such pattern of social relations is the level of social solidarity that characterizes the various groups to which you belong.

Sociologists call relatively stable patterns of social relations **social structures.** One of the sociologist's main tasks is to identify and explain the connection between people's personal troubles and the social structures in which people are embedded. This work is harder than it may at first seem. In everyday life, we usually see things mainly from our own point of view. Our experiences appear unique to each of us. If we think about them at all, social structures may appear remote and impersonal. To see how social structures operate inside us, we require sociological training.

An important step in broadening our sociological awareness involves recognizing that three levels of social structure surround and penetrate us. Think of these structures as concentric circles radiating out from you.

Microstructures are patterns of intimate social relations. They are formed during face-to-face interaction. Families, friendship circles, and work associations are all examples of microstructures.

Understanding the operation of microstructures can be useful. Let's say you are looking for a job.

You might think you would do best to ask as many close friends and relatives as possible for leads and contacts. However, sociological research shows that people you know well are likely to know many of the same people. After asking a couple of close connections for help landing a job, you would therefore do best to ask more remote acquaintances for leads and contacts. People to whom you are weakly connected (and who are weakly connected among themselves) are more likely to know *different* groups of people. Therefore, they will give you more information about job possibilities and ensure that word about your job search spreads farther. You are more likely to find a job faster if you understand "the strength of weak ties" in microstructural settings (Granovetter, 1973).

Macrostructures are patterns of social relations that lie outside and above your circle of intimates and acquaintances. Macrostructures include class relations and **patriarchy,** the traditional system of economic and political inequality between women and men in most societies. Understanding the operation of macrostructures can also be useful. Consider, for example, one aspect of patriarchy. Most married women who work full-time in the paid labour force do more housework, child care, and eldercare than their husbands do. Governments and businesses support this arrangement insofar as they give little assistance to families in the form of nurseries, after-school programs for children, senior homes, and so on. Yet the unequal division of work in the household is a major source of dissatisfaction with marriage, especially in families that cannot afford to buy these services privately. Thus, sociological research shows that when spouses share domestic responsibilities equally, they are happier with their marriages and less likely to divorce (Hochschild with Machung, 1989). When a marriage is in danger of dissolving, it is common for partners to blame themselves and each other for their troubles. However, it should now be clear that forces other than incompatible personalities often put stresses on families. Understanding how the macrostructure of patriarchy crops up in everyday life, and doing something to change that structure, can thus help people lead happier lives.

The third level of society that surrounds and permeates us comprises **global structures.** International organizations, patterns of worldwide travel and communication, and the economic relations between countries are examples of global structures. Global structures are increasingly important as inexpensive travel and communication allow all parts of the world to become interconnected culturally, economically, and politically.

Understanding the operation of global structures can be useful, too. For instance, many people are concerned about the world's poor. They donate money to charities to help with famine and disaster relief. Some people also approve of the Canadian government giving foreign aid to poor countries. However, many of these same people do not appreciate that charity and foreign aid alone do not seem able to end world poverty. That is because charity and foreign aid have been unable to overcome the structure of social relations among countries that have created, and now sustain, global inequality.

As we will see in Chapter 9, Development and Underdevelopment, Britain, France, and other imperial powers locked some countries into poverty when they colonized them between the seventeenth and nineteenth centuries. In the twentieth century, the poor (or "developing") countries borrowed money from these same rich countries and Western banks to pay for airports, roads, harbours, sanitation systems, basic healthcare, and so on. Today, poor countries pay far more to rich countries and Western banks in interest on those loans than they receive in aid and charity. Foreign aid equals about one-tenth of interest payments (Jubilee Debt Campaign, 2010: 6; Organisation for Economic Co-operation and Development, 2008: 6). It thus seems that relying exclusively on foreign aid and charity can do little to help solve the problem of world poverty. Understanding how the global structure of international relations created and helps maintain global inequality suggests new policy priorities for helping the world's poor. One such priority might involve campaigning for the cancellation of foreign debt in compensation for past injustices. Some government officials in Canada and other countries have been promoting this policy for the past decade.

As these examples illustrate, personal problems are connected to social structures at the microlevel, macrolevel, and global level. Whether the personal problem involves finding a job, keeping a marriage intact, or figuring out a way to act justly to end world poverty, social-structural considerations broaden our understanding of the problem and suggest appropriate courses of action.

THE SOCIOLOGICAL IMAGINATION

In the 1950s, the great American sociologist C. Wright Mills (1959) called the ability to see the connection between personal troubles and social structures the **sociological imagination.** He emphasized the difficulty of developing this quality of mind. His language is sexist by today's standards, but his argument is as true and inspiring today as it was in the 1950s:

> When a society becomes industrialized, a peasant becomes a worker; a feudal lord is liquidated or becomes a businessman. When classes rise or fall, a man is employed or unemployed; when the rate of investment goes up or down, a man takes new heart or goes broke. When war happens, an insurance salesman becomes a rocket launcher; a store clerk, a radar man; a wife lives alone; a child grows up without a father. Neither the life of an individual nor the history of a society can be understood without understanding both.
>
> Yet men do not usually define the troubles they endure in terms of historical change. ... The well-being they enjoy, they do not usually impute to the big ups and downs of the society in which they live. Seldom aware of the intricate connection between the patterns of their own lives and the course of world history, ordinary men do not usually know what this connection means for the kind of men they are becoming and for the kind of history-making in which they might take part. They do not possess the quality of mind essential to grasp the interplay of men and society, of biography and history, of self and world. They cannot cope with their personal troubles in such a way as to control the structural transformations that usually lie behind them.
>
> What they need ... is a quality of mind that will help them to [see] ... what is going on in the world and ... what may be happening within themselves. It is this quality ... that ... may be called the sociological imagination. (Mills, 1959: 3–4)

The sociological imagination is a recent addition to the human repertoire. It is only about two centuries old. True, in ancient and medieval times, some philosophers wrote about society. However, their thinking was not sociological. They believed God and nature controlled society. They spent much of their time sketching blueprints for the ideal society and urging people to follow those blueprints. They relied on speculation rather than on evidence to reach conclusions about how society works.

The sociological imagination was born when three modern revolutions pushed people to think about society in an entirely new way. First, the **Scientific Revolution** began about 1550. It encouraged the view that sound conclusions about the workings of society must be based on solid evidence, not just on speculation. Second, the **Democratic Revolution** began about 1750. It suggested that people are responsible for organizing society and that human intervention can therefore solve social problems. Third, the **Industrial Revolution** began about 1780. It created a host of new and serious social problems that attracted the attention of many social thinkers. Let us briefly consider these three sources of the sociological imagination.

ORIGINS OF THE SOCIOLOGICAL IMAGINATION

The Scientific Revolution

It is said that a group of medieval monks once wanted to know how many angels could dance on the head of a pin. They consulted ancient books in Hebrew, Greek, and Latin. They thought long and hard. They employed all their intellectual skills to debate the issue. They did not, however, resolve the dispute because they never considered inspecting the head of a pin and counting. Any such suggestion would have been considered heresy. We, in contrast, would call it the beginning of a scientific approach to the subject.

People often link the Scientific Revolution to specific ideas, such as Copernicus's theory that Earth revolves around the Sun and Newton's laws of motion. However, science is less a collection of ideas than a method of inquiry. For instance, in 1609, Galileo pointed his newly invented telescope at the heavens, made some careful observations, and showed that his observations fit Copernicus's theory. This is the core of the scientific method: using evidence to make a case for a particular point of view. By the mid-seventeenth century, some philosophers, such as Descartes in France and Hobbes in England, were calling for a science of society. When sociology emerged as a distinct discipline in the nineteenth century, commitment to the scientific method was one firm pillar of the sociological imagination.

The Democratic Revolution

The second pillar of the sociological imagination is the realization that people control society and can change it. Four hundred years ago, most Europeans thought otherwise. For them, God ordained the social order.

Consider the English engraving reproduced in Figure 1.4. It shows how most educated Europeans pictured the universe in Shakespeare's time. Note the cloud at the top of the circle. The Hebrew name of God is inscribed on it. God's hand extends from the cloud. It holds a chain, which is attached to a woman representing Nature. Nature also holds a chain in her hand. It is connected to "the ape of Nature," representing humankind. The symbolism is clear: God and his intermediary, Nature, control human action. Note also that the engraving arranges everything in a linked hierarchy. The hierarchy includes the mineral, vegetable, and animal kingdoms; the elements; heavenly objects; angels; and so on. Each level of the hierarchy corresponds to and controls some aspect of the level below it. For example, people believed Archangels regulated the movements of the planet Mercury and the movements of Mercury affected human commerce. Similarly, in the medieval view, God ordained a hierarchy of people. The richest people were seen as the closest to God and therefore deserving of great privilege. Supposedly, kings and queens ruled because God wanted them to (Tillyard, 1943).

The American Revolution (1775–83) and the French Revolution (1789–99) helped to undermine these ideas. These democratic political upheavals showed that society could experience massive change in a short period. They proved that people could replace unsatisfactory rulers. And they suggested that *people* control society. The implications for social thought were profound, for if it was possible to change society by human intervention, then a science of society could play a big role. The new science could help people figure out ways of overcoming various

FIGURE 1.4 THE ELIZABETHAN WORLDVIEW

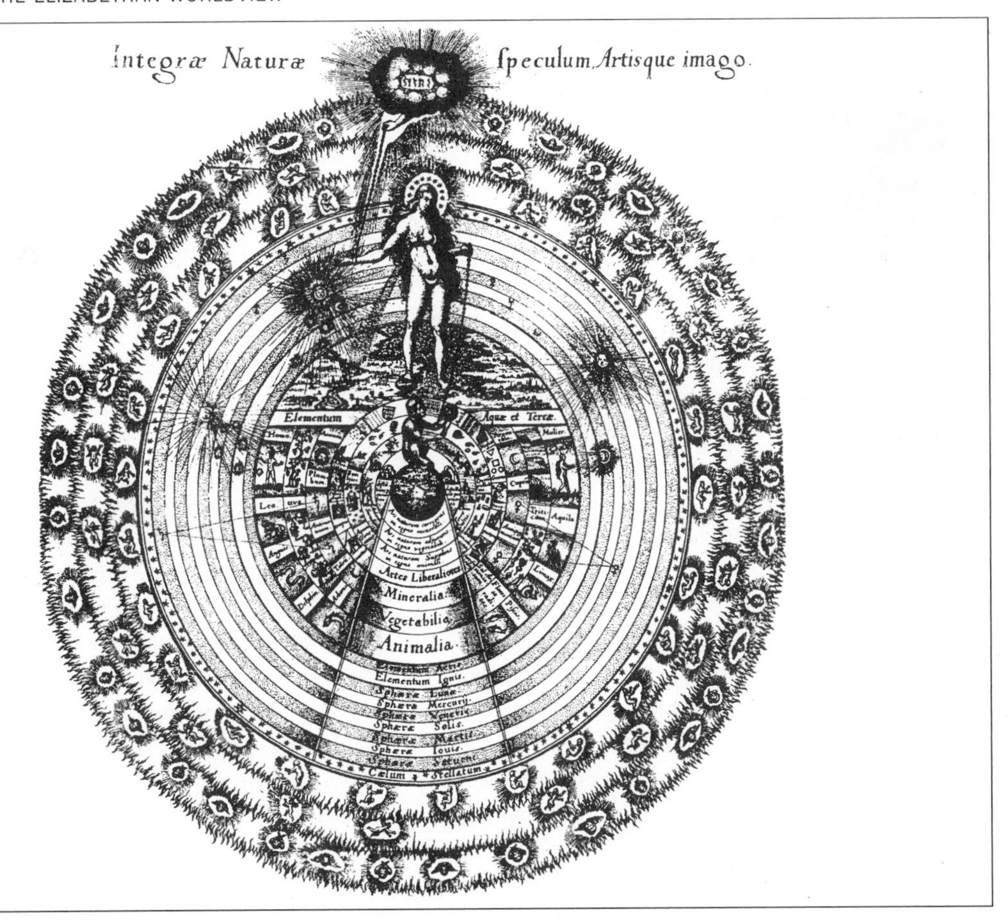

SOURCE: From Robert Fludd's *Utriusque* Cosmi *Historia* (1617–19). Photograph courtesy of Houghton Library, Harvard College Library.

social problems, improving the welfare of all citizens, and finding the most effective way to reach given goals. Much of the justification for sociology as a science arose out of the democratic revolutions that shook Europe and North America.

The Industrial Revolution

The third pillar of the sociological imagination was the Industrial Revolution. It began in England about 1780. Because of the growth of industry, masses of people moved from countryside to city, worked agonizingly long hours in crowded and dangerous mines and factories, lost faith in their religions, confronted faceless bureaucracies, and reacted to the filth and poverty of their existence by means of strikes, crime, revolution, and war. Scholars had never seen a sociological laboratory like this. The Scientific Revolution suggested that a science of society is possible. The Democratic Revolution suggested that people can intervene to improve society. The Industrial Revolution now presented social thinkers with a host of pressing social problems crying out for solutions. They responded by giving birth to the sociological imagination.

SOCIOLOGICAL THEORIES

THE ORIGINS OF SOCIOLOGY

The term *sociology* was coined by the French social thinker Auguste Comte in 1838 (Thompson, 1975). Comte tried to place the study of society on scientific foundations. He wanted to understand the social world as it is, not as he or anyone else imagined it should be. This was a highly original approach to the study of society. In ancient and medieval times, philosophers from diverse civilizations had sketched blueprints for the ideal society. We see evidence of this approach in the work of Confucius in China, Ibn Khaldun in Tunisia, and Plato and Aristotle in Greece. But Comte was swept up in the scientific revolution of his time. He was inspired by the astronomers and physicists of the modern era—Copernicus in Poland, Galileo in Italy, Newton in England. He wanted to test the validity of his ideas through careful observation of the real world rather than assuming that "God" or "human nature" determined the shape of society (see Box 1.1).

Despite Comte's breakthrough, there was a tension in his work, for although he was eager to adopt the scientific method in his study of society, he was a conservative thinker, motivated by strong opposition to rapid change in French society. His was a time not only of scientific but also of political and social revolution. Comte witnessed the democratic forces unleashed by the French Revolution, the early industrialization of society, and the rapid growth of cities. What he saw shocked and angered him because rapid social change was destroying many of the things he valued, especially respect for authority. He therefore urged slow change and the preservation of much that was traditional in social life. Thus, at its very origin, sociological research was motivated by adherence to scientific methods of research *and* a vision of the ideal society.

The same sort of tension is evident in the work of the most important early figures in the history of sociology: Karl Marx, Émile Durkheim, and Max Weber. These three men lived in the period from 1820 to 1920. They witnessed various phases of Europe's wrenching transition to industrial capitalism, and they wanted to understand and explain it. Like Comte, they were all committed to the scientific method of research. However, they also wanted to chart a better course for their societies. The ideas they developed are therefore not just diagnostic tools from which we can still learn much, but also, like many sociological ideas, prescriptions for combating social ills.

THEORY, RESEARCH, AND VALUES

To clarify the tension in sociology between analysis and ideal, diagnosis and prescription, we can usefully distinguish three terms: theory, research, and values.

Sociological ideas are generally stated in the form of theories. A **theory** is a tentative explanation of some aspect of social life. It states how and why certain facts are related. For example, in his theory of suicide, Durkheim showed how facts about suicide rates are related to facts about social solidarity. This enabled him to explain suicide as a function of social solidarity. In this broad definition, even a hunch qualifies as a theory if it suggests how and why certain facts are related.

After theories are formulated, the sociologist can conduct research. **Research** is the process of carefully observing social reality to assess the validity of a theory. It is because research can call the validity of a theory into question that theories are said to be only "tentative" explanations. The research process is discussed in detail in Chapter 20, Research Methods.

Before sociologists can formulate a theory, however, they must decide which problems are important

BOX 1.1 SCIENTIFIC VERSUS COMMONSENSE KNOWLEDGE

To better understand how scientific and non-scientific knowledge differ, consider the following statements, each of which represents a commonly accepted basis for knowing that something is "true" in our everyday lives:

1. "The proper place for women is in the home. That's the way it's always been." This statement represents knowledge based on tradition. Although some traditional knowledge is valid (sugar will rot your teeth), some is not (masturbation will not blind you). Science is required to sort out valid from invalid knowledge.
2. "Apparently, weak magnets can be used to heal many illnesses. I read all about it in the newspaper." This statement represents knowledge based on authority. We often think something is true because we read it in an authoritative source or hear it from an expert. But authoritative sources and experts can be wrong. For example, nineteenth-century Western physicians commonly "bled" their patients with leeches to draw "poisons" from their bodies, often doing more harm than good. As this example suggests, scientists should always question authority to arrive at more valid knowledge.
3. "I was driving my bike last night when I saw the car accident. The car that caused it was dark brown." This statement represents knowledge based on casual observation. However, we are usually pretty careless observers. That is why good lawyers can often trip up eyewitnesses in courtrooms; eyewitnesses are rarely certain about what they saw. In general, uncertainty can be reduced by observing in a conscious and deliberate manner and by recording observations. That is just what scientists do.
4. "If you work hard, you can get ahead. I know because several of my parents' friends started off poor but are now comfortably middle class." This statement represents knowledge based on over-generalization. For instance, if you know a few people who started off poor, worked hard, and became rich, you may think any poor person can become rich if he or she works hard enough. You may not know about the more numerous poor people who work hard and remain poor. Scientists, however, sample cases that are representative of entire populations. This enables them to avoid overgeneralization. They also avoid overgeneralization by repeating research. This ensures that research findings are not idiosyncratic.
5. "I'm right because I can't think of any contrary cases." This statement represents knowledge based on selective observation. Sometimes we ignore evidence that challenges our firmly held beliefs. Thus, you may know people who work hard but remain poor. To maintain your belief that hard work results in wealth, you will have to ignore those cases. The scientific requirement that evidence be drawn from representative samples of the population minimizes bias arising from selective observation.
6. "Mr. Smith is poor even though he works hard but that's because he has a disability. People with disabilities are the only exception to the rule that if you work hard you can get ahead." This statement represents knowledge based on qualification. Qualifications or "exceptions to the rule" are often made in everyday life—and they are in science, too. The difference is that in everyday life, qualifications are easily accepted as valid, whereas in scientific inquiry, they are typically treated as hypotheses that must be tested as rigorously as the original hypothesis.
7. "The Toronto Blue Jays won 50 percent of their baseball games last month but 80 percent of the games they played on Thursdays. Because it happened so often before, I bet they'll win next Thursday." This statement represents knowledge based on illogical reasoning. In everyday life, we may expect the recurrence of events without reasonable cause, ignoring the fact that rare sequences of events often occur just by chance. For example, it is possible to flip a coin 10 times and have it come up heads each time. On average, this will happen once every 1024 times you flip a coin 10 times. In the absence of any apparent reason for this happening, it is merely coincidental. It is illogical to believe otherwise. Scientists refrain from such illogical reasoning. They also use statistical techniques to distinguish between events that are probably due to chance and those that are not.
8. "I just can't be wrong." This statement represents knowledge based on ego-defence. Even scientists may be passionately committed to the conclusions they reach in their research because they have invested much time and energy in them. It is other scientists—more accurately, the whole institution of science, with its commitment to publishing research results and critically scrutinizing findings—that strictly limits ego-defence in scientific understanding.

(*continued*)

BOX 1.1 ***(continued)***

9. "The matter is settled once and for all." This statement represents knowledge based on the premature closure of inquiry. It involves deciding that all the relevant evidence has been gathered on a particular subject. Science, however, is committed to the idea that all theories are only temporarily true. Matters are never settled.

10. "There must be supernatural forces at work here." This statement represents knowledge based on mystification. When we can find no rational explanation for a phenomenon, we may attribute it to forces that cannot be observed or fully understood. Although such forces may exist, scientists remain skeptical. They are committed to discovering real, observable causes of real, observable effects.

SOURCE: From Babbie, *Practice of Social Research*, 6E. © 1992 Cengage Learning.

enough to study and how the parts of society fit together. If they are going to recommend ways of improving the operation of some aspect of society, they must even have an opinion about what the ideal society ought to look like. As we will soon see, these issues are shaped in large measure by sociologists' values. **Values** are ideas about what is right and wrong, good and bad. Inevitably, values help sociologists formulate and favour certain theories over others (Edel, 1965; Kuhn, 1970). So sociological theories may be modified and even rejected because of research, but they are often motivated by sociologists' values.

Durkheim, Marx, and Weber initiated three of the major theoretical traditions in sociology: functionalism, conflict theory, and symbolic interactionism. A fourth approach, feminism, has arisen in recent decades

Before delving into social research, a sociologist must first develop hypotheses—testable claims about the social world. Testing hypotheses by means of research helps determine the validity of theories.
SOURCE: © Davidian/iStockphoto.com.

to correct some of the deficiencies of the three long-established traditions. It will become clear as you read this book that there are many more sociological theories than just these four. However, because these four traditions have been especially influential in the development of sociology, you will find it useful to read a thumbnail sketch of each one here at the beginning.[1]

FUNCTIONALISM

Durkheim's theory of suicide is an early example of what sociologists now call **functionalist theory.** Functionalist theories incorporate four features:

1. They stress that human behaviour is governed by relatively stable patterns of social relations, or social structures. For example, Durkheim emphasized how suicide rates are influenced by patterns of social solidarity. Usually the social structures analyzed by functionalists are macrostructures.
2. Functionalism underlines how social structures maintain or undermine social stability. Typically, Durkheim analyzed how the growth of industries and cities in nineteenth-century Europe lowered the level of social solidarity and contributed to social instability. One aspect of instability, said Durkheim, is a higher suicide rate. Another is frequent strikes by workers.
3. Functionalist theories emphasize that social structures are based mainly on shared values. Thus, when Durkheim wrote about social solidarity, he sometimes meant the frequency and intensity of social interaction, but more often he thought of social solidarity as a sort of moral cement that binds people together.
4. Functionalism suggests that re-establishing equilibrium can best solve most social problems. Thus, Durkheim said that social stability could be restored in late-nineteenth-century Europe by creating new associations of employers and workers that would lower workers' expectations about what they could expect out of life. If, said Durkheim, more people could agree on wanting less, social solidarity would rise and there would be fewer strikes, fewer suicides, and so on. Functionalism, then, was a conservative response to widespread social unrest in nineteenth century France. (A more radical response would have been to argue that if people are expressing discontent because they are getting less out of life than they expect, discontent can be lowered by figuring out ways for them to get more out of life.)

Although functionalist thinking influenced North American sociology at the end of the nineteenth century, it was only during the continent's greatest economic crisis ever, the Great Depression of 1929–39, that functionalism took deep root here (Russett, 1966). With 30 percent of the paid labour force unemployed and labour unrest reaching unprecedented levels, it is not surprising that sociologists with a conservative frame of mind were attracted to a theory that focused on how social equilibrium could be restored. Functionalist theory remained popular in North America for 30 years. It experienced a minor revival in the early 1990s but never regained the dominance it enjoyed from the 1930s to the early 1960s.

Sociologist Talcott Parsons was the foremost proponent of functionalism. He is best known for identifying how various institutions must work to ensure the smooth operation of society as a whole. For instance, when the family successfully raises new generations, the military successfully defends society against external threats, schools are able to teach students the skills and values they need to function as productive adults, and religions create a shared moral code among people, then, said Parsons, society is well integrated and in equilibrium (Parsons, 1951).

Parsons was criticized for exaggerating the degree to which members of society share common values and social institutions contribute to social harmony. This led North America's other leading functionalist, Robert Merton, to propose that social structures may have different consequences for different categories of people. Merton noted that some of those consequences might be disruptive or **dysfunctional** (Merton, 1968 [1949]). Moreover, said Merton, although some functions are **manifest** (visible and intended), others are **latent** (invisible and unintended). For instance, a manifest function of schools is to transmit skills from one generation to the next. A latent function of schools is to encourage the development of a separate youth culture that often conflicts with parents' values (Coleman, 1961; Hersch, 1998).

CONFLICT THEORY

The second major theoretical tradition in sociology emphasizes the centrality of conflict in social life. **Conflict theory** incorporates these four features:

1. It generally focuses on large, macrolevel structures, such as relations between or among classes.
2. Conflict theory shows how major patterns of inequality in society produce social stability

in some circumstances and social change in others.

3. Conflict theory stresses how members of privileged groups try to maintain their advantages while subordinate groups struggle to increase theirs. From this point of view, social conditions at a given time are the expression of an ongoing power struggle between privileged and subordinate groups.
4. Conflict theory typically leads to the suggestion that decreasing privilege will lower the level of conflict and increase the sum total of human welfare.

The conflict paradigm originated in the work of Karl Marx. A generation before Durkheim, Marx observed the destitution and discontent produced by the Industrial Revolution and proposed a sweeping argument about the way societies develop (Marx, 1904 [1859]; Marx and Engels, 1972 [1848]). Marx's theory was radically different from Durkheim's. Class conflict lies at the centre of his ideas.

Marx argued that owners of industry are eager to improve the way work is organized and to adopt new tools, machines, and production methods. These innovations allow them to produce more efficiently, earn higher profits, and drive inefficient competitors out of business. However, according to Marx, the drive for profits causes capitalists to concentrate workers in larger and larger establishments, keep wages as low as possible, and invest as little as possible in improving working conditions. Thus, in factories and in mines, a large and growing class of poor workers comes to oppose a small and shrinking class of wealthy owners.

Marx believed that workers would ultimately become aware of belonging to the same exploited class. Their sense of "class consciousness," he wrote, would encourage the growth of trade unions and labour parties. These organizations would eventually seek to put an end to private ownership of property, replacing it with a system in which everyone shared property and wealth. This was the "communist" society envisaged by Marx—a society in which there is no private property and everyone shares wealth in proportion to their need.

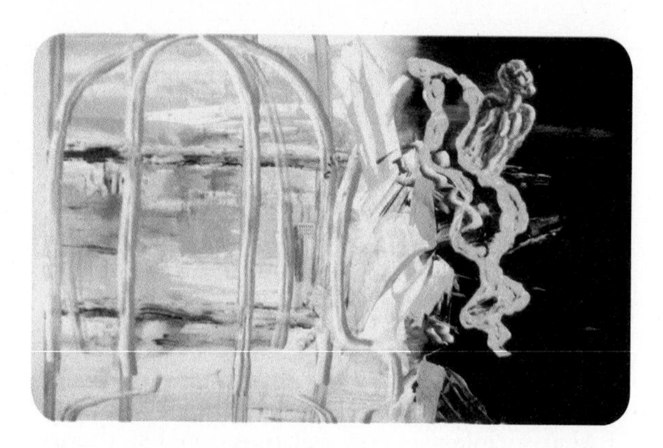

Max Weber wrote that the modern era is a bureaucratically organized "iron cage." Sociology promises to teach us both the dimensions of that cage and the possibilities for release.

SOURCE: Carol Wainio, *Untitled* (1985). Acrylic on canvas, 33" × 350". Photograph courtesy of the S.L. Simpson Gallery, Toronto. Courtesy Carol Wainio.

Weber

Although some of Marx's ideas have been usefully adapted to the study of contemporary society, his predictions about the inevitable collapse of capitalism have been questioned. Max Weber, a German sociologist who wrote his major works a generation after Marx, was among the first to find flaws in Marx's argument (Weber, 1946). Weber noted the rapid growth of the "service" sector of the economy with its many nonmanual workers and professionals. He argued that many members of these occupational groups stabilize society because they enjoy higher status and income than do manual workers employed in the manufacturing sector. In addition, Weber showed that class conflict is not the only driving force of history. In his view, politics and religion are also important sources of historical change (see the next section). Other writers pointed out that Marx did not understand how investing in technology would make it possible for workers to toil fewer hours under less oppressive conditions. Nor did he foresee that higher wages, better working conditions, and government benefits, such as employment insurance and medicare, would pacify manual workers. Thus, we see that many of the particulars of Marx's theory were called into question by Weber and other sociologists. Nonetheless, Marx's insights about the fundamental importance of conflict in social life were influential—and still are today.

SYMBOLIC INTERACTIONISM

Above we noted that Weber criticized Marx's interpretation of the development of capitalism. Among other things, Weber argued that early capitalist development was caused not just by favourable *economic* circumstances. In addition, he said, certain *religious* beliefs facilitated robust capitalist growth. In particular, sixteenth- and seventeenth-century Protestants believed their religious doubts could be reduced, and a state of grace ensured, if they worked diligently and lived modestly. Weber called this belief the **Protestant ethic.** He believed it had an unintended effect: People who adhered to the Protestant ethic saved and invested more than others did. Thus, according to Weber, capitalism developed most robustly where the Protestant ethic took hold. He concluded that capitalism did not develop because of the operation of economic forces alone, as Marx argued. Instead, it depended partly on the religious meaning individuals attached to their work (Weber, 1958 [1904–05]).

In much of his research, Weber emphasized the importance of empathetically understanding people's motives and the meanings they attach to things to gain a clear sense of the significance of their actions. He called this aspect of his approach to sociological research the method of *Verstehen* (pronounced Fer-SHTAY-en, meaning "understanding" in German).

The idea that subjective meanings must be analyzed in any complete sociological analysis was only one of Weber's contributions to early sociological theory. Weber was also an important conflict theorist, as you will learn in later chapters. At present, however, it is enough to note that his emphasis on subjective meanings found rich soil in North America, for here was an idea that resonated deeply with the individualism of North American culture. A century ago, it was widely believed that individual talent and initiative could achieve just about anything on this continent of opportunity. Small wonder, then, that much of early North American sociology focused on the individual or, more precisely, on the connection between the individual and the larger society. For example, George Herbert Mead at the University of Chicago was the driving force behind the study of how individual identity is formed in the course of interaction with other people. We discuss his contribution in Chapter 3, Socialization. Here we note only that the work of Mead and his colleagues gave birth to symbolic interactionism, a distinctively North American theoretical tradition that continues to be a major force in sociology today.

Functionalists and conflict theorists assume that people's group memberships—whether they are young or old, male or female, rich or poor—shape their behaviour. This can sometimes make people seem like balls on a pool table: They get knocked around and cannot determine their destinations. We know from our everyday experience, however, that people are not like that. You often make choices, sometimes difficult ones. You sometimes change your mind. Moreover, two people with similar social characteristics may react differently to similar social circumstances because they may interpret those circumstances differently.

Recognizing these issues, some sociologists focus on the subjective side of social life. They work in the symbolic interactionist tradition. **Symbolic interactionism** incorporates these four features:

1. It focuses on face-to-face communication or interaction in microlevel social settings. This feature distinguishes it from both the functionalist and the conflict paradigms.
2. Symbolic interactionism emphasizes that an adequate explanation of social behaviour requires understanding the subjective meanings people attach to their social circumstances.
3. Symbolic interactionism stresses that people help to create their social circumstances and do not merely react to them.[2]
4. By underscoring the subjective meanings people create in small social settings, symbolic interactionists validate unpopular and unofficial viewpoints, thus increasing our understanding and tolerance of people who may be different from us.

To understand symbolic interactionism better, let us return briefly to the problem of suicide. If a police officer discovers a dead person at the wheel of a car that has run into a tree, it may be difficult to establish with certainty whether the death was an accident or a suicide. Interviewing friends and relatives to discover the driver's state of mind just before the crash may help to rule out the possibility of suicide. But, as this example illustrates, understanding the intention or motive of the actor is critical to understanding the meaning of a social action and explaining it. Suicide, then, is not just an objective social fact but also an inferred, and therefore subjective, social fact. A state of mind must be interpreted, usually by a coroner, before the dead body becomes a suicide statistic (Douglas, 1967).

For surviving family and friends, suicide is always painful and sometimes embarrassing. Insurance companies often deny payments to beneficiaries in the case of suicide. As a result, coroners are inclined to classify deaths as accidental whenever such an interpretation is plausible. Being human, they want to minimize the family's pain after such a horrible event. Sociologists believe that, for this reason, official suicide rates are about one-third lower than actual suicide rates.

The study of the subjective side of social life reveals many such inconsistencies, helping us to go beyond the official picture, deepening our understanding of how society works, and supplementing the insights gained from macrolevel analysis. Moreover, by stressing the importance and validity of subjective meanings, symbolic interactionists also increase respect for and tolerance of minority and deviant viewpoints.

FEMINIST THEORY

Few women figured prominently in the early history of sociology, largely because the strict demands placed on women by the nineteenth-century household and the lack of opportunity outside the household prevented most of them from obtaining a higher education and finding work that could support sociological research. Not surprisingly, therefore, the women who did make their mark on the discipline in its early years had unusual social backgrounds. These exceptional people introduced into the discipline gender issues that were largely ignored by Marx, Durkheim, and Weber. Appreciation for the sociological contribution of these pioneer women has grown in recent years as concern with gender issues has come to form a substantial part of the modern sociological enterprise.

Harriet Martineau is often called the first woman sociologist. Born in England at the beginning of the nineteenth century to a prosperous family, she never married and was able to support herself comfortably from her journalistic writings. Martineau translated Comte into English. She undertook critical studies of slavery and factory laws. She also wrote about gender inequality and was a leading advocate of voting rights and higher education for women, as well as gender equality in the family. As such, Martineau was one of the first feminists (Yates, 1985).

Despite its auspicious beginnings, feminist thinking had little impact on sociology until the mid-1960s, when the rise of the modern women's movement drew attention to the many remaining inequalities between women and men. Since then, feminist theory has had such a big influence on sociology that it may now fairly be regarded as sociology's fourth major tradition. There are several variants of modern feminism (see Chapter 7, Gender Inequality: Economic and Political Aspects). However, the various strands of **feminist theory** share the following four features:

1. Feminist theory focuses on various aspects of patriarchy, the system of male domination in society. Patriarchy, feminists contend, is at least as important as class inequality in determining a person's opportunities in life, and perhaps more so.
2. The feminist paradigm holds that male domination and female subordination are determined not by biological necessity but by structures of power and social convention. From their point of view, women are subordinate to men only because men enjoy more legal, economic, political, and cultural rights.
3. The feminist paradigm examines the operation of patriarchy in both micro and macro settings.
4. The feminist paradigm contends that existing patterns of gender inequality can and should be changed for the benefit of all members of society. The main sources of gender inequality include differences in the way boys and girls are brought up; barriers to equal opportunity in education, paid work, and politics; and the unequal division of domestic responsibilities between women and men.

The theoretical traditions outlined above are summarized in Table 1.1. As you will see in the following pages, sociologists in Canada and elsewhere have applied them to all branches of the discipline (see Box 1.2). They have elaborated and refined each of them. Some sociologists work exclusively within one tradition. Others conduct research that borrows from more than one tradition. However, all sociologists are deeply indebted to the founders of the discipline.

THEIR REVOLUTION AND OURS

In the nineteenth century, the founders of the discipline devoted their lives to solving the great sociological puzzle of their time: the causes and consequences of the Industrial Revolution. However, the ideas that stirred them did not spring fully grown from their minds. Rather, their social experiences helped to shape their ideas. There is an important lesson to be learned here. In general, sociological ideas are influenced by the social settings in which they emerge.

This lesson immediately suggests two important questions. First, what are the great sociological puzzles of *our* time? Second, how are today's sociologists responding to the challenges presented by the social settings in which *they* live? We devote the rest of the book to answering these questions in depth. In the remainder of this chapter, we offer an outline of what you can expect to learn. To provide a context for this outline, we first say a few words about how the Industrial Revolution of the nineteenth century was transformed into the Postindustrial Revolution of our day.

TABLE 1.1 THE MAIN THEORETICAL TRADITIONS IN SOCIOLOGY

PARADIGM	MAIN LEVEL OF ANALYSIS	MAIN FOCUS	MAIN QUESTION	IMAGE OF IDEAL SOCIETY
Functionalism	Macro	Values	How do the institutions of society contribute to value consensus and, thus, to social stability?	A state of equilibrium
Conflict theory	Macro	Class inequality	How do privileged groups seek to maintain their advantages and subordinate groups seek to increase theirs, often causing social change in the process?	The reduction of privilege, especially class privilege
Symbolic interactionism	Micro	Meaning	How do individuals communicate so as to make their social settings meaningful?	Respect for the validity of minority views
Feminism	Micro and macro	Patriarchy	Which social structures and interaction processes maintain male dominance and female subordination?	The reduction of gender inequality

THE INDUSTRIAL REVOLUTION

The Industrial Revolution involved the application of science and technology to industrial processes, the construction of factories, and the formation of a large class of "blue-collar" workers. Within about a century, it took root throughout Western Europe, North America, and Japan. A century after that, industry had begun implanting itself in most of the rest of the world.

As noted in our discussion of Marx, the industrial working class protested long workdays, low pay, and dangerous working conditions. Workers went on strike, formed unions, and joined political parties. Their protests forced governments to tax citizens to provide at least minimal protection against ill health, unemployment, and poverty. Working-class protests also forced employers to limit the length of the workweek to 40 hours, improve working conditions, and raise wages. Employers were still able to increase their profits, however, by making the organization of work more efficient and introducing new technologies.

Collecting taxes, administering social services, providing healthcare, and investing heavily in technological innovation required the growth of government and business offices, hospitals, schools, universities, and research laboratories. Thus, alongside the old manufacturing sector of the economy, the new "service" sector was born. Its employees came to be known as "white-collar" workers. Highly trained professionals stood at the peak of the service sector. Secretaries and clerks were positioned near its base. By 1980, more than half of all people working in Canada's paid labour force were in nonmanual occupations (Ornstein, 1983: 252). Sociologists call this most recent transformation of human society the **Postindustrial Revolution.** Specifically, the Postindustrial Revolution refers to the technology-driven shift from manufacturing to service industries and the consequences of that shift for virtually all human activities (Bell, 1976; Toffler, 1990).

Especially since the early 1980s, the Postindustrial Revolution has been sped up by **globalization**—the process by which formerly separate economies, states, and cultures become tied together and people become increasingly aware of their growing interdependence (Giddens, 1990: 64; Guillén, 2001). In recent decades, rapid increases in the volume of international trade, travel, and communication have broken down the isolation and independence of most countries and people. Also contributing to globalization is the growth of many institutions that bind corporations, companies, and cultures together. These processes have caused people to depend more than ever on people in other countries for products, services, ideas, and even a sense of identity.

BOX 1.2 **THE FOUR PARADIGMS IN CANADA**

Each of the four major sociological paradigms has influenced research in Canada. This is evident from the following portraits of some of Canada's leading sociologists.

SOURCE: Photo courtesy of Ed Clark.

S. D. Clark (1910–2003) received his Ph.D. from the University of Toronto. He became the first chair of the Department of Sociology at that institution. Born in Lloydminster, Alberta, he is especially well known for his studies of Canadian social development as a process of disorganization and reorganization on a series of economic frontiers (Clark, 1968). The influence of functionalism on his work is apparent in his emphasis on the way society reestablishes equilibrium after experiencing disruptions caused by economic change.

SOURCE: Reprinted with permission from Carleton University Archives.

John Porter (1921–79) was Canada's premier sociologist in the 1960s and 1970s. Born in Vancouver, he received his Ph.D. from the London School of Economics. He spent his academic career at Carleton University in Ottawa. There he served as chair of the Department of Sociology and Anthropology, dean of Arts and Science, and vice-president. His major work, *The Vertical Mosaic* (1965), is a study of class and power in Canada. Firmly rooted in the conflict paradigm, it influenced a generation of Canadian sociologists in their studies on social inequality, elite groups, French-English relations, and Canadian–American relations.

SOURCE: Courtesy the American Sociological Association.

Erving Goffman (1922–82) was born in Mannville, Alberta. He studied sociology and anthropology as an undergraduate at the University of Toronto and completed his Ph.D. at the University of Chicago. He pursued his academic career at the University of California, Berkeley, and the University of Pennsylvania. Goffman developed an international reputation for his "dramaturgical" approach to symbolic interactionism. This approach highlights the way people present themselves to others, managing their identities to create desired impressions on their "audience," in much the same way as actors do on stage (Goffman, 1959).

SOURCE: Photo © Karyn Gorra. Courtesy Margrit Eichler.

Margrit Eichler (1942–) was born in Berlin, Germany. She did her Ph.D. at Duke University in the United States before beginning her academic career in Canada. She served as chair of the Department of Sociology at the Ontario Institute for Studies in Education and head of the Women's Studies Program at the University of Toronto. She is internationally known for her work on feminist methodology (Eichler, 1987). Her work on family policy in Canada has influenced students, professional sociologists, and policymakers for more than two decades (Eichler, 1988).

The causes and consequences of postindustrialism and globalization form the great sociological puzzles of our time. Much of this book is devoted to analyzing postindustrialism, globalization, and their effects. In concluding this chapter, a review of some of the sociological issues raised by the Postindustrial Revolution and globalization is therefore in order.

POSTINDUSTRIALISM AND GLOBALIZATION: OPPORTUNITIES AND PITFALLS

At the end of the twentieth century, many observers were wildly optimistic about the benefits that postindustrialism and globalization were supposedly going to bring to humanity. One commentator proclaimed "the end of history," by which he meant that liberal capitalism had become the unrivalled socioeconomic system in the world and its dominance was bound to usher in a long era of peace, freedom, and prosperity, leaving no corner of the world untouched (Fukuyama, 1992). Similarly, in a special issue of the *New York Times Magazine* devoted to technology, one staff writer gushed:

> Individuals are acquiring more control over their lives, their minds and their bodies, even their genes, thanks to the transformations in medicine, communications, transportation and industry. At the same time, these technologies are providing social benefits and undoing some of the damage of the past. Technology helps to conserve natural resources and diminish pollution. ... The Information Revolution, besides enabling us to visit Mars at will, is fostering peaceful cooperation on Earth by decentralizing power. Political tyrants and demagogic warmongers are losing control now that their subjects have tools to communicate directly with one another. People are using the tools to do their jobs without leaving their families. They're forming new communities in cyberspace and forming new bonds with their neighbors in real space. Technology has the potential to increase individual freedom and strengthen community. (Tierney, 1997: 46–7)

This and similar outpourings of optimism were written before the stock-market crash of 2000, the terrorist attacks of September 11, 2001, the second invasion of Iraq by the United States in 2003, and heightened fears about the consequences of climate change that surrounded the 2005 hurricane season. However, even before these devastating shocks changed the minds of all but the most starry-eyed observers, sociologists were more realistic about the prospects of humanity. On the whole, they agreed that postindustrialism and globalization promise many exciting opportunities to enhance the quality of life and increase human freedom—but they also saw many social-structural barriers to the realization of that promise.

The unresolved social issues that confront us in the era of postindustrialism and globalization fall under three headings. Each issue is addressed in later chapters.

Autonomy versus constraint. One of the major themes that emerges from *New Society* is that many people are freer to construct their own identities than ever before. Almost everyone used to retain their religious, ethnic, racial, and sexual identities for a lifetime, even if they were not particularly comfortable with them. In the era of postindustrialism and globalization, however, various social developments and technological advances—ranging from international migration to the World Wide Web to greater acceptance of sexual diversity—free people from traditional constraints. The theme of increasing personal autonomy is taken up in Chapter 2, Culture; Chapter 3, Socialization; Chapter 4, Gender and Sexuality; Chapter 5, Communication and Mass Media; and Chapter 13, Religion.

Some chapters, however, point out that we experience increased freedom only within certain limits. For example, we can choose a far wider variety of consumer products than ever before, but consumerism itself increasingly seems a compulsory way of life (Chapter 2, Culture). Moreover, it is a way of life that threatens the natural environment (Chapter 16, Sociology and the Environment). Meanwhile, new technologies, such as surveillance cameras, cause us to modify our behaviour and act in more conformist ways (Chapter 14, Deviance and Crime). As these examples show, the autonomy promised by postindustrialism is only half the story. The other half is that postindustrialism places new constraints on us.

Prosperity versus inequality. The second major theme that emerges from *New Society* is that postindustrialism opens up new economic, political, and educational opportunities. It makes work less onerous for many people. It raises the average standard of living. It enables women in particular to make rapid strides in all institutional spheres.

Again, however, we must face the less rosy aspects of postindustrialism. Tremendous economic and political inequality between women and men persists (Chapter 7, Gender Inequality: Economic and Political Aspects). So does inequality between Aboriginal and other Canadians (Chapter 8, Race and Ethnic Relations). Inequality between rich and poor in Canada has increased in recent decades (Chapter 6, Social Stratification). It is maintained partly by the educational system (Chapter 12, Education). By some measures, inequality between rich and poor nations has risen sharply (Chapter 9, Development and Underdevelopment). There are more good jobs at the top of the occupational structure, but many more bad jobs at the bottom (Chapter 11, Work and Occupations). The quality of the Canadian healthcare system is threatened at precisely the moment when our population is rapidly aging and most in need of healthcare (Chapter 17, Health and Aging). Although elections are regularly held throughout much of the world, it is an illusion to think that democracy has conquered the planet (Chapter 18, Politics and Social Movements). Thus, economic and political inequality persist despite growing prosperity and opportunity.

Diversity versus uniformity. The third major theme that emerges from *New Society* is that postindustrial society is more tolerant of diversity than any previous form of society was. Immigration policies no longer stipulate racial, ethnic, or religious criteria for entry into the country. As a result, our cities are more socially heterogeneous than ever before (Chapter 15, Population and Urbanization). The traditional nuclear family made up of mother, father, and children has given way to a wide variety of new family forms. Myriad radio stations, TV channels, newspapers, magazines, CD titles, books, and websites are now available to us.

Yet despite growing social diversity, there is a strong push to conformity in many spheres of life. For example, most of our diverse cultural consumption is governed by the tastes and the profit motive of vast media conglomerates, most of them American-owned (Chapter 5, Communication and Mass Media). Powerful interests are trying to shore up the traditional nuclear family despite its inappropriateness for many people in postindustrial society (Chapter 10, Families). The globalization of economic, political, and cultural affairs may be threatening the survival of distinct national cultures (Chapter 19, Globalization). The push to uniformity thus counters the trend toward growing social diversity.

WHY SOCIOLOGY?

Renowned English sociologist Anthony Giddens wrote that we live in an era "suspended between extraordinary opportunity ... and global catastrophe" (Giddens, 1982: 166). Because of the collapse of the Soviet Union in 1991 and the actions of international terrorists, nuclear, chemical, and biological catastrophes are more likely now than they were just a few years ago. A whole range of environmental issues, deep inequalities in the wealth of nations and of classes, racial and ethnic violence, and unsolved problems in the relations between women and men continue to stare us in the face and profoundly affect the quality of our daily life.

Despair and apathy is one possible response to these complex issues. But it is not a response that humans have often favoured. If it were our nature to give up hope, we would still be sitting around half-naked in the mud outside a cave.

People are more inclined to look for ways of improving their lives, and this period of human history is full of opportunities to do so. We have, for example, advanced to the point where for the first time we have the means to feed and educate everyone in the world. Similarly, it now seems possible to erode some of the inequalities that have always been with us and have always been the major source of human conflict. Students of sociology pursue careers that further such goals (see Box 1.3).

Although sociology offers no easy solutions as to how the goal of improving society may be accomplished, it does promise a useful way of understanding our current predicament and seeing possible ways of dealing with it. You sampled sociology's ability to tie personal troubles to social-structural issues when we discussed suicide. You reviewed the major theoretical perspectives that enable sociologists to connect the personal with the social-structural. When I outlined the half-fulfilled promises of postindustrialism and globalization, you saw sociology's ability to provide an understanding of where we are and where we can head.

I frankly admit that the questions raised in this book are tough to answer. Sharp controversy surrounds them all. However, I am sure that if you grapple with them, you will enhance your understanding of your society's, and your own, possibilities. In brief, sociology can help you figure out where you fit into society and how you can make society fit you. That, fundamentally, is sociology's goal.

BOX 1.3 CAREERS IN SOCIOLOGY

Students often ask, "Can I get a good job with a sociology degree?" "Exactly what kind of work could I do with a major in sociology?" "Aren't all the good jobs these days in technical areas and the natural sciences?" To answer these questions—and to help you decide whether a sociology or other social science major makes sense for you—consider the following data on the employment of Canadians with degrees in sociology and related fields.

A study based on 1988 data found that a higher percentage of Canadian sociology graduates were employed full-time than were graduates in the other social sciences (Guppy and Hedley, 1993). A study based mainly on 1996 data (Allen, 1999) showed the following in Canada:

- The unemployment rate among social science graduates was lower than among graduates in math, physics, engineering, agriculture, and biology.
- Between 1991 and 1996, there were more new jobs for people with social science degrees than for people with degrees in other fields.
- Although women earned less than men in all fields in 1996, the discrepancy between men's and women's income was smallest among social science graduates.

On the basis of these findings, it seems that sociology degrees promise more employment security for both men and women, and less income discrimination against women, than other degrees. It also seems that the postindustrial economy requires more new employees with a social science background than new employees with a background in some technical and scientific fields.

Tens of thousands of Canadians have undergraduate sociology degrees. A sociology B.A. improves your understanding of the diverse social conditions affecting men and women, people with different sexual orientations, and people from different countries, regions, classes, races, and ethnic groups. Therefore, people with a B.A. in sociology tend to be attracted to jobs requiring good "people skills" and jobs involved with managing and promoting social change (see Table 1.2). Often, people with a B.A. in sociology go on to graduate school and obtain professional degrees in other fields, including law, urban planning, industrial relations, social work, and public policy. You will therefore find many people with bachelor's degrees in sociology working as lawyers, urban planners, city managers, and healthcare and education administrators.

Most people with a graduate degree in sociology teach and conduct research in universities, with research being a more important component of the job in larger and more prestigious institutions. However, many sociologists do not teach. Instead, they conduct research and give policy advice in a wide range of settings outside the system of higher education. In many federal government agencies, for example, sociologists are employed as researchers and policy consultants. Sociologists also conduct research and policy analysis in trade unions, nongovernmental organizations, and professional and public interest associations. In the private sector, you can find sociologists practising their craft in firms specializing in public opinion polling, management consulting, market research, standardized testing, and "evaluation research," which assesses the impact of particular policies and programs before or after they go into effect.

One way of seeing the benefits of a sociological education is to compile a list of some of the famous practical idealists who studied sociology in university. That list includes several former heads of state, among them President Fernando Cardoso of Brazil, President Tomas Masaryk of Czechoslovakia, Prime Minister Edward Seaga of Jamaica, and President Ronald Reagan of the United States. The current first lady of the United States, Michelle Obama, also has a sociology degree. The former vice-president of the Liberal Party of Canada and former president and vice-chancellor of York University in Toronto, Lorna Marsden, is a sociologist. Anthony Giddens, former director of the London School of Economics and adviser to former British Prime Minister Tony Blair, earned a sociology doctorate. So do Martin Goldfarb, chairman, president, and CEO of The Goldfarb Corporation; and Donna Dasko, senior vice-president of Environics, two of Canada's leading public opinion firms with offices and affiliates around the world. Alex Himelfarb, former clerk of the Privy Council, holds a sociology Ph.D., too. So, for that matter, does British Columbia native Steve Nash of the Los Angeles Lakers, one of the best team players in professional basketball. His agent claims he is "the most colorblind person I've ever known" (Robbins, 2005). Arguably, Nash's study of sociology contributed to his team-building ability and his performance on the court by helping him to better understand the importance of groups and diverse social conditions in shaping human behaviour.

TABLE 1.2 JOBS COMMONLY HELD BY CANADIANS WITH DEGREES IN SOCIOLOGY

Government	Corrections
community affairs officer	corrections officer
urban/regional planner	criminology assistant
legislative aide	police officer
affirmative action/employment equity worker	rehabilitation counsellor
foreign service officer	criminal investigator
human rights officer	juvenile court worker
personnel coordinator	parole officer
Research	**Teaching**
social research specialist	college/university placement worker
consumer researcher	public health educator
data analyst market researcher	teacher admissions counsellor
survey researcher	**Business**
census officer/analyst	market analyst
demographer/population analyst	project manager
system analyst	sales representative
Community Affairs	real estate agent
occupational/career counsellor	journalist
homeless/housing worker	public relations officer
public health/hospital administrator	actuary
child development technician	insurance agent
public administration assistant	human resources manager
social assistance advocate	production manager
resident planning aide	labour relations officer
group home worker	administrative assistant
rehabilitation program worker	quality control manager
rural health outreach worker	merchandiser/purchaser
housing coordinator	computer analyst
fundraising director/assistant	data entry manager
caseworker/aide	publishing officer
community organizer	advertising officer
youth outreach worker	sales manager

SOURCE: Guppy and Hedley (1993). Reprinted with permission from the Canadian Sociological Association  Société canadienne de sociologie.

SUMMARY

1. Durkheim showed that social structures influence even apparently nonsocial and antisocial actions. Specifically, he showed how levels of social solidarity affect suicide rates.
2. Because of the rise in youth suicide, the pattern of suicide rates in Canada today is not exactly the same as in Durkheim's France. Nevertheless, Durkheim's theory explains the contemporary Canadian pattern well.
3. Sociologists analyze the connection between personal troubles and social structures.
4. Sociologists analyze the influence of three levels of social structure on human action: microstructures, macrostructures, and global structures.
5. Values suggest which sociological research questions are worth asking and how the parts of society fit together. Values underlie sociological theories. A theory is a tentative explanation of some aspect of social life. It states how and why specific facts are connected. Research is the process of carefully observing social reality to assess the validity of a theory.
6. There are four major theoretical traditions in sociology. Functionalism analyzes how social order is supported by macrostructures. Conflict theory analyzes how social inequality is maintained and challenged. Symbolic interactionism analyzes how meaning is created when people communicate

in microlevel settings. Feminism focuses on the social sources of patriarchy in both macro and micro settings.

7. The Scientific, Industrial, and Democratic Revolutions stimulated the rise of sociology.
8. The Postindustrial Revolution is the technology-driven shift from manufacturing to service industries and the consequences of that shift for virtually all human activities. Globalization is the process by which formerly separate economies, states, and cultures become tied together and people become increasingly aware of their growing interdependence.
9. The causes and consequences of postindustrialism and globalization form the great sociological puzzle of our time. The tension between autonomy and constraint, prosperity and inequality, and diversity and uniformity are among the chief interests of sociology today.

QUESTIONS TO CONSIDER

1. Do you think the promise of autonomy, prosperity, and diversity will be realized in the twenty-first century? Why or why not?
2. In this chapter you learned how variations in the level of social solidarity affect the suicide rate. How do you think variations in social solidarity might affect other areas of social life, such as criminal behaviour and political protest?
3. Is a science of society possible? If you agree that such a science is possible, what are its advantages over common sense? What are its limitations?

GLOSSARY

Altruistic suicide (p. 7) occurs in settings that exhibit high levels of social solidarity, according to Durkheim. Altruistic suicide results from norms very tightly governing behaviour.

Anomic suicide (p. 7) occurs in settings that exhibit low levels of social solidarity, according to Durkheim. Anomic suicide results from vaguely defined norms governing behaviour.

Conflict theory (p. 15) generally focuses on large, macrolevel structures, such as the relations between or among classes. It shows how major patterns of inequality in society produce social stability in some circumstances and social change in others. It stresses how members of privileged groups try to maintain their advantages while subordinate groups struggle to increase theirs. It typically leads to the suggestion that eliminating privilege will lower the level of conflict and increase human welfare.

The **Democratic Revolution** (p. 10) began about 1750. It suggested that people are responsible for organizing society and that human intervention can therefore solve social problems.

Dysfunctional consequences (p. 15) are effects of social structures that create social instability.

Egoistic suicide (p. 7) results from a lack of integration of the individual into society because of weak social ties to others.

Ethnomethodology (p. 26) is the study of how people make sense of what others do and say in terms of norms that exist independently of individual social actors.

Feminist theory (p. 18) claims that patriarchy is at least as important as class inequality in determining a person's opportunities in life. It holds that male domination and female subordination are determined not by biological necessity but by structures of power and social convention. It examines the operation of patriarchy in both micro and macro settings. It contends that existing patterns of gender inequality can and should be changed for the benefit of all members of society.

Functionalist theory (p. 15) stresses that human behaviour is governed by relatively stable social structures. It underlines how social structures maintain or undermine social stability. It emphasizes that social structures are based mainly on shared values or preferences. It suggests that reestablishing equilibrium can best solve most social problems.

Global structures (p. 9) are patterns of social relations that lie outside and above the national level. They include international organizations, patterns of worldwide travel and communication, and the economic relations between and among countries.

Globalization (p. 19) is the process by which formerly separate economies, states, and cultures are becoming tied together and people are becoming increasingly aware of their growing interdependence.

The **Industrial Revolution** (p. 10) refers to the rapid economic transformation that began in Britain in the 1780s. It involved the large-scale application of science and technology to industrial processes, the creation of factories, and the formation of a working class.

Latent functions (p. 15) are invisible and unintended effects of social structures.

Macrostructures (p. 9) are overarching patterns of social relations that lie outside and above our circle of intimates and acquaintances. Macrostructures include classes, bureaucracies, and power systems, such as patriarchy.

Manifest functions (p. 15) are visible and intended effects of social structures.

Microstructures (p. 8) are the patterns of relatively intimate social relations formed during face-to-face interaction. Families, friendship circles, and work associations are all microstructures.

Patriarchy (p. 9) is the traditional system of economic and political inequality between women and men.

The **Postindustrial Revolution** (p. 19) refers to the technology-driven shift from manufacturing to service industries and the consequences of that shift for virtually all human activities.

The **Protestant ethic** (p. 17) is the belief, originating in the sixteenth and seventeenth centuries, that religious doubts can be reduced, and a state of grace ensured, if people work diligently and live ascetically. According to Weber, the Protestant ethic had the unintended effect of increasing savings and investment and thus stimulating capitalist growth.

Research (p. 12) is the process of systematically observing reality to assess the validity of a theory.

The **Scientific Revolution** (p. 10) began about 1550. It encouraged the view that sound conclusions about the workings of society must be based on solid evidence, not just on speculation.

Social solidarity (p. 6) refers to (1) the degree to which group members share beliefs and values, and (2) the intensity and frequency of their interaction.

Social structures (p. 8) are relatively stable patterns of social relations.

The **sociological imagination** (p. 10) is the quality of mind that enables a person to see the connection between personal troubles and social structures.

Sociology (p. 5) is the systematic study of human behaviour in social context.

Symbolic interactionism (p. 17) focuses on face-to-face communication or interaction in microlevel social settings. It emphasizes that an adequate explanation of social behaviour requires understanding the subjective meanings people attach to their social circumstances. It stresses that people help to create their social circumstances and do not merely react to them. By underscoring the subjective meanings people create in small social settings, symbolic interactionism validates unpopular and nonofficial viewpoints, thus increasing our understanding and tolerance of people who may be different from us.

A **theory** (p. 12) is a tentative explanation of some aspect of social life that states how and why certain facts are related.

Values (p. 14) are ideas about what is right and wrong.

SUGGESTED READING

Brym, Robert J. (2011). *Sociology as a Life or Death Issue*, 2nd Canadian ed. Toronto: Nelson. A guide to the sociological craft for beginners. It focuses on the social causes of death—specifically, the social context of hip-hop, suicide bombing, "natural" disasters, and cancer—to show how sociology can help people live longer and better lives.

The *Canadian Review of Sociology* (www.csa-scs.ca/crs-home) and the *Canadian Journal of Sociology* (http://ejournals.library.ualberta.ca/index.php/CJS/index) will give you a taste of the practice of sociology in Canada. Visit the website of the Canadian Sociological Association at www.csa-scs.ca for sociological news and conferences.

Stephens, W. Richard, Jr. (1998). *Careers in Sociology.* New York: Allyn & Bacon. In this book, 18 sociology graduates talk about the diverse and fascinating careers they have pursued. It is available online at www.abacon.com/socsite/careers.html.

NOTES

1. You will find more detailed discussion of these theories throughout the book. For example, on functionalism, see Chapters 12 and 13. On conflict theory, see Chapters 6, 10, 13, and 18. On symbolic interactionism, see Chapters 3 and 14. On feminism, see Chapters 4, 7, 10, and 18.
2. By emphasizing how social reality is constructed during interaction, symbolic interactionists downplay the importance of norms and understandings that precede any given interaction. **Ethnomethodology** tries to correct this shortcoming. Ethnomethodologists study how people make sense of what others do and say but stress that norms exist independently of individual social actors. Indeed, in the ethnomethodological view, everyday interactions could not take place without preexisting shared norms. Say you pass an acquaintance on the street, who offers a friendly "How are you?" If you proceed to outline in detail your financial situation, your love life, interesting developments at work, and so on, the acquaintance will quickly become annoyed. Most people expect "How are you?" to be answered with an equally brief reply. Violate the norm, and communication quickly breaks down (Garfinkel, 1967).

SOURCE: © John Warburton_lee/DanitaDelimont.com

PART 2

CULTURE

CHAPTER 2

CULTURE

Robert J. Brym
UNIVERSITY OF TORONTO

SOURCE: © Tanner Productions/CORBIS.

IN THIS CHAPTER YOU WILL LEARN THAT

- Culture is the sum of ideas, practices, and material objects that people create to adapt to, and thrive in, their environments.
- Humans have been able to thrive in their environments because of their unique ability to think abstractly, cooperate with one another, and make tools.
- We can see the contours of culture most sharply if we are neither too deeply immersed in it nor too much removed from it.
- As societies become more complex, culture diversifies and consensus declines in many areas of life. These changes increase human freedom.
- As societies become more complex, the limits within which freedom may increase become more rigid. This change constrains human freedom.
- Although people create culture to solve problems, culture sometimes has negative consequences that create new problems.

CULTURE AS PROBLEM SOLVING

Tiger Woods wears a red shirt on the last day of every tournament in which he competes. Sidney Crosby won't sign a team jersey until he has worn it in a regular season game. When Woods and Crosby started these superstitious practices, they were taking the first step toward creating one aspect of culture, the socially transmitted ideas, practices, and material objects that people create to deal with real-life problems. Their superstitions help to reassure them and let them play better. Research shows that, in general, superstitious practices help athletes reduce anxiety and improve self-confidence and performance (Damisch, Stoberock, and Mussweiler, 2010).

Like soldiers going off to battle, university students about to write final exams, and other people in high-stress situations, athletes invent routines to help them stop worrying and focus on the job at hand. Some wear a lucky piece of jewellery or item of clothing. Others say special words or a quick prayer. Still others cross themselves. And then there are people who engage in more-elaborate rituals. For example, sociologists Cheryl and Daniel Albas of the University of Manitoba interviewed three hundred university students about their superstitious practices before final exams. One student felt she would do well only if she ate a sausage and two eggs sunny side up on the morning of each exam. The sausage had to be arranged vertically on the left side of her plate and the eggs placed to the right of the sausage so they formed the "100" percent she was aiming for (Albas and Albas, 1989). Of course, the ritual had more direct influence on her cholesterol level than on her grade. Indirectly, however, it may have had the desired effect. To the degree that it helped to relieve her anxiety and relax her, she may have done better in exams.

When some people say *culture*, they refer to opera, ballet, art, and fine literature. However, for sociologists this definition is too narrow. Sociologists define **culture** broadly as all the socially transmitted ideas, practices, and material objects that people create to deal with real-life problems. For example, when Crosby developed his superstitions and the university student invented the ritual of preparing for exams by eating a sausage and eggs arranged just so, they were beginning to create culture in the sociological sense. These practices helped Crosby and the student deal with the real-life problem of high anxiety. Similarly, tools help people solve the problem of how to plant crops and build houses. Religion helps people face the

Sidney Crosby
SOURCE: © REUTERS/Shannon Stapleton.

problem of death and how to give life meaning. Tools and religion are also elements of culture because they, too, help people solve real-life problems.

Note, however, that religion, technology, and many other elements of culture differ from the superstitions of athletes and undergraduates in one important respect. Superstitions are often unique to the individuals who create them. In contrast, religion and technology are widely shared. They are passed from one generation to the next. How does cultural sharing take place? Through human interaction, communication, and learning. In other words, culture becomes shared when it is socially transmitted. A **society** involves people interacting socially and sharing culture, usually in a defined geographical area.[1] Culture, then, is the sum of the *socially transmitted* ideas, practices, and material objects that enable people to adapt to, and thrive in, their environments.

THE ORIGINS AND COMPONENTS OF CULTURE

You can appreciate the importance of culture for human survival by considering the predicament of early humans about 100 000 years ago. They lived in harsh natural environments. They had poor physical endowments, being slower runners and weaker fighters than many other animals. Yet, despite these disadvantages, they survived. More than that—they prospered and came to dominate nature. This feat was possible largely because they were the smartest creatures around. Their sophisticated brains enabled them to create cultural survival kits of enormous complexity and flexibility. These cultural survival kits contained three main tools. Each tool was a uniquely human talent. Each gave rise to a different element of culture.

ABSTRACTION: CREATING SYMBOLS

Human culture exists only because we can think abstractly. **Abstraction** is the capacity to create **symbols** or general ideas that carry particular meanings. Languages and mathematical notations are sets of symbols. They allow us to classify experience and generalize from it. For instance, we recognize that we can sit on many objects but that only some of those objects have four legs, a back, and space for one person. We distinguish the latter from other objects by giving them a name: chairs. By the time a baby reaches the end of her first year, she has heard that word repeatedly and understands that it refers to a certain class of objects. True, a few chimpanzees have been taught to make some signs with their hands. In this way, they have learned some words and how to string together some simple phrases. However, even these extraordinarily intelligent animals cannot learn any rules of grammar, teach other chimps what they know, or advance much beyond the vocabulary of a human toddler (Pinker, 1994). Abstraction at anything beyond the most rudimentary level is a uniquely human capacity. The ability to abstract enables humans to learn and transmit knowledge in a way no other animal can.

COOPERATION: CREATING NORMS AND VALUES

The ability to cooperate is a second factor that enables human culture to exist. **Cooperation** involves creating a complex social life by establishing **norms** or generally accepted ways of doing things, and values or ideas about what is right and wrong, good and bad, beautiful and ugly. For example, family members cooperate to raise children. In the process, they develop and apply norms and values about which child-rearing practices are appropriate and desirable. Different times and places give rise to different norms and values. In our society, parents might ground children for swearing, but in pioneer days parents would typically "beat the devil out of them." By analyzing how people cooperate and

TABLE 2.1 THE BUILDING BLOCKS OF CULTURE

THE HUMAN CAPACITY FOR ⟶	ABSTRACTION	COOPERATION	PRODUCTION
Gives rise to these elements of culture	ideas	norms and values	material culture
In medicine, for example,	*theories* are developed about how a certain drug might cure a disease	*experiments* are conducted to test whether the drug works as expected	*treatments* are developed on the basis of the experimental results

SOURCE: Adapted from Robert Bierstedt, *The Social Order* (New York: McGraw-Hill, 1963).

produce norms and values, we can learn much about what distinguishes one culture from another.

PRODUCTION: CREATING MATERIAL AND NONMATERIAL CULTURE

Finally, culture can exist because humans can engage in **production**; we can make and use tools and techniques that improve our ability to take what we want from nature. Sociologists call such tools and techniques **material culture**. All animals take from nature to subsist, and an ape may sometimes use a rock to break another object or use a stick to keep its balance in a fast-flowing stream. However, only humans are sufficiently intelligent and dexterous to *make* tools and use them to produce everything from food to computers. Understood in this sense, production is a uniquely human activity.

Table 2.1 illustrates each of the basic human capacities and their cultural offshoots in the field of medicine. As in medicine, so in all fields of human endeavour: abstraction, operation, and production give rise to specific kinds of ideas, norms, and elements of material culture.

Note that people are usually rewarded when they follow cultural guidelines and punished when they do not. Taken together, these rewards and punishments, aimed at ensuring conformity, are known as **sanctions** or the system of **social control.** Rewards (or positive sanctions) include everything from praise and encouragement to money and power. Punishments (or negative sanctions) range from avoidance and contempt to arrest and physical violence.

Despite efforts to control people, we often reject elements of existing culture and create new elements of culture. Reasons for this phenomenon are discussed in Chapter 14, Deviance and Crime, and Chapter 18, Politics and Social Movements. Here it is enough to say that, just as social control is needed to ensure stable patterns of interaction, so resistance to social control is needed to ensure cultural innovation and social renewal. Stable but vibrant societies are able to find a balance between social control and cultural innovation.

LANGUAGE AND THE SAPIR-WHORF THESIS

Language is one of the most important parts of any culture. A **language** is a system of symbols strung together to communicate thought. Equipped with language, we can share understandings, pass experience and knowledge from one generation to the next, and make plans for the future. In short, language allows culture to develop. Consequently, sociologists commonly think of language as a cultural invention that distinguishes humans from other animals.

In the 1930s, Edward Sapir and Benjamin Lee Whorf proposed an influential argument about the connection among experience, thought, and language. It is now known as the **Sapir-Whorf thesis** (Whorf, 1956). It holds that we experience important things in our environment and form concepts about those things (path 1 to 2 in Figure 2.1). Then, we develop language to express our concepts (path 2 to 3). Finally, language itself influences how we see the world (path 3 to 1).

FIGURE 2.1 THE SAPIR-WHORF THESIS

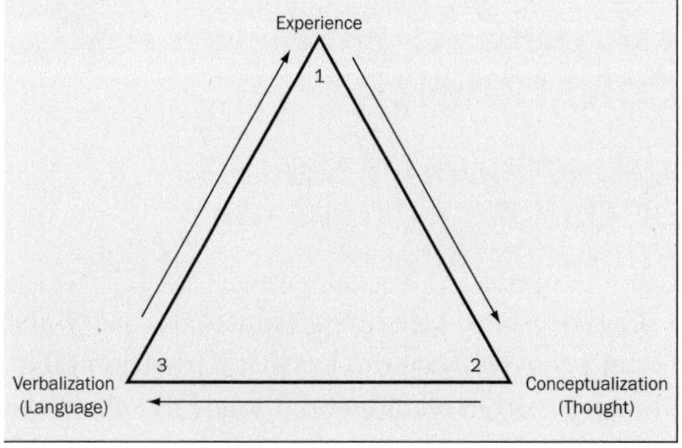

For example, different types of camels are important in the environment of nomadic Arabs, and different types of snow are important in the lives of the Inuit in Canada's Far North (path 1 to 2). Consequently, nomadic Arabs have developed many words for different types of camels and the Inuit have developed many words for different types of snow (path 2 to 3). Distinctions that these people see elude us because types of camel and snow are less important in our environment.

In turn, language obliges people to think in certain ways (path 3 to 1). If you're walking in a park, you will know whether a certain tree is in front of you, behind you, to the left, or to the right. When asked where the tree is, you will use such directions to describe its position. We think "egocentrically," locating objects relative to ourselves. However, egocentric directions have no meaning for speakers of Tzeltal in southern Mexico or of Guugu Yimithirr in Queensland, Australia. They lack concepts and words for "left," "right," and so on. They think geographically and will say that the tree is to the "north," "south, "east," or "west." Trained from infancy to attend to geographic direction, Tzeltal speakers are obliged to think in those terms. If a tree to the north is located behind them and they are asked where the tree is, they will point to themselves, as if they don't exist. Reportedly, a Tzeltal speaker can be blindfolded, put in a dark room, and spun around 20 times until he's dizzy yet still point without hesitation to the north, south, east, and west (Boroditsky, 2010; Deutscher, 2010). Or to take an example closer to home, income and power inequality between women and men encourages some men to use terms like *fox*, *babe*, *bitch*, *ho*, and *doll* to refer to women. However, the use of such words in itself influences men to think of women simply as sexual objects. If they are ever going to think of women as equals, gender inequality will have to be reduced, but the language such men use to refer to women will also have to change.

CULTURE AS FREEDOM AND CONSTRAINT

A FUNCTIONALIST ANALYSIS OF CULTURE: CULTURE AND ETHNOCENTRISM

I was once introduced to a woman at a party and began a conversation with her that started agreeably. However, within ten minutes, I found myself on the other side of the room, my back pressed against the wall, trying to figure out how I could politely end our interaction. I wasn't immediately aware of the reason for my discomfort. Only after I told the woman that I had to make a phone call and had left the room did I realize the source of the problem: She had invaded my culturally defined comfort zone. Research shows the average North American prefers to stand 75 to 90 centimetres (30 to 36 inches) away from strangers or acquaintances when they are engaged in face-to-face interaction (Hall, 1959: 158–80). However, this woman had recently arrived from her home in a part of the Middle East where the culturally defined comfort zone is generally smaller. She stood only about 50 centimetres (20 inches) from me as we spoke. Without thinking, I retreated half a step. Without thinking, she advanced half a step. Soon we had waltzed across the faculty club lounge, unaware of what we were doing, until I had no further room to retreat and had to concoct a means of escape.

As this example shows, despite its central importance in human life, culture is often invisible to people

Taking public transportation often forces us to abandon our culturally defined personal space. However, this abandonment of personal space is itself a cultural norm.
SOURCE: Andrew Benyei, *Commuters*.

who are immersed in it. That is, people tend to take their own culture for granted; it usually seems so sensible and natural that they rarely think about it. I was unable to understand how my culture was affecting me while I was in its grip. I understood its effect only when I removed myself from the faculty club lounge, the immediate context of its operation, and thought about how it was making me behave.

If people often take their own culture for granted, they are often startled when confronted by cultures other than their own. That is, the ideas, norms, and techniques of other cultures frequently seem odd, irrational, and even inferior. Judging another culture exclusively by the standards of our own is called **ethnocentrism.** Ethnocentrism impairs sociological analysis. This fact can be illustrated by Marvin Harris's (1974: 3–32) functionalist analysis of a practice that seems bizarre to many Westerners: cow worship among Hindu peasants in India.

Hindu peasants refuse to slaughter cattle and eat beef because, for them, the cow is a religious symbol of life. Pin-up calendars throughout rural India portray beautiful women with the bodies of fat white cows, milk jetting out of each teat. Cows are permitted to wander the streets, defecate on the sidewalks, and stop to chew their cud in busy intersections and on railroad tracks, causing traffic to come to a halt. In Madras, the police maintain fields where stray cows that have fallen ill can graze and be nursed back to health. The government even runs old-age homes for cows, where dry and decrepit cattle are kept free of charge. All this seems inscrutable to most Westerners, for it takes place amid poverty and hunger that could presumably be alleviated if only the peasants would slaughter their "useless" cattle for food instead of squandering scarce resources on feeding and protecting them.

According to Harris (1974), however, ethnocentrism misleads many Western observers. Cow worship, it turns out, is an economically rational practice in rural India. For one thing, Indian peasants can't afford tractors, so cows are needed to give birth to oxen, which are in high demand for plowing. For another, the cows produce hundreds of millions of kilograms of recoverable manure, about half of which is used as fertilizer and half as cooking fuel. With oil, coal, and wood in short supply, and with the peasants unable to afford chemical fertilizers, cow dung is, well, a godsend. What is more, cows in India don't cost much to maintain since they eat mostly food that isn't fit for human consumption. And they represent an important source of protein and a livelihood for members of low-ranking castes, who have the right to dispose of the bodies of dead cattle. These "untouchables" eat beef and form the workforce of India's large leather-craft industry. Thus, the protection of cows by means of cow worship is in fact a perfectly sensible and efficient economic practice. It only seems irrational when judged by the standards of Western agribusiness.

Harris's (1974) analysis of cow worship in rural India is interesting for two reasons. First, it illustrates how functionalist theory, outlined in Chapter 1, Introducing Sociology, can illuminate otherwise mysterious social practices that make social order possible. Second, we can draw an important lesson about ethnocentrism from Harris's analysis. If you refrain from taking your own culture for granted and judging other cultures by the standards of your own, you will have taken important first steps toward developing a sociological understanding of culture.

CULTURE AS FREEDOM

Culture has two faces. First, culture provides us with an opportunity to exercise our freedom. We use and elaborate elements of culture in our everyday life to solve practical problems and express our needs, hopes, joy, and fears.

However, creatively using culture is just like any other act of construction in that we need raw materials to get the job done. The raw materials for the culture we create consist of cultural elements that either existed before we were born or are created by others after our birth. We may put these elements together in ways that produce something genuinely new. However, there is no other well to drink from, so existing culture puts limits on what we can think and do. In that sense, culture *constrains* us. This is culture's second face. In the rest of this chapter, we take a close look at both faces of culture.

SYMBOLIC INTERACTIONISM AND CULTURAL PRODUCTION

Until the 1960s, most sociologists argued that culture is a "reflection" of society. Harris's (1974) analysis of rural Indians certainly fits that mould. In Harris's view, the social necessity of protecting cows caused the cultural belief that cows are holy.

In recent decades, the symbolic interactionist tradition we discussed in Chapter 1, Introducing Sociology, has influenced many sociologists of culture. Symbolic interactionists are not inclined to regard society as a cause and culture as a consequence. In their view, people do not accept culture passively. We are not empty vessels into which society pours a defined assortment of beliefs, symbols, and values. Instead, we actively produce and interpret culture, creatively fashioning it and attaching meaning to it in accordance with our diverse needs.

The idea that people actively produce and interpret culture implies that, to a degree, we are at liberty to choose how culture influences us.

CULTURAL DIVERSIFICATION

> This is a nice room tonight. When I look out, I see all kinds of different people. I see Black, White, Asian, everybody hangin' out, havin' a good time. ... This type of thing is not going to be able to happen about 300 years from now. You realize that? ... You realize there's not going to be any more white people? There's not going to be any more black people? Everyone's going to be beige. ... It's true, the whole world's mixing. There's nothing you can do about it. Eventually, we're all going to become some hybrid mix of Chinese and Indian. It's inevitable. They're the two largest populations in the world. So you can run from us now. But sooner or later, we're going to hump you. ... But I'm thinkin' if we're all going to mix anyway, let's start mixing people now that would never normally mix just to see what we'll get. You know, hook up a Jamaican with an Italian. They could have little Pastafarians. I'm Indian. I could hook up with a Jewish girl and we could have little Hinjews. A woman from the Philippines, a guy from Holland—little Hollapinos. A guy from Cuba, a woman from Iceland—little Ice-cubes. A French and a Greek—Freaks. A German and a Newfie—little Goofies. It's gonna happen. We might as well help it along.
>
> —Russell Peters (2009),
> Indo Canadian comedian

Part of the reason we are increasingly able to choose how culture influences us is that a greater diversity of culture is available from which to choose. Like many societies, Canada is undergoing rapid cultural diversification. Canada used to be composed almost exclusively of Christian northern Europeans and an Aboriginal minority. Then, in the 1960s, Canada eliminated overt racism from its immigration policies, and the country began to diversify culturally. In the 1970s, the Canadian government continued the trend by adopting a policy of multiculturalism, which funds the maintenance of culturally diverse communities (Fleras and Elliott, 2002).

Russell Peters
SOURCE: © ZUMA Wire Service/Alamy

About 95 percent of immigrants who arrived in Canada before 1961 came from Europe and the United States. In 2010, about 64 percent of immigrants came from *outside* Europe and the United States (see Table 2.2). Because of the inflow of immigrants from nontraditional sources, such as China, India, Pakistan, and the Philippines, more than a fifth of the population will be non-white by 2017 (excluding Aboriginal Canadians). Nearly three-quarters of non-white Canadians will reside in Toronto, Vancouver, and Montreal, with most of the rest in Edmonton, Calgary, and Winnipeg (Brym, 2009; Cardozo and Pendakur, n.d.).

MULTICULTURALISM

Some critics argue that our immigration and multiculturalist policies weaken Canada's social fabric. For one thing, they argue that multiculturalism encourages

TABLE 2.2 TOP SOURCES OF CANADIAN IMMIGRANTS (PERMANENT RESIDENTS), 2010

COUNTRY	PERCENTAGE OF TOTAL
Philippines	13.0
India	10.8
China	10.8
United Kingdom	3.4
United States	3.3
France	2.5
Iran	2.4
United Arab Emirates	2.4
Morocco	2.1
South Korea	2.0
Pakistan	1.8
Colombia	1.7
Haiti	1.6
Iraq	1.6
Bangladesh	1.6
Other	39.0
Total	100.0

SOURCE: Citizenship and Immigration Canada, *Facts and Figures 2010*, from http://www.cic.gc.ca/english/resources/publications/annual-report-2011/section2.asp. Reproduced with the permission of the Minister of Public Works and Government Services Canada, 2012.

cultural relativism. Cultural relativism is the opposite of ethnocentrism. It is the idea that all cultures and cultural practices have equal value. The trouble with this view is that some cultures oppose values that Canadians hold deeply. Should we respect racist and antidemocratic cultures, such as the apartheid regime that existed in South Africa from 1948 until 1992? Or female circumcision, which is still widely practised in Somalia, Sudan, and Egypt (see Box 2.1)? Critics argue that by promoting cultural relativism, multiculturalism encourages respect for practices that are abhorrent to most Canadians. (Multiculturalists reply that cultural relativism need not be taken to an extreme. *Moderate* cultural relativism encourages tolerance and should be promoted.)

Critics of multiculturalism also argue that it encourages immigrants to cling to their past rather than shrug off their old self-conceptions and create a distinctive *Canadian* identity (Bissoondath, 2002). This viewpoint has two problems. First, it is by no means certain that we lack a distinctive Canadian identity. In fact, as noted below, a defining element of our distinctive Canadian identity is precisely our deep respect for diversity. Second, contrary to the claims of the critics of multiculturalism, survey research shows that support for multiculturalism is *not* correlated with traditional attitudes (such as religiosity) that keep people rooted in the past. Support for multiculturalism *is* correlated with various modern trends, such as support for equality between women and men (Adams, 1997: 173).

GLOBALIZATION

Canada's multiculturalist policies are the latest stage in a long process of cultural evolution. In general, cultures tend to become more diverse or heterogeneous as societies become more complex, with important consequences for everyday life. Thus, in preliterate or tribal societies, cultural beliefs and practices are virtually the same for all group members. For example, many tribal societies organize puberty ceremonies to mark the end of childhood and the beginning of adulthood, fertility dances to pray for good crops and healthy babies, and other rites. These rituals involve elaborate body painting, carefully orchestrated chants and movements, and so forth. They are conducted in public. No variation from prescribed practice is allowed. Culture is homogeneous (Durkheim, 1976 [1915]).

In contrast, preindustrial Western Europe and North America were rocked by artistic, religious, scientific, and political forces that fragmented culture. The Renaissance, the Protestant Reformation, the Scientific Revolution, the French and American Revolutions—between the fourteenth and eighteenth centuries, all these movements involved people questioning old ways of seeing and doing things. Science

Globalization: Tim Hortons opened its first franchise in the United Arab Emirates in 2011.
SOURCE: © Robert J. Brym.

BOX 2.1 FEMALE GENITAL MUTILATION: CULTURAL RELATIVISM OR ETHNOCENTRISM?

The World Health Organization defines female genital mutilation (FGM) as procedures that intentionally alter or injure female genital organs for non-medical reasons (World Health Organization, 2012). It has no medical benefits. It typically results in pain, humiliation, psychological trauma, and loss of sexual pleasure. It often causes shock, injury to neighbouring organs, severe bleeding, infertility, chronic infections in the urinary tract and reproductive system, and increased rates of hepatitis B and HIV/AIDS infection. Between 100 million and 140 million girls and women worldwide have undergone FGM, the great majority of them in a handful of African countries.

Some people think FGM enhances fertility and that women are "unclean" and "masculine" if they have a clitoris. From this point of view, women who have not experienced genital mutilation are more likely to demonstrate "masculine" levels of sexual interest and activity. They are less likely to remain virgins before marriage and faithful within marriage.

One reaction to FGM takes a human rights perspective. In this view, the practice is an aspect of gender-based oppression that women experience to varying degrees in societies worldwide. Adopting this perspective, the United Nations defines FGM as a form of violence against women. Many international, regional, and national agreements commit governments to preventing FGM, assisting women at risk of undergoing it, and punishing people who commit it. In Canada, FGM is against the law.

Cultural relativists regard the human rights perspective as ethnocentric. They view interference with the practice as little more than neo-imperialist attacks on African cultures. From their point of view, talk of "universal human rights" denies cultural rights to less powerful peoples. Moreover, opposition to FGM undermines tolerance and multiculturalism while reinforcing racist attitudes. Cultural relativists therefore argue that we should affirm the right of other cultures to practice FGM even if we regard it as destructive, senseless, oppressive, and abhorrent. We should respect the fact that other cultures regard FGM as meaningful and as serving useful functions.

Which of these perspectives do you find more compelling? Do you believe that certain principles of human decency transcend the values of any specific culture? If so, what are those principles? If you do not believe in the existence of any universal principles of human decency, then does anything go? Would you agree that, say, genocide is acceptable if most people in a society favour it? Or are there limits to your cultural relativism? In a world where supposedly universal principles often clash with the principles of particular cultures, where do you draw the line?

SOURCE: World Health Organization. (2012). "Female Genital Mutilation." On the World Wide Web at http://www.who.int/mediacentre/factsheets/fs241/en/ (retrieved 16 March 2012).

placed skepticism of established authority at the very heart of its method. Political revolution proved there was nothing ordained about who should rule and how they should do so. Religious dissent ensured that the Catholic Church would no longer be the supreme interpreter of God's will in the eyes of all Christians. Authority and truth became divided as never before.

Cultural fragmentation picked up steam during industrialization, as the variety of occupational roles grew and new political and intellectual movements crystallized. Its pace is quickening again today in the postindustrial era under the impact of a variety of technological and globalizing forces (see Box 2.2).

Globalization has many roots (see Chapter 19, Globalization). International trade and investment are expanding. Members of different ethnic and racial groups are migrating and coming into sustained contact with one another. A growing number of people from these diverse groups date, court, and marry across religious, ethnic, and racial lines. Influential transnational organizations have been created, such as the International Monetary Fund, the European Union, Greenpeace, Amnesty International, and *Médecins sans frontières*. Inexpensive international travel and communication make contacts between people from diverse cultures routine. The mass media make Ryan Gosling and *Gossip Girl* as well known in Warsaw as in Winnipeg, while hip-hop is as popular in Senegal and Tunisia as it is in Chicago. Globalization, in short, destroys political, economic, and cultural isolation, bringing people together in what Canadian communications guru Marshall McLuhan (1964) called a "global village." Because of globalization, people are less obliged to accept the culture into which they are born and freer to combine elements of culture from a wide variety of historical periods and geographical settings. Globalization is a Mumbai schoolboy listening to Bob Marley on his MP3 player as he rushes to slip into his Levis, wolfs down a bowl of Kellogg's Basmati Flakes, and says goodbye to his parents in Hindi because he's late for his English-language school (see Box 2.3).

BOX 2.2 HOW TECHNOLOGICAL CHANGE SHORTENS YOUR ATTENTION SPAN

Young people's culture has always been faster than the culture of older people. Older people process information slower than young people do because, as we age, we have fewer and less efficient neurons. However, in recent years, technological innovation has encouraged young people's attention spans to shorten and the generational gap in processing speed to grow.

In particular, the electronic media make it possible to cater to the neurological advantages that young people have over older people. When *Sesame Street* became a huge TV hit in 1969, part of its appeal was that it made its story segments shorter than those on other children's programs. Decades of research by the Children's Television Workshop suggests that shows like *Sesame Street* condition children to regard brevity as normal. The widespread adoption of the personal computer and the Internet in the 1980s and 1990s reinforced the need for speed. Quick information gathering, instant communication, and rapid-fire gaming were once considered spectacular. Now they are routine.

The speed with which teenagers check Facebook, channel surf, listen to music, and engage in instant messaging often bewilders parents, who are unable to process what appear to them to be lightning-fast events. Many teenagers seem unable to listen to an entire song without becoming distracted. They often use MP3 players to skim songs, listening to each for less than a minute. A fast-paced media- and technology-rich environment affords plenty of opportunities to multitask. At clubs, DJs playing for a young crowd find it necessary to mix songs quickly to maintain a tight dance floor and excite people. In contrast, quick mixing represents information overload for an older crowd, which quickly becomes irritated unless the DJ plays songs in their entirety. Thus, although built on neurological foundations that have always separated younger from older generations, shortening attention spans have been nurtured by technological change in the electronic media. They quicken the pace of cultural fragmentation.

SOURCE: Peter Dazeley/Getty Images

SOURCE: Fox, Yale, and Robert Brym (2009).

A CONFLICT ANALYSIS OF CULTURE: THE RIGHTS REVOLUTION

Underlying cultural diversification is the **rights revolution,** the process by which socially excluded groups have struggled to win equal rights under the law and in practice. After the outburst of nationalism, racism, and genocidal behaviour among the combatants in World War II, the United Nations proclaimed the Universal Declaration of Human Rights in 1948. Its preamble reads in part,

> Whereas recognition of the inherent dignity and of the equal and inalienable rights of all members of the human family is the foundation of freedom, justice and peace in the world. ... Now, therefore The General Assembly proclaims this Universal Declaration of Human Rights as a common standard of achievement for all peoples and all nations, to the end that every individual and every organ of society, keeping this Declaration constantly in mind, shall strive by teaching and education to promote respect for these rights and freedoms and by progressive measures, national and international, to secure their universal and effective recognition and observance. (United Nations, 1998)

Fanned by such sentiment, the rights revolution was in full swing by the 1960s. Today, women's rights, Aboriginal rights, gay and lesbian rights, the rights of people with special needs, constitutional rights, and language rights are a key part of our political discourse. As a result of the rights revolution, democracy has been widened and deepened (see Chapter 18, Politics and Social Movements). The rights revolution is by no means finished—many categories of people are still discriminated against socially, politically, and economically—but in much of the world all categories of people now participate more fully than ever before in the life of their societies (Ignatieff, 2000).

BOX 2.3 THE GLOBALIZATION OF ENGLISH

The spread of English is a key marker of the extent of globalization. In 1600, English was the mother tongue of between four million and seven million people. Not even all people in England spoke it. Today, 750 million to 1 billion people speak English worldwide, more than half as a second language. With the exception of the many varieties of Chinese, English is the most widespread language on Earth, and it is by far the most important. More than half the world's technical and scientific periodicals are written in English. English is the official language of the Olympics, of the Miss Universe contest, of navigation in the air and on the seas, and of the World Council of Churches.

English is dominant because Britain and the United States have been the world's most powerful and influential countries—economically, militarily, and culturally—for more than two centuries. (Someone once defined language as a dialect backed up by an army.) In recent decades, the global spread of capitalism, the popularity of Hollywood movies and American TV shows, and widespread access to instant communication via telephone and the Internet have increased the reach of the English language. There are now more speakers of excellent English in India than in the United Kingdom, and when a construction company jointly owned by German, French, and Italian interests undertakes a building project in Spain, the language of business is English (McCrum, Cran, and MacNeil, 1992).

Even in Japan, where relatively few people speak the language, English words are commonly used and Japanese words that are badly translated into English often become popular. The result is what is commonly known as "Japlish." Sometimes the results are unintelligible to a native English speaker. "Push to my nose! I might be changing to you?" says the catchy sign in a T-shirt store in Tokyo's Ueno district. Certain computer terms are more comprehensible to a native English speaker. For example, when you learn to open a computer file's *ai-kon* (icon) you are told to *daburu-kurikku* (double-click) the *mausu* (mouse; Kristof, 1997).

In view of the extensive use of English in Japan, *The Japanese Times,* one of Tokyo's four English daily newspapers, ran a story a few years ago noting the pressures of globalization and suggesting it might be time for Japan to switch to English. However, it met with an official backlash. To limit the Anglicization of Japanese, the Ministry of Health and Welfare banned excessive use of English in its documents a couple of years ago. The Ministry of Education is now replacing many English words in official documents—such words as *sukeemu* (scheme), *eensenchibu* (incentive), *deribatibu* (derivative), and *identyityi* (identity). Whether official pronouncements will have much effect on the way English and Japlish are used in advertising and on the streets is, however, another question entirely. As one Japanese newspaper pointed out, given the popularity of English words, it's doubtful there will be much *foro-uppu* (follow-up).

For Japanese teenagers, English and Japlish are certainly considered the very height of fashion. "Japlish words are easy to pronounce. And English sounds very cool," says 11-year-old Mai Asai (quoted in Delmos, 2002). A 15-year-old girl, wearing her trademark *roozu sokusu* (loose socks), might greet a friend sporting new sunglasses with a spirited *chekaraccho* (Check it out, Joe). If she likes the shades, she might say they're *cho beri gu* (ultra-good) and invite her friend *deniru* (to go to a Denny's restaurant) or *hageru* (to go to a Häagen-Dazs ice cream outlet). Of course, the girl might also *disu* (diss, or show disrespect toward) her friend. She might come right out and inform him that the new shades look *cho beri ba* (ultra-bad) or *cho beri bu* (ultra-blue, depressing, or ultra-ugly). If so, the situation that develops could be a little *denjarasu* (dangerous). Terms of affection, such as *wonchu* (I want you), might not be exchanged. The boy might decide that he has made a *misu* (mistake) and that the girl is too *hi mentay* (high maintenance) to justify pursuing. The budding relationship might go nowhere. Nonetheless, we can be pretty sure that Japanese teenagers' use of English slang will intensify under the pressures of globalization.

Less humorously, the rise of English (as well as the influence of French, Spanish, and the languages of a few other colonizing nations) is eliminating several thousand languages around the world. These endangered languages are spoken by the tribes of Papua New Guinea; the native peoples of the Americas; the national and tribal minorities of Asia, Africa, and Oceania; and marginalized European peoples, such as the Irish and the Basques. An estimated five thousand to six thousand languages spoken in the world today will be reduced to one thousand to three thousand in a century. Much of the culture of a people—its prayers, humour, conversational styles, technical vocabulary, myths, and so on—is expressed through language. Therefore, the loss of language amounts to the disappearance of tradition and perhaps even identity. These are often replaced by the traditions and identity of the colonial power, with television playing an important role in the transformation (Woodbury, 2003).

The rights revolution raises some difficult issues. For example, groups that have suffered extraordinarily high levels of discrimination historically, such as Aboriginal Canadians, Jewish Canadians, Chinese Canadians, and Japanese Canadians, have demanded reparations in the form of money, symbolic gestures, and, in the case of Aboriginal Canadians, land and political autonomy.[2] Much controversy surrounds the extent of the obligation of current citizens to compensate for past injustices.

Another problem raised by the rights revolution concerns how we can achieve an acceptable balance between the right to be equal and the right to be different. For example, most residents of Quebec expect all Quebeckers to be able to compete on an equal footing for jobs, regardless of whether they are of French, English, or other origin. This is the right to equality. However, Quebeckers of French origin have also exercised their right to restrict non-francophones from expressing their right to be different. They have, for instance, passed laws restricting the use of English on public signs. These laws are controversial. Some English Quebeckers accept them as legitimate; others do not. Controversy therefore persists regarding the balance between the right to equality and the right to be different.

These problems notwithstanding, the rights revolution is here to stay and it affects our culture profoundly. Specifically, the rights revolution fragments Canadian culture by legitimizing the grievances of groups that were formerly excluded from full social participation and renewing pride in their identity and heritage. Our history books, our literature, our music, our use of languages, our very sense of what it means to be Canadian have diversified culturally. White male heterosexual property owners of British origin are still disproportionately influential in Canada, but our culture is no longer dominated by them in the way that it was just four or five decades ago.

POSTMODERNISM

In part because of the rights revolution, so much cultural fragmentation and reconfiguration has taken place in the last few decades that some sociologists think a new term is needed to characterize the culture of our times: **postmodernism.**

Postmodern culture has three main features. First, it involves *an eclectic mixing of elements from different times and places.* That is, in the postmodern era it is easier to create individualized belief systems and practices by blending facets of different cultures and historical periods. Consider religion. Surveys conducted by Reginald Bibby of the University of Lethbridge show that Canadians often supplement Judeo-Christian beliefs and practices with less conventional ideas about astrology, psychic powers, communication with the dead, and so forth (Bibby, 1987). People who attend church regularly are just as likely to hold such unconventional beliefs as nonattenders are. However, despite the widespread acceptance of unconventional beliefs, the overwhelming majority of Canadians still turn to established religions for **rites of passage,** or cultural ceremonies that mark the transition from one stage of life to another (e.g., baptisms, confirmations, weddings) or from life to death (funerals). Individuals thus choose their own mix of unconventional and conventional beliefs and practices. They draw on religions much like consumers shop in a mall; as Bibby says, they practise religion à la carte. Meanwhile, Canadian churches have diversified their menus to appeal to the spiritual, leisure, and social needs of religious consumers and retain their loyalties in the competitive market for congregants and parishioners. The mix-and-match approach we see when it comes to religion is evident in virtually all spheres of culture.

Second, postmodernism also involves *the erosion of authority.* Half a century ago, Canadians were more likely than they are today to defer to authority in the family, schools, politics, medicine, and religion. In fact, Canadians were often characterized as an especially deferential people, more respectful of authority than their individualistic, revolutionary, violent, and entrepreneurial cousins in the United States. In the second half of the twentieth century, however, Canadians grew skeptical about authority in many institutions, especially political institutions—even more skeptical than Americans in many respects (Brym with Fox, 1989; Nevitte, 1996; see Box 2.4). For example, voting and other forms of conventional politics are less popular than they used to be, while nonconventional political action, such as participating in demonstrations, is more popular (see Figure 2.2).

Finally, postmodernism is characterized by *the decline of consensus around core values.* Half a century ago, people's values remained quite stable over the course of their adult lives and many values were widely accepted. Today, value shifts are more rapid and consensus has broken down on many issues. For instance, half a century ago, the great majority of adults remained loyal to one political party from one election to the next. Today, people are more likely to vote for different parties in

BOX 2.4 AUTHORITY, IDENTITY, AND CULTURE IN CANADA AND THE UNITED STATES

Until the mid-1960s, the image of Canadians among most sociologists was that of a stodgy people: peaceful, conservative, respectful of authority, and therefore quite unlike our American cousins.

According to conventional wisdom, the United States was born in open rebellion against the British motherland. Its Western frontier was lawless. Vast opportunities for striking it rich bred a spirit of individualism. Thus, American culture became an anti-authoritarian culture.

Canada developed differently according to the conventional view. It became an independent country not through a revolutionary upheaval but in a gradual, evolutionary manner. The Northwest Mounted Police and two highly hierarchical churches (Roman Catholic and Anglican) established themselves on the Western frontier before the era of mass settlement, allowing for the creation of an orderly society rather than a "wild West." Beginning with the Hudson's Bay Company, large corporations quickly came to dominate the Canadian economy, hampering individualism and the entrepreneurial spirit. Thus, Canadian culture became a culture of deference to authority. That, at least, was the common view until the 1960s (Lipset, 1963).

Although the contrast between deferential Canadian culture and anti-authoritarian American culture may have had some validity 40 or 50 years ago, it is an inaccurate characterization today (Adams, 1997: 62–95). As we have seen, the questioning of authority spread throughout the Western world beginning in the 1960s. Nowhere, however, did it spread as quickly and thoroughly as in Canada. Canadians used to express more confidence in big business than Americans did, but surveys now show the opposite. Canadians used to be more religious than Americans, but that is no longer the case. Fewer Canadians (in percentage terms) say they believe in God and fewer attend weekly religious services. Confidence in government has eroded more quickly in Canada than in the United States. Americans are more patriotic than Canadians, according more respect to the state. Finally, Americans are more likely than Canadians to regard the traditional nuclear family as the ideal family form and to think of deviations from tradition—same-sex couples, single-parent families, cohabitation without marriage—as the source of a whole range of social problems. Thus, whether sociologists examine attitudes toward the family, the state, government, religion, or big business, they now find that Americans are more deferential to traditional institutional authority than Canadians are.

Because Canadians are less deferential to traditional institutional authority than Americans are, some commentators say that Canadians lack a distinct culture. For example, American patriotism sparks awareness of great national accomplishments in art, war, sports, science, and, indeed, all fields of human endeavour. Anthems, rituals, myths, and celebrations recognize these accomplishments and give Americans a keen sense of who they are and how they differ from non-Americans. Not surprisingly, therefore, a larger percentage of Americans than of Canadians think of themselves as "Americans" plain and simple rather than, say, Italian Americans. In Canada, a larger percentage of the population thinks of itself in hyphenated terms; compared with the Americans, our identity is qualified, even tentative.

Does this mean that Canadians lack a distinct national culture? Hardly. It means that although American culture is characterized by a relatively high degree of deference to dominant institutions, Canadian culture is characterized by a relatively high degree of tolerance and respect for diversity. We are more likely than Americans are to favour gender equality, accept gay and lesbian relationships, encourage bilingualism and multiculturalism, and accept the right of Aboriginal peoples to political autonomy. Characteristically, a large international survey by a condom manufacturer found that Americans have sex more often than Canadians do but Canadians are most likely to say that the pleasure of their partner is very important. As public opinion pollster Michael Adams writes,

> Twenty-five years of public-opinion polling in Canada has taught me a seemingly paradoxical truth. Canadians feel strongly about their weak attachments to Canada, its political institutions and their fellow citizens. In other words, they feel strongly about the right to live in a society that allows its citizens to be detached from ideology and critical of organizations, and not to feel obliged to be jingoistic or sentimentally patriotic. Canadians' lack of nationalism is, in many ways, a distinguishing feature of the country. (1997: 171)

In short, Canadian culture is distinctive, and its chief distinction may be that it qualifies us as the first thoroughly postmodern society.

FIGURE 2.2 CANADA: VOTING DOWN, DEMONSTRATING UP

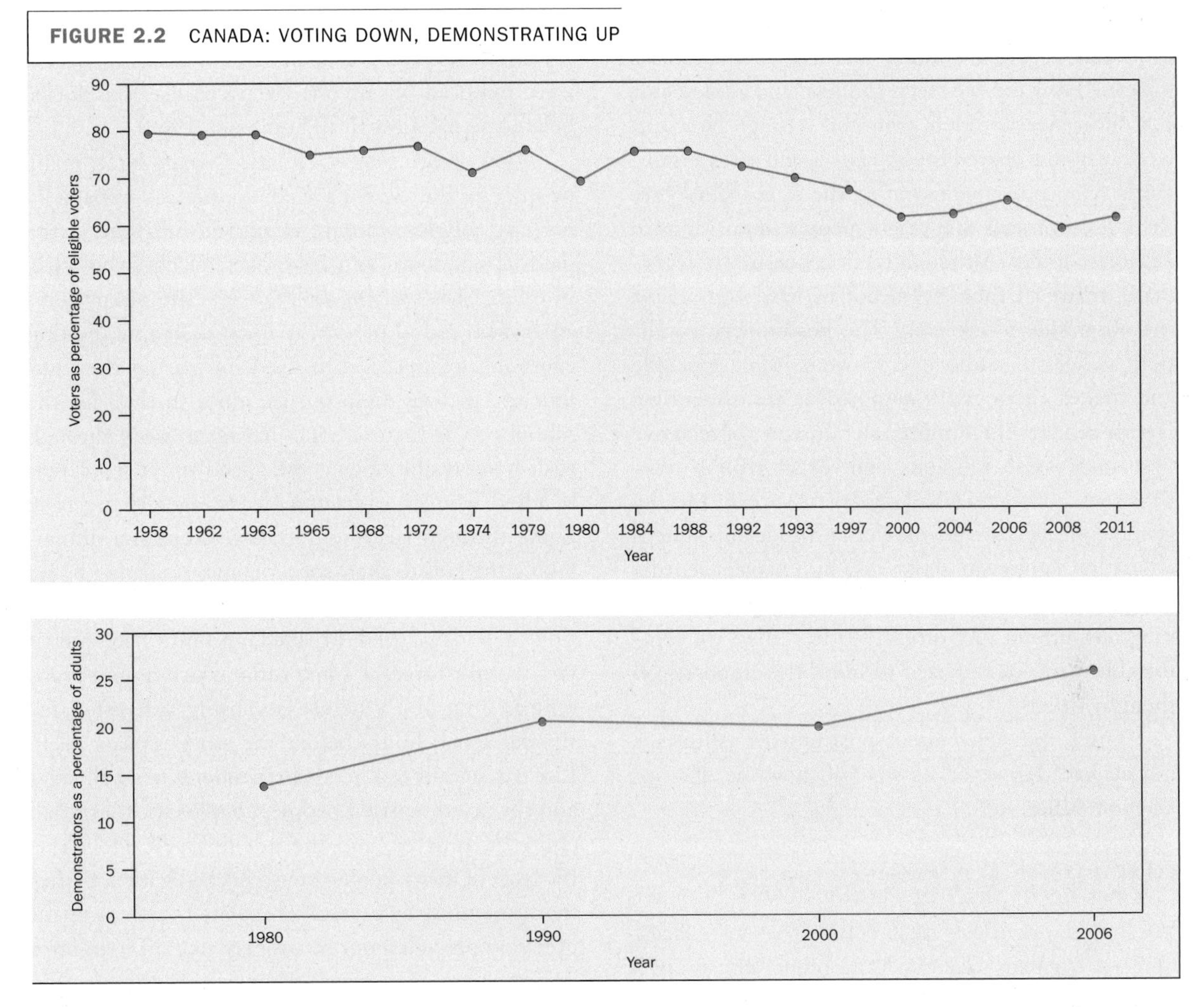

SOURCES: (top) Voter Turnout at Federal Elections and Referendums, Elections Canada, 1997. This is an adaptation of the version available at www.elections.ca. Reproduced with the permission of Elections Canada, but adaptation rests with the author; (bottom) *World Values Survey* (2012).

succeeding elections (Clarke, Jenson, LeDuc, and Pammett, 1996: 139–46).

The decline of consensus can also be illustrated by considering the fate of Big Historical Projects. For most of the past two hundred years, consensus throughout the world was built around Big Historical Projects. Various social movements convinced people they could take history into their own hands and create a glorious future just by signing up. German Nazism was a Big Historical Project. Its followers expected the Reich to enjoy a thousand years of power. Communism was an even bigger Big Historical Project, mobilizing hundreds of millions of people for a future that promised to end inequality and injustice for all time. However, the biggest and most successful Big Historical Project was not so much a social movement as a powerful idea—the belief that progress is inevitable, that life will always improve, mainly because of the spread of democracy and scientific innovation.

The twentieth century was unkind to Big Historical Projects. Russian communism lasted 74 years, German Nazism a mere 12. The idea of progress fell on hard times as 100 million soldiers and civilians died in wars; the forward march of democracy took wrong turns into fascism, communism, and regimes based on religious fanaticism; and pollution from urbanization and industrialization threatened the planet. In the postmodern era, more and more people recognize that apparent progress, including scientific advances, often has negative consequences (Scott, 1998).

The aspects of postmodernism listed previously—the eclectic mixing of cultural elements from different times and places, the erosion of authority, and the decline of consensus around core values—have many parents, teachers, politicians, religious leaders, and not a few university professors worried. How can we make binding decisions? How can we govern? How can we teach children and adolescents the difference between right and wrong? How can we transmit accepted literary tastes and artistic standards from one generation to the next? These are the kinds of issues that plague people in positions of authority today. Although their concerns are legitimate, many of them seem not to have considered the other side of the coin: The postmodern condition, as described above, empowers ordinary people and makes them more responsible for their own fate. It renders them more tolerant and appreciative of ethnic, racial, religious, and sexual groups other than their own—no small matter in a world torn by group conflict. The postmodern attitude encourages a healthy skepticism about rosy and naive scientific and political promises. And it frees people to adopt religious, ethnic, and other identities they are comfortable with, as opposed to identities imposed on them by others.

Thus, the news about postmodern culture is not all bad. However, as you will now see, it's not all good either.

CULTURE AS CONSTRAINT

We noted previously that culture has two faces. One we labelled "freedom," the other "constraint." Diversity, globalization, and postmodernism are all aspects of the new freedoms that culture allows us today. We now turn to an examination of two contemporary aspects of culture that act as constraining forces on our lives: rationalization and consumerism.

RATIONALIZATION

In fourteenth-century Europe, an upsurge in demand for textiles caused loom owners to look for ways to increase productivity. To that end, they imposed longer hours on loom workers and installed the first public clocks. The clocks, known as *Werkglocken* ("work clocks") in German, signalled the beginning of the workday, the timing of meals, and quitting time.

Workers were accustomed to enjoying many holidays and a flexible and vague work schedule regulated only approximately by the seasons and the rising and setting of the Sun. The regimentation imposed by the work clocks made life harder. Therefore, the workers staged uprisings to silence the clocks—but to no avail. City officials sided with the employers and imposed fines for ignoring the *Werkglocken*. Harsher penalties, including death, were imposed on anyone trying to use the clocks' bells to signal a revolt (Thompson, 1967).

Now, more than six hundred years later, many people in the world's rich countries—especially big-city couples who are employed full-time in the paid labour force and have preteen children—are, in effect, slaves of the *Werkglocke*. Life often seems an endless round of waking up at 6:30 a.m., getting everyone washed and dressed, preparing the kids' lunches, getting them out the door in time for the school bus or the car pool, driving to work through rush-hour traffic, facing the speed-up at work that resulted from the recent downsizing, driving back home through rush-hour traffic, preparing dinner, taking the kids to their soccer game, returning home to clean up the dishes and help with homework, getting the kids washed, brushed, and into bed, and (if you haven't brought some office work home) grabbing an hour of TV before collapsing, exhausted, for six-and-a-half hours before the story repeats itself. Life is generally less hectic for residents of small cities and towns, unmarried people, couples without small children, retirees, and the unemployed. However, the lives of many people are so packed with activities that time must be carefully regulated, each moment precisely parcelled out so we may tick off item after item from an ever-growing list of tasks that need to be completed on schedule (Schor, 1992). Women in particular are working more hours per week for pay, and overtime work is increasing, especially for senior managers (Statistics Canada, 2012).

After more than six hundred years of conditioning, it is unusual for people to rebel against the clock in the town square anymore. In fact, we now wear a watch on our wrist without giving it a second thought. This signifies that we have accepted and internalized the regime of the work clock. Allowing clocks to regulate our activities precisely seems the most natural thing in the world—which is a pretty good sign that the internalized *Werkglocke* is, in fact, a product of culture.

Is the precise regulation of time rational? It certainly is rational as a means of ensuring efficiency, that is, maximizing how much work you get done in a day. But is it rational as an end in itself? For many people, it is not. The precise regulation of time has gotten out of hand. Life has simply become too hectic for many people to enjoy fully. In this sense, rationality of means has led to irrationality of ends.

For American sociologist George Ritzer, the McDonald's fast-food restaurant epitomizes the rationalization process. Ritzer speaks of the "McDonaldization" of the world, by which he means that the organizational principles of the fast-food restaurant are coming to dominate everywhere (Ritzer, 1993, 1996).

At McDonald's, a set list of carefully weighed food portions with identical ingredients are cooked according to a uniform and precisely timed process. But, says Ritzer, the application of assembly-line procedures to meal preparation is dehumanizing for both employees and customers. Thus, the work is done by mainly nonunionized, uniformed, teenage workers who receive minimum wage. To boost sales, they are required to smile as they recite fixed scripts ("Would you like some fries or a drink with your burger?"). Nearly half of all McDonald's employees are so dissatisfied with their work, they quit after a year or less. To deal with this problem, McDonald's is field-testing self-service kiosks in which an automated machine cooks and bags French fries while a vertical grill takes patties from the freezer and grills them to your liking (Carpenter, 2003). Meanwhile, customers are expected to spend as little time as possible eating the food—hence the drive-through window, chairs designed to be comfortable for only about 20 minutes, and small express outlets in subways and department stores where customers eat standing up or on the run. In short, McDonald's executives have carefully thought through every aspect of your lunch. With the goal of making profits, they have rationalized food preparation, making it as inexpensive and as fast as possible.

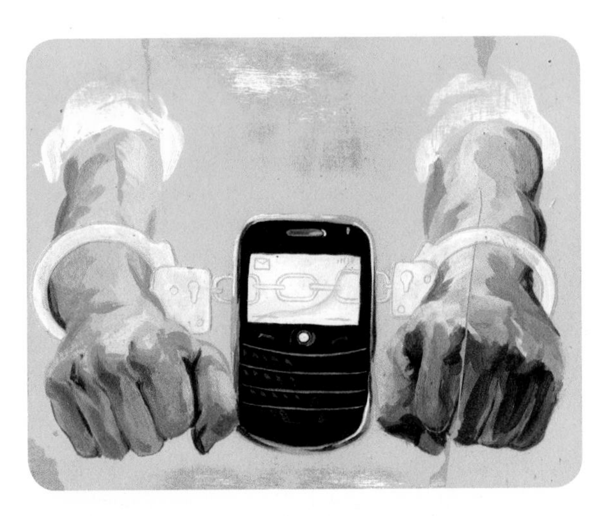

BlackBerrys and iPhones allow people to stay in touch with friends and work every waking moment. Many people have mixed feelings about these devices. Sometimes they seem pleasurable and efficient. At other times they prevent relaxation and intimacy. As such, they typify the two faces of culture.
SOURCE: © Dave Murray

Taking McDonaldization to a new extreme, one restaurant in Japan has even installed a punch-clock for its customers. The restaurant offers all you can eat for 35 yen per minute. As a result, "the diners rush in, punch the clock, load their trays from the buffet table, and concentrate intensely on efficient chewing and swallowing, trying not to waste time talking to their companions before rushing back to punch out. This version of fast food is so popular that, as the restaurant prepares to open at lunchtime, Tokyo residents *wait in line*" (Gleick, 2000: 244; emphasis in the original). Meanwhile, in New York and Los Angeles, some upscale restaurants have gotten in on the act. An increasingly large number of business clients are so pressed for time, they feel the need to pack in *two* half-hour lunches with successive guests. The restaurants oblige, making the resetting of tables "resemble the pit-stop activity at the Indianapolis 500" (Gleick, 2000: 155; Box 2.2).

As the examples of the *Werkglocke* and fast food show, rationalization enables us to do just about everything more efficiently, but at a steep cost. In fact, because it is so widespread, rationalization is one of the most constraining aspects of culture today. In Weber's view, it makes life in the modern world akin to living inside an "iron cage."

CONSUMERISM

The second constraining aspect of culture is consumerism. **Consumerism** is the tendency to define ourselves in terms of the goods and services we purchase. As artist Barbara Kruger put it: "I shop, therefore I am."

Advertising works by making it seem as if buying commodities will ensure that you gain desirable characteristics. For example, some years ago, the Gap hired Hollywood talent to create a slick and highly effective series of TV ads for khaki pants. According to the promotional material for the ad campaign, the purpose of the ads was to "reinvent khakis," that is, to stimulate demand for the pants. In *Khakis rock*, "skateboarders and in-line skaters dance, glide, and fly to music by the Crystal Method." In *Khakis groove*, "hip-hop dancers throw radical moves to the funky beat of Bill Mason." In *Khakis swing*, "two couples break away from a crowd to demonstrate swing techniques to the vintage sounds of Louis Prima" (Gap.com, 1999).

About 55 seconds of each ad featured the dancers. During the last 5 seconds, the words "GAP khakis" appeared on the screen. The Gap followed a similar approach in another ad campaign a couple of years later. Inspired by the musical *West Side Story*, the 30-second spots replaced the play's warring street gangs, the Jets and the Sharks, with fashion factions of their own, the Khakis and the Jeans. Again, most of the ad was devoted to the riveting dance number. The pants were mentioned for only a few seconds at the end.

As the imbalance between stylish come-on and mere information suggests, the people who created the ads understood that it was really the appeal of the dancers that would sell the pants. They knew that to stimulate demand for their product, they had to associate the khakis with desirable properties, such as youth, good health, coolness, popularity, beauty, and sex. As an advertising executive said in the 1940s: "It's not the steak we sell. It's the sizzle."

Because advertising stimulates sales, business has a tendency to spend more on advertising over time. Because advertising is widespread, most people unquestioningly accept it as part of their lives. In fact, many people have *become* ads. Thus, when your father was a child and quickly threw on a shirt, allowing a label to hang out, your grandmother might admonish him to "tuck in that label." Today, in contrast, many people proudly display consumer labels as marks of status and identity. Advertisers teach us to associate the words "Gucci" and "Nike" with different kinds of people, and when people display these labels on their clothes, they are telling us something about the kind of people they are and whom they associate with. Advertising becomes us.

SOURCE: © Barbara Kruger. Courtesy: Mary Boone Gallery, New York.

Recent innovations in advertising take full advantage of our tendency to define ourselves in terms of the goods we purchase. For example, when channel surfing and the use of personal video recorders spread, advertisers realized they had a problem on their hands. Viewers started skipping TV ads that cost millions of dollars and untold hours of creative effort to produce. As a result, advertisers had to think up new ways of drawing products to the attention of consumers. One idea they hit on was paying to place their products in TV shows and movies. They realized that when Brad Pitt or some other big star drinks a can of Coke or lights up a Marlboro, members of the audience tend to associate the product with the star. Wanting to be like the star, they are more likely to buy the product. Thus, sales of Travelpro luggage spiked in 2009, when the Oscar-nominated movie *Up in the Air* featured several travel scenes focusing on George Clooney's efficient and elegant suitcase. The product became part of who many audience members wanted to be.

Since the 1980s, there has been an explosion of advertising directed at children. Here, advertisers recognized, was a vast untapped market; children could be used to nag their parents to buy more products. The manipulation of children by advertisers soon became a sort of quasi-science. One advertising expert said seven basic types of nagging tactics can be unleashed by effective child-directed advertising:

> A *pleading* nag is one accompanied by repetitions of words like "please" or "mom, mom, mom." A *persistent* nag involves constant requests for the coveted product and may include the phrase "I'm gonna ask just one more time." *Forceful* nags are extremely pushy and may include subtle threats, like "Well, then, I'll go and ask Dad." *Demonstrative* nags are the most high-risk, often characterized by full-blown tantrums in public places, breath-holding, tears, a refusal to leave the store. *Sugar-coated* nags promise affection in

> return for a purchase and may rely on seemingly heartfelt declarations like "You're the best dad in the world." *Threatening* nags are youthful forms of blackmail, vows of eternal hatred and of running away if something isn't bought. *Pity* nags claim the child will be heartbroken, teased, or socially stunted if the parent refuses to buy a certain product. (Schlosser, 2002: 44)

Note that getting children to nag their parents to buy more products is only one aim of child-directed advertising. In addition, advertisers recognize that ads directed at children can be used to develop brand loyalty that will, in the ideal case, last a lifetime. A few years ago, executives at one large brewery must have been delighted to read the results of a consumer survey that found that the most popular ads among American children were a Taco Bell commercial featuring a talking Chihuahua and an ad for Budweiser beer.

The rationalization process enables us to produce more efficiently, to have more of just about everything than our parents did. However, it is consumerism, the tendency to define ourselves in terms of the goods we purchase, that ensures the goods will be bought. Of course, people living in the world's rich countries have lots of choice. We can select from dozens of styles of running shoes, cars, and all the rest. We can also choose to buy items that help define us as members of a particular **subculture,** adherents of a set of distinctive values, norms, and practices within a larger culture. But, regardless of individual tastes and inclinations, nearly all of us have one thing in common: We tend to be good consumers. We are motivated by advertising, which is based on the accurate insight that people will likely be considered social outcasts if they fail to conform to stylish trends. By creating those trends, advertisers push us to buy. That is why North Americans' "shop-till-you-drop" lifestyle prompted French sociologist Jean Baudrillard to remark pointedly that even what is best in North America is compulsory (Baudrillard, 1988 [1986]).

FROM COUNTERCULTURE TO SUBCULTURE

In concluding my discussion of culture as a constraining force, I want to note that consumerism is remarkably effective at taming countercultures. **Countercultures** are subversive subcultures. They oppose dominant values and seek to replace them. The hippies of the 1960s formed a counterculture and so do environmentalists today.

Countercultures rarely pose a serious threat to social stability. Most often, the system of social control, of rewards and punishments, keeps countercultures at bay. In our society, consumerism acts as a social control mechanism that normally prevents countercultures from disrupting the social order. It does that by transforming deviations from mainstream culture into means of making money and by enticing rebels to become entrepreneurs (Frank and Weiland, 1997). The development of hip-hop helps to illustrate the point (Brym, 2001).

Hip-hop originated in the American inner city in the 1970s. At the time, manufacturing industries were leaving the inner city for suburban or foreign locales, where land values were lower and labour was less expensive. Unemployment among African American youth rose to more than 40 percent. At the same time, many middle-class blacks left the inner city for the suburbs. Their migration robbed the remaining young people of successful role models. It also eroded the taxing capacity of municipal governments, leading to a decline in public services. Meanwhile, the American public elected conservative governments at the state and federal levels. They cut school and welfare budgets, thus deepening the destitution of ghetto life (Piven and Cloward, 1977: 264–361; Wilson, 1987).

With few legitimate prospects for advancement, poor African American youth in the inner city turned increasingly to crime and, in particular, the drug trade. In the late 1970s, cocaine was expensive and demand for the drug was flat. Consequently, in the early 1980s, Colombia's Medellin drug cartel introduced a less expensive form of cocaine called rock or crack. Crack was inexpensive, it offered a quick and intense high, and it was highly addictive. It offered many people a temporary escape from hopelessness and soon became wildly popular in the inner city. Turf wars spread as gangs tried to outgun each other for control of the local traffic. The sale and use of crack became so widespread, it corroded much of what was left of the inner-city African American community (Davis, 1990).

The shocking conditions described above gave rise to a shocking musical form: hip-hop. Stridently at odds with the values and tastes of both whites and middle-class African Americans, hip-hop described and glorified the mean streets of the inner city while holding the police, the mass media, and other pillars of society in utter contempt. Furthermore, hip-hop tried to offend middle-class sensibilities, black and white, by using highly offensive language.

In 1988, more than a decade after its first stirrings, hip-hop reached its political high point with the release of the album *It Takes a Nation of Millions to Hold Us Back* by Chuck D and Public Enemy. In "Don't Believe the Hype," Chuck D accused the mass media of maliciously distributing lies. In "Black Steel in the Hour of Chaos," he charged the FBI and the CIA with assassinating the two great leaders of the African American community in the 1960s, Martin Luther King and Malcolm X. In "Party for Your Right to Fight," he blamed the federal government for organizing the fall of the Black Panthers, the radical black nationalist party of the 1960s. Here, it seemed, was an angry expression of subcultural revolt that could not be tamed.

However, the seduction of big money did much to mute the political force of hip-hop. As early as 1982, with the release of Grandmaster Flash and the Furious Five's "The Message," hip-hop began to win acclaim from mainstream rock music critics. With the success of Run-D.M.C. and Public Enemy in the late 1980s, it became clear there was a big audience for hip-hop. Significantly, much of that audience was composed of white youths. As one music critic wrote, they "relished ... the subversive 'otherness' that the music and its purveyors represented" (Neal, 1999: 144). Sensing the opportunity for profit, major media corporations, such as Time/Warner, Sony, CBS/Columbia, and BMG Entertainment, signed distribution deals with the small independent recording labels that had formerly been the exclusive distributors of hip-hop CDs. In 1988, *Yo! MTV Raps* debuted on MTV. The program brought hip-hop to middle America.

Most hip-hop recording artists proved they were eager to forgo political relevancy for commerce. For instance, WU-Tang Clan started a line of clothing called WU Wear, and, with the help of major hip-hop recording artists, companies as diverse as Tommy Hilfiger, Timberland, Starter, and Versace began to market clothing influenced by ghetto styles. Independent labels, such as Phat Farm and Fubu, also prospered. Puff Daddy reminded his audience in his 1999 CD, *Forever*: "N—— get money, that's simply the plan." According to *Forbes* magazine, he became one of the country's 40 richest men under 40. By 2005, having renamed himself Diddy, he had his own line of popular clothing. The members of Run-D.M.C. once said that they "don't want nobody's name on my behind," but those days were long past by the early 1990s. Hip-hop was no longer just a musical form but a commodity with spin-offs. Rebellion had been turned into mass consumption. Hip-hop's radicalism had given way to the lures of commerce. A counterculture had become a subculture.

Diddy marketing "rebellion".
SOURCE: © REUTERS/Mike Blake.

Radical political currents in hip-hop still exist, but mainly outside the United States and other English-speaking countries. In Senegal, the playing of hip-hop that is highly critical of the government is widely believed to have helped topple the ruling party in the 2000 election. In France, North African youth living in impoverished and segregated slums use hip-hop to express their political discontent, and some analysts say the genre helped mobilize youth for anti-government rioting in 2005 (Akwagyiram, 2009). "*Rais Lebled* [Mr. President]," a song by a Tunisian rapper, became the anthem of young people participating in the democratic uprisings in Tunisia, Egypt, and Bahrain in 2011: "Mr. President, your people are dying/People are eating rubbish/Look at what is happening/Miseries everywhere, Mr. President/I talk with no fear/Although I know I will get only trouble/I see injustice everywhere" (Ghosh, 2011). However, in the

United States and Canada, hip-hop has become, for the most part, an apolitical commodity that increasingly appeals to a racially heterogeneous, middle-class audience. As one of hip-hop's leading analysts and academic sympathizers writes, "the discourse of ghetto reality or 'hood authenticity remains largely devoid of political insight or progressive intent" (Forman, 2001: 121). The fate of hip-hop is testimony to the capacity of consumerism to change countercultures into mere subcultures, thus constraining dissent and rebellion.

SUMMARY

1. Humans have been able to adapt to their environments because they are able to create culture. In particular, the ability to create symbols, cooperate, and make tools has enabled humans to thrive.
2. Culture can be invisible if we are too deeply immersed in it. The cultures of others can seem inscrutable if we view them exclusively from the perspective of our own culture. Therefore, the best vantage point for analyzing culture is on the margins—neither too deeply immersed in it nor too much removed from it.
3. Culture becomes more diversified and consensus declines in many areas of life as societies become more complex. This increases human freedom, giving people more choice in their ethnic, religious, sexual, and other identities.
4. So much cultural diversification and reconfiguration have taken place that some sociologists characterize the culture of our times as postmodern. Postmodernism involves an eclectic mixing of cultural elements from different times and places, the erosion of authority, and the decline of consensus around core values.
5. Underlying cultural diversification is the rights revolution, the process by which socially excluded groups have struggled to win equal rights under the law and in practice.
6. Although the diversification of culture increases human freedom, the growth of complex societies also establishes definite limits within which diversification may occur. This is illustrated by the process of rationalization (the optimization of means to achieve given ends), and the growth of consumerism (which involves defining one's self in terms of the goods one purchases).

QUESTIONS TO CONSIDER

1. We imbibe culture but also create it. What elements of culture have you created? Under what conditions were you prompted to do so? Was your cultural contribution strictly personal or was it shared with others? Why?
2. Do you think of yourself in a fundamentally different way from the way your parents (or other close relatives or friends at least 20 years older than you) thought of themselves when they were your age? Are your attitudes toward authority different? Interview your parents, relatives, or friends to find out. Pay particular attention to the way in which the forces of globalization have altered ethnic, racial, and religious self-conceptions, and how your attitudes to authority differ from those of your elders.
3. One of the main themes of this chapter is that rationality of means sometimes results in irrationality of ends. Select a sphere of culture (religion, education, the mass media, etc.) and illustrate the point.

GLOSSARY

Abstraction (p. 30) is the human capacity to create complex symbols, including languages, mathematical notations, and signs, in order to classify experience and generalize from it.

Consumerism (p. 43) involves defining ourselves in terms of the goods we purchase.

Cooperation (p. 30) is the human capacity to create a complex social life by establishing norms.

Countercultures (p. 45) are subversive subcultures. They oppose dominant values and seek to replace them.

Cultural relativism (p. 35) is the opposite of ethnocentrism. It is the idea that all cultures and all cultural practices have equal value.

Culture (p. 29) is the sum of socially transmitted practices, languages, symbols, beliefs, values, ideologies, and material objects that people create to deal with real-life problems. Cultures enable people to adapt to, and thrive in, their environments.

Ethnocentrism (p. 33) is the tendency to judge other cultures exclusively by the standards of our own.

A **language** (p. 31) is a system of symbols strung together to communicate thought.

Material culture (p. 31) comprises the tools and techniques that improve our ability to take what we want from nature.

Norms (p. 30) are standards of behaviour or generally accepted ways of doing things.

Postmodernism (p. 39) is characterized by an eclectic mixing of cultural elements, the erosion of authority, and the decline of consensus around core values.

Production (p. 31) is the human capacity to make and use tools. It improves our ability to take what we want from nature.

The **rights revolution** (p. 37) is the process by which excluded groups have obtained equal rights under the law and in practice.

A **rite of passage** (p. 39) is a cultural ceremony that marks the transition from one stage of life to another or from life to death.

Sanctions (p. 31) are rewards and punishments intended to ensure conformity to cultural guidelines.

The **Sapir-Whorf thesis** (p. 31) holds that we experience certain things in our environment and form concepts about those things. We then develop language to express our concepts. Finally, language itself influences how we see the world.

The system of **social control** (p. 31) is the means by which members of society ensure people conform to cultural guidelines.

A **society** (p. 30) involves people interacting socially and sharing culture, usually in a defined geographical area.

A **subculture** (p. 45) is a distinctive set of values, norms, and practices within a larger culture.

A **symbol** (p. 30) is anything that carries a particular meaning, including the components of language, mathematical notations, and signs. Symbols allow us to engage in abstraction.

SUGGESTED READING

Adams, Michael. (1997). *Sex in the Snow: Canadian Social Values at the End of the Millennium.* Toronto: Penguin. Adams is a sociologist and one of Canada's leading public opinion pollsters. Here he identifies and analyzes the core values of Canadian culture, highlighting differences by generation, gender, and country (Canada versus the United States).

Hall, John R., Laura Grindstaff, and Ming-Cheng Lo, eds. (2010). *Handbook of Cultural Sociology.* New York: Taylor & Francis. Sixty-five essays by leadings experts in the field comprehensively analyze the relationship of culture to social structure and everyday life.

Klein, Naomi. (2009). *No Logo: No Space, No Choice, No Jobs.* London, UK: Picador. Klein tells a story of rebellion and self-determination in the face of our new, branded world in the context of the Great Recession of 2007–09.

NOTES

1. New forms of society on the Internet ("virtual communities") show that physical proximity is not always a necessary part of the definition.
2. Many children of Aboriginal Canadians were put into residential schools in the twentieth century, and many of them were physically and sexually abused by the ministers, priests, and nuns who ran these schools. Many Aboriginal Canadians also claim that much land was taken from them illegally. Some 21 000 Japanese Canadians living within 160 kilometres of the Pacific Coast, three-quarters of them Canadian citizens, were forcibly moved to prisoner-of-war, internment, and work camps in 1942. They lost most of their property. Descendants of many Chinese Canadians were forced to pay an exorbitant "head tax" in the late nineteenth and early twentieth centuries, the purpose of which was to encourage them to leave the country. The Nazis enslaved and slaughtered millions of European Jews in World War II and stole their property. Survivors, a considerable number of them residing in Canada, later sought and received reparations from the German and Swiss governments.

CHAPTER 3

SOCIALIZATION

SOURCE: © Mark Richards/PhotoEdit.

William Shaffir

Dorothy Pawluch
McMASTER UNIVERSITY

IN THIS CHAPTER YOU WILL LEARN THAT

- Socialization is the social process that allow people to become members of society, develop a sense of self, and learn to participate in social relationships with others.
- Socialization takes place at all stages of the life cycle and in a variety of settings: families, schools, peer groups, the mass media, and occupational groups.
- Among the major contributors to socialization theory are Charles Cooley (who argued that individuals develop a sense of self as they interact with others), and George Herbert Mead (who focused on the way we create a sense of self by taking the roles of others).
- Socialization is a never-ending process. As people work, marry, divorce, raise children, and retire, they enter new relationships with others, learn new behaviour, and adopt new roles.
- Sometimes our self-concept undergoes abrupt change as we learn new role identities and negotiate a new self-image. Such "resocialization" occurs when we replace our way of life with a radically different one. It is most evident in jails, psychiatric hospitals, and boot camps, and in religious and political conversions.

WHAT IS SOCIALIZATION?

As well-entrenched members of society, most of us take for granted what we need to know to function easily in a variety of social contexts. A common language that allows us to communicate with others is essential, as is knowledge about norms, laws, attitudes, beliefs, and values. What we need to know ranges from the mundane to the serious. In an elevator, people typically face forward. Murder is outlawed. Picking your teeth in public is considered ill mannered, as are most acts of self-grooming. Diversity is valued. "Shouting" or using only capital letters in computer communications will likely upset those on the receiving end. Women and men are considered equal. Wear mismatched socks and people will wonder about you.

Even more basic to functioning in society, however, is some sense of ourselves as separate from others. In other words, to interact with others we need a **self,** a sense of individual identity that allows us to understand who we are in relation to others and to differentiate ourselves from them. This sense of self allows us to react to what we learn so that once we know what is expected of us in any given situation, we can choose whether or not to behave in ways consistent with those expectations. We are constrained by societal norms and values (shared ideas about right and wrong). At the same time, we are free to decide how to behave.

Nobody comes into the world pre-programmed with a sense of self and the knowledge necessary to act and interact appropriately with others. To learn the way of life in our society and develop an identity, we undergo a process of social interaction known as **socialization.** Socialization is the vital link between individuals and society. Neither can exist without the other. We would have no sense of ourselves as distinct and autonomous human beings without interaction with others. We would not be able to function without the tools that society provides to solve the problems of survival. Chapter 2, Culture describes symbols, norms, values, and everyday practices as examples of such tools. Their use allows us to master nature and build orderly societies. However, these tools must be acquired. They must become a part of us—internalized through socialization. At the same time, society would not be possible without human beings able to interact effectively with one another and to transmit the stock of knowledge that ensures continuity from one generation to the next. Socialization thus makes social interaction, social organization, and social order possible.

Since socialization occurs in a cultural context, the content of socialization differs from one society to the next. People in a particular society learn the norms, values, and lifestyles specific to their social environment. At the same time, in every society individuals differ in significant ways from one another. Individual differences, too, are to some extent the product of socialization. Each person is influenced by distinctive subcultures of family, friends, class, race, religion, and gender. (A subculture is a group within the larger culture that has distinctive values, norms, and practices.) Our unique personal histories permit us not only to share in the larger society, but also to participate in specific parts of it. Socialization helps to explain both similarities and differences among people in a particular society.

Primary socialization is the crucial learning process that occurs in childhood and initiates our entry into society. Since primary socialization is so important to becoming who and what we are, it is the focus of the first part of this chapter. However, we all know that we change over time as we encounter new situations and groups. Learning to be a student, spouse or parent; learning a job; making new friends; taking on new hobbies; joining new clubs; moving to another country; and if we are lucky, growing old—all involve socialization. This kind of learning is called **secondary socialization** because it occurs after people have already undergone primary socialization. However, it is not secondary in importance. We address the ongoing nature of socialization in considering socialization through the life cycle.

NATURE AND NURTURE

If we are products of socialization, does that mean that we are born as blank slates? Aren't we to some extent pre-programmed? Don't we have **instincts**? What about natural differences among people? Aren't some of us *naturally* more charismatic, brighter, and more compliant, while others are more aggressive or quieter?

The debate over whether biological inheritance ("nature") or social environment ("nurture") is more important in shaping our beliefs and behaviour is an old one. We can't deny that some human behaviour is the outcome of biological factors or that we seem to have certain predispositions from the moment we are born. Nor can we deny that whatever inclinations we might be born with as infants are developed in a social setting and influenced greatly by our social experiences. Someone who is aggressive might well become gentle—or at least less aggressive—if raised in a society that places great value on pacifism or under circumstances in which aggression is discouraged. Someone with intellectual potential is not likely to realize that potential without a stimulating environment or the appropriate educational experiences. It is apparent that the old nature versus nurture debate is futile because it sets up a false opposition. Nature and nurture are inseparable. The human brain provides the physiological apparatus required for interpreting experiences, but unless children have the opportunity to learn, reason, and solve problems in early life, the brain itself may not fully develop (Begley, 1995). Attempts to determine the relative importance of nature and nurture in human development are much like trying to establish whether width or height is more significant in determining area.

The evidence for just how critical social interaction and intimate relations with others are to our development as human beings is dramatic. Some evidence comes from studies of "feral" children—children who grow up alone in the wilderness or are raised by wild animals. While most accounts of feral children are either fictional (Tarzan and Peter Pan) or the stuff of legends (Rome is said to have been founded by Romulus and Remus, twins raised by wolves), there are cases that appear to be authentic (Newton, 2002). Among them is the story of Victor, the "wild boy of Aveyron." Victor was a young boy about 11 or 12 years of age whom villagers in southern France first noticed foraging for food in the local woods in 1797. He was

Most socialization takes place informally, with the participants unaware that they are being socialized. These little girls are unconsciously learning gender roles by playing dress-up.
SOURCE: Photo courtesy of Nurit Bodemann and Shira Brym.

caught several times but escaped each time, until his final capture in 1799. Victor was dirty, walked on all fours, and had no language. His hair was matted and a clean scar across his neck led to speculation that his throat had been cut while he was a young child and he had been left to die. He was eventually brought to Paris, where interest in the boy was intense and where great efforts were made to teach and "civilize" him. These efforts were largely unsuccessful. Victor never learned to speak and was largely apathetic to others. He died in 1828. His story was dramatized by French director François Truffaut in the 1970 film *The Wild Child.*

Studies of children raised in isolation by their families also provide convincing evidence for the need for interaction. One much-publicized case of long-term isolation involved a 13-year-old girl, referred to as "Genie," who came to the attention of authorities in 1970 in California. From the age of two until she was discovered, Genie was kept in a small room in the back of her family home, unclothed and strapped most of the time to a potty chair. Her father would not allow anyone, including Genie's mother, to communicate with her. The only sounds he used with Genie were menacing growls and barks. When she was found, Genie weighed just 27 kilograms (60 pounds) and was unable to talk. She had a strange bunny walk, spat constantly, sniffed, and clawed. She hardly made any sounds; she had learned to keep quiet because her father would beat her when she made noise. One of her caretakers described Genie as "unsocialized, primitive, hardly human" (Curtiss, 1977). As Genie was cared for and began to interact with others, she made slow but steady progress. She developed a considerable vocabulary, although she was never able to speak grammatically. Her years of social isolation also left their mark on her ability to relate to others. She was withdrawn and unable to form deep attachments. Genie is now living in an adult group home somewhere in Los Angeles.

The importance of social contact in the development of human infants is evident as well in research on institutionalized children. When the repressive regime of Nicolae Ceauçescu was toppled in 1989, the media was awash with images of Romanian children who had been raised in orphanages. They were in the third to tenth percentile for physical growth and grossly delayed in motor and mental development. As they grew, many of the orphans displayed clumsy and inappropriate social behaviours. Those who were adopted by families in the West, including Canada, fared better, but many of these children, too, displayed adjustment problems.

These examples raise the question of what it means to be human. It appears that people have a basic biological need for social interaction, communication, and intimate relations with others. In other words, we need each other. Without human contact, socialization is impaired, the individual is but a shell of a human being, and irreversible damage may be done to the person's sense of self.

THE SELF AND SOCIALIZATION

If socialization begins with the development of a self, what does that process look like? In this section, we first examine the ideas of Austrian psychoanalyst Sigmund Freud (1856–1939) because he was among the first scholars to emphasize the strong social roots of the emergence of the self. We then turn to the ideas of two American sociologists—Charles Horton Cooley (1864–1929) and George Herbert Mead (1863–1931)—whose work continues to influence how sociologists think about and study the self. We then briefly discuss the work of Paul Willis, who has extended Mead's ideas about the self in the 1990s.

SIGMUND FREUD

Sigmund Freud proposed one of the first social-scientific interpretations of the process by which the self emerges (Freud, 1962 [1930], 1973 [1915–17]). He noted that infants demand immediate gratification but begin to form a self-image when their demands are denied—when, for example, parents decide not to feed and comfort them every time they wake up in the middle of the night. The parents' refusal at first incites howls of protest. However, infants soon learn to eat more before going to bed, sleep for longer periods, and go back to sleep if they wake up. Equally important, the infant begins to sense that its needs differ from those of its parents, it has an existence independent of others, and it must somehow balance its needs with the realities of life. Because of many such lessons in self-control, the child eventually develops a sense of what constitutes appropriate behaviour and a moral sense of right and wrong. Soon a personal conscience crystallizes. It is a storehouse of cultural standards. In addition, a psychological mechanism develops that normally balances the pleasure-seeking and restraining components of the self. Earlier thinkers believed that the self emerges naturally, the way a seed germinates. In a revolutionary departure from previous thinking on the subject, Freud argued that only social interaction allows the self to emerge.

CHARLES HORTON COOLEY

In the early twentieth century, few scholars paid attention to the role of interaction in the development of a sense of self. In this respect, Cooley's work was groundbreaking. Cooley (1902) introduced the idea of the **looking-glass self,** suggesting that the gestures and reactions of others are a mirror or "looking glass" in which we see ourselves. Just as we look in a mirror to see a reflection of our physical body, we look to others to see a reflection of our social self. Cooley's emphasis was less on the actual responses of others than on our perception or interpretation of those responses. Just as we may be pleased or displeased with what we see when we look at ourselves physically in a mirror, so too are our conceptions about ourselves—our feelings about who and what we are—socially organized around our evaluation of how we believe ourselves to be judged by others.

This means that without the social mirror, there can be no sense of self. For Cooley, self-image emerges as a product of involvement in groups and communication with others. The first images of the self are received from **significant others**—those closest to children during the early stages of their lives, especially parents. Later, other images complement or supplant those first images, especially as the child's interaction network expands. Particularly important is the role played by an individual's **primary group,** the small group around us in which interaction is characterized by intimate, face-to-face association and cooperation. Typically, the primary group is a family.

GEORGE HERBERT MEAD

Following Cooley, Mead (1934) explored the interplay between the individual and society. His ideas became the foundation of symbolic interactionism (see Chapter 1, Introducing Sociology).

For Mead, society is essential to human development. That is because thinking is possible only if we can communicate symbolically, and we learn to do so by interacting with others. Symbols are gestures, objects, and sounds that stand for something else and whose meaning depends on shared understanding. A dove is a bird, but when we see a dove in a poster, we know it represents peace. Such symbols come from society and they enable us to think.

Our selves derive from society, too. The key to socialization, Mead wrote, is the ability to take the role of the other. **Taking the role of the other** involves anticipating how others will see and react to you. It is an essential skill that children must develop to be effective members of society. However, we are not born with this capacity; it must be acquired in three stages.

Three Stages in Taking the Role of the Other

The **imitative stage** comes first. Children younger than two years old have no real conception of themselves as separate social beings, and their language skills are insufficiently developed to allow them to communicate effectively. When they play, they often act out the behaviour associated with certain roles, such as mother, father, dancer, or firefighter—but what they are doing is not true role-playing, only mimicking or imitation.

In the second stage, the **play stage,** children begin to adopt the roles of significant others—a parent, a sports celebrity, a storybook hero—and their play shifts from imitative to imaginative. They learn to imagine how people will respond without actually having to act out the situation. Through language, children can now manipulate various roles without physical action. At this stage, the role need not be firmly rooted in reality, but can be defined according to the children's wishes or their desire to please significant others. Children do not yet see role-playing as a social necessity—they merely play at the social roles of life.

Moreover, children at this stage often experience difficulty coordinating their actions with others. If you've ever seen a group of four- or five-year-olds playing soccer, you know that a child at this age rarely pays much attention to the rest of the team. Each player cares only about getting the ball and kicking it. Four- or five-year-olds have a poorly developed concept of playing a particular position and cooperating with other team members according to defined rules in order to maximize the number of goals the team scores and minimize the number of goals scored by the opposing team. This capacity develops only in stage three.

The final stage in learning to take the role of the other is the **game stage**, during which children develop a generalized impression of the behaviour people expect and awareness of their own importance to the group and vice-versa. Mead used the metaphor of a game to describe the complex behaviour required at this stage. In an organized game, such as baseball, a player must continually adjust behaviour to the needs of the team as a whole and to the specific situations that arise in the game. If the batter is running to first base, the outfielder does not throw the ball to the second baseman because she likes him better than the first baseman. Instead, her actions are oriented to the general rules and practices that make up the game. At this point, Mead held, children are responding to the **generalized other,** a conception of how people in general—not someone specific—will respond. This generalized other is internalized. It comprises the values, attitudes, and beliefs that the individual understands to be a part of society and in terms of which the individual assumes others will react. In effect, taking the role of the generalized other means that we respond to our idea of the organized group or community of which we are a part. In any given situation, we observe the conduct and reactions of other people, ascertain their points of view, anticipate what is expected of us, and then plan, rehearse, modify, and perfect our own behaviour accordingly.

The "I" and the "Me"

In a way, then, we are not only subjects—thinking, knowing, and feeling beings—but also objects to ourselves—social and cultural beings whom we can evaluate, respond to, have feelings about, and try to modify. Mead called the subjective part of the self the "**I**" and the objective part of the self the "**me**." The "I" acts. The "me" reflects on our actions through the lens of social norms, values, and expectations. Thus, the self is both spontaneous (I) and conformist (me), active (I) and reflective (me), experiencing (I) and experienced (me). The two aspects of our selves engage in what Mead described as an "internal conversation." This internal conversation continues throughout our lives, which means that our sense of self continues to develop as we encounter new contexts and contacts.

PAUL WILLIS

While Mead focused on childhood socialization, British sociologist Paul Willis (1990) has emphasized the degree to which identity formation continues among teens and young adults. He also pays more attention than Mead did to variations in the social contexts within which teens and young adults forge, maintain, and transform their identities.

For Willis, class, racial, ethnic, gender, and regional differences are associated with differences in socialization patterns. In addition, the different institutions to which people belong provide them with relatively distinct symbolic resources that influence how they can express themselves and how others see them. These facts do *not* mean that people *automatically* learn the norms and values of the social contexts in which they happen to find themselves. They learn norms and values, but they also experiment and make choices from the variety of socialization opportunities they confront, and they are often helped by cultural industries, which seek to profit from the desire of young people to have fun, express themselves, and be stylish. Sometimes, young people even choose to push up against "the oppressive limits of established order and power" (Willis, 1990: 12). Yes, they may "consume" television but not necessarily passively. They shout out obscenities at politicians, insult people, and make rude comments about dress sense and personal mannerisms. Similarly with popular and rock music, young people read about and selectively excavate the history of pop and rock to control and produce their own collections. In the realm of style and fashion, Willis describes shopping as extremely hard work for young people. It is not a matter of simply going into a store and picking out an entire outfit. Great creativity is involved in selecting, combining, and recombining different clothing elements and achieving certain looks. Style and fashion are about experimenting with identity and making personal (and sometimes political) statements. Consider for example, the effect of wearing a Che Guevara shirt or a kaffiyeh (Arab headscarf)

In stressing the links among creativity, identity, and social context, Willis suggests that young people take advantage of every opportunity to make the everyday world around them meaningful. Like Mead, he reminds us that human beings are creative and strategic social actors, not pawns of vast, impersonal forces. Still, Willis acknowledges that social categories make a difference. The character of your socialization depends on the groups and institutions to which you belong and your **statuses** within those groups and institutions, that is, the culturally and socially defined positions you occupy in your social interactions.

GENDER SOCIALIZATION

Gender socialization is "the process through which individuals learn to become feminine and masculine according to expectations current in their society" (Mackie, 1991: 75). It has been the subject of much sociological attention in recent decades. Gender seems to most people to be such a natural part of everyday life that we typically take it for granted. We assume that people are either male or female. However, as we show here, and as discussed in Chapter 4, Gender and Sexuality, gender identity is learned.

To the extent that a culture defines male and female roles as sharply different, parents raise boys and girls so that they *will* be sharply different (for an exception, see Box 3.1). Moreover, boys and girls grow up *wanting* to be different, believing that gender role differences are normal and necessary. Patterns of gender role socialization reveal that, from the first days of life, an infant is not simply a child but a boy or a girl. Infant boys are usually addressed differently than infant girls are, the blankets in which they are covered are usually different colours, and the rooms in which they sleep are usually decorated to show their gender. One of the first things that a child learns is whether he or she is a "he" or a "she." From an early age, children show marked gender-specific preferences for certain toys and activities (Davies, 1990). These preferences are reinforced in later years. For example, among preteens femininity is constructed partly by means of shopping. Specialty stores and specialized departments in large department stories define (and, every season, redefine) certain clothing, hairstyling products, cosmetics, and accessories as appropriate and fashionable for girls. In this way, the meaning of becoming a woman is tied to various aspects of consumer culture (Russell and Tyler, 2002).

Parents are usually the first source of children's gender learning, and indications are that parents hold and communicate different expectations for males and females. One study of children's assigned household tasks found a clear gender division of labour (Cohen, 2004): Boys were expected to mow the lawn, shovel snow, take out the garbage, and do yardwork, while the girls were expected to clean house, wash dishes, cook, and babysit younger children. Although couples today enter parenthood with a stronger commitment to sharing household responsibilities than couples did in the past, most nevertheless develop a gendered division of labour (Fox, 1998, 2001).

The mass media, too, present idealized images and stereotypes of appropriate masculine and feminine characteristics. To the degree that females were portrayed in a narrow and biased way by the media for years, the impact of gender-role stereotypes negatively affected how children perceived

BOX 3.1 RAISING A GENDERLESS CHILD

Is Storm a boy or a girl? Storm's parents are not saying.
SOURCE: Steve Russell/The Canadian Press.

Is it possible to avoid gender socialization? A Canadian family has decided to find out. When their third child, Storm, came along, Kathy Witterick and her husband, David Stocker, made the decision to raise a genderless baby. They aren't telling anyone whether Storm is a boy or a girl. The only ones who know are Storm's two brothers, a close family friend, and the two midwives who helped with Storm's delivery. Instead, Witterick and Stocker sent an email to family and friends announcing Storm's birth: "We've decided not to share Storm's sex for now—a tribute to freedom and choice in place of limitation, a stand up to what the world could become in Storm's lifetime (a more progressive place?)."

This isn't the family's first experience challenging gender stereotypes. Storm's two brothers, aged five and two, have been encouraged to pick out their own clothing since they were 18 months old. Just last week, their Dad recounts, one of them found a pink dress at Value Village that he loved because "it really poofs out at the bottom." The boys also decide whether to cut their hair or let it grow. One of them prefers his long hair in three braids, two in the front and one in the back. The boys are encouraged to challenge how they're expected to look and act based on their sex.

Witterick and Stocker are receiving a lot of criticism. "Everyone keeps asking us, 'When will this end?'" says Witterick. "And we always turn the question back. Yeah, when will this end? When will we live in a world where people can make choices to be whoever they are?"

SOURCE: Poisson, Jayme. (2011). "Parents Keep Child's Gender Secret," *Toronto Star*, 21 May. On the World Wide Web at http://www.thestar.com/article/995112.

themselves (Adams and Bettis, 2003; Massoni, 2004). Oversimplified gender-role stereotypes affected children's self-concept and interaction with peers and adults (Kortenhaus and Demarest, 1993). When in 2001 researchers examined 83 leading children's books over the preceding 30 years in terms of the gender of the main character, illustrations, and title, they found that although gender stereotyping had decreased, it was still prevalent (Gooden and Gooden, 2001). Moreover, in recent decades, specifically sexualized forms of gender socialization have become more prevalent in the mass media (Box 3.2).

Stereotyping contributes to the streaming of males and females into traditional "male" and "female" jobs. More often than not, teachers and guidance counsellors wittingly or unwittingly encourage boys and girls to pursue occupational goals that are perceived as appropriate to their gender. This phenomenon becomes a self-fulfilling prophecy: Girls develop a self-image consistent with others' perceptions of them. Thus, one study of 150 Canadian teenagers found a tendency for girls to make traditionally feminine occupational choices and to express less confidence than boys do that they would realize their occupational goals (Baker, 1985). About three-quarters of the girls planned to hold paying jobs as adults. However, they tended to see responsibility for the household and for childcare as primarily theirs and to assume that paid work must fit in with these duties. Their expectations about the future fit the actual division of household tasks (Barber and Allen, 1992; Blau and Ferber, 1992; South and Spitze, 1994). Although more women are choosing

BOX 3.2 SEXUALIZING CHILDREN

A documentary film released by Canada's National Film Board raises the question of whether children are being pushed prematurely into adulthood by the media messages around them. A guide to the film *Sexy Inc.: Our Children Under Influence* refers to "the worrying phenomenon of the hypersexualization of our environment and its noxious effect on young people." The guide goes on to say,

> Marketing and advertising are targeting younger and younger audiences and bombarding them with sexual images.... [G]irls are being represented in a sexualized and sexist way, reducing children to mere consumers and conveying dispiriting stereotypes. From a young age, girls are treated as sexual objects, their development is not respected, and the lines between childhood and adulthood are blurred. (National Film Board of Canada, 2007)

Similar questions were raised when a controversy erupted in the summer of 2011 around an issue of *French Vogue*. Thylane Loubry Blondeau, a 10-year-old much in demand as a child model, appeared on the cover. She was lying on a tiger-skin rug and was heavily made up and seductively dressed in a red dress and leopard-print stilettos. Inside the magazine, another photo showed her draped across a bed dressed in a low-cut gold lamé gown and gold stilettos.

Other examples of the hypersexualization of girls by the mass media could be listed at will, illustrating that a type of socialization that would have been considered taboo just a few decades ago has now become widespread ("French Vogue Slammed," 2011).

How does this photo of Dakota Fanning contribute to the sexualization of children?

SOURCE: © Agencia el Universal/El Universal de Mexico/Newscom.

SOURCE: National Film Board of Canada. 2007. *Sexy Inc. Our Children Under Influence.* A Film by Sophie Bissonnette.

careers that are not traditionally feminine, women still tend to be concentrated in certain types of work and are underrepresented in other types. In Canada, as in most other parts of the world, women are more likely to take on clerical and service jobs, such as office work, nursing, and the care of young children, and are less likely to be involved in administration and management (Brooks, Jarman, and Blackburn, 2003).

The study of gender shows us that children and adults are socialized to respond to their social world by developing certain potentials and inhibiting others. It is certainly true that biological differences between the sexes have an impact on behaviour. For example, only men can impregnate; only women can produce an ovum, carry and nurture the developing fetus, and give birth. However, sociological findings have shown increasingly and convincingly that biological differences alone are insufficient to explain biological differences. Symbolic interactionists, in particular, have shown that gender is also acquired through interactions with parents, teachers, and peers as these unfold within the larger context of a society's cultural organization (Buysse and Embser-Herbert, 2004).

The importance of gender socialization, especially as men and women cross gender lines in work and leisure and participate more fully in previously gender-segregated activities, is examined in a recent study of how traditional gender roles are reproduced in modern wedding showers (Montemurro, 2005). Showers are ideal areas of social life in which to investigate shifts in gender socialization because they involve well-defined gender "scripts" and rituals that tend to celebrate heterosexuality. Based on in-depth interviews with 51 young women and participant observation at five bridal showers, the author concludes that men's presence at wedding showers does not reflect gender convergence or alterations in traditional marriage roles: "Rather, the fact that the co-ed shower was a supplement, that women still had traditional bridal showers, and that jokes were often made that reinforced traditional notions of husband and wife roles during the gift opening at co-ed showers all suggest a lack of change" (Montemurro, 2005: 33). Hence, the author concludes that bridal and co-ed showers perpetuate traditional gender roles in marriage.

SOCIALIZATION THROUGH THE LIFE COURSE

Sociologists refer to childhood socialization as primary socialization because it lays a foundation that influences our self-concept and involvement in social life for as long as we live. However, socialization continues throughout life, as we now show.

ADOLESCENCE AND YOUTH

Dramatic transformations of identity, status, and social relationships occur in adolescence. We enter adolescence as children and exit as young adults.

Socialization during adolescence requires that we find some balance between autonomy and conformity, freedom and constraint. As Brym and Lie (2003) have observed, adolescence in North America is characterized by a decline in adult supervision and guidance, the increasing influence of the mass media and peer groups, and the greater assumption of adult responsibilities. In fact, pointing to the experiences encountered by adolescents, analysts have long been wondering whether the adolescence stage in the life cycle is not in the process of vanishing altogether (Friedenberg, 1959; Wolf, 1977).

Unlike children, however, most adolescents are aware of the demands being placed on them by others and of the demands they place on themselves. This makes adolescence a challenging time of life, not only for adolescents, but also for parents, friends, and teachers. Adolescence is generally associated with emotional and social turmoil. Young people experience conflict with their parents and other adults as they attempt to develop their own identity, act on their own preferences, and form their own relationships. Much turmoil at this stage is attributed to physiological changes linked to the onset of puberty. "Raging hormones" no doubt play a part. But, as we emphasized in our discussion of gender roles, hormones and biology can only explain so much. A fuller appreciation of these phenomena requires that we think sociologically about what might be going on. In the case of teen angst, inconsistencies in the socialization process also play a part. For example, adolescents are repeatedly told by adults to "grow up" but are often treated as if they are still children. Sexuality is a case in point. Adolescents typically receive messages of encouragement from the mass media and restraint from parents. Although adolescents associate adulthood with freedom, they get the confusing message from adults that in order to "act like an adult," they must not decide for themselves but rather do exactly what adults tell them to do.

This predicament would not be such a problem if most adolescents did not live at home and under the authority of adults. Tellingly, adolescent identity crises are unknown in premodern societies, where adolescence does not exist as a separate and prolonged stage of life, and young people often marry by the age of 16 and either establish independent households or remain at home yet assume adult responsibilities.

Adolescence as a distinct period of life is a product of industrialization and the extension of education that it introduced. Mass education and compulsory school attendance altered the role of the family and helped give rise to adolescence. Because young people were required to remain in school, they were not expected to assume economic responsibilities as soon as they reached sexual maturity. Instead, they continued to live at home. It was in the modern high school, where students became educated in skills and knowledge that the family was not equipped to impart, that the distinctiveness of adolescence as a stage of life first crystallized (Burgess and Richardson, 1984; see Box 3.3).

Although many families subscribe to the ideal of democracy, the reality is different (Solomon, Warin, Lewis, and Langford, 2002). Parents and teenagers often claim that openness is the route to intimacy, but in practice young people experience rules imposed by parents who are often unwilling to compromise. Parents, in turn, exercise control and seek to monitor the adolescent's behaviour. This situation causes resentment among adolescents, who realize that parent-teenager relationships often lack open communication. As parents demand more and more information, the relationship moves further away from friendship.

We should not exaggerate adults' impact on adolescents. Although, on average, the family exerts more of an influence than peer groups do regarding such fundamental matters as religious orientation, political preferences, and career aspirations, occasions also arise when young people are less influenced by their families or teachers than by their peers. Peer influence promotes youthful autonomy. It is not that adults give young people freedom, but that the conflicting and confusing messages they receive from adults, peers, the media, and their own experience require them to make up their own minds. For those who are unable to reconcile the demands of the new and the old, adolescence may be a time of considerable confusion and turmoil (Hogan and Astone, 1986). Yet for all the turbulence and rebellion generally associated with adolescence, evidence suggests that most teenagers have good experiences of adolescence and believe they have positive relationships with their parents (Coleman and Hendry, 1990).

BOX 3.3 SOCIALIZATION INTO STUDENT ROLES

Research by University of Manitoba sociologists Cheryl Albas and Dan Albas (1994) explored how university students learn to perform a seemingly natural activity: studying. Based on data derived from their own observations, interviews, and logs obtained from students in their classes, Albas and Albas focused on the drama surrounding exam preparation. They described three types of students:

1. The diligently planning, high-achieving "Aces" recognized the importance of keeping their nose to the grindstone, were never satisfied with a grade lower than A, and planned their schedule to allow for adequate exam preparation.
2. The procrastinating, low-achieving "Bombers" made use of "wise nostrums, self-lulling mantras, and numerous convenient distractions, all of which are directed toward delaying serious study until the very last moment when guilt and fright force them into it" (Albas and Albas, 1994: 281).
3. The "Moderates" formed the largest category of students. They were most likely to have to juggle multiple roles (student, employee, member of a sports team, caregiver, and so on), so they had to ration their time and energy among roles.

Students seemed to fall into one of these three categories. Moreover, once they categorized themselves, or were categorized by others, as Aces, Moderates, or Bombers, their identity played an important role in structuring action. Students who viewed themselves as Aces and discovered their grades were faltering typically studied more or consulted with the professor. Bombers concluded they have little to lose by weak performance. "Give me a C and let me be free" was their motto. The authors observed that students who shared similar identities tended to be attracted to one another. They found that studying was easier if they interacted with others like themselves.

SOURCE: Albas, Daniel and Cheryl Albas. (1994). "Studying Students Studying: Perspectives, Identities and Activities." In Mary Lorenz Dietz, Robert Prus, and William Shaffir, eds., *Doing Everyday Life: Ethnography as Human Lived Experience* (pp. 273–89). Toronto: Copp Clark Longman Ltd.

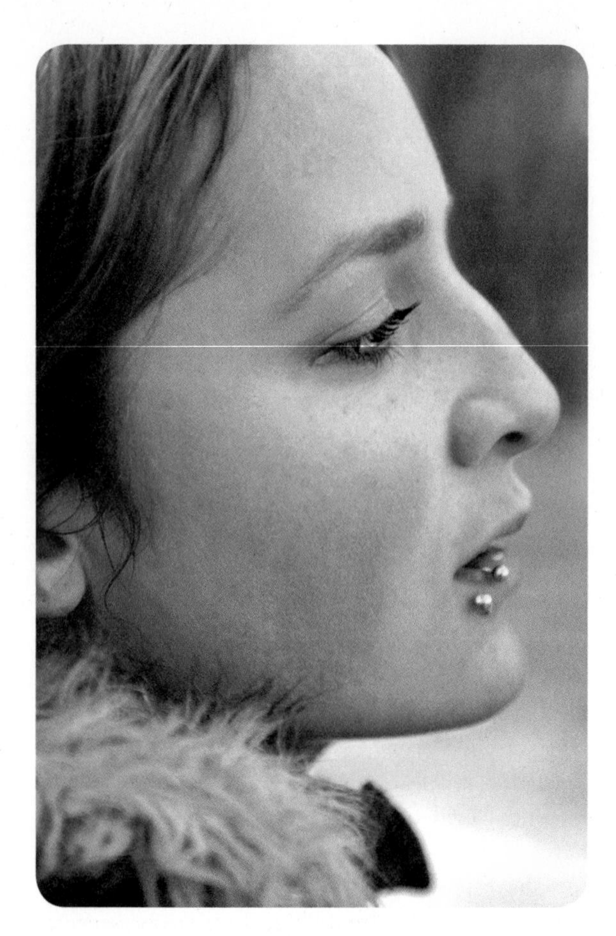

During adolescence, the most dramatic transformations of identity, status, and social relationships tend to occur.
SOURCE: © .shock/Shutterstock.

Why is this so? Adolescents may experience adolescence positively because much of it is exciting and fun. Friendships, for example, take on a different character in adolescence than in childhood. They often become intense, and people develop attachments that often last a lifetime. Many new interests arise in music, art, and fashion that adolescents use as symbols of group membership and indicators of personal taste and status. This allows them to develop passionate commitments and a sense of satisfaction and achievement when, for example, a favourite musical group has a number one song on the charts. Then, of course, there is the excitement of dating, the thrill of romance and sex, and the intense involvement in all of the accompanying activities, such as gossiping with friends, showing off a boyfriend or girlfriend, travelling together, and so on.

Finally, adolescence is also a period of **anticipatory socialization,** "the process by which aspirants to a particular social role begin to discern what it will be like to function in that position" (Stebbins, 1990: 99). Through interaction with people who act out various roles, and by observing how roles are portrayed in the mass media, adolescents learn to incorporate the perspectives and expectations of the larger society and imagine what it would be like to enact the roles to which they aspire (Stryker, 1980: 63). In effect, the individual "rehearses" for future positions, social relationships, and even occupations. For example, students intending to enter the legal profession try imagining how this experience, in its many aspects, will affect their next few years; and successful applicants for immigration to Canada try anticipating how this experience will influence the organization of family life, gender relations, occupational choice, and the like. Many young people experience anticipatory socialization as fun. Ahead of them, though, lie an uncertain future and the responsibilities of adulthood.

ADULT SOCIALIZATION

Adult socialization is the process by which adults take on new statuses and acquire new and different social identities. Adults frequently find themselves in new situations at work or in private life, meeting new people and taking on new responsibilities. To participate effectively in their society, adults must continuously undergo socialization (Clausen, 1986; Hogan and Astone, 1986; see Box 3.4).

Adult socialization differs from adolescent socialization in several important respects (Brim, 1968). Whereas adolescents seek to achieve autonomy, adults generally have control over the content and direction of their socialization. Although adolescents often have little choice but to participate in various activities, adults usually engage in socializing activities voluntarily. Because adults can often choose roles of their own free will, they can better understand and articulate their motives for new undertakings.

When we assume new statuses as adults, we need to become familiar with the expectations associated with them, learning how the statuses are best performed. Frequently such learning occurs over a considerable period as individuals interact with others in a similar situation.

Marriage constitutes one of the most important changes in anyone's life and is therefore perhaps the most important example of adult socialization. Although many of the traditional role expectations of marriage are no longer accepted uncritically, most people still choose to get married. In contrast to an

BOX 3.4 THE BOOMERANG GENERATION

Today, 51 percent of Canadians between the ages of 20 and 29 still live at home (Statistics Canada, 2011). That figure is double what it was 25 years ago. If we look at those between 20 and 24 years of age, the number jumps to 60 percent. Grown-up children leaving home to go to school or work, only to return to live with their parents, are sometimes called the boomerang generation or the failure-to-launch generation. Adult children living at home appear to be the new normal not only in Canada but also in much of the Western world, raising questions about whether typical patterns of transition to adulthood are changing.

Why do you think an increasingly large proportion of young adults live at home? Can you think of economic and noneconomic forces compelling them to do so? What implications does prolonging the time that young people live at home have for their adult socialization?

earlier period when tradition largely determined the choices new couples made, newlyweds and live-in partners are now more likely to chart their own course. This independence is highly valued by most people, but it can lead to strain in relationships with friends, family, and partners. There are no courses on how to adapt to married life. Most socialization consists of a couple learning, through trial and error, how to get along with each other and with members of the extended family.

A hugely important decision during adulthood is whether to become a parent, which, of course, involves acquiring a new set of skills and statuses. The statuses are conferred automatically, but the roles and expectations accompanying them must be learned. As parents inevitably discover, relationships with children require much negotiation and adjustment. Moreover, because children grow and change, adults cannot simply adjust to their new role as parents and then relax. They must continually adapt and accommodate to changing circumstances. No wonder many parents try to take control in rigid ways; they are simply trying to achieve some measure of stability in their lives and that of their family.

Socialization during adulthood also may involve the development of a career. As many postsecondary graduates discover, the difficulty of meeting this challenge successfully increases if employment prospects are uncertain. A set of "R words" serve as signposts of the changes taking place in the workplace—restructuring, reorganization, rationalizing, and reengineering—that strike fear in the hearts of employees and postsecondary students (Lawson, 1996). In addition, the type of employment offered to graduates is in flux. Many positions are now contracted for set periods, making employment less secure and stable (see Chapter 11, Work and Occupations). People can now expect to undergo career changes, with accompanying retraining, several times in their lives.

SOCIALIZATION AMONG OLDER ADULTS

Some of the most difficult socialization occurs in the later years of life. Our society extends little dignity to aging. Although medical advances have prolonged lives, there are relatively few meaningful roles and valued statuses for seniors. The mass media tends to present seniors as dependent if not helpless. Such portrayals reinforce **ageism,** or discriminatory practices based on age. Just as racists think of members of particular racial groups in stereotypical terms—as, say, inherently lazy or stingy or prone to crime—ageists emphasize the declining abilities of older adults rather than their talents. Such treatment can lead seniors to develop a diminished sense of self and in the extreme case can be devastating.

Ellie Berger (2009) explored how a group of Canadian workers between 45 and 65 years of age adapted to ageism in the workplace. Employers valued their experience and knowledge but also assumed that they were less flexible, in poorer health, less creative, less interested in technological change, and less trainable than younger workers were. In response to these attitudes, older workers develop strategies aimed at countering stereotypes, including changing their résumés to make their age less obvious, taking courses to keep their skills up, and using buzzwords to show that they are current with the jargon in their field.

Other transitions in later life also require adjustment. Although many people spend a good part of their working life looking forward to retirement from the paid labour force, the realities of retirement may create identity problems for the retiree. Many older people, particularly women, face the loss of a spouse. This period involves stress as the widow or widower seeks to accommodate a new status, identity, and set of life problems. Few norms govern when the survivor should resume normal functioning or how this should come about.

Finally, socialization in old age also involves facing death and dying. In our society, people talk little about death, making it difficult to prepare for the end of life (Kellehear, 1984). As one sociologist commented, "The status of a dying person is, like retirement and widowhood, a status almost devoid of roles" (Shepard, 1993: 153)

AGENTS OF SOCIALIZATION

Certain categories of people are especially likely to act as **agents of socialization**—individuals, groups, and institutions that impart the range of information we require to interact effectively and participate in society. In addition to parents and peers are social institutions, such as schools and the mass media, that have a significant impact on us. While we cannot interact with such institutions directly, we do interact with people, such as teachers and classmates, inside these institutions. Since they provide distinct contexts within which we take on new ideas and roles, institutions can thus serve as agents of socialization.

You may note that some agents of socialization, such as the family and the school, receive a mandate from society to "train" the next generation of members. In contrast, the peer group and the mass media do much of their "teaching" less formally and directly. Nonetheless, they profoundly influence how individuals perceive and respond to the people and the world around them.

FAMILIES

For young children in most societies, the family is virtually their entire world for the first few years of life. Parents are in a powerful position to influence their child. After all, the newborn is helpless, and his or her survival, physical and emotional, depends on the parents, who are the source of all rewards: security, love, affection, food, and approval. Through close interaction with parents and a small number of other people, the child learns to think and speak; internalizes norms, beliefs, and values; forms basic attitudes; develops a capacity for intimate and personal relationships; and begins to develop a self-image (Handel, 1990). Later experiences modify what children learn in the family, but it is not unusual for people to bring into adult life habits and expectations that characterized their childhood. Often, young people who rebelled against their parents' way of life and values as adolescents adopt the very same way of life and values when they become parents.

In some ways, the family is well suited to the task of socialization. It is a small group in which members typically enjoy frequent face-to-face contact. As a result, children's progress can be closely observed and adjustments made as necessary. Also, parents are usually well motivated. They have a strong emotional bond to their children, and the most meaningful and effective kind of social interaction for the purpose of socialization is fused with emotion.

However, the family is not always an effective agent of socialization. Some parents are negative role models. For instance, highly career-oriented parents may be surprised when their son opts to drop out of university "to enjoy life," rejecting a lifestyle requiring that enormous sacrifices be made for career success. Some parents have little understanding of parenting. They may be unprepared for it emotionally, and their dedication and commitment to the task may be offset by competing considerations. Some parents neglect, abuse, or even abandon their children. Some evidence suggests that parents may reproduce in their children the negative modelling they experienced in their own upbringing.

FAMILIES AND SOCIAL CLASS

At the same time, however, families bestow statuses on us that may significantly affect our lives and sense of self. Consider, for instance, how class status affects socialization styles. Research shows that middle-class parents tend to rear children differently from the way working-class parents do (Kohn, Naoi, Schooler, and Slomczynski, 1990). Middle-class parents are likely to instill in their children the desire to think independently and become high achievers, encouraging curiosity and initiative, while working-class and poor families are more likely to stress the need for obedience and authority. Often, children in poor and low-income families are socialized to believe that lofty educational and occupational ambitions are unrealistic in light of the family's economic situation. For that reason, children from such families are often inclined to think there is little point in heeding the advice of the educational establishment to study hard. Middle- and upper-income families tend to instill in their children a strong belief in the importance of economic success and professional careers (Ballantine 1997; Lareau, 1987). In this manner, the socialization styles characteristic of different classes strongly influence children's aspirations, educational attainments, and occupational trajectories.

FAMILIES AND ETHNICITY

Just as social class can influence how parents socialize their children, so too can ethnicity. Recently, a book titled *Battle Hymn of the Tiger Mother*, by Amy Chua, generated considerable controversy. A Yale law school professor, Chua maintains that the values of Chinese mothers—and Asian mothers more generally—are better for raising kids than "Western" parenting styles. The book begins as follows:

> A lot of people wonder how Chinese parents raise such stereotypically successful kids. They wonder what these parents do to produce so many math whizzes and music prodigies, what it's like inside the family, and whether they could do it too. Well, I can tell them, because I've done it. Here are some things my daughters, Sophia and Louisa, were never allowed to do: attend a sleepover, have a play date, be in a school play, complain about not being in a school play, watch TV or play computer games, choose their own extracurricular activities, get any grade less than an A, not be the No. 1 student in every subject except gym and drama, play any instrument other than the piano or violin. (Chua, 2011: 1–2).*

She explains that Asian culture and Western culture have completely different approaches to child rearing. As she points out,

> In one study of 50 Western American mothers and 48 Chinese immigrant mothers, almost 70% of the Western mothers said either that "stressing academic success is not good for children" or that "parents need to foster the idea that learning is fun." By contrast, roughly 0% of the Chinese mothers felt the same way. Instead, the vast majority of the Chinese mothers said that they believe their children can be "the best" students, that "academic achievement reflects successful parenting" and that if children did not excel at school then there was "a problem" and parents "were not doing their job." (Chua, 2011:2)†

Chua overgeneralizes about both Asian and Western culture. Within the same social class, few differences can be detected between families of Asian and Western origin in terms of educational achievement and economic attainment. Many differences between families of Asian and Western origin have to do with selective immigration: Immigration policy in Canada and other Western countries tends to select immigrants with higher education and the highest potential for economic success. Attributing ethnic differences exclusively to "culture" and "values" ignores such facts (Steinberg, 1981).

Still, the part played by ethnic culture, while difficult to tease out, should not be ignored. As we have seen, socialization unfolds against a cultural backdrop and the cultures of ethnic groups can and do shape socialization experiences. The issue of occupational choice offers an example. Few Jewish youth in Canada aspire to become police officers or firefighters. Why? It is surely not because they lack the physical stamina that such occupations demand. A more probable explanation lies elsewhere: For a variety of reasons, Jewish parents, and their parents and grandparents before them, did not encourage their offspring to consider these occupations as desirable, either economically or socially.

A study of Canadian Filipino youth (Salazar et al., 2001) provides interesting insights into the mechanisms by which ethnicity can affect school performance and educational attainment. Family, the study points out, is central in Filipino culture and provides the basis for both personal identity and a sense of self-worth. Most Filipinos are strongly linked to their families, which from their perspective extend beyond the nuclear family to a larger group of kin. A high value is also placed among the Filipino community on education. Moreover, education is understood not as a solitary, individual effort, but as a project or investment for the whole family. Everyone pitches in to provide help, encouragement, and as far as they can, financial support. Finally, Filipino culture understands success in school as the product of commitment and hard work, not just ability. These understandings and values come together to encourage Filipino adolescents to involve themselves in school activities and put effort into their studies. They are motivated in part by not wanting to jeopardize the family's reputation or to let down those who believe in them and support them. Ethnic cultures, then, do not determine educational and occupational success, but they do influence the range of possibilities that individuals are encouraged to consider (Dyson, 2005).

Of course, the degree to which an individual, or a family as a whole, is assimilated into the larger culture is important in the unfolding socialization drama. Thus it is not surprising that differences in socialization practices are gradually extinguished as individuals and families integrate and assimilate into the surrounding society. Yet considerable data indicate that ethnic culture frames socialization practices of day-to-day life even among individuals identifying minimally along ethnic lines.

DIVERSE FAMILY FORMS

Finally, it is important to note the ever-increasing diversity of forms taken by the family. Families today come in all shapes and sizes. Adoption, remarriage, and the growing availability of new reproductive technologies mean that children may not be biologically related to one or any of the adults who are raising them. Children may be raised by married or unmarried heterosexual couples, married or unmarried same-sex couples, single parents, either same sex or heterosexual, extended families, or grandparents. Researchers who have studied the impact of this increasing diversity on how well adjusted the kids grow up to be have concluded that the form a family takes is less important for the development of a healthy self than having adequate resources to raise and socialize children, including both financial resources and social support (Patterson and Hastings, 2007).

Dependence on parents declines as children grow up and start interacting with peers and adults other than their parents. Peers and other adults offer approval, emotional support, and views of reality that may differ from those of one's parents. This circumstance sets up new challenges in the socialization process, as we will now see.

SCHOOLS

Traditionally, schools have been seen as settings where social learning (cooperation, self-discipline, patriotism, and so on) is just as important as learning skills (reading, writing, arithmetic, and the like). The facade of one Canadian high school proclaims its mission in large letters carved above its main entrance, "To Build Character." One reason parents send their children to school is to be socialized, and schools are deliberately organized to achieve that goal.

Accompanying the formal curriculum of the school is a **hidden curriculum**—the informal teaching that helps ensure students' integration into society (Richer, 1988). School is usually the first setting in which children are supervised by adults who are not relatives or friends of the family. Moving from an environment of personal and intimate relationships to one that is impersonal is difficult for many children and something of a shock to almost all of them. Whereas parents often praise their children regardless of the talent they display, teachers typically seek to evaluate all students by a set of common standards. As a place where children are taught indirectly to be less emotionally dependent, the school serves as a model of much of the adult world, where many relationships are impersonal and defined by society with little emotional regard for the particular individuals who enter them. Of all the functions of the school, adjusting children to its social order—which offers a preview of what will be expected of them as they negotiate their way among the institutions of adult society—may be the most important (Bodine, 2003; Devine, 2002; Raby, 2005).

In a classic sociological paper on socialization titled "Learning the Student Role: Kindergarten as Academic Boot Camp," Harry Gracey (1967) emphasized the role schools play in teaching children how to fit into the social system, follow rules (even those that don't seem to make sense), respect authority, obey, compete, and achieve success. He compared kindergarten to military boot camps, which provide basic training for anyone entering the military. He quoted one teacher who said that she hated September because "everything has to be done rigidly, and repeatedly, until [the children] know exactly what they're supposed to do." However, by January, she said, "they know exactly what to do and I don't have to be after them all the time" (Gracey, 1967: 290). Routines are introduced from the first day of school and children are drilled in them for as long as it takes to achieve compliance. Kindergarten, Gracey concluded, is a training ground for not just the student role, but for life.

PEER GROUPS

Although the family is the most important socializing agent in the early years, peers often begin to influence even young children. Children eventually disengage from the family as their cast of significant others begins to shift to those of similar age and interests. A

peer group comprises individuals who are usually of the same age and enjoy approximately equal status. The earliest peer contacts often occur under the watchful eye of parents or adults, such as teachers in a nursery school or daycare centre. In time, however, the influence of the peer group may supersede, and even conflict with, parents and familial expectations.

In childhood, peer groups are formed largely by the accident of association. Members of the same peer group are not necessarily friends. For instance, all children in a given classroom constitute a peer group but rarely form a single friendship circle. Later in life, however, we *choose* peer groups based on such criteria as common interests and activities, and similar income level or occupation.

Significantly, the peer group is the only agent of socialization in childhood and youth that is not controlled mainly by adults (Corsaro, 1992). Although parents typically play the initial leading roles in the inculcation of basic values, peers seem to have the greatest influence in lifestyle issues, such as appearance, social activities, and dating (Sebald, 1992). Research shows that, especially during adolescence, peers can strongly shape the individual's aspirations and behaviour with respect to both acceptable and criminal behaviour (Giordano, Cernkovich, and DeMaris, 1993). Certainly, the peer group contributes to socialization by enabling children to engage in experiences that the family may not provide. Here they can interact in give-and-take relationships—relationships involving conflict, competition, and cooperation—that are not always possible at home. In this manner, children find many opportunities for self-direction and self-expression in peer groups (Adler and Adler, 1998). Peer groups allow young people to examine feelings, beliefs, and ideas that are unacceptable to the family. Peers share a vision of the world and allow young people to discuss sexual and emotional relationships and developments within their school and friendship circle.

Often, peer group socialization is harsh. Peers may pressure one another to conform to a standard deemed appropriate by the group. They may tolerate little deviation from group norms concerning speech, attitudes, and dress. Paradoxically, adolescents, preoccupied with gaining autonomy from their parents, and anxious about gaining acceptance from others like themselves, may find such demands for conformity difficult to resist (Thorne, 1993). In fact, by the teenage years, the peer group may demand behaviour that conflicts sharply with the norms and values of the parental generation.

The student's values are strongly influenced by his or her peer group, which consists of people of similar age and status, regardless of whether they are friends.

SOURCE: © Stockbyte Platinum/Alamy.

In this regard, it is understandable that parents often express concern about their children's friends, particularly during the teenage years.

If peer groups often reject the norms and values of their parents, where do the group norms and values come from? In large part, from the mass media. The mass media fascinate young people, who look to media heroes as symbols of identity. Taste in music, movies, television shows, and fashion express not only common preferences but also a common style that sets the group apart, both from parents and from other sets of peers (Hebdige, 1979). In fact, a "generation gap" may characterize relations between the peer group and parents, and the peer group's influence can rival that of parents.

For example, the structure and dynamics of the peer group may help us better understand bullying both in school contexts and online. Research shows that bullying does not happen in a social void. While the bully chooses who to target, peer groups consciously or unconsciously support bullying behaviour. Bullying typically starts with teasing. The bully initiates the teasing and others join in. One high school student describes the process as follows:

> There's a big crowd, "the gang," and then there's this one boy/girl on their own. Someone from the crowd starts to spout mean shit. That's when the bullying starts. There's more bullying going on in the crowd, because the gang also wants to show off to each other a bit. (Hamarus and Kaikkonen, 2008: 338)

The desire to be a part of the group can pressure others to participate, leading to the silencing and isolation of the victim. Bullying becomes a way to show status, power, or popularity within the school community. Once a bullying dynamic is established, the peer group is forced to adapt to the norms and values set up by the bully or they risk becoming targets themselves. As the bullying escalates, those participating in it become entangled in a collusive relationship, keeping what is going on a secret from teachers and parents.

During adolescence, peer groups take on particular significance. Adolescence is often a time of physical and emotional turmoil, but also of social turbulence as individuals develop new interests, new friendships, and a new identity. Given the dramatic and sometimes traumatic changes going on within and around them, adolescents often turn to peers for support since adults often have difficulty empathizing with adolescent concerns and are often likely to respond with anxiety of their own.

We often use the term *peer pressure* to emphasize the influence peers have on adolescents, but research by Cynthia Lightfoot (1997) suggests that the impact of peers is more complex than the concept of peer pressure implies. Lightfoot did research on risk-taking among adolescents and found that the impact of peers is less a case of pressure and more a matter of example. As one of her research subjects commented, "the idea of peer pressure is a lot of bunk. ... You go somewhere and everyone else is doing it and you'd think ... they seem to be having a good time—now why wouldn't I do this?" (Lightfoot, 1997: 36).

More generally, Lightfoot found that adolescent risk-taking may have multiple effects during adolescent development. It may generate a sense of individuality and self through opposition to others or established authority. It may create a bond among people who act together and share the thrill, sense of accomplishment, or feeling of relief that comes from engaging in reckless behaviour. It may generate a sense of pride or raise one's status with peers. Or it may just be fun to do. Telling someone not to do something because it is dangerous or reckless will not be effective, Lightfoot suggests, if the perceived benefits of the action are only possible because it is dangerous or reckless.

MASS MEDIA AND NEW COMMUNICATIONS TECHNOLOGY

Like the school and peer groups, the mass media have become important agents of socialization. The mass media include television, radio, movies, videos, CDs, the Internet, newspapers, magazines, and books. While the fastest growing mass medium is the Internet, TV viewing still consumes more of the average Canadian's time than any other mass medium. Indeed, television exhibits certain characteristics that distinguish it from the other socialization agents. Specifically, it permits imitation and role-playing. It is common for critics to express alarm about the TV shows children watch (and also about the content of popular music, especially rap, music videos, video games, and Internet websites; see Box 3.5). Depictions of violence and sex

BOX 3.5 THE TENDER CUT: SELF-INJURING AS LEARNED BEHAVIOUR

A study by Patricia Adler and Peter Adler (2011) on self-injurers showed the role that both the media and peers play in the rise of such behaviours as cutting, burning, branding, and bone-breaking. Although individuals have been self-injuring for centuries, up until the mid-1990s the behaviour was relatively rare and practised in isolation. Since then, however, self-injury has become much more common and has taken on a new meaning. Individuals are more likely to practise self-injury through what the Adlers call copycatting. They hear about these behaviours, see others engaging in them, and become curious. In some cases, they self-injure to be cool or to feel like they belong. In other cases, they turn to self-injury as a way of dealing with teenage anxiety or depression. For example, in Adler and Adler's study, Dana reported struggling with mood swings since she was a child. Asked why she started cutting herself, she recalled seeing a *Dateline* program on self-injury and reading about it in teen magazines. On a particularly difficult day, she decided to try it:

> I was like, other people have done it; I'll try it. Maybe I'll feel better. And like, I'll know what these people are talking about, because whenever I've heard these stories, these people have sounded like me, and so, maybe if I try something like them, it will feel better. I'd completely ignore the last part of the story where they'd be like, "Oh, I've recovered," you know, the happy ending. I was concerned with how they are feeling now and how they fixed it. (Adler and Adler, 2011: 58)

SOURCE: Adler, P. A. and P. Adler. (2011). *The Tender Cut: Inside the World of Self-Injury.* New York: New York University Press.

often worry them. However, the mass media are not always a negative influence. Thus, television viewing can make people more tolerant of unfamiliar and alternative lifestyles and cultures, while violent video games can help them let off steam, and popular music can help them cope with emotional problems.

In recent years, sociologists and other social scientists have invested considerable effort trying to understand the impact of new communications technology on socialization, particularly its influences on family life. In an era where vast distances may separate family members, new communication technologies—cellphones and the Internet—allow them to keep together in ways that were not possible just a few years ago. However, the technologies have both benefits and disadvantages. While they create new opportunities for family members to interact, they also create new opportunities for family members to live in isolation from one another (see Box 3.6).

A key feature of the mass media, particularly those offering access to the Internet, is that they offer adolescents in particular more say over which information will influence them. As sociologist Jeffrey Jansen Arnett (1995) observed, the mass media enable adolescents to engage in self-socialization by selecting socialization influences from a wide array of mass-media offerings. Accordingly, some ultra-orthodox and fundamentalist religious groups, fearing the erosion of their strict ideals of conduct, have challenged the intrusion of the mass media into the lives of their children and adolescents (Lapidus, 2006).

The degree to which cellphone technology can be used to bring together and influence otherwise largely unaffiliated youth to marshal resources toward common goals was apparent during riots that broke out in London, England, in 2011. Many of the rioters were angry about racism and social inequality in the United Kingdom, while others were simply trying to take advantage of the chaos for personal gain. Whatever their motives, their text messages helped them act collectively. For instance, "If you're down for making money, we're about to go hard in east London," one looter messaged (Yelaja, 2011). Other text messages directed looters to areas of untapped riches—stores selling expensive stereo equipment, designer clothes, alcohol, and bicycles. Messages were sent through regular texts and on Facebook. At the same time, social media provided information to fearful residents and shop owners. Twitter helped them pinpoint areas of violence, organize community clean-up groups, and alert people to alternative travel routes.

OTHER SOCIALIZING AGENTS

The family, school, peer group, and mass media are the main socializing agents, but other agents of socialization are important, too. Religious institutions, for example, may deeply affect the moral outlook of young people even in highly secular societies, such as Canada. Athletic teams may teach young people to compete, cooperate with others, follow rules, and make friends. Youth groups may be instrumental in teaching young people about group rules and expectations about conformity, and even about deviance.

BOX 3.6 TECHNOLOGY AND IDENTITY

Sociologist Sherry Turkle (2011) explored the impact of new communication technologies on social life in a book tellingly titled *Alone Together.* She argues that the new communication technologies—email messages, text messages, Facebook postings, Skype exchanges, role-playing games, and Internet bulletin boards—have made convenience and control a priority while diminishing the expectations we have of other human beings. Instead of real friends, we "friend" strangers on Facebook. Instead of meeting for coffee, we text message. Technology, she writes, makes it easy to communicate when we want and to disengage at will. The gains come in the greater connectivity that we enjoy. We can do anything with anyone, anywhere. At the same time, we can feel overwhelmed and isolated. Relentless technological connection can lead to a new kind of solitude. However, Turkle also sees reason for optimism, ironically, among those who are the greatest users of these technologies—the young. Young people, she insists, are increasingly raising fundamental questions about what authenticity and real human connection look like in an increasingly technological age, and how true connections can be achieved.

SOURCE: Turkle, Sherry. (2011). *Alone Together: Why We Expect More From Technology and Less from Each Other.* New York: Basic Books.

In such complex societies as ours, conflict among the agencies of socialization is almost inevitable.

Some socialization takes place in so-called people-processing institutions, whose primary goal is to change the lives of the clients they serve (Goffman, 1961). People-processing institutions include hospitals, correctional facilities, and organizations that provide programs for everyone from battered women and drug addicts to "at risk" children and people with cancer. While the services they provide are framed as help, support, or rehabilitation, these institutions also socialize clients to behave, think, and feel as prescribed by the institutions.

For example, Elizabeth Armstrong (2000) showed how hospital-based prenatal programs aimed specifically at poor, black, and immigrant women, try to teach women how to comply with the hospitals' white, middle-class values, as well as their institutional needs. For example, the programs expect that women will be accompanied by a "birth partner" or "labour coach"—someone who will support them through the birthing process. However, many women find the idea of having anyone but medical professionals present culturally alien. Others prefer "not to be seen like that," or think that their partners "couldn't handle it." There are also those for whom it would be difficult to count on the support of a partner or relative since those closest to them depend on jobs from which it would be difficult to take time off of. What many of the women would really like from the hospitals is to be able to come in as soon as they think they may be going into labour. Instead, the prenatal classes teach them how to time their contractions and estimate their stage of labour so as to avoid cluttering up the labour ward with false alarms. Women are made to feel bad about misjudging.

Other sociologists have investigated socialization into the world of the deaf. The claim that the deaf must be socialized may appear strange. A person does not, after all, learn to be deaf. Children who are deaf do, however, learn the behaviours and attitudes associated with being deaf, not so much at home as in institutions devoted to their education. Specifically, in schools for the deaf, the hearing world typically serves as the yardstick for what is considered normative. Thus, chewing gum may be forbidden because the sound of smacking lips, which children who are deaf cannot hear, may offend people who can hear: "The message is always the same: hearing people must not be offended or intruded upon by the noises of the deaf" (Evans and Falk, 1986: 157). In this sense, institutions created to educate deaf people often teach them to act in ways that suit those who can hear.

IDENTITY AND SOCIAL CHANGE

Are we free to become whomever we want, however we want? Of course not. Socialization is an active process in which we transform our identity as we take on new roles, but we do not always do so in conditions of our own choosing. It is important to remember that social circumstances powerfully influence identity. Premodern societies formed relatively cohesive groups in which most people could find solidarity and meaning in the family, the clan, and the community. Although such groups limited the range of personal experience, they conferred a strong sense of identity and purpose. Modernity expanded the range of personal choice and permitted a greater diversity of beliefs. Still, although modernization has emancipated people from the tyranny of tradition, it often leaves them without the comfort and security of heritage and roots. Modern societies, in general, offer more autonomy but less sense of purpose and fewer enduring social ties than did past societies. Not surprisingly, many people have difficulty establishing a stable and coherent sense of who they are in modern and postmodern societies.

The result is that some people shuttle from one identity to another, changing their lifestyle in search of an elusive "true self." They may join various social groups in search of purpose and belonging, and even experiment with various religions in the hope of finding a system of beliefs that "fits" them (Wuthnow, 1998). In sociological terms, the difficulty in developing a stable and coherent identity is rooted in the individual's social surroundings. The problem of answering the question "Who am I?" reflects not only a personal crisis but also the complexity and instability of modern and postmodern societies (Giddens, 1991).

Understanding the connection between personal development and social conditions calls for a view of human development that recognizes the constant possibility of change—even radical change. Some changes are minor or inconsequential, such as developing a new taste in clothes or exercising or "buffing up." However, there are also more profound life-altering experiences over which we may exercise relatively little control. A life-threatening illness, imprisonment, and severe depression that requires institutionalization are examples. In each instance, people must learn to adapt to fundamental alterations in daily routines. Although these changes may be temporary, they nevertheless strongly influence the individual's identity.

RESOCIALIZATION

A significant change in how we live, in the kinds of people with whom we interact, or in the way we understand others or ourselves often requires **resocialization.** Resocialization involves deliberately trying to instill particular values and behaviours in people who are members of tightly knit groups, such as fraternities or sports teams, or of **total institutions.** In total institutions, such as the military, convents, prisons, boarding schools, and psychiatric hospitals, people are isolated from the rest of society for a set period. All aspects of a person's life are strictly regulated. Authorities impose regimented routines on inmates with the goal of resocializing them into a new identity. The total institution attempts to achieve this objective by completely controlling and manipulating the environment, thus depriving its inmates of contradictory forms of social experience. Total institutions, in sociologist Erving Goffman's words, are "the forcing houses for changing persons; each is a natural experiment in what can be done to the self" (Goffman, 1961: 11–12).

People may at first join an organization willingly and then be subjected to resocialization against their will. For example, people who have joined religious cults have often found that cult leaders exercise a powerful hold over their everyday lives. Many followers develop blind obedience to their leaders, while others wanting to depart may be prevented from doing so, either by emotional pressure or in some cases by force. For most followers, however, the mental transformation they undergo suffices to keep them in the group (Beckford, 1985).

Resocialization in total institutions is a two-part process. First, the staff attempts to strip away the new inmate's established identity. This is accompanied by a series of experiences that include humiliations, degradations, and "mortification rituals," which may include physical pain. Second, efforts are made to reconstitute the inmate's sense of self by imposing a new identity and a new way of life on him or her. In a childlike condition of heightened ambiguity and stress created by degradation and humiliation, the person is ripe for conversion to the expectations of the more powerful group. The desire for security and acceptance often leads to imitation or adoption of the behaviour of authority figures (Light, 1980). The resocialized person often undergoes a symbolic ritual death and rebirth, shedding the old identity and taking on a new one.

A particularly shameful example of how total institutions function is the experience of Canadian Aboriginal peoples in residential schools. The residential school system started in Canada in the late nineteenth century and continued until the 1960s. At their height, 80 such schools operated across the country, with a peak enrolment in 1953 of more than 11 000 students. The students were often removed involuntarily from their homes. The schools were located in isolated areas, which typically did not allow for any contact with their families or communities. The children were subjected to strict discipline and intensive surveillance. They were punished for speaking their own languages and practising their cultural traditions. Many were physically and sexually abused (Kirmayer, Simpson, and Cargo, 2003). Aboriginal communities continue to struggle today with the legacy of these experiences in the form of high rates of substance abuse, suicide, depression, and other mental health problems.

Much less dramatic but often anxiety-provoking resocialization occurs outside total institutions when newcomers are inducted into professions, such as law, the ministry, and medicine. The transformative experience of medical students en route to becoming doctors is a case in point. Professionalization involves the moral and symbolic transformation of a layperson into an individual who can assume the special role and status claimed by a professional (Haas and Shaffir, 1987). The would-be professional must undergo public initiations involving testing and ritual ordeal before being elevated to the special status and role afforded by the profession (see Box 3.7).

A classroom in a residential school
SOURCE: Library and Archives Canada.

BOX 3.7 THE CLOAK OF COMPETENCE

A good example of socialization into a professional role is provided in research that Haas and Shaffir (1977) conducted on medical students at McMaster University. Haas and Shaffir found that medical students feel pressured to act as if they are in total command of what they are doing. They realize that the extent of their medical knowledge can easily be called into question by fellow students, tutors, interns, residents, faculty, and even patients. To reduce the possibility of embarrassment and humiliation, which at this stage in their medical career is easily their fate, students attempt to reduce the unpredictability of their situation by manipulating an impression of themselves as enthusiastic, interested, and eager to learn. At the same time, students seize opportunities that allow them to impress others.

The general strategy that students adopt is to mask their uncertainty and anxiety with an image of self-confidence. Image making becomes recognized as being as important as technical competence. As one student remarks: "We have to be good actors, put across the image of self-confidence, that you know it all." Referring to the importance of creating the right impression, another student said,

> Dr. Jones, who was my adviser or boss for medicine, he always came and did rounds on Wednesday mornings. Well, he didn't have very many patients on the service, but we always knew that his interest was in endocrinology, and ... if he had an endocrine patient ... we knew ... that he was going to pick that endocrine patient to talk about. And so, of course, ... any dummy can read up Tuesday night like hell on the new American Diabetic Association standards for diabetes or hyperglycemia ... and you can handle general medicine. So the next day you seem fairly knowledgeable.... That afternoon you forget about it because you figure Thursday morning hematology people make their rounds and, of course, you have to read up on hematology.

Students learn that to be a good student-physician is either to be or appear to be competent. They observe that others react to their role-playing. A student describes the self-fulfilling nature of this process when he says,

> To be a good GP you've got to be a good actor, you've got to respond to a situation. You have to be quick, pick up the dynamics of what is going on at the time and try to make the person leave the office thinking that you know something. And a lot of people, the way they handle that is by letting the patient know that they know it all, and only letting out a little bit at a time, and as little as possible. I think that they eventually reach a plateau where they start thinking themselves they are really great and they know it all, because they have these people who are worshipping at their feet.

SOURCE: From Hass, Jack and William Shaffir, "The Professionalization of Medical Students: Developing Competence and a Clock of Competence," *Symbolic Interaction 1* (Nov. 1977). Reprinted by permission of John Wiley and Sons.

The image of society Goffman (1961) presents in his research on total institutions is one in which large, impersonal institutions are gaining more and more control over people—over their actions, experience of the world, and sense of self. Resistance is possible in Goffman's view, and it is often successful, but only in the small events of everyday life, such as forming personal relationships with others or exchanging gifts and services. Yet today, with the advent of new forms of communication and technology, we find that new forms of autonomy and new sources of freedom and creativity have also emerged. Active, malleable, and innovative, human beings are not content to accept the world as they find it. They look for ways to transform the world and adapt it to their social needs and personal desires. Nothing better exemplifies this creative aspect of social life than the process of socialization.

SUMMARY

1. Socialization is an active process through which human beings become members of society, develop a sense of self, and learn to participate in social relationships with others. Through socialization we acquire knowledge, skills, and motivations for participation in society.
2. Each of us is born with a set of human potentials. Nature and nurture interact in contributing to human development.
3. Socialization is lifelong, typically involving relationships with family, school, peer groups, mass media, and occupational groups. Ours is an

age-graded society as well, and early childhood, adolescence, adulthood, and old age or retirement are significant stages; different roles and responsibilities are associated with each stage.

4. Because of the importance of socialization, many scholars have focused on examining it as an active, interactional process. Charles Horton Cooley was noteworthy for his concept of the "looking-glass self," which stressed that we view ourselves as we think others view us. George Herbert Mead emphasized how people assume roles by imagining themselves in the roles of others. Paul Willis, looking at the ways in which young people do not merely accept the world around them but transform it into a symbolic expression of their particular identity and their meaningful culture, has shown the intimate links connecting the acting individual and the broader social context.
5. Gender socialization is the learning of masculine and feminine behaviour and roles. From birth, and in every area of social life, the socialization of the sexes in terms of content and expectations makes the socially constructed gender role more significant than the biological role of male or female. Assumptions about appropriate male and female attributes limit the range of acceptable behaviour and options for both sexes.
6. The most important agent of socialization is the family. Initial warmth and nurturing are essential to healthy development. The self-concept formed during childhood has lasting consequences.
7. The central function of schools in industrial society is the teaching of skills and knowledge, but they also transmit society's central cultural values and ideologies. Schools expose children to situations in which the same rules, regulations, and authority patterns apply to everyone.
8. Peer groups provide young people with a looking glass unclouded by love or duty, and an opportunity to learn roles and values that adults do not teach.
9. The traditional mass media are impersonal and large-scale socializers. New forms of media are more interactive and allow people to play with and try out different identities.
10. During adulthood, individuals are socialized as they get jobs, marry, divorce, raise children, retire, and prepare for death. These many roles involve new and different relationships with others and guidelines for behaviour.
11. Sometimes there are abrupt changes in our self-concept, and we must learn new role identities and negotiate a new self-image. Resocialization occurs when we abandon or are forced to abandon our way of life and self-concept for a radically different one. This is most efficiently done in total institutions—for example, jails, psychiatric hospitals, and boot camps—or in religious and political conversions.

QUESTIONS TO CONSIDER

1. Consider the significant others in your life. Have they always been important to you? How have they shaped and influenced your sense of self?
2. Goffman's approach implies that "all the world's a stage" and all of us are merely "players." Do you agree with Goffman? Cite examples of impression management that you rely on and encounter in your life.
3. Prisons and psychiatric hospitals are socialization institutions organized to change, test, or "correct" people. How effective are these institutions and why are they not more successful in meeting their goals?
4. Think of any job you have had and consider the socialization that was required. Distinguish the formal and informal components of the socialization process.
5. What, if any, are the possible effects on personal identity of the use of the Internet? Could the consequences be greater separation and alienation from reality, others, and ourselves, or might the outcome for the user be a heightened sense of belonging, integration, and shared understanding? Are both extremes possible?

GLOSSARY

Adult socialization (p. 60) is the process by which adults take on new statuses and acquire new and different social identities.

Ageism (p. 61) refers to discriminatory practices based on age.

Agents of socialization (p. 62) are the individuals, groups, and institutions that impart, and from which we acquire, the range of information required to interact effectively and participate in society.

Anticipatory socialization (p. 60) involves beginning to take on the norms and behaviours of a role you aspire to but do not yet occupy.

In the **game stage** (p. 54) of development, children have developed a generalized impression of the behaviour people expect as well as awareness of their own importance to the group and vice-versa. This is the third and final developmental stage described by Mead.

Gender socialization (p. 55) is the process by which individuals learn to become feminine and masculine according to expectations current in their society.

The **generalized other** (p. 55) is a conception of how people in general will respond in a situation. It is internalized.

The **hidden curriculum** (p. 64) consists of informal teaching that helps ensure students' integration into society.

The **I** (p. 55) is the subjective or active part of the self, according to Mead.

In the **imitative stage** (p. 54) of development, children two years old and under do not interact effectively with others because they cannot take the role of the other. They merely imitate the behaviour of others. This is the first developmental stage described by Mead.

Instincts (p. 52) are inborn patterns of behaviour that are often responses to specific stimuli.

The idea of the **looking-glass self** (p. 54) suggests that the gestures and reactions of others are a mirror in which we see ourselves.

The **me** (p. 55) is the objective element of the self, according to Mead.

A **peer group** (p. 65) comprises individuals who are usually of the same age and enjoy approximately equal status.

In the **play stage** (p. 54), children begin to adopt the roles of significant others—a parent, a sports celebrity, a storybook hero—and their play shifts from imitative to imaginative. This is the second developmental stage described by Mead.

A **primary group** (p. 54) is a small group (especially the family) that is characterized by intimate, face-to-face association and cooperation.

Primary socialization (p. 52) is the crucial learning process that occurs in childhood and makes us members of society.

Resocialization (p. 69) is the deliberate attempt to correct or instill particular values and behaviours in an individual or group.

Secondary socialization (p. 52) is learning that occurs after people have undergone primary socialization.

The **self** (p. 51), a sense of individual identity, allows us to understand ourselves and differentiate ourselves from others.

Significant others (p. 54) are people, such as parents, who are of central importance in the development of the self.

Socialization (p. 51) is the social process whereby people undergo development by interacting with the people around them.

Status (p. 55) refers to the culturally and socially defined position a person occupies in an interaction.

Taking the role of the other (p. 54) involves anticipating in advance how others will see and react to you. It is an essential skill that children must develop to be effective members of society.

Total institutions (p. 69) are settings in which people are isolated from the rest of society for a set period and in which all aspects of a person's life are regulated under one authority.

SUGGESTED READING

Adler, Patricia A., and Peter Adler. (1998). *Peer Power: Preadolescent Culture and Identity.* New Brunswick, NJ: Rutgers University Press. Based on eight years of observation research, this is a first-rate sociological study of the role of peer groups in preadolescent socialization.

Becker, Howard S., Blanche Geer, Everett C. Hughes, and Anselm L. Strauss. (1961). *Boys in White: Student Culture in Medical School.* Chicago: University of Chicago Press. This is the classic study of professional socialization. It examines how medical students negotiate their transition into the medical profession and are transformed into physicians.

Ebaugh, Helen Rose Fuchs. (1988). *Becoming an Ex: The Process of Role Exit.* Chicago: University of Chicago Press. This excellent study examines the process whereby people learn to disengage themselves from previous roles and claims to identity.

Goffman, Erving. (1961). *Asylums: Essays on the Social Situation of Mental Patients and Other Inmates.* Garden City, NY: Anchor Books. This account analyzes life in total institutions and describes what such institutions make of inmates and how the latter organize their life inside them.

CHAPTER 4

GENDER AND SEXUALITY

Rhonda L. Lenton
YORK UNIVERSITY

SOURCE: Mosaic Hair Group. Stylist Peter Salituro. Colour Laura Brooks. Photographer Babak.

IN THIS CHAPTER YOU WILL LEARN THAT

- *Sex* refers to biological differences between males and females, while *gender* refers to the attitudes, beliefs, and behaviours we associate with masculinity and femininity.
- Individuals form a "gender identity" or a sense of biological, psychological, and social belonging to a particular sex. Individuals also learn to play a "gender role," that is, to act in accordance with expectations about how members of their gender are supposed to behave.
- *Sexuality* refers to activities intended to lead to erotic arousal and produce a genital response. Sexuality is guided by a set of social "scripts" that tell us whom we should find attractive, when and where it is appropriate to be aroused, when it is permissible to have sex, and so on.
- There are two major perspectives on the relationship among sex, gender, and sexuality. One (essentialism) holds that gender roles and sexual scripts develop naturally from biological differences between the sexes. The other (social constructionism) holds that gender roles and sexual scripts emerge in response to the different social positions women and men occupy.
- Because of the way gender and sexuality are structured in our society, intolerance for sexual minorities is widespread and male sexual aggression against women is common.
- A substantial decrease in gender inequality is now possible. Redefining sexuality is an important step in that process.

INTRODUCTION

GENDER, SEX, AND THE CASE OF DAVID/BRENDA

In April 1966, identical eight-month-old twin boys were brought to St. Boniface hospital in Winnipeg to be circumcised. They had developed a condition called phimosis, or closing of the foreskin. However, because of mechanical malfunction or doctor error, the electric cauterizing needle used for the procedure released a surge of heat. It burnt off the entire penis of one baby.

The parents sought expert medical advice but were given little hope. One psychiatrist summarized the baby's future as follows: "[H]e will be unable to consummate marriage or have normal heterosexual relations ... he will have to recognize that he is incomplete, physically defective, and that he must live apart" (quoted in Colapinto, 2001: 16). The baby's name was David Reimer.

Seven months later, now deeply depressed, David Reimer's parents happened to be watching a CBC television program featuring Dr. John Money of Johns Hopkins University in Baltimore. He was discussing how he had successfully assigned a male or female identity to children whose external sex organs and internal reproductive system were not clearly male or female. The main criterion he used for deciding the child's sex was expected "erotic functioning" as an adult. He recommended boys born with a penis shorter than 2.5 centimetres and girls born with a clitoris longer than 1 centimetre for sex reassignment, preferably within weeks of birth. According to Money, it was imperative, once the child's sex was decided, that doctors and parents never waver in their decision and never tell the child about his or her condition at birth.

Until David Reimer, Dr. Money had never had the opportunity to test his idea on a child born unequivocally a boy or girl. Therefore, when David's mother wrote to Dr. Money shortly after the television show, he urged her to bring the baby to his office in Baltimore. He considered it a bonus that David was a twin. This would allow him to compare the development of the two siblings. Dr. Money was eager to proceed. He believed that the "gender identity gate"—the time after which a child is "locked" into an identity as a male or a female—closes at two years of age. The parents nevertheless took several months to deliberate and consult with family and friends before giving the go-ahead. On July 3, 1967, David, now 22 months old, underwent surgical castration and reconstructive surgery. He became Brenda Reimer.

As the years passed, the parents tried their best to follow Dr. Money's instructions. Brenda was given dresses to wear, skipping ropes and dolls for presents, and regular doses of the female hormone estrogen at puberty.

In 1972, at a meeting of the American Association for the Advancement of Science in Washington, DC, Dr. Money unveiled the story of David/Brenda Reimer. He claimed that the experiment was an unqualified success. In *Sexual Signatures*, a co-authored book intended for the general public, he described David's sex reassignment as "dramatic proof that the gender-identity option is open at birth for normal infants." Money was equally optimistic in a 1978 journal article, where he reported that "[n]ow prepubertal in age, [Brenda Reimer] has ... a feminine gender identity and role, distinctly different from that of her brother" (quoted in Colapinto, 1997: 72).

Then, in March 1997, a bombshell: Dr. Money, it emerged, had doctored his reports. A biologist from the University of Hawaii and a psychiatrist from the Canadian Ministry of Health started a scientific scandal when they published an article in the *Archives of Adolescent and Pediatric Medicine* showing that David/Brenda had, in fact, struggled against his/her imposed girlhood from the start. In December, a long and moving exposé of the case in *Rolling Stone* magazine gave further details.

The authors documented Brenda's resistance to being a girl, including everything from tearing off her first dress to insisting on standing to urinate. According to her brother, Kevin, there was "nothing feminine about Brenda. ... She walked like a guy. Sat with her legs apart. She talked about guy things, didn't give a crap about cleaning house, getting married, wearing makeup. We both wanted to play with guys, build forts and have snowball fights and play army" (quoted in Colapinto, 2001: 57).

By the age of seven, Brenda announced she wanted to be a boy, and she refused to have further vaginal surgery because it would make her look more like a girl. She took estrogen only after being told that failure to do so would result in her limbs being disproportionate to her body. She refused to see Dr. Money after 1978. In 1979, Brenda made the decision to stop living as a girl.

In 1980, her father finally told Brenda what had happened to her. Brenda's first reaction was relief. She then resolved to become David again. By the age of 16, she started taking male hormone treatments and had her breasts removed and a penis surgically constructed. Subsequent surgeries allowed David to have sex with a woman at the age of 23. He married the woman two years later, in 1990, and adopted her three children. That did not, however, end his ordeal. In May 2004, at the age of 38, David Reimer committed suicide.

David Reimer, February 2001.
SOURCE: © Reuters/Corbis.

The story of David/Brenda introduces many of the issues raised in this chapter. How do we define *female* and *male?* What is the relationship between biological sex and the attitudes and behaviours that we associate with being male or female? What are the implications of this relationship for our sexual identity and sexual relations? I will touch on all these questions here. The answers, it will emerge, are not as obvious as they may at first appear.

DEFINING MALE AND FEMALE: SEX AND GENDER

While preparing to write this chapter, I asked my then six-year-old the difference between boys and girls. She answered: "Boys have a penis, girls have a vagina." Like most people, she distinguished men and women on the basis of biological **sex.** Your sex depends on whether you were born with distinct male or female genitalia and a genetic program that released either male or female hormones to stimulate the development of your reproductive system. Table 4.1 gives a more complete version of this common view by summarizing four key sex differences.

At the point of conception, a newly formed zygote has 46 chromosomes. If the last chromosome has an XX pattern, the zygote becomes a female.

TABLE 4.1 SUMMARY OF BIOLOGICAL SEX DIFFERENCES DURING TYPICAL FETAL DEVELOPMENT

VARIABLE	FEMALE	MALE
Chromosomal pattern	XX	XY
Gonadal	Ovaries	Testes
Hormonal	More estrogens than androgens	More androgens than estrogens + MIH
Sex organs	Uterus, fallopian tubes, vagina, clitoris, labia	Epididymis, vas deferens, seminal vesicles, prostate, penis, scrotum

SOURCE: Adapted from *Gender in Canada* by E. D. Nelson and Barrie W. Robinson, 1999, p. 48, Pearson Education. Reprinted with permission by Pearson Education Canada Inc.

If it has an XY pattern, it becomes a male. About 1 in 400 children is born with an unusual 46th chromosome pattern caused by the failure of the sperm to divide properly (Berch and Bender, 1987). Most of these combinations are never diagnosed.

Around the sixth or seventh week of gestation, the gonads or sex glands begin to develop—testes in the case of a male, ovaries in the case of a female. The testes and ovaries subsequently produce various hormones in varying amounts. These hormones contribute to the development of the sex organs. Differences between the sex organs are noticeable by the fourteenth week after conception. The scientific community appears to agree about only one sex difference in the brain (Blum, 1997): The part of the brain known as the hypothalamus makes the female brain sensitive to estrogen and is responsible for creating menstrual cycles in women.

Being male or female involves more than just biological sex differences, however, as the case of David/Brenda shows. Recalling his life as Brenda, David said, "[E]veryone is telling you that you're a girl. But you say to yourself, 'I don't *feel* like a girl.' You think girls are supposed to be delicate and *like* girl things—tea parties, things like that. But I like to *do* guy stuff. It doesn't match" (quoted in Colapinto, 1997: 66; my emphasis). As this quotation shows, being male or female involves not just biology but also certain "masculine" and "feminine" feelings, attitudes, and behaviours. Accordingly, biological sex must be distinguished from sociological gender. **Gender** comprises the feelings, attitudes, and behaviours associated with being male or female. Identification with, or sense of belonging to, a particular sex—biologically, psychologically, and socially—is known as **gender identity.** When people behave according to widely shared expectations about how males or females are supposed to act, they adopt a **gender role.**

Research shows that North Americans' expectations about how men and women are supposed to act have changed only somewhat since the 1960s (Bergen and Williams, 1991; Broverman, Vogel, Broverman, Clarkson, and Rosenkratz, 1972; Rosenkrantz, Vogel, Bee, Broverman, and Broverman, 1968; Williams and Bennett, 1975; Williams and Best, 1982). This is true despite significant changes in women's lives in particular. For example, in the 1960s and 1970s, males were generally expected to act tough and hide their emotions. This is still true today, albeit to a lesser extent. Boys still tend to learn at a young age that crying or displaying their feelings in public is likely to result in taunts and accusations of being a "sissy." As a result, they curb their nurturing abilities, thus fulfilling gender expectations.

Great pressure can be brought to bear on individuals who do not conform to gender expectations. Brenda is a case in point. She was ostracized and tormented by her peers for not acting feminine. Transgendered people report similar experiences of rejection (see Box 4.1). People are **transgendered** when their gender identity does not exactly match the sex assigned to them at birth. They blur widely accepted gender roles by, for example, cross-dressing. According to Dr. Diane Watson, a psychiatrist who heads the gender-identity clinic at Vancouver Hospital, 1 in every 5000 to 10 000 Canadians is transgendered (quoted in Nolen, 1999: D1). Moreover, says Dr. Watson, 1 in 30 000 Canadians is fully transsexual. **Transsexuals** identify with the opposite sex from that assigned to them at birth, causing them to change their appearance or resort to a sex-change operation. The apparent contradiction between biological sex and gender experienced by these individuals brings us back to the question of how we define males and females.

We typically accept "masculine men" and "feminine women" as normal. That is, we expect individuals to possess unambiguous sex organs and to adopt the gender role that is consistent with their biological sex. In fact, the World Health Organization classifies transgendered individuals as having a psychiatric disorder. As Canadian sociologist Margrit Eichler points out, however, if our notions of masculinity and femininity were less rigid, sex-change operations would be unnecessary since someone with a "gender identity problem" would not be defined as "sick." From Eichler's point of view, transgendered individuals represent a "problem" for most people only because our society does not recognize the validity of intermediate sexes (Eichler, 1980: 31).

In the case of David/Brenda, the rigidity of gender roles probably contributed to the failure of the first sex-change operation. David had, after all, been raised as a boy for nearly two years. He had seen boys treated differently from girls on television and in storybooks. He had played only with stereotypical boys' toys. After the sex reassignment, however, he got new clothes and new toys. He was also expected to behave differently. The contrast must have been all the more evident because the constant presence of his twin brother reinforced David's early understanding of how boys ought to behave. Evidence suggests that if gender reassignment takes place before the age of 18 months, it tends to be "successful" (Creighton and Minto, 2001; Lightfoot-Klein, Chase, Hammond, and Goldman, 2000).

The rigidity just described fosters the view that gender roles are entirely natural and spring fully formed from human physiology. But no one-to-one relationship exists between sex and gender. The two may be in discord, as transgendered individuals and transsexuals demonstrate. The picture becomes still more complicated when we consider sexual

Being male or female involves not just biology but also certain "masculine" or "feminine" feelings, attitudes, and behaviours.
SOURCE: Susan G. Scott, *The Princess.* Courtesy Susan G. Scott.

BOX 4.1 THE THIRD WAY: REFUSING TO GENDER IDENTIFY

It's not that Matt Lundie wants to be a man, particularly. He just doesn't want to be a woman.

"Just enough so people won't pick me out as being a freak"—that's his goal for the next year.

He has done two years of engineering at Carleton University in Ottawa, and he is taking the next year off to start another project. Next week, he moves to Winnipeg. In six months, he will begin to take male hormones and, a few months after that, he will have a mastectomy: both of his 38C breasts will be removed and his chest reshaped in a male contour. That will be it for the scalpel, though: "I don't have any need to modify my genitals."

He's having just enough surgery to get him what he wants: not a facsimile of a male body, just a less female one.

Matt was born Fiona, in a small southwestern Ontario town. For 21 years, he lived confused. "Even as a child I knew the expectations placed on me weren't realistic," he says, calm and resolute. "Until puberty, I thought I was a boy. The social messages of my whole childhood, of being told the boy's washroom was down the hall, was that I didn't fit, not in either mould."

Then he arrived at university and began to encounter variations on gender identity in the gay community. Last year, he tried something new: "I didn't gender identify."

He was still Fiona, but offered no other clues. That felt better, better than being a woman, anyway, but it wasn't great. When people couldn't figure him out, they reacted with confusion, awkwardness and often hostility. He got sick of dealing with that every day. So now, at 23, he's starting a new life as Matt.

"I don't believe gender is concrete, and people shouldn't be limited by their biological sex. But I can't really live in between."

Yet if he feels neither concretely male nor female, then why Matt over Fiona? "I like male clothes," he says with a small chuckle, then turns serious. "And the box you put men into has a bit more room."

He tried life in the other box. "Around Grade 11, I made an honest effort to be a traditionally gendered girl. I grew my hair; if you saw my prom picture, you'd think I was my sister or something." It didn't work. "I knew I didn't fit the mould of a woman, but I didn't know I had options. Now I know that neither of those two options fit who I am, so I'm going to stake out a third."

SOURCE: Excerpted from Stephanie Nolen, "The Third Way," *The Globe and Mail,* September 25, 1999, p. D1. Reprinted with permission of *The Globe and Mail.*

behaviour. Expectations about sexual behaviour are arguably among the most rigid of our gender norms, yet sexual behaviour often departs widely from biological sex and sociological gender.

SEXUALITY

Sexuality refers to activities that are intended "to lead to erotic arousal and produce genital response" (Reiss, 1986: 20). Some people think such activities are idiosyncratic. In fact, sexual behaviour is guided by a set of **sexual scripts** that tell us whom we should find attractive, when and where it is appropriate to be aroused, what is permissible, and how to behave sexually. These scripts are linked to gender roles. Men are usually expected to be the sexual aggressors, typically more experienced and promiscuous than women are. Women are expected to desire love before intimacy. They are assumed to be sexually passive, giving only subtle cues to indicate their interest in male overtures. Lacking the urgent sex drive that preoccupies males, women are therefore often held accountable for moral standards and contraception (Jensen, 1984).

For a long time, sexuality was assumed to be heterosexuality. The term *heterosexuality* was coined about 30 years after the term *homosexuality* made its appearance in the 1860s. Homosexuality was considered a serious psychiatric disorder until 1974, when it was finally dropped from the *Diagnostic and Statistical Manual of Mental Disorders*, the standard diagnostic tool used by North American psychiatrists (Shorter, 1997: 304). Even today, many people assume that individuals should desire only members of the opposite sex. Sociologists call this assumption **compulsory heterosexuality.**

The assumption of heterosexuality has negative implications for non-heterosexuals (including lesbian, gay, bisexual, and transgender people, discussed later in the chapter). They face discrimination, are denied basic civil rights (such as access to spousal benefits) in most countries, and risk abuse, including "gay-bashing." In addition, some feminists say that heterosexuality puts *all* women at a disadvantage, because heterosexuality is based on unequal economic, political, legal, and social relations between women and men. Adrienne Rich (1996: 132–33) thus defines compulsory heterosexuality as "the ideologically and materially enforced insistence that women see themselves entirely as the complements of men and live under male control or risk severe sanctions ranging from social stigma to death." Rich says that the institutionalization of heterosexuality in marriage and the family is a way of ensuring males' rights to physical, economic, and emotional access to women. Some feminists even take the extreme position that women should reject heterosexuality altogether since all such relationships are based on inequality. Below, I present an opposing view—that it is not women's heterosexual practices and identities that need to be criticized but rather the institution of heterosexuality *insofar as it is a system of male domination.* First, however, let us examine some research on sexual behaviour.

SEXUAL ATTITUDES AND BEHAVIOUR

Traditional sexual scripts expect each of us to meet a member of the "opposite" sex, fall in love, get married, and then have intercourse with our spouse. However, surveys reveal some departure from tradition and considerable diversity in sexual attitudes and behaviour. For example, 80 percent of Canadians do not disapprove of premarital sex and 75 percent do not disapprove of an unmarried couple living together (Bibby with Russell and Rolheiser, 2009: 44, 146).

Acceptance of premarital sex extends even to young people. Nearly all Canadians agree that birth control information should be available to teenagers who want it (Bibby, 1995: 65). By the time they are 15 years old, half of Canadian males and a third of Canadian females say they have had sexual intercourse at least once. By the time they are 19 years old, the figure for both males and females rises to more than 80 percent (Bibby with Russell and Rolheiser, 2009: 52; Hobart, 1996: 150; Rotermann, 2008). However, men seem to be more willing than women are to participate in unconventional sexual activities (Hatfield, 1995).

A 2007–08 survey of 26 032 people over the age of 16 provides data on sexual behaviour in 26 countries, including Canada (Durex, 2012; see Table 4.2). Two-thirds of the respondents said they had sexual intercourse at least once a week. At one extreme are the Greeks (87 percent). At the other extreme are the Japanese (34 percent). Canadians ranked 22nd at 59 percent. In terms of sexual satisfaction, Canadians do better, ranking 9th at 48 percent. Nigerians are the most satisfied (67 percent), while the Japanese are by far the least satisfied (15 percent). On average, the lifetime number of sexual partners is more than twice as high for heterosexual men (17) as it is for heterosexual women (8). New Zealand is the sole exception to this pattern. It is also the country in which heterosexual women have the most lifetime sexual partners (20). In several Asian countries (China, India, Malaysia, and Thailand), heterosexual women have the fewest number of lifetime sexual partners on average (2). Heterosexual Canadian women are above average on this indicator, with 10 lifetime sexual partners. For heterosexual men, Austrians lead the pack with 29 lifetime sexual partners, and Chinese men are at the bottom with 4. Heterosexual Canadian men rank 7th at 23.

Table 4.3 shows the frequency of sexual activity by gender and age in Canada. Not surprisingly, sexual activity declines with age. However, a considerable number of people over the age of 70 say they engage in sexual activity at least once a week. This finding challenges the myth that seniors are asexual.

Also of interest are male-female differences. For nearly all age groups, men report more frequent intercourse than women do, while women more often report abstention than men do. For instance, in the 50–59 age cohort, 13 percent of women say they never have sex compared with only 1 percent of men. In the 70+ age cohort, 22 percent of men say they have sex once a week or more, compared with only 7 percent of women. These figures probably reflect a tendency on the part of men to exaggerate their virility to conform to gender stereotypes.

Men and women differ in terms of the standards they use to justify sexual activity. Hobart (1996: 148) distinguishes the "love standard," according to which sexual activity is acceptable as long as the partners are in love, from the "fun standard," according to which sexual activity is acceptable as long as both partners want it. He shows that, in Canada, men and francophones are more likely than women and anglophones to endorse the fun standard. For example, almost 52 percent of Canadian francophone men and more than 37 percent of francophone women believe it is appropriate to engage in heterosexual sexual activity

TABLE 4.2 INDICATORS OF SEXUAL ACTIVITY, 26 COUNTRIES (n = 26 000)

	INTERCOURSE ONCE/WK OR MORE, IN PERCENT	SEXUALLY SATISFIED, IN PERCENT	LIFETIME SEXUAL PARTNERS, HETEROSEXUAL WOMEN	LIFETIME SEXUAL PARTNERS, HETEROSEXUAL MEN
Australia	60	42	10	25
Austria	70	43	17	29
Brazil	82	42	11	27
Canada	**59**	**48**	**10**	**23**
China	78	42	2	4
France	70	25	7	17
Germany	68	38	9	17
Greece	87	51	10	28
Hong Kong	62	29	4	14
India	68	61	2	6
Italy	76	36	7	19
Japan	34	15	8	14
Malaysia	74	38	2	9
Mexico	71	63	6	14
Netherlands	63	50	8	14
New Zealand	63	43	20	17
Nigeria	53	67	3	9
Poland	76	54	5	12
Russia	80	42	17	28
Singapore	62	35	3	8
South Africa	71	50	7	18
Spain	72	49	8	21
Switzerland	72	42	14	24
Thailand	65	35	2	12
United Kingdom	55	40	10	16
United States	53	48	9	13
Average	67	43	8	17

SOURCE: Durex (2012). "Sexual Wellbeing Global Survey 07/08." On the World Wide Web at http://www.durex.com/en-CA/SexualWellbeingSurvey/pages/default.aspx (retrieved February 20, 2012). Used courtesy of Reckitt Benckiser Group plc.

TABLE 4.3 FREQUENCY OF SEXUAL INTERCOURSE AMONG CANADIANS BY AGE AND SEX

AGE		NEVER	SOMETIMES, BUT LESS OFTEN THAN ONCE A WEEK	ONCE A WEEK OR MORE	TOTAL
18–29	men	26	35	39	100
	women	26	27	47	100
30–39	men	2	37	61	100
	women	4	29	67	100
40–49	men	1	38	61	100
	women	5	34	61	100
50–59	men	4	37	59	100
	women	16	45	39	100
60–69	men	9	52	39	100
	women	50	29	21	100
70+	men	28	59	13	100
	women	68	26	6	100

SOURCE: Adapted from Reginald W. Bibby, *Project Canada 2005 National Survey Data*. Reprinted with permission of the author.

for casual, recreational reasons. The comparable figures for anglophone men and anglophone women are 36 percent and 20 percent, respectively. Hatfield (1995) similarly reports that men are somewhat more concerned than women are with sex. Women are somewhat more concerned than men are with love. American research shows that women are more likely to cite "affection for partner" as the major reason for their first intercourse experience (48 percent), followed by "curiosity/readiness for sex" (24 percent). Men most often mention "curiosity" (51 percent), followed by "affection" (25 percent). A small percentage of women (3 percent) report having their first sexual experience for physical pleasure. In contrast, 12 percent of men cite this reason (Michael, Gagnon, Laumann, and Kolata, 1994: 93–94). One study of 1479 Canadians over the age of 18 found that men have sexual thoughts more often than women do, are more likely to have oral sex, have first intercourse at a younger age, have more sexual partners, and are more in favour of casual sex (Fischtein, Herold, and Desmarais, 2007).

Attitudes about extramarital affairs are quite conservative, and they are becoming more so over time. Between 1975 and 2000, adult endorsement of extramarital sex fell from 21 percent to 14 percent, while among teenagers, the drop was from 12 percent to 9 percent (Bibby with Russell and Rolheiser, 2009: 47). As far as actual behaviour is concerned, in a survey of 13 countries, 30–39 percent of Canadians between the ages of 16 and 45 admitted to sexual infidelity. This puts Canadians in the same league as South Africans, Australians, French, Italians, and Thais. By comparison, 40 percent or more of Americans, Russians, British, and Germans between the ages of 16 and 45 admitted to sexual infidelity. For Spaniards, Poles, and residents of Hong Kong, the comparable figure was in the 20–29 percent range (Mackay, 2000: 36–37).

Changing attitudes toward extramarital affairs are part of a tendency for people to have fewer sexual partners. Although there are undoubtedly several reasons for this tendency, one of the most important is the spread of sexually transmitted infections, HIV/AIDS in particular, since about 1980. Sexual attitudes were relatively liberal in the 1960s and 1970s. During those decades, contraception and abortion were legalized. The youth counterculture successfully promoted the idea of "free love." Thus, the culture of the times encouraged people to have multiple sexual partners, while changes in the law minimized the reproductive consequences of doing so. In contrast, once the dangers of HIV/AIDS and other sexually transmitted infections became widely known in the early 1980s, many people became more cautious in their sexual relations. Of those Canadians who took precautions against sexually transmitted infections in 2003, the most common method was to use a condom with a new partner. Still, 49 percent of Canadians had unprotected sex without knowing their partner's sexual history in 2005 (Durex, 2005; see Figure 4.1).

Canadians are becoming more tolerant of homosexuality and same-sex marriage (see Box 4.2). For example, in 1975 fewer than 3 in 10 Canadians agreed that sexual relations between two adults of the same sex were "not wrong at all" or only "sometimes wrong." Today, that figure is more than 6 out of 10. Acceptance of homosexuality is strongly correlated with age, gender, and region; young adults, women, and residents of Quebec and, to a lesser degree, British Columbians are more accepting of homosexuality than are other Canadians (Bibby, 2006: 21–22; Bibby with Russell and Rolheiser, 2009: 46–7).

Research shows that while men are somewhat more concerned with sex than women are, women are somewhat more concerned with love.
SOURCE: © Shutterstock.

SEXUAL ORIENTATION AND QUEER THEORY

People sometimes assert that 1 in 10 North Americans is gay or lesbian. Research shows that this view is an oversimplification. Based on a sample of nearly eight thousand university students in Canada and the United States, researchers found that different measures

FIGURE 4.1 PREVENTATIVE MEASURES TAKEN BY CANADIANS AGAINST SEXUALLY TRANSMITTED INFECTIONS (IN PERCENTAGE)

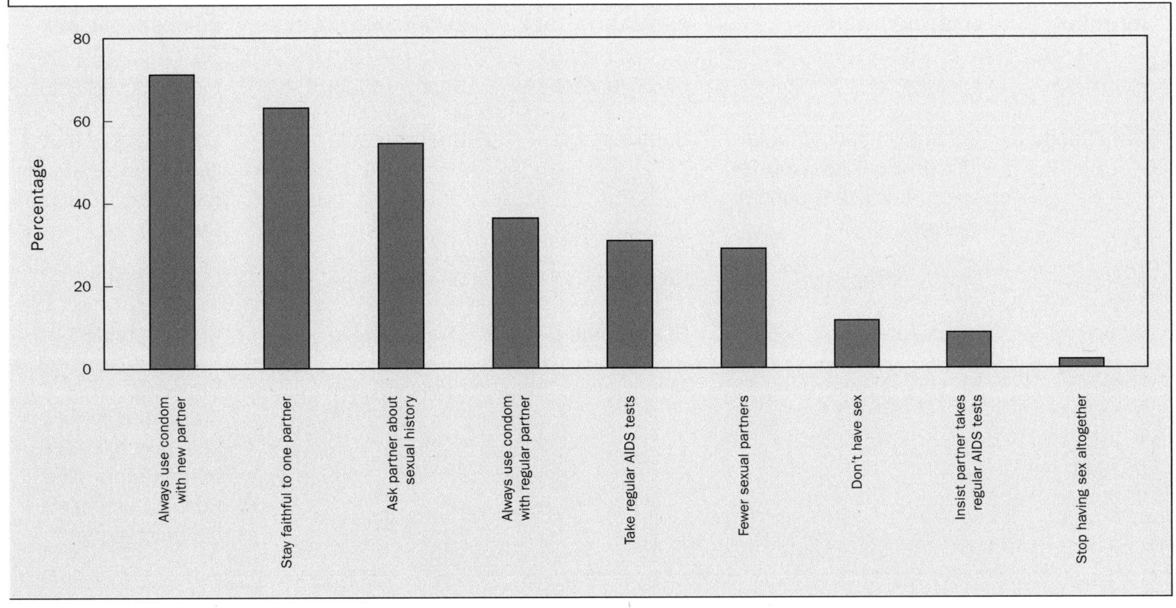

SOURCE: Durex (2005). "Give and Receive: 2005 Global Sex Survey Results." On the World Wide Web at: http://www.durex.com/en-jp/sexualwellbeingsurvey/documents/2003_global_report_phase_2.pdf (18 June 2012). Durex Global Sex Survey, 2003. Used courtesy of Reckitt Benckiser Group plc.

BOX 4.2 SAME-SEX MARRIAGE AND CIVIL UNION

In July 2005, Canada became the third country, after the Netherlands and Belgium, to legalize same-sex marriage. Argentina, Iceland, Norway, Portugal, South Africa, Spain, and Sweden subsequently passed same-sex marriage laws.

By May 2006, 7465 Canadian same-sex couples had tied the knot. (An additional 37 890 same-sex couples were living common-law.) Forty-six percent of the married same-sex couples were men, 54 percent were women. Just over a quarter of the men and nearly 11 percent of the women had children living with them (Statistics Canada, 2011b).

Canadians are becoming more tolerant of homosexuality.
SOURCE: © Jupiter Images.

The major world religions officially disapprove of homosexuality for the most part (see Table 4.4), so it is not surprising that several Canadian church leaders spoke out strongly against the same-sex marriage law. Canadian public opinion remains divided, although by 2006, 59 percent of Canadians agreed that "same-sex couples should have the same right to civil marriage as opposite-sex couples," and 62 percent considered same-sex marriage to be "a settled matter" that should not be reopened and debated again in Parliament." Younger Canadians, women, and people living outside Alberta and Ontario are more likely to support same-sex marriage than are older Canadians, men, and people living in Alberta and Ontario ("Same-Sex Marriage," 2005, 2008).

Many governments have dealt with such splits in public opinion by distinguishing between marriage and "civil union." A civil union grants some of the rights and privileges of marriage to a same-sex couple. At least some jurisdictions in more than a dozen countries allow same-sex couples to enter civil unions. Canadian law goes a step further by making no distinction between heterosexual and same-sex marriage. At the same time, Canadian law respects the right of religious organizations to discriminate against gays and lesbians who want to marry. No religious organization is required by law to marry a same-sex couple.

TABLE 4.4 THE OFFICIAL POSITION OF THE MAJOR WORLD RELIGIONS ON SEXUAL ISSUES

RELIGION	MASTURBATION	PREMARITAL SEX	EXTRAMARITAL SEX	HOMOSEXUAL SEX
Buddhism	Acceptable	Mostly acceptable	Unacceptable	Mostly acceptable
Christianity	Generally unacceptable (but no clear position for some Protestant denominations)	Unacceptable	Unacceptable	Unacceptable (but generally tolerated in the United Church of Canada)
Hinduism	Mostly acceptable	Unacceptable	Unacceptable	Unacceptable
Islam	Unacceptable	Unacceptable	Unacceptable	Unacceptable
Judaism	No clear position	Mostly acceptable	Unacceptable	Generally unacceptable (but generally tolerated in the Reform and Reconstructionist denominations)

SOURCE: Adherents.com (2001); Mackay (2000: 73).

of sexual orientation produced widely different results (see Table 4.5). Some 3.4 percent of men and 2.4 percent of women did define themselves as gay or lesbian, bisexual or other, but 12.0 percent of men and 13.4 percent of women expressed at least occasional attraction to members of their own sex, 21 percent of men and 25.8 percent of women said they had sexual fantasies about members of their own sex at least sometimes, and 12.5 percent of men and 8.0 percent of women said they had at least one intimate sexual experience with a member of the same sex.

These findings suggest that estimates of the prevalence of homosexuality depend on how homosexuality is measured. An estimate based on sexual identity results in a lower percentage than does an estimate focusing on **sexual orientation.** (Sexual orientation refers to the way a person derives sexual pleasure, including whether desirable partners are of the same or a different sex.) I conclude that it is inaccurate to think about sexuality in terms of a strict dichotomy between heterosexuality and homosexuality. It is more appropriate to conceptualize sexuality as comprising four continua: sexual attraction, sexual desire, sexual behaviour, and sexual identity (Michael et al., 1994: 174–79).

Research not only confirms that sexuality is multidimensional but also calls into question whether the conventional characterization of people as heterosexual, bisexual, or gay or lesbian adequately captures the range of sexual orientations in human populations. The provocatively labelled stream of thought known as **queer theory** denies the existence of stable sexual orientations altogether (Green, 2007). From the queer theorist's point of view, when we apply labels like heterosexual, bisexual, gay, and lesbian to ourselves or others, we are adopting official or at least socially accepted labels that fail to capture the fluidity and variability of people's actual identities and performances. Such labels impose social conventions on people, thus acting as forms of control and domination, and drawing attention away from the uniqueness of each individual.

Supporting these assertions, researchers recently asked a sample of 1784 Americans, half women and half men, to choose one of seven labels to define their sexuality: heterosexual, mostly heterosexual,

TABLE 4.5 MEASURES OF SEXUAL ORIENTATION AMONG CANADIAN AND AMERICAN UNIVERSITY STUDENTS

	MEN	WOMEN
Self-reported sexual orientation		
Heterosexual	96.6	97.6
Homosexual, bisexual, other	3.4	2.4
Total	100.0	100.0
Attraction		
Only to one's own sex	88.0	86.6
At least partly to other sex	12.0	13.4
Total	100.0	100.0
Sexual fantasies		
Always involving only the other sex	79.0	74.2
Sometimes involving the same sex	21.0	25.8
Total	100.0	100.0
Same-sex intimate sexual experiences (for those with intimate experiences)		
Only with other sex	87.5	92.0
At least once with same sex	12.5	8.0
Total	100.0	100.0

SOURCE: Reprinted with kind permission from Springer Science + Business Media: *Archives of Sexual Behavior, 34*, 2005, pp. 569–81, Ellis, Lee, Brian Robb and Donald Burke, "Sexual Orientation in United States and Canadian College Students."

bisexual, mostly gay/lesbian, gay/lesbian, questioning/uncertain, and other (Vrangalova and Savin-Williams, 2012). Table 4.6 shows the distribution of women and men who responded positively to the first five categories.

To understand better the differences among the various sexual orientations, the researchers also asked respondents to situate themselves along two dimensions: sexual attraction to men and women, and number of male and female sexual partners. They measured sexual attraction by asking respondents to indicate on a scale of 1 to 5 how sexually attracted they are to men and to women. They measured the number of sexual partners by asking respondents the total number of male and female partners with whom they have had a genital sexual experience. Figure 4.2 illustrates the results for women. It shows that, for all five sexual orientations, women are on average *simultaneously* attracted to same-sex and other-sex partners (albeit to varying degrees). For example, women who define themselves as heterosexual (signified by green squares) scored 4.86 out of 5 on other-sex attraction and 1.49 out of 5 on same-sex attraction. It also shows that, for all five sexual orientations, women have had on average more than one male *and* at least one female sexual partner. For example, heterosexual women (signified by green squares) had on average 10.2 other-sex partners and 1.7 same-sex partners. The pattern for men differs only in detail.

Our discussion demonstrates the existence of wide variation in attitudes toward sex, sexual identity, sexual orientation, and sexual conduct over time and place. It therefore helps to dispel myths about sexuality as natural or "fixed" and about men and women as sexual "opposites." However, they do not answer questions about the *origins* of sexual scripts or why inconsistencies exist between norms and behaviour. The next section addresses these issues by examining the relationship among sex, gender, and sexuality.

TABLE 4.6 SELF-REPORTED SEXUAL ORIENTATION BY SEX (IN PERCENTAGE)

	MEN	WOMEN
Heterosexual	81	71
Mostly heterosexual	9	20
Bisexual	3	6
Mostly gay/lesbian	2	1
Gay/lesbian	5	2
Total	100	100

Note: Information for this figure has been taken from a U.S. Facebook sample and is not representative of the U.S. population.

SOURCE: With kind permission from Springer Science + Business Media: *Archives of Sexual Behavior*, "Mostly Heterosexual and Mostly Gay/Lesbian: Evidence for New Sexual Orientation Identities," Volume 41(1), 2012, p. 5, Zhana Vrangalova and Ritch C. Savin-Williams.

FIGURE 4.2 SAME/OTHER SEXUAL ATTRACTION AND NUMBER OF SAME/OTHER SEX PARTNERS FOR WOMEN OF FIVE SEXUAL ORIENTATIONS

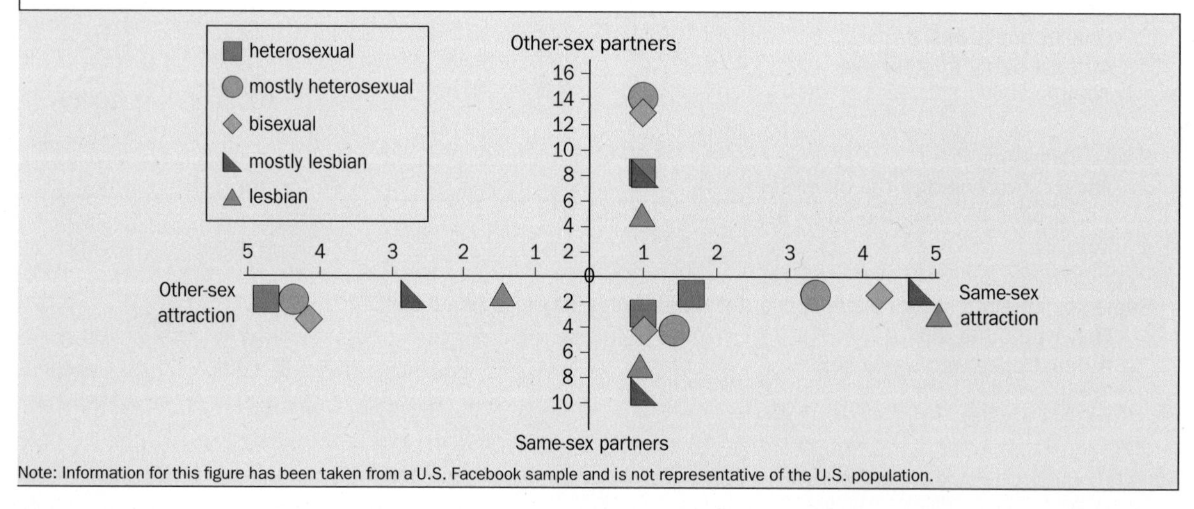

Note: Information for this figure has been taken from a U.S. Facebook sample and is not representative of the U.S. population.

SOURCE: With kind permission from Springer Science + Business Media: *Archives of Sexual Behavior*, "Mostly Heterosexual and Mostly Gay/Lesbian: Evidence for New Sexual Orientation Identities," Volume 41(1), 2012, pp. 7 and 9, Zhana Vrangalova and Ritch C. Savin-Williams.

DOES SEX DETERMINE DESTINY?

ESSENTIALISM

Most arguments about the origins of gender differences in human behaviour adopt one of two perspectives. Some analysts see gender as a reflection of naturally evolved dispositions. Others see gender as a reflection of the different social positions occupied by women and men. Sociologists call these two perspectives, respectively, essentialism and social constructionism. I now summarize and criticize essentialism. I then turn to social constructionism.

Essentialists first observe male–female differences in sexual scripts, the division of labour at home and in the workplace, mate selection, sexual aggression, jealousy, promiscuity, fidelity, and so forth. They then interpret these differences as natural and universal. According to essentialists, child rearing may exaggerate differences between men and women, but nature is the ultimate force at work in shaping them.

Essentialism has many variants, most of which originate in biology and psychology. Here we briefly consider three of the most popular variants: brain studies, sociobiology, and Freudian theory.

Brain Studies

Male–female differences in brain structure are sometimes said to account for male–female differences in behaviour and achievement. The brain comprises two hemispheres of about equal size, connected by a bundle of fibres. The left hemisphere is generally associated with language abilities, the right with nonverbal perception and visual and spatial skills. About this, little controversy exists in the scientific community. However, some brain researchers argue that the two hemispheres develop differently in boys and girls, as do the fibres connecting the hemispheres. Specifically, they claim that when the male fetus starts to secrete testosterone (the hormone responsible for furthering the sexual development of the male), it washes over the brain and briefly inhibits the growth of the left hemisphere. As a result, use of the *right* hemisphere becomes dominant in men. This supposedly allows men to excel in mathematical, artistic, musical, and visual-spatial abilities. Meanwhile (the theory continues), the bundle of fibres connecting the left and right hemispheres is bigger in women. This supposedly allows women to use the hemispheres more symmetrically, giving them an edge in feelings, intuition, language skills, and quick judgments (Bleier, 1984: 92; Blum, 1997: 36–63; Tavris, 1992: 45–46).

Such presumably innate differences in brain structure allegedly give rise to male–female differences in behaviour and achievement. For example, some proponents of this line of thought claim that men are best at jobs requiring logic and visual-spatial manipulation. Hence the disproportionately large number of men who work as scientists, mechanics, pilots, and so forth. For their part, women are presumably best at jobs requiring empathy, intuition, and language skills. Hence the disproportionately large number of women who stay home to raise children and who work outside the home as teachers, secretaries, social workers, and nurses. It follows from this line of reasoning that the gender division of labour is perfectly natural, structured by our brains rather than by society.

Sociobiology

Sociobiology is a second variant of essentialism, and E. O. Wilson (1975) is its leading exponent. Wilson argues that all human beings instinctually want to ensure that their genes get passed on to future generations. However, the different reproductive status of men and women means they have had to overcome different adaptive problems and develop different adaptive strategies. This gave rise to patterns of behaviour we now call "masculine" and "feminine." Individuals who possessed the characteristics that best resolved these problems—the most feminine women and the most masculine men—had a better chance of surviving and passing their genes to their offspring. Thus, over time, masculine and feminine behaviours became genetically encoded. According to sociobiology, genetic factors also trigger biochemical processes that further enhance sex differences through varying levels of hormone production in women and men.

David Buss, a well-known evolutionary psychologist, argues that four adaptive strategies or "universal features of our evolved selves" govern the relations between the sexes and contribute to the preservation of the human species (Buss, 1994: 211; see also Buss, 1995a, 1995b, 1998; Dawkins, 1976; Wilson, 1978). First, men want casual sex with women. Second, men treat women's bodies as men's property. Third, men beat or kill women who incite male sexual jealousy. And fourth, women are greedy for money.

Buss bases his argument on the claim that a woman has a bigger investment than a man in ensuring the survival of their offspring. That is because the woman produces only a small number of eggs during her reproductive life. Specifically, she releases fewer than 400 eggs during her reproductive years. At most, she can give birth to about 20 children. Men, however, typically release between 200 million and 500 million sperm every time they ejaculate. This number of sperm can typically be produced every 24 to 48 hours (Saxton, 1990: 94–95). It is thus adaptive in an evolutionary sense for a man to be promiscuous yet jealously possessive of his partners (Wilson and Daly, 1998) insofar as a promiscuous yet jealous man maximizes the chance that his, and only his, offspring will be produced. Moreover, since men compete with other men for sexual access to women, men evolve competitive and aggressive dispositions that include physical violence. In contrast, Buss says, it is in a woman's best interest to maintain primary responsibility for her genetic child and to look around for the best mate with whom to intermix her genes. He is the man who can best help support the child after birth. Hence women's alleged greed for money in contemporary society.

Research certainly supports the view that men and women emphasize different characteristics in selecting a mate. Simon Davis, for example, conducted a content analysis of personal advertisements in the *Vancouver Sun*. He discovered that attractive physical features were the most frequently mentioned desirable characteristic in a partner for both men and women. However, women were more likely than men were to list professional status, employment status, financial considerations, intelligence, commitment, and emotion. Men, conversely, were more likely to list attractiveness, physique, and sexiness, and to require a picture (Davis, 1990: 43–50). These results do not, however, establish that sex-typed mating preferences are *genetically* determined. As we will see, the results are also consistent with differences in how we assign status to masculine and feminine gender roles.

Freud

Freud (1977 [1905]) offered a third influential essentialist explanation of male–female differences. He believed that sexuality is the main human instinct. In his view, it motivates human behaviour and accounts for the development of distinct masculine and feminine gender roles.

According to Freud, children around the age of three to five begin to pay attention to their genitals. As a young boy becomes preoccupied with his penis, he unconsciously develops a fantasy of sexually possessing his mother. He begins to resent his father because only his father is allowed to sexually possess the mother. However, because he has seen his mother or another girl naked, the boy also develops anxiety that he will be castrated by his father for desiring his mother. To resolve this fear, the boy represses his feelings for his mother. That is, he stores them in the unconscious part of his personality. In due course, this repression allows him to begin identifying with his father. This leads to the development of a strong, masculine personality.[1]

In contrast, the young girl begins to develop a feminine personality when she realizes she lacks a penis. According to Freud,

> [girls] notice the penis of a brother or playmate, strikingly visible and of large proportions, at once recognize it as the superior counterpart of their own small and inconspicuous organ, and from that time forward fall victim to envy for the penis. ... She has seen it and knows that she is without it and wants to have it. (Quoted in Steinem, 1994: 50)

Because of her "penis envy," the young girl soon develops a sense of inferiority, according to Freud. She also grows angry with her mother, who, she naively thinks, is responsible for cutting off the penis the girl must have once had. She rejects her mother and develops an unconscious sexual desire for her father. Eventually, however, realizing she will never have a penis, the girl comes to identify with her mother. This is a way of vicariously acquiring her father's penis in Freud's view. In the "normal" development of a mature woman, the girl's wish to have a penis is transformed into a desire to have children. However, says Freud, since women are never able to completely resolve their penis envy, the feminine gender identity is normally immature and dependent on men. This dependence is evident from the "fact" that women can be fully sexually satisfied only by vaginally induced orgasm. Thus, a host of gender differences in personality and behaviour follow from the anatomical sex differences that children first observe around the age of three.[2]

A Critique of Essentialism

Essentialist arguments, such as those described earlier, have six main problems. First, *essentialists ignore the historical and cultural variability of gender and sexuality.* In some cultures, men are socialized to be nurturing and sensitive. Rape is incomprehensible. For example, anthropologist Margaret Mead reports that the Arapesh, a preliterate people in New Guinea, "know nothing of rape beyond the fact that it is the unpleasant custom of the Nugum people to the southeast of them" (Mead, 1935: 110). More generally, rates of rape vary widely across cultures (Sanday, 1981). This variability deflates the idea that biological constants account for innate behavioural differences between women and men, such as male aggressiveness and violence. Moreover, societies and cultures often change rapidly without any apparent genetic change taking place. Essentialist arguments have a difficult time explaining, for example, recent changes in child-care arrangements, women's increased participation in the paid labour force, and other aspects of women's lives, given the absence of any documented shift in male or female genetic structure that might account for such change.

Second, *essentialists ignore the fact that gender differences are declining rapidly and in some cases have already disappeared* (Caplan and Caplan, 1999). Hundreds of studies have shown that women are developing traits that were traditionally considered masculine. For example, research shows that women have become more assertive, competitive, independent, and analytical since the early 1970s. They play more aggressive sports, choose more mathematics and science courses, perform better in standardized tests, take more nontraditional jobs, and earn more money than they used to (Twenge, 1997). In what must be considered a serious blow to brain research on alleged male–female differences, a review of 165 studies of verbal ability representing tests of more than 1.4 million people found no gender differences in verbal skills. A review of one hundred studies of mathematics performance representing tests of nearly four million students showed small differences favouring *females* in the general population. (Larger differences favouring males were, however, found in samples of precocious individuals.) A review of dozens of studies on spatial ability reported that some studies found no gender differences, while other studies found only small differences in favour of men (Tavris, 1992: 52). Taken as a whole, this body of research suggests that few gender differences in ability remain to be explained, the few remaining differences are small, and those few small differences are disappearing.

Third, the research evidence employed by essentialists is often deeply flawed. Consider the sociobiologists' observation that men are more independent than women are. Research shows that, in fact, girls are more dependent than boys *only at certain ages*. Thus, although infant girls seem to behave in a more dependent fashion than infant are boys, girls at the age of two are more independent than are boys (Feiring and Lewis, 1979; Goldberg and Lewis, 1969). Evidence from studies purporting to find a genetic cause of homosexuality is also problematic. Hamer and Copeland (1996), for example, claim to have found a possible genetic marker for homosexuality in 33 of 40 brothers who were both gay. As Peele and De Grandpre (1995) point out, however, the study did not check for the frequency of the supposed marker in *heterosexual* brothers. Nor has anyone been able to replicate the findings. More generally, sociobiologists and evolutionary psychologists have not been able to identify *any* of the genes that, they claim, cause male jealousy, female nurturance, or the unequal division of labour between men and women. Meanwhile, brain researchers have had great difficulty showing how observed physical differences between male and female brains might be related to (nonexistent or small and shrinking) differences in male and female abilities. That is one reason several brain theories make contradictory arguments. For example, the theory reviewed previously says that men have greater right hemisphere specialization. However, a second theory holds that men have greater *left* hemisphere specialization, which gives them an intellectual advantage over women. Meanwhile, a third theory agrees that men have greater right brain specialization but insists that this gives men superior artistic and musical abilities; yet this contradicts the first theory, which says that women have the edge in musical and artistic skills, which rely on intuition and empathy (Tavris, 1992: 45–49). Lack of hard evidence encourages such unsubstantiated speculation.

Fourth, *essentialists tend to generalize from the average, ignoring variations within gender groups.* On average, women and men do, of course, differ in some respects. For example, one of the best-documented average differences between women and men concerns aggressiveness. Men are on average more verbally and physically aggressive than women are. However, when sociobiologists say men are *inherently* more aggressive than women are, they make it seem as if this is true of all men and all women. As Figure 4.3 shows, however, it is not. When verbal or physical aggressiveness is measured by trained researchers, scores vary widely within gender groups. Aggressiveness is distributed so that considerable overlap occurs between men and women. Thus, many women are more aggressive than the average man, and many men are less aggressive than the average woman.

Fifth, *essentialists exaggerate the degree to which gender differences are unchangeable.* For example, evolutionary psychologist David Buss and colleagues (1990) used data from 37 cultures to show that women consistently prefer older men with high earning capacity as partners. In contrast, men prefer women with good domestic capabilities. Buss claims that this demonstrates a genetic basis for mate selection. But Eagley and Wood (1999) reexamined Buss's data. They show that women's tendency to stress the "good provider" role in selecting male partners and men's tendency to stress women's domestic skills decrease in societies that have more gender equality. Similarly, women express less preference for older men, and men less preference for younger women, in more gender-egalitarian societies. As this example shows, gender differences vary with social conditions, a fact that essentialists ignore. Another example of how social conditions affect gender differences: The "male" hormone testosterone is associated with greater aggressiveness. However, Deborah Blum (1997: 158–88) notes that social situations involving competition and threat stimulate production of testosterone in *women* and cause them to act more aggressively (compare Caplan and Caplan, 1999). For example, when women take jobs that maximize competition and threat—when they become, say, corporate lawyers or police officers—they undergo hormonal and behavioural changes, thus decreasing behavioural differences between men and women.

FIGURE 4.3 THE DISTRIBUTION OF MALE AND FEMALE AGGRESSIVENESS

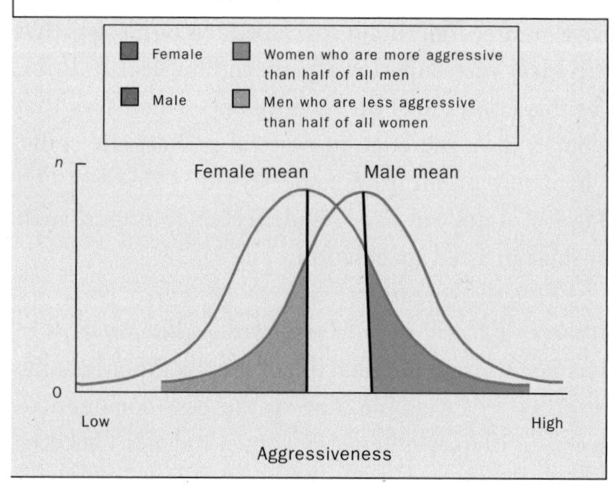

Finally, *essentialists offer explanations for gender differences that ignore the role of power.* Sociobiologists assume that existing behaviour patterns help ensure the survival of the species because they are the patterns that endured as humans evolved. However, their assumption overlooks the fact that some groups (such as men) are in a position of greater power and authority than are other groups (such as women). Behavioural differences between men and women may, therefore, result not from any biological imperative but from men's ability to establish their preferences over the interests of women. Indeed, from this point of view, sociobiology may be seen as an example of the exercise of male power, that is, a rationalization for male domination and sexual aggression. The same may be said of Freud's interpretation. *Must* young girls define themselves in relation to young boys by focusing on their lack of a penis? *Do* they define themselves that way? Freud offers no evidence to support his case. There is no reason why young girls' sexual self-definitions cannot focus positively on their own reproductive organs, including their unique ability to bear children. Freud simply assumed that men are superior to women and then created a speculative theory that justifies gender differences.

SOCIAL CONSTRUCTIONISM

Social constructionism is the main alternative to essentialism. Social constructionists argue that gender differences are not the product of biological properties, whether chromosomal, gonadal, or hormonal. Instead, gender and sexuality are products of social structure and culture. *Culture* is composed of shared systems of meaning. It incorporates people's values and beliefs. Although many systems of meaning coexist and compete at any one time, patriarchy, or male domination and belief in its validity, is widely accepted in nearly all societies today. *Social structure* refers to the way major institutions, such as families, the economy, and the political system, are organized. Social structures in most societies today are patriarchal in that they reinforce inequalities between women and men.

Social constructionists stress three main socio-historical changes that led to the development of gender inequality. The first was *long-distance warfare and conquest.* Anthropologists have shown that a high level of gender equality existed in foraging or hunting-and-gathering societies, the dominant form of society for 90 percent of human history. Rough equality between women and men was based on the fact that women produced a substantial amount of the band's food, up to 80 percent in some cases. Archaeological evidence from "Old Europe" tells a similar story. Old Europe is a region stretching roughly from Poland in the north to the Mediterranean island of Crete in the south, and from Switzerland in the west to Bulgaria in the east (see Figure 4.4). Between 7000 and 3500 BCE, men and women enjoyed rough equality throughout the region. The religions of the region gave primacy to fertility and creator goddesses. Kinship was traced through the mother's side of the family. Then, sometime between 4300 and 4200 BCE, all this began to change. Old Europe was invaded by successive waves of warring peoples from the Asiatic and European northeast (the Kurgans) and the deserts to the south (the Semites). Both the Kurgan and Semitic civilizations were based on a steeply hierarchical and patriarchal social structure. Their religions gave primacy to male warrior gods. They acquired property and slaves by conquering other peoples and imposed their religions on the vanquished. They eliminated, or at least downgraded, goddesses as divine powers. God became a male who willed that women should be ruled by men. Laws reinforced women's sexual, economic, and political subjugation to men. Traditional Judaism, Christianity, and Islam all embody ideas of male dominance, and they all derive from the tribes who conquered Old Europe in the fifth millennium BCE (Eisler, 1987).

FIGURE 4.4 APPROXIMATE AREA FOR EARLY CIVILIZATION OF OLD EUROPE

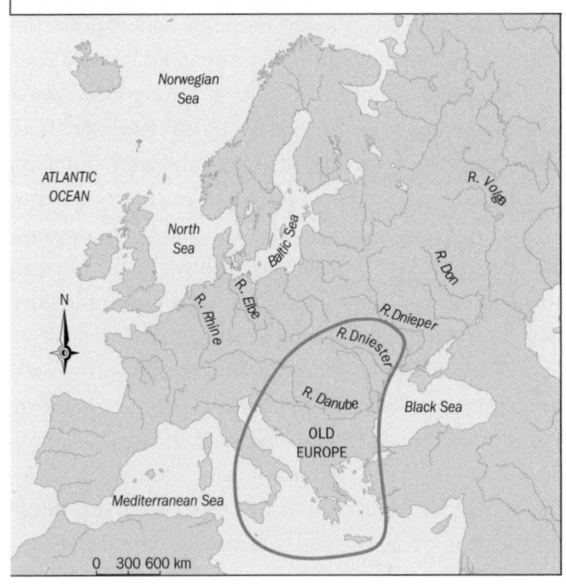

SOURCE: Reprinted with permission of University of California Press. Adapted from *Goddesses and Gods of Old Europe: 6500–3500 B.C.: Myths and Cult Images* (1982). Permission conveyed through Copyright Clearance Center.

The second change was to *plow agriculture*. Long-distance warfare and conquest catered to men's strengths and so greatly enhanced male power and authority. Large-scale farming with plows harnessed to animals had much the same effect. Plow agriculture originated in the Middle East around five thousand years ago. It required that strong adults remain in the fields all day for much of the year. It also reinforced the principle of private ownership of land. Since men were on average stronger than women, and since women were restricted in their activities by pregnancy, nursing, and childbirth, plow agriculture made men more powerful socially. Thus, land was owned by men and ownership was typically passed from father to son (Coontz and Henderson, 1986).

Third came *the separation of public and private spheres.* In the agricultural era, economic production was organized around the household. Men may have worked apart from women in the fields, but the fields were still part of the *family* farm. In contrast, during the early phase of industrialization, men's work was moved out of the household and into the factory and the office. Most men became wage or salary workers. Some assumed decision-making roles in economic and political institutions. But while men went public, most women remained in the domestic or private sphere.

The idea soon developed that this was a "natural" division of labour. This idea persisted until the second half of the twentieth century, when a variety of social circumstances, ranging from the introduction of the birth control pill to women's demands for entry into university, finally allowed women to enter the public sphere in large numbers.

So we see that, according to social constructionists, gender inequality derives historically from three main circumstances: the advent of long-distance warfare and conquest, the development of plow agriculture, and the assignment of women to the domestic sphere and men to the public sphere during the early industrial era.

Although gender inequality is decreasing somewhat in many societies today, it still persists. It is supported by a variety of economic and political arrangements discussed elsewhere in this book (see especially Chapter 7, Gender Inequality: Economic and Political Aspects). In what follows, I fill out the social constructionist perspective by outlining just two dimensions of contemporary gender inequality. First, I show how socialization still pushes girls to act in stereotypically feminine ways and boys to act in stereotypically masculine ways. I then discuss eating disorders and male violence against women to show that the social construction of gender has far-reaching implications for women, men, and the relations between them.

CONSTRUCTING GENDER THROUGH SOCIALIZATION

PRIMARY SOCIALIZATION

Research shows that, from the moment of birth, infant boys and girls are treated differently by parents, particularly fathers, and especially if the parents are heterosexuals. Girls are more likely to be characterized as delicate, weak, beautiful, and cute; boys as strong, alert, and well coordinated (Rubin, Provenzano, and Lurra, 1974; Sutfin et al., 2008). Interpretations of behaviour vary by sex. For example, when viewing a videotape of a nine-month-old infant, experimental subjects tend to label startled reactions to a stimulus as "anger" if the baby has been previously identified as a boy, and as "fear" if the baby is identified as a girl, *regardless of the baby's actual sex* (Condry and Condry, 1976). Parents also tend to encourage their sons to engage in boisterous behaviour and competitive play. They tend to encourage their daughters to engage in cooperative play (MacDonald and Parke, 1986). Boys are more likely than girls are to be praised for assertiveness, and girls are more likely than boys are to be rewarded for compliance (Kerig, Cowan, and Cowan, 1993). Parents reinforce gender-specific behaviour by the design of the child's room, the clothes they buy, and the toys they provide. Boys' toys, for example, are more likely to emphasize aggressive competition and spatial manipulation. Girls' toys tend to be more passive and oriented toward the home (for example, dolls, kitchen sets, washers and dryers; Hughes, 1995). Most parents encourage their children to play with gender-stereotyped toys. Preschool boys are just as likely to play with a dish set as a tool set if given a choice—unless they are told that the dish set is a girl's toy and they think their fathers will view playing with it as "bad" (Raag and Rackliff, 1998).

SECONDARY SOCIALIZATION

The process of channelling girls into roles culturally defined as appropriately feminine and boys into roles culturally defined as appropriately masculine continues in school. In most schools, teachers still tend to assume that boys will do better in the sciences and mathematics, girls in languages. Parents reinforce these expectations at home (Eccles, Jacobs, and Harold, 1990; Gunderson et al., 2012).

By the age of about 14, interaction with peers becomes an important factor in reinforcing gender-typed attitudes and behaviours. That is because the subcultures of male and female peer groups emphasize gender-stereotypical values. Boys tend to establish less intimate friendships than girls do. Moreover, boys' friendships tend to be based on such activities as team sports, which focus on independence, emotional control, and conquest. Girls tend to form less extensive friendship networks than boys do and focus on sociability, popularity, and attractiveness (Elkin and Handel, 1989; Udry, 1971: 76, 82).

THE MASS MEDIA

The symbolic representation of gender in the mass media also creates and reinforces gender stereotypes. The social construction of gender in the mass media begins when small children learn that only a kiss from Snow White's Prince Charming will save her from eternal sleep. It continues in magazines, romance novels, advertisements, and music, and on television and the Internet. It is big business. For example, Harlequin Enterprises of Toronto dominates the production and sale of romance novels worldwide. The company sells more than 175 million books a year in 23 languages in more than 100 national markets. Most readers of Harlequin romances consume between 3 and 20 books a month. A central theme in these romances is the transformation of women's bodies into objects for men's pleasure (Grescoe, 1996). As such, romance novels may be seen as a less extreme form of the pornography industry for men.

GENDER SOCIALIZATION AND SEXUALITY

In our society, we receive little systematic instruction regarding sexuality. That is probably because of our rather prudish history and the popular assumption that sexuality is a natural instinct that does not have to be taught. By default, therefore, as adults we tend to express our sexuality in a framework defined by our early, informal gender socialization.

Boys and girls do not always accept gender socialization passively; they sometimes resist it. For the most part, however, boys and girls try to develop the skills that will help them perform conventional gender roles (Eagley and Wood, 1999: 412–13). Of course, conventions change. It is important to note in this regard that what children learn about femininity and masculinity today is less sexist than what they learned just a few generations ago. For example, comparing *Cinderella* and *Snow White* with more recent Disney movies, such as *Tangled*, we see that girls going to Disney movies today are sometimes presented with assertive and heroic female role models rather than the passive and, by today's standards, quite pathetic heroines of the 1930s and 1940s. However, the amount of change in gender socialization should not be exaggerated, nor its effects on sexuality. *Cinderella* and *Snow White* are still popular movies for girls. Moreover, for every *Tangled* there is a *Little Mermaid*, a movie that simply modernizes old themes about female passivity and male conquest. As we saw in our discussion of sexual behaviour, survey research shows that men are still more likely than women are to adhere to sexual scripts emphasizing fun, conquest, and orgasm rather than love, tenderness, and emotionality. The fact that girls learn that sexuality is something they must fear—think of unwanted pregnancy and sexual assault—also serves to perpetuate passive sexual scripts for women today (Nelson and Robinson, 1999: 351).

Murray Warren, a teacher in Port Coquitlam, B.C., displays two of three children's books featuring children with same-gender parents at the Supreme Court of Canada in Ottawa, June 2002. The books were banned by the Surrey School Board in which Warren teaches. What gender stereotypes do these kinds of books seek to offset?
SOURCE: Fred Chartrand/The Canadian Press.

The social construction of gender and sexuality has far-reaching implications for men and women. As we have just seen, the social construction of gender during childhood socialization influences the way men and women express their sexuality. You will learn in detail later in this book how the social construction of gender also helps determine the kind of formal education men and women pursue, the kinds of jobs they get, and the way domestic work is divided between men and women. As you will now see, the standards of physical attractiveness that are internalized through gender socialization and sexual scripts have also contributed to dieting and eating disorders.

BODY IMAGE AND EATING DISORDERS

The social construction of gender involves defining standards of physical attractiveness for women and men. These standards are reinforced by the mass media.

Physical attractiveness is especially important for women. That is because they are judged on the basis of appearance more often than men are. Moreover, unattractive women are described in more negative terms than are equally unattractive men (Wolf, 1991). Masculinity is more likely to be assessed in terms of status and power than in terms of physical attractiveness.

Weight has become an increasingly important dimension of body image since the 1960s. Research shows that *Playboy* centrefold models and Miss America contestants have grown substantially thinner since 1959. A 1997 survey shows that 89 percent of North American women want to lose weight (Garner, 1997). Canadian women list "being overweight" as one of their major health problems

(Walters, 1992). Many men are concerned about their body image, too, but among women the emphasis on being thin is especially common. The "cult of thinness" has spawned major industries, including diet and self-help, cosmetic surgery, diet foods, and fitness (Hesse-Biber, 1996).

Standards of breast size pose a special problem for women. Although thin is in, large breasts have been popular since the 1960s (Koff and Benavage, 1998). Breasts, however, are composed mainly of fat; and the amount of breast fat is associated with total body fat. Thus, it is virtually impossible for most women to achieve the ideal standard of beauty.

Many women and men resent the thin models they see in the mass media. Nonetheless, dieting to lose weight and fear of being fat are common in girls as young as nine. One study found that half of all teenage girls are on diets (Pipher, 1994: 184–85).

Body image is associated with self-esteem and behaviour. People who are dissatisfied with their bodies are less likely to desire and engage in sexual activity. Conversely, bad sexual experiences contribute to a poor body image. For example, sexual abuse is an important cause of body dissatisfaction. In the 1997 survey cited previously, 23 percent of women and 10 percent of men viewed sexual abuse as having been moderately to very important in shaping their body image in childhood or adolescence (Garner, 1997).

At the extreme, concern with body image may result in anorexia nervosa (refusal to eat enough to remain healthy) or bulimia (regular, self-induced vomiting). Most estimates of the percentage of young women with such eating disorders are in the 2 to 6 percent range. For young men, most estimates are in the 1 to 3 percent range (Averett and Korenman, 1996: 305; Garner, 1997; Lips, 1993: 254; Pipher, 1994: 184–85). Some women and men have changed their body shape by means of surgical procedures, such as liposuction and cosmetic surgery. More than 90 percent of cosmetic surgery patients are women (Hesse-Biber, 1996: 51, 53).

There are cultural variations in standards of beauty. For instance, in the United States, black women are more likely to be above the recommended body weight than are non-black women. At the same time, they are less likely to see themselves as overweight. Obesity also results in fewer social penalties in the case of black women. Thus, obese white women have smaller family incomes than non-obese white women because they are less likely to be married and more likely to face job discrimination. This is not the case for obese black women compared with non-obese black women (Averett and Korenman, 1996).

MALE VIOLENCE AGAINST WOMEN

The way in which gender and sexual scripts are socially constructed also affects the frequency with which men sexually assault and harass women. Let us consider this issue in detail.

SEXUAL ASSAULT

The sexual assault of women is common. One in eight girls in Canada will be a victim of serious sexual abuse before the age of 16 (Bagley and King, 1990; Gadd, 1997). Perpetrators of child sexual assault are typically male, known to the victim, and in a position of authority over the child. Research demonstrates that, in general, victims of sexual assault are selected less because of sexual desirability than because of their availability and powerlessness (Duffy, 1998). One survey found that 60 percent of high school boys approve of forcing sexual activities on a girl, at least in some circumstances (Davis, Peck, and Stormant, 1993).

A survey of Canadian college and university students asked a series of questions about male violence against women during elementary school, during high school, since high school, and in the year preceding the survey (DeKeseredy and Schwartz, 1998). The researchers found that psychological or emotional abuse of women is most common, followed by sexual and then physical abuse. Males consistently reported lower levels of sexual, psychological, and physical violence against women than did women. However, even the percentages reported by males are disturbingly high. Moreover, the percentages grow as boys turn into men and advance from high school to post-secondary education. For example, 1.5 percent of boys said they forced girls to engage in sexual activities with them in elementary school, and 2.3 percent said they forced girls to engage in sexual activities with them in high school. For the year preceding the survey, the percentage was 11 percent. Fully 19.5 percent of men in Canadian colleges and universities said they had forced a woman to engage in sexual activities with them at least once since high school (see also Table 4.7).

Of course, men are the victims of violence, too. Like women, they are far more likely to be assaulted by men than by women. Some studies show that female partners are as likely as male partners to participate in

TABLE 4.7 INTIMATE VIOLENCE IN CANADA, 1993–2009

	1993	1999	2004	2009
Prevalence of self-reported spousal assault, preceding five years (percentage)				
Male victims	n.a.	7	6	6
Female victims	12	8	7	6
Spousal homicide (per 100 000 men and women)				
Male victims	0.3	0.1	0.1	0.2
Female victims	0.8	0.7	0.7	0.5
Sexual assaults reported to police (per 100 000 pop.)	120	78	70	71
Prevalence of criminal harassment (stalking) reported to police				
By current or ex-husband or boyfriend	n.a.	1300	2125	7755
By current or ex-wife or girlfriend	n.a.	100	200	1242

Note: Some of these figures are approximate because they were read from graphs. The enormous increase in the prevalence of stalking between 1999 and 2009 is largely a result of increased reporting.

SOURCES: Milligan (2011); Statistics Canada (2006; 2011a).

abusive acts—with the exception of sexual assault, which is almost exclusively a male domain (Straus, 1995). Note, however, that women are more likely to use violence as a response to their own powerlessness, attacking partners out of self-defence or lashing out at their children following abuse by their husbands. Men, conversely, are more likely to use force to retain control and power over their partners and children. Moreover, abusive men are far more likely to cause serious physical injuries than are abusive women, and abused men are therefore far less likely than abused women are to report their partners' violent acts to the police (Fitzgerald, 1993; Koss et al., 1994; see Figure 4.5).

The most severe form of sexual assault involves rape. Research shows that some rapists are men who were physically or sexually abused in their youth. They develop a deep-seated need to feel powerful as emotional compensation for their early powerlessness. Other rapists are men who, as children, saw their mothers as potentially hostile figures who needed to be controlled, or as mere objects available for male gratification, and saw their fathers as emotionally cold and distant. Raised in such a family atmosphere, rapists learn not to empathize with women. Instead, they learn to want to dominate them (Lisak, 1992). Significantly, rates of rape are highest in war situations, when some conquering male soldiers feel justified in wanting to humiliate the vanquished, who are powerless to stop them (Human Rights Watch, 1995). This suggests that, in general, rape involves using sex to establish dominance. The incidence of rape is highest in situations where early socialization experiences predispose men to want to control women, where norms justify the domination of women, and where a large power imbalance between men and women exists.

SEXUAL HARASSMENT

Two types of sexual harassment occur in the workplace. **Quid pro quo sexual harassment** takes place when sexual threats or bribery are made a condition of employment decisions. **Hostile environment sexual harassment** involves sexual jokes, comments, and touching that interferes with work or creates an unfriendly work setting. Surveys show that between 23 and 51 percent of women have been sexually harassed in the workplace (Gruber, 1997; Welsh and Nierobisz, 1997). When semi-public and public settings are included, up to 87 percent of women report being sexually harassed (see Table 4.7; Lenton Smith, Fox, and Morra, 1999). Based on available research, it seems clear that relatively powerless women are the most likely to be sexually harassed. Moreover, sexual harassment is most common in work settings that exhibit high levels of gender inequality and a culture justifying male domination of women. Specifically, women who are young, unmarried, and employed in

FIGURE 4.5 SEVERITY OF SPOUSAL VIOLENCE BY SEX OF VICTIM, CANADA, 2009

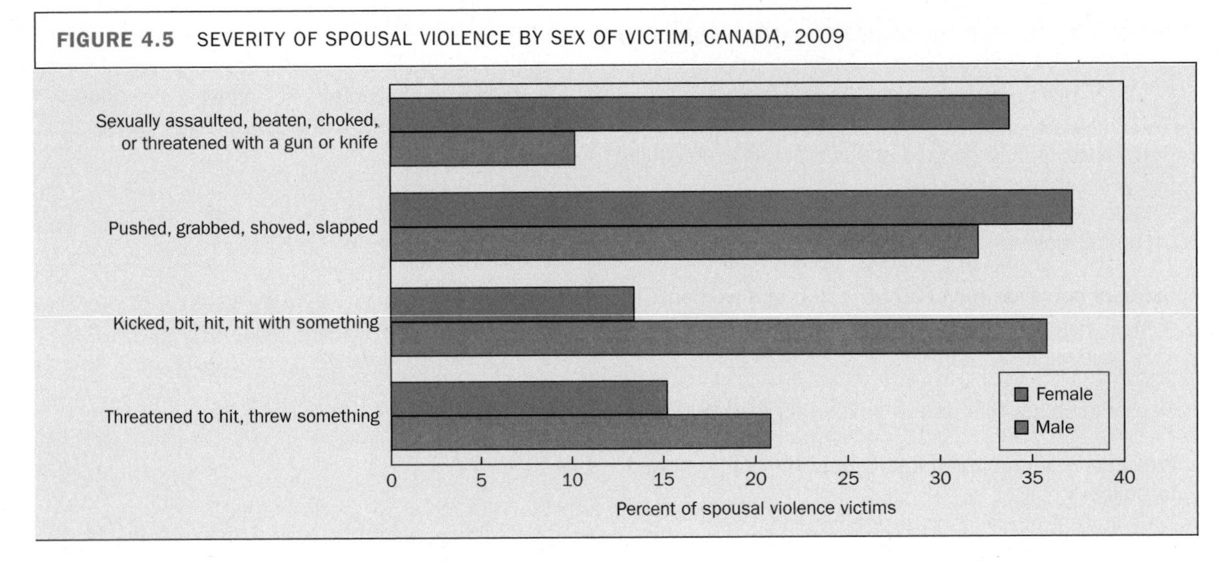

SOURCE: Statistics Canada. (2011a). "Family Violence in Canada; A Statistical Profile," Catalogue no. 85–224-X, p. 10.

nonprofessional jobs are most likely to become objects of sexual harassment. They are particularly likely to be sexually harassed if they are temporary workers, the ratio of women to men in the workplace is low, and the organizational culture of the workplace tolerates sexual harassment (Welsh, 1999).

As the foregoing discussion makes clear, large power imbalances between men and women and a culture that supports patriarchy are associated with high rates of sexual assault and harassment. Where men are much more powerful than women are, and where gender inequality is justified culturally, gender is socially constructed to permit and even encourage violence against women. The research literature is clear on this point. It shows, for example, that men who most enjoy sexist jokes are most likely to report engaging in acts of sexual aggression against women (Ryan and Kanjorski, 1998). Men who link sexuality with social dominance are more likely to sexually harass women (Pryor, Giedd, and Williams, 1995). And both men and women who abuse their intimate partners value control and dominance more than harmony in interpersonal relationships (Thompson, 1991).

LOOKING AHEAD: TOWARD A NEW SEXUAL ETHIC

For the past 40 years, most sociologists of gender have criticized the essentialist view that sexual scripts are part of "human nature." Rather than seeing sexuality as natural, they have examined how it is socially constructed. They do not deny the biological basis of sexuality. They simply appreciate that the form sexual expression takes is not inevitable and immutable. In the preceding pages, I illustrated the social constructionist case by examining the historical factors that shaped the emergence of sexual scripts, the relationship between gender socialization and sexuality, the ways in which sexual relations reflect and reinforce power differentials, the privileging of heterosexuality, the marginalization of other sexual identities, and the implications of gender roles for the sexual assault and harassment of women by men. There remains the task of discussing the implications of these insights for the new sexual ethic that is emerging in much of the world and the role that feminism has played in advancing it.

FEMINISM AND SEXUALITY

Feminism has been chiefly responsible for the social constructionist turn in the study of gender and sexuality. Its influence has been multifaceted.

In the 1970s and 1980s, some feminists took what many scholars now regard as an extreme position on the question of sexuality. For example, Catherine Mackinnon argued that heterosexual sex, even when it is consensual, necessarily involves a man *dominating* a woman. Why? Because, according to Mackinnon, men enjoy the power to define the meaning of sexuality, even for women. By sexualizing hierarchy and defining domination as pleasure, they limit the way women are allowed to experience and express their sexuality (Mackinnon, 1997: 158, 167; see also Jeffreys, 1990; Kitzinger and Wilkinson, 1994).

Mackinnon and others found abundant evidence of this process in the male-controlled pornography industry. According to one estimate, in 2006 pornography generated $97 billion in revenue, more than Microsoft, Google, Amazon, eBay, Yahoo, Apple, and Netflix combined (Ropelato, n.d.). Pornography oppresses women in three ways (Dworkin, 1981, 1987). First, it exploits women who work in the pornography industry by paying them low wages and requiring that they engage in demeaning acts of submission and abuse. Second, it teaches men how to treat women sexually. Specifically, by eroticizing and normalizing the degradation of women, pornography contributes to sexual harassment and the sexual and physical abuse of women, including rape. Third, pornography teaches women what men supposedly want—how they should dress, act, and have intercourse in ways that please men. In all these ways, then, pornography helps to turn heterosexual sex into male domination.

Some feminists have criticized the view that men control the meaning of sexuality and have turned heterosexual sex into a form of male domination. They point out that while *gender* inequality tends to favour male domination of women, *sexual* inequality tends to favour heterosexuality over homosexuality (Rubin, 1993: 33). Lesbians are discriminated against and oppressed as women *and* as members of a sexual minority; gays, male transvestites, and other male erotic minorities are discriminated against and oppressed despite the fact that they are men. Sexuality, the critics conclude, is rooted not just in gender stratification but also in sexual stratification.

A second feminist criticism of Mackinnon's view that men control the meaning of sexuality and have turned heterosexual sex into a form of male domination cites contradictory data. It is a matter of historical fact that pornography has not always involved male domination of women. For example, between the 1910s and 1950s, many pornographic films were playful, even silly depictions of a wide variety of sexual acts involving laughter, sweet expressions, and moments of shared affection (Power, 2009: 52–3). They were not the humiliating and often sadistic medium of women's oppression we know today so much as attempts to encourage sexual freedom. They support the idea that pornography and, more generally, sexuality, have not always expressed, and do not necessarily express, gender and sexual inequality. Pornography and, more generally, sexuality can be a means for women and men to create and disseminate their own sexual scripts based on female and male sexual fantasies, both heterosexual and non-heterosexual (Matrix, 1996).

Sexual Pluralism

In reality, more and more people accept that sexuality does not have to be expressed in traditionally feminine or masculine ways. An attitude of **sexual pluralism** is growing (Weeks, 1986). For most people, sexual pluralism does *not* mean "anything goes." Most sexual pluralists recognize that there will always be a need to regulate sexual behaviour. For example, they oppose the abuse of power in sexual relations and see the need for the state to punish, and help prevent, incest, rape, and other forms of sexual abuse. Sexual pluralism *does* mean judging sexual acts only by their meaning for the participants. Are power relations at play? If so, are they harmful to the participants? These are the sorts of questions that sexual pluralists use in evaluating the validity of sexual acts. They do not automatically condemn a sexual practice because it is, say, "homosexual" or "heterosexual." From a sexual-pluralist perspective, heterosexuality is not inherently about men dominating women any more than it is inherently about strict adherence to traditional masculine and feminine sexual scripts. The sexual expression of heterosexuality may involve the perpetuation of harmful relations of domination or it may not. Sexual pluralists would judge only the former negatively. Sexual pluralism, then, fosters a view of sexuality as something more than a form of victimization because of unequal power relations. It also encourages people to see sexuality positively, as a means of achieving greater pleasure, freedom of expression, and self-realization.

Riane Eisler (1987) convincingly argues that, for the first time in seven thousand years, social conditions now make it possible for humanity to return to the state of rough gender equality that existed before the invasion of Old Europe by conquering hordes from the north, east, and south. At least in the world's rich countries, nothing prevents us from adopting social policies that would create gender equality in the workplace, the home, and other spheres of life (see Chapter 7, Gender Inequality: Economic and Political Aspects). As this chapter demonstrates, the examination and redefinition of sexuality is an important step in the process of achieving gender equality.

SUMMARY

1. *Sex* refers to biological differences between males and females while *gender* refers to the attitudes, beliefs, and behaviours that we commonly associate with each sex.
2. Although it is popular to trace the origins of masculine and feminine gender roles to biological differences between the sexes, most sociologists focus on the ways in which gender is socially constructed.
3. Three major sociohistorical changes have led to the development of gender inequality: long-distance warfare and conquest, plow agriculture, and the separation of public and private spheres during early industrialization.
4. Conscious sexual learning begins in adolescence in the context of firmly established gender identities.
5. Although we receive little formal training regarding sexuality, sexual relationships tend to be male-dominated as a result of the character of gender socialization and men's continuing dominant position in society.
6. The social construction of gender and sexual scripts has defined standards of beauty that are nearly impossible for most women to achieve. This contributes to widespread anxiety about body image, leading in some cases to eating disorders.
7. Gender inequality and a sociocultural context that justifies and eroticizes male sexual aggression contribute to the widespread problem of male sexual violence.
8. The mass media reflect and reinforce the relationship between heterosexuality and male domination.
9. Social constructionism encourages sexual pluralism, which assesses sexual activities in terms of the meanings of the acts to the participants.

QUESTIONS TO CONSIDER

1. Do you think sexual orientation is genetically programmed or a function of social experience? On what do you base your opinion? What type of evidence would persuade you one way or the other?
2. Design a study to test whether gender roles are inherent or socially constructed.
3. What policy recommendations would you make to lower the level of sexual assault and sexual harassment? Why do you think these policies would be effective?

GLOSSARY

Compulsory heterosexuality (p. 79) is the assumption that individuals should desire only members of the "opposite" sex.

Essentialists (p. 87) observe male–female differences in sexual scripts, the division of labour at home and in the workplace, mate selection, sexual aggression, jealousy, promiscuity, fidelity, and so on. They then interpret these differences as natural and universal.

Gender (p. 77) encompasses the feelings, attitudes, and behaviours that are associated with being male or female as conventionally understood.

Gender identity (p. 77) refers to identification with, or a sense of belonging to, a particular sex, biologically, psychologically, and socially.

Gender roles (p. 77) comprise the repertoire of behaviours that match widely shared expectations about how males and females are supposed to act.

Hostile environment sexual harassment (p. 95) involves sexual jokes, comments, and touching that interfere with work or create an unfriendly work setting.

Queer theory (p. 85) denies the existence of stable sexual orientations and argues that when we use terms like "heterosexual," "gay," lesbian," and so on, we are adopting official or at least socially acceptable labels that fail to capture the fluidity and variability of people's actual identities and performances.

Quid pro quo sexual harassment (p. 95) involves sexual threats or bribery used to extract sexual favours as a condition of employment decisions.

Sex (p. 76) refers to being born with distinct male or female genitalia and a genetic program that releases either male or female hormones to stimulate the development of one's reproductive system.

Sexual orientation (p. 85) refers to the way a person derives sexual pleasure, including whether desirable partners are of the same or a different sex.

Sexual pluralism (p. 97) assesses sexual acts only by their meaning for the participants.

Sexual scripts (p. 79) are assumptions that guide sexual behaviour by telling us whom we should find attractive, when and where it is appropriate to be aroused, what is sexually permissible, and so on.

Sexuality (p. 79) involves actions that are intended to produce erotic arousal and genital response.

Social constructionism (p. 90) is the main alternative to essentialism. Social constructionists argue that gender differences are not the product of biological properties, whether chromosomal, gonadal, or hormonal. Instead, gender and sexuality are products of social structure and culture.

Sociobiology (p. 87) is a variant of essentialism. It holds that all human beings instinctually want to ensure that their genes get passed on to future generations. However, the different reproductive status of men and women means that they have had to develop different adaptive strategies. This gave rise to "masculine" and "feminine" patterns of behaviour that presumably became genetically encoded because of their adaptive value.

People are **transgendered** (p. 77) when their gender identity does not exactly match the sex assigned to them at birth. They blur widely accepted gender roles by, for example, cross-dressing.

Transsexuals (p. 78) identify with the opposite sex from that assigned to them at birth, causing them to change their appearance or resort to a sex-change operation.

SUGGESTED READING

Kimmel, Michael. (2008). *Guyland: The Perilous World Where Boys Become Men.* New York: Harper Collins. Based on interviews with more than four hundred boys and men between the ages of 16 and 26, this book analyzes the rules, restrictions, peer pressures, and gender policing involved in learning male identity today—and the disappointment and anger that often accompany male gender socialization.

Nelson, Adie. (2010). *Gender in Canada,* 4th ed. Toronto: Prentice-Hall Canada. The definitive Canadian work on the subject.

Weeks, Jeffrey. (2003). *Sexuality,* rev. 2nd ed. London: Routledge. A concise and authoritative introduction to the field.

NOTES

1. Freud called this set of emotions the "Oedipus complex" after the ancient Greek legend of Oedipus.
2. Psychoanalytic theorists since Freud have provided more nuanced explanations about how an oedipally produced ideology and psychology of male dominance and repression occurs. For example, Chodorow (1997) argues that because women play the mother role, girls develop a different type of Oedipus complex than boys do. A boy must repress his attachment to his mother, whereas a girl is more likely to seek to become a mother and to reproduce the mother-child relationship.

CHAPTER 5

COMMUNICATION AND MASS MEDIA

Josh Greenberg
CARLETON UNIVERSITY

Graham Knight
MCMASTER UNIVERSITY

SOURCE: © John Warburton_lee/Danitadelimont.com.

IN THIS CHAPTER YOU WILL LEARN THAT

- The mass media may be examined in terms of their economic and political organization, their representation of ideas, and their effects on people.
- Media ownership is highly concentrated, and dependence on advertising limits the range of views available in the press and on radio and television.
- English-speaking Canadians watch mostly American television programming, especially prime-time drama and comedies. Nationalists view this as a threat to Canadian culture, but others regard it as an effect of globalization that does not undermine the cultural fabric of society.
- Some analysts claim that news coverage has a left-liberal political bias, while other analysts argue that news coverage is conservative.
- Many analysts believe that a causal link exists between media violence and violent behaviour, but studies that demonstrate this alleged connection have been criticized on the grounds of flawed methodology. Even those who believe that media violence causes aggressive behaviour disagree about how it does so.
- Studies reveal that men tend to use TV in a more planned way than women do and watch more intently, whereas women are more likely to use TV as a focus for social interaction.
- Changes in media technology are transforming how people watch television, creating new cultural patterns of media consumption.
- Access to, and use of, the Internet reflects broader patterns of social inequality, although unequal access appears to be declining as the technology becomes less costly and more widely available. Use of the Internet for social interaction creates online communities that act as sources of identity and social support but that also pose new risks to personal privacy and safety.

INTRODUCTION

In 2010, the average Canadian spent 17.6 hours a week listening to radio, and Canadians aged 18 and over reported watching television 29.2 hours a week or more (Canadian Radio-television and Telecommunications Commission [CRTC], 2011a). The total number of hours Canadians spend watching television has been declining, while the hours we spend listening to the radio have remained stable. Newspaper circulation is also dipping, particularly in Ontario, the country's most populous province; in 2008, newspaper readership in Ontario dropped by 12.5 percent and by an additional 7.5 percent on an average day in 2009. Tabloid newspapers registered the biggest loss in numbers of copies sold per publishing day.

These facts point to several changes in media technology and use. Since the early 1990s, Internet use has grown rapidly, especially in the home. By 2010, 76 percent of Canadians aged 16 and over connected to the Internet from their homes daily (Statistics Canada, 2010). Initially, television viewing and news reading suffered because of the Internet, as people spent more of their leisure time doing other things online (watching videos, playing games, and so on). Nevertheless, with the emergence of digital video recorders (DVRs), as well as streaming and torrent software, people are watching more television, often at times outside the broadcast schedule. And while fewer people are buying and reading a daily newspaper today, they are still consuming lots of news online through their Google readers, Twitter feeds, and Facebook accounts. Conversely, as we will discuss later, the emergence of mobile and social media are changing the culture of watching TV such that more people are watching and commenting on television programs in real time.

Media is the plural of *medium*, or "middle"—hence the idea of media as the means for connecting two or more points. Media are commonly associated with communication. **Communication** means bringing together or unifying by establishing shared meanings and understandings between groups and individuals. Such unification occurs through the transmission of information, knowledge, or beliefs by means of language, visual images, and other sign systems, such as music. People once commonly distinguished **mass media** from **interactive media.** With mass media, communication flows are unidirectional, going from a transmission point, such as a television or radio station, to an audience whose members remain anonymous and isolated from one another.

Socioeconomic factors still greatly determine Internet access in Canada (Statistics Canada, 2011a). Ninety-seven percent of households in the top income quartile ($87 000 or more) had an Internet connection, compared with 54 percent of households in the lowest income quartile ($30 000 or less) (Statistics Canada, 2011a).
SOURCE: © Szefei/Shutterstock.

With interactive media, like the telephone or social networking websites, such as Facebook and Twitter, communications flow back and forth; people interact in the transmission and reception of communication.

In this chapter, we explore how communications media influence individuals, groups, and institutions. We also examine how we affect the media—how does society influence and shape communications industries, organizations and technologies? To address these questions, we have organized the chapter in four main sections that deal with the political economy of the mass media, representation and ideology, media effects and audiences, and issues relating to the Internet and new and emergent technologies. We focus mainly on newspapers, television, and the Internet.

We begin by considering two theoretical approaches in media studies: technological and critical perspectives. Technological theories hold that different media technologies determine social perceptions, interactions, and institutional arrangements. Critical theorists argue that social values, interests, and conflicts shape the technological development, use, and impact of media.

THE TECHNOLOGICAL PERSPECTIVE

The technological perspective derives primarily from the work of two important Canadian scholars, Harold Innis and Marshall McLuhan. From his survey of the history of human communication, Innis (1951) distinguished time-biased from space-biased media. **Time-biased media** are modes of communication that endure over time but are relatively immobile across space, such as writing on stone or clay tablets. **Space-biased media** can cover much greater space but are less durable over time—for example, writing on paper or transmitting sounds over the airwaves.

The two types of media foster different arrangements of institutions and cultural values. Time-biased media are conducive to a strong sense of tradition and custom, which promote religious forms of power and belief. Space-biased media assist territorial expansion, empire building, and secular forms of power and culture, such as the dominance of military institutions and the growth of the state. These different forms of power, in turn, create different types of social division and conflict. The elite groups that control the means of communication often try to use it to preserve their own privilege and interests. People who lack power struggle against elite control and in the process stimulate the development of new, alternative forms of communication. Historically, such a struggle over the means of communication resulted in the shift from time- to space-biased media.

Innis's ideas influenced the work of Marshall McLuhan (1964), who explored how changes in media technology over time affect people, their cultures, and ways of life. McLuhan argued that the relationship between communication, on the one hand, and institutions and culture, on the other, was mediated by the way that forms of communication alter the ways we experience the world and how we think. His famous statement, "the medium is the message," captures this idea. The invention of printing, for example, undermined oral communication and its emphasis on hearing, and ushered in a more visually oriented culture. Because print consists of visually separated words strung together in a linear sequence, it encourages us to see the world as comprising separate objects and to interpret that world in a linear, cause-and-effect way. Print removes communication from face-to-face interaction and so makes information more abstract. The abstracting effect of print, in turn, fosters individualism, privacy, rationality, and social differentiation. Historically, these effects of print coincided with the rise of nationalism and the weakening of social ties. Print, then, served to standardize national languages and became a principal mechanism of social identity.

The invention of the printing press reduced the influence of oral communication as it lessened face-to-face interaction and made information more abstract.
SOURCE: © Kevin Foy/Alamy.

For McLuhan, the spread of electronic media, particularly television, marked the end of the era of print dominance. The impact of TV is crucial for two reasons. First, unlike print, TV does not rely exclusively on one sense (sight). It integrates sight and sound and achieves balance between them. For McLuhan, the effect of this balance is to make TV a kind of tactile medium in the sense that it "touches" its audience more easily than print does. Second, TV allows communication to be almost instantaneous; there is no significant delay between transmission and reception of the message. These differences make TV more socially inclusive than print is and shrink social distances and time, creating a "global village" in which the expanded capacity for information gathering and transmission help to make us more aware of, and familiar with, life in other parts of the world. It is remarkable that McLuhan's argument that electronic media would create a "global village" predated the arrival of the Internet and the explosion of social networking platforms by more than two decades.

McLuhan's views, however, have proven controversial because he tended to see media technologies as an autonomous force that operates outside social and human control. Although he famously stated that "we shape our tools, thereafter our tools shape us," McLuhan has been characterized as a technological determinist for encouraging us to think that social change is shaped primarily by the nature and function of technology, and not by conscious human action. Those who subscribe to the critical perspective have developed this argument most forcefully.

THE CRITICAL PERSPECTIVE

According to the **critical perspective,** institutions such as the news media, and processes such as socialization and social control cannot be understood from the viewpoint of society as a whole, but only from that of unequal and conflicting groups and classes. In fact, the critical perspective has two variants, one emphasizing the relationship between media and inequality, the other emphasizing the relationship between media and social conflict.

The first variant of the critical perspective derives from orthodox Marxism. From this perspective, media corporations serve the economic interests and political power of those who own and control the means of material production (the dominant class). To maintain and consolidate its power and interests, the dominant class also exercises control over the production of ideas, beliefs, values, and norms that constitute a society's **dominant ideology.** The media, by disseminating the dominant ideology, create acceptance and legitimization of the status quo.

Max Horkheimer and Theodor Adorno (1972 [1947]) first developed this argument. They saw the mass media as part of a broader "culture industry" that functions to create "mass deception" about the exploitative and oppressive character of capitalist society. In their view, the role of the mass media is to distract and pacify people by feeding them standardized images and messages that stifle the capacity for independent, critical thought. A contemporary example of this perspective, the "propaganda model," argues that the media serve the interests of the leading political and economic class by "filtering" information to reduce or eliminate radical or subversive views. Herman and Chomsky (1988) identify five main filters: (1) the media's orientation to profit making, (2) their dependence on advertising for revenue and profit, (3) their reliance on powerful institutions and individuals as sources of information, (4) negative reaction—what they call flak—if the media deviate from promoting elite interests and values, and (5) their adherence to anti-communism as an overarching belief system. With the decline of communism, the fifth filter has morphed into the "war on terrorism."

The second variant of the critical perspective also acknowledges that the capitalist class and other powerful groups use dominant ideology to reinforce their position and maintain the status quo. They do so through the establishment of **hegemony**—the use of the media and other cultural institutions, such as the school system, to represent and establish their interests, values, and understandings as natural and universal. However, proponents of the second approach note that inequality can also spawn resistance and struggle, which create critical perspectives that allow people to interpret and criticize social reality and the dominant ideology. Although the mass media usually promote understandings that conform to the dominant ideology, their messages are always at least partially open to the challenge of competing interpretations. To be successful, hegemony has to be flexible enough to accommodate and incorporate a range of different viewpoints (Knight, 1998).

POLITICAL ECONOMY OF THE MEDIA

The critical perspective draws attention to how the social and cultural roles of the media depend on their role as agents of political and economic interests. The principal approach that sociologists take to analyzing this relationship empirically is that of *political economy*. Political economy focuses on the ownership and control of economic resources, and the effect of technology and economic power on cultural values, social structure, and political decision making. Media are organizations that are usually owned and controlled by large corporations or the state and that function like other bureaucracies. They have to sustain themselves economically through commercial revenue, government funding, subscriber fees and donations, or some mixture of these. What, then, are the primary goals of media organizations? Are they to inform and entertain or to capture market share and make money? In whose interests do they operate—owners, advertisers, or audiences? These questions are especially pertinent in democratic societies where such values as freedom, diversity of opinion, and the promotion of minority and national identities are strong.

Ownership and control of the mass media are generally becoming more concentrated in a smaller number of giant corporate hands. This trend is part of the wider process of economic globalization, and it is leading to the creation of large **multimedia chains**—corporations that own a diversified array of media operations and outlets in different fields, such as radio, TV, and publishing, and operate worldwide. One of the world's best-known multimedia corporations is the Walt Disney Company, whose total revenues in 2010 stood at US$38 billion (see Figure 5.1). The world's dominant media corporations are primarily U.S.-based. Only two of the top six media giants—Bertelsmann and Vivendi—are headquartered outside the United States, and these are located in Western Europe (Rupert Murdoch's News Corporation is a joint American–Australian company). While Canada is typically seen as a minor player in the global mediascape, the Canadian media economy has grown larger and more complex during the past few decades and now represents the eighth largest media economy in the world (Winseck, 2011a; see Table 5.1).

To secure and enhance their market position, multimedia chains practise horizontal and vertical integration. **Horizontal integration** refers to the sharing of facilities and resources between different plants and outlets. **Vertical integration** involves the control of resources and assets at different stages of production and distribution. The recent development of digital technology has enhanced both horizontal and vertical integration, and has led to a series of corporate mergers that have strengthened the position of multimedia chains as the dominant form of organization. These mergers unite delivery conduits (cable, satellite, telephony) and content (news, information). For example, in December 2011, Bell Canada and Rogers, the country's two biggest telecom companies, teamed up to buy a $1.07 billion majority stake in Canada's largest sports franchise company, Maple Leaf Sports and Entertainment. The companies (which are rivals in the cellular and Internet service sector) now own major shares of the Toronto Maple Leafs (NHL), Toronto Raptors (NBA), and Toronto FC soccer club. According to Rogers CEO Nadir Mohamed, this deal was all about achieving synergy in content and distribution, the company that owns the content (hockey, basketball, and soccer games) also owns practically all the distribution network: Bell Mobility, Bell TV, *The Globe and Mail* newspaper, CTV, TSN, NHL Network, Rogers Sportsnet, and so on.

Critics argue that consolidation of media properties and convergence of media platforms reduce the range of voices and perspectives that the mass media represent, leading to greater homogenization of ideas and cultural products. Although the names of the top owners may change from year to year, "the domination of the media by entertainment conglomerates exerts a consistently corrosive effect ... undermining debate when we need it most" ("The Big Ten," 2002). Moreover, the focus of mainstream corporate media on profits impedes progressive social change by favouring the interests of the powerful (Parenti, 2004). Finally, mergers demonstrate that the

FIGURE 5.1 THE WALT DISNEY COMPANY

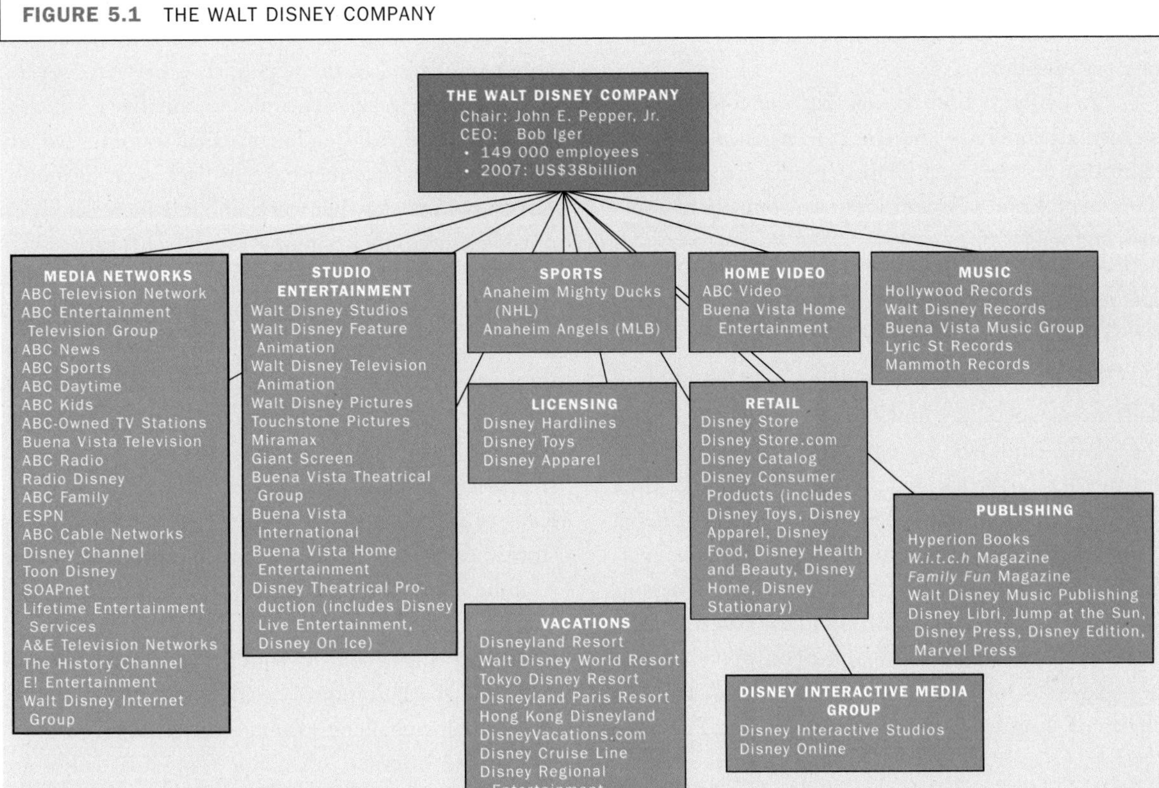

The Walt Disney Company wants to extend the Disney experience well beyond the theme parks, reaching every form of media delivery, and, in Celebration, Florida, creating environments for people to live within.

TABLE 5.1 TOP 10 NETWORK MEDIA, ENTERTAINMENT, AND INTERNET MARKETS BY COUNTRY (US$ MILLIONS), 1998–2010

	1998	2000	2004	2008	2009	2010 (EST.)
United States	336 885	395 695	395 936	420 397	406 733	411 357
Japan	94 255	100 799	114 330	141 340	156 120	157 985
Germany	59 919	68 981	79 877	84 635	84 100	89 905
China	23 057	27 599	32 631	66 310	72 024	81 005
United Kingdom	56 738	65 319	75 637	72 346	70 478	72 605
France	39 984	46 031	53 302	63 863	58 841	59 587
Italy	29 626	34 107	34 494	41 528	39 890	39 924
Canada	**15 399**	**18 203**	**25 842**	**31 287**	**30 701**	**31 229**
S. Korea	17 687	18 492	22 760	26 672	27 394	28 589
Spain	19 219	22 132	25 622	28 736	27 200	27 479
Total	692 770	797 358	860 431	977 114	973 481	999 665

SOURCES: Winseck, Dwayne. (2011). On the World Wide Web at http://dwmw.wordpress.com/2011/08/20/the-growth-of-the-network-media-economy-in-canada-1984-1010; data compiled from CRTC, Communication Monitoring Report, 2009 and various years; Canadian Newspaper Association, Ownership of Canadian Newspapers, 2009 and various years; Internet Advertising Bureau, Canada Online Advertising Revenue Survey, 2009; Corporate Annual Reports.

traditional distinctions between print and electronic media are disappearing, at least at the level of corporate organization.

Closer inspection reveals that the consolidation of media properties and the convergence of media platforms do not affect all mass media the same way. This fact becomes evident when we compare newspapers and television.

NEWSPAPERS: CONCENTRATION, MONOPOLY, AND ADVERTISING

In Canada, corporate ownership and control of daily newspapers has undergone rapid change since the 1970s and has become highly concentrated. Postmedia Network Inc., Quebecor Media Inc., and Torstar dominate the field today. Postmedia Network Inc. owns daily newspapers in Vancouver, Calgary, Edmonton, Saskatoon, Regina, Windsor, Ottawa, Montreal, and Halifax, and has control of the Toronto-based *National Post*, one of only two national newspapers. Quebecor Media Inc. controls the *Sun* chain of English-language tabloids in Toronto, Ottawa, Calgary, and Edmonton, as well as French-language tabloids in Quebec City and Montreal. Torstar controls the *Toronto Star*, the largest circulation newspaper in Canada, dailies in Hamilton, Kitchener-Waterloo, and Guelph, and a minority interest (20 percent) in Bell Globemedia, the parent company of *The Globe and Mail.*

The concentration of ownership in the hands of a few multimedia chains has raised serious questions about freedom of the press and the diversity of opinion, which are widely regarded as necessary for a democratic society. And while Canada is often considered to have a more liberal and progressive media environment than the United States does, the level of media concentration in Canada is high by global standards and more than twice as high as in the United States (Winseck, 2011b; see Table 5.2).

In 2006, daily newspapers earned $2.85 billion in advertising revenue, 75 percent of their total operating revenue (Statistics Canada, 2008a). By 2010, that number had dropped to $2.4 billion, approximately two-thirds of operating revenue (Statistics Canada, 2010). As newspapers have become more advertising dependent, the scale and costs of operation have also grown, reducing competition, creating local newspaper monopolies in all but large urban areas, and reducing the total amount of published news content. Even in big cities like Toronto, which has four large daily newspapers, papers have to specialize and appeal to particular market segments to survive. Although there are 94 "daily" newspapers across Canada, only about one-third of them publish every day; several have cut their weekly schedules to only five or six days in the past two years, and many small to mid-sized city "daily" papers have merged, cut back even further to just one or two days per week, and rely increasingly on outside sources for content (Winseck, 2011a).

The critical perspective sees multimedia chain ownership, local monopolies, advertising dependence, reductions in production scheduling, and increased reliance on outside content as resulting in the decline of diversity in news topics and viewpoints. However, evidence supporting the link is inconclusive. Some studies have found that monopolization leads to a decline in the volume and length of news stories, especially national and international coverage (Candussi and Winters, 1988; Trim with Pizante and Yaraskavitch, 1983). Other research finds that monopolization brings about no significant change and may even lead to small improvements (McCombs, 1988).

A major challenge facing conventional newspapers is the Internet. All major Canadian dailies are available over the Internet, though some charge for access. While this situation does not increase the diversity of local news sources, it does make it easier for people to gain access to different newspapers from different regions and countries. In addition, the Internet has spawned a host of Net-only news and information media, ranging from the general, such as Huffington Post, to outlets that have a particular political or ideological perspective, such as the Canadian alternative news website Rabble.ca. Net-only news media are also facing the challenge of how to raise revenue by attracting subscribers, donors, advertisers, or some mixture of these. In general, however, Net media lack the news-gathering capacity of conventional media, which means their role is still primarily one of aggregation, interpretation, and commentary.

TELEVISION: ECONOMY, CULTURE, AND IDENTITY

Commercialization and advertising dependence have also had a significant impact on the content and role of television. Rather than being driven by cultural goals, such as promoting Canadian national identity, private television companies are motivated essentially by profit. Income and profits come largely from advertising, and this means having to cater to large audiences with programming that will be informative and entertaining. To attract audiences and

TABLE 5.2 GLOBAL ENTERTAINMENT MEDIA CORPORATIONS

"About six players now own virtually everything, all aspects of the media experience."

— Drew Marcus, Deutsche Bank media sector analyst

RANK	REVENUE (US$ BILLION)
Top Six (2010)	
1. Disney (U.S.)	38.0
2. Comcast (U.S.)	37.9
3. Universal (France)	37.7*
4. News Corp. (U.S./Australia)	33.2†
5. Time Warner (U.S.)	26.9
6. Bertelsmann (Germany)	20.5‡
Top Four Canadian Companies (2010§)	
1. BCE	17.7
2. Rogers	11.9
3. Quebecor Media	3.9
4. Shaw	3.7

Notes: * Estimated US$ equivalent; original financial data given in euros
† Estimated US$ equivalent; original financial data given in AUD$
‡ Estimated US$ equivalent; original financial data given in euros
§ Values reported are converted from Canadian to U.S. dollars by using exchange rates (1 CAD = 0.979519 USD) at time of writing.

SOURCES: Bertelsmann (2008); CanWest Global (2007); Comcast (2008); Disney (2007); News Corporation (2008); Quebecor (2007); Shaw Communications (2007); Time Warner (2008); Vivendi (2008); Winseck (2008).

advertisers, private Canadian television, particularly English-language television, relies heavily on imported, mainly American, programming. Although the cost of licensing American programming has been increasing, it is still far less expensive to purchase than it is to produce comparable Canadian content.

The issue of Canadian content pertains largely to entertainment programming, particularly English Canadian drama. Audiences have long shown a strong preference for American dramatic television and, as a result, the audience for domestic programs is not large enough to make Canadian drama attractive in economic terms. Indeed, in 2010, 81 percent of English-language drama and comedy programs viewed in Canada were not made in Canada (CRTC, 2011b). Reaction to this situation is split. Cultural nationalists argue that broadcasting should be an instrument of Canadian culture and identity, actively promoting Canadian content (Collins, 1990). They single out drama because of its popularity and capacity to promote and reinforce cultural myths and values that solidify a distinct national identity. Strong support for the argument that TV drama enforces cultural identity can be found in Quebec, with its commitment to francophone drama and other entertainment programming on the part of both public and private TV. The strong national and cultural identity of francophone Quebeckers matches this commitment. Francophones not only watch more Canadian programming, but also watch proportionately more television drama than anglophones do.

The federal government has addressed the issue of television drama production by establishing content requirements, offering financial inducements, such as production subsidies, sheltering the national broadcaster (CBC/Radio-Canada) from market pressures and priorities, and erecting regulatory barriers preventing foreign companies from owning too large a slice of the Canadian media pie. Although production has been increasing, economic pressure means creating the kind of programming that will attract advertisers and foreign buyers, and this often means programs lacking a distinct Canadian character. Canadian television production is increasingly part of a global market dominated by the American television industry. For critical theorists in particular, the dominance of American entertainment programming amounts to a form of **cultural imperialism,** in which one society's media exert an overwhelming and unilateral influence over another society's culture (Tomlinson, 1997). As evidence of cultural imperialism, critical theorists point to the uneven flow of television and other cultural products between countries. Canada is one of the world's largest importers of cultural products—in 2010, Canada's cultural trade deficit was $1.8 billion (Statistics Canada, 2011b; see Table 5.3). The bulk of our cultural imports come from the United States.

On the other side of the debate, critics of the cultural nationalist position argue that although dramatic television is important, Canadians also develop a sense of collective national identity through their overwhelming preferences for domestic news and public affairs programming. *Grey's Anatomy* and *American Idol* may attract a larger Canadian audience than *Republic of Doyle* or *Little Mosque on the Prairie* do, but Canadians also overwhelmingly prefer to get their news and public affairs information from the CBC and CTV than they do from Fox News or CBS. This situation contributes strongly to Canadian national identity.

The concern that Canadian culture is under siege by American-style programming also overlooks the fact that many of the high-profile faces in American popular culture, from news to comedy and music, are originally Canadian. Think of TV news anchors like Fox's John Roberts (previously an anchor at CNN), who got his television start as a MuchMusic VJ in the 1980s, or the late Peter Jennings, anchor on *ABC News*. Canada has also produced a long list of A-list Hollywood stars, including Sandra Oh, Rachel McAdams, Jim Carrey, Kiefer Sutherland, Mike Myers, and Ryan Gosling. *Saturday Night Live*'s co-creator and long-time producer Lorne Michaels got his media career started as a writer and broadcaster for CBC Radio. And Chuck Tatham, a writer and executive producer for the hit TV shows *Arrested Development* and *How I Met Your Mother*, is a native of Guelph, Ontario. Ivan Reitman of *Meatballs*, *Ghostbusters*, and *Old School* fame, directors and screenwriters like Paul Haggis (*Crash*, *Million Dollar Baby*,

TABLE 5.3 VALUE OF INTERNATIONAL TRADE IN CULTURAL GOODS, CANADA, 2010 (THOUSANDS OF DOLLARS)

IMPORTS		EXPORTS	
Written and published works	2 702 748	Written and published works	416 738
Film and video	349 990	Film and video	495 136
Sound recording/music publishing	39 999	Sound recording/music publishing	126 284
Visual art	218 603	Visual art	73 177
Architecture	1 003	Architecture	3 802
Advertising	230 757	Advertising	164 007
Heritage	32 367	Heritage	27 937
Photography	154 429	Photography	93 226
TOTAL	3 730 096	TOTAL	1 295 936

SOURCE: Adapted from Statistics Canada (2011b). "Culture Goods Trade 2010; Culture Trade-Goods: Data Tables, 2003 to 2010," Catalogue no. 87-007.

Casino Royale), David Cronenberg (*The Fly*, *A History of Violence*), and James Cameron (*The Terminator*, *True Lies*, *Titanic*), and even major studio heads, such as Louis B. Mayer, a co-founder of MGM Studios, are all Canadians. Canadian musicians have also made major inroads as top-grossing performers not only at home and in the United States but internationally: Neil Young, Bryan Adams, and Justin Bieber are just a few examples.

Arguably, Canadians have strongly influenced American media culture just as Canadian culture has been subject to processes of Americanization. Along with Collins (1990), we might also question the supposed Americanization of Canadian identity through the mass media by noting that Canada is quickly becoming a "postnational" society. Because of economic and cultural globalization, a strong, unified, and permanent sense of national identity may be a thing of the past. Canadians' sharing of institutions and practices seems undiminished by the fact that English Canadians can't get enough of *CSI* or *Jersey Shore*.

Collins's (1990) argument is similar to the postmodernist view that, in affluent societies, identities and experiences are becoming increasingly fragmented, disconnected from one another, and amenable to individual reconstruction and reinterpretation, especially on the basis of ideas and images that people consume via the mass media (Fiske, 1987). Fragmentation is also occurring at the level of political economy and technology, with the proliferation of new TV services, such as specialty channels, superstations, pay-per-view channels, and home-shopping channels, in addition to over-the-top services like Netflix and AppleTV, and more conventional broadcast TV stations and networks (Ellis, 1992). As television becomes more differentiated, audiences become more fragmented, a process that is captured by the term *narrowcasting*. With this development, the role of TV as an agent of common culture is open to question.

REPRESENTATION AND IDEOLOGY: THE MEANING OF THE MESSAGE

Media analysis from the perspective of political economy alone is limited, because it takes for granted the nature of the messages that the mass media communicate. We emphasize the plural—*messages*. Mass media communicate on multiple levels—the pleasurable as well as the meaningful, the entertaining as well as the informative. Such communication involves the process of **representation**—that is, the use of language, visual images, and other symbolic tools to create messages people can understand and draw from as they go about their lives. Representation, however, is a selective process. It involves countless decisions about what is to be included and what is to be left out, what is to be emphasized and what is to be downplayed, and about the sequence in which the elements are to be connected into a coherent message. Sociologists use the term **framing** to denote the selective, organized nature of representation (Gitlin, 1980; Goffman, 1974). To frame is to set up boundaries that define where the representation begins and ends, and to organize the contents in a way that distinguishes what is being emphasized (the foreground) from what is treated as secondary (the context or background). The framing of any media product or object—a news report, an advertisement, a political cartoon, or a TV drama—has ideological effects inasmuch as it entails a particular inflection or bias. Every frame is only one of several different ways of seeing and interpreting something.

NEWS AND IDEOLOGY

Outside our immediate experience, news media are among our principal sources of information about social reality. Conservative and critical writers disagree on how news is framed and the ideological effects of news framing. Conservatives argue that news media have a "left-liberal" bias that runs counter to the views and interests of society's mainstream (Miljan and Cooper, 2003). According to conservative observers, bias operates in three related ways. First, the media have an anti-corporate bias and are critical of market-oriented solutions to social problems. Second, journalists give greater or more favourable attention to the views of interest groups and constituencies that share their personal liberal or left-wing political views—for example, unions, environmentalists, social welfare organizations, and, in the case of foreign news, socialist regimes and left-wing political movements (Miljan and Cooper, 2003). Third, the mass media concentrate on negative events, issues, and news angles, ignoring the positive aspects of social life (National Media Archive, 1993). The launch in Canada of Sun TV News in 2011 was intended as a corrective to what many conservative activists, politicians, academics, and some journalists saw as a systemic liberal bias in the Canadian media (see Box 5.1).

BOX 5.1 AN ARGUMENT FOR CONSERVATIVE NEWS

Since the head of the media conglomerate Quebecor, Pierre Karl Péladeau, made his announcement earlier this month that his company would be launching Sun TV News—an English-language all news channel that spotlights small 'c' conservative perspectives—assorted pundits have been debating the need for such an entity.

Not surprisingly, those who think a new conservative voice is a good idea tend to work at existing conservative media outlets or are public figures known for their conservative leanings. Conversely, those disparaging the notion are known to congregate on the left side of the socio-political spectrum.

Pundits on both sides of the issue have been bolstering their position by referencing the state of Canadian media today. Some claim that, in the main, a left-wing bias exists; particularly, when it comes to television news. As such, Sun TV News is a needed corrective. Others insist fairness, balance, and objectivity are, in large part, the order of the day.

As someone who studies media bias in Canada, what surprised me the most about the ongoing debate has been the absence of empirical data. Some commentators have even suggested that valid research on the topic doesn't exist. For example, in a column in the *National Post*, radio personality and self-described "liberal" John Moore argued left-wing media bias is "one of those gut things conservatives feel but can never prove." But, the fact is, the conservatives' collective "guts" are onto something.

Ryerson University professors Marsha Barber and Ann Rauhala explored the demographic and political leanings of Canada's television news directors. The results of their survey were published in 2005 in the *Canadian Journal of Communication*. The researchers found that the news directors, whom they describe as the people "with the most direct responsibility for programming the news on any given day," were more socially liberal than the rest of the Canadian population. Politically, news directors at private broadcasters were not significantly more left-leaning; however, those at Canada's public broadcaster were. Barber and Rauhala state, "It should be noted that journalists at Canada's public broadcaster, the CBC, share a different profile and are more likely to hold left-of-centre political views."

Barber and Rauhala's findings echo researchers David Pritchard and Florian Sauvageau's survey results from years earlier. Regarding Canadian TV journalists, they found that most felt the news organizations they worked for were "slightly left of centre" when it came to political outlook while they themselves were ideologically more left-leaning than their employers.

Other peer-reviewed studies have shown that the personal values Canadian journalists hold and the ideologies they subscribe to influence the coverage they produce. In their 2003 Donner Prize nominated book, Hidden Agendas: How Journalists Influence the News, the University of Windsor's Lydia Miljan and the University of Calgary's Barry Cooper show strong evidence of this link. They found when it comes to reporting on issues connected to social values, Canada's national journalists regularly "slant" their coverage in order to favour liberal views over socially conservative perspectives. When the researchers turned their attention to television news alone, they found that coverage by the CBC was most critical of conservative positions.

My own research has produced similar findings. For the last few years I've been examining the national news media's relationship with evangelical Christians—a group well known for their highly conservative social values. In one study, published in the *Journal of Communication and Religion*, I analyzed content from 11 years of national television news reports featuring those on the religious right. Like Miljan and Cooper, I found evidence of negatively slanted coverage. Journalists, particularly those working for CBC-TV, used omission, exaggeration, or misrepresentation of information to present evangelicals and the positions they held in the worst possible light.

Much of my research on evangelicals was published as the book, *Through a Lens Darkly: How the News Media Perceive and Portray Evangelicals*. In the introduction, I provide some particularly dramatic examples to illustrate how Canadian journalists can manipulate information to ensure a particular point of view comes across. One case involved a report filed by Neil Macdonald, a senior TV reporter for CBC's flagship news program *The National*. The story aired early in September 2008 and was a backgrounder piece on Sarah Palin, the evangelical politician who had just been named the Republican Party's vice-presidential candidate. Macdonald's report was supposed to reveal to the Canadian public who Palin really was and what she was all about. What it seemed to reveal was Macdonald's own biases.

At one point in his story, Macdonald ran a snippet from a speech Palin had delivered to a local church earlier that year. It showed her telling those in the pews that she believed America's war against Iraq was endorsed by God. The interview clip was meant to convince viewers that, as a staunch evangelical, Palin was dangerously jingoistic. The problem was Macdonald had edited off the beginning of the clip and in doing so had changed the meaning completely.

A posting on YouTube where Palin's complete speech can be viewed let's one compare Macdonald's version to the real McCoy. The portion of interview that Macdonald included in his report began with Palin saying, "Our leaders, our national leaders are sending them out on a task that is from God."

BOX 5.1 ***(continued)***

However, what Palin had actually said was this: "Pray for our military men and women who are striving to do what is right. Also, for this country [pray] that our leaders, our national leaders are sending them out on a task that is from God."

Someone watching or reading the full quote in its true context could see that Palin was not raising a war cry, she was raising a question: "Is this war a task from God?" It's a question to which she does not have an answer and advises praying for divine guidance in the hope of finding the right path.

I'm no fan of Palin myself. Clearly, she has been a party to numerous, *verifiable*, indiscretions. Regardless, that doesn't give a journalist license to "independently produce" additional negative examples.

There are other examples from my own research and that of others that lead me to personally support the launch of Sun TV news. I think Canada needs journalists and news outlets as diverse in their values as Canadians themselves. Simply put, when it comes to television news in Canada, a move in the "right" direction is also a move in the correct direction.

SOURCE: Adapted from the *Ottawa Citizen*, "An argument for conservative news." July 8, 2010. Used with permission of David Haskell.

In contrast to the conservative perspective, those who employ a critical perspective believe that the news media function chiefly to reproduce the values, interests, and perspectives of dominant social groups. Critical media scholars maintain that the news is ideological because corporate media organizations must make money, and therefore they depend heavily on elite sources (such as politicians, police, and corporations) for the news. This is seen not as a conscious conspiracy but as the unconscious effect of the values and practices that journalists employ when they define and gather news. Let us consider the critical perspective in greater detail.

Defining the News

How is news framed? To answer this question we must begin by asking what are the criteria, or **news values,** that the media use to determine what is newsworthy. They have three major criteria: immediacy, personalization, and extraordinariness.

Immediacy By definition, news is about what is recent or immediate. Although news organizations are often unable to capture events as they actually happen, the aim is to report them as quickly as possible after they occur. In many ways, this news value has been strengthened by the emergence of mobile and social media technologies, which enable journalists to access and report on events as they happen. For example, during Hurricane Irene's assault on the U.S. eastern seaboard in 2011, the *Wall Street Journal* experimented with Foursquare, a mobile geo-location service, to interact with social media users to provide details of New York City evacuation centres. In another example, *New York Times* journalist Brian Stelter covered the aftermath of the F5 tornado that destroyed Joplin, Missouri, in the summer of 2011. Because Internet connectivity was a problem, Stelter used his iPhone and Twitter account for reporting, showing people not only the immediacy of events on the ground, but also how social media can be used to connect with newsreaders in real time to provide information and create a shared experience. Immediacy has always been a major element in the competition among different mass media, and the goal of making communication faster dominates the history of media technology. Whenever possible, reporters write news in the present tense to convey the sense that events are ongoing.

The emphasis on immediacy goes beyond the present to the future. To generate interest and curiosity on the part of the audience, news stories often create a sense of uncertainty about what will happen next. The effect of this approach is that news tends to be concerned with the consequences of events and issues at the expense of their causes and development (Knight, 1982). Causes belong in the past, and news generally lacks a sense of historical perspective and context.

Personalization When news does deal with causes and explanations, it often reduces them to the level of individual motives and psychology. This is an effect of personalization. To communicate with an anonymous audience, news has to enable the reader or viewer to identify with news events that are often remote from everyday experience by making them more concrete and familiar. The emphasis on personalities has been intensified by the growth of TV news, where the need to be visual makes it more difficult to deal in abstract issues, such as unemployment, and easier to deal with people, such as the unemployed. Personalization is especially strong in political news coverage, as the mass media focus on party leaders and other prominent politicians and their popularity in the opinion polls. Critics often charge that this focus detracts from a fuller understanding of the political system and the more substantive aspects of political policy (Taras, 1990).

Extraordinariness Above all, news concerns events and issues that are out of the ordinary and that entail conflict, confrontation, deviance, or disorder (Knight, 1982). As conservative critics point out, this means that news is normally about the negative. For critical theorists, however, the negative emphasis of news does not undermine mainstream values and beliefs but in fact reinforces dominant ideology in at least two ways. First, by dwelling on the negative, news invokes and reproduces dominant definitions of what is normal. It identifies certain events and actors as dangerous, bizarre, or disruptive, and represents them as a threat to what is socially desirable (Knight, 1982; see Figure 5.2). Second, news coverage of deviance and conflict tends to focus on the actions of the appropriate social control authorities—the government, the police, the experts—to restore order. The threat of bad news is offset by reassurance that someone in authority is responding to the problem.

Gathering the News

Initially, newsworthy events come to the attention of the media via news releases, tips, and the routine monitoring of institutional power centres that generate media content, notably the police, the courts, Parliament, and academia. Further information is then gathered from key sources, usually by means of interviewing. In choosing their sources, news media also take account of a fourth news value: objectivity or fairness (Knight, 1982). In practice, objectivity translates into an attempt to achieve a balance of sources representing the different, often antagonistic, viewpoints that are involved in the event or issue being reported. These sources include authority figures (such as police, politicians, and experts), but also eyewitnesses, victims, and the representatives of groups and organizations ranging from big business to social activist groups that may have a stake in the event or issue.

However, just as news framing tends to focus on the activities of certain social actors, so too does it tend to rely on certain sources of information. A hierarchy of access exists to and for the media, and this has important ideological implications, as it reflects the general distribution of power in society. For example, elected politicians have a much greater obligation to speak to the media than do private

FIGURE 5.2 TORONTO'S "DAYS OF ACTION" HEADLINES: DISRUPTION-RELATED THEMES IN A LOCAL NEWSPAPER, 1996

These headlines illustrate the way the media emphasize the disruptive or confrontational effects of news events rather than their causes or effects on social solidarity. They also highlight the way labour and other social movements are often portrayed as the source of social disruption and conflict.

October 24: "Brace yourself for tough tomorrow"
October 25: "Don't be intimidated by protesters: Harris"
"Ambulances, police go on high alert" (continuation of previous report)
"No mail, trash but beer's on. TTC in doubt as protest affects many services"
"Days of action hits many services" (continuation of previous report)
"Parade, rallies expected to jam city tomorrow"
October 26: "Days of Disruption"
"Day of frustration, frayed nerves" (continuation of previous report)
"Shut out: pickets block mayor from city hall"
"Protest a pain for many StarPhone callers"
"TTC workers didn't ask for help: police chief says heavy police presence kept trouble to a minimum"
"Barely a blip. The labour protest pretty much failed to disrupt Bay Street. The TSE hummed along nicely."
"Protestors failed to tarnish Metro's image"
"Employers cope with disruptions"

sector officials, such as corporate executives, who can invoke the values of private property as a way to justify their own and their organization's privacy. At the same time, because of their power and status, corporate officials can easily gain access to the news media when they choose to do so. Labour activists, students, and anti-poverty groups, conversely, often have to "act up" to gain attention from news media because they possess considerably less institutional authority and power.

This hierarchy of access is reflected in the division of labour among three broad types of news source—official, ordinary, and alternative (Knight, 1998). **Official news sources** are representatives of dominant institutions—for example, politicians, police officers, professionals, experts, and corporate spokespeople. They appear more frequently and prominently than other sources do and are usually treated by the media as authoritative and credible. Official sources are offset by **ordinary news sources.** These sources play a double role in the news as eyewitnesses or, more important, as victims of newsworthy events or problems. As victims, ordinary sources personalize the harmful effects (actual and potential) of bad news. They are the ones adversely affected by deviance, conflict, and disruption. They speak more subjectively of personal experiences, feelings, and emotions—anger at what has happened to them and fear of what may happen next. **Alternative news sources** are the representatives of social movements and of social advocacy and activism groups. They stand between official and ordinary voices. Alternative sources address the social problems that underlie the harm that ordinary victims suffer. In this respect, they compete with official sources over the definition of victimhood: who is a victim, who is responsible, who should act, and what should be done. Alternative sources attempt to reframe the experiences and emotions of victims into a critical, normative, and political perspective of injustice and inequity (Carroll and Ratner, 1999).

The three types of source appear in the media to varying degrees. Although official sources represent the interests and values of particular institutions or organizations, they are often used to speak on behalf of society as a whole. This gives them an advantage in defining the news frame and establishing what the terms of the event or problem are. Deviance and disorder thus tend to be framed from a police perspective as a series of discrete events that are explained in terms of individual motives, rather than as structural phenomena caused by political or economic forces. Conversely, ordinary and particularly alternative sources are used to represent specific points of view. These may often contradict what official sources are saying, but they normally do so on the grounds that have already been determined by the news frame. In the case of news about mental illness, for example, news media tend to rely on representatives from the legal and medical establishments (such as criminal prosecutors and psychiatrists) rather than on mental health advocacy groups, social workers, or people with mental illness as their *primary* source of information and interpretation. When the latter groups are included in the coverage, their views are usually framed in response to the claims of those in positions of authority. This typically helps to construct a dominant interpretation of mental illness as a threatening condition associated with violence and other forms of unpredictable or dangerous behaviour. Media coverage tends to emphasize the risks and threats people with mental illnesses pose to themselves, their families, and their communities (Greenberg, 2006).

Alternative sources often face a dilemma in their relationship with the media. On the one hand, they are used simply as a reaction to official sources. In this case, their voice is a negative one of grievances and complaints, rather than a constructive one of analysis and proposals. On the other hand, they can attempt to draw the media's attention to their own framing of an issue or a problem. However, to do so, they may have to engage in public protests or other media stunts, events that associate their views with disruptive behaviour and can undermine their legitimacy (Hackett, 1991).

Although critical theorists see the media as generally representative of dominant ideology, they also recognize that relations between journalists and their sources involve an ongoing struggle for control (Ericson, Baranek, and Chan, 1989). The outcome depends chiefly on the status of the sources and the power they can exercise over the flow of information. In the case of crime news, the police enjoy an effective monopoly over the supply of information because there is no competing source on which the media can rely for credible, timely information. With politics, however, journalists have more leverage over sources by virtue of the adversarial structure of the political process, at least in democratic societies. This does not alter the fact that the government exercises the greatest control over the flow of information because of its political authority and control over policy. What the government does or says is intrinsically newsworthy, and governments attempt to use this fact to manage the media and mobilize popular consent and support for their actions. Governments employ various tactics to maximize favourable news coverage and minimize unfavourable coverage, such as providing news releases, freezing out hostile media by limiting access to information, staging events to attract media attention, timing the release of information to improve positive and limit negative coverage, and leaking information as a way of testing the waters or manipulating public expectations (Taras, 1990).

It is also important to note that the boundaries among official, ordinary, and alternative news sources can change and that there can be diversity and competition within each of these source categories. For example, university professors are often included in news reports to provide expert interpretation and analysis, and this can sometimes place them in a position of opposition or antagonism to other official sources, such as government or police. Academics can also assume an advocacy role, using their status as authoritative experts to agitate for changes in public policy, in terms similar to social movement activists or NGOs. Finally, alternative sources can become less oppositional and more "mainstream" over time as they increase their influence over how issues are framed and represented (Gillett, 2003).

MEDIA EFFECTS AND AUDIENCES

What is most striking about research on media effects is its focus on socially problematic aspects of the media's relationship with its audiences. There has been little research on the "prosocial" effects of the media. Even in the area of child socialization, research has tended to focus on the way the media reproduce and disseminate negative stereotypes of, for example, gender roles, seniors, or racial and ethnic minority groups (Buckingham, 1998: 135–36). Research shows nonetheless that the impact of the media is usually shaped by social context, as well as by the psychological predispositions that children bring to their use of the media.

For example, many politicians, activists, teachers, and parents have argued that television advertising is to blame for the growing problem of childhood obesity in North America. The food industry is a major advertiser, dominating television airtime with promotions for everything from breakfast cereals to soft drinks and fast-food restaurants. Fast-food restaurants spent $4.2 billion in advertising in 2009. The average preschooler (2–5 years old) saw 2.8 television ads for fast food every day in 2009; children (6–11 years old) saw 3.5 ads; and teens (12–17 years old) saw 4.7 ads. Young people's exposure to fast-food advertising has increased. Preschoolers viewed 21 percent more fast-food ads in 2009 than in 2003, children viewed 34 percent more, and teens viewed 39 percent more (Harris, Schwartz, and Brownell, 2010). Children's food knowledge, preferences, and behaviours are also influenced by their class, gender, age, race, and viewing strategies (Livingstone, 2005).

We next examine two approaches to the study of media effects. The first is the study of *media violence*, and it deals most directly with the negative aspects of the media's influence. The second offers a critique of the media effects model by focusing on *audience interpretation*, the way viewers make sense of what they see and hear on television.

MEDIA VIOLENCE

The effects of portrayals of crime and violence in the media have been a longstanding topic of public policy and debate. Concerns about the effects of media violence overshadow concerns about its causes. Focusing on effects suggests the need for social control to resolve the problem by limiting or eliminating the supply of violent imagery and overlooks the need to understand what creates demand for it.

Early research on the psychological and behavioural effects of the media swung between two poles of opinion. In the 1930s and 1940s, the effects of the media were generally thought to be harmful, direct, and strong. By the early 1960s, however, the prevailing view had been revised and media influence came to be seen as more innocuous. Media effects were thought to be minimal, mediated by a diversity of intervening social and psychological factors, and confined largely to reinforcing existing beliefs and habits (Klapper, 1960). This shift in views suggests that the issue of media effects is complex, and this is especially true in the case of media violence. Recent research on the effects of media violence, particularly on TV and in films but, increasingly, in video games marketed to youth, has generated much controversy. There has been extensive debate about what constitutes violence, how to measure its extent and intensity, and how to account for possible intervening factors, such as personality differences and social environment.

Most researchers believe that media violence has some real-life effects. Current research can be broken down into two main approaches. The first examines the effect of media violence on attitudes. The principal perspective here is known as **cultivation analysis.** It stems from research by George Gerbner and his associates. Gerbner argues that long-term exposure to television tends to cultivate perceptions that are often at odds with reality (Gerbner, Gross, Morgan, and Signorielli, 1994). One of the main arguments of the cultivation perspective is that people who watch a lot of television (or play a lot of video games) will be more exposed to violent imagery and more likely to perceive society as more violent and dangerous than it really is. This tendency is what Gerbner and his colleagues call the "mean world syndrome."

This argument has stimulated considerable research. Some of it disputes the view that a causal relationship exists between the amount of time people spend watching television or playing video games and their beliefs and emotions. Other research provides qualified support but argues that the relationship is affected by intervening factors, such as the type of programming people watch (Wober, 1998). A Canadian study suggests that what may be the central issue in cultivation analysis is the fundamental relationship among perceptions of violence, danger, and fear. The researchers found evidence to support the view that people who watch TV a lot believe the world is more dangerous than other viewers do, regardless of age and sex. However, although they found that women who thought the world was dangerous were also more likely to be fearful, they did not find this to be true for men. Moreover, for women, they could not explain the relationship between perception and fear of danger by the influence of television (Gosselin, DeGuise, Pacquette, and Benoit, 1997).

The second approach focuses on the media's effects on behaviour. The predominant view in studies about television is that media do play a limited role in generating real-life violence (Friedrich-Cofer and Huston, 1986; Geen and Thomas, 1986; Huesmann and Malamuth, 1986; Perse, 2001). Those who advance this view claim that the evidence is consistent with a link between TV and real-life aggressiveness, though the strength of the evidence varies according to the methodology (Huesmann and Malamuth, 1986; Perse, 2001). In 2005, the American Psychological Association passed a resolution naming video games as a cause of aggression, and in 2009 the American Academy of Pediatrics argued that violent video games represent a significant risk to the health of children and adolescents. Those who advance this view claim that the evidence is consistent with a link between TV and real-life aggressiveness, though the strength of the evidence varies according to the methodology used. The strongest support for a causal link comes from laboratory experiments (Friedrich-Cofer and Huston, 1986). Various measures of aggressiveness have been used, among them physical and verbal aggressiveness, aggressiveness toward people and objects, actual and fantasized aggressiveness, and reduced self-discipline (lack of patience and perseverance in

Many researchers argue that media violence has some real-life effects.

SOURCE: © John Garrett/CORBIS.

trying to accomplish tasks or dealing with others). The lab experiments have shown that television violence has an effect on real-life violence *independent* of the intervening factors that have been shown to affect overall levels of aggressiveness (such as personality, age, gender, and social background).

Studies of the effects of television on behaviour have been subject to a variety of criticisms, the most significant of which have been methodological. Laboratory experiments have been strongly criticized for their inability to replicate the normal social conditions under which people, particularly children, watch TV (McCormack, 1994). Children, like adults, normally watch a mixture of violent and nonviolent programming that blend together in an ongoing flow (Freedman, 2002). Younger children watch more television than older children do, and they also watch it more intermittently because of their shorter attention span and because the social setting provides an easy distraction. As a result, although the TV set may be on for long periods, the children are not paying attention to it much of the time. The question of what exactly counts as an "act of violence" is also poorly defined and could include a host of examples, from shooting police officers in *Grand Theft Auto* to repeated broadcasts of the terrorist attacks on the World Trade Center in 2001. It is questionable that the effects of video game violence will be as hard-hitting and forceful as the effects of watching real acts of terrorism repeatedly play out on the evening news. Third, laboratory experiments have been criticized for providing research subjects with an artificial social environment. At home, if children act aggressively, their parents may punish them, or their siblings or friends may retaliate; in most cases, the possibility of such a response is eliminated in the laboratory. Last, many stimuli influence aggressive thoughts or behaviours in laboratory settings, from pictures and the names of weapons to the colour of clothing, to violent passages from the Bible and hot temperatures (Ivory and Waddell, in press).

Despite these criticisms, the belief that a link exists between media images and aggressive behaviour has generated several theories about how the relationship functions. The most sociological of these is social learning theory, according to which violence must be learned like any other behaviour, and media violence provides scripts that teach children how and when to act aggressively. Social learning, however, does not occur in isolation from psychological factors. One of the most important findings of studies examining TV viewing in natural social settings is that the relationship between TV and real violence is bidirectional (Friedrich-Cofer and Huston, 1986). In other words, watching violent TV fosters aggressiveness, but those who prefer to watch violent TV already have more aggressive tendencies.

AUDIENCE RESEARCH: INTERPRETATION AND MEDIA USE

The effects of TV and other media on attitudes and emotions depend on how these media are used and on how they are related to other activities and interests. Audiences filter, interpret, and often challenge what they see and hear according to their social context, experiences, and beliefs. These contexts, experiences, and beliefs are themselves influenced by media use.

Researchers have examined the audience in many ways, with each approach based on particular theoretical assumptions. These approaches fall along a continuum between theories about the passive audience and the active audience. At one extreme, researchers see media audiences as vulnerable to the power and control of those who own the means of communication. In this view, the media are either responsible for the erosion of traditional values or for creating false consciousness in the service of capitalist values.

In contrast, other media researchers have explored audience reception and focused more on what people do with the media they consume. Where theorists who focus on the passive audience are concerned primarily with the messages that are encoded in media content, those who focus on the active audience are more interested in issues of reception and the processes of decoding (Hall, 1980).

In the 1980s, many researchers began studying television use in its "natural" social settings, especially the home. For instance, research in the United Kingdom found that men and women differed in the way they watched television and what they preferred to watch. Men were more likely to use TV in a planned way, selecting programs beforehand and watching attentively, whereas women had a more "take-it-or-leave-it attitude" to program choice and a generally less attentive way of viewing (Morley, 1986: 153). Men enjoyed sports and information programming, whereas women found little they liked except soap operas. Women were also much less reluctant than men were to admit that they talked about TV with their friends and co-workers, which suggests that television plays a greater role in women's patterns of sociability than in men's. Morley (1986: 155) attributed this to the fact that women felt guilty about watching TV while "surrounded by their domestic obligations." Making it a topic of conversation gave it greater legitimacy. Today, women typically watch more TV than men do, and outside of sports, shows with a high percentage of female viewers also tend to be among television's most successful programs (such as *American Idol*, *Dancing with the Stars*).

Television has been the primary focus of audience research because it has played a central role in the definition of the private sphere in modern society—family, domesticity, gender relations, consumption, and suburban living—since World War II. During the 1950s and 1960s, the TV set became the central point of the household around which family members gathered to share a common experience, delivering images from the outside world into the heart of the primary social group (Morley, 2000). This symbolic role has gone through periods of decline and reemergence. TV has spread to other social settings, such as bars, malls, classrooms, and sports stadiums. TV has also become more dispersed within the household (in the kitchen, bedroom, and even bathroom), allowing more autonomy and privacy in viewing habits. Personalized watching has also been encouraged by the proliferation of specialty channels and services catering to particular tastes and interests. And new interactive technologies, such as mobile phones, personal computers, and so-called third screens (iPods and other portable media devices), combined with over-the-top media services like Netflix, are creating a more complex communications environment that mediates the role and tempers the impact that any single medium can have at home, work, or school.

THE INTERNET AND WEB 2.0

The shift in audience research toward an interest in the wider media culture is partly due to the rapid growth and use of the Internet. The Internet is a term that is now used generically to refer to a variety of different forms of **computer-mediated communication (CMC),** such as email, instant messaging (IM), blogs and chat rooms, video-sharing sites, such as YouTube, and social networking applications, such as Facebook and Twitter. The fact that these media have given rise to a host of new terms, like *cyberspace*, *online communities*, *virtual reality*, *digital culture*, *Web 2.0*, and so on, suggests that the primary definition of CMC is uncertain and under continual development. The fact that the Internet continues to change technologically and socially, and that research on its structure, use, and effects have produced divergent findings and interpretations, compounds the uncertainty.

Early research and commentary on the Internet polarized optimists and critics. Optimists understood these new media as a vehicle for greater democracy, *globalism*, and identity experimentation. They believed that the growth of the Internet in the 1990s promised to revive civic culture by providing broad, diverse forums for discussions. The Internet, they argued, was going to revolutionize civil society by enabling citizen-to-citizen interaction through online debate, deliberation, consultation, decision making, administration and scrutiny, as well as facilitating online mobilizing, organizing, petitioning, and protesting.

Critics focused on such negative effects as disengagement from "real" social relations and the detrimental effects of online communication on attention, learning, and productivity. They understood the Internet as a site of danger for both youth who made themselves vulnerable to online predators and consumers who input home addresses and credit card numbers into databases accessed by third-party marketers and hackers.

In many ways, while research has become more methodologically sophisticated and nuanced, these broad themes have remained remarkably stable (see Box 5.2).

As the Internet has developed, research has tended to paint a more complex picture of its role and how it is changing. Macrolevel research has focused not only on inequalities in terms of Internet access, usage, and scope, but also on the ways in which new media technologies challenge our understanding of what CMC *means*. Microlevel research has been concerned with the reciprocal effects between offline and online interaction. These studies have addressed issues of individual and collective identity, surveillance, and social action in situations where individuals bring their offline information and interaction into their online activities.

BOX 5.2 SOCIAL MEDIA RISKS DESENSITIZING US TO OTHERS' TRAGEDIES

YouTube can turn a small-town choir singer into a viral hit overnight. But not all viral hits are because of hidden talents.

Take 14-year-old Jonah Mowry, who posted an emotional video on YouTube entitled "Whats goin' on."

In the video, Mowry, with tears running down his face, holds up cue cards with words about his struggles with bullying. The video was posted in August and has had almost nine million views. Young people around the world have submitted their own touching versions of "Whats goin' on," creating something of a support system for Mowry.

Many would agree this is a positive outcome of social media: allowing someone in trouble to seek help from the public while gaining an enormous amount of positive feedback. However, as an average YouTube browser, I felt quickly overwhelmed by all the responses to Mowry's video.

I even caught myself thinking that some of the videos people had posted appeared to be cries for attention. Does that mean I'm unsympathetic?...

Nowadays, sharing anything—your problems, your talents, your food photos, or your shoe collection—is possible with the touch of a button. It's so easy for everyone to vent online that viewers may turn a blind eye.

After the recent suicides of two teenagers who were bullied, Jamie Hubley of Ottawa, and Marjorie Raymond of Ste. Anne des Monts, Quebec, traditional and social media pumped up their efforts to build awareness of bullying. At one point, my Facebook feed was coated with links to articles about bullying or re-posts of the Mowry video.

I believe social media networks are an excellent way for people to express their opinions and emotions; we know it's healthier to talk than to keep our emotions bottled up. However, if we continue at the current rate, everyone will be using social media as a tool for venting, and fewer people will respond to each post.

Social media will become saturated with rants, complaints and cries for help, and people will stop caring....

A University of Southern California study came to a similar conclusion. The researchers suggested that receiving constant digital updates could desensitize people because their brains don't have enough time to process the information.

When you get too much information, you tend to just scan it and not fully understand or respond to it.

The campaigns to raise money for breast cancer and prostate cancer awareness go full force only one month a year—October for the former, and November for the latter. Why? Because the organizers know that if they constantly try to raise funds, potential donors will be overwhelmed and tune out.

Think of homeless people. How often do we ignore the man slumped on the street begging for change? He has become an accessory to our environment because there are so many like him everywhere we look. Many of us tune them out and turn a blind eye because we feel we can't help them all....

Social media are about community-building. We add childhood friends on Facebook, we follow celebrities or news outlets on Twitter, and we watch videos on every subject imaginable on YouTube. Social media allow us to find others with similar interests, and that's a positive outcome. But could they also cause future generations to become desensitized to human suffering?

SOURCE: Partsinevelos, Kristina. (2012). *The Calgary Herald*, 8 January. On the World Wide Web at http://www.calgaryherald.com/technology/Social+media+risks+desensitizing+others+tragedies/5963463/story.html. Used with permission of Kristina Partsinevelos.

THE DIGITAL DIVIDE: TECHNOLOGY AND SOCIAL INEQUALITY

Digital divide is a term that is commonly used to explain how access to and use of media technologies exacerbate and reproduce structural inequities. While access to the Internet has grown rapidly, not only in developed nations but also in developing countries, disparities persist.

Inequality of Access

In 2000, about 420 million people were estimated to be online; in 2008, the number of people online across the world surpassed 1.46 billion (or 21.8 percent of the world's population); by 2011, more than 2 billion were online (approximately 30 percent of the world's population) (Internet World Stats, 2008, 2011). The vast majority of people online are located in the affluent, developed nations, such as Canada, the United States, and Japan, where more than 78 percent of the total population of these countries has access to the Internet (Internet World Stats, 2011). By contrast, in more populous but less economically developed countries, such as India and China, Internet users number in the range of 8 to 36 percent of the total population

(Internet World Stats, 2011). Statistics on broadband access also suggest a global digital divide. While rates of access are high for such countries as Canada (29.8 percent), the Netherlands (38.1 percent), the United States (27.6 percent), and Sweden (31.9 percent), the figure is significantly lower for such countries as Pakistan (0.3 percent), Algeria (2.5 percent), Sudan (0.4 percent), and Zimbabwe (0.3 percent)—rates that hold across much of Africa, the Middle East, and Asia (International Telecommunication Union, 2011).

Despite less broadband access in the developing world, changes in technology associated with the rise of mobile telephony provide some optimism for narrowing the global digital divide. Take India, which has just a 7 percent Internet penetration rate. India also boasts the second largest telecom sector in the world, enjoys 63 percent mobile phone market penetration, and plans expansion of third-generation (3G) services that will enable high-speed Internet browsing on affordable mobile phones. The future for digital access thus looks much brighter than traditional Internet data suggest (Ghosh, 2011). Indeed, in March 2010, approximately 177 million people in India accessed the Internet through wireless networks; just one year later, that number had spiked to more than 381 million (Press Information Bureau, 2011).

The development of online access and use mirrors that of earlier media, such as television—originating in developed countries and then spreading to the developing world as the technology changed and became more readily available. In this process, a software gap also tends to develop. Just as global television content continues to be dominated by programming produced in the developed world, so the Internet is dominated by content produced in the developed world. In 2010, five countries—the United States, Japan, Germany, the United Kingdom, and Italy—owned 67 percent of all Internet hosts worldwide (Network Wizards, 2011).

Social class also tends to be a strong predictor of who is online. Between 2005 and 2009, Internet access grew fastest for the poorest 25 percent of Canadians, increasing from 58.7 to 76.2 percent of people in this income category. Nevertheless, as noted earlier in this chapter, almost all top-quartile-income Canadian households have Internet access at home. Unequal access to the Internet (and broadband, specifically) reflects several factors, particularly cost, occupation, and education. High-income households are likely to contain adult members who are familiar with computers because of their work, and this makes home use easier in terms of operating skill. People with higher levels of education are also more likely to be online, a pattern that holds independently of income and occupation (Dickinson and Ellison, 2000). In 2009, the percentage of Internet users among Canadians with university degrees increased to 94.7 percent. For those users with less than high school education, Internet access stood at 50.7 percent (Statistics Canada, 2011c).

In Canadian universities, student use the latest electronic technologies in classrooms, dorms, and pubs.
SOURCE: © Michaeljung/Shutterstock.

Web 2.0: A New Paradigm for Communication

Media institutions, organizations, and technologies are undergoing a paradigm shift, and while we should not conclude that the age of mass media is over, new and emergent media are shaping and being shaped by new forms of social organization. Traditional mass media, such as the press and television, continue to play a key role in the democratic life of Canadian society. However, where these types of media were based on a dissemination model in which communication flowed mostly in one direction from a single source to many sources, a more open, many-to-many networked media environment has begun to take shape (Greenberg and MacAulay, 2009). With this paradigm shift in media organization and technology, the relations between different social actors are also undergoing change. The notion that there exists a national public sphere in which individuals come together to debate issues openly and construct public opinion has been replaced by a more fragmented mediascape and the emergence of segmented spheres of assimilation in which individuals come together around narrower shared interests.

The first generation of the Internet (Web 1.0) was based on a paradigm of communication not unlike that of traditional broadcasting, though with greater access for users. In the early days of public Internet use (early to mid-1990s), users primarily downloaded text and images that others had posted online. Web 2.0 encourages users to be digital collaborators, building webpages and blogs, co-creating content by uploading and mixing videos on YouTube, and editing, deleting, and adding to information on Wikipedia. Web 2.0 facilitates participation, creativity, and open platforms that enable users not only to consume content but to generate and produce it as well (O'Reilly, 2005; Zimmer, 2008). Some critics are skeptical of the new technology, believing that Web 2.0 is a way for media corporations to exploit users by replacing skilled labour, such as web design, with the "free" labour of audiences who spend time and energy building content for others to consume (Banks and Humphreys, 2008).

IMPACT OF NEW MEDIA: BUILDING COMMUNITY ONLINE AND THE RISK TO PRIVACY

As was the case with radio and TV, the rapid growth of the Internet has prompted concern about its supposedly negative effects. For example, some studies link television watching and Internet surfing with obesity, inactive leisure time, poor diet, and declining reading rates, while others see the Internet as addictive (Hilts, 2008; National Endowment for the Arts, 2007; Kaiser Family Foundation, 2010; Statistics Canada, 2008b).

Other studies, however, point out that the Internet can be a source of valuable information that can inform and promote active and healthy lifestyles to at-risk populations, and that social media opens possibilities for civic engagement and activism (Kann, Berry, Grant, and Zager, 2007; Lewis, 2007; Anderson and Rainie, 2010). Instead of being seen as an isolating activity, the growing number of people online and the widespread use of email, instant messaging, and blogging by Canadians suggests that people are using the Internet to connect with others, thus enhancing social interaction and identity expression. As boyd (2007) notes, social networking sites are important spaces for youth to perform "identity work" at a time when the availability of physical social spaces, such as community centres, is declining. As such, online social networking communities can be as socially and emotionally supportive for their members as communities that are based on face-to-face interaction. Even online forums, such as newsgroups like Reddit and Digg, can have socially supportive side effects, as news stories permit participants to comment on and share information with others. Although virtual communities lack the kind of interpersonal cues available in face-to-face relationships, new technologies, such as webcams and Voice over Internet Protocol (VoIP) software, such as Skype, can *promote* interaction by removing risks and status or identity barriers that might normally inhibit the development of real world ties.

Surveillance and Privacy 2.0

Social networking sites such as Facebook raise concerns about online privacy and surveillance. Some scholars note the dangers of social networking sites as spaces of digital voyeurism. Because of the ways these sites encourage users to document and publish their daily activities, they enable users to monitor one another and can be havens for those preying on unsuspecting youth (Albrechtslund, 2008; Marwick, 2008). The anxieties associated with these possibilities have led to proposals for more Internet regulation, intervention, and education about the invisible risks and dangers associated with Internet use in general and of Web 2.0 in particular.

Others approach the issue of online privacy and surveillance differently. Some researchers cite a lack of empirical evidence that links the use of social networking to increased youth predatory behaviour and note that this "technopanic" obscures the more pressing issue of the sexual exploitation of youth that occurred long before Internet use became prevalent (boyd and Jenkins, 2006; Marwick, 2008). Accounts vary of how much personal information users actually disclose on their profiles. Some research shows that adolescents frequently display evidence of their risky personal behaviour, such as accounts of their sexual exploits and drug use, on their social media profiles (Moreno, Parks, Zimmerman, Brito, and Christakis 2009). Other research shows that young people are savvy when it comes to protecting their privacy online. A 2011 study by the Office of the Privacy Commissioner of Canada found that those aged 18 to 34 are more likely to use social media sites, but are also more likely to be aware of and to use restrictive privacy controls than older Canadians are (Hembrey, 2011). Furthermore, online surveillance is not always or only dangerous. Most young people use social media like Facebook to keep in touch with friends they infrequently see offline, so "participatory surveillance" becomes a way of maintaining relationships by mediating and reading about what your friends are doing and where they have travelled, what music they're listening to, and what movies they have recently seen (Albrechtslund, 2008; Lenhart and Madden, 2007). Moreover, police and other criminal investigations have used social networking sites to track down the locations of offenders (Zimmer, 2008; see Box 5.3). Finally, social media are used increasingly in emergency response, enabling first responders to collect very useful information that helps save lives. After the 2010 earthquake in Haiti, victims who had been trapped under rubble used Facebook on their mobile phones to identify their location and call for help, while healthcare providers drew on crowd-sourced information from Ushahidi, an open-source Web platform, to deliver aid and other support services to those who needed them. During the 2009 H1N1 pandemic, public health departments across Canada and the United States used Twitter to post real-time updates about lineups at vaccination clinics, in addition to using social media for making broader public health announcements. Following the BP oil spill in the Gulf of Mexico in 2010, residents texted photographs of oil-soaked birds to the Louisiana Bucket Brigade, whose maps helped volunteers identify areas most in need of cleanup (Merchant, Elmer, and Lurie, 2011). In sum, research shows a mixture of risks and rewards of participating in Web 2.0 technologies.

Social Activism 2.0

In 2010, *Time Magazine*'s "Person of the Year" was Facebook CEO Mark Zuckerberg. In 2011 this honour was given to the unnamed "Protester," in reference to the pro-democracy activism in the Middle East and North Africa and the Occupy Wall Street movement in the United States and elsewhere in the developed world. The fragmentation of the modern mediascape, embodied in many ways by new media corporations, such as Facebook, has created new opportunities and risks for social activism. Opportunities to participate in the coordination of collective mobilization and political action enable citizens to demand changes to society and politics in ways that were previously unthinkable (Greenberg and Gilberds, 2011). Consider the political revolution in Egypt in 2011.

BOX 5.3 USING SOCIAL NETWORKS AND DIGITAL SURVEILLANCE TO TRACK DOWN A STOLEN COMPUTER

Sean Power, using Prey, a free tracking program, tracked down his laptop to a bar in Brooklyn, where he saw that a man, Skype alias "Paolo Votano," was using his computer to browse the web and call friends. Power, however, was in Canada. Enter Twitter.

"Prey sent me a report & pic of a guy playing with my stolen laptop. What should I do? http://awe.sm/5J8hu," Power tweeted.

Soon enough, the Twitter world jumped in to help. They discovered that the man was in fact a part owner of the bar. One woman even went down to the bar herself to check out the situation.

"I am sure we can virtually arrange a geek squad intervention to go reclaim your gear. You need help rounding up a posse?" tweeted pfasano.

Power called the police instead. But they told him that they couldn't do anything unless he filed a report in person. Meanwhile, Power was able to get pictures of the man's face, his Gmail account, and his Chase bank account. He directed his followers not to get too involved.

"please please please don't get directly involved. I don't want any of you to get hurt for a stupid laptop," he tweeted.

But the girl at the bar decided to go:

"Apparently, the girl that went there has befriended two of the bartenders and is doing shots with them. Wow," Power tweeted.

Power called "Paolo." A long Twitter silence ensued during which followers wondered whether Power was pulling a viral stunt for Prey (he said he was not). Finally, the story came to an end:

"So ... Paolo freely gave it up. I'm not about to accuse anyone of anything. I'd rather forget that that place exists and just move on," Power tweeted (a friend of his went to go get the laptop). "But yes, Internet—I'm about 800 km away, and I got my stolen laptop back."

SOURCE: Lee, A. (2011). "Sean Power Tracks down Stolen Laptop Using Twitter, Prey from Hundreds of Miles Away." *Huffington Post* 14 May. On the World Wide Web at http://www.huffingtonpost.com/2011/05/14/sean-power-prey-stolen-laptop-twitter_n_861895.html (retrieved 21 December 2011).

Using a variety of social media platforms (Facebook, Twitter, YouTube, Flickr), activists in Egypt orchestrated a mass movement, involving youth in particular, against the regime of Hosni Mubarak. The availability of these media reduced the cost of sharing information and allowed Egyptians to be heard and supported by others around the world.

While it is difficult to measure the effect that social media have on political participation or social change, they have certainly given rise to new forms of civic discourse and generated new opportunities for mass mobilization. These predate the so-called "social media revolutions" of 2010–11. In January 2001, the Philippine Congress agreed to ignore crucial evidence against its country's President Joseph Estrada during his impeachment trial. Within a few hours of that decision, thousands of angry citizens took to the streets of Manila to protest political corruption and demand Estrada's resignation. Although word of mouth and existing social relationships enabled the protestors to come together, the demonstration was facilitated by the use of text messages reading: "Go 2 ESA. Wear blk." Within a few days, more than a million people had arrived, bringing business and traffic in the capital city to a halt. Similarly, in May 2004, both television and the Internet circulated images of U.S. soldiers abusing Iraqi prisoners in an attempt to hold U.S. military and political administration accountable. While these images were rapidly transmitted on television and other traditional broadcast media, it was the "manner in which they were proliferated and archived on blogs that may make them stand as some of the most influential images of all time" (Kahn and Kellner, 2005). In these and other cases, new technologies were used to organize, inspire, and amplify outrage against the anti-democratic actions of the authorities.

Despite the potential of the Internet and other technologies to enhance democracy, a few cautionary notes are important. First, as the essayist Malcolm Gladwell (2010) pointed out, social media do not support the kinds of "strong ties" that are typically required for high-stakes political change. While a protest against an oppressive regime can be mobilized quickly by a Facebook group or Twitter hashtag, the main drivers of political change are the material conditions in which people find themselves and their interpersonal connections and values. Social media are most effective in mobilizing and coordinating activism aimed at specific, short-term goals, such as toppling a tyrant or tracking an offender, rather than broader, longer-term projects, such as establishing democracy or reducing crime rates. Second, technology is not a tool used only by social movements to bring about political reform. Authoritarian regimes have the ability to leverage the Internet to enhance their repressive capacity (Morozov, 2011). The Internet has been used to identify, trace, and jail activists; it is not just a benevolent force that can free any society from the shackles of its oppression. Third, we would do well to heed U.S. media critic Robert McChesney's reminder that, historically, the development of new media was always met with enthusiasm that was later tempered by commodification: "Once the technologies proved profitable ... they were turned over to private interests" (McChesney, 1996: 8). Still, despite the attempts of economic and political power centres to control the Internet and other new avenues of communication, struggles by oppositional groups to elude or puncture the dominant informational infrastructure will always remain.

SUMMARY

1. Technological theory emphasizes the role played by media technologies on both individual psychology and social organization, and originates largely with the writings of two Canadian scholars, Harold Innis and Marshall McLuhan. Technology theory is also useful for understanding new forms of social interaction, networking, and surveillance that have resulted from the development of computer-mediated forms of communication.
2. Critical theory focuses on the impact of different interests and social inequalities on the organization (political economy) and content (ideology) of communications media. Some critical theorists emphasize the role of the media in reinforcing and sustaining dominant relations of power, wealth, and other valuable resources, whereas others see the media as an arena in which conflict occurs over the meaning of social reality. The two variants of critical theory

are particularly evident in research on the representation of social reality found in the news media.

3. Canadian newspapers exhibit high levels of ownership concentration, are usually part of large multimedia chains, and function largely as local monopolies. Arguably, the factor that has the greatest impact on news content is dependency on advertising.
4. In the case of television, advertising dependency, the high costs of production, and audience preferences mean that much of the programming Canadians watch is American. This is especially so for drama and sitcoms, less so for news and public affairs programs. Cultural nationalists view the situation as a threat to Canadian culture, whereas others see it as part of the general effect of globalization and do not believe that it undermines the institutional structure or cultural fabric of Canadian society.
5. Conservatives claim that news coverage has a left-liberal political bias that is unrepresentative of society's mainstream. Critical theorists argue that news coverage is ideologically conservative in that it defines reality from the perspective of elite political and economic interests. At the same time, some critical theorists argue that the media are not completely closed to alternative voices and viewpoints, and that these can challenge, to some extent, the hegemony of dominant social groups and interests.
6. Many observers believe that a causal link exists between violent media content and violent behaviour, particularly among children. However, the studies that support this view have been criticized on the grounds of flawed methodology.
7. Studies of audiences indicate that TV viewing and the responses to it vary by gender. Men and women tend to prefer different types of programming. Men are more likely to watch attentively and privately, whereas women watch in a more interactive, social way. Women also tend to be more open about their TV viewing and use it as a topic of casual social interaction and conversation. Changes in media technology have also begun to shift the culture of television consumption. Where the development of VCRs and DVRs led audiences to time-shift their TV viewing, social and mobile media have brought media audiences back to the broadcast schedule—using Twitter and other social media platforms, audiences are beginning to watch and talk online about their favourite shows in real time.
8. Although early views about the development of computer-mediated communication and the Internet tended to polarize optimists and pessimists, recent research has yielded a more complex, nuanced view. Inequalities of access (especially globally) and differences of use persist; however, the former show signs of declining as the technology becomes less costly. Research on the impact of the Internet shows that there are mixed opportunities and risks, from enhancing the potential for collective mobilization to increasing vulnerability to violations of personal privacy. A sophisticated theoretical understanding of the effects of the Internet and social media must balance this range of perspectives.

QUESTIONS TO CONSIDER

1. Despite the lack of strong, consistent, and unequivocal evidence confirming a direct link between violence in the media and in real life, why are many people convinced that such a link exists?
2. Critics of media imperialism often point to Canada as an example of a country overwhelmed by American popular culture—movies, magazines, music, and television. What is so appealing about American popular culture, not only in Canada but in other countries as well? Are Canadians vulnerable to becoming Americanized by the gross imbalance between the amount of domestic and U.S. dramatic programming we watch?
3. As more young people tune out the mainstream media and plug in to Web 2.0, what are the challenges this poses to democracy and issues of personal privacy, and what are the potential benefits to community development and the development of individual identity?

GLOSSARY

Alternative news sources (p. 113) are representatives of social movements and of social advocacy groups whose viewpoints often diverge from those of dominant social groups and their representatives.

Communication (p. 101) denotes the transmission of knowledge, ideas, meanings, and understandings.

Computer-mediated communication (CMC) (p. 117) refers to social interaction or information gathering through the use of computer technology.

The **critical perspective** (p. 103) takes the view that the media reinforce dominant ideology and the position of the dominant class and other powerful groups.

The theory has two variants. One sees dominance as more open to challenge and resistance than does the other.

Cultivation analysis (p. 115) examines the long-term effects of television viewing on beliefs about social reality. People who watch TV a lot tend to see the world as more violent and dangerous than it really is, and tend to be more fearful.

Cultural imperialism (p. 108) involves one society's media exerting an overwhelming and unilateral influence over another society's culture.

The **dominant ideology** (p. 103) comprises the interests, perspectives, viewpoints, and understandings of the dominant class and other powerful groups.

Framing (p. 109) is the process of defining the boundaries of a representation and the organization of its contents. Framing pertains to the selection of what is included and excluded, what is accentuated, and what is played down.

Hegemony (p. 103) is the exercise by the dominant class of cultural leadership by using the media to naturalize and universalize dominant ideology, and to absorb the challenge of alternative and oppositional points of view.

Horizontal integration (p. 104) is the ownership of different outlets in a media chain for purposes of sharing resources.

Interactive media (p. 101) are technologically mediated means of communication in which the flow of messages is two way—between actors who transmit and receive messages.

Mass media (p. 101) are technologically mediated means of communication in which the flow of messages is largely one way, from a single point of transmission to a large, anonymous, dispersed audience of receivers.

Multimedia chains (p. 104) are corporations that own and control a string of media operations or outlets in different fields of mass communication, such as television, radio, and magazines.

News values (p. 111) include such criteria as immediacy, personalization, and extraordinariness, in terms of which news media define and represent events and issues.

Official news sources (p. 113) are authoritative voices—for example, politicians, police officers, and professional experts—that the media often use to define the meaning of an event or issue.

Ordinary news sources (p. 113) are news sources that do not represent organizations or groups, and include eyewitnesses and victims of news events.

Representation (p. 109) is the use of language, visual images, or other means of communication to portray something in a coherent and meaningful way.

Space-biased media (p. 102), such as print, radio, and television, enable communication over extended distances. The messages, however, are not long lasting. Space-biased media promote territorial expansion, secular beliefs, and military-political forms of power.

Time-biased media (p. 102), such as stone carvings or inscriptions on clay tablets, convey durable messages but are relatively immobile.

Vertical integration (p. 104) refers to a media corporation's ownership and control of the means of production at all stages of the production process—for example, from producing newsprint to delivering newspapers.

SUGGESTED READING

Hamilton, James F. (2008). *Democratic Communications: Formations, Projects, Possibilities*. Lanham, MD: Lexington Books. Presents a critical analysis of Anglo-American historical and cultural traditions and alternative media practices as modes of "democratic communications." The book argues for "new possibilities" in democratic communications, and challenges the claim that creating alternative media is time and cost prohibitive.

Hugill, David. (2010). *Missing Women, Missing News.* Halifax, NS: Fernwood. The book critically examines how the establishment media reported the disappearance and murder of numerous prostitutes in Vancouver's downtown eastside and the subsequent murder trial and conviction of Robert Pickton. In contrast to the media storm that surrounded the trial, the author argues that Canadian media coverage of the murders itself was limited. However, even the trial coverage was superficial, drawing on stereotypes and a dominant ideology that pathologized the lives of the victims instead of critically exploring the social and political contexts of the murders and the media's unwillingness to cover them.

Jackson, John D., Greg M. Nielsen, and Yon Hsu. (2011). *Mediated Society: A Critical Sociology of Media.* Don Mills, ON: Oxford University Press. Provides a sociological perspective on media industries, content, and audiences, introducing students to key theoretical and methodological issues and debates.

Shirky, C. (2008). *Here Comes Everybody: The Power of Organizing Without Organizations.* New York: Penguin Press. Examines how changes in media technology associated with the rise of social networking sites alter social interaction and the balance of power among institutions, organizations, and individuals.

PART 3

INEQUALITY

SOURCE: BEN STANSALL/AFP/Getty Images/Newscom.

CHAPTER 6

SOCIAL STRATIFICATION

Harvey Krahn
UNIVERSITY OF ALBERTA

SOURCE: © BEN STANSALL/AFP/Getty Images/Newscom.

IN THIS CHAPTER YOU WILL LEARN THAT

- Persistent patterns of social inequality are based on statuses assigned to individuals at birth and on how well individuals perform certain roles. Societies vary in the degree to which mobility up and down the stratification system occurs.
- Explanations of the origins and impact of social stratification include the theory of Karl Marx, which emphasizes the exploitation of the working class by owners of land and industry as the main source of inequality and change; the theory of Max Weber, which emphasizes the power that derives from property ownership, prestige, and politics; functionalist theory, which holds that stratification is both inevitable and necessary; and several revisions of Marx's and Weber's ideas that render them more relevant to today's society.
- Although there has been considerable opportunity for upward occupational mobility in Canada, wealth and property are concentrated in relatively few hands, and one in seven Canadians is a low-income earner. Because of labour-market changes, income and wealth inequality have been increasing. Thus, the stratification structure of the future will probably not resemble the pattern that emerged in the affluent middle of the twentieth century.
- A person's position in society's stratification system has important consequences, both for lifestyle and for the quality of life. Those who are situated higher in the economic hierarchy tend to live better and longer.

INTRODUCTION

While bundling up old newspapers for recycling, I flip through them quickly. Although the news writers don't use the term, I find myself reading about **social stratification**—that is, persistent patterns of social inequality within society.

A headline catches my attention: "20,000 more Alberta children living in poverty." The reporter writes that, between 2008 and 2009, the number of Alberta children living below the poverty line (a measurement we will discuss later in this chapter) increased by almost 40 percent, from 53 000 to 73 000 (Kleiss, 2011). The Canadian economy went into recession during 2008–09, so an increase in poverty rates is understandable. But how is it possible for 73 000 children to be living in poverty in a province with the highest average income in Canada? Perhaps their parents are unemployed or unable to work? The reporter notes, however, that more than half of these children have at least one parent who is employed full-time for the whole year. While, on average, Albertans have high incomes, some of the province's residents earn little although they work hard.

Another article reports that immigrant Canadians are more likely than other Canadians to be earning low incomes and to be unemployed even though they enjoy higher-than-average education (Hansen, 2011). In fact, while the education level of immigrants has been increasing over the past three decades because Canada gives priority to applicants who are highly educated, immigrants have been falling further behind in terms of income and unemployment rates. This seems odd since, after all, one of the reasons you attend university is to obtain an education that, you expect, will lead to a good job.

A third article about awful housing conditions in the northern Ontario community of Attawapiskat—many residents live in unheated houses without any running water—highlights another irony (Mackrael, 2011). It quotes a United Nations official who compares the poverty and poor living conditions in many First Nations communities in Canada to the situation in developing countries, the very countries emigrants are leaving to come to Canada for a better life!

However, not all of Canada's poor and unemployed are immigrants or First Nations. Some have seen their previous financial security disappear quickly because of economic restructuring. A newspaper story describes how the closing of a paper mill in Point Tupper, Nova Scotia, after 49 years of operation will lead to six hundred employees being laid off (Canadian Press, 2011). In addition, many retired mill workers are worried that their pensions will shrink if a new company does not buy and re-open the mill. I find another example of how economic restructuring is affecting workers (Hagerty and van Hasselt, 2012). In London, Ontario, 420 unionized employees of Caterpillar Inc. were "locked out" of their factory. Their employer wouldn't let them return to work unless they accepted a new contract that will cut their hourly wages from $34 to $16.50.

Although the very poor catch our attention, so do the very rich. A news item reminds me of just how rich some people are. By noon of the first working day in 2010, the one hundred most highly paid chief executive officers (CEOs) of companies operating in Canada had already earned as much as the typical Canadian worker earns in the whole year (Abma, 2012). Imagine working for half a day to earn an average $44 366 and then going on vacation for the rest of the year! However, these one hundred very rich individuals worked all year and reported average incomes of more than $8 million in 2010. The article goes on to observe that the gap between the earnings of the average Canadian worker and the earnings of the top Canadian CEOs was almost twice as high in 2010 as it was in 1998.

It's time to take the newspapers out to the curb, but one more headline can't be ignored: "Baby boomers living good life, while their children struggle." The author notes that, taking inflation into account, young couples today are earning only 5 percent more than their counterparts earned in 1976 (Pratt, 2011). In contrast, those aged 55 to 64 are earning 33 percent more than they did 35 years ago. In the meantime, housing prices in Canada have soared, and it now typically takes two earners per household to earn a decent living compared with only one earner three decades ago. The reporter quotes a University of British Columbia professor who is studying this shifting pattern of intergenerational inequality: "While the boomers retire richer than any generation before, their grandchildren are growing up in families that are poorer than [the baby boomers] were."

The common theme in these quite different stories is the existence of groups—the unemployed and low-income workers, First Nations, immigrants, young adults—that rank lower than others in the social stratification system. A low position in this ranking typically means having little power, little wealth, and little prestige, whereas a higher position generally implies the opposite. In this chapter, I begin

Caterpillar employees protest proposed wage cuts in London, Ontario, 2012. In reaction to the protests, Caterpillar shut down the plant permanently. It was widely expected that the plant's jobs would be moved to comparatively low-wage Indiana, where Caterpillar's head office is located; Caterpillar announced the plant closing just 36 hours after Indiana governor Mitch Daniels signed legislation making it more difficult for unions to organize in that state.

SOURCE: © Dave Chidley/The Canadian Press.

by discussing some of the ways in which sociologists study social stratification. I then examine a variety of theories of social stratification that attempt to explain its origins and impacts. The last section focuses on occupational and class structures and material inequality in Canada, and concludes by asking whether social inequality has been increasing.

STRATIFICATION: A CORNERSTONE OF SOCIOLOGY

Sociologists have four basic areas of inquiry. We study social structure, or the way in which society is organized, both formally and informally. We ask questions about social order. What is it that holds together a society comprising individuals with different interests, and when and why does social order break down? Inquiries about social change form a third key area in the discipline. How and why do societies, the institutions and power structures within them, and the values and beliefs held by individual members change? Finally, sociologists spend a lot of time studying social stratification, the manner in which valued resources—that is, wealth, power, and prestige—are distributed, and the way in which advantages are passed from generation to generation.

It could easily be argued that the study of social stratification is the cornerstone of sociology. Descriptions of social structure that ignore the stratification system are clearly inadequate. Imagine describing Canadian society to someone from another country without referring to some features of stratification. Would the listener really understand our society if she or he did not know that most large corporations are run by men, that the working poor continue to struggle to make ends meet even though the majority of employed Canadians earn a decent living, that First Nations are much more likely than most others to be living in poverty, and that immigrants are doing less well today than they were several decades ago, even though they are better educated?

Furthermore, inequalities in wealth can threaten social stability (the poor resenting the wealthy, for example, and demanding more equality), and inequalities in power can be used to maintain social order. For example, powerful corporations might lobby provincial or territorial governments for changes in the labour laws that would make it more difficult for unions to organize company employees. In less democratic countries, direct control of the police and military by a powerful political minority can lead to the quick and violent suppression of unrest among the masses. We have seen many examples in the past few years in the Middle East as the Arab Spring uprisings, fuelled by high levels of social inequality, were sometimes brutally suppressed (Al-Momani, 2011).

An understanding of social stratification is also essential for studying social change, since, frequently, it is the stratification system that is undergoing change. For example, changing gender roles and the slow movement of women into positions of power and authority in North America in the past few decades are really features of a changing stratification system. The massive social, economic, and political changes that began in the former Soviet Union in the late 1980s and in China a decade earlier are, among other things, changes in stratification systems, as the main sources of power come to include both the political system and the emerging capitalist economy.

SOCIAL HIERARCHIES IN STRATIFIED SOCIETIES

Imagine a society in which stratification did not exist, in which all things of value were distributed equally. Even if you picture a very small group, perhaps a preindustrial society with only a few hundred members, living on some isolated island where the necessities of life are easily obtained, it is still difficult to imagine a nonstratified society. A social hierarchy might emerge as a result of skill differences in fishing, in nursing the ill back to health, or in communicating with the spirits, for example. Inequalities in wealth might develop simply because some families were fortunate enough to have a larger number of children, providing more of the labour needed to accumulate valued possessions. And once accumulations of wealth began to be passed from generation to generation, a structured and relatively permanent pattern of inequality would emerge.

Perhaps you imagined some contemporary society comprising adults who, believing strongly in equality, decided to live and work together in some kind of urban or rural commune, sharing all their possessions. Again, it is easy to imagine how a social hierarchy could emerge, as those with more useful skills found themselves playing a more central role in this small-scale society. No doubt, when important decisions needed to be made, these individuals would be more likely to influence the outcome.

We do not need to repeat this mental exercise too many times before we see that social stratification in one form or another exists in all societies. However, our hypothetical examples are far from typical. In most societies, stratification is much more pronounced, and basic skills are seldom the foundation of primary social hierarchies. Nevertheless, cross-cultural variations exist in the criteria by which individuals and groups are ranked, the degree to which they can move from one position to another within the hierarchy, and the extent of inequality in wealth and power that exists within the hierarchy.

ASCRIBED AND ACHIEVED STATUS

Let's begin by defining the rank or position that a person has within a social hierarchy as that person's **status.** We can further distinguish between an **ascribed status** and an **achieved status.** The former is assigned to individuals, typically at birth. An ascribed status can be a function of race, gender, age, and other factors that are not chosen or earned and that cannot be changed (a few people do choose their gender status, but they are rare exceptions). In contrast, an achieved status is precisely that—a position in a hierarchy that has been achieved by virtue of how well someone performs in some role. The most obvious example is that of occupational status—for instance, individuals who have performed well in law school are entitled to become lawyers, and high-performance athletes strive to achieve the status of "professional athlete." By the same logic, someone could achieve the status of "bum" by performing poorly in educational, employment, family, and other social roles.

Although we may accept that a completely non-stratified society is impossible, most of us would probably agree that a stratification system in which higher positions were achieved, not ascribed, would be preferable. In a **meritocracy,** everyone would have equal chances to compete for higher status positions and, presumably, those most capable would be awarded the highest rank. Such a society would exhibit a considerable degree of **social mobility,** as those who were more qualified moved up the social hierarchy to replace those who were less competent and who were consequently compelled to move down.

OPEN AND CLOSED STRATIFICATION SYSTEMS

When we compare Canada with other societies, or look back at our history, we find that this country has what appears to be a fairly **open stratification system,** in which merit, rather than inheritance (or ascribed characteristics), determines social rank and in which social change is therefore possible. For example, dramatic changes in the status of various groups have occurred in this country over time. Although the practice was not nearly as widespread in Canada as in the United States, slaves (most of them black people from Africa but also some First Nations) were bought and sold in Canada from the 1630s till the 1830s (Derreck, 2003). Chinese labourers, brought into the country to help build the railways, were kept out of most "white" jobs by law until well into the twentieth century (Li, 1982). Similarly, it was not until the 1960s that black Canadians were allowed to compete for much more than the lowest-level positions in the Canadian railway industry (Calliste, 1987). However, by the 1830s, slavery had disappeared in Canada, and we now have laws against racial discrimination.

Comparing ourselves with other contemporary societies, we note that Canada does not have an aristocracy, such as the one that exists in Britain, where children of wealthy and powerful families of long standing inherit positions and titles. The degree to which Canadians compete for higher status occupations (in the education system and, later, within the workplace) stands in clear contrast to the situation in India, for example, where the caste into which an individual is born largely determines the type of work that he or she will be allowed to do. Although discrimination on the basis of caste membership has been illegal in India for many decades, the **caste system** continues to underpin a relatively **closed stratification system.** Compared with India, Canada offers many more chances for upward social mobility, an indication of a more open stratification system.

Ascribed and achieved statuses

SOURCES: © Gouhier-Guibbaud-JMP/ABACAPRESS.COM/Newscom (l); © Ronald Martinez/Getty Images (r).

It is all too easy, however, to overlook the extent to which ascribed statuses continue to limit opportunities for many Canadians as well. Discrimination against members of First Nations and visible-minority groups continues to occur in Canada today. So, too, does discrimination against members of the gay community, against seniors and people with disabilities, and against women. These people are in lower status positions not because they competed poorly for some higher ranking in the social hierarchy, but because they are gay, are old, have disabilities, or are female.

These are fairly obvious examples of the ways in which ascribed statuses continue to play a prominent role in Canada's social stratification system. But what about the child from a wealthy family who graduates from an excellent high school in a wealthy neighbourhood, completes a degree or two in a prestigious and costly university, and then begins a career in a high-status, well-paying profession? Is this simply an example of someone achieving a deserved high-status position, or did the advantages of birth (ascribed status) play some part in this success story? Similarly, when we hear of large companies laying off hundreds of workers, does their sudden downward mobility reflect their failure to compete in an open, merit-based stratification system, or were they simply unfortunate enough to be employed in a corporation that was being downsized?

As these examples illustrate, the social stratification system consists of a number of different hierarchies, some based on ascribed characteristics, others on achievement. Elsewhere in this book, you will read chapters devoted to various dimensions of stratification and inequality, such as gender, race, and ethnicity. Other chapters address activities (for example, work) and institutions (for example, education) in which stratification processes are extremely important, and still others focus on inequalities among regions and countries. Once you have read all these chapters, you will, I expect, be convinced of the central importance of social stratification in the discipline of sociology.

SOCIAL CLASS

You will also notice that, even though studies of gender, race, ethnicity, and work take you in quite different directions, all frequently share an emphasis on inequalities in income, wealth, or property, and on resulting inequalities in power. On average, women earn about 75 percent of what men earn. Older women are much more likely than are older men to be living in poverty. Immigrants and, particularly, First Nations are more likely to be unemployed or, if they are employed, to be in low-paying jobs. Owners of large workplaces are wealthier than most other members of society, and employees in professional and managerial occupations typically earn much more than lower-level employees. Recognizing, then, the extent to which such material inequality (that is, differences in income and wealth or property) parallels and overlaps with other social hierarchies, the rest of this chapter will focus primarily on material inequality or, after we define the terms, on social class and class structure.

Definitions of the concept of **class** vary considerably, as we will see in the next section, which outlines different theories of social stratification. I prefer to use the term in a general sense to indicate the position of an individual or a family within an economic hierarchy, along with others who have roughly the same amount of control over or access to economic or material resources. For example, an individual can be said to be a member of a class of large landowners, a class of wage-labourers and salaried workers (that is, the "working class"), or a "professional/managerial class." It is their similar economic situation and opportunities, a result of their shared position within a society's system of economic production, that makes these individuals members of the same class. In turn, we can use the term **class structure** to refer to the overall economic hierarchy comprising all such classes, choosing the word *structure* deliberately to indicate the relative stability and permanence of this social ranking.

Do you think of yourself as a member of a specific social class? Probably not very often, if at all. Like most North Americans, you probably have a reasonably good idea of how well off you are compared with others in your community. You probably have some sense of where your education, occupation, and income (or the education, occupation, and income of your parents) fit in some general hierarchy of **socioeconomic status.** "Class," however, is unlikely to be part of your everyday vocabulary. Nor is it typically part of the media's vocabulary. The newspaper stories I examined earlier, for example, identified a number of different dimensions of stratification, but social class was not among them.

This, however, does not make class a useless concept. As I have already suggested, pronounced patterns of material inequality exist in our society and overlap with most other dimensions of social stratification. The economic hierarchy is obviously not completely closed, but it is relatively stable and permanent, and it comprises some fairly distinct categories of individuals with similar amounts of control over material resources. Hence, it is useful to try to identify the classes that make up the stratification system (or class structure), to seek to understand their origin, and to examine the effects of membership in them on individuals and families. Rather than discarding the concept of class because few people think in these terms, we should perhaps ask why few people think about social classes despite their prominence. This is one of the topics discussed in the next section.

EXPLANATIONS OF SOCIAL STRATIFICATION

Now that you have considered some examples of social stratification and learned some new concepts, it is time to examine theories (or explanations) of social stratification elaborated by a number of important social thinkers, including some who were analyzing society many decades ago and others who have written about it more recently. As you will see, it is important to take into account the time and place in which a social theory was developed, since theorists construct their social explanations on the basis of what they see around them and expect to see in the future.

KARL MARX: CAPITALISM, EXPLOITATION, AND CLASS CONFLICT

Karl Marx had an immense impact on how we think about social stratification. He was born in Germany in 1818 but lived in England from 1849 until he died in 1883. His writings about the social and economic forces that brought about economic change look back over history but focus particularly on the rapidly changing European world that he observed during his lifetime. This was a time when industrial capitalism was transforming the economy and society. Large, mechanized, factory-based systems of production were emerging; cities were growing rapidly as peasants were being forced off the land or attracted to the city by the possibility of jobs in factories; and material inequality was extreme, as factory owners and merchants made huge profits while labourers lived in poverty. Trade unions, labour laws, and other arrangements that offer some protection to workers did not yet exist. Thus, as Marx observed, the Industrial Revolution was a time when both the level of economic production and the degree of inequality in society increased tremendously.

Modes of Production and Social Classes

Marx called the system of economic activity in a society its **mode of production.** In turn, its major components were the **means of production** (technology, capital investments, and raw materials) and the **social relations of production** (the relationships between the main classes involved in production). Slavery had been the primary mode of production in some societies in earlier times, and feudalism, an economic system in which peasants worked for landowners, not for a wage but for some share of the produce, was the mode of production that gave way to industrial capitalism in Europe.

Within industrial capitalism, Marx identified two major classes: the capitalist class, or **bourgeoisie,** which owned the means of production; and the **proletariat,** or working class, which exchanged its labour for wages. He also described a middle class—the **petite bourgeoisie**—comprising independent owners/producers (farmers, for example) and small-business owners. Marx expected this middle class largely to disappear as capitalism matured and drew some of its members up into the bourgeoisie but pushed most down into the proletariat. Of much greater importance in his theory of class inequality and social change was the relationship between workers and owners.

Marx reasoned that the value of a product sold was directly proportional to the average amount of labour needed to produce it. Thus, for example, an elegant piece of furniture was more valuable than its component pieces mainly because of the labour invested in it by the worker(s) who built it. Marx argued that the value of goods produced by wage-labourers far exceeded the amount needed to pay their wages and the cost of raw materials, technology, and other factors of production. Marx referred to this excess as **surplus value.** According to Marx, when commodities were sold, their surplus value was turned into profits for the owner. Marx viewed this as an exploitive relationship but one that differed from the exploitive relationships that characterized slavery or feudalism. After all, factory workers were paid a wage for their labour and were not legally forced to stay with the job. However, because most workers had few other options for making a living, and because owners controlled all aspects of the work, the legal freedom of wage-labourers to change jobs was, in practical terms, an illusion.

Class Conflict and Class Consciousness

The idea of **class conflict** among the major classes in a society was the driving force behind Marx's theory of social change. He argued that previous modes of production had collapsed and been replaced because of class conflict. Feudalism in Europe had given way to capitalism as a result of the growing power of the merchant class relative to the traditional alliance of landowners and the aristocracy, and the deteriorating relationship between landowners and peasants. Furthermore, Marx argued, capitalism would eventually be replaced by a socialist mode of production, in which private ownership of property would disappear, along with the exploitation and inequality it produced. The impetus for this massive change would again be widespread class conflict, this time between wage-labourers and the owners of the means of production, as inequality between these two classes became more pronounced.

Marx held that this revolution would take place only when members of the working class began to recognize that they were being exploited. In other words, Marx did not take it for granted that members of a class would see how their interests were similar. Whereas capitalists might be conscious of their group interests, wage-labourers needed to become aware of their common enemy. They needed to be transformed from a "class in itself" to a "class for itself." Thus, **class consciousness** was an important social-psychological component of Marx's theory of social inequality and social change. His vision of the future was that of a revolutionary upheaval in which the oppressed working class would recognize its enemy, destroy the institutions of capitalism, and replace them with a classless society based on collective ownership of the means of production.

Responses to Marx

During much of the twentieth century, critics of Marx's ideas pointed to the communist countries, with their apparently socialist system of government and absence of private property, and noted that inequality had not disappeared there. Instead, a new hierarchy had emerged, in which control of the political and bureaucratic apparatus was the main basis of power. These observations were largely correct. As a Russian joke from the 1970s noted, under capitalism man exploits man, but under communism it is the other way around.

In fact, I expect that Marx himself would have been highly critical of the Soviet communist system, given the degree to which individual citizens were exploited and harshly treated by a powerful minority. However, it is slowly becoming apparent that the emergence of a capitalist economy in Eastern Europe over the past two decades is leading to increased material inequality but from a different source (Silverman and Yanowitch, 2000). Today, individuals with control over some form of production or access to some marketing system are accumulating wealth while the majority of citizens appear to be no better off than before—indeed, many are worse off. The same pattern of growing social inequality has been observed in China where, despite the continued control of the economy by the Communist Party, some forms of free enterprise have been encouraged (Wu and Xie, 2002). In other words, while Marx's predictions about the inevitable emergence of a classless society have not been borne out, his type of class analysis still has considerable relevance for understanding the changing stratification system in North America, Eastern Europe, and even communist China.

Most theories of social stratification developed after Marx's were essentially a "debate with Marx's ghost" (Zeitlin with Brym, 1991: 117). Some social philosophers and sociologists elaborated on Marx's ideas, while others attempted to refute them. Among the critics, some focused on the absence of widespread class conflict, the growth of the middle class, and the relative decline in material inequality in Western Europe and North America in the twentieth century. I will examine some of these theories below, along with others that tried to develop more complex models of the contemporary class structure while basically following Marx's form of class-based analysis.

MAX WEBER: CLASS AND OTHER DIMENSIONS OF INEQUALITY

Max Weber was born in Germany half a century after Marx—in 1864. Like Marx, he built his analysis of social stratification on a careful reading of history and a thorough analysis of the economic and political events of his day. But because he was only beginning his university studies about the time Marx died, Weber had the advantage of seeing the direction in which a more mature industrial capitalism was taking European society. He continued to write about many aspects of social stratification and social change until his death in 1920.

Class, Status, and Party

Weber shared with Marx a belief that economic inequalities were central to the social stratification system and that the ownership of property was a primary determinant of **power**, or the ability to get others to do what you want them to do. However, he argued that power could lie in controlling other types of resources as well (Weber, 1948 [1922]). Specifically, he proposed that structures of social stratification could be better understood by looking at economic inequalities, hierarchies of prestige (or social honour), and political inequalities (control of power blocs, such as political parties or other organizations)—or, in his words, at "class, status, and party." Although these different hierarchies often overlap, they need not. For example, suddenly wealthy individuals might not receive the prestige they desire, being rejected in "high society" by those with "old money." Similarly, a politician might have considerable power through control of government resources, but might not be very wealthy or, for that matter, have much prestige.

Since Weber lived to see the emergence of white-collar workers, the growth of large private- and public-sector bureaucracies, and the growing power of trade unions, he was able to write about these alternative sources of power in a stratified capitalist society. He provided an insightful analysis of how power resided in the control of top positions in large bureaucratic organizations, even if the officeholder was not an owner of the organization. He recognized that well-educated wage-labourers might not be as powerless as were the factory workers of an earlier era. He also saw that a new class of middle-level, educated workers might not necessarily align themselves with blue-collar workers, and he was less inclined to conclude, as had Marx, that the middle class would disappear (Zeitlin with Brym, 1991: 118–19). In fact, he expected that the number of educated technical and professional workers in bureaucratic capitalist society would increase.

What Weber saw, compared with what Marx saw, was considerably more complexity in the social stratification system because of the growing diversity of the occupational structure and of capitalist enterprises. And although Weber was sometimes pessimistic in his writings about the future of democracy in a bureaucratic capitalist society, he did not link inequality and class conflict to the ultimate demise of capitalism itself, as did Marx. Similarly, although Weber, like Marx, commented on how members of a class might or might not recognize their shared interests, he did not conclude that it was the inevitable destiny of the working class to become a "class for itself."

Social Class and Life-Chances

Despite these divergences in their thinking, Weber, like Marx, placed primary emphasis on the economic underpinnings of social stratification. However, he defined class more broadly than Marx did. Rather than insisting that a limited number of class positions were based on an individual's relationship to the means of production, Weber saw a larger variety of class positions based both on ownership of property and on other labour-market statuses, such as occupation and education. Furthermore, he emphasized the **life-chances** that class positions offer, noting that a higher position in the economic hierarchy, however obtained, provides more power and allows an individual and his or her family to enjoy more of the good things in life.

Thus, the general approach to studying stratification that I outlined earlier, one that recognizes the central importance of class while acknowledging that

Mark Carney, Governor of the Bank of Canada. Weber believed that power resided in the control of top positions in large bureaucratic organizations, even if the officeholder was not an owner of the organization.

SOURCE: © REUTERS/Chris Wattie.

gender, race, and other dimensions of social inequality can also be very important, is in the Weberian tradition. Similarly, my general definition of class as a relatively stable position within an economic hierarchy held by an individual or a family, along with others with roughly the same amount of control over or access to material resources, follows Weber's use of the term.

DAVIS AND MOORE: A FUNCTIONAL THEORY OF STRATIFICATION

Twentieth-Century Affluence and Functionalist Theory

Although a number of other social theorists in Europe and North America wrote about social stratification in the early decades of the twentieth century, I will skip ahead to 1945, when Kingsley Davis and Wilbert Moore published their short but much-debated "principles of social stratification." In Chapter 1, Introducing Sociology, you read about **functionalist theory**, which emphasizes consensus over conflict and seeks to explain the function, for society as a whole, of social institutions and various aspects of social structure. Davis and Moore were part of this intellectual tradition, which arose in reaction to the conflict-oriented and socially radical theories of Marx (and, to a lesser extent, of Weber).

The emergence of functionalism as an alternative theoretical approach can be better understood if we view it as reflecting the highly optimistic view in mid-twentieth-century North America that, because World War II was over and the economy was expanding rapidly, affluence was increasing, social conflict was decreasing, and a harmonious future for society was dawning. Thus, during the several decades following World War II, an era some describe as the golden era of North American capitalism (Marglin and Schor, 1990), many social scientists were attracted to theories that downplayed conflict and emphasized the benefits to all of what seemed like an ever-expanding economy.

The Functional Necessity of Stratification

Davis and Moore (1945) argued that, because inequality exists in all societies, it must be a necessary part of society. All societies, they noted, have a variety of occupational roles that need to be filled, some requiring more training than do others, some having more functional importance, and some being less pleasant and more difficult to perform. To get people to fill important roles and to perform critical tasks well, and to spend time training for high-skill occupations, societies must ensure that the rewards for performance are greater. Thus, for example, doctors and school teachers need to be paid more than factory workers and truck drivers, and thus also rank higher than the latter in terms of social honour and prestige.

In short, according to Davis and Moore, social inequality is both inevitable and functionally necessary for society. But theirs was not a class-based and conflict-prone stratification system. Rather, Davis and Moore described a much more fluid socioeconomic hierarchy, with many different occupational statuses into which individuals are slotted on the basis of their effort and ability. The system is held together by consensus and shared values (not torn apart by conflict, as Marx theorized) because members of society generally agree that the hierarchy is fair and just. It follows that efforts to reduce social inequality will be ineffective and might even be harmful to society.

Criticisms of Davis and Moore

Many criticisms have been levelled against Davis and Moore's theory. For example, although some differences in pay might be justified to reimburse those who spend more years in school preparing for a specific occupation, are the huge income and wealth inequalities we see in our society really necessary? Why do women often earn less than men do, even if they are equally educated and do the same type of work? Are movie stars, professional athletes, and chief executive officers with multimillion-dollar annual incomes really so much more important to society than nurses, daycare workers, prison guards, and most other low-paid workers? And how does a theory like this account for inherited wealth and for the fact that wealth leads to power and the ability to accumulate still more wealth?

Given these criticisms, what accounts for the appeal of this theory? Perhaps it is the kernel of truth at its core that is so attractive—namely, the recognition that, to some extent, differences in income and prestige are based on different amounts of effort and ability. After all, we can easily think of examples of better-paying occupations that require long years of education and training. Nevertheless, this is far from the complete story about inequality in our society, which is much more pronounced than what such differences in effort and ability might lead us to expect. In fact, the theory's appeal probably lies more in its apparent justification of these large inequalities. You might test this hypothesis by explaining the theory, first to someone with a high income or inherited wealth, and then to someone who is unemployed or earning very little. Chances are that the functionalist explanation of stratification would sound much more plausible to the wealthier person.

GERHARD LENSKI: TECHNOLOGY AND STRATIFICATION SYSTEMS

Writing in the 1960s, a time of economic expansion and growing prosperity in North America, Gerhard Lenski (1966) developed a theory of "power and privilege" that attempted to explain the extent of material inequality in both contemporary and past societies. Lenski's explanation recognized power and conflict much more explicitly than had the Davis and Moore functionalist explanation of stratification. And, like Weber, he identified a number of different dimensions of social stratification, such as education and ethnicity, while emphasizing the centrality of economic inequalities. Although he used the term *class*, Lenski did not define it precisely, choosing instead to talk about the ruling elites in society in general terms and about how they managed to maintain their wealth and power at the expense of the masses.

Lenski reasoned that a society's technological base largely determines the degree of inequality within it. In simple hunting-and-gathering societies, he argued, the few resources of the society were distributed primarily on the basis of need. But as societies became more technologically complex, resources in excess of those required to fulfill basic needs were produced. Control of those surplus resources, or privilege, came to be based on power, allowing ruling elites to take a much larger share of these resources for themselves. Thus, the more complex agricultural societies, such as that of precolonial India, developed highly structured governing and tax-collecting systems, through which the privileged ruling elites accumulated immense amounts of wealth, while the masses lived in poverty.

As a result of industrialization and the complexity of modern technology, this "age-old evolutionary trend toward ever-increasing inequality" (Lenski, 1966: 308) was reversed. Owners of the means of production could no longer control the production process directly and had to rely instead on well-educated managerial and technical workers to keep the complex system operating. Education broadened the horizons of these middle-level employees, introducing them to ideas of democracy, encouraging them to demand a larger share of the profits they were helping to produce, and making them more articulate in their demands for equality.

Thus, Lenski's theory proposed a causal link among complex industrial technology, the higher education of workers, and workers' insistence on sharing the growing wealth of an industrial society. But why would employers give in to such demands? Because, argued Lenski, the industrial elite needed educated workers—they could not produce wealth without them. Equally important, the much greater productivity of industrial societies compared with preindustrial societies meant that the elite could "make economic concessions in relative terms without necessarily suffering any loss in absolute terms" (Lenski, 1966: 314). Because the economic pie was so much bigger, everyone could have a larger slice.

In one obvious sense, Lenski's theory resembled the functional theory of stratification—both noted that better-educated and more highly skilled workers are paid more. However, unlike the functionalist approach, Lenski's theory clearly took power differences into account, emphasizing how the extent of accumulation of wealth by elites, or the degree of material inequality, depends on the power and bargaining ability of middle-level workers. In fact, Lenski placed material inequality at the centre of his theory of stratification. But in contrast to Marx's nineteenth-century predictions of growing inequality as industrial capitalism matured, Lenski, writing in the middle of the twentieth century, saw a movement toward a more equal distribution of society's wealth.

ERIK OLIN WRIGHT: A NEO-MARXIST APPROACH

In reaction against functionalism, Lenski (1966) brought power and conflict back into his explanation of social inequality. He placed material inequalities resulting from one group's domination of another at the centre of his model, thus coming closer to the approach taken by Marx and Weber. But he did not carry through with a traditional Marxist analysis built around the relationships of different classes to the means of production. In contrast, a number of neo-Marxist scholars, writing in the 1970s and 1980s, attempted to update the original Marxist model so it could be applied to the late twentieth century. We will discuss only one theorist from the neo-Marxist camp, Erik Olin Wright.

Although Marx acknowledged the existence of a middle class comprising several distinct groups, including independent producers and small-business owners, he predicted that this middle class would disappear and so spent much more time writing about the relationship between the two primary classes (capitalists and workers). Wright's contribution lies in recognizing that as industrial capitalism matured, the middle class had grown and become more diverse, and in trying to understand the class dynamics of our more complex capitalist system of production. Of particular importance in Wright's theory is his notion of **contradictory class locations**—that is, occupational groupings that have divided loyalties within a class structure. For example, although managers work for capitalists, supervising lower-level employees and trying to get them to produce as much as possible, managers are themselves employees, potentially exploited by owners. Considering the substantial numbers of people in such contradictory locations, we can begin to understand why the widespread class conflict envisioned by Marx has seldom emerged.

Wright (1985) also argued that exploitation of one class by another can occur through control of property or the means of production (as Marx had insisted), as well as through ownership of skill or credential assets and control of high positions within organizations. Thus, he identified three classes of owners (the bourgeoisie, small employers, and the petite bourgeoisie with no employees), and nine classes of wage-labourers (nonowners), differentiated on two dimensions: the possession of organizational assets and of skill/credential assets (Wright, 1985: 88). For example, "expert managers" (such as engineers or lawyers in senior management positions within large companies) fill a class location characterized by extensive organizational assets and high skill/credential assets, in contrast to basic "proletarians," who have no specific skill/credential assets and no management or supervisory responsibilities (see Figure 6.1).

Despite his intention of developing a neo-Marxist theoretical model updated to the late twentieth century, Wright's theory is similar to Weber's view of class structure in some ways (Grabb, 2007). Specifically, the different class locations created by the intersection of organizational and skill/credential assets remind us of the different classes Weber described as he commented on how similar educational and occupational statuses resulted in similar control over and access to material resources. Even so, Wright's theory of class structure and his observations about contradictory locations within it are useful, because he deliberately attempted to incorporate the complexities of modern capitalist society into his explanation of social inequality.

FIGURE 6.1 ERIC OLIN WRIGHT'S TYPOLOGY OF CLASS LOCATION IN CAPITALIST SOCIETY

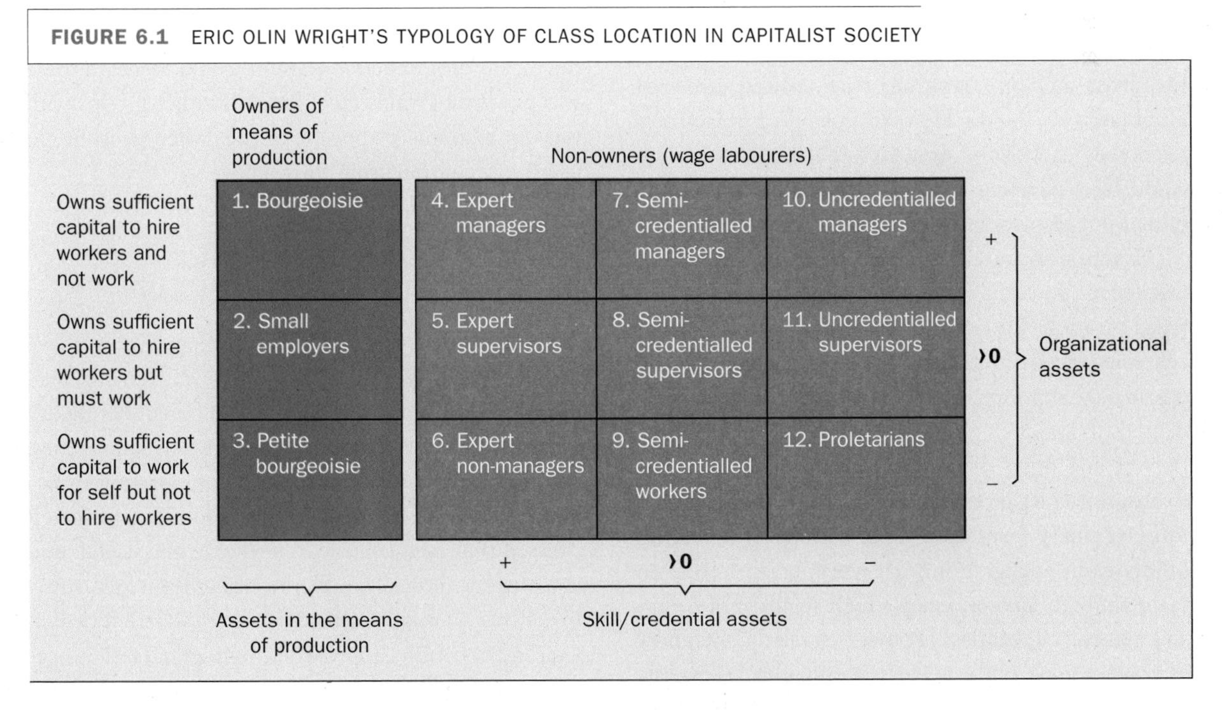

SOURCE: From Erik Olin Wright, *Classes*. 1985, p. 88. Reprinted with permission from Verso Books.

FRANK PARKIN: A NEO-WEBERIAN APPROACH

Wright attempted to bring Marx's class analysis back into the discussion of contemporary forms of social stratification. Frank Parkin (1972, 1979) was equally explicit in stating his intellectual debts to Max Weber's discussions of power, class, and social stratification (Grabb, 2007). In fact, Parkin went so far as to argue that neo-Marxist scholars, espousing what he calls "professorial Marxism" (1979: x), were merely putting forth dressed-up Weberian arguments. As a neo-Weberian, Parkin criticized traditional Marxist and contemporary neo-Marxist analyses for failing to take into account gender, race, religious, and other forms of social stratification that do not grow out of the relations of production in capitalist society but clearly have an origin and a permanency all of their own (1979: 4–5). Nevertheless, like both Weber and Marx before him, Parkin continued to emphasize the importance of property relations in contemporary stratification systems (Grabb, 2007).

Among Parkin's most useful contributions to stratification theory is his explanation of how patterns of structured inequality, whether based on class, gender, race, or some other ascribed or achieved status, are maintained or changed. To do so, Parkin returned to a concept introduced by Weber, that of **social closure.** Parkin defines this term as "the process by which social collectivities seek to maximize rewards by restricting access to resources and opportunities to a limited circle of eligibles" (1979: 44). He then goes on to elaborate two types of closure strategies that help us understand how patterns of social inequality are maintained but also sometimes altered.

Exclusion refers to the organized efforts of privileged, powerful groups to maintain their advantaged position. Processes of exclusion can range from centuries-old caste systems in closed societies to the use, in contemporary open societies, of educational credentials to maintain power and privilege. For example, lawyers and other professional groups have managed to ensure, via legal restrictions, that only they can perform certain types of work in our society. By excluding others from engaging in such work, it is possible to maintain high income, enjoy a high standard of living, and exercise a great deal of power. Similarly, members of trade unions can use legal sanctions to keep non-members, who might have the same skills, from taking on some well-paying jobs.

In contrast, **usurpation** refers to the efforts of excluded groups in a stratification system to gain advantages and power. As Parkin put it, all such actions have as their goal "biting into the resources and benefits accruing to dominant groups in society" (1979: 74). As with exclusionary practices, usurpation efforts range from lobbying and voting for social change to outright revolt against groups in power. Thus, over the past several decades, we have seen successful efforts by women's groups, First Nations groups, and other disadvantaged groups to change the balance of power and privilege in Canada. Going back further, labour unions took even stronger, sometimes illegal, actions to gain new powers and a more equitable distribution of resources for their members.

Thus, like Lenski, Parkin took a keen interest in the power struggles in society between groups with more and less power (Grabb, 2007). However, Parkin's neo-Weberian theory does not contain a premise of inevitability, either one of increased inequality and eventual social revolution as Marx predicted, or one of reduced inequality resulting from technological change and economic growth as Lenski predicted. Parkin did see a clear trend with respect to processes of social closure. With the growing emphasis on education in modern society, the use of educational credentials to maintain power and privilege has become more widespread. As a result, well-educated professionals have become a powerful class grouping, sometimes almost as powerful as wealthy capitalists who control the means of production (Grabb, 2007). Beneath these two powerful groups are a range of other groups with varying amounts of power, trying, when possible, to usurp more power from those above.

EXPLANATIONS OF SOCIAL STRATIFICATION: SUMMING UP

There are other theories of social inequality we have not discussed (Grabb, 2007). However, having been introduced to Marx and Weber, the functional theory of stratification, and several more recent approaches, you now have a sense of the range of existing explanations. Davis and Moore's functionalist approach stressed that inequality was inevitable and useful, and it downplayed social conflict resulting from inequality. In contrast to this consensus approach to stratification, a variety of conflict approaches highlighted differences in power resulting from and contributing to material inequality, the exploitation of some groups by others, and the social conflict that could result.

The theories we have reviewed differ in the assumptions they make and the conclusions they draw about the future of material inequality. Marx clearly saw inequality and exploitation of the working class increasing, and he predicted that class conflict would lead to the death of capitalism. Although Weber was not convinced that a socialist society would eventually emerge, neither did he argue that inequalities would gradually decrease (Grabb, 2007). As a neo-Weberian, Parkin takes a similar stance. Wright's emphasis on the growing number of middle-class locations also does not suggest an increasing level of material inequality, but neither does it imply the opposite. However, the functionalists and Lenski, writing in an era of economic growth and widespread optimism about the ability of capitalism to raise the overall standard of living, clearly felt that material inequalities were shrinking in Western industrial societies.

The various explanations also differ in the degree to which they emphasize class differences in access to and control of material resources. For Marx, class was the primary determining factor in this regard. Weber, using the term *class* somewhat more broadly, emphasized its central role but recognized other important dimensions of social stratification. So, too, did Parkin, who explicitly discussed the independent effects of gender, race, and religion. Davis and Moore basically ignored the concept of class. Although Lenski again focused more directly on economic inequality, he did not really describe society in terms of distinct classes, as Wright, in his neo-Marxist approach, did. Thus, if you view these theories in temporal order, it appears that social class, at least as defined in the Weberian sense, has made a comeback as an explanatory concept. In the following section, we turn from theories of social inequality to data on occupations and material inequality in Canada to see if the concept of social class still has relevance in contemporary society.

OCCUPATIONS, SOCIAL CLASS, AND INEQUALITY IN CANADA

OCCUPATIONAL SHIFTS OVER TIME

Some of the explanations of social stratification we reviewed above, such as Lenski's, focus directly on occupations while others, such as Wright's, rely on occupational data to discuss social class. Consequently, it would be useful to begin this section by examining occupational shifts in Canada over the past century. Table 6.1 displays the types of occupations most common near the beginning (1911) and in the middle (1951) of the last century, and near the beginning of the twenty-first century (2006). The biggest change was the decline in agricultural occupations, from 34 percent of all labour force participants in 1911 to only 2 percent in 2006. Other natural resource-based occupations (forestry, fishing, mining) also declined, but not as steeply. Manufacturing occupations increased in relative terms (from 14 to 17 percent) between the beginning and middle of the last century, but by 2006 had dropped to only 7 percent of the total labour force. The decline in manufacturing jobs has continued since then, intensifying in 2009 as the Canadian economy shrank as a result of global financial and economic instability (Usalcas, 2010).

Manufacturing, construction, transportation, and resource-based occupations are typically called blue-collar occupations, in contrast to white-collar occupations in the managerial, professional, clerical, sales, and service categories. Table 6.1 shows that white-collar occupations have come to greatly outnumber blue-collar occupations as industrial capitalism has matured. In 2006, 13 percent of Canadian labour force participants were in managerial/administrative occupations, up from only 5 percent in 1911.

Professional/technical occupations had multiplied by almost six times in relative terms, from 4 to 23 percent. Clerical, sales, and service occupations also had become much more common, from a total of only 17 percent in 1911 to 37 percent of all occupations in 2006.

What do these occupational changes tell us with respect to our previous discussion of the bases of social stratification? First, as various theories have indicated, the proportion of occupations requiring higher education has increased, while the proportion of traditional blue-collar, "working-class" occupations has declined. With the expansion in white-collar occupations, average incomes rose, at least until the early 1980s. Thus, to the extent that occupational data can inform us about class structure in the Weberian sense, occupational shifts over the past century suggest greater class diversity, rather than a polarization of classes, as a strict reading of Marx's theory would predict, and a rising standard of living for Canadian workers, rather than increasing poverty and exploitation.

And what do the numbers in Table 6.1 not tell us? First, they do not distinguish between the

TABLE 6.1 OCCUPATIONAL DISTRIBUTION OF LABOUR FORCE PARTICIPANTS,* CANADA, 1911, 1951, 2006

OCCUPATION TYPE	1911	1951	2006
Managerial/ administrative	5%	8%	13%
Professional/ technical	4	7	23
Clerical	4	11	12
Sales	5	7	11
Service	8	10	14
Manufacturing	14	17	7
Transportation	6	8	9
Construction	5	6	6
Agriculture	34	16	2
Forestry/ fishing/mining	5	4	2
Other occupa-tions	10	6	1
Total	**100**	**100**	**100**

*Labour force participants include both the employed (paid employees and the self-employed) and the unemployed (those who want a paid job but who are unable to find one). These data are based on the population aged 15 and older.

SOURCES: 1911 and 1951 data adapted from 1911 and 1951 Census results, presented by O'Neill (1991); 2006 data adapted from 2006 Census results, Statistics Canada (2006).

occupations typically held by women and those typically held by men. Since the middle of the last century, a rising proportion of women have been entering the labour force and moving into better jobs. But, as you will see (Chapter 7, Gender Inequality), women are still more likely to be employed in clerical, sales, and service occupations (what might be called a "pink-collar sector") than in blue-collar occupations or in higher-status and better-paying managerial and professional occupations. Thus, gender-based labour-market stratification continues to exist, intersecting with class-based stratification.

Second, the data in Table 6.1 do not directly describe workers' relationships to the means of production, in Marx's terms. Statistics Canada has never collected and categorized national data along these lines, but since the early 1980s a series of Ontario-wide surveys have used Erik Olin Wright's typology (Figure 6.1) to profile the class composition of that province (Livingstone, 1999: 158). In 1996, the Ontario employed labour force comprised corporate capitalists (1 percent), small employers (8 percent), the own-account self-employed or petite bourgeoisie (14 percent), managers (8 percent), supervisors (4 percent), professional/semi-professional employees (19 percent), and service and industrial workers (46 percent). The small sample size in this study (about six hundred respondents) means that these estimates are not precise, and the single-province focus does not allow for generalizations to all of Canada. Even so, this study clearly shows that the large class of paid workers contains several distinct types with varying amounts of decision-making authority and substantial differences in income, status, and occupational power.

Third, neither Table 6.1 (which displays occupational change over time) nor the 1996 Ontario study (which uses class data from only one point in time) can show how the Canadian class structure might be changing. But we can get one indication of change from other data on self-employment. Between 1946 and 1981, a period of significant decline in the number of people employed in agriculture, the proportion of self-employed Canadians dropped dramatically, from 33 percent to 10 percent. However, beginning in the 1980s, a slow reversal of the trend began in Canada, the United States, and other Western industrialized countries. By 2008, 10 percent of employed Canadians were own-account self-employed (without any employees) and 5 percent employed others (Krahn, Lowe, and Hughes, 2011: ch. 2). Researchers are uncertain whether more Canadians are voluntarily choosing self-employment or are being pushed into it as a result of higher levels of unemployment and growing corporate and public-sector downsizing. Nevertheless, the reversal of the decline in self-employment—the increase in the size of the petite bourgeoisie—is something theorists are trying to explain as they attempt to further update Marx's ideas of class-based stratification (Myles and Turegun, 1994).

Finally, the data in Table 6.1 do not reflect some of the dramatic changes in employment opportunities and outcomes that have been occurring in the past four decades. I will return to this topic later, but for now I will simply note that unemployment rates have risen and fallen and are now rising again, part-time and temporary work have become much more common, and income growth appears to have stopped, while income and wealth inequality have increased. Consequently, the higher standard of living that accompanied occupational changes in the second half of the twentieth century is no longer guaranteed for all those in middle-status occupations. Thus we need to look carefully at the distributional side of the occupation and class structures, at "who gets what" in return for their employment (Westergaard, 1995). But before examining changing patterns of material inequality in Canada, I will first discuss another important feature of stratification systems in modern societies—opportunities for occupational mobility and status attainment.

OCCUPATIONAL MOBILITY AND STATUS ATTAINMENT

Many people move up the occupational and income ladders during their careers, frequently after investing in higher education of some kind. Some move down, often because of economic circumstances beyond their control. Sociologists have conducted a great deal of research on such **intragenerational occupational mobility** (mobility within an individual's lifetime) and on **intergenerational occupational mobility,** the process of reaching an occupational location higher or lower than the location your parents held. Such research is interesting in itself, since we all like to compare how well we have done relative to others. It is also theoretically important since it tests hypotheses derived from theories of inequality (the functionalist perspective, for example) that propose that higher positions in society are generally filled by those most qualified.

If the only intergenerational occupational mobility we observed was a result of better-qualified people moving up to replace those who were less qualified, we should also see an equivalent amount of downward mobility. Such a scenario of "musical jobs" or, to use the technical term, **circulatory mobility,** does not really describe the Canadian situation over the past half-century, however, because of the pronounced parallel process of **structural mobility** resulting from a significant change in the shape of Canada's overall occupational structure. As noted earlier, over the past half-century, industrial societies, including Canada, experienced a great deal of growth in white-collar occupations (clerical, managerial, and professional positions) as traditional agricultural and blue-collar industrial jobs declined in relative importance. Hence, with an increase in the number of higher-status jobs, each generation had more chances than the preceding one to improve the status of their jobs.

Even so, Canadian studies conducted over the past several decades indicate that Canada, like the United States, has a relatively open stratification system, more so than countries like Sweden, the United Kingdom, France, and the Netherlands (Wanner, 2009). In other words, in Canada relatively more people have been able to move up the occupational ladder relative to their parents. During the second half of the last century, the Canadian occupational structure opened up for women and men in different ways. The steep decline in agricultural employment meant that many men moved out of the agricultural occupations held by their fathers. For women, the major shift was away from the housework that had been the main female occupation for their mothers' generation. For both sexes, expansion of postsecondary educational opportunities, leading to higher status occupations, played an important role (Wanner, 2009). However, most of this opening of the stratification system occurred between 1973 and 1986. Little changed in terms of mobility opportunities in the following decades.

Thus, overall, Canadian mobility studies find only a limited amount of direct occupational inheritance across generations. Yet those at or near the top of the occupational hierarchy are still more likely to pass their advantages on to their children. As Richard Wanner (2009: 129) concludes, "Canada is still a stratified society characterized by a considerable amount of inheritance of privilege." This intergenerational transfer of advantage takes place primarily through different levels of access to the postsecondary education system.

Research in Canada and other Western countries examining the process of **occupational status attainment** has shown, not surprisingly, that the most important influence on the status of an individual's current job is the status of that person's first job. Individuals who enter the labour market as articling lawyers, for example, typically make their way higher up the occupational ladder than do those who began as unskilled labourers. In turn, the status of that first job is heavily influenced by the level of education completed. Such findings obviously lend some support to theories suggesting that more-qualified people, as indicated by higher education, end up in higher-status and better-paying occupations.

However, many studies have also traced education-job linkages back to the previous generation, showing that those who obtain more education and hence better jobs are more likely to come from families with better-educated parents. For example, a 14-year longitudinal study of high-school graduates in Edmonton, Alberta, showed that young people from families in which one or both parents had completed university were almost three times more likely than others were to complete university themselves (Krahn, 2009). For a variety of reasons (for example, more money for higher education, more well-educated role models), children from more advantaged backgrounds can build on their initial advantages.

THE DISTRIBUTION OF WEALTH

Evidence from various sources demonstrates that a small number of people continue to own or control a very large portion of the wealth in Canada. For example, in 2011, 54-year-old David Thomson and his family were estimated to be worth $23 billion. While only number 17 on the *Forbes Magazine* list of "The World's Billionaires" (2011), they were Canada's wealthiest family. In contrast, in 2009, the median net worth (the difference between the total assets owned by a family, including a home, and its debt) for Canadian low-income families (excluding seniors) in which at least one person was employed was only $19 000, compared with $257 700 for non-low-income families in which someone was employed (Luong, 2011).

These statistics highlight the wealth gap between low-income and average-income families, and the wealth chasm between these two groups and very rich Canadian families, such as the Thomsons, the Westons, and the Irvings, who have business holdings spread around the globe as well as in Canada. Together with highly paid CEOs and corporate directors, these wealthy families clearly form a distinct upper class, the haute (or high) bourgeoisie in Marx's terms. By way of example, in 2010, the CEOs of the top one hundred companies listed on the Toronto Stock Exchange received a median compensation package (earnings, bonuses, and stock options) of $8.38 million (Mackenzie, 2012). It would take the average Canadian worker (employed full-time and year-round), with annual earnings of about $44 300 in 2010, 189 years to earn as much money as any of these one hundred CEOs receive in one year.

At the other end of the wealth scale are the 7 percent of Canadian families (excluding seniors) with low income and no wage earners who reported a median net worth in 2009 of only $1000. These families (about 1.2 million people in total) typically relied on government transfer payments (for example, employment, welfare, or disability support payments) and had trouble making ends meet. Three out of 10 (29 percent) were at least two months behind in paying bills, and almost one in 10 (8 percent) was at least two months behind on loan payments (Luong, 2011).

Over the long term, the economic growth experienced in Western industrialized countries, along with some income redistribution efforts by governments, have had an equalizing effect on the distribution of household wealth. Wolff (1991), for example, showed that inequality in household wealth decreased between 1920 and the 1970s in Sweden, Britain, and the United States. Although comparable data are not available for Canada for the same period, it is likely that a similar decline occurred here as well. However, Wolff also noted that, in the mid-1970s, wealth inequality began to increase again in the United States and Sweden (it remained constant in Britain). What about Canada?

A recent study reveals that, on average, Canadian families were considerably wealthier in 2005 than they were in 1970 (Morissette and Zhang, 2007). However, there is more to this story. Wealth inequality declined between 1970 and 1977, remained steady until 1984,

SOURCE: © Artizans Entertainment.

and then increased considerably in the next 20 years. Thus, back in 1984, the top 10 percent of Canadian families owned 51.8 percent of total family wealth. By 2005, this figure had increased to 58.2 percent (Morissette and Zhang, 2007). In other words, the wealth gap between rich and poor families has been growing over the past two decades in Canada.

INCOME DISTRIBUTION

High-Paying and Low-Paying Occupations

Although most people have virtually no contact with the wealthiest families in Canada, we are much more aware of, or perhaps are even members of, a larger, not quite as wealthy but still very affluent group of households containing one or more individuals in high-paying occupations. By way of example, 2006 census data for individuals working full-time year-round revealed Canadian dentists earned an average of $142 100 (in 2005), while medical specialists earned even more ($201 847). Judges earned almost as much ($192 448) while lawyers had to be content with average yearly earnings of $142 345 (Statistics Canada, 2006). In contrast, cashiers working full-time year-round earned only a fraction of this ($20 140), as did hotel clerks ($23 790), hair stylists and barbers ($19 746), and pet groomers and other animal-care workers ($20 898).

Using the term *class* in the Weberian sense, you could label individuals in well-paid managerial and professional occupations as members of an upper-middle class, given their high incomes and their access to and control of material resources through their employment positions. In contrast, retail workers and those employed in some service occupations (for example, food and beverage services, child-care and home-support services) work in the low-paying, insecure occupations that we might describe as the lower working class.

These occupational earning patterns hide large gender differences. Thus, among people working full-time and full-year, women's earnings were 71 percent of men's in 2007, a figure that has not changed significantly since 1995 (Krahn, Lowe, and Hughes, 2011: ch. 4). Female dentists earned, on average, 63 percent of what their male counterparts earned in 2005 ($100 047 and $158 094, respectively). Among senior managers, women earned 60 percent of what men earned. Female university professors, however, reported 2005 earnings of $78 798, more than 80 percent of the earnings of male professors ($96 281). Among the lower-paid occupations, male janitors reported annual 2005 earnings of $35 439, considerably higher than the earnings of their female counterparts ($26 980). Similar gender differences are observed in all occupational groupings (Statistics Canada, 2006) but, as these examples demonstrate, the female–male earnings ratio does vary considerably by occupation.

Income Inequality

The 2006 census data discussed above give some indication of the distribution in Canada of employment earnings, the largest component of total income, which also includes income from investments, government assistance, and all other sources. Studies of income tax data show that the level of total income inequality in Canada has increased dramatically over the past seven decades. In 1945, at the end of World War II, the most advantaged 10 percent of Canadians (the top decile) received 37 percent of all income (Yalnizyan, 2010). While this figure fluctuated over the next four decades, income inequality in Canada slowly declined. In 1985, the top decile received 35 percent of all income. However, the long-term trend then reversed, and income inequality increased steadily during the next two decades—in 2007, the top 10 percent received 41 percent of all income (Yalnizyan, 2010; see Box 6.1).

THE POOR

Defining and Measuring Poverty

Poverty can be defined in different ways. We could talk about **absolute poverty,** arguing that the poor are those who have barely enough to stay alive, like many of the inhabitants of poor countries. Or we could conclude, as most Canadians do, that **relative poverty** is really what matters. If your neighbours own their homes, drive cars, eat in nice restaurants, put money into pension plans, and take vacations outside the country, while you rent a small apartment, ride the bus, look forward to a meal at McDonald's, have no savings, and read about foreign countries in the public library, you probably consider yourself poor. According to this definition, Canada does have a considerable number of poor people.

Most discussions of poverty in Canada rely on the **low-income cutoff** or **LICO** (commonly, though unofficially, known as the "poverty line"),

BOX 6.1 CANADA'S RICHEST 1 PERCENT

In 2007, a Canadian in the richest 1 percent of tax filers made a minimum of $169 300. The average income of this class was $404 500.

Tax records for Canada's richest 1 percent go back to 1920. They show that the top 1 percent of tax filers increased their share of total income from the mid-1920s to the mid-1930s. Their share declined only after Canada went to war. From the beginning of World War II to 1977, the income share of the richest 1 percent was cut almost in half, falling from 14 percent in 1941 to 7.7 percent in 1977. Then the trend reversed direction. The share of all income going to the richest 1 percent almost doubled between 1982 and 2007, rising from 7.9 percent to 13.8 percent. By 2007, the 246 000 Canadians lucky enough to be among the richest 1 percent claimed a bigger piece of the income pie than at any time since 1941 (see Figure 6.2).

A recent study shows that, in the early 1990s, the average income of the top 10 percent was eight times as high as the average income of the bottom 10 percent (Organisation for Economic Co-operation and Development [OECD], 2011). By 2008, the top decile reported 10 times as much income as the lowest decile. Income inequality has increased in most rich countries over the past two decades, but income inequality in Canada has been above average. Inequality was lower in Sweden, Norway, and Switzerland than in Canada, and higher in the United States and the United Kingdom.

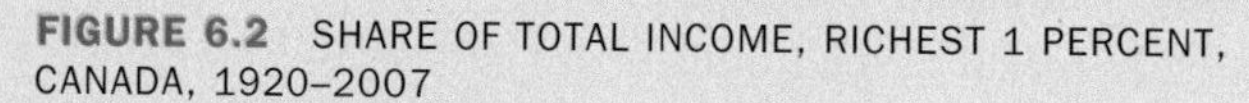

What accounts for increasing income inequality since the mid-1970s? As in most other Western industrialized countries, part-time and temporary work became much more common in Canada, leading to lower total income for a larger proportion of workers in many industries (Fuller and Vosko, 2008). At the same time, the most highly paid corporate CEOs and managers were given ever-larger compensation packages while the Canadian income tax system was altered so that the highest earners paid a lower rate of income tax than they had paid in the past. Back in 1948, the super-rich could expect to pay 80 percent income tax on annual earnings over $2.37 million (in today's dollars). Today, the top marginal tax rate is 43 percent (Yasnizyan, 2010: 4). With less money collected through income taxes, there has also been less money for the government to redistribute to the poor.

FIGURE 6.2 SHARE OF TOTAL INCOME, RICHEST 1 PERCENT, CANADA, 1920–2007

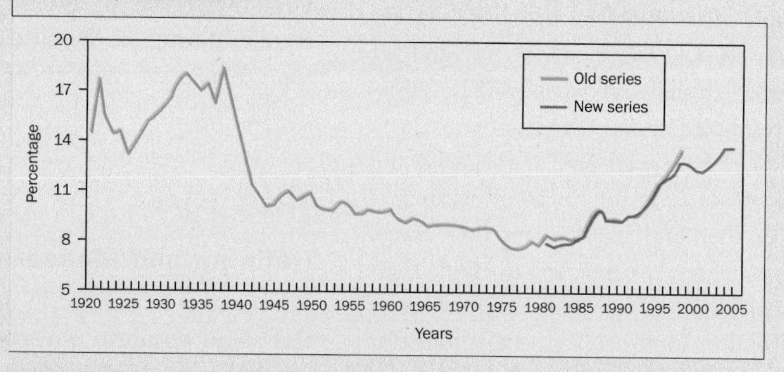

SOURCE: Yalnizyan, Armine. (2010). *The Rise of Canada's Richest 1%*. Ottawa: Canadian Centre for Policy Alternatives, pp. 11–12.

estimated by Statistics Canada on the basis of data obtained from its ongoing *Survey of Labour and Income Dynamics*. According to this survey, the average Canadian spends about 43 percent of after-tax income on the basic necessities (food, shelter, and clothing). To establish the LICO, Statistics Canada adds 20 percent to this figure (Statistics Canada, 2011). Hence, anyone spending more than 63 percent of after-tax income on the basic necessities is considered a low-income earner (see Box 6.2). Obviously, some people budget better than others do, so these are average cost estimates. However, there is no denying that the cost of living is higher in larger urban centres and that it takes more money to feed and clothe additional people, so different LICOs are calculated for communities of various sizes and for families of various sizes within those communities (National Council of Welfare, 2010). For example, based on 2009 income data, Statistics Canada sets the after-tax LICO for a single person living in a city with more

BOX 6.2 MEASURING POVERTY: A CHALLENGE FOR CANADA

Who is poor in Canada? It depends on the measure used, and that depends on who is measuring. Different researchers use different criteria. If poverty is defined as including only those whose physical existence is endangered, then a very small percentage of Canadians are poor—about 5% according to the Fraser Institute. If poverty is considered in relation to community norms and standards and being poor means that a person cannot fully participate in society, then the poverty rate is around 12% to 15%. This definition is used by anti-poverty organizations.

Canada does not have an official poverty line—an income level below which someone is considered poor, depending on family size and where they live—adopted by federal and provincial/territorial governments. The closest thing to an official poverty measure [is] ... the Low-Income Cut-off or LICO (before and after taxes).

LICOs set an income threshold based on spending on necessities as a percentage of income (people on low incomes spend a higher percentage of income on necessities than people with higher incomes). LICOs have a long history, but they are increasingly out-of-date because Statistics Canada has not updated them and no longer collects the data that would allow them to be updated. LICOs reflect 1992 spending patterns. ...

There are two other measures of poverty levels that have been used widely in Canada. Low-Income Measures (LIMs) set an income threshold relative to median family income. The median means half of family incomes are above it and half are below it. A poverty level of 50% or half that median income is commonly used for the LIMs (before and after tax).

Market Basket Measure (MBMs) are based on the cost of a basket of goods. What is in the basket was developed by officials at the federal department of Human Resources and Social Development Canada. The basket includes food, shelter, clothing, transportation, and other necessary household goods or services. The cost of a basket of goods varies depending on where you live. The cost of a basket of goods is compared to disposable income to determine low income.

The LIM is relatively straightforward and is useful for comparisons with other countries. An assumption behind this kind of comparison is that being poor is relative to a nation's standard of living. Half the median income in a developing country will be much lower than half the median income in Canada. The Market Basket has the advantage of clarity in describing a basket of goods, but the validity of what is in the basket is arguable (e.g., five pairs of long underwear, but no computer access). ...

These poverty measures (LICO, LIM, and MBM) do not lead to dramatically different poverty rates at the national level. But there can be important differences between these measures when considering geography (by municipality or province, for example) and family composition (single individuals, families with children, etc.).

SOURCE: Shillington, Richard and John Stapleton. (2010). *Cutting Through the Fog: Why Is It So Hard to Make Sense of Poverty Measures?* Toronto: Metcalf Foundation. On the World Wide Web at http://metcalffoundation.com/wp-content/uploads/2011/05/cutting-through-the-fog.pdf (retrieved 12 July 2012).

than half a million residents at $18 421, compared with $12 050 for a single person living in a rural area. The low-income line for a family of four in a large city was $34 829, substantially higher than that for a similar-sized family in a rural area ($22 783).

Who Are the Poor?

Rising unemployment causes the number and proportion of people living below the poverty line to increase. In 1980, for example, 11.6 percent of all Canadians were below the after-tax poverty line but, with the recession of the early 1980s, that figure climbed to 13.7 percent by 1984. As the economy recovered, the proportion of poor Canadians dropped again to 10.2 percent in 1989 but then rose steeply to 15.2 percent in 1996 following the recession in the early 1990s. Over the next decade, the proportion of poor Canadians rose and fell. In 2009, the most recent year for which data are available, 9.6 percent of Canadians were living below the after-tax LICO (National Council of Welfare, 2011).

Although poverty rates tend to follow unemployment rates, not all of Canada's poor are unemployed or out of the labour force. Using the market basket measure (MBM) of low income (see Box 6.2), which provides slightly higher estimates than the LICO measure (10.1 percent versus 9.2 percent in 2007, for example), more than half a million Canadians (34 percent of all low-income Canadians) were supported mainly by someone who held a job (Human Resources and Skills

Development Canada [HRSDC], 2012). More than 75 percent of these **working poor** Canadians worked full-time for the full year. They were poor not because they were not working but because they earned so little. Overall, as part-time and temporary work have become more common in Canada, the working poor have come to make up a much larger proportion of Canada's poor (Sauvé, 2006).

First Nations are among the poorest citizens of our country (see Box 6.3). The most recent census data (Statistics Canada, 2008b) show unemployment rates among 25- to 54-year-old First Nations Canadians that are more than twice as high as among non-First Nations in the same age category (13 percent versus 5 percent, respectively, in 2006). First Nations living on reserves have the highest unemployment rates (23 percent in 2006). Consequently, the poverty rate (LICO) for First Nations living off-reserve in 2007 was 13.7 percent, compared with 9.9 percent for all Canadians (HRSDC, 2012). The comparable rate for First Nations living on reserves, if available, would be much higher (see Box 6.3).

On average, recent immigrants are younger and more educated than are native-born Canadians (see Chapter 8, Race and Ethnic Relations). Even so, in 2007, 16.4 percent of immigrants who had arrived in Canada in the previous decade were living below the LICO. Over the past decades, immigrants have come to be significantly over-represented among Canada's working poor (Wallis and Kwok, 2008). Between 1980 and 2005, the earnings (in 2005 dollars) of recent immigrants declined 21 percent, while the earnings of Canadians in general stayed roughly the same (Statistics Canada, 2008a: 40).

BOX 6.3 AFTER ATTAWAPISKAT, WHAT?

When Canadians first saw the news about Attawapiskat they knew that no matter who is at fault, nobody in Canada should be using a plastic bucket for a toilet and have to dump it outside on a regular basis. Nobody should be calling a shack with mould on the walls home. And nobody in Ontario should be paying $23.50 for six apples and four small bottles of juice. ...

No one's hands are clean on this issue. The federal government has woefully underfunded the housing, educational and health needs of First Nations for years. The First Nations leadership has not been aggressive and honest enough about the conditions on many reserves. The provincial government has not ensured that the economic benefits from development on traditional lands flowed more equitably to First Nations. And the news media have ignored the reality of Third World conditions in Canada for far too long. ... This is not the first time there has been a crisis at Attawapiskat.

In 1979, 30,000 gallons of diesel fuel (the largest spill in Northern Ontario) leaked under the elementary school. The school was finally closed in 2001 because of ongoing health problems suffered by students and teachers. Ten years later, the federal government pledged (for the third time) to fund a new school. Meantime, the children remain in inadequate portables.

In May 2008, hundreds of people were evacuated from the community because of flooding caused by ice jams in the Attawapiskat River. In July 2009, a massive sewage flood dumped waste into eight buildings that housed 90 people. As a stopgap measure, De Beers (the diamond mine is 60 kilometres away) donated and retrofitted two construction trailers to house 90 people until the damaged homes could be fixed or replaced. Two years later, this "short-term solution" still houses the 90 people—who share six washrooms and four stoves. ...

Some may ask, "Why don't the people of Attawapiskat just move?" That's like asking: Why don't the people of Vancouver, Los Angeles and San Francisco move out of the San Andreas/Queen Charlotte Fault zone where earthquakes can occur? Why don't people in the Caribbean move out of the hurricane zones?

The people of Attawapiskat happen to live on inhospitable land on the fault line between advancing western civilization in pursuit of mineral wealth (mainly diamonds and chromite) and their own hunter/gatherer civilization. Many do not live in Third World conditions. About a third of them do actually get a real living and cultural identity from trapping and harvesting caribou, geese and fish. Another hundred work at the nearby De Beers diamond mine. Many still live on the land, coming into the settlement only at Christmas or other "gathering times." They don't move because it's their land. It's home.

SOURCE: Excerpt from J. F. (Jim) Foulds (2011), "After Attawakispat, What?" From http://www.thestar.com/opinion/editorialopinion/article/1108609-after-attawapiskat-what.

Several decades ago, senior citizens were more likely than younger Canadians were to be living below the poverty line. However, higher proportions of recent cohorts of retirees have had employer-provided pensions and personal retirement funds (Gougeon, 2009), and the federal government has maintained old-age pension levels, even though they are quite small. Consequently, in contrast to the working poor, among whom poverty rates have risen, the poverty rate for seniors has declined. In 2007, only 4.8 percent of seniors were living below the LICO, compared with 9.9 percent of the total Canadian population (HRSDC, 2012). In contrast, 21.3 percent of Canadian single parents were living below the LICO in 2007. Four out of five (82 percent) of these single parents were female. Many of these young women were completely dependent on social assistance, since it is almost impossible for a single young mother to look after children and hold down a job.

FIGURE 6.3 TOTAL WELFARE INCOME AS A PERCENTAGE OF (AFTER TAX) POVERTY LINE (LICO), ONTARIO, 1992 AND 2009

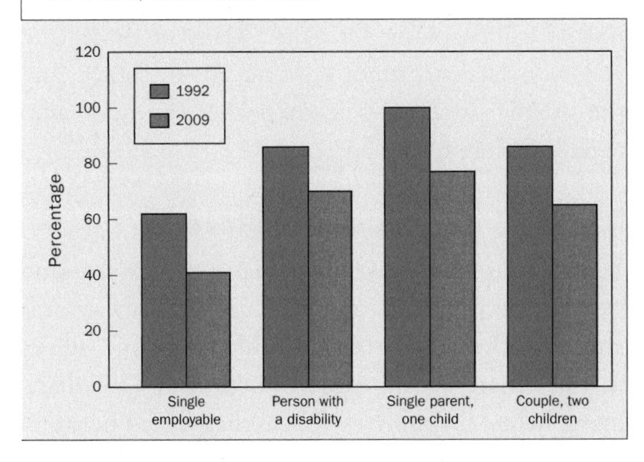

SOURCE: Data reported in National Council of Welfare. (2010). *Welfare Incomes: 2009*, specifically Table 13: Welfare Incomes as a Percentage of the After-Tax LICOs, 1992–2000, p. A-46; and Table 13: Welfare Incomes as a Percentage of the After-Tax LICOs, 2001–2009, p. A-47. Reproduced with the permission of the Minister of Public Works and Government Services Canada, 2012.

Social Assistance for the Poor

Many people believe that "welfare" (social assistance) and employment insurance are too easy to obtain and that the amount of money received is enough to encourage people to avoid seeking work (Swanson, 2001). Is this true? Because welfare regulations vary across provinces and territories, we will examine data from Ontario, the largest province and among the provinces with the highest welfare incomes, for 1992 and 2009.

Figure 6.3 shows that, in 1992, a single, employable adult (an adult who did not have a disability, was not a senior, and was not considered unable to seek work because of family responsibilities) who was eligible for Ontario social assistance received 62 percent of the after-tax poverty line (LICO). Almost two decades later, in 2009, the same type of person receiving welfare would have received only 41 percent of the poverty line. Recall that the poverty line is lower than the median income. Thus, the $7501 this single employable adult would have received from welfare in 2009 was exactly one-third of the median income for single adults in the province (National Council of Welfare, 2010).

People with disabilities who are receiving welfare have generally been treated a bit more generously by provincial governments. Thus, in 1992, such an individual would have received total annual transfer payments that were 86 percent of the poverty line. Here again we see that welfare payments have been reduced. In 2009, the $12 905 that a person with a disability would have received from the provincial government was only 70 percent of the poverty line and only 57 percent of the median income for all single adults in Ontario.

Single parents and couples with children, like adults with disabilities, have also been treated somewhat better by the welfare system, compared to single, employable adults. However, for both groups, we see in Figure 6.3 that their total annual welfare payments, as a percentage of the appropriate low-income line for their family type, declined over the past two decades. In 2009, a single parent with one child would have received $17 372, exactly half the median income for a two-person family in Ontario that year. The $22 695 that a couple with two children would have received from welfare that year was only 29 percent of the Ontario median income for four-person families (National Council of Welfare, 2010).

Summing up, in Ontario, and also across Canada, the amount of welfare assistance is very low. Furthermore, in every province and territory, welfare incomes have been cut over the past two decades, sometimes substantially, for almost all types of recipients. As the National Council of Welfare (2010: vii) concluded, after reviewing similar data for all provinces and territories, "[r]egardless of the measure used, welfare incomes were consistently far below most socially accepted measures of adequacy." Consequently, it is difficult to accept the argument that overly generous welfare systems discourage people from looking for work. Many of those who receive assistance cannot work outside the home, and the money provided seldom pushes the poor who receive it close to the poverty line.

Moving Into and Out of Poverty

Discussions of poverty can leave the impression that the poor and the nonpoor are separate groups and that there is little mobility from one status to the other. While the proportion of Canadians living below the after-tax LICO has varied between 9 and 15 percent over the past two decades, Statistics Canada data show that, between 1993 and 1998, one in four Canadians (24 percent) lived in a low-income family for at least one year (Morissette and Zhang, 2001). A similar but more recent analysis, also using pre-tax LICO calculations, showed that, even with a strong economy, this picture had not changed: Between 1996 and 2001, 25 percent of all Canadians lived below the poverty line for at least one year (Statistics Canada, 2005: 122).

The earlier study provided a more detailed multi-year analysis, showing that 8 percent of the total population experienced poverty (were in the low-income group) for four or more years out of a possible six. However, among Canadians living in lone-parent families, 38 percent experienced poverty for at least four years between 1993 and 1998. More recent data show that, for a single year (2003–04), about 4 percent of all Canadians slide below the poverty line while a similar proportion move above it (National Council of Welfare, 2008b). Thus, poverty is not a static status. Individuals and families move into and out of poverty each year. Nevertheless, a sizable minority remain stuck in poverty year after year. Losing a job, having to take a lower-paying job, becoming a single parent, or being widowed can drastically increase the chance of falling into, and remaining stuck in, poverty. In addition, welfare regulations in many provinces "claw back" social assistance benefits as soon as welfare recipients start earning even a small income (National Council of Welfare, 2008a). This predicament creates a "welfare trap" that further increases the chances of poor Canadians, particularly single-parent families, remaining poor (see Box 6.4)

MATERIAL INEQUALITY IN CANADA: SUMMING UP

Is Inequality Increasing in Canada?

Compared with some other countries, and compared with the situation in Canada a century ago, the level of material inequality in this country today is relatively low. Even so, you have seen evidence of a great deal of inequality in wealth and income. Furthermore, there are indications that, for at least several decades, the level of inequality has been slowly rising. Corporate concentration has been increasing as a small number of huge business enterprises, many of them family owned or family run, have gained control over a larger share of the assets of Canada's biggest corporations. Wealth inequality in general appears to be increasing, income inequality has risen, and the number of working poor in Canada has increased.

Looking more closely at the labour market, we see that unemployment rates have been rising slowly but steadily for several decades. Although these rates

BOX 6.4 ONE STEP FORWARD, ONE STEP BACK: WELFARE "CLAWBACKS"

A single mother with two children aged 15 and 19 living in subsidized housing gets $13 873 annually from welfare, GST credit, and federal child benefits. The mother takes a part-time job that pays $14 000 a year and her 19-year-old enrolls in university part-time and gets a part-time job that pays $2400. Both must now take public transit. The son has a $1000 bursary. On paper, the family's income per year is $31 273. The mother's and student's earnings reduce their welfare by $8200 (half of her pay and half of his). Their earnings also cause their subsidized rent to rise by $2268 per year. Payroll taxes eat up another $815. TTC and GO Transit passes for both cost $4728 and work-related clothing another $1000. The family is now left with $14 262 ($31 273 minus $17 011) or just $389 more before taxes than they had at the start.

SOURCE: "Case Study: Why A Job Doesn't Pay." *Toronto Star* 6 December 2007: A1. Reprinted with permission—Torstar Syndication Services.

have gone up and down a number of times, and are lower now than they were in the 1990s, the long-term trend since the mid-twentieth century has been upward. Hence, in 2011, the average annual unemployment rate was 7.4 percent, representing 1.12 million unemployed Canadians (HRSDC, 2012), a number almost equal to the populations of Saskatchewan and Prince Edward Island combined. With increasing global financial and economic uncertainty, we can expect the national unemployment rate to stay at this level over the next several years. Comparisons across provinces in 2011 reveal the extent of regional inequality in Canada, with unemployment rates of 12.7 percent in Newfoundland and Labrador, 9.5 percent in New Brunswick, 7.8 percent in Ontario, and only 5.0 percent in Saskatchewan.

Part-time employment rates have also been rising over the past few decades. Forty years ago, fewer than 4 percent of employed Canadians worked part-time. In 2008, 18.4 percent had a part-time job. Since the 1980s, the number of temporary jobs has significantly increased, as employers have begun to cut long-term wage costs by offering more limited-term contract positions. By 2008, one in eight working Canadians had a job with a specific end date (Krahn, Lowe, and Hughes, 2011: ch. 2). Real wages are no longer increasing, and inequality in earnings has been rising as a result of these part-time and temporary employment trends, as well as declines in employment in traditionally higher-paying industries and occupations.

A More Polarized Society?

It is difficult to avoid the conclusion that, in Canada, the gap between the advantaged (those with full-time, permanent jobs) and the disadvantaged (those with part-time, temporary, or no jobs) is slowly increasing (Fuller and Vosko, 2008). A similar pattern has been observed in Britain (Dorling et al., 2007) and in the United States (Cavanagh and Collins, 2008). This is not to suggest that a new era of massive inequalities is dawning. However, the evidence is clear that material inequalities are rising, not declining, and that society is becoming more polarized in terms of access to and control over economic resources (OECD, 2011; Yalnizyan, 2010). Using Weber's definition of class, I conclude that class differences in Canada and many other countries are becoming more pronounced.

Obviously, many interrelated factors have contributed to the growth in material inequality (Krahn, Lowe, and Hughes, 2011). Although some new high-skill and well-paying jobs emerged over the past several decades in Canada, the overall outcome has still been a net reduction in employment opportunities. Globalization, the process whereby goods and services are produced by business enterprises operating in many different countries, has led to a more competitive and cost-cutting economic environment. Business enterprises have responded by shifting many of their activities to countries in which lower wages and less rigorous environmental and labour laws allow them to earn higher profits. In North America, layoffs and downsizing were a frequent response, along with the replacement of full-time permanent jobs with part-time and temporary positions. Labour unions, which traditionally resisted attempts to cut wages and jobs, have lost some of their power. At the political level, an ideology emphasizing that "the market knows best," and that people need less rather than more government intervention in the economy and the labour market, has led to fewer government efforts to reduce material inequalities and reduced transfer payments to the poor (National Council of Welfare, 2008a). Tax cuts for the highest income groups have exacerbated patterns of income and wealth inequality (Yalnizyan, 2010; OECD, 2011). It remains to be seen how the global financial and economic uncertainties that arose in late 2008, which had significant impacts on Canada's political, economic, and financial institutions, will further affect long-term patterns of social inequality in Canada.

CONSEQUENCES OF MATERIAL INEQUALITY

Other chapters in this textbook will go into more detail about the many consequences of material inequality for individuals and families. You will see that position in the class structure has an effect on belief systems, behaviours, and lifestyles, and that the poor, the middle classes, and the very wealthy frequently hold different opinions on various subjects, may vote differently, and certainly enjoy different lifestyles. But, much more important, people in different positions in society's economic hierarchy experience different life-chances, to use Weber's term.

Consequences for Individuals and Families

Children from poorer families typically do not do as well in school as children from more affluent families do (Davies and Guppy, 2006). They are more likely to be enrolled in nonuniversity academic streams (Taylor and Krahn, 2009) and to drop out before completing high school (Tanner, Krahn, and Hartnagel, 1995). They are also much less likely to go to university (Krahn, 2009). As noted earlier in the discussion of occupational mobility, such effects of poverty are largely responsible for the perpetuation of class inequalities from one generation to the next.

For a variety of reasons, including better nutrition, access to better health care, and less hazardous working conditions, those who are situated higher in the economic hierarchy are typically healthier than are poor people (Raphael, 2011). Consequently, on average, the poor do not live as long as those who are better off (Wilkinson and Pickett, 2010). Similarly, when dealing with the criminal justice system, those with greater access to and control over economic resources tend to fare better (King and Winterdyk, 2010). As a result, the poor are overrepresented in jails. First Nations and visible-minority Canadians with low incomes are particularly disadvantaged when dealing with the criminal justice system (Fitzgerald and Carrington, 2008). I could go on, but these examples are probably sufficient to make the point that life-chances are a function of position in the class structure and that those higher up in the economic hierarchy enjoy a better quality of and, often, a longer life.

Consequences for Society

In addition to these substantial consequences of material inequality for individuals and families, can material inequality have other broader social outcomes? Specifically, given the relatively high and increasing level of inequality in Canada, can we expect more social unrest? Will conflict between the "haves" and the "have-nots" increase? Those committed to a classical Marxist theory of social change might welcome such conflict; for them, it would indicate that capitalism was finally beginning to give way to a socialist society. Others might view such conflict much more negatively. Whatever the response to such a possibility, it is clear that values and beliefs directly influence the way the people respond to evidence of inequality and its consequences.

But returning to the question, can we expect an increase in social unrest and conflict as a result of higher levels of inequality? During the early 1980s, for example, the solidarity movement in British Columbia brought together members of trade unions, social-welfare organizations, and various community-based groups in opposition to the Social Credit government's cutbacks in government programs and attempts to change labour legislation. Bryan Palmer (1986) described the protests and rallies that took place as evidence of growing class conflict. However, these events were exceptional. Much more often, the poor and the near-poor put up with their less advantaged position because they have few of the resources (for example, money, education, organizations) that make it possible to fight for social change (Brym, 1979). In fact, in the past decade, we have seen more opposition from a better-organized middle class, in response to government cutbacks in health and education funding, and in support for the seniors, than from the poor in response to welfare cutbacks. And we have seen intensified negative stereotyping of the poor and those on welfare, a process that Jean Swanson (2001) calls "poor-bashing."

However, we have also seen the emergence of a remarkable new social movement, Occupy Wall Street, that brought together a wide range of individuals and groups, including middle-class, university-educated social activists, and the homeless, all concerned about the growing level of social inequality in North America. It remains to be seen whether this movement, sparked by an online suggestion from a Vancouver-based nonprofit organization (Adbusters), will have an impact on patterns of social inequality in Canada and elsewhere (see Box 6.5).

Thus, while it is unlikely that growing social inequality and fewer opportunities for upward mobility will translate into widespread social unrest in Canada, it remains possible that coalitions of concerned citizens will have an impact on this long-term trend. As for the long-term consequences for global peace and security as a result of a growing gap between rich and poor countries, they are difficult to predict. Even so, as Paul Krugman, an influential American economist, noted, "The ultimate effects of growing economic disparities on our social and political health may be hard to predict, but they are unlikely to be pleasant" (Krugman, 1994: F9).

RESPONDING TO INEQUALITY

Some people believe that more equal distribution of society's resources would be preferable to the current level of inequality. They believe that existing differences in life-chances are unjust and look for ways in which social institutions, laws, and tax systems might be

BOX 6.5 THE PROCESS IS THE POINT: THE OCCUPY MOVEMENT IN CANADA

Since the Occupy movement arrived in Canada, pundits and media commentators have been scratching their heads, asking the same question in different ways: what is the point? Critics of the nascent movement highlight a lack of coherent goals, the apparent disorganization of those involved, and the pointlessness of camping out to create more equity. ...

The reason that public commentators are having such trouble with the Occupy movement is because it defies conventional categories. "Social movement" is the best descriptor that can be applied, but it also looks different than other social movements that Canada has seen. ... [I]t involves people setting stakes in the ground, both metaphorically and literally, indicating through that act of claiming space that they plan to stay put for the long haul. It involves experiments in direct and radical democracy. In short, it involves trying out things that are neither familiar nor widespread under our current system.

Theorists of democracy have long understood that democracy itself is a process, not an end. Hannah Arendt famously described the public sphere as a shared table, around which we gather in order to relate to one another and find our common ground. This involves much more than going to the ballot box every four years; it requires human relationships, wrought through time spent together struggling over dilemmas and finding solutions to the problems that collectively face us. As the pressure mounts on individuals—not just young people but perhaps felt more keenly by young people—to seek out scarce jobs, pay off mounting debt, and struggle to survive under increasingly unforgiving economic circumstances, the opportunity to come together so as to share frustrations and seek solutions within the public realm is one that is rarely offered. The Occupy movement offers just such an opportunity: a genuine moment of democratic engagement not mediated through the interests of pre-existing political parties or NGOs. It represents a chance to experience the actual human relationships that lie at the root of democracy.

SOURCE: Kennelly, Jacqueline. (2011). "The Process is the Point: The Occupy Movement in Canada." This article first appeared in Carleton University's monthly online publication, *Carleton Now*. On the World Wide Web at http://carletonnow.carleton.ca/november-2011/the-process-is-the-point-the-occupy-movement-in-canada (retrieved November 2011).

SOURCE: © Tomas Abad/Alamy.

changed to reduce material inequality. Others, equally offended by inequality and its consequences, reject this reformist approach in favour of a more radical position, advocating the replacement of capitalist society by some kind of socialist or social-democratic alternative. Still others respond to evidence of extensive inequality with little ambition to change it, believing, simply, that this is "the way things are." Although perhaps bothered by its consequences, members of this group might still conclude that the existing level of inequality is inevitable and that well-intentioned efforts to reduce it will, in the long run, have little effect. They might even conclude that inequality is functional, as Davis and Moore (1945) argued nearly 70 years ago, and that efforts to reduce it will be counterproductive. In short, reactions to inequality, and recommendations about what, if anything, should be done about it, reflect personal values and political orientations.

Assuming that a lower level of inequality is a goal worth striving for, it is clear that the government has a role to play in trying to reach that goal. The Canadian state has a significant impact on the distribution of wealth and income through tax systems that redistribute wealth from the rich to the poor (Yalnizyan, 2010); through minimum-wage and other types of legislation; and through transfer payments, such as pensions for seniors and those with disabilities, social assistance for low-income individuals and families, and employment insurance. Even so, compared with some other industrialized countries, Canada spends considerably less on attempts to reduce poverty (Raphael, 2011).

Canada's welfare policies place more faith in the power of a free market, unregulated by government legislation and policies, to produce wealth and jobs that should, it is expected, trickle down to the poor (Esping-Andersen, 1990). Unfortunately, as my review of labour-market trends indicates, there is little evidence that the free market has performed successfully in this regard. Instead, unemployment rates have risen, precarious employment has become more common, and social inequality has increased. Furthermore, during the past several decades, the political mood has changed, and concerns about reducing government deficits, streamlining government, and making Canada more competitive in the global marketplace appear to have been influencing government policy more than concerns about reducing inequality. In fact, some deficit-reducing initiatives (for example, reductions in social-assistance payments) have led to increases in material inequality in Canada, as have tax reform initiatives that have favoured the very rich.

But twenty-first-century government policies do not necessarily require this trade-off. For example, government-funded job-creation strategies may continue to be useful in the future, as they were during the aftermath of the global financial crisis of 2008–09. Revised tax policies that would raise corporate income taxes, increase the marginal tax rate for Canada's highest paid citizens, and eliminate some of the tax write-offs enjoyed by the upper and middle classes could also be useful.

A large part of the problem lies, of course, in the fact that any serious effort to redistribute the wealth and income from the well-off to the poor would probably be opposed by the former. If we really want to do something about material inequality in Canada, and globally, if we want a different kind of society and a different kind of world, many of us—and that would include me—have to be willing to accept less so that others can have more.

SUMMARY

1. Social stratification refers to persistent patterns of social inequality. Some social hierarchies are based on ascribed statuses, such as gender, race, and age, which are typically assigned to an individual at birth. Other social hierarchies are based on achieved statuses, which index how well an individual has performed in some role. A society in which considerable social mobility between statuses is possible is said to have an open stratification system.
2. Social theorists have proposed a variety of explanations of the origins and effects of social stratification systems. In his class-based theory of social stratification, Karl Marx emphasized the exploitation of the working class by the owners of the means of production and the potential for class conflict to generate social change. Max Weber also put considerable emphasis on the power that resides in ownership of property but argued that hierarchies of prestige and political power are influential as well.
3. The functional theory of social stratification suggests that inequality is both inevitable and necessary insofar as it ensures that the most qualified individuals are selected to fill the most important and rewarding roles. Power differences are downplayed in this theory, as is conflict between social classes. A number of more recent theories of social stratification, including those put forward by Gerhard Lenski, Frank Parkin, and Erik Olin Wright, have placed more emphasis on power and conflict. Wright developed a class-based theory of stratification that adapts many of Marx's ideas to contemporary circumstances. Parkin's approach follows in the footsteps of Weber.
4. Occupational shifts in Canada over the past century reveal some of the changing features of Canada's stratification system. Studies of occupational mobility show that Canada is a relatively open society. Even so, there is strong evidence that class-based advantages are often passed from one generation to the next.

5. Ownership of wealth and property in Canada is highly concentrated, and income inequality is relatively high and growing. Statistics Canada's low-income cutoff line (LICO) reveals that about one in ten Canadians is currently living below the "poverty line." There is considerable evidence that the poor and others near the bottom of the social hierarchies in our society enjoy fewer life-chances than do the well-off. The poor are less likely to do well in school and to continue on to higher education. They are also less healthy and have a shorter life expectancy, and they do not fare as well when dealing with the criminal justice system. Because of their limited access to social and material resources, the poor have seldom become an active force for social change.
6. Some theories of social stratification developed in the middle of the twentieth century suggested that material inequality was declining as the North American economy expanded. However, the period of rapid economic growth that characterized the middle decades of that century appears to have ended. As unemployment rates have risen, as part-time and temporary work become more common, and as governments cut back on social-assistance programs while reducing taxes for the very wealthy, evidence accumulates that material inequality is slowly increasing in Canada.

QUESTIONS TO CONSIDER

1. Does social class play a more or less significant role than do ascribed statuses (such as race, gender, and age) in determining patterns of inequality in Canadian society?
2. How are social and material advantages passed from one generation to the next, resulting in persistent patterns of social inequality?
3. What role, if any, should governments play in addressing persistent patterns of social inequality?
4. What does *poverty* mean, and how should we measure it?
5. As Canada becomes a more culturally diverse country, what are the implications of high levels of poverty among immigrants and First Nations?
6. The 2011 Occupy Wall Street movement involved extended public protests about social inequality in many North American cities and around the world. Did this social movement have a lasting effect?

GLOSSARY

Absolute poverty (p. 143) is the state of existence of those who have so little income that they can barely stay alive.

Achieved status (p. 129) is a changeable status that is acquired on the basis of how well an individual performs a particular role.

Ascribed status (p. 129) is a status, such as age, gender, or race, that is assigned to an individual, typically at birth, and is not chosen by the individual.

The bourgeoisie (p. 132), according to Marx, is one of the two main classes in the capitalist mode of production. It comprises the owners of the means of production.

A **caste system** (p. 130) is a closed stratification system, most common in India, with strict rules regarding the type of work that members of different castes (the strata of Indian society into which people are born) can do.

Circulatory mobility (p. 141) is the occupational mobility that occurs within a society when better-qualified individuals move upward to replace those who are less qualified and who must consequently move downward.

Class (p. 131) is a position in an economic hierarchy occupied by individuals or families with similar access to, or control over, material resources.

Class conflict (p. 133), according to Marx, is conflict between major classes within a mode of production. It eventually leads to the evolution of a new mode of production.

Class consciousness (p. 133), according to Marx, is the recognition by members of a class of their shared interests in opposition to members of another class.

Class structure (p. 131) is the relatively permanent economic hierarchy comprising different social classes.

A **closed stratification system** (p. 130) is a stratification system in which little or no social mobility occurs, because most or all statuses are ascribed.

Contradictory class locations (p. 137), according to Erik Olin Wright, are the locations within a class structure populated by occupational groupings with divided loyalties (for example, managers who supervise others yet report to owners).

Exclusion (p. 138), according to Frank Parkin, is the organized effort by privileged, more powerful groups to maintain their advantaged position.

The **functionalist theory of stratification** (p. 135) views social organization as analogous to a biological organism in which the parts (or organs) exist because of the functions they perform in maintaining the whole. In this theory, stratification exists because of vital functions it presumably performs in maintaining social equilibrium.

Intergenerational occupational mobility (p. 141) refers to an individual's occupational mobility, either upward or downward, in relation to her or his parents' occupational status.

Intragenerational occupational mobility (p. 141) refers to an individual's occupational mobility, either upward or downward, within his or her own lifetime.

Life-chances (p. 134), according to Weber, are the opportunities (or lack thereof) for a higher standard of living and a better quality of life that are available to members of a given class.

The **low-income cutoff (LICO)** (p. 143), known unofficially as the "poverty line," is an estimate of the income level below which a person or family might be considered to be living in relative poverty. It is defined by Statistics Canada as the level of income at which more than 63 percent of income is spent on basic necessities.

The **means of production** (p. 132), according to Marx, are one of the main components of a mode of production, consisting of the technology, capital investments, and raw materials used in production.

A **meritocracy** (p. 130) is a society in which most or all statuses are achieved on the basis of merit (how well a person performs in a given role).

The **mode of production** (p. 132), according to Marx, is the system of economic activity in a society, comprising the means of production and the social relations of production (the class system).

Occupational status attainment (p. 141) refers to the process whereby an individual attains a particular occupational status and the factors that influence that process.

An **open stratification system** (p. 130) is a stratification system in which merit, rather than inheritance (or ascribed characteristics), determines social rank.

The **petite bourgeoisie** (p. 132), according to Marx, is a secondary class within the capitalist mode of production, including independent owners/producers (for example, farmers) and small-business owners.

Power (p. 134) is the ability to impose one's will on others.

The **proletariat** (p. 132), according to Marx, is one of the two main classes in a capitalist mode of production, comprising workers who exchange their labour for a wage.

Relative poverty (p. 143) is a state of existence in which individuals have significantly less income than do most others in their society, causing their lifestyle to be more restricted and their life-chances to be substantially curtailed.

Social closure (p. 138), according to Max Weber and Frank Parkin, refers to the methods used by relatively powerful groups to maintain their unequal access to status and resources, and to exclude others from such access.

Social mobility (p. 130) is the process whereby individuals, families, or other groups move up or down a status hierarchy.

Social relations of production (p. 132), according to Marx, are one of the main components of a given mode of production—specifically, the relationships between the main classes involved in production.

Social stratification (p. 127) refers to persistent patterns of social inequality perpetuated by the way wealth, power, and prestige are distributed and passed from one generation to the next.

Socioeconomic status (p. 131) refers to a person's general status within an economic hierarchy, based on income, education, and occupation.

Status (p. 129) is a culturally and socially defined position that a person occupies in a group.

Structural mobility (p. 141) refers to the occupational mobility in a society resulting from changes in the occupational structure (for example, the upward mobility of many individuals resulting from the creation of more middle- and upper-level jobs in the economy).

Surplus value (p. 132), according to Marx, is the value of goods in excess of the cost of production, which takes the form of profit when the product is sold.

Usurpation (p. 138), according to Frank Parkin, is the effort of excluded groups within a stratification system to gain advantages and power at the expense of more powerful groups.

The **working poor** (p. 146) are individuals who work but whose income leaves them below a designated low-income, or poverty, line.

SUGGESTED READING

Grabb, Edward and Neil Guppy, eds. (2009). *Social Inequality in Canada: Patterns, Problems, and Policies*, 5th ed. Toronto: Pearson. A comprehensive collection of readings on various dimensions of stratification in Canada.

McQuaig, Linda and Neil Brooks. (2010). *The Trouble with Billionaires*. Toronto: Penguin Canada. Have the super-rich really earned their wealth and esteem? Read this fascinating book and draw your own conclusion.

Raphael, Dennis. (2011). *Poverty in Canada: Implications for Health and Quality of Life*, 2nd ed. Toronto: Canadian Scholars' Press. An excellent interdisciplinary examination of the causes and extent of poverty in Canada, what it feels like to live in poverty, and what might be done to alleviate it.

Swanson, Jean. (2001). *Poor-Bashing: The Politics of Exclusion*. Toronto: Between the Lines. A social activist takes a critical look at how the poor and people receiving welfare in Canada are stereotyped and mistreated by the media and government, and offers useful suggestions for social change.

Wallis, Maria A. and Siu-ming Kwok, eds. (2008). *Daily Struggles: The Deepening Racialization and Feminization of Poverty in Canada*. Toronto: Canadian Scholars' Press. A collection of research papers examining the impact of race, gender, and immigrant status on poverty and social exclusion in Canada.

CHAPTER 7

GENDER INEQUALITY: ECONOMIC AND POLITICAL ASPECTS

Monica Boyd
UNIVERSITY OF TORONTO

SOURCE: © Barry Deutsch.

IN THIS CHAPTER YOU WILL LEARN THAT

- A major source of inequality between women and men is that many women are excluded from public economic and political activity. The persistent tendency of many women to be relegated to domestic affairs leads to less income, prestige, and power.
- Although women have entered politics and the paid labour force in increasing numbers over the past century, they still tend to be chiefly responsible for meal preparation, cleaning, laundry, and child care.
- In the paid labour force, women and men still tend to be segregated in different kinds of jobs; "women's jobs" typically pay less, carry less prestige, offer less security, and bestow less authority.
- Although women make up more than half the Canadian population, only one in five members of Parliament is a woman.
- In recent years, employment equity policies and policies requiring equal pay for work of equal value have been implemented to help lessen gender inequalities, but much research and political action are still required before gender equality is achieved.

INTRODUCTION

In the twentieth century, enormous changes occurred in the attitudes, expectations, and behaviours of women and men. Compare the lifestyle of typical men and women born in 1925, 1950, and 1975. The pair born in 1925 would have been 25 years old in 1950. During the 1950s, they would almost certainly have married and had children. In the 1950s, most women were expected to work exclusively in the home and take complete responsibility for domestic affairs. **Social roles** are the behaviours that are expected of people occupying particular social positions. In the 1950s, women's main roles were those of wives and mothers. In contrast, men were expected to have paying jobs, and their responsibilities were to meet their family's needs for food, clothing, and shelter. Their roles were those captured by the terms "provider" and "head of household."

In contrast, by the time the pair born in 1950 turned 25, the belief that women should marry and work exclusively in the home was rapidly eroding. The average age at marriage had increased, indicating that many women and men were postponing marriage. After divorce laws were revised in 1968, divorce rates rose, signalling that fewer women and men would have a single spouse for the duration of their adult lives. Other changes were blurring the line between work in the home and work in the labour force. Men were starting to become more involved in household maintenance and child rearing, and more women were joining the paid labour force.

The scenario for the pair born in 1975 and turning 25 in 2000 is different again. Most people born during the mid-1970s still saw themselves as eventually having spouses or partners and raising children. Unlike the generation born in the 1920s, however, they probably also saw themselves as sharing domestic responsibilities with their spouse or partner and as both holding paid jobs.

A changed world does not, however, mean an equal world. Although we often hear about the "revolution" in gender equality that has taken place in recent decades, the revolution is not finished. As I show in this chapter, gender inequality still exists: In your lifetime, you have probably seen and are likely yet to see at least some of the gender inequalities discussed here. At the same time, you are also likely to witness a variety of interventions aimed at reducing those inequalities.

I begin with a definition of gender inequality and then explore its major aspects and the three main arenas in Canadian society in which gender inequality is evident: the home, the labour force, and politics. I end with a review of the actions, policies, and laws that could reduce gender inequality in the future.

UNDERSTANDING GENDER INEQUALITY

GENDER INEQUALITY DEFINED

Social scientists usually refer to inequalities between men and women as "gender inequalities" rather than "sex inequalities." They favour *gender* because it refers to the *social* meanings associated with being a man or a woman, whereas *sex* refers to the *biological* characteristics of men and women. Gender is found in social roles, in daily interactions, and in institutions (Andersen, 2005; Martin, 2003; Wharton, 2000).

Gender Stereotypes

To better understand the gendered nature of roles, think about such words as *provider* and *caregiver*. They do more than describe the expected behaviour associated with being a partner in a marriage; they also cause people to evaluate types of behaviour as "masculine" or "feminine." Once in place, these images of masculinity and femininity influence how people see themselves and how they experience the world. The observation that "it's a boy" often causes Canadian parents to decorate the child's room in bold colours, or at least in pale blue as opposed to pink. A male child is likely to receive stuffed animals, trucks, and play toolkits rather than the dolls, play dishes, and play makeup that are likely to be given a girl. Through parental behaviour, television, movies, and print media (including schoolbooks), children learn to define certain social behaviours as being inherently, chromosomally male or female, even when such traits are largely learned. By the time children have grown into adults, they have adopted and identified with many "masculine" or "feminine" personality traits and behaviours. In turn, they are likely to treat others around them through the lenses of their own identities and understandings of masculinity and femininity. In many instances, these conceptualizations are **gender stereotypes**—that is, oversimplified beliefs about how men and women, by virtue of their physical sex, possess different personality traits and, as a result, may behave differently and experience the world in different ways.

Gender-related identities and behaviours are largely socially constructed. They are outcomes of the way we interact with others and encounter taken-for-granted rules and ways of doing things in

Through parental behaviour and the media, children learn to define certain social behaviours as inherently male or female. A male child is likely to receive trucks and play toolkits, while a girl more often receives dolls, play dishes, and play makeup.
SOURCE: © Jupiter Photos.

families, schools, the legal system, politics, and the paid workplace (West and Fenstermaker, 1993).

The fact that gender is largely learned and that its content is continually renewed and altered through social interaction has three implications:

1. Gender identities and behaviours are not stable and fixed (see Chapter 4, Gender and Sexuality). What people take to be masculine or feminine varies from one society to the next and, within a given society, over time.
2. Gender identities—the internalized sense of being a man or a woman—and gender-specific behaviours need not be congruent with the sex assigned to individuals at birth.
3. Just like sexuality and sex, gender identities and behaviours are not polar opposites (Gagne and Tewksbury, 1998; Segal, 1998). Images of masculinity and femininity often emphasize opposites, but there are in fact *degrees* of masculinity and femininity.

A fixation on the allegedly opposed characteristics of men and women is evident in such phrases as the "opposite sex" and "*vive la différence*." Psychological studies of gender stereotypes also lead us to conclude that most people think of men and women as opposites. In one famous study, psychologists asked respondents to indicate which traits, from a checklist of 122 adjectives, characterized average men and women. They found that men were described as very aggressive, very independent, very active, very competitive, very logical, able to make decisions easily, and almost always acting as leaders. Women were described as not at all aggressive, not at all independent, very emotional, very passive, not at all competitive, very illogical, able to make decisions only with difficulty, and almost never acting as leaders (Broverman, Vogel, Broverman, Clarkson, and Rosenkranz, 1972).

These results were obtained from respondents in the late 1960s; a study today would almost certainly have some different results. But contemporary studies show that people often still view women and men as having different, and opposite, personality traits (Kite, Deaux, and Haines, 2008). The persistence of stereotypical thinking about feminine and masculine characteristics as polar opposites should sensitize you to two things. First, the idea of difference is apparently a powerful one and hard to dispel even when it is contradicted by research. Second, in these polarized depictions, feminine traits are viewed as less desirable than masculine ones.

Dimensions of Inequality

Gender stereotypes shape our attitudes about girls and boys, men and women, and they are often important factors in determining the ideologies that perpetuate gender inequalities. Sociologists usually define **gender inequalities** as hierarchical asymmetries between men and women with respect to the distribution of power, material well-being, and prestige (as recognized through deference or honour). This definition does not imply that men as individuals always have greater prestige, wealth, and power than do individual women. It does imply that, *on average*, compared with women, men have more wealth, greater power, and positions that are accorded higher prestige.

Power is the capacity to impose your will on others, regardless of any resistance they might offer. It thus refers to the capacity to influence, manipulate, and control others. Power is exercised not only in the overt imposition of the will of one individual on others, but also in the control or support by groups or organizations of agendas that either uphold or challenge existing conditions (Duffy, 1986). For example, professorial power over students not only reflects professors' capacity to assign grades, but also the authority that the university gives them in the classroom.

Material well-being involves access to the economic resources necessary to pay for food, clothing, housing, and other possessions and advantages. Two important sources of material well-being are work-related earnings and accumulated wealth.

Prestige is the average evaluation of occupational activities and positions that are arranged in a hierarchy. It reflects the degree of respect, honour, or deference generally accorded to a person occupying a given position. Commonly, two or more differently evaluated positions are described as having higher or lower prestige. How would you rank someone who works as a physician and someone who works as a cashier at a fast-food outlet? Mostly people rank the former above the latter.

The three dimensions of inequality just defined—power, material well-being, and prestige—are found in discussions of social stratification, the unequal ranking of groups in society in terms of prestige, material possessions, and power (see Chapter 6, Social Stratification). Stratification is the result, achieved over time, of routine and frequently recurring practices and often unstated rules. Gender inequality is social stratification based on gender.

What explains gender inequalities in prestige, material well-being, and power? What form do these inequalities take? I will now examine these issues in turn.

EXPLAINING GENDER INEQUALITY

As sociology developed during the twentieth century, the earlier neglect of gender by the fathers of sociology ceased. New theories emerged that explained gender inequality and its persistence. It was mainly women who developed these theories, and they frequently included insights taken not just from sociology but also from other disciplines (Chafetz, 2006; Lengermann and Niebrugge-Brantley, 2001; Lorber, 2010). **Feminism** refers to the body of thought on the cause and nature of women's disadvantages and subordinate position in society and to efforts to minimize or eliminate that subordination. Because many different perspectives exist on the sources of gender inequality, we can discuss a variety of feminist theories.

Liberal, Marxist, socialist feminist, and multiracial feminist perspectives are among the most popular explanations for gender inequality in Canada (Newman and White, 2006). Liberal feminism is rooted in the liberalism of the 1700s. It assumes that human beings are rational and will correct inequalities when they know about them. Liberalism assumes that a good society is one in which men and women enjoy equal rights and opportunities. According to liberal feminism, gender inequalities are caused and perpetuated by gender stereotyping and the division of work into "women's" and "men's" jobs. Accordingly, the two main ways to achieve gender equality are by (1) removing gender stereotyping and discrimination in education and paid work, and (2) changing laws so that men and women have equal opportunities in the labour force and in politics (Lorber, 2010).

A different perspective on gender inequality derives from the writings of Karl Marx. According to Marxist feminists, women's unpaid work in the home maintains and reproduces the labour force. Capitalists benefit because they obtain refreshed workers at the beginning of each day and mothers raise children who will become future labourers. They also benefit from women's paid work because women in the paid labour force, like men, help capitalists earn profit and because they act as a "reserve army of labour" that can be hired and fired as labour demands change. Marxist feminists believe that gender equality is possible once socialism replaces capitalism.

Socialist feminists build on Marxist feminism. They agree that gender inequality is caused by the gendered division of labour and its exploitation by capitalism. However, they argue that classes constitute only one set of social relations that oppress women. The second set of social relations that performs this function is that of patriarchy, the system of male domination over women. Patriarchy predates capitalism. The forms it takes vary across time and within societies. But generally, childbearing and the sexual activities of women are the foundation of gender inequality. Moreover, because domestic and public spheres intersect, inequalities in one sphere can create disadvantages for women in the other sphere. (The "public sphere" refers to government and the world of paid work.) For socialist feminists, the steps required to decrease gender inequality include government-subsidized maternal benefits and child care, and the payment of equal wages and salaries to people who do equally valued work. Removing inequality altogether requires the eradication of male dominance as expressed in the legal system, the educational system, the family, and the economy (Chafetz, 2006; Lorber, 2010).

Finally, multiracial feminism emphasizes the importance of race in understanding gender inequality. This approach modifies the socialist feminist perspective by observing that hierarchical systems of domination incorporate race. For sociologist Patricia Hill Collins (1990), race, class, and gender combine to form a "matrix of domination." All three intersect, so the way that people experience gender inequality depends on their location within class and racially defined structures (Chafetz, 2006; Lorber, 2010; Zinn with Dill, 1997). Multiracial feminism contributes to our understanding of gender inequality in three ways. First, it highlights differences among women in terms of gender inequality. Second, it points out that women of specific races and in certain class locations are in positions of power and domination over other groups of women. Third, it emphasizes that solutions to gender inequality vary according to the location of groups of women in the matrix of domination.

EXERCISING POWER

Most sociologists describe the power relations between men and women as those of male domination and female subordination.

Male influence and control over women is broadly defined. It does not, for example, refer just to the predominance of men rather than women in political positions or in the military. Instead, power pervades all social relations, routine behaviours, and commonly accepted practices. For example, denying women the right to vote clearly denied them a voice in choosing who would govern them and, equally important, denied them direct input into the formulation of laws that would affect them, bestowing that right on men instead. Similarly, a workplace regulation that encouraged or compelled women to quit work upon marriage, such as the one that existed in the federal civil service until 1955, made it difficult for married women to earn income and forced many of them to depend on their husbands for money.

Power is also evident in day-to-day situations, such as when a young woman becomes the object of sexual innuendo or leering by her male classmates, co-workers, or strangers. During a safety forum at Osgoode Hall Law School in Toronto, a police officer said, "women should avoid dressing like sluts in order not to be victimized" (quoted in Pilkington, 2011). He thus blamed the victim for sexual assault and took responsibility away from the typically male perpetrator. The comment sparked outrage and resulted in SlutWalk, a movement in which mostly young women took to the streets across Canada and the United States to protest against the rape culture that the police officer's comment typified.

In Canada, behaviour such as the police officer's is often considered "normal." It draws on notions of femininity and masculinity that define women as "sexy" or "available" and men as sexual aggressors. If she protests such attention, a woman may discover that she is the object of further derision and that no rules or formal appeal mechanisms exist to stop or penalize the offenders. In short, she often cannot prevent or protest unwanted attention that arises from the social meanings attached to her biological sex.

Sexual harassment is essentially a display of power in which one person attempts to control, and often succeeds in controlling, another through sexual overtures. Although isolated cases of women harassing men have received attention from the press, in most cases of sexual harassment, it is the man who makes the sexual overtures. When the capacity or incapacity to control and influence becomes routine and patterned, we can speak of power as a *system* of dominance and exploitation.

Sexual harassment is the result of the general belief that men are superior to women and may impose their will on them. It is also the outcome of patterned ways of behaving that are based on this belief and that serve to reinforce it. For example, because of our society's higher evaluation of men (and its corresponding devaluation of women), men are more likely to be employed in positions in which they are the bosses and women are supervised by them. The harassment potential that is associated with this imbalance of power is evident in such situations as a female secretary working for a senior-level male manager or a female assembly worker supervised by a male foreman.

Gender inequalities in power also combine with racial inequalities. As a result, minority-group women experience the most harassment because they are both women and members of a minority group (Berdahl and Moore, 2006). For these women, the experience of harassment is doubly problematic since it includes not only sexual harassment but racial harassment as well. It also is problematic for immigrant women who, as recent arrivals, are uncertain of their rights and may have had different understandings in their home country as to what constitutes sexual harassment (Welsh, Carr, MacQuarrie, and Huntley, 2006).

SEPARATE SPHERES

Power relations are important for understanding inequality because power, prestige, and material well-being are often interrelated. For example, although the ability to control others does not necessarily depend on having a higher income or being wealthy, wealth and high income normally bestow power, just as power normally enhances the capacity to be wealthy and earn high income. In seeking to understand gender inequalities, researchers point out that, historically, women have been excluded from certain types of activities that create opportunities for acquiring power, prestige, and wealth. During the late nineteenth and for much of the twentieth century, the "proper place" of Canadian women was thought to be in the home, where they would be responsible for producing and raising the next generation (Ursel, 1992). They were not expected to participate in politics, to enact legislation, or to be employed. The denial of voting rights for women until the end of World War I and the existence of legislation that limited the hours and times when women could be employed limited their participation in the public sphere. The public sphere was viewed as the domain of men, who were expected to be the breadwinners and heads of households.

What have been the consequences of the separation of the public sphere for men and the private sphere for women? To answer this question, consider what is implied by work in the home. For family members, work in the home, including child

Women normally shoulder the burden of dual responsibility—for child care and for wage earning. Women also spend more time than their male counterparts do on housework and child care.
SOURCE: © iStockphoto.com/Fertnig Photography.

care, is unpaid, and, all too frequently, the amount of skill, effort, and energy expended is not widely noticed because most housework is not done in the presence of husbands. Adding to the devaluation of work in the home is the tendency to view nurturing and caregiving activities as biologically determined traits rather than acquired skills.

Restricting women to the home reduces their access to power, prestige, and material well-being. Although a woman who works only in the home may receive part of the income of another household member, she is dependent on the person who hands over the money. Economic dependency, in turn, is likely to produce asymmetries in power between the woman and the income earner, who, after all, can withhold money for the purposes of control or influence. Similarly, if all her activities are limited to the private sphere, a woman cannot obtain direct access to power through political representation, political office, or favourable laws.

Finally, because material well-being and power are so closely connected to deference and respect, the societal evaluation of work done in the home is not high. One classic indication of the devaluation of housework is the phrase "just a housewife." Sociological research shows that many activities done in the home, such as cooking, cleaning, and babysitting, are not high in prestige (Armstrong and Armstrong, 1994: Table 16).The low regard for housework is also evident from interviews conducted with 1200 17-year-olds in Hamilton, Halifax, and rural Nova Scotia. Sociologists Dianne Looker and Victor Thiessen found that young people view housework as women's work. They consider it tiring since it involves long hours, high pressure, and much boredom. It generates few financial rewards. It is unimportant for the community. And young men consider housework—especially if it is full-time—to be a job at the bottom of the occupational hierarchy (Looker and Thiessen, 1999).

In short, the belief that a woman's place is in the home disadvantages women relative to men in the distribution of prestige, power, and economic resources. Recognition of these disadvantages has elicited two main responses. First, some people have tried to eliminate the devaluation of domestic labour by having women's unpaid work recognized officially and having a dollar value assigned to it. In Canada, women's unpaid work was recognized officially in the 1996 census. After intense lobbying, questions on unpaid child care, unpaid home maintenance, and unpaid eldercare were included in the 1996, 2001, and 2006 censuses, but dropped in 2011 (Luxton and Vosko, 1998). Assigning a dollar value to women's unpaid work was raised in feminist discussions in the 1970s and there is still interest in measuring the value of unpaid work today. One Statistics Canada economist estimated that unpaid domestic work, if done in the market for wages, would be worth about one-third of the gross national product (the total value of market-produced goods and services produced in the country over a year). He also found that women do about two-thirds of all unpaid domestic work (Jackson, 1996).

The second response to the recognition of women's disadvantages emphasizes the entry of women into the public sphere. Women's growing labour-force participation and their political activities are often viewed optimistically because many people think these developments generate more money and power for women. Liberal feminists are especially likely to hold this view. Yet the fact that women are now part of the public sphere of paid work and politics does not mean that gender equality exists. Women's **labour-force participation rate** is still lower than men's is. (Women's labour-force participation rate is the proportion of women over the age of 14 who work for money, are seeking to work for money, or do unpaid work for a family business, expressed as a percentage of all women over the age of 14. It does not include women who do unpaid domestic work.) Women are still less likely to become elected politicians than men are. Paid work does not mean liberation from unpaid work, as you have seen. And substantial gender inequality remains in the labour force and in the political sphere. In the remainder of this chapter, I examine the movement of women into the public sphere, their continuing disproportionate involvement in unpaid work in the home, and the inequalities that still exist today in the public sphere.

SITES OF WORK

FEMALE LABOUR-FORCE PARTICIPATION

In the past, most work done by women was unpaid domestic labour. In the early days of Canadian settlement by Europeans, women processed food, wove fabric, sewed clothing, tended the sick, and produced the next generation of labourers. Women also took in boarders, did laundry, and prepared meals for others in their homes (Phillips and Phillips, 1983).

Canadian women continue to work in the home, but in the past 50 years, they have increasingly done work that is paid and usually performed outside the home. At the beginning of the twentieth century, only 14 percent of women were economically active in the paid labour force, compared with 78 percent of men (Leacy, 1983). By 2011, 62 percent of women were in the labour force, compared with 71 percent of men (Ferrao, 2011: Chart 2).

The marital status of female labour force participants also changed dramatically during the twentieth century. Until the 1960s, the typical female worker in the paid labour force was a never-married woman, but today married women constitute the majority. The labour-force participation rate of women with young children has also increased substantially. By 2009, almost two-thirds of women with a youngest child under the age of three were employed in the labour force, more than double the proportion in the mid-1970s (Ferrao, 2011).

Explaining the Increase

Three factors caused these changes in the women's labour-force participation rate: change in Canada's economy that increased the demand for workers in service jobs, decrease in the number of children born, and increased financial pressure on families. These factors altered attitudes toward the paid employment of women and helped remove barriers to such employment. Let us review each of them in turn.

Canada's Changing Economy In the early twentieth century, most Canadian jobs were in agriculture or manufacturing. Starting in the 1920s, more and more jobs became available in firms that provided services: telephone communication, financial assistance, medical care, educational instruction, and so forth. Women were often considered suitable employees for the new service jobs. By the early twentieth century, women—albeit mainly young and single women, in accordance with the prevailing belief that married women belonged in the home—had already supplanted men as office workers (Lowe, 1987) and teachers (Prentice, 1977). With respect to office work, this development was made possible by the introduction of the typewriter, which was thought to lower the skill requirements of secretarial work. Hiring women as teachers and secretaries was also appealing because they could be paid lower wages than men were on the strength of the belief that women were economically supported by the men in their household anyway.

Fertility Decline and Labour Supply Declining fertility also facilitated women's entry into the paid labour force, since it created an imbalance between the labour demands of the expanding service economy after World War II and the available labour supply. Canada's fertility rate dropped substantially during the 1930s and early 1940s as a result of the Depression and World War II. Consequently, the supply of new workers was relatively small when the postwar Canadian economy boomed. There were too few men and young, single women—the traditionally preferred source of labour—to meet the growing demand for labour in Canada's new service-based economy. In response to labour scarcity and the desire to minimize wage costs (Connelly, 1978), employers began loosening restrictions against the hiring of married women. The fact that married women were not averse to working for wages—indeed, they were eager to do so—had been proved by the experience of their employment during World War II (Pierson, 1977). As a result, female labour-force participation rates increased rapidly in the postwar years.

Family Finances Family finances also influenced the rise in female labour-force participation. Despite the idea that a woman's proper place was in the home, women's employment had always been an important source of income for low-income families. To meet economic needs, many working-class women laboured as domestics and in factories during the late nineteenth and early twentieth centuries. After World War II, women's paid employment became an important source of family income for single-parent and two-adult families alike. Today, one in five families with children under the age of 25 is headed by women who are single parents (Milan, Keown, and Urquijo, 2011: 12), most of whom work in the labour force. My analysis of 2006 census data shows that when single-parent mothers are employed, average family income is more than twice as high as that reported by families without earnings from the mother. In husband-wife families, family incomes are 1.3 times as large as when both partners are employed (Statistics Canada, 2011a, 2011b).

DOMESTIC LABOUR

The exclusion of women from the public sphere was part of a more general predicament in which women were almost solely responsible for unpaid domestic production and for work associated with reproduction (bearing and rearing children). Canadian women cooked, cleaned, and took care of children, and men provided the money necessary to sustain the family. Has this structure changed with the rising labour-force participation of women?

If you think that the answer is "no," you are correct. My analysis of 2006 census data shows that women are still more likely than men are to do unpaid work involving home maintenance and child care. Women also spend more hours than men do on these activities. Both women and men are less likely to be caring for seniors than to be doing home maintenance or child care, although women are more often caregivers for seniors than men are.

Even when they are in the paid labour force, women continue to spend more time than men do on housework and child care. Figure 7.1 shows that, compared with married men, a higher percentage of married women spend 15 hours or more on housework and on child care among those who have at least one child under age 15 in the household (see Chapter 10, Families for more on housework). Lone-parent women also spend more time on housework and child care than do lone-parent men. Not surprisingly, women report spending less time than men do watching television and playing sports and games (Statistics Canada, 2011d: Table 1.1).

The greater amount of time spent by women on unpaid work illustrates the phrase "the double day." Entering the labour force may mean fewer hours spent on work in the home, but it increases the hours of total work, paid and unpaid, performed by women. In fact, the demand on women to provide unpaid care likely will increase because the number of senior Canadians in need of care will increase substantially. Past caregiving patterns suggest future providers of care are most likely to be women (Cranswick and Dosman, 2008).

In addition to increasing hours of unpaid work, caregiving responsibilities alter the way women and men lead their lives. Consider Grace, who is in her early 50s, has teenage children, and also has an 80-year-old ailing parent living nearby. She represents what is called the "sandwich" generation—individuals caught between the demands of caring for children and older relatives. As she cares for her children and parent, Grace is likely to cut back on her social activities, move closer to her parent, report that her own health is affected, and experience altered sleep patterns. The strongest impact, however, is on paid work. Grace is likely to find that caregiving activities cause her to arrive late at work, leave work early, or miss work occasionally (Williams, 2004). Clearly, the domestic sphere and the public spheres intersect. What people do or don't do in one sphere affects their activities in the other.

FIGURE 7.1 PERCENTAGE SPENDING 15 HOURS OR MORE A WEEK ON UNPAID HOUSEWORK AND ON CHILD CARE, WOMEN AND MEN AGES 25–54 IN THE LABOUR FORCE WITH AT LEAST ONE CHILD UNDER AGE 15 IN THE HOUSEHOLD, CANADA, 2006

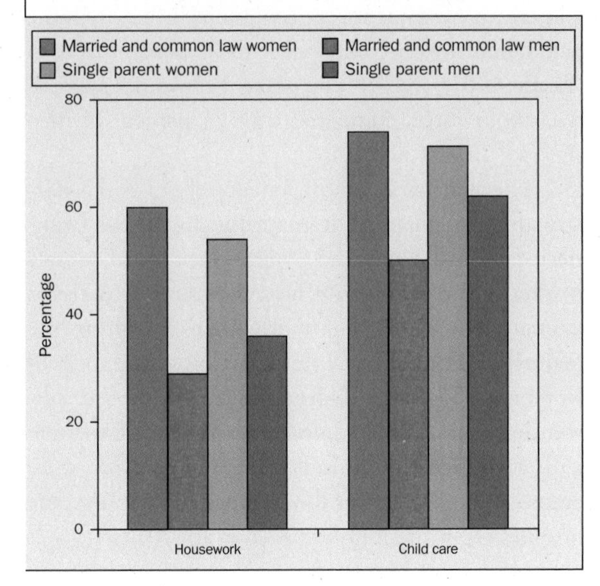

SOURCE: Adapted from Statistics Canada (2011g).

LABOUR-FORCE INEQUALITIES

OCCUPATIONAL SEGREGATION AND SEX TYPING

Liberal feminists explain the fact that unpaid caregivers tend to be women by referring to gender stereotypes and gender roles. Gender stereotypes imply women are more caring and therefore better caregivers. Gender roles emphasize that good daughters, wives, and mothers are women who care for their parents, partners, and offspring. Socialist feminists note that caregiving is consistent with other activities that maintain male wage workers and disproportionately benefit men.

The equation of women and caregiving is also found in paid work. Although more and more Canadian women are now paid workers, they are frequently in jobs that involve caregiving, nurturing, and the sort of management functions typically found in the home. Women tend to be secretaries ("office wives"), nurses, social workers, teachers, seamstresses, and wait staff. In contrast, men tend to be managers, doctors, professors, and factory and construction workers. The concentration of men in some occupations and women in others is often called the **sex segregation of occupations,** and the notion that a given occupation is appropriate for one sex versus the other is referred to as the **sex typing (or sex labelling) of occupations.**

Occupational Segregation

Men and women can be compared across occupations in a given place (a firm, a city, or a country). If men and women are concentrated in different occupations, the occupational structure is considered sex segregated. Figures 7.2 and 7.3 show that, according to the 2006 census, sex segregation exists in Canada. For women, the 10 most frequent jobs include secretary, registered nurse, elementary schoolteacher, babysitter, and receptionist. For men, the 10 most frequent jobs include truck driver, janitor, retail trade manager, farmer, carpenter, and so on. The only occupation that both men and women occupy in large numbers is retail salesperson.

The figures show only the top 10 occupations. The census collects information on more than five hundred occupations. These longer lists confirm that women and men often are concentrated in different occupations. The degree of occupational segregation by gender has, however, declined somewhat since the 1960s. The decline is attributable mainly to the movement of women into previously male-dominated occupations, not the entry of men into female-dominated occupations.

Sex labelling of occupations usually accompanies occupational segregation. Certain occupations are seen as jobs that are more appropriate for women. Other occupations are seen as jobs that are more appropriate for men. Often these views are so ingrained in our thinking that we recognize sex typing only when unstated expectations are contradicted. Consider the terms *woman engineer* and *male babysitter*. We frequently use these terms to indicate a departure from the implied norm—that men are engineers and women are babysitters. We rarely say "female babysitter" Or "male engineer." Or consider the list of the 10 most frequent occupations for men and women. What gender comes to mind for secretary, nurse, or receptionist or for truck driver, farmer, or carpenter? These occupations are strongly sex-typed both in imagery and in reality.

The fact that women now compose about 47 percent of the labour force is a yardstick by which occupations are female sex-typed or male sex-typed. In such occupations as actor, cook, dispatcher and radio operator, journalist, optometrist, financial and

FIGURE 7.2 TEN MOST COMMON JOBS FOR WOMEN, CANADA, 2006

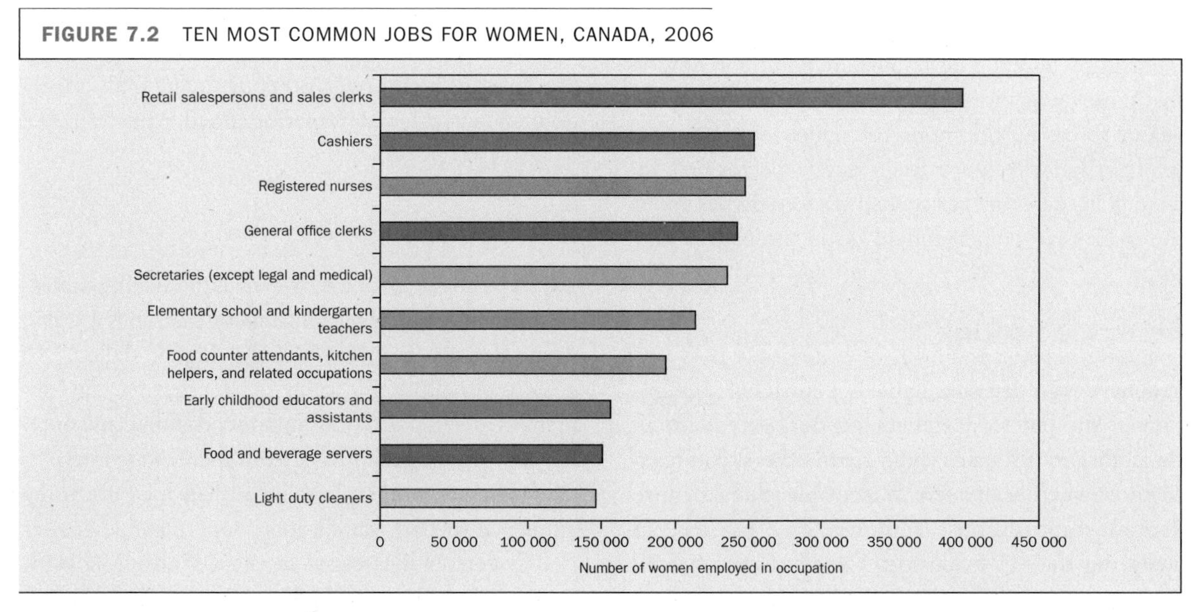

SOURCE: Adapted from Statistics Canada (2008: Table 3).

FIGURE 7.3 TEN MOST COMMON JOBS FOR MEN, CANADA, 2006

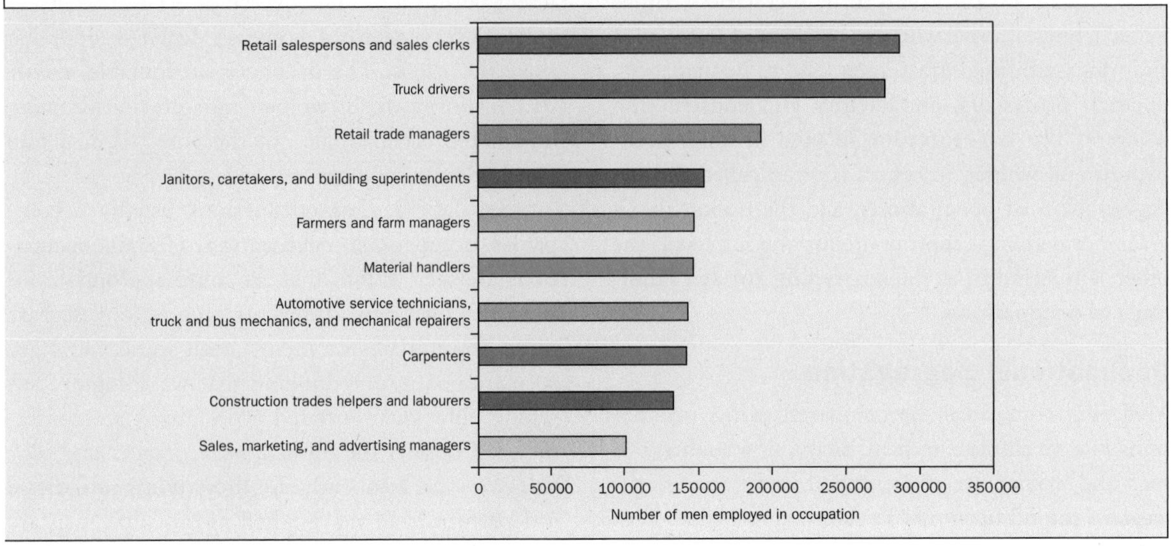

Retail salespersons and sales clerks
Truck drivers
Retail trade managers
Janitors, caretakers, and building superintendents
Farmers and farm managers
Material handlers
Automotive service technicians, truck and bus mechanics, and mechanical repairers
Carpenters
Construction trades helpers and labourers
Sales, marketing, and advertising managers
0 50000 100000 150000 200000 250000 300000 350000
Number of men employed in occupation

SOURCE: Adapted from Statistics Canada (2008: Table 3).

investment analyst, and veterinarian, 45 percent to 50 percent of workers are women. These occupations are not sex-typed (Statistics Canada, 2011e).

Why Care?

Why should you be concerned about sex typing and sex segregation? Because the occupations in which women are concentrated are often lower than those held predominantly by men in terms of authority, responsibility, skill requirements, mobility opportunities, and earnings. I will discuss many of these inequalities later. The important point for now is that these inequalities indicate male advantages in the labour force. Furthermore, the nature of sex typing implies that the work traditionally performed by women in the home has created sex stereotypes about the work that women should do in the paid labour force.

POWER AT WORK

You have seen that substantial occupational segregation exists, but to document gender asymmetry in the ability to influence and control others, you need to know whether men are indeed able to make more decisions and exercise authority over women. In analyzing the 1994 Statistics Canada *General Social Survey*, my colleagues and I found that men were more likely than women were to describe their jobs as managerial or as supervising others. Specifically, 25 percent of women and 40 percent of men described themselves as supervisors. Male supervisors managed more employees than did female supervisors. Male managers were more likely than female managers were to hold top positions and plan the activities of all parts of the business (Boyd, Hughes, and Miller, 1997). This pattern illustrates the **glass ceiling** effect: Women face invisible barriers that prevent them from penetrating the highest levels of organizations where power is concentrated and exercised (see Box 7.1). Finally, men often supervise women; when women supervise, they usually exercise authority over other women. Only rarely do men have a female superior (Boyd, Mulvihill, and Myles, 1991: 424).

GENDER AND SKILL

Jobs typically held by women have lower skill requirements than do jobs typically held by men (Boyd, 1990; Myles and Fawcett, 1990). Since higher-skilled jobs usually pay more and offer more security, employment in lower-skilled jobs implies economic and quality-of-work inequalities between men and women.

Why are women less likely than men are to be employed in high-skilled jobs? One possible answer is that gender bias exists in the definition of **skill.** Sex typing and a general devaluation of work done by women influence commonsense evaluations of what is or is not "skilled" work. For example, nursing

BOX 7.1 WOMEN STILL HITTING GLASS CEILING

The number of women breaking into the top executive jobs at Canadian companies remains small, growing at a snail's pace, according to a new survey by Catalyst Canada. As of June 1, 2010, women held 17.7 percent of top officer positions, up from 16.9 percent in 2008, an improvement of less than a percentage point. ... "It's a number that most business leaders would not be happy with if they were talking about any other aspect of their business," said Deborah Gillis, senior vice-president of Catalyst Canada, which released a report of the number of senior officers in top executive positions of the *Financial Post* 500 companies. Of the 468 companies that participated in the Catalyst Canada census count, 144 had 25 percent or more women in top positions, while 142 had no women in those jobs.

SOURCE: Lu, Vanessa. (2011). "Women Still Hitting Glass Ceiling," *Toronto Star* 3 March. On the World Wide Web at http://mmsearch.com/html/research/women_still_ceiling.php (retrieved 9 March 2012). Reprinted with permission—Torstar Syndication Services.

occupations may require high levels of interpersonal skill in dealing with relatives of dying patients, but because the ability to handle distraught people is widely considered natural in a woman, it is not recognized as a professional skill in a nursing occupation. In contrast, plumbing jobs, usually performed by men, require knowledge of toilets and sinks, soldering, and pipe fitting—so-called technical skills.

When women supervise, they usually exercise authority over other women; only rarely do men have a female superior.
SOURCE: © Monkey Business Images/Shutterstock.

Bias in the evaluation of skills occurs when such technical knowledge is considered more valuable than knowledge about personal interaction and caregiving.

This example indicates that our definitions of skill are socially constructed. What we define as skill reflects other social evaluations and hierarchies—in this case, hierarchies based on gender (Gaskell, 1986; Steinberg, 1990). If people think of women as being worth less than men are, they are inclined to let their attitude influence how they define the skill requirements of jobs held primarily by women or primarily by men. Jane Gaskell (1986) suggested that women are disadvantaged in the skill definitions assigned to jobs sex-typed as female because, historically, women have not been represented by strong unions that have lobbied in their interest. Furthermore, women are less likely to be trained on the shop floor as apprentices. Instead, the training required for "female" jobs is often incorporated into high-school curricula, with the result that the skill-training component is less visible than it is in occupations in which training is provided on the job.

Skill undervaluation of female sex-typed occupations is a concern for two reasons. First, wage levels are associated with skill requirements. Thus, if the skill requirements of jobs in which women predominate are undervalued, the pay rates in those jobs are likely to be lower. Second, current pay equity policies often ask whether men and women are receiving equal pay for performing jobs of comparable worth. The "worth" of a job, however, includes its skill requirements. If the skill requirements of jobs employing predominantly women are already devalued, then fair comparisons between appropriate sets of jobs may not be made (Steinberg, 1990).

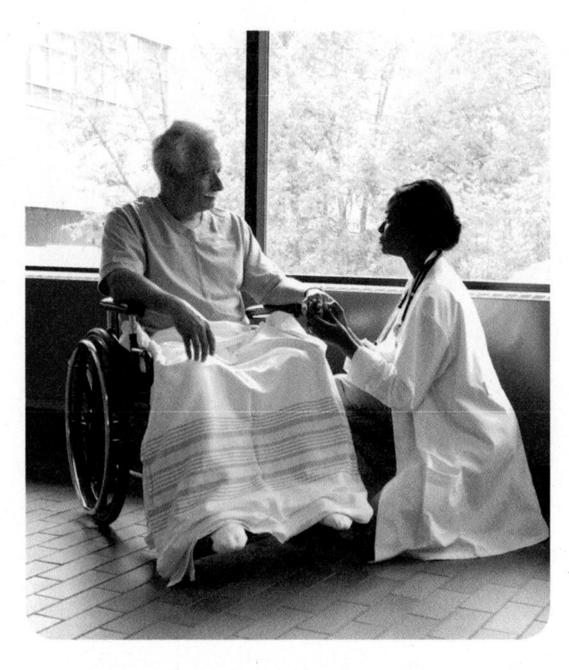

Nurses may be required to deal with dying patients and their relatives, but because the ability to handle distraught people is considered natural in a woman, this high level of interpersonal skill is not recognized as a professional skill in a nursing occupation.
SOURCE: © Jupiter Photos.

NONSTANDARD WORK

Another example of gender inequality can be seen in **standard** and **nonstandard work.** If asked to describe a typical job in the labour market, you would probably mention full-time, full-year employment with job-related benefits. This is usually what we mean by standard work. In contrast, nonstandard work includes **part-time work,** part-year employment, limited-term contract employment, employment through temporary-help agencies, self-employment, and multiple job-holding (Krahn, 1995). Nonstandard work, also called precarious employment, is more common for women than for men (Cooke-Reynolds and Zukewich, 2004; Cranford, Vosko, and Zukewich, 2003).

Women and Part-Time Work

Compared with men, women in the labour force are much more likely to be part-time workers—more than twice as likely as men were in 2011 (Statistics Canada, 2011c). This is significant because part-time work has been increasing as a share of all employment. Many workers now take part-time employment because they cannot find full-time employment; many women take part-time employment so they can take care of their children (Ferrao, 2011: Table 9).

Women and Nonstandard Work

Since the 1970s, women have made up more than two-thirds of the part-time labour force. Part-time work can thus be seen as an employment ghetto for women. Women are also overrepresented in nonstandard work defined more broadly. Using a definition of nonstandard employment that includes self-employment, temporary work, part-time work, part-year work, and multiple job-holding, a 1994 Canadian study found that 40 percent of all currently employed women, compared with 27 percent of men, were working in nonstandard employment (Krahn, 1995). These levels of nonstandard work remained stable through the 1990s and early 2000s (Vosko, Zukewich, and Cranford, 2003: Chart A).

Concerns about Nonstandard Work

Employment in nonstandard work is of concern for two reasons. First, it is becoming more common, especially among young people. Second, compared with full-year, full-time jobs, nonstandard jobs generally provide less job security, lower pay, and fewer benefits, such as pension plans (Duffy and Pupo 1992; Fuller and Vosko, 2008). Thus, nonstandard employment in general and part-time work in particular imply a marginal workforce—marginal in terms of earnings, benefits, and job security.

EARNINGS

In addition to gender inequalities in occupations, power, skill, and type of work, women in Canada earn less than men do on average—about 65 cents for every dollar earned by men in 2008. As you can see from Figure 7.4, this ratio represents gradual improvement from earlier times.

EXPLANATIONS OF WOMEN'S LOWER PAY

Observers have explained the pay gap between women and men by focusing on four factors:

1. Gender differences in the characteristics that influence pay rates
2. Gender differences in the type of work performed
3. Discrimination
4. Societal devaluation of women's work

Explanations that focus on gender differences in the characteristics that influence pay rates usually

FIGURE 7.4 RATIO OF WOMEN'S TO MEN'S EARNINGS, CANADA, 1976–2008

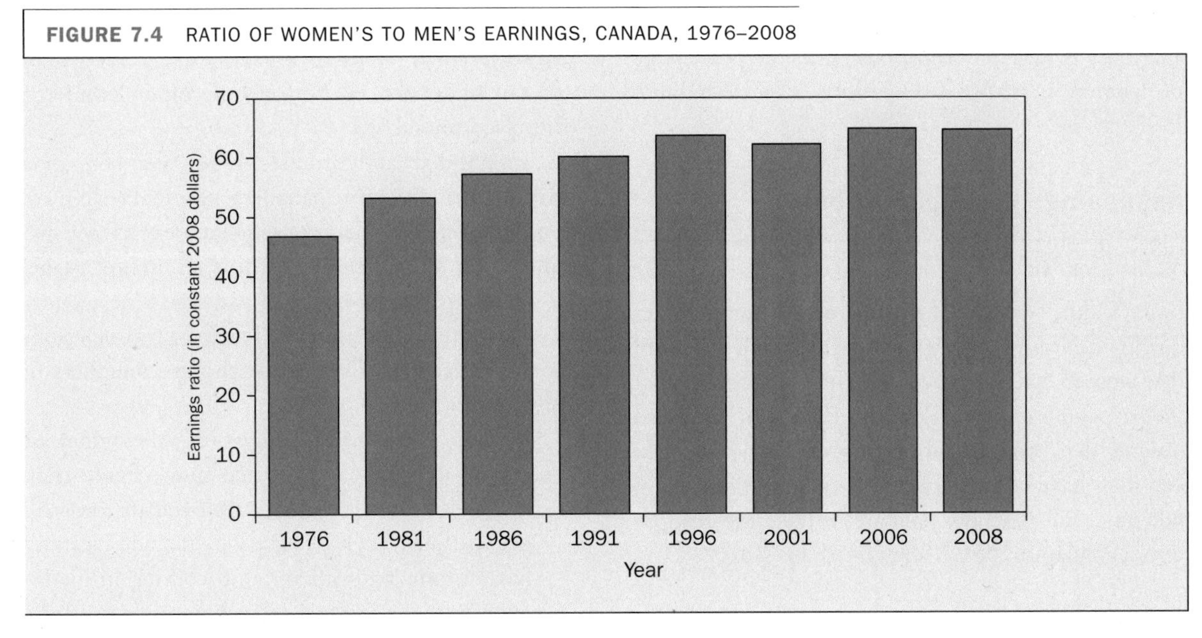

SOURCE: Adapted from Williams (2011: Table 7).

assume that earnings reflect the productivity of workers and that productivity is increased by more education, labour-force experience, and length of time on the job. Advocates of this explanation argue that the lower wages of women are caused by lower productivity resulting from women's lower educational achievements, and labour-force interruptions because of women's family responsibilities.

Explanations that focus on gender differences in the type of work performed assume that the gender gap in pay reflects the concentration of women in certain occupations and industries characterized by low wages, including nonstandard (particularly part-time) work.

Explanations that focus on discrimination argue that women are paid less than men are because of their gender. Such discrimination can be personal and deliberate, but it is often impersonal, produced by standard, unquestioned practices, such as assigning women to certain jobs and men to other jobs, and paying men and women different wages even when they hold the same job. Much of this impersonal discrimination is called **statistical discrimination,** the process whereby employers make decisions about whether to hire and how much to pay any given woman on the basis of the employers' perceptions of the average characteristics of *all* women. For example, if an employer believes that women typically leave the labour force for long periods to raise children, or will not travel extensively or work overtime because of family responsibilities, the employer may impose those generalized beliefs on particular women. Thus, a single woman with no children might find herself being paid less than a man because of the employer's belief that women in general are less productive than men are. Alternatively, she might find herself denied opportunities for job training or advancement because of her employer's belief that women in general will leave their jobs to have families or will not perform certain tasks, such as long-distance travelling, because of family obligations.

Finally, explanations of the gender earnings gap that focus on the societal devaluation of women's work hold that the lower earnings of women reflect a general devaluation of "women's work"—that is, of tasks initially performed in the home—and the incorporation of that devaluation into pay practices. As we have seen, the work women perform in the home can be invisible and often is not viewed as work. Accordingly, people who do domestic work for money receive low wages. The devaluation of women's labour is rooted in the historical image of every woman having a male breadwinner to provide for her and not "needing" to be paid the same wage as a man who, after all, has a family to support! Once in place, pay practices persist and fuel a faulty logic that not only sustains pay differences between men and women in the same jobs, but also provides a rationale for the lower wage rates paid in sex-typed occupations and jobs. Wages in occupations fall as the percentage of women in those occupations rises (England, 1993: ch. 3).

Assessing the Explanations

Most sociologists emphasize discrimination and the devaluation of work performed by women (explanations 3 and 4) as the main reasons for gender inequality in earnings. They point to the absence of proof that women are less productive than are men or that they expend less effort (England, 1993: 27). They also observe that earnings gaps persist even when women and men have comparable levels of education, are in full-time, full-year jobs, and are in the same occupations (Williams, 2011: Tables 8–10; see Box 7.2).

BIRTHPLACE AND COLOUR MATTER

So far, my discussion of gender inequality in work has proceeded as if all women were alike and all men were alike. This is, of course, not the case. Some women and men are young and others are older. Some are married or living with a partner; others are not. Some women are born in Canada; others are born elsewhere. In addition, women differ in their colour and ancestral origins, as do men.

The intersection of gender inequality with inequalities stemming from birthplace and colour is of interest to many Canadians. That interest is fuelled by the changing ethnic and colour composition of Canada's population, initiated by changes in Canada's immigration policies starting in 1962. It has become evident since then that foreign-born women and women of colour experience not only gender inequality but also the inequalities that arise in a society that allocates privileges to certain groups and not to others on the basis of colour, ethnicity, birthplace, and class.

In popular and official usage, members of a **visible minority** are Canadian residents who are non-white and who may consequently experience discrimination. However, the term is an umbrella label for diverse groups.

Government statistics lead us to four conclusions about the earnings of women who are members of visible minorities:

1. Women who are members of Aboriginal or visible-minority groups are more likely than are white women to be employed in low-skill occupations. Such occupations include cleaning hotel rooms and offices, and working in manufacturing jobs in food-processing plants and the textile industry. Many workers in Canada's garment firms are immigrant women of colour, and their jobs are often characterized by irregular employment, bad lighting, poor ventilation, and low pay (Das Gupta, 1996; Yanz, Ladd, Atlin, and Maquila Solidarity Network, 1999).
2. Foreign-born women who are permanent residents of Canada and who are members of visible minorities earn less on average than their Canadian-born counterparts do (Chui and Maheux, 2011). My research shows that the earnings gap increases between Canadian-born and foreign-born women when foreign-born women of colour have no knowledge of English or French (Boyd, 1999).
3. Overall, women who are members of Aboriginal or visible-minority groups earn less than women

BOX 7.2 WOMEN CONTINUE TO EARN FAR LESS THAN MEN

"Women across the country earn far less than men," Statistics Canada has just reported. Canadian women earned $30,100 on average in 2008, only 65 per cent of the amount earned by men. That women are less likely than men to work full time is one reason for that disparity, the report says. But even women working full time made only 71 per cent of what men made." Jamie Peck, a professor of economic geography at the University of B.C., says that "It's not just straight gender discrimination, although that's clearly present in the workplace. Men and women tend to be located in different parts of the economy, by industry and occupation." The report reveals some progress, with women's earnings rising 13 per cent between 2000 and 2008. Education, according to the report, appears key to that improvement, with many women using schooling to climb out of the realm of sales, service, and clerical jobs into higher-paid positions in health care and education.

SOURCE: Baron, Ethan. (2010). "Equal Work is Still Resulting in Unequal Pay," from http://www2.canada.com/theprovince/news/story.html?id=cd1db504-6b8a-4c2d-a56c-8a5c1ef61092. Material reprinted with the express permission of *The Vancouver Province*, a division of Postmedia Network Inc.

who are not members of visible-minority groups. My research and that of others show that earnings differentials persist between women who are and women who are not members of visible-minority groups, even when we account for the fact that differences between groups can exist with respect to age, education, and other factors that influence the levels of earnings (Pendakur and Pendakur, 2011). This means we cannot rule out discrimination as a factor, and that at least part of the lower earnings of women who are members of visible-minority groups and Aboriginal women may be caused by employers not hiring these women for certain jobs, promoting them slowly, or paying them less.

4. Considerable diversity exists among women in their labour-force characteristics. Thus, we should not think of women as a homogeneous group.

These findings reaffirm the criticisms voiced by women who are members of minority groups and by foreign-born women—namely, that, for them, inequality issues are not restricted to gender but also include race and immigrant status, and that each group is unique in the kinds of disadvantages and subordinations it experiences. These criticisms are consistent with multiracial feminism.

WOMEN'S GROUPS: ORGANIZING FOR CHANGE

So far, I have discussed the increasing movement of women out of the home and into the labour force. The economy, however, is only one of several arenas in the public sphere from which women have historically been excluded and in which their participation remains very limited. Politics is another important arena that initially excluded women and that women have now begun to penetrate. The political arena includes more than voting or running for political office. It can be broadly defined to include any activity that mobilizes people to make their views known, to press for change, and to achieve objectives.

Collective actions aimed at such change are called **social movements.** The **women's movement** is a social movement that takes action to improve the status of women. Feminism is an important part of the women's movement. However, as I observed earlier, many different forms of feminism exist, each with a different understanding of the causes of gender inequality and subordination and of the actions required to improve the situation.

Over time, changes have occurred in feminist thought and in the nature of the women's movement. Both before and immediately after women were granted the right to vote, early efforts focused on improving the quality of life in the home for women and their families (O'Neill and Young, 2010). The large-scale entry of women into the paid labour force during the 1960s and 1970s elicited a different set of concerns. Based on a model of equal rights between women and men, women pressed for gender equality in employment opportunities and earnings.

Beginning in the 1960s, advocacy groups, some closely affiliated with the federal government, such as the Canadian Advisory Council on the Status of Women, and others receiving substantial government funding, presented agendas for change to parliamentarians, ministers, and key civil servants in government departments. Such direct interaction with the agencies and members of the state achieved some successes, depending on the party in power and how robust the economy was. For example, through the lobbying efforts of various groups, women's rights are now enshrined in the 1982 Canadian Charter of Rights and Freedoms, and legislative changes ensure a fairer division of assets in divorce cases. However, the efforts of women's groups have been limited by at least two factors (Newman and White, 2006). First, because many women's groups rely on governments for funding, their roles as critics of government policy can be easily compromised. They may change their agendas or adopt a conciliatory style. The heterogeneity of women's groups is a second factor limiting their impact. There are many different women's groups, and not all of them agree on what should be done for women. For example, diverse opinions exist among women's associations on child-care issues and on access to abortion; it is often impossible to create a coalition to lobby for one clear policy.

Women's groups still lobby governments for change, but from the 1980s on, three factors changed the interaction between women's groups and governments: the electoral success of more conservative parties; the federal government's calls for economic restraint and increased provincial, territorial, and private-sector responsibility; and the dissatisfaction within women's advocacy groups on agendas reflecting the concerns of white, largely middle-class women (Tremblay and Andrew, 1998). By the mid-1990s, political representatives and departments of federal and provincial governments (which in the case of Quebec and Ontario had also taken leadership on certain issues, such as pay equity) were no longer as responsive to lobbying efforts by women's groups. They reduced funding. In 1995 the federal government reorganized their units dealing with women's issues and disbanded the Canadian Advisory Council on the Status of Women, which had been mandated to inform the public and the Canadian federal government on issues of concern to women. In 2006 the federal government reduced the annual budget of the federal department of the Status of Women Canada, removed the word "equality" from the mandate of the Status of Women Canada, and closed 12 of the organization's 16 offices. Alongside these changes, a different model of advocacy emerged in which women's groups operated in coalition with other social-movement-based groups, often rejecting networking and direct contact with political parties (Newman and White, 2006).

Recently, associations that represent the interests of women of colour, immigrant women, and lesbians have added much to the landscape of women's associations in Canada. The attention they have directed to issues of racism, sexual identity, and class inequality has forced mainstream groups representing primarily white, heterosexual, middle-class women to become more inclusive in their membership base and agendas. Women of colour have argued that these groups fail to acknowledge concerns other than those of white middle-class women. The mainstream argument that gender subordination reflects the restriction of women to the private sphere fails to recognize that many women of colour have long engaged in paid work and that issues of racism in employment are of equal importance to them. Furthermore, to the extent that women of colour work as domestics, it is white women who have power over them as their employers; women of colour tend to see both gender oppression and racial oppression as important issues. Immigrant women have their own concerns, including language training, job-skill training, culturally sensitive child care, and culturally sensitive assistance in situations of domestic violence. For lesbians, areas of interest include gay rights and related issues, such as the inclusion of sexual orientation in human rights codes and the prohibition of employment discrimination on the basis of sexual orientation.

GENDER IN POLITICS

> The voice of government, as the [1971] Royal Commission on the Status of Women observed, is still a man's voice. Women remain governed rather than governors, legislated rather than legislators. (Brodie, 1991: 9)

Formal politics is an important area of gender inequality because that is where laws determining rights and entitlements are formulated and public policies set. Politics and political representation are the mechanisms that translate the interests of groups into political demands and actions (Brodie, 1991: 9). If some groups are politically disenfranchised or face barriers to the representation of their interests, their needs may not be met and the premise that democratic governments represent all the people is falsified. For the first 50 years after Confederation, the notion that the private sphere was the appropriate place for women went hand in hand with the exclusion of women from politics. During the twentieth century, however, women moved into the political arena. They obtained and exercised the right to vote. They participated in political parties and were elected to political office. And they created associations to represent the interests of women, including access to abortion and child care; equality in the labour force and pensions; the prevention of family violence (including spousal violence and child abuse), prostitution, and rape; and participation in politics.

VOTING RIGHTS

Before 1916, Canadian women did not have the right to vote. Without that right, they could not elect candidates to represent their interests in government. Between 1916 and 1925, however, all provinces and territories except Quebec and the Northwest Territories enfranchised women. Quebec granted women the vote in 1940, and the Northwest Territories did in 1951. The federal government granted voting rights in 1917 to women who were British subjects and had served with the military or had a close relative in the military. It extended those rights to women not connected to the military in 1918. However, voting rights were not given to women or men of Chinese, East Indian, or Japanese ancestry until the late 1940s, to male and female Inuit until 1950, or to all registered Indians until 1960.

The suffrage movement in English Canada was a factor in winning the vote for women (Bashevkin, 1993: ch. 1). However, the vote was granted on the premise that women would use it only to improve the quality of home life, and that enfranchisement would not divert women from their "natural and sacred" duties in the domestic sphere (Burt, 1993: 216).

Such sex stereotyping of women also led to the expectation that women would not be interested in politics. Most men believed that women would not vote at the same rate as men. Most men also believed that women would vote in a politically naive and parochial way as a result of being isolated at home. These stereotypes proved false. In Canada today, the percentage of eligible voters who cast a ballot is about the same for women and men. The political agendas of men and women differ but not because women's views are parochial. Research shows that women are more likely than men are to oppose free markets and military spending and to be more concerned with social-welfare policies (Bashevkin, 1993: ch. 2; O'Neill and Young, 2010). Gender differences in voting interests may be due to the fact that women and men operate in different political cultures (which have been moulded by gender differences in political socialization) and have different opportunities to participate in politics. Again and again, women hear that "politics is a man's world." Excluded from political life, women are more likely to be concerned with moral and community-based political issues than with issues pertaining to the acquisition and exercise of power (McCormack, 1975: 25–26). However, women do not act as a cohesive voting bloc on any issue (Brodie, 1991; O'Neill and Young, 2010).

TABLE 7.1 NUMBERS AND PERCENTAGES OF FEDERAL POLITICAL REPRESENTATIVES WHO ARE WOMEN, MARCH 2012

	TOTAL	WOMEN	WOMEN AS A PERCENTAGE OF TOTAL
HOUSE OF COMMONS			
Conservative Party of Canada	165	39	24
New Democratic Party	101	28	28
Liberal Party	35	7	20
Bloc Québécois	4	1	25
Independent Conservative	1	0	0
Green Party	1	1	100
Vacant	1		
Total	308	76	25
SENATE			
Conservative Party of Canada	59	21	36
Liberal Party	41	16	39
Independent	2	1	50
Progressive Conservative	1	1	100
Vacant	2		
Total	105	39	37

SOURCE: Compiled from Parliament of Canada (n.d.).

PARTICIPATING IN THE WORLD OF POLITICS

In the mid-1970s, women composed fewer than 4 percent of Canada's members of Parliament (MPs). After the May 2011 federal election, 25 percent of MPs were women, as were 38 percent of senators (Table 7.1). However, enthusiasm over such progress should be tempered by the recognition that women represent more than half of Canada's electorate (Box 7.3). Table 7.1 shows variations by party in the percentages of federal MPs who are women, with the highest percentages in the New Democratic Party (NDP) and the Conservative Party of Canada. These differences reflect such factors as the recruiting strategies of parties and barriers to women in politics, both of which are discussed later in this chapter. Other variations exist. My analysis of women who were sitting in the House of Commons in March 2012 shows that 17 of the 76 (22 percent) women were foreign-born, which is slightly above the percentage in the female Canadian population as a whole and certainly greater than the 10 percent foreign-born among male MPs. However, visible minorities in general, and visible-minority women in particular, are underrepresented in politics (Black, 2008; Trimble and Arscott, 2003).

When elected, women are seldom found in the upper ranks of political parties. Although Kim Campbell served briefly as prime minister of Canada in 1993, the presence of women in the upper echelons of power is rare enough to be newsworthy. If gender made no difference, why would the cover of *Maclean's* run a photo of Kim Campbell over the caption "When the Boss Is a Woman" (October 4, 1993), and why would newspaper articles describe what MP Belinda Stronach was wearing (Bashevkin, 2009)? Former Governor General Michaëlle Jean and former U.S. Secretary of State Condoleezza Rice are also exceptions who demonstrate the scarcity of women, particularly women who are members of visible minorities, in the top echelons of power.

BOX 7.3 WOMEN: HALF THE POPULATION, A FIFTH THE SEATS IN PARLIAMENT

Think of a country where the majority of citizens are relegated to just a fifth of the seats in the government. Think of Canada.

Nearly 90 years after Agnes MacPhail became the country's first female MP, women have failed to gain more than a secondary role in the halls of power.

Canada lags behind Angola, Ecuador, Mozambique, Guyana, and even Afghanistan when it comes to the representation of women in its parliament.

In Rwanda, 56 per cent of the federal seats are held by women. By those standards, Canada's performance has been dismal.

Just 22 per cent of this country's federal politicians are women—a proportion that has remained all but unchanged through five elections.

And the numbers are not much different at the provincial and municipal levels.

So what's wrong with that? Can't men adequately represent the interests of women? Well, no, say those who have studied the issue.

The taxpayers of Canada, including women, help political parties pay the bill for elections through tax breaks for donors, campaign-expense refunds, and per-vote subsidies.

So "how can we allow parties to present us with a group of so-called representatives who are not at all mirroring the representation of the country as a whole?" asks Sylvia Bashevkin, the principal of University College at the University of Toronto whose recent book *Women, Power, Politics* explores the political gender gap.

Young girls need to see female politicians to know that they can become the prime minister of Canada, said Dr. Bashevkin. Young boys, she said, need to see that women can be effective leaders.

And an increase in the number of women in Parliament would lead to different policy decisions, said Dr. Bashevkin. "Because, on average, across political systems in the democratic world, women politicians are the ones who move forward on issues that relate to their experiences, whether it's childcare, whether it's violence against women, whether it's equal pay, or whether it's government funding on research against breast cancer."

Anne McLellan, a former Liberal cabinet minister, embarked on a process of party renewal in 2006. She travelled the country looking at, among other things, ways to draw good women into federal politics.

It won't be easy, Ms. McLellan said in summing up her findings.

The women she spoke to expressed concerns about finding a balance between work and family life. They said they were discouraged by the hyper-partisan atmosphere in Ottawa and the "men playing silly games." And they were turned off by the media's sexist depiction of female politicians. "They say 'why would I put myself through that,'" said Ms. McLellan.

Political parties need to solve those problems before Canada's Parliament and legislatures become a true reflection of Canadian society.

But just getting women to run is only half the battle. The other half is getting them elected. And carrots or sticks may be required to push the parties to act.

Some countries have adopted quotas—and they have been effective. But quotas present a whole new set of problems, including the fact that they cast doubts about qualifications of women who are elected.

Some countries have introduced subsidies for parties that nominate women. Subsidies can be—and often are—ignored.

In the end, Canada can opt for the status quo. Or it can have a conversation.

But Kim Campbell, the only woman to hold the office of prime minister, said getting women into Parliament matters.

"Because, if they are not there, then people do not learn that they belong," said Ms. Campbell, "and they do not keep the doors open for all the generations of young women yet to come."

SOURCE: Galloway, Gloria. (2010). "Women: Half the Population, a Fifth of the Seats in Parliament." *Globe and Mail October* 12: A16.

Table 7.1 illustrates the truth of the saying "the higher, the fewer" with respect to the participation of women in Canadian political parties. Sylvia Bashevkin (1993: ch. 3) found that women are more likely to be local riding secretaries (as opposed to presidents), and that they do the necessary clerical work, paralleling the "pink ghetto" of female-typed clerical work found in the labour force. In the 90 years since most women gained the vote federally, only five women have served as party leaders of Canada's major parties, all since 1989: Audrey McLaughlin served as leader of the NDP between 1989 and 1995; Kim Campbell was leader of the Progressive Conservatives between June and December 1993; Else Wayne served as interim

Michaëlle Jean, 27th Governor General of Canada, 2005–10
SOURCE: © Robert Wagenhoffer/The Canadian Press.

leader of the Progressive Conservatives in 1998, Alexa McDonough was leader of the NDP from 1995 to 2003; and Elizabeth May has led the Green Party since 2006, winning a seat in the 2011 election.

EXPLAINING THE POLITICAL PARTICIPATION OF WOMEN

We have seen that a quarter of Canada's federally elected representatives are women. This low proportion cannot be explained by differences between female and male candidates in getting elected. My research on the results of the 2011 federal election finds that 20 percent of all male candidates were elected compared to 17 percent of all female candidates. The main reason for the gender difference is that women were underpresented in the pool of candidates who ran for office; just 28 percent of all candidates in the 2011 federal election were women.

Four major explanations exist for the underrepresentation of women in Canadian politics. The first focuses on sex-role stereotypes. It argues that certain characteristics of women keep them from participating in politics. According to this argument, women are less assertive than men are, more oriented to family than to politics, and conditioned through childhood socialization to view politics as an inappropriate activity (Brodie, 1991). This explanation is less popular than it once was because it stereotypes all women, failing to acknowledge that the traits of men and women often overlap and that women have diverse traits. Moreover, this explanation invokes the behaviour of men as the standard, implying that women are "deficient," and that the problem is to be found in women rather than in the characteristics of political life.

A related explanation for the underrepresentation of women in Canadian politics reverses the emphasis by arguing that the culture of politics is "male" and therefore hostile to the participation of women. Descriptions of political life as "gladiatorial" create the image of a blood sport in which the stakes are the acquisition and display of power (Bashevkin, 2009). Such an environment creates a chilly climate for women, who may have interests beyond domination and who may prefer to resolve conflicts in nonconfrontational ways.

Second, women may quickly learn the negative consequences of public life. Media coverage of female candidates and elected representatives often pays far more attention to the personal appearance, marital status, and sexuality of women politicians compared with men (Bashevkin, 2009; Trimble and Arscott, 2003). Sylvia Bashevkin (2009) argues that the attention on the personal characteristics of women politicians and the accompanying harsh scrutiny of their appearance and behaviour results from the "women + power = discomfort" equation. When stereotypes about women relegate them to the private sphere of the home, or at best see them as less than men, the presence of women where political power is exercised creates unease. One response to this ambivalence is to reaffirm the more traditional roles of women, and this is accomplished when the media discuss the age, dress, weight, boyfriends, and marital histories of female politicians. This framing of women politicians draws attention away from the work that women undertake as elected political representatives. Three additional consequences of media accounts are that (1) they fail to recognize the prior political activities of female politicians, with the result that women's histories of acquiring competency remain largely unknown; (2) they suggest that female politicians are responsible for women's issues, when, in fact, gender interests may not be on the agenda of any politician, male or female; and (3) they use the term *feminism* or *feminist* to denote negative personal characteristics (Trimble and Arscott, 2003).

The third reason for women's underrepresentation in politics is gatekeeping. By controlling the nomination of candidates for elected office, political parties influence the gender composition of their electoral slate and the ridings that nominees represent. In the past, women candidates were often "sacrificial lambs," allowed to run mainly in ridings in which the chances of winning were small. In today's climate of striving for gender equality, few parties can afford to provide a slate of candidates with few or no women. But sometimes parties still assign women to ridings in which their chances of winning are poor.

Insufficient resources are the fourth reason for the lack of gender parity in Canadian politics. Money is an important resource for winning nominations and mounting publicity campaigns. Even though there are limits on what candidates may spend in an election, my research finds that the average upper limit in the 2011 election was $102 000. Women may be at a disadvantage to the extent that they earn less than male candidates do and consequently have less to put into a campaign. Whereas men who enter politics tend to come from law and business, women candidates tend to come from social work, journalism, and education, where earnings are lower (Newman and White, 2006: Table 5.2). Social networks are also an important resource needed for contesting nominations and elections. They are useful for obtaining financial contributions and recruiting volunteers to lobby voters. Yet to the extent that politics is "an old boys' club," women may not have access to insider or "old boy" networks (Cool, 2011).

Finally, the clash between political and family life influences the participation of some women in politics. The culture that emphasizes politics as a man's world fails to recognize that politicians also have personal lives and family responsibilities. Indeed, the lifestyle that is part of this culture is almost anti-family. Ignoring the family needs and responsibilities of politicians affects both men and women. However, because women more than men are designated as primary child-care providers, their participation in politics can require greater personal and child-care costs.

REPRESENTATION BY WOMEN, REPRESENTATION FOR WOMEN

Until recently, most research on women in politics focused on the question of how many women held party positions or were elected legislators. However, representation *by* women is not the same as representation *for* women. Although both men and women may use their legislative roles to place women's issues on the political agenda and to support party policies and legislation that reflect women's situations and concerns, they may not.

Jane Arscott and Linda Trimble (1997) summarize the views of numerous social scientists and women's groups when they call for "representation by women as if women mattered"—that is, the election of women who will act in the interests of women. They raise a second issue, too: How are differences of class and race among women to be represented? Specifically, can women legislators and party officers understand and speak for women who are different from them and who may have different experiences and concerns? The great majority of Canadian female legislators are white, middle-class, publicly heterosexual, and well educated.

Do they understand, stand for, and speak for other women, including Aboriginal women, women of colour, immigrant women, senior women, poor women, homeless women, lesbians, and women who are victims of spousal abuse (Vickers, 1997: 28)? Furthermore, if mainstream women cannot speak for all women, then should targets or quotas be set for women of colour, poor women, lesbians, and so on? These questions are now being debated but Canadian governments at all levels appear unwilling to exercise the political will, spend the money, and change the electoral laws and party practices that would accommodate such differences.

ELIMINATING GENDER INEQUALITY

In this section, I consider the mechanisms that can be used to lessen the degree of gender inequality, starting with a review of general approaches and then looking at specific interventions designed to reduce inequality in the labour force and political representation.

MODELS OF CHANGE

The choice of mechanism for bringing about change depends on how we explain gender inequality. If we see gender inequality as arising out of personality differences between men and women, we are likely to prefer a mechanism that influences personality traits—for example, we may seek ways of altering the messages that people receive about masculinity and femininity in schools and through the mass media. If we see inequalities as resulting from organizational rules and practices governing recruitment and promotion, we are likely to emphasize the need to change those rules and practices.

Starting in the 1970s, North American research on inequality began to shift away from perspectives that attributed unequal outcomes to individual differences in talent, educational achievement, and opportunity. That viewpoint resulted in social programs and public policies oriented to individuals, such as efforts to increase access to education and training for members of less privileged groups. By the 1980s, people were becoming more aware of power relations and the influence of workplace cultures and practices as sources of gender inequality. This awareness was fuelled partly by feminism, with its twin emphases on the undervaluation of women and men's domination of women in diverse areas of social life. Accompanying such changing perspectives was growing impatience with organizations slow to change their practices voluntarily. Increased pressure was put on governments to develop public policies that lessened or eliminated gender inequalities.

Public policy refers to the statements made and the actions taken—or not taken—by governments with respect to a given problem or set of problems (Pal, 1989: 4). State intervention influences the magnitude of gender inequality and sustains or minimizes male domination of women in reproduction, family, and the labour force. In the category of reproduction are government actions pertaining to medical care, new reproductive technologies (such as in vitro fertilization), contraception, and abortion. In the category of the family are government policies regarding family law (including regulations governing divorce and property division) and child care. Government intervention in the labour force affects gender inequality through employment insurance policies, maternity- and parental-leave policies, job-training programs, employment policies, and pay policies. So far, no government policy targets gender inequality in politics.

PUBLIC POLICY AND GENDER INEQUALITY IN THE LABOUR FORCE

Two areas of policy development that bear on gender inequality in the labour force are **employment equity,** including **affirmative action,** and pay equity, as expressed in the principle of **equal pay for work of equal value** (or "work of comparable worth"). Policies in both areas seek to correct inequalities in paid work by removing barriers that handicap certain groups, including women. Many of these barriers are seen as systemic. Rather than reflecting deliberate and conscious decisions to discriminate, systemic barriers refer to organizational practices, such as informal methods of recruitment or weight and height requirements for designated jobs. These practices often privilege members of one group while handicapping others. They differ in the populations they cover, the mechanisms they employ to determine and eliminate inequalities, and the aspects of labour-force inequality that they address.

Assessing the Impact

Many publications outline the specifics of Canadian employment-equity and equal-pay policies (Agocs, 2002; Haq and Ng, 2010). Do such policies work? Have related programs succeeded in moving women into jobs from which they were previously excluded? Is the real monetary worth of women's work in female job ghettos being acknowledged? In answering these questions, there is good news and bad news. The good news is that legal action has been taken against some cases of inequality. In the late 1980s, for example, litigation forced CN Rail to hire women in the St. Lawrence region. At the time of the complaint, women held fewer than 1 percent of blue-collar jobs in the company, and a pattern of discriminatory hiring practices was revealed. The company was ordered to discontinue a number of these practices and to adopt new recruiting and hiring practices. Similarly, equal-pay-for-work-of-equal-value legislation has resulted in pay adjustments in a number of cases. For example, nurses' pay has been raised to match that of orderlies, and the federal court upheld the right of pay equity for federally employed women in selected female-dominated occupations. In the fall of 2005, Canada Post was ordered to pay an estimated $150 million in back wages to clerical workers who were in a mostly female bargaining unit and who were paid substantially less than workers, most of them men, were, performing equivalent tasks sorting mail. Following an appeal by Canada Post, the Supreme Court of Canada upheld the original decision in 2011.

A few isolated victories do not, however, amount to winning the war. Critics of employment-equity policies note three types of "bad news." First, the legislation is limited in its jurisdiction and does not apply to a large part of the population. For example, the federal Employment Equity Act of 1995, which replaced the Employment Equity Act of 1986, covers only the public service, federally regulated employers, and portions of the public sector specified by orders in council, such as contractors who have 100 or more employees and who are doing business with the government. Second, failure to comply with the legislation is penalized lightly. Although the federal Employment Equity Act of 1995 imposes fines on employers who do not report the required data or who knowingly provide false or misleading information, the amount cannot exceed $10 000 for a single violation and $50 000 for repeated or continued violations (Canada, 1995: s. 36[2]). Finally, in 2009, the federal government passed the Public Sector Equitable Compensation Act that prevents public servants from filing complaints with the Canadian Human Rights Commission and thus accessing the court system to obtain settlements in pay-equity cases. Instead, female public service workers must use collective bargaining in the workplace to achieve wage parity with their male colleagues.

Numerous criticisms have been voiced about equal-pay-for-work-of-equal-value policies. First, many of the policies exclude small firms. Second, they compare men and women within the same firms, so they do not apply to women employed in firms in which the labour force is all female. Third, the method of establishing the comparable worth of two jobs is based on existing job descriptions. Jobs that are considered similar by virtue of pay or classification are evaluated on the basis of knowledge and skills, effort, responsibility, and working conditions (England, 1993; Steinberg, 1990). But such evaluation does not correct for the a priori undervaluation of certain skills, as discussed earlier.

For many feminists, these and other criticisms suggest that limited change can be expected from employment-equity and pay-equity policies in their current forms. Supporters are likely to press for stronger policies and broader coverage in the decades to come. However, government and business support for such changes is not assured. Business owners may argue that such equity is unaffordable in tough economic times.

CORRECTING THE BALANCE: WOMEN IN POLITICS

No federal policy is aimed at reducing gender inequality among elected politicians. But numerous actions could increase the percentage of women in Canadian politics in the future. All have to do with reducing barriers erected by social roles and changing organizational aspects of political recruitment and elections:

- *Expressing good intentions.* Commonly taking the form of party statements indicating commitment to the principle of gender parity, such displays have little impact.
- *Reducing the economic barriers to winning nominations and running for office.* Reducing the financial burden facing women and some men can be achieved by introducing legislation that would allow candidates the right to take unpaid leave from employment to contest party nominations and elections; setting spending limits for nomination contests and party leadership campaigns; making contributions for nomination contests tax deductible; reimbursing money spent on nomination contests if the candidate gets a minimum level of support (say, 15 percent of the vote); using centralized party funds for nomination battles; and treating child-care and housekeeping costs as part of the campaign costs, thereby making them subject to reimbursement (Brodie, 1991: 49–50).
- *Recognizing family needs and responsibilities and the social roles of women.* Julie Cool (2011) suggests that Parliaments could implement more gender-sensitive practices, such as ending parliamentary business at a reasonable time, allowing for "family days," or spreading parliamentary business over a number of shorter days.
- *Weakening or eliminating the gatekeeping tradition.* This reform could be accomplished by basing the amount of the government subsidy paid to political parties for their campaign expenses on an upward sliding scale according to the proportion of their elected candidates who are women (Brodie, 1991:50). Under this system, the amount of the subsidy would vary with the number of women elected.
- *Engaging in affirmative action.* Affirmative action measures include setting quotas to ensure that a certain percentage of women are on riding nomination lists, and establishing guarantees that a certain percentage of women are nominated for and are present in the party organization.
- *Centralizing decision making in political parties.* Research suggests that affirmative action measures can be difficult to implement in a single-member electoral system. Under the single-member system in Canada, a person

running for office in a riding wins by getting the most votes. This approach is conducive to the control of nominations by local party organizations. However, attempts to increase the number of women holding office are most effective in electoral systems that place decision making about nominations and party representation at levels higher than the local riding. A more centralized decision-making structure gives party elites more control over the representation of women and other minority groups. Modifying Canada's single-member system is another area in which action could be taken to increase the percentage of women politicians (Newman and White, 2006).

Which, if any, of these reforms will be adopted remains to be seen. It is highly likely, however, that debate over gender inequalities in politics and the economy will remain an important issue in Canadian social life for a long time.

SUMMARY

1. Many sociologists view the segregation of women and men in the private and public spheres as an important source of gender inequality. Exclusion from the economic and political arenas of Canadian life can mean disadvantages in access to income, prestige, and power. Restricted in the past to the domestic sphere, women have been economically disadvantaged and have had little or no opportunity to influence legislation directly. In addition, their unpaid work in the home has been considered low in prestige, or at least lower in value than their spouses' paid work.
2. During the twentieth century, women entered the labour force and the political arena in ever-increasing numbers. Today, more than half of all women are in the labour force. Politically enfranchised, women have also entered the political arena, either as politicians or in connection with groups associated with the women's movement. Many of these changes have occurred—or, at least, have accelerated—in recent decades. Between the 1970s and the early 1990s, the labour-force participation rate of women more than doubled, and the number of elected women MPs quadrupled.
3. Although they do paid work, many women are still responsible for most of the meal preparation, cleaning, and laundry needs of their families. Women still tend to be considered the primary caregivers for children and seniors.
4. In the labour force, women and men are occupationally segregated, with women concentrated in jobs stereotyped as "women's jobs." Women are more likely than men are to be employed in jobs that are part-time or otherwise nonstandard. They earn less than men do, on average, and their skills tend not to be fully recognized or fairly evaluated. These issues affect women to varying degrees, depending on their birthplace, race, and ethnicity. Nevertheless, the overall picture is one of gender inequality in the labour force, with women disadvantaged relative to men.
5. There is evidence of a gender gap in politics. Women represent more than half of Canada's adult population, but only 25 percent of federally elected legislators. This imbalance notwithstanding, substantial gains have been made in recent elections. And as agents pressing for improvements in their own status, Canadian women have left a considerable legacy of influence and change.
6. Future generations will have to combat not only gender-role stereotypes but also ideologies and structures that privilege men and handicap women. In recent years, employment-equity and equal-pay-for-work-of-equal-value policies have been developed to remedy some of the inequalities in the paid labour force. Analysts have also documented the various ways in which women's participation and influence in the political arena can be enhanced.

QUESTIONS TO CONSIDER

1. If you grew up in a two-parent household, describe the types of activities that each parent did around the house. Were they different? Did the amount of time each spent on activities in the home vary? Why? Alternatively, if you grew up with brothers and sisters, how did your parent(s) delegate household chores? Did boys and girls have different chores, and if so, what were they?
2. Think back to jobs you have held in the past three years that involved working with other people. Reflecting on the type of work you did compared with the work of others, would you say that sex segregation or sex typing existed? Why or why not?
3. In some of the occupational skill assessments that have been conducted in recent years, the job of dogcatcher was deemed more skilled than the job of child-care worker. Why do you think such an evaluation was made? Do you agree with the ranking? Why or why not?
4. This chapter discussed the principles of political "representation by women," "representation for women," and "representation of difference." Should women legislators be elected only if they champion women's causes? Should electoral rules be changed to allow for the proportionate or even disproportionate election of women of colour and other disadvantaged women in order to represent their interests and experiences?

GLOSSARY

Affirmative action (p. 177) comprises the policies and programs designed to create opportunities for, and to further the achievements of, historically disadvantaged groups in the labour force. One form of action to correct past inequalities involves setting targets and quotas for the hiring and promotion of members of groups that have faced barriers and discrimination in the past. The term is often used interchangeably with employment equity; strictly speaking, it is one aspect of employment equity.

Employment equity (p. 177) is the principle of equal treatment of all groups in the paid labour force. Employment-equity policies and programs seek to dismantle barriers and alter workplace cultures to create opportunities for and further the advancement of historically disadvantaged groups.

Equal pay for work of equal value (p. 177), also known as "equal pay for work of comparable worth," is a principle supported by policies and programs that seek to equalize the wage rates offered for different jobs that are of comparable worth or value in terms of such factors as knowledge, complexity, responsibility, and skill.

Feminism (p. 159) refers both to the body of knowledge about the causes and nature of women's subordination to men in society, and to the various agendas, often involving political action, for removing that subordination.

Gender inequalities (p. 159) are inequalities between men and women in the distribution of prestige, material well-being, and power. They are also inequalities in relations of male domination and female subordination.

Gender stereotypes (p. 158) are a set of prejudicial generalizations about men and women based on the oversimplified belief that sex determines distinct personality traits and, as a result, causes men and women to experience the world and behave in different ways.

The **glass ceiling** (p. 166) is the level in an organization above which women and members of minorities are seldom found.

The **labour-force participation rate** (p. 162) for women is the proportion of women over the age of 14 who work for money, are seeking to work for money, or do unpaid work for a family business, expressed as a percentage of all women over the age of 14. It does not include women who do unpaid domestic work.

Material well-being (p. 159) refers to having access to the economic resources necessary to pay for adequate food, clothing, housing, and possessions.

Nonstandard work (p. 168) refers to one or a combination of the following types of employment: part-week employment (reduced hours per week), part-year employment, limited-term contract employment, employment through temporary-help agencies, self-employment, and holding of multiple jobs.

Part-time work (p. 168) refers to jobs involving fewer hours of work than is the norm for full-time work.

Power (p. 159) is the capacity to influence and control others, regardless of any resistance they might offer.

Prestige (p. 159) is the social evaluation or ranking, by general consensus, of occupational activities and positions in a hierarchical order that reflects the degree of respect, honour, or deference the person engaged in the activity or occupying the position is to be accorded.

Public policy (p. 177) refers to the government's stance on issues and problems, as expressed through its statements and actions or its silence ans inaction.

Sex segregation of occupations (p. 165) refers to the concentration of women and men in different occupations.

Sex typing (or sex labelling) of occupations (p. 165) is the designation of an occupation as "female" or "male," depending on the sex for which it is considered appropriate.

Skill (p. 166) is ability or expertise in performing a given technique or task. Researchers describe tasks as requiring more or less skill on the basis of their complexity and the degree of autonomy required to perform them. Existing rankings, incomes, and levels of education associated with various occupations are often accepted by researchers as indicators of skill.

A **social movement** (p. 171) is an enduring collective attempt to change part or all of society by means of rioting, petitioning, striking, demonstrating, or establishing pressure groups, unions, and political parties.

Social roles (p. 157) are the expectations and behaviours associated with particular positions in society.

Standard work (p. 168) is full-time, full-year employment, usually accompanied by job-related benefits, such as vacation leave, sick leave, and parental leave, as well as by health and pension benefits.

Statistical discrimination (p. 169) is the discrimination that occurs when negative decisions concerning the hiring or promotion of an individual are made on the basis of the average characteristics of the group to which the individual belongs.

A **visible minority** (p. 170) is a category of people (other than Aboriginal people) who are non-white and who, because of their race, may face discrimination in hiring and promotion.

The **women's movement** (p. 171) is a social movement that takes action to improve the conditions of women.

SUGGESTED READING

Agnew, Vijay, ed. (2009). *Racialized Migrant Women in Canada: Essays on Health, Violence and Equity.* Toronto: University of Toronto Press. This edited collection examines issues concerning immigrant women's health and experiences of family violence and labour market discrimination, with considerable discussion about racialized immigrant women.

Bashevkin, Sylvia. (2009). *Women, Power, Politics: The Hidden Story of Canada's Unfinished Democracy.* Don Mills, ON: Oxford University Press. This highly readable book provides evidence on the differential representation of women and men in politics by the mass media. Suggestions are provided for how to remedy this situation and how to encourage greater political engagement by Canadian women.

Newman, Jacquetta and Linda A. White. (2006). *Women, Politics, and Public Policy: The Political Struggles of Canadian Women.* Don Mills, ON: Oxford University Press. Chapters in this book focus on types of feminist theories, the women's movement in Canada, women in politics, policies with respect to families, paid work, and reproductive regulation and rights.

Statistics Canada. (2011). *Women in Canada: A Gender-based Statistical Report,* 6th ed. Ottawa: Minister of Industry. Catalogue No. 89-503-X. This report contains textual overviews and data on women, covering such topics as their family status, health, educational patterns, paid and unpaid work characteristics, and treatment by the criminal justice system. Separate chapters deal with Aboriginal, visible minority, and immigrant women.

CHAPTER 8

RACE AND ETHNIC RELATIONS

Vic Satzewich
MCMASTER UNIVERSITY

SOURCE: © REUTERS/Robert Galbraith.

IN THIS CHAPTER YOU WILL LEARN THAT

- The study of race and ethnic relations involves several sociological approaches. Among the most important are the frustration-aggression, sociobiology, socialization, and power-conflict approaches.
- *Ethnicity* and *race* are terms used to categorize groups on the basis of cultural and physical criteria. Although the concept of race has little basis in biology, and although ethnic identities and boundaries are situational and flexible, race and ethnicity are important parts of social reality.
- Aboriginal people in Canada are Indians, Métis, and Inuit. There are two main sociological interpretations of Aboriginal people's socioeconomic status in Canada: the culture of poverty thesis and the internal colonial model.
- The nationalist movement in Quebec has deep historical roots. The contemporary nationalist movement is united around the goal of maintaining the French character of Quebec. One of the main problems facing the nationalist movement in Quebec is exactly how to define the boundaries of the nation.
- Immigration played a central role in both the early and the later phases of Canadian development. Canada accepts refugee, family class, and independent immigrants. Each category is subject to different selection criteria.
- John Porter's description of Canadian society as a vertical mosaic is not as accurate as it once was.

INTRODUCTION

It started as a peaceful protest aimed at grabbing the government's attention over a dispute about an old burial ground. It ended with what journalist Peter Edwards (2001) referred to as "one dead Indian." On September 5, 1995, just after the Labour Day long-weekend when campers had gone home, about 30 Kettle Point and Stoney Point band members from the Kettle Point Reserve near Sarnia occupied Ipperwash Provincial Park. Some band members believed that an ancient burial ground in the park was being desecrated and they wanted to protect their ancestors' resting place. A few weeks earlier, a group of reserve members had reclaimed land that was part of a nearby military base. That land had been lent temporarily to the federal government during World War II for military training purposes. Various provincial and federal governments had dragged their feet over the return of the land that was part of the military base for nearly 50 years, and the occupants of Ipperwash did not feel like waiting another 50 years for their concerns about the graves in the park to be dealt with.

Dudley George was shot and killed by an Ontario Provincial Police officer in a chaotic altercation the day after the occupation of Ipperwash started. The officer who shot George was eventually convicted

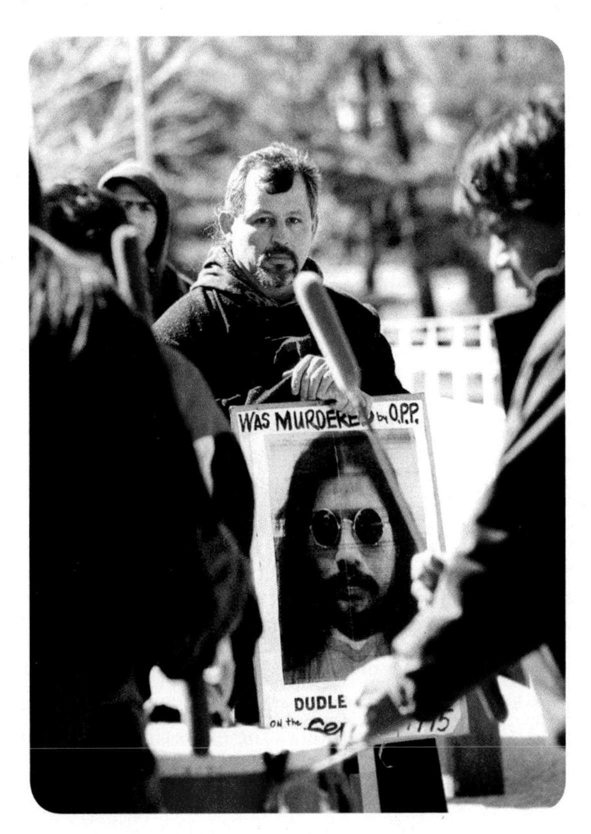

Native protester Dudley George was shot and killed by an Ontario Provincial Police officer during the occupation of Ipperwash Provincial Park near Sarnia in 1995.
SOURCE: © Nora Penhale/Sun Media.

of criminal negligence causing death, and the larger circumstances surrounding the incident were investigated at a public inquiry in late 2005 and early 2006. Both the trial of the OPP officer and the public inquiry turned up unpleasant facts about racism within the OPP and within the provincial Conservative government of the day. For instance, the day before George was shot, two OPP officers were posing as a television crew. The lens of their camera was covered, but the audio was turned on. One officer, responding to his colleague's question about whether any members of the media were in the area, said, "No, there's no one down there. Just a big fat-fuck Indian." After a few minutes, another voice is heard: "We had this plan, you know. We thought if we could get five or six cases of Labatt's 50, we could bait them. And we would have this big net and a pit." People are heard laughing in the background. The officer calls the plan "creative thinking" and adds that it "works in the South with watermelons" (Gray, 2004: A7).

According to Murray Klippenstein, the lawyer for the George family, "the reference to baiting Indians with alcohol and the reference to the South and the watermelon are the kind of poisonous, racist talk I thought we had put behind us in Ontario.... The reference to blacks in the South is the kind of talk you would hear when people are dehumanizing someone, and that attitude makes it easy to lynch or shoot them" (Gray, 2004).

In November 2005, the Ipperwash inquiry into the death of Dudley George turned up some equally ugly racist views expressed by provincial government officials. Former provincial attorney general Charles Harnick told the inquiry that at a top-level meeting to discuss how the provincial government ought to handle the occupation of the park, then premier Mike Harris, in a moment of anger, shouted, "I want those fucking Indians out of the park" (Harries, 2005: A1). Although Mr. Harris has denied saying this, Mr. Harnick insists that "I heard what I heard" (Appleby, 2006: A7).

We may never know with certainty whether racism played a central role in why Dudley George died. Some say that although the expression of racism by some OPP officers was regrettable, it was incidental to the way the events surrounding George's death unfolded. Others say that the police do not take their marching orders from politicians, so whatever the premier might have said at the meeting was irrelevant to how the police eventually dealt with the situation.

Ethnic and racial tensions in Canada do not often end in physical violence or violent death. And, in comparison to many other countries, ethnic and racial relations seem peaceful here. But other kinds of ethnic and racial problems exist. In Ontario, the 2001 Safe Schools Act, which mandates a policy of "zero tolerance" for violent and disruptive behaviour in schools, is alleged by some to work to the disadvantage of black students (Henry and Tator, 2006: 211). In 2008, Toronto school trustees voted to establish a black-focused elementary school in the city. Critics argued that this was a step backward to racial segregation (Brown and Popplewell, 2008). The same debate rekindled in Toronto in 2011 with a proposal to establish a black-focused high school. As of 2007, there were eight hundred outstanding land claims filed by First Nations against the federal government. At the current pace of resolution, it will be 2100 before most of them are dealt with (Frideres and Gadacz, 2012: 226). Former Toronto mayor Mel Lastman's 2001 racist jest that he was reluctant to travel to Kenya because he feared being put in a pot of boiling water by "dancing natives" probably did not help Toronto's bid to host the 2008 Summer Olympic Games (Walcott, 2003). Arab Canadians complain that they have faced increased stereotyping and discrimination in Canada and at the Canada-U.S. border since September 11, 2001 (Li, 2003). In 1995, the country was on the verge of collapse after nearly half the voters in Quebec voted in favour of separation. And some observers claim that the federal government's policy of multiculturalism undermines the unity of our country (Bissondath, 1994), creates disloyalty to Canada, undermines foreign policy (Granatstein, 2007), and causes "more overt hostility in Canada to those of European ancestry ... than to the non-white minority" (Stoffman, 2002: 126).

These examples all touch in some way on the issue of what different ethnic and racial groups are allowed and able to do in our society, and how they are treated. In other words, they all say something about the distribution of power and resources in Canada. The sociology of ethnic and racial relations concerns primarily the study of how power and resources are unequally distributed among ethnic and racial groups. Sociologists who are interested in race and ethnic relations ask a number of interrelated questions: What are the conditions under which ethnic and racial groups come into contact? Which ethnic and racial groups hold most of the power in a society? How do they exercise power? Are there social and economic advantages associated with having a particular ethnic or racial background? What are the social consequences of the unequal distribution of power and resources? How have ethnic and racial groups challenged inequality and power imbalances? How have governments tried to manage and contain ethnic and racial conflict?

My aim in this chapter is to provide some sociological answers to these questions. I begin by examining what sociologists mean by *ethnicity*, *race*, and *racism*, and then discuss various theoretical approaches to the study of ethnic and racial relations. Next, I examine the three main forms of ethnic and racial relations in Canada: Aboriginal/non-Aboriginal relations, French/English relations, and immigrant/nonimmigrant relations. In each case, you will see how power and resource imbalances play important roles in structuring relationships among groups.

ETHNICITY AND RACE: THE SOCIAL CONSTRUCTION OF DIFFERENCE

We use the terms *race*, *racial*, *ethnic*, and *ethnicity* in a variety of ways in our everyday lives. Some students in my classes talk about how they are under pressure from their parents to marry someone of the same "race" or "ethnicity." Others are concerned that "race relations" in Canada seem to be getting worse. Yet others describe the joys of living in a "multiethnic" country, of eating meals in a variety of "ethnic" restaurants, and of observing and participating in the rituals and festivals of "ethnic" groups from around the world.

The assumption underlying our commonsense understandings of these terms is that race and ethnicity are *ascribed* characteristics. That is, we assume that we are born with a certain race or ethnicity that cannot be changed. Sociologists, however, recognize that, although we cannot change our birth parents, and generally cannot change our skin colour, we do not necessarily have fixed and unalterable ethnic and racial characteristics or identities. Instead, sociologists believe it is more useful to see race and ethnicity as certain kinds of *achieved* statuses—statuses that are acquired by virtue of social definition. In contrast, Box 8.1 shows how Statistics Canada used ascribed characteristics for its measurement of ethnicity and race in the 2011 *National Household Survey*.

ETHNICITY AND RACE

Ethnicity

Sociologists do not agree on how to define and measure ethnicity. *Objective definitions of ethnicity* assume that ethnic groups exist because of people's social attachments (Isajiw, 1999). From this point of view, ethnicity is something that people possess because of differences in language, culture, customs, national origin, and ancestry. *Subjective approaches to ethnicity* focus on the process of ethnic identification. Sociologists who emphasize the socially constructed nature of perceived reality insist that ethnicity is a "transactional" process. Ethnic groups are made up of people who identify themselves, or who are identified by others, as belonging to the same ancestral or cultural group. Whether they display any of the cultural characteristics of the group with which they identify, or whether they are merely born into that group, is largely irrelevant. When subjective definitions are used, then, "ethnicity" is self-defined and reflects "a shared 'we-feeling' within a collectivity (groupness) whose symbolic components can vary [over] time and place" (Fleras and Elliot, 1996). From this perspective, ethnic identities and boundaries are situational, variable, and flexible.

Most of the ethnic categories that we take for granted are actually recent historical creations. The ethnic category "English" would have been unthinkable to the person who lived in the British Isles eight hundred years ago. People defined themselves, and were defined by others, as Celts, Saxons, Normans, and so on. Only some of those people came to be known as "the English" (Lieberson, 1991). Similarly, the people whom we now think of as "Germans" did not exist 150 years ago. As these examples suggest, the way in which people define themselves, and are defined by others, is in constant flux (Lieberson, 1991: 444). If we take a long view, it is common for ethnic categories and identities to be recast and created anew.

This is what seems to be happening in Canada now. A feeling of commonality has crystallized that is the basis for a common ethnic identification. In preparing for the 1991 census, Statistics Canada held meetings, organized focus groups, and tested different ways of posing questions that tried to measure the ethnicity of our population. One thing that Statistics Canada found "was a strong tendency [for respondents] to report Canadian as their ethnic origin and as their ethnic identity" (White, 1992: 166). Largely because of political pressure, "Canadian" was included

BOX 8.1 THE ETHNICITY AND "RACE" QUESTIONS IN THE 2011 NATIONAL HOUSEHOLD SURVEY

Statistics Canada has collected information on the ancestral origins of the population for more than a century. The *National Household Survey,* which replaced the Long Form Census in 2011, tries to measure the composition of Canada's diverse population by asking the following questions:

ETHNIC ORIGIN

17. What were the ethnic or cultural origins of this person's **ancestors**?

An ancestor is usually more distant than a grandparent.

For example, Canadian, English, French, Chinese, East Indian, Italian, German, Scottish, Irish, Cree, Mi'kmaq, Salish, Métis, Inuit, Filipino, Dutch, Ukrainian, Polish, Portuguese, Greek, Korean, Vietnamese, Jamaican, Jewish, Lebanese, Salvadorean, Somali, Colombian, etc.

SPECIFY AS MANY ORIGINS AS APPLICABLE USING CAPITAL LETTERS.

RACIAL ORIGINS

19. Is this person:

Mark more than one or specify, if applicable.

This information is collected in accordance with the Employment Equity Act and its Regulations and Guidelines to support programs that promote equal opportunity for everyone to share in the social, cultural, and economic life of Canada.

- White
- South Asian (e.g., East Indian, Pakistani, Sri Lankan, etc.)
- Chinese
- Black
- Filipino
- Latin American
- Arab
- Southeast Asian (e.g., Vietnamese, Cambodian, Malaysian, Laotian, etc.)
- West Asian (e.g., Iranian, Afghan, etc.)
- Korean
- Japanese

Other–Specify

SOURCE: Adapted from Statistics Canada (2010).

as a response category in the ethnicity question for the next census. "Canadians" are now the numerically largest ethnic group in Canada (see Table 8.1).

Why do some of us define our ethnic roots or ethnic identity as "Canadian"? Some of us may simply be unaware of or uninterested in our ancestral roots and, hence, by default define ourselves as Canadian. For others, defining ourselves as Canadian is a political act used to express our dissatisfaction with the government's policy of multiculturalism (White, 1992: 168–69). At the same time, though, many of us insist that we are Canadian because that is simply the group with which we identify and with which we share a sense of belonging (Angus Reid Group, 1991; Howard, 1998). According to Rhoda Howard-Hassmann (1999: 528), the emergence of this sense of community means that "the ethnic English-Canadian is a new social creation."

Race

For much of the twentieth century, there was little difference between commonsense understandings of **race** and the way that race was analyzed in the social and natural sciences. Most scientists believed that races were real and objective subdivisions of *Homo sapiens.* These divisions were supposedly based on a combination of unalterable physical and genetic characteristics. Features, such as skin colour, hair texture, body and facial shape, genetic diseases, metabolic rates, and distribution of blood groups, were used to construct various racial typologies. The most common typology was the division of humanity into "Caucasoid," "mongoloid," and "negroid" races (Montagu, 1972).

During the 1930s, scientists began to raise doubts about the scientific validity of the concept of race (Barkan, 1992). Since the 1950s, the scientific consensus has been that racial classifications of humanity are arbitrary, that genetic differences between groups are tiny, and that genetic differences are behaviourally insignificant (Montagu, 1972). Racial classifications based on a characteristic such as skin colour are as illogical as racial classifications based on the length of index fingers (Miles, 1982). Moreover, only a fraction of 1 percent of all human genes are necessarily shared

TABLE 8.1 TOP 25 ETHNIC ORIGINS IN CANADA 2006

ETHNIC ORIGIN	SINGLE AND MULTIPLE RESPONSES	SINGLE RESPONSES	MULTIPLE RESPONSES
Canadian	10 066 290	5 748 725	4 317 570
English	6 570 015	1 367 125	5 202 890
French	4 941 210	1 230 535	3 710 675
Scottish	4 719 850	568 515	4 151 340
Irish	4 354 155	491 030	3 863 125
German	3 179 425	670 640	2 508 785
Italian	1 445 335	741 045	704 285
Chinese	1 346 510	1 135 365	211 145
North American Indian	1 253 615	512 150	741 470
Ukrainian	1 209 085	300 590	908 495
Dutch (Netherlands)	1 035 965	303 400	732 560
Polish	984 565	269 375	715 190
East Indian	962 665	780 175	182 495
Russian	500 600	98 245	402 355
Welsh	440 965	27 115	413 855
Filipino	436 190	321 390	114 800
Norwegian	432 515	44 790	387 725
Portuguese	410 850	262 230	148 625
Métis	409 065	77 295	331 770
British Isles, n.i.e.[1]	403 915	94 145	309 770
Swedish	334 765	28 445	306 325
Spanish	325 730	67 475	258 255
American	316 350	28 785	287 565
Hungarian (Magyar)	315 510	88 685	226 820
Jewish	315 120	134 045	181 070

[1] Not included elsewhere.

SOURCE: Adapted from Statistics Canada (2009).

by members of the same race, genetically defined. Thus, from a strictly genetic point of view, Stephen Harper may have more in common with black hockey star P.K. Subban of the Montreal Canadiens than with white businessman David Thomson, the richest person in Canada.

In sum, genetic differences between races are arbitrary, extremely small, and without behavioural consequences. Ethnic boundaries and identities are flexible, negotiated, and historically variable. We should not conclude, however, that race and ethnicity are unimportant aspects of modern society. According to W. I. Thomas's famous sociological dictum, if people define situations as real, they are real in their consequences (Thomas and Znaniecki, 1918: 79). Even though race is a hollow biological concept, and even though ethnic identities and boundaries are neither fixed nor unchanging, many people believe in the existence of ethnicity and race, and organize their relationships with others on the basis of those beliefs. Therefore, race and ethnicity are important parts of our social reality.

Racism

If race is a biological myth, what is racism? Is a school racist if it puts on hot dog days but not chow mein days? Are black people in Toronto subject to racist policing? Is Don Cherry a racist because he denigrates European hockey players who compete in the National Hockey League? Is Professor Philippe Rushton of the University of Western Ontario a racist because he believes that black people have smaller brains than whites and Asians do? Is a black woman racist if she wants to marry only a black man? Is a white man racist if he wants to marry only a white woman? Was the Bush administration in the United States racist for the way that it managed the aftermath of Hurricane Katrina in New Orleans in September 2005?

Before we can begin to answer these kinds of questions, we need to define racism. Sociologists define racism as both a certain kind of idea and a certain kind of institutional practice. I will consider each of these definitions in turn.

Traditionally, sociologists defined racism as "the belief that humans are subdivided into distinct hereditary groups that are innately different in their social behaviour and mental capacities and that can therefore be ranked as superior or inferior" (Marger, 1997: 27). Some scholars have suggested that because ideas about the inherent superiority and inferiority of groups have been so thoroughly discredited, racism has taken new forms (Omi and Winant, 1986). Biological versions of racism may be dead, but researchers have developed the concept of **new racism** as a way of analyzing its changing manifestations.

The concept of new racism was developed by Martin Barker (1981) to analyze the way that racist ideas were being expressed in the 1970s by British members of Parliament (MPs) when they were speaking out against British immigration policy. That policy permitted people from former British colonies in Asia, Africa, and the Caribbean unrestricted entry to the country. In their speeches, the MPs did not refer to British *biological* superiority or to Indian, African, or Caribbean *biological* inferiority. Instead, they regarded immigrants from these areas as *culturally* different from British people and alleged that the ability of British people to continue to advance the moral level of humanity was being undermined by immigration policy. The MPs' statements could not be considered "racist" by the traditional definition of the term. However, the statements had the consequence of helping to stop almost all nonwhite immigration from those countries.

These events suggested that the definition of racism had to be broadened. Accordingly, Barker (1981: 21) argued that the new racism involves the beliefs that although races of people cannot be ranked biologically, they are different from each other and that social problems are created when different groups try to live together. These beliefs should be considered racist because of their underlying intent: to socially exclude, marginalize, and denigrate certain groups of people but to do so without reference to unalterable biology. People may even believe in abstract virtues, such as equality, justice, and fairness, yet still hold negative attitudes, and engage in discriminatory behaviour, toward minority group members (Henry and Tator, 2006: 19).

How widespread is racism? A 2006–07 survey conducted by Léger Marketing and Sun Media found the following:

- 9 percent of Canadians considered themselves strongly or moderately racist.
- Men are more likely than women are to describe themselves as moderately racist (10 percent versus 6 percent of women).
- 21 percent of Canadians believed that some races are more gifted than others are.
- 9 percent of Canadians would react negatively if their child married someone of a different race.
- 92 percent of Canadians have witnessed racist comments or behaviours.
- 17 percent of respondents believe that their city is more racist than it was 10 years ago (Léger Marketing, 2007)

However, Canada fares well in international comparisons. For example, although 18 percent of Canadians who were polled in a 2002 international survey felt that immigrants have a bad influence on the country, 43 percent of Americans and 50 percent of respondents in the United Kingdom said that immigrants had a bad influence on their countries (Parkin and Mendelsohn, 2003: 5).

A different indicator of the scope of racism in Canada is given in Table 8.2, which focuses on *perceived* discrimination. Table 8.2 shows the

TABLE 8.2 PERCEPTIONS OF DISCRIMINATION BY GENERATION AND VISIBLE MINORITY STATUS, CANADA, 2002

		Frequency of Discrimination		
DISCRIMINATION	**TOTAL POPULATION**	**SOMETIMES OR OFTEN**	**RARELY**	**DID NOT EXPERIENCE**
	000s	%	%	%
Total population	22 444	7	6	86
Not a visible minority	19 252	5	5	90
Visible minority	3 000	20	15	64
First generation	5 272	13	10	77
Not a visible minority	2 674	5	6	89
Visible minority	2 516	21	14	65
Second generation or more	16 929	6	5	89
Not a visible minority	16 349	5	5	90
Visible minority	480	18	23	59

SOURCE: Adapted Statistics Canada (2003).

results of the *Ethnic Diversity Survey* conducted by Statistics Canada in 2002. Among other things, the survey asked Canadians whether they had experienced discrimination or unfair treatment during the past five years. The survey found that 64 percent of visible-minority Canadians reported that they "did not" experience discrimination or unfair treatment because of their ethnocultural characteristics in the past five years. Another 15 percent reported that they "rarely" experienced discrimination, and 20 percent of respondents reported that they had "sometimes" or "often" experienced discrimination. In contrast, just 5 percent of those who were not visible minorities reported experiencing discrimination or unfair treatment because of their ethnocultural characteristics during the past five years.

Institutional racism refers to "discriminatory racial practices built into such prominent structures as the political, economic and education systems" (Doob, 1996: 6). Institutional racism can take three forms. First, some institutional practices are based on explicitly racist ideas. Canadian history has plenty of examples of this form of institutional racism (Bolaria and Li, 1988). Chinese people were excluded from certain jobs and were denied the right to vote in federal elections until 1947. Japanese Canadians were denied their basic civil rights, were forcibly expelled from the west coast of British Columbia, and had their property confiscated during World War II (Bolaria and Li, 1988). Most status Indians were denied the right to vote in federal elections until 1960. Residential segregation was widespread for black people living in Canada. Restrictive covenants in wills, deeds, and leases were used to ensure that property could not be sold or leased to blacks and Jews. Blacks were frequently refused service in restaurants, theatres, and recreational facilities (Henry and Tator, 2006: 69). Canada had the worst record of all Allied countries in allowing Jewish immigration during World War II, when millions of Jews were being gassed in Europe (Abella and Troper, 1982). In each case, ideas about the alleged inferiority of certain groups underpinned institutional practices.

Second, some institutional practices arose from, but are no longer sustained by, racist ideas (Miles and Brown, 2003). For example, in 1966, the federal government admitted a small number of black workers from the Caribbean to work on Canadian farms. Now, more than 20 000 migrant workers from the Caribbean and Mexico enter Canada each year to harvest fruits, vegetables, and tobacco in Ontario and other agricultural areas in Canada during the summer months. Canadian government officials originally justified this practice partly by arguing that black workers are racially suited to back-breaking labour under the hot sun but racially unsuited to the cold Canadian winters (Satzewich, 1991). The present migrant-labour policy had its origins in racist thinking, but racist ideas are no longer used to justify this migration stream.

Third, institutions sometimes unintentionally restrict the life-chances of certain groups through a variety of seemingly neutral rules, regulations, and procedures. This is sometimes referred to as *systemic discrimination.* For example, height and weight requirements for jobs with police forces and fire departments did not necessarily originate in racist ideas, but these requirements meant that for many years certain Asian groups could not get jobs as police officers or firefighters. Word-of-mouth recruiting in organizations and inflated educational requirements for nontechnical jobs are also forms of systemic discrimination because they unintentionally put minority groups at a disadvantage in the distribution of scarce resources, such as jobs (Special Committee on the Participation of Visible Minorities in Canadian Society [Special Committee], 1984).

The debate about racial profiling in policing is also about this kind of institutional racism (Satzewich and Shaffir, 2009). According to a study conducted by University of Toronto criminologist Scott Wortley (2005), black people in Kingston, Ontario, are nearly four times as likely to be pulled over by police as white people are. Aboriginal peoples are 1.4 times as likely to be pulled over as white people are. When the study results were announced, the chief of the Kingston Police Force tearfully apologized, saying "especially to the black community and the aboriginal community where there are disparities, we apologize. I apologize. I'm not asking any police officer to apologize. ... My police officers have the right to ... walk tall with pride. What we're doing wrong, if we're doing anything wrong, is systemic and that's my problem. So I apologize to the black community, the aboriginal community and we'll do better" (Farmer, 2005).

Originally, racist thinking was used to justify allowing Caribbean and Mexican agricultural workers into Canada during the hot summer months but not during the cold Canadian winters.
SOURCE: Richard Thornton/Shutterstock.

THEORIES OF RACE AND ETHNIC RELATIONS

There are a number of sociological approaches to the interpretation of race and ethnic relations (Rex and Mason, 1986). In this section, I discuss four approaches that seek to explain various forms of ethnic and racial hostility. Such hostility is multifaceted and, depending on the circumstances, is described as racism, prejudice, ethnocentrism, or xenophobia.

Social Psychology

Social-psychological approaches to the interpretation of race and ethnic relations focus on how **prejudice**—an unfavourable, generalized, and rigid belief that is applied to all members of a group—and racism satisfy the psychic needs of certain people. *Frustration-aggression* is a popular variant of social-psychological theory. It explains prejudice and racism as forms of hostility that arise from frustration. The theory suggests that people who are frustrated in their efforts to achieve a desired goal—a better-paying job, for example, or entry to a university—respond with aggression (Marger, 1997). Since the real source of frustration is usually too powerful to confront directly, or may not be known, people take out their frustrations on the less powerful. From this perspective, minority ethnic and racial groups are convenient and safe targets of displaced aggression. This displacement is also referred to as scapegoating. The concept of scapegoating is sometimes used to explain anti-Semitism—negative attitudes and everyday discrimination directed against Jews (Brym and Lenton, 1993).

This kind of explanation has a commonsense appeal. We all have bad days at work or at school, and when we get home, we sometimes lash out at the people close to us. However, the theory has limitations. First, people respond to frustrating circumstances in a variety of ways. Displaced aggression does not always follow frustration. We sometimes internalize frustrations and end up giving ourselves an ulcer, or we may direct our frustrations at the real source of our problems. The theory does not say why we respond to frustrating circumstances in different ways. Second, the theory does not explain why some groups, and not others, are chosen as scapegoats.

Primordialism

The **primordialist thesis** suggests that ethnic and racial attachments reflect an innate tendency for people to seek out, and associate with, others who are similar in terms of language, culture, beliefs, ancestry, and appearance (Scott, 1990). From this point of view, ethnic prejudice and racism are ways of maintaining social boundaries. Sociobiologists offer a popular form of primordial theory. They suggest that prejudice and **discrimination**—practices that deny members of particular groups equal access to societal rewards—stem from our supposedly biologically grounded tendency to be nepotistic. Sociobiologists argue that the process of natural selection does not operate at the level of individuals, but rather at the level of kin groups. Clusters of genes are assumed to be passed on through kin selection (Wilson, 1978). Ethnic and racial groups are seen to be nothing more than large extended families. Since people have a "natural" tendency to want to pass on their genes, they favour their own "families." Thus, people are inherently both altruistic (prepared to sacrifice their own individual interests for the sake of the group) and ethnocentric because they want to pass on their genes to their own group. Humans, therefore, naturally favour members of their own ethnic or racial group—their "relatives"—and have a natural distrust and dislike of "nonfamily" members (van den Berghe, 1986: 255).

Are racism, prejudice, and discrimination programmed by our genes? It seems unlikely. The first problem with sociobiology is that shared ethnicity or race does not prevent conflict from erupting. White workers have struck against white-owned factories, and people have killed members of their own ethnic or racial group without concern for common ethnicity or race (Bonacich, 1980). Second, sociobiology is not able to explain how and why we frequently break out of our supposed genetically programmed nepotism. For example, Canadians of diverse ethnic and racial origins participate together in various kinds of anti-racist social movements (Henry and Tator, 2006). Ethnic and racial relations, therefore, are not necessarily zero-sum games in which one group wins at the expense of another.

Normative Theories

Normative theories of ethnic and racial prejudices concentrate on the way in which prejudices are transmitted through socialization and the social circumstances that encourage discriminatory behaviour (Marger, 1997). For example, the *socialization approach* focuses on how we are taught ethnic and racial stereotypes, prejudices, and attitudes by our families, peer groups, and the mass media. For instance, as a teenager in Saskatchewan in the 1970s, I remember watching the TV show *All in the Family*. People in Saskatchewan at the time held many prejudicial attitudes, particularly toward Aboriginal peoples. However, the television program *All in the Family* exposed my generation to a repertoire of ethnic and racial slang and stereotypes that we had not heard before. Archie Bunker, the show's central character, was supposed to be a caricature of an American "bigot," but he also taught us terms like "wop," "dago," "spic," and "nigger," and the corresponding stereotypes. Similarly, as Box 8.2 shows, the English language places different values on the colours black and white in subtle ways. Our language, in turn, shapes how we perceive and socially evaluate different racial groups.

Socialization theories are superior to social-psychological and primordialist approaches because they emphasize the way in which ethnic and racial prejudices and attitudes are learned through social interaction. The limitation of socialization theories is that they are unable to explain how prejudicial ideas, attitudes, and practices arise in the first place. This is where power-conflict theories come into play.

Power-Conflict Theories

Karl Marx (1967 [1867]: 751) wrote that "the turning of Africa into a warren for the commercial hunting of black-skins signaled the rosy dawn of the era of capitalist production." Marx did not take his analysis of slavery and racism much farther than that. Later generations of Marxist scholars, however, have sought to link racism to the structure of capitalist societies.

Orthodox Marxists argue that racism is an *ideology*—a set of statements shaped by economic interests about the way the social world works. Racism is ideological insofar as it is used by capitalists to mystify social reality and justify the exploitation and the unequal treatment of groups of people.

This justification can take many forms. For example, in the seventeenth century, American and Caribbean plantation owners justified the use of

BOX 8.2 LANGUAGE, COLOUR OF RACE

Language is an integral part of our culture. Language not only expresses ideas but shapes our thought. Our childhood socialization involves, in part, the ability to use language. In the following "Short Play on 'Black' and 'White' Words," Robert Moore shows how aspects of our language help unwittingly to reproduce both negative and positive racial imagery:

"Some may blackly (angrily) accuse me of trying to blacken (defame) the English language ... I may become a black sheep (one who causes shame or embarrassment because of deviation from the accepted standards), who will be blackballed (ostracized) by being placed on a blacklist (list of undesirables) in an attempt to blackmail (to force or coerce into a particular action) me to retract my words. But attempts to blackjack (to compel by threat) me will have a Chinaman's chance of success, for I am not a yellow-bellied Indian-giver of words, who will whitewash (cover up or gloss over vices or crimes) a black lie (harmful, inexcusable). I challenge the purity and innocence (white) of the English language. I don't see things in black and white (entirely bad or entirely good) terms, for I am a white man (marked by upright firmness) if there ever was one. ... While many may be niggardly (grudging, scanty) in their support, others will be honest and decent—and to them I say, that's very white of you (honest, decent).

"The preceding is of course a white lie (not intended to cause harm), meant only to illustrate some examples of racist terminology in the English language."

SOURCE: "Racist Stereotyping in the English Language" by Robert B. Moore (pp. 269–297). Reprinted from *Racism in the English Language* by Robert B. Moore, Council on Interracial Books for Children, 1976.

Africans as slaves by denying the humanity of Africans (Williams, 1964). In Marxist terms, the existence of racist ideas did not cause slavery; rather, slavery was a particular system of labour control that was justified by racist ideology.

In the case of advanced capitalism, racism is viewed by Marxists as an ideology that justifies the especially intense exploitation of racial minority and immigrant workers (Bolaria and Li, 1988; Castles and Kosack, 1984). From this point of view, racist ideas are used by employers as a means of creating artificial divisions in the working class so as to prevent the formation of a class consciousness that would threaten the social and economic order (Bolaria and Li, 1988; Castles and Kosack, 1984; Nikolinakos, 1973). Racist ideas can also help to justify the allocation of certain groups to low-wage, socially marginal jobs.

Race and the Split Labour Market **Split labour-market theory** was developed by Edna Bonacich (1972, 1979) because of the limitations of orthodox Marxism in analyzing racism. She argues that orthodox Marxism tends to assume that the capitalist class is all-powerful and that other classes play no role in the development of racist thinking. This is inaccurate; racism is found in all classes to varying degrees. Second, orthodox Marxism portrays racism in overly conspiratorial terms. Little evidence demonstrates that capitalists sit around plotting new and devious ways of using racism to stop workers from developing class consciousness. Third, orthodox Marxism has trouble explaining why racialized conflict so often results in *exclusionary practices*—practices that deny employers access to cheaper, more exploitable labour. In 1885, for example, the Canadian government instituted a "head tax" on new immigrants from China. Chinese immigrants had to pay $50 to the federal government. In 1900, the tax was raised to $100, and in 1903 to $500. The Chinese Immigration Act of 1923 completely barred Chinese immigration and was in force until 1947 (Li, 1988: 30). If racism is developed by capitalists to justify exploitation, then why does it so often result in efforts to block the entry of new immigrants and limit the job opportunities of those already in the country? Bonacich feels that more attention has to be paid to the way in which the competition for jobs and other scarce resources among the working class creates and sustains racism.

Split labour-market theory suggests that racial and ethnic conflict is rooted in differences in the price of labour. For historical reasons—mainly involving military conquest—non-white workers have often received low wages and white workers high wages. Employers try to replace high-paid white workers with low-paid non-white workers. Meanwhile, high-paid workers, faced with displacement or the threat of displacement, try to protect their own interests by limiting capitalists' access to cheaper non-white workers. Thus, cheaper non-white workers are the victims of a complicated process of class struggle between expensive labour, cheap labour, and capitalists.

The theory applies well to Canada. During the late nineteenth and early twentieth centuries, the presence of Chinese workers and merchants in British Columbia provoked a negative response on the part of various segments of the white working class and white shop owners. As split labour-market theory predicts, the hostility of whites was rooted in differences in the price of labour. According to evidence presented at the Royal Commission on Chinese and Japanese Immigration in 1903, Chinese workers earned about one-half of the wages that white workers earned in the same jobs (Li, 1988: 44). A number of racist organizations emerged whose aim was to limit the number of places where Chinese people could work, which helped stop additional Chinese immigration (Roy, 1989).

Split labour-market theory makes three other points that are relevant to the analysis of ethnic and race relations in general. First, it argues that individual racism, ethnic prejudice, and institutional racism emerge from intergroup conflict. Second, the theory maintains that prejudicial ideas and discriminatory behaviour are ways of socially marginalizing minority groups that the dominant group sees as threats to their position of power and privilege. Third, the theory suggests that to understand ethnic and racial relations, we need to look beyond individual personalities and sociobiological processes and analyze processes of economic, social, and political competition among groups (Marger, 1997: 98).

Keeping these three observations in mind will help you understand the three main patterns of ethnic and racial relations in Canada: Aboriginal/non-Aboriginal relations, French/English relations, and immigrant/non-immigrant relations. These are the topics that we turn to next.

ABORIGINAL PEOPLES

Have you ever fumbled trying to find the right way to refer to someone who is ethnically or racially different from you? Are we supposed to say that a person is a "Native," an "Indian," an "Aboriginal," or a member of the "First Nations"? Are you sensitive about how you want others to refer to your ethnic or racial origins? You may think that this sensitivity is an indication that political correctness has run amok. However, you should not dismiss the issue of labels and names easily.

Ethnic and racial labels are about power. Take the term *Indian*. A hopelessly lost Christopher Columbus thought he had found a sea route to India when he was discovered in 1492 by people indigenous to this part of the world. He mislabelled them "Indians." Britain's military, political, and economic domination of North America in the eighteenth century meant that it had the power to ignore the linguistic and cultural differences among indigenous groups and define them in any way they saw fit. They chose the term *Indian*.

As indigenous people have acquired more power, they have begun to challenge externally imposed labels. In the 1980s, for example, the National Indian Brotherhood renamed itself the Assembly of First Nations, and people in Alberta who were called Sarcee Indians by Europeans for most of the twentieth century now refer to themselves as Tsuu T'ina, which means "Earth People" in English (Steckley 2003: 7). Groups have rejected externally imposed labels as part of a search for forms of consciousness, identity, and culture that are untainted by the colonizing power's definition of the situation (Jenson, 1993).

One, albeit imperfect, way to navigate through the complex issue of naming is to use the definition of "Aboriginal peoples" in the 1982 Canadian Charter of Rights and Freedoms. In the Charter, the "Aboriginal peoples" of Canada include Indians, Inuit, and Métis. In 2007, there were 778 050 Indians, and in 2006 there were 389 780 Métis, and 50 480 Inuit in Canada, who together made up nearly 4 percent of the total population.

At its simplest level, the term *Indian* (or *status* or *registered Indian*) refers to people who are recognized as "Indians" by virtue of the federal government's Indian Act. Many people now use the term "First Nations" to refer to Indians. But deciding who is an Indian under the Indian Act is a much more complicated question. Until 1985, Indian women who married non-Indian men, along with their children, lost their federally recognized Indian status; they became *non-status Indians*. In 1985, Bill C-31 was passed. It allowed these women and their dependent children to regain their Indian status. Indian bands, however, now have the power to develop their own membership codes. This means that not all individuals who have had their Indian status reinstated are members of an Indian band (Frideres and Gadacz, 2012).

There are two definitions of *Métis*. Métis organizations in Western Canada tend to focus on a person's objective "roots" as the condition for being considered Métis. Thus, the Métis National Council defines the Métis as "descendants of the historic Métis who evolved in what is now Western Canada as a people with a common political will" (Métis National Council, 1983). The Congress of Aboriginal Peoples uses a broader definition, suggesting that the Métis should include descendants of the historic Métis in Western Canada *and* anyone of mixed European-Indian ancestry who defines himself or herself as Métis (Congress of Aboriginal Peoples, 2008). Thus, subjective definitions of ethnic group membership are more important for groups like the Congress of Aboriginal Peoples.

Finally, *Inuit* are part of a diverse group of people who have lived for many centuries north of the tree line. In Canada, the name *Inuit* has replaced the earlier name *Eskimo.* The language of the Inuit is Inuktitut (McMillan, 1988: 240).

EXPLANATIONS OF ABORIGINAL CONDITIONS

The socioeconomic conditions of Canada's Aboriginal peoples represent a national tragedy (Royal Commission on Aboriginal Peoples, 1996). Canada has made admirable efforts to condemn social inequality and the denial of human rights in other countries, such as South Africa when apartheid—the policy of legalized ethnic separation and inequality—was still in force. Ironically, though, the commitment to social justice for Aboriginal peoples in our own country has not been as strong. In the 1980s, the South African government routinely defended itself against our criticisms of apartheid by saying that we should first clean up our own backyard (Bourgeault, 1988; York, 1989). Statistical evidence shows that Aboriginal peoples are the most socially and economically disadvantaged groups in the country. In 2006, 44.4 percent of housing units on reserves in Canada needed to be replaced or were in need of major or minor repairs, and one quarter of the population on reserves were living in overcrowded houses. (Frideres and Gadacz, 2012: 124). Though government statistics indicate that 98 percent of houses on reserves have adequate water supplies (Department of Indian Affairs and Northern Development, 2004: 63), the October 2005 mass evacuation of the Kashechewan reserve in northern Ontario because of water supply problems shows that decent water supplies are not available to all reserve communities; indeed, 98 other reserve communities were also under boil water advisories at the time (Curry, 2005). In 2006, 17 percent of reserve communities had water-quality issues that required immediate attention (Frideres and Gadacz, 2012: 126).

On average, Aboriginal peoples have much lower family incomes, lower rates of labour-force participation, and higher rates of unemployment than non-Aboriginal Canadians do (Frideres and Gadacz, 2012: 104–08). They are also significantly overrepresented in provincial and federal jails. The overall death rate for Aboriginal people in Canada is now similar to that of the rest of Canada, although Aboriginals between 15 and 44 years of age are more than twice as likely to die as the average Canadian is (Frideres and Gadacz, 2012: 84). In 2005, the life expectancy of status Indian men was 71.1 years, six years lower than the Canadian average. Life expectancy for status Indian women was higher than that for Indian men but still below life expectancy for other Canadian women: 76.3 compared with 82.4 years. The infant mortality rate (the number of deaths of children under one year old per thousand live births) for status Indians is 20 percent higher than it is for other Canadians (Frideres and Gadacz, 2012: 84).

For many years, Canadian politicians, bureaucrats, and social scientists have puzzled over where these differences and inequalities come from, how and why they persist, and what can be done about them. Indeed, when the federal government announced in 1991 the establishment of the Royal Commission on Aboriginal Peoples, Ovide Mercredi, then chief of the Assembly of First Nations, caustically commented that "Indians have been studied to death." I want first to consider the federal government's historical explanation of these conditions and then examine two sociological accounts of them: the culture of poverty thesis and conflict theory.

The Government's View

Throughout the first half of the twentieth century, government Indian policy was premised on the belief that Aboriginal culture was both different from and inferior to European culture. Armed with this ethnocentric attitude, the federal government sought to assimilate Aboriginal people into mainstream Canadian society (Gibbins and Ponting, 1986). In 1920, this approach was summed up as follows by Duncan Campbell Scott, the deputy minister of the federal government's Department of Indian Affairs: "[O]ur object is to continue until there is not a single

Indian ... that has not been absorbed into the body politic and there is no [longer an] Indian question" (quoted in Titley, 1986).

The government, therefore, forcibly tried to Europeanize Aboriginal people and culture. Traditional cultural practices, such as the potlatch, a winter exchange of gifts and property on the British Columbia coast, and the sun dance, a summer solstice religious ceremony on the Prairies, were outlawed. Such practices were regarded as pagan, anti-capitalist rituals that inhibited the development of both Christianity and a capitalistic work ethic (Cole and Chaikin, 1990; Pettipas, 1995). The federal government also tried to assimilate and Christianize Aboriginal children by establishing a series of residential schools. These boarding schools were located far from the children's families and home communities. While in school, the children were forbidden to speak in their mother tongue and to speak with siblings of the opposite sex, and they had their hair shorn. Boys were given extensive training in manual labour and girls were taught domestic labour skills. The goal of this schooling was to resocialize Aboriginal children and to instill in them a new European identity (Titley, 1986). The government's legislative, regulatory, and educational approach to Aboriginal people reflected the view that inequality, poverty, and poor social conditions were rooted in Aboriginal cultural and racial inferiority.

The Culture of Poverty Thesis

In the 1960s and 1970s, many sociologists also saw Aboriginal culture as the source of the "Indian problem." To account for the origins and persistence of the problem, some sociologists proposed a variant of the **culture of poverty thesis.** The concept of a culture of poverty was first developed by Oscar Lewis (1961), an American anthropologist interested in explaining the slow pace at which Mexican Americans and Puerto Ricans were being assimilated into U.S. society. He suggested that some ethnic groups do not readily assimilate, and hence are poor, because their culture does not value economic success, hard work, and achievement.

Kazemipur and Halli (2000) have applied Lewis's framework to the issue of ethnic poverty in Canada, and Nagler (1972) has applied it to the conditions of Aboriginal people. More recently, Frances Widdowson and Albert Howard (2008) have argued that because many Aboriginal peoples participate in modern society as consumers rather than producers, they remain stuck at an earlier, "Neolithic" stage of human development:

> Isolation from economic processes has meant that a number of Neolithic cultural features, including undisciplined work habits, tribal forms of political identification, animistic beliefs, and difficulties in developing abstract reasoning, persist despite hundreds of years of contact. (Widdowson and Howard, 2008: 13)

They argue that the cultural gap between Aboriginal peoples and the rest of the Canadian population prevents the integration of Aboriginal peoples and is responsible for many of the social problems and pathologies in their communities.

Some sociologists, such as Stephen Steinberg (1981), criticize culture of poverty explanations by arguing that groups generally do not get ahead or lag behind because of their cultural values. Instead, they are born into certain stations in life and adopt the values and attitudes that are consistent with their life-chances. If Aboriginal peoples have low aspirations, it is likely the result of a realistic assessment of their dismal job prospects and a resignation born out of bitter personal experience. For Steinberg, the culture of poverty is the consequence, not the cause, of poverty.

Conflict Theory

Since the 1970s, sociologists have focused on blocked opportunities rather than culture as the explanation for inequalities between Aboriginal and non-Aboriginal peoples. The *colonization model* is the most popular variant of the conflict approach (Frideres and Gadacz, 2012). The colonization model analyzes the problem of inequality in terms of power imbalances and the exploitation of Aboriginal peoples and lands by white society.

Theorists of colonization argue that the Indian Act, which outlines the federal government's policies and procedures for dealing with Indian issues, is a paternalistic document that disempowers Indian people (Frideres and Gadacz, 2012). It places limits on the actions of both individual Indians and their band councils. When Indians from Brantford, Ontario, wanted to sue the federal government over unfulfilled treaty promises in the 1920s, the government passed a law making it illegal for them to use band funds to hire lawyers to pursue their claims (Titley, 1986).

Indians did not get much help from federal or provincial/territorial politicians either. Since most Indians could not vote in either federal or provincial/territorial elections until the 1960s, politicians had no need to stand up for the interests of Indians who lived in their constituencies. Chiefs who failed to cooperate with the government's designs were routinely removed from their positions (Satzewich and Mahood, 1994). Band councils are still required to have their decisions approved by the federal minister of Indian Affairs. Thus, rather than helping to create the social conditions that would afford Indian people greater autonomy over their lives, government policy has fostered social marginality and dependence. This is why many Indian leaders have called for the abolition of the Indian Act.

Furthermore, most of the present-day conflicts between Aboriginal peoples and various levels of government originated in the past misuse of power by government officials. Present-day land-claim disputes sometimes go back a hundred years, when government officials could arbitrarily lop off chunks of Indian reserve land and sell it to whites (Frideres and Gadacz, 2012). The Canadian government and private business have derived tremendous economic benefits from the exploitation of land appropriated from Aboriginal communities.

A significant proportion of Aboriginal men and women are owners and managers of both small and large businesses. John Kim Bell, for example, put his musical career on hold to set up the Canadian Native Arts Foundation.

SOURCE: The Canadian Press (Colin McConnell).

CLASS AND GENDER DIVERSITY

Criticisms of the internal colonial model have focused on its tendency to overgeneralize about the conditions of Aboriginal people in Canada. As significant as inequalities between Aboriginal and non-Aboriginal peoples are, conflict and feminist sociologists argue that it is worth remembering that socioeconomic diversity also exists within Aboriginal communities. These sociologists analyze class and gender differentiation within Aboriginal communities and the implications of such differences for both individual life-chances and wider community life (Satzewich and Wotherspoon, 2001; Voyageur, 2008).

Feminist sociologists have been interested in the role of gender in recent debates about the inclusion of the right to self-government in the Canadian Constitution. During the debate over the Charlottetown Accord in 1992, many Aboriginal women were concerned that the proposal for self-government, which was advanced by the predominantly male leadership of Aboriginal organizations, did not contain any guarantees of gender equality (Fiske, 1996; Krosenbrink-Gelissen, 1994: 357–60). The Native Women's Association of Canada, therefore, fought against the accord in the months leading up to the referendum.

Other conflict theorists are interested in the political and economic implications of socioeconomic differentiation within Aboriginal communities. Researchers challenge the stereotype that all Aboriginal people are either poor, unemployed, living on welfare, or working in low-skill, dead-end jobs. In fact, a small but significant proportion of Aboriginal men and women work in skilled professional and technical occupations, and others are owners or managers of small and large businesses (Gerber, 1990). Menno Boldt (1993: 124) argues that most Indian reserves are characterized by a two-class social order (see also Alfred, 1999). One class consists of "a small, virtually closed élite class comprising influential landowners, politicians, bureaucrats, and a few entrepreneurs," while the second consists of "a large lower class comprising destitute, dependent, powerless [and wage-earning] people" (Boldt, 1993: 124). Boldt argues (1993: 125) that this two-class structure has important consequences for community life and politics:

> With the élite class controlling the political agenda, lower-class interests get neglected.
>
> Elite class interests tend to be primarily "power" not "problem" oriented; that is, such interests are related to expanding their jurisdiction and control over band/tribal political and administrative structures. ... [These] are given preference over the problems that afflict the Indian lower class: high unemployment; excessive rates of family disintegration; alcohol and substance abuse; extraordinary levels of violence, suicide, incarceration, and so on.

Researchers are also studying the formation of a capitalist class within Aboriginal communities. Land-claim settlements, although ostensibly earmarked for the benefit of all community members, are frequently controlled by small ruling elites. In the case of the Inuit, Marybelle Mitchell (1996: 449) argues,

> The state's acknowledgment in 1973 of its responsibility to negotiate land settlements with Native people led to the formation of an Inuit ruling class. Created by the state to facilitate access by the multinationals to the Arctic's natural resources, these leaders, a wholly new kind of talking chief, are signing away the land and aboriginal rights of their fellow Inuit in return for limited entitlement to land, some managerial powers and varying amounts of cash channeled through development corporations.

The members of this new capitalist class are different from other Canadian capitalists in that they do not personally own all the wealth and capital that is at their disposal. They do, however, control the compensation that communities receive from land-claims settlements. They establish development corporations, hire and fire employees, make capital-planning and investment decisions, and decide what and how much to produce. The unanswered sociological question is whether members of this capitalist class will make decisions about the future that are in their own material interests or in the interests of the community as a whole.

QUEBEC: NATIONALISM AND IDENTITY

On the evening of October 30, 1995, many adult Canadians were tuned to TV or radio coverage of the Quebec referendum on separation. I followed the results that night with mixed emotions. On the one hand, as a second-generation Canadian with no ethnic roots in the old British Empire, I could empathize with people in Quebec. On the other hand, as a child of the Trudeau years, I was socialized to believe in a vision of Canadian unity. Many on the "no" side believed that a lot of Quebeckers were just bluffing in the pre-referendum rhetoric; when it came to the crunch, they would vote in favour of staying in Canada. Then the results came in. In some parts of Quebec, 90 percent of voters were in favour of separation. As the results from around Montreal were tabulated, the "no" side gained ground. When the final count was tallied, 49.6 percent of Quebeckers voted for separation. Across Canada, people were both exhilarated and downcast because Canada had "won."

Will the issue of separation go away? Despite the ebb and flow in support for separation, the answer is clearly "no." As with other areas of ethnic relations in Canada, an understanding of the contemporary scene must begin with an appreciation of history and of power relations. In this section, I examine three main sociological questions: (1) What is the historical basis for the emergence of Québécois nationalism? (2) Who is a Québécois? (3) What does the close 1995 vote mean for ethnic relations in Quebec and the country?

THE SOCIAL BASIS OF QUÉBÉCOIS NATIONALISM

Even though the 1867 British North America Act asserted that there were two founding peoples of Canada, the English and the French, and that they had equal places in Canadian Confederation, *les Québécois* are one of the oldest colonized peoples in the world (Milner and Milner, 1973). The French government controlled the colony of New France from the early 1600s to 1763. The inhabitants of New France were expected to serve the interests of France. The colony was established in part to pursue the fur trade and to transfer economic resources to the mother country. Much of the French commercial and political elite left the colony following the British victory over France in 1763. When New France was transferred to British control—what the Québécois refer to as "The Conquest"—a new colonizing power came to dominate the society.

An anglophone—unilingual, English-speaking—elite gradually took over the economic and political affairs of the province. Most French Canadian peasants (*habitants*) remained subsistence farmers. During the nineteenth century, some of them immigrated to the northeastern United States to work in the expanding cotton and linen mills; others moved to other provinces in Canada; and still others became part of the urban industrial working class in the province (Ramirez, 1991). By the late nineteenth century, Quebec was a province where "capital speaks English and labour speaks French" (Whitaker, 1993: 22)—a telling description of the way in which linguistic and class structures overlapped. The French Canadians in Quebec, who formed a numerical majority, were worse off than the anglophone minority in virtually every material way (Whitaker, 1993: 22).

The Catholic Church occupied a unique position as a social, political, and religious intermediary between the two groups. In addition to attending to the religious needs of its French-speaking parishioners, the Catholic Church acted as an agent of social control over French Canadian workers and farmers. The church promoted ideologies that were conservative and anti-modern. It devalued the importance of formal education for the masses, discouraged workers from forming and joining secular trade unions, encouraged married couples to have large families, and vigorously discouraged French Canadians from taking up professions or establishing businesses of their own. These ideas were not in the best material interests of French Canadian workers and farmers, but they helped ensure the survival of French Canadian culture (Latouche, 1993).

This social structure began to change very quickly during the rapid industrialization stimulated by World War I, as the industrial working class became a significant player on the political scene. One of the biggest changes in the 1940s and 1950s was the rise of a new francophone middle class of technical workers and professionals. The upper echelons of the corporate world, still under the control of anglophones, remained hostile to the advancement of francophones, even if they were bilingual. The new francophone middle class, therefore, faced a situation of blocked social mobility, which was partly responsible for the Quiet Revolution in Quebec.

The **Quiet Revolution** was the social, political, and cultural transformation of Quebec in the 1960s, in part because of the initiatives of this new middle class. These changes included the secularization of the educational system, reform of the civil service, growth in the provincially controlled public sector, greater involvement of the Quebec provincial government in the economic affairs of the province, and questioning of the Catholic Church's authority in all areas of life. Facing blocked mobility in the corporate world, francophones created their own economic opportunities by expanding the power of the provincial government.

Social scientists and political pundits have pored over referendum and federal and provincial election results over the past 30 years in an effort to determine which social forces are responsible for sustaining the push for sovereignty. Some see the present-day sovereignty movement as an expression of middle-class nationalism that is a continuation of the Quiet Revolution. From this perspective, separation is promoted by middle-class professionals as a way of furthering their material interests. Emboldened by the success at expanding the activities of the provincial government during the Quiet Revolution, they desire even more control over their affairs (Whitaker, 1993).

However, likening the sovereignty movement to a massive job-creation project is too simplistic. First, francophone professionals are no longer shut out of the corporate sector in Quebec. Over the past 30 years, middle-class francophones have achieved upward mobility in both the public and private sectors. Second, a diversity of class interests exists within the sovereignty movement. Many francophone professionals support sovereignty, but there is also a social democratic tradition within the movement that is trying to mobilize working people against foreign (anglophone and U.S.) capitalist domination. Their vision of a sovereign Quebec involves a reorganization of power relations between francophones and non-francophones, and between workers and capitalists. Some francophone capitalists also support the sovereignty movement (Whitaker, 1993).

Clearly, the contemporary sovereignty movement is not based on the support of only one social class. According to Fleras (2012), the nationalist movement is sustained by a broadly based desire among most francophone Quebeckers to achieve a common goal—to create the conditions that will allow them to preserve the French language and culture and "*voler de ses propres ailes* (fly on their own wings) by acquiring the freedom to make their own decisions on everything from cultural policy to social development" (Turp, 2005: A25). Fleras argues that, rather than defining support for the sovereignty movement in class terms, it is more useful to conceptualize the movement as made up of groups who have differing views about how best to maintain their language and culture. Thus, the present-day sovereignty movement consists in part of moderates who want to strengthen Quebec's position within the federal system. This involves a new constitutional division of powers that has yet to be settled. Radical supporters, however, argue that the best way for the French language and culture to survive is for the people of Quebec to have their own state. They argue that they will always be a minority if they stay in Canada and that they will always be subject to the tyranny of the majority. As Louise Beaudoin of the Parti Québécois put it, "I want to be a majority in my own country" (Fleras, 2012: 242).

WHO IS QUÉBÉCOIS?

The population of Quebec is ethnically and linguistically heterogeneous, with 20.5 percent of the population made up of people whose mother tongue is not French: Jews, anglophones, allophones (people whose mother tongue is neither French nor English), visible-minority immigrants, and Aboriginal peoples (Fournier, Rosenberg, and White, 1997: 282). One of the central issues facing the nationalist movement in Quebec is the definition of a Québécois. This question cuts to the heart of ethnic relations in the province.

Benedict Anderson (1983) regards nations as "imagined communities." They are imagined in the sense that, even though members of the smallest nation can never know everyone in the community, there is still a common feeling of fellowship with others in the nation. People in Shawinigan do not personally know all other Quebeckers. Nevertheless, they have a comradeship that extends beyond personal relationships. Nations also possess physical and symbolic boundaries that define who is a member and who is not. Sociologists interested in nationalism want to identify the symbolic boundaries of the nation. In the case of the nationalist movement in Quebec, this issue is translated into the question of who is "in" and who is "outside" the imagined community. And if some groups are "out," will they ever be accepted as Québécois?

A majority of nationalists define the imagined community as all people who now live in the province of Quebec. For them, the social and symbolic boundaries of the nation correspond to present-day provincial boundaries. Sociologists call this a form of **civic nationalism** (Balthazar, 1993).

A minority of nationalists reject civic nationalism in favour of cultural and linguistic criteria for membership in the nation. *Ethnic nationalists* define the Québécois as people who share a common history, culture, ancestry, or language. This is where the concept of *pure laine* ("pure wool") Québécois becomes important. Some nationalists regard the true Québécois as only those who are the direct descendants of the French people who settled in the colony of New France before the conquest of 1763. Other groups in the province are regarded as "cultural communities" (Groupe de recherche ethnicité et societé, 1997: 107). According to the province's policy of interculturalism, these cultural communities must learn to accommodate themselves to the dominant francophone culture and language.

The debate about how to define a nation is not academic hairsplitting. Then premier Jacques Parizeau commented on referendum night in 1995 that the pro-sovereignty forces were defeated by "money and the ethnic vote." After his resignation, Parizeau commented further that it was the first time in Canadian history that the majority (60 percent) of francophone Quebeckers voted in favour of sovereignty. These statements implied that ethnic minorities were not

With 19.4 percent of Quebec's population made up of people whose mother tongue is not French, one of the central issues facing the nationalist movement in Quebec is the definition of a Québécois.

SOURCE: © Megapress/Alamy.

really part of the nation and that *pure laine* votes should be worth more than the votes of others. At the time, Parizeau's remarks also confirmed the worst fears of ethnic minorities—namely, that sovereigntists are not civic nationalists but rather ethnic nationalists at heart and that ethnic minorities will never be considered full and equal citizens in a sovereign Quebec (Ha, 1995).

Many people in the sovereignty movement distanced themselves from Parizeau's comments, and the movement has sought to repair the damage that they caused to ethnic relations. Yet polls conducted in 2005 indicated that just more than half of Quebeckers would vote in favour of sovereignty in a new referendum ("A Dream," 2005: 8). A possible reason for the resurgence in support for sovereignty is that the "children of Bill 101" are coming of age. Bill 101 was enacted in 1977 and requires that the children of immigrants attend francophone schools. Immigrant children educated in francophone schools are now entering the political arena and many believe that their interests would be better served in an independent Quebec (Laforest, 2005: A25; Turp, 2005: A25).

Even though some of the children of immigrants may be buying into the sovereignty movement, the nature of Quebec identity continues to be hotly debated. In 2007, the government of Quebec established the Consultation Commission on Accommodation Practices Related to Cultural Differences to investigate public discontent over the nature of change in Quebec society occurring as a result of immigration and increasing cultural and religious diversity. The "Reasonable Accommodation Commission," as it came to be known, held public forums around the province. Quebeckers from all walks of life participated in these forums. Some embraced the new diversity and called for renewed effort to welcome newcomers and ethno-religious communities. Others expressed anxiety over the future of Quebec's core secular values and the status of the French language and French culture in North America (Bouchard and Taylor, 2008: 37). As Commissioners Gerard Bouchard and Charles Taylor suggested:

> The main danger we are facing is that the groups that make up our society combine their mistrust and (largely unfounded) reciprocal fears and thus jeopardize the *rapprochment* process now under way. In other words, there is a risk that our imaginary fears will engender a genuine danger. We are thinking, in particular, of the still fragile Quebec identity that has taken shape in recent decades and continues to grow despite our differences, or more precisely, from our differences. Moreover, and quite rightly, it is abundantly but freely sustained by the French-Canadian heritage, a very rich heritage that is thus enjoying a new life not by closing in on itself but by opening up the creative, fruitful contribution of the Other. This is precisely what it has done repeatedly in the past. In short, it is the future of the Quebec nation that is at stake here. (Bouchard and Taylor, 2008: 242)

Quebeckers, and Canadians more generally, intently followed the work of the Reasonable Accommodation Commission. As Augie Fleras (2012: 234) puts it, "Quebec must strike a balance between securing its future identity as a francophone and secular-liberal society with remaining a welcoming community for ethno-religious minorities." Though less politicized, the rest of Canada also faces a balancing act between maintaining "Canadian" values and identity and becoming a more hospitable place for newcomers.

IMMIGRATION: STATE FORMATION AND ECONOMIC DEVELOPMENT

The third aspect of ethnic and racial relations in Canada that I consider is immigrant/non-immigrant relations. In 2006, 6.2 million immigrants were living in Canada, representing 19.8 percent of the population. In large cities, the impact of immigration is even greater. In 2006, immigrants made up 20.6 percent of the population of Montreal, 24.3 percent of the population of Hamilton (Ontario), 39.6 percent of the population of Vancouver, and 45.7 percent of the population of Toronto (Statistics Canada, 2008). Canada accepts more immigrants and refugees in proportion to our population than virtually any other country in the world (Li, 2003).

Migration has been a feature of our history for more than three hundred years. However, the nature, sources, determinants, and consequences of immigration have varied through history. In the nineteenth century, immigrants contributed to the processes of capitalist state formation—the process of creating a capitalist system of production and governance. They did this in a number of ways. The early working class in Canada was made up largely of immigrants (Avery, 1995; Pentland, 1981). Immigrant workers helped build the canals, railways, and roads that became part of our economic infrastructure. Many nineteenth-century immigrants were farmers. Their crops were used to feed Canadian workers and, as productivity increased, were exported to feed people in other countries. Those farmers helped to stimulate capitalist industry through their roles as consumers of goods. A significant proportion of the corporate elite in nineteenth-century Canada were made up of immigrants (Clement, 1975; Macmillan, 1985), as was a large segment of the early political elite. Canada's first prime minister, Sir John A. Macdonald, was an immigrant from Glasgow, Scotland.

Immigrants continue to make important contributions to Canadian society. Demographers predict that, in the absence of new immigrants, the population of Canada would begin to decline by 2015. Without new immigrants to replenish our population, the next generation of taxpayers would have to pay far more in taxes and Canada Pension Plan contributions. Retiring at the age of 55, or even 65, would become a pipe dream for many older workers, as employers and governments would need to take steps to retain enough workers. Employers would face serious shortages of workers, and manufacturers would face a smaller consumer market in which to sell their goods (Economic Council of Canada, 1991).

FACTORS THAT SHAPE CANADIAN IMMIGRATION

No single variable can explain the complex pattern of immigration to Canada. Over the past 100 years, six main variables have influenced which groups of people have been let into the country as immigrants.

The first variable is social class. Most immigrants are admitted to Canada because they fill job vacancies, have certain skills that are in demand, or because they create jobs for other Canadians. Indeed, one of the central objectives of Canadian immigration policy is to contribute to the economic prosperity of the country. As such, the flow of immigrants to Canada has been closely linked to the overall structure of the Canadian economy. Between 1947 and the early 1960s, for example, immigrants were regarded by the Canadian government as "factory fodder" (Collins, 1988). Immigrants were recruited to fill unskilled and semiskilled manual jobs in agriculture, construction, mining, logging, the garment industry, and heavy manufacturing. During this time, it was common for individual employers to demand that the government recruit as many as three hundred immigrant workers at a time to fill job openings (Avery, 1995).

In the early 1960s, immigration policy began to place more emphasis on the recruitment of highly skilled professional and technical workers, and on immigrants with large amounts of investment capital. Canada still wants highly skilled workers, but it also admits large numbers of unskilled workers for jobs that Canadians do not want to do.

The second determinant of immigration is ethnic and racial **stereotypes**—exaggerated, oversimplified images of the characteristics of social groups. Before 1962, Canadian immigration policy had a racialized hierarchy of desirability. Immigration policy was based on the assumption that European immigrants were racially and culturally superior to all other potential immigrants. Non-Europeans were stereotyped as racially and culturally inferior and, therefore, were not welcome. In the 1950s, for example, immigration officials could bar groups from entering Canada on the grounds that the groups were "unsuited to climatic and economic conditions" or that they were "unable to assimilate" (Bolaria and Li, 1988). These phrases were thinly veiled excuses for racial preferences in the selection of immigrants.

Since 1962, ethnic and racial stereotyping in selecting new immigrants has become less important. Canadian immigration policy is now more open in terms of the ethnic and racial origins of immigrants (see Table 8.3). Before 1961, Europeans made up more than 90 percent of total immigrants to Canada. Now, immigrants from Europe make up about 17 percent of the yearly flow of immigrants to Canada.

The third variable that shapes immigrant selection consists of a variety of geopolitical considerations stemming from Canada's relationships with other countries. Racist selection criteria were taken out of immigration regulations in the 1960s, in part because they interfered with Canadian international diplomacy. In the early 1960s, Canada began to assert itself as a middle power in world politics that could mediate social conflicts in and between other

TABLE 8.3 TOP 10 SOURCE COUNTRIES OF IMMIGRANTS (PRINCIPAL APPLICANTS AND DEPENDENTS) TO CANADA, 1966, 2010

1966		2010	
COUNTRY OF ORIGIN	**NUMBER**	**COUNTRY OF ORIGIN**	**NUMBER**
United Kingdom	63 291	Philippines	36 578
Italy	31 625	India	30 252
United States	17 514	China	30 197
Germany	9 263	United Kingdom	9 499
Portugal	7 930	United States	9 243
France	7 872	France	6 934
Greece	7 174	Iran	6 815
The Netherlands	3 749	United Arab Emirates	6 796
Australia	3 329	Morocco	5 946
Switzerland	2 982	Korea, Republic of	5 539

SOURCE: Manpower and Immigration. (1967). *Immigration Statistics, 1966,* Ottawa: Queen's Printer, p. 5; Citizenship and Immigration Canada. (2010). "Immigration Overview—Permanent and Temporary Residents." On the World Wide Web at http://www.cic.gc.ca/english/resources/statistics/facts2010/permanent/10.asp (retrieved 28 July 2010).

countries. Outside of Europe, though, our diplomats did not have much credibility because our immigration policy implied that certain groups were inferior and therefore not suited to life in Canada (Hawkins, 1989).

In the 1980s, the Cold War also played a role in shaping who was let in. According to Whitaker (1987), a double standard was at work in the admission of refugees. People who managed to escape from the Soviet Union or other Eastern Bloc countries were routinely granted refugee status in Canada. In 1985, for example, it took a day for the brother of a Czech hockey star who played for the Toronto Maple Leafs to be granted refugee status. Canadian immigration bureaucrats were much more cautious, however, about admitting "socialist" refugees who were fleeing right-wing dictatorships in various Central American countries. More recently, in the context of the U.S.-led war in Iraq, Canada agreed to accept several thousand Iraqi refugees as a way of helping the American government manage tensions in the Middle East.

The fourth variable affecting immigrant selection is humanitarianism. Canada accepts immigrants and refugees partly on humanitarian and compassionate grounds. In 1986, Canada was the first country to be awarded the Nansen Medal by the United Nations for its generosity and commitment to international refugee programs (Fleras, 2012).

The influence of the fifth variable, public opinion, is more difficult to determine, in part because Canadians do not speak with one voice regarding immigration (Wilkes, Guppy, and Farris, 2008). A 1991 poll found five distinct segments of opinion regarding immigration. Twenty-three percent were "protagonists" who supported increased levels of immigration and believed that immigrants made important contributions to the betterment of Canadian society; 22 percent were "concerned supporters" who approved of current levels of immigration but who were concerned that immigration had certain negative effects on Canadian institutions; 21 percent were "indifferent" in their attitudes toward immigration and ambivalent about the contributions that immigrants make; 19 percent were "reactionaries" who felt that the government has lost control over immigration and that immigration was largely negative for Canada. The size of this segment seems to rise when cases of people who appear to be abusing the immigration system come to light. This happened during the summer of 1999, when four boatloads of what appeared to be economic migrants from China

After the terrorist attack on the United States of September 11, 2001, Canada introduced a new Permanent Resident Card and a number of new measures to increase security at Canadian borders.
SOURCE: © george green/Shutterstock.

were dumped on the Vancouver Island coastline. The remaining 15 percent of Canadians in the poll had no opinion on immigration (Holton and Lanphier, 1994). Holton and Lanphier (1994; see also Zong, 1994) suggest that these findings point to a hardening of Canadian attitudes toward immigration.

The sixth variable, security considerations, has become more important since the terrorist attacks on the United States on September 11, 2001. In the aftermath of the attacks, Canada introduced a new Permanent Resident Card and a number of new measures to increase security at Canadian borders. In addition, Canada and the United States are increasingly discussing the harmonization of immigration policies, particularly in the area of security screening of immigrants and refugees. Some commentators refer to this harmonization as a move toward a "Fortress North America" (Satzewich and Wong, 2003).

CONTEMPORARY IMMIGRATION CATEGORIES

Immigrants in Canada fit one of three main categories: refugees, family class, and economic immigrants. Altogether, 280 681 immigrants entered Canada in 2010.

Refugees

Nearly 25 000 refugees and their dependents were admitted to Canada in 2010. There are three categories of refugees that Canada accepts through its immigration program. *Convention refugees* are people who are defined as refugees by the 1951 Geneva Convention Relating to the Status of Refugees and its 1967 protocol. They are people who, by reason of their race, religion, nationality, membership in a particular social group, or political opinion, live outside of their country of nationality or their country of habitual residence and who are unable or unwilling, because of fear of persecution, to return to their country of origin (Citizenship and Immigration Canada, 1996: 28).

Country of asylum class refugees are people who are outside their country of citizenship or residence who are seriously and personally affected by civil war, armed conflict, or massive violations of human rights. Finally, *source country class* refugees include people who would meet the definition of a Convention refugee but who are still in their country of citizenship or residence. This category also includes people who have been detained or imprisoned and are suffering serious deprivations of the right of freedom of expression, the right of dissent, or the right to engage in trade union activity.

Family Class Immigrants

About 60 000 *family class immigrants* arrived in Canada in 2010. Family class immigrants have close family members already living in Canada who are willing and able to support them. A sponsor must be a Canadian citizen or a permanent resident who is over 18 years of age and who is living in Canada. Depending on the circumstances, a sponsor must be able to provide for the lodging, care, maintenance, and normal settlement needs of the family member(s) for between three and ten years (Citizenship and Immigration Canada, 2002).

Economic Immigrants

Economic immigrants numbered about 187 000 in 2010. The government recently increased the size of this category in total immigration flows and decreased the number of family class immigrants because it believes that the former are of greater economic benefit to Canada. There are six subcategories of independent immigrants. *Skilled workers* have to either have an offer of employment from an employer in Canada or be a skilled worker with one year of continuous full-time paid work experience in an occupation that is deemed to be short of Canadian-born workers by the Minister of Citizenship and Immigration. In 2011, the 29 occupations on the list of eligible occupations included architects, dental hygienists, cooks, plumbers, and crane operators. Skilled workers are also assessed on the basis of merit as measured by the **points system.** As Table 8.4 shows, applicants are awarded points for various attributes that the Canadian government deems important in determining an immigrant's economic and settlement prospects. An applicant has to earn a minimum of 67 out of 100 points to "pass" and potentially gain admission to Canada as a skilled worker. The amount of money immigrants need to have when they arrive in Canada depends on the number of family members they have. For example, an immigrant who brings three family members to Canada needs to have $20 654.

Immigrant investors are capitalists who have a personal net worth of at least $1.6 million and who plan to invest at least $800 000 in Canada. *Self-employed immigrants* must have the intention and ability to create their own employment. They are expected to contribute to the cultural or artistic life of the country. They can also qualify under this program if they purchase and manage a farm in Canada.

Provincial Nominees and the Canadian Experience Class

Provincial nominees and the *Canadian experience class* are recently established fourth and fifth categories. Provinces may fast-track individuals for admission to Canada based on specific provincial labour shortages. The Canadian experience class allows temporary workers and international students who have studied in Canada to apply for permanent residency. *Live-in-caregivers*, the sixth category, are admitted as housekeepers and nannies for upper-middle-class and wealthy families.

TABLE 8.4 THE POINTS SYSTEM FOR THE SELECTION OF SKILLED WORKERS AND PROFESSIONALS, CANADA, 2011

CRITERIA	UNITS OF ASSESSMENT (MAXIMUM)
Education	25 points
Proficiency in English and/or French	24 points
Work experience	21 points
Age	10 points
Arranged employment in Canada	10 points
Adaptability	10 points
PASS MARK	**67 POINTS**

SOURCE: *Skilled workers and professionals: Who can apply—Six selection factors and pass mark, 2010*, URL: http://www.cic.gc.ca/english/immigrate/skilled/apply-factors.asp. Citizenship and Immigration Canada. Reproduced with the permission of the Minister of Public Works and Government Services, 2012.

ETHNIC INEQUALITY AND THE CANADIAN LABOUR MARKET

JOHN PORTER AND THE VERTICAL MOSAIC

What happens to immigrants after they come to Canada? How are they sorted and placed in the socio-economic structure? John Porter's answers to these questions in *The Vertical Mosaic* (1965) have had a profound impact on Canadian sociology. Since the book's publication, Canadian sociologists have been interested in whether ethnicity and race affect the operation of the labour market, social mobility, and the composition of elites.

Porter argued that Canada is a **vertical mosaic,** a society in which ethnic groups tend to occupy different and unequal positions in the stratification system. He called the first ethnic group to take control of a previously unoccupied or newly conquered territory the "charter group" of that society. One prerogative that goes to a charter group is the ability to decide "what other groups are to be let in and what they will be permitted to do" (Porter, 1965: 62). Canada has two charter groups, the English and the French. Although their power was, and is, unequal, Porter argued that the two charter groups have been able to set the terms by which other immigrants are admitted to Canada. These charter groups reserved for themselves the top positions in the occupational hierarchy. They also made up the upper ranks of the labour, political, bureaucratic, religious, and media elites.

Immigrants who arrived after these charter groups were assigned to less preferred positions. Non-English and non-French immigrants were assigned an entrance status that was linked in part to the social evaluation of their cultural and racial capacities. Groups from Northern and Western Europe were considered more racially and culturally like the English and French, and were accorded a higher entrance status than Southern and Eastern European immigrants were. The latter were regarded as culturally, if not racially, inferior to the charter groups and were therefore placed in lower levels of the occupational hierarchy and excluded from elite positions. Non-Europeans were defined as unable to assimilate and were virtually barred from entry (Woodsworth, 1972).

Porter argued that once the vertical mosaic was established, it took on a life of its own. Immigrants and their descendants who were initially allocated a subordinate entrance status faced limited prospects for upward social mobility. He thought two factors accounted for the rigidity of the vertical mosaic. One was blatant prejudice and discrimination by charter groups. The other was the retention by ethnic groups of cultural practices that were incompatible with economic success in modern, industrialized societies. In other words, certain immigrants and their descendants were caught in an *ethnic mobility trap* because of their continued identification with a subordinated and marginalized ethnic group (Wiley, 1967).

In the context of its time, Porter's analysis was powerful and insightful. As we have seen, before 1962, the selection of new immigrants was based on ethnic and racial stereotypes. These stereotypes also shaped charter group perceptions of what kinds of jobs immigrants were fit to do. In the 1950s, for example, Italian immigrant men were regarded by immigration bureaucrats and members of the economic elite as culturally willing and able to "tolerate irregular employment, low wages and physically demanding work." They were recruited specifically for work in agriculture, mining, domestic service, the metal trades, and logging (Iacovetta, 1992: 28). Black women from the Caribbean were recruited specifically as housekeepers and nannies for middle-class families in the 1950s and 1960s, in part because they were believed to be nurturing and passive (Daenzer, 1993).

THE DECLINING SIGNIFICANCE OF THE VERTICAL MOSAIC

Does the vertical mosaic still exist? Is the distribution of economic rewards still based on ethnicity? Over the past 25 years, debates have raged among Canadian sociologists about whether race and ethnicity continue to shape our stratification system (Brym with Fox, 1989). Gordon Darroch (1979) and

The storefront of a downtown Toronto pharmacy reflects the ethnic diversity of most large Canadian cities.
SOURCE: © Dick Hemingway.

Edward Herberg (1990) argue that the vertical mosaic is no longer a useful way of describing our society. Later in his life, John Porter also had doubts about its relevance (Pineo and Porter, 1985). Other scholars argue that, although we may be moving in the direction of greater equality, the vertical mosaic is still a useful metaphor for describing our society. Some analysts suggest that the vertical mosaic has been recast along racial lines (Fleras, 2012); others argue that immigration status is the key to understanding patterns of inequality within the "new vertical mosaic" (Nakhaie, 2006).

What is the evidence for the view that "race" (visible minority status) and/or immigration status constitute fundamental dividing lines in Canadian society? One way to answer this question is to compare the earnings of visible minorities with the earnings of those who are not visible minorities; and the earnings of the Canadian-born with the earnings of the foreign-born. Table 8.5 provides information on the earnings of people between the ages of 25 and 65 who were working full time in Canada in 1986, 1991, and 2001. It shows that native-born visible minorities and native-born non-visible minorities earned about the same amount over the three census periods. For example, in 2001, Canadian-born non-visible minorities earned on average $40 030 and Canadian-born visible minorities earned $40 060—an earnings ratio of 0.999:1. However, larger earnings differences can be found when comparing the Canadian-born with the foreign-born. Thus, Canadian-born visible minorities earn substantially more than foreign-born visible minorities, with an earnings ratio of 1.22:1. Conversely, immigrants who are not visible minorities do better than Canadian-borns who are not visible minorities; those who were not visible minorities and were Canadian-born earned $40 030 in 2001 compared with $43 163 for those who were not visible minorities and were foreign-born Canadians, a ratio of 1.08:1. These findings suggest that the most economically disadvantaged category in Canada are visible-minority immigrants (Nakhaie, 2006).

These findings should lead us to be cautious about concluding that "race" constitutes a fundamental socioeconomic dividing line in Canadian society. Canada does not have a single, clear-cut pattern of ethnic or racial economic disadvantage, and significant differences exist in the relative positions of visible minority men and women.

Note that the categories "visible minority" and "white" are made up of diverse groups of people. "Visible minority" Canadians have different immigration histories, histories of settlement, and times of

TABLE 8.5 EARNINGS* OF VISIBLE AND NON-VISIBLE ETHNO-RACIAL GROUPS, 1986–2001

	1986	1991	2001
Visible			
Native-born	$36 928	$36 892	$40 065
Foreign-born	$32 310	$31 654	$32 952
Not Visible Minority			
Native-born	$36 439	$36 541	$40 030
Foreign-born	$36 850	$39 947	$43 163
Not Visible Minority/Visible Ratio			
Native-born	0.987:1	0.990:1	0.999:1
Foreign-born	1.14:1	1.26:1	1.31:1
Native-born/Foreign-born Ratio			
Non-visible	0.989:1	0.915:1	0.927:1
Visible	1.14:1	1.17:1	1.22:1

*Adjusted to 2001 Consumer Price Index. All are age 25–64 and working full time.

SOURCE: Adapted from M. Reza Nakhaie, "Earnings of Visible and Non-visible Ethno-racial Groups 1986-2001," *Canadian Ethnic Studies, 38* (2), June 2006, pp. 19–46. Reprinted with permission.

arrival in Canada, so some do better economically in Canada than others do. Furthermore, when looking only at those born in Canada, some "visible minority" groups do as well as, or better than, their white counterparts. For example, Canadian-born Chinese and South Asian-origin men and women in the public sector, and South Asian and Chinese women in the private sector, do as well as or better than comparable Canadian-born white men and women (Hou and Coulombe, 2010).

Notwithstanding these cautions, at the very least the vertical mosaic metaphor seems to describe accurately the position of visible minority immigrants as a whole in Canada. Most visible minority immigrants are struggling economically, with higher rates of unemployment, lower earnings, and higher rates of poverty than their white immigrant counterparts and the Canadian born (Fleras, 2012: 139–44). Differences between immigrants who are members of visible minorities and white immigrants have been explained by the devaluation of immigrant credentials. Some suggest that education credentials of immigrants from visible minorities are devalued in the labour market and by certification authorities. In one celebrated case, an evaluation officer of the Ontario Ministry of Education wrote to a Jamaican immigrant that his honours degree from Harvard University and his Ph.D. from Stanford were equivalent to "at least Grade Thirteen in the Ontario school system" (Special Committee, 1984). Although this may have been a bureaucratic error, evidence shows that many immigrant teachers, doctors, nurses, and engineers find that their non-Western university degrees and diplomas are of little value in Canada (Basran and Zong, 1998; Henry and Tator, 2006). Some say that this devaluation of credentials is a reflection of racism in Canadian society. Others are more hopeful, suggesting that as time spent in Canada increases, so too will their economic success.

Other research on employers' hiring practices has documented the influence of racial discrimination in employment. Henry and Ginsberg (1985) conducted a study in Toronto in which they sent two groups of actors with virtually identical résumés to apply for various jobs. The only difference between members of the two groups was the colour of their skin or their accent: One group consisted of actors who were white and who had Anglo-Canadian accents, and the other group consisted of visible-minority group members, some of whom had non-Anglo-Canadian accents. The researchers found that, in both face-to-face interviews and approaches over the telephone, whites received three job offers for every job offered to applicants from visible minority groups. Applicants from visible-minority groups were five times as likely to be told that the job had been filled when a subsequent white applicant was invited for an interview (Henry and Ginsberg, 1985).

A follow-up study conducted in 1989 showed no racial discrimination in job offers following face-to-face contacts between applicants and employers. Blacks and whites received equal numbers of job offers. When it came to approaches over the telephone, however, callers with foreign accents were less likely to be invited for an interview and more likely to be told that the job was filled when, in fact, it was not (Henry, 1989). A more recent study suggests that having an "ethnic-sounding" name affects the hunt for jobs. Employers in Toronto, Montreal, and Vancouver are about 40 percent more likely to interview applicants for jobs with English-sounding names than someone with a "foreign-sounding" name, even when they have the same credentials (Oreopoulos and Dechief, 2011; Immen, 2011: B12).

SUMMARY

1. Ethnic categories and identities are not fixed and unchanging; they evolve socially and historically. Canadians may now be considered an ethnic group, as many of them display a strong desire to define their ethnicity as "Canadian."
2. Racism refers to ideas and institutional practices that discriminate against members of groups that are perceived as racially distinct. Institutional racism refers to circumstances in which social institutions operate, or once operated, on the basis of racist ideas.

3. Racism, prejudice, and discrimination have been analyzed from different sociological perspectives. Social-psychological theories, primordialism, normative theories, and power-conflict theories each offer different interpretations of ethnic and racial hostility.
4. The term "Aboriginal peoples" includes people who are defined in the Constitution as "Indian," "Métis," and "Inuit." The terms used to describe Aboriginal peoples are socially negotiated and change because of shifts in power relations among groups.
5. The culture of poverty thesis was used in the 1970s as a way of explaining the poor socioeconomic conditions of Aboriginal people. Problems with the culture of poverty thesis led to the development of the internal colonial model, a variant of conflict theory. Conflict and feminist sociologists are beginning to be more interested in class and gender diversity within the Aboriginal population.
6. Material inequalities between French and English in Quebec provided the historical basis for the emergence of nationalism in Quebec. The contemporary nationalist movement has a diverse class base.
7. Debates exist in the nationalist movement about who is Québécois. Tensions exist between ethnic and civic nationalists.
8. During the nineteenth century, immigrants contributed significantly to the formation of Canada. Now, immigrants contribute substantially to the social and economic reproduction of Canadian society.
9. Six main variables have shaped immigrant selection in Canada: social class, ethnic and racial stereotypes, geopolitical considerations, humanitarianism, public opinion, and security considerations. Immigrants are categorized as refugees, family class, or independents. Independent immigrants are selected on the basis of the points system.
10. John Porter argued that Canada was a vertical mosaic, a social structure in which ethnic groups occupy different and unequal positions within the stratification system. Evidence suggests that the vertical mosaic is declining in importance, at least for European immigrants and people born in Canada. Discrimination against visible-minority immigrants is still a problem.

QUESTIONS TO CONSIDER

1. What are the strengths and weaknesses of different sociological approaches to the study of race and ethnicity?
2. To what extent do racist attitudes and behaviour affect the life-chances of people in Canada?
3. What obligations do societies have to accommodate themselves to the presence of ethno-religious diversity?
4. Do you think that the importance of class and gender diversity within Aboriginal communities will increase or decrease in the future? Why?
5. Are Canadians an ethnic group? Why or why not?

GLOSSARY

Civic nationalism (p. 199) is a form of nationalism in which the social boundaries of the nation are defined in territorial and geographic terms.

The **culture of poverty thesis** (p. 195) holds that some ethnic groups do not readily assimilate and hence are poor because their culture does not value economic success, hard work, and achievement.

Discrimination (p. 191) refers to practices that deny members of particular groups equal access to societal rewards.

Institutional racism (p. 189) refers to discriminatory racial practices built into the political, economic, and education systems.

New racism (p. 188) is a theory that suggests that it is natural for groups to form bounded communities. One group is neither better nor worse than another, but feelings of antagonism will be aroused if outsiders are admitted.

The **points system** (p. 204) is used by the Canadian government to select independent immigrants. Applicants are awarded points for various attributes that the Canadian government deems important in determining an immigrant's potential economic contribution to Canada.

Prejudice (p. 190) is an unfavourable, generalized, and rigid belief applied to all members of a group.

The **primordialist thesis** (p. 191) is the theory that ethnic attachments reflect a basic tendency of people to seek out, and associate with, their "own kind."

The **Quiet Revolution** (p. 198) refers to the social, political, and cultural modernization of Quebec in the 1960s, in part because of the emergence of a large francophone middle class.

Race (p. 186) is a socially constructed label that has been used to describe certain kinds of physical differences between people.

The **split labour-market theory** (p. 192) holds that racial and ethnic conflicts are rooted in differences in the price of labour.

Stereotypes (p. 201) are exaggerated, oversimplified images of the characteristics of social categories.

The **vertical mosaic** (p. 204) is a social structure in which ethnic groups occupy different and unequal positions within the stratification system.

SUGGESTED READING

Fleras, Augie. (2012). *Unequal Relations: An Introduction to Race, Ethnic and Aboriginal Dynamics in Canada,* 7th ed. Toronto. Pearson. A comprehensive and accessible source for understanding patterns of ethnic and "racial" dynamics in Canada.

Frideres, James and René Gadacz. (2012). *Aboriginal People in Canada: Contemporary Conflicts,* 9th ed. Toronto: Pearson. A thorough historical and contemporary overview of Aboriginal and non-Aboriginal relations in Canada.

Miles, Robert and Malcolm Brown. (2003). *Racism,* 2nd ed. London: Routledge. One of the best theoretical discussions of the meaning of race and racism in modern Western societies. The authors argue for a critical, social-constructionist approach to race and racism.

Simmons, Alan. (2010). *Immigration and Canada: Global and Transnational Perspectives.* Toronto: Canadian Scholars Press. A well-argued and critical analysis of contemporary immigration issues.

Tanovich, David. (2006). *The Colour of Justice: Policing Race in Canada.* Toronto: Irwin Law. The first comprehensive look at racial profiling in Canada, this book shows that justice in Canada is driven partly by stereotypical assumptions about crime and those who commit it.

CHAPTER 9

DEVELOPMENT AND UNDERDEVELOPMENT

SOURCE: © Christie's Images/CORBIS.

Anthony Winson
UNIVERSITY OF GUELPH

IN THIS CHAPTER YOU WILL LEARN THAT

- Global inequality is one of the most pressing issues of our times.
- A historical approach to global inequality helps us understand divergent development in different parts of the world.
- Some development theorists argue that the pursuit of economic growth by the International Monetary Fund and the World Bank has led to the *under*development of much of the world, undermining rural livelihoods, for example.
- While identifiable factors have allowed the rapid development of a few formerly poor countries, the associated social and environmental costs have been high.
- War and military aggression sponsored by developed countries have negatively influenced development in many poor countries.
- Global inequalities are staggering, and new evidence indicates that the gap between rich and poor countries is wider than earlier believed.

COMMONSENSE THEORIES OF DEVELOPMENT

Many people entertain pet theories or working hypotheses about why some parts of the world are poor and others are rich. A personal example may help illustrate this point. My parents lived for several years in countries that were poor by Canadian standards, and my mother held a theory that was popular at the time. She told me about living in a small South American jungle mining camp in what was then the British colony of British Guiana and commented that "if you had lived in that heat and humidity you would know why they are so poor." It was perhaps not surprising that a young woman who had lived through 20 Saskatchewan winters would find the tropics an obstacle to productive activity. It was just common sense to her that the climate explained why British Guiana was underdeveloped.

Decades later, my experiences and observations in Mexico and Central America challenged my mother's views. I confronted the architectural evidence of a wealthy colonial past and the archaeological wealth of complex indigenous civilizations that predated the invasion of Europeans. Excavations in Mexico City had just unearthed evidence of the rich city-state of Tenotitchlán that existed when Hernán Cortés and his Spanish soldier adventurers arrived on horseback from the Atlantic Coast in 1519. Just to the north lay the pyramids of Teotihuacán, structures that dwarf the fabled pyramids of Egypt. This city-state reached its peak between 500 and 600 CE, encompassed 21 square kilometres, and had a population 10 times larger than that of contemporary London (Waldman, 2005). To the south, I encountered the imposing ancient hilltop city of Monte Alban near present-day Oaxaca City and evidence of several other precolonial settlements of considerable size and development along the highway leading farther south into the mountains of the mist-shrouded Lacandon forest in the Mexican state of Chiapas that borders Guatemala. In the lowland regions of this zone, I came across some of the most impressive archaeological finds in the Western Hemisphere, relics of the extensive Mayan civilizations that existed from approximately 50 BCE to 1000 CE. Over time, the Mayans constructed a series of cities that boasted ornate architecture, elaborate irrigation infrastructure and palatial structures for their nobility, and massive platforms to accommodate elaborate religious rituals. Between 600 and 800 CE, this civilization reached the highest development of its arts and sciences. By then, the Mayans had invented an elaborate system of hieroglyphic writing, a complex calendar for predicting the seasons, accurate computations of time, and detailed astronomical observations. All of this 1500 years ago in the midst of a part of the world notable for its heat and humidity. So much for my mother's climate theory of development.

Climate is not completely insignificant in understanding the origins and development of human civilizations. Regions with year-round permafrost or great deserts do not allow dense human settlement and the agriculture it depends on, let alone the accumulation of wealth. Or at least they did not in the past. Today, as the example of the desert kingdom of Dubai shows, oil wealth can help spur impressive development in formerly inhospitable places. The key word here is *can*; other oil-rich countries, such as Nigeria, have failed to mobilize their wealth to realize development goals. They remain mired in poverty. Why? With this question we enter ongoing debates that animate the study of development and the explanations for global inequalities that flow from these debates. One of the goals of this chapter is to introduce you to key explanations or theories of development and the controversies they have engendered.

But why study development at all, you might ask? What relevance does it have for my life? What *is* development anyway? It makes sense to address these questions before we examine key debates in the field.

WHAT IS DEVELOPMENT?

The idea of development dates from the eighteenth century, when scholars in Scotland and France formulated the idea of progress. They promoted the industrialization and democratization of society based on the equal rights and freedoms of its citizens.

At first, development was just an idea. It was not until after World War II that the idea crystallized into a full-blown project or, more accurately, a series of projects that became part of state policy and the policy of some non-state organizations (Parpart and Veltmeyer, 2003). After World War II, development came increasingly to mean a process that generated economic growth, industrialization, and modernization in regions and countries perceived to be poor, traditional, and undeveloped. More recently, development has had a broader, more complex meaning, incorporating such notions as progress for women, empowerment of the underprivileged, and environmental sustainability.

Two main factors motivated interest in development after World War II. First, the Cold War broke out between the developed capitalist countries led by the United States and the communist countries led by the Soviet Union. Among other things, the Cold War involved intense competition between the two rival blocs to amass power by gaining influence and control over less developed countries. Second, businesses in the developed West, particularly the United States, were interested in new markets outside their traditional spheres of operation. Latin America, Africa, and Asia were thus of great interest to the Western powers for geopolitical and economic reasons.

Given the context just described, it may not surprise you to learn that some analysts have argued that development, and the study of development, have served to support world **capitalism,** an economic system based on competitive enterprises seeking to maximize profits by using wage labour. However, as we will see, other analysts deny that that genuine development can occur within the confines of capitalism. They have promoted a non-capitalist road to development.

THE RELEVANCE OF DEVELOPMENT AND GLOBAL INEQUALITIES: SOCIAL JUSTICE AND SECURITY

Earlier I asked why you should care about development. We can look at this question from two perspectives, one involving morality and social justice, the other involving self-interest and the need for security.

Development is an important issue for many people because they find it morally repugnant that more than a billion people earn a dollar or less a day (see Figure 9.1). They consider it a matter of social justice that the world's desperately poor be lifted out of a life of illiteracy, disease, and hopelessness. They regard it as unacceptable that a Canadian student buys a coffee at Starbucks for three times the average daily wage of more than a billion people, or spends more on a laptop computer than the per capita gross domestic product of the world's 51 poorest countries (less than US$1000; Milanovic, 2009; United Nations, 2009).

Other people are more concerned with the practical implications of having so many people in the world with so little to sustain them. Few of us would feel comfortable living in a luxurious house with expensive furnishings and two luxury cars in the driveway if several of our immediate neighbours lived in a one-room shanty with a tin roof, owned virtually

FIGURE 9.1 PERCENTAGE OF GLOBAL POPULATION BY REGION LIVING BELOW $1/DAY (PPP*)

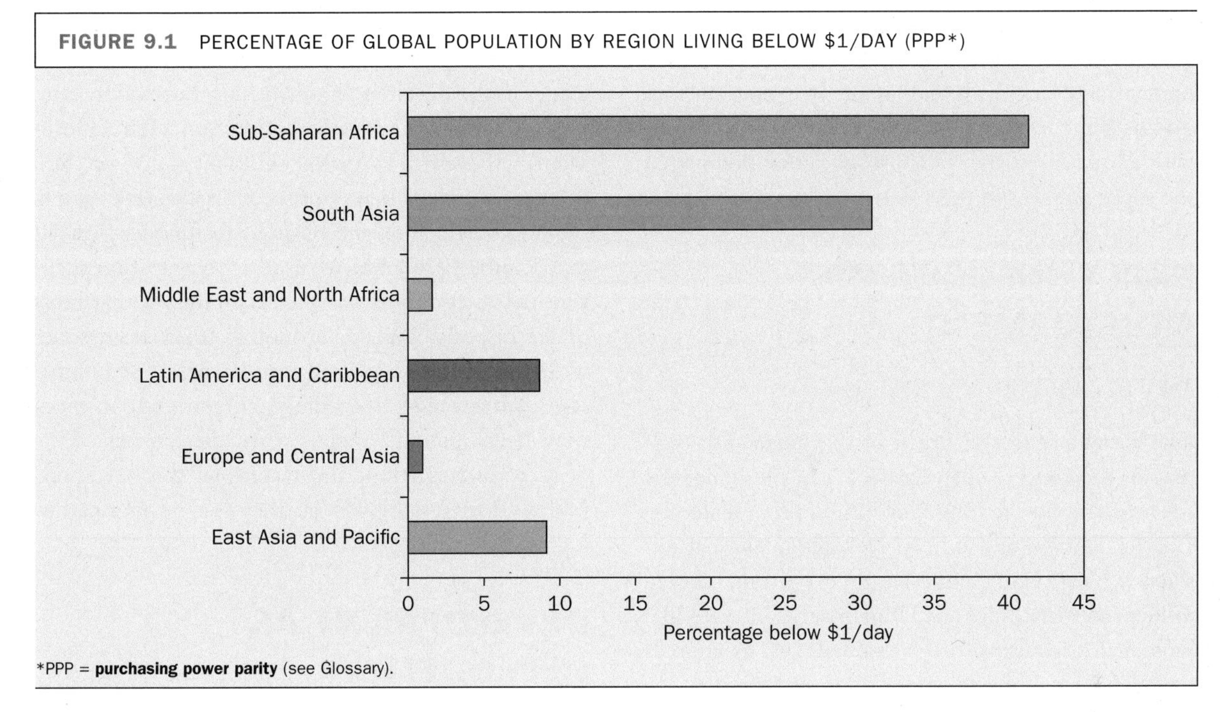

*PPP = **purchasing power parity** (see Glossary).

SOURCE: Based on data from 2005 World Development Indicators, World Bank, March 2005, page 67.

nothing, lacked regular employment, and spent much of their time staring enviously at our lifestyle and property. Eventually, our neighbours' poverty would have unpleasant implications for us.

The higher levels of violence and unrest that accompany poverty would likely wash over to our side of the street. We would have to pay higher taxes to bolster police forces to maintain order and deal with those who decide that it's not fair for us alone to have all the nice things in life. We would soon come to realize that our personal security cannot be divorced from the living conditions of our neighbours, and our failure to help raise their living standard must inevitably have serious, negative implications for us.

Life today is like the scenario painted above, but with added complications. Our poor neighbours might, for example, be living on land we own or land we took from them by using to our advantage property laws and the fact that our neighbours didn't have formal title to the land they had been living on for generations. We might allow our poor neighbours to grow crops, but they would have to give us most of their harvest for the privilege of living on our land. We might select a few of the poor neighbours to supervise the land and reward them with a disproportionate amount of the crop and some extra money under the table. We might also provide the chosen few with firearms and training so they could protect the property and especially the production of fruits and vegetables, dealing appropriately with anyone who might want to challenge existing property rights.

Challenges would likely arise because most households enjoy only a bare subsistence and grow rapidly, making less food per person available over time. Unrest would mount. We would therefore be forced to send some of our family members to help our managers keep order, and some of them would come back with injuries from the skirmishes. Before long, it would be necessary to lock up and occasionally kill people in the poorer households to maintain the status quo, and some of our own family members would undoubtedly get killed trying to police the growing violence.

When we add these complications to our fictitious neighbourhood economy, we have a model that better mirrors the world as it has existed for some time. It is a model that not only describes huge differences in income between our neighbours and us but also points out the inequality that exists *within* poor neighbourhoods. Importantly, the model also establishes that the neighbourhood economy is maintained by a system of power relations backed up by disproportionate wealth and, ultimately, our willingness to exercise violence when all else fails.

Social scientists who study development have proposed radically different theories to explain development and lack of development. It is now time to outline some of the most important of them. I begin with a brief discussion of approaches that dominated the social sciences in the 1960s.

EARLY THEORIES OF DEVELOPMENT

DEVELOPMENT IN STAGES

The social sciences emerged in the nineteenth century in the context of lively debate in the biological sciences around theories of evolution propounded by Charles Darwin and others. Debates in the natural sciences, especially concerning evolution, deeply influenced social thinkers. Human societies were like biological organisms, they reasoned. Just as animals and plants pass through stages of development, so do societies; and like animals and plants, societies are susceptible to pathologies or diseases.

Such ideas were still influential in the 1960s, when W. W. Rostow argued that societal development follows several necessary **stages of development** (Rostow, 1960). According to Rostow, in the beginning, a society might be traditional, undifferentiated, and undeveloped. When it comes into contact with a developed society, however, science and technology spread, and the traditional society enters a stage of possible "takeoff." Takeoff occurs when and if an increase in market transactions, manufacturing, and trade takes place. The faster society moves along the path to development, the more quickly barriers to the spread of market relations are removed and the more efficiently scientific and technological diffusion occurs.

DEVELOPMENT AS A STATE OF MIND

Another popular approach in the 1960s was **modernization theory**, which emphasizes the importance of values and norms as drivers of development. David McClelland (1961), for example, argued for the importance of entrepreneurship and what he called the "need for achievement," the desire for feelings of accomplishment and personal satisfaction. People who enjoy a high need for achievement are more likely to become successful entrepreneurs, McClelland argued, and societies that encourage entrepreneurial behaviour and competitiveness are the most likely to develop economically and socially. Other writers in this tradition emphasized the importance of other values in the development process—the need for savings, investment, innovation, education, high achievement, self-control in having children, and so on. Still others recognized that poor societies also lack capital, stable governments, and business techniques (Inkeles and Smith, 1976). But what all modernization theories had in common was their assumption that most of the responsibility for economic backwardness lies with the societies of the "third world" or "global south" themselves. According to modernization theorists, development happens when the citizens of the poor countries adopt the virtues of the developed North. If they fail to do so, they remain in a pathological, undeveloped state.

DEVELOPMENT AS DEPENDENCY

Dependency theory sharply challenged the notion that lack of development is due to the deficiencies of less developed countries. It did so by taking a holistic view—recognizing that each part of the world is shaped by, and helps to shape, a wider, global reality—and attending to the history and structure of relations between countries.

Dependency theorists produced abundant evidence of strong and enduring economic and social relationships between "metropolitan powers," such as Spain, Portugal, Britain, and France, and "satellite regions" of the global south. First focusing on Latin America and the Caribbean (Cardoso and Faletto, 1979; Frank, 1966), they established that it was precisely the nature of the relationship between metropolitan powers and satellite regions that blocked economic progress in the global south. Let us consider the implications of this argument in detail.

FROM CONTACT TO CONQUEST

Evidence contradicts the notion that the societies of the global south existed in an undeveloped state, as stage and modernization theories suggest. From China through the Middle East and the Mediterranean to Central and South America, great civilizations rose and fell. For example, between 1200 and 200 BCE, Carthage flourished on the northern shores of Africa, while the later naval, military, commercial, and cultural advances of the Muslim people of the Maghreb region of northwestern Africa allowed them to invade and dominate Spain and Portugal until the twelfth century. In the area of east Africa now known as Zimbabwe, we find great stone constructions and evidence of extensive metallurgical development and trade across vast distances. Africans had developed a great deal on their own before Europe began asserting its dominance over the continent (Rodney, 1972).

Initial contact between Europe and the societies of the global south took place around 1500. For the next several hundred years, the Europeans engaged in wholesale pillage and plunder, causing massive death, migration, and economic upheaval—unpleasant facts that stage and modernization theories ignore. Before Europeans could exploit the global south for its riches, they had to conquer existing civilizations. Superior technology in the form of gunpowder and firearms helped to secure the conquest, as did diseases borne by the Europeans. Europeans had evolved resistance to smallpox, influenza, and other diseases that they introduced into the global south. In Mexico alone, the population was reduced from 20 million to 2 million in the first century of contact with Europe. A population collapse of similar magnitude occurred in North America, and among the Inca of Peru. Overall, some 95 percent of the New World's population was wiped out in a fairly short period after European contact (Diamond, 1999: 210–11).

Following their conquest of the New World, the Spanish established a feudalistic landholding system based on hierarchical relationships imported from Europe and subordinated to the power of the Spanish Crown. Its purpose was to support a local European landed elite and funnel valuable minerals, principally gold and silver, and agricultural commodities to the mother country. The Spanish monarchy appropriated much of the profit.

THE SLAVE TRADE

Another disruptive aspect of the relationship between Europe and the global south involved the West African slave trade. It undermined traditional state structures and forms of governance in West Africa and created deep-seated ethnic animosities.

Forced labour had existed for centuries in Europe. Muslim pirates from North Africa had undertaken raids as far afield as southern England to enslave captives. However, the trans-Atlantic slave trade, initiated by Europeans after 1500, established slave economies of unprecedented size, with dire consequences for West Africa in particular.

African slaves taken on board HMS Daphne, November 1, 1868.
SOURCE: The National Archives of the UK, ref. 84/1310.

The Portuguese initiated the trans-Atlantic slave trade near the mouth of the Congo River around 1500. Taking advantage of the custom of local African chiefs to buy household slaves, the Portuguese began trading European merchandise for human lives and shipping enslaved Africans across the Atlantic to work in the vibrant Portuguese colony of Brazil, where they produced first sugar, then coffee. By 1530, five thousand slaves a year were being removed from their homelands for shipment to Brazil (Hochschild, 1999: 12).

Slavery soon became a major disruptive force in West Africa. The ruler of the Kingdom of the Congo, Nzinga Mbemba Alfonso, a convert to Christianity who learned Portuguese, wrote to the King of Portugal to protest what was happening to his people:

> Each day the traders are capturing our people—children of this country, sons of our nobles and vassals, even people of our own family. ... Corruption and depravity are so widespread that our land is entirely depopulated. ... We need in this kingdom only priests and schoolteachers, and no merchandise, unless it is wine and flour for Mass. ... It is our wish that this kingdom not be a place for the trade or transport of slaves. (quoted in Hochschild, 1999: 13)

The King of Portugal was unmoved. Slave trading accelerated, and before long, Dutch merchant traders began introducing slavery to the English Caribbean, initially on the island of Barbados. Later, the English established a major Caribbean sugar colony in Jamaica and the Spanish followed suit in Cuba. Later still, American rice and cotton plantations stimulated demand for still more slave labour. By the early nineteenth century, some 12 million Africans and their descendants worked on the plantations of the Caribbean and the United States.

The societies of entire regions of Africa were thus ruined, and the foundation was set for the deep, enduring impoverishment of Africa. Matters worsened when, in the nineteenth century, England, Belgium, France, and Germany carved up much of Africa for its resource wealth. They established artificial boundaries that ignored traditional ethnic spheres of influence, thereby increasing ethnic antagonism and warfare. In some areas, such as the territory that the British named Rhodesia, the colonizers imposed heavy taxes on peasant farmers, forcing them off the best agricultural lands and into wage labour for white farmers (Arrighi, 1970). Later, some dispossessed Africans began a mass migration to South Africa for work in the expanding gold and diamond mines.

Meanwhile, across the Atlantic, the slave economies of the Caribbean and the United States flourished, generating unheard of wealth for slave traders, slave owners, and the European aristocracy and royalty. Slavery enabled capital to accumulate—capital that industrialists would later use to spur European development.

THE STRUCTURAL ROOTS OF UNDERDEVELOPMENT

Dependency theory shows how social and economic structures established by European colonizing powers since about 1500 distorted local societies for the benefit of European traders and merchants, and later blocked the emergence of industrial capitalism in the global south. In the words of Andre Gundar Frank, a leading dependency theorist, "the historical development of the capitalist system generated **underdevelopment** in the peripheral satellites" (Frank, 1966: 3). At the same time, the extraction of resources from the global south propelled the rapid development of industry in Western Europe and, later, North America. What remains unclear is whether European *countries* or *classes* were responsible for underdevelopment in the global south.

Slave labour on a Caribbean sugar plantation in the 1830s
SOURCE: © HIP/Art Resource, NY.

COUNTRIES VERSUS CLASSES AS CAUSES OF UNDERDEVELOPMENT

During the 1970s, debates on development and underdevelopment focused on the *mechanisms* through which metropolitan powers exploited the global south. Originally, dependency theorists conceived of underdevelopment as a process involving one area—Western Europe—extracting surplus from other areas—Latin America, Africa, and Asia. Some scholars argued that, in recent times, it was primarily through unfavourable **terms of trade** that exploitation took place. They held that prices of agricultural exports primarily from the underdeveloped south declined over time relative to prices of industrial goods made in the developed countries and imported by the poor countries. However, they still imagined that one area was exploiting another.

Robert Brenner (1977) challenged the geographical version of dependency theory and revived interest in a Marxist approach that emphasized class relationships. He argued that dependency theory ought to focus on exploitation occurring at the level of *class relationships*. In his view, by analyzing the nature of the class interests that shape underdevelopment and the types of class conflict that underdevelopment engenders, we can gain a fuller and more precise understanding of the process of underdevelopment. Following Marx, Brenner argued that the struggle among classes to achieve dominance is the prime mover of social change. Accordingly, identifiable classes in the metropolitan countries—merchants, traders, shippers, and the aristocracies and monarchies of Spain, Portugal, Holland, Belgium, France, and England—orchestrated the plunder of the global south. Moreover, these social actors counted on elites in the global south to establish mechanisms for extracting valuable commodities by using the forced labour of indigenous peoples and imported slaves. Brenner further argues that, in more recent times, the mechanisms of underdevelopment changed as England and then the rest of Western Europe began to industrialize under the direction of a new class of industrial capitalists. As industrialization occurred, so too did the nature of demands on the global south (for example, see Box 9.1).

NOT ALL COUNTRIES ARE ALIKE: CLASS ALLIANCES AND STATE CONTROL

The global south is not homogeneous. Each country has a unique history. In particular, different class alliances came to control the states of the global south, with widely different consequences for the pattern of underdevelopment that ensued (Cardoso and Faletto, 1979). For example, in Argentina and Brazil, the large export-oriented economy that developed under the control of foreign capitalists allowed local elites and a sizable middle and industrial working class to emerge by the late nineteenth century (Murmis and Portantiero, 1969). Especially in periods when foreign influence was weakest (during global recessions, for instance), internal elites and their allies were able to establish local industrial enterprises and internal markets that deepened the process of development and strengthened local economies. In contrast, foreign capital was so dominant in small countries, such as Honduras, Costa Rica, and Guatemala, that middle and industrial working classes of much political significance failed to develop, and the economy was based almost exclusively on the exports of just a few commodities, such as bananas and coffee (Ellis, 1983; Handy, 1985; Stone, 1975; Winson, 1983, 1989).

BEYOND DEPENDENCY: AGRARIAN CLASS STRUCTURE AND UNDERDEVELOPMENT

In the 1980s and 1990s, researchers focused increasingly on the role of class structures, class alliances, and state policies to better understand the processes of development and underdevelopment. Consider, for example, research on estates—large, privately owned agricultural enterprises employing many agricultural workers to produce export crops, such as coffee, wheat, and cotton, in societies as diverse as Chile, Brazil, and Egypt. Analysts found that, for three reasons, estate agriculture was more of an impediment to development than were agrarian structures dominated by small family farms (the North American model in the nineteenth and early twentieth centuries). First, estate owners tended to compensate their workers with small plots of land rather than substantial money wages. This greatly restricted the purchasing power of rural workers and therefore the demand for goods that small manufacturers could have produced locally. Second, with a ready supply of cheap labour at hand, estate owners had little incentive to employ advanced agricultural machinery on their estates. This limited the local market for manufacturers of agricultural machinery, who in North America were central to early industrialization. Third, estate owners exercised enormous political power. They influenced governments to maintain

BOX 9.1 THE DESTRUCTION OF THIRD WORLD DOMINANCE IN MANUFACTURING

Before the Industrial Revolution of the late nineteenth century, many goods other than foodstuffs were produced in both Europe and the global south by traditional industry. Small workshops produced a huge variety of metal goods and wooden implements, and all manner of luxury goods made from glass, silver, gold, and so on. Grain was ground in stone grinding mills powered by water or animals. People wove textiles at home on looms from yarn or thread spun on hand-operated spinning wheels. While productivity was low, many people worked in these ways, so output was considerable. Paul Bairoch (1982) estimates that in 1830, the global south (including Japan) accounted for 63 percent of world manufacturing, compared with just 37 percent for Europe and North America. Levels of productivity differed little by region. This would soon change, however.

In England, the rising influence of modern industrialists challenged the longstanding dominance of old merchant families whose fortunes relied on trade. The old "mercantilist" system relied on protected markets and trade monopolies within them. For example, the British East India Company was allowed to block the import of European manufactured goods into India, which was good for traders but bad for industrialists. In 1813, however, the monopoly of the British East India Company was ended by the British Parliament. Now, Birmingham textile manufacturers could export cheap textiles produced by modern machinery to India. This devastated millions of Indian domestic textile producers. Similar events took place elsewhere. As Bairoch argued, it was "in the years 1830 to 1860 that this division between the future developed world and the Third World ... began to take shape. The industrialization of the former led to the deindustrialization of the latter, and the proportional contribution of each region to the total [world] output of manufacturing production was almost exactly reversed" (Bairoch, 1982: 274).

Even relatively wealthy countries are not immune to the distortions of capitalist development. For example, the Maritime Provinces were the first locus of industrial development in Canada, with a thriving shipbuilding and steel industry (Alexander, 1978). By the 1890s, the proportion of people employed in manufacturing was about the same in Nova Scotia, New Brunswick, and Ontario (Winson, 1985: Table 1). Despite this promising early start, and in some ways reminiscent of the impact of British manufacturers on Third World industry described by Bairoch, Maritime industries were disadvantaged by federal policies and the actions of central Canadian financial institutions that control Canadian industry. Maritime industry went into decline, negatively affecting the regional farming economy and resulting in a long-term legacy of high unemployment, underemployment, and lower average income for the Maritime population (Acheson, 1972; Winson, 1985).

free trade policies so they could export agricultural products and import whatever machinery they needed, unhindered by tariffs. This made it difficult for local industry to develop. In contrast, in Canada and the United States, tariffs protected local manufacturing in the early stage of industrialization (Richards, 1976; Winson, 1989).

DEVELOPMENT IN CANADA

Canada achieved independence in 1867. Before then, it consisted of a number of British colonies and a vast western and northern territory controlled by the Hudson's Bay Company, which was incorporated by British charter in 1670. How did Canada become a prosperous country despite its colonial past?

First, like Australia, New Zealand, and the United States, Canada was settled by large numbers of Europeans who soon overwhelmed the Aboriginal population. The European settlers were determined to reproduce or improve the standard of living they enjoyed in the old country. Much of the wealth they produced was therefore reinvested locally. In contrast, when the European powers colonized most of Africa, they set up only small enclaves of white settlers. Their main aim was to exploit local resources and populations, sending nearly all of the wealth back to Europe.

Second, Canada's geopolitical position helped it overcome its colonial past and develop economically. Canada served as a major supplier not just of raw materials but also of manufactured goods, such as airplanes, to the Allies during World War II. Canada's favourable geopolitical position gave its industry a major boost.

Third, Canadian state policy sometimes protected and stimulated Canadian industrial growth. For example, the 1879 National Policy established a duty on imported manufactured goods. The National

Policy sheltered the growth of Canadian industry, then in its infancy, by making foreign-made manufactured goods more expensive. Similarly, the 1965 Auto Pact required that foreign automobile companies wanting to sell cars in Canada duty-free manufacture cars in Canada and use a certain proportion of Canadian-made components. The Auto Pact stimulated the growth of an industry that, directly or indirectly, is now responsible for the employment of one-sixth of Ontario's labour force (Brym, Roberts, Lie, and Rytina, 2012: 232).

GEOGRAPHY AND BIOLOGICAL RESOURCES

A recent, provocative contribution to the study of development and underdevelopment is Jared Diamond's examination of the early history of human civilization. Diamond set out to understand why wealth and power are distributed as they now are rather than in some other way. For Diamond, the answer is complex but boils down to the following idea: "History followed different courses for different peoples because of differences among peoples' environments" (Diamond, 1999: 25).

To make his case, Diamond (1999) distinguished between proximate (or immediate) and ultimate (or fundamental) causes of development. He found that the development of firearms and modern metallurgy by Europeans, along with lack of resistance to deadly diseases in the peoples of the Americas, were the *proximate* causes of the defeat of established, complex civilizations by the marauding Spanish army in Latin America in 1520. The conquest set the stage for the emergence of commercial, administrative, military, and industrial structures over the next several hundred years—structures that helped to enrich Europe while retarding progress in the Americas, Australia, Africa, and much of Asia.

Why did the Europeans alone enjoy such early advantages as firearms, modern metallurgy, and resistance to diseases that proved deadly to the peoples they subjugated? What, in other words, were the *ultimate* causes of European development? Diamond (1999) argues that the geographical features of different continents and the biological resources available to early peoples were fundamentally important. Europe (and the adjacent Middle East) was especially rich in plants and animals that could be domesticated. Moreover, their east–west axis facilitated the intermingling and dissemination of a wide variety of species because geographical barriers were few and climate was roughly similar across the region. In contrast, relatively few animals were available for domestication in the Americas. Moreover, the Americas, Africa, and most of Asia ran along a north–south axis with physical barriers and climatic differences that made the dissemination of species difficult. Australia was isolated and had no animal species that could be domesticated. The wealth of species available for domestication in Europe and the Middle East allowed for the accumulation and storage of large food surpluses, which in turn enabled the growth of large, complex, hierarchical societies. The first cities emerged in the Middle East and so did technological advances beyond the stone tools of the pre-agricultural period, including the refinement of metal, the manufacture of implements and arms, and the construction of oceangoing vessels. These advances spread to Europe relatively easily. Dense population centres and proximity to domesticated animals also allowed germs to spread and cause the first mass epidemics. However, the survivors developed resistance to these germs. For Diamond, then, the early domestication of plants and animals made agriculture possible and was a prerequisite for the development of the guns, germs, and steel that eventually ensured the dominance of European colonizers in the Americas and later in Asia and Africa.

CRITICISMS OF DIAMOND'S THESIS

Diamond's thesis has sparked much debate. Some critics argue that he ignores the mountain ranges and deserts that surely impeded the diffusion of domesticated plants and animals across Europe. Others point out that corn, a major staple, *was* disseminated from Central to South America (Blaut, 2000). Still others note that Diamond ignores crucial political factors. For example, the Ottoman Empire cut off Europe's trade with Asia in the fifteenth century, so European merchants were encouraged to develop marine transportation technology and navigational and cartographic knowledge to reach the East by travelling around the southern African coast. Their technological advantage later allowed them to dominate the seas, exploring and exploiting much of the rest of the globe (Pickover, 1997). Despite the criticisms of Diamond's work, the broad scope of his argument and the eloquence with which he makes it have proven attractive to a wide audience.

THE NEOLIBERAL ERA: DEBT, STRUCTURAL ADJUSTMENT, AND UPHEAVAL IN THE SOUTH

THE RISE OF NEOLIBERALISM

In recent years, the **neoliberal theory** of economic development has become influential in the highest policy circles. It is worth analyzing because the most important institutions affecting development policies in the global south adopted it and still apply it today. A central idea of neoliberal theory is that only in societies where markets are free of government interference can competitive entrepreneurs maximize economic growth for the benefit of themselves and the rest of society. This idea was not always popular. A "hands off" approach by governments contributed to the severity of the Great Depression of the 1930s, when the North American unemployment rate reached 30 percent. Thereafter, desperation brought a strong desire for a new approach to economic thinking. In the United States, the Democratic Party under Franklin Delano Roosevelt, inspired by the economic thinking of the British economist John Maynard Keynes, took the view that government *should* intervene in the market. Its policies, and those of likeminded governments in Canada, Britain, and elsewhere, favoured massive government spending to stimulate the economy and the establishment of public enterprises where the market had failed to provide viable alternatives.

The "Keynesian" approach to economic development worked well for four decades. Then, in the 1970s, it too began to run into difficulties—specifically, high inflation coupled with low or stagnant economic growth. This situation provided the context for American economist Milton Friedman and his allies to advocate a return to policies that would drastically restrict the role of government in the economy in favour of private market solutions.

What implications did the spread of Friedman's ideas have for the global south? In the 1970s, international banks and lending institutions had gone on a lending spree. Many governments in the global south were eager to accept low-interest loans to assist in the industrialization of their nations. The election of Republican president Ronald Reagan in 1981 brought a dramatic change in monetary policy along the lines advocated by Friedman. Among other things, the change entailed a drastic increase in interest rates to deal with inflationary tendencies in the economy. Interest payments on loans made by the countries of the global south soared, and a debt crisis, especially acute in South America, ensued. As governments faced defaulting on their loans, international lending agencies put in place a new set of policies poor debtor countries would have to follow to be bailed out of their dilemma. These policies reflected Friedman's neoliberalism.

The new policy, often called the **Washington consensus,** united the International Monetary Fund (IMF), the World Bank, and the U.S. Treasury around Freidman's neoliberalism. The chief economist at the World Bank, Joseph Stiglitz, wrote that the three pillars of this consensus are austerity, privatization, and market liberalization (Stiglitz, 2003: 53).

In practice, **structural adjustment programs (SAPs)** became the basis of the bailout of the countries of the global south facing a debt crisis. The IMF and the World Bank offered to help the debtor countries financially if they met a set of harsh conditions: Privatize state-owned enterprises, such as telephone and oil companies and national banks; let in international corporations and goods produced in the developed countries; end tariff protection of local industry and agriculture; radically curtail social welfare programs; encourage new lines of agricultural exports—these were key aspects of SAPs. Proponents of SAPs claimed they were necessary to provide needed economic discipline and achieve economic growth. Critics argued that SAPs would cause social upheaval and misery. As we will see, the critics were right.

Neoliberals assumed that markets work perfectly if left free to do so. Demand for labour, capital, and commodities will equal supply. There will be no unemployment. The only thing that could prevent this ideal outcome is market interference. If greedy unions constrain the workings of free markets by demanding and receiving excessively high wages, or if meddling politicians encourage the growth of social policies (employment insurance, welfare, universal health insurance, and so on), then the market will not be able to work its magic. By implication, if economic problems exist, markets must be unleashed. By this logic, the solution to unemployment, for example, is a reduction in wages.

NEOLIBERALISM AND SAPS AS SOLUTIONS TO POVERTY

Proponents of neoliberal reforms in developing countries argue that they have raised incomes in poor countries and lifted millions of people out of poverty

(Neilsen, 2007). Critics have argued that neoliberalism has produced a dramatic increase in global **income inequality**, widespread misery, and social dislocation. Who is right? Let us consider the conflicting evidence.

Clearly, there have been winners in the neoliberal global economy. For example, after Mexico opened its economy to foreign capital and free trade, and privatized publically owned companies, a new class of billionaires emerged. Some benefited from the sale of public sector enterprises at low prices. Others managed to monopolize lucrative new markets. Notably, Carlos Slim Helu became the richest man in the world in 2007—richer than Bill Gates. Large commercial agricultural producers also benefited from the development of new agro-export industries oriented to the U.S. market.

India and China also opened their economies to foreign corporations and trade, helping them realize exceptional rates of economic growth. New industries have rapidly expanded to serve overseas and domestic markets. New entrepreneurial and professional middle classes have arisen in these countries, while masses of rural poor flood into cities to take up work in new factories that provide incomes considerably higher than those available in rural areas.

Do these examples not prove the success of the neoliberal economic model? The answer depends partly on how we define success. In narrow economic terms, policies associated with neoliberalism have succeeded in some places. The wealth of some countries has increased, as has the standard of living. New infrastructure, including hydroelectric stations, rail networks, highway systems, and air transportation facilities, has been built. These facts suggest development is indeed taking place.

Nevertheless, even among the success stories, glaring problems have emerged. And then there are the many countries that have benefited little or not at all from neoliberalism or have suffered because of it. Let us consider these issues in detail.

Level of Consumption versus Quality of Life and the Environment

An increase in monetary income in India and China does not mean that the average quality of life has necessarily improved in those countries. Life in rural areas often provided nonmonetary benefits—personal security, tranquility, better air quality, the benefits of having family close, and so on—that are not captured by economic indicators of well-being. Life in the city for new immigrants often brings increased personal insecurity with dramatic increases in crime and violence, negative health outcomes associated with polluted air and water, dangerous work environments, and deterioration in diet associated with the consumption of fast food and low-quality street foods.

The kind of unregulated development seen in India and China in recent years has also brought with it massive environmental destruction. For example, to power its expansion, China constructed the massive Three Gorges electric dam project on the Yangtze River. The lake it created has displaced more than a million people and destroyed 13 cities and 140 towns, including historical sites and valuable agricultural land. Lack of regulation means that dangerous and

Workers stretch as far as the eye can see in the Cankun Factory, Xiamen City, China.

SOURCE: © Edward Burtynsky, courtesy Nicholas Metivier, Toronto/Howard Greenberg & Bryce Wolkowitz, New York environmentally destructive industries, such as the scavenging of waste from electronic devices and the breaking up of decommissioned ships in vulnerable marine environments, are commonplace.

Agricultural expansion has denuded vast territories and resulted in the rapid spread of deserts. China is rapidly exceeding the carrying capacity of its ecosystem. Winds carry soil from highly eroded land in the northwest as far away as South Korea and Japan, while air and water pollution affect the health of hundreds of millions of families. At the same time, industrial development has claimed tremendous water resources previously devoted to agriculture. The Yellow River no longer reaches the sea for part of the year or even the downstream agricultural province of Shandong. This situation has imperilled agriculture in an important food-producing region. As renowned environmentalist Lester Brown concludes, "China is on the verge of a massive ecological meltdown" (2003: 11, 37).

Absolute Poverty and Global Income Inequality

Many parts of the world have not witnessed the kind of income growth that China and India have enjoyed. In fact, as Stiglitz notes, in the last decade of the twentieth century, "the number of people living in poverty has actually increased by almost 100 million. This occurred at the same time that the total world income increased by an average of 2.5 percent annually" (Stiglitz, 2003: 5).

Measuring the gap at the global level between people with high and low income is difficult. Various experts use different methods and come up with different results. Nevertheless, as a leading researcher states, "the most basic fact about world inequality is that it is monstrously large; that result is inescapable, whatever the method or definition" (Sutcliffe, 2005; see Box 9.2). Branko Milanovic, a leading economist with the World Bank, notes that the top 5 percent of individuals in the world receive about one-third of total world income, while the top 10 percent get one-half. On the other hand, the bottom 5 and 10 percent of people in the world get just 0.2 and 0.7 percent of world income, respectively. Looked at another way, the ratio of the richest 5 percent compared with the poorest 5 percent of world citizens is 165 to 1. The richest 5 percent earn in 48 hours about what the poorest 5 percent earn in an entire year (Milanovic, 2005: 15).

A recent international project to measure the direction of change in global inequalities provides us with a more accurate estimate of global inequalities than we have had up to now. The International Comparison Program includes data from 146 national statistical agencies and major financial and development organizations, including the United Nations, the World Bank, and the International Monetary Fund. A key finding of the project is that price levels in most Asian countries, notably China, India, Indonesia, and the Philippines—countries with about 38 percent of the world's population—are much higher than was formerly assumed. This means that they have many more poor people than previously thought, with new estimates bringing incomes down some 40 percent in China and India, 17 percent in Indonesia, 41 percent in the Philippines, 32 percent in South Africa, and 24 percent in Argentina. Average incomes did not

BOX 9.2 IF 100 PEOPLE LIVED ON EARTH

If the earth's population was shrunk to exactly 100 people, and all proportions were kept the same, there would be:
58 Asians,
10 East and West Europeans,
14 North and South Americans, and
12 Africans.

About one-third would have access to clean, safe drinking water.

One-third of the population would be children, only half of which would be vaccinated against preventable infectious diseases such as measles and polio.

Of the 67 adults, one-third would be illiterate.

20 people would receive 75 percent of the entire world's available income.

Only 7 people would own an automobile.

One person would have control over nuclear weapons.

One-third of the available land would be desert, tundra, pavement, and other wasteland; about one-eighth would be suitable for crops.

SOURCE: Reprinted with permission from the Sustainability Institute.

decline in all of the poorer economies, but increases in Russia, Egypt, Nigeria, and Lebanon were more modest than declines in the Asian countries. Milanovic (2008) concludes that global inequality is much greater than even the most pessimistic analysts thought.

Trends in Inequality within and between Countries

What is the *trend* in global income inequality? Is it decreasing or increasing, and if so, for what time period? Scholars have marshalled evidence that gives us a good idea of inequality trends since the 1930s. The data are better for the developed countries, but trends are apparent for the global south, too.

Considering inequality within developed countries, the gap between the rich and poor decreased from the 1930s to the 1960s. This was the period when the welfare state was being constructed and Keynesian economic policies were being implemented (Bornschier, 2002: 102). For the global south, the same trend is apparent for only some countries. Brazil and Mexico saw increased gaps between rich and poor between 1950 and 1970. The gap between rich and poor countries was quite stable during these decades.

After the 1970s, when neoliberal policies were implemented, the picture becomes less rosy. Inequalities within countries substantially increased. Between countries, the gap also increased, especially during the 1980s (Bornschier, 2002: 108–10; Braun, 1997). Neoliberal policies were probably not the only factor contributing to this outcome. Other causes of the growing gap between rich and poor include the increasing penetration and integration of national economies by transnational corporations and the ongoing massive technological shift away from industrial production to the digital information economy, especially in the developed countries. Nevertheless, neoliberalism helped to widen the gap between rich and poor.

Growth Needs Strong States

Neoliberal policies have not stimulated growth in the global south. To the contrary, growth rates were higher in the decade before the introduction of SAPs (an average of 2.5 percent between 1960 and 1979) than in the era when SAPs were imposed by international lending agencies (0.0 percent between 1980 and 1998; Brym et al., 2005: 1). But what does history teach us about the policies the *rich* countries followed to encourage industrialization? Did they follow the tenets of neoliberalism? Aside from Britain, the first industrializing country, they did not. As French political economist François Chesnais (2004) notes, "the United States, France, Germany and the other industrialised countries [including Japan] benefited from selective *protection* of their home market for over a century or more" (my emphasis). This gave them time to grow until they could compete with Britain in world markets. Only the countries of the global south that fell under the sway of neoliberalism have lacked the opportunity to nurture their industrial and technological base. "Time has been denied to them," writes Chesnais.

Contrary to neoliberal theory, minimal state involvement is about the last thing industrializing countries need. In recent decades, the rapid industrialization of the "Asian tigers"—South Korea, Taiwan, Singapore, and, later, China and India—depended on strong states and considerable state involvement in the economy. For example, governments in South Korea and Taiwan after World War II were highly centralized and authoritarian. They succeeded in carrying out sweeping land reforms that eliminated the class of powerful landowners—the same class that opposed protectionist policies in Latin America. The governments of these two countries opted for a strong industrial policy that marshalled the resources of the state to develop infrastructure and use state credit to fund investment in key industrial sectors. They kept control of industrial development by preventing foreign corporations from taking over their expanding industries. They also used their power to repress labour movements, which kept wages down and made emerging industry highly competitive in the world market.

China followed suit. The all-powerful Communist Party organized a top-down transformation of the economy to encourage foreign investment—but on their terms rather than terms dictated by neoliberal institutions. The Communist Party organized massive infrastructure projects that encouraged industrial investment. It kept wages low and used violence to prevent the formation of independent labour organizations.[1]

Women under Neoliberalism

Other signs exist that neoliberalism has failed to produce the results claimed by its advocates. The dismantling of many national banks by IMF policy prescription undermined cheap credit to small farmers and imperilled rural incomes in many poor countries (Rodriguez Gomez and Torres, 1996: 157–58). Trade liberalization encouraged the import of heavily subsidized agricultural commodities from the developed countries. They undermined rural incomes, as prices for food produced by small farmers plummeted in the face of an incoming tide of low-cost food. Because of such policies, millions of rural poor have been forced off the land and into already overcrowded towns and cities. Millions more migrated to the developed world, some illegally and at great danger to themselves. Such migrants have become the source of a huge global economy in recent years. They typically do menial work and send money back to family members in Mexico, the Philippines, and elsewhere.

In some parts of the global south, such as India and Thailand, neoliberal policies have been especially hard on women, partly because women form the bulk of the agricultural workforce (Shiva, 1993: 232). Elsewhere, in countries as diverse as Nicaragua and Nigeria, women have had to raise families on their own as their husbands are forced to migrate to the cities or to the developed world in search of cash income. Evidence suggests that these circumstances are breaking down longstanding patriarchal structures and forging new ties of solidarity among women as they strive to cope with the new realities, but the change involves much suffering.

Since 1999, the World Bank and the IMF have implemented policies that they believe promote gender equity. However, critics point out that these new policies have been weakly implemented and have done little to eliminate gender barriers for women wanting to access the paid workforce or engage in production for export markets. Nor do they tackle the substantial gender inequality that exists in the households of the global south (Brym et al., 2005).

STATE VIOLENCE, WAR, AND THE PRODUCTION OF POVERTY

Military aggression and war have helped undermine development in much of the post–World War II era, and they therefore deserve to be discussed at some length. During the Cold War, mutually assured destruction by nuclear weapons made military confrontation between the Soviet Union and the United States out of the question. Nevertheless, both countries used their economic and military might to reshape the world during this period.

Under the guise of making the world "safe for democracy" and "fighting communism," the United States was directly or indirectly involved in a series of military *coups d'état* in Latin America and elsewhere from the 1950s to the late 1970s, beginning with the CIA-organized invasion of Guatemala in 1954. The government it had installed at that time prepared the ground for a series of pro-American regimes that have carried on continual campaigns of **state terrorism** that have killed many tens of thousands of Guatemalans, often with unspeakable brutality (Falla, 1994). More than a million citizens have been forced to flee the violence in their country. For most of the decades that followed, Washington provided military aid, training, and diplomatic support for these regimes (Gareau, 2004: 63). When it became politically impossible for Washington to provide such assistance because of the Guatemalan military's gross human rights abuses, the Israeli government stepped in to provide military aid and training (Marshall, Scott, and Hunter, 1987).

The "domino theory" held that if one country fell under communist influence, its neighbours would soon follow suit. Operating with the domino theory in mind, the United States began a decade-long military intervention in Vietnam in the 1960s. This intervention followed years of French colonial domination. America's undeclared war killed more than a million North Vietnamese military personnel, between 500 000 and two million civilians, and more than 58 000 American military personnel. The war destroyed Vietnam's economic infrastructure; the country has only recently shown signs of recovery and economic expansion.

The main American rival on the world stage at this time was the Soviet Union, which also sought to extend its influence and promote the economic model it favoured. In so doing, it used military force to block efforts to democratize and liberalize authoritarian communist regimes within its sphere of influence (Hungary in 1956, Czechoslovakia in 1968) while lending its support to pro-Soviet governments elsewhere in Eastern Europe with strong authoritarian tendencies. Throughout the Cold War, the Soviet Union provided military equipment, training, and in-country advisers to various authoritarian regimes in the Middle East, notably Syria, Algeria, and Iraq under Saddam Hussein, as it competed with the United States for influence in the region. It refrained from supplying the most advanced weaponry to these states, however, for fear that doing so would drag it into direct military confrontation with the Americans (Antonenko, 2001).

Soviet economic and military aid also assisted the struggles of different movements around the globe to remove colonial and neocolonial domination. It bolstered the Vietnamese war effort against the United States, helped the Cubans resist the American economic blockade of that country, and provided arms and materiel to Angola, Mozambique, and Nicaragua in their war against "contra" mercenary armies and the apartheid South African government. Such countries as Cuba and Nicaragua turned to the Soviet Union for military aid only after the United States had fostered economic destabilization and engaged in covert military operations with the intention of bringing down these governments.

In the 1970s the United States, with the help of allies, such as France, provided military equipment, extensive training, and expertise to help install military governments in Brazil, Uruguay, Chile, Argentina, and the Dominican Republic. When these oppressive military regimes came to power, they typically forged strong ties with multinational corporations while suppressing trade unions and popular organizations and groups that opposed them. The oppression they unleashed was brutal. In Argentina, the number of citizens killed by the pro-American dictatorships exceeded 30 000 people, with members of the younger generation the principal victims (Marchak, 1999). Increasingly, the tactics of repression developed by these dictatorships in Latin America are being used in other part of the world to stamp out dissent.

In the 1970s, popular struggles against a staunchly pro-American dictatorship in Nicaragua, and European colonial regimes in Angola and Mozambique, were successful in establishing governments that sought to redistribute land and wealth, and establish more democratic forms of popular participation. Indeed, in their first years in power, they made dramatic strides in combating illiteracy and expanding healthcare (Vilas, 1986).

In the 1980s, the U.S. government sponsored illegal arms deals to covert armies to fight the revolutionary government in Nicaragua and support the South African government in its campaign to destabilize Mozambique and Angola (Gareau, 2004; Marshall, Scott, and Hunter, 1987). In Mozambique, the South African strategy of destabilization was responsible for destroying 718 health facilities and schools accommodating 300 000 students between 1981 and 1986 (Gareau, 2004: 139–40). In Nicaragua, more than 50 000 people were killed or wounded in what was called the "contra war." In southern Africa, a task force appointed by the secretary general of the United Nations estimated that damage to Mozambique, Angola, and Zimbabwe from South Africa's destabilization campaign amounted to $60 billion (1988 prices) between 1981 and 1988, an immense sum for such desperately poor countries. Moreover, 1.5 million people died from violence or violence-related disease and famine, and half the population of Mozambique and Angola was displaced (Gareau, 2004: 141).

In the twenty-first century, war has continued to plague parts of the global south, particularly sub-Saharan Africa and the Middle East, and has undermined the benefits that might come from development assistance. Post-communist Russia has become a major arms vendor. The Russian defence industry now depends on arms exports for its survival, and private interests in Russia increasingly act without government support to penetrate the lucrative Middle East arms market (Antonenko, 2001). New actors have also emerged to pursue self-serving policies that fuel war, economic turmoil, and social disruption and dislocation, China chief among them. For example, China's pursuit of oil in Sudan has led it to support the Sudanese regime, which is responsible for the ongoing genocide in Darfur.

RESISTANCE TO THE NEOLIBERAL NEW WORLD ORDER

GOVERNMENT RESISTANCE

We end our discussion by considering how governments and people in the global South, and most recently in the developed North as well, have resisted neoliberal policies.

Such resistance has been particularly acute in Latin America. Since 2000, Argentina, Brazil, Bolivia, Ecuador, and Venezuela have elected governments that oppose neoliberalism. These governments have been deeply concerned with the increasing concentration of land ownership, the concomitant spread of landlessness, and skyrocketing urban poverty in recent decades. They have sought to aid the landless and the urban poor, and in some cases to nationalize key resource industries and capture the profits that for decades went largely to transnational companies with little local benefit. The Chavez government in

Women members of the Movimento Sem Terra (MST), Brazil's Landless Workers Movement, protest against then United States president George W. Bush's visit to Brazil. The march also marked support of International Women's Day, and thousands of protesters participated.
SOURCE: © Cazalis/Corbis.

Venezuela has used its oil wealth to provide substantial aid to other poor countries in Latin America. In fact, it has provided more aid than has the United States, which has an economy 90 times the size of Venezuela's ("Chavez," 2007).

POPULAR RESISTANCE

In civil society as well, broad-based organizations have challenged the neoliberal development model. Most prominent among these is the World Social Forum, which first brought together representatives from around the world in Porto Alegre, Brazil, in 2001. Their statement of principles set out their aims as follows:

> The alternatives proposed at the World Social Forum stand in opposition to a process of globalisation commanded by the large multinational corporations and by the governments and international institutions at the service of those corporations' interests, with the complicity of national governments. They are designed to ensure that globalisation in solidarity will prevail as a new stage in world history. This will respect universal human rights, and those of all citizens—men and women—of all nations and the environment and will rest on democratic international systems and institutions at the service of social justice, equality and the sovereignty of peoples. (World Social Forum, 2009)

Another notable example of popular resistance to neoliberalism is *Via Campesina*, an international organization of peasant farmers, rural women, and landless workers that seeks to achieve social justice and gender parity in the context of sustainable agricultural production (Borras, 2008). In 2007, hundreds of delegates from 86 countries met in the small village of Nyéléni in the African nation of Mali and set out their principles (see Box 9.3).

Popular resistance to neoliberalism worldwide often takes the form of sit-ins, demonstrations, and strikes by students, nongovernmental organizations, unions, peasant associations, and trade unions. Increasingly, however, resistance to neoliberalism has entered formal politics. For example, the 2008 American presidential race sparked debate over the damage done to people and the environment by the North American Free Trade Agreement, and the 2012 campaign raised the question of whether the level of economic inequality had grown too high. It is impossible to know where such debate will lead or what it will eventually achieve. However, the aftermath of

BOX 9.3 EXCERPT FROM THE *DECLARATION OF NYÉLÉNI*, MALI, 2007

What are we fighting for?

A world where ...

... all peoples, nations and states are able to determine their own food producing systems and policies that provide every one of us with good quality, adequate, affordable, healthy, and culturally appropriate food;

... recognition and respect of women's roles and rights in food production, and representation of women in all decision-making bodies;

... all peoples in each of our countries are able to live with dignity, earn a living wage for their labour and have the opportunity to remain in their homes;

... where food sovereignty is considered a basic human right, recognised and implemented by communities, peoples, states and international bodies;

... we are able to conserve and rehabilitate rural environments, fish stocks, landscapes and food traditions based on ecologically sustainable management of land, soils, water, seas, seeds, livestock and other biodiversity;

... we value, recognize and respect our diversity of traditional knowledge, food, language and culture, and the way we organise and express ourselves;

... there is genuine and integral agrarian reform that guarantees peasants full rights to land, defends and recovers the territories of indigenous peoples, ensures fishing communities' access and control over their fishing areas and eco-systems, honours access and control over pastoral lands and migratory routes, assures decent jobs with fair remuneration and labour rights for all, and a future for young people in the countryside;

... where agrarian reform revitalises interdependence between producers and consumers, ensures community survival, social and economic justice and ecological sustainability, and respect for local autonomy and governance with equal rights for women and men ... where it guarantees the right to territory and self-determination for our peoples;

... where we share our lands and territories peacefully and fairly among our peoples, be we peasants, indigenous peoples, artisanal fishers, pastoralists, or others;

... in the case of natural and human-created disasters and conflict-recovery situations, food sovereignty acts as a kind of "insurance" that strengthens local recovery efforts and mitigates negative impacts ... where we remember that affected communities are not helpless, and where strong local organization for self-help is the key to recovery;

... where peoples' power to make decisions about their material, natural and spiritual heritage are defended;

... where all peoples have the right to defend their territories from the actions of transnational corporations;

What are we fighting against?

Imperialism, neoliberalism, neo-colonialism and patriarchy, and all systems that impoverish life, resources and eco-systems, and the agents that promote the above such as international financial institutions, the World Trade Organisation, free trade agreements, transnational corporations, and governments that are antagonistic to their peoples;

The dumping of food at prices below the cost of production in the global economy;

The domination of our food and food producing systems by corporations that place profits before people, health and the environment;

Technologies and practices that undercut our future food-producing capacities, damage the environment and put our health at risk. Those include transgenic crops and animals, terminator technology, industrial aquaculture and destructive fishing practices, the so-called white revolution of industrial dairy practices, the so-called 'old' and 'new' Green Revolutions, and the "Green Deserts" of industrial bio-fuel monocultures and other plantations;

The privatisation and commodification of food, basic and public services, knowledge, land, water, seeds, livestock and our natural heritage;

Development projects/models and extractive industry that displace people and destroy our environments and natural heritage;

Wars, conflicts, occupations, economic blockades, famines, forced displacement of people and confiscation of their land, and all forces and governments that cause and support them; post disaster and conflict reconstruction programmes that destroy our environments and capacities;

The criminalization of all those who struggle to protect and defend our rights;

Food aid that disguises dumping, introduces GMOs into local environments and food systems and creates new colonialism patterns;

The internationalisation and globalisation of paternalistic and patriarchal values that marginalise women, diverse agricultural, indigenous, pastoral and fisher communities around the world.

SOURCE: *La Via Campesina*, 2007.

the 2008–09 global financial meltdown suggests that the neoliberal model may have run its course and that new opportunities for constructing a sounder and more just global economic system are at hand.

A telling sign that people are questioning the legitimacy of the neoliberal order emerged in 2011. A blog posted by the Vancouver-based magazine *Adbusters* called for the occupation of Wall Street, the centre of American finance, demanding that "Barack Obama ordain a Presidential Commission tasked with ending the influence money has over our representatives in Washington. It's time for Democracy Not Corporatocracy; we're doomed without it" (Chappel, 2011). In just a few months, the Occupy Wall Street Movement saw protests spread from a few major North American cities to more than 750 locations around the globe ("Occupy Protests around the World," 2011).

The Occupy Wall Street movement resonated not only with the poor but also with broad sections of the middle class. Many Americans were disgusted by the failure of government to prosecute any of the wealthy people believed to be at the heart of decisions that brought on the financial crisis in 2008, while millions remained unemployed or lost their homes. Elsewhere, government austerity measures in the face of economic slowdown and skyrocketing unemployment were the most prominent motivators. Everywhere, stark economic inequalities brought on by three decades of neoliberal policies provoked anger and spurred tens of thousands to demonstrate in the streets.

The Occupy Wall Street movement, together with the democracy movement that swept much of the Middle East and North Africa in 2011, suggest that, despite the seemingly overwhelming power of global elites and the economic model they have imposed, it is ultimately people who make history.

SOURCE: Artist rendering by Katherine Ball.

SUMMARY

1. Global inequality is perhaps the most pressing issue of our times.
2. Stages of economic growth theory posits that societies proceed through various stages of development much as biological organisms do. Contemporary American market society is considered the ultimate stage.
3. Modernization theory argues that value orientations determine the success of development in a particular country. Countries in which people have a high need for achievement and value competitive behaviour are said to have a higher likelihood of success in the development process.
4. Dependency theory stresses the role of structural relationships of exploitation between rich and poor regions of the globe as important in blocking the development of the latter.
5. According to Jared Diamond, environmental factors, including the geographical features of different continents and the biological resources available to early peoples, were fundamentally important in determining which part of the globe came to dominate other parts of the globe.
6. Marxist development theory places particular weight on class structure and conflict between fundamental classes within each historical epoch as central to determining development outcomes.
7. A historical and holistic approach helps us understand the divergent development of different parts of the globe.
8. Significant structural barriers have blocked or retarded the economic development of many countries.

9. Not all countries in the global south are the same; different class structures and political arrangements have produced different development outcomes.
10. Policies promoted by the International Monetary Fund and the World Bank have helped to undermine rural livelihoods in some parts of the world and have not effectively addressed the severe disadvantages women face in several regions of the global south.
11. Certain factors have allowed for the rapid development of a few formerly poor countries, but the associated costs for society and the environment have often been high.
12. War and military aggression, often sponsored by developed countries, have had a major negative impact on development in the global south.
13. Today there is general agreement that global inequalities are staggering, and new evidence indicates that the gap between rich and poor countries is wider than earlier believed.
14. Resistance to the dominant development model is growing and is particularly strong in Latin America. The Occupy Wall Street movement suggests this resistance is taking on global dimensions.

QUESTIONS TO CONSIDER

1. Do you think global inequality will change over the next 25 years? In what ways? Why do you think these changes will occur? If you think global inequality will remain the same, explain why.
2. Should Canadians do anything to help alleviate global poverty? Why or why not? If you think Canadians should help end global poverty, then what should we do?
3. What circumstances allowed some countries to escape underdevelopment in the late twentieth and early twenty-first centuries?

GLOSSARY

Capitalism (p. 212) is an economic system based on profit seeking in competitive markets. It is associated with dynamic technological development, the development of class inequality, and accelerating environmental destruction.

Deindustrialization (p. 230) is a process, linked to neoliberal policies, that facilitates businesses moving to the lowest wage jurisdictions nationally or abroad, resulting in social dislocation and economic decline in older industrial regions.

Dependency theory (p. 214) is an explanation of uneven global development that stresses the exploitative relationships that have existed between Europe and the global south, to the detriment of the latter (see underdevelopment).

Income inequality (p. 221) is the difference in income earned by high and low income earners, whether within a country or among countries.

Modernization theory (p. 214) argues that economic growth and development can best be achieved if the values underlying market capitalism are aggressively fostered.

Neoliberal theory (p. 220) calls for the elimination of government involvement in the economy, which-presumably allows free markets to achieve economic growth and development.

Purchasing power parity (p. 213) is the number of units of a country's currency needed to buy the same amount of goods and services in the domestic market as a U.S. dollar would buy in the United States.

Stages of development (p. 214) in W. W. Rostow's theory are the developmental phases through which societies supposedly pass. Rostow believed that modern American capitalism represents a final developmental stage characterized by sustained economic growth.

State terrorism (p. 224) is a deliberate act of physical or psychological violence perpetrated by state organizations (the army, secret police, etc.) to intimidate and coerce certain groups by causing fear, anxiety, panic, and horror.

Structural adjustment programs (SAPs) (p. 220) are policies imposed on debtor countries by the World Bank that entail privatization of state enterprises, opening of debtor economies to imports and capital from developed countries, eliminating social poverty reduction programs, and meeting debt obligations to the financial institutions of the rich countries.

Terms of trade (p. 217) refers to the ratio of the price of exports to the price of imports.

Underdevelopment (p. 216) is the idea that the development of Europe required the exploitation of the global south and undermined its economic development.

The **Washington consensus** (p. 220) is the shared view of the International Monetary Fund, the World Bank, and the U.S. Treasury Department that emerged in the late 1970s promoting a neoliberal approach to economic development and stabilization in the global south.

SUGGESTED READING

Collier, Paul. (2008). *The Bottom Billion: Why the Poorest Countries Are Failing and What Can Be Done about It.* Toronto: Oxford University Press. Argues that the challenge of lifting the world's poorest billion people out of poverty is akin to rebuilding Europe after World War II, requiring not only immediate aid but also trade and security effectively promoted by multilateral institutions.

Griesgraber, Jo Marie, and Bernard Gunter, eds. (1996). *Development: New Paradigms and Principles for the Twenty-First Century (Rethinking Bretton Woods).* London: Pluto Press. A critique of the Washington consensus approach to development and a detailed proposal for equitable, sustainable, and participatory development.

Veltmeyer, Henry, ed. (2008). *New Perspectives on Globalization and Antiglobalization: Prospects for a New World Order.* Aldershot, UK: Ashgate. Eleven specialists in the political economy of international relations and globalization analyze the diverse dimensions of the globalization process.

NOTE

1. As transnational manufacturing firms shifted investment to low-cost labour markets, the **deindustrialization** of many developed countries took place, devastating communities in the north of England and the north-central United States (Bluestone and Harrison, 1982, 1988). Canadian workers and communities in Ontario and Quebec have not been immune to these forces (Winson and Leach, 2002). Investment has not shifted to all low-wage countries, however, because few can offer the massive infrastructure, disciplined low-cost labour force, and political stability that China can.

PART 4

INSTITUTIONS

SOURCE: © ABC/Photofest.

CHAPTER 10

FAMILIES

SOURCE: © ABC/Photofest.

Sandra Colavecchia
MCMASTER UNIVERSITY

IN THIS CHAPTER YOU WILL LEARN THAT

- Our definitions of family and marriage are embedded in social policies that influence personal decisions about intimate relationships.
- Functionalism, conflict theory, symbolic interactionism, and feminism view families through different lenses. Each provides a unique perspective on the relationship between families and the larger society, and on how individuals experience family life.
- Family forms vary historically and across societies, as do ideas about ideal marital relationships and parent-child relationships. Sociologists therefore argue that families are socially constructed; social contexts influence seemingly personal decisions about intimate relationships.
- Industrialization changed family life and redefined men's and women's roles. Increasingly, women—especially middle- and upper-class women—came to be identified with the private sphere of the family, and men came to be identified with the public sphere of politics and work for wages.
- Families, and intimate relationships in general, have undergone dramatic change in the past several decades. Family structures are more diverse. Divorce, cohabitation, lone-parent families, delayed home-leaving, same-sex families, transnational families, and one-person households are more common. Myriad social, economic, political, and ideological factors have shaped these trends.
- Compared with family policy in Western Europe, Canadian family policy does not provide sufficient support, particularly for working parents in need of high-quality child care.

INTRODUCTION

Whether you are male or female, single or in a relationship, childless or a parent, living on your own or still living with your parents, heterosexual, lesbian, gay, bisexual, or transgendered, the choices you make about your intimate relationships are probably markedly different from those your parents and grandparents faced. Like an increasing number of young Canadians, you may have decided to delay marriage and family and live with your parents while pursuing your education and career goals. You may be in a same-sex relationship or living with a girlfriend or boyfriend or raising a child as a single parent. You may have made decisions for or against premarital cohabitation; getting involved with someone of a different race, culture, or faith; or balancing full-time employment and parenthood. If you've delved into the life histories of your parents or grandparents, or talked to them about your plans, you may have concluded that, when they were young, they faced a much narrower set of choices about how their lives would unfold. Two sets of statistics illustrate the magnitude of the change. First, divorce rates have shot up in the past century. In 1925, fewer than 1 percent of marriages ended in marital dissolution, but the divorce rate rose steadily until 1987 and then levelled off. Today, 38 percent of Canadian couples divorce by their 30th anniversary and 30 percent of Canadian children experience a parental separation or divorce before the age of 16 (Ambert, 2012; Juby, Marcil-Gratton, and Le Bourdais, 2004; Sev'er, 1992; Wu and Schimmele, 2009). Second, families have become smaller as many women delay childbearing to pursue postsecondary education and paid employment. In 2009, Canadian women had an average of 1.67 children, compared with 3.5 children in 1921 (Statistics Canada, 2007; 2011).

This chapter examines how and why families and intimate relationships have undergone change and diversification, particularly in the past several decades. While you enjoy a wider range of choice than your parents and grandparents did, you also face more uncertainty and more challenges. You may be confused by intense public debate about what a family is, what role the government should play in defining family and marriage, and how governments might best support families. The main goal of this chapter is to clarify the often-confusing array of family-related structures, choices, debates, and policies that you confront by outlining sociological insights on family life.

The 1950s TV classic *Father Knows Best* (top) portrayed smoothly functioning, happy, white, middle-class, mother-householder, father-breadwinner families. *Modern Family* (bottom) reached the TV screen in 2009. Jay, a white Anglo-Saxon man in his 60s, is divorced and married to Gloria, who is Colombian, divorced, and in her 30s, and has a young son (Manny) from her first marriage. Jay has two adult children—Claire (married with three children) and Mitch (who, together with his male partner, have adopted a Vietnamese baby). Comparing sitcoms from the 1950s with today's sitcoms, we see that age, ethnicity, race, sexual orientation, and marital status have been transformed from constants into variables.

SOURCE: © John Springer Collection/CORBIS (t); © ABC/Photofest (b).

I begin by discussing definitions of families and marriage. I describe why these definitions are important, not just for sociologists and policymakers but for individuals as they navigate intimate relationships. I note that, historically, definitions of families were narrow, while recently sociologists have developed more inclusive definitions that recognize historical and cross-cultural variations in family life. I then show how functionalists, conflict theorists, symbolic interactionists, and feminists understand families. Different theoretical interpretations of family structure, family diversity, and the mechanisms connecting families to the wider society deepen our understanding of the social roots of family life. Next, I offer a brief history of families to show how major economic transitions, notably industrialization and postindustrialization, have transformed them. The chapter wraps up with an analysis of contemporary social policy, situating Canadian family policy in the international context. This discussion highlights how policy is informed by political ideology and how, in turn, family policy constrains the personal decision making of Canadians, particularly working parents.

DEFINING FAMILIES

Just 50 years ago, most sociologists and nonsociologists defined *the* family as mom, dad, and their children—as if only one family form existed. The standard sociological definition of the family was something like "a cohabiting man and woman who maintain a socially approved sexual relationship and have at least one child." Today, we define families (now in the plural) more broadly to capture a wide range of family structures. Many sociologists now define **families** as sets of intimate social relationships that people create to share resources to ensure their welfare and that of their dependants. Social scientists prefer the broader definition partly because they recognize that definitions have big implications for government social policy and inform the decisions we make about how to live. Governments deny some people certain rights, government services, and benefits if they fall outside the definition of what constitutes a family, and people may make marital or other choices partly because of such exclusions. The traditional, narrow definition of family harms many people.

Implications for Social Policy

To understand the importance of definitions, consider the Compassionate Care Program, established in 2004. The program provides government benefits to Canadians to help them care for a gravely ill family member. Initially, the government said you could receive benefits to care for only one of the following family members: your child or the child of your spouse or common-law partner; your wife, husband, or common-law partner; your father or mother; your father's wife or mother's husband; or the common-law partner of your father or mother. The definition excluded grandparents; siblings; in-laws; same-sex partners and their extended family; other extended family members, such as aunts and uncles; and people who live in other kinds of unconventional families, such as individuals who live with a friend and consider that friend to be a family member. Because of public criticism, the government has since expanded the criteria so that all Canadians can apply for benefits as long as they can make the case that the person who is gravely ill is someone they consider a family member, even if he or she is a close friend or neighbour. The expanded definition of family thus had far-reaching consequences for the care of gravely ill Canadians.

Government policies do not just rely on *explicit* definitions. They depend on *implicit* expectations of the kind of support that individuals receive from family members. Take loan programs for postsecondary students. Eligibility criteria for student loans are based on parental income. It is assumed that parents support their children financially. Children whose parents' incomes are above a certain threshold are ineligible for loans even if they are in a situation where their parents do not provide financial support. Many of my students have been in this position or have friends in this situation. They must rely on part-time employment or other means of support.

People receiving government assistance in the form of welfare or disability payments are also constrained by government policy insofar as they may have their assistance reduced or taken away if they are found to be cohabiting. Typically, rules governing welfare receipt assume that a man living with a woman on social assistance automatically provides financial support to the woman and her children. However, research shows that this assumption is false. Many such relationships involve men who are not the biological fathers of children. In **blended families**—two parents and the child or children from their former marriages or intimate unions—partners are less likely to pool resources than they are in other family types (Colavecchia, 2009; Burgoyne and Morison, 1997). Thus, welfare eligibility rules deter relationship formation because some women are reluctant to get involved with a man for fear of losing government benefits. It follows that the high frequency of single-parent households among black families in North America may be at least partly the result of government policy (Calliste, 2001; Sudarkasa, 1993; Wilson, 1987). Welfare rules have effectively dissuaded single mothers from living with and receiving financial and nonmaterial support from parents, extended kin, friends, and unemployed male partners, thus weakening black families and communities. This example, too, illustrates how definitions of the family strongly influence families and the provision of government services.

DEFINING MARRIAGE

Traditionally, sociologists defined **marriage** as a socially approved, presumably long-term sexual and economic relationship between a man and a woman involving reciprocal rights and obligations between spouses and between parents and children (Murdock, 1949: 2). Government definitions of marriage were similarly restrictive, excluding, for example, long-term, intimate, same-sex relationships. Many countries prohibited interfaith and interracial marriages, and even when they did not, citizens often disapproved of them. I once asked a friend's mother about her experience in an interracial marriage in Canada in the mid-1960s. She noted that while interracial marriages were legal in Canada at the time, people still looked at her and her husband askance when they walked down the street. In some other countries, interracial marriage was against the law even if the prohibition was not enforced. Consequently, at home and abroad, the couple faced tremendous social disapproval.

Another example of how government definitions of marriage can exclude certain relationships is that of cohabiting or common-law marriages, in which a couple lives together but is not legally married. In the past, governments did not recognize such relationships. Consequently, many cohabiting spouses were denied access to government benefits. Today, many cohabiting couples consider themselves no different from married couples, and they have access to the same benefits as formally married spouses. However, unlike married couples, cohabiting couples often face a one-year probationary period before they can gain access to a partner's benefits.

Definitions have become a matter of heated debate with respect to same-sex marriage. In 2001, the Netherlands became the first country in the world to legalize same-sex marriage. Belgium, Spain,

Reverend Brent Hawkes performs North America's first legal same-sex marriage at Toronto's Metropolitan Community Church in 2001. Pictured are Elaine and Anne Vautour.
SOURCE: © REUTERS/Andy Clark

Canada (in 2005), South Africa, Norway, Iceland, Sweden, and Argentina followed suit. Other countries do not recognize same-sex marriage, although some American states, such as New York, do. Other U.S. states and many Western European countries allow same-sex couples to register their partnerships under the law in so-called civil unions. Civil unions recognize the partnerships as having some or all of the legal rights of marriage.

Groups favouring same-sex marriage argue that it is a civil and human right, and that religious gay men and lesbians have the right to make a religious commitment in a place of worship that permits same-sex blessings (Abbott, 2010). Same-sex marriage helps to challenge systemic, institutionalized homophobia and affords gays and lesbians legal protection and greater social legitimacy (Green, 2011). Pragmatically, it ensures equal access to pensions and medical benefits, and extends other legal rights, such as the right to make medical decisions for a partner. Other groups oppose same-sex marriage, usually on the religious grounds that it is "unnatural" or "immoral." In the United States, opposition has been fuelled by the Christian Evangelical Right, which has used vast economic resources, including ownership of important media outlets, to raise funds, mobilize supporters, and campaign for the support of public and government opinion against gay and lesbian rights and same sex-marriage (Fetner, 2008).

Questions about how to define marriage have also surfaced in recent debates over polygamy (the marriage of a man to more than one wife) as Mormons in British Columbia and Utah face state prosecution for the practice (Javed, 2008).

Implications for Personal Decision Making

About 10 years ago, I had a conversation with Lucy, a woman in her nineties. Lucy told me that when she was growing up in the early 1900s, only two real options were available to her—getting married or joining a convent. Lucy got married. Her younger sister, Catherine, joined the convent. At the time, people considered it odd if adult women lived independently, with roommates, or in any kind of arrangement outside marriage for any more than a few years.

My mother's history resembles Lucy's. She, too, faced few choices when she married my father in the 1960s. Lucy and my mother were constrained not just by government definitions and policies but also by cultural and religious norms and expectations. As a Roman Catholic Italian immigrant, my mother could not even dream of remaining single and living independently—even though she had the financial resources to do so because she had worked full-time ever since coming to Canada as a young teen. Similar constraints exist today for some young Canadians, particularly women, who are discouraged from living independently because of the religious or cultural norms of their communities. These examples illustrate how the social context in which people find themselves, not just political regulations, mould individual destinies.

Beginning in the late 1960s, women and men started to enjoy more options. Increasing secularism meant that support for the institution of marriage and traditional gender roles that underpinned religious doctrine started to erode. The women's movement of the 1960s gave women a political voice to challenge the idea that women belonged in the domestic sphere. The expansion of postsecondary institutions and the service sector provided women with the economic resources needed to become more independent.

As new family types flourished beginning in the late 1960s, so did sociological definitions of families. They became more inclusive, allowing that many different types of family structure exist. For example, Canadian feminist sociologists Bonnie Fox and Meg Luxton offer a broad definition that centres on **social reproduction**—the physical, emotional, and mental work of caring for others. It defines

> family as the relationships that bring people together daily to share resources for the sake

> of caring for children and each other ... [and families as] the relationships that mobilize resources especially for the sake of generational and daily production—for social reproduction. ... [Family is also] the emotional connection that ... ties people of different generations and households together. (Fox and Luxton, 2001: 29)

SOCIOLOGICAL PERSPECTIVES ON FAMILIES

More inclusive definitions deflect our attention from presumably fixed roles and structures, and toward the actual goals of, and activities within, families. When sociologists describe families as socially constructed, we convey the idea that families are neither static, universal, nor biologically determined (Baker, 2009a; Eichler, 1983). Although change in family structures and roles has been especially rapid since the late 1960s, families have *always* evolved along with broader economic and political change. For instance, the transition from agriculture to industry in Western Europe in the late eighteenth and nineteenth centuries redefined women's relationship to production and their role within the family. In the agricultural and artisanal households of the preindustrial era, women's productive labour was valued because it was visible and central to daily subsistence. Under this system, husbands and wives were economic partners and women's caregiving was bound up with their daily productive work. In contrast, industrialization entailed mass production in factories, the disappearance of households as units of production, and the necessity of working for a wage to support a family. The public sphere of work separated from the private sphere of the family. Among the poor and members of the working class, wives also worked for a wage. However, in the more affluent classes, women were relegated to the domestic sphere alone. Here they became financially dependent on breadwinning husbands. Their unpaid housework and caregiving became less visible and less socially valuable. Thus, the separation of the public and private spheres that accompanied industrialization increased the level of gender equality.

Historical information on family change has been useful to sociologists interested in developing theories of the family. In the next section, I describe four theoretical perspectives that elucidate the inner workings of families and how families relate to the wider society. Each theory has its own point of emphasis, and while each theory is not entirely satisfactory in its explanatory power, each contributes to our understanding of the way families operate and change.

FUNCTIONALISM

Functionalists draw an analogy between the human body and society. The human body comprises different parts, each with a unique function, and these parts depend on one another to maintain a state of equilibrium and well-being for the entire body. Similarly, functionalists view society as consisting of interdependent parts. The family is one part that is central to the well-being of the entire society.

Talcott Parsons held that the **nuclear heterosexual family** is optimally functional for society and the ideal social unit in which to raise children. He premised his argument on the supposed efficiency of a strict sexual division of labour between husbands and wives. Ideally, he wrote, husbands take on the "instrumental" role of breadwinner and wives take on the "expressive" role of caregiving (Parsons, 1951). He claimed that this division of labour holds families together because it makes men and women interdependent. Without such interdependence, marriages would become unstable, harming society.

Apart from providing a stable structure for economic cooperation, emotional support, and the socialization of children, Parsons identified two other functions that families perform. They provide a framework for reproduction and sexual activity. In Parsons's view, the biological requirements of reproduction necessitate heterosexuality, and marriage norms regulate heterosexual sex.

Parsons believed that over time, the family performed fewer functions because schools, nursing homes, the medical profession, and other institutions took on more of the work that was once done exclusively by the family. For instance, preschool programs now help to socialize children and nursing homes care for seniors. In essence, the scope of families has shrunk.

Since Parsons thought that the heterosexual nuclear family is the only family form that benefits society, he implicitly criticized families that diverge from this ideal, such as dual-earner families, single-parent families, and nonheterosexual families. Like other functionalists, he emphasized husbands' and wives' presumably shared values and interests.

He did not address the possibility that their values and interests might not always coincide, that economic inequality and power differentials might lead to conflict. In general, by advocating a traditional gender division of labour, functionalists justify gender-based inequality insofar as it promotes women's financial dependence on men and therefore family stability. However, they fail to see that financial dependence influences marital dynamics by reducing women's leverage in negotiating a wide range of family issues and preventing women from leaving marriages that are conflict ridden and harmful to them and their children. The financially coercive nature of traditional nuclear families can thus compromise the successful socialization of children and the provision of emotional support.

Functionalism also promotes an ahistorical view of families. Many middle- and upper-class North American families in the two decades after World War II fit the functionalist ideal, but many did not. Moreover, especially after the early 1960s, only a minority of North American families conformed to the functionalist ideal (Coontz, 1992). Functionalists do not examine how historically specific factors, notably the deprivations of the Great Depression (1929–39) and World War II (1939–45), followed by high levels of state support for nuclear families and growing affluence, supported the proliferation of traditional nuclear families. The plain fact is that in the two decades following the horrors of the 1930s and early 1940s, when the economy was booming and housing was inexpensive, when governments encouraged childbirth by paying out substantial "baby bonuses" and supported the building of single-family homes in the suburbs with massive road construction projects, conditions were ideal for the proliferation of traditional nuclear families.

A less well known example of state involvement to support heterosexual nuclear families occurred in the late 1940s and 1950s. During this period, fear of communism led to political and educational campaigns promoting heterosexuality, marriage, and childbearing (Adams, 1997). Conforming to traditional nuclear family ideals became a show of patriotism and support for democracy. Difference was equated with dissent; nonconformists were regarded as potential security threats. Consequently, the RCMP subjected some gays and lesbians and childless married couples to surveillance because they were regarded as potentially sympathetic to communism and a threat to national security (Adams, 1997).

CONFLICT THEORY

Conflict theory corrects functionalism's ahistorical bias by underscoring how developing economic forces structure family life. Karl Marx proposed an early variant of conflict theory, and in the hands of Marx's best friend and lifelong collaborator, Friedrich Engels, the theory came to highlight how "modes of production" shape family life and living arrangements. (A mode of production, you will recall from Chapter 6, Social Stratification, consists of the form of labour and tools that characterizes an entire historical era and the type of class structure that is associated with it.) Engels (1972) observed that in preindustrial times, families were "units of production" in the sense that they produced most of the goods and services needed for daily survival. Agricultural and artisanal families worked and lived in their homes, where no clear distinction existed between the private sphere of the family and the public sphere of work and citizenship. Accordingly, productive labour and caregiving were easily combined because they were accomplished in the same physical space.

With industrialization, production moved outside the family. Working-class families came to depend on wages earned by factory workers, male and female adults and children. A clear distinction emerged between the public sphere of work and the private realm of family relations. Households were no longer units of production.

Among the middle class and the affluent, women did not need to work for wages, and the view emerged that the home was a haven from the horrors of the workplace. Middle class and affluent people increasingly saw women as the guardians of this new sanctuary. The notion emerged that "a woman's place is in the home" (Cott, 2009; Margolis, 2009).

Based on the anthropological research of his day, Engels argued that preliterate societies lack private property. Land ownership becomes a feature of societies only when bands or tribes became wealthy enough to settle down and produce more than their members needed for bare subsistence. When someone takes control of this surplus production, that person becomes relatively rich. However, a problem then emerges, Engels wrote—the problem of how to transmit wealth to offspring. Historically, the problem has been solved by requiring female fidelity and male control of property. If men control property, they can ensure it is not squandered. If they enforce the fidelity of their wives, they increase the probability that their sons are in fact *their* sons. These two principles—male control of property and female fidelity—were the foundations of the nuclear family, according to Engels.

If, for Marx and Engels, private property gave rise to the nuclear family, then the nuclear family in turn supported capitalism insofar as it produced, nurtured, socialized, fed, clothed, and housed people who would become workers. However, Marx and Engels paid little attention to social processes within families, such as the social relations and interactions that structure unpaid work in the home. In prioritizing class relations, Marx and Engels largely ignored gender relations and gender-based inequalities—precisely the topics that are of principle interest to feminists.

FEMINISM

In the 1960s, some feminist researchers attempted to extend Marxist theory by studying gender relations in families and how women's unpaid labour in the home is essential for the smooth functioning of capitalism (Luxton, 1980). While the term "feminist scholarship" is an umbrella encompassing many specialized theories, there are some recurring themes across all feminist scholarship. The goal of much feminist research is to render visible women's "hidden" experiences—experiences that, despite their significance in family life, are commonly ignored by nonfeminist researchers (DeVault, 1999). These experiences include housework, meal preparation, and the transition to parenthood (Oakley, 1975; DeVault, 1991; Walzer, 1998, Fox, 2009).

In their examination of such subjects, feminists introduced the concept of patriarchy, the social system by which men control women, and identified the consequences of men having more power than women do in families. Unlike functionalists, who argue that the gendered division of labour produces family stability, feminists see the gendered division of labour as hierarchical, coercive, nonfunctional, and a potential source of conflict. For feminists, the division of labour between women and men in the family crystallized when men started to exercise economic and political dominance and developed a patriarchal ideology justifying their authority. At its most extreme, it results in male violence against women; in the feminist view, when men engage in physical, emotional, psychological, and financial abuse, their aim is to control women (Ambert, 2012; Cory and McAndless-Davis, 2008; Gartner, Dawson, and Crawford, 2001).

A second important difference between functionalism and feminism concerns the issue of the uniformity or diversity of family forms. Functionalists regard the traditional nuclear family as universal. In contrast, feminists recognize that diverse family structures have always existed to satisfy a wide range of human needs that are influenced by the social environment (Stacey, 2011). For instance, women tend to become more domestic when opportunities for work in the paid labour force are relatively scarce and less domestic when such opportunities are abundant (Gerson, 1985; Luxton, 1980). By the same logic, cultural norms of femininity and masculinity change over time and differ from place to place, influencing the diverse ways in which people enact gender roles (West and Zimmerman, 1987).

Late-nineteenth- and early-twentieth-century feminists, and "second-wave" feminists from the 1960s and 1970s, have been criticized in recent decades for focusing too much on the concerns of young, professional, affluent, white, heterosexual, able-bodied women, and ignoring the experiences and interests of marginalized women, including Aboriginal women, women of colour, immigrant women, poor and working-class women, older women, women with disabilities, and lesbians. Recent feminist scholarship has sought to correct this imbalance by paying more attention to the unique issues and experiences affecting less privileged women (Nelson, 1996).

SYMBOLIC INTERACTIONISM

The theories I examined earlier offer mainly macrolevel analyses of the family. In contrast, symbolic interactionists focus on families at the microlevel, exploring how people fashion a meaningful family life out of their everyday interactions. It analyzes how our sense of self develops in interaction with others, particularly parents and other family members. For symbolic interactionists, it is above all the use of symbols and rituals, such as the rings, houses of worship, and ceremonies associated with weddings, that create the meaningful experiences that hold families together (Ambert, 2012: 14).

As noted in Chapter 3, Socialization, the development of the self extends beyond childhood and primary socialization. With respect to the family, research has found, for example, that the birth of a baby changes a new mother's sense of self in ways that are different from the changes new fathers experience. In a study of first-time parents, Walzer (1998) found that mothers spent more time than their husbands did taking care of the baby's physical needs and also thinking about, and being preoccupied with, the newborn. Moreover, women's worries were different from those of their husbands. For instance, while mothers worried that maternal absence might deprive the baby of something important, men viewed paternal absence as more of a loss for themselves, in that they might miss an important milestone, such as the first time the baby crawls. In a study I conducted on family finances, I found that husbands and wives reported that wives experienced more worry, anxiety, and guilt over personal spending, and were more focused on the family in their spending, and that these differences emerged during the transition to motherhood (Colavecchia, 2009).

The main criticism levelled against symbolic interactionism is that by emphasizing microlevel interactions, it neglects how larger structures influence families. Consider the emergence since the 1970s of neoliberal government economic policy as it relates to the family. By emphasizing the need to privatize child care and eldercare, neoliberalism seeks to place the burden of responsibility for the care of children and seniors on individual families rather than on the state (Baker, 2009b). Doing so would increase the burden on women since they do a disproportionate amount of child care and eldercare.

HISTORICAL AND CROSS-CULTURAL VARIATION

EARLY HUNTING AND GATHERING SOCIETIES

The influence of the social environment on families has been evident ever since foraging societies first emerged. Foraging societies were nomadic bands or tribes of up to about a hundred people who roamed the countryside to harvest edible wild plants and hunt animals.

The nuclear heterosexual family living in a privatized household with specialized gender roles is a new creation. It was not the norm for most of human history and prehistory. Humans have been around for about 100 000 years, and foraging societies predominated during the first 90 000. Because women spent much of their time gathering the food that constituted a large part of the band's needs, the care of children in foraging societies was not the responsibility of an individual household but of a wider group that included men. Men hunted more than women did, but the unpredictability of hunting meant that women's economic contributions were highly valued.

PREINDUSTRIAL SOCIETY

When nomadic tribes finally settled in permanent communities, they turned to agriculture and the domestication of animals. Family households were premised on assumptions and practices quite different from those we are familiar with. Today, families are based on ideas of love and caring, and of the special bonds and expectations of support between spouses and between parents and children. Love as a prerequisite or main motivator of marriage is a relatively recent social development. For millennia, marriage was a social contract that served to join two families and advance their mutual economic and political interests (Coontz, 2005).

In the preindustrial era, the composition and size of households was based almost exclusively on its economic and labour needs. Husbands and wives were economic partners. Women did not focus exclusively on caregiving. Spouses continually made economic calculations about how much labour was required to run the farmstead or artisan shop. Household size fluctuated, depending on labour needs. For instance, more people would typically live in the home during

Preindustrial families were the economic units of production. This scene shows a husband weaving at his loom and the wife spinning yarn.

SOURCE: © Culver Pictures/The Art Archive at Art Resource, NY.

harvest season as people were brought in to help with the harvest. A sharp line of demarcation between the public and private spheres did not exist because preindustrial families were economic units of production and nuclear families lived alongside relatives and hired help to maintain the family "corporation."

There was no expectation that children would live with their parents until adulthood. Parents often saw children as an economic liability—another mouth to feed—if their labour was not required. Households could not afford to sustain many nonproductive members, so children as young as six or seven were expected to do chores and they were routinely sent to live and work in other households if their labour was not required at home. Given today's ideas about the special bond between parents and children, it is hard to imagine the practice of sending young children to live with others, yet the economic structure and ideology of the day supported this arrangement. Moreover, since husband-wife partnerships were essential for the economic survival of a household, widowhood was often followed by immediate remarriage. Given today's ideas about the special bond of intimacy between spouses, it may be hard to imagine immediate remarriage, but, again, the economic structure of preindustrial households demanded it.

INDUSTRIALIZATION

Industrialization began in the late eighteenth century in England. A hundred years later, North America, Western Europe, and Japan had followed suit. Industrialization had a profound effect on family life. Production by individual family households was replaced by large-scale factory production. As wage labour in factories and offices supplanted labour on farms and in small workshops, households shrank and increasingly contained just parents and their children, while the separation of public and private spheres transformed men's and women's family roles.

As noted, among the poor and the working class, it was generally necessary for all family members, some as young as six or seven, to work for a wage. Things were not as jolly as the young chimney sweeps dancing on the rooftops in *Mary Poppins* make it seem. Young boys in the early industrial era were recruited to crawl up narrow chimney flues and clean out the soot. They would have to strip off their clothes to be able to wriggle up and down the chimneys, scraping their knees, elbows, and other protruding body parts against the sooty chimney walls in the process. The first recorded cases of industrial cancer (known at the time as "soot wart"), date from this era. Similarly, Charles Dickens's story was not in the least unusual. When the police arrested his father in 1824 for failure to pay a debt, Dickens was set to work in a shoe polish factory, a dreadful ordeal that coloured much of his writing. He was 12 at the time.

For four reasons, the preference was to keep women at home if possible. First, domestic labour—preparing meals, washing clothes, cleaning, and so on—was time intensive because households did not have modern conveniences, such as running water and electricity. Second, factory work was often dirty and dangerous, and workers were often subject to physical (and, in the case of women, sexual) abuse. Parents, worried about their daughters' safety, preferred to send sons out to the factories. Third, men's wages were generally higher than women's wages. Fourth, some opportunities existed for women to earn money in the home, for instance by taking in other people's laundry or doing sewing in the home for textile factories (Bradbury, 1993).

Among the middle and upper classes, women focused exclusively on homemaking and caregiving. New ideologies about femininity, motherhood, and children emerged to support the relegation of more affluent women to the private sphere, including the idea that "a woman's place is in the home" and that women are biologically and uniquely predisposed to caregiving because of their "maternal instinct." A burgeoning medical and scientific literature and religious doctrine supported such notions. New psychological and child development theories promoted "intensive mothering," asserting that children need intensive and exclusive maternal care to ensure their long-term psychological well-being and avoid delinquency. This literature stirred up women's fears and guilt, helping to keep them away from the public realm of wage labour and politics.

Under the new industrial regime, children required substantial economic investment for education and training. As a result, families became smaller, particularly in the more affluent classes, as parents, largely mothers, poured time, energy, and resources into ensuring that their children would succeed in the new economic order. Thus, the economic transformation of society gave rise to a new set of ideas about the socialization of children and the responsibilities that parents, and mothers in particular, needed to undertake.

THE 1950S AND BEYOND

ECONOMIC PROSPERITY AND THE TRADITIONAL NUCLEAR FAMILY

In North America and Western Europe, the **fertility rate** (the number of live births per 1000 women of childbearing age) continued to decline until the 1950s, when an unprecedented rise in the standard of living and the emotional response to the losses of World War II gave rise to a dramatic shift in family trends. Incomes were sufficiently high that a man could earn a "**family wage**"—enough money to support a family on his own. Government offered relatively generous child allowances. This situation facilitated early marriage and childbearing, and led to increases in home ownership, the expansion of suburbs, and the enthusiastic embrace of family life.

Today, when politicians, writers, and others argue that the modern family is in crisis and give us an idealized image of the family, they use the 1950s as their point of comparison (Popenoe, 1993). However, marital and fertility trends were anomalous compared with the decades leading up to and following the 1950s. Moreover, considerable evidence shows that observers who idealize the 1950s ignore the dark underside of family life (Coontz, 1992; Luxton, 1980). Many people were trapped in unhappy and abusive marriages. Some marriages resulted in divorce, and divorce rates would undoubtedly have been higher if women had been less economically dependent on their husbands and divorce laws had been more liberal.

ECONOMIC CRISES AND THE EMERGENCE OF THE DUAL-EARNER FAMILY

The tide quickly turned as economic affluence gave way to repeated recessions stretching from 1973 to, most recently, 2008–09. During this period, the growth of low-wage manufacturing in China and other countries caused the Canadian manufacturing sector to shrink. Unionized jobs that at one time paid a family wage became scarcer. More wives found it necessary to take jobs in the paid labour force to make up for the declining wages of their husbands. The great majority of these jobs were in the service sector. Although many were part-time, and therefore associated with relatively low pay and few benefits, they helped to alleviate the economic squeeze that families experienced. Today, there are nearly as many women in the paid labour force as there are men. It is common even for women with preschool children to be employed in the paid labour force.

Some people urge a return to the male-breadwinner/female-homemaker nuclear family, ignoring that this model fails to address the economic needs of most families and the widespread desire of women to become educated, hold jobs, and pursue careers. Such critics find it acceptable that caregiving is a privatized responsibility assumed disproportionately by women. They criticize the alternative: new social policies, including support for high-quality, affordable, and universally accessible child care, that would enhance the ability of parents to juggle paid employment and caregiving.

In sum, much of what we take for granted about families—how they are organized, the views we hold about children and marriage, and what we deem to be appropriate roles for men and women—is a consequence of change in the larger society. Contemporary trends in family life, outlined in the next section, further demonstrate this important fact.

CONTEMPORARY TRENDS

I now want to outline major trends in contemporary families and some of the economic, social, political, and ideological factors underlying them. Specifically, I examine marriage, divorce, cohabitation, fertility, single-person households, delayed home-leaving, and transnational and multi-family households.

MARRIAGE

Most people marry. Following divorce, most remarry. Consequently, married-couple families, although declining as a proportion of all households, remain the most common family form in Canada (see Figure 10.1). The major changes we have seen in marriage include a growing number of Canadians deciding to forgo marriage altogether to remain single and live alone; people opting to cohabit rather than marry formally; commuter marriages where couples live apart, often to pursue jobs in different cities; the legalization of same-sex marriages; and the growth of single-parent households. Canadians are also delaying marriage, as evidenced by a higher age at first marriage for males and females (now more than 30 for men and more than 28 for women). The pursuit of educational and career goals leads to the postponement of marriage, and the attainment of economic security allows women to forego marriage and live independently.

FIGURE 10.1 MARRIED-COUPLE FAMILIES WITH CHILDREN AGED 24 AND UNDER, CANADA, 1986–2006

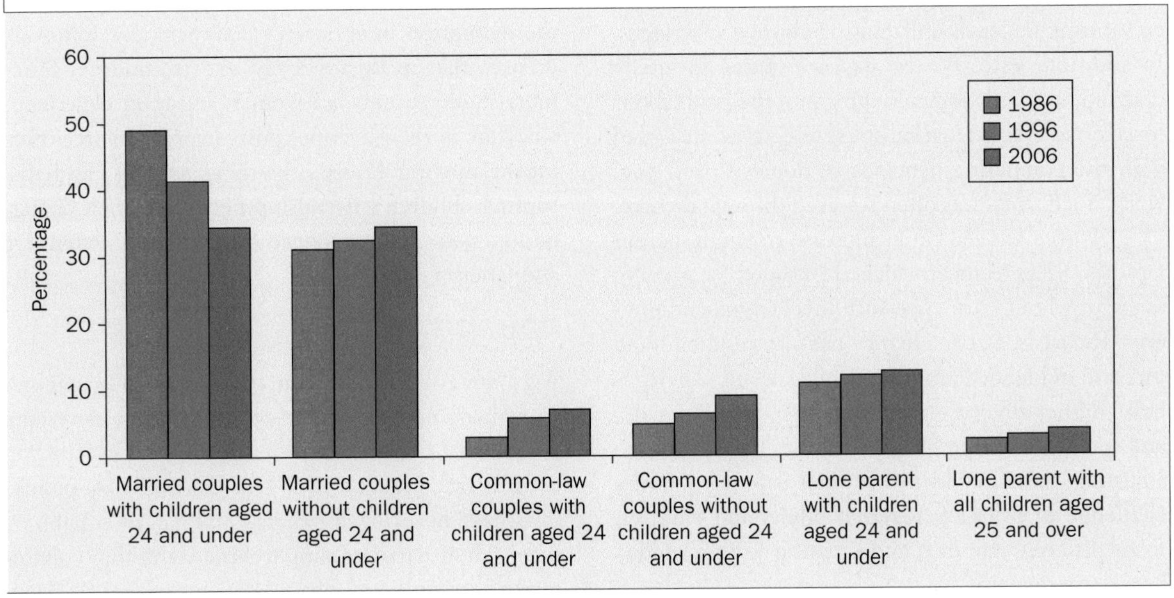

SOURCE: Statistics Canada (2009a).

Social movements and ideological changes (outlined later) have contributed to the increase in cohabitation and same-sex marriage.

DIVORCE

An understanding of the increasing prevalence of divorce requires a rethinking of what marriage means. Today, most Canadians choose a marriage partner based on love and romance. Yet for most of human history, people married to advance the economic and political interests of two families (Abbott, 2010; Coontz, 2005). Since love requires work and commitment if it is to endure, we can understand how marriages based on love might be more fragile than those based on economic, political, and family obligations.

Many scholars link rising divorce rates to legal reforms that have made divorce easier. Historically, the Canadian divorce rate was suppressed until legislation was liberalized in 1925, 1968, and 1985. It was not until 1925 that Canadian women could petition for divorce on the grounds of adultery (Sev'er, 1992). Before 1968, however, divorce was inaccessible to most Canadians because a person wanting a divorce had to apply to the Canadian Senate to have the divorce granted by an Act of Parliament (Wu and Schimmele, 2009). The Divorce Act of 1968 introduced the concept of marriage breakdown as a ground for divorce, meaning that spouses who were separated for three years could now seek a divorce. Consequently, the 1968 divorce rate was almost ten times higher than the 1925 rate. The 1968 law retained fault-based grounds for divorce, including adultery, cruelty, and desertion, but the divorce rate soared to 124 out of 1000 marriages in 1969.

The Divorce Act of 1985 instituted no-fault divorce, meaning that a person wanting a divorce no longer needed to show any wrongdoing, such as adultery or cruelty, on the part of their spouse. The 1985 legislation shortened the period of separation from three years to one year. Changes in legislation reflected changes in social demand. The divorce rate continued to increase, by 1980 reaching 260 out of 1000 marriages (Wu and Schimmele, 2009). The divorce rate peaked in 1987 and then levelled off. Recent marriages have a nearly 40 percent chance of ending in divorce (Statistics Canada, 2005). The fact that 30 percent of children will experience a parental separation or divorce before reaching the age of 16 means that family change is normative for many young Canadians (Juby, Marcil-Gratton, and Le Bourdais, 2004).

Higher divorce rates were also a by-product of shifts in the economy. As we have seen, the decline of the manufacturing sector squeezed many families economically, motivating women to take jobs in the expanding service sector. Increased participation of women in the paid labour force gave them the financial means to leave unhappy or abusive marriages. In addition, with too few daycare spaces to satisfy demand, married women's entry into the paid labour force often created marital stress as couples struggled with the competing demands of domestic and paid work. Such stress was often resolved through divorce.

Divorce has led to an increase in single-parent families, 82 percent of which are headed by women, many of whom must cope with low income and poverty (Richards, 2010). Divorce has also resulted in an increase in blended families. While second marriages have higher divorce rates than first marriages do, and some children in blended families have problems adjusting, in many blended families parents meet the challenge of bringing together adults and children from different families and creating a harmonious home environment.

The effect of divorce on children's well-being has been the focus of much public concern. Social science research offers two important conclusions about how children are affected by parental divorce. First, children are most adversely affected by divorce when there is a high degree of conflict between parents. In fact, children suffer more in high-conflict *intact* families than in low-conflict divorced families. Divorce provides a solution to the problem of high parental conflict. Second, it is not divorce per se, but the disruption in children's daily routines following divorce that more adversely affects children. Since most single parents are women and most experience a decline in their incomes post-divorce, divorce often means moving house, changing schools, and disrupting children's friendship networks. Such change undermines children's need for routine (Furstenberg and Cherlin, 1991).

COHABITATION

A growing number of couples, particularly younger Canadians, are deciding to cohabit, and an increasing number of children are being born to cohabiting couples (see Figure 10.2). The fact that most cohabiters have never been married and half of cohabiters marry their partners supports the claim that cohabitation is often a trial phase before marriage (Wilson, 2009). For others, cohabitation is an alternative to marriage (see Box 10.1). In Canada, rates of cohabitation are exceptionally high in Quebec, which enjoys relatively generous family support policies (notably, widely available, inexpensive, government-funded daycare), and where many people reject Catholic traditions. Cohabiting relationships tend to be less stable than marital relationships, partly because

FIGURE 10.2 PERCENTAGE OF COMMON-LAW UNIONS IN EACH AGE COHORT, CANADA, 1986–2006

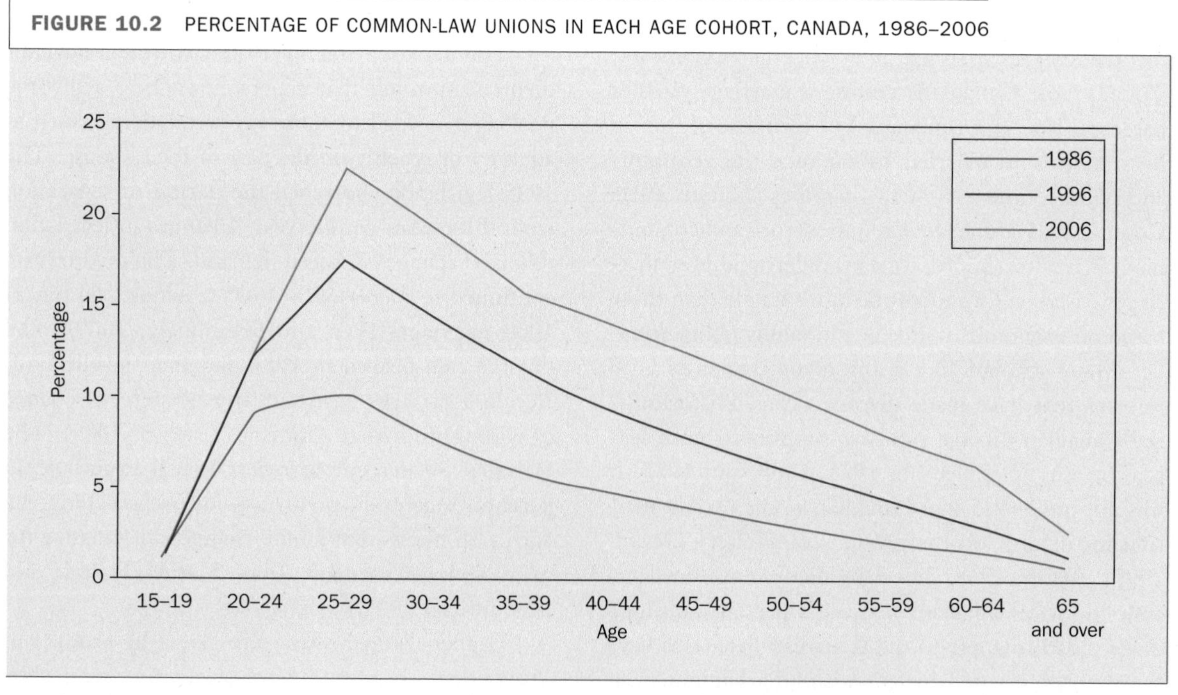

SOURCE: Statistics Canada (2009b).

BOX 10.1 FIRST COMES LOVE, THEN COMES COHABITATION

Jessie Skinner has a slew of reasons for not wanting to get married. At the top of his list is the fact that, having lived with his girlfriend, Eva Bowering, for three years now, he simply doesn't see the point of it. "I'm not a religious person," the 24-year-old writer and blogger adds. "I also don't like big family gatherings, which is what a wedding would be."

Then there's the possibility of divorce, something his own parents went through when he was a student at York University. "If they hadn't been married, maybe they wouldn't have felt the need to separate themselves."

Skinner and Bowering are part of a growing demographic that's choosing to live with their significant others before marriage—or simply instead of it. In the 2006 census, Statistics Canada found there were more unmarried Canadians than legally married ones for the first time ever. Two decades ago, about 7 per cent of families were common-law; by 2006, that number had grown to almost 19 per cent.

In this brave new world of premarital bliss, common-law couples are rewriting the rules—or making them up as they go.

After dating long-distance between Toronto and St. Catharines for a year, Skinner and Bowering squeezed into a bachelor apartment along the Danforth. ... Although they don't necessarily have their future planned out—Skinner doesn't want kids, for example, but Bowering, 25, is undecided—right now life is in the details: supporting each other, keeping the apartment clean and taking care of their cat, Joni, named after Joni Mitchell.

"That's the thing you have to worry about when you move in with someone," Skinner says. "It's not the relationship, it's what are you going to do when you don't have a fridge for two weeks?"

While directing and producing the doc *Thoroughly Modern Marriage*,... Sue Ridout found many reasons for this shift toward cohabiting, including the fact that young people today are cautious about divorce. She says some couples opt out because of the high cost of weddings, which have in many cases become elaborate consumer affairs.

These people are not breaking new ground, like the rebellious "living in sin" couples of previous generations. "There's some positive role models out there for them, of people who have been living together successfully for a long period of time," Ridout says. ...

Common-law relationships have long been thought of as high-risk, but even that is starting to change. According to a recent study by Steffen Reinhold, a post-doctoral researcher at the Mannheim Research Institute for the Economics of Aging in Germany, the adage that couples who live together before marriage are more likely to divorce no longer holds true, even though it was grounded in statistics in the '80s and '90s.

Using data from various editions of the U.S. National Survey of Family Growth, Reinhold found that Americans who cohabit do not have a higher risk of divorce.

"My favourite explanation would be that it used to be the case that cohabitation was something of a fringe phenomenon, that only a few people did it in the United States," Reinhold says. These people, he adds, may have been less attached to the institution of marriage in general. But now that more than 50 per cent of marriages in the U.S. are preceded by a period of living together, the association no longer holds. ...

SOURCE: Nicole Baute. (2011). "First Comes Love, Then Comes Cohabitation." *Toronto Star* 20 January. On the World Wide Web at http://www.thestar.com/living/article/925521–first-comes-love-then-comes-cohabitation (retrieved 18 August 2011). Reprinted with permission—Torstar Syndication Services.

cohabiters tend to hold less traditional ideas about family life and are less likely to believe in marital permanence (Wilson, 2009).

FERTILITY

Long-term fertility decline is associated with the economic, social, and ideological changes that accompanied industrialization. Every year, I poll my students to find out how many siblings they have to illustrate the trend toward smaller family sizes. Most of my students are only children or have one sibling, which mirrors what we see among Canadian families generally. The number of live births in Canada per 1000 people dropped from 45 in 1851 to 10.5 in 2004 (Baker, 2009a).

How can we explain the trend toward small families? When I pose this question in class, students usually point to birth control and women's paid labour-force participation as the major causes. The decriminalization of contraception, the availability of the birth control pill, and the legalization of abortion certainly gave women more control over childbearing. Yet historical evidence also shows that women have always attempted to prevent pregnancy and limit childbearing by means of withdrawal, self-induced abortions, and even infanticide.

Declining fertility in the past several decades is also a consequence of women's rising level of education, which leads to the postponement of marriage and childbearing, and shortens the reproductive years. Both of my grandmothers began childbearing in their late teens and continued into their early forties, but many women today go to university until their mid- to late-20s and have their first child in their 30s. Many go on to pursue careers in which professional obligations, such as training and business travel, discourage them from having many children.

Marriage and fertility are becoming increasingly uncoupled. More people have children outside of marriage, either as single-parents or in a cohabiting relationship (see Figure 10.3), and some married couples are deciding not to have children. New reproductive technologies, such as in vitro fertilization, offer new possibilities for creating life and in the process transform how we define and understand parenthood. Increasingly parenthood is becoming unhitched from biology as individuals and couples who cannot reproduce biologically use adoption, sperm and egg donors, and surrogates to become parents (Baker, 2009a). People who have no biological connection to a child, either because they are stepparents or adoptive parents, can still define themselves as parents. An example of how parenthood is being defined in social rather than biological terms can be seen in the popular television comedy series, *Modern Family*. It follows three families that are interrelated through the biological father, Jay Pritchett, and his grown children, Claire and Mitchell. Jay has remarried a younger woman and is helping to raise her son, while Jay's grown son Mitchell is gay and raising an adopted daughter with his partner.

SAME-SEX MARRIAGE AND SAME-SEX COUPLES RAISING CHILDREN

Same-sex cohabitation and marriage, with and without children, have increased in Canada. The raising of children by same-sex parents predates same-sex marriage legislation in 2005, but it has only been recently that same-sex parents have been able to foster and adopt children through the Children's Aid Society. The question of how children raised by lesbian and gay parents fare compared with children raised by heterosexual parents has been important for family law, specifically judicial decision making in post-divorce litigation involving disputes over child custody.

Opponents of same-sex marriage have often argued that children are adversely affected by being raised by same-sex parents and have argued that the sexual orientation of parents should be considered in child custody cases. Research comparing children raised by lesbian and gay parents and by heterosexual parents finds no differences that would warrant discrimination against a parent based on their sexual orientation. Children raised by lesbian and gay parents are similar to children raised by heterosexual parents in terms of various outcomes, such as mental health, academic achievement, behavioural issues, and quality of parent-child relationships (Stacey and Biblarz, 2001).

FIGURE 10.3 PROPORTION OF CHILDREN AGES 14 AND UNDER LIVING WITH MARRIED PARENTS, CANADA, 1986–2006

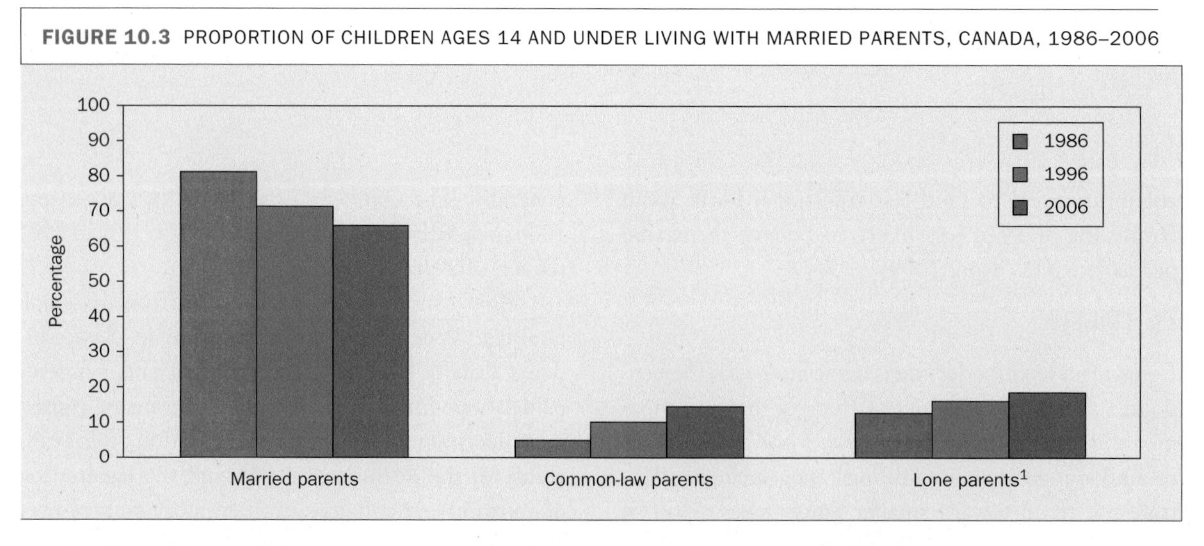

SOURCE: Statistics Canada (2009c).

The fact that children raised by gay and lesbian parents have done so well despite the social stigma and discrimination they often face is a testament to the quality of parenting by gays and lesbians. Much of the explanation for why children of lesbian and gay parents do well is related to the fact that same-sex parents tend to differ from heterosexual parents in ways other than sexual orientation that make them good parents. Children born to heterosexual parents are more likely to have been unplanned. Heterosexual parents are also likely to be younger and have fewer economic resources than do gay and lesbian parents.

Research also shows that gay and lesbian parents are more successful in sharing housework and child care than heterosexual parents are (Nelson, 1996; Dunne, 1997). Despite their increasing labour-force participation, women continue to do a disproportionate amount of housework and child care in heterosexual relationships. The term "second shift" has been coined to describe the domestic labour that women do after putting in their "first shift" in the paid labour force (Hochschild, 1989). The "third shift" describes the emotional work that women perform to keep family life harmonious in the face of time shortages and the frantic pace of life most working parents face (Hochschild, 1997). The greater sharing of unpaid labour in gay and lesbian relationships points to the salience of gender ideologies in sustaining inequalities in heterosexual relationships.

SINGLE-PERSON HOUSEHOLDS

Increasingly, Canadians are living alone (see Figure 10.4). The most recent census shows that lone-person households outnumber families for the first time in Canadian history. Some people who live alone were once married or cohabiting. Higher divorce rates, greater financial stability, and improved health for older widows and widowers helps to explain this trend. In addition, more people are remaining single. This trend is largely the result of increased financial independence for women and the weakening of the stigma once associated with remaining single.

DELAYED HOME-LEAVING

In attempting to reach their educational and career goals, young adults are remaining in their parents' home longer than they used to (see Figure 10.5). In addition, some young adults return to their parents' home after living independently for a time. Young adults may return after divorce or separation to receive emotional support or assistance with child care, or because they want to upgrade their educational qualifications and need their parents' financial support. Cultural and gender factors influence these patterns. Some ethnic groups place a strong emphasis on adult children, particularly daughters, remaining in the parental home.

FIGURE 10.4 FAMILY STRUCTURE, CANADA, 1996–2006

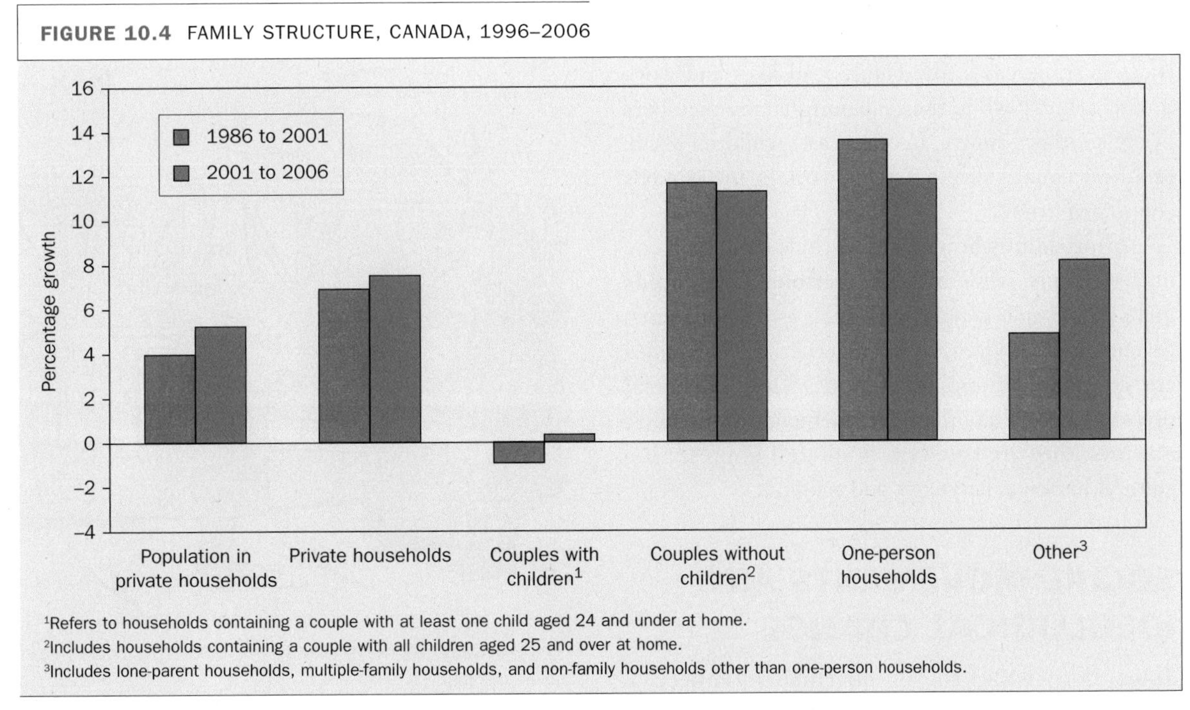

[1]Refers to households containing a couple with at least one child aged 24 and under at home.
[2]Includes households containing a couple with all children aged 25 and over at home.
[3]Includes lone-parent households, multiple-family households, and non-family households other than one-person households.

SOURCE: Statistics Canada (2009a).

FIGURE 10.5 CANADIANS IN THEIR TWENTIES LIVING IN THEIR PARENTS' HOME, 1986–2006

Percentage

70
60
50
40
30
20
10
0

20 to 24 years
25 to 29 years

1986
1996
2006

SOURCE: Statistics Canada (2009e). "Figure 15: More young adults in their twenties live in the parental home in 2006." http://www12.statcan.ca/census-recensement/2006/as-sa/97-553/figures/c15-eng.cfm (retrieved 18 August 2011).

TRANSNATIONAL AND MULTI-FAMILY HOUSEHOLDS

Since the 1980s, the world has witnessed unprecedented levels of international migration and travel. At the same time, new communications technologies have made it easier for families to stay in touch across international borders. These developments explain the increasing prevalence of **transnational families,** in which family members reside in different countries. In some cases, the family lead lives and work in one country while the remaining family members live in another country. In other cases, children reside in a host country while parents work in the family's country of origin.

Multi-family households include more than one nuclear family, while **intergenerational households** include multiple generations, such as grandparents, parents, and children, living together. Such families are common among immigrants. Often financial pressures necessitate these arrangements. Sometimes, however, they are based on an interest in preserving cultural heritage, language, and religion.

SOCIAL MOVEMENTS AND IDEOLOGICAL CHANGE

Since the 1960s, social movements—collective attempts to change the social order—have changed people's attitudes about families significantly. For example, the civil rights movement extended political, social, and economic rights to people of colour, making interracial marriages more socially acceptable. The gay and lesbian social movement successfully promoted the extension of economic and political rights to people involved in same-sex relationships, paving the way for the legalization of civil unions

"Empty-nesters. They're hoping to sell before the flock tries to move back in."

SOURCE: © www.CartoonStock.com.

and same-sex marriage in some jurisdictions (Fetner, 2008). The women's movement helped enormously in women's struggle for the right to higher education, paid employment, equal pay for doing the same work as men, and so on. As women's education, income, and independence increased, the fertility rate fell and the divorce rate rose because women now had the capacity to limit childbirth and leave unsatisfying marriages. The women's movement also supported the sexual revolution, which gave women more freedom to have sex outside of marriage. Radical feminism in particular embraced the rights of gays and lesbians and brought attention to the problem of violence in intimate relationships.

Long-term trends, such as increasing secularism and individualism, had implications for family life, too. Growing secularism eased religious strictures against divorce, cohabitation, and same-sex relationships. Today, cohabitating couples may joke about "living in sin" but their humour is rooted in a history of severe condemnation of people living together without being married. Similarly, remaining single was met with far more curiosity and condemnation than is the case today, particularly for single women.

Individualism involves prioritizing personal happiness over social obligation, including the responsibilities bound up with marriage and family. One consequence of growing individualism is that we have higher expectations of our partners than our parents or grandparents had of theirs. Our higher expectations create more fulfilling relationships as we seek compatible partners and are less likely to remain in unsatisfying relationships. However, they also lead to higher rates of relationship dissolution and people deciding to live alone when partners or spouses fall short of expectations. These cultural shifts partly explain the increasing number of voluntarily childless married couples. While the stigma surrounding voluntarily childless couples has not disappeared, in rejecting the traditional expectation that having children is integral to marriage, voluntarily childless couples challenge the conventional view that children are a prerequisite to personal happiness and fulfillment (Basten, 2009; Carroll, 2000).

Sociologists, politicians, religious leaders, and others differ in their evaluations of the changes I have just reviewed. Social conservatives assert that the family is in crisis and is undermined by feminism, secularism, and individualism (Popenoe, 1993). Social liberals contend that these changes are not harmful. Rather, they promote equality and choice, thus leading to happier and more fulfilling lives. The following discussion of family policies shows that such ideologies and assumptions about family life are important as they become concretized in family policy.

SOCIAL POLICY

Family policies encompass marriage and divorce laws, income security programs, such as maternity and parental leaves, child welfare programs, and child-care services. Given Canada's universal health care system and high standard of living, we might assume that the state generously supports families in this country. However, in many ways Canadian family policies fall short of those in Western Europe. Imagine a family policy continuum, one pole of which signifies that families are a *collective* responsibility and the other of which signifies they are an *individual* responsibility. Canada and Western Europe lie close to the opposite poles (although the United States lies even closer to the ideal of individual responsibility; see Figure 10.6).

INCOME SUPPORT POLICIES

Some of the shortcomings of Canadian family policy are evident if we compare income support plans in Canada with those in Western Europe. **Income support payments** include cash transfers to families in the form of direct payments and tax deductions, maternity and parental leave benefits, and maintenance payments, which involve child support for children whose parents have divorced.

FIGURE 10.6 THE CONTINUUM OF FAMILY POLICIES

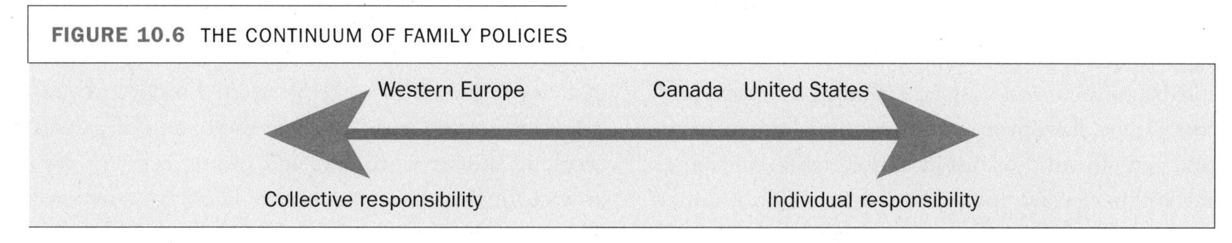

NOTE: Family policies encompass income support, maternity and parental leave and benefits, and child care.

In Canada, the main forms of support include the Universal Child Care Benefit, the Canada Child Tax Benefit, the Family Supplement (paid when one parent is receiving employment insurance), and the Parental Leave Benefit. Benefit levels in Canada are lower than levels in Sweden, Denmark, Germany, and Norway, among other Western European countries (Phipps, 2009). In fact, they are even lower than levels in some poorer Eastern European countries, such as Romania, Lithuania, and Slovenia (McGill Institute for Health and Social Policy, 2012). Moreover, Canadian policy uses stricter eligibility criteria, making it more difficult for families to qualify for support. Looser eligibility criteria in many European countries make it easier for a larger number of families to qualify for support (Phipps, 2009). Unlike our Universal Child Care Benefit, which the government considers taxable income, many European programs offer tax-free income support programs.

Western European countries, including Finland, Sweden, Germany, and France, have implemented advanced maintenance payments that provide economic support to children of divorced parents where the absent parent does not pay child support (Phipps, 2009). This system does not exist in Canada. Instead, we require that noncustodial parents pay child support and put measures in place to try to enforce it when a parent is not voluntarily providing the support. Often these measures are insufficient to meet the economic needs of children.

MATERNITY AND PARENTAL LEAVE AND BENEFITS

Leave

Maternity and parental leave provide job protection for Canadians while parents care for their newborns. In Canada, we distinguish maternity from parental leave and allow provincial and territorial differences in the length of leave. Maternity leave varies from 15 to 18 weeks depending on the jurisdiction. Only biological and surrogate mothers are eligible for such leave. Parental leave varies from 35 to 52 weeks, depending on the province or territory. It is available to mothers and fathers, including adoptive parents. Many European countries offer longer leave, paid and unpaid. For instance, the Netherlands provides unpaid leave for parents with children under the age of eight, and Spain offers three-year unpaid leave (Organisation for Economic Co-operation and Development, 2011).

Our system offers fathers parental leave, but it is mostly mothers who take it. In other countries, fathers are more strongly encouraged to take parental leave. In addition to parental leave for mothers, such countries offer "take it or lose it" leave for fathers only. The fact that so few men take parental leave stems from societal attitudes about men's and women's appropriate roles, and also from the fact that women on average earn less than men do; gender disparities in the labour market channel the lower-earning spouse, typically the woman, into parental leave. For most couples, the decision about who should take parental leave is made on a purely economic basis rather than taking into consideration the aptitudes, dispositions, and desires of individuals.

Benefits

Benefits refer to the money parents receive from employment insurance and sometimes from employers during their leave. Residents of Quebec enjoy higher benefit levels than other Canadians do and there are other provincial and territorial variations as well. Some Canadians receive a "top-up" of their benefits from their employer. Some observers therefore suggest we have a two-tier system, with higher benefits going to employees who are already the most advantaged in the labour market.

One of the main criticisms of how Canadian maternity and parental benefits are determined is that we require recent labour-force participation and link benefits to earnings in the previous year only. Our laws preclude women from receiving benefits for second and third children if they have not been working in the year before giving birth. This eligibility requirement forces many women to decide between (1) returning to work sooner than they would like to so they can qualify for benefits for a subsequent child, or (2) forgoing benefits altogether so they can stay at home with their children.

In France and Germany, the state allocates leave benefits to new parents even if they lack a recent history of paid employment. This approach results in more families qualifying for benefits. Other family-friendly policies that exist in some Western European countries but not in Canada include the option of parents working shorter work days and taking paid sick days to care for sick children at home. These cross-national differences underscore how the larger social context shapes ostensibly private decisions, such as the decision of whether to stay at home to take care of a sick child.

CHILD CARE

Canada lacks a system of universally accessible, affordable, high-quality, regulated daycare. Some analysts argue that universal child care would provide short- and long-term benefits to our economy; others say that the costs are prohibitive. Our government's willingness to provide daycare during World War II to entice women to work in munitions factories and take other jobs to help the war effort suggests that universal child care can be implemented if there is sufficient political will. This is most evident when we consider how Quebec has made child care a political priority. In Quebec, parents have access to regulated, licensed, and affordable childcare for $7 a day. In the rest of the country, child care in licensed, regulated daycare centres is expensive and scarce. Parents must often wait a year or two to get a spot in a daycare centre (see Box 10.2). Consequently, most Canadian

BOX 10.2 LACK OF CHILD CARE COSTS CANADA

Unless more men start raising babies Canada is going to be a poorer place, says a new report that looks at problems facing mothers in the workforce.

The alternative is to launch a national child-care program, says the report by YWCA Canada....

"The prosperity of the nation is intimately tied to the labour force participation of an educated, skilled workforce that is becoming increasingly female," says the report. "Barring a major shift of men into child-rearing, provision of early learning and child-care services [are] essential to the nation's future economic prosperity."

The issue hits home with Ryerson University student and new mother Jennifer Kim, 29, who has a university degree in science and a college diploma. She hopes to return to class next fall to complete a degree in early childhood education and eventually work in the field of music for young children.

Kim's husband has a good job as a computer software developer. But the couple can't afford both her school expenses and regulated child-care fees of up to $60 a day. With more than 18 000 children on Toronto's waiting list for subsidized child care, Kim's options are limited.

Fortunately, her mother is willing to help care for her daughter. But Kim knows that's an option most families don't have.

"It astounds me that in this day and age most women are unable to find high-quality, affordable child care in their communities."

It shocks YWCA Canada's Paulette Senior too.

She notes that a national daycare program was one of the key recommendations of the 1970 Royal Commission on the Status of Women. And yet regulated child care today is available for just 20 per cent of children under age 5.

"More than 40 years later, women are still waiting. Given the huge advances of women in other areas since then, we feel the need for a national child-care plan is an important issue to highlight. ..."

The YWCA's report ... notes the number of women employed in Canada more than doubled between 1976 and 2009, to more than 7.7 million.... Employment for women with infants and toddlers hit 64.4 per cent in 2009, up from 27.6 per cent in 1976. That number jumped to almost 79 per cent for women with children between the ages of 6 and 15—almost the same rate for women without children, says the report.

The education picture has changed dramatically, too. In 1971, men made up 68 per cent of university graduates between the ages of 25 and 29. By 2006, the rate had almost reversed, with young women making up 60 per cent of graduates.

These trends indicate that the Canadian labour force will soon have more women than men with university education.

Women's workforce and education advances represent an "unstoppable movement toward equality" that needs a national child-care policy to help women combine these gains with motherhood, the report urges. ...

Volumes of research show that quality child care helps children become lifelong learners, supports the social needs of families, and is a powerful tool in reducing child poverty, the report says. It can also help drive the economy. A recent Canadian study on the cost-benefit of public investment in quality child care shows a return of $2.54 for every dollar invested.

"A national plan to ensure comprehensive access to quality, affordable early learning and child care services is not a luxury, a frill, or a threat to Canadian families," the report concludes.

"It is essential to Canadian prosperity, a crucial support for children and parents, and should become as normalized in our social structure as the public school system as a choice for parents."

SOURCE: Laurie Monsebraaten. (2011). "Lack of Child Care Costing Canada: Report." Toronto Star 6 March. On the World Wide Web at http://www.thestar.com/news/article/949585--lack-of-child-care-costing-canada-report (retrieved 18 August 2011). Reprinted with permission—Torstar Syndication Services.

children are cared for in informal and unregulated settings—by relatives, by friends, in home daycares, and by nannies.

In the absence of a universal child-care system, some relatively well-off Canadians have relied on the Temporary Live-In Caregiver program. This program allows women from foreign countries to work as nannies with the objective of receiving permanent resident status after two years of such work. Faced with dire economic need in their countries of origin, many women who come to Canada under this program have left their own children to care for Canadian children. Some of these women are exploited and abused by their employers but unable to do anything about their situation because of their immigration and economic status (see Box 10.3).

IMPLICATIONS OF SOCIAL POLICY

Family policies strongly influence the economic security of families. In many European countries, poverty rates are substantially lower than in Canada. The lack of policy support for working parents in Canada means that women—single mothers in particular—are less likely than their Western European counterparts are to work in the paid labour force. Apart from economic security, family policies influence the quality of care that children receive. In the absence of sufficient government support, families must navigate the daily dilemmas of juggling paid labour and caregiving by relying on individual rather than collective solutions.

CONCLUSION

Sociology helps us appreciate how social forces influence our intimate relationships and family life. The chapter began with a discussion of why definitions of family and marriage matter. We saw that the definitions embedded in policies include some categories of people and exclude others from various forms of support. We also saw how definitions provide a framework for individual decision making about the kinds of relationships and families we might pursue. Most sociologists argue for a more inclusive definition of family than currently exists in Canadian legislation. This inclusive definition emphasizes that social reproduction—the physical, emotional, and mental work of caring for others—lies at the basis of family life. It does not designate particular family structures as falling within the definition.

We also saw that each of the four main sociological perspectives offers a different interpretation

BOX 10.3 PLAN TO CURB NANNY ABUSE PRESENTED TO PARLIAMENT

Foreign caregivers should be granted "conditional" permanent resident status upon their arrival in Canada and employers [should] undergo briefings on their rights and responsibilities before they can start working, a parliamentary committee has recommended.

Nannies would see the conditions lifted after completing 24 months of work within a 36-month period, the immigration committee has recommended in a report tabled in the House of Commons yesterday.

Caregivers would also be entitled to interim health benefits and would be allowed to go to school.

"Having permanent resident status upon arrival in Canada would enable caregivers [to have] the same rights as other permanent residents: mobility, the right to live where they wish, to bring their family members or to change employers. Further it would be easier than under the present system for caregivers to escape abusive situations," the report says. ...

Before they can hire a nanny, employers would have to attend a "briefing on the live-in-caregiver program and the rights and responsibilities of all concerned." ... The briefings would stress the following conduct is unacceptable and in many cases subject to sanction:

- Confiscating passports.
- Failing to comply with the Canada Revenue Agency rules regarding pay and record of employment.
- Failing to make the required deductions.
- Employing a caregiver without a work permit.
- Paying less than the provincial minimum wage.
- Requiring caregivers to work longer than reasonable work hours.
- Assigning caregivers tasks unrelated to their prescribed roles.

SOURCE: Dale Brazao. (2009). "Plan to Curb Nanny Abuse Presented to Parliament." *Toronto Star* 11 June. On the World Wide Web at http://www.thestar.com/news/canada/article/649043 (retrieved 18 August 2011). Reprinted with permission—Torstar Syndication Services.

of families. The most diametrically opposed are the functionalist and feminist perspectives. Functionalists regard the traditional heterosexual nuclear family, consisting of a male breadwinner and female homemaker, as the ideal family form. Feminists seek to demonstrate that this type of family is by no means universal and is characterized by a high level of gender inequality and frequent failure to satisfy the needs of all family members. Our overview of the social history of families from foraging societies to the present revealed enormous variation in family structure, men's and women's roles, and changing ideologies surrounding marital and parent-child relationships. The interplay between economic forces and family life continues. Many contemporary trends in family life, including delayed marriage, fertility, and home-leaving, reflect broad economic shifts.

What might Canadian families look like in a hundred years? Will our children and grandchildren face life options similar to ours or will their futures look entirely different? Imagining the future reminds us of the plasticity of families and the need to implement social policies that address the needs of diverse Canadian families. While the term *policy* may seem remote and complex, in fact what we are talking about is finding ways to ensure that children whose parents are working in the paid labour force enjoy high-quality child care and that policies are set up to minimize child poverty. These are not lofty goals or a luxury we cannot afford. The examples of many other countries, and the province of Quebec, provide clear evidence that thoughtful family policy is essential for children and their families, whatever form the family might take.

SUMMARY

1. The government uses definitions of family and marriage to formulate social policy. Historically, these definitions have excluded many types of families, denying them government services and benefits. In formulating social policy, governments also make assumptions about the kinds of support that should exist within families, so social policy has repercussions for many aspects of families, including relationship formation and dissolution.
2. Definitions of family and marriage shape personal decision making. As definitions broaden, people have more choice in how they want to organize their family life.
3. The four main theoretical perspectives in sociology provide different interpretations of families. Functionalists view the traditional nuclear family as the ideal unit within which to raise children. Conflict theorists focus on how family life is shaped by larger economic structures. Feminist approaches systematically examine women's experiences and the consequences of gender-based inequality in families. Symbolic interactionism advances a microlevel perspective by examining how families are produced and reproduced through everyday interactions.
4. Family forms vary over time and place and are socially constructed. In foraging societies, families were immersed in the larger group. Privatized households did not exist. Caregiving was shared by all members of the group.
5. In preindustrial societies, households were economic enterprises and household composition was determined by labour requirements. The economic needs of the household took priority over the emotional bonds between spouses and between parents and children.
6. Industrialization and the need for wage work brought about a separation of public and private spheres that led to the emergence of the nuclear family living in a privatized household. During this period, ideas about women and children changed dramatically. Among the affluent, domesticity and intense child care became the widespread norm for women.
7. The traditional nuclear family is a relatively recent phenomenon.
8. Intimate relationships and families have undergone tremendous change in the past several decades. Some of the most significant trends in family life include delayed marriage and home-leaving, lower fertility, and higher rates of same-sex marriage, cohabitation, divorce, lone-parent families, single-person households, transnational and multi-family households, and unconventional families.

9. Myriad social, economic, political, and ideological factors explain recent change in family forms. They include the influence of the civil rights movement, the women's movement, and the gay and lesbian social movement. Family trends have also been influenced by increasing secularism, individualism, and declining social stigma for nontraditional family choices.
10. Compared with family policy in Western Europe, Canadian family policy does not provide sufficient family support, particularly for working parents in need of high-quality child care. Family policies provide inadequate economic security to Canadian families, which accounts for the relatively high rate of child poverty and of single-parent families living in poverty in this country.

QUESTIONS TO CONSIDER

1. How have definitions of family affected you directly, either in terms of formal state policy and programs or in terms of personal decision making?
2. Reflect on the social, historical, and cultural factors that shaped the choices your parents and grandparents made about their intimate relationships and families. In what ways were the life options available to your parents and grandparents different from the options available to you?
3. Many argue that the nuclear family is ideal because it is based on human biology. How might you refute that argument based on what you have learned about families in this chapter?
4. Imagine that you have been elected to public office and have influence over family social policy. What social programs would you reform or establish to best support Canadian families?
5. If you had to offer a prediction of what intimate relationships and families will look like in 100 years, what would you imagine? Will some family types remain? Will some disappear entirely? Speculate on what marriage, divorce, cohabitation, and fertility will look like 100 years from now.

GLOSSARY

Blended families (p. 235) include two parents and the child or children from their former marriages or intimate unions.

Family, in the traditional sociological definition, is a cohabiting man and woman who maintain a socially approved sexual relationship and have at least one child. Today, we define **families** (p. 234) (now in the plural) more broadly to capture the wide range of family structures we encounter—as sets of intimate social relationships that people create to share resources to ensure their welfare and that of their dependants.

The **family wage** (p. 242) refers to the wage men traditionally received that was sufficient to support a family.

The **fertility rate** (p. 242) is the number of live births per one thousand women of childbearing age.

Income support payments (p. 249) include cash transfers in the form of direct payments or tax deductions, and maternity and parental leave benefits. In Canada, the main forms of support include the Universal Child Care Benefit, the Canada Child Tax Benefit, the Family Supplement (paid when one parent is receiving employment insurance), and Maternity and Parental Leave Benefits.

Intergenerational households (p. 248) are families that include multiple generations such as grandparents, parents, and children living together.

Marriage (p. 235) was traditionally defined as a socially approved, presumably long-term, sexual and economic relationship between a man and a woman involving reciprocal rights and obligations between spouses and between parents and children. Today, many countries recognize common-law marriage and some allow marriage between people of the same sex.

A **multi-family household** (p. 248) includes more than one nuclear family.

A **nuclear heterosexual family** (p. 237) includes a father, mother, and children living in a privatized household.

Social reproduction (p. 236) refers to the physical, emotional, and mental work of caring for others that is typically done in families.

Transnational families (p. 248) are families whose members are geographically separated for extended periods.

bureaucratic organization. Although we still see vestiges of the first and second industrial revolutions in our working lives, many things have changed. Most prominent is the movement from a manufacturing-based economy to a service economy.

Contextualizing the Canadian Labour Market

Before discussing the shift to a service economy, it's useful to have some background information about the Canadian labour market. Since 1970, the labour force has changed dramatically. Some of the changes reflect demographic trends, such as the aging of the population. Some changes are due to a combination of economic and political factors, such as the increasing participation of women in the labour force. And some changes are the result of government policy to deal with predicted labour shortages, such as the increasing prominence of immigrants in the labour market.

So how exactly has the labour force changed? Compared with 30 years ago, Canada's labour force is now older. Workers over 55 years old have increased their participation, including those 65 and over who are now delaying retirement. Workers over 55 now represent 32 percent of the labour force, compared with 22 percent in 1976 (Carriére and Galarneau, 2011: 5). For their part, younger workers, ages 15 to 24, are entering full-time work later in life than previous generations did, primarily because of their increased level of education (Carriére and Galarneau, 2011).

Canada's population is also more educated than it was 30 years ago. In 1971, about 16 percent of Canadian-born workers between the ages of 25 and 34 had less than a high school diploma. Almost 9 percent of this age cohort had some postsecondary education. Three decades later, just 3.5 percent of workers in this age cohort had less than a high school diploma, while nearly 18 percent had some postsecondary education. The trend toward higher levels of education holds across age groups. The increased emphasis on education has made it more difficult for workers who have not completed high school to do well in the labour market. In 2009, 82 percent of those with a postsecondary education were employed, compared with 55 percent of those with high school education or less (Statistics Canada, 2012a). Thus, while the increased importance of education is a good news story for those who are well educated, it is a bad news story for those who are less well educated.

A third key change in the Canadian labour market is the growing reliance on immigration to meet the demand for skilled workers (Statistics Canada, 2003). In the 1980s, approximately 125 000 immigrants arrived in Canada annually. By the 1990s, this figure soared to about 220 000. Immigrant workers today, like Canadian-born workers, are more highly educated than those who arrived earlier. The rise in the educational status of immigrants is partly explained by the federal government's immigration policy in the 1990s. This policy emphasized bringing skilled immigrants to Canada to "foster a strong and viable economy in all regions of Canada" (Statistics Canada, 2006a: 87). Recent immigrants are also more likely to be members of a "visible minority" compared with those arriving earlier. Recent arrivals face increasing difficulty in the labour market from discrimination and a lack of recognition of their educational credentials (see Chapter 8, Race and Ethnic Relations).

Women's participation in the labour force is the final important labour market change since the 1970s. Women now make up just under half of the paid workforce, compared with only 37 percent in 1976 (Statistics Canada, 2006b; Statistics Canada, 2011a; see Chapter 7, Gender Inequality: Economic and Political Aspects for details).

The Canadian economy has experienced four big recessions since the 1970s—one in the mid-1970s, one in the early 1980s, one in the early 1990s, and one beginning in 2008. During each of these periods, the economy shrank and unemployment rose, particularly in the manufacturing sector. Young workers were particularly susceptible to layoffs because the last hired are usually the first fired when a company struggles in a difficult economy. Recovery from the 1991–92 recession was particularly sluggish. It was not until the end of that decade that the Canadian labour market began to fire on all cylinders. By 2008, the unemployment rates had dropped below 6 percent—a level not seen since the 1960s. Then, all hell broke loose. The housing and credit markets collapsed in the United States, and the shock was soon felt globally. Manufacturers started shutting down factories. In Canada, the auto sector was particularly hard hit. By all accounts, Canada weathered the global recession better than other countries did, and by early 2011, the employment rate bounced back to where it was at the start of the 2008 recession (Gilmore and LaRochelle-Côté, 2011).

Keeping this overview in mind, we can now turn to an analysis of the rise of the service economy, what it means for where Canadians work, and the quality of the jobs they hold.

The second industrial revolution started in the early 20th century. Henry Ford's assembly line and other mass-production technologies transformed the workplace.
SOURCE: Ellen Griesedieck, *Rouge Assembly Line.* Courtesy Gallery Henoch.

WORK IN THE SERVICE ECONOMY

Since 1976, Canada has experienced a shift away from goods-producing industries and a rapid growth in service industries (see Figure 11.1). Employment in services more than doubled while employment in manufacturing increased less than 20 percent. Economic downturns affected employment in goods-producing industries more strongly than employment in services; you can plainly see the big drops in manufacturing employment in the early 1980s and the early 1990s, the two recessions covered by Figure 11.1 (Statistics Canada, 2009). The effect of the recessions on service employment was much less pronounced. From 1976 to 2010, the percentage of Canadians employed in service industries grew from 65 to 78 percent (Statistics Canada, 2011a, p. 315).

There are many reasons that Canada, like many industrialized countries, experienced massive growth in the service industry. Chief among them is that increased global competitiveness facilitated the movement of much manufacturing to low-wage, less-developed countries. Since the 1990s, free-trade agreements with the United States and Mexico have facilitated the migration of manufacturing jobs out of Canada. Proportionately fewer manufacturing jobs mean proportionately more service jobs.

In 2010, retail and wholesale trade was the largest segment of the economy; retail trade accounted for three-quarters of all trade (Statistics Canada, 2011b). By far the largest category of retail trade is food and beverage stores, including grocery stores; specialty food stores; and beer, wine, and liquor stores. Lower-tier service jobs in such stores are characterized by low pay and nonstandard work hours: features of bad jobs (Presser, 2003).

FIGURE 11.1 EMPLOYMENT IN GOODS AND SERVICES, CANADA, 1976–2011

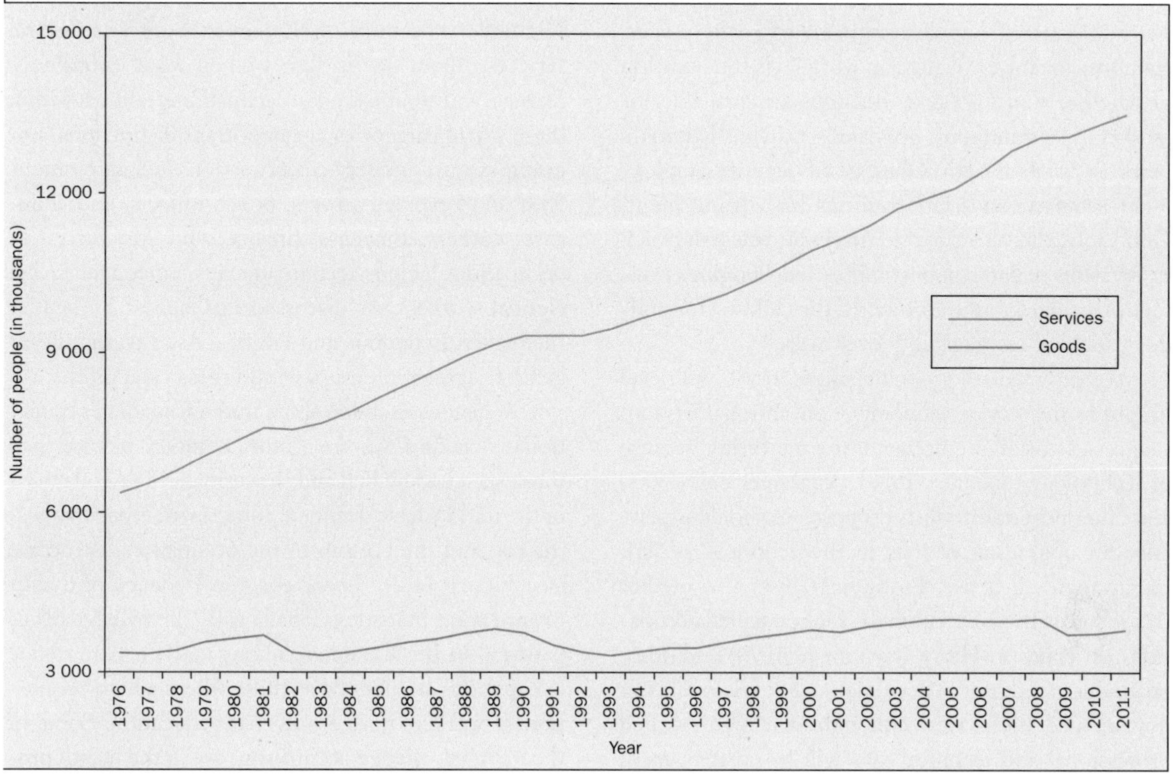

SOURCE: Statistics Canada (2012d).

From the early twentieth century until 1990, manufacturing industries employed more Canadians than did any other segment of the labour force. By 2010, manufacturing industries ranked second. Considered part of the upper tier of the service industry, healthcare and social service industries ranked third, employing nearly 12 percent of the paid labour force in 2010 (Statistics Canada, 2011b). Much of this growth is due to increased demand for health care by an aging population.

Given that manufacturing is the second-largest employer of Canadian workers, you may wonder why there is so much concern about the decline of manufacturing. While manufacturing, along with retail and wholesale trade, and health and social services represent the largest categories of employment, they are not necessarily the industries experiencing the highest rate of growth. Professional, scientific, and technical services, along with business, building, and other support-service industries, experienced the highest rate of growth from 1987 to 2011. Manufacturing is far down the list in terms of growth, surpassing only the resource-based industries of forestry, fishing, mining, oil and gas, and agriculture.

Sociologists are concerned about the decline of jobs in manufacturing industries because these jobs have long represented good jobs in terms of wages, benefits, and security. These jobs also represented the best opportunities for young workers, especially young men, with high school education or less. In December 2011, wages were significantly higher in manufacturing industries (on average, $22.53 an hour) compared with those in retail trade (on average, $15.59 per hour; Statistics Canada, 2011b: 119–20).

Sociologists often refer to the shift from a goods- to a service-based economy as **deindustrialization.** Deindustrialization began in Canada and the United States in the 1970s and continues today. It reduced the number of unionized, well-paying, full-time manufacturing jobs and increased the number of "bad" jobs located in the lower-tier service industries. The process of deindustrialization also caused a host of long-term economic and labour market difficulties, such as a rise in unemployment and increasing income inequality.

GOOD JOBS OR BAD JOBS?

At the centre of our discussion of what the service economy means for Canadian workers is the question of whether more good or bad jobs are available for workers. At minimum, good jobs provide **extrinsic rewards,** such as high wages, good benefits, employment security, and opportunities for advancement. Good jobs can also provide **intrinsic rewards,** such as decision-making opportunities; challenging, non-repetitive work; and autonomy that allows for self-direction and responsibility over tasks.

Debate revolves around changes in the skill level of jobs in the service economy. Conventional wisdom suggests that skill requirements are increasing because of technology (Spenner, 1983). As Daniel Bell (1973) and other postindustrialists propose, we should experience an upgrading of jobs in the economy as skill requirements increase. Postindustrialists also predict that job growth will occur in the higher-skilled occupations. In contrast, Harry Braverman (1974) and other postindustrial critics believe that skill levels are being downgraded. In this view, although some highly skilled professional and technical jobs will be created, most jobs will be lower-skilled industrial and service jobs.

So which is it? Are we moving to the postindustrial world of Bell or the downgraded world of Braverman? One way to answer this question is to look at which occupations are held by Canadians. About one in four men is employed in the construction trades and as transport and equipment operators. Another one in five men is employed in sales and service occupations. Just under one-third of all women work in sales and services. About one in four women work in business, finance, and administrative occupations. Hidden within these broad categories are important distinctions. For example, sales and service occupations include cashiers, food and beverage servers, police officers, and child-care workers. Business, finance, and administrative occupations include accountants, insurance agents, and clerical workers. As discussed in Chapter 7, Gender Inequality: Economic and Political Aspects, significant gender segregation exists within these categories.

When we examine shifts in the Canadian occupational structure, we see a more complex picture than those sketched by Bell and Braverman. Blue-collar jobs in the middle have declined. Job growth is occurring at the top and the bottom of the occupational structure (see Figure 11.2). There is some evidence of a shift toward what Statistics Canada calls "knowledge occupations" in the Canadian labour market. Knowledge occupations are defined as those where a high proportion of workers have a university education. Some of the main knowledge occupations are in the health professions, science and engineering, and management. The percentage of Canadians in knowledge occupations increased from 14 to 25 percent between 1971 and 2001 (Baldwin and Beckstead, 2003). Whether this is indicative of a shift to a larger knowledge-based economy is something still debated by sociologists.

FIGURE 11.2 CHANGE IN EMPLOYMENT BY OCCUPATIONS, CANADA, 1987–2011

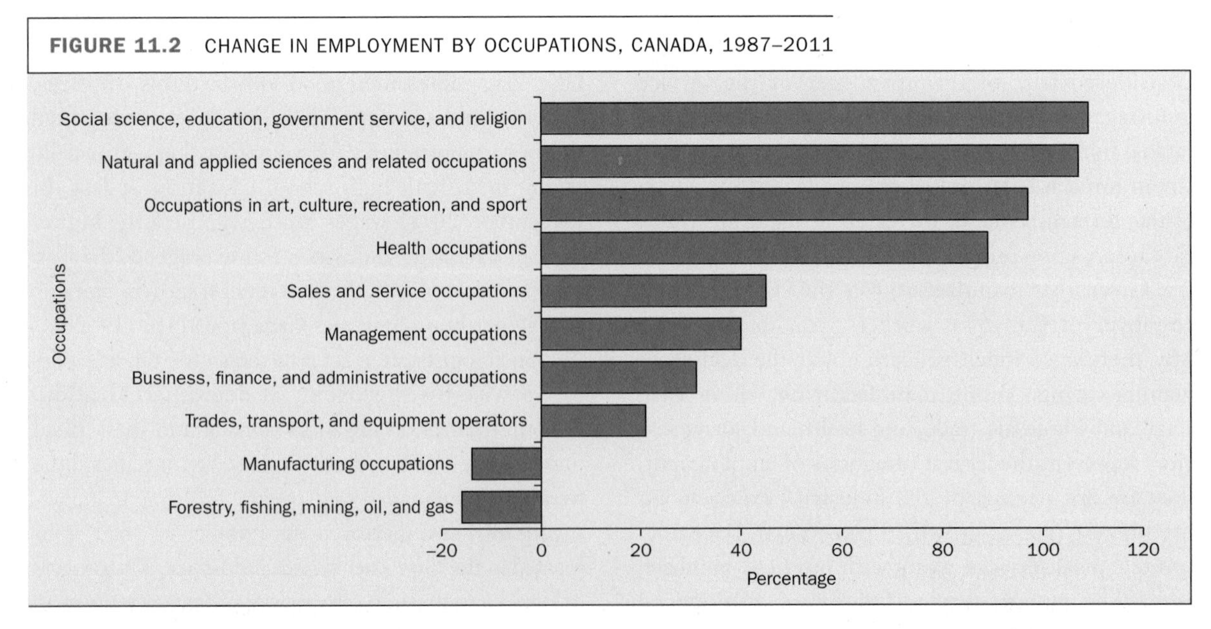

SOURCE: Statistics Canada (2012d).

A service-based economy does not necessarily involve bad jobs for everyone. A misconception about the service economy is that the service sector creates only bad jobs and that the goods sector is the source of good jobs. This scenario assumes that all service jobs are alike. Instead, we should think of the service sector as having a lower tier made up of traditional services, such as retail trade, food, and personal services, and an upper tier consisting of other services, such as finance and business, utilities, health, education, and public administration. Whether you find yourself in a lower- or upper-tier service job has implications for your wages, job security, and the skill content of your work (Economic Council of Canada, 1991; Krahn, 1992).

However, these statistics are partly misleading. Statistics Canada points out that driving the growth in service occupations is an increase in part-time work and self-employment. So although business and other services have the potential to create good jobs, some of those jobs may not be full-time. The movement to a service economy has affected the types of jobs available in Canada. Some good jobs are created in financial services and health services, while bad jobs with nonstandard hours are also created, primarily in sales and service. I now explore the issue of nonstandard work more fully.

NONSTANDARD JOBS

Twenty years ago, sociologists of work did not spend much time researching nonstandard jobs. That has changed with increasing numbers of temporary, part-time, contract, and self-employed workers. Nonstandard work is now a central part of the economy. Most of us know people who work in a nonstandard job. You may have a part-time job at a local retail store that helps you pay your tuition and other bills, while giving you (almost) enough time to study. One of your parents may have been laid off because of company restructuring, only to be hired back later as an independent contractor. One of your friends may have used a "temp" agency to find work when her other attempts didn't work out.

Part-time jobs, temporary jobs in which people are hired through a temporary agency, self-employment, contract work, outsourcing, and seasonal work are all considered nonstandard jobs. Some sociologists call them "precarious" jobs because they do not provide stable, long-term employment or adequate pay (Cranford, Vosko, and Zukewich, 2003). In most industrial countries, including Canada, one-quarter to one-third of all jobs are now nonstandard (Chaykowski, 2005; Cranford et al., 2003; Krahn, 1995).

It is not always clear what defines a job as nonstandard. Often, nonstandard jobs are defined in terms of what they are not: They are not jobs in which workers have a full-time, year-round job with one employer, located at the employers' premises, and under the supervision of that employer. In a standard job, workers also have a reasonable expectation that employment will continue indefinitely (Cranford et al., 2003: 459; Kalleberg, 2011; Kalleberg, Reskin, and Hudson, 2000).

Nonstandard jobs, conversely, may lack some or all of the characteristics of a standard employment relationship. First, some nonstandard jobs lack an employer; self-employed workers do nonstandard work. They take on all the risk of their employment, including ensuring they make money, withhold taxes, and save for retirement. Second, in many nonstandard jobs, like contract and temporary work and some kinds of self-employment, workers are hired on short-term contracts and cannot assume their employment will continue indefinitely (Cranford et al., 2003; Kalleberg et al., 2000). Third, many nonstandard jobs offer fewer than full-time hours. Fourth, in many nonstandard jobs, the legal employer, who is responsible for hiring and paying the employee, is not the employer who oversees daily work. This is the case for temporary help agency and contract jobs. For example, a worker hired by a temporary agency is legally employed by the agency but does not work for the agency (Kalleberg, 2011; Vosko, 2000). Rather, the temporary employee works for a client organization. When the job for which she is hired is completed, she must wait to receive payment and a new assignment from the temporary agency, not the company where she was working. This is similar to the experience of Zainab Taiyeb, whom we learned about at the beginning of this chapter. Although she was selling products for Rogers Cable, a Rogers' subcontractor hired her and was responsible for paying her.

To understand nonstandard work, it is useful to look at part-time and temporary employment, two of the more common and widely discussed forms of nonstandard work. In 2011, just under 20 percent of Canadians worked in part-time jobs. Since 1976, the part-time rate has more than doubled for young workers ages 15 to 24. Young workers, similar to women, often prefer the flexibility of part-time work as a way to balance school attendance or family responsibilities. The part-time rate has also grown for workers over the age of 55. This increase may be due to older workers opting for part-time work as a steppingstone to retirement (Pold, 2004). Alternatively, it could signal that older workers are unable to find full-time work to replace a full-time job they lost because of downsizing or corporate restructuring.

Employment in part-time work can mask serious problems in the labour market. A sign of a poor labour market is having substantial numbers of people who would prefer full-time work working part-time. This phenomenon is called the *involuntary* part-time rate. In 2011, one in four part-time workers in Canada stated they would prefer to be working full-time (Statistics Canada, 2009). They are *involuntary* part-time workers. Involuntary part-time jobs are especially common in the Atlantic provinces where the unemployment rate is higher than the national average (Statistics Canada, 2009).

To respond to changing demand for products and services, employers increasingly rely on temporary workers, ranging from clerical help to computer programmers, hired on contract or through temporary-employment agencies. Statistics Canada's data on temporary workers include seasonal labourers, contract workers, and those working for temporary employment agencies. Nonstandard workers are usually hired for a predetermined period or until a project is completed. In 2011, 14 percent of Canadian workers were employed in temporary or contract positions (Statistics Canada, 2012c). Slightly more than one-third are young workers between the ages of 15 and 24. Immigrants who arrived in Canada within the past five years are twice as likely to work in temporary jobs as the Canadian-born and immigrants who arrived more than 10 years ago (Gilmore, 2009). Temporary workers, who often work alongside full-time permanent workers, earn substantially less per hour than their full-time counterparts do. The average hourly wage for a full-time permanent worker was $23.72 in 2011, compared with $18.40 for temporary workers.

WHY THE RISE OF NONSTANDARD WORK?

Scholars link the increase in nonstandard work to the rise of the service economy, instability in the global economy, privatization of government services, and organizational restructuring that occurred in the late twentieth century (Vosko, 2000).

From an employer perspective, nonstandard work is attractive since it allows for the creation of more flexible organizations. We can think about flexibility in two ways. First, there is **functional or internal flexibility** that allows employers to move workers from one job to another within an organization. However, it is a second type of flexibility—**numerical or external flexibility**—that drove employers to create nonstandard jobs. Numerical flexibility enables employers to adjust the size of their workforce by easily hiring and firing workers in response to fluctuations in labour demand (Kalleberg, 2003).

The downsizing of the 1980s and 1990s also drove the rise of nonstandard work—and not just in the private sector. In the 1990s, governments saddled with large deficits slashed jobs and privatized work previously carried out by government employees. Advances in telecommunications and information technology made it easier for private and public organizations to rely on outside suppliers and to quickly mobilize (and demobilize) temporary workforces (Kalleberg, 2000). As well, some of the movement to nonstandard work is associated with the increased participation of women in the labour force. Some women, especially those with young children, prefer part-time and other nonstandard work arrangements. People commonly assume that because standard jobs predominate now, they have been the most common form of work for centuries. In reality, the standard employment relationship as we know it arose after World War II (Fudge and Vosko, 2001). Insecure jobs, such as seasonal and casual labour, have always been a big part of the Canadian economy (Smith, 1999). In addition, linking the increase in nonstandard work only to the rise of the service economy overlooks the historic use of nonstandard work by manufacturing and other goods-producing industries. Automobile manufacturers have a long history of contracting out the production of auto parts. Agriculture has long relied on day labourers and seasonal employees. Immigration policy allows Mexican men to work as temporary farm labourers in Ontario. They are expected to return to Mexico when harvesting ends. Thus, when discussing the rise of nonstandard work, we should remember that, historically, standard employment is unique.

Most employers view the recent increase in nonstandard jobs positively. Employers reduce costs associated with full-time employees and they gain flexibility in competitive markets. For employees, there are more downsides. Research documents increased job insecurity, loss of benefits, and wages that are too low to allow a decent standard of living.

ARE NONSTANDARD JOBS BAD JOBS?

Much of the early literature on nonstandard jobs referred to them as bad jobs. Evidence shows that nonstandard workers are worse off than are workers in standard employment relationships (Cranford et al., 2003; Kalleberg et al., 2000). However, just how bad they are varies by type of nonstandard employment. Some nonstandard jobs are low paid (e.g., jobs secured through a temporary worker agency) while others are not (e.g., independent technical contractors; Houseman, Kalleberg, and Erickcek, 2003; Kunda, Barley, and Evans, 2002). The experience of nonstandard work is complicated and variable.

When we compare how nonstandard workers are treated by full-time employees, we find evidence for the negative evaluation of nonstandard jobs. Temporary workers placed by an agency in an organization for a short time often feel like "nonpersons" who are isolated from full-time employees (Rogers, 1995). As one temporary worker said,

> There was no Christmas present under the tree like the rest of the company would get [at the office party].... There were some places where it was just blatant, just terribly blatant. Whenever there was going to be a company party or something the temps had to stay and work. You know, cover the phones so the regular people got to go. You could tell where the second-class citizenship started. (quoted in Rogers, 1995: 150)

Compared with standard workers, nonstandard workers are at greater risk of experiencing alienation, isolation, and abuse.

In some European countries, strict regulations control the use of nonstandard workers. For example, in Norway, the use of fixed-term contracts and temporary help agencies is severely restricted (Olsen and Kalleberg, 2004). Some European Union countries have implemented the European Union's Framework Directive on equality of treatment for part-time and fixed-term workers. This means that part-time and fixed-term workers in these countries should enjoy the same employment and working conditions, such as sick pay, pensions, and other benefits, as full-time workers receive. Although some countries limit the reach of the EU Directive (in Britain only 10 percent of part-time workers are covered), there is some hope that it will result in an increase in quality and stability for some forms of nonstandard work (Preisler, 2011).

WORK HOURS AND WORK ARRANGEMENTS

At the same time as nonstandard jobs are becoming more numerous, many workers are increasingly concerned with the number of hours they are working. Most of the focus is on overwork, with references to a "24-hour workday," needing to be available "24/7," and an "escalation in expectations" in terms of how many hours employees should be working (Epstein and Kalleberg, 2001: 6). The mass media, corporate executives, and students in my sociology of work course often discuss work-life balance and time for life outside work. Are we really working more than people did in previous generations, or has work changed in other ways?

To answer these questions, we first need to know how many hours per week Canadians are working. In 2011, Canadians worked approximately 36.4 hours per week on average. In 1976, Canadians worked approximately 38.6 hours (Usalcas, 2008). Contrary to the hype, Canadians are not working longer hours.

Canada is not alone in the decline in average hours worked per week. Most rich countries have experienced a decline in average work hours in recent decades. The rise of part-time work and reduction in the proportion of people working more than 50 hours per week account for most of the decline.

However, while on average Canadians today are no more overworked than their predecessors were, we are seeing another trend in work hours. As Figure 11.3 shows, a higher percentage of workers now work either longer or shorter hours compared with 30 years ago. While the 40-hour workweek was still the most common in 2011, the proportion of Canadians working a 40-hour week has declined since 1976. Proportionately more Canadians work fewer than 40 or more than 40 hours a week. Some analysts refer to this trend as the **polarization of working hours;** some workers are experiencing overwork while others have the opposite problem.

Many explanations exist for this polarization. Some have to do with choice. Certain groups of workers, such as students and those with young children, may choose to work fewer hours to balance competing demands. In addition, the rise of service industries has increased the number of people working nonstandard schedules and hours (Presser, 2003). Other explanations for the polarization of working hours point to the effect of economic restructuring and the increase in part-time, temporary, and other forms of nonstandard work.

FIGURE 11.3 DISTRIBUTION OF EMPLOYMENT BY HOURS WORKED PER WEEK, 1976 AND 2011

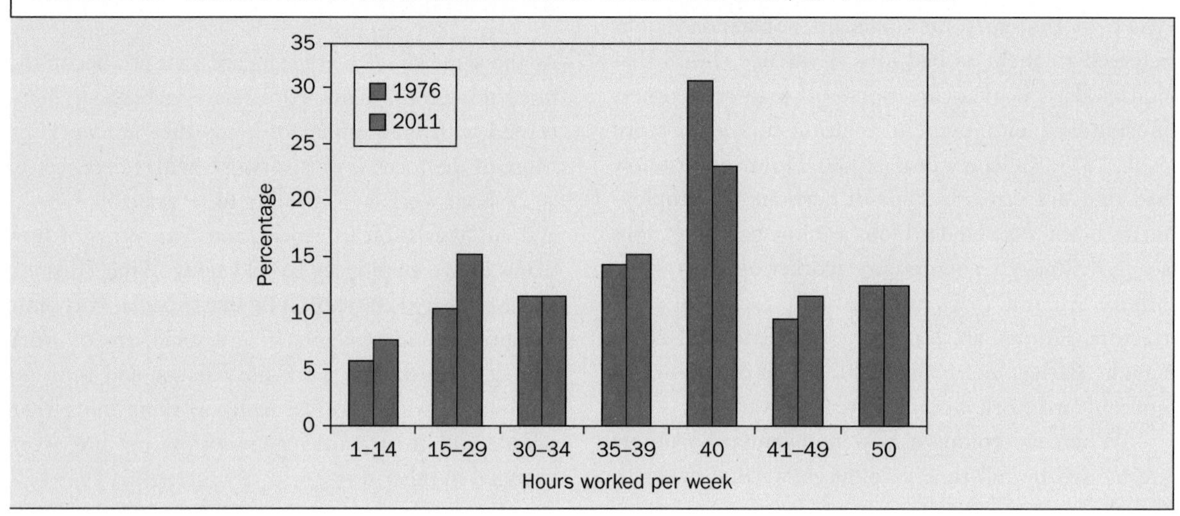

SOURCE: Statistics Canada (2012b).

According to sociologist Harriet Presser (1999, 2003, 2004), all the attention paid to changes in work hours has ignored the other way that work schedules have shifted. Presser says the issue is not just how many hours are worked, but *which* hours of the day and days of the week are worked. She focuses on **nonstandard work schedules,** defined as either working nonstandard hours that fall outside the 9-to-5 workday (shift work) or working non-standard days, such as Saturday and Sunday. Her research shows that nonstandard work schedules have increased because of three interrelated factors. First, the service sector demands nonstandard schedules to a much higher degree than manufacturing industries do. Linked to this is the increasing participation of women in the labour market. With more and more women working during the day, there is an increased demand for stores, restaurants, and other businesses to stay open later and on weekends. Second, demographic changes such as the postponement of marriage and the rise in family income (mainly because of the increase in dual-earner couples) have increased the demand for recreation and leisure activities during the evenings and on weekends. The aging of the population has also increased demand for 24-hour services, especially in terms of the need for round-the-clock medical services. Third, technological changes and globalization processes have created a "24-hour economy" in which workers are on call at all hours. Email, fax machines, and cellphones enable workers to be connected at all times and allow companies to require their workers to stay connected. As well, the head office in one country may need to be in contact with branch offices in another. Working across time zones in the global economy increases the number of employees working nonstandard schedules.

In 2005, about 28 percent of Canadians worked nonstandard hours (Williams, 2008). For example, shift work can consist of evening or late-night work, rotating shifts (where the time of shifts changes daily, weekly, or monthly), split shifts (working part of the day in the morning and part later in the day), and irregular shifts. Although women make up only about 37 percent of full-time shift workers, almost 70 percent of part-time shift workers are women (Williams, 2008). Women are also more likely than men are to work rotating shifts, evenings, and weekends, while men are more likely to work irregular shifts. Overall, evidence suggests that nonstandard schedules have increased since 1991 (Shields, 2002).

Why do employees work nonstandard schedules? The great majority of Canadians working evening shifts—65 percent of men and 53 percent of women—say they do so because they have no choice or the hours are mandated by their employers (Shields, 2002: 17). Sixteen percent of men and 20 percent of women state they work evenings because of demands from school. Caring for family is cited by 3 percent of men and 11 percent of women (Shields, 2002), with women more than men using nonstandard schedules to balance work and family needs (Presser, 2004). Thirteen percent of men and women state they work evenings because they like it. I conclude that most employees working nonstandard schedules are doing so because of the nature of their job, not by choice.

Why should we be concerned about people working nonstandard schedules? First, a variety of health and social issues are linked to shift work. Shift workers, especially those on night and rotating shifts, are more likely to experience disturbance of the natural circadian rhythm of their bodies as sleep is disrupted (Shields, 2002). Shift workers engage in more unhealthy behaviours, such as smoking, compared with other workers. Psychosocial problems, such as stress and depression, are also more common among shift workers than other workers (Shields, 2002). Shift workers can also become isolated from friends and family as their life is on a different schedule. The World Health Organization has conducted research showing that working the night shift is associated with increased risk of cancer—a finding that gives an entirely new meaning to the term "graveyard shift" ("Graveyard Shift," 2007).

Second, nonstandard work schedules create a hidden form of inequality (Presser, 2003; Shields, 2003). Workers who do not have a postsecondary degree are more likely to work nonstandard schedules. Nonstandard schedules are more common among women and men working fewer than 30 hours per week and among men working more than 40 hours per week. In the United States, black workers are more likely to work shifts compared with Hispanic and white workers. The workers most likely to work shifts are those that are already disadvantaged in the workplace—workers of colour, workers lacking higher education, and those working part-time or fewer than 40 hours per week. In Canada, shift work is more common among blue-collar and sales and service occupations than professional and clerical jobs. Those most likely to work nonstandard schedules have some of the lowest-paying jobs, working as cashiers and salespeople.

We are also seeing other changes in work arrangements. Multiple-job holding, or "moonlighting," more than quadrupled between 1976 and 2011. In 1976, more than three-quarters of multiple-job holders were men. By 2011, more than half of multiple-job holders were women. It seems that to make ends meet, an increasing number of women have to cobble together more than one part-time job. While the growth in multiple-job holders may seem alarming, it's useful to keep in mind that moonlighters represented just around 6 percent of the paid labour force in 2011. The vast majority of Canadians continue to work at one job.

Some changes to work schedules and arrangements are more positive. Evidence suggests that many employers are providing workers with more choice and flexibility, usually under the guise of creating more "family-friendly" workplaces. In 2005, just over 34 percent of Canadians worked flexible hours. Flexible hours are most common in large firms and in the information and culture industries, business services, and retail trade and consumer industries. Flexible hours are less common in manufacturing, where individualized start and stop times are not possible. Men are more likely to report working flexible hours than women are. Some 43.5 percent of university-educated workers work flexible hours (Statistics Canada, 2009). Thus, who works how many hours and when they work those hours are part of the way that inequality is structured in the Canadian labour market.

THE IMPACT OF BLACKBERRYS, iPHONES, AND LAPTOPS

BlackBerrys, iPads, laptops, and other Internet-connected mobile devices allow today's employee to work anywhere at any time. These devices can complement flexible work schedules and arrangements by making it technologically possible to stay connected to work without being at the office. These devices have changed not only how we work but also how we balance our work and nonwork time (Boswell and Olson-Buchanan, 2007).

We are starting to gain a better understanding of both the advantages and the disadvantages of using smart phones and other devices and from having nearly constant access to the Internet. Some studies point to increased productivity deriving from the ability of users to answer emails sooner than nonusers can (Mazmanian, Orlikowski, and Yates, 2005), and to take advantage of free moments to get work done. How many times have you responded to your email while waiting in the checkout line of a store or in the few minutes before your professor starts class? Previously nonproductive time can now be productive—there is no need to stop working just because you've left work. These devices also allow workers to stay connected with family throughout the workday and may help balance family obligations. Sick kid? No worries. You can stay home and take care of your child while Skyping into meetings and communicating with co-workers over email.

However, the very advantages of mobile devices point to their disadvantages. Users of these devices report a heightened need to stay connected and be responsive, adding to the pressure to be accessible at all times. As one BlackBerry user stated:

> The biggest advantage is far more frequent, rapid responses to largely business-related inquires and the ability to do that in a very convenient way. Clearly the negative is there are some expectations. I know if my coworkers didn't get a response from me ... they'd be like, "Geez, what's he doing at 11:00pm? Why isn't he responding to my emails? (Matusik and Mickel, 2011: 1016)

In this same study, workers reported that they were expected to respond quickly not only to co-workers and supervisors but also to family members who called during the workday (see Box 11.1).

Sociologists have begun to question whether these devices really help workers achieve work-life balance. What is emerging is a picture of blurred boundaries, where the line between work and the rest of life is disappearing (Olson-Buchanan and Boswell, 2006; Schieman and Glavin, 2008). As work permeates home life, concern grows about increased stress and conflict with family members. Recently, some companies have decided employees need help reigning in their off-hour email time. Starting in late 2011, the servers at Volkswagen in Germany were prohibited from sending employees email more than 30 minutes before or after work. It's not clear if other companies will follow suit. What is clear is that workers will continue to use their smart phones and other devices outside work, and will need to learn to cope with the ongoing collision of work and nonwork time.

BOX 11.1 ALWAYS CONNECTED, ALWAYS WORKING

In their study of working professionals, Matusik and Mickel (2011) wanted to know how BlackBerrys, iPhones, and other mobile devices affected workers and how workers set boundaries around the use of these devices. Based on their interview data, they discovered three types of mobile device users: enthusiastic users, balanced users, and those who saw mostly trade-offs (professional benefits versus personal costs).

Nearly one-third of the employees were enthusiastic users. They were most likely to emphasize the personal and professional benefits of their devices. Because they perceived few downsides, they did not feel the need to engage in boundary-setting behaviours to limit their use. As one user said,

> The biggest advantage is that I have this comfort level that I know that I'm always gonna be connected ... you know I hate to feel I'm missing something. I hate that feeling. Biggest disadvantage, it doesn't do everything I want it to do. (quoted in Matusik and Mickel, 2011: 1015)

Balanced users also accounted for fewer than one-third of the respondents. These users described both the benefits and the costs of using their devices. They also had the highest level of boundary-setting behaviours to limit the negative effect of mobile communications devices on their lives. Indicative of the need to set limits, one IT consultant said,

> From a personal perspective, it's a lot about setting limits. It's really easy to start reading email and get sucked into responding to people. It can start eating into your personal time. I'll check to see if there are burning issues. They have to be red-hot-on-fire before I'm going to take some of my personal time to deal with it on the weekend or at night. (quoted in Matusik and Mickel, 2011: 1016)

Members of the trade-off group, about 40 percent of respondents, experienced professional benefits and significant personal costs. They also engaged in boundary-setting behaviours but experienced more struggles with such strategies than balanced users did. One such user reported,

> I have recently instituted a time-management strategy for personal balance. The BlackBerry is left at home when I want to be left alone. ... I can't live without it and I can't live well with it. The difference between today and the past is you have to do so much. So it's a great tool to leverage your efficiency. Problem is I don't have the self-control to turn it off, and therefore, I hate it. ... (quoted in Matusik and Mickel, 2011: 1016)

SOURCE: Adapted from Matusik, Sharon F. and Amy E. Mickel. "Embracing or embattled by converged mobile devices? Users' experiences with a contemporary connectivity technology." *Human Relations 64* (8), pp. 1001–1030.

LABOUR-MARKET SEGMENTATION

You know from your study of social stratification that people with higher education and people from upper-class families are more likely than less-advantaged people are to end up in good jobs. Another factor that affects your life-chances is the structure of the labour market. Although some economists think of the labour market as a single, open competition in which people are rewarded in proportion to their education and skills (Becker, 1975), **labour-market segmentation** theory offers a different perspective. Instead of assuming that we all have an equal chance of getting good jobs, labour-market segmentation theory shows that *where* you enter the labour market may limit your chances of getting a different, better job.

Labour-market segmentation theory emphasizes that jobs are divided according to their location in the "core" or "periphery" of the economy. A core industry is a group of companies in a relatively non-competitive market, such as the automobile industry. Core industries tend to be capital-intensive, large, and unionized, and they tend to exert control over their environment—for example, by influencing governments to limit foreign competition. For a variety of reasons, such as the need to maintain skilled workers who can operate expensive equipment, and in response to the presence of unions, jobs in core industries tend to be stable and to offer good wages and access to benefits (Morissette, 1991).

The periphery, in contrast, is characterized by lower-tier service jobs and jobs in highly competitive markets. Firms in this sector tend to be smaller, labour-intensive, and nonunionized, and the employment they offer lacks security and pays low wages. Work is also characterized by high turnover rates, owing to product-demand fluctuations and seasonal work cycles, such as in the fisheries on the east and west coasts.

Your chance of finding a good job is determined not only by the sector of the economy you enter but also by the existence of **primary labour markets,** both external and internal to firms. Internal primary labour markets provide opportunities for advancement by providing the chance to climb up the job ladder as you gain skills and knowledge (Althauser, 1989). Secondary labour-market jobs do not offer much of a job ladder. These jobs are sometimes referred to as "dead-end jobs" because of the lack of upward mobility associated with them. Workers at McDonald's may be able to move from being on the crew to assistant manager, but unless they buy their own franchise (which is rare), that is the extent of their mobility.

Employers often create primary labour markets for some employees but not for others. In a single firm, managers can have access to mobility through an internal labour market while their clerical, production, and maintenance staff may have little room to move up. In today's service economy, employers' increasing use of temporary and part-time workers is another way in which secondary labour markets are created within companies. Increasingly, these types of secondary markets are found outside the lower-tier service industries. At Canadian universities, departments have full-time professors to do research and teach. In addition, "sessional" instructors are hired to teach one or two classes. Substantial differences exist between these two groups in terms of pay, job security, and mobility opportunities. As a full-time professor, I have a multiyear contract and may be promoted if I fulfill my job duties. My colleague, who is a part-time instructor, has no access to promotions or job security. Instead, she receives year-to-year contracts only if the department needs her to teach a specific course. Although having secondary labour-market positions gives organizations the "flexibility" to unload employees when they are not needed, it increases the insecurity of these employees and decreases their chances of getting ahead, both in their jobs and in life. Geography also plays a role in the chances of ending up in the primary or secondary labour market. Alberta, thanks to the oil and gas industry boom, has experienced lower than average unemployment rates in recent years. The Atlantic provinces have a high proportion of seasonal jobs, such as fishing and logging, and have a higher unemployment rate than the rest of Canada does (see Figure 11.4). Even if you are a highly skilled and motivated worker, you will have more trouble finding a good job in Newfoundland and Labrador than you would in Alberta because there are fewer jobs to go around. Those of us who live in urban and industrial areas are more likely to end up in a better job simply because there are more such jobs in the regional labour market (Statistics Canada, 2009).

I conclude that whether you end up in a good job or a bad job is the result of more than your individual characteristics or the occupation you choose. Your chances of landing a rewarding job depend on what sector of the economy your job is in and whether your

FIGURE 11.4 UNEMPLOYMENT RATE BY PROVINCE, CANADA, JULY 2012

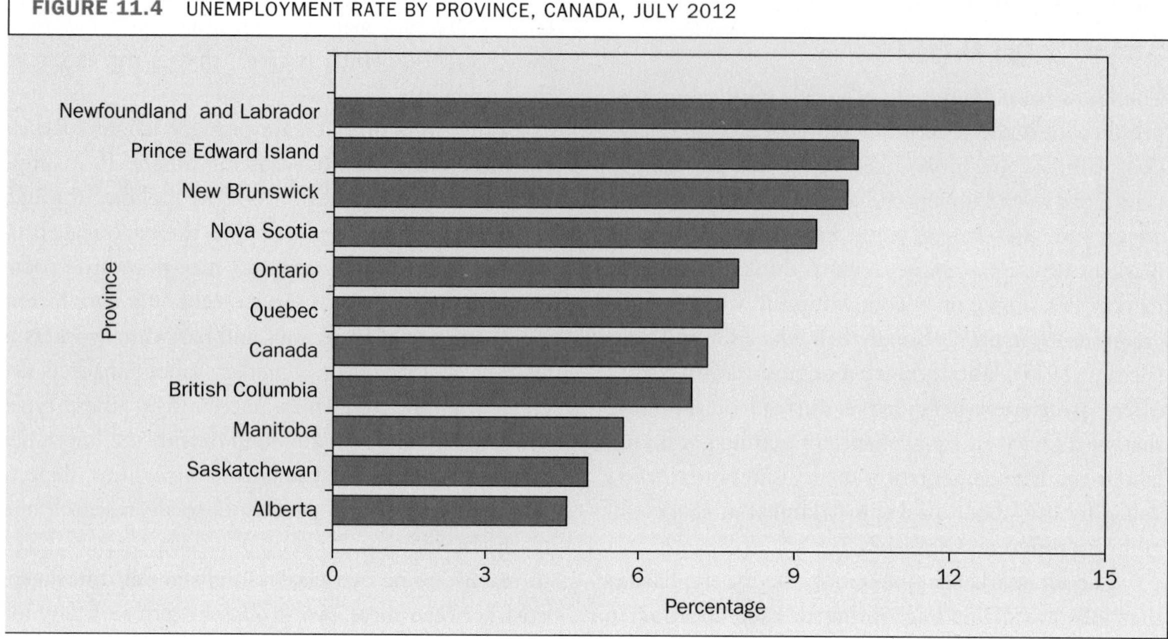

SOURCE: Statistics Canada. 2012. "Labour Force Survey, July 2012." http://www.statcan.gc.ca/daily-quotidien/120810/dq120810a-eng.htm (retrieved September 2, 2012).

job has an internal labour market associated with it. In the next section, I develop this idea by showing how some groups of workers find themselves stuck in job ghettos.

JOB GHETTOS AND DISADVANTAGED GROUPS

Job ghettos are parts of the labour market that prevent certain groups of workers from experiencing upward mobility. Structural barriers based on stereotypes work to keep some individuals from entering the primary labour market and the best jobs. The labelling of occupations as "female" or "male" jobs is one such example. In the healthcare industry, women are still more likely to become nurses than doctors, and, as doctors, women are more likely to be found in pediatric and family medicine than the higher-paying specialties of neurology and cardiology. Chapter 7, Gender Inequality discusses how female job ghettos are formed through occupational sex segregation, sex typing, and other forms of discrimination.

Ethnic job ghettos exist throughout the world. For example, in Canada, between 1860 and 1960, black railway workers were restricted to sleeping-car porter jobs and were not allowed to compete for the higher-paid jobs of sleeping-car conductor and dining-car steward (Calliste, 1993). Today, employer prejudice can keep qualified minorities from being hired. Since many visible minorities are also recent immigrants, their ability to move into better jobs is constrained by this dual status, unless they are entrepreneurs. Often, employers will request "Canadian work experience" before hiring white-collar workers. Some professional occupations, like doctor and veterinarian, require additional training for professionals emigrating from certain countries. Highly educated members of visible minorities in these situations may find themselves forced to take low-level service jobs, such as taxi driver or restaurant worker. (For more on this topic, see Chapter 8, Race and Ethnic Relations).

People with disabilities face barriers to good jobs because of the inaccessibility of education and workplaces. In 2000, only 45 percent of men and 39 percent of women with disabilities were employed, compared with 79 percent of men and 69 percent of women without disabilities (Statistics Canada, 2004). Lack of financial resources to attend school, inflexible workplace schedules, and lack of employers' commitment to hiring workers with disabilities are some of the reasons people with disabilities have trouble getting good jobs. Jamie Hunter, a 29-year-old with minimal

Geography affects a person's chance of finding work. For example, it is more difficult to find a good job in Atlantic Canada than in Saskatchewan.
SOURCE: David Blackwood, *For Edgar Glover: The Splitting Table Etching*, 1999. Courtesy The Edward Day Gallery.

control over his limbs because of a diving accident, experiences these barriers first-hand. Speaking about looking for work, he states,

> I recall one fellow, from the personnel department of a major corporation, who was so uncomfortable he couldn't even bring himself to take me to his office. So we sat in the lobby and he read me back my resume. "You're Jamie Hunter? You graduated from York University? You worked for a summer at Ontario Hydro?" Then he said thanks and left. That was it. The interview was over and I never heard from him again. (quoted in McKay, 1993: 170)

Hiring workers who have disabilities is not as costly as some employers believe. Only a fifth of people with disabilities require changes to the physical accommodations of workplaces (Shain, 1995). Until more employers make the effort to hire people with disabilities, these workers will continue to face barriers to good jobs.

Aboriginal people face formidable barriers in their search for employment. Living in remote areas limits both their job opportunities and their access to education and work training. Even when Aboriginal people move to areas where jobs are more readily available, they often lack crucial work experience. Aboriginal workers are especially vulnerable to the "bad-work syndrome" (Krahn and Lowe, 1998). Having access only to low-skill and part-time work gives individuals a spotty work history. They are then caught in a cycle where one low-skill job leads to another. For many, the "bad-work syndrome" makes it impossible to get better jobs.

Finally, the *youngest and oldest workers* may find themselves trapped in job ghettos based on age. Some employers view young workers as less serious and less interested in full-time jobs than more mature workers are. Because of downsizing and early retirement incentives, older workers may find themselves out of a job before they are ready to stop working. Access to better jobs is also limited by the prejudices of employers, who tend to view older workers as less productive and more resistant to new work methods. As the population of older Canadians grows, it is increasingly difficult to ignore the effects of age discrimination.

Labour-market segmentation creates areas of better and worse jobs in the labour market. Although we would like to think that we all have an equal chance of getting good jobs, research shows that some groups of workers may be trapped in bad jobs. Moreover, as I show next, some workers are able to protect their good jobs through the labour-market shelters of professional occupations and unions.

Although most Canadian women in the paid labour force are segregated in jobs traditionally dominated by women, they are making advances in traditionally male-dominated jobs.
SOURCE: © iStockphoto.com/Lisa F. Young.

PROFESSIONS

The occupations of doctor, lawyer, and other professions are some of the most desirable jobs in the labour market. High pay, autonomy, and respect from the outside community are some of the advantages bestowed on members of professional occupations. Many of us consider these occupations to be different from other occupations. This special status has caught the attention of sociologists.

Early studies of professions attempted to delineate their general characteristics. First, all professional occupations control a unique body of knowledge. Second, professional occupations are autonomous. Third, professionals generally have authority over their clients and subordinates because of the special knowledge they possess. Finally, professional occupations are supposed to be altruistic because of their focus on helping clients.

Many sociologists believe that this description of professionals is an "idealized model that imperfectly describes reality" (Hodson and Sullivan, 1990: 266), and that it provides only a checklist for determining which occupations are more or less professional. Overlooked by this approach is how certain occupations became professions in the first place. To address this issue, we need to consider power and the contested nature of professions. Doing so will uncover how professions act as **labour-market shelters,** protecting their members' access to good jobs.

Doctors, dentists, and lawyers were not always considered professionals. Which occupations are viewed as legitimate professions changes historically. For example, nineteenth century Ontario had few dentists as we know them today. Many different occupations provided dental services. Itinerant "tramp dentists" travelled from town to town servicing most Ontarians. If citizens needed teeth pulled or false teeth constructed, they could go to their local blacksmith or gunsmith. When a patient came to visit, the blacksmith would "leave the forge, wipe his hands on his apron, get the old turnkey wrench, and his brawny arm would soon draw not only the sufferer's tooth, but often the screaming patient himself from the old kitchen chair" (Wood, 1989: 266, quoted in Adams, 2000: 22).

To get to where they are today, dentists, like people in other occupations, engaged in a *process* of professionalization, which involved establishing professional dominance and securing legitimacy from the public (Friedson, 1970; Pescosolido, Tuch, and Martin, 2001: 3). Professional dominance occurs when the government acknowledges an occupation's knowledge claims and expertise, and then grants an occupation the right to be the only (or one of a few) types of practitioners allowed to apply this body of knowledge. Professions also require public approval. If the public refuses to follow the instructions of members of the profession or views them as illegitimate or just one among many types of experts, then the profession will have difficulty establishing its authority.

Sometimes, battles between different professions erupt, with each profession claiming expertise over the same "turf" (Friedson, 1970). For example, until recently, only doctors had the authority to deliver babies in Canada. Doctors maintained their authority because of their monopoly over relevant knowledge. They used their national association to lobby provincial and federal governments to deny others the right to deliver babies. However, the public and other healthcare practitioners questioned whether doctors ought to be the only legitimate deliverers of babies. In recent decades, because of public demand for access to midwives and the development of professional midwifery schools, doctors have lost some control over the birthing process and have lost their monopoly over this body of professional knowledge.

Some occupations are continually striving for professional status. "Semi-professions" are occupations that have only some characteristics of a profession (Hodson and Sullivan, 1990). Examples include nurses, engineers, accountants, pharmacists, and teachers. Although we may call these occupations "professions" in our everyday use of the term, the sociological definition of professions requires us to view them as semi-professions. Often, semi-professions do not have full control over their body of knowledge, or their autonomy may be constrained by a more powerful profession, as is the case with nurses. Furthermore, female-dominated semi-professions, such as teachers and librarians, face additional barriers to professionalization because of occupational sex segregation.

Third parties, such as the government, can threaten professional power by intervening in the decisions of professional organizations. We become most aware of such threats when the government pays for part or all of the services received by clients, as is the case for the Canadian healthcare system. During the summer and fall of 1996, doctors in Ontario fought the provincial government over who had the right to decide where doctors work. Doctors wanted to maintain their professional autonomy to work and live where they choose, while the Ministry of Health believed it had the right to force doctors to work in underserviced areas. Some doctors did not accept new patients to protest what they saw as government interference with their autonomy. They made some gains in terms of their salaries and partly satisfied the government's demand for more doctors to work in northern areas of the province. How this battle continues to play out will determine who is the legitimate authority over doctors: their own profession or the provincial government of Ontario.

UNIONS

Like professions and their associations, unions also attempt to attain or maintain good jobs for their members. Workers have organized unions to gain respect, increase wages, reduce working hours, and gain more control over their working day. In fact, the presence of unions has helped all of us. Without union efforts, we would not have such things as the eight-hour workday, child-labour laws, and occupational health and safety standards. I return to the state of unions in Canada and the role they play in the Canadian labour market when I discuss alienation later in this chapter.

Unions and professional associations are alike in a number of respects. They both shelter members from loss of jobs, pay cuts, and other employment-related risks. Legislation that mandates the hiring of union workers, such as exists on some construction sites, protects the jobs of union members. Likewise, when the professional association of lawyers restricts access to law school and the number of new lawyers, they too are protecting the jobs and incomes of existing members. Groups of workers who organize—whether it is a local union of flight attendants or a national association of doctors—increase their ability to keep their jobs.

TECHNOLOGY

The use of technology has long been a part of the employer–employee relationship. One of the most famous technologies, the assembly line, was used to control the pace of work (Edwards, 1979). In today's service economy, managers are more likely to invest in computers and information technology than other forms of work reorganization to improve their firms' productivity and efficiency (Osterman, 1995). Computerized office systems can reduce the time-consuming work of filing. Robots can do heavy and dangerous work. Advanced telecommunications systems make the globalization of work possible.

When employers introduce new technology in the workplace, skills are upgraded *and* downgraded. People must be trained to repair and maintain computer networks, but technology also simplifies some jobs, replaces workers, and allows work to be shifted to regions where labour is inexpensive. For example, automated bank machines not only made personal banking convenient but also sharply reduced the number of tellers while creating a small number of jobs for those who maintain the machines (Burman, 1997). More recently, Air Canada used computer and telecommunications technology to contract out the work of full-time Air Canada sales and service workers to private travel agency employees. This strategy had the effect of changing the "good" jobs at Air Canada into insecure, "bad" jobs (Shalla, 2002). New technologies often create a small number of skilled jobs but degrade or eliminate a larger number of jobs.

Technology also reduces geographic constraints as employers search for inexpensive labour or market expansion. Today, many companies have factories in Asia and product-development labs in the United States. For example, in recent decades, work in call centres grew quickly in bilingual, low-wage Moncton, New Brunswick, but growth slowed when call centres in even lower-wage India came online.

Although technology is changing the face of work, it does not mean that we have no control over what happens. Various social and technological factors affect the way new technologies are implemented (Zuboff, 1988). For example, much depends on the outcomes management wants, the type of technology that companies can afford, and whether unions and workers have a say in technological change (Shalla, 2002). According to Shoshana Zuboff (1988), management can design computer-based jobs either to increase or decrease the need for workers to use knowledge and judgment on the job. In her analysis of health insurance workers, she provides examples of job enhancement, in which managers gave workers the opportunity to use computers in complex ways. However, she also found that if management was interested only in productivity and efficiency, technology had detrimental effects on the quality of work.

New technologies require job retraining, even for middle-aged and older workers.

SOURCE: © iStockphoto.com/Chris Schmidt.

BUREAUCRACIES AND WORK ORGANIZATIONS

We live and work in a bureaucratic society. According to Max Weber, bureaucracies are the most efficient and rational type of organization that people have created. In bureaucracies, written rules provide guidelines for handling routine situations. A complex division of labour ensures that workers know what is required of them and helps to identify who is responsible when something goes wrong. Weber also saw bureaucracies as a mechanism for overcoming arbitrary decisions and corruption. For example, by having written rules about how decisions should be made and having a hierarchy of authority that clarifies who makes decisions, it is less likely that decision makers can decide to hire someone out of loyalty or obligation. Yet Weber was the first to admit that bureaucracies are not without their problems. Referring to bureaucracies as "the iron cage of the future," Weber was concerned about the potential for bureaucracies to limit creativity and initiative (Hodson and Sullivan, 1990: 184). Bureaucracies also can be rigid, tied down by "red tape," and lead to communication problems between managers and workers (Jones, 1996).

Weber believed that increased bureaucratization was the fate of modern society. Building on Weber, sociologist George Ritzer (1993) argues that society is now undergoing a new kind of rationalization process that he calls "McDonaldization." Today, writes Ritzer, the fast-food restaurant has surpassed bureaucracy as the organizational ideal. This means that our workplace, schools, leisure activities, and culture are taking on the characteristics of the fast-food restaurant.

There are four components to McDonaldization:

1. Creating the most *efficient* way to accomplish a task
2. Emphasizing things that can be *calculated*
3. Creating a *predictable* product and experience
4. Setting up systems of *control* to standardize the work of employees (Ritzer, 1993: 9–12)

Consider how we might apply Ritzer's ideas to universities. Ritzer would criticize the textbook that you are reading as part of the drive for increased efficiency, predictability, and standardization. Chapters are written by experts in each area. Instead of one author taking years to learn all of sociology, the book can be produced quicker because, presumably, each expert knows his or her area inside-out (Ritzer, 1993: 57). Conversely, you could also argue that chapters are actually better because they are written by experts. If you are like my students at the University of Toronto, your introductory sociology class is probably a large class that uses multiple-choice exams. Gone are the days of inefficient and unpredictable one-on-one examinations of students and, in many places, essay exams (Ritzer, 1993: 55). Multiple-choice exams take less time to mark compared with other ways of testing student's knowledge. I would be doing my colleagues who are teaching you a disservice if I said that the only value of multiple-choice exams is their efficiency over other testing methods; evidence shows that a well-written multiple-choice exam does a good job of capturing student's knowledge. Still, Ritzer's thesis is correct in that as universities have increased in size, faculty have been pushed to look for ways to increase the efficiency and the predictability of what they produce. This mimics some of the trends in the fast-food industry. Standardizing textbooks and exams are just two examples. If you look at other aspects of society, you will see other examples, such as vacationers who travel to other countries and stay at places like Sandals and Club Med, which offer a standard resort experience with little regard for the local culture.

If you look around at the organizations that touch your life, you will see evidence that Weber and Ritzer are correct. However, bureaucratic structure is not enough to ensure that organizations achieve their goals. As I discuss in the following section, management has also been developing strategies to organize how work is done by their employees.

MANAGERIAL STRATEGIES FOR ORGANIZING WORK

Over the past century, several approaches to organizing work in bureaucracies have come and gone. Some have endured (Braverman, 1974). Although early strategies were geared toward removing the need for workers to think on the job, more recent strategies have paid more attention to the ability and desire of workers to participate in workplace decisions. Whether these strategies offer real participation is a question to keep in mind as you read the following sections.

Taylorism

Frederick Taylor, an American industrial engineer, was the founder of scientific management or **Taylorism.** Originating in the 1890s, scientific management was an attempt by management to regain direct control of the labour process. Based on his own experience in factories, Taylor discovered that workers knew more than their managers about the work processes. As long as that was the case, workers could control how fast they worked and how much they produced. To shift control back to management, Taylor recommended a detailed division of labour that broke complex tasks into several subtasks. To do this, management needed to learn how workers did their jobs and then convert this knowledge into formal procedures. Using time and motion studies, managers documented the exact movements of workers and the length of time required to complete the task. Taylor also believed that conceptual work should be separated from the execution of tasks. It was management's job to design work procedures and the workers' job to follow those procedures. By breaking jobs into their smallest components and removing the need for workers to think, Taylorism opened the door for management to reduce its reliance on skilled labour. Cheaper, unskilled workers could now be hired to perform simplified tasks. Managers and intellectuals worldwide, including Russian communist leader Lenin, hailed Taylor as a pioneer in the rationalization of work.

Fordism is often discussed in relation to Taylorism. **Fordism** refers to the bureaucratically organized mass production of standardized goods by assembly-line methods. Although Henry Ford was not the first to use assembly-line technology, he was one of the most successful at using it to change the way things were made. Ford used assembly-line technology to implement many of the principles of Taylorism. This allowed him to create a division of labour in which workers stood in one place on the assembly line to do their assigned job and produce large numbers of standardized products.

Taylorism is not limited to factory work. Lowe (1987) shows how Taylorist principles rationalized office work in early twentieth-century Canada. And Taylorism is still around in many service industry jobs. Making hamburgers in a fast-food restaurant is broken down into minute tasks, and telephone reservation agents for airlines are given scripts to follow when dealing with clients. But today, as in the past, workers complain about the limited opportunities for creativity and self-fulfillment when working under scientific management.

Human Relations

One shortcoming of Taylorism is its assumption that workers are motivated only by desire for their paycheques (Bendix, 1974; Jones, 1996). In reaction to this simplistic view, the **human relations school of management** pushed management to rethink the Taylorist image of workers by showing the importance of the social aspects of work. Based on a series of experiments at the Western Electric Company's Hawthorne plant in Chicago, Elton Mayo and others found that friendly supervision and attention to the social environment increased workers' cooperation and productivity. The "Hawthorne studies" started the movement to consider how employers can fulfill employees' social needs, increase their satisfaction, and make them feel better about their jobs.

Although the validity of the Hawthorne studies has been called into question (Carey, 1967), most researchers agree that management strategies today still incorporate and build on elements of the human relations school. From suggestion boxes to workplace participation programs, organizations are trying to find the right "human touch" to decrease worker resistance and increase productivity. The following section takes a brief look at the rise of quality control and worker participation programs.

Quality Control and Worker Participation

In the 1990s, such concepts as "total quality management" (TQM), "Japanese management," "lean production," and "just-in-time" production were promoted as the solution for the productivity and quality problems of management. These programs emphasize quality control through communication and teamwork between management and workers. The rhetoric surrounding these programs promoted the potential for increased worker participation and workplace democratization.

Many North American manufacturing companies, like Saturn in Tennessee, CAMI in Ingersoll, Ontario, and Subaru-Isuzu in Lafeyette, Indiana, were part of the initial movement to total quality management programs. Initial reactions to these programs were positive. "Just-in-time" production cut costs as companies reduced their parts inventories and the need for warehouses. The use of participatory work teams led some academics and industry experts to consider these new management techniques a valuable new way of organizing work that enhanced workers' skills and participation and promoted the use of workers' mental capacities (Womack, Jones, and Roos, 1990). However, subsequent research in Canada and the United States suggested that many of these programs do little to promote worker empowerment because they tend to break down tasks like scientific management and assembly-line production did (Dassbach, 1996; Robertson et al., 1993).

Just as the service industry incorporated Taylorism, we now see the use of total quality management programs in service industries, including hotel chains, grocery stores, and airlines. Often these programs come with names like "service excellence." Most of these programs focus on improving customer service and may allow employees some discretion in dealing with customer complaints. For example, as part of a program to increase sensitivity to individual customers, one grocery store in England encourages staff to accompany customers to products rather than just give directions and to send flowers to customers in the event of a service lapse (Rosenthal, Hill, and Peccei, 1997). Employees are given greater discretion in the hope that this will lead to improved service.

Have worker-participation schemes resulted in empowered workers? Results from the service industry are mixed. Some evidence shows that employee empowerment schemes can increase the development of workers' interpersonal and problem-solving skills because employees have to deal with customers' problems and requests (Smith, 2001). As one employee of a copier service states, "[before the employee involvement program] I used to say [to customers] 'Here's your copies, now get out of here.' Now I have to make sure I'm communicating, *to understand their needs....* I'm trying to have more sensitivity to their needs" (Smith, 2001: 44). Whether or not these strategies will lead to increased empowerment on the part of workers depends on management's attitude. As long as these programs continue to be linked solely to management's desire for productivity increases and "the bottom line," their participatory potential will be limited. Alternatives, such as worker-owned companies, may bring us closer to real worker participation (Livingstone, 1993).

"WILL I LIKE MY JOB?" JOB SATISFACTION AND ALIENATION

The service revolution has changed the structure of work in Canada and across the world. There are more part-time jobs and increased use of computer surveillance, as well as some increases in knowledge-based jobs. Given these changes, how do Canadians feel about their jobs? According to a 2001 survey, 93 percent of Canadians reported they were satisfied with their jobs (McKenzie, 2001). Surveys show that getting respect from their bosses and feeling in control of their job mattered most to Canadian workers. Less important was the amount of money they made (see Figure 11.5). This finding reflects much of what we know about job satisfaction. To be satisfied at work, intrinsic rewards, such as autonomy and challenging work, are at least as important as extrinsic or material rewards.

Are 93 percent of Canadians *really* satisfied with their jobs? What do sociologists mean by **job satisfaction**? These are important questions. Job satisfaction is usually determined by a survey

FIGURE 11.5 WHAT CANADIANS SAY IS VERY IMPORTANT IN A JOB

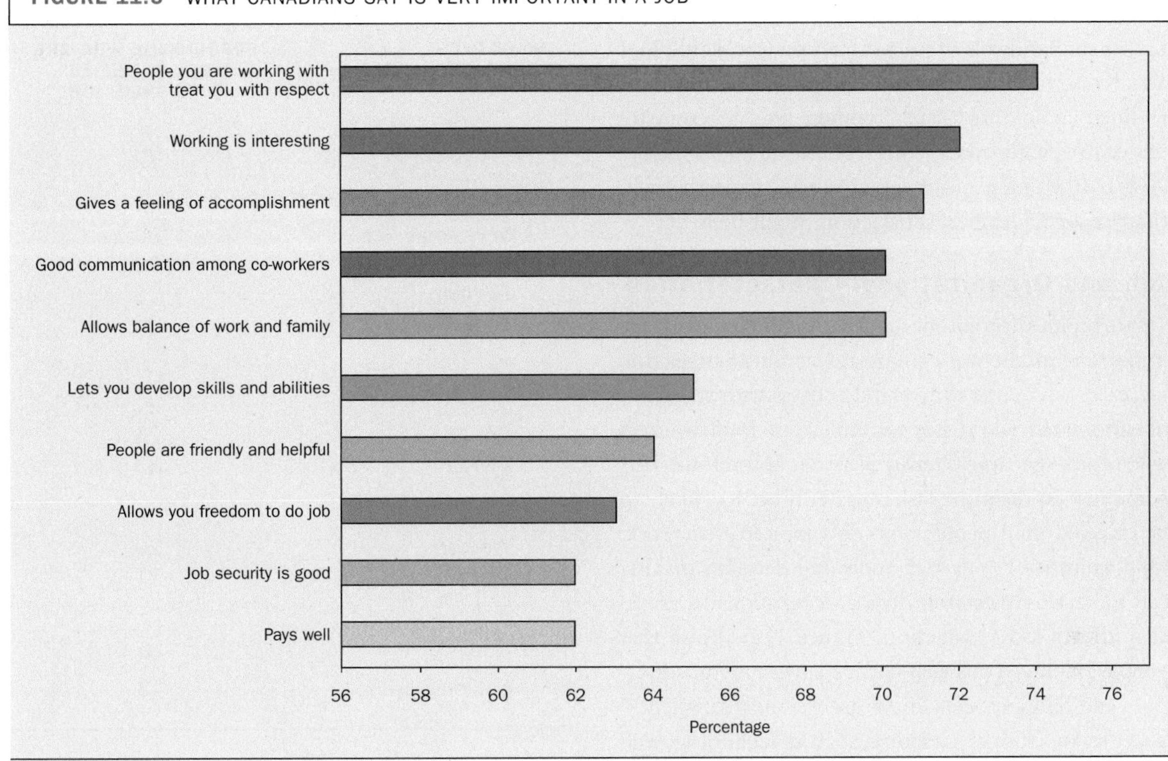

SOURCE: Canadian Policy Research Networks. 2006. "It's More than the Money—What Canadians Want in a Job." On the World Wide Web at http://www.jobquality.ca/indicator_e/rew001.stm (9 March 2006). Reprinted with permission of Canadian Policy Research Network.

question, such as, "How satisfied are you with your job?" In many ways, the responses to job satisfaction questions are similar to replies to the question "How are you today?" (Krahn and Lowe, 1998: 408). Most of us would answer "fine" to such a general question. Similarly, many workers respond that they like their jobs when asked how satisfied they are. Some analysts believe, however, that most workers do not want to admit that they do not like their jobs.

One solution to this problem is to use more specific job satisfaction measures, especially measures that refer to behaviours or behavioural intentions (e.g., Hodson, 1991). For example, the 2001 survey found that 22 percent of Canadians interviewed said they planned to change their job in the near future (Canadian Press/Leger Marketing, 2001). When we discuss alienation, we will look more closely at workers' behaviours to understand workers' negative reactions to their job. For now, we'll spend a bit more time on job satisfaction. Even though it is a problematic measure, it is still used by management to gauge how happy and productive their workers are.

WHAT DETERMINES JOB SATISFACTION?

A multitude of factors affect how we feel about our jobs, ranging from our individual characteristics to the size of the firm we work in. To give you an idea of this range, I'll discuss some of the major predictors of job satisfaction.

Individual Characteristics

Based on what we know about job ghettos, it might be a safe bet to predict that women, older workers, and younger workers will be some of the least satisfied groups of workers. Although it is true that younger workers are some of the most dissatisfied workers (see Table 11.1), older workers—at least those who have stable jobs—are actually a relatively happy group (Krahn, 1992). The higher job satisfaction reported by older employed workers may be the result of reduced expectations about work, more meaningful lives outside of work, or past advancement in jobs (Krahn and Lowe, 1998).

When you consider occupational sex segregation and the differences in jobs held by women and men, you might expect women to be less satisfied than men are. In most studies, though, women and men report similar levels of job satisfaction (see Table 11.1 and Krahn, 1992). However, when evaluating their feelings about their work, women tend to compare themselves with other women (Hodson and Sullivan, 1990). If women compared themselves with men, their reported level of satisfaction might be lower.

Job and Organizational Characteristics

Opportunities for autonomous and complex work are important predictors of job satisfaction: Satisfaction increases with autonomy and decreases with repetitive or automated work. For example, fast-food workers who repeat the same phrases every day and autoworkers who must do the same task repeatedly are less likely to be satisfied than people who do more creative work. Opportunities for participation and decision making can increase satisfaction. What occupation we are in also affects job satisfaction. Figure 11.6 shows that people employed in social science, government, education, and religion occupations are the most satisfied.

Organizational structure, such as technology and firm size, affect how happy we are at work. Blauner's (1964) classic study *Alienation and Freedom* shows how workers' alienation increased as technology shifted

TABLE 11.1 JOB SATISFACTION OF CANADIANS, 2000

EMPLOYEE CHARACTERISTICS	PERCENTAGE WHO ARE "VERY SATISFIED" WITH THEIR JOB
All Canadians	28
Size of company	
Very small	30
Small	23
Medium	18
Large	26
Age	
18–25	22
26–45	26
45+	33
Gender	
Women	29
Men	27
Employment status	
Full-time	25
Self-employed	43

SOURCE: Canadian Policy Research Networks. 2006. "Job Satisfaction." On the World Wide Web at http://www.jobquality.ca/indicator_e/rew002.stm (March 9 2006). Reprinted by permission of Canadian Policy Network.

FIGURE 11.6 WORK SATISFACTION BY OCCUPATION

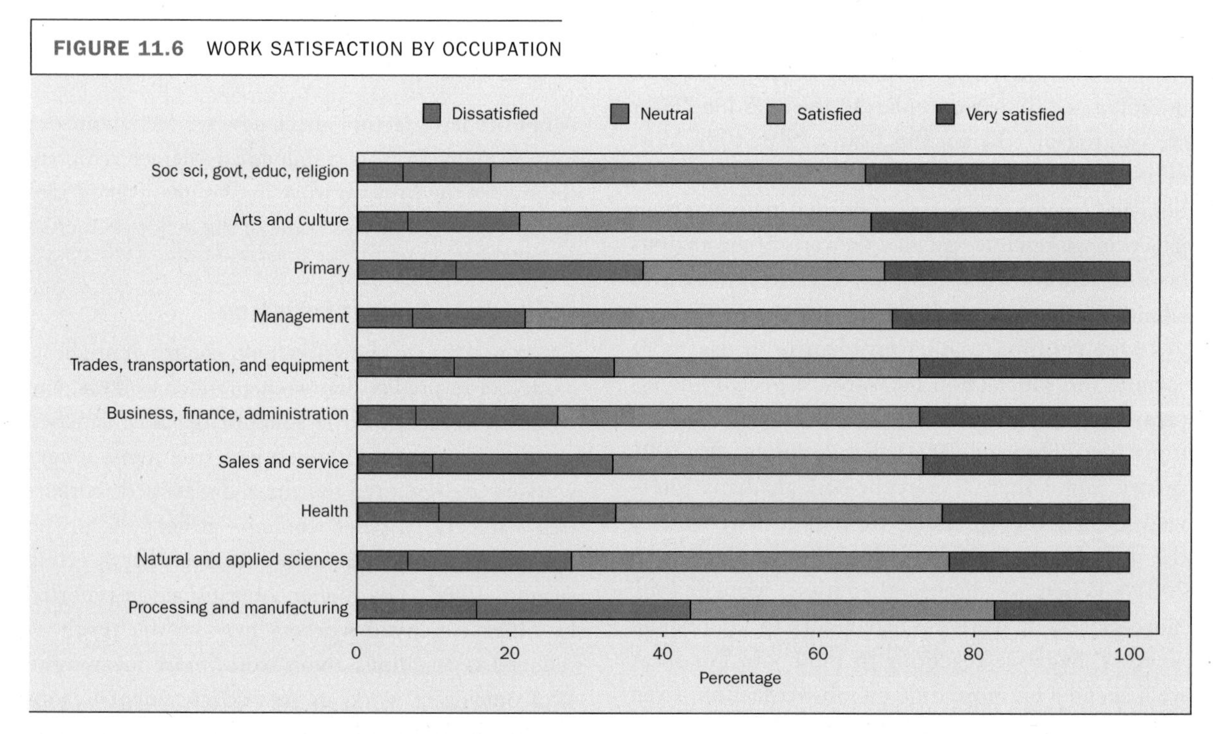

SOURCE: Canadian Policy Research Networks. 2006. "Satisfaction Most Common in Social Sciences, Arts/Culture and Management Occupations." On the World Wide Web at http://www.jobquality.ca/indicator_e/rew002_1.stm#2 (9 March 2006). Reprinted with permission.

from craftwork to machine tending and assembly-line work. In contrast, technology that requires the use of conceptual skills increases job satisfaction.

Employees in small companies experience a relatively high level of satisfaction. In 2000, 30 percent of Canadians who worked in very small companies were very satisfied, compared with 23 percent who worked in small companies and 18 percent who worked in medium-sized companies (see Table 11.1). As company size increases, so do workers' feelings of isolation and powerlessness. However, large companies offer benefits and opportunities that boost job satisfaction almost to the level found in very small companies.

When I consider all the individual, job, and organizational factors that influence job satisfaction, I am struck by the realization that much of our satisfaction at work is determined by things over which we have little or no control. Our employers determine how much we are paid and how challenging and autonomous our jobs will be. And the chance to work in a small, locally owned company or a large national or multinational corporation has much to do with the employment opportunities where we live.

ALIENATION

If job satisfaction focuses on the individual worker's feelings about his or her job, alienation is linked to the lack of control or powerlessness an individual experiences in relation to his or her job. Originating in the work of Karl Marx, the concept of **alienation** examines how the structural conditions of work lead to workers' lack of power over their work and lives (Rinehart, 1996). For Marx, alienation is an "objective condition" that stems from capitalism. Marx argued that capitalism robs workers of control over the means of production and the products of their labour and puts control in the hands of owners.

According to Marx, alienation of workers under capitalism has four sources:

1. Workers are alienated from the products they produce. They do not own them, and they have no say over how they will be used. Rather, under capitalism, work is a means to an end—work provides a paycheque so workers can buy things they need, but workers no longer directly produce what they need.
2. Workers do not control the process of production. The advanced division of labour is indicative of this condition. Decisions about how fast to work, the order in which to complete tasks, and the use of equipment are made by someone other than workers. Workers lose control over their daily work activity.
3. Workers are alienated from engaging in creative activity and thus from themselves.
4. Workers are alienated from others as they have fewer opportunities to talk and connect with co-workers. Also, work is not a collective process that can help the whole community. Overall, the division of labour under capitalism physically and emotionally isolates workers from one another.

Some sociologists conceptualize alienation as a way to think about how workers' psychological and emotional states are linked to the organization of work (Rogers, 1995). For example, when work is repetitive and does not allow for interaction between co-workers, workers may experience a high level of alienation. Some sociologists conceptualize alienation as a subjective state that arises from the reality of capitalist working conditions. Here the emphasis is on workers' feelings of powerlessness and lack of control or connection to their work and fellow employees.

Fighting Alienation: Individual and Collective Responses to Work

To understand alienation, we also need to look at how workers resist it (Schmitt and Moody, 1994). This can shed light on their negative feelings toward work.

When a worker engages in sabotage or repeatedly skips work, management may define the worker as destructive or lazy. Yet, in the minds of workers, these seemingly insubordinate behaviours may be an attempt to gain control over their job or reduce the amount of alienation they experience. To overcome a boring job where she was not assigned enough work, one temporary clerical worker stated, "I used to sleep there. Yes there's nothing to do. I always bring my book. When I get sick and tired of reading, I sleep. Sometimes, OK, you're not supposed to make phone calls, but what am I going to do with 8 hours?" (Rogers, 1995: 157). If management had provided enough work, this temporary worker might have exhibited good work habits.

When viewed as potential resistance to alienating conditions, the "misbehaviour" of workers appears in a different light. Some researchers argue that the alienating conditions of work lead some workers to "fight back" or react to these conditions (Edwards and Scullion, 1982; Rinehart, 1996). You may have had similar reactions to work, such as slacking off if you believed your supervisor required you to work too hard, or turning your work into a game to make the time go faster. Engaging in these behaviours does not mean you are lazy or incompetent. Rather, they are typical reactions to alienating work.

To cope with poor working conditions, some workers quit their jobs. Those who cannot quit may respond passively by socializing with co-workers, playing games, or reducing their productivity (Burawoy, 1979). Management often devises strategies to prevent these types of behaviours. For example, Taylorism was motivated in part by management's desire to reduce opportunities for workers to restrict their output.

For management, theft and destruction of company property is a particularly bothersome behaviour. But these criminal acts may be motivated by poor working conditions. A few years ago, an undergraduate student in my class confessed that, while working in a small T-shirt design factory, she purposely poked holes in some shirts. Because management had a policy of giving damaged T-shirts to employees, you might think she did this only to take advantage of her situation. As it turns out, though, employees were paid low wages and worked under conditions of extreme heat. This student saw her behaviour as a protest against the inadequate pay and difficult working conditions. Other workers engage in sabotage to gain concessions from management or to gain control over the work process. Factory workers may damage the assembly line to slow down the pace of work and clerical workers may hide files to reduce their workload (Hodson and Sullivan, 1990; Rinehart, 1996).

Do these individual acts of resistance change the amount of alienation workers experience? The answer to this question is complex. Many sociologists, beginning with Marx, illustrate how alienation is a condition of objective powerlessness that exists regardless of whether workers themselves consciously recognize it. Some workers become aware or conscious of the alienating conditions they experience at work. As predicted by Marx, these workers may respond to these conditions by forming unions, going on strike, or engaging in revolutionary behaviour focused on overthrowing capitalism. However, most workers do not develop "class-consciousness." Sociologists Harvey Krahn and Graham Lowe state, "In the absence of a well-defined alternative to the current economic system, we would not expect most workers to be able to clearly articulate their alienation and act on it. Apathy, or an attempt to forget about work as soon as one leaves it behind, are the common responses of many workers to a situation in which there is no viable alternative" (1998: 419).

Workers often resist alienating work conditions. Forms of resistance include striking, being absent, quitting, slacking off, and committing industrial sabotage.

SOURCE: Juan Manuel Sanchez. Courtesy of Nora Patrich and Joan Sanchez.

This means that hiding files or poking holes in a shirt may make the worker feel better and thus make it possible to get through the day. These types of activities may reduce the subjective feeling of alienation: Workers may feel less powerless or may feel they have more control over their working conditions. But these types of individual strategies do not change the structural conditions of work. Collective responses to workplace conditions are more likely to lead to lasting changes in how work is organized. These collective responses, such as forming a union, may not "overthrow" the economic system, but they can improve working conditions. Although playing games and stealing may momentarily increase workers' feelings of control over their jobs, most researchers agree that, for lasting change to occur, collective responses are needed. Chapter 18, Politics and Social Movements provides more details about the role of strikes in the Canadian labour movement's struggle for economic and social rights.

Unions play an important role in facilitating collective action by workers. Today, just under 30 percent of the nonagricultural paid labour force are in unions (Uppal, 2011). Compared with the experience in some other countries, such as the United States and Australia, **union density,** or the percentage of nonagricultural paid workers who are unionized, has not significantly declined in Canada over the past 30 years (Adams and Welsh, 2008). Over the past 150 years, the characteristics of unionized workers have shifted, however. During the late nineteenth century, craft workers organized; during the 1930s and 1940s, workers in the goods-producing sectors followed suit. Public-sector workers began to organize in the 1960s and 1970s. In 2011, public-sector industries had the highest rate of unionization (Uppal, 2011). Contrary to the image of the male unionized factory worker, today's unionized worker is more likely to be a woman with postsecondary education working in education or healthcare (Uppal 2011). Some union supporters warn that union density will stagnate if union organizing does not expand to cover new groups of workers, particularly young workers in service industries (White, 1993).

Whether the number of unionized workers in Canada will grow or decline depends on how unions deal with changes in the labour market and the economy. The rise of nonstandard work and the ease with which companies can move their businesses to other countries challenge union growth.

FINDING WORK

One of the buzzwords of twenty-first-century job seekers is "networking." Networking is sometimes referred to as the "art of talking to as many people as you can without directly asking them for a job" (*New York Times*, quoted in Flap and Boxman, 2001: 159). Potential job applicants are often advised to "network, network, network" (Ehrenreich, 2005; see Box 11.2).

This advice derives from the common belief that networking matters and is useful for finding a job, a belief with which sociologists concur. Sociologists define a **social network** as a bounded set of individuals linked by the exchange of material or emotional resources, everything from money to information to friendship. The patterns of exchange determine the boundaries of the network. Network members exchange resources more frequently with one another than with nonmembers. Individuals in a network think of themselves as network members. The people you know personally form the boundaries of your personal network.

One measure of the quality of a personal network is the number of ties or connections in the network. Someone with many ties has a "dense" network; he or she is connected to many people. Moreover, ties may be strong or weak. Frequency of interaction, emotional intensity, and reciprocity between individuals defines the strength of ties (Yakubovich, 2005). Strong ties exist between you and family members and close friends. You see such people regularly, care deeply about them, and would help them if they needed it. Weak ties exist between you and others in your personal network—say, the friend of a friend, someone you met via Facebook, or one of your parents' co-workers. You would not see such people often, nor would you count on them to help you in times of trouble.

In his study of professional, technical, and managerial workers in a Boston suburb, sociologist Mark Granovetter (1995 [1974]) found that 57 percent of his respondents found their job through personal contacts. Some 83 percent of these people said the contact who helped them get their job was someone they saw infrequently; they represented a weak tie. At the time his study was first published, Granovetter's finding was surprising and provocative. Common sense suggests that people to whom you are strongly tied would be most useful in helping you find a job because they are most motivated to help you. But it turns out what matters most in finding a job is good and unique information about jobs. Acquaintances who are one step removed from you are in a position to provide new (or nonredundant) information about jobs. These weak ties serve as "bridges" to "new parts of a social universe" or new parts of the labour market (Yakubovich, 2005: 410). In other words, the people you see frequently, such as your friends, probably have the same information about job openings that you do. But someone who is a weak tie in your network, such as your mom's best friend or your cousin's boss, may have information about job openings that your strong ties do not have. Because this information comes through personal contacts, it may not be readily available to the public, which decreases the amount of competition for the job opening. Thus, information from acquaintances or weak ties is most likely to lead to a new job. Granovetter calls this phenomenon "the strength of weak ties."

Since Granovetter's study, sociologists have continued to examine how personal contacts or networks

BOX 11.2 LOOKING FOR WORK IN THE INFORMATION AGE

Workopolis, Monster.com, Canjobs.com: these are all examples of internet job search sites available to all those looking for work. But does the proliferation of internet job search sites (and all the advice they provide) really make a difference? Or are they merely the old newspaper classified job ads wrapped up in a new technological package? In her book on the experiences of the white collar unemployed, Barbara Ehrenreich finds that job searching, thanks to the internet, has become "if not a science, a technology so complex that no mere job seeker can expect to master it alone" (Ehrenreich, 2005, p. 16). She posted her résumé on Monster.com and Hotjobs.com only to find that after two months she had yet to receive a legitimate inquiry, even from the health and biomedical companies she electronically "pelted." She concluded that the internet alone will not get you a job.

So why use the internet for job searches? First, using the internet gives employers and job applicants cheap access to information. Job applicants can find out about job openings more easily, compared to the past in which they had to go door-to-door to companies to look at job posting boards. Second, employers can easily obtain a pool of résumés and potential workers. Also, sending a résumé to an employer over the internet may be a signal that the job applicant is computer and internet-savvy. On the other hand, employers report that they are overloaded with résumés, especially from people who are not qualified and who they have no intention of hiring (Fountain, 2005: 1243).

Does the internet help people find jobs? Using data from two American surveys, Fountain (2005) found that, in 1998, using the internet increased searchers' chance of finding a job by 164 percent. By 2000, searchers using the internet were 28 percent *less* likely to find a job than other non-internet searchers, even after controlling for age, race, education, gender, length of unemployment, local unemployment rate and income. Fountain offers two explanations for this dramatic shift. First, if only a small number of people are using the internet, as was the case in 1998, then this group has access to information about job openings that others, who are probably equally qualified, do not have. Second, when only a small number of workers apply through the internet, employers may use this as a marker of the skill of workers, such as being more technologically savvy or resourceful than others: useful information that may affect their hiring decision. By 2000, when the number of people using the internet for job searches doubled, these advantages disappeared. Fountain concludes that even though the internet has changed the way people search for jobs, the change has been more about form than substance. The internet may provide a new way for workers to find information about employers and vice versa, but it is unclear whether the information on the internet is better than information obtained elsewhere. It may simply be that there is just more of it. The absolute quantity of information on the internet may not necessarily be better than the information found through other means of job searching. What seemed to work for the job searchers in Fountain's study was finding a job the old-fashioned way. Placing or answering a job ad more than doubled the chances a searcher would find a job.

SOURCE: Christine Fountain, "Finding a Job in the Internet Age," *Social Forces*, 2005, Vol. 83 (3), pp. 1235–1262, by permission of Oxford University Press.

help people find jobs. Recent studies emphasize the role of social capital or resources in your personal network (Flap and Boxman, 2001). Having contacts in your network with good or high-status resources improves your chances of finding a better job (Marsden and Hurlbert, 1988): "good networks help to get people good jobs" (Erickson, 2001: 156).

THE FUTURE OF WORK

At the end of any discussion of work, one question remains for most students: "Where will the jobs be when I graduate?" While I do not have a crystal ball, it is possible to make some projections about future jobs.

Education and retirement play key roles in determining which job openings are growing and which are not. Almost three-quarters of the new jobs that will be created in the near future are expected to require some form of postsecondary education. They are in the fields of health, natural and applied sciences, education, social science, government service, and business and professional services. In the United States, 10 of the 20 fastest-growing occupations between now and 2018 will be related to healthcare, similar to Canada (U.S. Bureau of Labor Statistics, 2010). These projections also highlight that the economy will continue to generate both good and bad jobs: While many of these jobs, such as doctors and biomedical engineers require postsecondary education, others, such as home healthcare aides, require only short-term training.

Different forms of nonstandard work will continue to proliferate. One form of nonstandard work of particular interest to many undergraduates is self-employment, which will represent an ever-growing percentage of the labour force, partly because companies find outsourcing a good way to reduce labour costs. Although only 16.7 percent of Canadian workers were self-employed in 2010, the growth rate of self-employment since the 1970s has outpaced that for workers in the public and private sector (Statistics Canada, 2009; LaRochelle-Côté and Uppal, 2011). Even during economic downturns, self-employment grows. Some workers who lose jobs because of corporate restructuring are pushed into self-employment as their only employment option. Other workers are drawn to self-employment because of a desire to have more control over their work. Regardless of why people become self-employed, the future appears to involve an increase in self-employment.

In the immediate future, we can expect employers to continue looking for ways to reduce operating costs. As in the past, one focus will be on reducing the cost of labour. Employers continue to move factories to countries with the lowest labour costs. Along with labour-reducing uses of technology, this tendency may further the trend toward the use of temporary and contract employees. What the head of production for the PowerPC microchip said in 1994 still rings true for many current workers: "I'm here for the duration, five years or so" (quoted in Osterman, 1995: 72).

Two decades ago, analysts debated two divergent futures for work. On the one hand, optimists emphasized the "end of the job" as we know it and the rise of self-employed, autonomous entrepreneurs (Bridges, 1994). Part of the optimistic scenario is based on the hope that the service industry will continue to create good jobs in finance, medicine, and the like. Pessimists, on the other hand, predicted the "end of work." Based on an analysis of jobs in the United States, Jeremy Rifkin (1995) believed that as many as three-quarters of white- and blue-collar jobs could be automated, with no jobs to replace the ones lost to automation. In Rifkin's view, the unemployment level was going to rise and leave more of us scrambling for the few remaining jobs. By the middle of the twenty-first century, millions of workers could be left permanently idle, he said. As I write this chapter, it is clear that neither prediction is completely right or wrong. As we discussed in this chapter, the service industry has created good jobs while also continuing to churn out lower-paid nonstandard ones. And while certain occupations, such as bank tellers and travel agents, have declined because of automation, we are far from reaching the end of work. As you've learned in this chapter, employers and employees have some control over whether technology creates good or bad jobs, reducing or increasing alienation. An important issue for the future of work is whether employers or employees will set the terms by which such changes will be judged. One thing is certain. The battle between workers and management will probably continue, as employees like Zainab Taiyeb try to organize their co-workers so they can improve their chances of having a say in what work looks like in the years to come.

SUMMARY

1. In the Industrial Revolution, large segments of the population moved from being peasant farmers to being wage-earning factory workers living in urban areas. During the second industrial revolution, companies increased in size and developed administrative offices with a complex division of labour.
2. The rise of the service economy is changing the types of jobs available in the labour market. The types of jobs available in the service economy are being polarized into good jobs in upper-tier industries and bad jobs in lower-tier industries.
3. The proportion of Canadians employed in nonstandard jobs is growing. Nonstandard jobs capture a variety of forms of work including part-time, temporary jobs, contract work, and self-employment. Young workers and older workers are overrepresented in some kinds of nonstandard jobs.
4. On average, Canadians are not working longer hours than they were 30 years ago. The proportion of Canadians working a 40-hour work week has declined over the past 30 years. However,

work hours are becoming polarized, with more Canadians working fewer than 40 hours per week and more working more than 40 hours per week.

5. With the rise of the "24-hour economy," increased demand for consumer services, and the aging of the population, an increase in those working nonstandard work schedules has occurred since the 1970s.
6. BlackBerrys, iPhones, and other mobile devices that connect to the Internet are changing the way we work. They increase productivity as workers can respond to email and other requests faster. Some users report downsides to these devices, such as a heightened need to be connected to work and the blurring of boundaries between work and nonwork time.
7. The labour market comprises different segments. Good jobs are located in core industries and firms with primary labour markets, while bad jobs may be found in peripheral industries and firms with secondary labour markets. Job ghettos are areas of the labour market that trap disadvantaged groups of workers. Labour-market shelters, such as professional associations and unions, help their members maintain access to good jobs.
8. Work and organizational characteristics are the primary predictors of job satisfaction.
9. Alienation is a structural condition of powerlessness that arises from the organization of work in the capitalist economy. Workers respond to alienating conditions in various ways, such as engaging in sabotage and quitting their jobs. Strikes and other forms of collective resistance may have some success in changing the conditions of work.

QUESTIONS TO CONSIDER

1. Thinking about your own work experience, do you see evidence of the service economy creating good jobs or bad jobs? Do you see evidence of an increase in nonstandard work schedules?
2. Research points to three types of smart phone or mobile device users: "enthusiastic," "balanced," and those seeing serious personal costs to using the devices. What type of mobile device user are you? Have you experienced difficulty separating work from non-work time?
3. What is the difference between job satisfaction and alienation? Is Marx's concept of alienation relevant for understanding work today? Why or why not? Have you ever engaged in workplace behaviour that could be interpreted as a reaction to alienating conditions? Did this behaviour change the alienating conditions? Why or why not?
4. Think about how you or your friends have found jobs. What role have personal contacts played in your search for a job? What other ways have you or your friends found work?

GLOSSARY

In Marxist theory, **alienation** (p. 279) is a structural condition of "objective powerlessness." Workers do not have power or control over their work situation and are separated from the means of production. This situation is a characteristic of work in a capitalist economy.

Deindustrialization (p. 261) refers to the shift from a goods- to a service-based economy.

The **division of labour** (p. 258) refers to the specialized tasks performed by different categories of workers. The division of labour increases when work is broken down into smaller components.

Extrinsic rewards (p. 262) are the material benefits of working. Adequate pay, benefits, and opportunities for advancement are examples.

Fordism (p. 275) refers to the bureaucratically organized mass production of standardized goods by assembly-line methods.

Functional or internal flexibility (p. 264) in nonstandard employment allows employers to move workers from one job to another within an organization.

The **human relations school of management** (p. 275) emphasizes the importance of the social aspects of work. Proponents argue that more satisfied workers are more productive workers.

Intrinsic rewards (p. 262) are the social-psychological benefits of working. They are derived from challenging work, nonrepetitive work, autonomy, and decision-making opportunities.

Job ghettos (p. 270) are parts of the labour market that prevent groups of workers from experiencing upward mobility.

Job satisfaction (p. 276) is determined by asking workers in a survey, "How satisfied are you with your job as a whole?"

Labour-market segmentation (p. 269) involves the division of the labour market into sectors of good and bad jobs.

Labour-market shelters (p. 272) are organizations that protect the jobs of certain groups of workers. Professional associations and unions are examples.

Nonstandard jobs (p. 258) include part-week employment, part-year employment, limited-term contract employment, employment through temporary-help agencies, self-employment, and multiple-job holding.

Nonstandard work schedules (p. 266) are characterized by either working nonstandard hours, which fall outside the 9-to-5 workday (shift work), or working nonstandard days, such as Saturday and Sunday.

Numerical or external flexibility (p. 264) in nonstandard employment enables employers to adjust the size of their workforce by easily hiring and firing workers in response to fluctuations in labour demand.

Polarization of working hours (p. 265) occurs when many workers in the labour market are working either too many hours (overwork) or too few hours (underwork).

Primary labour markets (p. 269) are where most good jobs are found. They have an internal labour market that provides a job ladder and the opportunity for upward mobility.

A **social network** (p. 281) is a bounded set of individuals linked by the exchange of material or emotional resources, everything from money to information to friendship. The patterns of exchange determine the boundaries of the network. Network members exchange resources more frequently with one another than with nonmembers. Individuals in a network think of themselves as network members. The people you know personally form the boundaries of your personal network.

Taylorism (p. 275), also known as scientific management, is named after its developer, Frederick Taylor. This style of management breaks job tasks into their smallest components. Work is also separated into conceptual and manual tasks, removing the need for workers to make decisions about their work.

Union density (p. 281) is the percentage of paid workers in a country who are unionized.

SUGGESTED READING

Adams, Tracey and Sandy Welsh. (2008). *The Organization and Experience of Work.* Toronto: Nelson. A thorough, up-to-date overview focusing on the Canadian experience.

Ehrenreich, Barbara. (2005). *Bait and Switch: The (Futile) Pursuit of the American Dream.* New York: Metropolitan Books. Provides a provocative and humorous look at networking.

Rinehart, James W. (2006). *The Tyranny of Work: Alienation and the Labour Process,* 5th ed. Toronto: Thomson Nelson. A Canadian classic.

CHAPTER 12

EDUCATION

Scott Davies
MCMASTER UNIVERSITY

SOURCE: AFP/Getty Images.

IN THIS CHAPTER YOU WILL LEARN THAT

- Sociologists study links between schools and society, focusing on inequality, socialization, and social organization. Theoretical approaches include structural functionalism, Marxism, human capital theory, feminism, credentialism, and institutional theory.
- Canadian schooling has been marked by three broad trends. First, to fulfill a mandate to retain the vast bulk of students in secondary levels, schools have *expanded.* Second, this expansion has necessitated a greater variety of *accommodations*, as educators attempt to address a range of student abilities and exceptionalities. Third, demands for postsecondary credentials are generating a simultaneous trend toward more intense forms of *competition.*
- Canadian school-level attainment shows a pattern of inequality, in that it varies by class, gender, and race.
- Socialization through education has become less religious and now lacks the hard-edged, prescriptive tone it had in the past. Reflecting trends in pedagogical philosophy, today's schools have a more indulgent quality, with teachers using less punitive tactics to elicit compliance from students.
- Canadian schools have changed from wielding traditional authority to wielding legal-rational authority, and in the process have become more bureaucratic. Today, schools are being pressured to become more "accountable" and "market-like."

INTRODUCTION

Go to the education section in any bookstore and what will you see? Dozens of titles declaring schools to be in some sort of crisis: *The Catastrophe in Public Education*, *Public Education: An Autopsy*, *Failing Our Kids: How We Are Ruining Our Public Schools*, *The University in Ruins*, and so on. Newspapers decry the quality of schooling with headlines like "Johnny Can't Read and He's in University." Such drama! Is it really that bad?

Not if you consider several facts about schools. Until quite recently higher education was deemed to be a waste for common people. Early in the twentieth century, most people did not complete high school. But the past half-century has brought a change in ideologies. In Canada and elsewhere, advanced levels of education are seen to be not only suitable but also necessary for many people. Over 50 years, high-school attendance has become almost universal, and attaining a secondary-school diploma the norm. University enrolments have never been higher. Further, public opinion surveys show that most Canadians rate our public schools favourably and believe they are effective teachers of our youth (Canadian Council on Learning, 2007).

This highlights a key paradox. Modern schooling has been a success story in many respects, having grown immensely, reshaped the lives of most Canadians, and received billions in government funds. Yet as schools become more central to society, they attract more and more criticism. This chapter will illuminate this paradox by exploring the transformation and changing connections between schools and Canadian society over the past century.

HOW SCHOOLS CONNECT TO SOCIETY: CLASSICAL AND CONTEMPORARY APPROACHES

Sociologists examine three major ways that schools connect to society. First, schools shape society by **selection.** Education systems have long channelled students into different types of schools and programs. This process creates stratification when programs are designated as "higher level" or "lower level" and link to better or worse job opportunities. The endless grading, judging, marking, and testing in schools sorts and certifies students with different

Schools socialize students by fostering the development of attitudes, knowledge, and skills that are necessary in adult society.
SOURCE: © Monkey Business Images/Shutterstock.

"badges of ability." This may seem self-evident, since we have all written hundreds of tests in our lives. But a sociological approach sets this process within a bigger picture: Schooling connects to societal-level inequality. In a society marked by disparities in wealth and income, and where more people go to school for longer periods, never before has the pursuit of educational credentials been as consequential for income, occupational success, and other life-chances. Sociologists ask *who* is selected for *what*, and *why?*

These kinds of questions can be traced back to the ideas of Karl Marx and the structural functionalists. Although Marx wrote little on schooling, his twentieth-century followers have examined the role of schooling in maintaining patterns of economic inequality. They have argued that schools are stratified in ways that reflect workplace hierarchies, with basic forms of schooling teaching youth to be punctual and compliant, and with higher levels encouraging students to internalize orders and the expectations of authority figures. In contrast, structural functionalists see school selection as an increasingly meritorious process in which the brightest and hardest working are identified, rewarded, and selected for training in professional work and high-level management.

Second, schools shape society as they *socialize* people. They help prepare new adults for the next generation, passing along values and knowledge. This too may seem glaringly obvious, but decisions on *which* values and knowledge are passed on can be contentious. When Émile Durkheim (1961 [1925]) was writing, industrialization and the rise of democracy were promoting individualism, and people felt freer to develop their talents to their fullest extent. As individualism flourished, Durkheim sought to understand how modern societies could replace the binding and authoritative voice of religion, which had traditionally prescribed norms to guide people's thoughts and actions. What would now keep individuals from being self-centred and acting only in their own interest? Durkheim cared deeply about "moral education," the normative element of schooling that he hoped would become society's prime tool to combat the rising culture of individualism.

When Canada was more religious, schools imparted old-fashioned virtues and moral codes. But society has changed, so contemporary sociologists now ask these questions: Do schools still impart a clear set of values? Is socialization better understood as a series of unintended consequences that are beyond anyone's control? Just how successful are schools at socializing students? Do they treat everyone the same, or does school socialization differ by class, gender, and race?

Third, education shapes society through *social organization*. Schools affect how we learn and help define different types of occupations. This was a core interest of another classical theorist, Max Weber, who was fascinated by "rationalization," supposedly the main "logic" of modern societies, embodied in bureaucratic organizations. For him, modern schooling was changing society by teaching knowledge in a systematic fashion and creating credentials to forge more formal pathways to labour markets.

Why do employers seek and hire employees with school credentials? The conventional wisdom is that schools teach skills, employers hire the most skilled, and school credentials are signals of skills. But Weber's contemporary followers have questioned whether the school–labour market connection is so simple. They contend that most school content is only loosely connected to what is demanded in most jobs. They see schools as largely serving to distribute legitimate access to jobs.

Let us now examine in depth each of the three roles of education: selection, socialization, and social organization.

SELECTION

When Canada was an agricultural society, land was a prime economic resource, and affluent families strove to pass their property to their children. When manufacturing and commerce became the key economic activities, upper-middle-class children could inherit business fortunes. But today, most youth earn their living through employment and need credentials. "Class reproduction," the passing of advantage from one generation to the next, does not operate through direct inheritance in education. No one can legally inherit his or her parents' law degree, medical licence, MBA, or teaching certificate. These things must be earned. Now that most positions of power and status require some sort of school credentials, how do the affluent pass on their advantages?

School selection occurs in two ways. First, schooling itself is structured in a stratified manner, though this structuring takes different forms across countries and over time. Second, within that structure students from different backgrounds have unequal rates of success. Families navigate their way through this structure, searching for ways to boost their children's educational success for the most prized credentials. Most parents expect their children to receive a postsecondary education (see Figure 12.1).

CHANGING SCHOOL STRUCTURE

In Canada, the traditional form of educational selection is known as "streaming." Streaming consists of splitting students into curricular groupings, one typically bound for postsecondary schooling, one headed for general training. Students in the upper tier are exposed to advanced mathematics and works of literature, while those in the lower tiers focus on the rudiments of literacy, numeracy, and practical workplace skills. Although Canada ranks near the top of the world in reading literacy (see Figure 12.2), Canadian sociologists have long condemned streaming for limiting educational opportunity, particularly for students from working-class backgrounds. Streaming is

FIGURE 12.1 PERCENTAGE OF CANADIAN PARENTS EXPECTING THEIR CHILDREN TO ATTEND POSTSECONDARY INSTITUTIONS, 2002

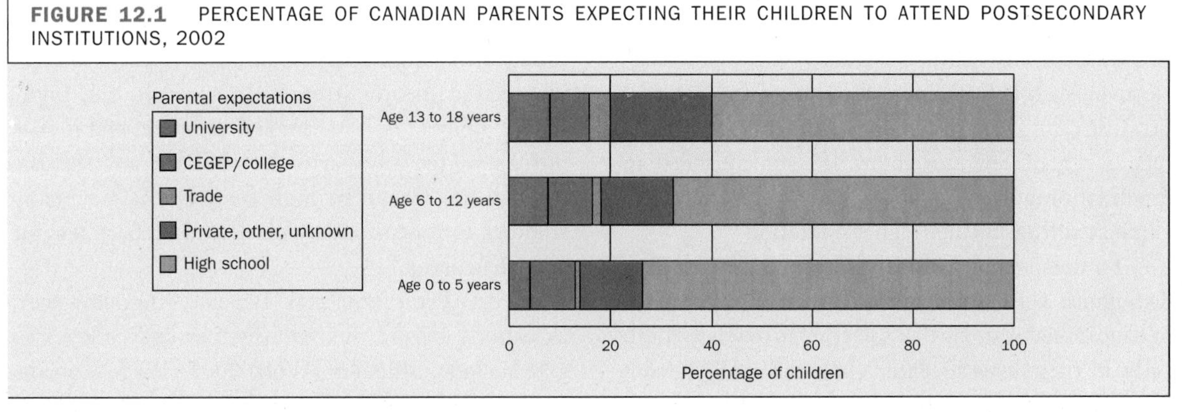

SOURCE: Statistics Canada (2002).

FIGURE 12.2 RESULTS FROM PISA INTERNATIONAL LITERACY TEST, 2000 AND 2009

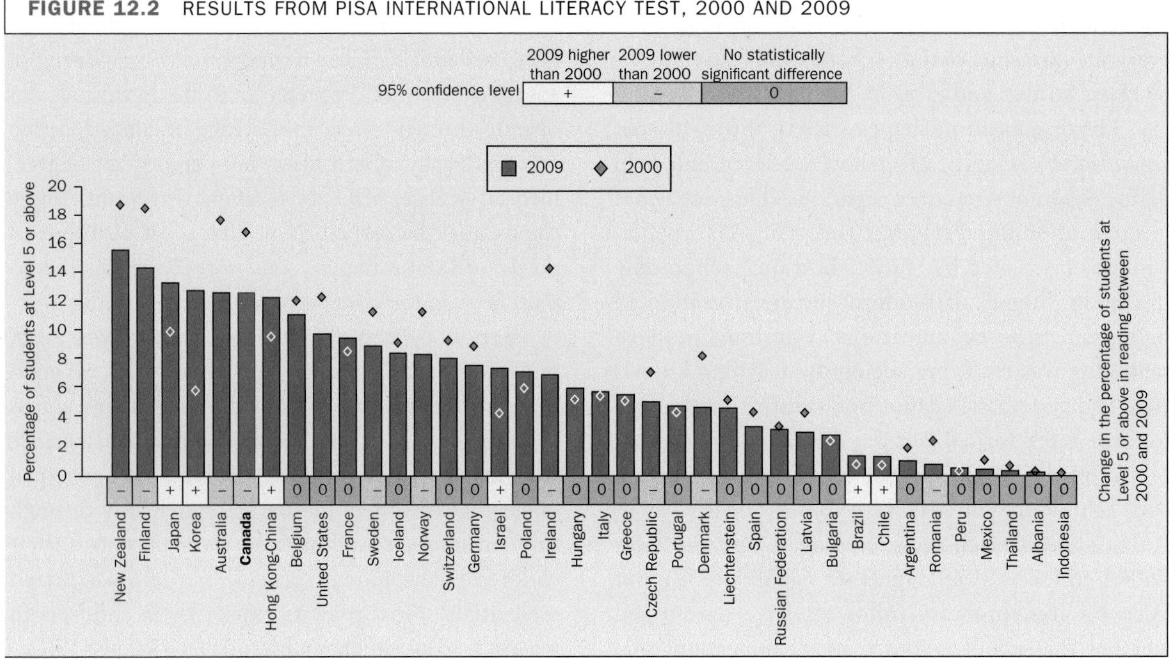

SOURCE: OECD (2010), PISA 2009 Results: Learning Trends: Changes in Student Performance Since 2000 (Volume V), PISA, OECD Publishing (http://dx.doi.org/10.1787/9789264091580-en).

seen to dampen their aspirations, manage their ambitions, and discourage them from moving on (Krahn and Taylor, 2007). To understand Canada's form of educational stratification, we need to set streaming in an international context.

Compared with that in many European countries, Canadian education has actually been relatively open and flexible. For decades, schools in Britain, France, and Germany sorted students into entirely academic or entirely vocational schools at relatively young ages (Kerckhoff, 2002). European academic secondary schools were oriented to prepare elites and preserve a heritage of classic literature, philosophy, and rigorous exams. "Excellence" was equated with high culture. Until recently it was inconceivable for French secondary-school students to study "practical" electives, such as business or accounting, for instance. Stratification was rigid; once students entered a type of school, few moved out. If a student failed an examination at age 15 or 16, they were effectively eliminated from further higher education.

To understand national differences, sociologists distinguish **sponsored mobility,** which takes place in educational systems that select relatively few youth early in their lives to enter elite universities, from **contest mobility,** which takes place in educational systems that group the bulk of youth into the same school, expose them to the same curriculum, and send larger numbers to higher education (Turner, 1960). Sponsored mobility uses highly structured streaming to restrict access to higher education, while contest mobility promotes more competition within a unitary structure. Canada is an example of a contest system, while many European countries have had sponsored systems. For most of the twentieth century, Canadian schooling did not sharply separate a "gifted" minority from the rest by creating separate schools. Academic curricula were instead given to almost everyone. From the 1960s until recently, proportionately more Canadian youth flowed into Canadian universities than European youth flowed into European universities, and even lower streams were not strongly vocational; little high-school content has been directly job-related in any stream. As a result, the high-school diploma lacks vocational meaning, and it does not guarantee any particular skill for any specific occupation. Canadian high schools channel many students to postsecondary levels and prepare few for any particular job.

This distinction may be changing, however, as nations expand their universities and colleges to take in more students (Wolf, 2002). As in Canada, European policymakers want more youth to study in university, claiming that more graduates will generate wealth and improve their nation's economic competitiveness. Most European nations are removing barriers, creating more alternative channels for youth, and moving toward an ever-more streamlined contest model. As such, the form that inequality takes in education is changing.

As more youth enter higher education, competition shifts to higher levels, and stratification *within* universities and colleges becomes increasingly important. Higher education can be seen as stratified along two main dimensions: selectivity of institution and field of study (Davies and Guppy, 1997). Universities and colleges with the best reputations offer their graduates access to elite jobs, higher wages, contacts, and other advantages. In some countries, higher education institutions differ greatly in prestige. In Europe, ancient universities, such as Oxford, Cambridge, and the Sorbonne, have much more exclusive student bodies, and they more readily provide their students with access to elite positions. In Canada, universities are generally more selective and academically intensive than are community colleges, whose vocational mandates give them a subordinate position within higher education (Dennison, 1995).

Fields of study also differ in their prestige, selectivity, access to resources, and payoffs for their graduates. High prestige was once attached to humanistic fields (such as philosophy and English) that enjoyed elite patrons, but in recent decades this has changed. Fields linked to powerful professions or commercial markets, such as medicine, law, engineering, and business, have now gained the upper hand. These fields offer students pathways to lucrative job markets (Walters, 2004).

As colleges and universities are flooded with an unprecedented number of applicants, school selection moves upward to higher education. Students in different institutions and fields face unequal prospects. Universities and colleges sort these larger masses for vastly different occupational and social opportunities. Since there are simply not enough high-paying jobs for all graduates, entry into the most advantageous slots in higher education is becoming increasingly valuable. Required high-school grades—the prime currency for entrance to universities—have steadily risen over the past decade. Many universities are boosting their entrance standards and tuition fees, gaining repute not only by admitting top students but also by rejecting large numbers of qualified students. Institutions that were already highly exclusive are increasingly selective, while the less discriminating are expanding their enrolments.

Fields linked to powerful professions or commercial markets, such as medicine, law, engineering, and business, offer students pathways to lucrative job markets.

SOURCE: © Andresr/Shutterstock.

The degree of stratification in higher education differs across nations. For instance, the American system is a mix of private-sector and public institutions that are arrayed on a steep prestige hierarchy. American higher education has famous Ivy League universities, elite liberal arts colleges, and flagship public universities that greatly overshadow less-renowned entities. This steep, entrenched system makes the name of elite institutions important to employers. Canadian higher education, in comparison, not only lacks a private sector but also lacks a steep institutional hierarchy (Davies and Hammack, 2005). Until recently, Canadian governments have allowed only publicly funded universities. The resources allocated to these institutions have been fairly equal, while their American counterparts are much more unequal. Although the top American colleges and universities select from a national and international pool of applicants, only small numbers of Canadian undergraduates cross provincial or territorial borders, and most commute to their local institution. Canada has a relatively small national market for undergraduate credentials. Although degrees from top-ranked colleges in the United States can offer great opportunities there, few employers in Canada value the name of any one Canadian university over others.

Accordingly, Americans have long ranked their universities, but the practice is relatively new in Canada. The best-known Canadian rankings are compiled by *Maclean's* magazine. The magazine gives high scores to institutions with such attributes as large libraries, incoming students with top high-school grades and from other provinces and territories, faculty with research awards, and small classes. Although popular, this practice has been criticized for using questionable measures and for creating an artificial image of hierarchy and competition among our universities. However, university administrators take them seriously and strive to improve their relative position. In 2011, the top three "primarily undergraduate" universities according to *Maclean's* were Mount Allison (Sackville, New Brunswick), Acadia (Wolfville, Nova Scotia), and the University of Northern British Columbia (Prince George, British Columbia). The top "comprehensive" universities were Simon Fraser (Burnaby, British Columbia), Victoria (Victoria, British Columbia), and Waterloo (Waterloo, Ontario). The top three "medical/doctoral" universities were McGill (Montreal, Quebec), the University of Toronto (Toronto, Ontario), and the University of British Columbia (Vancouver, British Columbia) (*Maclean's*, 2011).

Canada may be developing a more pronounced hierarchy in higher education. As our universities and colleges increasingly generate more of their own revenue, whether via large external research grants, corporate funds, alumni donations, or steeper tuition, some universities and colleges will likely enjoy advantages. If wealthier institutions are perceived by students and employers to offer a superior education, it may bring a steeper pecking order to Canadian higher education.

INEQUALITY AMONG STUDENTS

Within sociology, a debate has raged since the 1960s over whether schools create equal opportunity for all. Functionalists believed that schools were increasingly rewarding the best, allowing any bright students, regardless of their social backgrounds, to enter high-paying professional and managerial positions. In contrast, neo-Marxists contended that the very design of mass public schooling ensures that people who are born disadvantaged remain disadvantaged. In recent years, this claim has been extended to race and gender, with many analysts arguing that female students and those who are members of minority groups are treated poorly in school and are given little choice but to enter low-paying jobs in female and minority-group "job ghettos." The claim here is that schools worsen existing inequalities by stereotyping disadvantaged youth, devaluing their cultures and skills, and steering them into lower streams. Sociologists have conducted research on this topic for decades. The early research focused mostly on social class, but it has since broadened to include gender and race. This research has consistently uncovered the following patterns.

First, educational attainment for youth from all class backgrounds has steadily risen over the past half century. As Table 12.1 shows, more Canadians from all walks of life attend school for more years than did their fathers. Second, despite this expansion, student success has been found to be consistently related to socioeconomic background. This has been true not only across time but also across the world, and, indeed, it is one of the "iron laws" in the sociology of education. Youth from less advantaged backgrounds are repeatedly overrepresented in lower streams, get lower grades, drop out of school at higher rates, and are underrepresented in higher education. Inequalities along socioeconomic lines were evident when such data were first collected and they have persisted ever since, not only in Canada but also in other Western nations (Anisef, 1974; Blossfeld and Shavit, 1993; De Broucker and Lavallée, 1998; Gamoran, 2001; Guppy and Arai, 1994; Knighton, 2002; Krahn, 2004; Porter, Porter, and Blishen, 1982; Ryan and Adams, 1999; Wanner, 2000).

To illustrate these inequalities, we can examine Table 12.1, which shows the proportion of Canadians who were age 21 in 2006 who had ever attended a postsecondary institution. The top row of Table 12.1 shows that 74.7 percent of Canadians of that age had attended a university, community college, or CEGEP. However, this percentage differs for different levels of parental schooling. For example, the likelihood of someone attaining a university degree was 24.3 percent if neither parent had any postsecondary education, but it rose to 49.2 percent if at least one parent had a postsecondary education. We see a clear socioeconomic effect in Table 12.1; the likelihood of attaining a university degree more than doubles across levels of parental education. These findings are typical of dozens of studies on this topic.

However, a different picture emerges when we compare the school success of males and females. Males once had a virtual monopoly on higher education, but this imbalance began to change in the late 1950s. By the 1980s, more women than men were attending university. Females now drop out of high school in fewer numbers, graduate more often, enter universities in greater numbers, and score higher on many standardized tests (Frenette and Zeman, 2008). Today, women have surpassed men on most measures of education attainment.

TABLE 12.1 POSTSECONDARY PARTICIPATION OF CANADIANS AGE 21 IN 2006 (IN PERCENTAGE)

	ATTENDED A POSTSECONDARY INSTITUTION	ATTENDED COMMUNITY COLLEGE OR CEGEP	ATTENDED UNIVERSITY
All Canadians	74.7	33.0	41.7
Family income			
Below $50,000	66.2	34.8	31.4
$50 000+	79.0	32.1	46.9
Aboriginal status			
Aboriginal	51.1	28.0	23.1
Non-Aboriginal	75.4	33.2	42.2
Parents' education			
No postsecondary	60.9	36.6	24.3
Some postsecondary	80.7	31.5	49.2
Immigration status			
First generation	86.6	29.6	57.0
Second generation	83.0	30.0	53.0
Nonimmigrant	71.2	34.2	37.0

SOURCE: Adapted from Statistics Canada data in McMullen (2011), "Postsecondary Education Participation among Underrepresented and Minority Groups," Table 1. Reproduced with permission.

What explains this reversal? It partly reflects the success of the women's movement; partly the entry of women into traditionally male-dominated professions, such as law and medicine; and partly how some "female-dominated" occupations, such as teaching, nursing, and social work, not only grew but also demanded higher-level educational certificates. Men's attainment has not kept pace, partly because substantial numbers of men continue to work in blue-collar jobs, such as mining and construction, which rarely require postsecondary schooling (Guppy and Arai, 1994).

Although higher numbers of women are going to university, they often enter different fields from their male counterparts. Figure 12.3 shows the distribution of university graduates among selected fields of study in 2007. While the majority of all students in Canadian universities are female, women do not form the majority in fields that are related to math, computer science, or engineering. Of course, these numbers are *very* different from those of previous eras. For instance, in the early 1960s, about 25 percent of university graduates were women; in some fields, such as forestry, *no* women graduated, and several others, such as law, had only a handful of female graduates (Statistics Canada, 2001). But while this pattern has certainly changed, and while such fields as business, law, and medicine have seen dramatic change, women continue to be underrepresented in several dynamic and well-paying fields (see also Buchmann, DiPrete, and McDaniel, 2008).

Patterns of educational attainment by Aboriginal and immigration status show that on average, second- and especially first-generation immigrants exceed nonimmigrants in postsecondary participation, particularly in attending university (Table 12.1). Meanwhile, Aboriginal Canadians have a much lower participation rate in postsecondary education and university attendance than do non-Aboriginal Canadians. Other data show that Aboriginal, black, and Hispanic Canadians have lower-than-average participation rates (Davies and Guppy, 2006). What accounts for these variations? An explanation must take three legacies into account: differences in socioeconomic status, colonization, and immigration policy.

The large variation among minority groups is partly a product of Canada's changed immigration policy. Whereas recruitment in previous eras targeted Europeans with relatively low levels of schooling, since the late 1960s Canada has targeted Asians with advanced educational credentials. As a result, living conditions for immigrants vary widely. Some of them enter the country with profiles that typically promote

FIGURE 12.3 PERCENTAGE OF MALE AND FEMALE UNDERGRADUATE STUDENTS WITHIN EACH PROGRAM, 2007

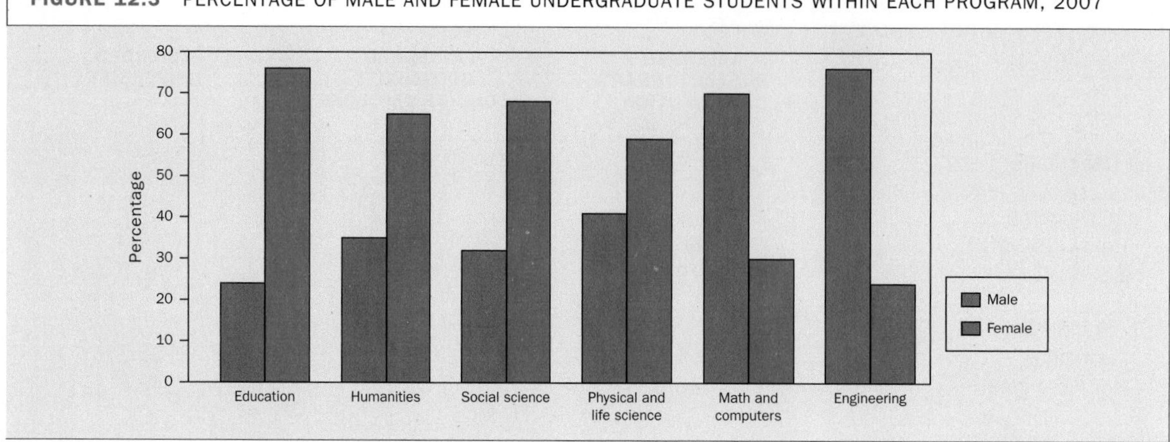

SOURCE: Statistics Canada, *Education Indicators in Canada: Report of the Pan-Canadian Education Indicators Program*, October 2009 (http://www.statcan.gc.ca/pub/81-582-x/81-582-x2009003-eng.htm).

educational success—high levels of parental education, comfortable incomes, urban residence—while others do not. Thus, Canada's educational rankings partly reflect the "inputs" from the immigration system as well as its own internal processes. Meanwhile, Aboriginal Canadians are products of colonialism, segregation, and discrimination, which render them the most impoverished ethnic group in Canada.

Given these patterns of attainment, a question arises: Do schools ameliorate inequalities in society, maintain them, or make them worse? This question is difficult to settle empirically because almost everyone goes to school. If there were some groups or regions where youth didn't go to school, then researchers could see whether the presence of education worsens or improves rates of inequality. For something that resembles these conditions, sociologists have looked to the time of the year in which few students are in school: summer. Although such research is scant in Canada, a large American literature is available (Alexander, Entwistle, and Steffen-Olsen, 2007; Burkam, Ready, Lee, and LoGerfo, 2004; Downey, von Hippel, and Broh, 2004). Its basic logic runs like this: If schools gave superior treatment to middle-class children, then student learning gaps (as measured by standardized test scores) would grow over the school year and would either stagnate or shrink during the summer months. Alternatively, if such gaps grow in the summer and narrow during the school year, then schools probably do not disadvantage youth of lower socioeconomic standing and may even mitigate the effects of home and neighbourhood. This research is almost unanimous in its basic conclusion: Schooling *reduces* learning gaps along socioeconomic lines, while these gaps widen in the summer when students are not in school. Researchers conclude that schools indeed function as equalizers, at least in terms of measured learning.

The near-mountain of empirical research on school inequalities thus lends support to a more nuanced position. Schools can be seen as progressive institutions that offer opportunities for all youth but are limited in their power to eliminate inequalities. Contemporary schools have enjoyed some success in reducing inequality, but they have not come close to totally eliminating such disparities. Affluent children have many more advantages and fare better in school because of their advantaged home environments.

SOCIALIZATION

Contemporary sociologists offer different depictions of how schools socialize their students. According to structural-functionalist theory (Dreeben, 1967), schools teach modern values. As societies industrialize, urbanize, and become more cosmopolitan, schools provide a common culture to compensate for the declining influence of religion. Schools are said to transmit such values as universalism (which involves treating everyone as equal, rights-bearing individuals) and meritocracy (a system in which social rewards go to people with talent who exert effort in open competitions). But rather than teaching these new values overtly, the functionalists contend that schools teach them a **hidden curriculum.** Teachers do not repeatedly lecture students on universalism and meritocracy but instead teach these values by running schools in a universalistic and meritocratic fashion—students learn by doing. By treating all students equally before common rules, schools are seen to embody the values of universalism, and by rewarding deserving students, they are seen to teach the value of meritocracy. Thus, modern schools teach core values by virtue of their very structure.

Other sociologists see a darker side to school socialization. For instance, Marxists also claim that schools impose a hidden curriculum—but one that promotes obedience to authority, not cheery modern values (e.g., Bowles and Gintis, 1976; see Box 12.1). They contend that public education is structured to support capitalism by creating a disciplined labour force. By organizing student learning in a competitive manner and having students vie for grades and rewards, schools are said to mirror capitalist competition and individualism. Likewise, feminists and many students of race claim that schools impose subordinate identities on their students. (This argument is elaborated below.)

Functionalists claim that schools teach universalism and meritocracy, while Marxists assert that schools impose obedience to authority.
SOURCE: PhotoDisc.

To assess these theories, it is useful to think of school socialization as a continuum. At one extreme are boarding schools, where the institution regulates virtually all facets of life—not only lessons but also how and when students sleep, eat, dress, and play. The school becomes the student's entire social universe, resembling what sociologists call a *total institution*, an all-controlling organization that remakes people's identities, where people are isolated from the larger society and are strictly controlled by a specialized staff. In boarding schools, teachers become powerful socializing agents, forging identities and having an almost singular impact on how pupils speak, look, and act. At the other extreme of the continuum is online education. If a person's education consists solely of online courses taken at home, the school's position in that

BOX 12.1 WILLIS'S LEARNING TO LABOUR

One of the most famous books in sociology is Paul Willis's *Learning to Labour* (1977). Willis observed a working-class school in England's industrial north in the mid-1970s, when many working-class boys dropped out of school at age 16 and took jobs in factories. He set out to explain why they would enthusiastically accept factory jobs that other youth would reject as inferior, degrading, and low paying. Willis reasoned that it was too easy to say that these boys simply had no choice, since they experienced no physical coercion and actually exercised a degree of self-direction. To get his answer, Willis probed the cultural life of the school.

In his study, Willis found two male peer groups. One, nicknamed "the lads," was antagonistic toward teachers, lessons, school rules, and students who were diligent, deferent, and obedient. The second subculture, the "ear'oles," accepted school authority and strove to be upwardly mobile. The lads called them "ear'oles" because they saw these boys as overly passive, like a human ear, never *doing* anything, and always on the receiving side of orders. Crucially, the lads felt *superior* to the ear'oles because the lads made their own fun and excitement in school.

Although *Learning to Labour*'s description of classroom antics is rich and entertaining, the book became famous as an account of how school "resistance" helps "reproduce" the class structure. That is, when youth reject what schools have to offer, their only remaining options are bottom-level jobs. The book was also controversial for its contention that the lads embodied the culture of the working class. Since most school rebels were from working-class backgrounds, Willis saw their conflict with school as a form of *class* conflict, full of unarticulated ideological meanings. For Willis, the lads' belief that school activities were useless in the workplace was an insight into the deskilled nature of work in capitalism. Their constant denigrating of teachers' advice, he felt, signalled a recognition of the capitalist hidden curriculum. Subsequent research has questioned whether Willis's ideas can be generalized to contemporary Canada, but many remain fascinated by his depiction of male peer groups' bravado and aggression.

person's life can be marginal, something that merely appears on a computer screen, to be ignored at will. School becomes just one socializing force among many, like a television program that can be turned on or off. Most Canadian students experience school socialization somewhere between these extremes. Few attend boarding schools or take only online courses from home. Most attend public schools full-time, Monday to Friday. Bearing this reality in mind, we next explore how schools socialize students, contrasting the ways socialization in schools has changed over the past 150 years. We then consider the ways in which schools treat different groups of students differently.

CHANGING FORMS OF MORAL EDUCATION

The history of Canadian schools is one of declining religious influence and altered moral content. Canadian public schools were originally organized by churches, with Roman Catholics being granted separate schools in Ontario, and Protestants being granted separate schools in Quebec. Similar denomination-based arrangements were made in all provinces. In the mid-nineteenth century, few people questioned the proclaimed need for public schools to provide Christian teaching. The earliest schools were nominally secular, but their religious character was overt.

Egerton Ryerson, the father of public schooling in what is now Ontario, wanted schools to create literate, religious, and devoted citizens. He and other school promoters believed that religious schooling could curb an array of perceived problems, such as the rising incidence of youth crime and general ignorance (Prentice, 1977: 128). Christianity occupied a central place in public school missions for a century. Even in the 1950s, public authorities demanded strong religious influence in public schooling, with some calling for public schools to teach "cardinal virtues" and "Christian ideals" (Government of Ontario, 1950: 36–37). By the late 1960s, educators had very different ideas. Fewer educators saw their role as passing on religiously inspired wisdom, time-honoured truths, and a sense of moral duty. Instead, school socialization was to become much more individualistic. Educators increasingly sought new ways of teaching for a new age. Consider this quotation from a 1968 provincial committee report:

> Learning by its very nature is a personal matter. There is virtually a metabolism of learning which is as unique to the individual as the metabolism of digestion. Parents and teachers may create conditions with learning in mind, but the actual learning experience is intimate and subjective, for each human being reaches out to the world in his own idiosyncratic way. (Ontario Department of Education, 1968: 49)

After the late 1960s, schools saw their role less as providing moral guidance and more as creating forums for thinking about moral issues. This created a different type of moral education, at least in emerging theories of pedagogy. Students were to be exposed to a fuller range of contemporary controversies, beliefs, and ideals than before. Teachers aimed to enable students to make informed choices, rather than have them accept moral edicts. Ideals from Christianity were replaced by ideals of critical thinking, science, and multiculturalism. Educators wanted less to tell students what was unambiguously true or false and more to nurture a deeper understanding of various subject matters, based on discovery rather than repetition. More educators saw their mission as taking a critical stance toward society, exposing injustices, and questioning established interpretations of history (Hurn, 1993: 191).

What has been the impact of these changing ideals? Although both functionalist and Marxist theories can be compelling, what do empirical studies tell us about *actual* socialization in current schools?

In partial support of functionalist theory, schooling does appear to make people more "progressive," in the sense of supporting civil liberties, tolerating minorities, appreciating social justice and ethnic diversity, and embracing nontraditional roles for women (Kingston, Hubbard, Lapp, Schroeder, and Wilson, 2003; Pallas, 2000). However, schools do so in a relatively neutral and individualized manner, and they offer rather ambiguous moral messages. That is, although students are encouraged to identify with various progressive causes, such as protecting the environment, helping the homeless, fighting racism, and fundraising for overseas children, schools do this by having students relate their own experience and venture their own opinions. Classrooms increasingly have "feel-good" posters that exhort children to read and stay in school, a form of "bumper-sticker morality" containing catch phrases for quick consumption rather than deep discussion and reflection. Yet, in support of Marxist theory, schools spend most of their time on mundane matters of personal conduct, striving to get students to be orderly and task-oriented. Much of teachers' time is spent on urging students to be respectful of one another, to participate in class, and to be cooperative (e.g., Brint, Contreras, and Matthews, 2001; Jackson, Boostrom, and Hansen, 1998).

Although studies tend to support elements of both functionalist and Marxist theory, they also suggest that modes of shaping students are changing. Teachers now treat students in a more indulgent fashion than in previous eras. They see self-esteem as essential for learning and control their classes with a lighter touch than in the past. They increasingly rely on "token economies," giving small rewards to get children to comply, rather than using overt authority. They use group projects, not just individual assignments, and especially in elementary schools, students work in rotating activity centres, freely moving around the classroom and choosing their tasks. Today's schools are making less use of classic styles of enforcing obedience. Further, teachers try to inspire *all* students. Whereas schools in the past would give up on those students deemed hopeless, whether too poor, too troubled, or too slow, today's schools work hard to engage the entire student body, even the least able performers. Indeed, the law demands that schools do so.

In some respects, the socializing power of Canadian education weakens as students progress from elementary and secondary to postsecondary levels. As Mullen (2010) notes, research comparing commuters to students who reside on campus concludes that university life has a far greater impact on the values, attitudes, and psychological growth of the latter. This is especially the case for students at elite universities in the United States. However, in Canada, most college and university students are commuters. They attend classes for 10 to 15 hours per week, so are not immersed in an intensive, all-encompassing educational environment. Further, Canadian higher education institutions are not arrayed on a steep prestige hierarchy, and so are less likely to breed social elites that are relatively homogeneous and cohesive, as American Ivy League colleges and England's Oxbridge do. Nevertheless, Canadian higher education influences students in more subtle forms by reshaping their social networks (Stevens, Armstrong, and Arum, 2008). Higher education can greatly alter the number, quality, and type of social ties students enjoy, and thereby influence their subsequent job, choice of marriage partner(s), and lifestyle opportunities.

To summarize, the morality taught in public schools has shifted from religious indoctrination to a more individualized and indulgent approach that encourages students to learn by reflecting, not reciting. This change reflects the diversification of Canadian society, where moral reference points are numerous and where the sentiment exists that schools should address social problems but should not preach a monolithic doctrine. Within this secular and individualized form of education, do schools treat everyone the same? That is the question to which we now turn.

The diversification of Canadian society has influenced the way morality is taught in school.
SOURCE: Nelson Collection.

CREATING IDENTITIES? GENDER AND RACE

Historically, Canadian education prepared girls and boys for different roles in adult society. Traditional school systems were premised on the notion that most young women should be homemakers or schooled for a narrow range of "nurturing" occupations, such as nursing and elementary-school teaching. Though boys and girls were mostly grouped together at lower ages, they were often segregated at older ages, with the expectation that a select few boys would move to advanced studies (Prentice, 1977: 111–12). Although both sexes attended school, their experiences were dissimilar. Few people challenged gender traditionalism until the 1960s.

Women's educational attainment has changed since then, matching and even outpacing male attainment in many areas. But despite this apparent change, critics continue to accuse schools of continuing to reinforce traditional gender roles (American Association of University Women Educational

Foundation, 1998; Bennett DeMarrais and LeCompte, 1995; Kelly and Nihlen, 1982). They detect a hidden curriculum that quietly subordinates women, prepares them for a gendered division of labour, and sends messages about their inferiority. The explicit gender stereotyping of the late nineteenth century has only been masked, they argue, and they support their argument by pointing to several indicators beyond standard measures of school attainment.

First, feminist critics examine school staffing, noting that despite some change, most positions of power remain in the hands of men. Some observers have even called schools "academic harems." For instance, an elementary school can be staffed almost entirely by women, save for the most powerful position—the principal—who is often a man. While teaching positions in lower grades are held almost entirely by women, higher-level teaching and administrative positions are held by men. A second indicator of gender bias pertains to curriculum. For several decades, feminists have charged school textbooks with being loaded with sexist language, illustrations that depict most active characters as male, and stories that depict women in nurturing occupations and as stay-at-home moms. They also contend that high-school literature courses ignore female authors and that history textbooks disregard the contributions of women. Here there has been change, especially as most provincial governments have curriculum guidelines that monitor gender representation in most course material.

A third indicator of gender inequity is the fact that schools tolerate the conduct of male students that, in the adult world, would be considered sexual harassment. Feminist critics decry schools' "hostile hallways" in which sexual comments, touching, jokes, and leers are deemed "normal" and "natural" and are therefore tacitly permitted. Schools are said to accept such behaviour when they rationalize such acts as "boys being boys." Such rationalizations are linked to inequities in extracurricular programs. Schools continue to be accused of considering it natural that men's sports teams should receive higher priority and more funding than women's teams, an imbalance said to send a message of female inferiority. Finally, teachers stand accused of treating female students unfairly, directing girls toward stereotypical nurturing fields, such as teaching, nursing, and administrative studies. Others claim that girls' self-esteem is damaged in the classroom when teachers ignore them in favour of boys (this particular accusation has been controversial, since research suggests teachers only give males more attention for disciplinary reasons). The sum total of these inequities, it is argued, is a gendered "hidden curriculum" that alienates females from course material, dampens their aspirations, and ultimately reinforces gender inequality.

Similarly, some analysts argue that Canadian schools sometimes socialize minority students into racial identities. The historical episode of residential schools for Aboriginal children is the most blatant. In the nineteenth and twentieth centuries, the Canadian government set out to mould Aboriginal identities by sending up to half of all Aboriginal children to these schools with the intent of making them "modern Indians" who would speak English or French, convert to Christianity, and learn skills for menial jobs. The residential school was a total institution that separated Aboriginal children from their families and communities, interrupted the rhythms of their home lives, and implanted more regimented cultural norms. The legacy of this racism is felt in Aboriginal communities to this day. Likewise, young black children in some cases were singled out for discriminatory treatment in the nineteenth and early twentieth century, labelled as "coloured," and segregated in black-only schools (Axelrod, 1997: 79).

Since the 1980s, Canadian schools have responded to such problems in two ways. First, they have reworked curricula to make them more multicultural and inclusive of minority groups. Policymakers have overseen the rewriting of history and literature textbooks to better reflect the experiences of immigrants and racial minorities, and have introduced anti-racist measures to encourage students to be more accepting of diversity. For multiculturalists, schools should also cultivate cosmopolitan world citizens who identify more deeply with the global community and its concern with peace, ecological health, and the developing world's advancement, and see themselves not only as national citizens but also as members of the human race, with obligations to all people everywhere.

Although overt segregation laws have been long removed, and although multicultural curricula have been adopted in a variety of forms, some sociologists continue to charge Canadian schools with being insensitive to the needs of youth from minority groups (Dei, 2005). Schools, they contend, "racialize" children from minority groups by making them assume racial identities and experience themselves as "different" (Lewis, 2003). In this view, schools actively reinforce racial identities and inequalities. Students who are members of minority groups are seen to be ill-treated by school practices, particularly "colour-blind" policies that ignore the disadvantages of children from these groups. School multiculturalism, it is held, only superficially addresses historical legacies of racism, while white teachers are seen to be blind to experiences that are actually colour-coded and unwilling to challenge dominant understandings of race. For instance, a commissioned report accused the Ontario government's Safe Schools Act and "zero tolerance" policy of being culturally insensitive and of singling out black males for punishment (Ontario Human Rights Commission, 2003).

Partly in response to these changes, Canadian schools have attempted to accommodate minorities in a second and more controversial fashion: through greater school choice. "School choice" refers to the use of public funds that give parents more discretion in their children's education. It usually entails making available to parents a wider variety of educational options beyond a standard, local public school.

Each province has developed its own mix of support for religious and linguistic minority schools, and some sociologists support the move, reasoning that public schools have failed to meet the needs of minority youth (Dei, 2005). On these grounds, the Toronto District School Board narrowly approved the opening of a black-focus school in 2007. It will undoubtedly receive much attention in the coming years from educators and the public, not only because race is a hot-button issue in Canadian education, but also because it signals a key debate about school socialization. Underlying choice reform is a more pluralist and less individualistic vision of nation building than currently exists. Reformers see the nation as a community of communities, with schools playing a vital role in its construction. From their point of view, students' ethnicity, race, religion, and gender mediate their relationships to the national community, creating "unity through diversity." Accordingly, separate schools are needed to socialize minority groups into their own culture, defined by race, language, or religion. For opponents, however, pluralist schooling segregates students. Opponents favour multicultural education as a means of integrating all groups into society. At present, insufficient evidence exists to settle the debate.

THE LIMITS OF SCHOOL SOCIALIZATION

Although claims that schools mould gender and racial identities are very popular, one difficulty is that they assume that schools have a great deal of socializing power, rather than providing convincing evidence of their effects. It is conceivable that some educational institutions, such as residential boarding schools, may wield great socializing power, but the average public school today is far more limited in its reach. We need to recognize other socializing influences. Students clearly are influenced by forces well beyond the school—their families, neighbourhoods, workplaces, and, of course, peer groups (Looker and Thiessen, 1999).

Sociologists have long examined high-school peer groups, believing they set limits on schools' socializing sway, and how varying degrees of student autonomy may *hinder* school goals. Sociologists in the 1950s and 1960s became interested in peer cultures when they found that student populations were less deferential than in previous decades. Although most school deviance was mild, consisting of minor rule-breaking, irreverence, apathy, or truancy, it still subverted educational goals by disrupting classrooms and interrupting learning. James Coleman (1961) argued that, among adolescent peers, learning and achievement mattered less than popularity and looking good. Moreover, in the peer group, being a top student did little for a person's reputation. Coleman's ideas have since spawned a large body of research on the formation of student subcultures. This research has examined how the very structure of schooling encourages youth to respond in ways that can frustrate the socializing efforts of educators (Coleman, 1961; Tanner, 2001).

Specifically, over the decades, sociologists have interpreted youth's obsession with physical appearance, hairstyles, clothing brands, and cliques as no mere by-product of their relative immaturity. Instead, sociologists see them as responses to particular social conditions. Schools segregate youth by age, give youth little power, and require their attendance by law. Yet students do have some degree of autonomy. High school is not overly challenging for most youth. Most students have some disposable income. These conditions, sociologists argue, encourage youth to be status-conscious. Status groups emerge when social structures offer few alternative avenues for social mobility. Students become a status group because they lack power and authority but have enough autonomy to invent their own social realm within schools. By this logic, Murray Milner (2004) has likened high-school cliques to Indian castes. Castes emerged in traditional India when there was little democracy or economic mobility for people of low social rank. Upper castes obsessed about appearance, social ranking, and maintaining social distance from inferiors. They created elaborate rituals and pressures for conformity, especially for intimacies such as eating and romantic relationships.

So how are high-school cliques like castes? According to Milner, teens risk social demotion if they are seen eating or dating someone with low status. They use small cruelties and put-downs to uphold their dominance. A jock pesters a nerd to maintain his own status at the nerd's expense. Status also explains why some teens are so concerned with conforming to brand-name clothing fashions. The isolated world of high school creates pressures for cliques to display their status through consumer commodities. Since teens are largely excluded from "producer" roles in prestigious workplaces but are freely granted "consumer" roles, the latter become their main source of reputation.

Sociologists have also traced a second, more antagonistic element of student subcultures to schools' very own selection function (Cohen, 1955; Stinchcombe, 1964). In this view, since schools reward only some students and deem others to be academically unfit, they create disincentives for unsuccessful students. Low-ranked students suffer an inglorious status and get labelled as "underachievers" and channelled into streams that lead neither to postsecondary education nor to useful job-training programs. These students suffer emotional injury in schools and hunger for a more positive self-image. Accordingly, low-achieving students form anti-school subcultures as an alternative source of social recognition. These subcultures invert the values that schools try to promote, rejecting students who are rule-abiding, obedient, and hardworking, and celebrating the rule-breaker, the insolent, and the hedonist. Among males, this rebellion is epitomized by confrontations with teachers, fighting, smoking, drinking, and sexual bravado. Among females, it is marked by a flaunting of their sexuality and a preoccupation with dating. In both cases, subcultures are seen to be a youthful expression of frustration with school selection processes that thwart upward mobility.

Since the 1980s, sociologists have argued that oppositional subcultures can also take racialized forms. Fordham and Ogbu (1986) claim that African Americans criticize their high-achieving peers for "acting white," that is, for adopting the culture and language of white America and being disloyal to their own community. Such pressures are said to discourage black students from identifying with schooling. The "acting white" thesis has become very influential, but is it true? Several American sociologists have put it to the test, but most cast doubt on it. Some suggest that only a small portion of black students take oppositional stances to schools (Downey and Ainsworth-Darnell, 2002). Others argue that generic peer pressures are felt by *all* high-achieving students, regardless of race, and those who earn top grades are similarly labelled *geeks, nerds,* or *brainiacs.* Only in schools where student achievement is starkly unequal by race, they speculate, will this pressure take a racialized form (Tyson, Darity, and Castellino, 2005).

Does the "acting white" phenomenon exist in Canadian schools? Far less systematic research on the topic exists here, but some researchers claim that black Canadians sometimes form oppositional subcultures. In a field study of a Toronto high school, Patrick Solomon (1992) claimed that black males were increasingly drawn toward sports, and saw academics as a "white activity." Other sociologists, such as George Dei (2005), similarly contend that black youth are increasingly alienated from the mainstream curriculum and require alternative "black-focus" schools to nurture a more positive cultural identity.

Studies of peer groups suggest that school selection provokes at least a mild form of antagonism from lower-achieving students and that this can frustrate the efforts of educators. However, the very existence of oppositional subcultures similarly suggests that some theories may exaggerate the extent to which schools mould gender and race identities. Students learn roles in their neighbourhoods, families, media, and places of employment (which can be highly segregated), and these are competing sources of socialization that may be partly counteracted by schools.

For instance, some feminists (Holland and Eisenhart, 1990; Weis, 1990) contend that peer groups, not school officials, divert female students toward established gender roles and discourage educational advancement. Some suggest that embracing a student role may actually erode gender traditionalism. In a field study of an English secondary school, Lynn Davies (1984) found that youth in university-bound streams were relatively more "androgynous" and less conforming to gender stereotypes. In contrast, girls who were about to drop out looked forward to motherhood rather than to careers, and would-be male dropouts were more traditionally masculine. A similar pattern was found in a Canadian study that employed survey research. In a large sample of Ontario high-school students and dropouts, I found that both girls and boys in academic streams were less traditional than those in nonacademic streams, and those differences widened in later grades (Davies, 1992). Since new career opportunities for academically oriented males and females may weaken traditional conceptions of gender, it is not clear that schools continue to enforce gendered and racial identities. Though schools certainly treated females and minority students differently in the past, contemporary research shows that public schools promote more liberal and progressive views about gender and race and that schools have long been among the few places in society where boys and girls are grouped together to perform the same role.

These findings force us to think more about the *limits* of schools' socializing role. Paradoxically, as more people go to school for more years, the socializing impact of schooling may become *weaker*. More than in any previous era, schools now compete with other socializing agents. More youth are employed part-time, popular culture is everywhere, and today's parents are spending more time on developmental activities, hiring more tutors, and purchasing more extracurricular lessons for their children (Adler and Adler, 1994; Aurini, 2004; Daly, 2004; Davies, 2004; Quirke, 2006; Sayer, Bianchi, and Robinson, 2004). Schools are losing their monopoly on structured lessons and developmental activities, at least among the middle class. The upshot is that their unique impact on students may be on the wane. Rather than being a total institution, schools are moving toward the weaker end of the socializing continuum, no longer imparting a cohesive ideology and now competing with more socializing agents than before.

SOCIAL ORGANIZATION

For Weber, modern schooling reflected the emergence of a rationalized worldview in the organizational form of bureaucracy. With schools now being one of Canada's largest expenditures, costing at least $60 billion per year, they need to be seen as legitimate organizations that generate useful skills in a relatively efficient manner. Contemporary theorists offer widely differing accounts of whether schools are indeed efficiency-seeking organizations. Some see schools as converging with Weber's ideal type of bureaucracy; others do not.

THEORIES OF SCHOOL ORGANIZATION

The most straightforward account is offered by economists. **Human capital theory** asserts that the school's role is primarily economic: to generate needed job skills. The theory assumes that both individuals and governments "invest" their time and dollars in schools because they believe it will lead to prosperity. The costs of schooling—books, buildings, teacher salaries—are "inputs," and student learning is the "output" or product. Human capital theorists see schools as organized to maximize student skills. If the value of the output exceeds its cost, schooling becomes a worthwhile investment, such as when individuals' expenditures in schooling early in their life eventually raise their earnings or improve their health. Schooling is thus seen as a form of capital—*human* capital—since people cannot be separated from their knowledge and skills in the same way that they can be distinguished from their financial and physical assets (Becker, 1964).

Indeed, research consistently shows that education *does* pay. On average, people with more years of schooling earn higher wages and have better employment rates (Walters, 2004). School pays, but why? Although some analysts point directly to the skills that are generated through education, many sociologists question the extent to which schooling improves useful job-related skills and whether jobs use what schools teach.

"Credentialists" like Randall Collins (1979) are generally skeptical of human capital theory for at least two reasons. First, usually far fewer high-skilled jobs are available than there are graduates from high schools, colleges, and universities. Employees are often overqualified; available jobs often do not require their learned skills (Livingstone, 1998). Second, Collins sees weak connections between school content and the workplace. Much schooling—hours of essay writing, studying quadratic equations and periodic tables, practising the tuba—has little to do with most job realities. School curricula develop according to their own dynamics, he argues, and seldom in response to employers' demands. Further, employers rarely bother to look at student grades when hiring. With the exception of a few professions, merely possessing a diploma, certificate, or degree will suffice. If school content were really connected tightly to the job market, Collins reasons, employers would surely use grades as vital indicators of a candidate's suitability. So why do employers seek graduates with credentials if little of their learning actually connects to job demands? Collins offers several answers.

One is **credential inflation.** Just as monetary inflation devalues money, modern education devalues credentials. Just as a dollar cannot purchase the same goods it could 30 years ago, a high-school diploma does not lead to the same job it did

30 years ago. Inflation results from intense competition in the labour market. When hiring, managers in large corporations and in government are often flooded with job applicants. The sheer number of candidates makes careful and personal consideration of each one impossible. Hence, managers need a bureaucratic screening device, a procedure to reduce the applicant pool that is seen to be fair and efficient. Over the past few decades, employers have increasingly used credentials for this purpose, even for jobs that are not complex or demanding. Hiring someone with credentials may not reflect a need for specific skills. Seeking a leg up on competitors, people comply by obtaining an educational credential. This inflation creates a growing gap between the competencies required in jobs and the level of education possessed by job occupants.

Another reason that employers seek graduates with credentials concerns **professionalization.** Professional associations, such as the Canadian Medical Association, control occupational standards by setting the educational requirements for their profession. By demanding higher levels of education, these occupations can limit the number of eligible competitors. Over the decades, many occupations have raised entry requirements—school teachers, nurses, accountants, and social workers, to name a few. Sociologists see this as part of a process of professionalization in which an occupation tries to raise its standing and command higher wages. Think of all the requirements that didn't exist 40 years ago: M.S.W., M.B.A., B.N., and so on. What fascinates Collins is that teaching, nursing, social work, and business easily survived in past generations without demanding these credentials, and little evidence suggests that these occupations have become so much more complex as to necessitate these higher levels of schooling.

Collins also contends that some employers prefer to hire employees with advanced credentials just because they are prestigious. According to Collins, many employers hire university graduates for jobs to gain trust from clients and customers. Firms want to appear serious, businesslike, and trustworthy and not "fly-by-night." For Collins, well-educated employees are the human equivalent of a nice piece of office furniture: They signal that the firm is honourable. Advertising a workforce with many letters trailing their names (B.A., B.Sc., L.L.B., M.B.A, M.A., Ph.D., etc.) can be a mark of status in a world where business transactions can be highly uncertain and in which clients seek signals of high repute.

SCHOOL AUTHORITY: FROM TRADITION TO RATIONALITY TO MARKETS?

Premodern schools were typically small and informal, and educational authority was decentralized. Canada had thousands of school boards, most of which controlled only a few small schools. Each teacher had little formal training and enjoyed wide discretion over his or her classroom. Lessons were taught without many formal guidelines. There was little large-scale planning and there were few educational laws. Teachers had parental-like authority over students. They could discipline largely as they pleased, often resorting to corporal punishment, with little fear of reprisal. Curricula were justified in terms of passing on time-honoured doctrine and cultural traditions. Teachers were proclaimed to be moral trustees of society.

All this changed during the twentieth century. In Weber's terms, modern institutions like schools were rationalized. Public education was justified less in moral terms and more by its social utility. Canadian schools cut "irrelevant" subjects like ancient languages and adopted new ones, usually justified in terms of their necessity for daily living. Teachers were seen less as trustees of the common good and more as semi-professionals with skills and responsibilities.

Rationalization was accompanied by a change in organizational form. Schools grew and looked less like little red houses and more like office buildings. They were increasingly governed by general rules. Lines of control were formalized from top to bottom, with hierarchical chains of command and clearly defined responsibilities. Regulations delegated authority to credentialed officials in a more specialized division of labour, particularly at upper-grade levels. Personnel were selected for their advanced training rather than for personal ties to highly ranked officials. Public schools hired certified teachers with university diplomas. Curricula were standardized, approved by higher-ranking bodies, and arranged in uniform age-graded levels. Modern schools became bureaucracies.

After World War II, governments across Canada saw education as increasingly necessary for prosperity and the development of the citizenry. Consequently, they gave public high schools a new mandate: to retain as many youth for as many years as possible. Seeing only a few students as suitable for advanced education became passé. A new norm emerged: Virtually everyone ought to complete high school. Those who did not were to be deemed either deviant or proof of a failing system. The big challenge for schools was how to translate these new ideals into new realities.

The expanded mission for schooling transformed secondary schools within a generation. School officials interpreted their mandate as delivering a broadly comparable education to all students. They further standardized schooling, from physical plant, to teacher training, to curricula. Authority and power were increasingly wielded in distant hierarchies rather than in local communities, an approach that has been dubbed, somewhat derisively, as the "one best system" (Tyack, 1974), faulted for being indifferent to the needs of individual pupils. Critics commonly portrayed schools as resembling nineteenth-century industrial factories, a "one-size-fits-all" institution.

However, with a new mandate, schools needed to devise ways to motivate an increasingly wide range of students. That was not easy. In earlier times, high schools could steer students who were uninterested in academic work into jobs. But now schools were expected to retain the vast bulk of youth, including those with learning disabilities or little academic ambition. Since teachers encountered many youths who found academic work neither appealing nor absorbing, the big challenge for modern secondary schools was to accommodate a wider range of student aptitude, preparedness, abilities, and motivation than any high school had ever faced before. Again, that was not easy. Unlike the monetary incentives that some organizations offer their employees, the incentives that schools offer their students can be weak. Their most obvious reward is a grade—the prime currency for higher-education admissions. But for youth who do not seek studies beyond high school, grades can be nearly useless. Schools have other organizational constraints, too. Teachers would love to have students who enrol on a fully voluntary basis, but many students attend school only through compulsion. Many teachers want to deal individually with students, but current funding levels force most classes to consist of 20 to 30 students. As it stands, teachers face large classes of captive students with greatly varying abilities and levels of motivation.

This has been the core challenge for reformers. **Progressive pedagogy,** rooted in the ideas of John Dewey in the early twentieth century, has been a force in Canadian schools since the 1960s. Progressives do not want schooling to be merely utilitarian for students and aim instead to nurture intrinsic forms of motivation, to engage students and have them work voluntarily. Modern teachers want to entice students to do their work not just for grades or to evade sanction, but out of true curiosity. Dewey called for schools that catered to the interests of the learner. By having students direct their own learning, schools could unleash students' intrinsic motivation, he reasoned. Over the decades, many reforms have attempted to engage students within the parameters of schools' organizational constraints (Tyack and Cuban, 1995).

Progressives reformed schools by destructuring classrooms, creating curricula with fewer rote and memory-based exercises, and relaxing discipline. Traditional classrooms strictly regulated student talk and movement by arraying student desks in straight rows. But in the 1970s, progressives saw such regimentation as stifling student imaginations. They encouraged more interaction and tolerated some chatting and freer movement in the classroom. They also decorated classrooms, adorning walls with student art work and colourful posters, often next to traditional emblems like the flag. Corporal punishment was largely abandoned in favour of notions of student rights. The binding idea was that departures from traditional schooling were needed to motivate students (see Box 12.2).

After witnessing these changes, sociologists in the 1980s offered a different take on bureaucratic schools (Powell, Farrar, and Cohen, 1985). In their eyes, decades of reform had made schools more like "shopping malls" than factories. They were struck by the transformation of schools into human service organizations that strove to accommodate their students. Schools became mall-like, they argued, by differentiating courses by degree of difficulty and creating electives to cater to student choice. They created "specialty shops" for students with different abilities, whether "gifted," ESL, or specially able. Schools bolstered extracurricular activities and devised services to address a wide variety of social, physical, and emotional problems. Educators became sensitized to different kinds of learning styles, as proclaimed by theories of "multiple intelligences," which claim that student ability in, say, dance, should be valued as much as student ability in math (Gardner, 1999; see Table 12.2).

The theory of multiple intelligences was developed by Dr. Howard Gardner (1998), who contends that the traditional notion of intelligence based on IQ testing is an overly narrow model of human potential. Gardner instead proposes that there are eight different kinds of intelligence. Some Canadian schools have embraced this theory and are designing curricula to match each type of intelligence. By doing so, they

BOX 12.2 FREE SCHOOLS

"Free schools" took the experimental attitude of the progressives further by destructuring all aspects of schooling. Inspired by Summerhill, an English private school founded in the 1920s, free schools rocketed to prominence in the 1960s and early 1970s, when hundreds of them were opened across North America. These schools were founded on the belief that only self-motivated, self-regulated, and self-evaluated education could nurture true learning. In many free schools, daily activities were chosen by students. There was no mandatory attendance. Most school exercises were optional. Standard methods of evaluating students with grades or report cards were condemned, since true learning was thought to be too personal to be measured, and since grading could create power inequities between staff and students.

Free schools were to be pressure-free places for students to develop their own interests and talents, without any compulsion to compete with others or to comply with some external standard. Yet despite generating an incredible amount of excitement, most free schools closed in a few short years. Without the benefit of clear and enforceable rules for student conduct, many became unmanageable, and teachers quickly became disillusioned and fatigued. Lacking the bureaucratic trappings of education, such as standardized curricula, certified teachers, timetables, and formal courses, the public grew skeptical of whether they were schools at all, and therefore free schools appeared to be illegitimate in the eyes of politicians. Some survived in the form of "alternative schools." Operated by public boards of education, these schools are less structured than regular schools but still use mandatory rules of attendance and approved curricula.

Free schools, popular in the 1960s and 1970s, were so unstructured that many people questioned whether they were schools at all.

SOURCE: © Roger Hutchings/Alamy.

illustrate how schools are attempting to accommodate a wide range of student needs.

Although secondary schools in the past had openly promoted academic achievement, the shopping-mall high school eased expectations. Mastery of core subjects was no longer expected from all students. Students who desired a more enriched curriculum could still find it, and lower-achieving students could pass from grade to grade in return for little more than orderly attendance. High schools had evolved unwritten rules about how tough certain courses should be. These informal rules unofficially designated elective courses to be easier than required math and science courses. Teachers in the latter subjects could legitimately demand much effort and time, but other teachers could face rebellion from students, parents, and even administrators if they dared to expect anything comparable.

The idea of the shopping-mall high school was introduced in the mid-1980s and it accurately depicted how schools were then striving to accommodate students. This effort has since sparked controversy, however. Over the past decade, educators have been stung by emerging demands to raise standards and become "accountable." Canadian policymakers are promoting higher standards as they understand them, usually in the guise of standardized performance indicators.

Today, critics are claiming that public schools are too bureaucratic. For instance, Chubb and Moe (1990) see public bureaucracies as aloof and slow to change, and requiring a mechanism to inject quality-orienting dynamics. These reformers condemn public education as an inefficient monopoly that is unresponsive to its clients, and they hail "market" reforms for their potential to create competitive pressures, similar to those faced by for-profit businesses. Under the banner of "school choice," these reformers want to force schools to survive only by collecting funds directly from fee-paying clients. The imperative to attract clients, they contend, has many advantages. It can match the tastes of parents and educators. It can encourage new providers to enter the educational field, bringing innovation to schooling, and devising customized programs

TABLE 12.2 THE THEORY OF MULTIPLE INTELLIGENCES

INTELLIGENCE	END-STATES	CORE COMPONENTS
Logical mathematical	Scientist, mathematician	Sensitivity to, and capacity to discern, logical or numerical patterns; ability to handle long chains of reasoning
Linguistic	Poet, journalist	Sensitivity to sounds, rhythms, and meanings of words; sensitivity to the different functions of language
Musical	Composer, violinist	Abilities to produce and appreciate rhythm, pitch, and timbre; appreciation of the forms of musical expressiveness
Spatial	Navigator, sculptor	Capacities to perceive the visual-spatial world accurately and to perform transformations on one's initial perceptions
Bodily kinesthetic	Dancer, athlete	Abilities to control one's body movements and to handle objects skillfully
Interpersonal	Therapist, salesperson	Capacities to discern and respond appropriately to the moods, temperaments, motivations, and desires of other people
Intrapersonal	Person with detailed, accurate self-knowledge	Access to one's own feelings and the ability to discriminate among them and draw upon them to guide behaviour, knowledge of one's own strengths, weaknesses, desires, and intelligences
Naturalist	Biologist, naturalist	Abilities to recognize and categorize objects and processes in nature

SOURCE: Adapted from Gardner, H. and Hatch, T., 1989, "Multiple Intelligences Go to School: Educational Implications of the Theory of Multiple Intelligences," *Educational Researcher, 18*, (8), 4–10, American Educational Research Association.

for their clients. And it can boost school performance in the form of standardized test scores, since market-based schools will presumably be motivated to raise their quality to attract customers (Ouchi, 2003).

School choice is indeed growing in Canada in at least two forms. One creates more choice within the public school system, expanding the menu of programs beyond standard school offerings. For instance, the City of Edmonton has largely reinvented its school system by offering a smorgasbord of pedagogical choice and offering a variety of special-theme schools, including those that specialize in sports, science, language, arts, intensive academics, alternative pedagogy, and multiple intelligences (Taylor and Woollard, 2003). Another Alberta initiative has been to create "charter schools," independently run but government funded, each pursuing a special theme, whether ESL, traditional academics, Suzuki music and philosophy, science and math, or programs aimed at gifted, Aboriginal, female, or at-risk students (Bosetti, 2001). The second type of choice is private schooling. The proportion of Canadian students enrolled in private schools is growing, particularly in affluent locales. For instance, in Toronto, 10 percent of students are enrolled in private schools, higher than the 7 percent national average (Davies and Quirke, 2005). More than 60 nonreligious private schools have opened in the city in the past 15 years. These schools attempt to appeal to their customers by developing specialty programs and small classes. Almost all offer some sort of specialty, creating an astonishing array of programs and philosophies of teaching, each seeking a niche in a competitive marketplace. Similarly, home-schooling is growing in Canada, as more parents are turning to themselves to provide educational options for their children (Arai, 2000; Aurini and Davies, 2005).

Are Canadian families embracing more competitive educational strategies? Traditionally, private education has been reserved either for elites or for members of religious minorities. But various forms of private education are now expanding. The proportion of Canadian students enrolled in private schools grew from 5 percent to 7 percent over the past decade. The number of Montessori schools is growing (Aurini, 2002). The tutoring industry has also undergone a staggering transformation over the past 30 years, with the number of tutoring businesses growing between 200 percent and 500 percent in major Canadian cities (Aurini and Davies, 2004). In 2007, a third of Canadian parents reported that they had hired tutors for their children (Canadian Council on Learning, 2007; Box 12.3).

Although these private alternatives certainly create more variety in education, there is still no evidence that they offer higher-quality schooling than regular public schools do, taking into account the socioeconomic advantages of their students. Indeed, rather than being more academically intensive, many of these schools have strong "shopping-mall" and "progressive" elements, like those that have inspired public educators for decades. Proud of their customized offerings, they prize pedagogical freedom and intimate relations above all. Yet, as tuition-charging schools, they lack any mandate to ensure equal access. Despite good intentions, only wealthier families can afford them. These schools illustrate the tension between satisfying yearnings for choice and providing equity.

Indeed, a flip side of market reasoning is that the customer should pay. Such thinking has permitted Canadian universities to deregulate tuition fees for their professional schools, such as dentistry, law, medicine, and M.B.A. programs. Administrators of these professional programs believe student demand will not be deterred by soaring costs, since professional degrees often lead to high incomes. Accordingly, they have raised fees well above the Canadian average for undergraduates of $5366 in 2011-12, charging up to $37 501 in 2011-12 for a year's tuition in an executive M.B.A. program (Statistics Canada, 2011).

BOX 12.3 THE GROWING NICHE FOR TUTORING CHAINS: PREKINDERGARTNERS' ACADEMIC PREP

Merrick is 5. On this crisp October afternoon, he'd just finished a flashcard drill of simple words, and the children next to him were following suit. "Cap. Lap. Map. Trap," they recited. "Cat. Fat. Rat." Academic tutoring has dropped down to the sandbox-and-nap-time set. In recent years, early-childhood education experts and industry analysts say, more parents have started sending their 3- to 5-year-old children to for-profit tutoring centers to give them an academic edge in elementary school.

Tutoring for tots, some say, has been spurred by increased academic accountability in schools, heightened competition to get into top-ranked colleges, and new research that links early exposure to books, music, and language to better academic performance in later years. And the convenience and recognizable brand names of some established tutoring companies seem to attract parents, some industry-watchers say. While pre-K tutoring is now just a tiny segment of the $2.5 billion K–12 tutoring industry—about 1 percent—that share is likely to grow as more parents and policymakers emphasize early-childhood education. There is an annual growth rate of roughly 15 percent in the K–12 tutoring industry overall in the past few years.

Yet while some companies wax enthusiastic about pre-K tutoring, many early-childhood experts decry the trend. Tutoring 3- to 5-year-olds in a classroom setting with flashcards and workbooks can be overly prescriptive, dampen enthusiasm for learning, and even spur developmental problems, some scholars say.

"Parents have the idea that education is a race, but it is not," said David Elkind, the author of the 1981 book *The Hurried Child* and a child-development professor at Tufts University in Medford, Mass. "However well-intentioned, [pre-K tutoring] is a moneymaking thing that builds on parental anxieties, with no research or support."

"Are [parents] damaging their kids for life? Hardly," said Barbara A. Willer, a deputy executive director of the Washington-based NAEYC. "But there's a larger issue. As a society, do we make sure that tutoring is available just to those who can afford it, or do we ensure that there are high-quality pre-K programs for all?"

Merrick's mother, Mary Jansen, would agree. She says the program encourages her son to achieve beyond his grade level. And that, she says, is necessary for Merrick to succeed in school. "Kids can't only be little kids anymore," she said, after her son finished his half-hour tutoring session here. "I want him to go to the college he wants. As long as it's Ivy League."

SOURCE: Rhea R. Borja, 2005, "Growing Niche for Tutoring Chains: Prekindergartners' Academic Prep," *Education Week, 25* (8), 10. Reprinted with permission from *Education Week*.

Although these fee hikes may not have discouraged student demand, they do appear to be influencing the composition of student bodies in these programs. A recent study suggests that when programs deregulate their fees, they become more likely to accept students who have highly educated parents and to have students from poorer backgrounds who are eligible for bursaries and scholarships. The losers in the process appear to be middle-class students, who lack advantageous family backgrounds, yet are often ineligible for income-contingent loans and bursaries (Frenette, 2005).

These tuition trends reflect broad changes in the organizational form and governance of postsecondary schooling. In 1850, Canadian higher education consisted of a scattering of small and mostly religious institutions. Between 1850 and 1990, the system was expanded, secularized, socialized, rationalized, coordinated, and "massified." Since 1990, most provinces have significantly reduced per-student funding, while at the same time raising performance expectations. In response, universities and colleges have become more attuned to market and government forces. In finding ways to secure new revenue sources, they have transformed themselves. For instance, to attract and accommodate new kinds of students, colleges and universities have moved far beyond their conventional weekday timetables on their main campuses and are offering courses in evenings, on weekends, at branch campuses, and with online technologies—much as a business enterprise would change to pursue new customers. To engage in large-scale fundraising, most universities and colleges now have large public relations offices that court would-be donors and corporate sponsors. To compete with rivals, some are even engaging in "image makeovers," using consultants to "rebrand" themselves, sometimes by replacing traditional coats of arms with corporate logos and slogans (Kirp, 2004). These activities signal the encroachment of traditional missions of teaching and research by new competitive pressures, a trend decried by some as "academic capitalism" (Slaughter and Rhoades, 2004; Box 12.4).

At the same time, provinces are expecting colleges and universities to demonstrate their effective and efficient use of tax monies by participating in quality

BOX 12.4 IS CANADA SINGING THE "IVORY TOWER BLUES"?

In *Ivory Tower Blues,* sociologists James Côté and Anton Allahar (2006) warn of a crisis in Canadian higher education. They describe how universities enrol unmotivated students and inflate their grades, with some students attaining B's with minimal levels of effort and skill. Much of their discussion draws on their own experiences at the University of Western Ontario, but they also cite findings from the National Survey of Student Engagement. The NSSE suggests that even though only 10 percent of all undergraduates are highly engaged with their studies, and 40 percent are largely disengaged, the vast majority report regularly earning A's and B's. The loss of academic integrity is tolerated by administrators who, Côté and Allahar argue, regard students as "consumers" who pay much-needed tuition and accept the situation as the inevitable by-product of university expansion. These ideas have sparked controversy. Supporters have championed *Ivory Tower Blues* for fearlessly exposing one of higher education's dirty secrets. Critics accuse Côté and Allahar of exaggerating problems, romanticizing the students of yesteryear, and failing to acknowledge the need for new instructional methods to inspire today's youth (for a warehouse of these debates, see www.ivorytowerblues.com).

Which side in the debate is correct? *Ivory Tower Blues* acknowledges that many students in past generations opted to coast toward a "Gentleman's C" rather than exert themselves for a higher grade. But Côté and Allahar contend that today's disengaged students, unlike those of yesteryear, now receive inflated grades, and on this point they are supported by other researchers (e.g., Anglin and Meng, 2000). In addition, new American research suggests that some students can graduate from university without learning very much (Arum and Roska, 2010). Moreover, Côté and Allahar and their critics all agree that universities need new strategies to involve students. But does this combination of disengagement and grade inflation amount to a full-blown crisis? At this time, there is little evidence that Canada's universities are suffering from a loss of legitimacy, but Côté and Allahar are referring to another kind of "crisis": a longstanding erosion of liberal ideals of higher education. For them, universities should strive to transform students' hearts and minds, broaden their intellectual horizons, and create exemplary citizens. *Ivory Tower Blues* laments the declining authority of those ideals, along with the tendency for many to champion higher education only for its economic utility. Their sequel *Lowering Higher Education* (Côté and Allahar, 2011) responds to their critics and suggests practices that might halt further decline in standards.

assurance programs. Politicians increasingly want closer links between these institutions and local industries and labour markets, and to justify their receipt of public funds by meeting "key performance indicators" that signal compliance with standards of hiring, course content, and graduate placement. Importantly, however, these "KPIs" do not include any measures of student learning, but instead consist of bureaucratic formalisms that are easily counted, such as ensuring that faculty have Ph.D.s or that courses fulfill required numbers of hours. British Columbia, Alberta, Ontario, and New Brunswick have also passed legislation allowing the opening of private degree-granting bodies, reasoning that the marketplace has a role to play in helping meet new demands for higher education. These pressures are spawning greater organizational variety in higher education, one marked by private and for-profit universities, international branch campuses, transnational enrolments, corporate involvement, and online technologies. Venerable ideals of intellectual elites retreating in quiet contemplation are giving way to a new image of bustling "learning organizations" that can teach the masses by responding to ever-shifting market and political winds.

CONCLUSION

The enterprise of Canadian schooling has grown immensely. Almost all Canadians attend high school, most graduate, half now go on to postsecondary school, and many will return to some sort of educational institution later in life, as ideologies of "lifelong education" become reality. But what has been the impact of this monumental expansion? Schools partially compensate for pre-existing inequalities in student preparedness, but their selection role ensures that expansion does not bring greater equity, at least along socioeconomic lines. Further, the singular socializing impact of school in our lives actually shrinks. School becomes a weaker socializing agent as it integrates into our lives, competing with many other agents. Some forms of schooling have become more competitive. Prestigious programs that offer the most recognition and best rewards are increasingly exclusive. Other programs are more accommodating, treating students in more progressive ways and offering more choice than ever before.

These trends remind us of the paradox discussed at the outset of this chapter. Canadian schools now serve unprecedented numbers of students for longer periods of their lives, yet they are a lightning rod for more and more criticism. This is a prime instance of "disenchantment" in Max Weber's definition: As schooling becomes ever more central to society in the modern era, it loses its "magical" quality to command deference. As all citizens attend school for most of their youth, more are familiar with schooling and have higher expectations for what schools should do for them. Education has become a "motherhood" issue that everyone supports in the abstract, yet in the process it loses its overtones of elite rituals, aristocratic cultures, and time-honoured pageantry. The caps and gowns, the great halls, and Latin-inscribed coats of arms have largely disappeared, replaced by rationalized bureaucracies that merely promise access to labour markets.

This disenchantment shouldn't cloud a sunnier accomplishment: School systems now offer unparalleled opportunities for individuals. Schooling helps extend human rights and literacy to even the poorest segments of society. Who today reminisces for bygone eras in which schooling was a privilege for the few? Such ideas now provoke a sense of outrage and are rightfully seen to deny basic rights. Schooling may be demystified, yet we cannot manage without it.

SUMMARY

1. The selection function of school systems is being transferred from secondary to postsecondary levels. In past decades, secondary-level streaming played an important gate-keeping role, so an adolescent's life-chances were shaped largely by his or her performance in high school. However, as higher education expands, life-chances are determined increasingly by where a person graduates in a stratified structure of higher education.
2. As more Canadians attain advanced levels of education, formerly valuable credentials, such as the high-school diploma, have become devalued. Devaluation generates demand for more schooling, leading to a spiral of educational expansion as groups jockey for advantages in the labour market.
3. A pattern of inequality exists in Canadian school attainment. Along social class lines, students from more affluent backgrounds continue to

enjoy considerable advantages. In terms of gender, women now outpace men on many indicators, though considerable gender segregation remains in certain fields of study. The legacy of conquest for Aboriginal peoples and their history of discrimination and segregation continue to be evident in schools, while changing immigration selection policies have created a partial reversal in patterns of attainment for other racial groups.

4. Today's moral education is less religious and explicit than before. Schools now mostly aim to have students understand key issues, rather than having a hard-edged, prescriptive tone. The hidden curriculum continues to emphasize the orderly completion of tasks, punctuality, and neatness. But today's schools have a more indulgent quality than they did in the past, trying to shore up students' self-esteem and capture rather than command their interests.
5. Canadian schools have changed from informal institutions that wielded traditional authority to legal-rational bureaucracies. In the latter form, progressive educators have pursued strategies to spark intrinsic learning and cater to students in ever-more accommodating ways. In the 1970s, this involved lessening teacher power in favour of students. Today, it sometimes involves the use of market-like mechanisms to treat students as if they are "customers."

QUESTIONS TO CONSIDER

1. Compare your schooling experience so far with that of one of your grandparents by using the themes of selection, accommodation, competition, and sponsored and contest mobility.
2. From what you have experienced in school, how would you motivate students to be effective learners? What organizational reforms might best inspire students? Be honest and give examples.
3. Observe a classroom. Do you see socializing messages in operation? Cite examples. Sort out the socializing influences of schools from those of families, neighbourhoods, labour markets, and peer groups.

GLOSSARY

Contest mobility (p. 290) is a form of educational competition in which most youths are grouped into the same school and exposed to the same curriculum, and in which relatively large numbers are directed to higher education.

Credential inflation (p. 301) takes place when labour-market competition encourages individuals to acquire schooling, and employers raise required credential levels for reasons that are not connected to their needs for skilled employees.

The **hidden curriculum** (p. 294) comprises elements of school content, such as rules, procedures, structures and norms, that can shape students in covert ways.

Human capital theory (p. 301) emphasizes how schooling can enhance productive skills and thereby generate wealth for both individuals and society.

Professionalization (p. 302) is the process by which an occupation attempts to raise its social standing, often including the creation of formal educational credentials.

Progressive pedagogy (p. 303) is an educational movement that emphasizes student-directed learning, less structured curricula, and an emphasis on inspiring students to be intrinsically motivated in their studies.

Selection (p. 287) is the process by which the structure of schooling feeds into broader patterns of social stratification.

Sponsored mobility (p. 290) is a form of educational competition in which relatively few youths are selected early in life to enter elite universities.

SUGGESTED READING

Baker, David, and Gerald LeTendre. (2005). *National Differences, Global Similarities: World Culture and the Future of Schooling.* Stanford, CT: Stanford University Press. An international examination of schooling trends, focusing on the curriculum and student achievement.

Grubb, W. Norton and Marvin Lazerson. (2004). *The Education Gospel: The Economic Power of Schooling.* Cambridge, MA: Harvard University Press. This book reveals the allure of Americans' longstanding faith in schooling as a remedy for all sorts of economic and social problems.

Levine-Rasky, Cynthia. (2009). *Canadian Perspectives on the Sociology of Education.* Toronto: Oxford University Press. This collection of original essays examines the complex relationship between schooling and Canadian society.

CHAPTER 13

RELIGION

REGINALD W. BIBBY
UNIVERSITY OF LETHBRIDGE

SOURCE: © Morgan Danveau

IN THIS CHAPTER YOU WILL LEARN THAT

- Religion has been studied by sociologists since the beginnings of sociology.
- Religion has both individual and social components—people display a wide range of levels of commitment, but groups play a major role in instilling and sustaining personal religiosity.
- Since religious groups are organizations, they can best be understood by using organizational concepts and frameworks.
- For the vast majority of people, religious commitment and involvement are rooted in social institutions, particularly the family.
- Religion's influence on individuals tends to be noteworthy but not unique, while its broader role in most societies is to support social structure and culture.
- Despite the problems of some groups, religion's future in Canada and elsewhere is secure, grounded in ongoing spiritual interests and needs.

INTRODUCTION

Religion is very much alive today. In recent years, religion has received worldwide attention in such varied developments as the death of Pope John Paul II, the phenomenal sales of Dan Brown's *The Da Vinci Code*, and the exposure given to the so-called atheist books of such authors as Richard Dawkins and the late Christopher Hitchens. Religion's presence and importance is blatant in the conflict, terrorism, and peacemaking efforts in the Middle East. In 2006 it was centre stage in the clash of values and perhaps even civilizations as European countries and their leaders experienced the protests and threats of Muslims for allowing their newspapers to publish cartoon depictions of Muhammad (Ghafour, 2006). Even more daunting in light of September 11, 2001, was the 1998 directive of "fundamentalist"/"extremist" Osama bin Laden that "in compliance with God's order ... every Muslim who believes in God and wishes to be rewarded" is to "kill the Americans and plunder their money wherever and whenever they find it"—thinking that, in turn, has been widely condemned by most Muslim leaders.

In North America, religion's presence is also readily evident in the God-laced responses to such militancy on the part of U.S. political leaders, whose supporters frequently include large numbers of the so-called Christian Right. Apart from its links to global issues, religion in the United States is pervasive. Attendance at services is extremely high and the majority of people say that religion is very important to them. The organizational health of American religion can be seen in the emergence of a growing number of very large and influential "megachurches," such as Joel Osteen's much-publicized Lakewood Church that occupies a 16 000-seat former basketball arena in Houston. Far from having only a local focus, many function as religious multinational corporations—spreading the message of "how to do ministry" to other parts of the world, including Canada. Spirituality has joined religion in going public and become part of pop culture, read about in books, such as Rhonda Byrne's *The Secret* and Eckhart Tolle's *A New Earth*, and talked about on *Oprah*.

In Canada, beyond such media offerings, the reality of religion is readily apparent in the tendency of the vast majority of people to continue to identify with a religious tradition; in the growing numbers of individuals identifying with faiths that include Islam, Hinduism, Sikhism, and Buddhism; in the widespread interest in spirituality; in debates about same-sex marriage and polygamy; in the efforts of Catholics and mainline Protestants to resolve problems relating to the legacy of residential schools; in the imminent prime minister of the day ending his 2006 election victory speech with the words "God bless Canada," and in the national publicity given to Toronto's Catholic Archbishop being elevated to the status of Cardinal in early 2012.

Many early social scientists were convinced that religion's days were numbered, that it would be just a short time before it was discarded in favour of science. Through the 1990s, the widespread consensus was that religion's influence was declining and that Canadians and people in most other technologically advanced countries were leaving religion behind—although the United States stood out as a puzzling anomaly.

We now know that such observers were wrong. In the early decades of the twenty-first century, religion lives on, embraced by large numbers of people in virtually all cultures, however "advanced" or "nonadvanced." Moreover, interest in religion and spirituality is actually on the upswing in many parts of the world, including North America, Russia, and Asia. In many Islamic countries, it is not clear that the importance of religion has ever been in doubt. Today, religion is frequently associated with conflict and division. But it also continues to bring meaning, sustenance, and hope to billions of people.

I begin the chapter by taking a brief look at what some of the early and influential social scientists had to say about religion, and then discuss how sociologists go about studying religion in both its individual and group forms. After clarifying what sociologists mean by religion, I look at "how much of it" we have in Canada and proceed to examine its sources and consequences—what kinds of factors contribute to people being religious and the influence that religion has on both individuals and societies. In concluding the chapter, I reflect on the kinds of religious developments we can expect in the future.

I'll be giving particular attention to Canada, in large part because I have spent much of my life examining religious developments here and have some fairly unique research findings I can tell you about. However, while focusing on Canada, I will keep my eyes on the rest of the world, starting with the United States.

Contrary to the opinion of some people, religious belief is not disappearing in Canada. In fact, in urban areas most people have many options for worship.
SOURCE: © Dick Hemingway.

SOCIOLOGY AND RELIGION

A number of years ago, an American evangelist who was holding services in Edmonton was asked by a fairly strident television interviewer, "How do you know there is a God?" The evangelist immediately responded, "Because I talked to Him five minutes ago." It was an interesting claim but one that a sociologist is not in a position to verify. A basic rule of science is that "what counts" as real is what we can detect through our senses—what we refer to as "empirical" knowledge. In contrast, proponents of religion have traditionally asserted that the world we know through the senses is only part of a greater reality that, because of the limitations of sense perception, can only be known through faith.

In principle, science and religion are compatible. Science limits itself to what is perceivable, and religion maintains that reality includes the nonperceivable. Conflict between the two should only arise when one oversteps its boundaries and invades the other's territory.

Still, for the most part, science is in the driver's seat. As Émile Durkheim (1965 [1912]: 479) pointed out many years ago, religion "can affirm nothing that [science] denies, deny nothing that it affirms." Try though it might, religion cannot overrule science in refuting basic evolutionary claims or dismissing sound medical diagnoses. At the same time, since science is limited to conclusions about the observable, it too can only go so far. Sociologists cannot address the evangelist's claim that he had actually spoken to God, any more than it can evaluate the claim that a person whose cancer has gone into remission was healed by God.

Sociology consequently suffers from one serious methodological limitation in studying religion: It cannot probe the supernatural claims that religion so often is about. Sociologists nonetheless can offer considerable insight into "the observable part" of religion. For example, they can examine the following:

- Who tends to think they have experienced God
- Who believes in life after death and what individuals think will happen when they die
- The extent to which people have spiritual needs, and what they mean by "spirituality"
- How many and what kinds of people are involved in religious groups
- The impact that religious involvement has on individuals and societies

In short, sociologists cannot address everything when it comes to religion; but they can address much, without getting caught up in the issue of religion's ultimate truth or falsity. Max Weber summed up the focus of sociological explorations into religion this way: "The essence of religion," he wrote, is not the concern of sociologists, since "we make it our task to study the conditions and effects of a particular type of social behaviour" (1963 [1922]: 1). For our purposes, whether or not religious ideas are true is not as important as the fact they are *believed* to be true. As W. I. Thomas and Dorothy Swaine Thomas noted in their classic theorem, if we define things as real, they are real in their consequences (Thomas and Znaniecki, 1918: 79). The very fact that religious ideas are held means they potentially can have an important impact on individuals and social life.

THEORETICAL TRADITIONS

Three early theorists—Karl Marx, Émile Durkheim, and Max Weber—have had a strong influence on the sociology of religion.

MARX AND CONFLICT

Karl Marx grew up in a Jewish environment but came to believe that religion is a human creation. Using the language of the day, Marx (1970 [1843]: 131) wrote, "Man makes religion; religion does not make man." He argued that man has "found only his own reflection in the fantastic reality of heaven, where he sought a supernatural being," and that being religious characterized "the self-consciousness and self-esteem of a man who has either not yet gained himself or has lost himself again."

It has been argued that we can resolve undesirable conditions by either changing them or reinterpreting them. Peasants, slaves, and the marginalized in our day theoretically can rise up and revolt; they also can minimize the importance of "this world" by looking heavenward, singing spirituals, and dreaming of walking streets of gold after they die. According to Marx, religion constitutes the latter response, resulting in people who are economically and politically deprived redefining reality, rather than changing their oppressive conditions. Religion, Marx wrote, soothes the disadvantaged like a narcotic—functioning as "the opium of the people" (Marx, 1970 [1843]: 131), in the process blinding them to the inequalities at hand and bottling up their creative energies. So it is that some observers today would argue that many socially and financially deprived individuals who are unable or unwilling to play an active role in altering social conditions or even their own lives substitute religious status for social status. A taxi driver by day is the head of a temple committee by night; the housekeeper in the hotel during the week is the star soloist in the church choir on the weekend. Religious status supplants social status; the next world supplants this world.

But Marx did not see such a redefining of reality as a chance happening. On the contrary, he maintained that those who hold power encourage religious belief among the masses as a subtle tool in the process of exploiting and subjugating them. Aligned with the interests of the dominant few, religion serves to hold in check the potentially explosive tensions of a society. Consistent with his thinking, respected social historian H. Richard Niebuhr (1957 [1929]: 51) has been among those who have claimed, for example, that a widely held belief among nineteenth-century American slave owners was that religion helped African Americans to become "better" slaves. He cites one advocate of "negro missions" who asserted that "slaves well-instructed in the Christian faith were less likely to develop revolutionary inclinations than the half-educated, such as [revolt leader] Nat Turner."

Historically, said Marx, society and religion were so intertwined that attacks on feudalism, for example, were attacks on the church, while revolutionary social and political doctrines were simultaneously viewed as theological heresies (Marx and Engels, 1964: 132). We might argue that we see similar fusion between politics and religion today, not only in theocracies, such as Iran, but also in such a country as the United States, where the dominant religion, according to some observers, is "the American Way of Life," supported by the country's primary religious groups. We'll return to this issue shortly.

For Marx (1970 [1843]: 131), religion was an inadequate salve for a sick society—"the sigh of the oppressed creature, the heart of a heartless world and the soul of soulless conditions." When the sickness was remedied, there would be no need for the salve. Using another metaphor, Marx (1970 [1843]: 132) wrote that his criticism of religion was an attempt to remove "the imaginary flowers from the chain, not so that man shall bear the chain without fantasy or consultation, but so that he shall cast off the chain and gather the living flowers." Freed from the panacea of religion, individuals would be able "to think, act, and fashion their reality with illusions lost and reason regained" (Marx, 1970 [1843]: 132).

If you are someone who is personally religious, you understandably are not particularly excited to have Marx suggest that you may well be disadvantaged in some way and need to open your eyes and give your energies to changing your current situation. But before you reject his thinking altogether, it is worth noting that, at minimum, Marx seems to offer considerable insight, even today, into why some people join extreme religious groups that downplay the importance of this life—encouraging them to give up what possessions they have and, in some instances, give up their lives as well.

DURKHEIM AND COLLECTIVITY

Émile Durkheim was the son of a rabbi but was raised in a Catholic educational tradition. He himself was an atheist and an anti-cleric, who believed that a scientific understanding of society has the potential to raise the quality of social life.

In his classic work *The Elementary Forms of the Religious Life* (1965 [1912]), Durkheim argued that religion's origin is social. People who live in a community come to share common sentiments, and as a result a **collective conscience** is formed. When they gather together, they have a feeling of being in the presence of something beyond themselves that is experienced by each member, yet is greater than the sum of their individual consciences. The feeling is not unlike "the electricity in the air" we experience at an exciting playoff hockey game or a big rock concert, where that feeling "out there" seems to transcend the sum of individual emotions. Durkheim maintained that the experience is so vivid that people have felt the need to label it. In reality, Durkheim asserted, "God" is the group experiencing itself. The experience *is* real, he argues; it's just that it isn't what those involved think it is.

Once people experience such an alleged supernatural reality, they proceed to designate some related objects as **sacred** and others as **profane.** Christians have accorded special status to the cross, the Bible, and holy water, in contrast to almost everything else. Symbols of the sacred are many and diverse: Jews have assigned sacred status to the Torah and Star of David, Muslims to the Qur'an and the Saudi Arabian city of Mecca, Hindus to the Vedas and the sacred syllable "Aum"(or "Om"). In Durkheim's view, religious beliefs articulate the nature of the sacred and its symbols, and religious rites provide guidelines as to how people should act in the presence of the sacred. So it is that Muslims, for example, are expected to pray at specific times five times a day, facing Mecca,

In Durkheim's view, religious rites provide guidelines as to how people should act in the presence of the sacred. Muslims, for example, are expected to pray at specific times five times a day, facing Mecca, and to make a pilgrimage to Mecca at least once in their lifetimes.

SOURCE: © Shutterstock.

and to make a pilgrimage to Mecca at least once in their lifetimes; Hindus offer daily devotional prayers in the morning and evening, sometimes accompanied by ritual bathing. Sikhs, when they enter their temples, must cover their heads and remove their shoes, and, where the opportunity is provided, wash their hands and feet.

Because all groups feel the need to uphold and reaffirm their collective sentiments, people come together as what he refers to as a "church." According to Durkheim (1965 [1912]: 62–63), "the idea of religion is inseparable from that of the Church," since it is "an eminently collective thing." Even when religion seems to be entirely a matter of individual conscience, it still is nourished by social sources. Besides meeting needs at the individual level, he claimed, religion creates and reinforces social solidarity. Collective life is consequently both *the source* and *the product* of religion. Accordingly, Durkheim (1965 [1912]: 62) defined religion as "a unified system of beliefs and practices relative to sacred things ... which unite into one single moral community called a Church, all those who adhere to them."

Durkheim (1965 [1912]: 475–76) observed that "we are going through a stage of transition and moral mediocrity. The great things of the past which filled our fathers with enthusiasm do not excite the same ardour in us." He added poetically, "The gods are growing old or are already dead, and others are not yet born." But despite the problems of traditional Catholicism in particular, Durkheim didn't believe that religion would disappear: "There are no gospels which are immortal, but neither is there any reason for believing that humanity is incapable of inventing new ones." The dominant groups and forms of expression might change, but the social sources that give rise to religion obviously will remain and, with them, religion. Durkheim also contended that there would always be a place for religious explanations. The reason? Science is fragmentary and incomplete, advancing too slowly—life cannot wait. Religion will therefore continue to have an important "gap-filling" role.

Durkheim's legacy has been important. You don't have to agree with his assertion that the gods are socially created to realize that God and ethical conceptions, for example, frequently reflect social and individual characteristics. In fact, an age-old concern among people valuing faith has been the inclination of humans to create the gods in their own images. What's more, Durkheim's acknowledgment that science moves too slowly for many of us anticipated the ongoing "market" for alternative explanations on the part of religious leaders and just about anyone else, including—to use just one illustration—psychics. The vast market for explanations of the unknown is evident from the fact that in 2012, Google listed more than 20 million entries for "psychics."

WEBER AND IDEAS

Max Weber was born in Germany. His grandparents were Protestants who had been refugees from Catholic persecution and eventually became successful in business. He was interested in religion from an early age but never shared the deep commitment of his Calvinist mother. His background was reflected in one of his most important works.

Weber's interest in the origin and nature of modern capitalism led him into extensive debate with Marx's ideas and stimulated much of his work in the sociology of religion. Unlike Marx and Durkheim, Weber had little interest in the question of whether religion is ultimately true or false. Rather, he maintained that religion, in addition to having a supernatural component, is largely oriented toward this world. As a result, religious ideas and behaviour should frequently be evident in everyday conduct. In *The Protestant Ethic and the Spirit of Capitalism* (1958 [1904–05]), for example, Weber examined the possibility that the moral tone that characterizes capitalism in the Western world—the *Protestant ethic*—can be traced back to the influence of the Protestant Reformation. His hope was that his work would contribute "to the understanding of the manner in which ideas become effective forces in history" (Weber, 1958 [1904–05]: 90).

Weber took the position that ideas, regardless of whether they are objectively true or false, represent a person's definition of reality and therefore have the potential to influence behaviour. Accordingly, he emphasized the need to interpret action by understanding the motives of the actor (a method he called *Verstehen*, or understanding). To achieve such awareness, he said, researchers should place themselves in the roles of those being studied.

Weber understood the need to study diverse societies, present and past, to examine culture's influence on religion. He therefore embarked on comparative and historical studies of religion and its relationship to social and economic life in China, India, and ancient Israel. A compilation of his writings,

Sociology of Religion (1963 [1922]), illustrates the way that Weber approached religion. He noted that god-conceptions are strongly related to the economic, social, and political conditions in which people live. The gods of light and warmth and of rain and Earth have been closely related to practical economic needs; heavenly gods that rule the celestial order have been related to the more abstract problems of death and fate. In political conquest, the gods of the conquered are fused with the gods of the conqueror and reappear with revised characteristics. Furthermore, the growth of **monotheism** (belief in one god) is related to goals of political unification.

Beyond the social sources of the gods, Weber dealt with such major themes as the relationship between religion and social class, and the nature of religious organizations. He reflected on religious leadership and the important process whereby a personal following is transformed into a permanent congregation, which he referred to as "routinization." He noted that different groups in society vary in their inclination to be religious: Peasants are religious when they are threatened; the nobility find religion beneath their honour; the middle class sees religion largely in ethical terms; the working class supplants religion with other ideologies.

Over the years I have found that students, whether religious or otherwise, appreciate the way in which Weber attempted to take religion seriously and not become embroiled in attacking it or dismissing it. His approach has become fairly typical in the contemporary study of religion. Still, along with Weber, some of the ideas of Marx and Durkheim have remained insightful.

THE NATURE OF RELIGION

Are you religious? If you are like many Canadians, you may promptly say, "Yes" or "No, I'm not," perhaps adding, "I'm not religious but I am spiritual." The term *religion* is widely used, but obviously people have different ideas in mind when they use it. Up to now, I have been assuming that we have a consensual understanding of what we mean by "religion." But before we go much further, and particularly before we look at research on religion, we need to clarify what we actually mean by the term.

"Religion" can be a blurry concept. Many people use it in a functional sense: What people value most becomes their religion—money, career, family, sports. A young boy allegedly told a Canadian religious doorknocker, "My mother is RC; my dad is NHL." The problem with such functional definitions of religion, sociologist Peter Berger (1974: 129) once observed, is that they become like grey cats on a dark night. If religion is everything, then it is nothing.

In a pioneering work published some five decades ago, Charles Glock and Rodney Stark (1965) offered some thoughts that continue to be helpful. They pointed out that, in defining religion for social scientific purposes, we should begin by recognizing that humans develop systems of meaning to interpret the world. Some systems—commonly referred to as "religions," including Christianity, Judaism, and Islam—have a supernatural referent. Others, such as a science-based system (scientism) or political "isms" (communism, fascism), do not. The latter systems, they suggested, might be viewed as human-centred or **humanist perspectives,** in contrast to *religious perspectives,* which are succinctly referred to here as **religions.**

The two types of perspectives differ on one critical point: Religion is concerned with discovering life's meaning, and humanist perspectives are concerned with making life meaningful. Humanist Bertrand Russell stated the difference well: "I do not think that life in general has any purpose. It just happened. But individual human beings have purposes" (in Cogley, 1968: 171). Religious perspectives suggest that our existence has meaning, preceding that which we, as humans, decide to give it. In contrast, humanist perspectives assume that life has no "ultimate meaning" and therefore focus on giving it meaning.

The dichotomy is not perfect; some would say that such criteria might lead us to see Buddhism, for example, as a humanist perspective. Here I would simply defer to commonly understood thinking and place Buddhism in its familiar religion category for the sake of communication. However, for the most part, I think the religious perspectives/humanist perspectives approach is helpful.

PERSONAL RELIGIOSITY

Now that I've clarified things a bit, let's go back to the pointed question: How religious are you? And to be less pointed, how religious are Canadians as a whole? Sociologists have not believed that the answers are arbitrary or simply subjective. They have given much effort to finding ways of defining and measuring what they have called **personal religiosity.**

Much of the early research used one of three basic indicators to determine the religiosity of a person.

All three assumed group involvement: identification, membership, and attendance. In surveys, people were asked questions, such as "What is your religious preference?" "Do you belong to a congregation?" and "How often do you attend religious services?" People who indicated that they had a religious preference, belonged to a local group, or attended services with regularity were viewed as religious.

However, as you know well, simply knowing that someone is "Protestant" or "Hindu," "Jewish" or "Mennonite," tells us very little about a person's actual commitment to his or her faith. Similarly, people might be group members, but members may be active or inactive, committed or uncommitted. And service attendance, although measuring participation in a group, excludes people who could be very committed yet, for such reasons as age, health, work schedule, and geographical location, are not overly active in a religious organization.

Since the mid-1960s, social scientists have responded to the limitations of these three measures by viewing religious commitment as having a variety of dimensions. In one of the more helpful frameworks devised, Stark and Glock (1968) suggested that the religions of the world typically expect their most devoted followers to hold key beliefs, engage in certain practices, have supernatural experiences, and be aware of the central tenets of their faiths. Stark and Glock refer to these belief, practice, experience, and knowledge components of commitment as **dimensions of religiosity.** It is not enough to believe *or* practise *or* experience *or* know; all four traits are expected of the committed.

My ongoing Project Canada national surveys, which to date span 1975 through 2005, provide comprehensive data on personal religiosity in this country. The surveys have found that Canadians continue to exhibit relatively high levels of religious belief, practice, experience, and knowledge (see Table 13.1). Indeed, some eight in ten say they believe in God, close to seven in ten maintain there is life after death, six in ten acknowledge that they pray privately at least once a month, and about five in ten think they have experienced the presence of God. Almost half also exhibit some basic knowledge of Islam, Judaism, and Christianity. On the surface,

TABLE 13.1 RELIGIOUS COMMITMENT ALONG FOUR DIMENSIONS, CANADA, 2005 (IN PERCENTAGE)

DIMENSION	RESPONSE	PERCENTAGE
Believe in God	Yes, I definitely do	49
	Yes, I think so	33
	No, I don't think so	11
	No, I definitely do not	7
Believe in life after death	Yes, I definitely do	36
	Yes, I think so	31
	No, I don't think so	21
	No, I definitely do not	12
Practise private prayer	Daily	27
	Several times a week	11
	About once a week	7
	Once or more times a month	8
	Hardly ever/never	47
Experience God	Yes, I definitely have	26
	Yes, I think so	23
	No, I don't think I have	30
	No, I definitely have not	21
Knowledge	The name of the sacred book of Islam (Qur'an)	53
	The first book in the Old Testament (Genesis)	47
	Who denied Jesus three times? (Peter)	41

SOURCE: Derived from Reginald W. Bibby, *Project Canada 2005 National Survey.*

then, early twenty-first century Canadians seem to be a fairly religious people.

However, the surveys have also found that although around 50 percent claim to be committed to Christianity or another religion, less than half of the committed demonstrate the belief, practice, experience, and knowledge characteristics that Stark and Glock (1968) saw as central to commitment. Among the other 50 percent of Canadians, about three in ten indicate that they are interested in but not committed to any religion, and the remaining two in ten simply say that they are not religious (Bibby, 2004a). According to the 2005 Project Canada survey, 25 percent of Canadians say that religion is "very important" to them, with most having fairly conventional ideas of religion in mind. Regional variations are striking, with the levels ranging from a high of about 40 percent in the Atlantic region, through around 30 percent to 35 percent in Ontario and the three Prairie provinces, to lows of 15 percent in British Columbia and 10 percent in Quebec.

An interesting footnote is worth pondering: Pollsters are continually reminding us that Americans are more religious than Canadians are (Kiefer, 2004; Ray, 2003; Winseman, 2004). However, New Brunswick sociologist Samuel Reimer (2003) has been arguing for some time now that we must not overlook an important qualitative difference in religious belief and commitment in the two countries. Reimer maintains that it is easier to be highly committed in the American religious environment than it is in Canada since, in his words, higher levels of religiosity in the United States have "more to do with cultural supports for religiosity than with deeper religious conviction." Since it is more difficult to be religiously committed in Canada, religious devotion, among Canadians, he argues, "is more likely to be based on conviction."

COLLECTIVE RELIGIOSITY

How many times have you heard people say, "I don't have to go to church to be religious"? Increasingly the generalization has been expanded to include temples and synagogues as well. It may be a common argument, but it doesn't have much sociological support.

Most social scientists, beginning with Durkheim, have maintained that personal religiosity is highly dependent on **collective religiosity**, or group support of some kind. Such dependence is not unique to religion. It stems from a basic fact of life: The ideas we hold tend to come from our interaction with other people. However creative we might like to think we are, the fact is that most of the ideas we have in our heads right now can be traced back to the people with whom we have been in contact—family, friends, teachers, authors, journalists, and any number of other so-called experts. Moreover, if we are to retain those ideas, they have to be continually endorsed by at least a few other people whose opinions we value. Ideas are sustained by relationships.

Consequently, it is not surprising that researchers find that evangelicals, for example, one of the most numerically vibrant "religious families" in the country, have learned that they need to "grow their own and keep their own." They have more children than members of most other groups do, provide them with positive church-life experiences from the time they hit the church nursery, make sure they have youth-friendly programs when they are teens, and encourage them to marry each other—or if worst comes to worst, marry an outsider and bring the partner into the group—and then continue to be part of young adult and adult activities. To fail at any of those three crucial points in the biography of their daughters and sons is to run the risk of seeing them abandon evangelical faith. People cannot hold ideas or commitment for long without a measure of social support.

Seem like a strong claim? Try it on your own biography.

The Church-Sect Typology

Those who have examined religious groups in predominantly Christian settings have recognized two major kinds of organizations. First, there are numerically dominant groupings—the Roman Catholic Church in medieval Europe, the Church of England, the so-called mainline denominations in Canada and the United States (Anglican, United, Presbyterian, Lutheran), and so on. Second, smaller groups have broken away from the dominant bodies. For example, in the sixteenth century, Protestant groups, including the Church of England, broke away from the Roman Catholic Church; but Methodists in turn broke away from the Church of England, and the Salvation Army emerged as a breakaway group from the Methodists. Today, additional emerging groups include an array of Baptist and Pentecostal denominations and nondenominational "grassroots" congregations that are found in virtually every North American city.

From this pattern of dominant groups and breakaway groups, sociologists who try to make sense of religious groups developed an analytical scheme known as the **church-sect typology.** This framework attempted to describe the central characteristics of these two types of organizations, as well as account for the origin and development of sects.

In perhaps its earliest formulation, Max Weber distinguished church from sect primarily on the basis of theology (churches emphasize works, sects stress faith) and relationship to society (for churches, accommodation; for sects, separation). Weber noted the irony in the sect's development: Initially a spinoff from an established church, the sect gradually evolves into a church itself (Gerth and Mills, 1958). The sect at first is characterized by spontaneity and enthusiasm. In time, however, these traits give way to routinization and institutionalization.

Although the church-sect typology has been used extensively, alternative ways of understanding religious groups have become increasingly popular.

Organizational Approaches

In sociological terms, religious organizations are no different from other social organizations. Therefore, there has been a growing tendency to analyze religious groups by making use of the same frameworks we use in studying social organizations in general.

Led by the work of respected American sociologist Rodney Stark and his associates (Finke and Stark, 1992; Stark and Bainbridge, 1985; Stark and Finke, 2000), a market model for understanding religion has become prominent in recent years. Religious groups are seen as "firms" or "companies" competing for "market share."

- Seen through such eyes, the Roman Catholic, Anglican, and Eastern Orthodox churches are part of multinational corporations; so is the Salvation Army.
- A number of groups, including the United Church and the Pentecostal Assemblies of Canada, are companies that are "Canadian-owned and -operated."
- Many smaller evangelical Protestant denominations have been "branch plant" operations of American groups—not unlike "Ford Canada" or "Wal-Mart Canada"—that, over the years, have become increasingly autonomous. Some other groups, including Presbyterians and some Lutherans and Baptists, have similarly evolved from overseas operations.
- Despite the fact that Jews, Muslims, Hindus, Sikhs, and Buddhists all have worldwide roots and ongoing ties with those roots, none have developed official international or national structures that oversee their Canadian businesses. They have lobby groups and other organizations that address some common interests. But their "business outlets" are typically highly autonomous, with their synagogues, mosques, and temples owned and operated by their local congregations.
- Similarly, large numbers of other religious firms operate as privately owned companies. They are started by religious entrepreneurs who are convinced that a market exists for their particular product. The early days are often modest, with operations launched in homes, schools, and warehouses. Some are successful; many are not.

Apart from provocative marketing language and corporate analogies, a general organizational approach to religious groups sheds new light on basic features of religious groups, including (1) the nature and the sources of their members, (2) their formal and informal goals, (3) the norms and roles that are established to accomplish their purposes, (4) the sanctions that are used to ensure that norms are followed and roles are played, and (5) the degree of success that groups experience in pursuing their goals. Let me briefly illustrate.

Membership When studying the membership of religious groups, it readily becomes apparent that the vast majority of those involved are following in parental footsteps. Canadian census data show that when two parents have the same faith, 95 percent of their children are also raised in that faith. As a result, new additions to almost any given congregation are primarily active members who are on the move geographically. These include people coming to Canada from other countries. For example, during the 1980s and 1990s immigrants contributed most of the growth to Hindu, Sikh, Muslim, and Buddhist groups. Given the extensive worldwide growth of Roman Catholicism, Pentecostalism, and Islam, "immigration pipelines" are going to favour those traditions in the immediate future (Allen, 2009). Conversely, the "pipelines" have narrowed for members of the United and Presbyterian Churches (Bibby, 2011a: 30–31).

Congregations frequently compete with one another for members and staff, especially in urban areas where some "outlets" are larger and more affluent than others are. The more attractive congregations typically have the resources to search farther for their leaders and hold them longer.

During the 1980s and 1990s, immigrants contributed most of the growth to Hindu, Sikh, Muslim, and Buddhist groups in Canada.
SOURCE: © iStockphoto.com/David P. Lewis.

They also have better physical facilities. It's not just a Protestant or Catholic phenomenon: Muslims, Hindus, Sikhs, Buddhists, and Jews typically define their meeting places as important centres for social activity. Consequently, groups tend to build structures as lavish as their resources will permit. In recent years, a number of Protestant "megachurches" have come into being in Canada and the United States. They typically have seating for one thousand to four thousand people, are serviced by many full-time staff members, and have annual budgets in the millions of dollars. They are found in major cities, such as Toronto, Montreal, Winnipeg, Edmonton, Calgary, and Vancouver. But they also are appearing in smaller communities, such as Abbotsford, Red Deer, and St. Catharines. They typically co-opt technology and culture. PowerPoint and worship bands, cellphones and texting are part of services, with Starbucks coffee commonly found both outside and inside sanctuaries. These megachurches make it difficult for other congregations to compete. Catholics are showing signs of following suit, recognizing that one way of dealing with the priest shortage and the need for specialized ministries is to have larger, regional parishes.

Congregations, like secular businesses, also expand their services and personnel in keeping with their economic means. Some of the megachurches, for example, offer many of the typical worship and educational opportunities of more traditional, older groups. But they also have extensive programs aimed at children, teenagers, young adults, and seniors. The programs range from small but sophisticated groups studying in homes ("cell groups"), through well-developed music and drama programs, to multimedia education, entertainment, and elaborate Web activities that often include podcasts. A room in one well-known British Columbia megachurch resembles a 1950s diner—complete with a car front, jukeboxes, booths, and stools. As the church's head youth minister told me, "The young people love this room; but the seniors love it too."

An obvious point of tension involves maintaining integrity while providing products that attract customers.

Goals The conscious and unconscious goals of local religious groups vary by congregation and members. Like the goals of other social groupings, these conscious and unconscious goals commonly appear to be in conflict. For years observers have noted that the formal goals derived from religious doctrine, such as spiritual growth, frequently exist in tension with "survival goals" relating to numerical growth that translate into necessary human and financial resources (Metz, 1967).

Similarly, congregations frequently have difficulty in reconciling their pastoral or "comfort" function with their prophetical or "challenge" function (Glock, Ringer, and Babbie, 1967). For example, the national leadership of the United Church of Canada viewed itself as prophetic in its call during the mid-1980s to allow gays and lesbians to be eligible for ordination as ministers. In taking such a controversial position, the denomination lost a sizable number of dissenting members and, in some cases, entire congregations (O'Toole et al., 1993). Prophecy has its organizational price.

There is an additional point of tension: how to satisfy the needs of the existing clientele while reaching out to new people who are not involved yet have important needs themselves. For example, as the twenty-first century began, the most divisive issue in U.S. Protestant congregations was whether church music should be traditional and oriented toward *insiders* or contemporary and aimed at *outsiders*. It is a dilemma that congregations of virtually all religious stripes are not particularly adept at resolving, with obvious negative implications for growth.

Norms, Roles, and Sanctions If groups, like companies, are to achieve their official and unofficial goals, they have to be able to establish norms for what has to be done and assign roles for their members to play. An examination of congregational roles reveals that most groups in Canada—led by Catholics, evangelicals, Muslims, Hindus, and Sikhs—often have a human resource problem for two main reasons. The first is that they are top-heavy with men and often inadequately tap the resources of women, a reality that has been variously met with acquiescence, resistance, and a measure of change (Nason-Clark, 1993; Nesbitt, 1997; Speaker-Yuan, 2005; Stackhouse, 2005). The second problem is that groups typically rely on volunteers to carry out key roles. These are the same people who congregational leaders have to work hard to recruit and retain—people on whom they depend for involvement and financial support. They are not hired and they can't exactly be fired. It adds up to a situation in which religious groups are frequently fragile and inefficient companies (Bibby, 1993; Brannon, 1971; Monahan, 1999).

Success In their studies of religion in Canada, researchers have tended to emphasize "the numerical bottom lines" of religious groups and to focus on such indicators of success as attendance, membership, and finances.

Through the early 1990s, the research news was not particularly good for organized religion. Overall, attendance and membership were down, with some groups feeling great hardship as a result of inadequate finances. The mainline Protestant groups—the United, Anglican, Presbyterian, and Lutheran churches—were the most severely hit, along with Roman Catholics in Quebec. Despite some attendance and membership losses, the Roman Catholic Church outside Quebec appeared to be relatively healthy. And although their numbers were not as large as many people think, conservative Protestant groups were at least able to hold their own and grow modestly—a significant accomplishment, given that they have represented only about 8 percent of the population since 1871 and could have readily been absorbed by larger competitors. Other faith groups, such as Hindus, Muslims, Sikhs, Jews, and Buddhists, were having a difficult time growing, primarily because they were having considerable difficulty holding on to their offspring, who all too frequently were marrying Catholics, Protestants, and people with no religion (Brym, Shaffir, and Weinfeld, 2010).

The size of a group is largely a function of immigration, birth, and mortality factors. What was disconcerting for religious leaders in Canada through the early 1990s was that most groups were top-heavy with older people, and many did not seem able to replace them with comparable numbers of younger people. As a result, it was estimated that, by 2015, weekly attendance would drop dramatically for mainline Protestants and Quebec Catholics, decline slightly for "Other World Faith" groups, and remain fairly stable for conservative Protestants and Roman Catholics elsewhere in Canada (Bibby 1993: 103ff). There was a very real possibility that the dominant players on the Canadian religious scene would be Roman Catholics and evangelical Protestants.

Religious groups are increasingly recognizing the importance of connecting with culture. Here Toronto Roman Catholic Archbishop Thomas Collins wears a Maple Leafs sweater in St. Peter's Square at the Vatican in February 2012, during the week when he was elevated to Cardinal.

SOURCE: Emanuel Pires/Archdiocese of Toronto.

Such projections are proving accurate. However, as we will see shortly, there is good reason to believe that the "old story" of *secularization* needs to be replaced by a "new story" of polarization. **Religious polarization** refers to the growing tendency of some people in a given setting to embrace religion and the tendency of others to reject it. A solid and growing core of Canadians are choosing to live life without religion. Simultaneously, a solid and durable core continues to see faith as important. The ongoing significance of religion for many people appears to reflect the efforts of groups to be more effective in addressing the needs and interests of children, teenagers, and young adults.

The Canadian Situation

Affiliation with religious groups has been widespread in Canada since the founding of this country. Close ties have always been apparent between Canadians of British descent and the Church of England, Methodism, and Presbyterianism; between the French and the Roman Catholic Church; and between other ethnic groups and the churches of their homelands (see, for example, Bramadat and Seljak, 2008). As noted earlier, Islam, Hindu, Sikh, and Buddhist growth in recent years has been directly related to immigration from Asia.

In the 2001 census, 84 percent of Canadians indicated that they have a religious preference. Nationally, Catholics compose 45 percent of the population; Protestants, 29 percent; and unspecified Christians, 3 percent. Seven percent consist of those with other religious preferences, and 16 percent have no specified religion (Table 13.2). A 2010 update offered by Statistics Canada's *General Social Survey* (GSS) of more than 15 000 people found the preference level remained high but had slipped a bit to 76 percent, with Catholics and Protestants composing 67 percent of the national population.

Such data suggest that it is an exaggeration to think of Canada as a highly diversified religious mosaic. As Statistics Canada (2003: 5) noted in releasing the 2001 census findings, Canada is "still predominantly Roman Catholic and Protestant." It's true that Muslim, Hindu, Sikh, and Buddhist populations all doubled in size between 1991 and 2001, and they have added diversity and vitality to the Canadian religious scene. Yet, measured against the Canadian population, their numbers are still relatively small. It is also premature to assume that their numbers will continue to grow, given the tendency of many of their offspring to socialize with and marry people outside their groups—a reality and challenge well known, for example, to Canada's Jewish community. Christian groups not only continue to hold a large monopoly but are frequently the primary beneficiaries of such intermarital "religious defection" (Bibby, 2002: 82–85). Time will fill out the story.

The Christian faith also continues to be pervasive in the United States, where surveys show that about 85 percent of Americans identify with Christian groups (Gallup, 2012). However, the numerically dominant groups in the United States are not the same as those in Canada. While one in two Canadians is Catholic, the same is true of only one in four Americans. Furthermore, just one in ten Canadians identifies with conservative Protestant (evangelical) groups, in contrast to more than three in ten Americans. A tipoff on the difference is that some

TABLE 13.2 RELIGIOUS IDENTIFICATION, CANADA AND THE PROVINCES AND TERRITORIES, 2001 (IN PERCENTAGE)

	CANADA	BC	AB	SK	MB	ON	QC	NB	NS	PE	NL	YT	NT	NU
Catholic	45	19	28	33	29	37	84	54	37	48	37	22	46	24
Roman	43	18	26	31	27	34	83	54	37	47	37	22	46	23
Eastern Orthodox	2	1	2	2	2	2	1	<1	<1	<1	<1	<1	<1	<1
Protestant	29	32	39	48	45	35	5	37	49	43	60	34	31	67
United	10	9	14	20	16	12	<1	10	16	20	17	9	6	1
Anglican	7	8	6	7	8	9	1	8	13	5	26	15	15	58
Presbyterian	1	1	1	<1	<1	3	<1	1	3	6	<1	1	1	<1
Lutheran	2	3	5	8	5	2	<1	<1	1	<1	<1	2	1	<1
Baptist	3	3	3	2	2	3	<1	11	11	5	<1	4	2	<1
Pentecostal	1	1	1	2	2	1	<1	3	1	1	7	2	3	4
Other	8	7	9	9	12	5	3	4	4	6	10	1	3	4
Christian: Other	3	5	4	3	4	3	1	1	1	2	1	4	3	3
Other faiths	7	8	6	<1	3	9	4	<1	<1	<1	<1	1	2	<1
Jewish	1	<1	<1	<1	1	2	1	<1	<1	<1	<1	<1	<1	<1
Muslim	2	2	2	<1	<1	3	2	<1	<1	<1	<1	<1	<1	<1
Hindu	1	<1	<1	<1	<1	2	<1	<1	<1	<1	<1	<1	<1	<1
Buddhist	1	2	1	<1	<1	1	1	<1	<1	<1	<1	<1	<1	<1
Sikh	<1	4	<1	<1	<1	<1	<1	<1	<1	<1	<1	<1	<1	<1
Other	<1	<1	<1	<1	<1	<1	<1	<1	<1	<1	<1	<1	<1	<1
No religion	16	36	23	16	19	16	6	8	12	6	2	39	18	6

SOURCE: Adapted from Statistics Canada. (2003). "Religions in Canada," Analysis Series, 2001 Census. Catalogue no. 96F0030XIE2002015.

40 percent of Americans claim that they are "born again" (Gallup, 2012); the term itself is not even particularly common in Canadian religious group circles, even among many of today's evangelicals. In fact, 31 percent of Canadians in our 2005 survey told us that if they were in the presence of someone they didn't know who was "born again," their immediate reaction would be to feel uncomfortable. They'd better not wander too far into the United States.

When Canadians are asked about actual *membership* in religious groups, as opposed to mere affiliation or identification, more people—about 30 percent—claim to belong to churches than to any other single voluntary group. About one in four attends services at least once a month, and roughly the same proportion of parents with school-age children expose their children to Sunday schools or similar kinds of religious instruction on a fairly frequent basis.

However, between approximately the 1940s and 2000, church attendance in Canada declined sharply, documented by Gallup poll findings summarized in Figure 13.1. Gallup had been asking Canadians if they attended a service "in the last seven days"—the phrasing of the inquiry adds sporadic attendees to those who claim they attend every week. Using such a measure, Gallup found that Protestant weekly attendance dropped from around 60 percent to about 30 percent between the 1940s and mid-1970s, rebounding to around 40 percent by the mid-1990s. The decline in Roman Catholic attendance appears to have started around 1965, dropping from roughly 85 percent to 40 percent by the late 1990s—led by low church-going in Quebec (for details, see Eagle, 2011; Bibby, 2011b). No such dramatic decline in attendance has taken place in the United States: Weekly attendance has remained remarkably steady at just over 40 percent dating back to the late 1930s when polling began (Newport, 2010; Newport, Moore, and Saad, 1999).

On the surface, evidence suggests that attendance has levelled off in Canada (Figure 13.2). In 1984, 23 percent of the country's 15- to 19-year-olds were attending services weekly. By 1992, the figure had dropped to 18 percent. Surprisingly, teenage

FIGURE 13.1 ATTENDANCE AT RELIGIOUS SERVICES, CANADA, 1946–2001

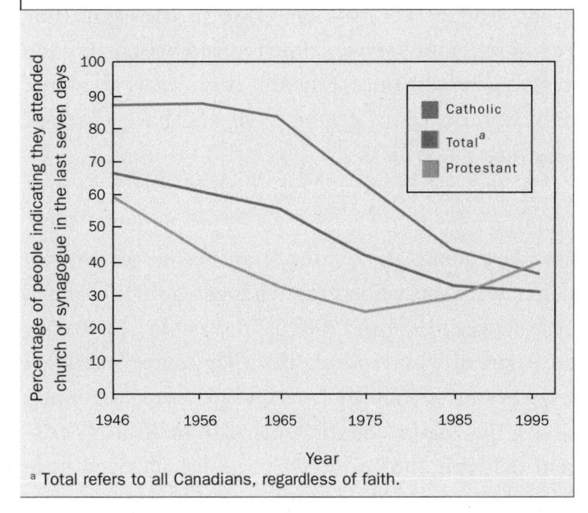

[a] Total refers to all Canadians, regardless of faith.

SOURCE: Gallup Canada, Inc., surveys, 1946–1995. Gallup's national figure for 2001 is 31 percent, for 2010 26 percent; no Protestant-Catholic breakdowns are available (Bibby, 2011a).

FIGURE 13.2 ATTENDANCE IN CANADA, 1975–2010

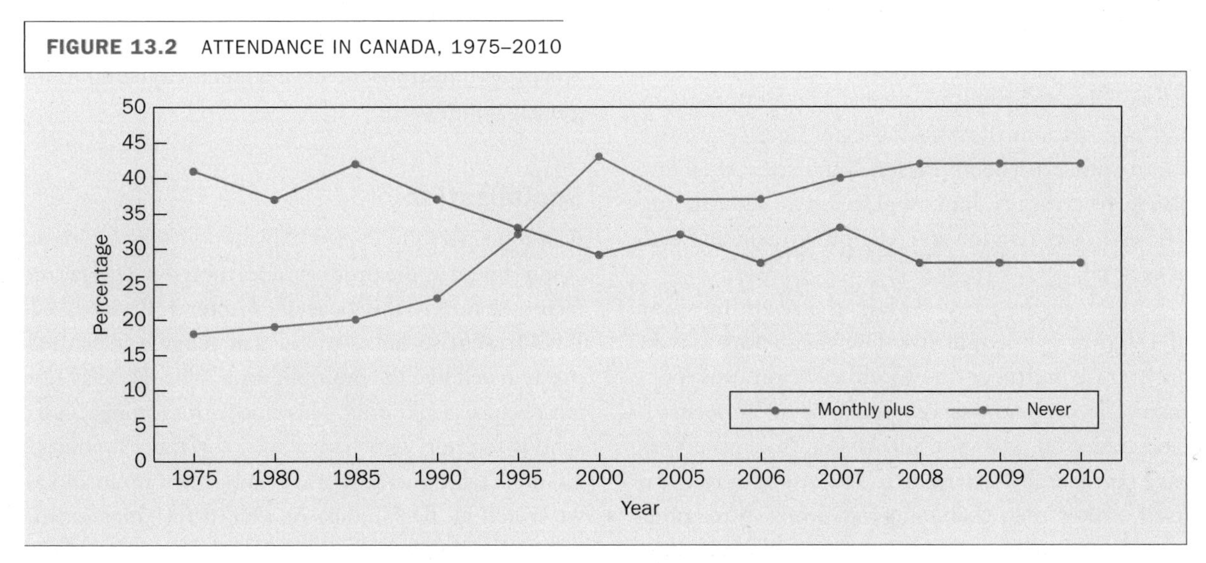

SOURCES: Reginald W. Bibby, *Project Canada Surveys*, 1975–1980; *General Social Surveys*, Statistics Canada, 1985–2010.

attendance rebounded to 21 percent in 2000, where it remains today (Bibby, 2009). Close to the same proportion of adults—some one in five—say they attend religious services close to every week, and one in three, at least once a month. Both levels are down only slightly from around 1990 and have changed very little since 2005.

What can be missed when we look only at how often people attend is how many people never show up. The findings are very important. While the proportion of teenagers who were attending regularly changed little between 1984 and 2008 (23 percent to 21 percent), the segment who reported that they "never" attended services almost doubled, from 28 to 47 percent. Among adults, the "never" figure doubled from 20 to 40 percent between 1985 and 2007, and has changed little since then (*General Social Survey*, 1985, 2010).

These attendance patterns point to an intriguing emerging religious situation in Canada: polarization. A fairly stable and durable segment of the population, comprised of both younger and older people, continue to value faith. However, for another growing segment, faith is unimportant. A significant proportion—like undecided voters—constitute something of an ambivalent middle who, in the longer run, "are up for grabs" (Bibby, 2011a: 51ff). Polarization, rather than secularization, captures the reality of these three important population components in Canada and elsewhere.

THE SOURCES OF RELIGION

More than a few religious leaders over the years who have seen their best efforts to involve people come up empty have murmured, "There is only so much we can do." It's an insightful lament. The best programs and ministries in the world will not hit a responsive chord with everybody. Personal and societal factors also play critically important roles in determining who embraces religion and religious groups, and who does not.

Much of the early work in the scientific study of religion by people like Durkheim focused on preliterate cultures in which religion was pervasive. Everyone was religious, or so it seemed. Consequently, it's not surprising that observers gave considerable attention to the origin of religion itself, rather than examining variations in religious commitment.

However, individual differences in religion's importance in contemporary societies have called for explanations as to why some people are religious and others are not. The explanations tend to focus either on individuals or on social structure.

INDIVIDUAL-CENTRED EXPLANATIONS

At least three dominant "person-centred" explanations of religious commitment have emerged. See to what extent you see yourself and others in what the experts have had to say.

Reflection

The desire to comprehend reality is widespread among humans. In reflecting on the meaning of existence, people have commonly concluded that life has a supernatural, "transempirical" dimension. As Weber (1963 [1922]: 117) put it, religion is the product of an "inner compulsion to understand the world as a meaningful cosmos and take up a position toward it."

There is little doubt that Canadians, like people elsewhere, reflect on life's so-called big questions. Some 80 percent say they think about such issues as the origin and purpose of life, the meaning of suffering, and what happens after we die. Such questions take on particular urgency when people have to come to grips with such events as the attacks on September 11, 2001, or a devastating tsunami—or have to deal with the suicide of a friend or the loss of a parent. Still, although such times of reflection may provide religious groups with an opportunity to respond, reflection in itself does not usually lead to religious commitment and involvement. Fewer than one in three Canadians who often raises these meaning questions gives evidence of being religiously committed.

Socialization

A second person-centred explanation sees religious commitment as the product of learning—socialization factors that were the focus of Chapter 3. Freud (1962 [1928]) went so far as to say that religion is learned pretty much like the multiplication table. He may not have been exaggerating. I have never forgotten a high-school teacher who had played for the Edmonton Eskimos telling us that if we had grown up in India, we would all be Hindus. As Durkheim emphasized, personal religiosity has social origins and, consequently, will strongly reflect the social environments from which we come, beginning with our family.

Why is an Iraqi a Muslim, a Londoner Church of England, a Ute (as in Utah) a Mormon, a Quebecker a Catholic? The answers are obvious. What is less clear is why some of those four people take their religion more seriously than the others do. To address the question, we probably would start by looking at the commitment level of their parents. Beyond family, we would expect that individuals who are devout have been exposed to additional social sources that are positive toward religion—friends, an ethnic group, an institution, a community or region, perhaps an entire society. Religion is very much a learned phenomenon.

Accommodation to social pressures, notably those of primary groups, seems to be a related source of religious group involvement. For example, one marriage partner may become more active in response to the hopes and expectations of the other, friends in response to friends, parents in response to having young children, children in response to their parents. As John McEnroe of tennis fame once put it, "I can go to church once in a while, just for Mom." In small communities where religion is pervasive and normative, accommodation would be expected to be an important source of religious involvement.

It's important to keep in mind that socialization appears to be a *necessary* but not a *sufficient* cause of religiosity. That is to say, to the extent that Canadians are currently involved in religious groups, most had parents who also were involved. However, the fact that Canadians had parents who were involved does not ensure that their sons and daughters will follow suit. Although about eight in ten of today's weekly attendees had parents who attended weekly, only about three in ten Canadians whose fathers or mothers attended weekly have followed their example.

With a decreasing number of parents actively involved in religious groups in recent decades, fewer have been passing the experience of organized religion on to their children. For example, in 1975, some 35 percent of Canadians with school-age children claimed that they and their children were attending services on a regular basis. By 2000, that figure had dropped to around 20 percent. Such a pattern, if it had continued, obviously would have had devastating numerical consequences for organized religion. But as of 2005, it had increased to 23 percent. The fact that the pro-religious proportion of parents remains fairly stable points to religion continuing to be important for a significant core of people, at the same time as it is becoming less salient for others.

One of the strongest predictors of adult religiosity is childhood religious practice. When parents participate in religious observance with their children, the early socialization experience is often imprinted for life.
SOURCE: © iStockphoto.com/Sean Locke.

If religious involvement and commitment are to last a lifetime, they need to receive ongoing social support. Our surveys have found that the commitment level of a partner is strongly related both to personal involvement and to the importance placed on religion. In more than seven in ten cases, if one partner is a weekly attendee, so is the other. In fewer than three in ten cases does a person attend weekly or view religion as "very important" if the partner does not.

Deprivation

A third person-centred explanation of religious commitment is that the devout are drawn primarily from the ranks of society's deprived or disadvantaged. Religion provides them with compensation, sometimes in this life, sometimes later. The roots of such thinking, of course, are found in the work of Marx and Freud.

The deprivation argument was developed more fully by Glock and Stark (1965), whose work has been influential. They maintained that five types of deprivation are predominant in the rise and development of religious and secular movements: economic, social, organismic (that is, physical or mental), psychic, and ethical. The first three types of deprivation are self-explanatory. Psychic deprivation refers to the lack of a meaningful system of values, and ethical deprivation refers to having values that are in conflict with those dominant in a society.

Research in the 1970s and 1980s using objective indicators, such as income, health, and social relationships, did not find deprivation to be a particularly good predictor of broad religious participation in either the United States (Roof and Hoge, 1980) or Canada (Hobart, 1974). The learning perspective seems to have had far more applicability.

Since 2000, suicide bombing has received considerable world attention. Because such attacks are often religiously inspired, and because they are so violent, you might expect the attackers to be driven by extreme deprivation. And, in fact, some observers initially hypothesized that suicide bombers must be poor, unemployed, uneducated, unmarried, socially marginal young adults with little to lose. Analysts assumed that people with such characteristics could be relatively easily convinced to exchange their lives of suffering in the here-and-now for promises of glory and martyrdom in the hereafter.

Research has demonstrated, however, that the deprivation argument does not hold in the case of suicide bombers. Sociologists Robert Brym of the University of Toronto and Bader Araj of Birzeit University in Palestine note in their study of suicide bombings in Israel, the West Bank, and Gaza from 2000 to 2005 that suicide bombers typically come from working-class and middle-class backgrounds, and they are generally better educated than the populations from which they are drawn. For example, the suicide bombers who were responsible for the attacks of September 11, 2001, were all well-educated, middle-class men (Brym and Araj, 2006). Studies of extreme forms of religious participation thus lead us to the same conclusion as studies of general populations: Deprivation does not appear to be systematically associated with religious commitment. This leads us to look for additional explanations of religious commitment.

STRUCTURE-CENTRED EXPLANATIONS

Suicide bombers hardly exist in social isolation. On the contrary, they typically are members of political and military groups found in the Middle East and, in the case of the Tamil Tigers, Sri Lanka. The groups to which they belong in turn are committed to getting rid of occupying forces, overthrowing existing regimes in their own countries or, in the case of a group like Hamas—the largest Palestinian resistance movement—obliterating Israel and creating an Islamic theocracy. Structural conditions clearly play an important role in such "religio-political" organizations coming into being and in individuals being recruited as members.

Such realities remind us that, in addition to personal characteristics of the reflection, socialization, and deprivation variety, religious commitment is strongly influenced by the broader national, regional, and group contexts in which people find themselves. You might immediately think of a theocracy, such as Iran, where the president and legislature are subject to clerical supervision. However, in virtually every society, Canada included, history and culture combine to create milieux that, to varying degrees, do or do not support religion.

Those proclivities often vary not only along national lines but also by the region in which people live and the groups of which they are a part. Historically, Canada's "Bible Belt" has been viewed as Alberta, when by every conceivable measure it probably has actually been the Atlantic region (Bibby, 1987; Hiller, 1976). Regardless, to grow up in either of these two regions results in being exposed to environments that are far more "pro-religious" than people experience in a province like British Columbia. Social environments are important determinants of religious commitment and involvement.

Two early prominent Canadian sociologists, S. D. Clark (1948) and W. E. Mann (1962) argued that, historically, the emergence of sect-like groups, such as indigenous Baptists and Pentecostals, in Canada was tied to the existence of unstable conditions, which were produced by such factors as immigration and economic depression. With industrialization and increased prosperity and stability, some of these smaller, independent evangelical groups evolved into denominations—a process referred to as **denominationalism.**

A further example of the impact of societal factors on religion can be found in Quebec. Much of the drop-off in Roman Catholic attendance between 1965 and 1980 was related to the accelerated modernization of Quebec, including the Church's relinquishing of much of its important role in education and social services to the provincial government (Beyer, 1993, 1997; Rouleau, 1977).

The climate that present-day societies provide for religion is the subject of considerable debate. Some observers maintain that increasing industrialization and postindustrialization contribute to a decline in the pervasiveness and importance of religion. This widely held **secularization thesis** has been prominent in the social sciences, largely because of the influence of Durkheim, Marx, and Freud. It's a framework that seems particularly appropriate to developments in much of Protestant Europe. It also is the dominant explanatory framework the media and Statistics Canada use in making sense of religious developments in Canada (see, for example, Catto, 2003; Statistics Canada, 2004a, 2004b; Valpy and Friesen, 2010).

But there is also another take on religious developments—what we might call the **persistence thesis.** Proponents of this position, among them Daniel Bell (1977) and Rodney Stark and William Bainbridge (1985), claim that religion—traditional or otherwise—persists in industrial and postindustrial or postmodern societies, continuing to address questions of meaning and purpose, and responding to widespread interest in spirituality. Stark maintains that some religious groups or companies will fail, but because of ongoing market demand, new ones will emerge to pick up the slack. What is in doubt is not the persistence of religion, only the identity of the key players.

In Canada, we can readily explore the relationship between religious involvement and commitment and some of the correlates of social and cultural change, such as age, urbanization, education, and employment status. If the secularization thesis is correct, we would expect religiosity to be pretty low for everyone by this point in our history, particularly so for Canadians who are younger, are living in larger communities, are well educated, and are part of the paid work force. Conversely, if the persistence thesis is correct, we would expect some variations in these anticipated patterns.

Here are the main findings:

- Differences in religious group involvement are readily apparent, with attendance lowest among people under 35, somewhat higher for those 35 to 54, and highest among Canadians 55 and older (Table 13.3). There is also some support for the idea that secularization is most advanced in those parts of Canada that were first to experience extensive economic development—central Canada and the west coast.
- Religious participation varies little by community size, education, gender, and employment status. However, full-time employment is associated with a noticeable decline in attendance for women, presumably related to time pressures. The post-1950s increase in dual-employed parents may, in fact, be largely responsible for the decline in mainline Protestant and Catholic attendance in Canada in the last half of the twentieth century (Bibby, 2011a: 262. Robert Putnam (2000: 195) makes a similar point with respect to the impact on service attendance in the United States, while Callum Brown (2009) has drawn attention to the same pattern in Britain. Religious groups needed to adapt by providing "ministries" that responded to changing family life. Few have.
- It is intriguing to note that, while just fewer than one in three Canadians currently attends services monthly or more, one in two people across the country says that he or she engages in personal religious practices or spiritual activities at least once a month, while two in three tell Statistics Canada that their religious or spiritual beliefs are either very important" or "somewhat important" to how they live their lives. While there are some variations by age, region, and gender, differences are minor by community size, education, and employment. A majority of Canadians in every demographic and social category, for example, report that their religious or spiritual beliefs have significantly influenced how they live.

Such findings about the ongoing personal importance of religion and/or spirituality are consistent with what observers from Durkheim to Stark have expected. Many Canadians are religious and spiritual, many are spiritual but not religious, but only a minority appears to be *neither* religious *nor* spiritual (Bibby, 2011a: 124–26. The data also point to the fact that an extensive market for religion and spirituality persists.

THE CONSEQUENCES OF RELIGION

In today's increasingly pragmatic world, Canadians face what seem like unlimited choices and limited resources. We need to sort out what is worth our time and what is not. Religion gets no exemption from such selective consumption.

TABLE 13.3 SERVICE ATTENDANCE, PERSONAL PRACTICES, AND THE IMPORTANCE OF RELIGION AND SPIRITUALITY BY SOCIAL CHANGE CORRELATES, CANADIAN ADULTS, 2010 (IN PERCENTAGES)

	SERVICE ATTENDANCE *MONTHLY-PLUS*	PERSONAL RELIGIOUS PRACTICES OR SPIRITUAL ACTIVITIES *MONTHLY-PLUS*	RELIGIOUS OR SPIRITUAL BELIEFS *VERY OR SOMEWHAT IMPORTANT TO HOW YOU LIVE YOUR LIFE*
Nationally	28	51	66
Age			
55 and over	37	61	78
35–54	25	50	66
18–34	22	41	53
Community Size			
Larger urban centres	24	48	62
Rural areas	25	49	65
Region			
Atlantic	33	54	71
Prairies	33	55	72
Ontario	31	54	69
British Columbia	25	47	64
Quebec	20	44	56
Education			
High school or less	29	52	67
Some postsecondary	26	49	65
Degree or more	31	52	66
Gender and Paid Employment (under 65, non-students)			
Female	27	56	69
Not employed outside the home	33	62	74
Employed outside the home	24	53	68
Male	23	40	57
Not employed outside the home	25	41	57
Employed outside the home	22	39	56
Not employed outside the home (male and female)	32	58	71
Employed outside the home (male and female)	23	46	62
Women (all)	24	53	68
Men (all)	22	39	56

SOURCE: Derived from Statistics Canada, *General Social Survey*, 2010.

Gone is the day when religious leaders could expect people to become involved in their groups because it's "their duty." Our 2005 national survey found that 61 percent of Canadians believed that their parents "felt they were supposed to go to church." Eighty-seven percent of respondents maintained that, today, "people who attend religious services should not go because they feel they have to but because they find it to be worthwhile."

Is religion "worthwhile"? On balance, does it enhance personal and social life?

PERSONAL CONSEQUENCES

Research findings on religion and what we might refer to generally as "mental health" are contradictory. Important early work carried out by social psychologist Milton Rokeach (1965: 2) led him to conclude, "We have found that

Canadians of every social and demographic stripe tend to acknowledge that they have spiritual needs.
SOURCE: © Shutterstock.

people with formal religious affiliation are more anxious [than others are]. Believers, compared with nonbelievers, complain more often of working under great tension, sleeping fitfully, and similar symptoms." Yet research dating back to the 1970s has consistently found a negative relationship between religious commitment and *anomie*—valuelessness and rootlessness (Lee and Clyde, 1974). Over the years a number of researchers have argued that involvement in groups, such as sects and cults, has contributed to upward mobility, providing an improved self-image and hope in the face of economic and social deprivation (e.g., Johnson, 1961; Whyte, 1966). During the 1970s and 1980s, considerable literature emerged warning against the psychological and emotional damage that could be inflicted by the alleged "brainwashing" of cults (Dawson, 2006: 95ff).

Gale Frankel and W. E. Hewitt (1994) of the University of Western Ontario are among the researchers who have found a positive relationship between religious group involvement and good mental health. Research into the "Toronto Blessing" congregation has even maintained that physical healing sometimes occurs (Poloma, 1997; Poloma and Hoelter, 1998). National denominational surveys that I have carried out for the United Church of Canada and the evangelical Christian and Missionary Alliance document a fairly predictable conclusion: People who are highly involved in established religious groups claim that their involvement significantly enriches their lives (Bibby, 2012; in the United States, Newport, 2007).

What seems apparent from all this is that some forms of religiosity are connected with well-being, while others are not.

My own analyses of our survey data dating back to 2000 suggest that, overall, Canadians who exhibit religious commitment are slightly more inclined than others to claim a high level of happiness; to find life exciting; to express a high level of satisfaction with family, friends, and leisure activities (Bibby, 2004a: 128–29, 2011a: 98ff; Figure 13.3). However, when the impact of other factors, such as age, education, community size, and region, is taken into account, the apparent modest influence of commitment typically disappears or at least has to be qualified. For example, Gee and Veevers (1990) found that religious involvement and life satisfaction were positively related nationally, but not in British Columbia.

In short, religious commitment by itself appears to have a fairly limited influence on valued personal characteristics. Moreover, it is often less important than such variables as age, education, or employment in predicting personal well-being.

An important word of caution: this "no difference" finding does not mean that faith is not adding something to the lives of people who value faith. Rather, in light of the high levels of happiness and contentment reported by Canadians generally, it suggests that large numbers of other people are finding alternative pathways to personal well-being. Religion is having an impact—but not necessarily a unique impact.

INTERPERSONAL CONSEQUENCES

One of the first attempts to examine the relationship between religious commitment and compassion was carried out by Clifford Kirkpatrick in Minnesota in 1949. He found that religiously committed people

FIGURE 13.3 PERSONAL WELL-BEING AND RELIGIOUS SERVICE ATTENDANCE, 2005

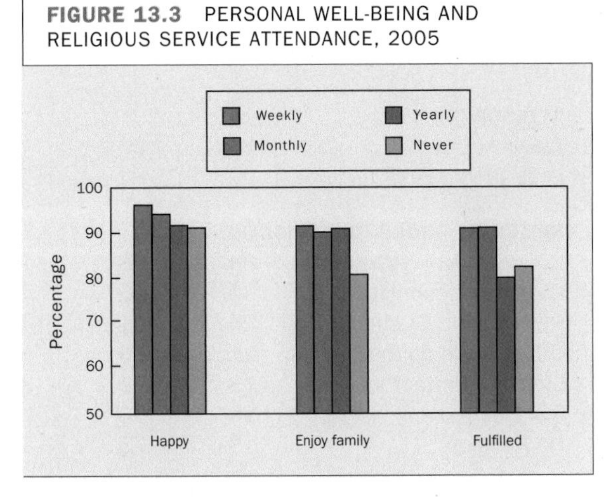

SOURCE: Reginald W. Bibby, *Project Canada 2005*.

were somewhat less humanitarian in their outlook than were others.

Some 20 years later, Rokeach (1969), drawing on U.S. national data, observed that religious commitment was *negatively* related to social compassion; in the case of Roman Catholics, no relationship—positive or negative—existed. Rokeach concluded that "the results seem compatible with the hypothesis that religious values serve more as standards for condemning others ... than as standards to judge oneself by or to guide one's own conduct" (Rokeach, 1969: 35).

These findings have not gone unchallenged. Research conducted on specific religious groups and in certain locales has found a positive relationship between commitment and compassion. In a more immediate relational sense, Wilcox (1998) has found that, although conservative Protestant parents are more likely than others are to use corporal punishment in disciplining their children, they also are more likely than other parents were to praise and hug their children. Extensive research on religion and racial prejudice, such as Smith's (1999) look at anti-Semitism and "the Religious Right," has yielded contradictory results.

However, some three decades ago, Richard Gorsuch and Daniel Aleshire claimed to have found the key reason for the discrepancies. Church members often appear to be more prejudiced than those who have never joined a church. But, they say, it is not because of religious involvement. On the contrary, when involvement level is taken into account, the people who turn out to be the most prejudiced are the "marginally involved" members. Gorsuch and Aleshire concluded, "The highly committed religious person is—along with the nonreligious person—one of the least prejudiced members of our society" (Gorsuch and Aleshire, 1974: 287). If this is the case, then, as with personal characteristics, religion may be making a difference interpersonally—but it is not a unique difference.

Ongoing analyses of Project Canada data have found that religiously committed people in this country do not differ significantly from others with respect to their interpersonal relationship attitudes (Bibby, 1987, 1995, 2004a). They hold a similar view of people, claim a comparable level of compassion, and appear to be no more or less tolerant of deviants, members of minority groups, and people of other religious faiths than are other Canadians. Furthermore, in contrast to the findings of Rokeach and Stark and Glock, no noteworthy differences appear in the interpersonal attitudes held by Roman Catholics and Protestants.

There is, however, one area in which religion still appears to speak with a fairly loud if not unique voice—the area of personal morality, notably sexuality. With few exceptions and with varying degrees of explicitness, religious groups tend to oppose "moral innovation." Examples include opposition to changing sexual standards, legal abortion, and distribution of pornographic materials (see Table 13.4).

That said, there is considerable variation in the position that religious groups take on many sex-related

TABLE 13.4 PERCENTAGE OF CANADIANS OPPOSED TO SELECTED ISSUES BY SERVICE ATTENDANCE AND GROUP IDENTIFICATION, 2005

	PRE-MARITAL SEX	EXTRA-MARITAL SEX	HOMO-SEXUALITY	SAME-SEX MARRIAGE	ABORTION: RAPE	ABORTION: CHILD UNWANTED	DISTRIBUTION OF PORNOGRAPHY
ATTENDANCE							
Weekly	60	96	75	62	45	79	69
Less than weekly	7	82	25	20	4	36	31
RELIGIOUS GROUP IDENTIFICATION							
Conservative Protestants	64	98	74	64	41	82	69
Christian Unspecified	30	92	45	44	28	65	44
RC: Outside Quebec	25	91	47	37	25	62	47
Other World Faiths	21	86	38	33	12	46	39
Mainline Protestants	13	89	35	28	6	40	43
RC: Quebec	10	78	33	22	6	40	35
No Religion	3	73	10	7	1	19	17

SOURCE: Derived from Reginald W. Bibby, *Project Canada 2005 National Survey.*

issues, as well as in the inclination of average people who identify with those groups to "follow the party line." Generally speaking, evangelical Protestants are the most likely to be opposed to changes in the sexual realm, Quebec Catholics—despite the official position of their Church—the most receptive, with their openness exceeded only by Canadians with no religion.

But this just in. Two recent analyses that I have carried out on adults and teens show that there is a consistent, positive relationship between holding clear-cut belief in God and endorsing interpersonal values that make for civility—such traits as honesty, concern for others, politeness, and the like. Canadians who "definitely believe in God" consistently differ from atheists (Bibby, 2009, 2011a; see Table 13.5). That's not to say that theists necessarily come through behaviourally, or that there is no social compassion, for example, among atheists. The findings do suggest, however, that belief in God is one, if only one, potential source of civility. To the extent that that is the case, there could be some significant social value in people believing in God. Recent atheist media blitzes in Canada and elsewhere—using such catch lines as, "There's probably no god. Now stop worrying and enjoy your life"—may, in the end, have limited interpersonal payoffs.

SOCIETAL CONSEQUENCES

I've looked at some personal and interpersonal consequences of religious involvement and commitment.

TABLE 13.5 VALUES OF THEIST AND ATHEIST TEENS, PERCENTAGE INDICATING "VERY IMPORTANT"

	NATIONALLY	THEISTS	ATHEISTS
Trust	84	88	78
Honesty	81	86	75
Concern for others	65	72	54
Politeness	64	71	57
Forgiveness	60	72	44
Working hard	55	61	49
Patience	44	55	35

SOURCE: Bibby, Reginald W. (2009). *The Emerging Millennials.* Lethbridge, AB: Project Canada Books.

But what about the net consequences for societies more generally? On balance, is religion a plus or a minus—or simply irrelevant?

A cursory look at the historical evidence in Canada provides mixed reviews. Many would argue that religion has played and continues to play an important role in helping immigrants adjust to life in Canada, providing resources in the form of both personal faith and social support. Others would quickly add that many religious groups, notably the United, Anglican, and Roman Catholic churches, along with the Jewish community, have played important roles in helping to establish a just society, where diversity and inclusiveness today are valued on a level matched by few countries anywhere in the world. In addition, the claim can be made that religious groups are among the few organizations in Canada that explicitly attempt to instill morality, ethics, and compassion, thereby making an important contribution to civility.

Those things said, you hardly need me to remind you that other views of religious groups are not so charitable. For example,

- In the course of taking their place in the country, a number of Christian groups were anything but just and compassionate in their treatment of Aboriginal peoples, including their complicity with government goals in running residential schools.
- The "Quiet Revolution" in Quebec in the 1960s that saw the province take over many services from the Catholic Church was not accompanied by an overt revolt. However, covertly, large numbers of Catholics had found the Church to be highly oppressive and began to stay away (Graham, 1990: 114ff).
- A variety of highly publicized sexual abuse cases that spanned the country—from the Mount Cashel orphanage in Newfoundland and Labrador, through the "Orphans of Duplessis" in Quebec and the Christian Brothers in Ontario, to the Catholic Diocese in Prince Rupert, B.C.—left many Canadians stunned and disenchanted with organized religion (see Bibby, 1993: 68ff).
- Catholics, Jews, and Muslims, along with smaller religious bodies, including Mennonites, Hutterites, Jehovah's Witnesses, Scientologists, and Doukhobors, have been on the receiving end of hostility and discrimination at various points in our nation's history.

Clearly the evidence to date is mixed. Religion adds to the quality of life in the country and sometimes subtracts. What does seem to contribute to a fairly unique religious situation in Canada is the entrenchment of pluralism. Religious groups here have to play by the rules of diversity, being respectful of one another—not making excessive claims of uniqueness, not being overly aggressive in raiding each other's ranks, not being exploitive of vulnerable categories, such as immigrants, children, and seniors. And they have to respect individual rights, in keeping with the Charter of Rights.

So contained, religious organizations that might otherwise have a detrimental effect on collective life in Canada are kept in check. We have no effective "Moral Majority," as the United States does. The same-sex marriage issue was not allowed to become an unrestrained and uncivil debate, and if someone tested the boundaries—as one Alberta bishop was tempted to do on occasion—public opinion tended to result in public relations retreats. This is not a country where Christians can call other people "heathen," but they also cannot be ridiculed as "bigoted Bible-thumpers." This is not a country where Muslims can call for the heads and hands of artists who draw caricatures of Mohammed, but it also is not a place where artists can insult and incite Muslims. Some groups don't always like the rules, but that's the way the religion game is played in Canada. So contained, religion—it seems to me—is positioned to contribute positively to our individual and collective life (Box 13.1).

More than half a century ago, Peter Berger (1961) noted that Durkheim's assertion that religion functions primarily to integrate societies seems to offer a good description of religion in the United States. Religion, or at least the mainline segment of organized Christianity that historically has embraced the largest number of members, has tended to endorse American culture rather than to challenge it, to endorse the status quo rather than call for social transformation. So intense has been the bond between religion and American life that for some time observers such as Robert Bellah (1967) have described the phenomenon as American **civil religion.** In an influential book, *Protestant, Catholic, Jew*, Will Herberg (1960: 75) put it this way:

> Americans, by and large, do have their "common religion" and that "religion" is the system familiarly known as the American Way of Life. ... By every realistic criterion the American Way of Life is the operative faith of the American people. ... To be a Protestant, a Catholic, or a Jew are today the alternative ways of being an American.

Canada, committed as it is to diversity and a downplaying of overt nationalism—except for the occasional international hockey championship—has no such civil religion. As the University of Regina's William Stahl (1986: 16) has colourfully put it, "Other than a few bands and firecrackers, Confederation was not attended by much emotional outpouring." And religious groups have done little to add fervour to our rather lifeless expressions of nationalism. Still, Harold Fallding (1978) reminds us that, historically, "Canadian Protestant churches have reflected the British position of legitimizing authority through supporting government, offering prayers, for example, for its success in securing order and justice." The fusion of Catholicism with life in Quebec, Anglicanism with the status quo in southern Ontario, and conservative Protestantism with political and social life in Alberta are obvious examples.

On occasion, of course, religion has challenged North American culture. The civil rights movement in the United States received much of its leadership and impetus from African American evangelical churches. American Catholic bishops and the National Council of Churches have frequently spoken out against perceived injustices, including poverty, racism, and war. Jerry Falwell's "Moral Majority," which peaked in the 1980s, contributed to a very vocal "Christian Right," committed to altering the nature of American life by influencing the country's major institutions.

In Canada, religious groups have had and continue to have the freedom to address governments. To varying degrees they have availed themselves of the opportunity—and responsibility. Protestant churches, for example, have received mixed reviews for their concern about the plight of Jews during World War II; some churches and individuals were silent, while others were not (Davies and Nefsky, 1997). In the 1940s, a radical effort was made by the Roman Catholic Church to support striking workers, a preview of the ongoing inclination of the Canadian Conference of Catholic Bishops to support average Canadians and to be vocal in criticizing the profit orientation of the nation's economy. Protestant groups, often led by the United Church, along with a growing number of ecumenical consortia and initiatives, and, more recently, evangelical churches, have been making concerted efforts to bring about

BOX 13.1 WHY THE GLOBAL RAGE HASN'T ENGULFED CANADA: MULTICULTURALISM AND MEDIA LIKELY MUTED PROTESTS

Why haven't Muslims in Canada taken to the streets in large numbers to protest against cartoons of the Prophet Mohammed? It's not because everyone in Canada is so nice to each other, say Canadian Muslim leaders and Islamic scholars. It's because Canada's multiculturalism is complex.

They say Muslim immigration into Canada has been different. So has Muslim integration into Canadian society. And so has the political action of Canadian Muslim organizations around the highly sensitive issue of Islamic religious fundamentalism.

The difference is illustrated by events in France in 2004 and Canada in 2005, said Tarek Fatah, a leader of the Muslim Canadian Congress.

In France, few if any representative voices within the French Muslim community were heard in the news media speaking in favour of a law banning conspicuous religious symbols, such as the traditional Muslim head scarf, in public schools.

This was the case even though a significant percentage of French Muslims had no problem accepting the law within the cultural context of French secular society.

The powerful Muslim opposition that was heard, Mr. Fatah said, came from "the mosque structure" but "the mobilization of moderate Muslim voices never happened."

In contrast, in Canada in 2005, the news media pointedly reported that the most vociferous opposition to an Ontario law permitting Islamic religious tribunals to arbitrate family and marital disputes came from Muslim organizations themselves.

In Mr. Fatah's view, the mainstream Muslim community in Canada has recognized the need to take what he calls "ownership of the word Muslim." It has become actively involved in Canadian political life and not marginalized as is the case in many Western countries.

"It's a shift, for Canadian Muslims, that has not happened anywhere else."

Mohamed Elmasry, president of the Canadian Islamic Congress, said violent demonstrations simply aren't a fit with the Canadian Muslim community—which, because of Canada's immigration requirements, he said, is the most highly educated Muslim community in the world.

"They would find legal and peaceful means of protest far more productive," said the imam and professor at the University of Waterloo. "With demonstrations, you cannot have full control over who does what."

His organization, the largest Muslim umbrella group in Canada, has actively discouraged demonstrations over the cartoons and has spoken publicly against the violent protests—as has the Muslim Canadian Congress.

Earle Waugh, a University of Alberta Islamic scholar, said most Muslim immigrants to Canada do not feel sidelined, a factor significantly fuelling the protests in European countries.

"There is no sympathy within the Canadian Muslim community for a radical approach," he said. "No sympathy for the fundamentalists."

Canada has had no legacy of Muslim colonies like that of the British and French, and no history of migrant Muslim guest workers like that of Germany.

SOURCE: Michael Valpy, 2006, "Why the Global Rage Hasn't Engulfed Canada: Multiculturalism and Media Likely Muted Protests," *Globe and Mail* 8 February, p. A14. Reprinted with permission from *The Globe and Mail.*

social change (Crysdale, 1961; Lewis, 1993; Stiller, 1997). Religious coalitions, such as the national Citizens for Public Justice and, in Ontario, the broad-based Interfaith Social Assistance Reform Coalition (ISARC), have been among those calling for greater and more effective attention being directed toward social programs, the environment, and Aboriginal issues.

It is important to note that locally, nationally, and globally, religion clearly has the potential both to bring people together and to tear them apart. Religion's role in contributing to conflict, past and present, is well known. Globally, what seems like never-ending conflict in the Middle East and elsewhere provides further contemporary examples of religion playing a role in contributing to divisiveness. At times I—along with many others—wonder about the long-term outcome of what seems to be a deepening chasm between the West and the Muslim world.

Yet in the aftermath of both the September 11, 2001, attacks and the fury over the publishing of the Mohammed caricatures in 2006, significant numbers of Muslim leaders were among the first to decry violence and bloodshed, and to call on people worldwide to find peaceful means of resolving their differences. Therein lies the paradox of religion: It can both enrich and destroy social life.

THE FUTURE OF RELIGION

One thing is certain: Religion is not going to disappear. Proponents of the secularization thesis expected religion to be replaced by science and reason as societies evolved. Opponents of the secularization thesis countered that humans have needs, notably the need to come to grips with death, that only religion can satisfy. It is noteworthy that one unique contribution religion brings to the Canadian religious and spiritual marketplace is hope in the face of death (Bibby, 2011a: 174–76). Consequently, even if secularization leads to the demise of some religious groups, new providers are bound to appear. Ironically, rather than signalling the end of religion, secularization stimulates innovation (Stark and Bainbridge, 1985).

Emerging religious forms will include sects—groups that break away from established religions, and new religious movements (**cults**) with origins outside of older religions. From this point of view, shifts in the overall "religious economy" over time involve "the rising and falling fortunes of religious firms, not the rise and fall of religion per se" (Finke and Stark, 1992: 275).

As we glance around the globe, there is no need to spend time debating religion's future with the wise social scientists of old. Religion is simply everywhere (see, for example, Cox, 2009; Allen, 2009; Mead, 2010; Reynolds, 2011; Thomas, 2010; Table 13.6).

In Canada, there are signs that a modest rise in religious involvement is taking place that will continue in the immediate future. However, it is due not so much to the arrival of new religions as it is to the rejuvenation of the older, well-established ones.

Census and survey data reveal that fairly small numbers of Canadians have opted for new religious groups in recent decades. The proportion of Canadians who identified with such groups as Jehovah's Witnesses and Mormons has never been more than one-half of 1 percent. In a country of some 35 million people, newer, sect-like groups remain on the margins of the Canadian religious scene.

Further, we now know that relatively few people have been switching from one group to another—apart from a fair amount of movement *within* conservative Protestantism, where people who are Pentecostal move to a Baptist church, for example. The amount of "inter-family" switching—such as Roman Catholics becoming Protestants, or Jews or Muslims opting for Catholicism—has been grossly exaggerated.

TABLE 13.6 THE WORLD'S 16 LARGEST RELIGIONS

RELIGION	NUMBER OF ADHERENTS WORLDWIDE
1. Christianity	2.1 billion
2. Islam	1.5 billion
3. Hinduism	900 million
4. Chinese folk	395 million
5. Buddhism	375 million
6. Sikhism	23 million
7. Juche	19 million
8. Spiritism	15 million
9. Judaism	14 million
10. Falun Gong	10 million
11. Bahäi	7 million
12. Cao Dai	5 million
13. Confucianism	5 million
14. New Age	5 million
15. Jainism	4 million
16. Shinto	4 million
No Religion, secular	1.1 billion

SOURCE: Bibby, Reginald W. (2011a). *Beyond the Gods & Back: Religion's Rise and Demise and Why It Matters*. Lethbridge, AB: Project Canada Books, p. 201. Drawn from www.adherents.com 2010 and www.religionfacts.com 2010.

A big surprise? Despite the fact that the proportion of Canadians who say they have "no religion" increased from 4 percent in 1971 to 16 percent in 2001, most haven't really been dropping out permanently. The majority of people in this category are young and single. About one-third have come from mainline Protestant homes, another one-third from Catholic homes; only about one in three have parents who also have no religion. As they get a bit older, marry, have children, and want religious weddings, baptisms, and the like, lo and behold, many proceed to tell pollsters that they are "Catholic" or "United" or "Jewish"—again. Using the panel component of our national surveys, we have found that, within five years, one in three people who said he or she had "no religion" proceeds to have one; within ten years that figure jumps to two in three. The "no religion" category is a temporary residence for most people—sort of like living in an apartment before moving into a house (Bibby, 2004b: 29–51).

We consequently have a situation in which Canada's established religious groups find themselves with lots of "affiliates" who identify with the group and aren't about to turn elsewhere. I'm not talking only about adults. Our national surveys of teenagers between the ages of 15 and 19 have found that the country's "emerging generation" closely resembles adults when it comes to current service attendance levels. About 90 percent of teens claim the same group affiliation as their parents, and only about 2 percent indicate any strong interest in new religions. Their belief, practice, experience, and knowledge levels, while typically lower than those of adults, are appreciable and, in at least some instances, can be expected to rise as teens move into their 20s and beyond. Some three in ten say religious involvement is important to them and their level of enjoyment of religious groups is on par with that of adults. In addition, more than half acknowledge that they have spiritual needs (see Table 13.7).

So let's add all this up: Canadians are not doing much switching or dropping out. The overwhelming majority continue to hold beliefs, engage in practices, experience the gods, and express spiritual needs. Perhaps they just aren't interested in organized religion? Not so. Our surveys over the past few decades have been documenting a consistent finding: More than one in two people who attend services less than once a month say they are receptive to greater involvement if it is worthwhile for themselves or their families (Figure 13.4). What do these people see as "worthwhile?" Having their spiritual needs met, getting some insight into how they might have better relationships with partners and children and friends, and maybe finding some emotional resources to help them cope with the needs they face in living everyday life. Likewise, about 40 percent of seldom-attending teens say they are open to greater involvement—"if I found it to be worthwhile" (Bibby, 2009, 2011a, 2012). In short, many people in Canada haven't given up on religion—and haven't even given up on religious groups. However, in the midst of living lives that are full, where time and other resources are often being severely stretched, they have to find significance in religious participation. Otherwise, why bother? The research suggests that, to the

TABLE 13.7 A PROFILE OF RELIGION AND SPIRITUALITY IN CANADA: TEENAGERS AND ADULTS (IN PERCENTAGE)

	ADULTS	TEENAGERS
Beliefs		
God	82	67
Atheism	7	16
Life after death	67	75
Spirit world contact	46	46
Practice (weekly)		
Pray privately	45	30
Attend religious services	25	21
Read the Bible/ other scriptures	19	9
Experience		
Have experienced God	49	39
Knowledge		
Denier of Jesus	41	23
Sacred book of Islam	53	30
Religious Involvement		
Is important	53	30
Is enjoyed	25	26
Spirituality		
Have spiritual needs	72	54

SOURCES: Bibby (2006, 2009).

FIGURE 13.4 RECEPTIVITY TO GREATER INVOLVEMENT IN RELIGIOUS GROUPS BY AGE COHORT, PROTESTANTS AND CATHOLICS ATTENDING LESS THAN ONCE A MONTH, 2005

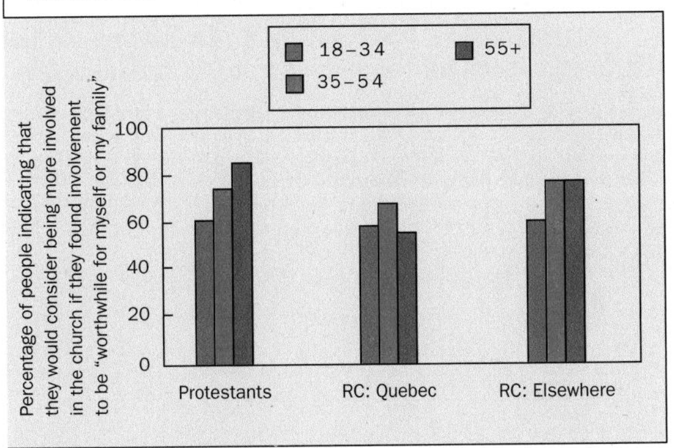

SOURCE: Bibby (2006: p. 202).

extent that groups literally find "their affiliates" and succeed in touching their lives in significant ways, many will become involved. There's no doubt that the proportion of Canadians who are tuning out of religion has been increasing in recent decades. They may compose about one-third of the population. But another one-third or so continue to value faith. The remaining one-third are "religiously undecided"; they haven't dropped out and occasionally drop in.

Assuming that the need for religion will persist for large numbers of people, the three central academic questions that need to be answered are (1) Which "religious companies" will be the most prominent? (2) How effective will be they be in responding to Canadians? (3) To what extent will the population tend to gravitate toward the religious and nonreligious ends of "the polarization continuum."

SUMMARY

1. Sociology uses the scientific method to study religion. Religion explores reality beyond what can be known empirically.
2. The sociology of religion has been strongly influenced by the theoretical contributions of Marx, who stressed the compensatory role of religion in the face of economic deprivation; Durkheim, who emphasized both the social origin of religion and its important social cohesive function; and Weber, who gave considerable attention to the relationship between ideas and behaviour.
3. Religion can be defined as a system of meaning with a supernatural referent used to interpret the world. Humanist perspectives make no such use of the supernatural realm, attempting instead to make life meaningful.
4. Personal religious commitment increasingly has come to be seen as having many facets or dimensions. Four such dimensions are commonly noted: belief, practice, experience, and knowledge. Personal commitment is created and sustained by collective religiosity. In Canada, religious polarization has been increasing in recent decades, resulting in solid cores of people both valuing religion and rejecting it—trends with critical implications for commitment at the individual level.
5. Variations in the levels of individual commitment that characterize complex societies have led to explanations that emphasize individual and structural factors. Reflection, socialization, and deprivation have been prominent among the individual explanations, while the dominant structural assertion has been the secularization thesis.
6. Religion appears to be, at best, one of many paths leading to valued characteristics, such as personal happiness and compassion. Although religion can be socially disruptive, Canada's emphasis on social and cultural diversity functions to put limits on how religion can be expressed, thereby optimizing the possibility of religions contributing positively to social and collective life.
7. Although proponents of secularization saw religion as being replaced by science and reason, it is now apparent that religion continues to be important throughout the world, including Canada. Its future is not in doubt.
8. The search for alleged religious switchers and dropouts in Canada reveals that few have turned elsewhere or permanently opted for "no religion." Most still identify with the country's established groups.
9. Canadians young and old, in large numbers, continue to hold religious beliefs, claim religious experiences, and express spiritual needs. Many also say they are receptive to greater involvement with religious groups.
10. The inclination for Canadians to embrace religion or reject it will depend largely on how religious groups respond to ongoing interests and needs.

QUESTIONS TO CONSIDER

1. Which of the three key theorists do you find to be the most helpful in understanding religion: Durkheim, Marx, or Weber?
2. What does it mean to be religious?
3. Do you see yourself as (a) religious and spiritual, (b) spiritual but not religious, (c) religious but not spiritual, or (d) neither religious nor spiritual?
4. What kinds of people do you find are interested in (a) spirituality and (b) organized religion? Do you think there are any noticeable differences by age?
5. Does religion make any difference in the lives of the people you know? How would Canadian society be different if organized religion disappeared?
6. Do you think it is true that secularization stimulates religious innovation—that the decline of old groups provides the opportunity for new groups to surface and prosper?
7. Imagine that you are serving as a consultant to a major Canadian religious group. What might you suggest it consider doing to (a) keep the people it has and (b) gain the interest of people who are not actively involved?

GLOSSARY

The **church-sect typology** (p. 319) is a framework, originating with Weber, in which religious organizations are studied in terms of ideal-type characteristics. (churches emphasize works and stress accommodation to society, while sects stress faith and separation from society).

Civil religion (p. 332) refers to the tendency for nationalistic emphases to be nurtured by a society's religions, so that a culture takes on many religious-like characteristics. The term is most often used with respect to the United States.

Collective conscience (p. 314) is Durkheim's term referring to awareness that a group is more than the sum of its individual members and the belief that such awareness is experienced as the supernatural.

Collective religiosity (p. 318) is religious commitment as manifested in and through religious groups; it is key to the creation and sustenance of personal religiosity.

Cults (p. 334) are religious groups that have their origins outside older religions. Sects, in contrast, are groups that have broken away from established religions.

Denominationalism (p. 326) refers to the tendency for a wide variety of Protestant religious groups to come into being, seemingly reflecting variations not only in theology but also—and perhaps primarily—in social characteristics.

Dimensions of religiosity (p. 317) are the various facets of religious commitment, including belief, experience, practice, and knowledge.

Humanist perspectives (p. 316) are systems of meaning that do not have a supernatural referent and that are used to interpret the world.

Monotheism (p. 316) refers to belief in one god.

The **persistence thesis** (p. 327) is the assertion that religion will continue to have a significant place in the modern world because it has never actually declined or because people continue to have interests and needs that only religion can satisfy.

Personal religiosity (p. 316) refers to the level of religious commitment characterizing an individual.

Profane See Sacred and profane.

Religions (p. 316) are systems of meaning for interpreting the world that have a supernatural referent.

Religious polarization (p. 321) refers to the growing tendency of some people in a given setting to embrace religion and the tendency of others to reject it.

Sacred and profane (p. 314) are the two categories by which Durkheim claimed all things are classified; the sacred represents those things that are deemed to warrant profound respect, and the profane encompasses essentially everything else.

The **secularization thesis** (p. 327) holds that religion as it has been traditionally known is continually declining, resulting in a loss of religious authority, societally and individually, as well as changes in religious organizations themselves.

SUGGESTED READING

Beaman, Lori G., ed. (2012). *Religion and Canadian Society* (2nd ed.). Toronto: Canadian Scholars Press. A collection of valuable, wide-ranging articles on religion in Canada by many of the country's top thinkers in sociology and religious studies.

Bibby, Reginald W. (2011). *Beyond the Gods & Back: Religion's Demise and Rise and Why It Matters.* Lethbridge, AB: Project Canada Books. This work draws on the author's extensive surveys and newly available international data in maintaining that the current religious situation in Canada is characterized by polarization. It features an examination of the implications for personal and social life, and religion's future.

Bramadat, Paul and David Seljak, eds. (2008). *Christianity and Ethnicity in Canada.* Toronto: University of Toronto Press. A superb reader by leading Canadian scholars examining the relationships between religious and ethnic identity in nine major religious traditions. Complements their earlier reader (2004), *Religion and Ethnicity in Canada*, Toronto: University of Toronto Press.

Brym, Robert J., William Shaffir, and Morton Weinfeld, eds. 2010. *The Jews in Canada* (Toronto: Oxford University Press).

Christiano, Kevin J., William H. Swatos, Jr., and Peter Kivisto. (2008). *Sociology of Religion: Contemporary Developments*, 2nd ed. Walnut Creek, CA: AltaMira Press. An excellent overview of theory, methods, and up-to-date findings on religion and society from an American point of view.

Clark, S. D. (1948). *Church and Sect in Canada.* Toronto: University of Toronto Press. This Canadian classic examines the social factors contributing to the rise of different types of religious groups in this country.

Dawson, Lorne L. (2006). *Comprehending Cults: The Sociology of New Religious Movements*, 2nd ed. Toronto: Oxford University Press. A succinct overview of cults that have emerged from the 1970s onward, dealing with such issues as why cults emerge, who joins, and their social significance.

Noll, Mark. (2007). *What Happened to Christian Canada?* Vancouver: Regent College Publishing. This is a short but detailed and invaluable essay in which a renowned American historian examines religious change in Canada since the 1950s and contrasts the religious histories of Canada and the United States.

SOURCE: © Victor Tangermann

PART 5

CHANGE AND CONFLICT

CHAPTER 14

DEVIANCE AND CRIME

SOURCE: © Dan Lacey

Julian Tanner
UNIVERSITY OF TORONTO

IN THIS CHAPTER YOU WILL LEARN THAT

- The study of crime and deviance is about the behaviour itself and societal reaction to that behaviour.
- Many deviant and criminal incidents never become known to the police.
- Official crime statistics are not just a record of criminal behaviour. Many other factors influence their composition.
- The crime rate in Canada is falling.
- The more serious the crime, the less likely it is to occur.
- The correlates of crime and deviance include age and gender.
- Numerous, often competing, explanations of criminal behaviour exist.
- Society responds to crime and deviance in diverse ways.
- Much of the public concern with crime centres on young people. Extreme and disproportionate reactions to crime and deviance have been conceptualized as moral panics.

INTRODUCTION

For much of our everyday lives, we take for granted that our routine activities will follow an orderly and predictable pattern. When we drive on the highway, we can rely on the fact that others will also be driving on the right-hand side of the road and will stop their vehicles at a red light. If they did not, the result would be chaos—or worse. Likewise, when we want our morning cup of coffee, we expect to join the lineup at Tim Hortons—and we don't like other patrons pushing in front of us. Everyday life depends on people following agreed-upon rules, however unconsciously.

A good part of the sociological enterprise is concerned with explaining the orderliness of human behaviour (Giddens, 1991; Robertson, 1989). And yet just a moment's reflection will tell you that human behaviour is not always predictable, that the rules are not always obeyed, and that we don't always live up to other people's expectations. People do jump the queue and break the speed limit on the highway. They also do much worse things; they steal, cheat, rape, and murder. How and why people break rules—why they deviate from the expectations of other people—is an important part of the subject matter of the sociology of crime and deviance.

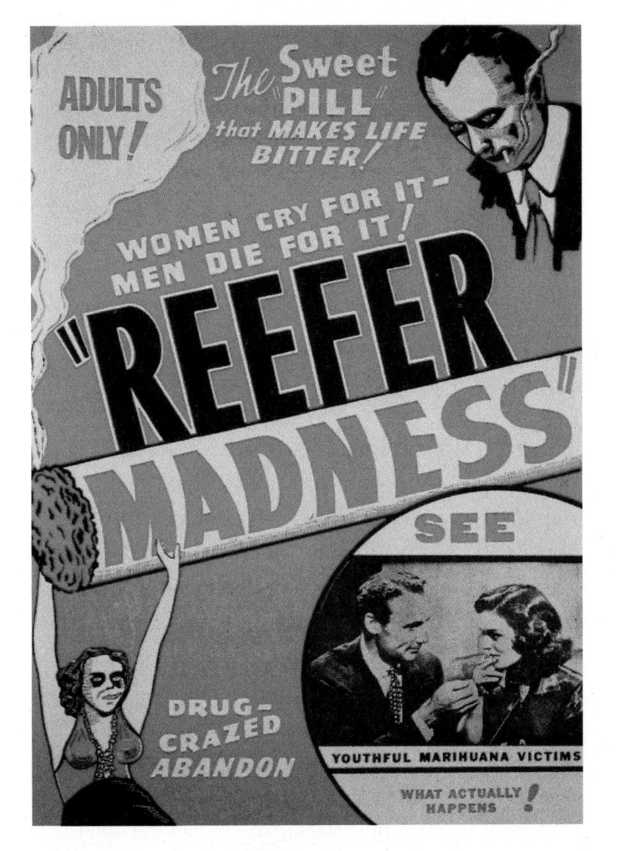

This 1936 movie poster illustrates how relative deviance is. The movie suggests that people go insane after smoking marijuana.
SOURCE: *Reefer Madness*, 1936. Directed by Louis Gasnier.

We have a complicated relationship with crime and deviance. On the one hand, survey after survey confirms that deviance—particularly violent interpersonal crime—is one of the major discontents of our society. Many people, especially seniors, live in fear of crime. On the other hand, crime and deviance fascinate us. Crime stories constitute an important part of our entertainment culture. No new TV season would be complete without its roster of programs like *CSI* and *Flashpoint.* Movies, books, and newspapers also rely on crime and deviance for much of their content. In fact, this dependency seems to be increasing—crime coverage in the mass media has expanded substantially over the past decade or so (Sacco, 2005: 80).

Real-life crime stories are no less likely to grip the public imagination. Indeed, few fictional representations can compare with the courtroom drama of Amanda Knox, the American student in Italy accused, convicted, and, finally, acquitted of the killing of her British female roommate in October 2011. Her trial attracted a global audience, captivated by a story of sexual intrigue involving attractive female protagonists, prosecutorial incompetence, and the denouement of a successful appeal. The very ambiguity of our feelings about crime and deviance makes it fertile ground for exercising the sociological imagination.

Amanda Knox comforted by her parents after she was set free from an Italian prison in 2011.

SOURCE: © Ted S. Warren/AP Photo.

CONCEPTIONS OF CRIME AND DEVIANCE

CRIME AND DEVIANCE AS NORM-VIOLATING BEHAVIOUR

If I were to ask you what you consider examples of crime or deviance, you would probably include such acts as murder, rape, bank robbery, and theft, perhaps hockey riots in Vancouver, British Columbia, and race riots in London, England. You might also mention drug use, some types of sexual behaviour, drunk driving, and a host of other acts of seemingly lesser importance: speeding on the highway, talking in theatres, jaywalking, and—increasingly—cigarette smoking.

These acts are all examples of rule-breaking behaviour. One way of conceptualizing crime or deviance is to emphasize its rule-breaking qualities, focusing in particular on its behavioural dimensions. Sociologists refer to the rules in question as **norms,** or generally accepted ways of doings things. The most important norms are written *laws*, or norms that the state enforces. **Deviance** involves breaking a norm. **Crime** involves breaking a law.

All human societies have norms about appropriate behaviour. Some norms have wide scope, applying to more or less everybody in the community—prescriptions against murder and armed robbery, for instance. Other norms may apply only to particular subgroups of society. For example, there are prohibitions on the behaviours of adolescents that do not apply to adults. They involve some types of sexual behaviour, for example, and alcohol use. In the United States, some jurisdictions have laws prohibiting young people from being in a public place after a certain time in the evening. Such curfew regulations (which some people would like to see introduced in Canada) do not apply to adults. Normative behaviour can be gendered, too. When I first visited Canada from the United Kingdom in 1970, I was surprised to find that women had to have a male escort if they wanted to enter a bar in Ontario.

Norms are enforced in many ways. The most important of them are laws, which are regulated by a **criminal justice system** that includes police, courts, prisons, and so on. The criminal justice system responds to law violators in legally prescribed ways, with the most grievous offences evoking the most severe sanctions. In Canada and all of Western Europe, life imprisonment is the most severe sanction afforded by the criminal code. In other parts of the world—the United States and China, for instance—capital punishment (the death penalty) remains the ultimate sanction.

Many of the norms that control everyday life do not require legal intervention. They are more likely to be enforced informally. People who insist on talking in a theatre are liable to be admonished by the people around them. Communal pressure is enough to regulate such behaviour.

How might we distinguish between diverse kinds of rule-breaking behaviour? One answer has been provided by John Hagan (1991), who suggests that norm violations can be differentiated by how serious they are, as gauged by three different measures of seriousness: (1) how harmful the act in question is deemed to be, (2) how much agreement there is that the behaviour in question is wrong, and (3) the severity of the sanction, or punishment, imposed on that behaviour (see Figure 14.1).

We have the sense that more harm is inflicted by, say, physical violence than soft drug use. The brutal murder of a small child grievously affects not just the victim but also her family, friends, and neighbours. In some high-profile cases—the decapitation of a passenger on a Greyhound bus in Manitoba in August 2008, for instance—the broader society shares a communal sense of horror and outrage. Sometimes the grief and condemnation is global: witness the reaction to the mass killing of 77 young people in Norway by a solitary gunman in July 2011. Contrast these examples with the case of the person who occasionally uses marijuana. Many (though not all) people would say that marijuana has little or no harmful effects; and even if there are harmful effects, the only victims are the users themselves. Similarly, whereas most of us would agree that deliberately hurting somebody by physically assaulting him or her with a weapon is morally wrong, there is significant disagreement about how inherently wrong using marijuana is. Finally, we punish acts that we regard as very harmful and wrong more severely than those deemed less harmful and wrong. These days, convicted marijuana users are unlikely to receive a prison sentence (they are more likely to receive a fine or a probation order). By contrast, those convicted of physical assault with a weapon are likely to receive a lengthy prison term.

Hagan employs his conception of "seriousness" to identify different kinds of deviance. He designates a small group of offences as **consensus crime**—acts that are felt to be very harmful and wrong, and for which the harshest criminal sanctions are reserved. What he calls consensus crimes are referred to in legal philosophy as crimes *mala in se*—crimes that are evil in themselves. Homicide, attempted homicide, violent assault with a weapon, violent sexual assault, armed robbery, kidnapping, and theft are all examples of crimes *mala in se*.

A second group of illegal behaviours is what Hagan calls **conflict crime.** Here, "conflict" means not that they involve acts of interpersonal violence or aggression, but that members of the community disagree over whether the behaviours in question are harmful, wrong, or deserving of severe criminal sanction. In legal terminology, these acts are referred to as crimes *mala prohibita*—crimes wrong by definition. In the conflict crime category, we find such offences as euthanasia, gambling, prostitution, drug use, and public drunkenness—all examples of what are sometimes referred to as morality offences.

The important point about conflict crime is that its presence in the Criminal Code is loaded with controversy. A decade ago, much public debate surrounded the appropriateness of a lengthy prison term for Saskatchewan farmer Robert Latimer, who killed his daughter, who had severe disabilities, in what he regarded as an act of mercy. Some people regularly call for the decriminalization of marijuana use, or even of prostitution, much to the horror of other people.

FIGURE 14.1 TYPES OF DEVIANCE AND CRIME

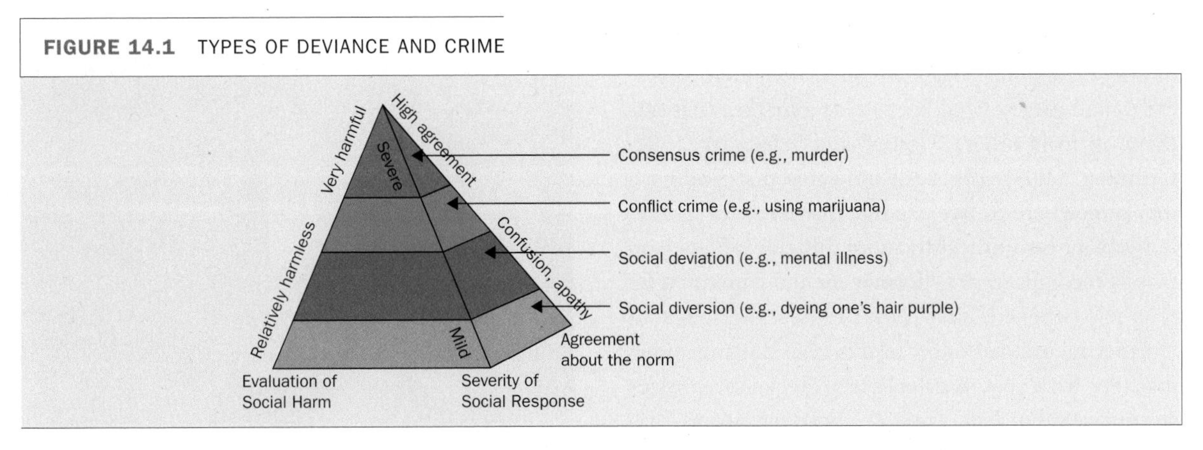

SOURCE: Hagan, 1991. Reprinted with permission from John Hagan.

Same-sex marriage became legal in Canada in 2005, but only after decades of political and legal battles.
SOURCE: © Paul Chiasson/The Canadian Press.

The public is divided about how wrong, harmful, and deserving of strict punishment these offences are. With marijuana use, for example, we have a situation in which large numbers of people, particularly young people, have used it and believe that they, as well as other people, should be allowed to use it.

Not all norm-violating behaviour is illegal. While we may condemn the person who refuses to come to the assistance of somebody involved in a road accident, there is no law requiring that person to be a good Samaritan (Siegel and McCormick, 2006: 6–7). Nor is it illegal to have a mental illness, be gay, be obese, be addicted to drugs, or attempt suicide. Nonetheless, people who have a mental illness, are gay or lesbian, are obese, or are alcohol- or drug-dependent are still subject to varying degrees of **social stigma**; they may be condemned, ostracized, and medicalized because of a marker that sets them off from others (Conrad and Schneider, 1992; Goffman, 1963). Research indicates that finding a job, somewhere to live, a circle of friends, or a marital partner is significantly more difficult for a person who is recognized as a "former mental patient" than it is for others (Link, 1982). The experience of "former mental patients" in this regard is not much different from that of ex-convicts. Hagan categorizes stigmatized, but legal, acts as "social deviations."

On occasion, victims of stigma fight back. Longstanding equal rights campaigns by gays and lesbians are one example; what have become known as "slut walks" are a more recent one. Young women who fail to conform to dominant normative expectations about their sexual behaviour—who engage in casual sexual relationships, for example—risk condemnation and stigmatization as "sluts." For the most part, avoiding the slut identity requires individual commitment to a stable relationship leading to marriage and children (Dunn, 2008). Slut walks, however, represent a collective form of resistance.

In January 2011, a police officer speaking in a university classroom in Toronto proposed that "women should avoid dressing like sluts in order not to be victimized."

In response to this statement, a public slut walk was organized, with participants invited to dress in deliberately provocative clothing. After the Toronto event, slut walking went global, with other large cities around the world hosting similar protests.

What is it that slut walks do? First, by mocking the disreputable and demeaning label, they are draining it of its spoiling and hurtful effects. Second, they are a collective rejection of the inference that women invite their own sexual victimization.

Hagan reserves the term "social diversion" for minority heterosexual and same-sex activities—phone sex is a contemporary example—as well as forms of symbolic or expressive deviance involving adolescents. About the latter, the important point to remember is that young people often find themselves condemned as antisocial, threatening, or dangerous not because of what they do or don't do, but because of how they appear to others by virtue of the clothes they wear, the music that they listen to, and their hairstyle. It is not illegal to shave your head, colour

Toronto slut walk takes to city streets.
SOURCE: © Graham Hughes/The Canadian Press/AP Photo.

your hair purple, cover your body in tattoos, have a stud in your nose, wear saggy pants, or listen to gangsta rap, but doing so often invites a censorious response from adults. Billie Joe Armstrong of the rock group Green Day, for instance, was thrown off his scheduled airline flight in August 2011 because he chose to wear saggy pants.

Particular clothing or hairstyles or musical choices are interpreted as signs of putative deviant or criminal behaviour. Before the rampage shooting at Columbine high school in April 1999, few people noted, or cared, that some adolescents wore long trench coats to school. After Columbine, trench coats were immediately banned from high schools across North America; students who wore them faced suspension (Tanner, 2010).

Generally speaking, the more serious the form of deviance, the less likely it is to occur. The most serious criminal acts—homicide and other violent interpersonal assaults—do not happen often. In 2007, violent crime accounted for 13 percent of all crime committed in Canada, and homicide for less than 0.2 percent of all violent crime (Dauvergne, 2008; Li, 2008) Conversely, other deviant acts occur routinely—so much so, in fact, that some commentators ponder whether the behaviours in question (speeding on the highway, for instance) actually warrant characterization as deviant.

I must make one more point about Hagan's typology: it is subject to change. The acts, behaviours, and conditions that constitute his various categories vary over time. For instance, there was a time when drunk driving was not regarded as a serious offence, when it was inconsistently enforced and rarely punished with a prison sentence. Nowadays, we regard it as a more serious offence—indeed, it has become a consensus crime. In September 2011 Jack Tobin, the son of prominent Canadian politician Brian Tobin, was sentenced to three years imprisonment for the drunk driving death of his best friend. It is doubtful that he would have received a prison sentence 30 years ago. Violence against women is also treated more seriously than it was in the past.

One of the biggest changes in societal definitions of acceptable behaviour involves cigarettes. While it has long been known that smoking is addictive and dangerous to health, it is only relatively recently that legal restrictions have been placed on the practice. In the recent past, smoking was normative—socially acceptable behaviour—and in some quarters seen as a sign of adult sophistication and maturity. Change also works in the opposite direction. For example, abortion is no longer illegal in Canada. The law prohibiting abortion was repealed in 1988. In July 2008, the decision was made to award the Order of Canada to Dr. Henry Morgentaler, who started performing abortions in Canada in 1969, before it was legal. Likewise, while the use of marijuana has not been decriminalized, it is not the serious crime that it once was, and mental illness has become a medical problem rather than a criminal problem, with those affected by it treated, not punished.

We should note, however, that opinion is still divided about marijuana. While some academics now regard its use as a normalized feature of everyday youth culture (Aldridge, Measham, and Williams, 2011), the Canadian government recommends mandatory prison terms for those convicted of trafficking the drug.

CRIME AND DEVIANCE AS LABELS AND SOCIAL CONSTRUCTS

Labelling Theory

Because some acts that were once illegal are now legal, and vice versa, you should understand that while the study of crime and deviance is about rule-breaking behaviour, it is *not just* about rule-breaking behaviour. It is also about how members of society react to some behaviours. This understanding is the starting point for a second approach to the study of deviance and crime, one that sees deviance and crime as a matter of definitions or labels that have been applied to some behaviours but not others. **Labelling theorists** believe that publicly recognizing somebody as criminal or deviant is an important cause in itself of criminal or deviant behaviour.

From a definitional perspective, crime and deviance are not distinctive types of human behaviour. We cannot divide human activity into its criminal and noncriminal variants based on behaviour alone (Becker, 1963). Few if any acts are viewed as wrong under all circumstances. On the one hand, all known human societies identify some activities as morally reprehensible and worthy of condemnation and punishment. In this sense, crime and deviance are universal. On the other hand, different human societies pronounce different acts and behaviours criminal or deviant. In other words, crime and deviance may be universal, but there are no universal forms of crime and deviance (Conrad and Schneider, 1992: 5–6).

That what counts as deviant or criminal behaviour varies by time and place is well illustrated by cases in which the argument about the universality of crime and deviance appears strongest. Take, for instance, the intentional killing of one person by another. You might think that murder would be universally acknowledged as a serious offence. However, intentional killing is not defined as murder in the context of war, when those doing the killing are our own soldiers, acting in the line of duty. Similarly, the fatal shooting of suspects by police officers rarely results in criminal charges. When the state (or government) kills on our behalf (in those nations that still have the death penalty, for instance), those doing the killing are not called murderers; they are public executioners.

Incest is another interesting example. While most societies have legal prohibitions against incest, significant variation exists regarding what counts as incest. Some jurisdictions forbid sexual relationships only between brothers and sisters, while others extend the ban to include third cousins (Conrad and Schneider, 1992: 5–6). Note too that while prostitution is legal in the state of Nevada in the United States and the city of Amsterdam, Holland, it is illegal in Canada. Similarly, while adult alcohol use is a legal and normal feature of Canadian lifestyles, in parts of the Middle East it is treated as a serious offence requiring a severe penalty—in some cases, corporal punishment.

Turning to drug use, we find that opiates have been illegal in Canada only since 1908. Before then, no legal prohibitions on their use existed. Opiate-based cough syrups and tonics were routinely prescribed by doctors and sold in pharmacies in a variety of forms. People who were dependent on opiate-based drugs were not stigmatized as criminal or deviant, nor was opiate dependency seen as a sign of mental illness.

Opiate drugs were also used for recreational purposes in smoking dens on Canada's West Coast. Their main users were Chinese immigrants who were brought to Canada to build the transcontinental railroad and received much lower wages than their European counterparts did. Public concern about the morality of recreational drug use served as a conduit for anti-Asian sentiment rooted in stiff competition for jobs after the Canadian Pacific Railroad was completed. The first Canadian anti-narcotics legislation introduced in 1908 targeted the opium dens, making the recreational usage of opiates a criminal offence for which there were heavy penalties. No such penalties accompanied the medicinal use of opiates (Cook, 1969).

Sociologists who study the social reaction to drug use conclude that the legality of a drug is determined as much by the status of its users as by the amount of harm done by the drug. The lower the status of the user, the more likely the drug will be criminalized (Becker, 1963). Consider that cocaine in its powdered form has been a drug of choice of sports stars and entertainment celebrities since the early 1970s. However, it became a significant social problem only when it became associated with poor, unemployed racial minorities in U.S. inner cities, who ingested it in small, precooked units as crack cocaine. Once cocaine travelled down from the Hollywood Hills to the inner city, it became a major crime problem, one measure of which is that penalties for crack cocaine convictions have been more severe in the United States than for other forms of cocaine use (Reinarman and Levine, 1989).

Social Constructionism

Social constructionism is similar to the labelling approach. In fact, in some accounts they are indistinguishable. They differ, if at all, in that social constructionism is broadly concerned with the genesis of all social problems—climate change, health risks, car accidents—whereas labelling theory applies specifically to crime and deviance. Both theories stand in contrast to the norm-violation approach that we began with—what constructionists like to call an objectivist approach to crime and deviance.

In contrast to labelling and social-constructionist explanations, objectivist accounts of crime and deviance focus on the behaviour itself. It is assumed that we know what crime and deviance is, how much damage and harm it causes, and what needs to be done about it (Sacco, 2005). Researchers working in this tradition are likely to pose the following kinds of questions: Are rates of crime and deviance increasing? What kinds of people become bank robbers, prostitutes, or murderers? What factors predict rampage school shootings, corporate crime, youth gang activity, and so on? Do people who break one kind of rule also break other kinds?

Labelling and social-constructionist theorists argue that crime and deviance become problematic because some people—usually the most powerful—define them as such. Sociologists working in this tradition focus on activities and claims that result in new

Whether certain subcultures are deviant is a source of much debate.
SOURCE: © Jupiter Images.

crimes being defined. They are more likely to ask, "Why do we care more about youth crime than corporate crime?" than "What causes youth crime and corporate crime?"

More generally, social constructionism advises that so-called objective facts are not always responsible for the criminal or deviance status of a particular condition. They like to remind us that alcohol—a legal drug—is more damaging and harmful to individuals and society than some illegal drugs are. They point out that the number of deaths associated with tobacco and alcohol is much larger than the number stemming from the use of illegal drugs. They sometimes use such evidence to support the decriminalization of illegal drugs. (Note, however, that their argument has been challenged by other analysts who say that because illegal drugs are not widely available, we do not yet know enough about their risks to reach valid conclusions; South, 2007: 811).

In some extreme cases, people have defined and reacted to social problems without showing that they exist. In the United States, satanic crime has received considerable media attention, even though not a shred of evidence supports repeated claims that it is a serious problem. Special crime units have even been set up to tackle the problem, and parental advisory groups formed to prevent the spread of satanic imagery and, presumably, satanic values and lifestyles in popular music (Sacco, 2005). Based on such cases, constructionists argue that while objective conditions and agreed-on facts play a role in the designation of deviance, they are rarely the decisive determinants of whether a particular behaviour is defined as such.

Thankfully, we do not have to choose between objectivist and constructionist perspectives. It is quite possible to study the same phenomenon and ask different but complementary questions about them. We could ask how and why hate crime has become a new crime problem (a constructionist question) and, at the same time, inquire about the characteristics of those who perpetrate hate crimes (an objectivist question). From an objectivist vantage point, you might ask, Does listening to rap music cause crime and deviance? From the constructionist perspective, the crucial question is, Why are we so concerned about the violent content of rap music but pay so little attention to the violent content of country music? Both are perfectly good research questions, and a full understanding of crime and deviance requires both the norm-violation and labelling/constructionist approaches (Thio, 2010).

It is also often the case that objectivist and constructionist researchers study different kinds of crime and deviance. Objectivists tend to study serious, or consensual, crime—murder, sexual assault, armed robbery and the like. Constructionists, conversely, are more inclined to study noncriminal deviance—binge drinking, lap dancing, prescription drug abuse (OxyContin—or criminal activities, the criminal status of which is fiercely contested (prostitution, for example). They are also more interested in new or emerging forms of deviance; in the early 1990s, sociologists of crime and deviance paid little attention to Internet-based child pornography, or telephone sex, for instance.

CRIME IN THE NEWS

How are crime and deviance represented in the news media and popular culture and why does it matter? You may have heard the expression "If it bleeds, it leads." It's a good summary of the importance of crime to news organizations. The public has a big appetite for crime stories that the news media are happy to accommodate.

However, the media do not report all criminal incidents. Violent crime is reported more regularly than property or **white-collar crime,** which may be defined as crime conducted by high-status individuals in the course of their occupation or profession. Research consistently shows that crimes of violence appear in news reports in numbers disproportionate to their incidence in official crime statistics (Reiner, 2007; Sacco, 2005).

The commonsense view about the relationship between the mass media and crime and deviance is that journalists simply record events as they happen. In this view, media accounts provide a more or less faithful reflection of objectively verifiable crime problems. However, news organizations do more than just record the facts. Whether they realize it or not, journalists shape how readers, viewers, and listeners feel and think about crime and deviance. Research on media institutions indicates that the news we consume is a result of a selection process (see Chapter 5, Communication and Mass Media). News items compete for time and space. Crime stories have an advantage in this competition because they are deemed highly newsworthy.

In his study of law and order reporting, British sociologist Steve Chibnall (1977) identified a number of informal criteria that are regularly used by journalists to select stories. Visible and spectacular incidents with political and sexual connotations rank highest. Similar rules determine how crime stories are presented—how many and which photographs will accompany a story, what headlines will be used, and so forth.

I am not suggesting that news organizations make up stories about crime or that crime problems would disappear if journalists chose to ignore them. My argument is that what we read in the newspapers and watch on TV is a result of a predictable selection process. The mass media typically exaggerate the nature and scope of crime, presenting rare cases as if they are typical or the start of a new and worrying trend.

How news organizations construct crime stories is of more than academic interest because it influences how citizens think about crime. For example, research shows that Canadians overestimate crime and **recidivism** (repeat offending) rates and underestimate the severity of criminal sanctions for crimes. Crucially, the same research also tells us that most people rely mainly on the mass media for their knowledge of crime (Roberts, 2004).

COUNTING CRIME AND DEVIANCE: NUMBERS AND MEANING

OFFICIAL STATISTICS

People naturally want to know about the amount of criminal and deviant activity in Canada, and whether or not it is increasing. One answer to these questions is provided by official statistics compiled by the government. Most accounts of crime and deviance are made persuasive by the use of data collected by the police, the courts, and other governmental agencies. Moreover, virtually every important theory of deviant behaviour, and especially criminal behaviour, relies on information about offences and offenders collected by or on behalf of the government. It is therefore important to know how these data are collected. For starters, note that the more serious the norm violation, the more comprehensive the data collection. Thus, we have considerably more information about crime and delinquency, and alcohol and drug use, than we do about the expressive or symbolic deviancy of adolescents (Tanner, 2010).

Since 1962, a system of uniform crime reports has provided the basic count of criminal infractions in Canada. According to an arrangement originally pioneered in the United States, police departments across the country file information on "crimes known to the police". The system is designed to produce consistent, comparable, nationwide crime statistics. For crime to become known to the police, one of two things must happen. Either members of the public experience or observe a criminal incident and pass that information on to the police, or the police themselves detect the incident.

One of the few incontrovertible facts about the official count of crime is that it underestimates the actual amount of crime occurring in any jurisdiction at any given time. This is not a comforting thought for people already concerned about the level of crime in society. There are well-documented reasons that citizens choose not to share their knowledge of some criminal events with the police. They may fear reprisals from offenders, particularly if they know them. They may feel that the incident is too trivial to bother the police. They may be too embarrassed to report the incident. They may mistakenly believe that stolen items were lost. Some crimes are never reported to the police because the crime in question is a commercial transaction between, say, a prostitute and her client or a drug dealer and a drug buyer. In each of these cases, neither party has an interest in reporting details of the deal to the police.

The public reports most of the crime that the police know about. No more than 10 percent of crime is discovered by the police in the course of their own patrols or investigations (Sacco and Kennedy, 20011). One of the difficulties that the police face is that many crimes are committed so as to avoid detection.

Most burglars, for instance, do not break into houses when they know that the police are in the area or when residents are likely to be at home.

The number of criminal incidents that remain unknown to the police is often referred to as the **dark figure of crime.** It is a large figure. How large? In one of my studies, I found that just 33 percent of robberies, 23 percent of rapes, and 21 percent of assaults with a weapon were reported by young victims to the police (Tanner and Wortley, 2002). A more recent survey of Toronto high-school students found that less than half of all self-reported deviant acts had been discovered by parents, teachers, or the police (Savoie, 2006).

What happens if, for any reason, members of the public become more inclined to report crime to the police—if, say, it becomes easier for them to report crime because of the widespread use of cellphones or because the organizations they work for require them to report incidents that were previously dealt with informally? What happens if police departments are allowed to hire more police officers and acquire improved information technology? The answer, of course, is that we would start to see an increase in recorded crime, regardless of whether or not there had been any real change in criminal behaviour in the population. The important lesson here is that official statistics are affected by more than just the deviant motivations and behaviour of perpetrators (Liska and Messner, 1999).

In Canada in 2010, roughly 2.1 million crimes were known to the police (Brennan and Dauvergne, 2011). A large proportion of these were classified as property crimes; a substantially smaller proportion was classified as violent crime. Note, too, that violent crime includes everything from homicide, attempted homicide, and sexual assault to minor pushing and shoving ("common assault").

Figure 14.2 reveals that both the overall volume of crime in Canada and its severity were down in 2010. In fact, the overall crime rate is the lowest since 1978.

Why is the crime rate down—and why don't our perceptions of safety always mirror that decline?

Although other factors are undoubtedly involved, part of the explanation of declining crime rates is demographic. Crime rates are higher when young people, young males in particular, represent a larger proportion of the population and lower when their numbers are fewer, as they are presently. An aging population means a declining crime rate.

Why then don't falling crime rates necessarily make us feel any safer? Again, a number of factors are probably at work. I would like to emphasise two. First, the growing preponderance of crime stories in news coverage probably increases fear of crime. Second, as Scot Wortley (2011) has suggested, both the private security industry—Alarm Force, ADT, and so on—and law enforcement agencies benefit from public anxiety about crime. The more anxious we are about crime, the more persuaded we are to buy home security devices and the more tolerant we are of expanding police budgets.

FIGURE 14.2 POLICE-REPORTED CRIME RATES IN CANADA, 1962–2010

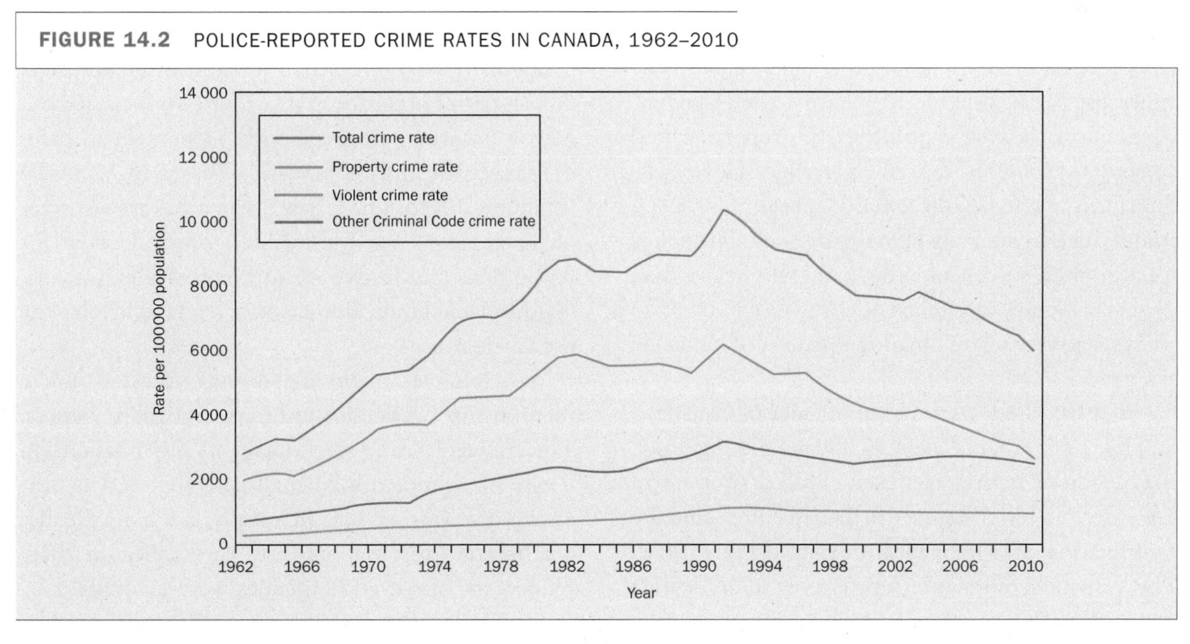

SOURCE: Brennan and Dauvergne (2011:2).

REGIONAL VARIATIONS IN CRIME RATES

Official crime figures reveal intriguing regional variations. Generally speaking, provinces and cities in the Western part of the country have higher crime rates than those in the East. This pattern has existed for a long time and applies to both the overall crime rate and specific types of crime.

Why is the West more crime-prone? Tim Hartnagel (2004) offers a persuasive answer. He suggests that, like its American counterpart, Western Canada encourages a "frontier mentality" favouring individualism, independence, and risk-taking. On occasion, risky behaviours lead to criminal ones. The Western provinces have more migrants from the rest of Canada than any other part of the country does (see Chapter 15, Population and Urbanization). Migration loosens the social controls that prevent law-violating behaviour. It is easier to break rules as a stranger in town than in the community where you grew up, where everybody knows your name and where informal social control is stronger. In addition, the populations of the Western provinces are relatively young, and crime is associated with youth. Finally, Aboriginal Canadians are proportionately more numerous in Western Canada than in the rest of the country, and Aboriginal Canadians have especially high crime rates (Brym, 2009), for reasons I will discuss later.

HOMICIDE RATES

Homicide rates are the most valid and reliable crime indicator, partly because it is hard to hide bodies. Homicide is less susceptible to the reporting and detection problems described earlier. Consensus about the gravity of the offence means that it is a crime with exceptionally high report rates. The police are also more successful at detecting homicides than most other kinds of criminal offences. What, then, do official statistics tell us about the pattern of homicide in Canada?

In 2010, there were 554 homicides in Canada—roughly 1.6 homicides per 100 000 people (Mahony, 2011). These figures represent both a short-term decrease—56 fewer homicides than in 2009—and the continuation of a long-term decline (Figure 14.3). The Canadian homicide rate is now at its lowest level since 1966. As has always been the case, men are more likely than women are to be both victims and perpetrators of homicide. Homicide rates are higher in the West and the North, with Western Canadian cities, such as Saskatoon and Regina, having higher rates than cities in the East (Beattie and Cotter, 2010). And Toronto, Canada's largest city? While Toronto had a larger *number* of homicides (80) than any other Canadian city in 2010, its homicide *rate* of 1.40 per 100 000 of the population is both below the Canadian average and lower than most other major metropolitan urban areas (Brennan and Dauvergne (2011) . However, research suggests that while Toronto does not have an especially high homicide rate, the nature of homicide in the city is changing. Gartner and Thompson (2004) have shown that homicide victims in Toronto have become younger over time and are increasingly likely to be male rather than female and black rather than white. In addition, they are likely to be residents of particularly disadvantaged neighbourhoods.

Homicide in Toronto has also increasingly become a crime committed in public places, such as bars, city streets, and parks, rather than in private. For many people, the increasingly public nature of homicide is what makes it especially frightening; it suggests growing victimization of innocent bystanders in seemingly random acts of violence. Exemplifying these fears is the case of Jane Creba, a 15-year-old high-school student who was shot and killed outside Toronto's Eaton Centre on December 26, 2005. She was caught in the crossfire of a gun battle involving male youth.

The Creba case also illustrates that death by handgun is a largely urban phenomenon. In 2010, 50 percent of homicides in Toronto were carried out with a firearm, compared with 44 percent of cases in Vancouver and 33 percent of cases in Montreal (Mahony, 2011). The larger urban areas are also sites of most gang-related homicides, which account for fewer than one in five of all homicides in Canada. Gang-related homicides are most likely to involve the use of firearms.

Sociologists of homicide are interested in the relationship between murderers and their victims. The frequent crime-story image of this relationship is one of a predatory killer dispatching victims otherwise unknown to him (it usually is a him). Reality is different. Most victims know their killer. In 2010, 83 percent of solved homicides were committed by someone familiar to the victim (Mahony, 2011). Most stranger homicide occurs during the course of another criminal incident—during a robbery or

FIGURE 14.3 HOMICIDES IN CANADA, 1961–2010

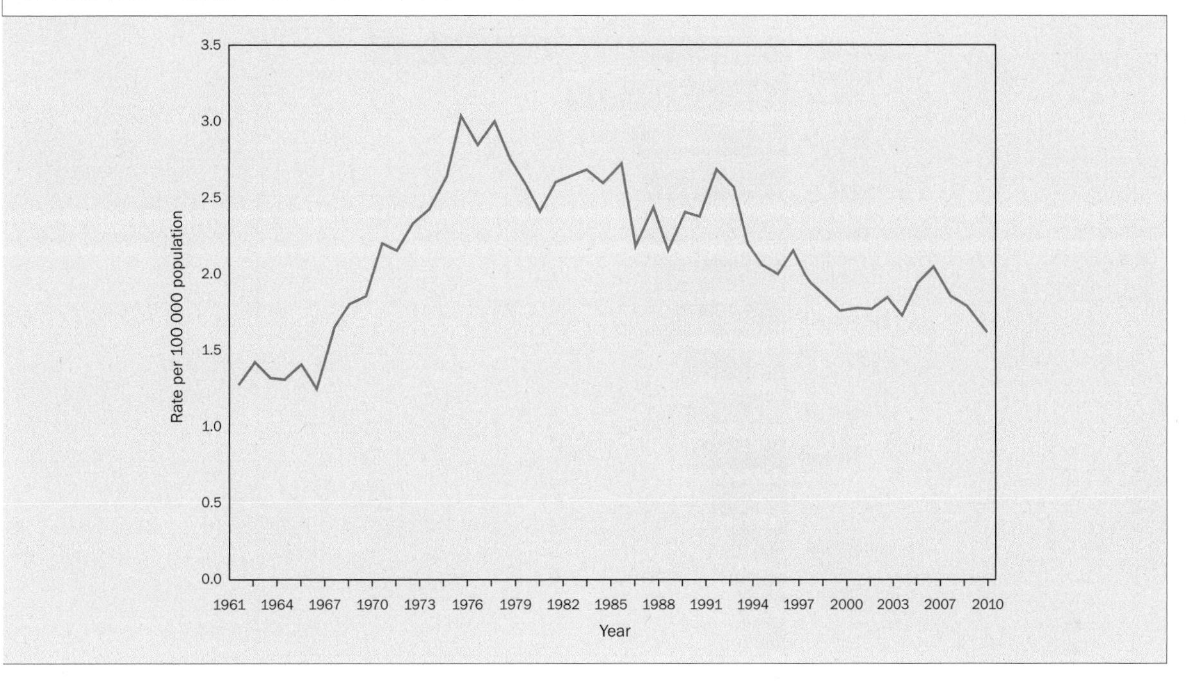

SOURCE: Mahony (2011).

as the culmination of a sexual assault, for instance. People we know as family members or acquaintances are a greater threat to our safety than strangers are. Acquaintances kill about one-third of homicide victims; family members kill another one-third.

A familial relationship of particular interest involves husbands and wives, and common-law spouses. Women are four times more likely to be victims of intimate partner homicide than men are. Likewise, women are at greater risk from the violent attentions of former spouses than men are. The rate of spousal homicide has, however, been decreasing over the past three decades and in recent years has remained relatively stable (Mahony, 2011).

Child victims of homicide are rare. They are killed primarily by women. Women who kill are, in fact, likely to kill children. Female killers tend to be under the age of 21 and single, and have a mental illness (Li, 2008).

We can also compare Canada's homicide rate with those of other countries. Looking at Figure 14.4, you can see that although Canada's homicide rate is similar to that of many European nations, it is much lower than the U.S. rate. According to Statistics Canada, the rate of homicide on this side of the border is roughly one-third of the rate on the other side (Beattie and Cotter, 2010). However, nonurban homicide rates are not that different in Canada and the United States, while urban differences are enormous. In 2010, according to FBI statistics, Baltimore had a homicide rate (per 100 000 population) of 34.8 and Detroit a rate of 34.5. By comparison, Vancouver had a rate of 1.50 and Montreal a rate of 1.27 (Mahony, 2011). Many people in Canada have easy access to American TV channels. Comparing Canadian and U.S. violent crime rates affords a splendid opportunity to examine one particularly popular explanation of violent crime, especially violent youth crime: that exposure to violent media contributes to real-life violence.

This is an argument with a long history. Beginning with dime store comics and continuing with movies, TV, and popular music—first, rock 'n' roll, now rap—popular culture has often been held responsible for crimes of violence. Many things are wrong with this argument. However, the point I want to concentrate on is that people in Canada watch much the same kind of entertainment and news programming as people in the United States do, yet there are big differences in patterns of violent crime, particularly homicide. While criminologists debate the factors responsible for cross-border differences, it is unlikely that media consumption has anything to do with them.

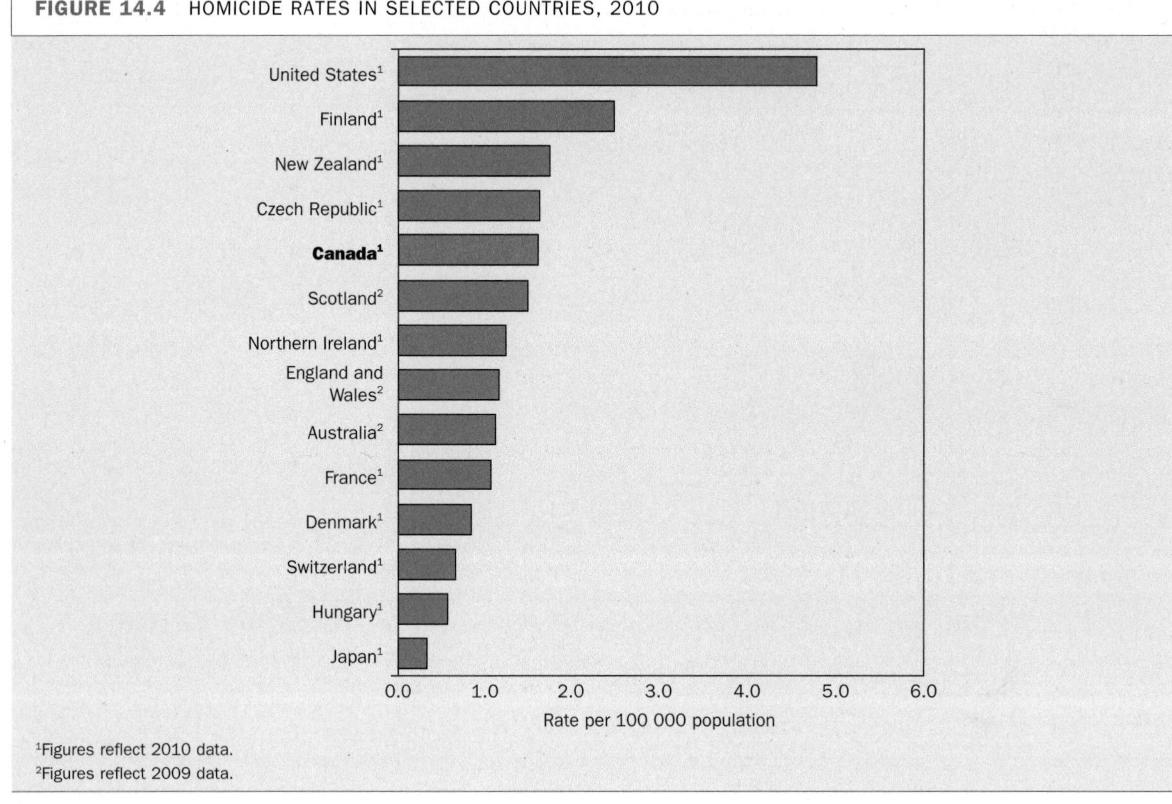

FIGURE 14.4 HOMICIDE RATES IN SELECTED COUNTRIES, 2010

SOURCE: Mahony (2011).

OTHER DATA SOURCES: SELF-REPORT SURVEYS AND DIRECT OBSERVATION

Because of the shortcomings of official crime statistics, sociologists have developed additional information sources, the most important of which are self-report and observational studies. Sociologists use **self-report studies** mainly to conduct research on deviance among young people, particularly those in high school. They ask students about their deviant behaviour and, less often, their experiences of victimization. Respondents complete a questionnaire that asks them to report on their own deviant activities or experiences of victimization. Statistics Canada also conducts surveys of adult victimization periodically. Self-report studies have their drawbacks. As with any survey on a sensitive subject, researchers must be careful to ensure that respondents give truthful answers to questions about criminal activity, drug use, and sexual assault. However, self-report studies have served sociologists well. First, they give a sense of the amount and type of crime and deviance that does not find its way into the official record. Second, their findings force us to abandon the idea that we can neatly divide the adolescent population into deviants and nondeviants; self-report studies show that many more adolescents are involved in activities that could get them into trouble with the law than are known to the police. Third, they show that young people who are charged by the police and prosecuted by the courts differ from "hidden" delinquents insofar as they are more likely to be repeat offenders and to commit serious crimes.

Researchers use **observational studies** to collect information about crime and deviance by watching it happen, either as outside observers or as participant observers. Many gang researchers have engaged in observational studies. A good example is Venkatesh's (2008) study of a Chicago street gang. While observational studies provide texture and detail to our understanding of deviance, they too have their downside. The very act of observing people can sometimes change their behaviour. Researchers studying prostitution might station themselves on a street corner to watch the action, but prostitutes, seeing the researchers, might conclude that they are police officers or investigative journalists and discontinue negotiations with potential customers (Liska and Messner, 1999: 24).

Police and court data, self-report surveys, and observational studies are different ways of collecting information about crime and deviance, but they are not necessarily alternative methods. Some investigations of crime and deviance combine different methods, gathering some information from surveys and official statistics, and additional information from observational or self-report research.

The overall profile of crime and deviance documented by the different sources is similar in many crucial respects. Students of crime and deviance are often interested in the characteristics of populations and individuals most involved with rule-breaking behaviour. Official police and court statistics and self-report studies often paint a roughly similar picture of these characteristics, as we will now see.

CORRELATES OF CRIME

A correlate is a phenomenon that is associated with another phenomenon. Factors associated with criminal and deviant activity are correlates of crime. When we ask about the characteristics of people most likely to engage in crime—are they old or young, male or female, rich or poor?—we are posing questions about the correlates of crime.

Age is one important correlate of crime. Irrespective of whether crime rates are high or low in a particular time or place, people in their teens and early 20s will be disproportionately represented. Arrests typically begin in early adolescence, increase steadily throughout the teenage years, and then taper off when individuals reach their 20s. Some criminologists have argued that the age basis of crime is universal and the single most important fact about crime requiring explanation (Gottfredson and Hirschi, 1990).

Crime also correlates with gender. Crime is not simply a young person's game; it is a young man's game. Again, this is a universal and enduring characteristic of all modern societies, and it is especially evident with respect to violent crime. Debate exists, however, over the degree to which the gender gap in criminality may be narrowing.

Two other correlates of crime are mired in controversy. Official police, court, and prison data often indicate an inverse relationship between social class and criminality—that is, the lower people's social and economic standing, the more likely they are to be involved in crime. However, this relationship is considerably less likely to manifest itself in self-report studies, leading some experts to conclude that the relationship between class and crime is a myth and to recommend that class not be considered an explanation of crime.

This argument does not persuade everybody in the criminology community. Detractors suggest that self-report studies fail to find a connection between class and crime because they neglect to ask questions about serious crime—murder, armed robbery, and rape, for example. Instead, they pose questions about relatively minor offences. Moreover, self-report studies often focus on students, but the most disadvantaged and marginal people are the least likely to attend school. Crucially, they are also the people most likely to be involved in criminal behaviour. When surveys include both school and street populations, and contain measures of serious crime, class re-emerges as a significant correlate of crime.

Significantly, which class is most involved with crime depends on what type of crime we are talking about. **Street crime**—robbery, burglary, and the like—involves mainly people from low-status backgrounds. White-collar or business crime is more likely to involve people from more privileged backgrounds. This observation stands as a corrective to the suggestion that only the poor and disadvantaged are criminals.

The second controversial correlate of crime is race. Unlike the United States, Canada does not officially record details about the racial characteristics of offenders or their victims. People who oppose the collection of race-related crime statistics argue that any evidence showing the overrepresentation of particular racial or ethnic groups in crime might result in increased public hostility toward those groups. People who support collecting race-based crime statistics argue that if racial and ethnic minorities are treated differently by the criminal justice system—if they are more likely to be stopped, searched, arrested, and charged by the police, and more harshly punished by the courts—then the only way such bias can be exposed and changed is by gathering racial data.

Aboriginal peoples and blacks are overrepresented in Canada's prison population. Does this mean that members of those groups are actually committing more crime or that they are more likely to come to the attention of the police and the courts? Research on Aboriginal peoples in Western Canada suggests both racial bias in the treatment of Aboriginal offenders and greater criminal activity by Aboriginal peoples. Sociologists typically explain high crime rates among Aboriginal Canadians by the fact that Aboriginal peoples were a subjugated, colonized people who suffered enforced cultural assimilation and abuse in residential schools. As a result, they now experience relatively low levels of educational achievement, dysfunctional families, high rates of substance abuse, severe estrangement from Canadian society—and high crime rates (Grekul and LaBoucane-Benson, 2008).

Research with ethnically and racially diverse high-school students in Toronto indicates that their encounters with police officers are predicted by their own self-reported criminal activity. That is, youth who report offending most often are the most likely to be stopped, searched, and charged by the police, regardless of racial background. However, researchers have also discovered racial disparities in police apprehension among students who report little or no deviant activity.

Black youth uninvolved in crime were at significantly greater risk of arrest than their innocent white counterparts. The researchers conclude that these findings are consistent with what has become known as **racial profiling,** or targeting by police officers of members of particular racial or ethnic groups (Wortley and Tanner, 2005).

THEORIES OF CRIME AND DEVIANCE

When we hear about a criminal incident, especially a violent, dramatic one (a school rampage, for instance) the first question we usually ask is, Why did he do it? Sociological theories of crime and deviance drawn from the objectivist (norm violations) tradition are designed to answer these kinds of causal questions.

Sociologists are not alone in asking causal questions. Nor are they alone in answering them. Sociological explanations of crime compete with media accounts and biological and psychological explanations. A major difference between biological and psychological explanations of crime and deviance, on the one hand, and sociological explanations, on the other, is that sociologists are more interested in group-based variations in deviant and criminal activity. The psychologist will try to explain why particular individuals decided to end their lives, but sociologists, beginning with Émile Durkheim, will want to know why, for instance, Protestants are more inclined to suicide than Roman Catholics are, or why men are more likely to commit suicide than women are.

Different theories may explain the same deviant act. Do people steal because they have few other legitimate means of acquiring possessions or money? Because they have failed to develop strong social bonds to society? Because they pursue everyday routines that provide them with plentiful opportunities to do so with impunity? One of the tasks of sociological research is to determine which theory best explains the agreed-upon facts.

Many theories of crime and deviance exist, and I will now introduce you to the most important ones.

STRAIN THEORY

Strain theory holds that crime and deviance are the result of societal pressures to break rules. We may trace the theory back to Durkheim's concept of anomie. (Recall from Chapter 1, Introducing Sociology that, according to Durkheim, anomie exists when norms governing behaviour are vaguely defined.) Robert Merton (1938) modified the concept to explain patterns of crime and deviance in the twentieth-century United States.

All societies, wrote Merton, establish culturally approved goals for their members and socially approved means of achieving those goals. However, some societies, such as the United States, pay more attention to goals of wealth, power, and prestige than to appropriate ways of achieving them. The imbalance between goals and means creates stress for lower-class people. They want what all Americans want—a nice house, a big car, a steady job—but lack legitimate means of achieving them, notably school and work opportunities. Rebuffed, they respond in a variety of deviant ways to the resulting stress. One mode of adaptation (Merton called it "innovation") involves using criminal means to achieve economic success.

People involved in money-making criminal enterprises exemplify Merton's innovators. Gangsters like the fictional Tony Soprano or the real life Al Capone subscribed to the American dream. They believed in, and aspired to, power, wealth, and status. Where they differed from non-criminals is in their chosen means of achieving those goals. Instead of pursuing educational qualifications and legitimate careers, they opt for illegal strategies.

Several studies add weight to strain theory by examining the relationship between income inequality and rates of homicide. They find that people in the lowest income group are most inclined to homicidal activity. This finding is consistent with the view that pressure to deviate is strongest among people with the fewest conventional opportunities. Moreover, the relationship is strongest in societies that most strongly emphasize success goals and where material inequalities are greatest (Krahn, Hartnagel, and Gartrell, 1986).

Other strain theories of crime and deviance focus on thwarted ambition and its criminal consequences among lower-class male youth. Albert Cohen (1955) saw delinquency among working-class boys as resulting from school experiences. Encouraged to strive for success, they find their ambitions blocked because the sort of socialization they have received at home prepares them poorly for success in school. Frustrated because of their inability to measure up to what Cohen calls the school's "middle-class measuring rod," they react against the school system by engaging in activities that directly counter those valued and sponsored by the school. Hence, they commit delinquent behaviour that appears to be without purpose, such as vandalism. According to Cohen, destructive behaviour is its own reward, a way of subverting the middle-class measuring rod.

A third variant of strain theory combines elements from both Merton and Cohen. According to Cloward and Ohlin (1960), deviant motivation, in the form of limited opportunity, is not enough to explain criminal behaviour. Frustrated adolescents also need access to deviant opportunities in order to become delinquent. Not all would-be delinquents have the opportunity to become criminal innovators, as Merton supposes. Low-status people become involved in different types of deviant subculture depending on the opportunities available to them. Those who have the opportunity to learn from adult thieves gravitate to criminal gangs. Those without those networks but in possession of the necessary physical attributes and combat skills may join fighting gangs. Those without conventional or criminal opportunities may end up in drug-based subcultures.

Some contemporary applications of strain theory document the social pressures that result in higher rates of deviance among socially disadvantaged groups. Other extensions of classic strain theory seek to explain the frustrations that drive some individuals to crime and deviance. An important and influential example of the latter is Robert Agnew's (1992) general strain theory, which focuses on the stresses that ensue from different social relationships, not just those that result from chasing inaccessible success goals. Agnew argues that negative relationships generate negative emotions, such as anxiety, fear, and anger, that, in turn, generate deviant responses. First, relationships with others may hinder the achievement of a valued goal. Adolescents might see parents or teachers as barriers to desired outcomes, such as spending leisure time with friends. Second, adolescents may lose or be threatened with losing something or someone of value to them—a job, say, or a parent through divorce. The third type of toxic relationship involves situations from which adolescents find it difficult or impossible to extricate themselves, such as the clutches of bullies at school or an abusive father at home. Agnew suggests that these myriad strains sour relationships with others and can lead to deviant and disreputable behaviour of various kinds. Much research supports Agnew's claims. Among young people who are experiencing the sorts of strains listed above, delinquency provides more relief than do nondeviant solutions (Vold, Bernard, and Snipes, 2002).

Though white-collar criminals like Conrad Black, pictured here, often express contempt for the law, share an organizational or business culture that rewards rule breaking, and associate with others from whom they can learn both the skills and the rationalizations needed to carry out their crimes, sociologists have continued to focus on street crime more than "suite" crime.
SOURCE: © REUTERS/John Gress.

The dominant success goals that traditional strain theorists have in mind are usually material ones—wealth and possessions. Today we live in an age of celebrity, an age in which we attach inordinate significance to fame in all its manifestations. Is it possible that fame has become a dominant success goal, legitimate access to which, like material possessions, is unevenly distributed throughout the population? Do those unable to achieve fame in the sporting world or entertainment industry, for instance, turn to crime and deviance partly as a means of acquiring celebrity status?

Two Canadian scholars, Patrick Parnaby and Vince Sacco (2004), think so. They point out that gangsters like Al Capone and John Dillinger became celebrities in the 1930s, attracting huge amounts of media attention (Capone, for instance, was featured on the cover of *Time*), and that serial killers often have their own fan clubs.

Their argument is exemplified by the story of James Frey's bestselling autobiography, *A Million Little Pieces* (2003). Purportedly an account of his life of lurid crime and drug use, it was an official choice of the Oprah book club and, in 2008, was outsold only by Harry Potter books. However, the book was later discovered to have been an invention. The revelation of his true crime—cheating his readers—was, ironically, rewarded with more fame: the book became a bestseller again.

SOCIAL LEARNING THEORIES: EDWIN SUTHERLAND AND DIFFERENTIAL ASSOCIATION

The basic proposition of learning theories is that willingness to break rules is a consequence of the socialization experience to which individuals have been exposed. Some people are motivated to engage in crime because they have acquired favourable opinions about what others regard as deviant behaviour. The learning of antisocial conduct and practices takes place in a variety of settings, beginning with the family and continuing with the peer group and the neighbourhood. Within each of these contexts, people may see as normal what others regard as wrong, dangerous, harmful, and shameful.

The best-known proponent of the learning perspective is Edwin Sutherland (1947), who insisted that a process of **differential association** is primarily responsible for deviant or nondeviant behaviour. Specifically, if people experience more nondeviant than deviant associations as they grow up, they are likely to follow the straight and narrow. Otherwise, they are likely to become deviants. According to Sutherland, criminals need to learn the tricks of the trade—how to steal a car or rob a bank, for instance. No less importantly, they must also learn rationalizations that tell them that stealing other people's money or property is justifiable. More association with deviant than nondeviant lifestyles teaches people these two important sets of lessons. Moreover, learning continues later in life. For example, research that I conducted with Scot Wortley showed that ex-inmates often believe that their time in prison has been a learning experience. The ex-inmates we interviewed described how prison enabled them to become more immersed in gang culture, learn new skills, and develop additional reasons for hating the police (Wortley and Tanner, 2005).

CONTROL THEORY

Travis Hirschi (1969) pioneered **control theory.** Its basic argument is that a set of ties bind young people to the conventional world, and when those ties are weak, deviance and crime occur. No special motivation is required. According to Hirschi, we all have within us a natural inclination for rule breaking that is only kept in check because we have developed *attachments* to family and friends, *commitments* to conventional ambitions and activities in school and at work, prosocial *values and beliefs* that we share with people who are important to us, and conventional *activities* at school and at work. Individuals not constrained by such ties are likely to become involved in crime and deviance.

Control theory has a solid reputation as a predictor of relatively minor and occasional deviance involving adolescents. However, when more serious crime and delinquency is involved, and when the deviant behaviour in question appears more motivated or has a political underpinning, it is less plausible. In the fall of 2005, visible minority youth, mainly of Arab background, took to the streets of major French cities in protest against poor educational opportunities, inadequate housing, racial discrimination in the labour market, and heavy-handed policing. In Montreal in the summer of 2008, minority youth rioted when one of them was shot and killed by a police officer. Reference to weak ties alone cannot explain this sort of politically inspired collective action. Control theory fails to explain why members of disadvantaged groups fail to develop conventional attachments to society in the first place.

We can apply the same observations to the riots that erupted in different parts of London, England, in August 2011. While their meaning and significance (mindless criminality or social protest?) have been fiercely debated by both media commentators and politicians in the United Kingdom, the fact that major incidents were not randomly distributed throughout the city but were concentrated instead in neighbourhoods characterized by unemployment, poverty, and strained relationships with the police suggests more systemic determinants as well.

A more recent variant of control theory is the so-called general theory of crime, which argues that all deviance has a common cause in low self-control. Gottfredson and Hirschi (1990) propose that rule breaking of all sorts shares common features. It is easy to execute, immediately satisfying, risky, exciting, produces few long-lasting rewards, and is harmful to others. The personality characteristics of individuals with low self-control include impulsivity, a taste for risk, an action orientation, and short-term thinking. Low self-control presumably originates in early socialization when parents are too busy or unconcerned to police their children's behaviour and unable or unwilling to teach them the difference between right and wrong. Canadian research finds that low self-control predicts driving under the influence of alcohol and school-related behavioural problems among high-school students (Keane, Maxim, and Teevan, 1993; Nakhaie, Silverman, and Lagrange, 2000).

A tale of two riots. Same behaviour, different meaning? Is there a political purpose to the London rioting that is missing from the Vancouver hockey riots?

SOURCES: © Jason Payne/Vancouver Sun (t); © REUTERS/Luke MacGregor (b).

ROUTINE ACTIVITIES THEORY

Routine activities theory, by locating the source of crime in the structuring of everyday life, also downplays the significance of criminal motivation. It argues that much criminal behaviour is not dependent on complex causation. The presence of a suitable target and the absence of capable guardians suffice. Bring these conditions together with motivated offenders, and deviance and crime are likely to result.

Cohen and Felson (1979; Felson and Boba, 2010) suggest that the development of expensive and highly valued consumer goods has encouraged property crime because items like iPods, computers, and cellphones are easy to steal and transport. They also reason that residential property is harder to protect because increased labour force participation means that fewer homeowners are around during the day to deter burglars, and that, compared with earlier eras, the amount of leisure time that teenagers have at their disposal provides them with the opportunity and motivation for delinquent episodes.

Routine activities theorists argue that crime rates vary not just because of the number of individuals in the population willing and prepared to commit crime, but also because of the presence or absence of capable guardians, and because of the daily routines that people follow. Research shows that some routines are more closely linked to criminal offending and criminal victimization than others are. People who spend large stretches of time away from home each day at work and out on the town in the evening and on weekends report higher levels of victimization than those who live more home-centred lives. Teenagers who spend large stretches of time in unsupervised leisure activities with other teenagers are at particular risk of criminal victimization and offending.

A useful illustration of how daily routines structure deviant behaviour is Hagan and McCarthy's (1997) study of street youth and crime in Toronto. They demonstrate that a substantial amount of criminal activity by street youth is motivated by situational exigencies. Nothing very surprising about this observation, you might say—except for the fact that most theories of crime have looked to the past to explain the criminal present. Strain and learning theories identify the roots of crime in lack of opportunity and differential association; control theories explain deviance by the failure to develop prosocial bonds early on at home or in school. Hagan and McCarthy argue that while these theories do a good job of explaining why some young people leave home and are on the street in the first place, they are less useful for explaining patterns of crime that occur afterwards. Crime on the streets has more immediate causes. Street life thus becomes a relatively independent influence on such activities as theft and prostitution.

TYPES OF CRIME AND DEVIANCE

So far, I have looked at conceptions of deviance and crime, ways of measuring their incidence, and prominent theories of criminal deviance. I now turn to several subfields of the sociological study of crime and deviance.

GENDER AND CRIME

Sociological studies of female crime and deviance are a comparatively recent development. In the past, sociologists ignored female wrongdoers because they thought their numbers were small or assumed that all female deviants were prostitutes. They judged male deviance a law-and-order problem and female deviance a sexual problem. This sexualized view of female deviance derives from the criminal records of known offenders. Historically, most girls and women were arrested and incarcerated for prostitution or because they were suspected carriers of venereal disease.

Self-report studies have done much to dispel the notion of female offenders as sexual deviants. They show that girls and women are no strangers to deviant behaviour of all types. Official and unofficial measures of crime and deviance indicate that the major difference between males and females is largely one of volume. Males are more inclined than females to crime and deviance (especially violent crime), start their deviant activities earlier, and end them later.

Increasingly, however, some sociologists see female crime as a growing problem. Women and girls are becoming more violent, more involved in gang activity, and so on. High-profile cases, such as the murder in 1997 of 14-year-old Reena Virk in Victoria and the subsequent trials of one of the young females accused of the crime, have done much to consolidate this kind of argument.

The belief that we are witnessing shifting patterns of female crime and deviance has led to the development of theories that link these changes to the effects of changing gender roles in society. In the 1970s, sociologists proposed the "liberation hypothesis," suggesting that, as women less frequently perform traditional domestic roles as wives and mothers, and begin entering the paid labour force in larger numbers, their patterns of crime and deviance will come to resemble those of males (Adler, 1975; Simon, 1975). However, available evidence offers little support for the liberation hypothesis. Differences in male and female crime rates, particularly violent crime, are quite stable over time.

Recently, some sociologists have asserted that while young women may be less physically violent and aggressive than their male counterparts are, they are more likely to take part in psychological aggression directed against other girls, such as name calling, spreading harmful gossip, and rumour mongering. This argument, too, has been challenged by research showing that psychological aggression is not the exclusive prerogative of "mean girls," and that girls who are victims of relational aggression are targeted by boys too (Chesney-Lind, Morash, and Irwin, 2007).

Currently, two schools of thought exist about how to account for similarities and differences between the deviant activities of males and females. Some analysts think that female wrongdoing can be best explained by the same concepts and theories used to explain male wrongdoing. For example, Canadian research indicates that lower levels of deviance and criminality among young females than among young males can be explained by the concepts of control and opportunity (Hagan, Gillis, and Simpson, 1987). Conversely, sociologists influenced by feminist ideas are more likely to argue

Should squeegee kids' actions be considered criminal, a nuisance, or a form of subsistence work?
SOURCE: © Fred Thornhill/Sun Media.

for gender-specific theories of crime and deviance. They argue that it is unreasonable to suppose that theories devised with male behaviour in mind, and tested exclusively with information supplied by males, will prove equally applicable to female deviants. The idea that we might need different theories to explain male and female deviance receives partial support from a U.S. study. Researchers found that depression was a cause of female delinquency but not male delinquency. They also reported that playing sports increases male violence but not female violence (Daigle, Cullen, and Wright, 2007).

YOUTH, CRIME, AND DEVIANCE

Young people are at the heart of most people's concerns about crime and deviance (Tanner, 2010). It has been this way for a long time, with successive adult generations believing that the behaviour of young people has never been worse than it is now (see Box 14.1). Media coverage encourages such views, preferring bad news stories to more uplifting ones, and focusing on high-profile and unrepresentative crimes of violence, rather than more typical shoplifting incidents, for example.

Moral panics are extreme reactions to deviance and crime, and social constructionists have extensively examined them. Episodes of moral panic are characterized by the conviction that the deviance or crime in question is sufficiently dangerous that it constitutes a threat to the core values and well-being of society. Politicians, newspaper editors, and prominent personages clamour for immediate action. They typically say that something has to be done right away or the situation will only get worse. Some examples of moral panic in Canada have focused on raves (Hier, 2002) and so-called squeegee kids (Parnaby, 2003).

Most moral panics involve young people for two main reasons. First, many adults view them as vulnerable to corrupting influences from "satanic" adults to violent movies, video games, and rap music. Second, young people represent the future. If bad influences corrupt them now, what will become of the nation when they reach adulthood?

How can we spot moral panics? Moral panics exist when the public reaction to deviance or crime is out of proportion to the nature and scope of the problem—when, for instance, there is little or no factual basis to claims about increased levels of drug use among young people or incidents of lethal violence in schools (Ben-Yehuda, 1986; Lawrence and Mueller, 2003).

Youth Gangs

Youth gangs have emerged as a major crime problem in Canada over the past decade because of an apparent increase in gang activity in large cities. However,

BOX 14.1 COPS IN SCHOOLS

The prospect of uniformed police officers walking the halls of Toronto schools is bound to make some students and parents uneasy.

But after the shooting death last year of 15-year-old Jordan Manners at C.W. Jefferys Collegiate and a subsequent report on school safety that revealed disturbing levels of violence and fear in some schools, it is clear that a greater police presence has become a necessary, if unfortunate, reality. That's why the Toronto public school board and city police are working on a strategy to place "school resource officers" in some schools as early as this fall.

Board chair John Campbell says the plan is still "a work in progress." It is expected that 22 public high schools will "host" officers, who will spend two or three days a week at their designated schools. (Another five or six officers are expected to be placed in Catholic schools.) But the list of schools has not yet been determined. Neither has the precise nature of officers' duties, although a memo this week from education director Gerry Connelly to trustees suggests they could include co-ordinating lectures and anti-bullying programs, helping principals plan emergency procedures, and "being visible and active in the school community."

What is clear is that the school board wants police officers to take a more formal and proactive role in ensuring school safety. "They're really there to develop relationships with the kids," says Campbell.

That seems reasonable. One of the hard lessons of the school safety report is that many students are reluctant to report violence. That culture of silence provides fertile ground for bullying and crime.

Putting police in schools won't solve the problem entirely. But kids who see the same police officer day after day will be more likely to confide in them. And officers who get to know students and the surrounding community will be more likely to spot trouble before it happens.

SOURCE: "Cops in Schools." (2008). *Star.com.* On the World Wide Web at http://www.thestar.com/comment/article/450080 (retrieved 11 February 2012).

gang activity has attracted more media attention than academic research. Much of the research is several decades old and based on small samples of already-identified groups of young people in specific geographic locations—for instance, immigrant gangs in British Columbia (Gordon, 2000).

I conducted an investigation of youth gang activity in Toronto with Scot Wortley (Wortley and Tanner, 2004). We interviewed a sample of high-school students and street youth. We learned that many of our respondents who reported past or present gang membership were not involved in criminal activities at all. Their gang membership had more to do with the pursuit of legitimate leisure activities than deviant ones. Membership in organizations involved with crime and deviance, such as drug trafficking and violent conflict with other gangs, was more common among street youth than among high-school students.

We also found that poverty, race and ethnicity, family structure, and living arrangements influence gang membership. These factors reflect the patterns of inequality, disadvantage, and discrimination to which strain theorists draw our attention. Other recent Canadian research tells a similar story. For example, disadvantaged Aboriginal youth in the West are recruited into gangs who provide them with the status and the income (largely from the drug trade, where they work as low-level dealers) otherwise denied them in cities like Winnipeg and Regina or on the reserve. The larger American research literature documents the same pattern.

Serious and repetitive gang activity can result in incarceration for gang members. Evidence suggests that the prison system also functions as a recruiting ground for gang members. On occasion, gangs formed in prison extend their activities onto the street once members are released (Grekul and LaBoucane-Benson, 2008). American research has found a similar pattern with bike gangs and white supremacist groups.

NET EFFECTS: INTERNET DEVIANCE

The rapid development of computer technology—the Internet in particular—has significantly expanded opportunities for deviant and disreputable behaviour (Thio, 2010). The deviant purposes that computers have been used for include, but are not limited to, identity theft, cyber stalking, and the sale and distribution of pornography.

Identity theft has become the fastest-growing crime of the twenty-first century. Credit card, health card, and driving licence information is stolen and used to buy goods and services. It is easy to do and difficult to detect and is much more profitable than conventional property crime.

Pornography is not, of course, an invention of the Internet. The Internet has, however, made its consumption considerably easier, making it accessible to a wide range of buyers, including adolescents. Internet porn has the advantage of being a home-based activity, allowing users to indulge in it without surreptitious visits to adult bookstores and video stores that might reveal their disreputable tastes to others. The Internet has become a principal means by which the trade in child pornography has flourished (Jenkins, 2001).

The Internet has also become a medium by which people can target their dislike of, or hatred for, other people. In September 2010, an 18-year-old male student at Rutgers University in the United States used a webcam to secretly film his roommate kissing another male. The encounter was then video streamed over the Internet. That student, Tyler Clementi, subsequently killed himself.

On occasion, the Internet has been deployed not out of malice or for financial gain but for essentially political reasons. A case in point is the WikiLeaks phenomenon. Orchestrated by Internet activist Julian Assange, WikiLeaks is an organization that disseminates classified information over the Internet. It has been responsible for, among other activities, the downloading of secret military information detailing the Iraq war. While political and military elites in Washington and London are anxious to portray such leaks as wildly outrageous criminal acts, Assange and his supporters prefer to see themselves as courageous defenders of freedom of information. (We might also note that crime fiction has similarly embraced the idea of the computer hacker as hero in the form of Lisbeth Sander, the heroine of *The Girl with the Dragon Tattoo* [Larsson, 2008]).

Older modes of communication technology are similarly vulnerable to hacking. A recent example is provided by News International, the news empire owned by Rupert Murdoch and the activities, in particular, of his flagship organ, *News of the World*.

The news-gathering techniques of this tabloid newspaper in the United Kingdom included paying senior Scotland Yard police officers for information about crime stories and hacking the cellphones of politicians, celebrities, members of the British royal family, a missing teenager later found murdered, relatives of victims of the July 2007 tube bombings in London, and relatives of British soldiers killed in Afghanistan. While the news organization has sought to portray these crimes as the actions of a few rogue journalists, it is clear that they were operating under the clear (if perhaps only implicit) direction of their employer.

RESPONDING TO CRIME AND DEVIANCE

When sociologists study reactions to deviant behaviour, they are examining the ways in which societies try to prevent or control that behaviour.

INCARCERATION

The prison is the chief means by which we seek to control crime. Prisons are, however, a relatively recent invention. Canada's first prison was Kingston penitentiary, opened in 1835. Before then, convicted offenders received other forms of punishment, including hanging and deportation. Canada introduced prisons to incapacitate and punish offenders and discourage them (as well as other potential offenders) from committing additional crimes. Prisons were also expected to reform offenders, encouraging them to live law-abiding lives by teaching them work skills while serving time.

For more than a hundred years, Canada's prison population has varied very little in proportionate terms, fluctuating between 80 and 110 adults per 100 000 people (Brown, 2011). While the staggeringly high rate of incarceration in the United States and Russia is the main story told in Figure 14.5, it is worth noting that Canada is more likely to imprison offenders than are several Western European nations, as well as Japan and India.

Prisons do a poor job of rehabilitating prisoners. Many studies show that the recidivism rate among ex-prisoners is high, with a large proportion of the prison population at any one time made up of people who have been there before—sometimes, several times before (Morgan and Liebling, 2007).

Prison inmates suffer numerous deprivations (see Box 14.2). They are denied their freedom, required

FIGURE 14.5 WORLD PRISON POPULATION RATE (PER 100 000 OF THE NATIONAL POPULATION)

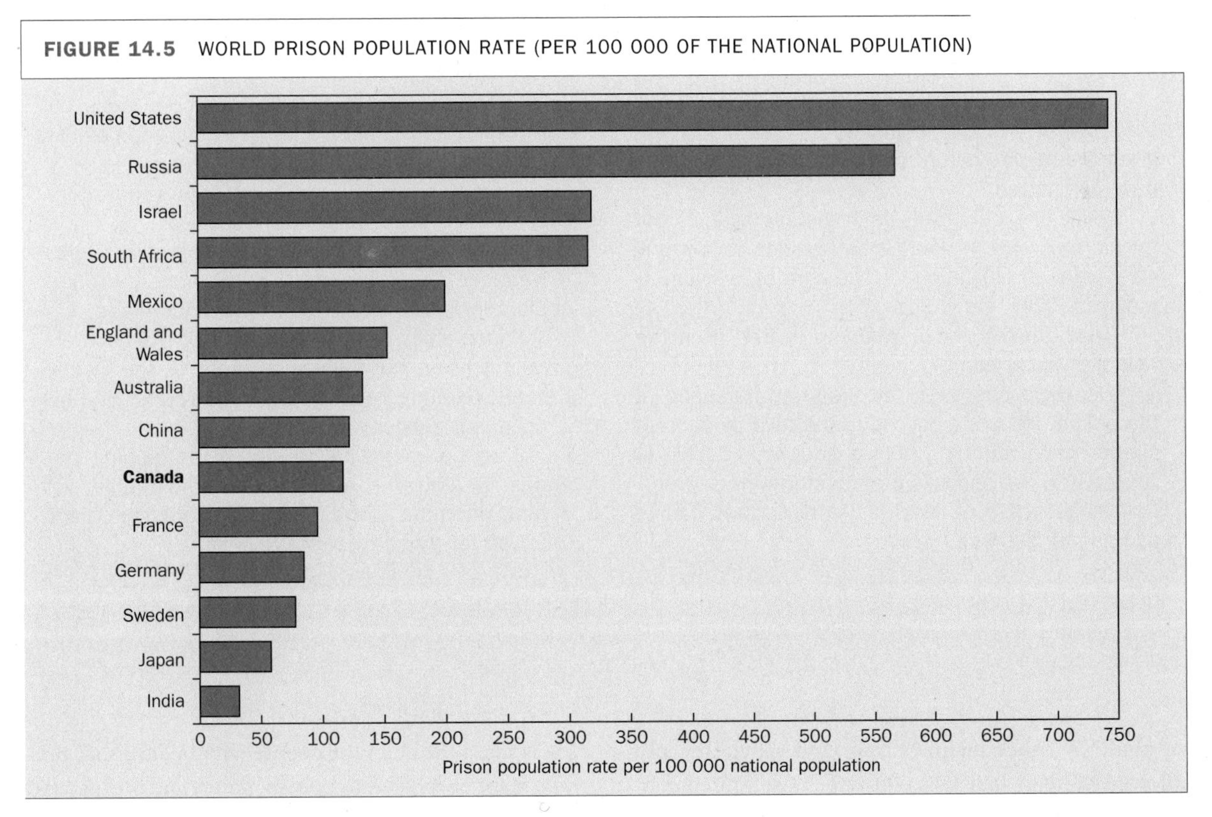

SOURCE: *World Prison Population List*, 9th edition, 2011. From http://www.prisonstudies.org/images/news_events/wppl9.pdf. International Centre for Prison Studies. Used with permission.

BOX 14.2 RUSSELL WILLIAMS ENTERS A "GRIM" EXISTENCE IN KINGSTON PENITENTIARY

From flying military jets and meeting dignitaries to living in a cell the size of a walk-in closet, Russell Williams has entered a "grim" existence at Kingston Penitentiary. The former commander of CFB Trenton turned sado-sexual killer was sentenced Thursday to life in prison with no chance of parole for 25 years for the slayings of Jessica Lloyd and Marie-France Comeau.

As Williams was being promptly whisked away to the maximum-security prison, the lead detective in the case said he'll serve his sentence in the segregation unit—home to some of Canada's most notorious inmates, including schoolgirl killer Paul Bernardo.

"In general people of his nature are taken down into solitary confinement, kept by themselves. They don't have access to any other inmates," Det. Insp. Chris Nicholas said outside the Belleville courthouse.

Defence lawyer Tony Bryant, who represented Bernardo, expects Williams will be on the same range as his old client, where the prison cells are 2.5 by 3 metres.

Bernardo's tiny cell—his home for the past 15 years—is not much larger than a typical household washroom, equipped with a cot, desk, and toilet.

Prisoners can talk to the inmate in the adjoining cell, but can't see them at the prison, which opened in 1835.

"It's a grim existence, no question about that," said Bryant. "Most people would say rightly so, given the horrific nature of the crimes these people have committed."

Williams would likely be in the segregation unit for his own safety, said Bryant, adding prison officials have an obligation to take care of everyone—they can't pick and choose.

That doesn't mean Williams is free from the risk of physical harm.

Bernardo has been attacked and harassed at the prison. He was punched in the face by another inmate while returning from a shower in 1996. In June 1999, five convicts tried to storm the segregation range where he lives and a riot squad had to use gas to disperse them.

Williams' military training gives him an edge in defending himself in prison, said lawyer and psychologist Patrick Baillie in an interview from Calgary.

But the former colonel's life behind bars is a stark contrast to the one of privilege he's experienced.

"That will be a huge adjustment. It is a massive change from the lifestyle he's had in the past which was independent, which was widely respected and which had with it all sorts of future possibilities," said Baillie.

"Now you're an individual who's going to be told what you eat, and when you eat and how many people are going to be living in your cell and which cell you're going to be in."

The transition will be particularly difficult for someone like Williams, who is used to having a large degree of control over others and who is very smart, said Baillie. He will have to adjust as well to the monotony.

"Some people will rebel and fight. Others will have an initial period of shock and then a decision that they need to get on with it," said Baillie.

Prisoners in the segregation unit get an hour outside their cell for exercise. For the other 23 hours a day, they are locked in their cells. They can watch television—if they buy a television. They can read and have writing materials. But there's no access to computers or the Internet.

Prisoners cannot receive telephone calls but can make them to people on an authorized call list, if they pay for the calls.

Offenders can hug and touch approved visitors, even have conjugal visits with spouses.

During his time at the Quinte Detention Centre in Napanee, Ont., since his February arrest, Williams could only speak to visitors from behind glass.

Prison officials will likely monitor Williams' state of mind, given his suicide attempt at the Quinte Detention Centre over the Easter weekend and his subsequent hunger strike.

Early psychological treatment or training programs for Williams are unlikely, said Baillie and Bryant, who note space in programs are limited and reserved for those closer to release.

SOURCE: Hewitt, Pat. 2010. "Russell Williams Enters a 'Grim' Existence in Kingston Penitentiary." *Star* October 24. On the World Wide Web at http://www.thestar.com/news/canada/article/880485–russell-williams-enters-a-grim-existence-in-kingston-penitentiary (retrieved 11 February 2012).

to abide by other peoples' rules and schedules, not allowed to wear their own clothing, have limited contact with friends and family from the outside, and required to live in an overcrowded, dirty, smelly, and violent environment. The unpleasantness of prison life is not a problem for people who believe that prison's main purpose is to punish, deter, and incapacitate offenders. It is a problem for people who adhere to rehabilitative ideals.

Prisons fail to rehabilitate for three reasons. First, commitment to the rehabilitative ideal has never been strong to begin with, with relatively few resources allocated to that goal. Second, in response to the harsh conditions that they encounter, prisoners have developed an inmate subculture with its own code of conduct that often challenges the regime imposed upon them. Third, prisoners learn new criminal skills from other prisoners and learn how to justify the use of violence (Sykes, 1958). Given immersion in the prison subculture, prison time is more likely to lead to more prison time than rehabilitation.

Prisons are the centrepiece of approaches to crime control that emphasize suppression. Calls for tougher law enforcement—more proactive policing, longer prison sentences for habitual criminals, mandatory minimum sentences for violent, gun, and gang-related crime—are all examples of suppressive strategies.

The "tough on crime" legislation proposed by the current government is likely to increase the size of the prison population in Canada. Because, as we have seen, crime rates are going down, this is a strange time for incarceration rates to be increasing; stranger still is that the rise will be a direct result of government policy that is unlikely to reduce the crime rate—an observation that brings us, appropriately enough, to deterrence theory.

Deterrence theory holds that getting tough on crime will lead to its eradication or at least reduce the probability of offending. Deterrence can take one of two main forms. *General deterrence* is the process by which the punishment of some law violators discourages other potential law violators from breaking the law. *Specific deterrence* is the process by which an individual who has been caught and punished for an offence will find the experience sufficiently costly that he or she will not repeat the wrongdoing again.

Deterrence, whether specific or general, has three elements. The first involves the severity of the penalty. Are offenders given jail time or just a fine? The second involves the certainty of punishment. When drivers consider the chance of getting caught speeding, they are considering the certainty of punishment. The final element is the speed of

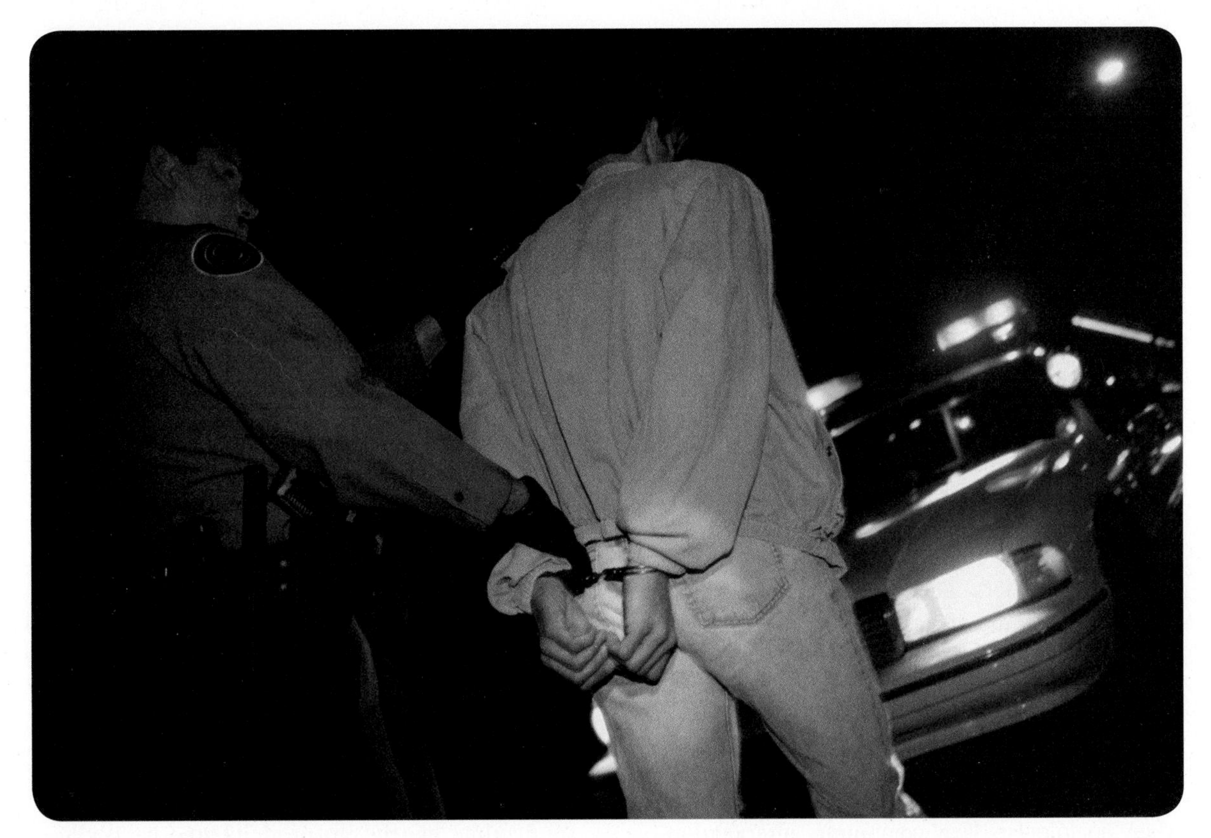

Contrary to the belief of many people, crime rates in Canada are declining. Nonetheless, Canada has a higher incarceration rate than most Western European Countries.
SOURCE: © Photodisc.

punishment. How long after law violators have been apprehended do they have to wait for punishment? Deterrence theory holds that law-violating behaviour will be low when severity, certainty, and speed of punishment are high.

Most practical applications of deterrence theory concentrate on the severity or harshness of legal sanctions. Hence the advocacy of capital punishment, long prison terms, and boot camp. However, most research does not support the proposition that harsh punishment deters. Where it exists, the death penalty has not reduced homicide rates (Fuller and Wozniak, 2006: 266). Boot camp has been less effective than other means of dealing with young offenders (Doob and Cesaroni, 2004). Longer prison terms are no more effective in reducing recidivism than are shorter terms (Doob and Webster, 2003).

The problem with deterrence theory is its assumption that criminals are rational calculators, carefully calibrating the costs of crime against its rewards. However, most criminals have only an imprecise understanding of the punishment they might receive for a given offence. Moreover, many violent crimes are prefigured by anger, which works against rational calculation. More evidence supports the **certainty principle,** which holds that potential offenders are more often deterred by the thought of certain but moderate punishment than by the guarantee of severe punishment for an act they believe they can get away with (Von Hirsch, Bottoms, Burney, and Wikstrom, 1999).

In addition to not necessarily producing lower crime rates, get-tough policies come with a high price tag. Keeping people in prison costs a lot. Mandatory minimum sentences mean that there will be more people in prison. More people in prison means that more people coming out of prison and trying to find a job and accommodation will be burdened with the stigma of being an ex-convict. In the United States, the "war on drugs" has resulted in the incarceration of bit players in the drug trade: addicted users and minor suppliers. The sheer expense of locking up minor criminals means that fewer tax dollars are available for other kinds of law enforcement and anti-crime policies that focus on prevention and intervention.

INTERVENTION

Many sociologists view community intervention on behalf of young offenders as an effective strategy for reducing crime. Interventionist policies assume that we can most effectively tackle crime by weakening motivations, and minimizing opportunities, for lawbreaking. Interventions include recreational programs for neighbourhood youth, counselling sessions, and the assignment of youth workers to neighbourhood street gangs. While programs of this sort have always commanded tremendous loyalty from their practitioners, they are expensive and have rarely been properly evaluated for their effectiveness.

PREVENTING CRIME

Too much of our thinking about crime focuses on catching and controlling offenders. Public policy debates about crime rarely discuss nonlegal solutions. Yet given what we know about the risk factors associated with serious and repetitive criminality among youth, one may reasonably suggest that expanded daycare, for example, might be a less costly and more effective investment of taxpayers' dollars than imprisonment is.

Evidence that some criminal justice policies do not work, or do not work as well as we would like them to, does not mean that they are going to be abandoned. Criminal justice policies are driven by political ideology, not criminological research. This is particularly true for juvenile justice policy.

Much if not most of the controversy surrounding criminal justice policy in Canada centres on young people. Over the past century, young people in trouble with the law have fallen under the provisions of the Juvenile Delinquents Act of 1908, the Young Offenders Act of 1984, and the Youth Criminal Justice Act of 2003.

The Juvenile Delinquents Act was replaced by the Young Offenders Act in large measure because critics felt that it was failing to deter or prevent rising rates of juvenile crime. The Young Offenders Act was, in turn, replaced by the Youth Criminal Justice Act because critics felt that it was failing to deter or prevent rising rates of youth crime.

The current Youth Criminal Justice Act emphasizes getting tough on serious, repeat young offenders while adopting less punitive strategies for the far more numerous minor offenders, including warnings and community-based diversionary programs. The most recently available crime statistics indicate that since the introduction of the new legislation, the rate of youth crime, like the rate of adult crime, has declined.

Nonetheless, the present government believes that more can and should be done to suppress, in the words of Justice Minister Rob Nicholson, "out-of-control young people" (Chase, 2011). Hence, it has introduced new crime legislation that, among other things, would make it easier to transfer young offenders who have committed serious crimes to the adult court, where they would be eligible for adult sentences, that is, lengthy prison terms. While the wisdom of sentencing a 14-year-old murderer to life imprisonment is not immediately apparent to sociologists, lawyers, and judges, the government remains firm in its resolve to deliver stricter juvenile justice policy. As Doob and Sprott (2004: 214) remark, "It is easier to be tough on crime than to be smart about crime."

BIG BROTHER IS WATCHING YOU: SURVEILLANCE IN EVERYDAY LIFE

Prisons and incarceration are not the only means by which contemporary societies seek to constrain the behaviour of its citizens. Nor are the lawbreakers their only concern. In postmodern societies, it has been suggested, both public and private institutions increasingly seek to monitor and control the behaviours of ordinary law-abiding citizens, as well as recognized deviants (Staples, 2008).

Consider the following: convicted offenders under house arrest are required to wear electronic bracelets, tracking their movements; some job seekers are required to comply with obligatory drug tests as a condition of employment; store owners use video cameras to observe customers and employees alike; companies trace the online purchasing habits of Internet users. These examples illustrate eroding differences between the criminal justice system's way of doing things and the ordinary, everyday culture of surveillance. Their common goal is to regulate everyday behaviour and establish conformity.

Staples suggests that everyday surveillance is distinguished from more formal kinds of social control, first, by its scope. The closed circuit television (CCTV) camera scans everybody—not just the suspicious looking shoppers in high-end stores, not just the teenagers lurking in the parking lot. Second, our behaviour is controlled less by the threat of punishment than by the certain knowledge that we are being watched. Third, surveillance is everywhere. Whereas, historically, criminals were confined to prisons, and those with mental illnesses to asylums, ordinary citizens are regulated, and encouraged to self-regulate, by the omnipresence of the all-seeing CCTV camera, the threat of random drug tests, and compulsory ID tags. Nowhere are these developments more apparent than in schools.

Increasingly—ever since the shootings at Columbine high school in April 1999—schools have begun to take on some of the characteristics of custodial institutions, places where safety and security issues have become as important as educational ones. Students are now confronted with a barrage of zero tolerance policies, metal detectors, practice lockdowns, random drug tests, CCTV cameras, police officers in the hallways, and mandatory uniforms. While there is little evidence that these policies work as intended—they do not actually make schools safer for students—research has identified some unintended effects: a climate of fear and anxiety and—in the case of zero tolerance policies—racial profiling in the classroom.

Critics wonder whether these practices undermine teaching and learning objectives in schools. They also consider them to be an affront to civil liberties. Some schools in the United Kingdom (one in seven according to a Guardian report; Harris, 2011) now fingerprint their students out of concern about the theft of library books and cafeteria food; there are now legislated proposals to extend the power of teachers to search students and confiscate phones and computers. These developments, for some people, suggest that George Orwell's Big Brother has now made his way onto school premises.

SUMMARY

1. While crime and deviance are universal phenomena, there are no universal forms of crime and deviance. What counts as crime and deviance varies by time and place. Crime and deviance also vary by how serious they are judged to be. The more serious the offence, the more severe the punishment.
2. Crime and deviance can be studied as objective behaviours and social constructs. Objectivist and constructionist perspectives tend to ask different, though not necessarily competing, questions about crime and deviance.

3. Official counts of crime and deviance underestimate the amount of crime and deviance occurring in society. There is an inverse relationship between the seriousness of crime and deviance and the frequency of their occurrence. The homicide rate is generally regarded as the most valid and reliable measure of criminal activity in the community.
4. Canada's crime rate has been declining over the past several decades. There are significant variations in rates of crime across the country.
5. The shortcomings of official crime statistics are well known. To reduce reliance on them, self-report and observational studies have been developed as additional data sources.
6. There are a number of important correlates of crime, including age and gender. However, correlation does not necessarily imply causation. Sociological theories of crime and deviance are designed to answer questions about causation.
7. Historically, the deviant and criminal activities of girls and women have been ignored or sexualized. Increasingly, however, sociologists are paying more attention to the forms and frequency of female crime and deviance.
8. Concern about youth crime and deviance has always been prominent.
9. Imprisonment and other deterrence-based policies have been a mainstay of the societal response to criminal behaviour. Research suggests that they are not very effective in reducing crime levels. Other anti-crime strategies focus on prevention. Much of the public debate about criminal justice policy in Canada concentrates on young offenders.

QUESTIONS TO CONSIDER

1. What are moral panics? Why do they often involve young people?
2. Why is studying reaction to crime and deviance often as important as studying criminal and deviant behaviour itself?
3. Choose a particular form of criminal or deviant activity (for instance, youth gangs, drug use, serial killers) and consider how it might be studied from both objectivist and social constructionist perspectives.
4. How do the mass media influence criminal and deviant behaviour?
5. What are the most important causes of crime?
6. Are girls and women becoming more violent and aggressive?

GLOSSARY

The **certainty principle** (p. 364) is a component of deterrence theory that argues that it is the probability of punishment, rather than its severity, that dissuades potential offenders from breaking the law.

Conflict crime (p. 343) involves criminal acts that are subject to disagreement about their wrongfulness, the amount of harm they cause, how wrong they are, and how severely they should be punished.

Consensus crime (p. 343) involves criminal acts that are generally agreed to be seriously harmful, wrong, and deserving of severe penalty.

Control theories (p. 356) argue that crime and deviance are likely to occur when internal and external controls are weak or absent.

Crime (p. 342) is a breach of the criminal law that is liable to prosecution and punishment.

The **criminal justice system** (p. 342) comprises the social institutions charged with the task of apprehending, prosecuting, and punishing known offenders.

The **dark figure of crime** (p. 349) is the number of criminal incidents that take place but are unknown to the police.

Deterrence theory (p. 363) argues that the threat of punishment discourages criminal violation.

Deviance (p. 342) is the breaking of a norm.

Differential association (p. 356) theory proposes that criminal behaviour is learned through contact with other individuals and groups.

Labelling theory (p. 345) argues that public identification of individuals as criminal or deviant leads to more crime or deviance by those individuals.

Moral panics (p. 359) are extreme reactions to crime and deviance.

Norms (p. 342) are rules that prescribe standards of everyday behaviour.

In **observational studies** (p. 352), information about crime and deviance is collected by observing it.

Racial profiling (p. 354) is a selective enforcement of the law based on racial or ethnic characteristics of those apprehended by police officers.

Recidivism (p. 348) is repeat offending, particularly following punishment or rehabilitation.

Routine activities theory (p. 357) argues that in addition to a motivated offender, criminal events require a suitable target and the absence of a capable guardian.

In **self-report studies** (p. 352), respondents report about their involvements with crime and deviance as offenders and victims.

Social constructionism (p. 346) is a broad theoretical perspective concerned with the subjective meanings of social problems.

Social stigma (p. 344) is a damaged reputation or status.

Strain theory (p. 354) argues that people are pressured into breaking rules because they have few opportunities to succeed in life by legitimate means.

Street crime (p. 353) refers to conventional violent and property crime. It is often contrasted with white-collar crime.

White-collar crime (p. 347) is crime committed by high-status people in the course of their occupational careers.

SUGGESTED READING

Cohen, Stanley. (2002). *Folk Devils and Moral Panics,* 3rd ed. New York: Taylor and Francis. A sociological classic. The story of how societal reaction ("moral panic") turned mildly deviant youth groups (the mods and the rockers) into "folk devils" in mid-1960s Britain.

Sacco, Vince. (2005). *When Crime Waves.* Thousand Oaks, CA: Sage. A stimulating examination of a wide range of crime and deviance issues, including media representations of crime, the use and abuse of statistics, and fear of crime, from a social constructionist perspective.

Tanner, Julian. (2010). *Teenage Troubles: Youth and Deviance in Canada,* 3rd ed. Toronto: Oxford University Press. A comprehensive overview of what is known about juvenile crime and deviance in Canada. It examines a number of themes—schools and delinquency, deviant subcultures, youth gangs—from both objectivist and constructionist perspectives.

Venkatesh, Sudhir. (2008). *Gang Leader for a Day: A Rogue Sociologist Takes to the Streets.* New York: Penguin. A fascinating account of how a young researcher came to study gang activity in a notoriously tough Chicago community. It is important for what it tells us about gang activity and the challenges and rewards of doing observational research.

CHAPTER 15

POPULATION AND URBANIZATION

SOURCE: © James A. Sugar/Getty Images.

John Hannigan
UNIVERSITY OF TORONTO

IN THIS CHAPTER YOU WILL LEARN THAT

- Especially rapid population growth occurs when (1) breakthroughs in hygiene, public health, nutrition, and medical knowledge cause the death rate to fall, and (2) lack of industrialization, urbanization, and modernization prevent the birth rate from falling.
- The choice of opportunities, experiences, and lifestyles available to urban residents is shaped and constrained by three sets of factors: those related to the physical environment; those associated with population size, distribution, and composition; and those dictated by the changing structure of the wider economy.
- Contrary to the theory that the core of Canadian cities is hollowing out, recent evidence suggests that city centres are remaining relatively stable economically and demographically. In contrast, the rings of older suburbs around city cores are stagnating, losing jobs and population to constellations of edge cities in the surrounding regions.
- The fastest-growing middle-class neighbourhoods are private communities, where control over local government, public services, and security rests in the hands of nonelected professional managers. One popular form of such neighbourhoods is the gated community, where nonresidents are considered intruders and are monitored and kept out by guards, alarm systems, and surveillance cameras.
- Cities are becoming multiethnic, with many neighbourhoods in the largest cities becoming home to members of visible minorities. This is generating racial and ethnic residential and commercial patterns that stand in marked contrast to the ecology of the older, industrial city.

INTRODUCTION

A few years ago, *Toronto Life* magazine published a cover story entitled "The New Suburbanites" about why some "diehard downtowners" are giving up on the city and moving to small towns within a 150-kilometre (95-mile) radius of Toronto (Preville, 2011). Profiled are Carrie Low, a corporate lawyer, Brian Porter, a firefighter, and their two daughters. Life in Toronto's east end neighbourhood, the Beaches, had become too stressful and "over-engineered" given the demands of two careers and a never-ending shuttle of kid drop-offs and pickups to lessons, play dates, and birthday parties. The couple felt like runners in a relay race, always passing the baton. They decided that the problem wasn't each other, or their careers or their children, "but the city itself." Living in Toronto, Carrie and Brian concluded, "required too many contortions," so they "decided to divorce it." Their solution was to purchase a 2700-square-foot detached house in Cobourg, 118 kilometres (73 miles) east of Toronto along Lake Ontario.

Nineteenth-century towns like Cobourg have delivered everything these escapees from the city are seeking. Carrie, who commutes to Toronto several days a week, contrasts her current Via train ride back to Cobourg, where "those of us who make that commute all know one another" to riding to work on Toronto's transit system, where "everyone is in their own bubble, no one makes eye contact, and even if you ride with the same people every day you never say hi to them." Simon Heath, a writer who moved to Creemore, 123 kilometres (75 miles) north of Toronto, reports that he and his wife, Lily, feel absolutely comfortable allowing their children to wander off at the local farmers' market, something they would never have done in the big city. "Outside the city," Heath says, "everyone knows who you are and what you're up to."

This profile of small-town life highlights a theme that has resounded through the discipline of sociology since its founding in the nineteenth century. Urban life, it is said, is qualitatively different from a rural or small-town existence: meaner, more stressful, more alienating. Obsessed as they are with efficiency and making money, urbanites are said to have no time for relating to others in a more holistic and humane way. Increasing population size and density bring with them a host of urban problems, from traffic gridlock and pollution to family breakdown and crime.

The tale of Carrie, Brian, and their daughters illustrates one of the most influential ways of looking at residential settings. Termed **environmental-opportunity theory** (Michelson, 1973), it posits that people actively choose where they want to live depending on the extent to which a particular place either meshes with or constrains their preferred lifestyle. Not all of us, of course, get to choose our community freely, but people will always strive to match their choices with their needs. This fact is also well illustrated in the case of "Prairie Edge," a small Alberta municipality where residents perceive the "rural advantage" as being directly linked to the reduced parental anxiety that comes from a "safe" everyday environment (see Box 15.1).

Is urban life meaner, more stressful, more alienating than small-town life?

SOURCE: © Al Harvey/The Slide Farm.

A second lens through which urban life can be viewed is that of *demography*—the study of populations: their size, distribution, and composition. As you will learn later in this chapter, in the preindustrial city significant growth was constrained by a high birth rate and a high death rate. Only when the death rate began to fall because of advances in hygiene, nutrition, medical knowledge, and public health did the industrial city thrive, bringing with it a distinctive spatial organization and way of life. Today, the social organization and character of cities are being powerfully influenced by flows of highly diverse groups of immigrants. This has resulted in the re-urbanization of the central city, the growth of the multiethnic city, and other urban changes.

A third approach asserts that the urban experience is constrained not just by the nature of the physical environment or by demographic forces, but also by the changing configuration of international, national, and local economic arrangements. In recent years, the emergence of a globalized economy has had profound implications for North American

BOX 15.1 PRAIRIE EDGE: A "RURBAN" COMMUNITY

"Prairie Edge" is a pseudonym for Camrose, Alberta, a community of 14 000 about 100 kilometres (62 miles) from Edmonton. In the early 1990s, a survey research firm, John Yerxa Research Inc., asked residents of Prairie Edge (and three other "rural communities") to compare their place of residence with that of Edmonton. Just more than 80 percent reported that they believed a rural setting was a better place to raise a family. Residents particularly appreciated a quieter and smaller setting for its easy social interaction and perceived high level of personal safety. However, they recognized that their community lacked the wide choice of shopping and entertainment opportunities that were more readily available in Edmonton.

Sociologist Kieran Bonner resided in Prairie Edge around the time of the survey and independently carried out his own study among the middle-class parents who were his neighbours. Bonner found that they stressed three interrelated themes—safety, convenience, and reduced parental anxiety—as the key benefits of the "life world" of a smaller centre. Each of these, in turn, flowed out of the high visibility and familiarity that resulted from smallness. However, some of his informants, especially those who had moved from a larger city, indicated that the familiarity resulting from high visibility (it was difficult to be a "stranger" in Prairie Edge) led to an ethic of helping and politeness but not to sociability and friendliness. In other words, people trusted their local environment more, especially with regard to potential dangers to children, but they did not necessarily share a strong sense of "community." Prairie Edge, Bonner concluded, possessed both rural and urban characteristics and thus could be described as being "rurban."

SOURCE: Adapted from Kieran Bonner, *A Great Place to Raise Kids: Interpretation, Science, and the Urban-Rural Debate,* Montreal and Kingston: McGill-Queen's University Press, 1997.

cities, changing both their physical form and their social-class patterns. In particular, it has resulted in an increasing polarization between rich and poor, affecting the homeless person sleeping in the park, the highly paid professional eating in the chic urban restaurant, and the suburban homeowner shopping in a "big-box" megastore on the fringes of the city (Kleniewski, 1997: 135).

Similarly, resource towns and farming communities have been hard hit by international trade agreements and a harsher rural-urban division of labour in the global economy. In this changing climate, the countryside comes to serve two new and very different purposes: vacation playground and toxic dumping ground. Thus, while towns in the British Columbia interior and the Alberta foothills are transformed into ski and golfing resorts linked to global tourism, other communities are forced to "grasp at environmentally dubious schemes like hazardous waste treatment, strawboard manufacture, tire incineration and mega-hog barns" (Epp and Whitson, 2001: xv).

In this chapter, I will look at this three-pronged influence of environment and structure on city life over the past century. In the course of the discussion, you will encounter three main types of cities: the industrial city, the corporate city, and the **postmodern city.** The industrial city originated in the nineteenth century and reached its zenith in the 1920s and 1930s, the corporate city arose after World War II and dominated during the 1950s and 1960s, and the postmodern city dates from the 1970s up to the present.

EARLY CITIES

Cities are "relatively large, dense, permanent settlements in which the majority of the residents do not produce their own food" (McGahan, 1995: 1). By most accounts, the city as a distinct form dates back five thousand or six thousand years to 3000–4000 BCE, when it first appeared in Mesopotamia (now southern Iraq) and Egypt. Initially, ancient cities were established largely as centres of religious worship and were not much larger than most single-industry towns in Canada today. For example, Memphis, at the head of the Nile River delta, had an estimated population of 40 000 in 3000 BCE. Cities later swelled: Babylon had a population of 200 000 during the reign of Nebuchadnezzar in the seventh century BCE; Alexandria, Egypt, surpassed 300 000 three centuries later; and Rome reached 800 000 at its peak in the second century CE (Chandler and Fox, 1974).

Three elements of prime importance characterized these preindustrial cities: the existence of a food surplus in fertile valleys, which permitted the specialization of labour in zones of dense settlement; the achievement of literacy among scribes, priests, and other elite members of society, which allowed for the keeping of financial and other records; and technological innovations, notably metallurgy, agricultural irrigation, and the harnessing of wind and water power for sailing and grain milling.

After the fall of Rome to Germanic tribes in the fifth century CE, cities stagnated and declined over large parts of Europe. They continued to flourish, though, in the rising Islamic empire, which, at its zenith, stretched from Spain to India. More decentralized than the Roman world, the Islamic empire contained a number of cities that reached impressive levels of size and sophistication. For example, more than 500 000 people lived in Cairo in the fourteenth century, when Egypt held a trade monopoly on the east-west spice route (Abu-Lughod, 1991: 38).

From the eleventh century on, a number of city-states along the Mediterranean—Florence, Genoa, Venice, Pisa—succeeded in reestablishing trade routes to Asia and the Middle East by means of the Crusades. The commercial revival that followed was felt even in the merchant towns of the North Sea and the Baltic, which themselves had begun to develop a brisk trade in wool and cloth. From this renaissance developed a distinct class of professional merchants who established their own municipal laws and institutions distinct from those in the surrounding feudal society; there also emerged a market for housing and a variety of other goods and services, which generated further urban growth (Golden, 1981: 120–22). Although preindustrial cities were important as centres of commerce, knowledge, and art, they never contained much more than a small fraction of the overall population. Even at their height, ancient and medieval cities were incapable of supporting urban populations of more than 5 or 10 percent of society, primarily because they could not generate a sufficiently large agricultural surplus to feed a huge urban populace. When the cities did begin to swell, periodic outbreaks of the bubonic plague (the notorious "Black Death"), spread by fleas from infected rats, killed as many as half the people in Europe's cities. Thus, by 1800, of the roughly 900 million people in the world, only about 3 percent lived in urban places of 5000 or more inhabitants (Hauser, 1965: 7). And despite significant changes in architectural styles and building materials, the physical layout of the communities in which they lived had not changed all that much from antiquity to the eighteenth century—they were still built up within protective walls and organized around a central market square and places of worship, such as cathedrals, temples, or mosques (Abu-Lughod, 1991: 49–50).

POPULATION ISSUES AND URBAN GROWTH

Urban growth is a product not only of technological progress and social invention but also of the broader patterns of population growth that shape a society. These demographic forces operate in conjunction with other social and economic factors to create a slow-moving but powerful current that relentlessly moves us in certain directions (McQuillan, 1994: 229).

THE DEMOGRAPHIC TRANSITION

For much of human history, societies hovered in a steady state in which both birth rates and death rates were high. As a result, the overall size of the population remained more or less stable from decade to decade.

In the absence of any effective form of birth control, women in preindustrial societies were destined to bear a large number of children. This was deemed necessary for several reasons. Infant and childhood mortality rates were high; routinely, only about half of the children born survived to adulthood. Thus, it was necessary to have large families in the hope that some would escape the grim reaper. Furthermore, in traditional societies offspring were viewed as having considerable economic value, especially in the poorer classes where children were expected to help with the farm work or were sent off to work as servants in the homes of the rich. In the absence of pension plans or retirement funds, parents fortunate enough to reach old age depended on their children to care for them.

The human lifespan was much shorter than it is today. For example, in 1867, the year Canada officially became a country, the average life expectancy at birth was 42 years (Beaujot, 2004: 446) as compared with 80.9 years for those born between 2006 and 2008 (Statistics Canada, 2011a). Even the most learned medical authorities did not understand the causes of and proper treatments for illnesses, attributing them to intangibles, such as "vapours" and the like. Those who fell ill were "bled" by leeches and subjected to other such treatments.

Beginning in the eighteenth century, this pattern began to change dramatically with breakthroughs in hygiene, public health, nutrition, and medical knowledge. Once it was understood that often-fatal maladies, such as cholera, were preventable by establishing a clean water supply, the death rate declined significantly. Now the causes of death were more likely to be degenerative diseases, such as cancer and heart disease. Especially important strides were made in reducing infant mortality. Note, for example, the declining infant mortality rate in Canada: in 1831, 1 in 6 children did not survive his or her first year; in 1931 it was 1 in 14, and by 1999 this dropped to 1 in 190 (Beaujot, 2004: 446). In 2008, infant mortality declined further to approximately 1 in 200 (Statistics Canada, 2011b).

While death rates plunged, birth rates, at first, remained relatively high. Deeply ingrained cultural traditions and beliefs remained stubbornly embedded. Large families remained the norm and the use of birth control was outlawed. The result was a period of rapid population growth, especially in urban areas.

Eventually, however, birth rates also began to fall. Contributing to this was a series of changes associated with increasing modernization, industrialization, and urbanization. One crucial factor was the offloading of responsibilities formerly attached to the family onto the state. Children now were required to remain in school until they were adolescents; consequently, child rearing became more costly. Primary care for seniors began to shift from adult children to government-operated programs and institutions. This change from high to low birth and death rates is known as the **demographic transition** (see Figure 15.1). Initially, this change was most characteristic of cities in Western Europe and North America, but ultimately it spread to rural districts as new health technologies and medical treatments expanded beyond the city limits.

FIGURE 15.1 THE DEMOGRAPHIC TRANSITION

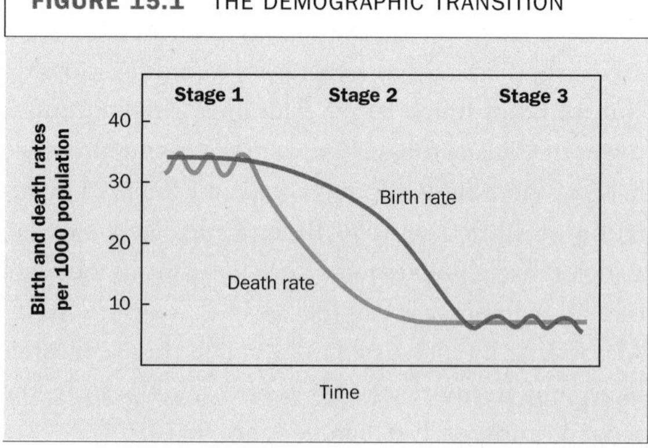

From the mid-1960s, wealthier nations in the developed world entered a new demographic era that differs in several ways from that associated with the demographic processes outlined above. First, fertility plunged below 2.1 births per woman—the **replacement level** at which births and deaths balance and the population level remains stationary, ignoring population inflows from other countries (immigration) and population outflows to other countries (emigration). This situation reflects a fundamental shift in contemporary values, especially among the middle class. Whereas previously the pressure to raise a family was paramount, now the emphasis shifted to equality of opportunity and freedom of choice. Increasingly, women entered the paid labour force on a full-time basis, not just out of economic necessity but also in pursuit of self-fulfillment. With declining fertility rates, the population as a whole is becoming older, especially in countries where immigration has concurrently slowed. Some analysts have described this as the "second demographic transition" (Champion, 1993; Van de Kaa, 1987).

Malthus versus Marx

As the initial demographic transition loomed, fears arose over the possibility of overpopulation. Alarm was first sounded by the British clergyman and political economist Thomas Malthus.

Under normal conditions, Malthus (1798) believed, there exists a natural "urge to reproduce" that flows from the attraction between the sexes. The resulting population growth is potentially limited by two checks. "Positive checks" are related to mortality: famine, epidemics, wars, and plagues, such as the Black Death. Positive checks are generally beyond human control. In contrast, "preventive checks" are related to fertility. Since Malthus condemned the use of contraception as immoral, the only remaining remedy was for couples to exercise "moral constraint." For all practical purposes, this meant postponing marriages as long as possible.

With declining fertility rates, the population as a whole is becoming older.
SOURCE: © Jupiter Images.

Of greater interest today are Malthus's comments about the relationship between population growth and resource (especially food) depletion. Malthus argued that population, if left unchecked, would increase geometrically or exponentially (as in the series 2, 4, 8, 16). Meanwhile, food supply would increase only arithmetically (as in the series 2, 4, 6, 8). Eventually, population would outstrip the food supply, resulting in widespread poverty, hunger, and misery. Malthus concluded that only grinding poverty would ultimately succeed in discouraging people from marrying early and raising large, healthy families.

Karl Marx was one of Malthus's most outspoken critics. According to Marx, Malthus was blind to the real cause of excess population: the capitalist economic system. Capitalism, Marx insisted, is organized to keep the working class in a perpetual state of poverty and unemployment. That is because it is to the financial advantage of capitalists to have more workers than jobs. The excess supply of workers allowed factory and mill owners to keep wages low and easily replace workers who created trouble. Furthermore, it facilitated the maintenance of a "reserve army of labour" that could be expanded or shrunk depending on whether the economy was expanding or in recession. Rapid population growth, then, was less a result of a mismatch between population and resources and more a case of deeply flawed social and economic arrangements.

The contrasting views of Malthus and Marx have reappeared in today's environmental debate. In the 1960s, several authors became widely known for their doomsday scenarios concerning overpopulation and dwindling resources. In the spirit of Malthus, conservation biologist Paul Ehrlich warns in his provocatively titled *The Population Bomb* (1968) that world population is expanding out of control, especially in Asia and Africa. At the same time, he holds, the unchecked consumption habits of people in the world's rich countries are depleting supplies of food, oil, and water. The result will be catastrophic, Ehrlich predicts. One notable critic of this viewpoint is economist Julian Simon, who argues that Ehrlich is wrong in identifying a pending population crisis. Simon notes that the price of most resources has been dropping, cities are becoming less polluted, and humans can be counted on to cope with population pressures through their technological ingenuity (Simon and Kahn, 1984).

THE INDUSTRIAL CITY

By the end of the eighteenth century, a new type of city had begun to emerge, first in England and later in continental Europe and America. This *industrial city* was larger, more complex, and more dynamic than any urban settlement that had preceded it. At century's end, more than 50 percent of the population of England and Wales lived in places with 20 000 or more people, compared with only 17 percent a century earlier (Weber, 1963 [1899]: 47). Global urbanization trends from 1800 to 2000 are shown in Figure 15.2.

What contributed to the growth of industrial cities? One popular theory emphasizes advances in transportation and agricultural technology, inasmuch as these factors contributed to the production and movement of agricultural surpluses from farm to city. Among the innovations were better methods of land drainage, the use of fertilizers, methods of seed selection, techniques of animal breeding, toll-road building, and the application of steam power to farm machinery and rail transport. Other scholars emphasize a boom in trade and commerce, which provided a powerful inducement to greater investment, technological improvements, and, ultimately, increased agricultural productivity.

FIGURE 15.2 PERCENTAGE OF WORLD POPULATION LIVING IN URBAN AREAS AND IN LARGE CITIES 1800–2000

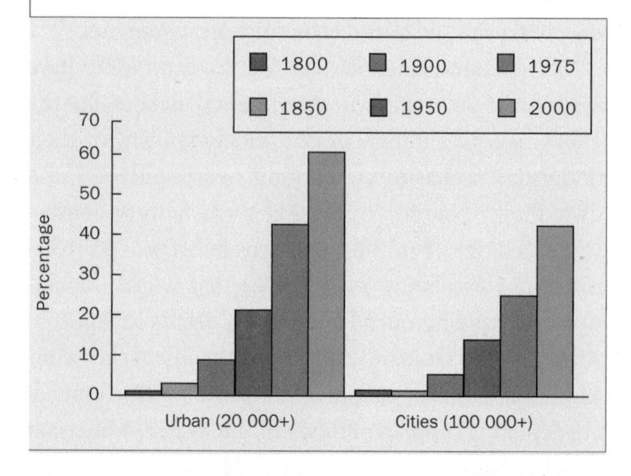

SOURCE: Adapted from Kingsley Davis, 1995, "The Origin and Growth of Urbanization in the World," *American Journal of Sociology*, 60, p. 430. Reprinted with permission from the estate of Jefferson Davis.

Another key factor appears to have been a shift in the sources of capital accumulation—that is, how factory owners raised the investment money needed to build and improve their manufacturing facilities. In England after 1850, capital investment was facilitated by the creation of the joint stock company, a business structure that pooled the capital of many investors and that had limited liability (the shareholders could not be held personally responsible for enterprises that failed).

Finally, urban growth has been linked to the invention of the factory. Previously, under the "putting-out" system, piecework was done in village or rural cottages and collected at regular intervals by the agents of merchant entrepreneurs. With the advent of the factory system, workers were required to work in a central location. Initially, factories had to be located next to rivers to run directly on water power. Then, as steam-powered machines became the standard, factories concentrated in cities because steam power could not be distributed economically over a wide grid, as electrical systems can be today.

THE DEVELOPMENT OF AN URBAN-INDUSTRIAL ECONOMY IN CANADA

At the time of Confederation in 1867, Canada lagged significantly behind both Britain and the United States in the development of an urban-industrial economy. The British North American colonies, both inside and outside the new political union, traded very little with one another, looking instead to the United States or Great Britain. According to the first manufacturing census in 1870, such localized activities as sawmilling, flour milling, shoemaking, and clothing manufacture accounted for almost half the value of the manufactured goods produced in Canada (Nader, 1975: 207). At the same time, only a tiny minority of Canadians lived in urban areas. In 1871, 18 percent lived in a town or a city (Stone, 1967: 29).

As the twentieth century dawned, Canada had a population of just more than five million, with two-thirds of these people living in rural areas and dependent for their livelihood on farming and the farm economy (Kremarik, 2000: 19). Soon however, industrial cities finally began to emerge. Although Toronto and Montreal were the largest industrial centres, factory towns also grew up elsewhere in Ontario, chief among them Windsor, because of its proximity to industry and markets in Detroit, and Hamilton, because of its port and strategic location on the Great Lakes. In addition to strategic location, the availability of investment capital played a significant role in directing where industry was established. The Canada Bank Act of 1871 was instrumental in concentrating economic power in a few national metropolitan centres, notably Toronto and Montreal. The act adopted the British model of a branch-banking system wherein a handful of major banks each established a network of branches. In contrast, under the U.S. unit-banking system, many more banks are independent. Investment capital was thus concentrated in a handful of urban centres rather than being widely dispersed across the country (Nader, 1975: 215).

Through various interventions by the federal government—the building of the transcontinental railroad, the imposition of a protective tariff system to encourage domestic manufacturing, a vigorous immigration policy that encouraged agriculture on the Prairies—a system of national economic markets was eventually established. In particular, at the turn of the twentieth century, these interventions found form in the expansion of wheat production for export. With cash from wheat sales jingling in their pockets, Prairie grain farmers were able to purchase manufactured goods from the factories of Ontario and Quebec, thus stimulating a marked upsurge in Canadian urbanization from 1891 to 1911 (Stone, 1967: 20–21). By 1911, four cities had populations exceeding 100 000: Montreal (470 480), Toronto (376 538), Winnipeg (136 035), and Vancouver (100 401). However, the formation of a national market led to the deindustrialization of the Maritime provinces (Brym, 1986).

As the twentieth century progressed, the proportion of the Canadian population classified as "urban" increased dramatically, crossing the 50 percent mark before 1931 and reaching 70 percent in 1961. By 2011, 81 percent of the Canadian population was living in towns and cities (see Table 15.1).

A handful of large urban regions account for most of the increase in urbanization in recent decades. As of 2011, more than one Canadian in three (35.0 percent) was living in one of the three largest census metropolitan areas (CMAs)—Toronto, Montreal and Vancouver—and these areas were growing at a faster rate (7.9 percent between 2006 and 2011) than were Canada's other 33 CMAs over the same period. Immigration was largely responsible for this growth pattern (Statistics Canada, 2012a).

While Toronto and Montreal continue to hold the largest number of Canadians, the fastest growth rates since 1951 have been in Western Canada. Between 1991 and 1998, Calgary's population grew by 18.4 percent and that of Vancouver by 21.2 percent. This compares with 8.1 percent for the nation as a whole (Little, 1999). By the first decade of the new millennium, Western Canada's growth rate had started to slow down. Nevertheless, between 2006 and 2011 Calgary's population grew by 12.6 percent, Vancouver's by 9.3 percent, and Edmonton's by 12.1 percent. According to the 2011 census, the population of Toronto's CMA now stands at 5.6 million, while 3.8 million people reside in Montreal, 2.3 million in Vancouver, and around 1.2 million in each of Ottawa-Gatineau, Calgary, and Edmonton (Statistics Canada, 2012b).

TABLE 15.1 URBAN-RURAL POPULATION, CANADA, 1931–2011

	1931	1961	1991	2011
Rural	46	30	23	19
Urban	54	70	77	81
Total	100	100	100	100

SOURCES: Adapted from Statistics Canada (2009); Statistics Canada (2012c).

A historical analysis of census data reveals interesting differences in the way Canada's largest cities grew at the end of the twentieth century. Net international migration (immigrants minus emigrants) has been the single biggest source of population increase in Toronto: 85 percent of the total between 1991 and 1997, compared with 68 percent in Vancouver. By contrast, migrants from the rest of Canada accounted for 29 percent of Vancouver's growth, whereas Toronto actually lost people to other provinces (2 percent of the city's population). Calgary fired on all cylinders, with natural increase (births minus deaths) accounting for 43 percent, net international immigration for 31 percent, and interprovincial migration for 22 percent of growth (Little, 1999). The last figures reflected the strong growth of Alberta's natural resources sector, coupled with a continuing decline in manufacturing in central Canada.

RESEARCHING THE INDUSTRIAL CITY: THE CHICAGO SCHOOL

By the final quarter of the nineteenth century, U.S. cities were seeing jumps in population that rivalled and even surpassed those in Britain. Nowhere was this more dramatic than in Chicago, which mushroomed from 122 000 people in 1860 to 1.7 million in 1900 and 3.4 million in 1930. Such rapid growth left in its wake social dislocation and human misery. Among those who sought to address these problems was the chairman of the sociology department of the University of Chicago, Robert E. Park.

Park and his colleagues believed that they could improve conditions for the disadvantaged by discovering what made the city "tick" and then using this knowledge to help solve its "social pathologies": crime, juvenile delinquency, family breakdown, and mental illness. To carry out this task, they employed an assortment of methods and models. On the one hand, Park argued that researchers should consider themselves urban anthropologists who would venture out into the field and study the natives, and their customs, beliefs, and practices. This inspired a rich ethnographic tradition of urban research in which Park's colleagues and students rendered finely detailed, first-hand accounts of homeless men, gangs, "taxi-dance halls," and so on. At the same time, Park also urged his students to consider the city of Chicago as a kind of social laboratory in which various natural processes took place. One way of documenting these processes was through the development of urban-growth models (discussed in the next section) by which the changing social and spatial structure of the city could be depicted visually. Another was to use "ecological spot maps" in which differences in the rate of various deviant behaviours, such as juvenile delinquency and schizophrenia, could be plotted geographically to discover underlying patterns. Some of the most memorable work to come out of the Chicago School tradition drew on personal documents and other biographical materials (Zorbaugh, 1929).

To put this mountain of data into some kind of theoretical order, Park and his colleagues used several approaches. First, they tapped into a long tradition of exploring the contrast between rural and urban life. In the latter part of the nineteenth century, German social philosopher Ferdinand Tönnies (1957 [1887]) had attempted to depict the difference between traditional and modern societies by introducing a distinction between a *Gemeinschaft*—the "community of feeling" that exists in villages, tribes, and small communities—and *Gesellschaft*—the characteristic feature of social relations in the city. Tönnies favoured *Gemeinschaft* and saw its decline as a loss of all that is natural and satisfying about small-town life. In contrast, he wrote, *Gesellschaft* denotes a lifestyle based on money, commercial contracts, individual interest, and class antagonism. Although he was more positive about the possibilities for individual freedom in modern urban life, German sociologist Georg Simmel (1950) used the same rural-urban contrast to interpret the shift to an urban society.

The rural-urban dichotomy runs through much of Chicago School theorizing. Thomas and Znaniecki (1918–20), for example, depict the city as being responsible for destroying the traditional institutions of Polish peasant life—family, neighbourhood, church—and substituting nothing but an empty well of social disorganization. Freed from the ties that formerly bound the community together, marriages dissolve, teenagers run wild, and even murder is not uncommon. In his modification of Simmel's social-psychological profile of urban life, Louis Wirth (1938) proposed that the city is characterized by the concurrent trends of increasing size, density, and heterogeneity. In his view, the city creates a distinct way of life—**urbanism**—that is economically efficient but socially destructive. Wirth's list of urban characteristics includes the decline of the family, the disappearance of the neighbourhood, and the undermining of traditional bases of social solidarity. Urbanites are said to be superficial, unable to step outside their narrow occupational roles to relate to people in a holistic and meaningful way, and guided by an all-consuming drive for success and money.

A century later, the rural-urban typology is still pervasive in the popular imagination. In the final weeks of December 2008, the Canadian media featured several stories from the British Columbia interior that accented small-town altruism and solidarity.

German philosopher Ferdinand Tönnies contrasted the community of feeling that exists in villages and small communities with the commercialism and individualism of the city.
SOURCE: Sheila Maloney, *Zephyr Ontario*. Courtesy Nancy Poole's Studio.

One of these stories cast the people of McBride, a village hard-hit by mill closings and job losses, as heroes for fighting freezing cold to dig a kilometre-long passageway through massive snowfalls to rescue two trapped and starving horses. In a second, more tragic case, residents of Sparwood, a coal-mining town 300 kilometres (185 miles) southwest of Calgary, came together at a candlelight vigil to remember seven local men who perished in an avalanche during a snowmobile ride in the backcountry. "Each and every one of us know them," Sparwood's mayor told the hundreds of mourners at the vigil (Montgomery, 2008). By contrast, a 28-year-old man was found dead on Christmas morning in the east-Toronto district of Scarborough. According to one press report, no one seemed acquainted with the victim, although a couple of people had heard loud arguments coming from his apartment. The 11-storey block of community housing units where he resided was described as "not a place where tenants know their neighbours" ("Slain Man Mystery to Tenants," 2008).

FIGURE 15.3 BURGESS'S CONCENTRIC ZONE MODEL APPLIED TO CHICAGO

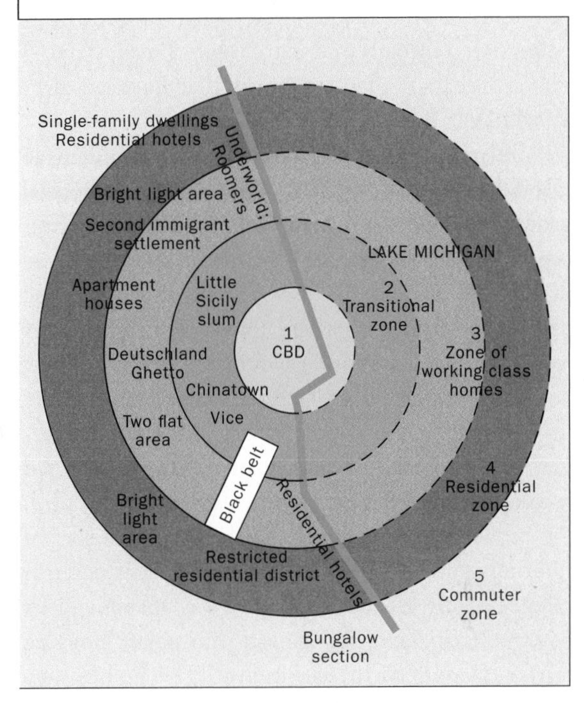

SOURCE: Redrawn from Ernest W. Burgess, 1961, "The Growth of the City: An Introduction to a Research Project," in George A. Theodorson, ed., *Studies in Human Ecology*, Evanston, IL: Row, Peterson, p. 41.

ECOLOGY OF THE INDUSTRIAL CITY

Industrial cities were also unique in their ecology—that is, their spatial layout, physical structure, and population distribution. To depict the spatial or ecological patterns of the city, a group of sociologists and geographers from the University of Chicago devised a set of urban-growth models in the 1920s and 1930s.

Burgess's **concentric-zone model** conceptualized the expansion of cities as a succession of concentric rings, each of which contained a distinct resident population and type of land use (Burgess, 1961). This concentric model of urban growth identified five zones (see Figure 15.3).

Zone 1, the central business district (CBD), is the commercial pulse of the city. It is the site of the major department stores, live theatres, hotels, banks, and office space. The land is the most valuable in the city, which means that residential and low-rent commercial uses are inevitably displaced in favour of big-money commercial enterprises.

Zone 2 is called the zone in transition. In the 1920s, large parcels of land in Chicago's transitional zone were being held by speculators who expected that the CBD would push outward, making them millionaires. In the meantime, Zone 2 stood as an area of cheap housing that became the initial resting point for each new wave of immigrants who took jobs in the nearby factories. Also located there were a variety of marginal businesses—pawn shops, tattoo parlours, second-hand stores—that could not afford the high rents of the city centre. The transitional zone also attracted a raft of illegal commercial activities—gambling, prostitution, drug dealing—that needed to be accessible to clientele in the CBD but that were considered socially unacceptable in the high-profile heart of the downtown area.

Zone 3, the zone of working-class homes, denotes the area settled by second-generation immigrants and rural migrants. In Burgess's time, Zone 3 was a neighbourhood of semi-detached, two-family homes where fathers still worked in inner-city factories but from which the upwardly mobile children aspired to escape, into the middle-class suburban zones.

Zone 4, the zone of better residences, was where the bulk of the middle class—small-business people, professionals, sales personnel, and office employees—could be found. Initially, it was an area of single-family detached houses, but by the mid-1920s, it was increasingly characterized by apartment buildings and residential hotels.

Finally, Zone 5, the commuter zone, was an area beyond the political boundaries of the city composed of satellite towns and suburbs. With the growth of commuter railroads and automobile travel, Zone 5 was a precursor of the suburbs that boomed after World War II.

Burgess's concentric-zone model made three interrelated assumptions. First, all commercial growth was said to emanate from the dominant city-centre nucleus and proceed outward in an orderly and predictable manner. Second, residential growth took place at the periphery, where it was easier and cheaper to obtain open land for development purchases. New housing was added here, but it was intended primarily for the middle and upper classes, who were increasingly able to take advantage of newly constructed commuter rail lines and, later, expressways. Third, the model was dynamic in that it assumed a sort of filtering-down process. As housing aged, it deteriorated, became less desirable, and was abandoned by better-off citizens, who moved into newer housing farther away from the city centre. The homes they left behind, some of them mansions, were subdivided into rooming houses, flats, and dormitories for artists and students. In recent years, many of these have been restored to a measure of their former glory, either by residential "gentrifiers" or by commercial users, such as restaurateurs or hair stylists. Furthermore, Burgess assumed that, as immigrant newcomers to the industrial city found their balance and began to prosper, they would want to upgrade their housing. For example, the second generation of "white ethnics"—the acculturated sons and daughters of those who had come as part of the Polish, Italian, German, and other European immigration around the turn of the twentieth century—could be expected to settle in the zone of working-class homes, which possessed superior housing to that occupied by their parents in the transitional zone.

Burgess's urban-growth model appears to have fitted Chicago in the 1920s reasonably well, but, as a scheme for understanding all cities in different places and times, it is not as successful. First, the notion of a single growth nucleus has not held up very firmly. Such cities as Calgary and Edmonton, which developed later in the century and which were shaped largely by the automobile, are more likely to possess more than one nucleus or growth centre. Similarly, Los Angeles is widely known as "the city without a downtown." This was first recognized in the 1940s by geographers Chauncey Harris and Edward Ullman (1945), who proposed a **multiple-nuclei model** of urban growth in which were located a series of growth centres—retail, wholesale, residential—each representing the concentration of a specific function or activity within the urban economy.

Second, Burgess seems to have underestimated the importance of transportation corridors as magnets for urban growth. Geographer Homer Hoyt (1939) developed a **sector model** of urban growth after studying 142 U.S. cities during the Depression years. He argued that cities grew not in concentric circles but in sectors or wedges along major transportation arteries, extending like the tentacles of an octopus from the CBD. Within each sector, the social character of the residential housing would remain constant. For example, upper-income groups would follow a northward progression, and working-class groups a southward path, thereby producing a distinct sectoral pattern to the developing city. Montreal and Vancouver seem to fit this sector model, because their populations tended to spread out along the natural shorelines of the bodies of water on which they are located (Driedger, 1991: 90).

Third, Burgess failed to appreciate that some resident groups would develop strong residential attachments to their neighbourhoods and refuse to move on, even in the face of an aging housing stock. This was first pointed out by Walter Firey (1947) in his study of Boston. Firey gives several examples that span the socioeconomic spectrum, from Beacon Hill, an elite area near the city centre, to the North End, a blue-collar Italian area where the residents chose to remain in their old neighbourhoods because the places were cherished as symbols of the residents' family connections, traditions, and culture.

URBANIZATION OF THE DEVELOPING WORLD

A century ago, most urban growth was concentrated in the rapidly industrializing countries of Europe and North America. Today, nearly two-thirds of the world's urban population resides in the less developed regions of Asia, Oceania, Africa, Latin America, and the Caribbean (Gugler, 1996: vii). In the Southern hemisphere, the demographic transition is moving faster and with far greater numbers than those experienced in the past (Ness and Law, 2000). Over the next three decades, cities in the global south are expected to double in size to about 4 billion people, with 19 cities reaching a population of more than 10 million by 2015 (see Figure 15.4).

FIGURE 15.4 MEGACITY GROWTH

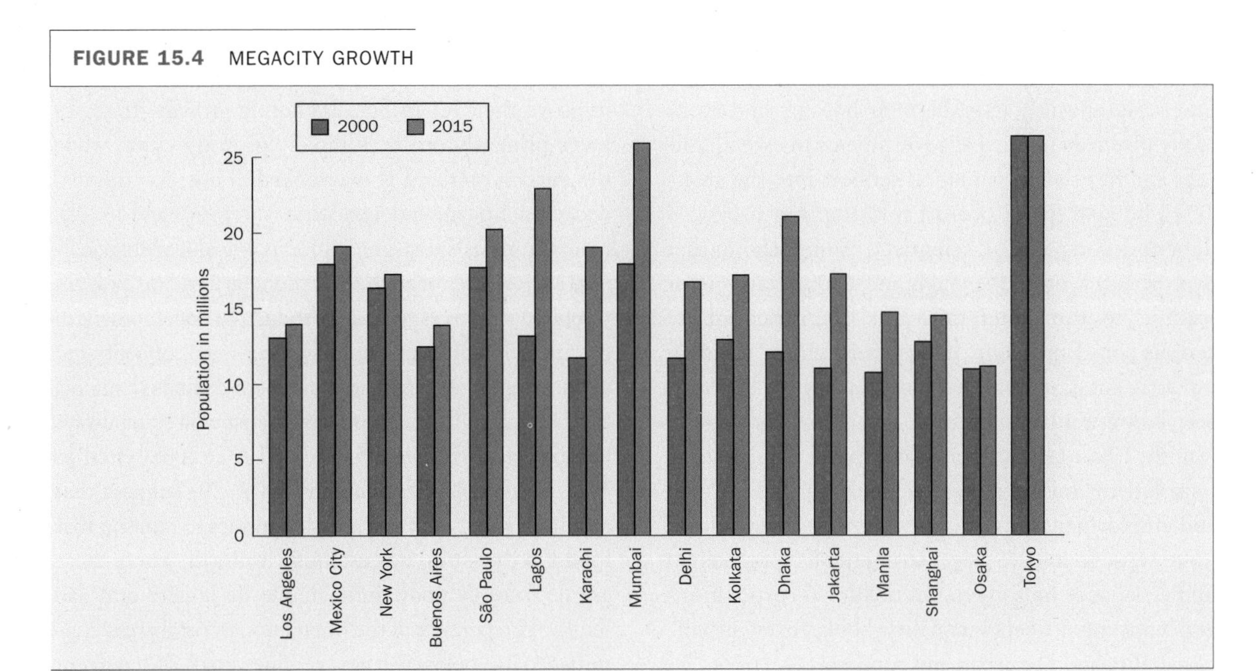

SOURCE: Reprinted by kind permission of the *New Internationalist*. Copyright New Internationalist, www.newint.org.

Although urbanization in the Southern hemisphere has followed sundry paths, it has displayed some common features. To a greater extent than with Northern cities, cities of the South are characterized by a high degree of **urban primacy.** This describes a situation in which one metropolitan centre, usually the capital city, is considerably larger and more dominant than any of the others. In Mexico, for example, this primacy is indicated by roadside markers throughout the country that indicate the distance to Mexico City, which is six times the size of its nearest rivals, Guadalajara and Monterrey (Flanagan, 1995: 154). In 1990, Mexico City's share of the national population was 18.5 percent, as against 3.5 percent for Guadalajara and 3.2 percent for Monterrey (Rowland and Gordon, 1996). Primacy is most evident on the African continent, where 11 out of the 20 most extreme examples of primacy systems occur (Clark, 1996: 27). In many cases, they are located along the sea coast, a legacy of colonial times when they operated as shipping points for raw materials on their way to Spain, France, England, and other imperial powers. Much the same pattern exists in present times; resource-producing regions funnel export commodities to big coastal cities, where the goods are subsequently shipped overseas. This is said to contribute to the underdevelopment of the interior, where provincial towns and cities tend to stagnate, unable to sustain a robust local industrial and commercial base.

In recent years, however, cities with populations between 100 000 and 500 000 have experienced remarkable growth, especially in some Latin American countries. In Argentina, for example, intermediate cities have grown faster than Buenos Aires has, while in Mexico, interior cities that have plugged into the international economy have outstripped the growth rate of Mexico City (De Oliveira and Roberts, 1996).

Cities of the South are often described as victims of **overurbanization.** This means that the population of urban areas is growing faster than the urban economy, services, and resources can absorb it. This creates an underclass of residents who live in illegal squatter settlements and employ themselves in marginal trades, such as selling food and lottery tickets on street corners (Flanagan, 1995: 153). Canadian cities have recently had a taste of this in the form of growing numbers of panhandlers, "squeegee kids," and other homeless urban people, but the numbers in Southern cities are much larger. With public housing scarce, "squatter settlements" are common. In such settlements, people occupy urban land without legal title, frequently organizing "invasions" at set times and places. Once they have staked out their plots, the squatters put up makeshift shelters and establish basic public services, such as water supply and sewage disposal. Some squatter settlements remain poor, but others significantly upgrade their housing and eventually persuade municipal governments to extend utilities and health and sanitation services into the area.

The concept of overurbanization has provoked debate among social scientists. Some claim that overurbanization is the single most important factor leading to the generation and intensification of serious social problems in Southern cities: grinding poverty, mass unemployment, inadequate services, social unrest, increasing crime, and political instability (Smith, 1996: 148). Others claim that it is misleading to isolate the mismatch between demographic growth and employment opportunities, arguing that it makes more sense to look to larger structural factors, such as undue reliance on foreign multinational corporations and continued deep inequality between an urban-based elite and the urban and rural masses.

Some countries in Asia, Africa, and Latin America have exhibited distinctive patterns of **peri-urbanization** whereby the rural and the urban have become blurred in unplanned settlements on the outskirts of large cities. The motivation for this is mostly economic: Land in these peri-urban zones is cheaper; shelter can be constructed economically by using locally available materials; and families can keep farm animals and cultivate subsistence crops without violating any of the restrictions of the formal planning system (Stren and Halfani, 2001: 478). In contemporary Asian cities, for example, urbanization is increasingly characterized by the *desakota* (from the Indonesian words for "village" and "city"). Here, most people continue to live in village settings and almost all the land is under cultivation, but most family income comes from non-agricultural sources. Some family members may even commute to work in the city, or live in the city and remit portions of their salaries to their families (Ginsburg, Koppel, and McGee, 1991). The linked processes of peri-urbanization and *desakota* challenge the conventional paradigm of the urban transition derived from the case of Western Europe and North America in the nineteenth and early twentieth centuries. Rather than remain strictly separated, the rural and the urban coexist in densely populated areas on the fringe of large mega-urban regions (McGee, 1991: 4–5).

Finally, sociologists who study urbanization in the South have been much concerned with urban bias, that is, uneven investment and development that favour urban over rural areas. Despite the problems generated by overurbanization, landless migrants continue to flow into cities, which they see as their best chance to improve their lot in life. Economic growth strategies focus primarily on these rapidly growing cities, while the rural hinterland is overlooked. Thus, for the two decades following independence (the 1960s and 1970s), many of Africa's first-generation political leaders penalized agriculture through their monetary and tax policies to obtain resources to finance industrial development in the cities. In addition, public services were concentrated in the large cities, especially national capitals (Lofchie, 1997: 24–25). Although poverty statistics are not always reliable, data from 2006–07 (ECLAC, 2008, cited in Winchester and Szalachman, 2009: 29) suggest that absolute poverty in rural areas continues to outstrip that found in the cities. For example, in Brazil, where there are notoriously poor slums in Rio de Janeiro and São Paulo, 45.6 percent of the population in rural areas continues to live below the poverty line versus 26.9 percent in the cities. In Mexico, the figures follow the same pattern (40.1 percent in rural areas versus 26.8 percent in cities). Much the same holds for most African nations. India, by contrast, shows more or less comparable levels of poverty in urban and rural areas (Drakakis-Smith, 1988).

While many explanatory factors are the same across urban and rural areas, some key specific attributes of poverty can only be found in cities. In particular, high rates of inequality and unemployment may lead to increases in crime and other forms of social and political conflict, especially for young men. High rates of violence make mobility within the community dangerous (Winchester and Szalachman, 2009: 11), especially in neighbourhoods where gang activity is prevalent.

THE CORPORATE CITY

Although the industrial city continued to exist in North America into the 1970s, it began to lose ground after 1945 to a new urban form. Simply defined, the **corporate city** denotes the perception and organization of the city as a vehicle for capital accumulation—that is, as a money-making machine.

The corporate city comprises five major elements (Lorimer, 1978; Reid, 1991): (1) the corporate suburb, (2) the shopping centre, (3) the suburban industrial park, (4) the downtown office tower, and (5) the high-rise apartment building.

Each of these five elements of the corporate city has evolved over the years. Some of their central features have recently changed. Facing the spectre of shopper boredom and increased competition from both revitalized downtown retail districts and exurban big-box stores (Home Depot, Costco, Wal-Mart, and the like), shopping centres have been undergoing a redesign that includes a more diverse mix of retail tenants. In the face of changing demographics, suburban developments have also been forced to include a greater variety of housing types, including more townhouses and row houses and such innovations as "granny flats" (separate quarters for aged parents). After years of being half-empty, some downtown office buildings have begun to convert to condominiums. Nevertheless, the process by which the corporate city has been assembled and maintained remains much the same and stands in marked contrast to that which undergirds the building of the industrial city. Nowhere has this been more evident than in the case of the corporate suburb.

THE CORPORATE SUBURB

Before World War II, North American cities, such as Toronto, were configured in a grid system, with residential avenues crossing long commercial streets at right angles. Since most urban residents lived within a few blocks of neighbourhood stores and services, pedestrian traffic constantly moved up and down the streets. This spawned a lively "front-yard culture" in which passers-by regularly interacted with porch sitters, since front yards and families faced the street rather than the house itself (Fowler, 1992: 205).

When cities expanded, they did so incrementally, often a dozen houses at a time. The cost of extending sewers, water lines, and other city services was assumed by the municipality and paid for over 20 or 30 years through tax increases or special bonds. Lots were narrow and houses two or three storeys high. Parking space was mostly on the street and, as auto ownership spread rapidly, increasingly scarce.

In the early 1950s, all this changed with the building of Don Mills, Canada's first mass suburb, on the northern fringe of Toronto. Don Mills emphasized a system of short curving roads in the form of circles and crescents. Initially, this layout was probably meant to convey a sense of privileged exclusivity, although over time it also came to reflect a desire to shield children from the perceived danger of through-traffic. In any case, it made public transit difficult, consigning buses to main arterial roads on the perimeter of the housing subdivision. Don Mills houses were placed on wider lots with larger setbacks from the streets. With no sidewalks, small front porches, and minimal pedestrian traffic (most residents drove to the nearby Don Mills Plaza to shop), the social action shifted to the fenced-in backyards, which were, in any case, favoured by parents, who appreciated being able to keep an eye on their toddlers from the kitchen window. Don Mills was one of the first residential areas in Canada to be planned completely from scratch and built all at once. In contrast to the development pattern in the central city, almost all the servicing costs, including that of a sewage treatment plant along the Don River, were assumed by the developer, E. P. Taylor. By doing so, Taylor changed the rules of urban development, relegating the municipality to a more passive role and introducing corporate success as a major planning consideration (Sewell, 1993: 95).

With the triumph of Don Mills, the corporate suburb spread rapidly across Canada and the United States. (The United States had already introduced its own early prototype of a planned, mass-produced suburb in Levittown, Long Island, 32 kilometres, or 20 miles, from New York City.) Although there were local differences, these first-generation postwar suburbs shared five main characteristics: a peripheral location, relatively low population densities, architectural similarity, a relatively low purchase price for houses, and a fairly high degree of economic and racial homogeneity (Jackson, 1985: 238–43).

Suburbanism as a Way of Life

In the 1950s, the suburbs were routinely disparaged as being sterile social and cultural wastelands where conformity ruled and individual taste and thought were stifled. This notion was given wide exposure in the 1956 best-seller *The Organization Man*, a study of Park Forest, Illinois, 48 kilometres (30 miles) south of Chicago (Whyte, 1956). Suburban dwellers were invariably depicted as living in mass-produced housing that was uniform in design and decoration. This image is bitingly evoked in folk singer Malvina Reynolds's 1950s ditty "Little Boxes" (Reynolds, 1964: 28):

> Little Boxes on the hillside
> Little Boxes made of ticky tacky,
> Little Boxes on the hillside,
> Little Boxes all the same.

Not only was the physical appearance of suburban areas said to be homogeneous, but life there was also said to revolve around a "dry-martini culture." During the workweek, fathers commuted in car pools or by rail to jobs at IBM, General Motors, and other corporate giants, while mothers ferried the children around in the family station wagon and socialized at coffee parties. On the weekend, the husbands washed the cars and tended well-manicured lawns, while the wives shopped for groceries at nearby plazas. At night, couples socialized in one another's homes, around the pool or the barbecue.

For sociological researchers, **suburbanism** represented an important trend. In a much-quoted 1956 article, "Suburbanism as a Way of Life," Sylvia Fava did a take on Louis Wirth's classic 1938 essay. Fava claimed that suburbanites were far more likely than their counterparts in the central city were to be both sociable and socially active. Similarly, in a much-cited before-and-after study of middle-class couples in Toronto who chose to relocate during the early 1970s, Michelson (1973) found that suburban movers increased their involvement with neighbours, while city relocators increased interactions with friends and relatives.

Another key feature of the suburban lifestyle was its emphasis on children and the family. Perhaps the most influential study with regard to the importance of children in suburban communities was that by Seeley and Loosley (1956) in *Crestwood Heights*, a profile of the affluent community of Forest Hill Village in 1950s Toronto. Although Crestwood Heights was more a neighbourhood on the northern edge of the city, its organization around the needs of its children (schools, camps, counselling) was said to be typical of the developing suburbs of the time.

Suburbanism was further depicted as a lifestyle choice rather than a strictly economic decision. City dwellers who packed up and left the central city were said to be embracing a new, family-oriented way of life, seduced by advertisements in the real estate section of the Saturday newspaper promising "bourgeois utopias" (Fishman, 1987). Not all residents, however, embraced this lifestyle with equal enthusiasm. Women in the suburbs frequently felt cut off from the social and cultural stimulation of the central city with its theatres, art galleries, restaurants, and shopping streets. Sociability in the corporate suburb was restricted to private gatherings in the home or the backyard with neighbours. Not surprisingly, a number of researchers found that women were less satisfied than their husbands were with their choice of residence, often having a sense of stagnation and isolation despite relatively frequent visiting and entertaining (Michelson, 1973).

Significantly, this lifestyle did not appear to be replicated in working-class suburbs, where people's values and social behaviours remained firmly anchored in blue-collar culture. Berger (1960) refers to the myth of suburbia, by which he means a standardized and stereotyped view of the suburbs as uniformly middle-class, homogeneous, conformist, child-centred, female-dominated hotbeds of sociability.

It is possible to discern three alternative interpretations of the relationship between suburban residence and lifestyle patterns (McGahan, 1995: 232–36). According to the *structural* interpretation, the environmental and demographic characteristics of the suburb encourage a distinct style of life. For example, by excluding stores and services, such as restaurants, bars, and movie theatres, from residential neighbourhoods and by discouraging public transit, the Don Mills model promoted greater reliance on private sociability, as evidenced by the weekday morning coffee klatches and weekend pool parties that came to be identified with suburban life in the 1950s and 1960s.

In contrast, the *selective migration* interpretation denies that the suburban environment exercises any independent effect on behaviour patterns. Rather, it is suggested that those who chose to move to the corporate suburbs after World War II were already primed to embrace **familism**—a lifestyle that places a high value on family living, marriage at a young age, a brief period of childlessness after marriage, and child-centredness of the type that Seeley and his colleagues observed in Crestwood Heights (Bell, 1968: 147).

Finally, the *class and life-cycle* interpretation proposes that what Berger had branded the "suburban myth" was nothing more than a snapshot of middle-class life at mid-century. Today, many of the same characteristics—child-centredness, commuting, backyard culture—can be observed in the second wave of gentrification in the central city. As the corporate suburb matured, it changed appreciably, with a new set of social activities replacing those that had prevailed at an earlier stage in the life cycle of both the suburb and the families who settled there. Whether it was the Don Mills–style suburb or downtown office towers, the corporate city did not just happen. It was the deliberate product of an alliance between government and business interests.

Logan and Molotch (1987) have termed this alliance an **urban-growth machine,** a loosely structured coalition of local economic and political interest groups with a commitment to sustained growth and development. Urban-growth machines can include an extensive cast of players: businesses, property owners, investors and developers, politicians and planners, the media, utilities, cultural institutions (museums, theatres), professional sports teams, labour unions, and even universities. Growth machines pursue a narrow band of interests, sacrificing the sentimental and symbolic value of places—which is associated with jobs, neighbourhood, home town, and community—in favour of a strict emphasis on land use as an investment and commodity to be bought and sold (Palen, 1995: 20) Although government and business may honestly believe that local communities thrive only if they continue to expand economically, it could also be said that the structure that growth machines impose on urban living gives people a minimum of freedom to live their lives in the corporate city as they choose (Lorimer, 1978: 220).

THE POSTMODERN CITY

In recent years, a new kind of urban form has appeared on the global landscape: the postmodern city. Although there is some debate over what exactly is meant by this term, several aspects do seem clear.

First, the postmodern city is the product of the simultaneous operation of the forces of re-urbanization and counter-urbanization.

Counter-urbanization occurs when people move from central cities and inner suburbs into the surrounding rural hinterland (Berry and Gillard, 1977). Writing a quarter century ago, respected Canadian urban planner Hans Blumenfeld (1982, 1983) ventured that, if sustained, counter-urbanization might well result in a new urban form—the exurb. A decade later, exurbs in Canada and the United States were already home to nearly 60 million people, making them the fastest-growing component of the continental landscape (Davis, Nelson, and Dueher, 1994). Initially entirely residential, exurbs today are increasingly likely to take the form of edge cities that include significant commercial, leisure, and entertainment components.

At the same time, the central city has been staging a comeback from the dismal days of the 1960s and 1970s, an era in which it was effectively abandoned by middle-class families who moved in large numbers to the corporate suburbs. In part this re-urbanization of inner city districts reflects the continuing gentrification of older neighbourhoods. Additionally, however, it has been powered by the global migration of immigrants from around the world (Fishman, 2005).

Second, cities are becoming multiethnic, with many ethnic neighbourhoods in the largest cities becoming home to visible minority groups. This development is generating racial and ethnic residential and commercial patterns that stand in marked contrast to the ecology of the industrial city that I discussed earlier. These new urban settlers can be found both in suburban subdivisions and in inner-city precincts. In Toronto, most of the recent growth in the foreign-born population has occurred in the "905" area—the ring of satellite towns and cities, named after the area code, that surrounds the urban core. For example, Brampton to the northwest of Toronto, once a symbol of small-town Ontario conservatism, attracted 42 900 immigrants between 2001 and 2006, roughly a tenth of all newcomers to the Toronto metropolitan area. Two-thirds of the new residents came from three countries: India, Pakistan, and the Philippines. In Vancouver, many recent immigrants headed for the suburban municipalities of Richmond, Burnaby, and Surrey. In Richmond, foreign-born people, about half from the People's Republic of China, made up 57.4 percent of the population in 2006, the highest proportion of those born elsewhere in all of Canada's municipalities (Statistics Canada, 2008).

Third, the postmodern city is characteristically fragmented, even chaotic. Elizabeth Wilson (1991: 136) describes it as resembling "a split screen flickering with competing beliefs, cultures and 'stories.'" Geographically and socially split, the postmodern city does not have a single "way of life" of the sort identified by Wirth for the industrial city and Fava for the corporate suburb.

Finally, the postmodern city is characterized by the privatization of public space. Privatization occurs across a wide spectrum of settings, from downtown malls and festival marketplaces to private, "gated" communities on the fringes of the city. Although suburban dwellers have always put a premium on private space, from the enclosed backyard to the drive-in theatre, this value is now washing over the city as a whole and, in the process, drastically reducing the number of public places where people can come together to shop or socialize (Goldberger, 1996: 139).

The postmodern city is characterized by the privatization of public space, as shown in this mall scene.
SOURCE: © Norman Chan/Shutterstock.

While some urban observers have applauded the changing contours of the postmodern city, especially those associated with re-urbanization, others have expressed serious reservations. In particular, they have displayed considerable unease over the escalating "suburbanization" of the inner city.

I next examine three overlapping components of the postmodern city: the edge city, the multiethnic city, and the dual city. Although each component has real-life spatial and demographic components, none exists in pure form. Instead, they are constructs, formulated by academic researchers or journalists, that help us visualize an important dimension of the globalized, privatized, and fragmented postmodern city.

THE EDGE CITY

Although they differed significantly in their patterns of housing, transportation, and shopping, the industrial city and the corporate city displayed more or less the same spatial configuration: an urban core containing the bulk of the office space, cultural institutions, factories, and a ring of suburbs where much of the more affluent middle class resided. Even with the growth of shopping centres and industrial parks in the 1950s and 1960s, the lion's share of jobs and services remained within the city itself, and suburbanites were daily commuters.

During the past quarter-century, however, this traditional pattern has been turned inside out with the rapid growth of **edge cities** (Garreau, 1991). Situated in exurbia—the rural residential area around the suburbs within commuting range of the city—edge cities have no dominant single core or definable set of boundaries; they are typically "clusters of malls, office developments and entertainment complexes that rise where major highways cross or converge" (Fishman, 1990: 18). Some edge cities are expansions of existing satellite cities, but others sprout up in unincorporated townships, lacking clearly definable borders and legal status as places (Palen, 1995: 187).

What has led to the growth of edge cities? Leinberger and Lockwood (1986) offer five reasons for edge cities' recent emergence. First, there has been a major shift in North American economies from manufacturing to a service and knowledge base. One result of this shift is that middle-class employees are now more willing to live near where they work than they used to be when jobs were located in factories that were dirty, noisy, and unattractive. An example of the older pattern can be found in Ontario's steel industry, where the managers and executives at Stelco and Dofasco traditionally settled on the other side of the Skyway Bridge in Burlington, while the mill workers remained in Hamilton. In contrast, Kanata, the outer suburban location of Ottawa's microchip computer industry, is solidly middle class.

Second, there have been significant changes in transportation patterns that favour trucks and cars over subways, streetcars, and trains. As a result, urban facilities have scattered over the exurban landscape, unfettered by the requirement of locating along established transportation corridors.

Third, recent advances in telecommunications technology have reduced the necessity for offices to locate downtown in close physical proximity. Some types of businesses—stock brokerages, banks—still prefer to be close to one another and to central city services. However, the tremendous growth of technology, such as fax machines, cellular phones, and email, has geographically freed many employees whose linkages to the workplace are now activated on the road or from home offices.

Fourth, as it has become increasingly expensive to operate in the city, offices, industries, and professional

The tremendous growth of technology, such as fax machines, cellular phones, and email, has geographically freed many employees whose linkages to the workplace are now activated on the road or from home offices.
SOURCE: © Jupiter Images.

practitioners (lawyers, accountants, and so on) have pulled up their roots and moved to cheaper locations. Among other things, parking is more plentiful and less expensive out of the city.

Fifth, the coming of age of dual-income, baby-boom families with one or two children has meant that people's lives are increasingly governed by considerations of time, convenience, and efficiency. The clustering of offices, shopping centres, and recreational facilities at the juncture of exurban highways meets the needs of this subpopulation, the members of which have little time in their lives to commute downtown to shop, eat, or be entertained.

These changes have shown up in new patterns of commuting to work in large urban areas. In Canada, census data from 1996 and 2001 point to several significant trends (Heisz and LaRochelle-Coté, 2005: 16). First, the number of workers who commute within a suburb or across the city from suburb to suburb has risen appreciably. Second, the growth of "reverse commuters" (those who travel from the city centre to the suburbs) has uniformly outstripped that of traditional commuters (those who travel from outside to inside the city centre).

Edge cities have been of particular interest to urban sociologists because they are neither suburbs nor centralized cities but a hybrid that incorporates elements of each. Unlike the typical suburb, which is primarily residential, edge cities contain many of the functions of the traditional city: shopping, office space, housing, entertainment facilities. Also, in contrast to suburbanites, who commute to work in the central city by rail or car, edge-city residents are inclined to live and work in the same geographic area. Commuting now means driving to an adjoining suburb or exurb, rather than heading downtown. This can be seen in the "905 belt" surrounding Metro Toronto, where a number of areas now function as "magnets." That is, more people travel to jobs there each day than journey out of the community to jobs elsewhere in the Greater Toronto Area. Finally, in contrast to the typical suburb, which lacks a well-developed infrastructure of sports, entertainment, and cultural facilities, the edge city is increasingly the site of a burgeoning number of performing arts centres, sports arenas, and entertainment complexes.

Nevertheless, it would be wrong to think that there are no real differences between edge cities and the older cities. Unlike the industrial city, the edge city lacks a single centre. In the former, it was always possible to start downtown and eventually reach the outer boundaries of the city. In contrast, the spatial logic of the edge city dictates that centres and boundaries are not needed. Instead, the edge city is made up of three overlapping types of socioeconomic networks: household networks, networks of consumption, and networks of production. Each of these runs on the guiding principle of convenience. Two-income families with children, who make up the largest demographic segment of the edge-city population, are increasingly pressed for time and, as a result, frequently create their own "personal cities" out of the destinations they can reach within a manageable time (Fishman, 1990).

THE MULTIETHNIC CITY

According to Statistics Canada's most recent population projections, by 2031, 31 percent of Canada's population are likely to be a member of a visible minority group (Statistics Canada, 2010). This contrasts with 13 percent in 2001 and less than 5 percent in 1981 (Bélanger and Malenfant, 2005). Just over 71 percent of visible minority people are expected to reside in the CMAs of Montreal, Toronto, and Vancouver. By 2031, it is estimated that the visible minority population will account for 63 percent of Toronto's population, up from 43 percent in 2006. In Vancouver, this figure will reach a comparable level (nearly 60 percent). In Montreal, visible minorities will constitute a somewhat lower proportion of the urban population (31 percent), although this is still nearly double the 2006 number (16 percent) (see Table 15.2). This new demographic makeup has important implications for our understanding of contemporary urban structures and processes (Fong and Shibuya, 2005).

In particular, we are likely to witness the growth of a new generation of residentially segregated neighbourhoods (Fong, 1996; Fong and Wilkes, 1999). Whereas newcomers from Northern and Western European nations tended to blend in residentially with Canadians from the charter groups (British and French), members of most Asian ethnic groups are likely to cluster together, apart from other groups. The evidence so far indicates that these visible minority neighbourhoods are formed when residents who are not visible minority members move out as large numbers of a visible minority group move into the neighbourhood (Hou and Picot, 2004).

Contrary to the classic urban-growth model proposed by the Chicago School's human ecologists, the postmodern city doesn't exhibit a simple pattern of first-generation immigrant settlement (in the zone of transition adjacent to the commercial core). Using data from New York and Los Angeles, Logan, Alba, and Zhang (2002) distinguish between two very different types of ethnic communities: the traditional immigrant enclave with dense concentrations of immigrants and high levels of poverty and other urban problems, and the more desirable ethnic neighbourhood whose residents are much better endowed both financially and socially. This dual pattern is especially evident in suburban neighbourhoods in major Canadian cities. Whereas some groups, notably the Chinese, settle here to take advantage of a more plentiful supply of new owner-occupied housing, others with fewer resources come for affordable subsidized social housing (Bourne, 1996). What is less well understood is the nature of social relations among multiple minority groups in a multiethnic context and how these relationships shape urban structures and processes between minority groups and members of charter groups (Fong and Shibuya, 2005). One thing we do know is that relatively little overlap exists in the minority neighbourhoods of different groups. In 2001, for example, among the 135 visible minority neighbourhoods in Toronto, only in three did both Chinese and South Asians combined represent at least 30 percent of the neighbourhood population (Hou and Picot, 2004: 11).

TABLE 15.2 PROPORTION OF FOREIGN-BORN AND VISIBLE MINORITY POPULATIONS BY CENSUS METROPOLITAN AREA, 2006 AND 2031 (SELECTED CANADIAN CITIES)

	FOREIGN-BORN (PERCENTAGE OF TOTAL POPULATION)		VISIBLE MINORITY (PERCENTAGE OF TOTAL POPULATION)	
	2006	**2031**	**2006**	**2031**
Canada	20	26	16	31
Census metropolitan area				
Toronto	46	50	43	63
Vancouver	40	44	42	59
Montreal	21	30	16	31
Ottawa-Gatineau (Ottawa part)	22	29	19	36
Calgary	24	30	22	38
Edmonton	19	22	17	29
Hamilton	24	27	12	25
Winnipeg	18	24	15	27
Windsor	23	28	16	33
Kitchener	23	28	14	28

SOURCE: Adapted from Statistics Canada (2010).

THE DUAL CITY

With the edge city increasingly becoming the occupational, residential, and commercial centre for the middle classes, what has become of urban downtowns? The central city, some analysts suggest, has become polarized between two starkly different realities that are spatially discrete and have only the name of the city and some public places in common. Situated just blocks or streets away from one another, the "city of despair and squalor" and the "city of hope and splendour" are light years apart. This split reality has been called the "dual city." The term **dual city** has come to refer to the urban expression of two increasingly divergent streams in the global economy. On the one hand, there is an information-based, formal economy rooted in financial services, telecommunications, and the microchip. Typically, those who are part of this upper-tier informational city live in a world of computer software, fax machines, cellphones, and Internet surfing. Residentially, they can be found in "gentrified" niches of the inner city (gentrification is discussed below) or in exclusive suburbs, where they isolate themselves both socially and geographically from the rest of the city. In Castells's (1989) description, these spaces constitute a microsociety with their own separate circuit of leisure, lifestyle, and services.

On the other hand, juxtaposed to the informational city is an "informal economy" that has been excluded from the main loop. Residents here rely not on high-technology communications but on face-to-face social networks, usually established on the basis of shared race and ethnicity. People are engaged in a wide range of activities, from labouring in immigrant sweatshops in the clothing trade to offering such services as furniture making, home renovation, and auto repairs (Gordon and Sassen, 1992). Although this informal economy cannot be equated with urban poverty per se, its participants stand relatively little chance of ever penetrating the upper-tier information economy.

Gentrification

In the 1970s and 1980s, considerable attention was paid by urban researchers to the phenomenon of **gentrification** in the dual city. By gentrification, I mean the transformation of working-class housing into fashionable downtown neighbourhoods by middle- and upper-income newcomers. Gentrification is neither anticipated nor accounted for by the ecological growth models discussed above. Similarly, it runs counter to predictions about mass flight to the suburbs that dominated urban sociology in the 1950s and 1960s. A comparison of the suburban lifestyle and the postmodern urban lifestyle as typified by gentrification is set out in Table 15.3.

Four primary explanations for gentrification have been advanced (Ley, 1991: 182–85). First, demographic changes led to gentrification in the 1970s and 1980s. At the time, baby boomers who were born and raised in the suburbs began to look for housing of their own. Facing high demand and short supply, they turned to inner-city housing, which was cheap but in

TABLE 15.3 COMPARISON OF SUBURBAN AND POSTMODERN URBAN LIFESTYLES

	SUBURBAN	POSTMODERN GENTRIFIED URBAN
Neighbourhood social involvement	Deliberate and sustained	Incidental
Lifestyle focus	Family	Consumerism
Typical activities	Home activities (gardening, entertaining)	Dining out, shopping
Typical occupation of resident	Middle manager	Architect, corporate lawyer, etc.
Housing type	Split-level, detached	Victorian, semi-detached
Social composition	Class-exclusive	Socially and culturally diverse
Ideology	Anti-urban	Pro-urban

SOURCE: John A. Hannigan, 1995, "The Postmodern City: A New Urbanization?" *Current Sociology*, *43* (1), p. 180.

dire need of rehabilitation. They opposed demolition, favoured by urban-renewal advocates.

Unlike suburban settlers in the previous period, many of these urban migrants were childless and career oriented. This meant that schools, playgrounds, and parks were not their major concerns and they were happy with smaller housing units lacking the big backyards and basement recreation rooms that were characteristic of Don Mills–type housing. Since many of these young professionals worked downtown, they were willing to trade space for proximity to their places of employment and to downtown cultural and entertainment facilities.

Second, gentrification may be accounted for by economic changes related to the flow of capital in and out of the housing market. In this view, gentrification functions as a "back to the city movement by capital, not people" (Smith, 1979). As you have seen, in the 1950s and 1960s, financial capital flowed into the building of the suburbs under the guidance of governments that viewed the construction of large-scale projects by development companies as the fastest, most efficient way of coping with the pressures created by the baby boom. Developers were encouraged by an array of incentives: tax breaks, government-backed mortgages, guarantees, and insurance with low premiums. By the 1970s, the profit levels in suburban building had begun to shrink, and capital flow switched back to the urban centre to take advantage of the rent gap—that is, the difference between the current value of land in its "depressed" state and the value that could be charged given a higher or better land use (Smith and LeFaivre, 1984).

Third, middle-class newcomers to the central city arrived in search of a lifestyle that was more distinctive and cosmopolitan than that available within the constraints of suburban conformity. In the central city, they could express a distinctive aesthetic and style of consumption, characterized by a dislike of mass-produced goods and a penchant for objects and buildings from a bygone era, notably the Victorian age (Filion, 1991: 554). This new lifestyle also extended to the surrounding neighbourhood, which filled up with wine bars, California-style restaurants, franchise coffee outlets, and trendy boutiques.

A fourth explanation of gentrification looks to the kinds of changes in the urban economy that were described at the beginning of the section on the dual city. With the tremendous boom in jobs in advanced service industries, such as those connected to the "globalized information economy," there has been a dramatic increase in the number of well-paying occupations located downtown. This growth has, in turn, produced a pool of middle-class workers interested in trying the experience of inner-city living.

It should be emphasized that the image of gentrifiers as returning from the suburbs is false; gentrification is, in fact, a "stay in the city" rather than a "back to the city" movement (Wittberg, 1992: 27). Ley (1991: 186) cites data from Canadian cities that indicate that only 2 to 3 percent of a sample of households moving into Toronto's Don Vale neighbourhood between 1966 and 1976 originated in the suburbs. Similarly, a high percentage of those in Ottawa's Centretown (55 percent); Vancouver's False Creek (78 percent); and Montreal's Milton-Parc, Plateau Mont-Royal, and Papineau (79 percent) neighbourhoods had previous addresses in the central city. This research suggests that gentrifiers are devoted to an inner-city lifestyle, even when they have reached a stage in the life cycle where they might have predictably moved to the suburbs.

Among those most likely to settle in gentrified areas of the inner city are women. Summarizing the empirical evidence available from these studies, Warde (1991: 228) lists the following as typical of gentrified enclaves:

> a female population increasing faster than the male population; an unusually high proportion of young and single women; very high proportions of women in professional and technical occupations; high levels of academic credentials; a high proportion of dual-earner households, but few families; presence of young professional women; and the postponement of marriage and childbearing.

Why do gentrified neighbourhoods appeal to the women described by Warde? One explanation is that inner-city communities help relieve some of the pressures of women's dual roles as both members of the paid labour force and mothers of young children. The advantages include relatively cheap housing, public transit, and readily available child-care and social-support systems. Travel time is an especially important consideration. Female gentrifiers tend to have jobs in downtown office buildings, so inner-city housing allows them to lead their lives on a tight schedule, with such services as shopping, schools, daycare, and medical clinics located nearby. In contrast, suburban residence requires long daily commutes, especially when the weather is bad, as well as the devotion of a good share of leisure time to travelling to widely scattered stores and services. Gentrification thus represents an environmental solution to a potential set of social problems (Rose, 1984: 66).

Private Communities

In recent years, another phenomenon—the rise of private communities—has been embraced by an even greater number of middle-class homeowners than has gentrification. Located in the newer suburbs and in edge cities, private communities compete with central cities for residents, offering as incentives a homogeneous middle-class population, physical security, stable housing values, local control, and freedom from exposure to the social problems of the inner city. In the United States, nearly four million residents are estimated to live in access-controlled developments (Sanchez, Lang, and Dhavale, 2005), and another 28 million in areas governed by private community associations. In Canada, although there are some gated communities around Toronto and cities in British Columbia's Okanagan Valley, the majority can be found in rural areas, usually in vacation, resort, or retirement sites. As can be seen in Table 15.4, only a small percentage of these are equipped with the guards and video surveillance that are more standard in gated projects in the United States.

In her detailed case studies of 10 gated communities in British Columbia, Ontario, and Nova Scotia, Grant (2005) found that the residents were less likely than their equivalents in other countries, such as the United States and Brazil, to cite security concerns as the major reason for moving there. Rather, they were in search of a privileged enclave where they could separate themselves from younger generations (many were seniors and empty nesters) and those who are less well off. The gates, Grant concludes, "function to secure homogeneity within a wider context of urban diversity" (p. 309).

The Fortress City

At the same time as middle-class homeowners are barricading themselves in private gated communities, the public-private partnerships that increasingly dictate what happens to postmodern cities are said to be systematically privatizing and militarizing public space to secure it against the homeless and the poor. Emerging from such alliances is the "fortress city" in which the urban disadvantaged are isolated socially and spatially from office workers, tourists, and suburban day trippers.

The fortress city has been described in *City of Quartz*, Mike Davis's (1990) sweeping examination of present-day Los Angeles. Los Angeles, Davis notes, is a city obsessed with urban security. What passes for a downtown, a series of billion-dollar, block-square megastructures around Bunker Hill, has been

TABLE 15.4 DOCUMENTED GATED PROJECTS IN CANADA, MARCH 2004

PROVINCE	TOTAL GATED PROJECTS	PROJECTS WITH 500 UNITS OR MORE	PROJECTS WITH GUARDS	VIDEO SURVEILLANCE	ADULT PROJECTS	SENIOR PROJECTS
British Columbia	228	3	5	5	44	36
Alberta	21	3	1	2	2	2
Saskatchewan	8	—	—	—	—	—
Manitoba	1	—	—	—	—	1
Ontario	49	8	9	5	10	7
Nova Scotia	7	—	—	2	1	1
Canada	314	14	15	15	57	47

Note: Adult communities discourage children—some suggest 19+ years, others say 25+ years. Those that use the word *senior* or have age limits over 40 are classified as seniors' projects.

SOURCE: Jill Grant, 2005, "The Function of the Gates: The Social Construction of Security in Gated Developments." *Town Planning Review*, 76, 291–313. Reprinted by permission of Town Planning Review, Liverpool University Press.

insulated by removing almost all pedestrian linkages to the poor immigrant neighbourhoods that surround it on every side. To make public facilities and spaces as unlivable as possible for the homeless and the poor, the city is engaged in a virtual war against them. Tactics and defences include the establishment of barrel-shaped, "bum-proof" bus benches that make sleep impossible, the random deployment of outdoor overhead sprinklers in Skid Row Park to discourage overnight camping, and the removal of public toilets and washrooms in areas patronized by vagrants. To secure its garbage, one popular seafood restaurant has spent $12 000 to build a "bag-lady-proof trash cage" out of three-quarter-inch steel rods with alloy locks and vicious curved spikes. To cope with a burgeoning inmate population, law-enforcement agencies are building downtown jails and prisons designed by celebrity architects to look like hotels, convention centres, or office buildings, thus camouflaging their real purpose.

Nor is the fortress city restricted to Los Angeles. In the late 1970s, Henry Ford II persuaded the heads of 50 large corporations in Detroit to put equity capital into the Renaissance Center, a $357 million megaproject along the Detroit River opposite Windsor, Ontario. Poorly planned, the hotel-office venture resembles a castle with virtually invisible pedestrian entrances. It is cut off from downtown Detroit by a wide road and railroad tracks. It stands as a "symbol of isolation: an extreme case of a self-contained, inward-facing complex, surrounded by fortress-like two-storey walls covering the heating and ventilating equipment" (Frieden and Sagalyn, 1989: 222). In 1996, General Motors purchased the Renaissance Center and moved their corporate headquarters there. Over the next decade, GM completed an extensive renovation that cost $1 billion. On the Jefferson Avenue side, the concrete berms that cut off the buildings from the sidewalk were removed, and a more pedestrian-friendly glass entryway installed. Most of the changes, however,

A homeless person carrying her cat is evicted from her dwelling in the shantytown on Toronto's waterfront on September 24, 2002. Home Depot, the company that owns the land, requested that police remove the squatters.

SOURCE: © Paul Chiasson/The Canadian Press.

were on the Detroit River side, where a five-storey Wintergarden atrium and the Detroit Riverwalk were constructed.

The clash between the guardians of the fortress city and the urban poor was highlighted in the "Tent City Eviction" in Toronto. Tent City was a two-hectare (five-acre) plot of polluted, abandoned industrial land near the shore of Lake Ontario. For five years, as many as 110 residents had been squatting on the waterfront property owned by big-box building supplies store Home Depot, making it Canada's largest homeless community. After a high-profile story in the *New York Times* described the site, which seemed to be increasingly hosting prostitution and drug-dealing activities, Home Depot abandoned any further pursuit of plans to erect safe, affordable housing and sent in private security guards accompanied by police to evict the squatters. Guards were posted and the former residents were given 72 hours to retrieve their belongings.

SUMMARY

1. Cities are relatively large, dense, permanent settlements in which the majority of the residents do not produce their own food.
2. Until the Industrial Revolution, cities were incapable of supporting more than about 5 percent of a society's population, largely because agricultural surpluses were not large enough to feed a big urban population. In addition, high mortality rates, especially among children under 10 years of age, dictated that, even with high birth rates, urban population growth was slow.
3. Demographic transition theory holds that the main factors underlying population dynamics are industrialization and the growth of modern cultural values. In the preindustrial era, both birth rates and death rates were high, and population growth was therefore slow. In the first stages of industrialization, death rates fell, so population growth was rapid. As industrialization progressed and people's values about having children changed, the birth rate fell, resulting in slow growth again.
4. Malthus argued that while food supplies increase slowly, populations grow quickly. Because of this presumed natural law, only war, pestilence, and famine can keep human population growth in check. In contrast, Marx argued that overpopulation is not a problem of too many people. Instead, it is a problem of too much poverty. Marx said that if the exploitation of workers under capitalism is ended, poverty will disappear along with the overpopulation problem.
5. The best-known urban-growth model in the social sciences is Ernest Burgess's concentric-zone scheme in which the expansion of cities is conceptualized as a successive series of rings, each of which segregates a distinct resident population and type of land use. Other, more recent models favour patterns of urban growth resembling pie-shaped wedges that develop along transportation routes or multiple nodes of economic activity, each with its own nucleus.
6. In contrast to the rise of the city in Western Europe and North America, cities of the South have grown at a much faster pace than the industrial economy. The resulting "overurbanization" has accelerated problems of poverty and unemployment, which are rooted in basic structural inequalities and uneven development.
7. The corporate city of the 1950s and 1960s was the product of an urban-growth machine in which a coalition of politicians, planners, real-estate developers, business people, and other interest groups joined forces to engineer economic development and progress. The main products of this alliance were (a) the corporate suburbs, (b) shopping centres, (c) suburban industrial parks, (d) downtown office towers, and (e) high-rise apartment buildings.
8. Three theories—structural, selective migration, and class and life-cycle stage—have been proposed to explain the relationship between suburban residence and lifestyle patterns. Although all three have merit, the suburban way of life observed by many researchers in the 1950s and 1960s appears to have been a unique product of a particular time and place.
9. In recent decades, the contemporary city has mirrored and incorporated a split global economy. On the one hand, the members of the upper-tier information city work in jobs related to financial services, telecommunications, and high technology, and live either in gentrified downtown neighbourhoods or in private communities

on the edge of the city. On the other hand, members of the informal economy are excluded from the information city and live in ethnic or racial ghettos that are often, but not necessarily, located in the inner city. Together, the information city and the informal economy constitute the dual city whose residents have little in common with each other.

10. Cities are becoming multiethnic, with many ethnic neighbourhoods in the largest cities becoming home to visible minority groups. This is generating racial and ethnic residential and commercial patterns that stand in marked contrast to the ecology of the industrial city.
11. One of the defining characteristics of the postmodern city is the increasing privatization of public spaces. Privatization is manifested in the booming growth of gated communities and other private residential enclaves where outsiders are not welcome, and in the construction of fortress cities where tourists and other affluent consumers are kept in while the homeless and the urban poor are kept out.

QUESTIONS TO CONSIDER

1. Map out your own "personal city" by keeping a record for a full week of all the trips you take to work, school, shopping, medical and dental appointments, friends' houses, restaurants and night clubs, and so on. What proportion of these trips occurs within your neighbourhood? Within the community in which you live? Across the wider metropolitan area?
2. To what extent does the big city in which you live or that you live closest to constitute a dual city?
3. How has suburban life been depicted in the mass media? Think, for example, of popular television series, such as *Desperate Housewives* and *The Simpsons*. To what extent do these depictions support the "myth of suburbia"?
4. Visit Statistics Canada's website (www.statcan.gc.ca). What kinds of questions about cities could you answer by using this data source?

GLOSSARY

A **city** (p. 371) is a relatively large, dense, permanent settlement in which most of the residents do not produce their own food.

The **concentric-zone model** (p. 377) is the classic urban-growth model proposed by Ernest Burgess in which the expansion of cities is visualized as a successive series of concentric rings, each of which contains a distinct resident population and type of land use. As social groups become more established and prosperous, they move farther away from the city centre.

The perception and organization of the city as a vehicle for capital accumulation create a **corporate city** (p. 380). The corporate city contains five major elements: the corporate suburb, high-rise apartments, suburban industrial parks, downtown office towers, and shopping malls.

The **demographic transition** (p. 372) is the change from high to low birth and death rates that characterized modernization, industrialization, and urbanization.

The juxtaposition and mutual isolation of an upper-tier information city and a lower-tier city creates a **dual city** (p. 387). Members of the upper tier work in jobs related to financial services, telecommunications, and high technology, and live in gentrified neighbourhoods and private communities on the edge of the city. A lower tier of people work in informal and low-technology jobs, and live in ethnic or racial ghettos.

Edge cities (p. 384) include self-contained entertainment, shopping, and office areas and have emerged in formerly suburban areas or just beyond the fringe of suburbia.

The **environmental-opportunity theory** (p. 370) proposes that people choose where they want to live depending on the extent to which a particular place meshes with or constrains their preferred lifestyle.

Familism (p. 382) is a lifestyle that places a high value on family living, marriage at a young age, a brief period of childlessness after marriage, and child-centredness.

In **gentrification** (p. 387), working-class houses are transformed into fashionable downtown neighbourhoods by middle- and upper-income migrants.

The **multiple-nuclei model** (p. 378) is a model of urban growth characterized by a series of growth centres—retail, wholesale, residential—each representing the concentration of a specific function or activity within the urban economy.

Overurbanization (p. 379) is the process whereby the population of urban areas is growing faster than the urban economy, services, and resources can absorb. It is especially evident in large cities in the southern hemisphere.

Peri-urbanization (p. 380) is a process of urbanization observed in Asia, Africa, and Latin America whereby the rural and the urban have become blurred in unplanned settlements on the outskirts of large cities. One instance of this is the *desakota* in Indonesia.

The **postmodern city** (p. 371) is a new urban form that is more privatized and more socially and culturally fragmented and globalized than the corporate city.

The **replacement level** (p. 373) is the number of children that each woman must have on average to sustain the size of a population, ignoring immigration and emigration. The replacement level is 2.1 children.

The **sector model** (p. 378) of urban growth proposes that the city expands outward from the centre in a series of sectors or wedges along major transportation arteries, such as highways and railroad lines.

Suburbanism (p. 382) is a way of life outside city centres that is organized mainly around the needs of children and involves higher levels of conformity and sociability than life in the central city.

The **urban-growth machine** (p. 383) is a loosely structured coalition of local economic and political interest groups that hold in common a commitment to sustained growth and development.

Urbanism (p. 376) is a way of life that involves increased tolerance but also emotional withdrawal and specialized, impersonal, and self-interested interaction.

Urban primacy (p. 379) is a situation in which one metropolitan centre in a country, usually the capital city, is considerably larger and more economically dominant than any other city in the country.

SUGGESTED READING

Bishop-Stall, Shaughnessy. (2004). *Down to This: Squalor and Splendor in a Big-City Shantytown.* Toronto: Random House. This is an engaging but disturbing first-person account by a journalist of a year spent residing in Tent City, located on a marginal property along Toronto's waterfront.

Brugmann, Jeb. (2009). *Welcome to the Urban Revolution: How Cities Are Changing the World.* Toronto: Viking Canada. An engaging discussion of the connections among globalization, economic development, city planning, and poverty. Brugmann, an international urban and environmental consultant, argues that progressive metropolitan centres, such as Barcelona, Vancouver, and Curitiba, Brazil, have developed new ways of designing, governing, and living in cities "from the sidewalk up."

Hannigan, John. (1998). *Fantasy City: Pleasure and Profit in the Postmodern City.* London and New York: Routledge. In this thoroughly researched and comprehensive account of the rise of the city as theme park in the 1980s and 1990s, Hannigan argues that megaplex cinemas, themed restaurants, casinos, and other large-scale entertainment spaces allow leisure and conviviality without real social interaction.

Hiller, Harry H., ed. (2005). *Urban Canada: Sociological Perspectives.* Toronto: Oxford University Press. The first new text in the field published in Canada in over a decade, this collection of 14 articles explores a broad range of topics in Canadian urban sociology, historical and contemporary.

Sewell, John. (1993). *The Shape of the City: Toronto Struggles with Modern Planning.* Toronto: University of Toronto Press. A generously illustrated history of urban growth and planning in Canada's largest city, by a well-known activist, author, and former mayor of Toronto.

CHAPTER 16

SOCIOLOGY AND THE ENVIRONMENT

SOURCE: © Fred Lum/The Globe and Mail/The Canadian Press.

S. Harris Ali
YORK UNIVERSITY

IN THIS CHAPTER YOU WILL LEARN THAT

- The analysis of the relationship of human beings to their natural and built envrionment forms the basis of environmental sociology.
- The rise of environmental awareness and concern has led to a questioning of the relationship among industry, the state, and the general public.
- The prominence of particular environmental problems depends on the interactions of scientists, representatives of industry, the state, environmental movement participants, and the mass media.
- Strategies to manage and govern the environment are based on regulatory approaches that are shaped by differences in the power and influence of various social groups.
- Environmental risks are unevenly distributed in society, and a disproportionate share of them falls on socially and economically marginal people.

INTRODUCTION

THE EARTH IN DANGER

Sometimes small, seemingly trivial changes may make huge differences. For instance, very small changes in the temperature of our planet—just a few degrees—may suddenly trigger an avalanche of large-scale environmental changes with enormous consequences for life on Earth. This example highlights our vulnerability to "tipping points." A **tipping point** is a critical threshold (Gladwell, 2002). When a slow and gradual process reaches a tipping point, it will, with little or no warning, rapidly accelerate, causing dramatic changes. Current scientific evidence indicates that the world's ecological systems are coming dangerously close to just such a tipping point. When that tipping point is reached, Earth's environmental system will collapse. Our planet will no longer be able to provide the natural resources we depend on to survive.

Global climate change is one example of how environmental problems may develop incrementally and almost imperceptibly until a tipping point is reached. Scientists have found that intensified industrial activity over the last century has added huge amounts of carbon dioxide and other greenhouse gases to the atmosphere. These gases trap heat, gradually warming Earth. However, once we reach a critical temperature increase, global warming will occur far more rapidly. Accelerated warming will, in turn, lead to the rapid onset of many environmental changes that have serious consequences, including greater frequency of hurricanes and storms, record flooding, reduced biodiversity, extensive droughts, shrinking river flows, extensive bush fires, the diffusion of bacteria and viruses to new areas, the scarcity of many natural resources, and the creation of large numbers of environmental refugees and large weather-related insurance losses that will destabilize global financial markets.

Greater understanding of the role tipping points play in environmental problems has led to the realization that we need to act fast to prevent catastrophe. Sociologists can contribute to these efforts because many environmental problems originate in the relationship between nature and society. For example, the industrial and consumer activities that contribute to climate change are based on collective decisions about how we should structure social institutions and policies. We have the capacity to change them if we want.

In this chapter, I begin by examining how environmental issues and problems are linked to the way societies are organized. I then address some of the chief questions environmental sociologists investigate. First, how do members of society think, feel, and act in relation to environmental issues? Which social factors influence their thoughts, feelings, and actions? Second, how do different social groups affect various strategies for addressing environmental problems? Third, why are environmental risks unevenly distributed in society? What are the implications of the uneven distribution of risk for our health and well-being?

INCORPORATING THE ENVIRONMENT INTO SOCIOLOGICAL ANALYSIS

Biology and geography were used in the nineteenth century to "explain" and thereby justify the superiority of certain classes, races, and civilizations. Sociology developed partly as a critique of conventional wisdom and an attempt to demonstrate the superiority of *social* explanations of such inequalities. Accordingly, sociologists were reluctant to consider the biophysical environment in their analyses until recently. The emergence of urgent environmental problems in the 1970s led them to reevaluate their bias. They came to appreciate that environmental problems have social *and* biophysical bases. Climate change is a case in point.

Climate Change as a Sociological Issue

Climate change is partly the result of human intervention in nature, such as industrial and transportation activities that burn fossil fuels (oil, coal, natural gas, and so on) which, in turn, release greenhouse gases. Most societies have developed large-scale institutional structures and a whole way of life based on cars and factories that require fossil fuels to function. To a degree, we are locked in to a high-carbon society, and the coal, petroleum, and automobile industries have helped to keep things that way (Urry, 2011). These powerful players curry the favour of politicians, criticize the science that supports climate change, and lobby against environmentalists who demand new industrial practices and environmental policies. Not surprisingly, therefore, much of environmental sociology focuses on the relationships among industry, the state, and the environmental movement, including the role the mass media play in these relationships. To help understand these matters, it is useful to consider "the tragedy of the commons" (Hardin, 1968).

The Tragedy of the Commons

The environmental commons consists of the natural resources that we share and depend on, such as the air, water, and soil. Tragedy arises when people try to maximize their personal economic gain by exploiting the commons. For example, industrial pollutants may enter the air and contaminate it. Currently, the cost of cleaning up the air falls not to the private company that caused the pollution but to the party responsible for taking care of the commons, namely the state (and, by extension, taxpayers and society at large). In this sense, the private company enjoys a "free ride." It profits from increased production but does not have to pay the costs associated with air pollution because all members of society share them. We refer to the pollution as an **externality** because its cost is externalized from the private company to the state and society. The tragedy of the commons grows when many companies engage in detrimental environmental pursuits. Motivated by profit, they all look for a free ride. If this practice is sufficiently widespread and enduring, the commons will be destroyed. Everyone will breathe foul air and pay the environmental and health consequences. Today, threats to the global commons are widespread.

THE DEVELOPMENT OF ENVIRONMENTAL AWARENESS AND CONCERN

Although environmental issues have always existed, they did not become prominent until the 1970s. Until then, analysts emphasized protecting natural resources. They did not question the industrial processes that threatened them. Their outlook began to change when Rachel Carson published *Silent Spring* (1962). Carson documented how chemicals in the environment could transform a world full of life and the sounds of the wilderness into a world enshrouded in silence. She focused in particular on the effects of the pesticide DDT on the food chain. DDT was used indiscriminately after World War II. Its pervasiveness, combined with strong evidence of its dangers, made the silent spring scenario feasible and frightening. A movement sprang up to protect the environment from chemical contamination and demand more government regulation of industrial activity. In response, the chemical industry mobilized resources to counter the movement's claims. The confrontation became a dispute that politicians could not ignore.

In 1968, the environmental movement gained impetus when a group of European industrialists, business advisers, and civil servants known as the Club of Rome became convinced that governments' environmental policies were short-sighted and dangerous. They commissioned researchers to develop computer models to extrapolate the effects of continued industrialization, technological development, natural resource depletion, pollution, food production, and population growth to 2010 based on existing trends. Published in 1972, the Club of Rome report painted a picture of total societal collapse because of inadequate food, too much pollution, and insufficient natural resources (Meadows, Meadows, Randers, and Behrens, 1972). These findings reinforced the idea that industrial growth had to be curbed to prevent catastrophe.

In 1973, war broke out between Israel and its neighbouring Arab states. Because the West supported Israel, the Arab states stopped the flow of oil to the West, causing a crisis that drove home the environmental movement's message: many natural resources are in short supply. In the following years, government agencies in Canada and abroad established new environmental laws and agencies in response to this message.

During the 1980s, governments and societies grappled with two environmental problems of global proportions: ozone depletion and climate change. A decade earlier, scientists had predicted that chlorofluorocarbons (CFCs), a class of chemicals used as a refrigerant and a solvent for cleaning metals, could rapidly destroy Earth's ozone layer. The ozone layer filters out ultraviolet radiation from sunlight and thereby protects us from such ailments as skin cancer, immune system disorders, snow blindness, retinal damage, and cataracts. In 1985, scientists verified the earlier prediction. They found an enormous hole in the ozone layer over the Antarctic. Action was swift. Coordinated international efforts led to the banning of CFCs in 1987.

During the same period, some people raised concern about other chemicals arising from industrial activity, namely carbon dioxide and methane, and the ensuing problem of global climate change.

Policies to curb carbon dioxide production are contentious because they affect so many industries and consumers. Sharp conflict has erupted between climate change supporters and industry-led skeptics, each side arguing the scientific basis of their claims. The existence of benign chemical alternatives for CFCs allowed governments to take quick action to solve that problem, but no quick fix is available for the carbon dioxide issue. The pervasiveness of carbon dioxide, produced by burning wood, coal, and oil, complicates matters.

In light of the magnitude of environmental problems, the United Nations World Commission on Environment and Development published *Our Common Future* in 1987. It introduced the idea of **sustainable development.** As an industrial strategy, sustainable development recognizes the dual needs of protecting the environment and allowing economic growth. The idea was to adopt industrial strategies that meet the needs of the present generation without compromising the ability of future generations to meet their own needs. Many of the policies and actions that are needed to move sustainable development forward can happen only if there is "buy-in" from the public. For this reason, it is important to determine the degree to which environmental attitudes and behaviours are changing in the direction of environmental sustainability.

ENVIRONMENTAL CONCERN

Environmental Attitudes

According to sociologist Ulrich Beck's (1992) **risk society thesis,** in the optimistic decades immediately preceding World War II, the developing welfare states of the Western world were preoccupied with issues related to the distribution of social goods, including wealth, educational opportunities, consumer goods, income, and property. In contrast, over the last few decades, we have become preoccupied with issues related to the distribution of social "bads," chief among them the environmental risks and externalities produced by industry. For Beck, this switch has served as an impetus for individuals and institutions to start questioning the industrial basis of people's relationship to the environment. Previously, the environment was not an issue because any risks that were produced were simply dismissed as the "price of progress" and ignored. In the risk society, we ignore such issues as global warming and ozone depletion at our peril.

Figure 16.1 shows that, although environmental concern has been on the upswing in Canada in recent decades, it appears to follow an **economic contingency** logic (Buttel, 1975). Specifically, a larger proportion of the population considers environmental issues important during good economic times, while a smaller proportion considers environ-

FIGURE 16.1 ENVIRONMENTAL CONCERN IN CANADA (1972–1985) AND ONTARIO (1986–2009)

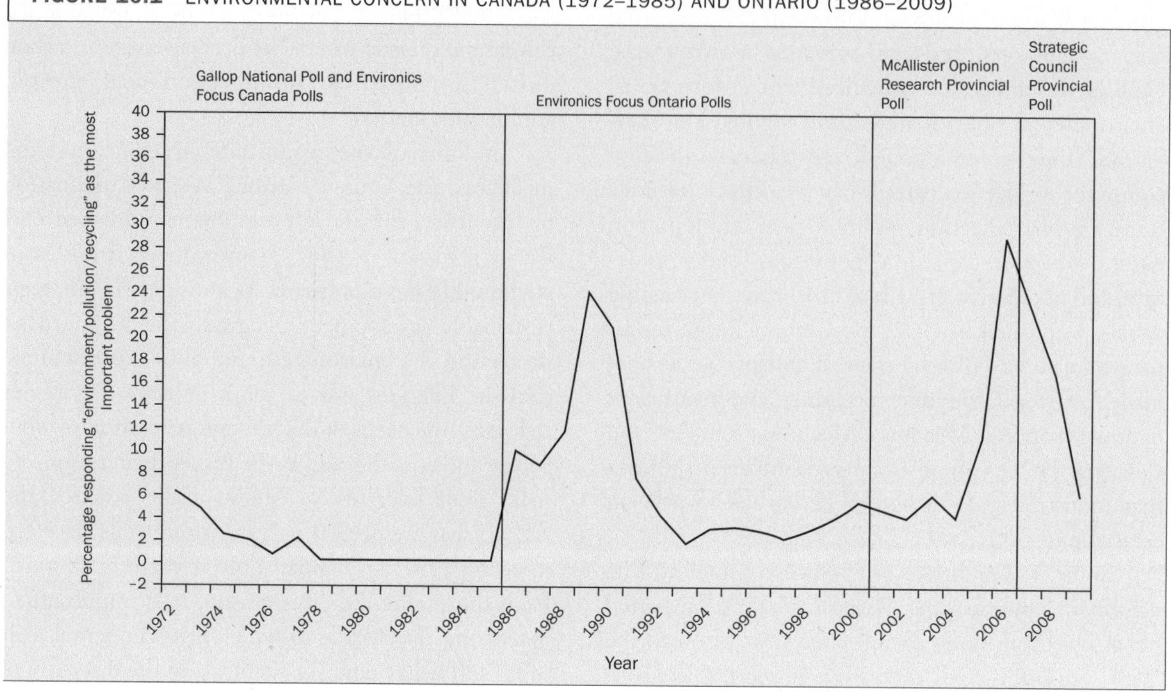

SOURCE: Data from Appendix 2 of *Blue-Green Province*. Reprinted with permission of the Publisher of *Blue-Green Province* by Mark Winfield © University of British Columbia Press 2012. All rights reserved by the Publisher.

mental issues important during times of economic hardship. Thus, Figure 16.1 reveals a decline in environmental concern during the recessions in the early 1990s and around 2007. Still, many Canadians regard environmental problems as important even in the worst of economic times (see Figure 16.2). The realization persists that we need to confront environmental issues no matter what.

Environmental Behaviour

Although surveys show that many people are sympathetic to environmental issues, they do not necessarily modify their behaviour accordingly. What accounts for inconsistency between environmental attitudes and behaviour? Sociologists have proposed several explanations.

Anthony Giddens (2009) argues that environmental issues are "back-of-the-mind" rather than "front-of-the-mind" issues because many environmental dangers, no matter how frightening they may appear, are not tangible, immediate, or visible in day-to-day life. Environmental issues are also kept on the back burner because of a psychological tendency known as **future discounting.** People find it difficult to give the same amount of consideration and thought to the future as they do to the present. Present reality hits home more than future possibilities do. The future is therefore discounted. As such, a small reward offered now will normally be taken in preference to a much larger one offered at some undetermined point later. Future discounting has big implications for how people act in response to environmental problems. It means that many people are not inclined to change environmentally dangerous behaviour because of the current benefits they receive from it.

The inconsistency between environmental attitudes and behaviour is further complicated by the influence of "Jevon's paradox"—as we become more efficient in the use of a natural resource, the cost of using it falls and we then use more of it (Cato, 2011: 153). Environmental savings are thus soon lost. For instance, people may switch to low-energy light bulbs but they may soon realize that using them saves money, so they leave their lights on longer. The same may happen with the introduction of more fuel-efficient cars. People save money on gas by purchasing such vehicles, so they feel justified in going on more frequent or longer trips. Consequently, the rate of gas consumption remains high.

The **framing** of an environmental problem also influences the relationship between attitudes

FIGURE 16.2 THE NEED TO FOCUS ON THE ENVIRONMENT

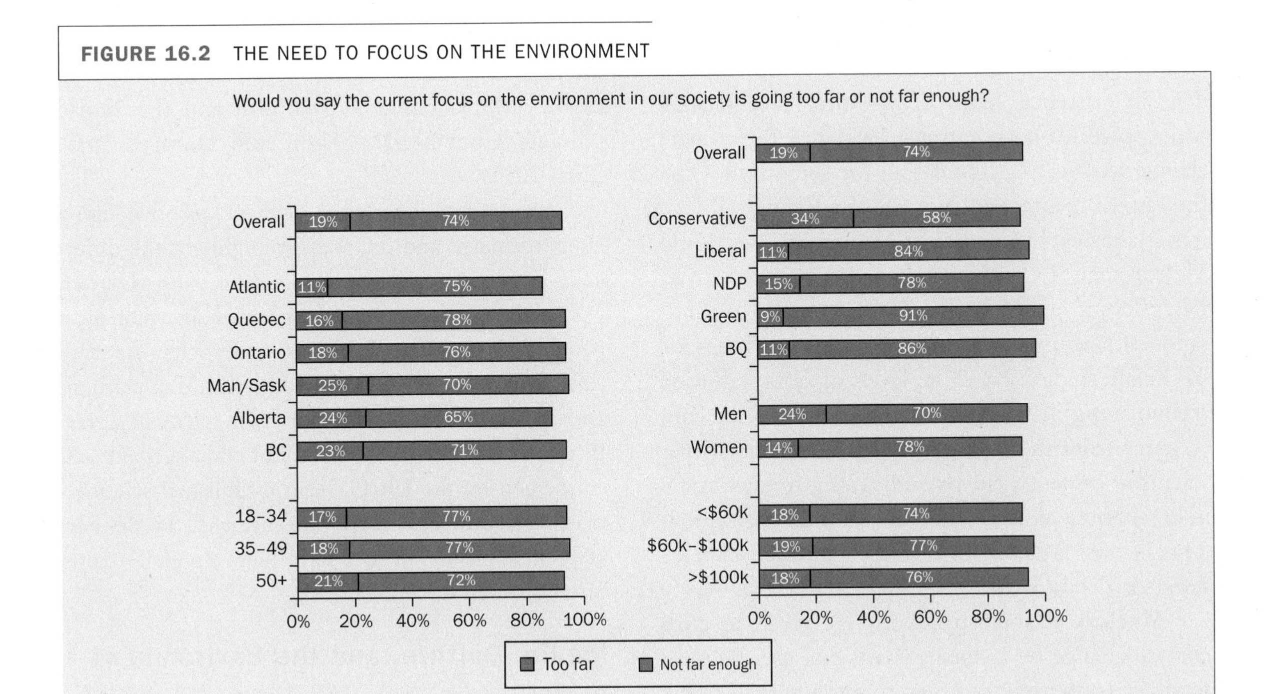

In December 2009, about three-quarters of the Canadian population felt that the current focus on the environment was not going far enough. Notice the variation among provinces and the political parties on this point. What do you think could account for this?

SOURCE: Harris/Decima. (2009). "In spite of recession, environment remains a high priority." On the World Wide Web at http://www.harrisdecima.com/sites/default/files/releases/2009/08/24/hd-2009-08-24-en275.pdf (retrieved 13 February 2012).

and behaviour. Framing refers to the way people interpret and give meaning to events and things in their social settings. When people enter a social setting, they frame it by asking themselves, in effect, "What's going on here?" (Goffman, 1974: 8). Framing renders what would otherwise be meaningless into something that we take into account when interacting. How something is framed therefore influences how people act. If people regard an environmental problem as significant, they may act on it. Otherwise they may not. For social constructionists, such considerations form the basis for analyzing environmental issues.

THE SOCIAL CONSTRUCTION OF ENVIRONMENTAL ISSUES

How is a problem transformed from a nonissue to an issue that attracts public attention and political interest? The social constructionist perspective focuses on the stages in that process (Hannigan, 2006). In the first stage, people *assemble* a claim or complaint about an environmental problem they regard as undesirable. Scientists typically assemble claims regarding environmental problems. Next, the claim must be brought to people's attention. Typically, the mass media serve as the platform for publicizing it. Popularizers, such as David Suzuki, and celebrities, such as Pamela Anderson, often play an important role in publicizing environmental claims because their fame allows them to grab the media spotlight. Environmental activists may also try to lure the mass media by drawing on dramatic visual images—for example, photographs of the clubbing of baby seals in Labrador. Coverage of high-profile events, such as the awarding of the 2007 Nobel Peace Prize to the Intergovernmental Panel on Climate Change and former U.S. vice-president Al Gore, serve much the same purpose.

THE SOCIAL CONSTRUCTION OF CLIMATE CHANGE

People often contest claims about environmental problems, especially if the claims have wide-ranging political and economic implications. Consider climate change. Reducing the emission of greenhouse gases requires massive change in the way industry and government operate, as well as the lifestyles we will be able to pursue. Conflict has been fierce between those calling for action on climate change and those who deny its existence. Many of the latter have backing from powerful corporations. Evidence for climate change has been accumulating for some time. The Intergovernmental Panel on Climate Change (IPCC) was established by the United Nations and the World Meteorological Organization to collect and summarize relevant evidence. The IPCC consists of thousands of scientists who interpret tens of thousands of climate studies. Based on levels of carbon dioxide accumulating in tree rings, coral reefs, and ice core columns from the Arctic, the IPCC concluded that scientific evidence clearly indicates a dramatic rise in greenhouse gas since the time of industrialization. This in turn is linked to increased surface temperature (see Figure 16.3).

Much is at stake if actions are taken to curb climate change by reducing fossil fuel use. Because fossil-fuel-intensive industry represents the largest contributor to climate change, it has a particularly strong responsibility to curb fossil fuel extraction and use. Sociologists have found, however, that fossil-fuel-intensive industries have organized to discredit scientific research on climate change, sow doubt among the public by claiming that the research is erroneous or a hoax, and influence politicians to avoid passing meaningful environmental legislation. Oil industry interests in particular have organized themselves covertly through front operations, such as the Global Climate Coalition and the World Climate Council (McCright and Dunlap, 2010; Urry, 2011).

The competing claims of those acknowledging climate change and the skeptics highlight the difference between popular and scientific truth (Derber, 2010). Popular truth refers to knowledge that most people in a society believe to be true. Scientific truth refers to knowledge established by scientific methods and on which the great majority of scientists agree. It is clear that the phenomenon of climate change, as confirmed by the IPCC, is an established scientific truth. Yet powerful corporate interests, by deliberately creating doubt, seek to influence popular truth, often through the mass media.

Media, Culture, and the Environment

Popular culture plays an important role in influencing people's environmental attitudes and behaviours. In the decades following the energy crisis of the mid-1970s, depictions of a dark environmental future proliferated in Western popular culture. Such films as *Blade Runner*, *Total Recall*, and *The Day After Tomorrow* painted a picture of a time when Earth's environment is ruined. Misery, poverty, oppression, violence, disease, scarcity, and pollution

FIGURE 16.3 VARIATIONS OF THE EARTH'S SURFACE TEMPERATURE

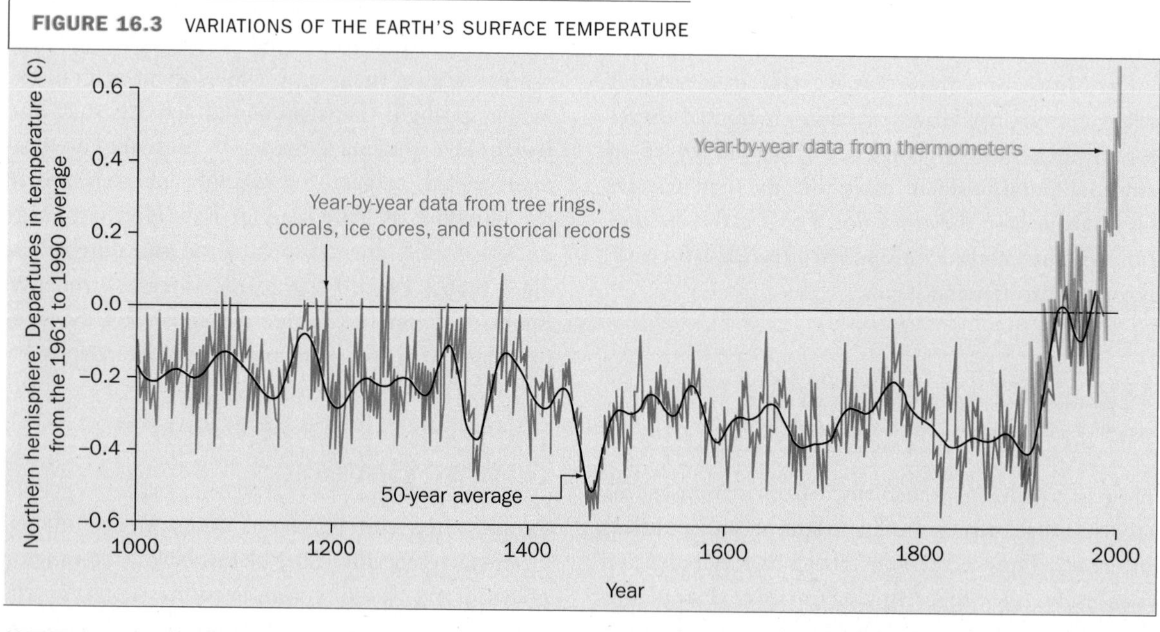

SOURCE: Pearce, Fred, 2010. "Controversy behind climate science's 'hockey stick' graph." On the World Wide Web at http://www.guardian.co.uk/environment/2010/feb/02/hockey-stick-graph-climate-change (retrieved 11 February 2012). Copyright Guardian News & Media Ltd. 2010.

are everywhere. The popularity of such films raised environmental consciousness among the public (Buell, 2004). More recently, *Avatar*, the highest-grossing film ever, had a strong environmental theme. Set in 2154, the film tells the story of a powerful corporation mining a faraway planet for a valuable mineral. In the process, the corporation seeks to eradicate the indigenous people and the natural environment. Events now taking place in northern Alberta's tar sands region apparently inspired the movie.

The news media also play a significant role in framing environmental issues. They often cover environmental problems and issues precisely because the controversy associated with them is filled with dramatic moments. Environmental movements sometimes deliberately employ sensationalistic techniques to draw media attention (Hannigan, 2006). For instance, they may stage "morality plays" in which environmental group members present themselves as the idealistic and morally good protectors of the environment, challenging whalers, loggers, and nuclear operators who are depicted as villains in a David-versus-Goliath confrontation. For their part, journalists may themselves be involved in the framing process by covering environmental issues in ways they know will resonate with a larger audience. Thus, the coverage of an environmental issue might, for example, be framed in terms of health and safety, bureaucratic bungling, or good citizenship.

Greenpeace activists confronting whaling ships.
SOURCE: © Rex Weyler

NATURAL RESOURCES

NONRENEWABLE RESOURCES

We can classify natural resources according to their quantity and ability to regenerate. Nonrenewable resources are finite in quantity and therefore exhaustible since they can only be used once. Oil is an example. The finite quantity of nonrenewable resources has significant economic implications because resource scarcity results in high prices for the commodity in question (see Box 16.1). No big oil discoveries have been made since the 1970s; we have reached **peak oil** production and can expect only declining production in the future. We are now consuming four barrels of oil for every new barrel discovered (Urry, 2011: 78). Oil extraction has become problematic because sources that are more difficult and expensive to exploit must now be tapped. For instance, some analysts believe that, if we factor in externalities paid by taxpayers, the cost of extraction will soon be higher than the price we pay for oil from the Alberta tar sands. The technical difficulties involved in extracting oil from the tar sands means that tar sands oil generates three times the greenhouse gas emissions of normal oil extraction while consuming huge amounts of water and energy (Nikiforuk, 2010: 3).

Peak oil represents a sociological tipping point. Beyond the peak, our entire way of life will change. Resource and energy struggles will become a defining feature of our society. Experts predict that the full force of peak oil will be felt within a few years (Urry, 2011; see Box 16.2).

RENEWABLE NATURAL RESOURCES

In contrast to fossil fuels, forests are renewable if we take care to ensure that new trees replace those that are harvested. In practice, renewal may not occur as quickly as needed. Some types of trees, such as those in the old growth forests of British Columbia, take centuries to grow. Similarly, overfishing may not allow fish stocks to replenish, as was the case with the cod fishery in Newfoundland in the early 1990s. The government had to impose a moratorium on cod fishing in 1992 to give the cod an opportunity to replenish, and only recently has hope been expressed that commercial fishing may soon resume. Some renewable natural resources—sunlight, gravity, wind power, and tidal wave power—are inexhaustible for all practical purposes. Such inexhaustible resources are widely considered to be critically important for sustainable development.

BOX 16.1 BOOMTOWNS: THE CASE OF FORT McMURRAY

Boomtowns are predicated on the exploitation of natural resources. Since natural resources are usually located in remote and sparsely populated areas, their extraction requires people to migrate to the boomtown. The resulting population increase typically results in rapid and dramatic social change. For example, a greater number of salaried workers may lead to an infusion of money in the local economy, but this in turn may cause inflation in prices and rents. The existing community infrastructure may not be able to accommodate the rapidly increasing population, leading to a housing shortage and strain on the resources available for medical treatment, education, law enforcement, and public assistance. Increased rates of crime, divorce, suicide, alcoholism, and stress often follow (England and Albrecht, 1984; Freudenburg, 1984; Gramling and Brabant, 1986).

The transformation of Fort McMurray, Alberta, the heart of the province's booming tar sands industry, is a case in point (Nikiforuk, 2010):

- Fort McMurray's population growth has been 9 to 12 percent annually. About 100 000 people now live in the regional municipality.
- Nearly half the city's population comes from poor fishing communities in Newfoundland and Labrador. In total, about 340 000 people from the east coast have migrated to Alberta in the past few decades to supply labour power for the petroleum industry.
- Housing in Fort McMurray is scarce and expensive. The price of a single-family home climbed from $174 000 to more than $600 000 in a decade—twice the average price of a home in Canada.
- Inflation is rampant.
- It takes 40 minutes to order a cup of coffee at Tim Hortons. Lineups at the banks on payday can be 60-people deep.
- In summer, homeless Aboriginal peoples and drug addicts sleep under cars or in tents amid piles of garbage by the Syne, a small channel of water near downtown.

Fort McMurray

SOURCE: © Larry MacDougal/The Canadian Press.

SOURCES: Nikiforuk, Andrew. (2010). *Tar Sands: Dirty Oil and the Future of a Continent*. Vancouver: Greystone Books; http://homeprosgroup.com/fort-mcmurray (retrieved 20 February 2012).

BOX 16.2 ENVIRONMENTAL MANAGEMENT ON EASTER ISLAND

Famous for its gigantic stone statues conspicuously sticking out from a dramatically desolate environmental wasteland, Easter Island is a 171-square-kilometre (66-square-mile) island in the South Pacific. Located 3700 kilometres (2300 miles) west of Chile, Easter Island is "the most remote habitable scrap of land in the world" (Diamond, 2011: 79). Because the island lacks significant natural resources, it is a mystery how nearly 400 statues, 4.5 to 21.3 metres (15 to 70 feet) high and weighing 9 to 245 metric tons (10 to 270 tons), could have been constructed or transported to the island.

However, archaeologists have found that the island was once thickly forested. Numerous tribes competed against one another to demonstrate their status by constructing and transporting bigger and bigger statues. Eventually, the competition required so much wood, rope, and food that everyone wound up losing. Natural resources became so badly depleted that the island could no longer sustain human life. With nowhere to flee, the Easter Islanders died off.

Is the world today's Easter Island, a worst-case scenario of what lies ahead for the planet?

Easter Island

SOURCE: © iStockphoto/Thinkstock.

Canada is a country of vast natural resources but abundance may not translate into wealth for all. Why not? To answer this question, we must understand how profits generated from resource extraction are unequally distributed across society and why this is allowed to occur.

THE RESOURCE CURSE

In Canada, natural resources are owned by the government. The government issues a licence for a private corporation to extract natural resources and is paid a royalty for this right. Usually, the royalty is a percentage of the revenue obtained through its use. In absolute terms, royalty rates for certain natural resources are very low. For example, at 39 percent of gross revenue, Alberta has one of the lowest royalty rates for oil extraction in the world (see Figure 16.4). Nevertheless, the amount of revenue generated from oil royalties enables Alberta to forgo imposing a provincial sales tax on its citizens and to collect income tax at a comparatively low rate. In fact, the province collects more revenue from oil than it does from taxpayers. This situation has significant social and political consequences.

One consequence is that the public is less likely to scrutinize how the government spends public funds than would be the case if they were taxed at a higher rate. Taxation, it turns out, strengthens democracy. In turn, the government is less inclined to feel that it has to answer to the public. This is seen, for instance, in the Alberta government's failure to measure oil production data and report oil royalties accurately (Alberta Royalty Review Panel, 2007). At the same time, heavy dependence on resource royalties obliges the government to please the petroleum industry. For example, not wanting to bite the hand that feeds it, the government is disinclined to strictly regulate the environmental impact of the petroleum sector (Nikiforuk, 2010).

Such situations as those just described have led sociologists to conclude that ownership and licensing

FIGURE 16.4 GOVERNMENT SHARE OF INDUSTRY OIL REVENUES COLLECTED THROUGH ROYALTIES

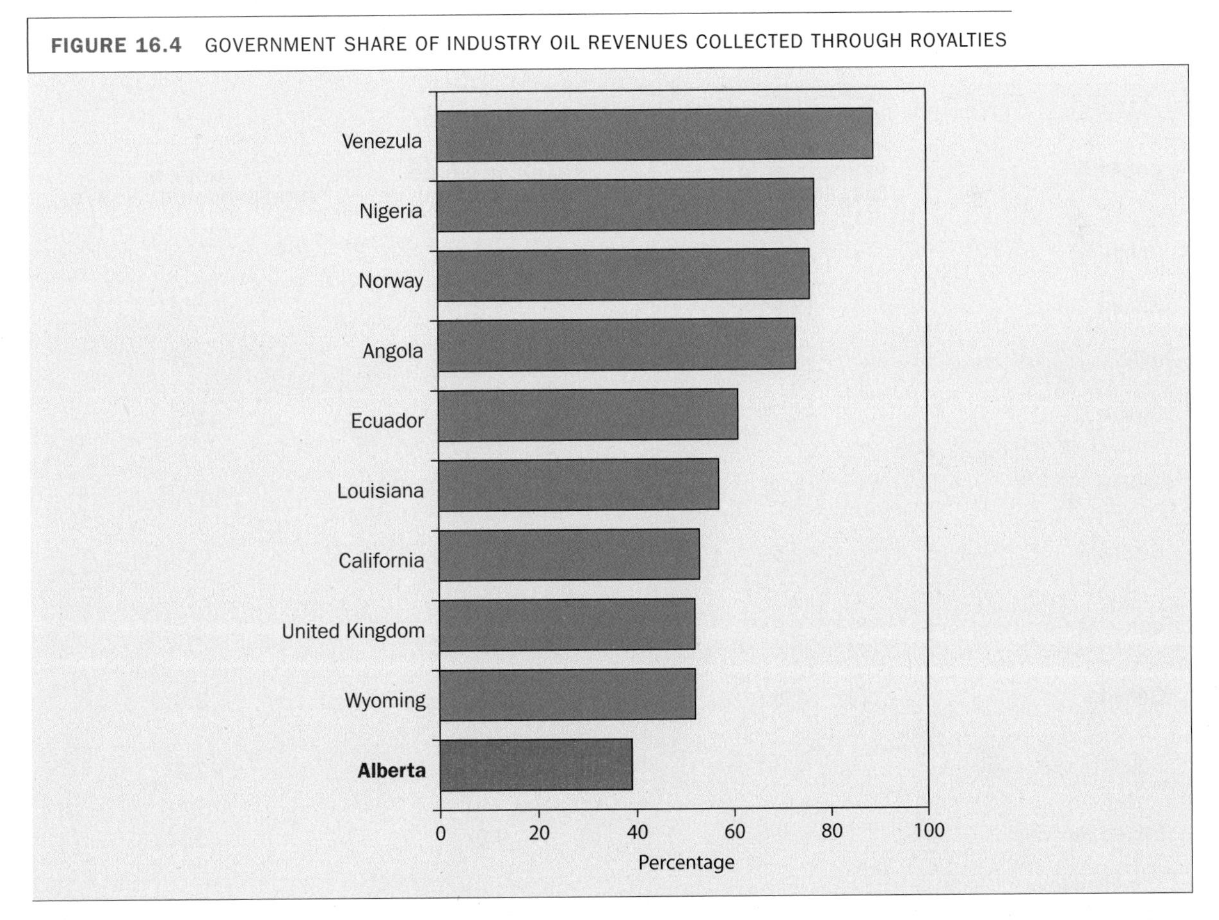

SOURCE: United States Government Accountability Office. Data supplied to the Alaska State Legislature, 2006. (GA0-07-676R).

arrangements used to govern natural resources in resource-rich countries amount to a **resource curse** that hampers democracy, increases corruption, and creates injustice (Friedman, 2006). In extreme cases, including those in Saudi Arabia and the other oil-rich Gulf states, autocratic government becomes firmly entrenched.

ENVIRONMENTAL GOVERNANCE

Environmental governance refers to attempts by those in power to regulate and alleviate environmental problems (Davidson and Frickel, 2004). Students of environmental governance explore how environmental policies are developed and implemented, and how government interacts with industry, social movements, and consumers in addressing environmental issues.

The capacity of a state to regulate activities that have environmental consequences depends partly on its sovereign power, or its ability to rule without external interference. Many environmental threats are not confined to a particular locality or jurisdiction; they are international in scope. Cooperation among states is required to address them. For instance, the need to regulate the emission of greenhouse gases on the part of each country led to heated disputes about sovereignty rights at the 1992 United Nations Conference on Environment and Development in Rio de Janeiro, the 1997 United Nations Framework Convention on Climate Change Conference in Kyoto, and the 2011 follow-up conference in Copenhagen. Some countries, including the United States, Canada, and Saudi Arabia, strongly oppose the imposition of regulations that would limit the extent to which their domestic industries are able emit greenhouse gases. Another example of this type of dispute occurred in 2008 when the Canadian government lobbied against proposed American legislation that would ban the United States from buying oil from the Alberta tar sands because extracting and refining it releases more pollutants than conventional petroleum production does. The Canadian lobby wanted to ensure a market for the oil despite its harsh environmental consequences (Nikiforuk, 2010).

As Table 16.1 and Figure 16.5 suggest, Canada has a poor record on the environmental front. The 1988 Canadian Environmental Protection Act could have been an important regulatory tool for the state.

TABLE 16.1 TOP CARBON DIOXIDE EMITTERS, 2011

COUNTRY	PERCENT OF GLOBAL CO_2 EMISSIONS (A)	SHARE OF WORLD POPULATION (B)	INDEX OF IRRESPONSIBILITY (A/B)
China	23.71	19.4	1.2
United States	17.91	4.6	3.9
India	5.47	17.1	0.3
Russia	5.28	2.1	2.5
Japan	3.77	1.9	2.0
Germany	2.59	1.2	2.2
Iran	1.84	1.1	1.7
Canada	**1.80**	**0.5**	**3.6**
South Korea	1.78	0.7	2.5
United Kingdom	1.61	0.9	1.8

SOURCE: Calculated from Germanwatch (2011: 2).

FIGURE 16.5 CANADA'S GREENHOUSE GAS EMISSIONS (1990–2007)

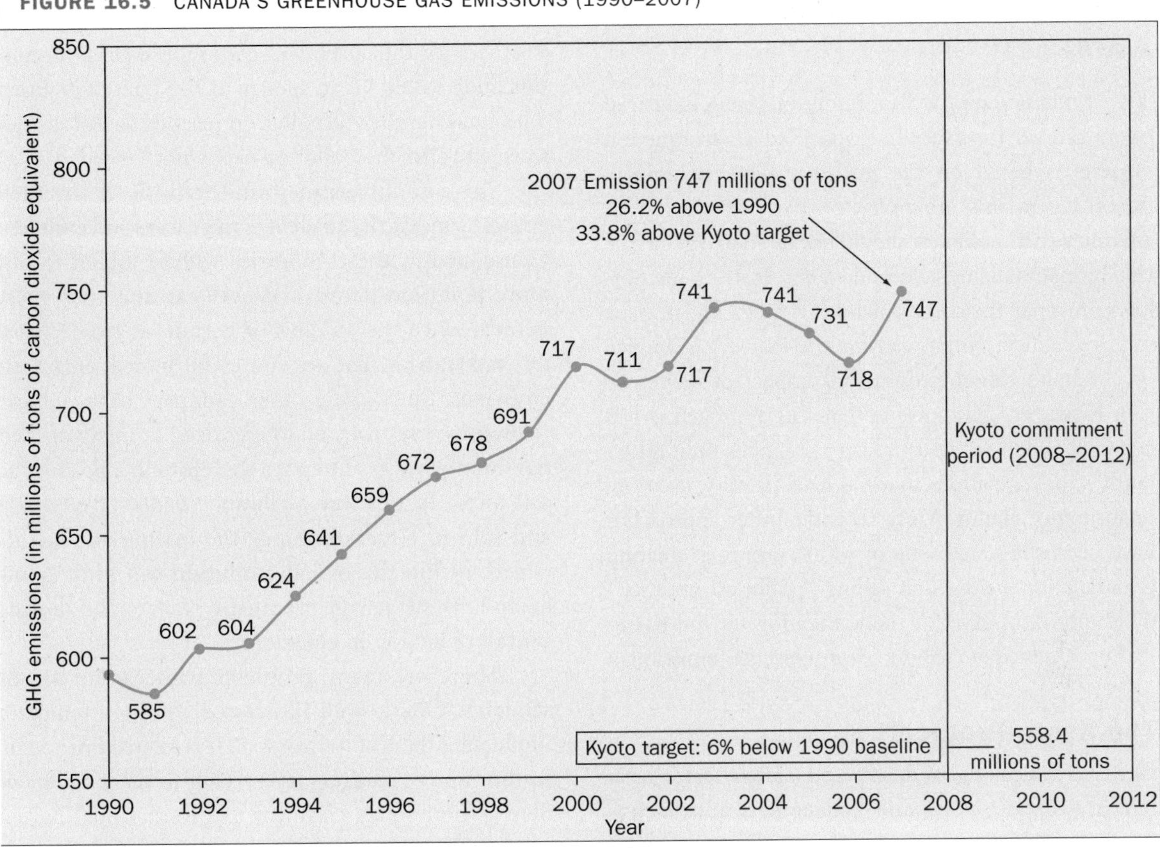

The greenhouse gas emission level that Canada committed itself to reach by 2012 under the Kyoto Agreement is 6 percent below the 1990 level. The graph shows that over the last two decades, the amount of greenhouse gas emissions has in fact increased dramatically.

SOURCE: Canada's 2007 Greenhouse Gas Inventory: A Summary of Trends (Environment Canada). Figure 1: Canada's GHG Emissions 1990–2007, on the World Wide Web at http://www.ec.gc.ca/ges-ghg/default.asp?lang=En&n=61B9E974-1 Environment Canada. Reproduced with the permission of the Minister of Public Works and Government Services, 2012.

However, because of consistent lobbying efforts by industry, the Act was revised in 1999 to emphasize the replacement of mandatory penalties with voluntary measures, self-regulation, and the establishment of regulations by nongovernmental bodies. An examination of investigations and inspections of possible Act violations from 1989 to 2008 found that the number of warnings increased but the number of persecutions declined (Girard, Day, and Snider, 2010). One factor accounting for this trend involves big budget cuts to Environment Canada over the years; warnings are cheaper and faster than investigations are.

INDUSTRY, ECONOMY, AND THE ENVIRONMENT

From an environmental point of view, the material basis of our economy is organized in a linear fashion. This means that raw natural resources are first extracted from the earth, processed and refined into purer form, and used to manufacture commodities. The commodities are then transported to retailers, where consumers buy them. Once they no longer satisfy consumer needs, the commodities are discarded. Waste products end up in landfills.

Each stage of this linear economy—resource extraction, processing, commodity transport, wholesale and retail sale, consumption, and postconsumption—has its own environmental impacts. For example, with resource extraction, such materials as fossil fuels and iron ore are taken from the environment, but farmland or forested areas may be destroyed in the process. During other stages, environmental impacts usually take the form of solid, liquid, and gas emissions. Governments direct much regulatory attention to controlling or limiting these emissions. Clearly, the environment and the economy are intimately linked.

THE BUSINESS SOLUTION TO ENVIRONMENTAL PROBLEMS: CREATE A MARKET FOR POLLUTION

The regulatory approach of fining or taxing industrial organizations for exceeding specified environmental impacts is based on the **polluter pays principle.** According to this principle, the party producing an environmental pollutant should not be able to get a free ride by externalizing associated costs. Instead, the polluter must pay the costs. The idea is that a fine or a tax serves as a disincentive, causing the industry to reduce or eliminate the environmental impact of its activities. However, critics argue that this approach is too coercive. They say that industry complies only reluctantly with regulations to avoid legal liability, taxation, or insurance claims. More recently, other approaches have been suggested, one of which proposes creating a market for buying and selling "pollution permits." This approach serves as the foundation for the Kyoto Protocol, aimed at curbing greenhouse gas emissions.

The Kyoto Protocol

Generally speaking, industry and nation states have tended to oppose **command-and-control approaches** to regulating their activities for the purpose of environmental protection. Such approaches are based on the government issuing commands to industry to adopt environmentally protective practices and to control environmentally harmful emissions by adhering to certain regulations. One of the objections to this approach raised by industry is that it fails to give industry any room to adopt environmentally better practices on their own terms. That is, if industry is to implement changes to their practices, they want to do so according to their own schedule and capacity. In theory, marketable pollution permit schemes—also called "cap-and-trade"—allow such flexibility.

Here is how cap-and-trade works in principle: National or international governmental bodies set an absolute limit on the total amount of a certain pollutant that can be emitted. This limit (or cap) is to be reached by a certain date. For example, the target of the Kyoto Protocol was to reduce overall global emissions of greenhouse gases by at least 5.2 percent below 1990 levels by 2012 (Giddens, 2009: 186). To reach this cap, each country must cut emissions by a certain amount. As such, each country is allowed or permitted to pollute, but at a level significantly lower than before. The right to pollute must be purchased in the form of a permit from the national or international agency that runs the newly created market. In the case of the 1997 Kyoto Protocol for the curbing of greenhouse gas pollution, this body would be an agency of the United Nations. The total number of pollution permits issued is fixed to ensure that the pollution cap is not exceeded.

Some countries may find it difficult for their domestic industries to change their ways and emit less. Consequently, these countries will be forced to buy more pollution permits. Where can they buy these permits since the amount of permits is fixed? From other countries that are successful in reducing their emissions. Since these other countries have reduced their emissions, they no longer need as many of their pollution permits. They are therefore in a position to sell them. In this way, pollution permits are bought and sold in a market. Since the buying and selling occurs within the overall pollution cap limit, some analysts think it will eventually lead to the desired overall reduction in emissions.

There are many problems with cap-and-trade schemes. One is well illustrated by the attempt to implement the Kyoto Protocol. It is related once again to the issue of sovereignty—trying to make independent nation states conform to international agreements. There is no worldwide sovereign to impose sanctions if individual countries violate regulations or do not agree to participate in the scheme. Thus, in 2001, United States President Bush withdrew his country from the Kyoto Protocol by refusing to send it to the Senate for ratification ("Kyoto and Beyond," 2007). Other problems arise as differences within a nation state make it difficult to ratify the protocol. For example, in Canada, regional differences made it difficult to come to a consensus on the Kyoto Protocol. Given their province's reliance on oil and natural gas, politicians from Alberta strongly opposed it, while Quebec was a strong supporter since that province draws mainly on hydroelectric power. Manitoba supported it because of the potential devastation that global climate change may wreak on agriculture in that province (Mitchell, 2010: 4).

MEASURING ECONOMIC VERSUS ENVIRONMENTAL PROGRESS

Concern about environmental protection and the economic interests of business and industry intersect in many ways, often to the detriment of the environment. Consider something as basic as how we measure the strength of the economy—by calculating gross national product (GNP). The GNP adds up the dollar value of all the goods and services produced in a country in a year. It does not distinguish economic activities that are bad for the environment from those that are benign. Let's say a mining operation produces a toxic liquid. A clean-up crew then collects the toxin and transports it to a landfill. The toxin leaks into groundwater and some of it enters a nearby community's water supply. Over the years, the cancer rate of residents and clean-up workers increases; the residents are consuming small quantities of the toxin and members of the clean-up crew were exposed to it when they collected it and took it to the landfill. Those afflicted require prolonged medical treatment and eventually die before they reach the average life expectancy for people in the country. All these activities add to the GNP, both the beneficial ones (producing a mineral and creating jobs) and the harmful ones (producing a toxin, exposing people to it, and causing the cancer rate to rise and people to die prematurely). In this manner, environmental destruction contributes to GNP. GNP figures suggest that the economy is growing stronger, but they give no indication of the environmental devastation that underlies development. Social scientists have proposed alternatives to the GNP that adjust for social and environmental costs, but to this point, they have not been influential in policymaking (Giddens, 2009).

Recently, the incorporation of the social and environmental aspects of economic activities has become a consideration for some businesses. This often takes the form of corporate social responsibility initiatives and eco-standards practices.

CORPORATE SOCIAL RESPONSIBILITY AND ECO-STANDARDS

Increasing public concern about the environment has forced industry to make concessions. Today, for instance, some companies say they exercise "corporate social responsibility" by ensuring that their practices are ethically and environmentally sound and in the public interest. The problem is that such measures are voluntary, so they may not be effective. In some cases, companies even claim they are engaged in environmentally protective practices when they are not. They promote a "green" image merely as a public relations ploy to attract more business—a practice sometimes called "corporate greenwashing."

People would be able to identify instances of corporate greenwashing more easily if the environmental practices of companies were made transparent to the public. One attempt to do this is with eco-standards and eco-labels. A company that conforms to established environmental standards for production and manufacturing would be able to apply for certification stating that its product or practice is environmentally friendly. The environmental standards themselves would be developed by another agency or sometimes by the government. An external auditor would ensure that the company complies with the standards and procedures, and issue a certificate on the basis of the assessment. The agency and auditor would therefore operate as watchdogs for the public, vouching for the company and ensuring it is not making false claims. The issued certificate could take different forms, such as the company or product being included in official green shopping guides or green mutual fund portfolios, or through the issuing of environmental stewardship certificates that can be displayed publicly in the storefront or factory. In addition, eco-labels could be displayed on products so consumers could see they conform to a standard before deciding whether to buy them.

The eco-standards approach has been used for a variety of products and processes, including organic food labelling, labelling of genetically modified food, energy efficiency certification, and marine certification and seafood labelling (to certify that only sustainable yields are being caught). But can these eco-labels be trusted? Toilet paper produced by J.D. Irving Limited of New Brunswick carries the Sustainable Forestry Limited (SFI) eco-label, yet investigation by CBC journalists found that forestry practices involved in manufacturing it violate important principles that the general population associates with sustainable forestry, including clear-cutting, herbicide use, lack of recycled material in the manufacturing process, and the replanting of just one tree species, which threatens the long-term survivability of the replanted forest ("Toilet Paper Chase," 2012). To address such false environmental claims, such groups as Greenpeace and CorpWatch have established websites and blogs to investigate and then inform the public of specific cases of greenwashing. This is just one sort of activity that environmental movement groups are involved with.

THE ENVIRONMENTAL MOVEMENT

At the turn of the twentieth century, the increasingly pervasive impact of industrialization on forests gave rise to concerns about preserving the natural beauty of wilderness areas. Consequently, national parks, such as those at Niagara Falls, Ontario, and Banff, Alberta, were established to protect areas of natural beauty. (Another incentive for the national park system was the promotion of tourism and the Canadian National Railroad; Paehlke, 2009). At the time, the environmental movement consisted of nature-based groups, such as the Sierra Club and the National Audubon Society.

With the publication of *Silent Spring* in the 1960s, the first wave of the modern environmental movement was born. It focused on environmental threats to human health, and it took a somewhat anti-industrial perspective. By the mid-1980s, a second wave of environmentalism could be discerned. It was less apocalyptic and more pragmatic and professional in tone, more willing to work with business and government in dealing with issues such as acid rain. In Canada, business-government-environmentalist round tables were established. The shift from an adversarial to a cooperative stance may have reflected broader changes in society, including aging members in the first wave, who now had families to raise and mortgages to pay; a growing number of second-wave members who had graduated from university programs in environmental studies; and recognition by business and government that environmentalism was not just a passing fad (Paehlke, 2009).

By 2002, global climate change was at the top of the political agenda, signalling the rise of a third wave of environmentalism. Addressing climate change requires large-scale alterations in the way society is organized. For this reason, the issue subsumes other types of environmental issues, such as increasing energy efficiency in manufacturing, building design, and transportation; switching to renewable energy sources; significantly increasing the recycling and reuse of materials; and adopting more effective forest and other resource management strategies. This third wave of environmentalism was also characterized by the emergence of the federal Green Party. In every election since 2004, the Greens have been able to run a candidate in all federal ridings. So far, they have elected just one MP, but their presence on the national stage has forced the other political parties to give greater prominence to environmental issues—if only to prevent supporters from being attracted to the Green Party (Paehlke, 2009).

SOCIAL BASE AND COMPOSITION

The social base of the environmental movement has shifted over time. During the early part of the twentieth century, the nature-orientated environmental movement consisted largely of the affluent. Modern environmental groups tend to draw disproportionately on the "new middle class" of young, well-educated people who often work in public, cultural, or social service occupations, including teachers, social workers, actors, journalists, artists, and academics—and their student apprentices (Brown, 2009). Such people may be attracted to the environmental movement for two reasons. First, they tend to have values that are incompatible with those of the business world and the idea of profit maximization at all cost. Second, they may be involved in jobs where they advocate for the rights of clients—such as a social worker involved in a campaign to improve environmental conditions in an inner-city community where she works. Both of these types of "new-middle-class" tendencies are in line with environmentally based values that call for social and political change to improve society (Kriesi, 1989).

The "new-middle-class" thesis only partly describes membership in Canada's Green Party (Camcastle, 2007). True, the Greens attract young, well-educated people—but an unusually large proportion of them are self-employed. Otherwise, the social profile of the Green Party is not hugely different from those voting for other parties. The Party itself has had some success with the electorate, indicating a small but broadening base of public support. In the 2011 election, the Greens won nearly 4 percent of the popular vote and well-known environmentalist and head of the Green Party

In the 2011 election, the Greens won nearly 4 percent of the popular vote.
SOURCE: © ZUMA Press/Newscom.

Elizabeth May became its first elected member of Parliament (Elections Canada, 2012).

Many issues that concern environmental activists are health related because they violate the core value of survival. Threats to health undoubtedly motivate some activists to become involved in health-related environment issues.

THE ENVIRONMENT AND HEALTH

You are what you eat—and what you touch and breathe. If the air, water, food, and physical surroundings in which we carry on our daily activities are contaminated, we too become contaminated. Environmental and health issues are thus intimately connected. All human beings alive today have some level of **body burden**—the sum of dangerous chemicals that accumulate in the human body over a given period. Human decision making and the resulting organization of society shape the way chemicals enter the human body.

For example, in the mid-1960s, the Ontario Department of Lands and Forests (now the Ministry of Natural Resources) and private timber companies collaborated to spray the chemical Agent Orange on northern Ontario forests (Zlomislic, 2011). Agent Orange killed shrubs and birch, maple, and poplar tress so that profitable spruce trees would be free to grow without competition. We now know that Agent Orange causes cancer, but in the mid-1960s, workers involved in the spraying program, many of them university students, were unaware of the risks. They mixed chemicals with little protection and stood in fields holding red, helium-filled balloons on fishing lines while low-flying planes flew over them and sprayed the chemical. Decades later, these workers are experiencing serious health effects.

The Agent Orange case is one of acute exposure, that is, high-dose exposure in a short period. Other examples of acute exposure include explosions at chemical factories and industrial accidents. However, many environmental health risks are chronic, involving low-dose exposure over an extended period. One example involves bisphenol A, which is found in many clear, hard plastic products, such as CDs and DVDs, water and baby bottles, eyeglass lenses, and hockey helmet visors. It is also used in epoxy resins and the lining of tin cans containing food. It is one of the most common chemicals in the world (Smith and Lourie, 2009). Consequently, most people are in contact with bisphenol A every day for most of their lives. With bisphenol A (and other chemicals that disrupt the body's hormonal system), low doses lead to potent health effects. Hence, low levels of such chemicals in the environment are of particular concern. Low levels of bisphenol A have been associated with a range of illnesses, including prostate and breast cancer, urogenital abnormalities in male babies, declining sperm quality in men, early onset of puberty in girls, insulin-resistant diabetes, obesity, and attention deficit hyperactivity disorder (Smith and Lourie, 2009). Because of such concerns, in 2008 Canada became the first country in the world to ban bisphenol A from baby bottles. There are, however, many other harmful chemicals that pervade the environment. How are these regulated? To address these questions we need to understand the process of risk management.

RISK MANAGEMENT

Body burden is influenced by how a country regulates chemicals in the environment. The state does this through **risk management**—the process by which a regulatory agency establishes the levels of chemicals that are allowed to enter the environment. Risk management uses information from animal experiments to help determine safe levels of exposure. This technical information is combined with environmental information to come up with a specific regulation (Ali, 2008). However, the terms of the regulation are subject to political pressure. It may be that the strict regulation of a chemical emission will be costly to industry. Industry will therefore lobby for a laxer and less costly regulation. The environmental lobby, in contrast, may call for stricter regulation. As such, risk management is hardly a politically neutral, technical exercise.

In 2008, Canada became the first country in the world to ban bisphenol A from baby bottles.
SOURCE: © The New York Times/REDUX.

In North America, risk management works on the principle that a chemical is assumed to be harmless until it is proven dangerous. Until then, the chemical will still be produced and allowed to enter the environment. This pro-industry orientation has been challenged by environmentalists calling for the adoption of the precautionary principle.

THE PRECAUTIONARY PRINCIPLE

The essence of the scientific method and the experimental approach is to establish the existence of cause-effect relationships. With respect to environmental health issues, this involves showing that exposure to a certain amount of a chemical in the environment (the cause) leads to a particular illness (the effect). In practice, causality is difficult to prove because environmental exposures take place while many compounding factors impinge on a given dose-response interaction. Laboratory experiments remove these confounding factors by manipulating the physical setting (see Chapter 20, Research Methods). However, researchers cannot remove compounding factors in the real world, where the cause of a disease may be due to many factors. Cancer, for instance, may result from several causes acting at different points in life, such as exposure to factory smoke during childhood, cigarette smoke during youth, and radon gas during adulthood. Ambiguity in what causes cancer exists; it may be one thing, or it may be several. Thus, the tobacco industry argued for decades that cigarette smoking might not be a cause of cancer because cigarette smokers tend to be overweight, have poor diets, live in polluted neighbourhoods, and so on—and all these factors are causes of cancer. (Only recently have researchers shown how exposure to tobacco smoke turns cells carcinogenic, thus silencing this particular line of defence.) Similarly, defenders of polluting industries have argued that just because a disease is found in laboratory animals exposed to a particular contaminant, this does not necessarily mean that it will lead to the disease in humans. In the end, polluting industries often argue that insufficient evidence proves conclusively the existence of a cause-effect relationship between a pollutant and a disease, so regulating or banning a pollutant is not justified. Chemicals are innocent until proven guilty beyond doubt in Canada and the United States.

In Western Europe, regulatory agencies take a different approach. They do not allow the introduction of a new chemical if statistical evidence shows a correlation between its use and a dangerous health effect. Underlying this approach is the precautionary principle—the view that, under conditions of uncertainty, it is better to err on the side of safety. Some researchers argue that the logic of the precautionary principle should be applied not just to the regulation of chemicals but also to other regulatory issues, including the use of genetically modified food, genetic engineering, nanotechnologies, global warming, and activities that lead to the loss of biodiversity (Raffensperger and Tickner, 1999).

Because of the inadequacies of risk management, environmental health risks persist. However, sociologists have found that these risks do not affect everyone in society equally. Some individuals and groups are disproportionately affected by these risks, depending on their race/ethnicity, social class, gender, and place of residence. In other words, the inequality exists in the distribution of risk. Certain organizations in the larger environmental movement have mobilized to address issues related to the unequal distribution of risk.

ENVIRONMENTAL INEQUALITY

Race and ethnicity, social class, and gender all influence how environmental risks are distributed and experienced. Generally, people in subordinate positions are more exposed to environmental risk than are people in dominant positions. Recognition of this fact spurred the **environmental justice movement**. The initial impetus for the movement was the work of sociologist Robert Bullard (1993). Based on quantitative evidence and mapping, his research showed that toxic waste sites were located disproportionately in African American and Hispanic neighbourhoods in the United States. For example, about 60 percent of African Americans live near toxic waste sites.

Today, many workers, members of racial minority groups, and women have been drawn into environmental justice organizations. They tend to engage in local campaigns focusing on the survival needs of the poor, in contrast to some national and international environmental organizations that tend to engage in "full-stomach" environmentalism (dealing with nature preservation for enjoyment and enhancing the quality of life; see Guha and Martinez-Alier, 1998). As such, environmental justice organizations make a concerted effort to link occupational, community, economic, environmental, and social justice issues. They combat racism by asserting people's civil and human rights. They engage in activities aimed at eliminating the unequal enforcement of environmental, civil rights, and public health laws; the different degree of exposure of different races and classes to harmful chemicals in the home, school, neighbourhood and workplace; and discriminatory zoning and land-use practices.

ENVIRONMENTAL JUSTICE AND CANADA'S FIRST NATIONS

Canadians do not have to deal with the historical legacy of slavery to the extent Americans do, which is why we have been less engaged in the struggle for human rights. Still, First Nations peoples in Canada face their own legacy of colonization and inequality (Agyeman, Haluza-DeLay, and O'Riley, 2009). For example, the rural area within the Sarnia-Windsor-London triangle of Southern Ontario hosts many harmful industries, including a regional landfill, numerous smaller landfills, a sewage treatment plant treating 15 million litres (4 million gallons) a day, and the country's largest concentration of heavy industry, much of it related to petrochemicals, called "Chemical Valley." It is also home to eight First Nations territories (Mascarenhas, 2009). From 1974 to 1986, this area experienced 32 major chemical spills and 300 smaller ones that poured about 9 metric tons (10 tons) of pollutants in the St. Clair River, which runs through the area (Walpole Island First Nation, n.d.). The waterways in the region are so polluted that they have been designated as "areas of concern" by the International Joint Commission (Environment Canada, 2010).

The Aamjiwnaang First Nations Reserve is located in Chemical Valley. Epidemiological studies of this community show that, over the past decade, a statistically significantly lower number of boys than girls have been born. The imbalance has been attributed to environmental endocrine disruptors present in the toxic chemicals emitted by area industry (Mackenzie, Lockridge, and Keith, 2005).

Many of the issues that environmental justice groups deal with in the United States relate to the urban setting. In contrast, the environmental justice issues many First Nations people face involve the distribution of environmental risks in more remote settings, such as mercury contamination in northern Ontario (Erikson, 1995), water quality problems on reserves (Indian and Northern Affairs Canada, 2003), contamination from radioactive materials from uranium mining at Great Bear Lake in the Northwest Territories (Blow, 1999), and chemical contamination in the Mohawk territory

A sign warning of toxic substances in Talfourd Creek on the Aamjiwnaang First Nation reserve near Sarnia, Ontario.
SOURCE: © AP Photo/Carlos Osorio.

of Akwesasne in eastern Ontario and western Quebec (Tarbell and Arquette, 2000).

Issues of environmental justice are even dealt with by those in some of the most remote parts of the country, such as Inuit in Nunavik. Since some dangerous chemicals found in the environment are fat soluble, they contribute to the body burden of women more than men. Mother's milk in particular is quite high in fat. Analysis of Inuit mothers' milk has shown that it contains five times as much polychlorinated biphenyl (PCB), a cancer-causing agent, than that of southern Canadian white women. In some cases, the concentration was even higher (Milly and Leiss, 1997). It is not permissible to feed cow's milk with this much PCB to infants.

PCB belongs to a set of chemicals known as persistent organic pollutants (POPs). POPs do not break down in the environment, even after centuries. They are produced for various industrial purposes in the southern areas of world. Over time, POPs are carried through wind currents to the northern regions, where they bioaccumulate in the fat of living things. Living things in the Arctic region are therefore threatened by environmental health risks they had no role in producing and from which they did not benefit. Such facts raise the issues of inequality and injustice.

THE UNEQUAL BURDENS OF ENVIRONMENTAL INEQUALITY

Inequalitiy in the distribution of environmental health risks take various forms. For example, poorer neighbourhoods in Canadian cities contain a disproportionate amount of polluting industry. Thus, the North End of Hamilton, Ontario, is host to many heavy metal and chemical industries that pollute the local environment (Ali, 2002). North End residents have the lowest socioeconomic status in the city and are exposed to much higher levels of particulate air pollution than are residents of higher socioeconomic status neighbourhoods (Jerrett et al., 2001). True, the establishment of polluting and environmentally damaging industry in relatively poor parts of the city provides much-needed jobs. However, it also reflects the fact that powerful and wealthy people make decisions about where to place dirty industry, and they are in a position to avoid living nearby. This, too, is a form of environmental inequality.

The flow of waste from the northern to the southern hemisphere illustrates yet another form of environmental inequality. Increasingly, North America and Western Europe dump toxic waste, industrial pollution, and discarded consumer goods in the southern hemisphere in exchange for fees and jobs (Faber, 2009). The countries of the southern hemisphere have weaker environmental regulations than those in the north do, and they often lack the expertise to evaluate and manage the risks of the hazardous waste they accept. In the end, we apply two standards of environmental health and safety—a relatively high standard for those in the north and a relatively low standard for those in the south, implying that human life in one region is worth less than that in the other. As a former World Bank's chief economist once wrote in a leaked memo, "I think the economic logic behind dumping a load of toxic waste in the lowest wage country is impeccable and we should face up to that. ... I've always thought that under-populated countries in Africa are vastly under-polluted" (Rich, 1994: 248).

As the world's second biggest exporter of asbestos, a mineral known for its fire-resistant properties, Canada upholds the double standard. For decades, we have known that asbestos causes serious lung-related ailments including mesothelioma, a rare form of cancer. Consequently, many countries have banned the import and export of the substance. Yet Canada refuses to list asbestos as a hazardous product and sends large quantities of it from Quebec to India, Pakistan, and China ("Canada Wins Battle," 2011).

Today, the problem of environmental inequality because of the trade in toxic waste is intensified because of the proliferation of computers. Soldered circuit boards contain various toxic heavy metals, while cathode ray tubes components release toxic compounds when burned—which happens when incineration is used as a waste disposal method. Computers quickly become obsolete and we tend to discard them quickly. Consequently, mountains of toxic "e-waste" accumulate and are shipped to developing nations, such as China, India, and Pakistan. There, the material is reused, recycled, or incinerated under largely unregulated conditions, endangering the environment and the lives of electronic waste workers (Markoff, 2002).

CLIMATE CHANGE AND INEQUALITY

Environmental inequality is also evident in the unequal burden created by climate change. Many analysts argue that climate change will have the greatest effect on those least responsible for causing the problem. One study based on an ecological mapping of climate change effects around the world found that countries producing the least amount of greenhouse gas per capita tend to be the most vulnerable to climate change (Shingler, 2011). For example, rising sea levels caused by climate change will entirely submerge South Pacific island nations, such as the Solomon Islands, Tongo, and Tuvalu. Furthermore, such poor nations have inadequate technical, financial, and administrative capacity, putting them at a disadvantage in international negotiations related to the regulation of climate change. Similar arguments have been made in international discussions on sustainable development. Developing nations argue that it is unfair to impose strict regulations on their greenhouse gas emissions because that would unjustly limit their industrial development—a limitation not faced by nations in the northern hemisphere when they underwent industrialization. The charge of the developing nations is that the countries of the northern hemisphere engaged in unrestricted industrialization using fossil fuels, induced climate change, and now want to penalize the countries of the southern hemisphere as they attempt to industrialize. As seen in Table 16.2, data support the claims made by developing nations concerning relative resource consumption and environmental impact.

Finally, environmental inequality has a generational component. Decisions made by the present generation that result in environmental degradation may jeopardize the survival chances of the unborn. The rights of the unborn deserve to be considered by today's decision makers and the world's citizenry, including you and me.

TABLE 16.2 AVERAGE CARBON DIOXIDE EMISSIONS AND RESOURCE CONSUMPTION IN CANADA, THE UNITED STATES, INDIA, AND THE WORLD

CONSUMPTION PER PERSON IN 1991	CANADA	UNITED STATES	INDIA	WORLD
CO_2 emission (in tons per year)	15.2	19.5	0.81	4.2
Purchasing power (in US$)	19 320	22 130	1150	3800
Motor vehicles per 100 persons	46	57	0.2	10
Paper consumption (in kilograms/year)	247	317	2	44
Fossil energy use (in gigajoules/years)	234–250	287	5	56
Fresh water withdrawal (in m^3/year)	1688	1868	612	644

Note the dramatic differences in the consumption of resources and the production of carbon dioxide between Canada and the United States compared with India and the world.

SOURCE: Wackernagel, Mathias and William E. Rees. (1996). *Our Ecological Footprint: Reducing Human Impact on the Earth.* Gabriola Island, BC: New Society Publishers, p. 85.

SUMMARY

1. Sociologists recognize that environmental problems have a biophysical basis. They consider the role of social and material factors in their analyses of environmental issues.
2. The origin of many environmental problems may be understood in terms of the tragedy of the commons. The central feature of this tragedy is that since environmental commons, such as air and water, are used by all members of society, the ownership and use of these resources are not clearly defined or delimited. Consequently, private corporations will try to maximize the economic benefits they receive from exploiting the commons, knowing that the environmental consequences of their actions will be shared by all, potentially leading to the destruction of the commons.
3. Public awareness of environmental issues increased from the 1960s onward, with the unfolding of a sequence of influential events, including the publication of *Silent Spring* and the *Limits to Growth Report*, the establishment of the environmental movement, and the oil crisis of 1973. In the 1980s, the identification of two global environmental problems further reinforced the public's environmental concern: ozone depletion and global climate change. During that period, the influential notion of sustainable development was proposed by the international community as a way to manage environmental impacts without derailing economic growth. From the 1990s onward, several high-profile international conferences were held to coordinate efforts to combat global environmental problems.
4. The social constructionist perspective analyzes how environmental issues garner public attention. It focuses on the claims-making process and how the interactions among various individuals and institutions, such as industry and government representatives, environmental movement activists, scientists, and the mass media are able to promote certain claims over others. Popular culture also plays an important role in the social construction process.
5. Members of the new middle class, particularly young, highly educated individuals involved in service and cultural occupations, are disproportionately attracted to the environmental movement. However, support for the Green Party is more broadly based.
6. The attempt by nation-states (or other jurisdictions) to alleviate environmental problems is generally referred to as environmental governance. The international nature of many environmental

problems makes environmental governance efforts of individual nation-states and jurisdictions difficult. This is because each nation-state has sovereign powers and cannot impose its will on other nation-states without violating the other's sovereignty rights.

7. State environmental governance initiatives may be directed at private industries. Traditionally in Canada, under the Canadian Environmental Protection Act, the government has pursued a top-down, "command-and-control" approach to regulating the environmental impact of manufacturing and production. This approach has been resisted by industry. Consequently, voluntary self-regulatory mechanisms have been introduced, including the establishment of a market for pollution permits.
8. A healthy biophysical environment helps ensure good human health, while a chemically contaminated environment means that human beings are exposed to illness-causing chemicals. To minimize or eliminate exposure to toxic chemicals, the precautionary principle has been favoured in Western Europe. According to this principle, a chemical should be banned if there is even the suspicion that it can cause illness.
9. The regulation of toxic chemicals occurs through risk management, which involves interpreting technical information from animal tests. Political and economic interests influence risk management. For example, to carry on business, industry tends to argue for more lenient regulatory standards for the chemical by-products they produce while environmental activists demand more stringent standards.
10. Inequality arises from the unequal distribution of environmental risks. Relatively low status groups tend to shoulder a disproportionate share of environmental risks. As this fact came to be more widely recognized, environmental justice groups emerged to address issues related to environmental inequality. First Nations communities face particularly difficult conditions stemming from government and industrial policies that do not sufficiently consider issues of environmental inequality and injustice.

QUESTIONS TO CONSIDER

1. Sociologist Ulrich Beck (1995: 140) writes that "the environmental problem is by no means a problem [only] of our surroundings. It is a crisis of industrial society itself, reaching deeply into the foundations of institutions; risks are produced industrially, externalized economically, legitimized scientifically, and minimized politically." Take an example of any environmental problem and construct an argument that supports or challenges the above statement.
2. Select an environmental issue and explain how it is socially constructed. Consider the different claims made by government officials, environmental movement actors, scientists, and industry officials. How did media coverage of the environmental issue you selected represent the various claims expressed? Was equal coverage given to all involved?
3. Search the Web to analyze the controversies that arose at the International Climate Summit held in Copenhagen in December 2009. What sort of issues arose and how can they be understood sociologically in terms of such concepts as the tragedy of the commons, sovereignty rights, environmental inequality and injustice, power relations, economic contingency, and framing? What were some of the reasons that the Canadian government gave for not agreeing on the protocol that the international community put forward as necessary for combating global climate change?

GLOSSARY

Body burden (p. 409) refers to the sum of all foreign chemicals that accumulate in the human body over a given period.

The **command-and-control approach** (p. 406) to environmental management is the top-down government strategy of issuing regulations to control the environmental impact of industry.

The **economic contingency** (p. 397) thesis holds that public environmental concern depends on the state of the economy. In good economic times, more attention will be given to environmental issues, while in bad times, environmental concern will lessen.

The **environmental justice movement** (p. 410) seeks to address issues associated with the unequal distribution of environmental risks caused by discrimination.

An **externality** (p. 396) is an environmental impact that is produced by one party (such as an industry) that does not take responsibility for the consequences of the environmental impact. Rather, the consequences are addressed by another party, such as the state or the general public, which bears the cost of addressing the environmental impact.

Framing (p. 399) refers to the process of how events and issues are interpreted based on how they are presented.

Future discounting (p. 398) refers to the psychological tendency to forgo future benefits in favour of immediate benefits.

Peak oil (p. 401) is the tipping point at which new oil reserves can no longer be found, thus forcing society to rely on depleting reserves.

The **polluter pays principle** (p. 406) addresses the externality problem by charging fines or taxes to force a corporation or country that causes pollution to pay the cost of environmental cleanup and protection.

A **resource curse** (p. 404) arises in regions where valuable natural resources are especially abundant. Such abundance discourages democracy because privately owned natural resource industries provide government with most of its revenue, allowing them to exert excessive political influence and rendering government insufficiently politically accountable to taxpayers.

Risk management (p. 409) is the process of establishing regulations for protecting the environment and health. Risk management is not a narrow, technical field so much as a political process.

The **risk society thesis** (p. 397) is that contemporary societies have become preoccupied with issues related to the distribution of social "bads," chief among them the environmental risks and externalities produced by industry.

Sustainable development (p. 397) is an industrialization strategy that attempts to address economic, social, and environmental concerns in a balanced way, by meeting the needs of the present generation without jeopardizing the ability of future generations to meet their needs.

A **tipping point** (p. 395) is a threshold beyond which a system unexpectedly, rapidly, and dramatically changes.

SUGGESTED READING

Hannigan, John. 2006. *Environmental Sociology*, 2nd ed. New York: Routledge. A definitive overview of the field.

Kolbert, Elizabeth. 2006. *Field Notes from a Catastrophe: Man, Nature and Climate Change.* London: Bloomsbury. An exceptionally clear and balanced analysis of the problem of climate change.

Nikiforuk, Andrew. 2010. *Tar Sands: Dirty Oil and the Future of a Continent.* Vancouver: GreystoneBooks. A comprehensive analysis of one of Canada's most pressing environmental issues.

CHAPTER 17

HEALTH AND AGING

Neena L. Chappell
Margaret J. Penning
UNIVERSITY OF VICTORIA

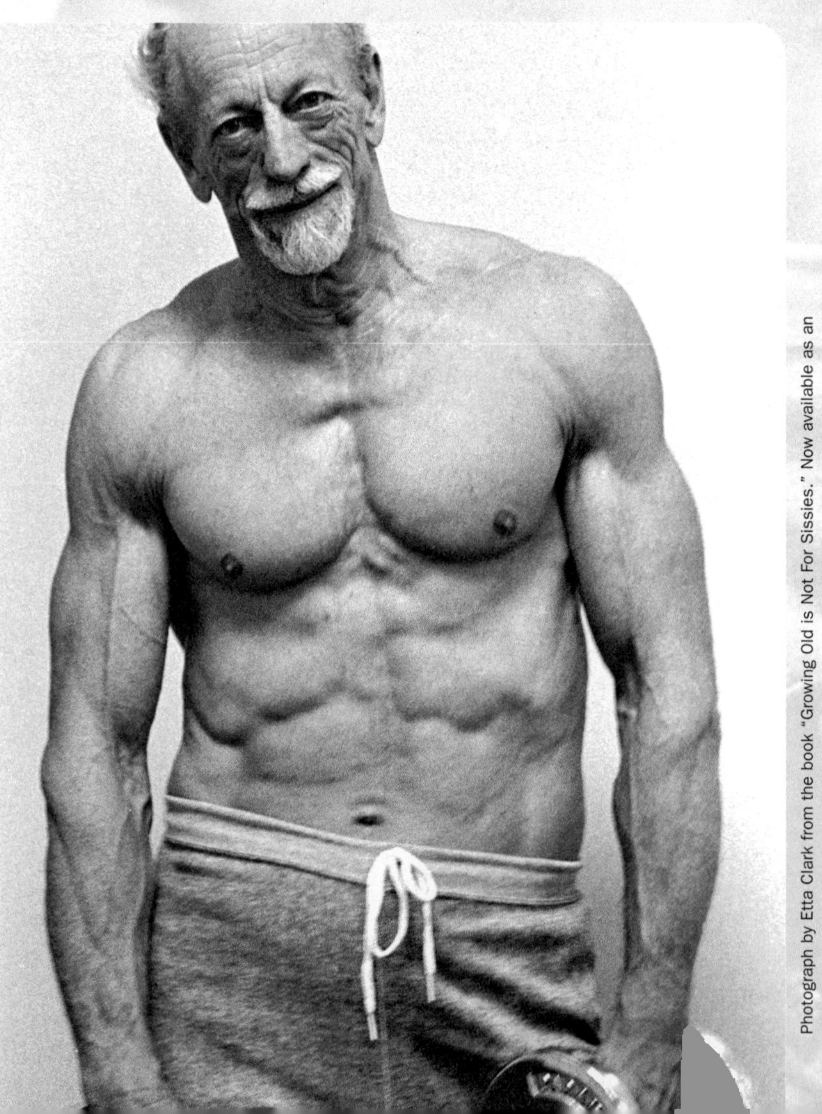

Photograph by Etta Clark from the book "Growing Old is Not For Sissies." Now available as an eBook in the iBook Library.

IN THIS CHAPTER YOU WILL LEARN THAT

- People are living longer and healthier lives than they did in the past. Although this is a triumph, we tend to consider the increasing size of the older population to be a social problem that has negative implications for demands on the nation's resources.
- Contrary to generally accepted beliefs, not all aspects of health decline as we age.
- In Canada, significant inequalities in health exist. Health varies with such factors as socioeconomic position, gender, Aboriginal status, ethnicity, race, and age.
- At all stages of life, the most common forms of healthcare include self-care and informal care, provided primarily by family members. Most people who provide healthcare are women.
- Recent years have seen an upswing in privatization and profit making in Canada's healthcare system, particularly for services that are most important to older adults. As a result, people who are most in need of care are the least likely to have access to it and the most likely to have to rely on themselves and their family members.

CHALLENGING COMMONSENSE BELIEFS ABOUT HEALTH AND AGING

We can learn much about health and aging from people's life stories. Each story has unique features, but we can find common elements in the social factors that influence them and provide the context within which they play out. For example, Jean was born in 1925 on a small farm, one of seven children of a Swedish immigrant mother and a Métis father. She graduated from high school, finished a year of teacher's college, and returned home to marry John, whom she had met a few years earlier. John had had a hard childhood and been forced to quit school after Grade 8 to work on the family farm. Together, they settled on a small farm across the road from his parents. John dreamed of the day when he could buy more land and make a good living for himself and his family. Until then, he worked in the local steel mill, tending to the farm during the evening and on weekends. Meanwhile, Jean supported him in his work, taking care of their children and his parents and doing various chores on the farm when she had time.

In 1953, John developed polio and spent the next year and a half in bed. Throughout his ordeal, Jean nursed him and cared for his parents. To make ends meet, she also worked the night shift as a nurse's aide at a local nursing home. Money was tight and there were numerous mouths to feed. With five children and another on the way, they were overjoyed when, after 12 years on the farm, they were able to add indoor plumbing. No more hand-washed diapers and no more running to the outhouse in the middle of winter! Living on a farm meant that although they could not afford much beyond necessities, there was always plenty to eat.

Over the years, economic circumstances improved as the children grew older and were able to help. Yet the years of poverty, hard work, and deprivation had left their mark. In 1991, at the age of 68, John died of a malignant brain tumour. Although no one was sure, family members speculated about whether it had anything to do with the years spent in the steel foundry and breathing in the chemical sprays that kept the weeds at bay on the farm. The pension that John earned at the steel mill did not provide Jean with an income so she was forced to sell the family farm and rent an old house close to one of her daughters, whose children she cared for as her daughter worked. However, helping became increasingly difficult as Jean's health declined. Although she had quit smoking as soon as she heard about the problems it caused, she had developed a cough that would not go away. It left her winded, and she was unable to walk very far. For several years, she had also battled weight problems and was eventually diagnosed with diabetes. A year after moving, Jean suffered a stroke and died before she could get to the hospital. She was 69—old from the point of view of someone in his or her 20s but not in terms of the life expectancy of women in Canada at the time. (**Life expectancy** is the number of years that the average person can expect to live.)

Jean's life story points to the many complexities we encounter when thinking about aging, health, and healthcare. When Jean died, people wondered, Why hadn't she taken better care of herself? Why did she let her weight go? Why hadn't she quit smoking before it became such a problem? Why didn't she get more exercise? Why had she opted to live in an area far from health services? After all, she was a bright and capable woman; if any woman could look after herself, it was Jean.

At Confederation, average life expectancy in Canada was 42 years. In 2008, it approached 81 years. The number of people aged 65 years and older has increased because of improved hygiene, sanitation, and nutrition, as well as healthcare.
SOURCE: © Monkey Business Images/Shutterstock.

The assumption that Jean should have been able to make choices that would have been more beneficial to her health ignores the complex role of social-structural factors, such as social class, gender, age, ethnicity, and rural-urban residence, in defining the available range of choices and their implications for health and longevity. During and after the Depression and World War II, living and working conditions were often harsh. Gender also played an important role. At the time Jean and John were married, family fortunes were generally tied to men's occupations and income levels. The fact that Jean's work was largely unpaid and that she assumed responsibility for the care of other family members, continually placing their needs (including their health) above her own, was typical of the experience of women at the time. As a Métis woman, Jean may also have experienced additional barriers in her ability to gain access to employment, healthcare, and other resources. By the time John died, Jean was experiencing the accumulated health effects of her earlier life circumstances. However, old age and its associated low status also appear to have played a role, possibly undermining her health further by limiting access to economic resources, affordable housing, and appropriate healthcare.

Sociology offers a lens through which to examine the social factors linked to people's health and longevity as they age. This chapter discusses these issues. In doing so, it brings together two areas of sociology often considered separately—the sociology of aging and the sociology of health and illness (also known as medical sociology). We can easily connect the two: aging tends to be equated with, and defined in terms of, ill health. Health tends to be a major problem in later life, and older adults account for much of the illness, disability, and healthcare use in any society.

We begin by focusing on individual and population aging and the role of social factors in influencing how people age. Next, we address health as people age, including the relations among social inequalities, health, healthcare, and aging. Finally, we examine health-related issues in Canada in the context of international and global trends in healthcare.

INDIVIDUAL AND POPULATION AGING

Today, most Canadians can expect to live to old age, barring accident and war. This was not always the case, as we can see in Table 17.1. In 1920, at birth, Canadian men lived to their late 50s on average, women to around 60. People can now expect to live more than 20 years longer than if they had been born in 1920. Once they reach age 65, they can expect to live even longer. In 2005, a 65-year-old could expect to live another 19.5 years (17.9 more if a man; 21.1 more if a woman) or to age 84.5. That is 4.1 years more than could be expected at birth. It is not until their 90s that men and women have approximately the same number of years left to live on average.

The fact that almost everyone can expect to live to old age distinguishes our era from earlier historical periods. In the past, some individuals lived as long as people live today, but never before has the vast majority lived to old age. With most of us now living to old age, it will not surprise you that older adults represent an increasing proportion of the Canadian population (see Box 17.1). In 1921, just over 5 percent of the population was age 65 and over; however, this cohort is projected to constitute 20 percent of the population by 2021 (Raina et al., 2009).

The main reason for the increasing proportion of older adults in the population is decreasing fertility. In Canada, the average number of children born per woman reached a peak of 3.9 in 1957 and subsequently declined; in 2011, it was 1.67 (Statistics Canada, 2011b). With declines in the number and proportion of children in the population, the proportion of older people necessarily increases. Fertility was the major predictor of population aging until the population reached a life expectancy at birth of 70 years of age. At that point, almost all young people survive. Further declines in mortality are now concentrated at the older ages (Chappell, McDonald, and Stones, 2008), resulting in relatively larger older age groups and thus contributing more to population aging. Deaths in old age usually result from chronic degenerative diseases. Cancer and circulatory diseases, including heart disease and stroke, are the major causes of death, followed by respiratory and infectious diseases (Statistics Canada, 2006a).

TABLE 17.1 LIFE EXPECTANCY IN CANADA, 1920–2005

YEAR	LIFE EXPECTANCY AT BIRTH FOR WOMEN	LIFE EXPECTANCY AT 65 FOR WOMEN	LIFE EXPECTANCY AT BIRTH FOR MEN	LIFE EXPECTANCY AT 65 FOR MEN	LIFE EXPECTANCY AT BIRTH FOR TOTAL POPULATION	LIFE EXPECTANCY AT 65 FOR TOTAL POPULATION
1920	61	77	59	76	60	76.5
1930	62	78	60	77	61	77.5
1940	66	79.7	63	77.7	64.5	78.7
1950	71	80	66	78	68.5	79
1960	74	80.5	68	78	71	79.3
1970	76	81.5	69	78	72.5	79.8
1980	79	82.5	72	78.5	75.5	80.5
1990	81	81.5	75	81.5	78	81.5
2000	82	85.6	76.9	82.2	79.3	84.1
2006-08*	83.1	86.5	78.5	83.5	80.9	85.0

*Computed by using data from these three years.

SOURCES: Human Resources and Skills Development Canada (2009); Munroe (2003); Organisation for Economic Co-operation and Development (2009); Statistics Canada (2003a, 2006b, 2011a).

BOX 17.1 DEFINING OLD AGE

In recent years, most of the world's developed countries, including Canada, have accepted the chronological age of 65 years as the definition of when old age begins. Otto von Bismarck, the late–nineteenth–century Chancellor of Germany, was the first to define a retirement age—at 70, workers were eligible to receive pensions. The decision increased the loyalty and productivity of workers but cost little because average life expectancy at the time was 45; Bismarck knew that most workers would die before receiving any pension payments. After von Bismarck, other countries (including the United States and the United Kingdom), followed suit, tending to adopt the age of 65 as the age at which people became eligible to retire with full social security benefits. In Canada, the age of 70 was first adopted but this was later changed to 65. In recent years, as people live longer and healthier lives, they increasingly question whether 65 should be the age of retirement. In Canada and the United Sates, most jurisdictions have now abolished mandatory retirement. In addition, the age at which people become eligible for full pension benefits is increasing in some countries.

We now live much of our lives assuming that an extended future is before us. Consequently, forward thinking has become realistic. Most of us now are members of multigenerational families. Unlike in the past, young people today often know their grandparents and even their great-grandparents. Increased longevity also means that the illnesses and disabilities accompanying old age are more prominent and that different demands are placed on the healthcare system than was the case when fewer people lived to old age. Longer life expectancy results in more healthcare and service jobs for the younger generation. It affects when people retire and what they do after they retire. Now that mandatory retirement has disappeared from virtually all Canadian provinces and territories, more people will likely continue to be employed into their 70s and 80s (see Figure 17.1).

FIGURE 17.1 CANADIAN POPULATION AGE STRUCTURE, 1851–2006 (POPULATION IN THOUSANDS)

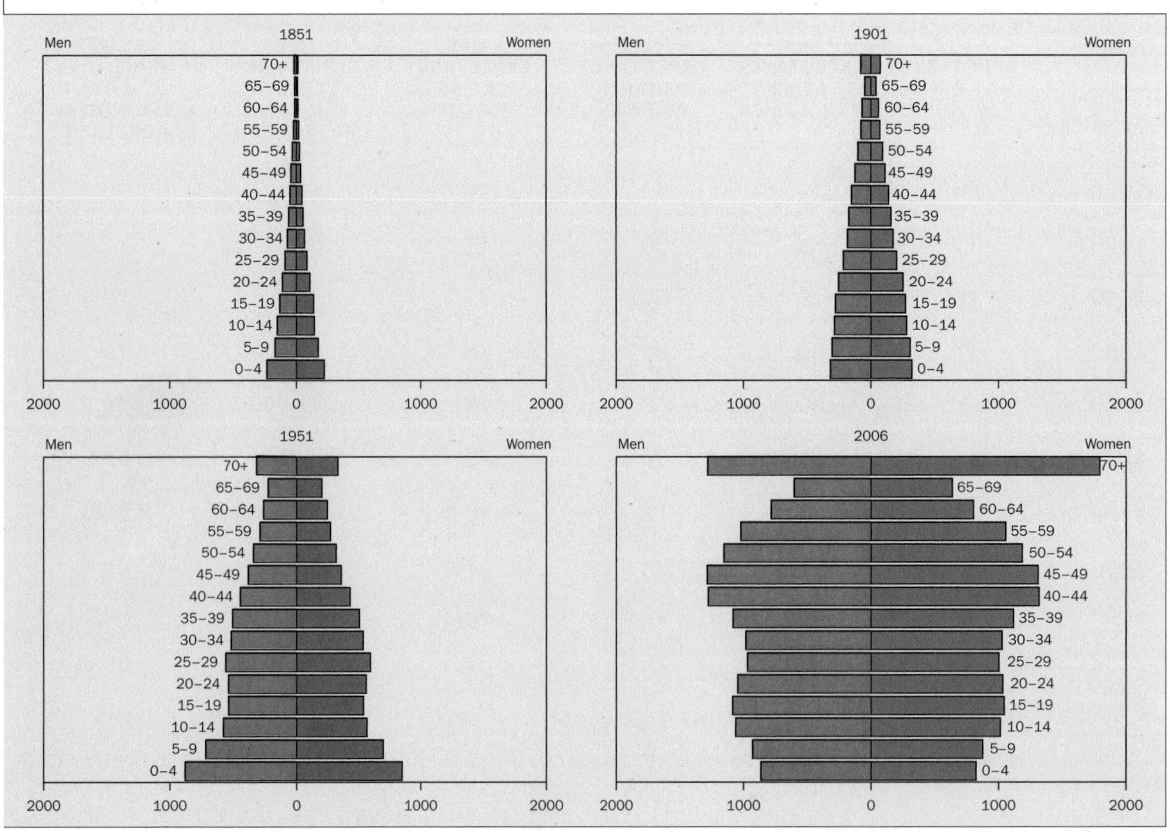

The social construction of old age—how society views older adults and the opportunities and constraints that are available to them—influences how older adults experience life. In contemporary Western societies, we tend to stereotype older people, a tendency referred to as **ageism.** We are inclined to see older adults as poor; frail; having no interest in, or capacity for, sexual relations; being socially isolated and lonely; and lacking a full range of abilities in the work place. Researchers have documented ageism in students' attitudes toward older people, healthcare treatment, literary and dramatic portrayals, humour, and legal processes (Chappell, McDonald, and Stones, 2008). They have called it a "quiet epidemic" that contributes to indifference (Stones and Stones, 1997). However, ageism speaks to our treatment of older people as a social category and not necessarily to interpersonal antagonism. We may treat our grandmothers well while also referring to and treating other older adults with indifference or even contempt.

Ageism exists for several reasons. Some analysts point to the importance of structural factors, such as the segregation of young and old cohorts in society and the fact that most older adults in Canada are outside of the paid labour force and therefore considered nonproductive members of society. This separation can also result in a lack of knowledge and interaction, which contribute to ageism (Hagestad and Uhlenberg, 2005). For example, students who have had positive interactions with older people and those who have learned about aging tend to have fewer negative attitudes toward seniors as a group (Ferraro, Freeman, Nellett, and Sheel, 2008; Palmore, 1988).

Other researchers attribute ageism to younger people's fears of their own future (Martens, Goldenberg, and Greenberg, 2005). Old age is associated with death and with declining health, including both physical and, in some instances, mental health. Indeed, old age has been medicalized, so that aging tends to be equated with disease. **Medicalization** refers to the social and political process whereby more and more areas of life come under the authority and control of medicine (Zola, 1983). Because of the legitimacy accorded to medicine in present-day society, the appropriate response to aging (when defined as disease) becomes treatment by physicians (Estes, 1979).

However, medicine often cannot cure much of what happens during old age, when chronic conditions are the most prevalent. For example, there is no definitive test for Alzheimer's disease (the most common type of dementia). Some older adults suffer from depression, which often has the same symptoms as dementia and is treatable, but if doctors diagnose them with dementia, they will face stigmatization and inappropriate pharmacological treatment.

Note too that not all cultures view the type of changed behaviour that tends to accompany dementia in the same manner. The Chinese, for example, view dementia as part of normal aging and less as a signal that the individual is ineligible for participation in social life. The West places high value on cognitive functioning and the ability to reason, Chinese culture embraces a dual concept of self that includes both mind and heart (affect). Affect is considered before, and as more authentic than, reason. Therefore, Chinese culture accepts people with dementia more readily (Ikels, 2002).

DIVERSITY IN AGING

Of course, not all people who are 65 or older are the same. Differences in age, class position, gender, race, ethnicity, rural-urban living environments, and other factors distinguish them. However, when we fail to recognize diversity and, instead, assume all older adults are the same, the result can be problematic. For example, it can lead to inaccurate beliefs and stereotypes, including belief in "apocalyptic demography." **Demography** is the study of the characteristics of populations and the dynamics of population change. The belief that population aging has drastic negative consequences for society is sometimes called apocalyptic demography (Gee, 2000). Apocalyptic demography reduces the complex issue of an aging population to the notion that society cannot afford a high and growing percentage of seniors. This judgment tends to be based on the view that nearly all older adults are poor, socially isolated, sick, and in need of medical services. Alternatively, others believe that most older adults are well off and can afford to pay for such services themselves; they presumably overuse publicly funded services. Either way, those who adopt such views argue that we should dismantle or at least cut back health and social services. Such sweeping generalizations of older adults are untrue and unhelpful, as will become clear later.

AGE DIFFERENCES

People who are considered seniors span about 30 years in age. Among them, age differences in health are evident, especially in terms of chronic conditions, functional disability, and injuries from falls. The older a person becomes, the more likely he or she is to have more chronic conditions and more severe functioning difficulties and to fall or sustain an injury from a fall (Chappell and Penning, 2012). Age also formally structures social relations in terms of when we can drive, marry, draw a pension, and so on. Informally, age-appropriate norms suggest that it is more acceptable for an older man to marry a considerably younger woman than for an older woman to marry a considerably younger man.

SOCIOECONOMIC AND CLASS DIFFERENCES

People who enjoy socioeconomic advantages tend to experience better health and live longer than others do. This fact is especially evident in middle age but extends into old age, when individuals generally are no longer part of the paid labour force (Mustard et al., 1997).

The prevalence of low income among seniors has decreased significantly in recent decades, from 30.4 percent in 1977 to 4.8 percent in 2007. Still, pockets of economic disadvantage persist. For example, in 2007, 13.9 percent of all older (65 and older) *unattached* adults in Canada lived below the low-income cutoff (see Chapter 6, Social Stratification). The figure was 13.0 percent for unattached older males and 14.3 percent among unattached older females (Colin and Jensen, 2009). The protection of living in a family is striking—only 1.1 percent of older adults living in families were living in poverty. Having few economic resources affects everyday life in profound ways: everything from the type of house and neighbourhood you live in to the schools you attend, the food you eat, the people you associate with, the leisure activities and vacations you can afford, and whether you have a car, a pension, investments, and much else. We carry these experiences into later life, with implications for our health.

GENDER

Some researchers consider aging a women's issue—for good reason. There are more senior women than senior men, and the gender imbalance increases in older age cohorts. In 2011, 56 percent of those aged 65 and over in Canada were women. The comparable figure for those aged 80 and over was 63 percent (Statistics Canada, 2011b). Women live longer than men do largely because of social and economic factors. Thus, the female-male difference in the **mortality rate** (deaths per thousand people in a population) is lower among more highly educated and wealthier people than among others (Rogers, Hummer, and Nam, 2000). This observation can be explained by a number of factors, including differences in smoking patterns (with men considerably more likely than women to smoke among those with lower, but not higher, education and income levels) and in work roles (with working-class men more often engaged in dangerous jobs, such as construction and mining, that increase the risk of an early death).

The gender difference in mortality rates has a number of important implications. It means that women are more likely to be widowed, not to remarry, and to live alone or in a nursing home in later life. They tend to be grandparents longer than men are and are more likely to be poor in old age, not only because of their general lower earning power when younger, but also because their savings have to cover a longer period. Women are likely to have more age peers in the same situation and are therefore able to maintain their social support networks into old age. Men tend to die before their spouses do because they have shorter life expectancies and because they tend to marry women younger than they are. Men who outlive their wives are more likely to remarry than are women who outlive their husbands. That is because, late in life, there are more unmarried women than men who are potential partners. Because it is socially acceptable for men to marry younger women, there is an even larger pool of potential partners from which senior men can choose. However, if they do not remarry, older men can be at greater risk of social isolation because they are less likely to maintain social support networks. Women are often the "kin keepers" in society, whereas men tend to rely on their wives for social connectedness.

ABORIGINAL STATUS

Aboriginal seniors compose fewer than 5 percent of Canada's total Aboriginal population because of high fertility rates and high mortality rates (and therefore shorter life expectancies; see Figure 17.2). However, it is expected that the number of Aboriginal seniors will more than double by 2017 and will represent about 6.5 percent of the Aboriginal population (Statistics Canada, 2005b). These older adults are more likely to live on reserves than are younger Aboriginal people, raising questions about the availability of appropriate care to older adults. Reserves, like most other rural locations across the country, see young adults leave for educational and employment opportunities in urban settings; most do not return.

FIGURE 17.2 ABORIGINAL AND NON-ABORIGINAL POPULATION AGE, 2006 (PERCENTAGE)

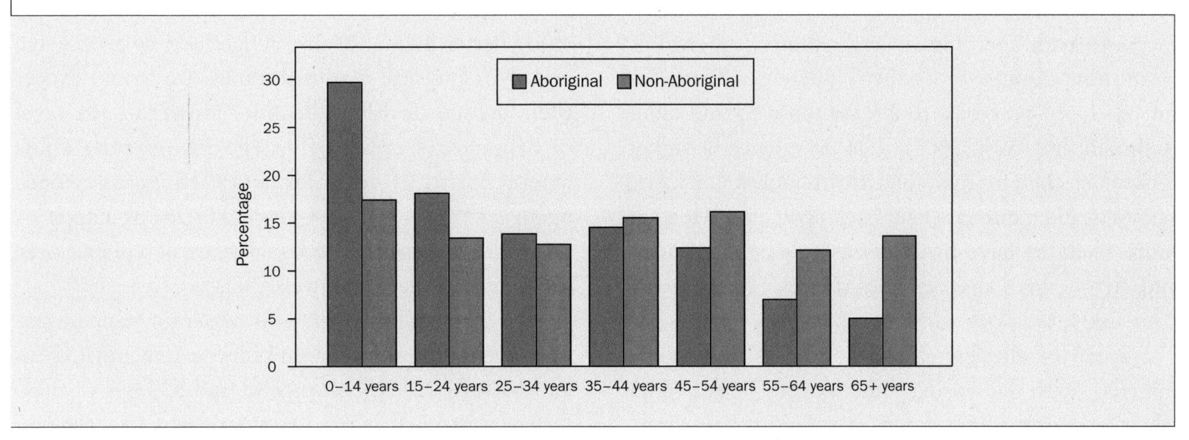

SOURCE: Statistics Canada (2008).

ETHNICITY AND RACE

Like gender and Aboriginal status, ethnicity and race represent fundamental organizing principles of society that are pervasive and socially constructed, and operate throughout the life course. Their effects are evident in the lack of social, economic, and political power of some racial and ethnic minorities. Among Canadian seniors, there are more foreign-born individuals than there are in the younger population. In 2006, 19.8 percent of Canada's total population was foreign-born, compared with 28 percent of the older adult (65 and older) population. Most foreign-born seniors immigrated to Canada when they were younger. Thus, the ethnocultural composition of our older adult population is heavily influenced by the immigration policies that were in effect in the past. For example, half a century ago, the government granted entry mainly to English- and French-speaking people from Europe and other Western countries. Most visible minority group members came to Canada only in recent decades. Thus, in 2006, only 8.5 percent of seniors were members of visible minority groups (see Box 17.2).

HEALTH AND OLD AGE

Old age tends to be associated with declining health. However, most older adults are not in poor health. Nor do psychological and emotional health and social well-being necessarily deteriorate in step with deteriorating physical health.

BOX 17.2 VISIBLE MINORITY SENIORS

Canadian immigration policy defines various categories of immigrants, including independent immigrants with educational and professional skills, close relatives of citizens and permanent residents of Canada, and business immigrants with substantial investment capital. In 2006, those born in Asia (including the Middle East) made up the largest proportion (58.3 percent) of newcomers to Canada, while those born in Europe made up the second largest group (16.1 percent). Europe used to be the main source region of immigrants. In 1971, Europe accounted for 61.6 percent of newcomers to Canada, while Asia accounted for only 12.1 percent (Statistics Canada, 2007b). This change means that future generations of Canadian seniors will be much more ethnically and racially diverse than is the case today.

Currently, more than 7000 older adults (65 and older) immigrate as permanent residents to this country every year, most often as family-class immigrants (Citizenship and Immigration Canada, 2011). Because members of their family sponsor them, their economic resources tend to be modest and they are not eligible for Old Age Security until after they have resided in Canada for 10 years. Many cannot communicate in English or French. For example, in one study of urban Chinese Canadian seniors, 83 percent chose to be interviewed in Cantonese, fewer than 25 percent spoke English well, and only 3 percent chose to be interviewed in English (Chappell, 2005).

The probability of having a long-term health condition and of having more than one such problem increases with age. The average number of chronic conditions ("multi-morbidity") increases from 1.9 for 65- to 74-year-olds to 2.5 for those 85 and older (Gilmour and Park, 2005). The prevalence is higher for women than for men for arthritis and rheumatism, cataracts and glaucoma, and back problems. Men are more likely to have heart disease, diabetes, cancer, and Alzheimer's disease (DesMeules, Turner, and Cho, 2004; Gilmour and Park, 2005).

Some of these conditions do not necessarily interfere with day-to-day functioning. Fewer older adults encounter limitations on activities than prevalence figures for chronic conditions suggest. For example, many people of all ages wear glasses because of deteriorating eyesight but function well with corrective lenses; when people with diabetes take their medication and follow appropriate nutritional and exercise regimens, they generally cope well. Many people with high blood pressure feel no effects; often they do not know they have the disease. A **functional disability** exists when a health problem interferes with day-to-day functioning. About 43 percent of adults aged 65 and older experience some restrictions in their daily activities, women more than men. This figure rises to 56 percent among those aged 75 and over (DesMeules, Turner, and Cho, 2004; Statistics Canada, 2004).

Pain is an important area of physical health that is not captured when examining disease, chronic conditions, and functional disability. Pain is a problem for many but certainly not all older adults. In Canada, 27 percent of people aged 65 and over living in the community suffer from chronic pain or discomfort; the figure is 38 percent for those living in institutions. This increases to 30 percent among those aged 75 and over. Women are more likely to suffer from chronic pain than are men. Some 84 percent of people suffering from chronic pain take some form of medication for their pain, either prescription or over-the-counter (Statistics Canada, 2004, 2008).

Mental disorders often have physical causes. Dementia is an example. In Canada, 6 to 8 percent of adults 65 years of age and older have dementia (Canadian Study of Health and Aging, 1994). About three-quarters of older adults with dementia live in long-term-care facilities. Rates increase the older a person becomes, rising to about 50 percent for people 90 years of age and older (Dubois and Hébert, 2006).

A correlation exists between mental and physical health. People in better physical health tend to enjoy better mental health. Therefore, as people age and their physical health declines, we would expect their mental health to decline. However, the level of happiness decreases after age 24, reaching a low among 35- to 44-year-olds, and then increases once again so that 55- to 64-year-olds are as happy as 18- to 24-year-olds. People 65 years of age and over are much happier (Helliwell, 2003).

In 2008, fully 79 percent of senior women and 77 percent of senior men said they were happy (Milan and Vézina, 2011). Self-esteem and feelings of mastery or control also seem to improve with age, peaking in middle age, followed by a modest decline in later life (Statistics Canada, 2001, 2007a). According to a recent national survey, fully 90 percent of adults aged 65 and over reported being satisfied with their lives. The figure was 84 percent among 15- to 24-year-olds (Statistics Canada, 2005a). It is unclear why older adults often have such good emotional health. Perhaps they have learned to cope with the exigencies of life or they compare themselves with those who are worse off (including those who have died). Perhaps the importance of material and physical matters wanes over time.

In a similar vein, the social lives of seniors tend to be healthy and characterized by social integration, not social isolation. A minority of older adults, particularly those who are poor, very old, or physically frail, are vulnerable to social isolation. However, most are embedded in a **modified extended family** (Litwak, 1960) characterized by mutual and close intergenerational ties, responsible filial behaviour, and contact between generations. Sociological research conducted over the past three decades has debunked the notion that families abandon their older members. Most seniors enjoy extensive social contacts, live close to at least one of their children, and can name friends and confidantes (Antonucci, 1990).

The conditions enjoyed by an increasingly large proportion of seniors have led sociologists to introduce the **compression of morbidity hypothesis** (Fries, 1983), which postulates that we will eventually postpone the age of onset of chronic disability so we will all be able to live relatively healthy lives until very shortly before death, when our bodies will deteriorate rapidly. Recent research suggests that although we are far from a dependency-free old age, many Canadians are experiencing a later age of onset of functional limitations. (However, the same is not necessarily true for people with chronic illnesses, such as diabetes.) This is good news, especially if the trend continues. Unfortunately, however, the vagaries of old age are not evenly distributed, as we will now see.

INEQUALITY, HEALTH, AND AGING

Research suggests that in recent decades the declining death rate has been steeper in some segments of the population than in others (Schalick, Hadden, Pamuk, Navarro, and Pappas, 2000). In general, people with more education, income, and wealth live longer than others do. They also tend to spend a greater proportion of their lives in good health.

Education

People with more education are able to avoid or postpone disability to a greater extent than are those with less education, although education may be of less benefit once disability is present (Huisman et al., 2005). People with a university degree often feel healthy and function well late into their 60s, 70s, and 80s, whereas those with less education do not (Ross and Wu, 1996). A recent Canadian study focused on changes in health over a three-year period among adults ages 50 and over, all of whom were in good health in the first year. It found that the likelihood of remaining in good health was greater among men and women in the highest educational and income groups (Buckley, Denton, Robb, and Spencer, 2005).

Income

Income is also important to health; it has been estimated that 23 percent of **premature mortality** (that is, years of potential life lost) among Canadians is linked to income differences (Raphael, 2005). One report shows that men with the lowest 5 percent of earnings before retirement are twice as likely to die between 65 and 70 years of age as are men with the highest 5 percent of earnings. High-income earners experience considerably more years of good health than those with lower incomes, with some reporting as much as a 12-year difference (Segall and Chappell, 2000). The pattern holds among older adults. Low-income seniors with disabilities tend to be more functionally disabled than are their high-income counterparts. As a result, even though people with low income are less likely to live to old age, those who do so are more likely to be institutionalized in long-term-care facilities than are those with higher incomes (Trottier, Martel, Houle, Berthelot, and Légaré, 2000).

Gender

Although women tend to live longer than men do, they are generally less healthy than men are. Thus, women report more multiple health problems associated with chronic conditions, such as arthritis and rheumatism, high blood pressure, back problems, and allergies (Chappell, McDonald, and Stones, 2008). The authors of one study found that 85 percent of senior women report one or more chronic conditions, compared with 78 percent of senior men. Although the likelihood of disability increases with age for both men and women, women are more likely to report limitations in activities of daily living or disability in later life than men are (Gilmour and Park, 2005). Women also report more severe disability than men do. That is, although men have lower life expectancy, they live a greater proportion of their lives without disabling conditions. While recent evidence suggests that men and women experience similar levels of mental health problems, they manifest them differently—for example, as depression in women and as alcohol and drug abuse and suicidal behaviour in men (Simon, 2000).

Aboriginal Status

In Canada, big differences exist between Aboriginal and non-Aboriginal adults in terms of health and well-being. Although the gap appears to have decreased somewhat in recent years, the life expectancy of Aboriginal Canadians currently remains six years less than that of non-Aboriginals (Cooke, Mitrou, Lawrence, Guimond, and Beavon, 2007). Differences are also evident *within* the Aboriginal population (see Figure 17.3). Aboriginal populations suffer from more chronic illnesses, including heart disease and diabetes, than non-Aboriginal populations do (Anand et al., 2001). They also have higher disability levels. In 2001, 70 percent of Aboriginal adults ages 65 and over living off-reserve reported one or more disabilities, including difficulties hearing, seeing, walking, climbing stairs, bending, and doing various other activities, nearly twice the rate for non-Aboriginal people of the same age (Statistics Canada, 2007b). Although most older Canadian adults rate their health as excellent or very good, fewer than half of non-reserve Aboriginal adults over the age of 64 report having excellent or very good health.

Reasons for these differences in health and life expectancy are numerous. In Aboriginal populations, death from infectious and parasitic diseases is

FIGURE 17.3 ABORIGINAL AND NON-ABORIGINAL CANADIANS' LIFE EXPECTANCY AT BIRTH BY SEX, 1991 AND 2001

Years: 90, 80, 70, 60, 50

Males 1991 | Males 2001 | Females 1991 | Females 2001

Total Canadian population | North American Indian population | Métis population | Inuit population

SOURCE: Statistics Canada (2007b).

associated with inadequate housing and unsanitary conditions. According to one government report, 75 percent of Aboriginal community water systems pose a high or medium risk to water quality (Indian and Northern Affairs Canada, 2003). Suicide rates are also high, as are death rates from drowning, fire, homicide, and motor vehicle accidents (Allard, Wilkins, and Berthelot, 2004). Racism and discrimination increase the risk of psychological distress, depression, and unemployment, and lack of access to opportunities and resources is conducive to poor health (Noh, Beiser, Kaspar, Hou, and Rummens, 1999).

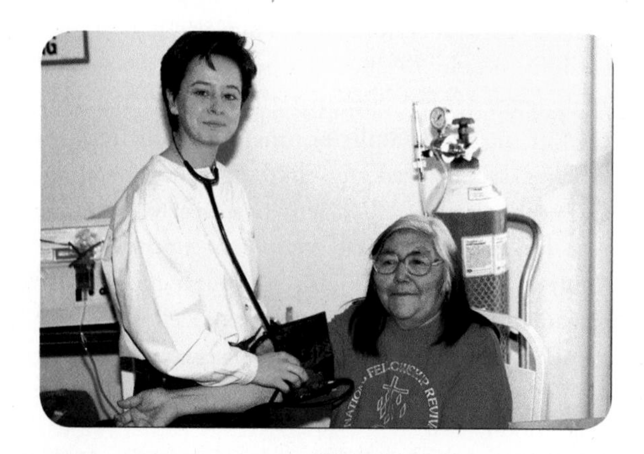

The life expectancy of Aboriginal Canadians is about six years shorter than that of non-Aboriginal Canadians.
SOURCE: © Photodisc.

Race, Ethnicity, and Immigration Status

Health inequities are also evident when we compare other ethnic and racial groups. Health and longevity vary widely from one country to the next (see Table 17.2). Less than one-quarter of Canadians aged 65 and over who were born in Canada, the United States, Europe, Australia, and Asia report fair or poor health. This percentage is considerably higher (about 33 percent) among those born in Central and South America and Africa (Chappell, McDonald, and Stones, 2008). Interestingly, however, immigrants, especially recent arrivals, generally enjoy better health than their Canadian-born counterparts do, a pattern observed to varying degrees for such health outcomes as chronic diseases, disability, dependency, life expectancy, and disability-free life expectancy (Chen, Ng, and Wilkins, 1996). This **healthy immigrant effect** may seem surprising at first glance. However, it likely reflects the Canadian government requirement that potential immigrants meet a minimum standard of health before being admitted to the country. Immigrants who have lived in Canada for a long period do not have a similar advantage. Does this mean that immigrants' health tends to decline after immigration? In fact, this seems to be what is taking place (Pérez, 2002). The search is on for explanations of this phenomenon. Most analysts focus on the negative health implications of changes in diet and activity

TABLE 17.2 LIFE EXPECTANCY AT BIRTH AND AT AGE 60 FOR SELECTED COUNTRIES WITH HIGH AND LOW LIFE EXPECTANCY, 2011

		LIFE EXPECTANCY AT BIRTH		REMAINING YEARS OF LIFE EXPECTED AT AGE 60	
Country or Area	**Year**	**Women**	**Men**	**Women**	**Men**
Afghanistan	2010–2015	49	49	15	14
Australia	2010–2015	84	80	26	23
Canada	**2010–2015**	**83**	**79**	**25**	**22**
Hong Kong	2010–2015	86	80	28	23
France	2010–2015	85	78	27	20
Japan	2010–2015	87	80	29	23
Kenya	2010–2015	59	57	18	17
Mozambique	2010–2015	52	50	17	16
Rwanda	2010–2015	57	54	17	16
Swaziland	2010–2015	49	50	17	15
Sweden	2010–2015	84	80	26	22
United Kingdom	2010–2015	82	78	25	22
United States	2010–2015	81	76	25	22
Zimbabwe	2010–2015	53	54	19	17

SOURCE: United Nations Department of Economic and Social Affairs, Population Division (2011).

levels, discrimination, declines in income and other resources, and difficulties in accessing healthcare services in the years immediately following immigration (Gee, Kobayashi, and Prus, 2004).

EXPLAINING SOCIAL INEQUALITIES IN HEALTH

What exactly is it about age, gender, Aboriginal status, ethnicity, race, social class, and other inequalities that result in poorer health? Early research focused on biological explanations and on differences associated with health services use, including differences in the likelihood that people would follow doctors' orders and inequalities in access to healthcare services. Indeed, the view that creating a universally equitable healthcare system would eliminate or at least reduce health inequalities was a major argument for the creation of a universal healthcare system in this country. More recently, evidence that inequalities in health and longevity have persisted despite the introduction of a universal healthcare system has led to renewed attempts to account for such differences (Crompton, 2000). Some researchers have offered explanations that are specific to one or another type of inequality. Others have focused on explanations associated with many sources of inequality. In general, the literature highlights three types of explanations: one focusing on individual health behaviours and lifestyles, one on social psychological resources, and one on material conditions and resources.

Many researchers argue that health inequalities reflect the impact of individual behaviours and lifestyles, including whether people smoke, consume excessive amounts of alcohol, eat foods high in fat and sugar, and lack regular exercise. People often consider lifestyles to be freely chosen. For example, one survey asked Canadians what the major determinants of health are. The most common responses referred to such factors as those just listed (Canadian Institute for Health Information, 2005).

Although research finds a link between social location and lifestyle factors, sociologists often criticize such explanations because they ignore how social inequalities can trump individual decisions in determining health outcomes (see Box 17.3). Thus, studies comparing the importance of individual decisions against social factors, such as income adequacy, often find that the latter are more important (House, 2001; Williamson, 2000). Moreover, when researchers focus on individual decision making, they often neglect the fact that people rarely make choices freely from a full range of possible options. We can criticize low-income earners for failing to exercise more, but only if we ignore that they may live in neighbourhoods where an evening jog is dangerous, affordable

When surveyed, Canadians identified a person's smoking, eating, weight, experience of stress, and exercise habits as the major determinants of health.

SOURCE: © Neil Roy Johnson/Shutterstock.

BOX 17.3 WHICH TIPS FOR BETTER HEALTH ARE CONSISTENT WITH THE EVIDENCE?

Governments, health associations, and health workers give the public a host of messages related to health issues. Traditional health tips focus on individual decision making and assume that ordinary people are entirely free to decide what to do with their lives. A second set of health tips takes a sociological approach and is more consistent with available evidence on the determinants of health. Contrast the two sets of messages below.

TRADITIONAL, INDIVIDUALISTIC TIPS FOR BETTER HEALTH:

1. Don't smoke. If you can, stop. If you can't, cut down.
2. Eat a balanced diet with plenty of fruits and vegetables.
3. Keep physically active.
4. Manage stress by, for example, talking things through and making time to relax.
5. If you drink alcohol, do so in moderation.
6. Cover up in the sun, and protect children from sunburn.
7. Practice safe sex.
8. Use cancer-screening opportunities.
9. Be safe on the roads.
10. Learn the first aid ABCs: airway, breathing, circulation.

TEN SOCIOLOGICAL TIPS FOR BETTER HEALTH:

1. Don't be poor. If you can, stop. If you can't, try not to be poor for long.
2. Don't have poor parents.
3. Don't own a car.
4. Don't work in a stressful, low-paid manual job.
5. Don't live in damp, low-quality housing.
6. Be able to afford to go on a foreign holiday.
7. Don't become unemployed.
8. Use all benefits you are entitled to if you are unemployed, retired, or sick or have a disability.
9. Don't live next to a busy road or near a polluting factory.
10. Learn how to fill in the complex housing benefit/asylum application forms before you become homeless and destitute.

By contrasting these two sets of health tips, we do not mean to suggest that people lack all choice, only that choices are socially structured.

SOURCE: D. Raphael, 2005, *Social Determinants of Health: Canadian Perspectives*, Toronto: Canadian Scholars' Press, p.13. Reprinted by permission of Canadian Scholars' Press Inc.

recreational facilities don't exist, and lack of child-care options means they have little time for such pursuits in any event. As this example shows, social inequalities structure choices. Attending only to individual decision making often amounts to blaming victims for structured inequalities.

A second explanation for how social location generates health inequalities draws attention to the role of stress and other psychosocial factors, including depression and perceptions of relative deprivation. From this perspective, inequality and lack of access to economic and other resources generate stress, leading to poor health. In addition, some analysts argue that more than poverty is at work here. They note that if poverty were the only problem, we would expect to find substantial differences in health between the poor and the nonpoor, but little or no difference between those who are only moderately well off versus those who are wealthy. Yet this is not the case. Instead, each increment in education and income brings additional health advantages. This finding suggests that it is not just poverty but the *perception* or *awareness* of inequality that leads to bad health. This is the **hierarchy stress perspective,** which suggests that when people compare their situation with that of others and see their situation negatively, they experience stress and their health declines (Link and Phelan, 2000). In addition to causing poor health, stress can operate indirectly by leading people to smoke tobacco, consume too much alcohol, eat too much or too little, sleep too little, and take dangerous drugs—all of which eventually have a negative impact on health in their own right (Link and Phelan, 2000).

Finally, some explanations emphasize resources and material conditions as the mechanisms linking people's social location to health outcomes. Such arguments hold that people's social class, age, gender, race, ethnicity, and so on, contribute to differential access to a range of resources that contribute to good or poor health. These resources include enough income to buy nutritious food, enough education to be aware of health issues (such as what constitutes a nutritious diet), access to means of illness prevention, the ability to avoid risk factors (such as living in environments where dangerous chemicals are present), and so on (Link and Phelan, 2000). Some researchers operating in this tradition insist that we should focus less on the resources that contribute to good or poor health and more on the way social class, age, gender, race, and ethnicity directly contribute to "systematic material, social, cultural, and political exclusion from mainstream society" (Raphael, 2005: 4). These structural factors are therefore considered to be fundamental causes of health status, influencing access to health-related resources, which, in turn, influence health (Link and Phelan, 2000; see Box 17.4).

BOX 17.4 WHY WE HAVEN'T WON THE WAR ON CANCER

Genes by themselves are responsible for just 5 to 10 percent of all cancers and a substantially smaller percentage of cancers in people over the age of 25. In other words, although genetic mutations cause all cancers, environmental factors cause more than 90 percent of the genetic mutations leading to cancer. "Environment" in this context means anything that people interact with, including exposures resulting from what we eat, drink, or smoke; natural and medical radiation; drugs; socioeconomic factors that affect exposures and susceptibility; and substances in air, water, and soil.

If environmental carcinogens cause more than 90 percent of the genetic mutations resulting in cancer, it follows that we can win the war on cancer by eliminating the offending substances or at least drastically reducing their prevalence and our contact with them. Unfortunately, the structure of our society makes it difficult for us to take preventive measures, partly because many people lack the resources that would allow them to, partly because industry and government resist change. This is the cancer paradox: although we know how to reduce the cancer incidence rate drastically, we have not been able to do so.

For example, tobacco consumption and poor diet (especially consuming too much red meat, animal fat, salt, sugar, and alcohol) cause more than 60 percent of cancers. Environmental pollution and exposure to hazardous substances at work account for another 10 percent or so. However, people who avoid these hazards tend to be comparatively well educated and well to do.

Even when low-income and less educated people know about the need to stop smoking and improve their diets, urging them to do so tends to have little effect. That is because the conditions of their existence conspire against them. At work, they are more likely to experience little control and

(*continued*)

BOX 17.4 ***(continued)***

high stress than higher income and better-educated people are. At home, they are more likely to face marital stress and divorce because of money problems. They are therefore more likely to turn to tobacco and alcohol to help them feel better in the short term. They are also more likely than better-educated and higher-income people are to be exposed to carcinogens at work. Miners, construction workers, people who work with asbestos, welders, petroleum refinery workers, rubber industry workers, textile industry workers, footwear production and repair workers, hairdressers, farmers, paint manufacturing workers, house painters, furniture and cabinet makers, machine shop workers, and garage mechanics all have elevated cancer incidence rates. In their neighbourhoods, they tend to suffer relatively high exposure to air and water pollutants that contribute to cancer risk because on average they live closer to dirty industries and industrial waste sites than others do. Because of their low income, they often find unhealthy foods within their budget and healthy foods too expensive. The notion that people in such circumstances are free to lower their cancer risk is naive to say the least.

Given the situation just described, you might think that governments and voluntary associations concerned with cancer would be investing heavily in research on how disadvantaged people can gain the educational, organizational, and political resources needed to change health, environmental, industrial, and social policy in a way that would lower their exposure to cancer risk. However, if we break down the $402 million that the Canadian government and voluntary associations spent in 2007 on cancer research, we find nothing of the kind. Some 55.1 percent of this sum went to investigating the biology and causes of the disease. Another 43.1 percent went to research on detection, diagnosis, prognosis, treatment, and related efforts. Just 1.8 percent—$7 million—was allocated to work on prevention. These sums refer just to research budgets. If we added the medical costs of dealing with cancer, the imbalance between the massive effort aimed at cure versus the paltry effort aimed at prevention would be even more glaring.

Funding priorities remain what they are because powerful industrial interests, governments, and segments of the population benefit economically from a bias toward finding cures rather than taking preventive action. A reorientation of policy would cause them financial harm. For example, cleaning up cancer "hot spots," such as Windsor and Sarnia, Ontario, Fort Chipewyan, Alberta, and Sydney, Nova Scotia, would involve massive expense and industrial dislocation on the part of major petrochemical and other companies. Or consider the cost of creating a string of "wellness centres" in low-income neighbourhoods across Canada to equalize opportunities across classes for good health and longevity. Such neighbourhood institutions could offer tasty and healthy meals for the same price as a Big Mac, medium fries, and a Coke, with menus formulated to suit the ethnic tastes of area residents. They could offer free nicotine patches and support groups for people wanting to quit smoking; free on-site cancer screening facilities; free counselling services for people facing marital or work-related stress; free competitive and instructional basketball, soccer, dance, and swimming activities for all age groups; and ads everywhere (multilingual where necessary) featuring famous role models promoting the new centres. How would McDonald's respond to the competition? How would taxpayers (most of them middle-, upper-middle, and upper-class) respond to the required expense?

SOURCE: Adapted from Brym et al. (2012: 81–102).

Debate continues regarding whether individual behaviours and lifestyle characteristics, stress and other psychosocial factors, or material conditions and resources are more important for understanding inequalities in health. The answer may well be "all of the above." As one study notes, "material conditions are intimately tied to psychological states, health behaviors, and social circumstances that also influence health," and we can see "these psychosocial states and health behaviors ... as responses to adverse conditions imposed by broader social and economic structures" (Lynch and Kaplan, 2000: 25).

INTERSECTING INEQUALITIES AND HEALTH OVER THE LIFE COURSE

Increasingly, sociologists are interested in the effects of multiple statuses on health outcomes. For example, the **age as leveller hypothesis** argues that age effects cut across all other statuses, in effect levelling inequalities from earlier in life. The competing **multiple jeopardy hypothesis** argues that the effects of membership in multiple low-status groups are cumulative. Thus, being female and old has more negative consequences than being either female *or* old (Markides, 1983).

More recently, researchers have argued that statuses cannot simply be added together to judge their effects. Instead, statuses interact, and we cannot fully understand them apart from one other (McMullin, 2004). For example, education and occupational status influence health but do so differently for men and women. Living in poverty has a stronger negative effect on women's health than on men's health (Prus and Gee, 2002). As a result, the greatest differences in life expectancy between men and women occur in the poorest areas (DesMeules, Manuel, and Cho, 2004). Similarly, the gap in perceived health status of Aboriginal peoples and the total Canadian population widens in older age groups (Statistics Canada, 2003b).

Conversely, some factors shrink health inequalities later in life. For example, the gap between upper- and lower-income groups increases as people reach their middle years (40s, 50, and 60s) and declines thereafter (Martel, Bélanger, Berthelot, and Carrière, 2005). Does this mean that socioeconomic inequalities in health diminish with age? This seems unlikely because many poor people die before reaching old age, a fact that comparisons of the health status of survivors ignores.

Finally, we note that, as a person ages, the social and economic factors that influence health change. According to the **life course perspective,** the circumstances experienced at all stages of life (including infancy, childhood, adolescence, young adulthood, and later adulthood) combine to influence what happens in later life. Some events and circumstances experienced earlier in life (for example, a car accident that leaves a person unable to walk) will affect that person's health for life regardless of what else happens later on. However, the impact of other events or circumstances is likely to accumulate gradually over the life course. Over time, a person may experience a number of events or situations (such as a car accident, subsequent unemployment, and the death of a spouse) that may have a negative impact on health. These events may be unrelated to one another. However, it is common for adverse exposures to be related. Children born into poor social and economic circumstances are more likely to have low birth weights, be exposed to poor diets, experience passive smoke exposure, and have below-average educational opportunities. These early life experiences are likely to continue in adulthood. Longevity and health in later life is likely to be a product of all these factors.

HEALTHCARE

How we view the causes of health problems influences how we deal with them. If we see the health problems of older adults as the result of what happens only in later life, we will target interventions to older adults. If we adopt a life course perspective and conclude that many of the health problems of seniors have their roots in lifelong experiences, we will want to address what happens early in life as well. If we attribute health problems to freely chosen personal behaviours, we will consider older adults responsible for their own health problems and will likely implement solutions aimed at educating people to make different choices in the future; or we will demand that people deal with the problems they themselves have created. If we attribute health inequalities to perceptions of stress, we may focus on altering how people view their circumstances rather than changing the circumstances themselves. If we see the organization of society and the distribution of economic and social resources as the main determinants of health, we will see economic and social policies as a means of improving health (Raphael, 2005). How then do Canadians deal with healthcare?

SELF-CARE AND INFORMAL CARE

Most people care for themselves most of the time; **self-care** is the primary form of care even when health declines and we require help from others and the healthcare system. We wash our hands, exercise, choose what to eat, establish any number of lifestyle practices, try to have a positive outlook on life, and select healthcare providers.

Except in emergencies, we generally turn first to family members and friends when we need help because of our health. This is true in old age and when we are young. Indeed, throughout history, networks of family members and friends have been the first resource for care.

Despite what you may hear about modern, Western societies such as Canada being individualistic, youth-oriented, and dismissive of older adults, we continue to care for older family members in need. In virtually all developed societies, about three-quarters of all care to seniors comes from family members and, to a lesser degree, friends (Cranswick, 2003; Kane, 1990). Typically, the spouse first provides care when the health of the other spouse fails; typically, the wife provides care for her husband.

Regardless of the resources that the healthcare system makes available, most older adults first turn to family members for care. SOURCE: © Shutterstock.

After the husband's death, the wife may enjoy a few more years of good health before she needs assistance. Her children, usually her daughters, provide most of the care before her death. Notice that informal caring comes primarily from wives and daughters. Sons provide mainly financial assistance and advice, while daughters provide mainly emotional support and hands-on care. However, if no daughter is available and a son is close by, then the son usually provides the necessary care (Keating, Fast, Frederick, Cranswick, and Perrier, 1999). This is possible because the great majority of older adults live close to at least one child

Usually, families readily assume responsibility for the care of seniors. Research has put to rest the myth that families in contemporary Western societies abandon seniors (Montgomery, Borgatta, and Borgatta, 2000). Moreover, despite what we have been hearing for many years about changing family forms, more women working in the paid labour force, fewer children being available to provide help, and greater geographic mobility, there is no indication that families are decreasing their involvement in senior care.

FORMAL MEDICAL AND HOME CARE

Often, family members cannot provide all the care loved ones need. Sometimes care calls for specialized knowledge, skills, medicine, and equipment that only physicians or other healthcare personnel can provide. Sometimes the sheer amount of time and effort required exceeds the family's capabilities. In such cases, people turn to the formal healthcare system. Canada's publicly funded healthcare system, like the healthcare systems of other wealthy countries (the United States excepted), offers universal access to physician and acute care hospital services for its citizens based on need rather than the ability to pay. In Canada, this system is known as medicare.

A Brief History of Medicare

Before the establishment of medicare, people needing healthcare were required to pay for it or do without. This situation was especially problematic for poor people whose health needs were often great—among them a disproportionately large number of older adults, the unemployed, and those with chronic disabilities. Gaps in access to healthcare were particularly apparent in the years following World War I and the Depression of the 1930s. With Tommy Douglas, the leader of the CCF party and premier of Saskatchewan, leading the way, Canada gradually introduced legislation to address these needs. In 1957, the Hospital Insurance and Diagnostic Services Act led to hospital care coverage for the entire population. In 1966, the Medical Care Act laid the groundwork for universal health insurance for physician services. By 1972, all Canadian provinces and territories had joined the program, with the federal government sharing physician and hospital services costs on a 50/50 basis with the provinces and territories.

From the outset, healthcare in Canada was structured as a provincial and territorial responsibility. The federal government develops policy and assists with funding, but each province and territory is responsible for delivering services. Through medicare, every province and territory offers publicly funded physician and acute care hospital services. This does not mean that we have "socialized medicine." Rather, a third party (the government) pays for most services on our behalf. Most physicians in Canada operate as private entrepreneurs; governments pay them for the services they decide are necessary and that they render. In other words, we publicly finance healthcare but physicians provide it privately, with payment guaranteed by the government. The more services physicians provide, the more they earn. They hold this privileged position because of the importance society attaches to their expertise, which makes them the gatekeepers to our healthcare system. Only physicians can order medical tests and prescription drugs, admit us to hospital, and certify that we are sick.

Historically, we defined health as the absence of disease, thereby excluding from coverage preventative measures and broad holistic views of health. We did not cover many types of healthcare, such as dentistry, home care, nursing homes, physiotherapy, counselling, podiatry, drugs prescribed outside hospital, chiropractic services, midwifery, and massage therapy. Coverage for such services varies within and across provinces and territories. Some jurisdictions provide some of these services as part of their healthcare system at no cost to the user. Others provide them at minimal cost or on a means-tested basis whereby people's finances are assessed. If they can afford a required service, they pay for it. Otherwise, government subsidizes the cost. Access to such services also varies. For example, some places require physician referral while others permit self-referral.

Home-Care Services in an Aging Society

Although different healthcare services are important to different people at different times, one type of healthcare service that is especially important in an aging society is home care. It brings services into people's homes, where they prefer to live, rather than requiring them to move to a nursing home. It is also much less expensive that maintaining them in nursing homes (Chappell, Havens, Hollander, Miller, and McWilliam, 2004; Chappell and Hollander, 2011).

Typically, home care includes personal care, nursing, and physiotherapy services. It can also include housekeeping, adult daycare, and respite services. Home care is not primarily about providing medical care. It offers social care that a medical condition prevents us from providing for ourselves, such as home support, housekeeping, and the company of others. For many older adults, staying in their own homes requires not only home care but also the presence of an unpaid caregiver. Despite its enormous importance, home care accounts for just 2 to 4 percent of public healthcare expenditures (Canadian Home Care Association, 2004). Today, most provinces are moving to more private, for-profit provision of home care.

HEALTHCARE SYSTEM CHANGE AND REFORM

In the years following the establishment of medicare, the cost of healthcare rose steadily. As a result, by the 1980s, the federal government had shifted away from its agreement to share the costs of healthcare 50/50 with the provinces and territories to a form of block funding, giving provinces and territories a set amount of money to cover healthcare services. In response, the provinces and territories began experimenting with user fees and extra billing to offset federal funding cuts. In response, in 1984, the federal government passed the Canada Health Act requiring the provinces and territories to maintain universal coverage, reasonable access to services, portability of benefits across provinces and territories, comprehensive services, and nonprofit administration by a public agency. It also banned user fees and extra billing.

Fiscal concerns remained. In the late 1980s and 1990s, the provinces, territories, and federal government further restricted healthcare spending and appointed commissions to review the system. Public debate erupted around the viability of a publicly funded healthcare system, and within government, the discussion broadened from concerns over financing to whether we need a different type of healthcare system. For the first time since the introduction of medicare, Canadian citizens and governments began to ask whether the right providers were providing the right services to the right people.

Without denying the importance of medical care by physicians, nearly all government reviews reached the same conclusion: we need to shift away from a system that is almost entirely biomedical and concerned only with the treatment and cure of disease, and acknowledge that health is "a state of complete physical, mental, and social well-being and not merely the absence of disease or infirmity" (World Health Organization, 1948). This definition implies a broad conception of care that incorporates health promotion, disease prevention, and attention to the social and environmental determinants of health. Deinstitutionalizing health services and providing more care outside hospitals was also recommended.

Major reforms followed. Most provinces regionalized healthcare services, fewer people received acute and extended care, hospital admissions fell, length of hospital stays dropped, and many surgical treatments moved to outpatient settings (Brownell, Roos, and Roos, 2001; Carriere, Roos, and Dover, 2000;

Canadian Institute for Health Information, 2007). However, a broadening of public healthcare did not occur (Lewis, Donaldson, Mitton, and Currie, 2001). To date, there is little evidence of an expanded focus on health promotion and disease prevention. Nor has attention shifted toward dealing with the social and environmental determinants, including poverty and inequality. Increases to home-care budgets were directed mainly to short-term post-hospital and nursing care, reinforcing a medical focus, rather than meeting the long-term chronic care needs of older adults (Penning, Brackley, and Allan, 2006). Indeed, healthcare reform is now narrowing the scope back to medical care. Why? As we will now see, the answer is linked to the internationalization of capital, often referred to as globalization.

GLOBALIZATION AND PROFIT MAKING

Economic globalization involves the use of a variety of technologies to boost transnational investment, finance, advertising, and consumption, thereby increasing the profits of multinational corporations (see Chapter 19, Globalization). Proponents of globalization emphasize the need for privatization and profitization. **Privatization** involves turning publicly owned organizations into privately owned companies, some of which can be not-for-profit. **Profitization** involves turning institutions into profit-making organizations. Both expand the opportunities available for big business but render low-income citizens less well protected.

Recent changes in Canada's healthcare system, including shortened hospital stays, removal of beds from the system, and the decline of long-term chronic home care, allow increasing profitization, the goal of the neoliberal agenda of globalization (Williams, Deber, Baranek, and Gildiner, 2001). Citizens, as consumers, are being asked to seek services privately that were once provided by the public sector. Private funding accounts for an increasing share of Canada's healthcare budget, including home-care expenses (Armstrong, Armstrong, and Coburn, 2001). Of concern is that the terms of the North American Free Trade Agreement (NAFTA) can be interpreted as meaning that once the Canadian government allows businesses to enter an area previously in the public sector, returning it to the public sector is permissible only if the government compensates for-profit firms for lost future profits—practically an impossibility. That is why a 2002 Royal Commission devoted an entire chapter of its report to arguing that Canada must state publicly and at every opportunity that our healthcare services are not to be included in NAFTA (Commission on the Future of Health Care in Canada, 2002). Government has failed to do so.

For-profit healthcare tends to be more expensive than universal public schemes. For-profit healthcare costs governments less, but people who use the services pay more. Much of the increased cost comes from administrative overhead charges (Marmor and Sullivan, 2000; see Figure 17.4). A for-profit system

FIGURE 17.4 ADMINISTRATIVE COSTS AS A PERCENTAGE OF HEALTHCARE SPENDING, SELECTED COUNTRIES

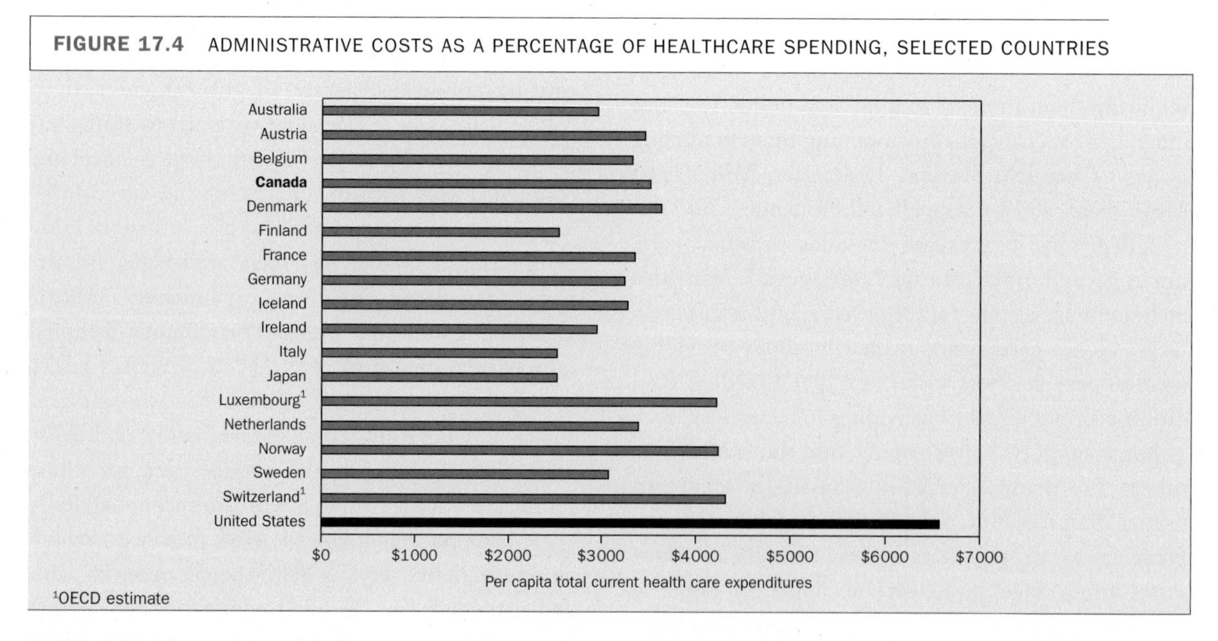

SOURCE: OECD (2011), Health at a Glance 2011: OECD Indicators. OECD Publishing. On the World Wide Web at http://dx.doi.org/10.1787/health_glance-2011-en.

also leaves many citizens without any health insurance. In the United States, one-sixth of the population lacked health insurance and another one-sixth lacked adequate coverage before President Obama's 2010 healthcare reform (DeNavas-Walt, Proctor, and Smith, 2010). In the period 2010-14, health insurance coverage will broaden, although tens of millions of Americans will remain uninsured or underinsured after 2014—most of them poor, illegal immigrants, or both. Canada's medicare system provides basic care to all people in need although some research suggests this is not the case for specialist services (Dunlop, Coyte, and McIsaac, 2000). People who earn low income, the senior population, and women receive more services because their needs tend to be greater.

The risk is that as more of our healthcare services are profitized, more people with healthcare needs will be disadvantaged. Access to needed care will increasingly vary by class, gender, and racial and ethnic inequalities. With fewer healthcare options available, people lacking economic resources will do without healthcare services or rely on self-care or care from family and friends (Arber and Ginn, 1991).

For this reason, many sociologists argue that economic globalization does not support the type of healthcare system that is appropriate for an aging society—a system that combines medical care *and* a strong long-term home-care program, including social services for older adults. Instead, globalization is dismantling many existing services, adding new inequalities in access to healthcare services to existing inequalities in healthcare needs. Disadvantaged seniors and their families are feeling most of the resulting pressure. It can be different, but whether Canada's citizens will demand greater equity in healthcare, and whether governments will listen, remains to be seen.

SUMMARY

1. Canada's seniors represent a highly socially diverse category of the population. Their health status varies by age, class, gender, Aboriginal status, race, and ethnicity.
2. Health is about physical, social, and psychological well-being, not just the absence of disease, and not all aspects of health status decline as we age. Older adults generally assess their health in positive terms and have good mental health and social well-being.
3. Despite the overall picture of good health in old age in Canada, significant inequalities in health exist. They are associated with such factors as socioeconomic position, gender, Aboriginal status, race, and ethnicity. Past increases in health and longevity have been concentrated in more advantaged social groups. Aboriginal and immigrant seniors, older women, and the poor continue to experience major health disadvantages.
4. Health-related inequalities have been attributed to individual health behaviours and lifestyle factors; psychosocial factors, such as stress; and material conditions and resources. Research findings suggest that economic circumstances, living conditions, and other material factors contribute much to health-related inequalities, and that health-related lifestyles and stress levels largely reflect these conditions.
5. We tend to equate healthcare with medical care provided by physicians in clinics or hospitals. However, the most common forms of healthcare are self-care and informal care by family members. When it comes to formal healthcare services, home care is particularly important to the health and well-being of seniors, yet it is not included in Canada's nationally insured healthcare system.
6. In recent years, increased emphasis has been placed on privatization and profit-making in Canada's healthcare system, particularly when it comes to services that are most important to older adults. As a result, people who are most in need of care have the least access to it and are the most likely to have to rely on themselves and family members for care.

QUESTIONS TO CONSIDER

1. What are the major myths about old age? How does the reality of old age in Canada compare with these myths?
2. How can we best account for inequalities in health among senior Canadians?
3. How well does Canada's healthcare system currently meet the healthcare needs of its senior population?
4. What are some of the consequences of economic globalization for Canada's healthcare system?

GLOSSARY

The **age as leveller hypothesis** (p. 430) holds that aging renders everyone disadvantaged, regardless of their other statuses.

Ageism (p. 421) is prejudice based on age.

The **compression of morbidity hypothesis** (p. 424) suggests that by postponing the onset of people's first chronic illness, the lifetime burden of illness may be compressed into a shorter period before death.

Demography (p. 421) is the study of the characteristics of populations and the dynamics of population change.

Functional disability (p. 424) is a long-term restriction or lack of ability to perform various activities of daily living (such as personal care and housework) because of a health condition or health problem.

The **healthy immigrant effect** (p. 426) refers to the tendency for recent immigrants to enjoy better health than do their Canadian-born counterparts. The effect dissipates over time.

The **hierarchy stress perspective** (p. 429) is an approach to understanding health inequality that emphasizes the stress associated with occupying a lower position in the social hierarchy and its negative impact on health.

The **life course perspective** (p. 431) draws attention to the interplay between individual life course change and larger societal changes.

Life expectancy (p. 418) is the number of years that the average person can expect to live.

Medicalization (p. 421) refers to the social and political process whereby more and more areas of life come under the authority and control of medical professionals.

The **modified extended family** (p. 424) is characterized by mutual and close intergenerational ties, responsible behaviour on the part of adult children, and contact between generations.

The **mortality rate** (p. 422) is the number of deaths per thousand people in a population.

The **multiple jeopardy hypothesis** (p. 430) holds that the effect of occupying multiple low statuses is cumulative.

Premature mortality (p. 425) refers to years of potential life lost.

Privatization (p. 434) involves turning publicly owned organizations into privately owned companies.

Profitization (p. 434) involves turning institutions into profit-making organizations.

Self-care (p. 431) is the range of activities that individuals undertake to enhance health, prevent disease, and restore health. Individuals may engage in these activities on their own or in conjunction with health professionals.

SUGGESTED READING

Armstrong, Pat, Hugh Armstrong, and David Coburn. (2001). *Unhealthy Times: Political Economy Perspectives on Health and Care in Canada.* Toronto: Oxford University Press. This collection of papers uses a political economy perspective to explore reforms that influence our health and healthcare.

Bolaria, B. Singh and Harley D. Dickinson. (2009). *Health, Illness, and Health Care in Canada,* 4th ed. Scarborough, ON: Nelson Education. This collection of critical articles examines key sociological issues in the areas of health, illness, and healthcare.

Bryant, T., Raphael, D., and Rioux, M., eds. (2010). *Staying Alive: Critical Perspectives on Health, Illness and Health Care***,** 2nd ed. Toronto: Canadian Scholars' Press. This collection of articles addresses key sociological issues in the political economy of health, illness, and healthcare, including globalization and privatization of healthcare.

Chappell, Neena L. and Margaret J. Penning. (2009). *Understanding Health, Health Care and Health Policy in Canada: Sociological Perspectives.* Don Mills, ON: Oxford University Press. This book provides a comprehensive sociological examination of health and healthcare in the Canadian context.

Wister, A. V. (2005). *Baby Boomer Health Dynamics: How Are We Aging?* Toronto: University of Toronto Press. This book examines whether Canadian baby boomers are more or less healthy than previous generations were and the implications of changing health patterns for the national healthcare system.

CHAPTER 18

POLITICS AND SOCIAL MOVEMENTS

Robert J. Brym
UNIVERSITY OF TORONTO

SOURCE: © Victor Tangermann.

IN THIS CHAPTER YOU WILL LEARN THAT

- The level of democracy in a society depends on the capacity of citizens to influence the state through their support of political parties, social movements, and other collectivities. That capacity increases as power becomes more widely distributed in society.
- The degree to which power is widely distributed influences the success of particular kinds of parties and policies.
- People sometimes riot, strike, and take other forms of collective action to correct perceived injustices. When they do so, they are participating in social movements.
- People are more inclined to rebel against the status quo when they are bound by close social ties to other people who feel similarly wronged and when they have the money and other resources needed to protest.
- For social movements to grow, members must make the activities, ideas, and goals of the movement congruent with the interests, beliefs, and values of potential new recruits.
- The history of democracy is a struggle for the acquisition of constantly broadening citizenship rights.

INTRODUCTION

I almost caused a small riot once. It happened in Grade 11, shortly after I learned that water combined with sulfur dioxide produces sulfurous acid. The news shocked me. To understand why, you have to know where I lived: in Saint John, New Brunswick, about 100 metres (110 yards) downwind of one of the larger pulp and paper mills in Canada. Acrid waves of sulfur dioxide billowed day and night from the mill's imposing smokestacks. The town's pervasive rotten-egg smell was a longstanding complaint in the area. But, for me, disgust turned to upset when I realized the fumes were toxic. Suddenly it was clear why many people I knew—especially people living near the mill—woke up in the morning with a kind of "smoker's cough." By the simple act of breathing, we were causing the gas to mix with the moisture in our bodies and form an acid that our lungs tried to expunge, with only partial success.

Twenty years later, I read the results of a medical research report showing that area residents suffer from rates of lung disease, including emphysema and lung cancer, significantly above the national average. However, even in 1968 it was evident a serious problem was brewing in my hometown. I therefore hatched a plan. Our high school was about to hold its annual model parliament. The event was notoriously boring, partly because, year in, year out, virtually everyone voted for the same party, the Conservatives. But here was an issue, I thought, that could turn things around. The pulp and paper mill was owned by K.C. Irving, an industrialist so powerful that his companies were said to control 40 percent of New Brunswick's economic output. *Forbes* magazine in the United States annually ranked Irving among the wealthiest men in the world. I figured that once I told my fellow students the political implications of the fact that water combined with sulfur dioxide produces sulfurous acid, they would quickly demand the closure of the mill until Irving guaranteed a clean operation.

Was *I naive*. As head of the tiny Liberal Party, I had to address the entire student body during assembly on election day to outline the party platform and mobilize votes. When I got to the part of my speech explaining why K.C. Irving was our enemy, the murmuring in the audience, which had been growing like the sound of a hungry animal about to pounce on its prey, erupted into loud "boos." A couple of students rushed the stage. The principal suddenly appeared from the wings and commanded the student body to settle down. He then took me by the arm and informed me that, for my own safety,

The year 1968 was one of student rebellion worldwide. Here students run from police in Paris, France.
SOURCE: © Bettmann/Corbis.

my speech was finished. So, I discovered on election day, was our high school's Liberal Party. And so, it emerged, was my high school political career.

This incident troubled me for many years, less because of the embarrassment it caused me than because of the puzzles it presented. Why did I almost cause a small riot? Why didn't my fellow students rebel in the way I thought they would? Why did they continue to support an arrangement that was enriching one man at the cost of a community's health? Why weren't they enraged? Couldn't they see the injustice? Other people did. The year 1968 was not just the year of my political failure at Saint John High School. It was also the year that student riots in France nearly caused the fall of the government of Charles de Gaulle. It was the year in which the suppression of student strikes by the Mexican government left dozens of students dead. It was the year in which American students at Berkeley, Michigan, and other universities fought with unprecedented vigour for free speech on their campuses, an end to American involvement in the war in Vietnam, increased civil rights for American blacks, and an expanded role for women in public affairs.

I didn't know it at the time, but by asking why students in Paris, Mexico City, and Berkeley rebelled while my fellow students did not, I was raising the main question that animates the sociological study of politics and social movements. Why are some groups more successful than others in formulating their demands and getting them carried out? In other words, who gets what and under what social circumstances? That is the main issue addressed by this chapter.

Power is the ability of an individual or a group to impose its will on others, even if they resist (Weber, 1946 [1922]: 180). In the first section of this chapter, you will learn that the power of a group may be widely recognized as legitimate or valid under some circumstances. If it is, raw power becomes legitimate **authority** (see Box 18.1). The people who occupy the command posts of institutions are then generally seen as **authorities.** Under other circumstances, however, power flows to nonauthorities. This situation undermines the legitimacy of authority. In this case, nonauthorities form **social movements,** or collective attempts to change part or all of the social order. They may riot,

BOX 18.1 THREE BASES OF AUTHORITY

Max Weber (1947) argued that authority can have one of three bases:

1. *Traditional authority:* Particularly in tribal and feudal societies, rulers inherit authority through family or clan ties. In such circumstances, people believe the right of a family or clan to monopolize leadership derives from a god's will.
2. *Legal-rational authority:* In modern societies, authority derives from respect for the law. Laws specify how a person can achieve office. People generally believe these laws are rational. If someone achieves office by following these laws, his or her authority is respected.
3. *Charismatic authority:* Sometimes, extraordinary, charismatic individuals challenge traditional or legal-rational authority. They claim to be inspired by a god or some higher principle that transcends traditional authority, such as the principle that all people are created equal. Their claim is widely believed. Charismatic figures often emerge during a **political revolution,** a concerted attempt by many people to overthrow political institutions and establish new ones. Political revolutions take place when widespread and successful movements of opposition clash with crumbling traditional or legal-rational authority (Skocpol, 1979).

petition, strike, demonstrate, and establish pressure groups, unions, and **political parties** (organizations that seek to control state power) to achieve their aims.

The terms defined above allow us to distinguish between "normal politics" and "politics beyond the rules." Normal politics is politics as it is practised when authorities are firmly in power. Politics beyond the rules is politics as it is practised when the legitimacy of authority grows weak. Sociologists have proposed various theories to explain the two types of politics. In the second and third sections of this chapter, I evaluate these theories using mainly Canadian data.

Finally, in the chapter's concluding section, I place our discussion in historical context. How has politics developed over the past 300 years? What developments can we reasonably expect in the near future? This section will help you to better understand your political options in coming years.

POWER FROM ABOVE: NORMAL POLITICS

In 1998, the RCMP used pepper spray to disperse Vancouver crowds demonstrating against visiting Indonesian President Suharto. The incident caused a scandal because it was widely seen as excessive use of force sanctioned by the prime minister. The solicitor general, who is responsible for the RCMP, was forced to resign over the incident.

This incident illustrates the use of **force** or coercive power by authorities. Paradoxically, the use of force by authorities is a sign of their weakness: If authorities are truly in a position of strength, their rule will be widely recognized as legitimate. They will not need to use force to impose their will because most people agree with their policies. Here, politics will be routine, nonviolent, or "normal." To be sure, minor outbursts of violence occur even under normal politics. However, such events are unusual in Canada today. They rarely result in fatalities. For the most part, Canadian politics today is normal politics.

Power is exercised in all social settings, from the family to the classroom to the workplace. However, the ultimate seat of power in society is the state. The **state** is a set of institutions that formulate and carry out a country's laws, policies, and binding regulations. Why is the state's power "ultimate?" Because its authority stands above all others, and if the state needs to use force to maintain order or protect its borders, most people will regard its actions as legitimate.

In democratic countries, such as Canada, the government is formed by the elected members of the political party that wins the most seats in a general election (see Figure 18.1). It comprises the head of the party, who becomes prime minister, and the cabinet ministers whom the prime minister selects to advise him or her. It is the job of the government to initiate policies, propose laws, and see that they are enforced. That is why the government is also called the *executive* branch of the state. Proposed laws are turned into operating statutes by the *legislature*, which consists of all the people elected to Parliament. It is the responsibility of the *judiciary* or court system to interpret laws and regulations, that is, to figure out whether and how particular laws and regulations apply in disputed cases. The state's *administrative apparatus or bureaucracy* undertakes

FIGURE 18.1 THE INSTITUTIONS OF STATE AND CIVIL SOCIETY

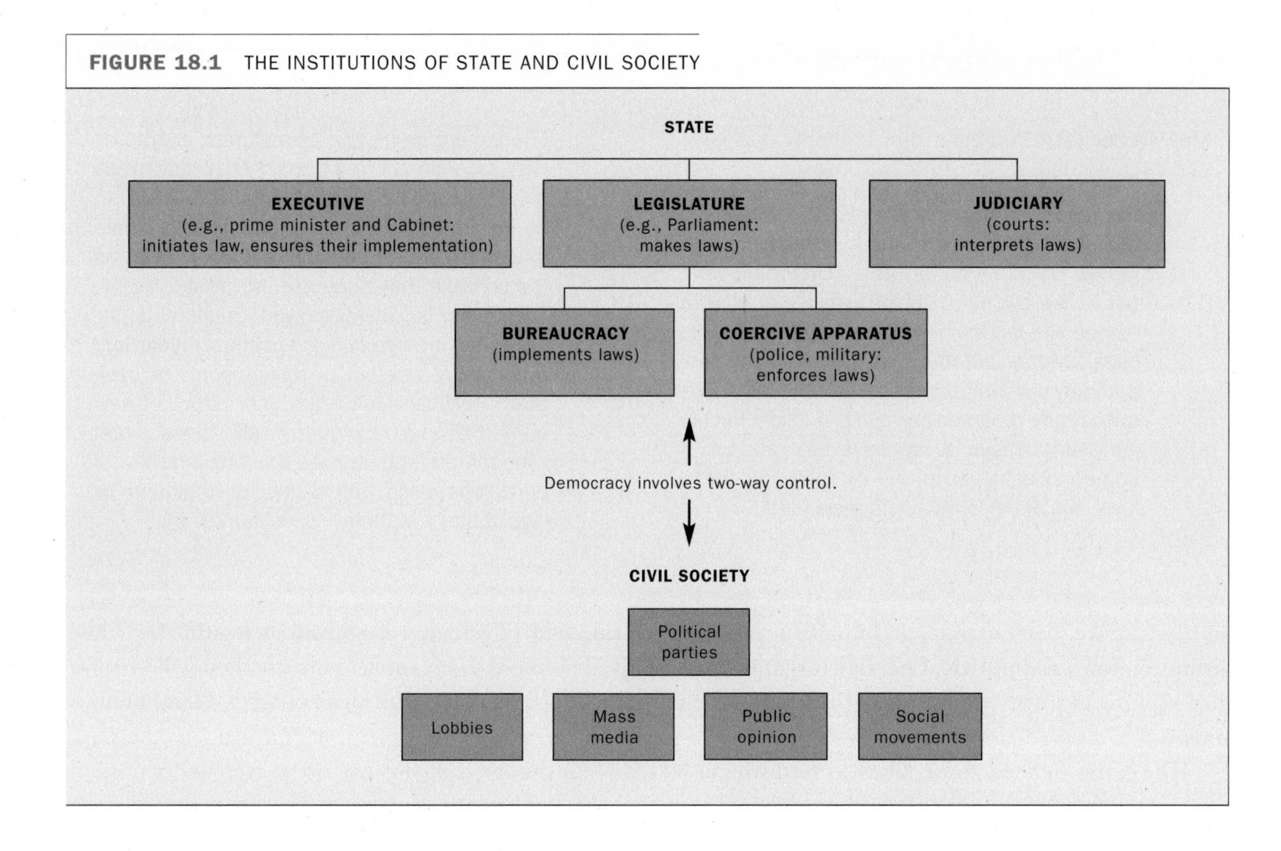

enforcement of laws. If laws are broken or the state's security is jeopardized, it is the role of the *coercive apparatus*—the police and military—to enforce the law and protect the state.

The state, then, is a set of institutions that exercise control over society. However, individuals in **civil society,** the private sphere of life, also exercise control over the state through a variety of organizations and institutions. We have already noted how social movements may influence the state. In addition, the mass media are supposed to keep a watchful and critical eye on the state and help to keep the public informed about the quality of government. Pressure groups or "lobbies" are formed by trade unions, manufacturers' associations, ethnic groups, and other organizations to advise politicians of their members' desires. Lobbies also remind politicians how much their members' votes and campaign contributions matter. Finally, political parties regularly seek to mobilize voters as they compete for control of government.

How democratic is the Canadian state? Does the interaction between state and civil society ensure that every citizen has a roughly equal say in the determination of laws and policies? Or, as George Orwell asked in *Animal Farm,* are some citizens more equal than others? Do we, as Abraham Lincoln claimed for the Americans, enjoy "government of the people, by the people, for the people?" Or is it more accurate to say, in the words of one wit, that we are subjected to "government of the people, by the lawyers, for the business owners"? These are among the chief questions asked by sociologists who study the state and its operations. It is now time to consider them in detail.

PLURALIST THEORY

Pluralist theory is one interpretation of the relationship between state and civil society (Dahl, 1961; Polsby, 1959). According to pluralists, we live in a heterogeneous society with many competing interests and centres of power. For example, the interests of parents with school-age children may differ from the interests of pensioners. Parents may want school budgets to grow. Pensioners may want them to shrink. Because of such heterogeneity, no one group can control politics, according to the pluralists. They argue that, over time, all voters and interest groups influence the political process almost equally. Sometimes one category of voters wins a political battle, sometimes another. Most often, however, politics involves negotiation and compromise among competing groups. According to the pluralists, because no one group of people is always able to control the political agenda or the outcome of political conflict, democracy is guaranteed.

ELITE THEORY

Elite theorists, C. Wright Mills (1956) foremost among them, sharply disagree with the pluralist account. According to **elite theory,** *elites* are small groups that occupy the command posts of a society's institutions. In the United States, the country that Mills studied, the most powerful elites are the people who run the country's several hundred biggest corporations, the executive branch of government, and the military. Mills wrote that the men who control these institutions (they are almost all men) make the important decisions that profoundly affect members of society. Moreover, they do so without much regard for elections or public opinion.

Mills showed how the corporate, state, and military elites are interconnected. People move from one elite to another over their careers. Their children intermarry. They maintain close social contact. They tend to be recruited from the upper-middle and upper classes. However, Mills denied that these similarities and interconnections turn the three elites into a **ruling class,** that is, a self-conscious and cohesive group of people, led by corporate executives and owners of big business, who act to advance their common interests. The three elites are independent of each other, Mills insisted. They may see eye-to-eye on many issues, but each has its own jealously guarded sphere of influence, and conflict between elite groups is therefore common (Mills, 1956: 277).

The Elitist Critique of Pluralism

Most political sociologists today question the pluralist account of democratic politics because research has established the existence of large, persistent, wealth-based inequalities in political influence and political participation.

John Porter's classic, *The Vertical Mosaic* (1965), was the first in a series of Canadian studies that demonstrate the weaknesses of pluralism and corroborate some aspects of elite theory (Brym, 1989; Clement, 1975; Olsen, 1980). These studies show that a disproportionately large number of people in Canada's political and other elites come from upper- and upper-middle-class families. For example, about 40 percent of Canadian prime ministers, premiers, and Cabinet ministers were born into the richest 10 percent of families in the country (Olsen, 1980: 129). In their youth, members of Canada's elites are likely to have attended expensive private schools. As adults, they tend to marry the offspring of other elite members and belong to exclusive private clubs. In the course of their careers, they often move from one elite to another. Arguably, people with this sort of background cannot act dispassionately on behalf of all Canadians, rich and poor.

Controversy persists over whether Canada's elites form a ruling class. Porter (1965), like Mills (1956), noted frequent conflict among elites. He argued against the view that a ruling class controls Canada. His top students disagreed. They argued that the interests of large corporations dominate Canadian political life (Clement, 1975; Olsen, 1980). However, both Porter and his students did agree on one point: contrary to pluralist claims, Canada's well-to-do consistently exercise disproportionate influence over political life in this country.

Studies of political participation in Canada add weight to the elitist view (Blais, Gidengil, Nadeau, and Nevitte, 1997; Frank, 1994; Mishler, 1979: 88–97). Many surveys show that political involvement decreases with social class. For example, the likelihood of voting falls with a person's class position. The likelihood of phoning or writing a member of Parliament, helping a candidate in an election campaign, contributing money to a political party, and running for office declines even more steeply as we move down the class hierarchy. As intensity of political participation declines, so does political influence. Consequently, although political apathy and cynicism are high among Canadians, the poorest Canadians are the most politically apathetic and cynical of any income category. They have less interest in politics than do the well-to-do, and they are more likely to think that government does not care what they think (see Figure 18.2). As a leading political sociologist wrote, "The combination of a low vote and a relative lack of organization among the lower-status groups means that they will suffer from neglect by the politicians who will be receptive to the wishes of the more privileged, participating, and organized strata" (Lipset, 1981: 226–27; see Box 18.2).

The Marxist Critique of Elite Theory

Although compelling in some respects, elite theory has its critics, Marxists foremost among them. Some Marxists, known as "instrumentalists," deny that elites enjoy more or less equal power. Actually, they say, elites form a ruling class dominated by big business. From their point of view, the state is an arm (or "instrument") of the business elite. Big business gains control of the state in three main ways. First, members of wealthy families occupy important state positions in highly disproportionate numbers. Second,

FIGURE 18.2 POLITICAL CYNICISM AND DONATIONS BY ANNUAL HOUSEHOLD INCOME, CANADA

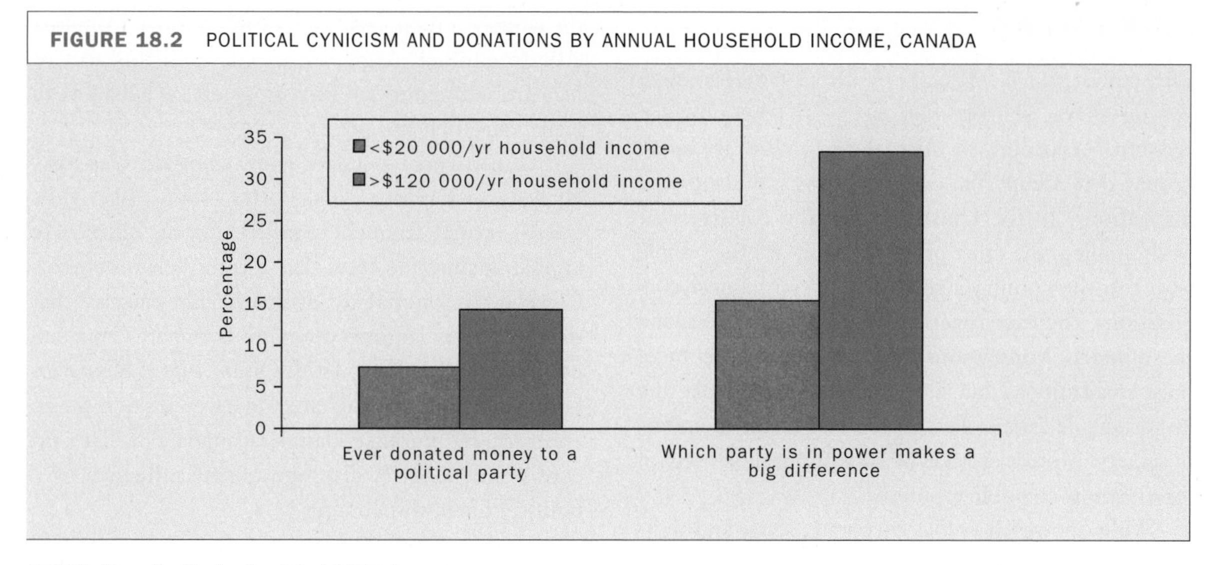

SOURCE: "Canadian Election Panel Study" (2010).

government officials rely mainly on the representatives of big business for advice. Third, political parties rely mainly on big business for financial support. According to some Marxists, members of different elites may disagree about specific issues. However, as a result of the three control mechanisms listed above, they always agree about one issue: the need to maintain the health of the capitalist system (Miliband, 1973 [1969]).

A second group of Marxists, known as "stucturalists" offers a somewhat different interpretation of why the state in capitalist society is necessarily biased in favour of big business. For the structuralists, it is not so much the social origins of high government officials or the social ties linking them with big business that encourages the state to act with a pro-capitalist bias. Rather, they argue, the capitalist state acts as an arm of big business because it is constrained to do so by the nature of the capitalist system itself. For example, if the Canadian government doubled the corporate tax rate, investment would be redirected to countries with regimes that are kinder to company profits. Such a move would cost Canada jobs and prosperity. It would be highly unpopular. The government could easily fall. Fearing such outcomes, governments in capitalist societies find their field of action restricted to policies that ensure the well-being of big business. According to the structuralists, it is the very fact that the state is embedded in a capitalist system that forces it to act in this way (Poulantzas, 1975 [1968]).

It follows from both the instrumentalist and the structuralist positions that ordinary citizens,

Karl Marx predicted that capitalism would create a large mass of impoverished workers who would eventually take over the state, eliminate private property, and forge a communist society. After the revolution of 1917, the Soviet Union became the first self-proclaimed communist society. This early May Day poster reads: "Workers of all countries unite. The 1st of May work holiday. Long live the international unity of the proletariat!"
SOURCE: © Corbis.

BOX 18.2 DEFEATING POLITICAL CYNICISM: TECHNOLOGY, ORGANIZATION, AND THE OBAMA EFFECT

Turnout in the American presidential election of 1996 reached an all-time low. Just 48 percent of the voting-age population went to the polls. However, in subsequent elections, turnout increased, reaching 56 percent in 2008. Why the upturn? At 61 percent in the 2011 federal election, Canadian voter turnout remains higher than voter turnout in the United States, but for more than a decade, Canadian voter turnout dropped while American voter turnout increased (see Figure 18.3). Why the different trends in the two countries?

The competitiveness of elections in the United States and Canada may be part of the answer. Big fights tend to draw big crowds, and recent American presidential elections have been intensely competitive. Over the same period, Canadians were arguably presented with less stark party alternatives than Americans were. Canadian cynicism about politics may have remained high because less seemed to be at stake in Canadian elections. The result: persistently declining voter turnout in Canada.

Another factor that has contributed to the recent American upturn in voter turnout is that technological and organizational improvements encourage more people to vote in the United States. Party organizers now use the Internet intensively to solicit donations, recruit volunteers, and communicate with them. They employ census and survey data to identify persuadable voters. Then, they send entire armies of the party faithful out to contact persuadable voters face-to-face and encourage them to vote (McDonald 2008a, 2008b). Canadian federal elections seem to be less technologically and organizationally advanced than American presidential elections are. Persistent declines in Canadian voter turnout may result from the technological and organizational lag.

Finally, the "Obama effect" is partly responsible for the most recent uptick in American voter turnout. President Barack Obama is, of course, a young, attractive, inspirational leader. In the 2008 presidential election, his message of hope and change appealed strongly to the most cynical age cohort: youth. Voters between the age of 18 and 29 supported Obama over McCain by a two-to-one margin, and they came out to the polls in droves ("United States," 2008). Meanwhile, voter turnout among Canadian youth is the lowest among all age cohorts (see Figure 18.3). We await our Obama.

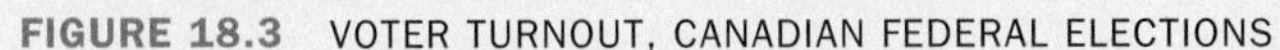

FIGURE 18.3 VOTER TURNOUT, CANADIAN FEDERAL ELECTIONS

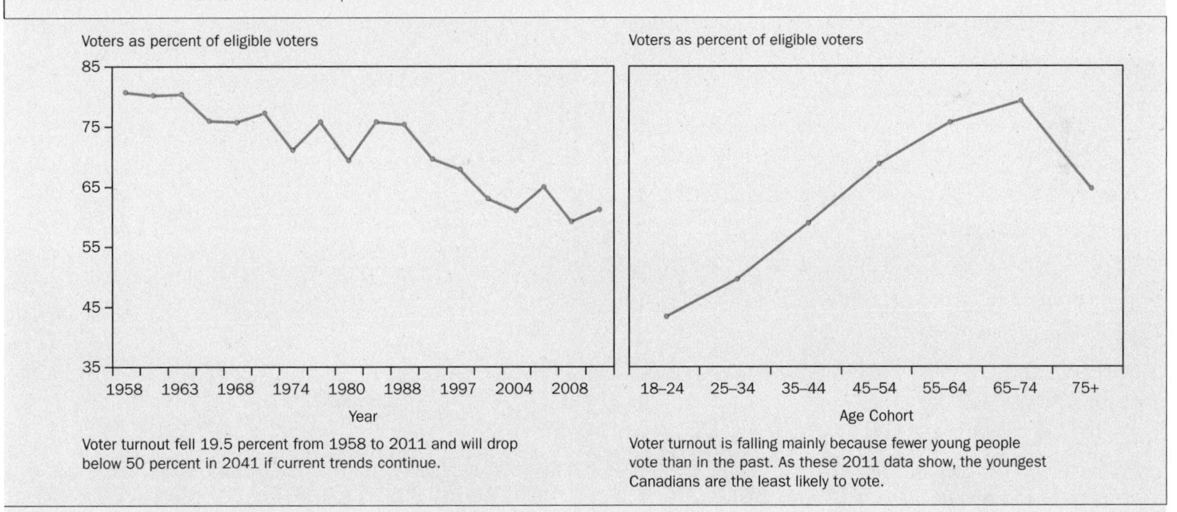

Voter turnout fell 19.5 percent from 1958 to 2011 and will drop below 50 percent in 2041 if current trends continue.

Voter turnout is falling mainly because fewer young people vote than in the past. As these 2011 data show, the youngest Canadians are the least likely to vote.

SOURCE: "Estimation of Voter Turnout by Age Group and Gender", Elections Canada, 2012. This reproduction is a copy of the version available at www.elections.ca. Reproduced with the permission of Elections Canada, but adaptation rests with the author.

and especially members of the working class, rarely have much influence over state policy. According to Marxists, true democracy can emerge only if members of the working class and their supporters overthrow capitalism and establish a socialist system in which economic differences between people are eliminated or at least substantially reduced.

POWER-BALANCE THEORY

Pluralists assume that all major groups in society enjoy approximately equal power. Elitists assume that members of the upper class enjoy the most power. Both approaches, however, assume that the distribution of power in society does not change much over time, except in those rare instances when revolutions take place.

In contrast, power-balance theorists argue that the distribution of power in society changes significantly more frequently. **Power-balance theory** allows that power is usually concentrated in the hands of the wealthy. However, adherents of this approach also note that other classes sometimes gain power. This has big implications for political life. Among other things, the distribution of power determines how democratic a society is.

To make their case, power-balance theorists first measure variations in the social distribution of power. They then show how those variations are reflected in the successes and failures of different political parties and the rejection and adoption of different state policies. Along with the pluralists, they recognize that society is truly democratic only when power is widely distributed. Along with the elitists, they recognize that society is not very democratic when power is highly concentrated in the hands of a few wealthy citizens. However, by treating the distribution of power as a variable, they improve our understanding of the relationship between power and democracy.

We can better understand power-balance theory by examining Canadian politics in comparative perspective. We first note that a group's power is partly determined by the degree to which it forms organizations to further its interests. For example, unionized blue-collar and white-collar workers are more powerful than their nonunionized counterparts are. That is because unions allow workers to speak with one voice. Unions enable workers to effectively bargain with employers and governments for improved wages, working conditions, and social policies. Moreover, if bargaining fails, they can go out on strike to try to force the issue.

If level of unionization increases working-class power, that should be reflected in the political behaviour of citizens and the policies adopted by governments. And, in fact, it is. Compare Sweden and Canada (Casper, McLanahan, and Garfinkle, 1994; Korpi, 1983; Myles, 1989; O'Connor, 1996; O'Connor and Brym, 1988; O'Connor and Olsen, 1998; Olsen, 2002; Olsen and Brym, 1996). In Sweden, more than three-quarters of blue- and white-collar workers are

The peak year of strike activity in Canada was 1919. In that year, 17.3 strikes took place for every 100 000 nonagricultural workers in the country. This photo was taken on "Bloody Saturday," June 21, 1919, during the Winnipeg General Strike. It shows a violent confrontation between rioters and Mounties and special police.
SOURCE: LAC C-33392.

union members. In Canada, about three in ten nonagricultural workers are members of unions. Several consequences follow:

- 61.4 percent of Canadians voted in the 2011 federal election, compared with 84.6 percent of Swedes in the 2010 Swedish federal election ("Voter Turnout," 2011; Statistics Sweden, 2011). The difference is largely due to the fact that working-class Swedes are more likely to vote than working-class Canadians are.
- The Swedish socialist party has formed the government almost continuously since World War II. In contrast, Canada's socialist party, the NDP, has never formed the federal government or even had a representative in the federal cabinet. The parties that have formed Canada's federal governments (Liberals, Progressive Conservatives, and Conservatives) are those that are most strongly supported by business (see Figure 18.4).
- Swedish governments have acted more vigorously than Canadian governments have to eradicate poverty and equalize incomes. Thus, fewer than 4 percent of Swedes are classified as living below the poverty line (as defined by the low income cutoff; see Chapter 6, Social Stratification). The comparable figure for Canadians is about 15 percent. In Sweden, about 20 percent of all income goes to the top 10 percent of income earners. The comparable figure for Canada is about 30 percent of all income. And in Sweden, a broader range of retired people receive more generous pensions and more frequent cost-of-living adjustments than do pensioners in Canada.
- Since women are disproportionately concentrated in low-income, low-status jobs (see Chapter 7, Gender Inequality), they benefit more than men do when the working class is more powerful. As a result, the ratio of women's to men's earnings is about 80 percent in Sweden and 67 percent in Canada. Moreover, in Sweden, the ratio of women to men who live below the poverty line is just above 90 percent, while in Canada the comparable figure is nearly 130 percent. Finally, parental benefits are superior in Sweden and child-care facilities are more widely available and affordable.

FIGURE 18.4 CONTRIBUTIONS TO FEDERAL POLITICAL PARTIES BY SOURCE

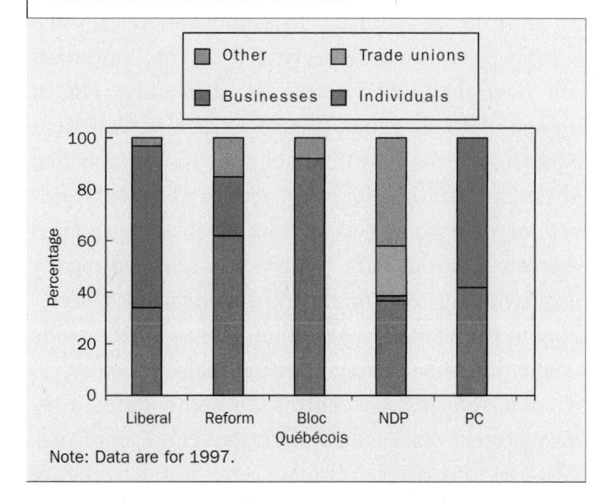

Note: Data are for 1997.

SOURCE: Elections Canada, "Contributions to Registered Political Parties, By Donor Category (Dollars)," from http://www.elections.ca/ecFiscals/1997/table03_e.html, 1997. Reproduced with the permission of the Minister of Public Works and Government Services Canada, 2011.

We thus see that elections matter a great deal in the lives of ordinary people. Elections determine the types of parties that get elected. Elected parties, in turn, shape government policies. The outcome of any particular election depends on the appeal of party leaders, their effectiveness in presenting issues to the public, and myriad other short-term factors (Clarke, Jenson, Le Duc, and Pammett, 1996; see Figure 18.5). However, when considering the types of parties that get elected over several decades, as we did previously, we see that the distribution of power between classes and other groups shapes the character of politics in a country.

The preceding analysis also implies that Sweden is more democratic than Canada is. True, citizens of both countries are legally free to vote and influence their governments. But because the working class is more powerful in Sweden, Swedes' legal right to vote and influence governments has been turned into real political influence on a wider scale. In general, only if more citizens wield more clout can society become more democratic.

STATE-CENTRED THEORY

Power-balance theory suggests that democratic politics is a contest among various classes and other groups to control the state for their own advantage. When power is substantially redistributed—when, for example, a major class gets better organized while another major class becomes less socially organized—old ruling parties usually fall and new ones take office.

Note, however, that a winner-take-all strategy would be nothing short of foolish. If winning parties monopolized the spoils of office, passing laws

FIGURE 18.5 RESULTS OF 2011 CANADIAN FEDERAL ELECTION

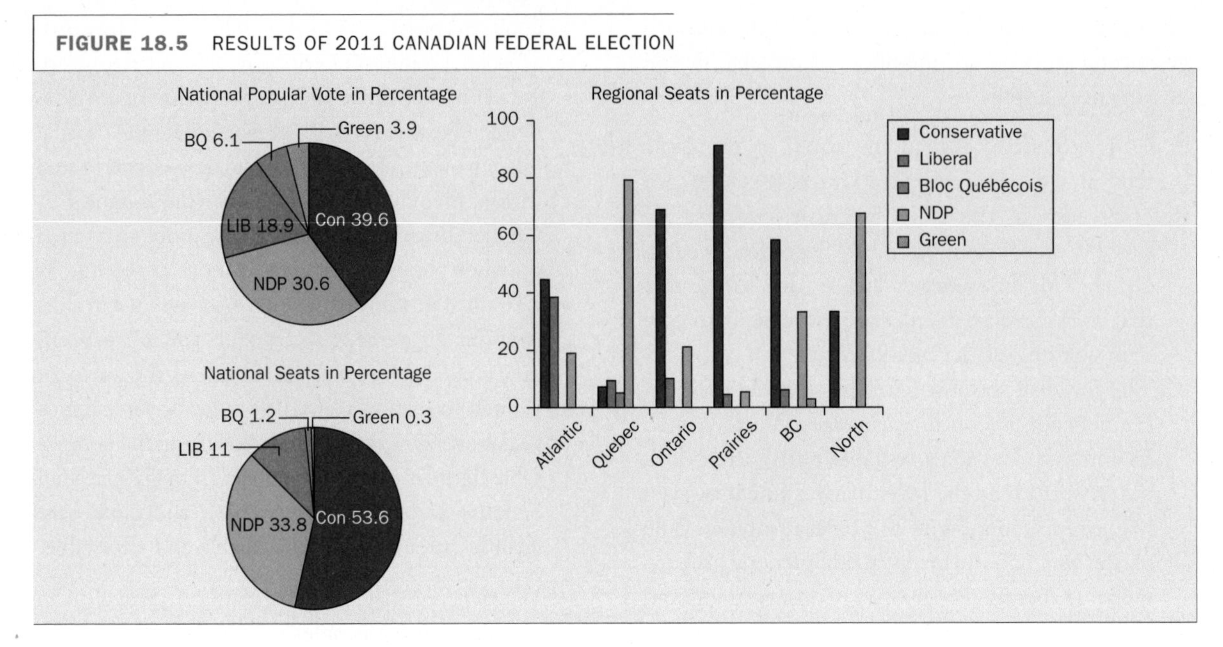

SOURCE: Data used to create the above chart was taken from the website of Elections Canada, www.elections.ca, 2011. It is used with the permission of the Chief Electoral Officer. Adaptation and analysis are the responsibility of the author.

that benefit only their supporters, they might cause massive outrage and even violent opposition. Yet allowing opponents to become angry, organized, and resolute would be counterproductive. After all, winners want more than just a moment of glory. They want to be able to enjoy the spoils of office in a stable political environment over the long haul. To achieve such stability, it is crucial that people who *lose* elections are given a say in government. To a degree, the party in power must attend to the wants of losing minorities. That way, even determined opponents are likely to recognize the legitimacy of the government and its right to rule. Pluralists thus make a good point when they say that democratic politics is about accommodation and compromise; they only lose sight of the fact that accommodation and compromise typically give more advantages to some than to others, as both elite theorists and power-balance theorists stress.

There is, however, more to the story of politics than conflict between classes and between other groups. Theda Skocpol and other **state-centred theorists** have shown how the state itself can structure political life independently of the way power is distributed among classes and other groups at a given time (Block, 1979; Evans, Rueschemeyer, and Skocpol, 1985; Skocpol, 1979). Their argument is a valuable supplement to power-balance theory.

To illustrate how state structures shape politics, consider the problem of nonvoting in the United States. In presidential elections, voter turnout fell more or less steadily between the end of World War II and 1996, when it stood at just 48 percent of the voting age population. Turnout increased in 2000 (50 percent), 2004 (55 percent), and 2008 (56 percent), but the United States still has one of the lowest voter turnouts of any rich democracy in the world (Piven and Cloward, 1989: 5). How can we explain this?

The high rate of nonvoting is largely a product of voter registration law—a feature of the American political structure, not of the current distribution of power. In every democracy, laws specify voter registration procedures. In some countries, such as France, citizens are registered to vote automatically once they receive state-issued identity cards at the age of 18. In other countries, such as Canada, a database of citizens who are eligible to vote was first created by state-employed canvassers who went door-to-door to register voters. The database is updated between elections with information supplied mainly by provincial, territorial, and federal data sources. Only in the United States do individual citizens have to take the initiative to go out and register themselves in voter registration centres. In some states, they must present state-issued ID (a driver's license or a passport) to register. Yet many American citizens are unable or unwilling to register. As a result, the United States has a proportionately smaller pool of eligible voters than the other democracies do. Only about 65 percent of American citizens are registered to vote (Piven and Cloward, 1989: 256–59).

Apart from shrinking the pool of eligible voters, American voter registration law has a second important consequence. Because some *types* of people are less able and inclined than others to register, a strong bias is introduced into the political system. Specifically, the poor are less likely to register than the better-off are. People without much formal education are less likely to register than the better educated are. Members of disadvantaged racial minority groups, especially African Americans, are less likely to register than whites are. Such people are less likely than others are to have the knowledge, time, and money needed to register, let alone a driver's license or a passport. Thus, American voter registration law is a pathway to democracy for some but a barrier to democracy for others. The American political system is less responsive than other rich democracies are to the needs of the disadvantaged. That is partly because, as state-centred theory suggests, the law requires citizen-initiated voter registration. As a result, many disadvantaged people are effectively disenfranchised.[1]

Big shocks sometimes rock state structures. In general, however, they are resistant to change. The foundations of state structures are anchored by constitutions, which can be altered only by large majorities of federally elected representatives and state- or provincial-level legislatures. Their upper stories are girded by laws, regulations, and policies, some of which help to keep potentially disruptive social forces at bay. American voter registration law is a case in point.[2] And then there are the many ideological reinforcements. All states create anthems, flags, ceremonies, celebrations, sporting events, and school curricula that stimulate patriotism and serve in part to justify existing political arrangements.

In sum, each school of thought reviewed above makes a useful contribution to our appreciation of normal democratic politics (see Table 18.1). Pluralists teach us that normal democratic politics is about compromise and the accommodation of all group interests. Elite theorists teach us that, despite compromise and accommodation, power is concentrated in the hands of higher-status groups, whose interests the political system therefore serves best. Power-balance theorists teach us that, despite the concentration of power in society, substantial shifts in the distribution of power often occur, and they have discernible effects on voting patterns and public policies. Marxists highlight the rare occasions when political power is rapidly redistributed by revolutionary upheavals. And state-centred theorists teach us that, despite the influence of the distribution of power on political life, state structures exert an important independent effect on politics, too.

POWER FROM BELOW: POLITICS BEYOND THE RULES

RELATIVE-DEPRIVATION THEORY

All five theories of democracy reviewed above focus on normal politics. We know, however, that politics is sometimes anything but normal. Routine political

TABLE 18.1 FIVE SOCIOLOGICAL THEORIES OF DEMOCRACY COMPARED

	PLURALIST	ELITE	MARXIST	POWER BALANCE	STATE-CENTRED
How is power distributed?	dispersed	concentrated	concentrated	concentrated	concentrated
Who are the main power holders?	various groups	elites	ruling class	upper class	state officials
On what is their power based?	holding political office	controlling major institutions	owning substantial capital	owning substantial capital	holding political office
What is the main basis of public policy?	the will of all citizens	the interests of major elites	capitalist interests	the balance of power between classes, etc.	the influence of state structures
Do lower classes have much influence on politics?	yes	no	rarely	sometimes	sometimes

processes can break down. Social movements can form. Large-scale political violence can erupt. As Vladimir Lenin, the leader of the Russian revolution of 1917, said, people sometimes "vote with their feet."

Until about 1970, many sociologists argued that social movements tend to emerge when people experience **relative deprivation.** People feel relatively deprived when they experience an intolerable gap between the social rewards they think they deserve and the social rewards they expect to receive. (Social rewards are widely valued goods, including money, education, security, prestige, and so on.) Accordingly, people are most likely to rebel against authority when rising expectations (brought on by, say, rapid economic growth and migration) are met by a sudden decline in social rewards (because of, say, economic recession or war; Davies, 1969). In addition, until about 1970, many sociologists held that the people who lead and first join social movements are likely to be outsiders who lack strong social ties to their communities.

A large body of research has now discredited these ideas. For example, we now know that the leaders and early joiners of social movements are usually well-integrated members of their communities, not socially marginal newcomers. In the 1930s, for example, Saskatchewan farmers and workers formed the Cooperative Commonwealth Federation (CCF) to protest federal government policy toward the West in general and Western agriculture in particular. The movement's leaders and early recruits were not outsiders. The workers were mainly local trade union activists. The farmers had been involved in the establishment of community-owned retail stores, credit unions, and marketing cooperatives (Lipset, 1971).

Much research also calls into question the idea that relative deprivation leads to the formation of social movements. For example, sociologists have compared measures of relative deprivation with the frequency of demonstrations, strikes, and acts of collective violence in France, Italy, Germany, and England. They have found that, in general, outbreaks of collective unrest do not increase with mounting relative deprivation (Lodhi and Tilly, 1973; Snyder and Tilly, 1972; Tilly, 1979a; Tilly, Tilly, and Tilly, 1975).

RESOURCE MOBILIZATION THEORY

Because of the inadequacies of relative deprivation theory noted above, an alternative approach to the study of social movements gained popularity. **Resource mobilization theory** is based on the idea that social movements emerge only when disadvantaged people can marshal the means necessary to challenge authority (Jenkins, 1983; McCarthy and Zald, 1977; Oberschall, 1973; Tilly, 1978). Foremost among the resources they need to challenge authority is the capacity to forge strong social ties among themselves. Other important resources that allow disadvantaged people to challenge authority include jobs, money, arms, and access to means of spreading their ideas.

You can appreciate the significance of resource mobilization theory by considering patterns of strike activity in Canada. When blue-collar and white-collar workers go out on strike, they are withholding their labour to extract concessions from employers or governments in the form of higher wages and improved social welfare benefits. When are workers most inclined to challenge the authority of employers and governments in this way? Research shows that in Canada since World War II, strike activity has been high when (1) unemployment is low, (2) union membership is high, and (3) governments have been relatively generous in their provision of social welfare benefits. Low unemployment indicates a strong economy. Workers are inclined to strike when business activity is robust because they know employers and governments can afford to make concessions. (Employers make bigger profits and governments collect more taxes during economic booms.) A high level of unionization is also conducive to more strike activity because unions provide workers with leadership, strike funds, and coordination. Thus, as resource mobilization theory predicts, strong social ties among workers (as indicated by a high level of unionization) and access to jobs and money (as indicated by a booming economy) increase challenges to authority (as indicated by strikes).[3]

Figure 18.6 shows the pattern of strike activity in post-World War II Canada. It supports the arguments of resource mobilization theory. Until 1974, the trend in strike activity was upward. (In the 1970s, Canada was, in fact, one of the most strike-prone countries in the world.) This was a period of growing prosperity, low unemployment, expanding state benefits, and increasing unionization. With increasing access to organizational and material resources, workers often challenged authority in the three decades after World War II. In 1973, however, economic crisis struck. Oil prices tripled, and then tripled again at the end of the decade. Inflation increased and unemployment rose. Soon, the government was strapped for funds and

FIGURE 18.6 WEIGHTED FREQUENCY OF STRIKES, CANADA, 1946–2008

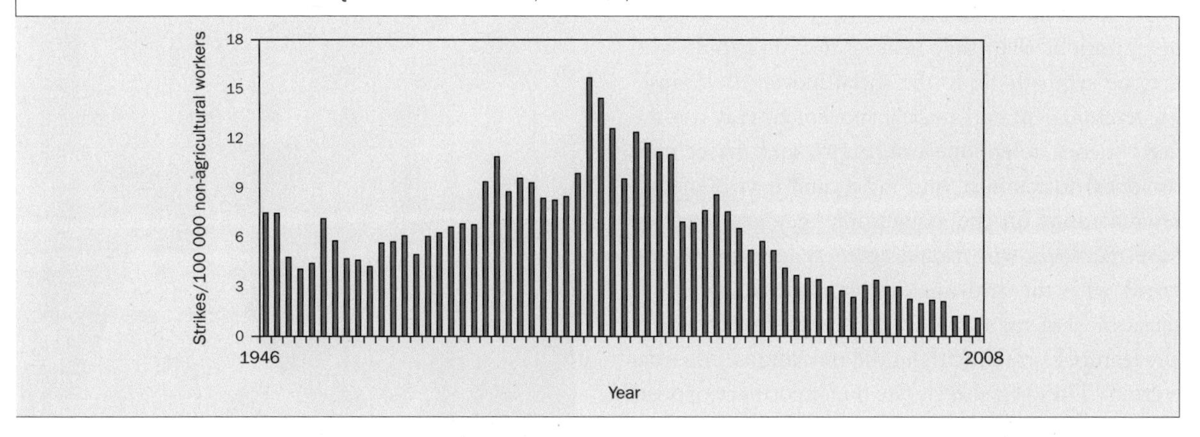

SOURCES: Canada Department of Labour (1970, 1973, 1985); Human Resources Development Canada (1995, 1998, 2006); International Labour Organization (2012).

had to borrow heavily to maintain social welfare programs. Eventually, the debt burden was so heavy that the government felt obliged to cut various social welfare programs. Unionization reached a peak in 1978, stabilized, and then began to fall (see Figure 18.7). Thus, in the post-1973 climate, the organizational and material resources of workers fell. As a result, strike activity plummeted. In 1974, nearly 16 strikes took place for every 100 000 Canadian workers. By 2006, that figure had fallen to just over 1 (Brym, 2008).

FRAMING DISCONTENT

As you have seen, resource mobilization theory is a useful approach to the study of social movements, such as the strike movement in Canada. Even so, the emergence of a social movement sometimes takes sociologists by surprise. In addition, the failure of an aggrieved group to press its claim is sometimes equally unexpected. And movements that do emerge are successful to varying degrees. It seems, therefore, that something lies between (1) the capacity of disadvantaged people to mobilize resources for collective action and (2) the recruitment of a substantial number of movement members. Sociologists call that "something" **frame alignment** (Goffman, 1974; Snow, Rochford, Worden, and Benford, 1986). Frame alignment is the process by which individual interests, beliefs, and values either become congruent and complementary with the activities, ideas, and goals of the movement or fail to do so. Thanks to the efforts of scholars operating mainly in the symbolic interactionist tradition (see Chapter 1, Introducing Sociology, and Chapter 3, Socialization), frame alignment has recently become the subject of sustained sociological investigation.

FIGURE 18.7 PERCENTAGE OF NONAGRICULTURAL WORKERS UNIONIZED, CANADA AND THE UNITED STATES, 1925–2010

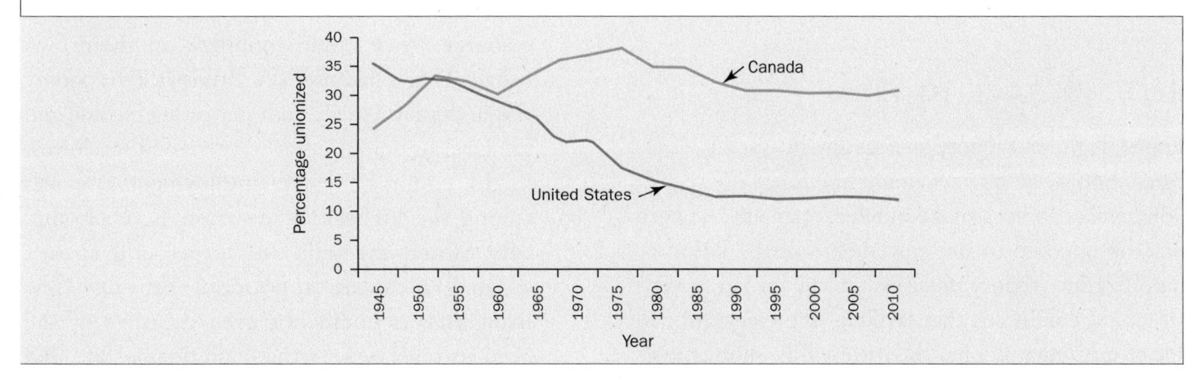

SOURCES: Bureau of Labor Statistics (2012); Canada Department of Labour (1973); Human Resources Development Canada (1995, 1998); Human Resources and Skills Development Canada (2011); Mayer (2004); Statistics Canada (2008).

Frame alignment can be encouraged in several ways. Social movement leaders can reach out to other organizations that, they believe, include people who may be sympathetic to the social movement's cause. For example, an anti-nuclear movement may use the mass media, telephone campaigns, and direct mail to appeal to feminist, anti-racist, and environmental organizations on the assumption they are likely to have members who would agree at least in general terms with the anti-nuclear platform. In addition, social movements can idealize values that have so far not featured prominently in the thinking of potential recruits. They can also elevate the importance of positive beliefs about the movement and what it stands for. For example, in trying to win new recruits, movement members might emphasize the seriousness of the social movement's purpose. They might analyze in a clear and compelling manner the causes of the problem the movement is trying to solve. Or they might stress the likelihood of the movement's success. By doing so they might increase the movement's appeal to potential recruits and win them over to the cause. Social movements can also stretch their objectives and activities to win recruits who are not initially sympathetic to the movement's original aims. This may involve watering down the movement's ideals. Alternatively, movement leaders may decide to take action calculated to appeal to nonsympathizers on grounds that have little or nothing to do with the movement's purpose. When rock, punk, or reggae bands play at nuclear disarmament rallies or gay liberation festivals, it is not necessarily because the music is relevant to the movement's goals. Nor do bands play just because movement members want to be entertained. The purpose is also to attract nonmembers. Once attracted by the music, nonmembers may make friends and acquaintances in the movement and then be encouraged to attend a more serious-minded meeting.

The Assembly of First Nations, which represents 633 Aboriginal groups, demands that Aboriginal Canadians have the right to formulate their own laws and reject some Canadian laws. Here, Aboriginal peoples protest certain taxes outside a government office.

SOURCE: © Dick Hemingway.

REFRAIN: BACK TO 1968

Frame alignment theory stresses the interaction strategies employed by movement members to recruit nonmembers who are like-minded, apathetic, or even initially opposed to the movement's goals. Resource mobilization theory focuses on the broad social-structural conditions that facilitate the emergence of social movements. One theory usefully supplements the other.

The two theories certainly help clarify the 1968 high school incident I described at the beginning of this chapter. It now seems clear that two main factors prevented me from influencing my classmates in New Brunswick when I spoke to them about the dangers of industrial pollution:

1. Disadvantaged people in New Brunswick were relatively powerless. They had access to few resources they could mobilize on their own behalf. That is because New Brunswick's economy was underdeveloped. Both per capita income and the level of unionization were among the lowest in the country. The unemployment rate was among the highest. In contrast, K. C. Irving, who owned the pulp and paper mill against which I railed, was so powerful that most New Brunswickers could not even conceive of the need to rebel against the conditions of life that he helped to create for them. He owned most of the industrial establishments in the province—the oil refinery and a network of gas stations, the dry

docks, the pulp mills, the mines, and the logging operations. Every daily newspaper, most of the weeklies, all of the TV stations, and most of the radio stations were his, too. Little wonder we rarely heard a critical word about his operations. Many people also believed that Irving could make or break provincial governments single-handedly. Should I therefore have been surprised that mere high school students refused to take him on? In their conservatism, my fellow students were only mimicking their parents, who, on the whole, were as powerless as Irving was mighty (Brym, 1979).

2. Many of my classmates did not share my sense of injustice. Most of them regarded K. C. Irving as the great provider. They thought his pulp and paper mill, as well as his myriad other industrial establishments, gave many New Brunswickers jobs. They regarded that fact as more important for their lives and the lives of their families than the pollution problem I raised. Frame-alignment theory suggests I needed to figure out ways of building bridges between their understanding and mine. I did not. I therefore received an unsympathetic hearing.

THE HISTORY AND FUTURE OF SOCIAL MOVEMENTS

I. THE RICH COUNTRIES

Three hundred years ago, social movements were typically small, localized, and violent. In Europe, poor residents of a particular city might riot against public officials in reaction to a rise in bread prices or taxes. Peasants on a particular estate might burn their landowner's barns (or their landowner) in response to his demand for a larger share of the crop. Then the reach of the state grew, soon encompassing most aspects of life. The state taxed nearly all its citizens at higher and higher rates as government services expanded. It imposed a uniform language and a common curriculum in a compulsory education system. It drafted most young men for army service. It instilled in its citizens all the ideological trappings of modern nationalism, from anthems to flags to historical myths. And in the process, social movements changed. They became national in scope, typically directing themselves against central governments rather than local targets. They grew in size, partly because potential recruits were now literate and could communicate using the printed word, partly because big new social settings—factories, offices, densely populated urban neighbourhoods—could serve as recruitment bases. And, in most cases, social movements became less violent. Their size and organization often allowed them to stabilize, bureaucratize, and become sufficiently powerful to get their way without frequent resort to extreme measures (Tilly, 1978, 1979a, 1979b; Tilly, Tilly, and Tilly, 1975).

Social movements often used their power to expand the rights of citizens. We can identify four stages in this process. In Britain, for example, rich property owners struggled against the king in the eighteenth century for **civil citizenship:** the right to free speech, freedom of religion, and justice before the law. The male middle class and the more prosperous strata of the working class struggled against rich property owners in the nineteenth century for **political citizenship:** the right to vote and run for office. In early-twentieth-century Britain, women and poorer workers succeeded in achieving these same rights despite the opposition of well-to-do men in particular. During the remainder of the century, blue- and white-collar workers struggled against the well-to-do for **social citizenship:** the right to a certain level of economic security and full participation in the social life of the country by means of the creation of the modern welfare state (Marshall, 1965).

In the last third of the twentieth century, the struggle to broaden citizenship rights entered a new phase, which we now examine in greater detail. The broadening of the struggle for citizenship rights was signalled by the emergence of so-called **new social movements** in the 1960s and 1970s (Melucci, 1980, 1995). What is new about new social movements is the breadth of their goals, the kinds of people they attract, and their potential for going global. I will consider each of these issues in turn.

Goals

Some new social movements, such as the peace movement, the environmental movement, and the human rights movement, promote the rights not of specific groups but of humanity as a whole to peace, security, and a clean environment. Other new social movements, such as the women's movement and the gay rights movement, promote the rights of particular groups that have been excluded from full social participation. Accordingly, gay rights groups have fought for laws that eliminate all forms of discrimination based on sexual orientation. They have also fought for the repeal of laws that discriminate on the basis of sexual orientation, such as anti-sodomy laws and laws that negatively affect parental custody of children (Adam, Duyvendak, and Krouwel, 1999).

Since the 1960s, the women's movement has succeeded in getting admission practices altered in professional schools, winning more freedom of reproductive choice for women, and opening up opportunities for women in the political, religious, military, educational, medical, and business systems (Adamson, Briskin, and McPhail, 1988; see Box 18.3).

The emergence of the peace, environmental, human rights, gay rights, and women's movements marked the beginning of a fourth stage in the history of social movements. This fourth stage involves the promotion of **universal citizenship**, or the extension of citizenship rights to all adult members of society and to society as a whole (Roche, 1995; Turner, 1986: 85–105).

Membership

New social movements are also novel in that they attract a disproportionately large number of highly educated, well-to-do people from the social, educational, and cultural fields—teachers, professors, journalists, social workers, artists, actors, writers—and student apprentices to these occupations. Such people are predisposed to participate in new social movements for several reasons. Their higher education exposes them to radical ideas and makes those ideas appealing. They tend to hold jobs outside the business community, which often opposes their values. And they often get personally involved in the problems of

BOX 18.3 THE WOMEN'S MOVEMENT AND ELECTORAL POLITICS

The women's movement was the first new social movement.

At the beginning of the twentieth century, women began to play a smaller role in domestic and farm work and started to enter the paid labour force in significant numbers. Owning more of their own economic resources, they became more independent-minded. They began to realize they might free themselves of oppressive authority in the home. They also started to understand there was nothing inevitable about their receiving less pay and working in worse conditions than men with comparable jobs did (Strong-Boag, 1986: 179).

Formulating a program for social change requires such resources as time, money, and education. Not surprisingly, therefore, the "first wave" of the women's movement comprised highly educated professionals. A group of women with just that social profile established the Canadian Woman Suffrage Association in Toronto in 1883. By demonstrating, petitioning, and gaining the support of influential liberal-minded men, women won the right to vote federally in 1918, in all provinces and territories but Quebec and Northwest Territories by 1925, in Quebec in 1940, and in the Northwest Territories by 1951.

Along with the right to vote, women won the right to run for public office. They immediately exercised that right, running mainly on the CCF and Liberal tickets. A woman was first elected to provincial office in Alberta in 1917 and to the federal Parliament in 1921.

In provincial and territorial legislatures and the federal Parliament, women sought institutional reform through government action. Specifically, they pursued equitable pay for women, easier access to higher education, protection from domestic violence, and a fair share of family assets and child support in case of divorce or desertion. However, progress was slow on all these fronts. That was partly because women's representation in the country's legislatures remained meagre. In 2012, women composed just 25 percent of federal MPs (Bashevkin, 1986; "Women in National Parliaments," 2012). Moreover, some female MPs were hardly advocates of women's rights.

Involvement in electoral politics requires time and money. Women are disadvantaged in this regard. On average, they have lower socioeconomic status than men do, and they are saddled with more domestic responsibilities. These factors prevent many women from running for office.

Public policy analysts note that female political participation can increase if such barriers are removed (Boyd, 2011: 175–76; Brodie, 1991). For example, laws could be passed that would allow candidates to take unpaid leave from their jobs to contest nominations and elections, set spending limits for nomination and election campaigns, make contributions for nomination campaigns tax deductible, treat child-care and housekeeping costs as reimbursable campaign expenses, and so on. Additionally, laws could be enacted that make government subsidies to political party campaigns dependent on

(continued)

BOX 18.3 (continued)

the proportion of their elected candidates that are women. In such a system, party subsidies would increase with the proportion of women elected.

Despite the existence of viable ideas for increasing women's participation in electoral politics, progress has been slow. Therefore, many feminists have developed a strategy that is oriented less toward established political institutions and more toward grassroots action. The new strategy sought to achieve change not just "from above," by means of party politics but also "from below," by creating a whole network of new organizations, such as study groups, consciousness-raising circles, women's bookstores, rape crisis centres, abortion clinics, shelters for battered women, and opportunities to publicize the importance of feminist aims, such as International Women's Day marches.

It was not only slow progress on the established political front that led women to create this network of new organizations. Many "second-wave" feminists were deeply involved in the student movement of the 1960s and 1970s. They were appalled to discover that, despite much rhetoric about liberation and equality, men controlled the student movement and often refused to allow feminist issues to become part of their agenda. To pursue their aims, they felt it was necessary to create new organizations run by women.

Today, the women's movement operates both at the grassroots level and within established political organizations to achieve its aims. It is internally differentiated. *Liberal feminists* believe that women can participate fully in society if they achieve equality of opportunity with men. They therefore advocate policies aimed at pay equity and the elimination of gender discrimination in the workplace. *Radical feminists* hold that male domination is rooted in the family. They champion free and safe contraception and abortion, an equitable division of domestic labour, and the like. *Socialist feminists* maintain that legal equality is not enough to ensure that women can participate fully in society. In addition, they argue, the state should provide affordable and accessible daycare facilities and other services. These services, they say, could alleviate the economic burdens that prevent most women, especially those from the working class, from taking full advantage of available opportunities for education and employment. *Anti-racist and postmodernist feminists* have criticized liberal, socialist, and radical feminists for generalizing from the experience of white women and failing to see how women's lives are rooted in particular historical and racial experiences. These new currents have done much to extend the relevance of feminism to previously marginalized groups. Thus, despite their different emphases, the various types of feminism share a strong desire to see members of a previously marginal group expand their citizenship rights and become full participants in society.

their clients and audiences, sometimes even becoming their advocates (Brint, 1984; Rootes, 1995).

Globalization Potential

Finally, new social movements possess more potential for globalization than old social movements did. In the 1960s, social movements were typically *national* in scope. That is why, for example, the intensity and frequency of urban race riots in the United States in the 1960s did not depend on such local conditions as the degree of black-white inequality in a given city (Spilerman, 1970, 1976). Instead, congressional and presidential action (and lack of action) on civil rights issues, national TV coverage of race issues, and growing black consciousness and solidarity helped to create the view among African Americans that racial problems are nationwide and can be solved only by the federal government.

Many new social movements that gained force in the 1970s increased the scope of protest still further. For example, members of the nuclear disarmament and environmental movements viewed federal legislation as a necessary but insufficient solution to the issues that troubled them. Once they recognized that, say, the condition of the Brazilian rain forest affects climatic conditions worldwide and that the spread of weapons of mass destruction can easily destroy all of humanity, movement activists pressed for international agreements binding all countries to stop environmental destruction and nuclear proliferation. Social movements went global.

The globalization of social movements was facilitated by the ease with which people in various national movements could travel and communicate with like-minded activists from other countries. In the age of CNN, inexpensive jet transportation, fax machines, and email, it is possible not only to see the connection between apparently local problems and their global sources but also to act locally and globally. Greenpeace, for instance, is a highly successful environmental movement that originated in Vancouver in the mid-1970s and now has offices in 41 countries, with its international office in Amsterdam ("Greenpeace," 1999). A more recent global initiative with roots in Vancouver is the Occupy Movement.

On July 13, 2011, Kalle Lasn, editor of the Vancouver-based anti-consumerist magazine *Adbusters*, created a hashtag on Twitter, #OCCUPYWALLSTREET, and designed a poster of a ballerina dancing on the back of the bronze sculpture of a bull (symbolic of a profitable market) racing up Wall Street in Manhattan (Yardley, 2011). The poster called for people to go to the centre of the financial universe and protest the growing wealth and greed of the richest 1 percent of society and their role in causing the world financial crisis of 2008–09. Thousands did, and within days, demonstrations and encampments were sprouting in cities around the world. It was the most remarkable evidence of the globalization of social movements ever observed. Although nearly all of the protests had died down by the end of 2011 (St. John's, Newfoundland and Labrador, was the last Canadian holdout), the movement succeeded in influencing global political discourse. One poll found that two-thirds of Americans surveyed in December 2011 believed that conflict between the rich and the poor was the main conflict in society—an increase of 19 percent since 2009 (Pew Research Center, 2012). The Occupy Movement helped to put class conflict back on the political agenda of the United States and other countries.

SOURCE: © Monica E/Occupy Together/www.occupytogether.org.

The globalization of social movements can be further illustrated by coming full circle and returning to the anecdote with which I began this chapter. In 1991, I visited my hometown. I had not been back in years. As I entered the city, I vaguely sensed that something was different. I could not define the change precisely until I reached the Irving pulp and paper mill. Suddenly, it became obvious: the rotten-egg smell was virtually gone. I subsequently discovered that in the 1970s a local woman whose son developed a serious case of asthma took legal action against the mill and eventually won. The mill owner was required by law to install a "scrubber" in the main smokestack to remove most of the sulfur dioxide emissions. Soon, the federal government was putting pressure on the mill owner to purify the polluted water that poured out of the plant and into the St. John River and the Bay of Fundy. Apparently, local citizens and the environmental movement had caused a change in the climate of opinion, influencing the government to force the mill owner to spend millions of dollars on a cleanup. It took decades, but what was political heresy in 1968 eventually became established practice because environmental concerns had been amplified by the voice of a movement that had grown to global proportions. In general, as this case illustrates, globalization helps to ensure that many new social movements transcend local and national boundaries and that many of them—but, as you will now learn, not all—promote universalistic goals.

II. THE OTHER 85 PERCENT

With variations, the pattern of social movement evolution sketched previously applies to the 20 or so rich countries of North America, Western Europe, Oceania, and Japan. As we have seen, social movements in these rich countries typically sought to broaden democracy through the expansion of citizenship rights. In contrast, social movements in the other 85 percent of the world (by population) developed differently. They focused less on broadening the bases of democracy than on ensuring more elemental human rights, notably freedom from colonial rule and freedom to create the conditions for independent economic growth.

The "other 85 percent" of the world is relatively weak economically, politically, and militarily because it began substantial industrialization only after World War I and in some cases after World War II. This circumstance allowed the early industrializers (Britain, France, Japan, Russia, the United States, and so on) to carve up most of Asia, Africa, and South America into colonies, protectorates, mandates, spheres of influence, and other administrative forms of subjugation. The nineteenth century was the age of imperialism. The early industrializers used the rest of the world as a captive market for their manufactured goods and a source of inexpensive raw materials and labour. They enriched themselves even as they limited economic growth and well-being in the less-developed countries.

Events in the Muslim world were, in many respects, typical and thus illustrate the problem (Hourani, 1991: 265–349). Already by the 1830s the armed forces of France had taken control of part of Algeria, those of Britain had taken control of part of the Arabian peninsula, and those of Russia had taken over the Muslim lands of the Caucasus. A century later, almost the entire Middle East and North Africa were under British and French control. Egyptian cotton fed the looms of Lancashire. Iraqi oil supplied half of France's needs. British and French ships brought European machinery and textiles to the region. British and French financiers profited handsomely from their control of local banking. Some indigenous merchants and landowners benefited from the new economic relations too. However, the growing number of peasants and urban workers remained poor and powerless.

In the world's rich countries, a strong bourgeoisie—an affluent and politically powerful class of merchants, industrialists, and financiers—did much to promote the growth of democracy in its early stages (Moore, 1967). In contrast, in the Muslim countries and the rest of the less economically developed world, the bourgeoisie was small, weak, and dependent on imperial interests. Consequently, democratic ideals had little chance to sink deep roots. Instead, European and (especially after World War II) American domination of less-developed countries bred resentment, resistance, and revolt. Peasants, urban workers, intellectuals, and military officers were increasingly attracted to anti-imperialist independence movements based on various forms and mixes of socialism and nationalism (Brym, 1980: 50–53; Wolf, 1999 [1969]).

In the Muslim world, Islam was an additional source of anti-imperialist sentiment. In 1928, the Society of the Muslim Brothers was formed in Egypt ("Muslim Brotherhood Movement," 2002). It served as a prototype for other, similar groups. The Muslim Brotherhood argued against Western values and imperialist domination. It called for a return to the teaching of the Qur'an, strictly interpreted, and demanded that Egypt become an Islamic state based on religious law (*shari'a*). This type of thinking became popular in Egypt and throughout the Muslim world in the twentieth century, gaining impetus especially in Iran from the 1960s on and then spreading to Algeria and as far afield as Afghanistan and Sudan by the end of the century.

Growing popularity did not translate into widespread political ascendance until recent times. After World War II, almost all Middle Eastern and North African countries were authoritarian regimes that suppressed the Muslim Brotherhood and forced its popularity to flow underground. There, it branched into several streams, two of the most notable of which were an extremist current exemplified by al Qaeda and a more liberal current exemplified by political parties that a plurality of Moroccans, Tunisians, and Egyptians favoured in national elections held in 2011 and 2012.

Extremist Political Islam: al Qaeda

A clear line of intellectual influence leads from the early Muslim Brothers to the assassins of Egypt's President Anwar Sadat in 1981 after he made peace with Israel to Osama bin Laden and al Qaeda (Worth, 2001). Al Qaeda's chief aims are to remove all Western (especially American) influence from areas with Muslim majorities, create in their place societies based on a fundamentalist interpretation of Islamic law, and destroy Israel as a Jewish state.

It is noteworthy that, however much al Qaeda is influenced by ideas dating back nine decades, it is every inch a global movement that relies on modern technology for its successes. Al Qaeda has placed operatives in as many as 60 countries. It finances itself through a complex international network of legitimate businesses, charitable and relief organizations, private donors, and opium trafficking operations (Shahar, 2001). Bin Laden communicated with his operatives via satellite telephone until U.S. law enforcement authorities inexplicably revealed they were tapping calls from his base in Afghanistan. Once he learned of these taps, he increased his use of another, more effective means of global communication—sending messages that are easily encrypted but difficult to decode via the Internet (Kelley, 2001; McCullogh, 2000).

Some analysts think such messages were used to help plan and coordinate the complex, virtually simultaneous jet hijackings that resulted in the crash of an airliner in Pennsylvania and the destruction of the World Trade Center and part of the Pentagon on September 11, 2001, killing some 3000 people.

Liberal Political Islam: Morocco, Tunisia, and Egypt

In late 2010, Mohamed Bouazizi, a 27-year-old Tunisian street vendor, set himself on fire to protest harassment and humiliation by local officials. His action catalyzed widespread and often violent anti-regime demonstrations that first overthrew the Tunisian government and then spread with similar effect to Egypt and Libya, while also rocking other governments throughout the region. Bouazizi and those inspired by him objected to the authoritarianism, corruption, economic stagnation, unemployment, and poverty that characterizes most of the Middle East and North Africa. They initiated what came to be called the "Arab Spring" (see Box 18.4).

The most popular political parties that emerged from national elections held in Morocco, Tunisia, and Egypt in 2011 and 2012 were those organized by the Muslim Brotherhood, now free to run for office. These parties are unlike anything most Westerners had expected, let alone seen. On the one hand, the parties now in the ascendant in the region insist that Islam should form the basis of politics and law. They are suspicious of Western intentions. On the other hand, they have repeatedly and publicly stated their support for democratic elections and their tolerance of religious and ethnic minorities. Exactly how such apparently liberal Islamic parties will act once in office is unclear as of this writing. However, they have given hope to many people in the region and beyond that the dark era of authoritarianism that characterized the Middle East and North Africa for so long is at last beginning to lift (Andersen, Brym, and Araj, 2012).

As recent events in the Middle East and North Africa illustrate, a wide range of reactions against Western power and influence now grips much of the developing world. In its extreme forms, the

BOX 18.4 WILL THE REVOLUTION BE TWITTERED?

Some observers claim that Facebook and Twitter made the Arab Spring possible because they allowed the powerless to express their grievances and coordinate their actions with ease. However, such claims probably overstate the beneficial effects of new communications technology on global social movements. Most Facebook friends are really acquaintances, and most Twitter followers don't know the people they are following personally. It is relatively easy to get such socially distant people on networking sites to participate in certain actions—but only if participation requires little sacrifice. Thus, the Facebook page of the Save Darfur Coalition has nearly 1.3 million members, but they have donated an average of just nine cents each to the organization (Gladwell, 2010). Big sacrifices in the name of political principles require strong social ties, not the weak ties offered by Twitter accounts and Facebook pages. Typically, when individuals join a movement, they attract clusters of friends, relatives, and members of the same unions, cooperatives, fraternities, college dorms, churches, mosques, and neighbourhoods. This pattern occurs because involvement in a social movement is likely to require big sacrifices, and you need to be close to others before you can reasonably expect them to share your ideas and willingness to sacrifice for a cause (McAdam, 1982).

A protester in Tahrir Square, Cairo, Egypt, in 2011, helping to overthrow the authoritarian regime of President Hosni Mubarak.
SOURCE: © Patrick Baz/Getty Images.

anti-Western reaction has no respect for minority rights, multiculturalism, elections, relatively open markets, and many of the other freedoms we enjoy and often take for granted in the West. In its more moderate forms, it shares many of the West's fundamental values. Yet regardless of its orientation, the anti-Western reaction is everywhere based on the desire of people to restore the independence and dignity they lost when the industrialized world showed up on their doorstep uninvited. One of the great tasks the West faces in the twenty-first century is to defend itself against violence while doing its utmost to remove the ultimate source of that violence: the gap between rich and poor countries that opened up at the time of the Industrial Revolution and that has widened ever since. Whether we are up to the task is anyone's guess.

SUMMARY

1. Democracy involves a two-way process of control between the state (the set of institutions that formulate and carry out a country's law, policies, and binding regulations) and civil society (the private sphere, consisting of social movements, political parties, and so on).
2. The level of democracy in a society depends on the capacity of civil society to influence the state through citizen support of social movements, political parties, and other groups. That capacity increases as power becomes more widely distributed in society.
3. Although pluralists correctly note that democratic politics is about negotiation and compromise, they fail to appreciate how advantaged groups tend to have more political influence than others do.
4. Although elite theorists are right to note that power is concentrated in the hands of advantaged groups, they fail to appreciate how variations in the distribution of power influence political behaviour and public policy.
5. While power-balance theorists focus on the effect of changes in the distribution of power in society, they fail to appreciate what state-centred theorists emphasize—that state institutions and laws also affect political behaviour and public policy.
6. The degree to which power is widely distributed influences the success of particular kinds of parties and policies. Widely distributed power is associated with the success of labour parties and policies that redistribute wealth.
7. Research does not support the view that social movements emerge when relative deprivation spreads.
8. Research suggests that people are more inclined to rebel against the status quo when they are bound by close social ties to many other people who feel similarly wronged and when they have the money and other resources needed to protest.
9. For social movements to grow, members must engage in frame alignment, making the activities, goals, and ideology of the movement congruent with the interests, beliefs, and values of potential new recruits.
10. The history of democracy is a struggle for the acquisition of constantly broadening citizenship rights—first the right to free speech, freedom of religion, and justice before the law, then the right to vote and run for office, then the right to a certain level of economic security and full participation in the life of society, and finally the right of marginal groups to full citizenship and the right of humanity as a whole to peace and security.
11. In the developing world, social movements have focused less on broadening the bases of democracy than on ensuring more elemental human rights, notably freedom from colonial rule and freedom to create the conditions for independent economic growth. In some cases these movements have taken extreme, anti-democratic forms.

QUESTIONS TO CONSIDER

1. Have you ever participated in a social movement or been actively involved in a political party? If so, explain how your political choices (which party you joined, your level of participation, the timing of your recruitment) were influenced by the sociological factors discussed in this chapter. If you have never participated in a social movement or been actively involved in a political party, explain how the sociological factors discussed in this chapter influence you to remain politically inactive.
2. How would you achieve a political goal? Map out a detailed strategy for reaching a clearly defined aim, such as a reduction in income tax

or an increase in university funding. Who would you try to recruit to help you achieve your goal? Why? What collective actions do you think would be most successful? Why? To whose attention would these actions be directed? Why? Write a manifesto that frames your argument in a way that is culturally appealing to potential recruits.

3. Do you think that social movements will be more or less widespread in the twenty-first century than they were in the twentieth? Why or why not? What kinds of social movements are likely to predominate?
4. Do you think that the twenty-first century will be more or less democratic than the twentieth? Why or why not?

GLOSSARY

Authorities (p. 440) are people who occupy the command posts of legitimized power structures.

Authority (p. 440) is power that is widely viewed as legitimate.

Civil citizenship (p. 453) recognizes the right to free speech, freedom of religion, and justice before the law.

Civil society (p. 442) is the private (nonstate) sphere of social life.

Elite theory (p. 443) maintains that well-to-do people consistently have more political influence than people who are less well-to-do have and that society is therefore not as democratic as it is often portrayed.

Force (p. 441) is coercive power.

Frame alignment (p. 451) is the process by which individual interests, beliefs, and values either become congruent and complementary with the activities, goals, and ideology of a social movement.

New social movements (p. 453) are post-1950s movements that attract a disproportionately large number of highly educated people in the social, educational, and cultural fields and universalize the struggle for citizenship.

Pluralist theory (p. 442) holds that society has many competing interests and centres of power and that no one interest or power centre predominates in the long run.

Political citizenship (p. 453) recognizes the right to run for office and vote.

Political parties (p. 441) are organizations that seek to control state power.

A **political revolution** (p. 441) is a concerted attempt on the part of many people to overthrow existing political institutions and establish new ones. Political revolutions take place when widespread and successful movements of opposition clash with crumbling traditional or legal-rational authority.

Power (p. 440) is the ability of an individual or a group to impose its will on others, even if they resist.

Power-balance theory (p. 446) suggests that social movement formation and success depend on how powerful authorities are, compared with partisans of change. It also holds that societies with widely distributed power are more democratic and more egalitarian than are societies with narrowly held power.

Relative deprivation (p. 450) is an intolerable gap between the social rewards people feel they deserve and the social rewards they expect to receive.

Resource mobilization theory (p. 450) holds that social movements crystallize and succeed in achieving their goals to the degree that they have access to scarce resources, such as money and effective communication facilities.

A **ruling class** (p. 443) is a self-conscious and cohesive group of people, led by corporate executives and owners of big business, who act to advance their common interests.

Social citizenship (p. 453) recognizes the right to a certain level of economic security and full participation in social life.

Social movements (p. 440) are enduring collective attempts to change part or all of the social order by means of rioting, petitioning, striking, demonstrating, and establishing pressure groups, unions, and political parties.

The **state** (p. 441) is a set of institutions that formulate and implement a country's laws, policies, and binding regulations. It consists of an executive branch (which initiates laws), a legislative branch (which makes laws), a judicial branch (which interprets laws), and an administrative and coercive apparatus (which enforces laws and protects state security).

State-centred theory (p. 448) shows how the state structures political life independently of the way power is distributed among classes and other groups at a given time.

Universal citizenship (p. 454) recognizes the right of marginal groups and the rights of humanity as a whole to full citizenship.

SUGGESTED READING

Baer, Doug, ed. (2002). *Political Sociology: Canadian Perspectives.* Toronto: Oxford University Press. This useful compendium of Canadian materials covers major issues and debates.

Tilly, Charles and Sidney Tarrow. (2007). *Contentious Politics.* Boulder CO: Paradigm Publishers. An accessible and innovative introduction to political sociology by two grand masters.

Wolf, Eric. (1999 [1969]). *Peasant Wars of the 20th Century.* Norman, OK: Oklahoma University Press. The best introduction to social movements in the developing world.

NOTES

1. In addition, fewer than 13 percent of the American working class are unionized, making it the least organized working class in any of the world's rich countries.
2. For example, in the 1890s, a coalition of white and black southern farmers threatened the established American political parties. It was precisely for this reason that American electoral laws were made more restrictive.
3. Some of these generalizations do not apply to countries with a long tradition of labour government. For example, since World War II, Sweden has experienced high levels of unionization and low strike rates. That is because Swedish workers and their representatives are involved in government policymaking. Decisions about wages and benefits tend to be made in negotiations among unions, employer associations, and governments rather than on the picket line.

CHAPTER 19

GLOBALIZATION

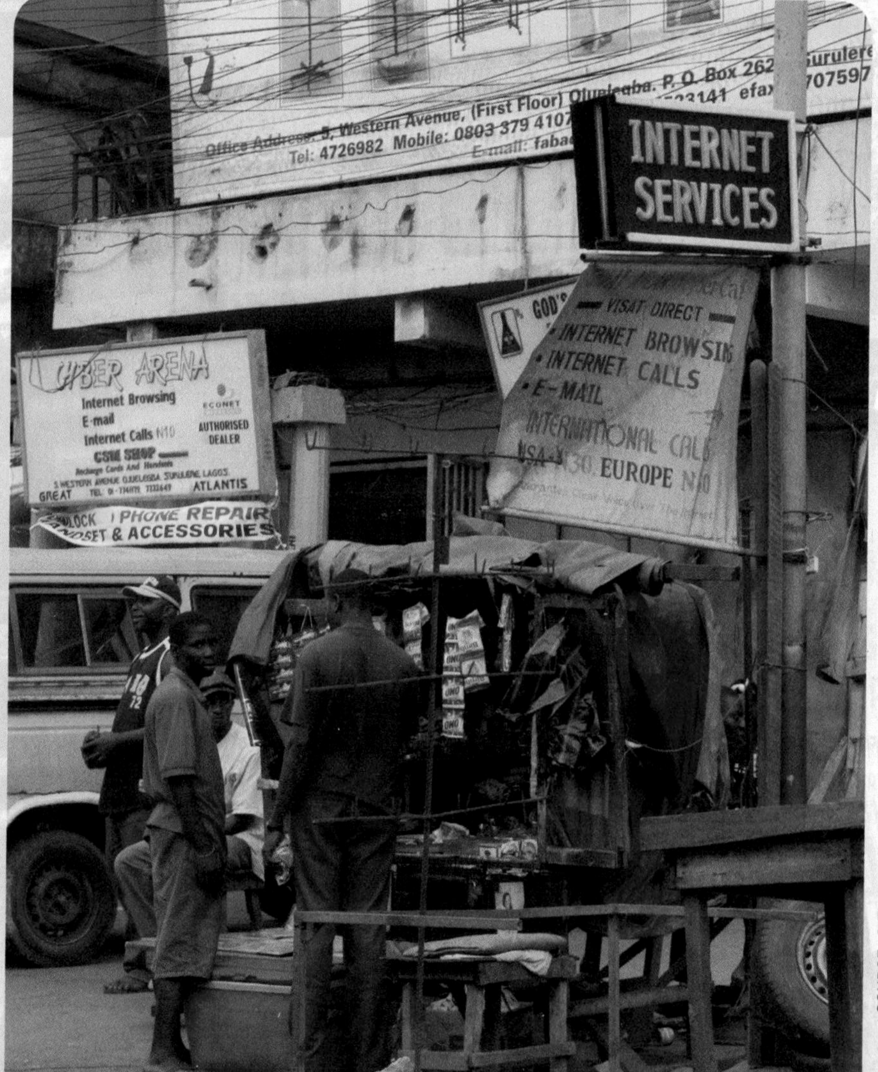

SOURCE: © Thomas Grabka/laif/Redux.

Josée Johnston
UNIVERSITY OF TORONTO

IN THIS CHAPTER YOU WILL LEARN THAT

- Globalization is a term used to describe how the world "shrinks" as capital, ideas, corporations, commodities, and workers rapidly cross vast distances. You will learn about the complexities of globalization, a term much used and abused, and acquire a working definition of it.
- Globalization is not a distant force but a real-world phenomenon that affects you daily as you eat, drink, work, and go shopping. By the end of the chapter, you will better understand how globalization relates to you as a consumer, a worker, and a citizen.
- Globalization is dynamic because it is contested by different social forces promoting different kinds of capitalist development and social organization. This chapter will give you a conceptual framework that will allow you to appreciate the "top-down" forces of globalization that promote the expansion of global markets and the "bottom-up" forces demanding greater democracy, social justice, and sustainability in the global system.

INTRODUCTION

THE BURGER AND FRIES GO GLOBAL

Think about your average fast-food meal: a burger, fries, and a pop. This is the food of North America—simple, greasy, fast, and familiar. Maybe fast food has something to do with the sociology of health or the sociology of food, but what does it have to do with the sociology of globalization?

It turns out that globalization has a lot to do with everyday events like eating fast food. The average North American meal travels more than 1600 kilometres to reach your dinner table, so there is a good chance that your burger and fries have been *globalized*.

Let's start with the burger. Although Canadian ranchers pride themselves on their cattle exports, at least 30 percent of the beef eaten in Canada is imported from the United States, Australia, New Zealand, and Uruguay. Even if the beef in your burger did originate in Canada, the process of transforming a cow into your hamburger was deeply affected by globalization processes. Because of global market pressures, the meatpacking industry in Canada was restructured in the 1980s and 1990s; the goal was to cut costs by centralizing production and finding cheaper labour supplies.

SOURCE: © Dwight Cendrowski/Alamy.

Today, just two slaughterhouse companies, Cargill Foods and XL Packers, account for more than 80 percent of Canada's beef-slaughtering capacity. The small town of Brooks, Alberta, is home to Lakeside Packers (XL Packers bought Lakeside in 2009, and controls 47 percent of meat packing capacity in Canada) (National Farmers Union 2009). Global restructuring in the meatpacking industry has also meant a shift in the global labour force. Thousands of people immigrated to work at Lakeside, and many languages are spoken inside the factory walls including Arabic, French, Spanish, Tagalog, Chinese, and Cambodian.

Even a vegetarian's fast-food choices are affected by globalization. In 2001, six vegetarians from British Columbia working with an American lawyer moved to sue McDonald's after it was revealed that McDonald's French fries use beef fat for "flavouring." After hearing the announcement, vegetarian activists in India held demonstrations and attacked a McDonald's in Bombay, demanding that McDonald's leave the country ("McDonald's Apologizes," 2001). McDonald's settled the lawsuit in 2002 by agreeing to donate $10 million dollars to Hindu and other consumer groups.

If our fast food is influenced by global forces, North American fast food also influences global eating. North American markets became relatively saturated with fast-food outlets in the 1980s, so McDonald's made a push in the 1990s for international expansion. The number of countries with a McDonald's went from 59 in 1991 to 119 in 2011 (McDonald's, 2011). Today, McDonald's operates more than 33 000 restaurants, and more than half of these are outside the United States (McDonald's, 2011). McDonald's opens a new restaurant every 17 hours and is the world's largest user of beef. Ronald McDonald himself is the second most recognized figure in the world, next to Santa Claus (Brownell and Horgen, 2004: 58), and by 2005, sales in the United States accounted for only 34 percent of McDonald's revenue (Workman, 2006). For these reasons, scholars now believe we should be studying not only the globalization of fast food but also the globalization of obesity (Sobal, 2001). The World Health Organization (WHO) estimates that 1.5 billion adults over the age of 20 are overweight; a third of them are obese (WHO, 2011).

It turns out, then, that everyday activities—like eating a hamburger and fries—have a lot do to with globalization. In an obvious way, the resources and labour that make up a fast-food meal originate from locations all around the globe. But even when the ingredients come from close to home, the food itself can be affected by global events, such as international trade agreements, European social movements, international labour migration, and faraway protests against McDonald's.

GLOBALIZATION OR "GLOBALONEY"?

But before going any further, let's raise perhaps our most difficult question in this chapter: What do we mean by *globalization*? It is a frequently heard buzzword, yet there is no consensus on its meaning. The term was coined in the late 1970s, and today there are thousands of globalization books, conferences, university courses, and references in newspapers and magazines, many of which contradict each other. This confusion has led some academics to dismiss the term altogether as a confused mixture of globalization and baloney—what some crankily refer to as "globaloney."

While it is hard to find agreement on a definition of globalization, you don't have to look hard to find controversy about whether globalization is good or bad. A common tendency on both the left and the right of the political spectrum is to depict globalization in simplistic terms. For right-wing free-marketers, globalization represents the welcome spread of capitalism throughout the world. For many left-wing social activists and politicians, globalization is more like a Death Star. In the words of Barry Lynn, former executive director of *Global Business* magazine,

> Globalization is many things, and much has been written about it and said. But throw all the tomes and studies and placards into a giant try-works, and you'll render two simple arguments:
>
> 1. Globalization is good because it spreads what is good in America, such as a liberal approach to business, and McDonald's.
> 2. Globalization is bad because it spreads what is worst about America, such as a liberal approach to business, and McDonald's. (Lynn, 2002: 34)

A primary objective of this chapter is to get beyond this kind of simplistic thinking and gain a more sophisticated sense of what exactly is meant by globalization. The objective is not to provide the ultimate definition of globalization that will ring true for all people until the end of time, but to understand how different political and economic interests struggle to promote their own brand of globalization.

DEFINING GLOBALIZATION

While figuring out exactly what we mean by globalization is a primary objective of the chapter, we need a neutral definition to get us started: **Globalization** is a social, economic, and political process that makes it easier for people, goods, ideas, and capital to travel around the world at an unprecedented pace (Waters, 1995: 3). Globalization makes the world look and feel smaller.

Of course, the world is not shrinking literally. What is instead occurring is that people, money, corporations, and ideas are travelling across the globe more quickly and efficiently than ever before. Distance no longer seems as relevant, and time lags that used to characterize our social relations are diminished. We no longer think it's crazy to have a romantic relationship with somebody across the country or even across the world. We can now communicate instantly through telephone, email, instant messenger, or a web-camera connection. If we want to see our girlfriend or boyfriend in person, we can take a relatively inexpensive plane trip rather than waiting for an ocean-going vessel to take us for a week-long journey across the seas. If our beloved is broke and needs money, we can transfer money instantly through electronic banking networks. And if you are single, you can systematically search the world for love through the thousands of online dating sites, some of which are devoted just to vegetarians, tattoo artists, and cat lovers.

One term for this shrinking world phenomenon is **time–space compression,** which suggests that we are no longer slowed down by long distances and time differences (Harvey, 1990: 284). Not only do we feel less constrained by time and distance, but some global phenomena also seem to transcend the idea of physical space altogether. The Internet has facilitated the creation of **virtual communities,** in which people can meet, share ideas, play games, and build relationships across borders without ever meeting face-to-face. Use of the Internet has not only increased dramatically but has also changed the patterns of our daily lives and interactions. In a survey of college graduates in 14 countries, including Canada, 40 percent felt that the Internet is more important to daily life than is music, dating, or spending time with friends (Cisco, 2011). While the Internet may seem indispensible to many readers of this textbook, it is important to note that the just 30 percent of the world's population is connected to the Internet (see Table 19.1).

There are many examples of time–space compression but there are also many instances in which time still passes slowly, and the limits of geography are still relevant. People may be more "wired" in

TABLE 19.1 WORLD INTERNET USERS AND POPULATION

WORLD REGIONS	POPULATION (2011 EST.)	POPULATION % OF WORLD	INTERNET USERS	USAGE GROWTH (2000–11)	INTERNET USERS AS % OF POPULATION	PERCENTAGE OF WORLD USERS	FACEBOOK USERS
Africa	1 037 524 058	15.0%	118 848 060	2 527.4%	11.4%	5.7%	30 665 460
Asia	3 879 740 877	56.0%	922 329 554	706.9%	23.8%	44.0%	152 957 480
Europe	816 426 346	11.8%	476 213 935	353.1%	58.3%	22.7%	208 907 040
Middle East	216 258 843	3.1%	68 553 666	1 987.0%	31.7%	3.3%	16 125 180
North America	347 394 870	5.0%	272 066 000	151.7%	78.3%	13.0%	167 999 540
Latin America/ Caribbean	597 283 165	8.6%	215 939 400	1 037.4%	36.2%	10.3%	121 192 460
Oceania/ Australia	35 426 995	0.5%	21 293 830	480.4%	60.1%	1.0%	12 881 560
WORLD TOTAL	6 930 055 154	100%	2 095 006 005	480.4%	30.2%	100.0%	710 728 720

SOURCE: Adapted from Internet World Stats (2011).

the global age, but they are often connecting with friends and family in their city—not necessarily making new friends around the world (Ghemawat, 2007). In fact, fewer than 2 percent of phone calls and less than 20 percent of data transmitted over the Internet cross national borders (Ghemawat, 2011). In addition, not all people and ideas have access to channels of globalization, such as the Internet or even the telephone. Inequality of access to means of communication is commonly called the **digital divide** (see Table 19.2).

There is a lot of academic debate about how recent globalization is. We won't venture far into this hotly contested territory, but it is important to note that the world has been shrinking for a long time. Time–space compression can be traced back at least to the sixteenth century with the beginning of trans-oceanic European exploration. The world became smaller with the invention of the steamship and the locomotive—two technologies that connected distant populations at a rate unimagined by previous generations. Colonial relationships in the eighteenth

TABLE 19.2 GLOBALIZATION AND TIME–SPACE COMPRESSION

EXAMPLE	HOW IT COMPRESSES SPACE AND TIME	LIMITS TO GLOBALIZATION
The telephone	Person-to-person communication is made possible across oceans and most national boundaries.	Many of the world's inhabitants do not have access to a telephone. In Africa, there are only 1.4 fixed telephone lines per 100 inhabitants, far below the world average of 16.6 telephone lines per 100 inhabitants (International Telecommunication Union, 2011a). Mobile telephony has greatly increased, but there are still significant differences around the globe: European consumers enjoy 119.5 mobile lines per 100 inhabitants, but Africa has only 53 mobile lines per 100 inhabitants (International Telecommunication Union, 2011b).
The Internet	Ideas, images, articles, videos, music, and text forms can be transmitted almost instantly across vast geographic distances.	On a global scale, access to the Internet is even more limited than access to the telephone. (See Table 19.1.)
Satellite television	Television is no longer restricted to local television stations; satellites allow transmission of programming from multiple points of production around the world.	Television ownership is concentrated in wealthy countries, television production is controlled by a small number of media monopolies centred in the industrialized North, and television content globally is fairly homogeneous and closely linked to consumer capitalism (McKibben, 1993). The top five media corporations in the world are concentrated in North America, and include Walt Disney Company, Time Warner, and Rupert Murdoch's News Corporation. Together, these conglomerates control hundreds of broadcasting, publishing, Internet, television and film companies ("Media Giants," 2011).
Electronic money markets	Capital can flow across national borders almost instantly.	The World Bank estimates that 2.7 billion people around the world do not have access to formal financial services, including bank accounts—let alone access to electronic financial markets (World Bank, 2011a).

and nineteenth centuries moved millions of people and shiploads of wealth around the world.

The current phase of time–space compression is not radically different in form, but its pace has grown especially quickly since the 1980s. A jet is much faster than a steamship. Email is less cumbersome than mail travelling by truck or ship. Ships moving silver, spices, and opium across the ocean can transfer wealth globally but not as quickly as the enormous and instantaneous flows of capital that move in and out of the stock market in seconds.

THE GLOBAL AND THE ETHICAL

Understanding globalization as a series of processes connecting people, resources, and capital across the globe gets us away from seeing it as either a blessing or an evil. Globalization is inherently neither good nor bad, but the consequences of globalization processes do affect human lives and the environment. These consequences generate strong opinions and ethical positions, particularly as they relate to economic processes and the role of the United States on the global stage.

Ethical debates surrounding global capitalism, and the global spread of insurrection, have become particularly pronounced in recent years. In December 2010, an incident in Tunisia sent shockwaves across this tiny country and the world. Mohamed Bouazizi, a young university graduate, could not find a job, so he began selling fruit and vegetables to make ends meet. When the authorities confiscated his produce because he did not have a licence, Bouazizi set himself on fire out of desperation and anger. In the days and weeks that followed, protests escalated across the country as Tunisians decried the bleak future they faced. In mid-January 2011, after a month of unrest, the Tunisian president, Zine al-Abidine Ben Ali, was overthrown. By late January, similar rumblings were occurring in nearby Egypt. Thousands began to gather in Tahrir ("Liberation") Square to protest the regime of President Hosni Mubarak. Egyptians rallied against difficult living conditions, increasing unemployment, corruption, and stagnation. Mubarak's 30-year rule ended in February. In the months that followed, similar uprisings took place in several Arab countries, including Libya, Bahrain, and Syria, as these countries' populations spoke out against the economic adversity they faced ("Egypt Protests," 2011; "Egypt Uprising," 2011; "Tahrir Square's Place," 2011; Whitaker, 2010).

Reclaiming public space and challenging inequality was also a common theme for the Occupy Wall Street movement that began in September 2011 in the United States. "Occupy" protests soon spread to many cities in Canada and around the world, including Toronto, Montreal, Tokyo, Tel Aviv, and Paris (see Figure 19.1). Like dissidents in the Middle East, the members of the Occupy movement criticized the inequalities generated by capitalism. However, unlike demonstrators in Tunisia, Egypt, and Syria, tent protesters did not seek to overthrow their leaders. They focused instead on glaring contrasts in the global economy: CEOs earn millions of dollars a year while middle-class families struggle to keep their homes. The movement resonated even among people who didn't protest. Former Canadian prime minister Paul Martin noted that he "[had] yet to talk to anyone who says [the protesters] aren't reflecting a disquiet that they themselves feel," and added, "the powerful thing is that Occupy Wall Street has hit a chord that really is touching the middle class—the middle class in Canada, the middle class in the United States, the middle class right around the world—and I think that makes it ... very, very powerful" (Freeland, 2011).

TOP-DOWN VERSUS BOTTOM-UP GLOBALIZATION

Questions of equality, security, and social justice are critical in the ongoing debate about globalization and will be explored in the rest of this chapter. These debates can be understood as part of the tension between top-down and bottom-up globalization. **Top-down globalization** involves the actions of groups promoting globalized capitalism and free trade. The term *globalization* was first widely used by the American Express credit card company, which boasted in the 1970s that its card was accepted worldwide (Harvey, 1990: 13). The term was then taken up in financial and business circles, where it came to represent hope for a world where capital could flow freely, uninhibited by national boundaries or governments insisting on national regulations and taxation.

Top-down globalization has been dominated by neoliberal economic policies, which have become prevalent in both rich and poor countries since the 1980s. **Neoliberalism** is associated with a retreat from state spending and regulation, a focus on individual responsibility for one's own welfare, less protection for labour and the environment, privatization of state resources, and faith in the power of the market and the profit motive to create wealth (see Chapter 9,

FIGURE 19.1 OCCUPY PROTESTS AROUND THE WORLD OCTOBER 2011

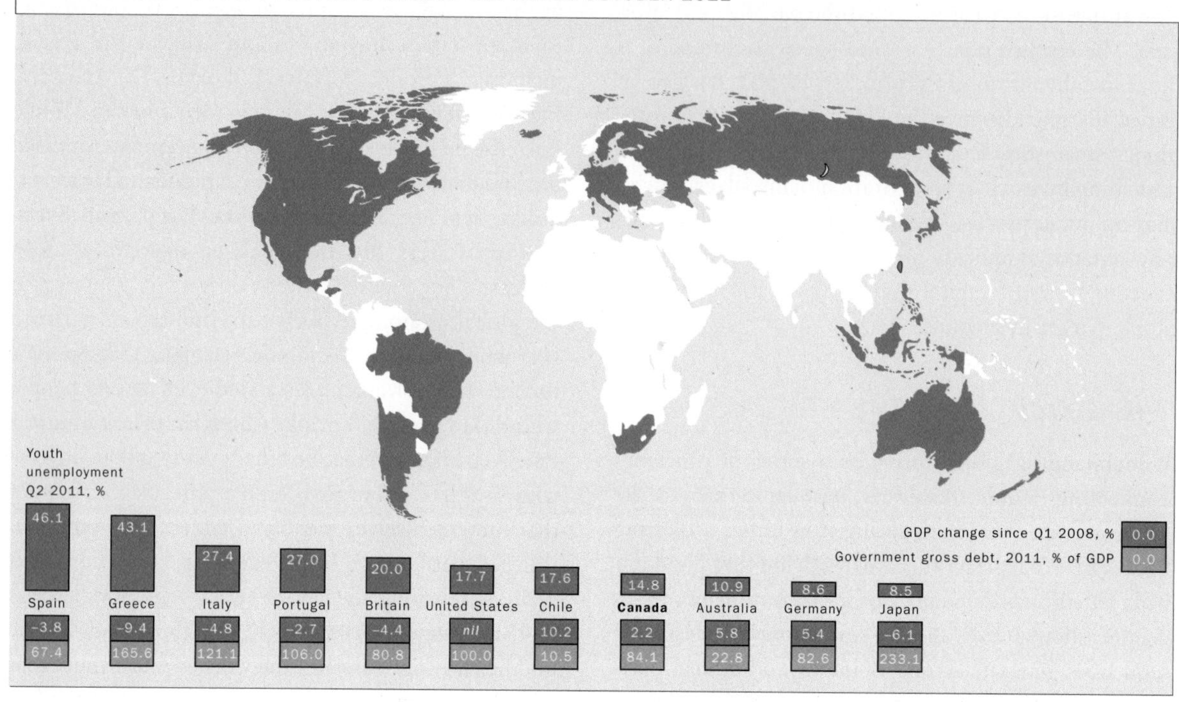

SOURCE: From http://www.economist.com/blogs/dailychart/2011/10/occupy-protests © The Economist Newspaper Limited, London (November 2, 2011).

Development and Underdevelopment). Top-down globalization is also strongly associated with the United States because of its role in promoting neoliberal policies globally through such institutions as the International Monetary Fund (IMF) and the World Bank, headquartered in Washington, D.C. For this reason, top-down globalization has also been referred to as the "Washington consensus." In addition, the United States is often perceived as an exemplar of neoliberal policy domestically, even though it seems to deviate on such key matters as a balanced budget (in part because of high levels of U.S. military spending).

Globalization from below describes the actions of groups that criticize the injustices that result from globalization processes, and in particular, the expansion of global markets. The mass media frequently describe these groups as being opposed to globalization. That is inaccurate. Many groups that criticize the injustices resulting from globalization actually support particular types of globalization, such as the spread of international human rights and global labour standards. Moreover, they use technologies, like the Internet, to help them organize and communicate internationally. In general, groups that support globalization from below advocate more democracy, environmental protection, and social justice in the global system. Bottom-up globalizers are against the neoliberal forms of globalization that put capital mobility, markets, and profits before people's basic needs, and they criticize the powerful economic, political, and military influence of transnational corporations and the United States government.

Top-down globalization has been targeted by environmentalists, peasant organizations, and farmers' unions, but it has also been criticized by capitalist insiders, such as world-famous economist and policy adviser Jeffrey Sachs, international financier George Soros, and Joseph Stiglitz, Nobel Prize winner and former chief economist and vice-president of the World Bank (Sachs, 2005; Soros, 1998; Stiglitz, 2003).

While everyone from rock stars to prime ministers demands greater justice in the global system, how to achieve it is not clear. There is no consensus on whether moderate capitalist reforms are sufficient, whether trade liberalization will help the poor, or whether the answer lies in partial or total withdrawal from global markets. Because of these differences, globalization from below should be understood less as a cohesive movement and more as a broad framework that encompasses multiple perspectives, including moderate critiques of neoliberalism, radical anti-capitalist positions, various forms of anarchism, armed peasant uprisings, and fair-trade coffee projects.

How then do the forces of globalization operate in our daily lives? People are involved with globalization processes as capitalists, consumer, workers, and citizen (Robbins, 2005: 2–4). In the remainder of this chapter, we explore the profound influence of time–space compression in each of these realms.

CAPITALISTS GO GLOBAL

THE RISE OF FINANCIAL CAPITAL

In economic terms, money used for investment, currency trading, and so forth is "financial capital." In the globalized economy, financial capital has grown much faster than production and trade. More than US$1.5 trillion flow through electronic financial channels every day, and an estimated 98 percent of these flows are purely speculative, meaning they are unrelated to the buying and selling of physical goods but involve short-term trading of such things as foreign currencies. Global trade in goods and services equalled $15.2 trillion in 2010. While this seems an impressive number, it is equal to only three days' worth of trade on foreign exchange markets (Bedell, 2010; United Nations Conference on Trade and Development, 2010). Using a fully computerized global financial system, traders can move around billions of dollars to profit from minuscule changes in currency rates.

The rise of financial capital has been labelled "casino capitalism" since financial speculators, like casino gamblers, stand to make or lose millions of dollars in short periods (Strange, 1986). The rise of casino capitalism has been facilitated by the financial deregulation that has occurred under neoliberal regimes since the 1980s as governments gave up regulatory powers. The danger with casino capitalism is that investor speculation (a process akin to placing a bet) makes financial systems unstable. Money floods into markets during periods of optimism, creating a financial "bubble" that drives markets up. The bubble bursts when investors realize that the market is overpriced relative to the value of real assets. This causes a period of panic involving an outflow of capital and, in due course, economic recession.

A snowball of financial panic is precisely what the world witnessed during the 1997 Asian financial crisis, which started in Thailand and went on to affect the currencies, stock markets, and asset prices of a host of Asian countries, including Indonesia, South Korea, and Hong Kong as well as the financial systems of Brazil and Russia. In 2008–09, a similar crisis occurred when the real estate market collapsed in the United States. Initially, inexpensive mortgages lured millions of Americans into the housing market. All was well while house prices rose. People felt richer, and they borrowed more and more money against the value of their homes. When people had to renew their mortgages at higher interest rates, many of them could not afford it. Foreclosures increased. With more houses on the market, house prices began to fall. The spiral of falling house prices and skyrocketing foreclosures soon put some large financial institutions in a position of not having enough cash on hand to continue operations. Some of them went bankrupt while others sought government assistance to stay in business. Because financial institutions around the world had invested heavily in U.S. debt, the financial crisis was global, not simply American. Some institutions, such as Iceland's three biggest private banks and Lehman Brothers, the fourth largest investment bank in the United States, went bankrupt, while governments had to lend money to keep other financial institutions afloat. Among other things, the crisis demonstrated how porous global financial borders are. In the words of the chief European economist at Deutsche Bank, "In this day and age, a bank run spreads around the world, not around the block" (Landler, 2008).

OVERCAPACITY AND CENTRALIZATION

The growth of casino capitalism is also linked to declining profits and overcapacity in the economy of goods and services. Put simply, global corporations can produce more things than the world's consumers can afford to purchase. Justin Lin, chief economist at the World Bank, noted in 2009 that, "unless we deal with excess capacity, it will wreak havoc on all countries," thus acknowledging the connection between recent economic downturns and the tendency towards overproduction (Evans-Pritchard 2009). In 2008, the car industry made about 94 million vehicles, over capacity by about 34 million cars (Welch, 2008). While financial markets boomed throughout the early 2000s, and wealth appeared to be growing exponentially for some people, a number of economists worried that excess capacity in the productive economy—accompanied by growing inequality and global poverty, which erode the worldwide consumption base—meant that a global recession was in the works (Bello, 2002). The 2008–09 U.S. financial crisis demonstrated both the overcapacity problem and the interpenetration of global financial markets. Global investors worried about the bankruptcy even of giants of the productive economy, such as General Motors and Chrysler, and the U.S. slowdown spread around the world. In 2008, the Indian high-tech and outsourcing industries, which rely heavily on business from the U.S. financial sector, began to freeze wages and announce layoffs for software programmers and workers in call centres (Kahn, 2008). Even China, whose rapid growth has been powered by exports, experienced a drop in exports at the end of 2008, leaving Communist Party officials worrying about employing the millions of workers in the export sector, which in turn depends heavily on American consumers (Jacobs and Barboza, 2008).

Besides creating complex webs of interdependence among national economies, the creation of a global economy has changed the way corporations look and operate. In short, these conditions have made corporations leaner, meaner, bigger, more diverse in terms of the goods they produce, and more involved in complex financial dealings and investments throughout the world.

To survive problems of overcapacity and economic slowdown, corporations have merged to trim operating costs. The Chinese automaker Geely bought Volvo from Ford (Nicholson, 2010). Renault took over Nissan, and Chrysler teamed up with Daimler-Benz (briefly) and then with Fiat. Chasing the high profits found in the financial sector, traditional corporations have gotten into the money-lending business, while banks have become involved in new kinds of businesses, such as securities trading. Today, transnational corporations find it hard to survive without diversifying into multiple goods in many countries, and this explains why the last decades have witnessed the greatest rate of mergers and consolidation in history (International Forum on Globalization, 2001: 6; see Figure 19.2). It also helps explain why the same handful of corporations can be found almost everywhere, offering a similar range of products in the world's shopping malls and airports (Box 19.1). These giant corporations trade with one another, but they also trade goods and services internally. Economists estimate that a third of all global trade involves transfers among different branches of the same corporation (Ellwood, 2001: 54).

GROWTH OF THE CORPORATE GIANTS

Corporations have become bigger and more powerful than many national governments (May, 2006). Consider just these two facts (White 2009):

- Of the largest 175 economic entities in the world, 109 (62.3 percent) are corporations (measured by sales), and 66 are countries (measured by gross domestic product).
- The world's biggest corporation, Wal-Mart earns annual revenue that is 2.24 times the size of the gross domestic product of Singapore (52nd on the list).

It will perhaps surprise you to learn that big corporations do not necessarily pay big taxes. In fact, corporations are paying less in taxes today than in the 1990s. Companies regularly play nation-states against one another, pressuring governments to lower taxes rates by threatening to move production to a more favourable location. The resulting decline in corporate taxes can be observed across all developed countries in the last two decades, as mobile individuals and corporations increasingly take advantage of global tax shelters, forcing governments to rely on taxes paid by less mobile individuals and small businesses (Figure 19.3). Recent trends in several countries show that tax rates for corporations are being maintained, and even lowered. In the midst of the economic crash in 2008, Ireland actually hiked tax rates to individuals, but maintained its corporate tax rate—one of the lowest among the wealthy countries at 12 percent. In Germany, corporate taxes were cut from 39 to 30 percent the same year ("Corporate Tax," 2009). In 2005, the U.S. Government Accountability Office reported that between 1998 and 2005, more than two-thirds of all corporations did not pay taxes every year (Borosage, 2008). These corporate tax breaks have taken place in spite of relatively high government debt.

Canadian corporations have also enjoyed big tax breaks, which they justify by their need to compete with the United States. Reductions in corporate taxes between 2000 and 2010 decreased the Canadian government's federal revenues by $12.5 billion a year (Jackson, 2005). Canada's own corporate tax rate was reduced from 50 percent in the early 1980s to just 29.5 percent in 2010 ("Canada's Corporate Income Tax," 2011). These corporate tax breaks have significant implications for income inequality. A recent report

FIGURE 19.2 FOREIGN DIRECT INVESTMENT AND ANNOUNCED MERGERS AND ACQUISITIONS, WORLDWIDE

NOTE: "Net direct investment position" is the difference between foreign direct investment in Canada and Canadian direct investment abroad.

SOURCE: Statistics Canada (2011).

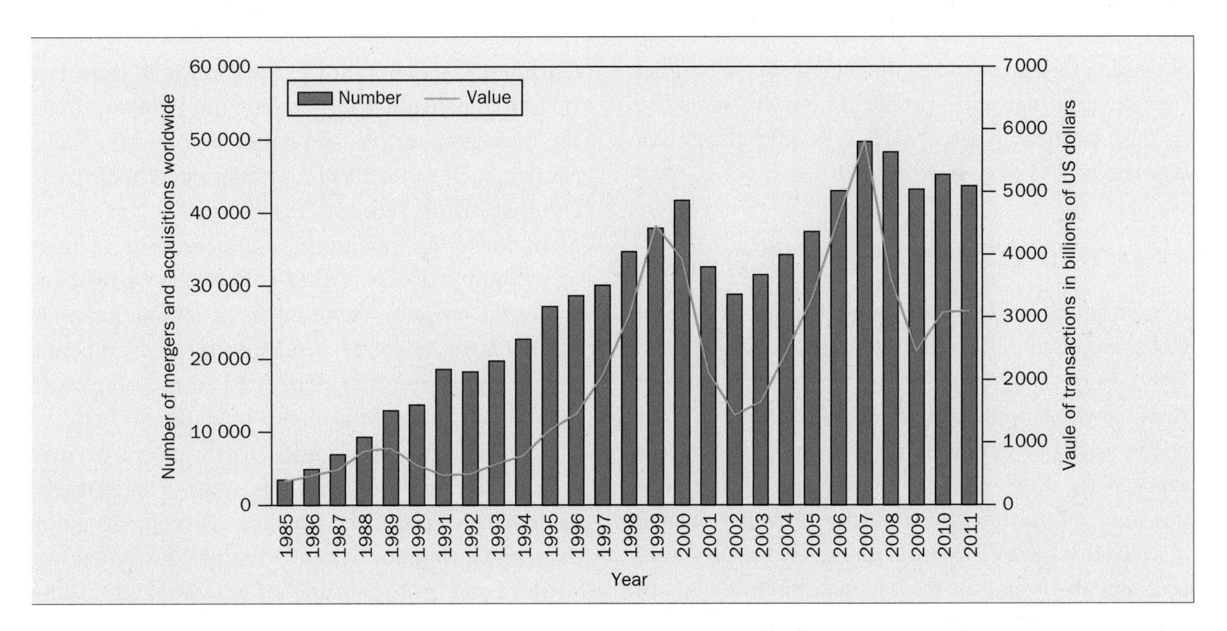

SOURCE: Institute of Mergers, Acquisitions, and Alliances. (2011). "Announced Mergers and Acquisitions, Worldwide 1991–2010." Thomson Financial, Institute of Mergers, Acquisitions and Alliances. On the World Wide Web at http://www.imaa-institute.org/statistics-mergers-acquisitions.html (retrieved 15 August 2012).

found that "taxes and benefits reduce inequality less in Canada than in most OECD countries" (Grant, 2011a). Before the mid-1990s, Canada's tax-benefit system used to be able to offset 70 percent of income inequality, with a redistributive effect similar to that of some Scandinavian countries. Today, this number has fallen to less than 40 percent (Grant, 2011a). The problems caused by tax imbalances because of corporate tax cuts and growing inequality in the redistribution of wealth have not gone unnoticed, even by Warren Buffett, one of the richest businessmen in the world. In an interview for ABC in November 2010, Buffett denounced the

BOX 19.1 KRAFT: YOUR FRIENDLY NEIGHBORHOOD MULTINATIONAL CHEESE CORPORATION (THAT ALSO SELLS BEER, SMOKES, AND CHOCOLATE)

The Kraft food brand demonstrates the complexity and expansiveness of a diversified transnational corporation. Today, it is difficult to go grocery shopping without buying a Kraft product, even if you are a vegan and don't eat cheese. Kraft Foods is the largest food producer in the United States and the second largest in the world, sells in 145 countries, has more than 200 production facilities, and has a global work force of more than 103 000. Even though Kraft is both large and omnipresent, it can be difficult to keep track of the many corporate structures linked to Kraft products. Kraft's story began simply enough, when it was founded as a wholesale cheese company in Chicago in 1903. Kraft's corporate genealogy quickly became very complicated as it acquired new products, took over other firms, and was in turn acquired by another corporation.

In 1988, Philip Morris—a multinational tobacco company—purchased Kraft Foods for US$12.9 billion. Some analysts speculated that Kraft's family-friendly image might offset the negative associations of Philip Morris being the world's biggest tobacco company. Philip Morris combined Kraft with General Foods a year later to form Kraft General Foods. Like other corporations in the early 1990s, Kraft General Foods experienced merger mania; Kraft gobbled up multiple companies around the world that sold coffee, candy, cheese, chocolate (including Toblerone), and cereals (including Shreddies and Shredded Wheat). In 1995, Kraft General Foods was reorganized and renamed Kraft Foods, while Kraft General Foods International became Kraft Foods International. In 2000, Philip Morris purchased Nabisco Holdings (a giant cracker and snack company), which it also merged into the Philip-Morris Kraft empire. In 2003, after negative publicity about a tobacco giant making food, as well as rising concern about the company's liability in tobacco and obesity class action suits, a company with the vague name of Altria became the parent company to the Kraft and Philip Morris family of food, cigarettes, and beer. In 2010, Kraft took over Cadbury, making it the largest confectionary company in the world (Jones and Dorfman, 2010).

overtaxing of the lower and middle classes, saying that "people at the high end—people like myself—should be paying a lot more in taxes. We have it better than we've ever had it" ("Warren Buffett," 2010).

CRITICS OF CORPORATE POWER

Bottom-up globalizers have reacted to the growth of global corporations in various ways (Bello, 2002; Starr, 1999). For example, the 1990s saw the emergence of an anti-sweatshop movement in North America after poor working conditions in the garment industry were exposed (A. Ross, 1997). Of particular importance was the 1996 Kathie Lee Gifford controversy, which, revealed that her Wal-Mart clothing line was produced by child labour and involved human rights abuses. In 2000, Naomi Klein's *No Logo* became an international best-seller. She argued that large corporate brands are vulnerable to a backlash against corporate power. "Today," she wrote, "more and more campaigners are treating multinationals, and the policies that give them free reign, as the root cause of political injustices around the globe" (Klein, 2000: 338). AdBusters, a rabble-rousing media organization headquartered in Vancouver, launched multiple campaigns to "un-cool" famous brand names associated with sweatshop labour and environmental degradation (Adbusters, 2005). Corporate Accountability International (formerly Infact) launched a Kraft boycott in 1994 to expose the business practices of its parent company, Philip Morris, such as its alleged promotion of tobacco to children. More recently, the Sierra Club criticized Kraft for using genetically engineered ingredients in its food products. Other corporations have been criticized on issues ranging from labour practices (particularly in coffee production), environmental sustainability, animal welfare, and relationships with the military-industrial complex operating in Iraq.

Corporations responded to this wave of anti-corporate criticism in various ways. For example, some have changed their names, diverting attention from their infamous brand. Philip Morris became Altria, much to the dismay of anti-smoking groups who argued this was an underhanded public relations move to obscure the company's roots in the tobacco industry. After receiving bad publicity about its genetic engineering, Monsanto became Pharmacia for most of its communications after merging with pharmaceutical giants Pharmacia and UpJohn.

Another way that global corporations are attempting to stem the tide of bad press is through a growing movement for corporate social responsibility, in which corporations voluntarily try to introduce best practices for labour and the environment.

FIGURE 19.3 CORPORATE TAX RATES WORLDWIDE

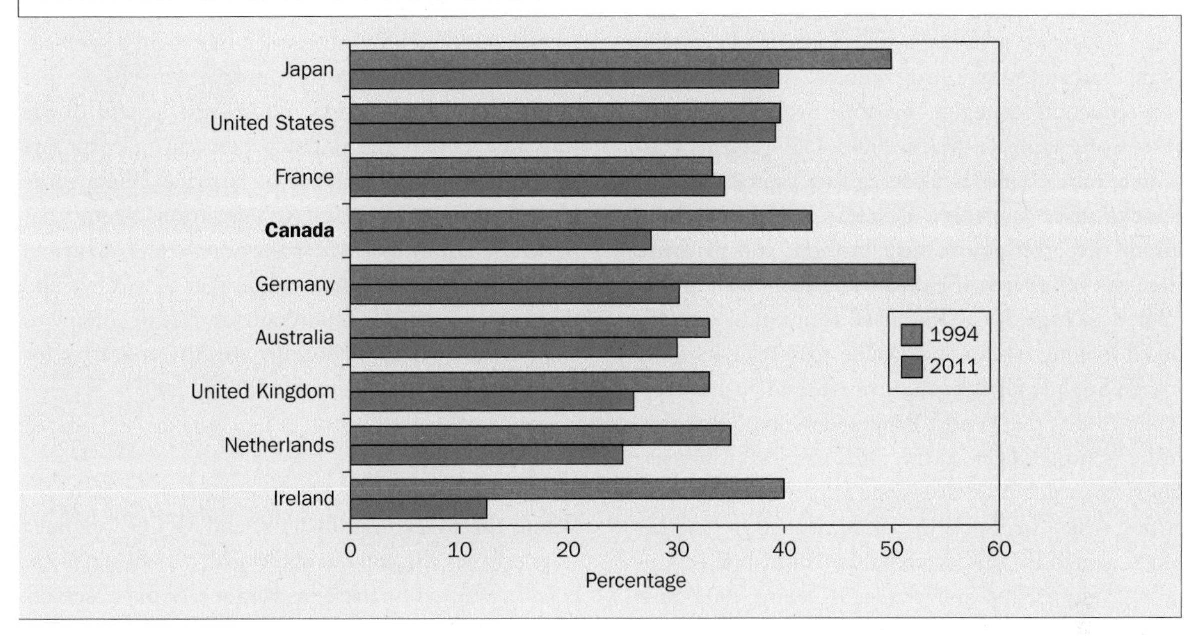

SOURCE: Organisations for Economic Co-operation and Development. (n.d.). OECD Tax database. On the World Wide Web at http://www.oecd.org/ctp/taxdatabase and http//www.oecd.org/dataoecd/26/56/33717459.xls (retrieved 15 August 2012).

The Gap, for example, released a report in 2004 that openly admitted a host of wage, health, and safety violations by its production subcontractors and promised to do better. Controversy exists over what is certified as responsible corporate behaviour and who is in control of the certification process. Philip Knight, CEO of Nike, withdrew a $30 million donation to the University of Oregon in May 2000 after the university endorsed a student-run regulatory organization (the Workers' Right Consortium) instead of the Fair Labor Association, a labour-rights group backed by the White House with corporate executives on its board of directors. Unfortunately, more than 15 years after the Gifford scandal, the institute for Global Labour and Human Rights reports that little has changed in terms of sweatshop labour. Such corporations as Wal-Mart, Target, J.C. Penney, and Macy's continue to sell goods from factories in which workers earn abysmally low wages, under-age labour is common, and supervisors routinely engage in physical and sexual abuse (Institute for Global Labour and Human Rights 2011).

The growing power of corporations has not emerged in a political vacuum. As corporations have grown in strength, some governments have lost ground, both to corporate power and to international institutions, such as the World Trade Organization. This change has led many analysts to wonder if the age of globalization means the end of the state system.

ARE STATES RELEVANT IN THE GLOBAL WORLD?

Critics of neoliberal policies have wondered about the extent to which states continue to be the main instrument of democratic governance. Has the state been replaced by a kind of "global governance?" Does real power rests in the hands of unelected officials in the world's three biggest international financial institutions: the International Monetary Fund (IMF), the World Bank, and World Trade Organization (WTO), sometimes called "the three sisters"? Because of pressure to meet the demands of these three very powerful international financial institutions, some critics argue that states have become less oriented toward meeting the demands of citizens. The result is a **democratic deficit** in which ordinary citizens are disenfranchised from the process of governance. Let's look briefly at how the three sisters challenge the capacity of states to make democratic decisions for average citizens.

THE THREE SISTERS

The IMF was established after World War II. Its official role was to maintain the stability of the international monetary system. Since the 1980s, the IMF has come to serve a different yet important role as the gatekeeper of the institutional financial system. IMF loans are conditional on the lending government following a package of reforms of known as "structural adjustment programmes" (renamed "poverty reduction strategies" in 1999; Brym et al., 2005; Woodroffe and Ellis-Jones, 2000). IMF reforms typically require countries to deregulate capital markets, remove price subsidies, decrease social spending, orient the economy toward exports, and privatize state-run industries. If a country refuses to adopt the reform package, it can find itself shut out of international lending circles and unable to service its debt. Joseph Stiglitz, former senior vice-president and chief economist at the World Bank and Nobel Prize laureate, is no stranger to the inner circles of international finance. Yet he is also one of the IMF's harshest critics, which he describes as imprisoned in "market fundamentalism" and as staffed by "third-rate economists from first-rate universities" (Denny, 2002). For Stiglitz, decisions made by the IMF to solve various financial crises show that "the IMF is not particularly interested in hearing the thoughts of its 'client countries' on such topics as development strategy or fiscal austerity," and that "[all] too often, the Fund's approach to developing countries has the feel of a colonial ruler" (Stiglitz, 2003: 40). Many poor countries have witnessed massive protests against the IMF.

Like the IMF, the World Bank was also established after World War II, and its job was to make loans to help postwar reconstruction. Most World Bank loans were made to poor countries and were often tied to large development projects, such as hydroelectric dams. As a condition of receiving loans, the World Bank required that certain structural adjustment criteria be met. Like the IMF, the World Bank has had its share of critics, both external and internal (Chapter 9, Development and Underdevelopment). In response, the World Bank increased its collaboration with local nongovernmental organizations (NGOs). While some observers applaud these efforts as part of the Bank's self-help approach to social problems, others argue that the Bank's NGO collaborations do not change its fundamentally undemocratic nature or the severity of its structural adjustment reforms.

The WTO emerged in 1995 out of the postwar trade treaty the Global Agreement on Tariffs and Trade (GATT). The WTO's job is to lower trade barriers, thereby increasing international trade and, presumably, prosperity. The WTO became known to many North Americans with the famous "Battle of Seattle" in 1999. WTO meetings in that city were met by huge, disruptive street protests. Every major meeting of the WTO since then has elicited protests, often from citizens of poor countries who charge that international trade works only to the benefit of the rich and ignores the unfair protection of corporate agribusiness at the expense of farmers. While some globalization-from-below organizations argue that trade liberalization will help the poor (e.g., Oxfam and Live 8 organizers), others argue that it will not and that entry to the WTO forces countries to comply to a set of trade rules written by wealthy countries for their own benefit (Bivens and Hersh, 2003).

A U.S. EMPIRE?

While the IMF, World Bank, and WTO influence state policies throughout the world, not all states are equally affected by these institutions. Some observers note that the age of globalization is also an age of more power for some states and relative powerlessness for states at the bottom of the global hierarchy. Critics of the United States sometimes accuse it of acting like an empire. Neoconservative thinkers in Washington acknowledge that the United States acts like an empire, although they argue that it uses its power benevolently to promote peace and democracy throughout the world.

Analysts debate whether the United States is a modern empire or a fading superpower (Ferguson, 2004; Wallerstein, 2002). The United States still enjoys enough political, economic, and military power to make unilateral foreign policy decisions (such as invading Iraq, which it did without United Nations endorsement), maintain a substantial global military presence (see Figure 19.4), and adopt unorthodox economic policies (like running huge fiscal deficits). Do these policies indicate the *decline* of U.S. hegemony? The United States is the world's biggest debtor, with a deficit of $16 trillion dollars in 2013. Especially after the 2008–09 financial crisis hit, some analysts argued that the power of the United States was waning relative to that of the countries that own its debt holdings, notably China (Fallows, 2008).

GLOBAL INEQUALITY AND THE "FOURTH WORLD"

Another feature of the global state system is a widening power gap between and within states. In the 1970s, analysts often divided the world into three

FIGURE 19.4 U.S. MILITARY FOOTPRINT ON THE WORLD

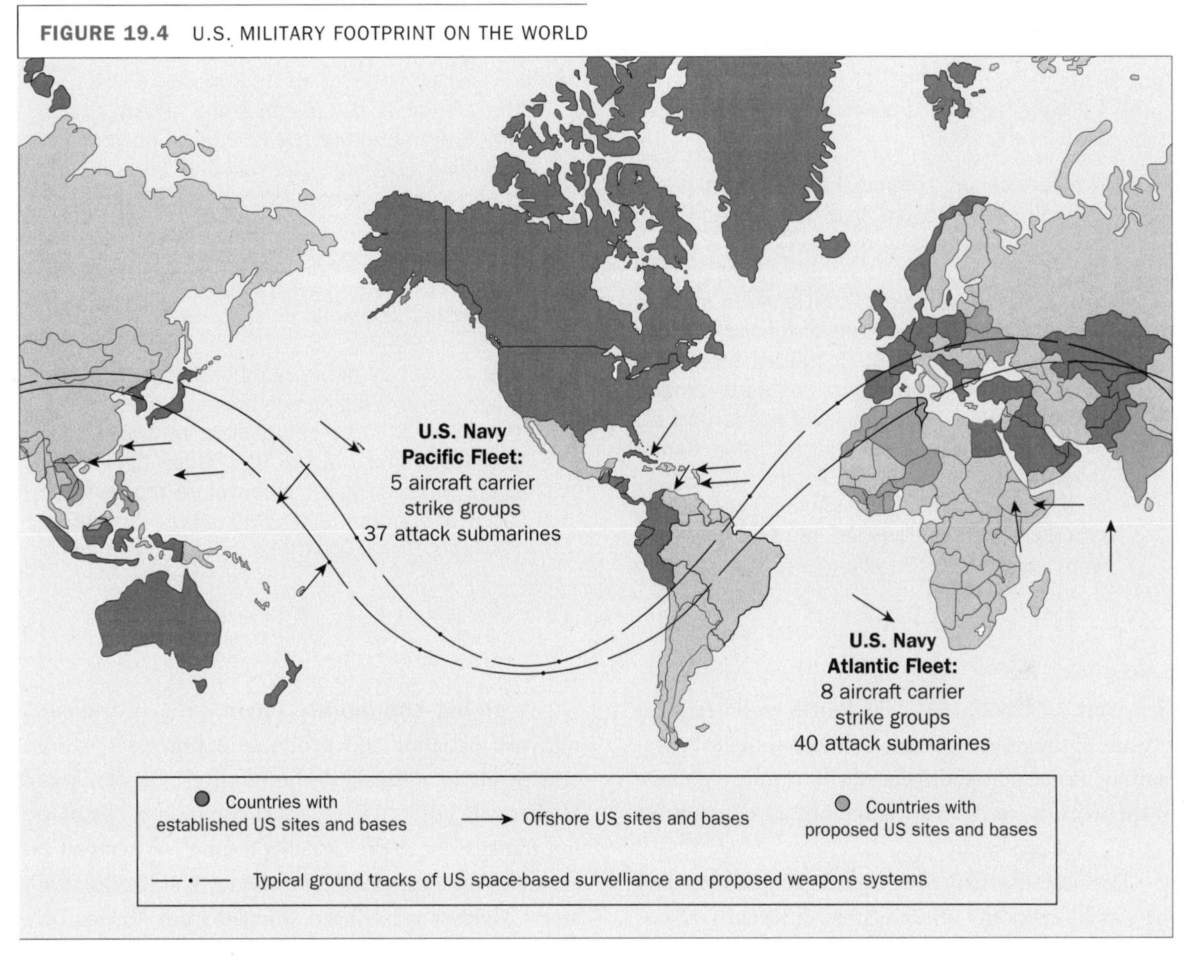

SOURCE: U.S. Department of Defense. *Base Structure Report, 2008*. On the World Wide Web at http://combatingglobalization.com/articles/combating_globalization4.html (retrieved 12 August 2012).

parts. The "first world" comprised the wealthy capitalist countries. The "second world" comprised the countries of the communist bloc. The "third world" comprised all the rest. This division is now inaccurate. The old third world now comprises a disparate assortment of nations that don't necessarily share common traits, the communist second world has for the most part collapsed, and it has become evident that widespread poverty exists even in the rich first world.

To meaningfully capture asymmetries among the world's countries today, analysts sometimes refer to the division between the "global north" and the "global south" or between developed and developing countries. Another useful terminological distinction is between the "majority world," which is generally poor and lacks basic social goods like housing, food, employment, and education, and the "minority world," which is generally well educated and has access to good jobs and public goods like healthcare.

People from the privileged minority world may live in wealthy countries like Canada, but they can also live in Mexico City or Hong Kong. Similarly, people from the majority world can be homeless and searching for adequate food and shelter in downtown Toronto. The majority world–minority world distinction serves as a valuable reminder that state borders do not always indicate who benefits and suffers in a globalized economic system and that the high living standard of the Canadian middle class is a global anomaly (Milanovic, 2005; see Box 19.2).

While the global economy has made a portion of the world's population wealthy, a large proportion of the world's people (at least 50 percent) are considered poor. The global economy operates independently of large populations and geographical areas, which are seen as irrelevant for its functioning. These marginalized populations and regions are sometimes called the **fourth world** (Cardoso, 1993; Castells, 1998;

BOX 19.2 GLOBAL EXTREMES

The following facts illustrate the extent of economic inequality in the world.

- A recent report showed that the wage gap in Canada is at a record high, with Canada's top 10 percent earners making ten times as much the bottom 10 percent.
- In 2006, the world's 497 billionaires (approximately 0.000 008 percent of the world's population) were worth $3.5 trillion, more than 7 percent of world gross domestic product (GDP; the total dollar value of goods and services produced in the world that year; Central Intelligence Agency, 2011; Forbes, 2011).
- In 2011, one family—the Waltons, heirs to the Wal-Mart fortune founded by Sam Walton—were worth US$93 billion net, making them the richest family in the world. The Waltons are worth more than the GDP of 154 countries, including Lebanon, Bolivia, and Luxembourg (Central Intelligence Agency, 2011; Forbes, 2011).
- In 2011, the world's 1210 billionaires enjoyed a total net worth of $4.5 trillion.
- Almost half the world lives on less than $2.50 a day.
- Impressive as these numbers appear, many investors on Wall Street are even richer than the CEOs of large companies. In 2007, it is estimated that the top five hedge fund managers on Wall Street made more money than all five hundred S&P 500 CEOs combined ("There's Rich," 2010).

Hoogvelt, 1997: 66, 162). The fourth world exists as a result of the new economic and technological paradigm of global competitiveness, where only a portion of the world's states and inhabitants are competitive in the global economy.

Recognizing that time–space compression and the global economy affect people differently allows our understanding of globalization to become more nuanced. Globalization does involve a number of intense connections within the core of the global system, as people in the minority world travel more, hold global investments, and integrate the Internet into their daily lives. At the same time, globalization also involves a process of *peripheralization* that marginalizes certain groups. Some people in rich countries like Canada—Aboriginal peoples, homeless populations, unemployed workers—are subject to exclusionary processes like those that affect people in parts of Africa, Asia, and Latin America (Hoogvelt, 1997: 129).

THE GLOBAL CONSUMER

Maybe you have yet to be convinced that globalization has anything to do with you. But have you gone shopping lately? If you consume commodities—meaning goods purchased in the marketplace rather than made from your own labour—then you are inevitably part of globalization. The tags on your clothing are more likely to read "Made in China" or "Made in Bangladesh" than "Made in Canada."

A **global commodity chain** is "a [worldwide] network of labor and production processes, whose end result is a finished commodity" (Hopkins and Wallerstein, 1986: 159). Global commodity chains are not transparent to the casual consumer. When you eat a tomato on a fast-food hamburger, you usually don't know whether it has been shipped from Mexico or a local greenhouse. When you buy a pair of running shoes, the price tag doesn't tell you much about the workers who made the shoes or the company's environmental track record. In this section, we will learn about the critical role consumption plays in the global economy, as well as some of the social and environmental critiques of globalized consumerism.

A GLOBAL GLUT

While consumers don't always understand the complexity of global commodity chains, consumption plays a critical role in driving growth in the global economy. High consumer spending increases economic growth, while a lack of consumer confidence is associated with economic slowdown and recession. Because North American and European markets are relatively saturated consumer markets, many corporations see expansion into global markets as essential for growth. **Consumerism**—a way of life in which a person's identity and purpose is oriented primarily to the purchase and consumption of material goods—is currently being exported to the world's middle and working classes.

As noted above, the global economy suffers from a problem of overcapacity that makes finding new consumer markets essential. In particular, many corporations are looking to expand sales to China, the world's most populous country, to solve the problem. So far, Chinese production has been focused mainly on export markets, thereby worsening the problem of global overproduction (Bello, 2002). This situation is beginning to change. In 2010, China was the third largest consumer market behind the United States and Japan, and by 2015, it is expected to be the second largest (Liao et al., 2010).

CULTURE AS COMMODITY?

Another characteristic of globalized consumerism is the tendency to treat culture like any other commodity. The United States has been instrumental in advancing this viewpoint—not surprisingly, given the tremendous size and power of the culture/entertainment industry in the United States. The biggest U.S. export consists of mass-produced products of popular culture (Barlow, 2001). While many countries have a tradition of protecting cultural products, the United States has used the WTO to prohibit states from using subsidies and quotas to protect domestic cultural products, like films, music, magazines, books, and music. For example, in 1997, the WTO supported a U.S. complaint and ruled that the Canadian government's usage of preferential tax and postal rates to protect the domestic magazine industry was unlawful. (U.S. magazines make up 85 percent of the magazines found on Canadian newsstands.)

A growing movement to resist the interpretation of culture as a commodity is centred around a 2005 UN treaty: the United Nations Educational, Scientific, and Cultural Organization's (UNESCO) Convention on Cultural Diversity (CCD). The UNESCO Convention was vehemently opposed by the United States, since the treaty will allow states to exclude cultural policies from free trade deals. As with most treaties, the devil will ultimately lie in the legal details, yet the CCD opens up the possibility for states legally to protect domestic cultural industries from the rules of trade.

CULTURAL IMPERIALISM?

The global spread of consumerism has been criticized as form of **cultural imperialism** (Barlow, 2001). From this viewpoint, global corporations, bolstered by sophisticated advertising tools, media monopolies, and declining trade barriers, are exporting a Western way of life throughout the world (Tomlinson, 1991). Cultural imperialism is often associated with liberal values around sexuality, feminism, and secularism.

Of course, people are not passive recipients of Western cultural products, which can be taken up in unique ways. A Japanese game show like *The Iron Chef*, for instance, represents a unique cultural hybrid that combines an American game-show format with Japanese cultural and culinary mores. When it was first shown in the United States, it was unlike any show made by American television producers, yet it was a huge hit on the American-based Food Network and inspired *Iron Chef America*, a highly successful English-language spinoff of the original Japanese show.

Western cultural products are transformed as they are consumed by different global cultures. However, this does not mean that the world's cultural products compete as equals. Free trade favours large economies and big economic actors. Canadians are more likely to eat in a McDonald's than they are to eat in a Jollibee, the leading fast-food restaurant in the Philippines. Because of the tremendous economic power of Hollywood, filmgoers in Canada are more likely to watch a movie made in Hollywood than we are to watch a film made in Denmark or even a film made in Canada (see Table 19.3). French political figures, such as former president Jacques Chirac, have been particularly vocal in criticizing the cultural power of Hollywood. He used the French state to protect and promote the French film industry. Chirac warned of a "catastrophe" for global diversity if U.S. cultural dominance goes unchallenged (Agence France-Presse, 2004).

Although tremendous economic and cultural power is centred in the corporate culture of the United States and Europe, there are important exceptions. The al-Jazeera television network counters the global prevalence of CNN, offering an Arab alternative to U.S.-produced news. An English-language channel of al-Jazeera went on air in 2006, making al-Jazeera's presence felt even more widely. The largest producer of movies in the world is not Hollywood, but Bollywood—the film industry based in Mumbai (formerly Bombay), India, which produces more than a thousand films a year and attracts more than 10 million Indians to the cinema every day. Bollywood films are seen in Russia, the Middle East, Africa, and Indian immigrant communities around the world. The cultural pervasiveness of

TABLE 19.3 U.S. MARKET SHARE OF FILM INDUSTRY FOR SELECTED COUNTRIES, 2008

COUNTRY OR REGION	PERCENTAGE OF FILM INDUSTRY BELONGING TO U.S. MOVIES
United States	91.5
Canada	88.5
United Kingdom	65
Australia	84.2
Spain	71.5
European Union	63.2
Poland	56.1
France	44
South Korea	48.8

SOURCES: Marché du film. European Audiovisual Observatory. *Focus 2009: World Film Market Trends.* On the World Wide Web at http://www.obs.coe.int/online_publication/reports/focus2009.pdf (retrieved 14 December 2011).

Bollywood films is so great that smaller Asian countries, like Bangladesh, have reacted against the perceived domination of Indian movies, which crowd out Bangladeshi films. In addition to Bollywood, a film industry arising out of Nigeria, called Nollywood, produces films with actors and themes that are wildly popular with African viewers, and which some Nigerians believe have "eliminated the cultural stranglehold of Hollywood" (Kennedy, 2004).

GLOBAL BRAND BACKLASH

While the term *cultural imperialism* may drown out the subtlety of global cultural exchange, visible signs of antagonism toward Western-style consumerism remain. One way that global consumerism is being contested is through a backlash against corporate brand names. Branded goods, like Coke, Barbie, and Nike, have a particular political, social, and cultural importance because of their connections to global corporations (Klein, 2000: 5). Just as transnational corporations have spread globally, so have their brands, and now McDonald's, the Gap, and Starbucks are all frequent targets of street protests around the world.

McDonald's has been the target of protests in more than 50 countries, and Hindu activists have demanded that the prime minister shut down all McDonald's because it offends traditional Indian vegetarian food culture (Brownell and Horgen, 2004: 61). Tens of thousands of Indians protested the opening of the first Kentucky Fried Chicken outlet in 1995, bringing together environmentalists, farmers, health officials, and anti-globalization activists (Wall, 2000). A global-brand backlash has also inspired greater attention to Coca-Cola's corporate practices throughout the world (see http://killercoke.org; Nestle, 2011). In some instances, consumption of Coke has dropped off in favour of domestic soft drinks, leading Coke to retool its sales strategy by focusing on specialized local drinks (Hays, 2000).

The idea that corporate globalization can be effectively fought by protesting against branded products is controversial. Many people argue that global corporations are geniuses at using social dissent to sell new consumer products (Frank, 1997; Heath and Potter, 2004). Just as 1960s radicals wore tie-dyed T-shirts and drove around in Boogie Vans, people today can purchase consumer products that express their disgust with the global capitalist system. You can wear a Che Guevara T-shirt while reading *Adbusters* and listening to K'Naan on your iPod. The extent to which countercultural consumption disrupts global flows of wealth is unclear. Marketing gurus are well aware of such consumer tendencies and advise global corporations to advance their brand by using

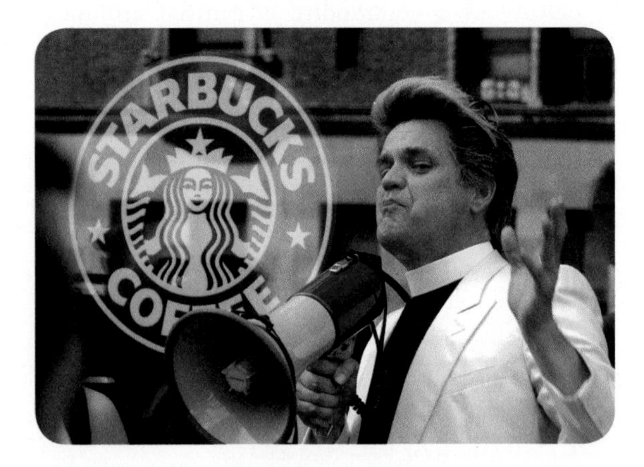

The Church of Stop Shopping, led by "Reverend Billy," promotes "retail interventions" into corporations like Starbucks. To see material on the Reverend's anti-consumer campaign and its intervention scripts, visit www.revbilly.com.
SOURCE: Reprinted by permission of Reverend Billy.

anti-establishment messages to sell products to young people around the world (Lindstrom, 2003: 132).

CONSUMER ALTERNATIVES: FAIR TRADE

Subverting corporate logos is not the only tactic used to disrupt global commodity chains. Bottom-up globalizers also focus on developing consumer products that are environmentally sustainable and produced by relatively well-paid workers. The fair-trade movement is one of the main proponents of this approach, arguing that producers should be paid a fair price rather than the free market price (Figure 19.5).

The fair-trade movement has paid special attention to coffee. Around the turn of the twenty-first century, the market for coffee plummeted to a 30-year low, leaving coffee prices below the cost of production for many farmers and causing heightened levels of poverty and debt for 25 million coffee-producing families worldwide (Oxfam, 2002). According to its proponents, fair-trade coffee is an important solution to the "sweatshops in the field" that characterize contemporary coffee production. Fair-trade coffee allows producers to earn a living wage and offer a guaranteed price that protects farmers against wild price fluctuations (see Figure 19.5). Fair trade also promises to protect the environment since most fair-trade coffee is "shade-grown" (that is, grown alongside trees that support wildlife and biodiversity).

While the market for fair-trade coffee is growing, it represents only a small fraction of the total coffee market. An estimated 6 percent of the coffee sold at Starbucks is fair-trade, and about 4 percent of all the coffee sold in the United States is fair-trade certified (Hickman 2008; Haight 2011). Fair-trade coffee organizations must convince consumers to pay more for their coffee—a choice that goes against the socialization of most consumers to shop for the best deal.

ECOLOGICAL CONSEQUENCES OF CONSUMERISM

Global consumerism has also been criticized for being based on a Western high-consumption lifestyle that is ecologically unsustainable, particularly if it is adopted by more people around the world. Twenty percent of the world's population (1.2 billion people) living in the industrialized developed world currently consume two-thirds of the world's resources and create 75 percent of all waste and pollution

FIGURE 19.5 FAIR TRADE AND FREE TRADE COFFEE PRICES, 1989–2011

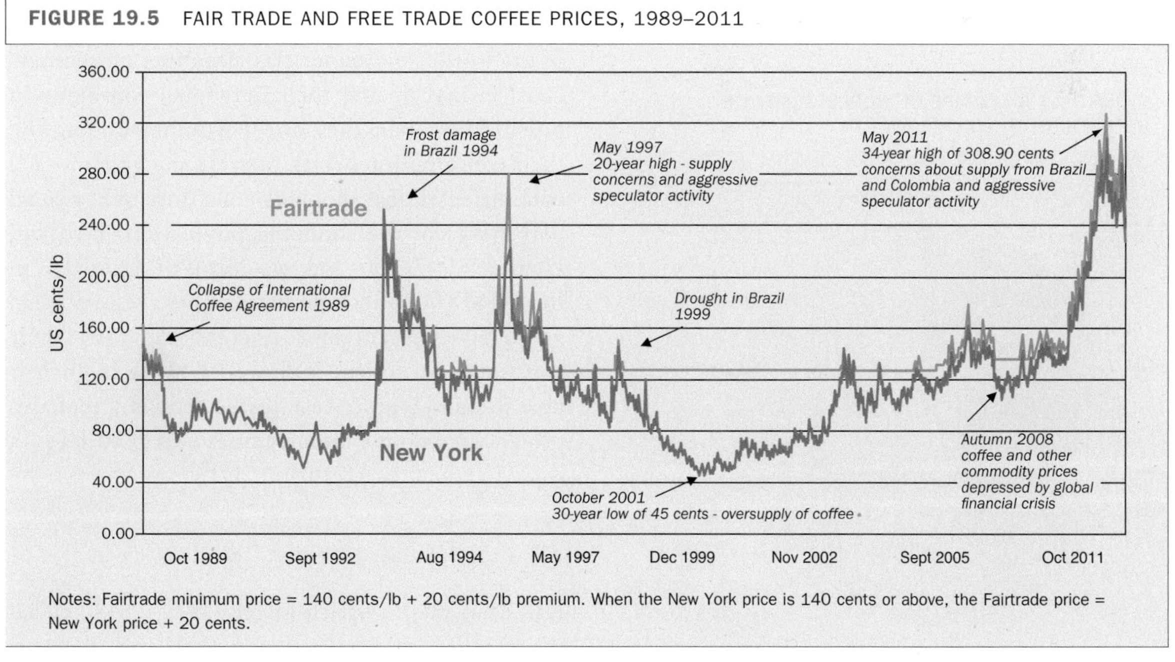

This graph shows a comparison of minimum Fairtrade price and the world market price for coffee, as measured on the New York Stock Exchange.

SOURCE: Fairtrade Foundation. (2011). *The Arabica Coffee Market, 1989–2011: Comparison of Fairtrade and New York Exchange Prices.* London, UK: Author. Reprinted with permission from the UK Fair Trade Foundation. http://www.fairtrade.org.uk/resources/reports_and_briefing_papers.aspx.

(Speidel, 2003: 5). What would be the implications if even a quarter of the remaining 80 percent of the world's people began to consume at the rate of wealthy Europeans and North Americans?

The size of China's economy has increased dramatically since it introduced free-market reforms in 1978, and it currently consumes more grain, meat, fertilizer, steel, and coal than the United States does (Speidel, 2003: 5). If China consumed as much oil per capita as the United States, China's total oil demand would be 80 million barrels a day—and currently the world produces only 60 million barrels a day (Speidel, 2003: 5). While some analysts say the solution to this problem is to find more oil, most experts believe that the world does not have enough reserves to sustain this level of consumption for long. Moreover, the current level of fossil fuel consumption is linked to global climate change. Sustainable consumption probably lies somewhere between the world's two extremes of overconsumers and underconsumers—at levels maintained by the roughly 3.3 billion people who eat moderate amounts of food (especially meat), rely primarily on sustainable modes of transportation, such as walking and public transportation, and consume minimal amounts of raw materials in their daily lives (Durning, 1992; see Figure 19.6).

While proponents of top-down globalization hope to turn the global middle-income stratum into overconsumers, the ecological challenge is to extend middle-income consumption habits to the world's poor underconsumers and the world's elite overconsumers. This will not be an easy political feat given the push to expand global consumption to address the problem of overcapacity in global production. The global economic system is currently organized around, and requires, high levels of consumption. In addition, it seems that members of the world's consumer class are often more interested in maximizing their individual consumption possibilities than they are in voluntarily curbing their consumption habits. Surveys show that totally committed ethical shoppers constitute only a small percentage of the shopping population (Bird and Hughes, 1997: 160) and two-thirds of Americans in the US$75 000+ income bracket believe they need 50 to 100 percent more income to satisfy their consumption desires (Schor, 1998). It is unclear how to build a more sustainable economy that also provides economic opportunities and good jobs—a topic to which I now turn.

Some observers think that a Western, high-consumption lifestyle is ecologically unsustainable if it is adopted by people around the world. For example, each passenger taking a round trip from Toronto to Vancouver on Air Canada (economy class) is responsible for putting nearly 533 kilograms of carbon dioxide into the atmosphere. What happens when hundreds of millions of additional people take to the skies?

SOURCE: © iStockphoto.com/EGDigital.

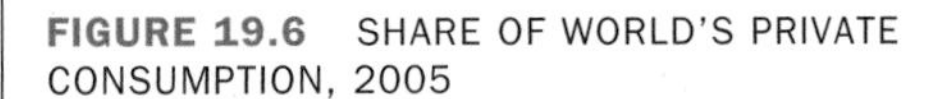

FIGURE 19.6 SHARE OF WORLD'S PRIVATE CONSUMPTION, 2005

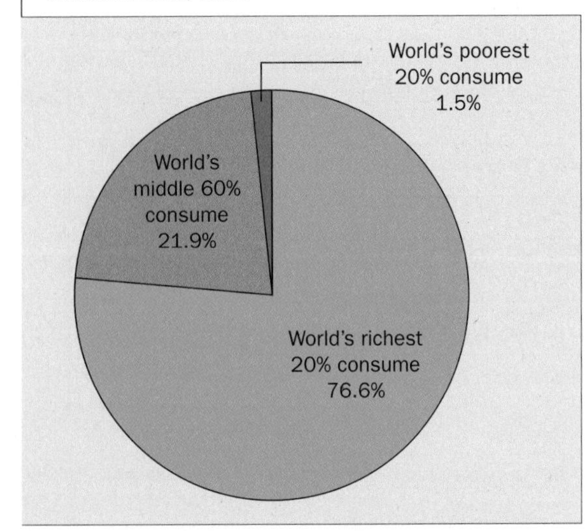

SOURCE: World Bank. (2008). "World Bank Development Indicators." © World Bank. On the World Wide Web at http://www.rrojasdatabank.info/wdi2008toc.htm (retrieved 19 August 2009). License: Creative Commons Attributiuon CC BY 3.0.

GLOBAL WORKERS

Karl Marx and Friedrich Engels (1972 [1848]) ended the *Manifesto of the Communist Party* with the now famous phrase, "Proletarians [workers] of all countries, unite." The political unification of working people across national borders is, however, relatively rare. Capitalists, in contrast, have proven adept at global planning and organization. Global capitalists have used numerous organizations and venues to formulate economic policy and interact with government policymakers, like the World Economic Forum held annually in Davos, Switzerland.

Global workers are relatively immobile and politically fragmented. Some of them cross international borders, but working abroad is constrained by international travel restrictions, work permits, and passports. When workers do move abroad to work, they are not always able to take their families with them and may be separated from loved ones for years at a time. Labour unions are struggling to protect workers in the competitive, footloose business environment of neoliberalism. While capital can move across borders with relative ease, unions are organized primarily within rather than across states. There have been attempts to increase the level of transnational union organization and solidarity, but most unions are oriented mainly to protecting domestic workers and wages against competition from foreign workers. In addition, many workers who travel abroad work in sectors that are relatively nonunionized and underregulated (e.g., nannying, the sex trade, agricultural workers), leaving them vulnerable to exploitation. While serious obstacles to organizing global workers remain, globalization processes have increased public awareness of sweatshop exploitation in factories around the world, leading some companies to ban the use of sweatshop labour. This section details some of the opportunities and challenges that globalization presents for global workers.

WAGE LABOUR AND WAGE INEQUALITY

The world of global labour might seem relatively mundane compared with the branded world of transnational corporations and global consumer goods. Yet without a global labour force there would be no goods for consumers to consume and no profits for capitalists. Most people exchange their labour for a wage, which they then use to pay their rent, buy groceries, and so forth.

Throughout the world, however, there is still a sizable section of the population for which the concept of wage labour is new. These people gain access to food, water, and shelter directly through their own work rather than receiving a wage and purchasing needed commodities. Many of the world's people still make a living off the land and subsist mainly on what they produce themselves; a little less than half the world's population lives in rural areas (World Bank, 2011b).

As urbanization increases and the use of wage labour spreads across the globe, so does the *segmentation* of labour markets. Women, people of colour, rural workers, and the people from the developing world in general are overrepresented at the bottom of the wage hierarchy. There is a tremendous disparity in global wages, particularly when we compare lower-level employees' salaries to CEO earnings (see Figure 19.7).

While income inequality in the United States is the most extreme among the world's rich countries, income and wealth inequality is a problem that worsened in Canada in the late 1990s (Picot and Myles, 2005). A 2007 study found the income gap between the richest 10 percent and poorest 10 percent of the population to be at a 30-year high (Yalnizyan, 2007). The average Canadian worker earned around $42 988 in 2009, while the average CEO earned $6.6 million (Grant, 2011b). Disparities in the Canadian labour market are based on class, as well as on race and country of birth. While many Canadians try to avoid minimum-wage work, thousands of migrants from Mexico and the Caribbean travel to Canada each year to work at agricultural jobs for minimum wages seven days a week with no overtime pay or statutory holidays (Basok, 2002).

While Mexicans working in Canada are denied labour rights granted Canadian citizens, minimum-wage jobs in Mexico are worse in terms of remuneration. Wages in Mexico remain stubbornly low despite the 1994 North American Free Trade Agreement (NAFTA) that Mexico signed with Canada and the United States. NAFTA was sold as a "rising tide" that would "lift the boats" of workers in the three countries. Yet the Mexican Labour Ministry reported that in 2003 workers earned an average of $360 a month, 16 percent less than they earned a decade earlier (Peters, 2004: 4; Jordan, 2003). Because per capita income is about one third that of the United States, the incentive to migrate (legally or illegally) remains higher than ever before, and cross-border migration remains a serious economic and political issue in both Mexico and the United States (CIA World Factbook, 2011).

Are low wages an age-old problem, or are they a unique result of globalization? The historical record shows that the search for cheap labour has been going on for hundreds of years. Indentured workers were

FIGURE 19.7 CEO'S AVERAGE PAY, 1990–2005

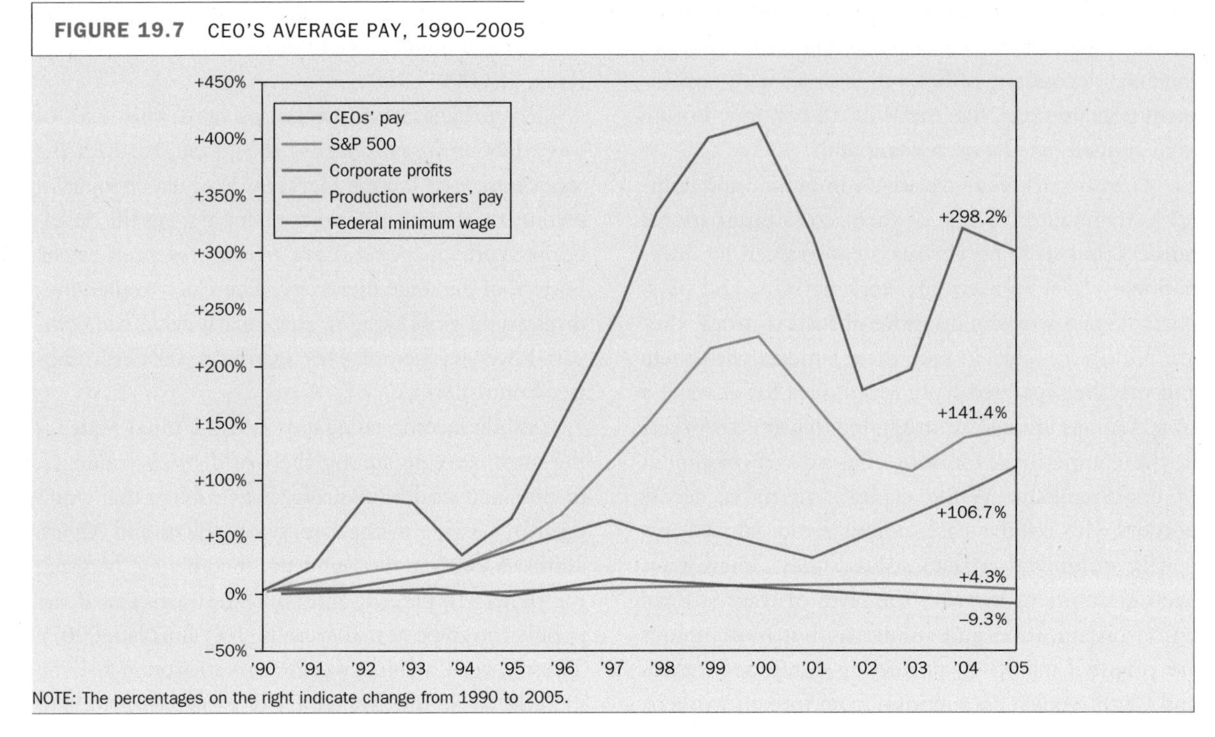

NOTE: The percentages on the right indicate change from 1990 to 2005.

SOURCE: Institute for Policy Studies and United for a Fair Economy. (2006). "Executive Excess 2006." On the World Wide Web at http://www.ips-dc.org/getfile.php?id=155 (retrieved 19 August 2009). Reprinted with permission.

brought from China to construct the North American railway system, while impoverished Irish immigrants competed with freed African American slaves for unskilled work in nineteenth-century North America. Globalization has heightened corporate competition for cheap labour. Firms use the threat of relocation as a way of keeping wages low. In effect, workers from different parts of the world compete against one another to attract foreign investment, driving wages down.

Given growing corporate competitiveness to find cheap labour, employment in a solid blue-collar job can no longer be taken for granted. Millions of North American workers in the manufacturing sector were laid off in the 1980s and 1990s (Beder, 2000: 132) and organized labour suffered serious setbacks, especially in the United States (Nissen, 2000: 3). Factory employment hit a 35-year low in Canada in 2011; while manufacturing was the number one sector of Canadian employment between 1976 and 1990, by 2011 it was only the third largest (Grant and Keenan 2011). Not only have North American manufacturing jobs declined since the 1980s, but corporations have also thinned out their management tiers, eliminating white-collar positions, **outsourcing** service jobs (e.g., call-centre jobs and computer programming) to South Asia, and making it unclear whether a university degree guarantees middle-class economic status (Anderson, Cavanagh, Lee, and the Institute for Policy Studies, 2005: 33; Ehrenreich, 2005). The solid blue-collar manufacturing job or white-collar office job that allowed men to support a stay-at-home wife and two children in a middle-class lifestyle is now relatively rare, and about two-thirds of Canadian mothers work outside the home. Economists report that a third of Canada's economic growth between 1997 and 2005 was due to the proliferation of two-income households ("Canadians Made Little," 2005).

Although manufacturing jobs were lost to lower-wage settings in the globalization period, service sectors jobs have mushroomed in the world's rich countries. Certain well-paying job sectors have expanded their ranks (e.g., teachers and nurses), but most new jobs are created in low-wage, temporary sectors of the service sector with median wages that fall near or below the poverty line (e.g., retail salespersons, cashiers, food preparers and servers, janitors, home care workers, and waiters; Anderson et al., 2005: 43–44). Economic analysts have identified the problem of "sub-employment" and the "working poor," terms that describe a situation in which workers have work but it is poorly paid, unstable, nonunionized, and fails to lift workers above the poverty line (Ehrenreich, 2001; "Paid to Be Poor," 2004; Sheak and Morris, 2002; Shipler, 2004). The number of such workers increased substantially in the 2007–09 recession, which drove the unemployment rate up to 9.7 percent in the United States and 8.6 percent in Canada by July 2009 (Statistics Canada, 2009; U.S. Bureau of Labor Statistics, 2009).

The growth in service jobs has been partially met by a rising number of migrant labourers who moved from developing countries to Europe and North America. Labour migration has increased the ethnic diversity of the labour force in the world's rich countries and, in turn, fuelled a racist, anti-immigrant backlash in some countries, raising questions about the meaning and practice of multicultural ideals. Despite these political conflicts, international migration is likely to continue to Europe and North America given that the baby-boom generation of workers is aging, birth rates are low, and a potential shortage of skilled workers looms in the future for most advanced industrialized countries. Together, these trends have increased competition among Canadian provinces and among highly industrialized countries to attract highly educated immigrants (Howlett, 2005: A7). The trend of south-to-north labour migration has raised questions in countries like Canada about how to recognize foreign credentials and integrate new immigrants into the economy, particularly since new immigrants experience a disproportionate degree of poverty and lower levels of unionization (Milkman, 2000; Picot and Myles, 2005: 20). Meanwhile, voices from less developed countries speak of a "global brain drain" in which skilled professionals leave their homeland to seek better opportunities in developed countries, a trend thought to cost India alone US$2 billion a year (United Nations, 2001).

SEARCHING FOR CHEAP LABOUR: "THE RACE TO THE BOTTOM"

Governments have reacted in different ways to the global competition to create jobs and attract corporate investment. In the less developed countries, some states have set up **export processing zones (EPZs)** where special financial deals—tax holidays, preferential rates for electricity and telecommunications, special exemptions from national labour laws, and the like—are used to lure corporations to set up shop and provide jobs. The most famous EPZ in North America is the *maquiladora* region in northern Mexico. *Maquiladoras* are factories that allow companies to assemble goods for export by using low-cost Mexican labour and imported high-tech machinery and parts.

Maquiladoras employ low-cost labour compared with the United States and Canada, but since 2001 hundreds of thousands of *maquiladora* workers have been laid off, threatened with layoffs, paid lower wages, and compelled to work in worse conditions. Why? Mexican labour is cheap, but not cheap enough in a global marketplace where transnational firms try to find the world's least expensive, least regulated, and least unionized labour supply. Although Mexican wages are a bargain by Canadian standards, low-cost manufacturing has increasingly moved to Indonesia, Vietnam, and China, where labour is even cheaper; the Chinese legal monthly minimum wage is around US$176 ("Seven Countries," 2011). Wage competition pits workers against one another in a "race to the bottom." Globalization has placed Mexico in a difficult position: wages are too low to alleviate poverty rates yet too high to continue to attract low-cost manufacturing.

Although working conditions in the factories of the developing countries are often wretched, some members of the world's labour force suffer in conditions that resemble slavery in the literal sense of the word. An estimated 27 million people worldwide are enslaved—more than at any other time in our history—and slavery generated $91.2 billion in profit in 2007 (Bales, 1999; Kara, 2008). We are connected to this extreme form of labour exploitation through global commodity chains. In the words of Kevin Bales, a sociologist and expert in global slavery,

> Slaves in Pakistan may have made the shoes you are wearing and the carpet you stand on. Slaves in the Caribbean may have put sugar in your kitchen and toys in the hands of your children. In India they may have sewn the shirt on your back and polished the ring on your finger. They are paid nothing. ... Your investment portfolio and your mutual fund pension own stock in companies using labor in the developing world. Slaves keep your costs low and returns on your investments high. (1999: 3–4)

The injustices of the global labour system have not gone unnoticed or uncontested, even though serious obstacles lie ahead for unions and workers.

In Canada, unionized workers as a percentage of nonagricultural workers fell from a high point of 38 percent in 1981 to 31.5 percent in 2010 (Human Resources and Skills Development Canada, 2011), while the American unionization rate fell to just 11.9 percent in 2010 (Bureau of Labor Statistics, 2011). Historically, unionism arose in large capitalist factories, yet globalized firms often decentralize and subcontract work to small, independent firms, making unionization and labour regulation more difficult. Unions have responded by developing new strategies that include cross-border organization, transnational solidarity campaigns, emphasizing the importance of good wages for all working people (not just union members), and drives to organize service-sector workers, such as janitors, hotel workers, and security guards (Babson, 2000; Frundt, 2000; Milkman, 2000; Nissen, 2000).

The anti-sweatshop movement of the 1990s also raised awareness of labour exploitation by transnational firms (A. Ross, 1997; R. Ross, 2004). Today, prominent retail corporations like Nike and the Gap must at least appear to take global labour issues seriously (reports suggest that working conditions are still abysmal in Nike's subcontracted operations; R. Ross, 2004: 42). Although it was unimaginable to promote a "sweatshop-free" clothing line in the early 1990s, the popular label American Apparel has proven that it is possible (albeit difficult) to run a successful business without the use of sweatshop labour. Although American Apparel rejects unions and does not consider itself an "altruistic company," it produces all of its garments and shoes in Los Angeles and pays its workers more than California's minimum wage (R. Ross, 2004: 1). Recently, American Apparel has become vocal about the fight to legalize undocumented workers in Los Angeles, launching the "Legalize LA" campaign. In a letter that introduced this campaign, Dov Charney, founder and CEO of American Apparel, says that "[American Apparel's] dream for Los Angeles is that the over 1 million undocumented migrant workers who live here, and contribute to the city economically, culturally, and socially will have the opportunity to become legal residents of the city, and the United States" (American Apparel, n.d.). Other clothing lines, such as No Sweat, use unionized labour in North America *and* developing countries. According to the No Sweat website, "We believe that the only viable response to globalization is a global labor movement" (No Sweat, 2005).

GLOBAL ECOLOGY

Consumers, workers, citizens, and nations all play critical roles in the globalization processes we have outlined. In turn, all these actors fit together in a larger global ecology that connects people, resources, and commodities. To better understand these ecological connections, I now examine the globalized food system.

GLOBAL FOOD

Global trade in agriculture allows relatively prosperous people to consume a wide variety of exotic fruits, imported bottled water, and distant marine life, such as shrimp and fresh tuna. Although the global trade in food products is a boon for discriminating eaters, critics of industrialized global agriculture question its environmental costs. Trade experts and environmental groups warn that agriculture is the largest contributor of greenhouse gas when food production and distribution chains are taken into account, and suggest that the global food system represents the biggest environmental challenge facing humanity (Clay, 2004; Shrybman, 2000).

One of the major environmental problems with the world's agricultural system is the immense amount of fossil fuel required to produce, package, and transport food. Fossil fuel consumption generates greenhouse gases, such as carbon dioxide, which is linked to global climate change. But why is food so closely linked with carbon dioxide emissions? The first and simplest answer is transportation. Today, most Europeans and North Americans eat foods that have travelled a long distance to get to their plate. Food's travel time is captured in the concept of "food miles," a measure of the distance food travels from production to consumption and an indicator of the amount of fossil fuels burned in the process. A Toronto study compared the distance travelled by conventional agricultural products purchased at a discount supermarket with the distance travelled by the same basket of goods purchased at a nearby farmers' market (Bentley, 2004). While the supermarket food travelled 5734 kilometres on average, the same farmers' market produce travelled an average of only 101 kilometres to get to the consumer (Bentley, 2004: 7).

Food transported from far away might add variety to our diet, but it frequently involves an unsustainable and irrational energy tradeoff. For a head of iceberg lettuce transported from California to the United Kingdom, 127 calories of nonrenewable fossil fuel energy are required to produce 1 calorie of food energy (Sustain/Elm Farm Research Centre, 2001: 1). The way that most of our foods are produced and packaged also relies heavily on fossil fuels. The food processing industry uses 10 calories of fossil fuel energy to produce 1 calorie of food energy. Intensive livestock operations are even more wasteful: 1 calorie of beef requires 35 calories of fossil fuel, and 1 calorie of pork requires 68 calories of fossil fuel. Because of these energy-intensive production techniques, food scholars estimate that if the entire world adopted North American food habits, fossil fuel reserves would be gone in just seven years (Manning, 2004: 42, 44).

Just as consumers in India and China move toward a meat-intensive diet, increasing demand for both animal feed and oil calls into question the stability of global food supplies. Despite short-term fluctuations, demand for oil is increasing while supply is just about stagnant. As a result, the price of oil increases, and agricultural crops, such as corn, are increasingly turned into biofuel to offset oil supply problems. However, the diversion of food crops into biofuel production causes food prices to rise. In 2007–08, news headlines reported food riots by poor people in many developing countries, ignited by sharply rising food prices (Walt, 2008).

Soil, Water, and Genetic Engineering

Besides relying heavily on fossil fuel, industrial methods of food production are associated with global environmental problems like deforestation, soil erosion, and declining water tables. In the past 40 years, soil degradation has caused farmers around the world to abandon about 430 million hectares of arable land. This area amounts to one-third of all cropland (Kindall and Pimentel, 1994; see Figure 19.8). Every year, 130 000 square kilometres of forest, an area four times the size of Switzerland, are destroyed to make way for agriculture. By 2020, an estimated 22 million hectares of savannah and forest, an area as large as the United Kingdom, will be cut down in South America to meet global demand for soya, a crop that is used largely for livestock feed and vegetable oil (World Wildlife Fund, 2004).

Even when adequate land can be found to grow crops, water is also needed. Seventy percent of world water usage is for irrigation, and food analysts worry about an emerging "world water deficit"

FIGURE 19.8 GLOBAL SOIL DEGRADATION

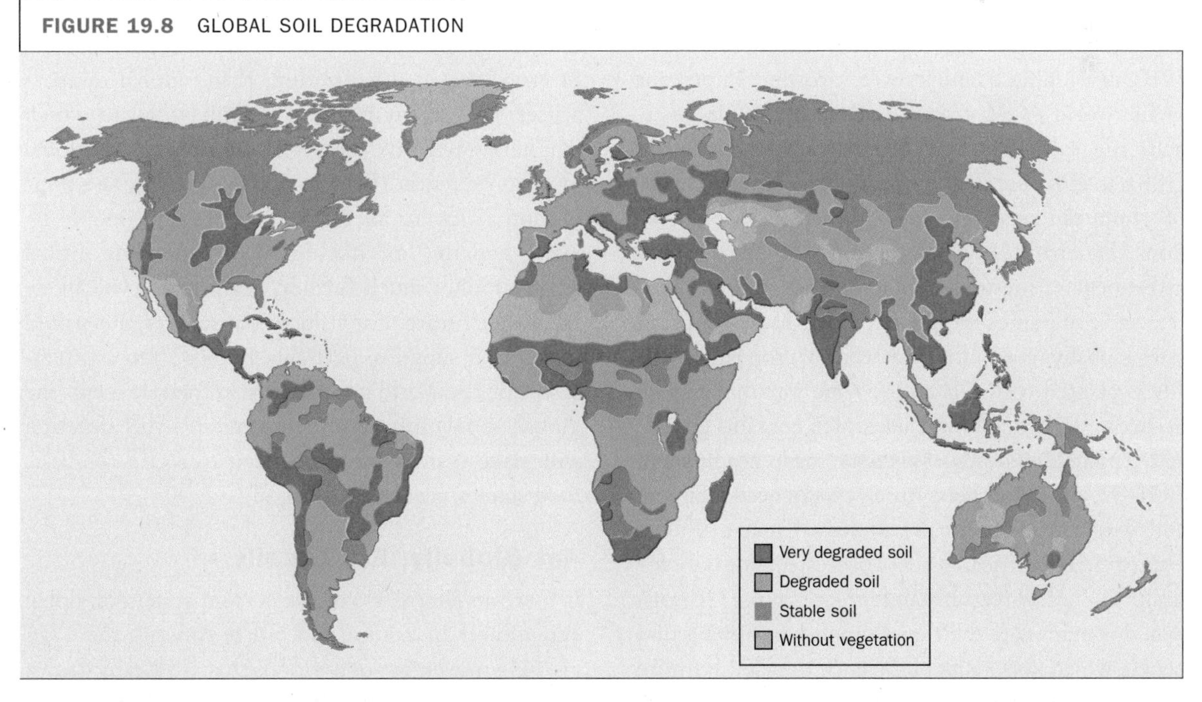

SOURCE: UNEP, International Soil Reference and Information Center (ISRIC), *World Atlas of Desertification, 1997.* In Philippe Rekacewicz. (2002). "Degraded Soils." UNEP/GRID-Arendal Maps and Graphics Library. Retrieved 17 May 2009. http://maps.grida.no/go/graphic/degraded.soils.

(Brown, 2005: 10). Underground aquifers refill slowly and are currently being pumped at rates that are unsustainable. In Northern China, for instance, groundwater levels are falling by at least one metre a year, while aquifers in the United States are being pumped at a pace that vastly exceeds replacement rates (Pimentel and Wilson, 2004).

Some scientists believe that global agriculture problems can be addressed by switching to genetically modified (GM) crops that have been designed to be drought- and pest-resistant by reengineering the plant's genetic structure. This technological solution is opposed by many environmentalists who worry about the long-term health and ecological impact of GE crops, particularly the negative impact on biodiversity, since GE crops tend to out-compete and contaminate related species. GE canola has already infected organic canola in Western Canada to such an extent that it is impossible for organic farmers to grow and market uncontaminated (GE-free) organic canola. Saskatchewan farmer Percy Schmeiser launched a lawsuit against seed giant Monsanto, suing for damages, and was awarded an out-of-court settlement. Activists in less developed countries are concerned that GE crops will permit large corporations to consolidate their control over agriculture and erode traditions of seed saving and innovation by farmers.

Although much of the world's (GM) crops have been grown in North America, their usage in the Global South has expanded considerably—by 2010, developing countries were growing 48 percent of the world's GM crops (ISAAA, 2010). One estimate suggested that by 2010, GM crops were being grown in 29 countries by 15.4 million farmers, many of whom ran relatively small, resource-poor operations (Federoff, 2011). Because of the huge capital investment in these technologies, multinational bioscience companies would like to expand adoption rates globally (currently 10 percent of crop land globally is planted with GE crops). One way this may be occurring is through food aid, which contains genetically engineered crops. This issue made headlines in 2001–02, when southern Africa experienced a famine and was given genetically modified maize by the United States. African leaders protested, not only for health and safety reasons but for fear that the GE corn would contaminate their own supplies (assuming that people would save some of the corn to plant in future harvests), and endanger export markets in Europe, where GE foods have faced bans and stiff consumer resistance (African Centre for Biosafety, 2005).

In 2005, scientists discovered that grain donated by the United States Agency for International Development (USAID) through the World Food Program (WFP) to Central American and Caribbean countries was heavily contaminated with genetically modified corn. Eighty percent of the samples tested included GE corn, including "StarLink," corn that is not authorized for human consumption in the United States (Organic Consumers Association, 2005). The UN Cartagena Protocol on Biosafety stipulates that genetically engineered crops can enter countries only with prior informed consent, but the WFP's heavy reliance on USAID grain supplies means that this right is currently not being enforced and that genetic contamination of the world's global grain supplies is likely to continue.

Global Hunger amid Plenty

The world grows enough grain to provide nearly three thousand calories per person per day (Lappé, 2005: 13), yet the number of undernourished people in the world has risen since the early 1980s, totalling at least 842 million people (Wheeler and Thompson, 2004: 212). World grain production is a general measure of global food security. Per capita grain production has been falling since 1984, while overall grain production was flat between 1996 and 2003 (Brown, 2005: 4).

It is especially troubling to consider these numbers in the context of widespread soil erosion, loss of crop land to urbanization, rising global temperatures, and shrinking water supplies—all of which will have a negative impact on the capacity of global grain production (Brown, 2005: 7). With the population rising to an estimated 9 billion people by 2050, and the low likelihood of expanding global grain supplies much further, grain prices will likely rise in the future. For affluent consumers, this would make food supplies, particularly meat, more expensive. For the world's malnourished people—half the global population by some estimates—this situation will make it increasingly difficult to access the basic food staples needed for survival.

Act Globally, Eat Locally

Is there an alternative to the current system of global agriculture? In Europe and North America there is a growing movement to eat foods that are locally grown and produced with organic farming techniques. Researchers in Britain estimate that if all farms in there became organic, an estimated $1.1 billion in environmental costs would be saved (Lang and Pretty, 2005; Lappé and Lappé, 2002).

The move to promote organic, locally grown food is not confined to the affluent minority world. The Nadvanya movement in India, for instance, aims to promote indigenous agricultural techniques to counter the presence of multinational agribusiness in ways that improve the environment and increase people's food security (Navdanya, 2005). Many organic farmers and food activists believe that organic farming techniques, not genetic engineering or food aid, are the answer to famines and food shortages (Hall, 2005), although not all food experts agree (Paarlberg, 2010).

The tension between local and global food represents the challenge and the paradox of bottom-up globalization. It is a challenge because most small-scale activists and food producers, like most of the world's workers, are rooted where they grow food and are not nearly as globalized as corporate agribusiness and its CEOs. It is a paradox because peasant and small farmer movements want to encourage *local* food consumption, defend *local* agricultural ecosystems, and, at the same time, use *global* networks to fight these battles. Their motto could be "act globally, eat locally."

Cuba: An Island's Isolation and Innovation

What would happen if globalization processes were reversed, and a country suddenly found itself isolated, without the ability to trade for food in global markets? Cuba provides a real-life answer to that question. It is literally an island, but is also a metaphorical island in that it is largely isolated from the major ebbs and flows of global food trade. The United States has refused to trade with Cuba since 1960, a year after the Cuban revolution in 1959. After the collapse of the Soviet Union, Cuba lost access to an extremely important source of food supplies and fossil fuels. Suddenly, the nation was hungry. Calorie consumption per person per day fell from 3000 in 1989 (the year the Soviet Union collapsed) to 1600 four years later.

Without fossil fuels or cheap grain supplies, Cuba's agriculture had to change, and change it did. Cuban agronomists began experimenting with more sustainable, low-input agriculture that used crop rotation to provide natural fertilization. They developed large urban gardens to feed and employ thousands of Cubans. Farmers began using oxen instead of tractors, saving fossil fuel. Today, almost completely cut off from global agricultural trade, Havana feeds itself from gardens within city limits. There are still problems ensuring adequate supplies of milk and meat, yet Cuban agriculture is remarkably successful, leading some analysts to suggest that the Cuban model is a possible future scenario for what agriculture could look like when fossil fuel supplies become scarce and the environmental consequences of globalized industrial agriculture become too onerous to ignore (McKibben, 2005: 69).

In an article profiling the costs and benefits of the Cuban agricultural experiment, environmental journalist Bill McKibben concludes with a provocative and difficult question that we would do well to ponder—a question that applies not only to Cuban agriculture, but to globalization more generally:

> Is it also possible ... that there's something inherently destructive about a globalized free-market society—that the eternal race for efficiency, when raised to a planetary scale, damages the environment, and perhaps the community, and perhaps even the taste of a carrot? Is it possible that markets, at least for food, may work better when they're smaller and more isolated? The next few decades may be about answering that question. (McKibben, 2005: 69)

SUMMARY

1. Globalization effectively shrinks the world; workers, commodities, ideas, and capital cross distances more quickly. Sociologists use the term "time–space compression" to describe this process.
2. Globalization processes have generated contradictory outcomes that benefit some groups but have also been linked to poverty, economic marginalization, democratic deficits, and the digital divide.
3. Developments in information technology have facilitated the economic integration of financial markets. Consequently, global flows of financial capital are much bigger than global flows of tangible goods and productive capital.
4. Corporations in the global era have become much bigger and are under pressure to become more competitive in the global marketplace. Local and even national competitiveness is no longer seen as sufficient for economic survival.
5. Politically, the globalization era has witnessed the creation of new international institutions of governance like the IMF, World Bank, and WTO, which have diminished the power and sovereignty of some states.
6. Globalization processes have allowed communities around the world to gain knowledge of the injustice and suffering inflicted by the global economy. Such awareness has inspired efforts to increase social justice in the global system. These efforts are known as "globalization from below."
7. Most of the goods Canadians consume connect them to workers and production processes thousands of kilometres away. The globalization process is almost impossible to escape given the extent of global commodity chains.
8. The period of globalization is associated with a shift in manufacturing employment out of the more developed countries. Competitive pressure is driving corporations to seek the lowest wages possible in the less developed countries (the so-called race to the bottom).
9. Global ecology is not something that exists separately from globalization processes. It is connected to the actions of citizens, consumers, workers, and states.

QUESTIONS TO CONSIDER

1. How do you benefit from globalization processes? What are the negative consequences of these processes? Consider your role as a worker, consumer, and citizen.
2. Do you think globalization has caused the Canadian state to lose sovereignty? Do you think Canadians suffer from a democratic deficit?
3. Do you think that consumer activism and social movement campaigns like the anti-sweatshop campaign are an effective way of making global commodity chains more equitable? Do you think that the corporate movement for social responsibility offers a more promising avenue for change? Is voluntary corporate action sufficient or are governments needed to make legislation and enforce corporate responsibility?

GLOSSARY

Consumerism (p. 476) is a way of life focusing on the purchase and acquisition of commodities. While traditionally thought of as a problem for North America and Europe, consumerism is also a cultural and ecological issue among affluent populations in the less developed countries.

Cultural imperialism (p. 477) is a controversial theory of cultural domination according to which powerful economic and political actors (primarily Euro-American) are thought to impose their values, norms, and lifestyles on other populations. Cultural imperialism often refers to the export of certain Euro-American cultural practices, such as materialism, consumerism, and sexual liberalism through the media of television, music, and film.

A **democratic deficit** (p. 473) involves the disenfranchisement of ordinary citizens from the decisions and process of governments. Democratic deficits are often attributed to the influence of corporate actors and international financial institutions on governments and the transfer of governance to institutions such as the IMF and WTO, which do not permit average citizens to vote or influence decisions.

The **digital divide** (p. 466) is the gap between people who are easily able to access communication technologies, such as the Internet and cellular phones, and people who lack the material resources, education, or infrastructure to access these technologies.

Export processing zones (EPZs) (p. 483) are manufacturing areas in which government programs provide special incentives to help promote export-oriented manufacturing. Sometimes EPZs are actual territorial zones demarcated by fences and borders, while in other cases they indicate programs that apply to all industries in a country. For instance, in 1991 Sri Lanka declared the entire country an EPZ.

The **fourth world** (p. 475) comprises marginalized populations and regions that are not competitive in the global economy.

A **global commodity chain** (p. 476) is a worldwide network of labour and production processes, the end result of which is a finished commodity.

Globalization (p. 465) is a social, economic, and political process that facilitates the movement of people, goods, ideas, and capital around the globe. With globalization processes, the world appears to shrink, although the ability to cross borders varies tremendously depending on one's position in the global economy.

Globalization from below (p. 468) is a short-hand way of describing a diverse range of projects seeking greater democracy, equality, and sustainability in globalization processes. These projects are generally opposed to neoliberal policies and U.S. hegemony in the global system and are also referred to as alternative globalization, the global social justice movement, and anti-globalization.

Neoliberalism (p. 467) refers to economic policies that became prominent in the late 1970s in both developed and developing countries. Neoliberalism is associated with a retreat from state intervention and regulation, greater focus on individual responsibility, less protection for labour and the environment, privatization of state resources, and faith in the power of the market and the profit motive to provide the greatest good for the greatest number.

Outsourcing (p. 482) occurs when firms contract production and services to smaller, independent firms. When outsourcing occurs on a global level, multinational corporations contract production and services to firms in less developed countries.

Time–space compression (p. 465) refers to the diminished importance of geography and time lags because of globalization.

Top-down globalization (p. 467) refers to the extension of capitalism globally, particularly as a result of the neoliberal policies and programs authorized by international financial authorities, such as the IMF and World Bank, and implemented by national governments. Top-down globalization is organized by elites in governments, corporations, and international institutions with little democratic input.

A **virtual community** (p. 465) is a group whose members share interests and meet primarily on the Internet.

SUGGESTED READING

Ehrenreich, Barbara and Arlie Russell Hoschschild, eds. (2002). *Global Woman: Nannies, Maids, and Sex Workers in the New Economy.* New York: Metropolitan Books. This captivating account offers personal and insightful analyses of how globalization affects women around the world. The economics of globalization come to life through the stories told in these chapters.

Sachs, Jeffrey. (2005). *The End of Poverty: Economic Possibilities for Our Time.* New York: Penguin. You may not agree with Sachs's hopeful analysis, but this is an undeniably influential account written by one of the world's most important economists (and endorsed by none other than Bono, who wrote the Foreword). The book is highly readable and combines economic analysis with personal stories from the author's travels in the world's poverty-stricken areas.

Smith, Jackie, ed. (2007). *Global Democracy and the World Social Forums.* Boulder, CO: Paradigm Publishers. This book provides a nonspecialist's account of the World Social Forum (WSF), one of the most exciting and important global activist events in recent decades. Each chapter is written by a scholar who has participated in the WSF, and together they show how the WSF is a critical part of the transnational movement for global peace, justice, and democracy.

PART 6

METHODS

SOURCE: © Robert Brym

CHAPTER 20

RESEARCH METHODS

Neil Guppy
UNIVERSITY OF BRITISH COLUMBIA

SOURCE: © Robert Brym.

To create this image, the 100 most frequently used words in this chapter were ordered alphabetically from left to right, and the font size for each word was made proportional to the frequency with which each word was used.

IN THIS CHAPTER YOU WILL LEARN THAT

- Science is one of several sources of knowledge. Like other sources of knowledge, it can be wrong. However, science uses methods of gathering theoretically relevant evidence that are designed to minimize error.
- Research methods are used by sociologists to gather evidence and test theories about recurring patterns of human activity. Underlying these techniques is a variety of assumptions about the nature of facts, objectivity, and truth.
- In comparison with the evidence available to natural scientists, an added complexity confronts social scientists: humans assign meaning to their actions, and interpreting meaningful action is complicated.
- Sociologists have devised many useful methods of obtaining evidence about the social world, including experiments, interviews, observational techniques, and surveys.
- Good sociological research adds to our knowledge of the social world, expanding opportunities and options by helping to solve social problems.

INTRODUCTION

Social research involves systematic, purposeful study. The systematic nature of sociological research comes, in part, from the methods sociologists use. Fundamental to methods is the careful, ethical collection of evidence. However, only evidence relevant to theoretical ideas is useful. The purposeful structuring of sociological inquiry comes from asking theoretically informed questions. Systematic sociological study integrates sound theory with careful methods.

This chapter introduces you to the principles of research methods. I begin by outlining some basic assumptions involved in social science research, including assumptions about personal values or bias, the nature of facts, and the sources of knowledge. Next, I explain how the subject matter of the social sciences—people—differs from the objects of inquiry in the natural sciences (e.g., molecules). People studying people adds complexity to social research. This added complexity comes from people interpreting their own behaviour, and the behaviour of others, by trying to understand meanings. Methods of observation and questioning lie at the heart of social research, and I review the strengths and weaknesses of each of these approaches in the final section of the chapter.

PERSPECTIVE

James Driskell and David Milgaard were convicted of murder. In 2005, 14 years after his conviction, after new DNA tests, James Driskell had his murder charges quashed. David Milgaard had to endure prison longer, but in July 1997, after 23 years in prison, he too was exonerated. Again, DNA testing was instrumental. Judges, juries, and prosecutors had weighed evidence that they believed demonstrated the guilt of these men. Circumstantial evidence, filtered by personal expectations and values, had led justice astray. Subjective judgments had seriously compromised these men's lives.

Gold (1998) claimed that "good science" exonerated Morin, but it was "not science that helped convict him." But what makes for "good science," the kind of science on which we can make serious decisions?

Wrongful convictions are rare. The criminal justice system minimizes such error through rules of evidence and presumptions of innocence. Likewise, science is organized to minimize error. Science is not perfect, however, and it is important not to put

Sociological theories were first proposed in the nineteenth century as secular accounts of rapid social change. By the early twentieth century, systematic methods for empirically testing hypotheses were being introduced.
SOURCE: Carol Wainio, *Untitled* (1985). Acrylic on canvas, 3300 × 5000. Photograph courtesy of the S. L. Simpson Gallery, Toronto. Reproduced with permission of the artist.

scientific practice on a pedestal, somehow immune to human foibles. Like all human activities, the social practice of science is influenced by subjectivity.

SCIENCE AS A SOCIAL PRACTICE

Science needs subjectivity but it cannot be overwhelmed by it. Subjectivity is important to certain phases in the practice of science but detrimental to other phases. Understanding the complexities of scientific methods requires distinguishing between times when subjectivity is beneficial and times when it is not. But just what is subjectivity? Most people would agree that our personal values and expectations are a core part of subjectivity. Frequently, people separate the world into facts and values; the real and objective versus the personal and subjective.

But what appears to us as reality is filtered or screened. Reality exists, certainly—it is no figment of the imagination. However, our values and expectations filter reality. While the saying "what you see is what you get" has an intuitive appeal, we know the claim is false. It exaggerates. Other things, especially our expectations and values, affect what we see.

Here is an example of filtering. The Sun is real. It is no figment of our imagination. We commonly speak about "sunsets" and "sunrises." But these terms deceive. Although we have all watched a "sunset," the Sun does not set. Our language conditions us to think of a moving Sun, but Earth rotates around the Sun. Earth's spin creates the *illusion* of a moving Sun.

Being skeptical of my claim about a filtered reality is important. Values and expectations influence our perceptions of reality, but they do not completely determine what we see. This is a critical point. The *extent* to which values and expectations influence what we see is debatable, but that is a secondary point. The key point is that *if* our perceptions of reality can be affected by our values, *then* how can scientists ever know for certain that what they "see" is true? Put another way, if observation cannot be a rock-solid foundation of scientific knowledge, then how is the practice of science to be understood?

An important claim of this chapter is that reality does not exist as some neutral scientific judge. Pure observation does not rule supreme. To think of an individual scientist as a detached, arm's-length observer of the physical or social world, making observations to test ideas, is to profoundly misunderstand science. The scientific method is not a mechanical process of collecting facts to prove things. Science is a much more complex social activity, and the methods of scientists are designed in the face of such complexity.

Here is an illustration of how values and expectations may creep into scientific work.

Recall from your high-school biology classes the work of Gregor Mendel. Mendel was the father of genetics. He cross-fertilized varieties of pea plants and noted that inherited traits followed consistent numerical ratios (i.e., the expression of dominant and recessive genes over successive generations). These experiments, demonstrating landmark principles of heredity, remain controversial (see Orel, 1996). R. A. Fisher, while a Cambridge University undergraduate, demonstrated that Mendel's results seemed fabricated. The likelihood that Mendel produced results conforming so closely to his hunches about heredity was, Fisher showed, in the order of 1 in 30 000.

Mendel may have been lucky, producing possible but very unlikely results. Alternatively, Mendel, or his assistant, may have unconsciously misclassified some pea plants. Classifications made by Mendel were not clear-cut, so his experimental results may have been interpreted as favouring his preconceived ideas. In this vein, Fisher (1966 [1936]: 123) claimed that Mendel's results were a "carefully planned demonstration of his conclusion."

"Observer bias" (making unconscious mistakes in classifying or selecting observations) is now commonly discussed as a danger to good methodological procedure. Mendel did not clearly and publicly describe his procedures. His data are no longer available for reexamination. Although it is impossible to know exactly why his results came out as they did, his ideas about genetics have proven invaluable.

Good research methods are designed to minimize the types of errors that have been attributed to Mendel's experimental evidence. These methods do not eliminate the biasing effect that values and expectations have on scientific research. They do, however, seek to minimize their impact.

MINIMIZING BIAS IN SOCIAL SCIENCE

Sociologists apply scientific practices to the study of human society. These practices incorporate several ways of reducing bias, especially the twin pillars of public (open) scrutiny and skeptical reasoning. Scientific ideas become provisionally accepted only after scrutiny by the scientific community. Individual scientists do not just proclaim a link between family background and children's school success or between HIV and AIDS; these links must be demonstrated by presenting research findings at scientific conferences, subjecting findings to peer review, and ensuring that research results can be replicated. The scientific community is organized to promote critical scrutiny.

Scrutiny is not enough, however. If the scrutiny is not rigorous and probing, then it is of little value. Scientific practice also encourages skeptical reasoning. New ideas are accepted only after others have critically examined them, only after they have withstood a barrage of questions from doubters. Examples of this doubting come from questions like this: Could something other than HIV cause AIDS? If HIV does cause AIDS, exactly how does the causal process work? Does HIV cause AIDS among all people? This process of doubting is built into the way science is conducted.

Scientists are also trained in methods of research designed to minimize the influence of their personal values and expectations on the results of their research work. They work to root out error in reasoning and observation. So, for example, scientists learn to collect and analyze information according to rules that reduce the risk that results will be affected by bias. Much of the latter part of this chapter focuses on these specific research techniques.

Science has prospered because of this healthy skepticism and public scrutiny. Both natural and social sciences have played a pivotal role in making our world a better place in which to live by helping to curtail malaria, improving the life chances of children with disabilities, and reducing gender inequity. Scientists are not infallible saints, however. The scientific community is not some sacred haven where only truth and enlightenment reign. Fraud and deceit are also part of science (Park, 2000).

It is also important to correct a possible misinterpretation about the role of values and expectations. I have portrayed these as "problems." This is too one-sided. Science would be substantially weaker, if not impotent, without values and expectations. Science is soaked through with individual judgments. Mendel's brilliance came from his expectation that dominant and recessive genes played a fundamental role in explaining inheritance. Mendel provided a new way of seeing the world, a new conceptual map for understanding.

Expectations and values are in tension within the scientific enterprise. Without them the spark of creativity and passion would be low, but with them we can be led to false conclusions (as judges and juries are occasionally misled). Put differently, objectivity and subjectivity each play an important role in science, including sociology. **Objectivity,** which is what courtroom judges and jurors strive for, stresses that observations should be free of the distorting effects of a person's values and expectations. Conversely, subjectivity is essential to change and innovation. Without people championing their own visions, we would have little creativity. A hallmark of science is its creativity. Mendel's was a beautiful solution to the mystery of inheritance, even if he may have been too exuberant in his experimental claims.

Science depends on both the creativity of new explanations and the assessment of whether these explanations are plausible. In sociology, this dual character resides in a division between theory (explanations of how the world works) and methods (ways of assessing the veracity of explanations).

This chapter is about assessing evidence. It explores how sociologists work within the rules of the scientific method. First, however, I contrast scientific knowledge with other forms of knowledge. The discussion moves next to the steps involved in the sociological research process. I then describe the main methods of gathering sociological data and the decisions that have to be made during the research process. Finally, I return in the conclusion to the role of subjectivity in research.

SCIENTIFIC VERSUS NONSCIENTIFIC THINKING

To differentiate good and bad science, consider what characterizes scientific thinking. Before the eighteenth century and the rise of science, our ancestors knew many things about the world. Much of this was custom or common sense—when to plant, what to plant, where to plant. Religious knowledge held centre stage in community life. Stories of creation, of how we came to be on Earth, were powerful tales that gave coherence to peoples' lives. Religious doctrine and common sense remain powerful in many societies, but scientific ways of knowing have increasing authority in industrial nations.

What characterizes this scientific way of knowing? A key contribution came from Scottish philosopher David Hume (1711–76). He disputed the popular argument of his day that science begins with observation. Hume argued that no matter how many observations you make, you cannot infer your next observation. This is the *problem of induction*. Put more graphically, no matter how many white swans you see, you cannot logically infer that all swans are white. However, observing one black swan is sufficient to refute the claim that all swans are white.[1] Hume was railing against Francis Bacon's claim that observation was the bedrock of science. For Hume, the collection of "facts" is useless unless you understand how to interpret them.

In Charles Dickens's *Hard Times*, Mr. Gradgrind demands facts: "What I want is Facts. ... Facts alone are wanted in life." Contrary to the popular saying, though, facts do not speak for themselves. Blue mould growing on spoiling food is a fact of life. It was only in 1928, however, that Alexander Fleming recognized this blue mould as a potent medical tool. Many people, perhaps even Mr. Gradgrind, had seen blue mould, but only Fleming understood it as penicillin. Science is not a collection of facts. However, among other things, it is a method of collecting facts.

Facts are bits of evidence, information that we can verify by using our senses. Because trillions of bits of human activity might be taken as facts, how do we select what should count as evidence? How do sociologists avoid idiosyncratic fact gathering? Sociological theory provides guidance for the hunting and gathering of facts. Evidence is gathered to test ideas, hunches, or theories. Only selected bits of human activity are used as evidence. Those selected bits are chosen because they relate to a sociologist's theory about how the world works.

In the twentieth century, Sir Karl Popper (1977 [1934]) improved this thinking with his ideas about falsification. As he claimed, observations refuting a well-conceived idea are always more important than evidence supporting or proving a theory (e.g., observing one black swan was more important than observing yet another white swan). For Popper, science does not start by gathering raw facts. It starts with a question or hunch, or in his words, a well-conceived conjecture.

Two core ideas about distinguishing scientific thinking from other ways of thinking have been presented earlier: public scrutiny and skeptical reasoning. Popper added the principles of testability and uncertainty. Testability is easy to understand. For an idea to be scientific it must have testable implications; it must be falsifiable (i.e., *if* an assertion is false, this can be demonstrated by evidence).

The concept of uncertainty may be more difficult to accept. Many people misunderstand science as a doctrine of certainty. As Park (2000: 39) puts it, "many people are uneasy standing on ... loose soil; they seek a certainty that science cannot offer." As Hume argued centuries before, observations cannot be the bedrock of science because of the problem of induction. Equally, however, science cannot proceed, as Popper correctly argued, without the possibility of observations that could refute a scientific claim. Observations based on well-reasoned methods can ferret out error and misunderstanding, although these same observations cannot guarantee universal truth or perfect certainty (see Box 20.1).

NATURAL VERSUS SOCIAL SCIENCE

The scientific practices of chemists and sociologists share many elements. The research methods of both disciplines help in understanding and explaining why certain patterns emerge. Furthermore, values are important in this process because these values underlie the creative imagination so central to scientific puzzle solving. Values also have the potential to bias or distort observations, and both the natural and the social sciences guard against distortion. If the scientific method is defined as a set of practices or procedures for testing knowledge claims, then both chemists and sociologists are doing science.

There is, however, a profound difference between the subject matter of the natural and the social sciences: Bacteria don't blush. This phrase neatly captures the key distinction. Human beings are conscious and creative; we can think, act, reason, and decide. As sociologists, we study "ourselves"—that is, our contemporaries and our ancestors. Bacteria, having no knowledge of social norms, do not blush when exposed to the beam of an electron microscope. Bacteria cannot think, act, reason, and decide; they cannot consciously control their surroundings or reactions in the same way human beings can.[2]

Perhaps the single most important difference is that, unlike chemists, sociologists study **meaningful action**—that is, activities that are meaningful to the people involved. For example, bacteria may not blush when studied, but people often react self-consciously when they know they are being observed. To study love, friendship, or charisma depends on learning something about the meanings people ascribe to actions. This has advantages and disadvantages. Unlike chemists, sociologists can ask questions of the people whom we study (bacteria don't talk either). But this advantage can also be a disadvantage. Interpreting people's answers is not easy.

BOX 20.1 SEEING SCIENCE SOCIOLOGICALLY

One of the most influential academic books of the twentieth century was Thomas Kuhn's (1962) *The Structure of Scientific Revolutions*. Before Kuhn, many people held a "brick-building" conception of science. They thought that individual scientists contributed to building a structure called scientific knowledge, one brick at a time. As scientific knowledge accumulated, the structure became taller and sturdier.

Kuhn challenged this view on several fronts. First, he held that science developed through contributions from a community of scholars who use "paradigms" as guiding tools about how the world is organized (Mendelian genetics is such a paradigm). Paradigms guide questions and answers. Evidence not fitting a paradigm is ignored. However, if anomalous evidence accumulates, a "scientific revolution" results. Scholars opt for a new guiding paradigm. The transition from Newton's mechanics to Einstein's relativity illustrates a paradigm shift, or a scientific revolution (Kleppner and Jackiw, 2000).

Second, Kuhn proposed a discontinuous view of scientific progress. The community of scholars did not keep building the Newtonian structure but shifted to a new structure defined by the Einsteinian paradigm. This discontinuous view of scientific progress also influenced debates about truth. Earth as the "third rock from the Sun" we now hold as a fundamental truth. But our ancestors were equally convinced that Earth was the universe's central rock. In the future, will our "third rock" conception seem equally odd? Kuhn's view suggests that truth is contextual. A new paradigm establishes a new context, showing us that beliefs we once held to be true were naive or misleading (like a setting Sun).

Finally, the argument about community was sociologically compelling. In Kuhn's hands, the practice of science was not understood as individual scientists ruthlessly questioning all ideas. To the contrary, paradigms provided a set of convictions about how the world was ordered. With faith in a paradigm, a community of scholars searched for what they were convinced existed. Paradigms had a disciplining effect, focusing attention on a delimited set of questions and answers. Notice also that Kuhn emphasized that scientific change was not gradual, but sudden (revolutionary) and that the change was organized or predictable (structured).

Because of this difference in subject matter, sociologists have developed an array of methods to help in understanding and explaining human activity. Since asking questions has advantages and disadvantages, good sociological research either employs a variety of ways to ask questions or relies on observational techniques to aid understanding and explanation.

METHODS OF SOCIAL RESEARCH

EXPLANATION

Sociologists have shown repeatedly that the years of schooling people receive is strongly influenced by family background. Children raised in poverty tend not to go as far in school as do children from upper-class families. Although this research demonstrates a link between family background and educational attainment, this link is, as I have reported it, descriptive, not explanatory. I have offered no reason *why* this relationship between family origin and educational destination exists. It is true that I have noted a potential cause (family background) and an effect (years of schooling), but I have failed to provide any mechanisms through which this implied causal process might operate. An **explanation** would be judged adequate only if it could show how family background actually influences educational outcomes.

The mere association or correlation between social origin and educational destination does not prove causality. The relationship between smoking and lung cancer is a good example of the rule that *correlation does not prove causation*. Smoking has long been linked to lung cancer, but only in the past few decades have we learned more about the causal mechanisms underlying this correlation. Cigarette companies, especially, have argued that the presumed connection was a **spurious relationship,** meaning that something other than smoking caused lung cancer (see Box 20.2). Accumulated evidence and more precise understanding and observation of the underlying modes of transmission have established that the original correlation is causal.

We might try to explain the link between family and schooling in several ways (Davies and Guppy, 2010). An obvious factor is money. Although public schooling is free, costs are incurred for field trips, tutoring, international tours, postsecondary education, and a host of other events. Children living in poverty may remain in school for fewer years than their upper-class peers because of these costs (and they may seek employment sooner to help with family income).

Money seems to be a partial explanation for the link, but other factors may be at work as well. Many skills and values taught in school may be more readily grasped by children from upper-class families, not because these children are smarter than are children living in poverty, but because the home environments of the children may expose them to different skills and values. The classroom culture may be more like the culture in upper-class homes (e.g., abstract word games are valued, reading and music are prized) and these children may therefore be advantaged.

The first explanation is largely about money and material resources. The policy implications of this explanation point to eliminating or reducing the costs of schooling. This has been accomplished in large measure in Canada. However, even when the costs of postsecondary education have also been reduced (e.g., in Quebec), social-class disparities in educational attainment remain. The second explanation points to cultural factors in the home (e.g., reading) as a reason for the family–school link. This explanation has influenced policies related to compensatory education, such as Head Start and After Four, educational programs designed to help disadvantaged children by giving them educational enrichment (see also Guppy and Davies, 2009).

The mechanisms by which causes have effects are essential for adequate explanation (Gross, 2009). You might think of these mechanisms as the social "cogs and levers" greasing the wheels that link causes with effects. Furthermore, multiple causes are involved in social-scientific explanations; a single unitary cause rarely provides a sufficient explanation. Sociologists search for the multiple factors that can help explain some particular state of affairs. So, in the family–school example, although only two explanations for the link are mentioned here, other explanations may also be tested and refined as sociologists attempt to see how greater equality of educational opportunity might be attained.

UNDERSTANDING

Sociologists must not be content merely to offer explanations for why a particular relationship exists. These explanations are often sterile unless they also address the meaningfulness of human activity. People make the social world happen, and in doing so they give meaning to their actions and to the actions of

BOX 20.2 CORRELATION AND CAUSATION

Where fires cause much damage, many fire trucks gather. This is a correlation; a lot of damage tends to go along with many trucks, while minimal damage tends to draw only a few trucks. But this "truck and damage" correlation does not prove that fire trucks cause fires. Consider Figure 20.1. The curved, double-headed arrow depicts the correlation between the amount of damage and the number of fire trucks. The single-headed, straight arrows show the direction of causation. The size of the fire is a common prior cause of both other variables (number of trucks and amount of damage).

FIGURE 20.1 AN EXAMPLE TO ILLUSTRATE THAT CORRELATION DOES NOT PROVE CAUSATION

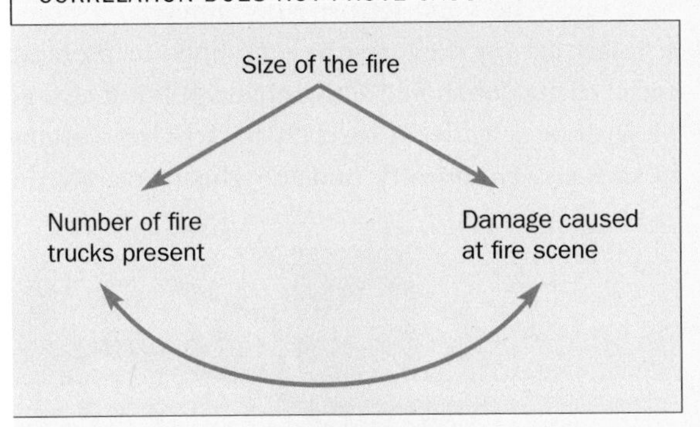

Causality is controversial because it often involves something we cannot observe directly. For example, no one can see lung cancer being caused by smoking. We infer that conclusion from assembled evidence that fits with theoretical conjecture.

Here is another example. Women living in poverty typically eat less nutritious meals and consequently are more likely than better-off women are to have premature babies. But not all women living in poverty have premature babies. There is a correlation between poverty levels and the incidence of premature births, and nutrition level has been identified as a key causal mechanism. Notice, however, that living in poverty does not guarantee premature births. Living in poverty only raises the probability that a mother will have a premature baby.

In a **causal relationship**, a change or variation in one thing produces a change or variation in another. If four basic conditions are met, causality may be established.

First, two variables must be associated or correlated. Consider again our two variables—the likelihood of premature births and poverty. Premature births must be more likely to occur among poor women than among women who are not poor if a causal relationship exists.

Second, the cause, or independent variable (poverty level), must precede the effect, or dependent variable (premature births), in time. (For more on independent and dependent variables, see p. 502.) Establishing that a woman is poor (or not) while she is pregnant confirms the causal ordering or temporal sequencing of the variables.

Third, the original association must not disappear once the effects of other variables on the dependent variable are examined. We need to verify that we have not made a false inference. Does the causal process really go from poverty to poor diet to premature babies?

Could it be that stress, and not poverty, is the causal agent? It may be that poor women are under more stress and that stress, not poverty, increases the likelihood of premature births. The initial causal relation between poverty and premature births would be spurious if stress was determined to be the operative factor (poverty may be correlated with stress, of course, but stress may still be the real causal agent).

Finally, we must offer a theoretical account of how one variable causes another. We must illustrate the social mechanism(s) through which causation operates. This theoretical reasoning also enables us to establish which variables are important to examine when we test to see whether a causal relation might be spurious. In the example, we theorize that poverty affects nutrition, which in turn affects the likelihood of premature birth.

others. A failure to address these meanings would leave sociology underdeveloped.

It is no simple matter, however, to understand what someone or some group means by their actions or utterances. One way to think about **understanding** is as follows. The first time I saw a cricket match, I could not fathom what was happening. To the extent that I have come to understand this complex social activity, I have learned *how to proceed with the activity*. To understand a cricket match means being able to participate fully in the activity, knowing what others mean by their actions and utterances, and knowing how others will interpret our actions and utterances.

A fundamental social process, called "taking the role of the other," nicely captures this idea of understanding. By imagining yourself in another person's role, you come to appreciate someone else's point of view. You come to understand, to reflect on, that person's ideas and issues. I do not mean that you must become Caesar to understand him; that would be impossible. Instead, sociologists focus on the web of relations in which people interact, paying attention to how people understand and interpret the views of others. They pay attention to "the definition of the situation," to the meanings of the people involved.

Erving Goffman's work in an insane asylum (as it was called then) is a good illustration of sociological understanding (Goffman, 1961). Goffman was interested in how the patterns of social activity in the asylum were organized. He came to see the mental hospital from the patients' point of view. By dispensing with the medical categories and scientific labels assigned to individual patients, Goffman began to understand the ways in which patients worked cooperatively to produce a coherent social structure. He learned to appreciate how the patients defined the routine activities of the asylum and how they coped with institutional procedures that denied them privacy and stripped them of their personal identities (e.g., by issuing institutional clothing and confiscating personal objects).

Goffman (1961: 129) also learned about what he calls the "careers" of patients with mental illnesses: "Persons who become mental-hospital patients vary widely in the kind and degree of illness that a psychiatrist would impute to them. ... But once [in treatment] they are confronted by some importantly similar circumstances and respond to these in some importantly similar ways. Since these similarities do not come from mental illness, they would seem to occur in spite of it." Although social life on the "inside" might seem unique or even bizarre at first, Goffman argues that anyone, patient or researcher, would, in time, come to find it much like many other communities in which he or she has participated, possessing an identifiable social organization and rhythm of activity.

Returning to the education example, explanations of high-school dropout rates that ignore the attitudes and values of the people who drop out are one-sided. An appreciation of the experiences of people who drop out is essential to a more complete account of the schooling process. Especially important here is the resistance of students to authority, often expressed through music and clothing. This resistance is not some idiosyncratic expression of random individuals, but represents part of a youth subculture that must be understood by anyone who wants to alter the schooling process to make it a better environment. How young school resisters define the situation of schooling is important to a full appreciation of dropping out.

Understanding and explanation work together. Although explanations of dropping out that ignore student values are deficient, merely reporting the stories of young resisters would be equally vacuous. A full appreciation of dropping out, or of any other social activity, requires both understanding and explanation. Often, different researchers pursue these two activities and their combined results contribute to fruitful research programs leading to social change.

Is it enough to just understand and explain? Most sociologists are progressive in the sense of wanting to see a better, more just world—a world with less human suffering and misery. Should sociologists be both researchers and activists? Put differently, should scholars act on their research findings to promote social change or should activism and political change be separate activities? Especially for scholars working in such areas as poverty, human rights or racism, the

Explanations of high-school dropout rates that ignore the attitudes and values of those who drop out are one-sided. An appreciation of the experiences of students who drop out is essential to a more complete account of the schooling process.
SOURCE: © iStockphoto.com/Rosmarie Gearhart.

urge to promote social change is pressing. Feminist scholars have been particularly adept at bridging the divide between research and social change advocacy.

Feminist research has done so by engaging in scholarship that disrupts traditional or accepted knowledge. Sociologists often ask questions from the vantage point of those on the margins of society (for example, the poor, the dispossessed, the victim). Feminist research has been pivotal in challenging traditional knowledge that excludes women, ignores discrimination or accepts the status quo as legitimate and proper. Further, feminist methodology has stressed minimizing harm and raising ethical standards. Academic feminism pushed against traditional social science that had helped to sustain the oppression of women by focusing exclusively on men or by examining issues of interest only to men (DeVault, 1996).

TECHNIQUES OF SOCIAL RESEARCH

Sociologists have developed a variety of techniques for gathering evidence. I will review three of the most important: experiments, survey research, and observational studies. As you read my accounts of research procedures, keep asking yourself these questions: How do sociologists go about developing insights about, or knowledge of, the social world? How do they come to know what they claim to know? What methods do they use and how believable are the results generated by these methods?

EXPERIMENTS

Experiments are the hallmark of scientific research and are commonly, though inaccurately, equated with science itself. Experiments are useful because they enable researchers to isolate causes and measure their effects. By no other method can researchers determine causation so precisely. An example is the best way to illustrate the point.

The shape of families has changed recently. At one time, the family was understood as a married couple—a man and a woman—with children. No longer. Single parent families have become more prevalent recently, as have common-law unions and same-sex couples. Nathan Lauster and Adam Easterbrook (2011) examined how successful people in these new types of families were in securing rental housing and, if they encountered resistance in renting, what the likely source of the resistance was.

A landlord could choose to rent to people in some types of family and not others. Landlords might judge new types of families as morally suspect or as violating the traditional family norms of existing tenants. Landlords also face the risk of damage to their premises and failure to pay rent, and they may judge people in new family types as riskier, less stable, or more likely to miss rent payments. These perceptions might vary with a landlord's previous experience with similar types of families, so there may be neighbourhood effects. That is, in neighbourhoods where people in new family forms are already renting, there might be less discrimination than in neighbourhoods where the traditional family form still dominates.

To explore these questions, Lauster and Easterbrook (2011) chose to conduct a field experiment. They wanted to compare the ability of people in different family configurations to find rental accommodation. They also wanted to know if their ability varied by neighbourhood.

The field experiment worked as follows. In Vancouver, such websites as craigslist.org and kijiji.com carry the largest volume of rental advertisements. The researchers wrote an email inquiry in which the only information they varied was the type of family that was inquiring and the size of the unit required. The family types were as follows: male-female couple; male-male couple; female-female couple; female adult, male son; male adult, male son. Five versions of the scripted email, with appropriate variations, read as follows:

> Hi, my name is [Matt/Melissa/Kate/Kevin], and [appropriate form; e.g., my son and I] saw your listing for a [#] bedroom [apartment/suite] on [website]. We are non-smokers and don't have any pets [or kids, if appropriate]. I'm a teacher and [she's/he's enrolled in a professional program; or he's enrolled in third grade]. Please let us know if the [apartment/suite] is still available and if we can view it. Thanks, [names of two people].

The scripted emails were sent to landlords who had advertised a one- or two- bedroom unit for less than $1700/month. Because the family forms existing in a neighbourhood might influence responses, they targeted nine different neighbourhoods. For example, they reasoned that in neighbourhoods with higher concentrations of same-sex couples, discrimination against same-sex couples would likely be lower than in neighbourhoods where traditional male-female couples predominated. By including nine neighbourhoods, the researchers were also able to see whether such neighbourhood factors as percentage of gay couples or lone-parent families, population under 15, and average monthly rent affected their findings.

The scripted emails ensured that all landlords received identical inquiries, save for the change in type of family. Sending emails asking about every one- or two- bedroom rental property advertised on a given day was ruled out because that would lead to a possible duplication of requests to the same landlord. Also, the experimenters wanted to code details of each advertisement, such as location, rent, and size, so they used a randomly selected set of advertisements. They also wanted to stagger their requests over two weeks to ensure no bias crept in from differences in the day of the week they inquired.

The results showed that heterosexual couples and female couples received the most positive responses (about 62 percent each), while male couples received positive responses only about 50 percent of the time. Single parents, either mother or father, received positive responses about 54 percent of the time.

Lauster and Easterbrook (2011) were interested in one other thing. They wanted to know if the likelihood of a positive response to the email sent for each family type varied by neighbourhood. For example, did male couples also receive significantly lower positive responses to their inquiries when the rental units were in traditionally gay neighbourhoods? The answer was no. As expected, male couples were more likely to receive positive responses when the email was directed to rental units in an area where male couples lived. While, overall, male couples experienced the greatest rental discrimination, it was lessened in neighbourhoods where many gay men already lived (although even in those neighbourhoods gay men were disadvantaged relative to heterosexual couples).

Female couples did not experience rental discrimination. Why not? Lauster and Easterbrook (2011) suggest two possible explanations. First, landlords could prefer women tenants, and this preference may override any negative views about family type. Second, perhaps landlords could accept female couples as an acceptable family form. The authors note that lesbian women experience other forms of discrimination and, in that light, it is surprising that they don't experience rental discrimination.

By dissecting the Lauster and Easterbrook (2011) experiment, we can examine more carefully several key research design features. The researchers began with a **hypothesis**—an unverified but testable knowledge claim. They hypothesized that "type of family" would affect "rental discrimination," with heterosexual couples more likely to receive favourable responses than the other family types.

To test this hypothesis, Lauster and Easterbrook (2011) examined the relationship between two **variables.** A variable is a measurable concept that can have more than one value. Age is a concept we use in referring to how long someone has lived. For newborns, we measure age in weeks or months, but for everyone else it is measured in years. In the language of research, Lauster and Easterbrook were interested in how type of family, their **independent variable** (the hypothesized cause), influenced rental discrimination, their **dependent variable** (the hypothesized effect). Lauster and Easterbrook used five different conditions or "treatments" for their independent variable: heterosexual couple, male couple, female couple, single mother, and single father. They reasoned that the likelihood of a positive response to the email about renting depended on which type of family the email was from. The dependent variable had three values: a positive response (yes, please come and see the unit), no response, or a negative response (rented already).

How did Lauster and Easterbrook (2011) know that only type of family and not another factor, such as a household size or social class, influenced rental discrimination? They were confident in their conclusion because, by design, they know that landlords received fictitious emails where only the type of family differed. By randomly sending the email to different landlords and referencing one of the five family conditions, they could compare how landlords responded, knowing that family type was the only factor that could have affected landlord responses. Household size was identical in each email. Social class was also constant since the reference was always to a teacher. It is true that rental units differed in price, and they could have been one- or two-bedroom units, but the researchers accounted for differences of this sort in their statistical analysis.

Random assignment or **randomization** lies at the heart of experimental design. Using a random procedure, such as flipping a coin or rolling a die, researchers assign people in an experiment to an experimental condition based on chance. If the coin comes up heads, a person is placed in experimental condition one; if the coin comes up tails, the person is assigned to condition two. Although in Lauster and Easterbrook's (2011) case, landlords differed by sex, age, income, and so on, the emails went to an approximately equal number of women and men, people with different annual incomes, and so on. The experiment was designed to ensure that the landlords receiving each type of email constituted a randomized group. Lauster and Easterbrook used this random assignment process to ensure that the only difference among the five conditions was family type.

Sociology experiments of the type conducted by Lauster and Easterbrook (2011) are relatively rare, largely because many social processes that interest sociologists are not amenable to experimentation. Ethical and practical problems also limit the use of experiments (see Box 20.3).

Laboratory experiments have been used in sociology although they have become less common in recent decades. A good example of a recent lab experiment is one undertaken by Martha Foschi and Jerilee Valenzuela (2008). They investigated the extent to which hiring decisions for junior engineering positions were influenced by the sex of the applicant and the sex of the decision maker. To do this, they had university students rate application files in which the applications were said to be from a short list (and hence very similar). The files contained a standard application form, a résumé, and an academic transcript. Precise details in the files differed but were nearly identical in terms of average grades across all courses, level of work experience, type of education, and so forth. The key difference was the sex of the applicant. Each person received two applications and were asked to choose the best candidate.

Foschi and Valenzuela (2008) found no difference between female and male applicants, nor any difference in outcomes whether the rater was male or female. That is, no bias toward male applicants being preferred occurred and indeed women raters tended to favour the female applicant. They conclude that (2008: 1034) "the social climate has been changing towards equality regarding views of men's and women's competence. This is particularly the case in experiments with university students as subjects, where recent work reveals that decisions do not always favor men."

As they note, using university students likely influences the results because people who are more educated tend to be more liberal in orientation. Also, university students might have been suspicious of the

BOX 20.3 ETHICS IN SOCIAL RESEARCH

Three groups share an interest in the conduct of sociological research: the sociological investigator, the people being observed or questioned, and the members of the larger society who enable such research to occur. Sociologists have a self-interest in their own research, but it is imperative that proper weight also be given to the interests of research participants and the public. Although primary responsibility for the rights and welfare of both participants and the public must reside with the sociologist as researcher, the self-interest of the sociologist requires that some arm's-length body review research designs and procedures to ensure the protection of all.

What are the typical risks involved in social research? These are of two broad types: risks to individuals and risks to communities or social groups. Understanding the first type—individual harm—is fairly straightforward. Social research can cause harm by asking people threatening questions that cause individual trauma (e.g., asking Aboriginal peoples about their memories of residential schools). Appreciating the second type—collective harm—may be less obvious. The results of social research can harm communities or groups by, for example, reinforcing stigmas and stereotypes (e.g., people living in poverty smoke more) or supporting policies that help some groups at the expense of others. Who sponsors the sociologist's research is an important issue, especially in this latter context. Here, too, relations between political advocacy and scientific research come to the fore.

Ethically responsible research must minimize threats or risks. Informed consent is key. Researchers must ensure that people not only consent but that they also consent after knowing what the research entails. Very occasionally in sociological research, deception is involved. This occurs in cases where the research requires that people not know exactly what is being studied (on the grounds that such knowledge may lead them to change their behaviour or lead them to respond in certain ways). For example, if you tell respondents your research is about the environment and then ask them what the most important problem is facing their region, many more will respond "environment" than if you did not provide this initial cue (Urmetzer, Blake, and Guppy, 1999).

In discussing a range of research projects in the remainder of the chapter, I will comment further on issues of ethics. An insightful sociological analysis of ethics is also provided by Kevin Haggerty (2004), who discusses "ethics creep" as a form of surveillance.

experiment and tried hard not to show any gender bias. They might have thought that this was a "study" and therefore they might not have acted naturally (but similar experiments in earlier decades did reveal male preference). As with any research, we must be cautious in generalizing the results. The latter problem is expressed technically as the issue of **external validity,** or the degree to which experimental findings remain valid in different contexts. External validity is often low; relationships discovered in experiments, especially lab experiments, do not always hold in more "real-life" settings. There is therefore good reason to be cautious about generalization. The field experiment, conducted in a natural as opposed to a laboratory setting, reduces the problem of artificiality. However, Lauster and Easterbrook (2011), in their field experiment could explore only a limited range of family types and family size, which was a complicating factor. They chose to keep family size constant at two, and so an alternative explanation for some of their findings might be the presence of childern as opposed to it being a single parent that influenced their results.

One field experiment that investigated the extent of job discrimination faced by people of different ethnic backgrounds found that whites had a 3-to-1 advantage over blacks in job offers.
SOURCE: © iStockphoto.com/DWlabs Inc.

As mentioned earlier, when people know they are being studied, they often become self-conscious. The very fact of being studied may influence their behaviour. This was demonstrated in productivity experiments conducted by Roethlisberger and Dickson (1939) at the Western Electric Company's Hawthorne factory. They found that productivity (the dependent variable) increased when they brightened the lighting but also when they dimmed the lighting. The researchers realized that people worked harder whenever the research team was studying them. Productivity increased in response to the researchers' presence, not because of changes they introduced. Social scientists have subsequently used the term **Hawthorne effect** when referring to changes in people's behaviour caused by their awareness of being studied. Sociologists have had to develop other techniques for collecting sociological evidence to avoid some of the problems associated with experiments.

SURVEY RESEARCH

The social survey is the primary means of collecting social science evidence. Researchers collect information through surveys by asking a sample of people identical questions. Political pollsters, market researchers, labour unions, governments, and university researchers all rely heavily on survey-based knowledge. Survey research is useful because it provides a method of systematically comparing answers to identical questions from a large sample of people, and it allows researchers to generalize the results to the larger population from which the sample was chosen. Questions can be posed either on a **self-administered questionnaire** or through a personal **interview.** Increasingly, the Internet is used as a way to conduct surveys (Brym and Lenton, 2001).

Rhonda Lenton (1990) used survey research to investigate parents' aggression toward their children. Because of strong taboos against child abuse, getting honest answers to questions about abusive behaviour is very difficult. The privacy surrounding child discipline makes observation or experiments inappropriate. Furthermore, asking blunt questions about "smacking your child" is unacceptable. Many alcoholics deny they have a drinking problem, just like many child abusers think of themselves as "strict disciplinarians." Parents use different strategies to influence their children, and Lenton wanted to examine the full range of this behaviour. Therefore, she chose to field a survey in which parents could be questioned by experienced and trained interviewers. She included questions covering an array of child–parent interactions, from praising and positive modelling through withholding privileges and love to spanking, slapping, and hitting.

A key problem facing Lenton was whether her questions about aggression and discipline would really measure child abuse. Child abuse is a theoretical concept. You and I may use the same term to mean different things. What types of maltreatment ought to be considered child abuse? Lenton (1990: 159) defines child abuse as "any act, excluding sexual mistreatment [which she separated as sexual abuse], carried out by a parent ... that has the intention of, or is perceived as having the intention of, hurting a child." Lenton wanted to include as "abuse" any act that a parent understands may hurt the child. To measure abuse, she asked parents whether they had done any of the following, ever, and in the past year: yell at a child, ridicule a child, withdraw emotionally from a child, hit a child with an object, withhold food from a child, and 24 other actions. Do these items provide an indication of what Lenton defines as child abuse? That is, are these valid indicators? **Validity** refers to accuracy or relevancy. Lenton's measurement of child abuse is valid to the degree that the items she uses as measures of abuse actually measure abuse as she defines it theoretically.

Lenton (1990) interviewed each parent and child separately. Each family member was asked to complete a child-discipline questionnaire, on which each of the 29 abuse items was listed. This sheet was completed privately and handed to the interviewer in a sealed envelope. By comparing the responses of all family members, Lenton could determine the consistency with which abuse was reported by different family members. This gave her confidence in the **reliability** of her measure. **Measurements** are reliable if they are consistent or repeatable. If different measures or indicators of the same concept give similar results, the measurements are reliable or, in other words, internally consistent.

Lenton (1990) faced another problem. She needed to find families with children. No publicly available list of such families exists. Lenton selected a random sample of Toronto families from the telephone directory. After first phoning to ensure that children lived in the household, members of the research team visited each eligible address to ask for permission to interview parents and children.

Surveys always involve **sampling.** Lenton's research team could never have interviewed all Toronto families (a complete enumeration of all families would be a *census*), nor would the expenditure of time and money have been efficient. Although the entire population could not be interviewed, it is this larger population about which Lenton wanted to draw conclusions. To use a different example, in doing research on urban household waste, interviewing all city dwellers is both unnecessary and impractical, even though the intention might be to use survey results to help design city policy. Information obtained from a subset of the population, the *sample*, is used to represent the views and characteristics of everyone. Samples selected by using rules of chance or probability provide random samples. Samples must represent the larger population from which they are drawn. For example, one or even a few kindergarten classes cannot be taken to represent all kindergarten classes, because not all kindergarten classes are alike. Therefore, if we want to generalize about social processes common to all kindergarten classes, we need to select a number of classes for study and we must know the probability of selecting each class.

Exactly how many kindergarten classes or, more generally, how many units must be included in a sample is a complex question. How many families should Lenton (1990) have selected? The precise answer depends mainly on the amount of variation or heterogeneity in the population and the degree of accuracy required in the study's conclusions. If you need very accurate results, you need a larger sample. Likewise, if the population is very variable, you need a larger sample to reflect that heterogeneity adequately. In studies of the Canadian electorate, very accurate forecasts of voting can be achieved with a random sample of about 1200 voters.

Selecting samples is not as easy as it might seem. How would you go about selecting a random sample of students in your faculty or program? Distributing questionnaires in classes would be one method, but many students do not attend every class. Students who attend regularly are, by definition, different from those who attend infrequently. A sample of students present in classes would therefore be biased. Using email addresses might seem practical, but many students do not let schools know their working addresses or filter Internet surveys out as junk mail. Registration lists give an approximation of the student population, but these lists are never perfect. Students drop out as the term progresses, while others change their address and phone number. If you were studying student retention or student financial needs, the people who might be hardest to find might be the very people to whom it would be most important to speak. Even with this severe limitation, however, student lists maintained by the registrar might be the best alternative available. The list from which a sample is selected is called the sampling frame. This frame must come as close as possible to including everyone in the population.

As noted, surveys that use the Internet have become popular. The same basic principles of design hold, and for targeted populations, such as university students or members of an organization, this can be an effective way of collecting data. However, for general populations, sampling issues are frequently a problem since sampling frames are next to impossible to establish. The result, then, is survey respondents who are volunteers, and these volunteers are not necessarily representative of the larger population. This creates the problems of external validity noted earlier.

Market-research firms use mainly telephone interviews in conducting their surveys. These firms usually rely on *random-digit-dialling* procedures to establish random samples. They select "banks" (i.e., lists) of working telephone numbers (e.g., 902-424-79xx), and let the computer randomly dial the last, or the last two, numbers. This method, used by Statistics Canada in some of its surveys, provides a random sample of households, including households with unlisted telephone numbers. Two important refinements are used. First, some households have more than one telephone number, increasing their chances of inclusion. Statistics Canada asks respondents how many working telephone numbers there are in a house so that it can correct for this small bias. Second, the person who is interviewed in the house must also be randomly selected (because, for example, women are more likely than men are to answer the phone even when both are at home). One popular strategy for obtaining a random sample of

Researchers collect information through surveys by asking people in a representative sample a set of identical questions. People interviewed on a downtown street corner do not constitute a representative sample of a country's adults. That is because the sample does not include people who live outside the urban core, underestimates the number of seniors and people with disabilities, does not take into account regional diversity, and so on.

SOURCE: © Janine Wiedel Photolibrary/Alamy.

household members is to interview the person who had the most recent birthday.

Telephone surveys require that people be interviewed. An alternative to interviewing is the use of self-administered questionnaires, which can be either mailed or delivered to members of the sample. Mailing questionnaires to people and handing them out to groups (e.g., students in a classroom, patients in a clinic) are less expensive than interviewing.

However, questionnaires lack the personal touch of interviewing. In an interview, misunderstandings can be clarified and responses can be expanded on. This cannot be done with self-administered questionnaires. Questionnaires work best with what are called close-ended questions, like those on multiple-choice exams, to which there are a limited number of set answers. Interviews, especially face-to-face as opposed to telephone interviews, allow for more open-ended questions, in which respondents can be encouraged to elaborate to ensure that they are properly understood. Lenton (1990), for example, chose to use personal interviews because she thought that the subject matter was best handled with face-to-face interaction. Notice, however, that she incorporated a short questionnaire on disciplinary techniques because she thought the questionnaire would be less threatening to people in that it was more anonymous. Once Lenton had established her sample and pretested her research strategy to ensure that she would obtain usable information, she set out to gather evidence that would allow her to evaluate the merits of three different hypotheses. A "cycle of violence" hypothesis holds that practices of child abuse are handed down from generation to generation. A "social-situational" hypothesis maintains that abusive parents may be reacting to stress and that stress itself may be linked to a family's socioeconomic status. Finally, a "cultural" hypothesis suggests that the attitudes of the family toward corporal punishment best differentiate the use of aggressive and nonaggressive behaviour in child discipline. Her research was designed to yield evidence that would help her decide which hypotheses were wrong. After analyzing the data, Lenton (1990: 176) concluded that "parents are inclined to use the disciplinary repertoires they learned when they were children—but only as long as certain current structural conditions are consonant with these repertoires." In particular, she pointed to structural conditions, such as unemployment in the family and low family income. To the extent that these structural conditions can be eliminated or reduced, the "cycle of family violence" can be arrested.

I mentioned earlier that the ability of sociologists to ask questions of people has both advantages and disadvantages. Lenton's (1990) work illustrates this. The physical punishment of children in the privacy of the home represents social activity that is not easily studied by any sociological method. Yet, as Lenton argues, child abuse is a public issue, not a private matter. By asking questions of people, she was able, first, to describe the extent of physical aggression used to discipline children and, second, to explain why some families were more likely than others were to use physical discipline. The disadvantage of asking questions of people, especially questions that people may find threatening, is that people may distort their responses. For example, Lenton found that in more than 75 percent of all families, children had been spanked or slapped in the previous year. Given current social norms about child abuse, this estimate of physical discipline is more likely to be an underestimate than an overestimate of such activity. If, however, different social classes subscribe to these norms to different degrees, people's responses to the 29 disciplinary measures might have altered. Lenton herself anticipated this criticism and asked people not just about their behaviour but also about their attitudes. She was therefore able to examine whether people from different social classes held different norms about child discipline.

This distinction between attitudes and behaviours, or words and deeds, is important. I always intend to give more money to charity than I do. Most people believe that littering is irresponsible, but most people still litter sometimes. When you read research focusing on people's attitudes, remember that thought is not easily translated into action. Interpreting the answers that people give to researchers' questions is complicated by more than this behaviour–attitude distinction. In asking people questions, either in interviews or on questionnaires, we must be careful about making assumptions (Guppy and Gray, 2008):

- *Do not assume that people understand what you are asking.* Language is notoriously ambiguous. How many friends did you see yesterday? This question may look simple at first, but people will differ in their understanding of "friends" and others will take "see" in the most literal way. The same words may mean different things to different people and in different contexts.

- *Do not assume that people know the answer to questions.* Most people do not want to appear ignorant when asked a question. This was illustrated nicely in a study of the prestige of occupations by Peter Pineo and John Porter (1967). They asked people to rate the prestige of two fictitious jobs: archaeopotrist and biologer. Most respondents cooperated and assigned these nonexistent jobs a prestige rating. When asked about their attitude on some issue, many people feel they must respond, even if they have no opinion on the topic or only a weakly formulated view.
- *Do not assume that people will admit the answer to themselves.* Alcoholics frequently claim that they can "quit any time." They refuse to admit that they are addicted. Similarly, child abusers may define themselves as strict disciplinarians. People routinely deceive themselves, sometimes only in minor ways, but "admitting the truth to ourselves" is a problem.
- *Do not assume that people will give valid answers to others.* People feel better about themselves when they are seen in a favourable light. In asking questions of people, researchers face the potential problem of "social desirability," because respondents may only give answers that reflect well on them. "What type of work do you do?" "Oh, I'm in public relations." Such a response could come from people working as telephone receptionists, tour guides, or corporate representatives.

Sociologists use many techniques in asking questions to gather valid and reliable evidence. For example, they will ask several questions rather than relying on a single question, use supplementary questions to expand on or clarify answers, and test questions before using them to improve any wording that is unclear or misleading (see Houtkoop, 2000).

Survey researchers do not focus only on individuals, although it is individuals who respond to survey questions. For example, it is possible to survey organizations, groups, corporations, electoral ridings, or job vacancies. Although people answer survey questions, the questions may apply to a unit or group of which someone is a member. For example, Janice Aruni (2004) studied private tutoring businesses by using a semi-structured interview survey to gather information about businesses that provide for-profit, supplementary instruction in academic subjects (e.g., K–12 school subjects).

I am making two points here. First, surveys can focus on different units of observation (individuals, businesses, workplaces, and so on). Second, individuals can act as informants to report information that pertains not to themselves but to some group or unit about which they have information. People can, for example, report on individual events (e.g., job vacancies), family composition, or corporate policy. Although each of these represents different units of observation, individuals are still answering the questions.

OBSERVATIONAL STUDIES

Another method commonly used by sociologists to gather information is observation. Sometimes sociologists act as outside observers; at other times they act as insiders and engage in **participant observation.** The obvious advantage of observation is that sociologists can see what people actually do, rather than relying on reports of what people say they do. One disadvantage is that gaining access to private actions or events can be difficult. For example, Lenton might have tried to observe parents disciplining their children rather than relying on what parents told her they did. But entering people's homes to make such observations would have been difficult. Furthermore, her presence may have influenced the type of discipline parents used (the Hawthorne effect).

In observation studies, examining the intentionality of social action is especially important. Max Weber (1949 [1904]) was one of the first sociologists to address the issue of intention as a focus of social research. Weber argued that in interacting with other people, we draw on meanings. For example, the clothing we choose to wear speaks to others. We attribute meaning to bow ties, jack boots, Laura Ashley scarves, and baseball caps. None of this is done naively, because what we wear helps define who we are. Skateboarders, for example, dress in a particular style; they wear a uniform of sorts. Making social life intelligible is part of what Weber thought sociologists must address. To understand skateboarding, it is essential to see how skateboarders "define the situation." It is important to learn about their culture and to understand their systems of meaning. The aim of such research is not to explain the behaviour of skateboarders from an outside point of view, but to investigate their shared values and beliefs—their "worldview."

Weber maintained that causal logic can be used to accomplish some of what sociologists want to explain. He thought, however, that sociology also had to make intelligible the subjective basis of social action. Weber used the German word *Verstehen*, or understanding, to refer to this mode of sociological analysis. To understand the meaning of social action requires being able, at least in principle, to fully engage in the social activity. An example is the best way to illustrate such understanding.

Youth subculture in Canada seems less influential and less prominent than in such countries as the United Kingdom or the United States. Sometimes this observation is expressed in the claim that youth culture in Canada is derivative of trends south of the border or across the Atlantic. However, as skateboarders and squeegee kids have risen in profile, as youth unemployment has grown, and as the plight of young criminal offenders has been debated, understanding Canadian youth subcultures has become increasingly important. For that reason, Brian Wilson (2002) undertook a study of the rave subculture in Southern Ontario.

Banishing squeegee kids or skateboarders to some less visible place, be it jail, another neighbourhood, or "just off the streets," is one reaction to youth considered deviant. Denouncing ravers as for amphetamine drug use and social disturbance is another. What these suggestions mainly reflect is a misunderstanding of youth culture and its social context. Gaining an appreciation of the rave subculture was Wilson's intent. Among the issues he pursued were the reasons for people participating in this activity—put simply, was it the lure of adventure and excitement in the rave scene or was it a push from family or school that led to involvement with the rave subculture?

To gain an understanding of this process, he chose participant observation as one of his methodological strategies. He attended more than a dozen raves, hung out in rave record stores, sat in on rave radio sessions, and attended public meetings focused on raves. He observed the rave subculture by participating in it, by being a part of the party. By participating with ravers in rave parties and in rave settings, he was able to learn, first-hand, about their lifestyles, values, and aspirations.

However, Wilson did more than just participate. He also interviewed 37 ravers. He used what he calls "in-depth, open-ended, semi-formal interviews" (Wilson, 2002: 301). An in-depth interview means that he explored specific topics in great detail, often pursuing nuances and tangents. They were open-ended in the sense that he allowed respondents to range widely

In participant observation, it is often necessary to "look" the part. Brian Wilson participated in rave parties to study first-hand the rave subculture of Southern Ontario.
SOURCE: © Alexandru/Shutterstock.

in their replies. Finally, they were semi-structured in that he had a set of general issues he wanted to discuss, but he did not ask every person he interviewed exactly the same questions in exactly the same order. His goal was to have a meaningful conversation with each person, guided by his interest in the subject but also by their knowledge, willingness, and interest in pursuing specific details.

He also did not interview a representative sample of rave participants. Such a sample would be difficult to define since no one has a list of regular rave members. Instead, Wilson (2002) sought to talk with a variety of people and he was careful not to draw all the people he interviewed from the same place. Diversity was more important to him than was representativeness.

Finally, Wilson (2002) paid particular attention to written materials that form part of the rave scene, including magazines (hard copy and ezines), flyers promoting specific raves, and rave recordings (complete with commentary by the DJ).

These materials provided another window into how ravers communicate with one another, what they stress and emphasize.

In essence, Wilson used a cluster of methods, with observation being his primary source of data. Participant observation was critical in giving him personal access to the subculture. He supplemented this by reading material and listening to rave productions. Finally, he also interviewed people to test out his interpretations of the rave subculture. In particular, he used the interviews to assess his own impressions of the rave scene.

Ethnographers study people in their own environment or their own natural setting. Although **ethnography** includes the researcher being immersed in a group or a subculture, it also typically involves a cluster of methods, including both in-depth, unstructured interviewing and the analysis of documents. Speaking with key informants who are central to the group or the subculture is crucial (Cresswell, 1998).

In part, Wilson (2002) came to understand the rave subculture in generational terms. Youth rebellion against perceived autocratic organizations (school, family, the justice system) leads to a lifestyle of resistance—to escaping authority, flaunting convention, and disregarding conservative norms. But it is a resistance that is not about political change or efforts to alter organizational forms. It is a resistance focused mainly on creating an autonomous space in which social identity can be fostered, nourished, and supported. In this sense the subculture has a "magical" quality where the reality of other worlds can be transcended or bracketed. Contrast this with, for example, the student-led demonstrations in many countries pushing for stronger democratic governance—China, Indonesia, Iran, Korea—or the resistance to globalization seen at World Trade Organization meetings (Tanner, 2001).

Wilson (2002) was able to gain an understanding of the rave lifestyle by participating in the life of the group. By hanging out with them, he gained an in-depth appreciation of their activity. As a participant observer, he was able to ask many questions of many different group members, gradually drawing a sociological portrait of the rave scene. In particular, he was able to contrast various interpretations of the rave scene—was it about resistance, pleasure-seeking, or escapism? As his work progressed, Wilson was able to refine his understanding. He could cross-reference his observations by seeing how other group members reacted to each new insight he gained, thereby increasing both the reliability and the validity of his conclusions. In short, he came to "define the situation" as rave participants themselves define it.

As with experiments, the external validity of ethnography can be problematic. How confident can Wilson be that his conclusions are not dependent on the impressions he formed from a single group of ravers? The intensive, in-depth nature of ethnography makes generalizability problematic. The key tradeoff is between the richly textured, "thick description" of ethnography and the insularity of detailed study of one or a few settings. Unlike survey researchers, ethnographers do not select different sets of random individuals or groups. The groups or settings they investigate are purposively chosen, sometimes because of easy access. For example, Wilson (2002) did not randomly choose rave subcultures; he made arrangements to participate with some rave scenes in Southern Ontario, and even then it was only one form of youth subculture. Imagine also, the ethical issues Wilson confronted (see also Haggerty, 2004).

Wilson's (2002) research portrays a subculture from its members' points of view. There are potential pitfalls of which Wilson had to be aware. First, how much did his presence influence his findings? Did people act differently when he was not around? In principle, there is no way to answer these questions, although ethnographers have tried to account for the effect of their presence in various ways. Some researchers conceal their research role; in effect, they try to be known to the other participants as one of them, rather than as a researcher (the ethics of this are dicey). Other researchers report that, with time, participants' awareness of their presence fades and they are treated as a member. Notice that this problem of presence is the Hawthorne effect in another guise. Whether in survey research, experiments, or observation studies, the researcher's presence can distort the domain of investigation. Researcher presence may undermine validity.

Beyond the potential pitfall of mere presence is the second problem: the findings of researchers may be ethnocentric. That is, researchers may impose their own values—their own worldviews—on the subject matter of their study. How do we know, for example, that Wilson (2002) depicted the ravers' point of view and not his own? One method of reducing personal bias is known as the "member test of validity" (Douglas, 1970: 21). For example, if the rave participants Wilson spoke with did not recognize themselves in his account—that is, if they saw Wilson's account as inauthentic—then we would worry about bias or distortion. Wilson was careful to "test" his tentative observations and insights on his informants by asking them questions and checking for observations that would falsify his impressions. Again, this is a research problem that extends well beyond ethnography. In fact, ethnography can be seen as the method that takes most seriously the task of understanding the members of a group from the members' point of view, stressing in particular their definition of the situation.

A third problem beyond presence and ethnocentrism is this: How do researchers know that the "tools" of their inquiry (e.g., questions, instructions, requests) did not in fact "create" or "generate" the resulting "findings"? For example, did Wilson (2002) create a finding by focusing attention on the ravers' resistance to dominant culture? Alternatively, did Lenton (1990) invent a relationship between social class and child discipline by asking questions that might be interpreted in different ways by the members of different classes? Again, this involves issues of reliability and validity. Lenton can be confident that she did not construct or create a pseudo-relationship between class and discipline to the extent that she shows that the basic pattern of findings is repeated across different questions about the disciplining of children. Wilson distinguished between (1) ravers' comments made in response to his questions and (2) statements his informants volunteered or that he overheard during his fieldwork. In addition, he used information provided to him by others on the margins of the rave scene: DJs, security guards, and radio station personnel. These alternative sources of information helped him avoid the problem of "creating" meaning. If ravers volunteered information that corroborated Wilson's impressions, and if these impressions were further reinforced by other knowledgeable observers, his faith in the authenticity of his account increased.

Not all observation can involve participation. Rik Scarce (2000) was interested in nature, and especially human domination of nature. His interest was in whether we could still speak of "wild salmon" or whether, like the cow and the dog, salmon were now domesticated. He argued that the very concept of "resource management" speaks to the idea of humans improving on nature, of scientists enhancing nature.

In studying the "domestication of salmon," Scarce (2000) used ethnographic methods. He could not participate as a scientist, but he could observe what scientists did, interview them, read their papers, and listen to their testimony at public inquiries. After doing all these things, he wrote an ethnographic account called *Fishy Business: Salmon, Biology, and the Social Construction of Nature*.

He was especially interested in how salmon had been manipulated to serve human ends. In the modern fishery, such phrases as *fish farming*, *aquaculture*, *genetic engineering*, *fish stocking*, and *fish hatcheries* are commonplace. We have engineered a new breed of salmon, mixing wild stocks and creating farmed salmon.

Scarce (2000) learned about this by hanging around fish hatcheries and asking questions, by visiting fishery research centres and watching what scientists were doing in their experiments, and by talking with scientists at their conventions and at public inquiries. He came to see the fish hatchery as a biological factory and to understand how salmon were increasingly "tooled" and "engineered." Observation was his staple method.

The believability of Scarce's (2000) research is enhanced by the fact that he observed events in their natural settings. He did not create a situation to see how people reacted (e.g., laboratory experiments) nor did he rely on people reporting on their own attitudes or behaviours (as in survey research). He was not a participant in the activity and so his involvement could not have distorted events (as may occur in participant observation). His presence as an observer may have influenced people, but he was often one of many observers (e.g., at scientific conferences and public inquiries).

OTHER METHODS OF RESEARCH

Historical Sociology

Many sociologists study social change. Max Weber, for example, attempted to explain the rise of capitalism by showing how Protestantism invigorated capitalist growth. Émile Durkheim was interested in how moral education helped to socially integrate a rapidly changing society. Both writers sought to answer sociological questions by examining historical change as evidence of significant social processes. Sociologists are more likely than historians are to use historical evidence to test theories of social change. Sociologists place less emphasis on history for history's sake.

Liliana Riga's (2008) work shows how sociologists make effective use of historical methods (see also Brym, 1978). Riga reexamined the nature of revolutionary Bolshevism among the leadership of the 1917–23 Russian Revolution. She wanted to understand the roots of the socialist ethic that inspired the revolution. This critical juncture in world history has often been contextualized within a framework stressing the class basis and "Russian" ethnicity of the revolutionary leadership. Riga argued that, in large measure, it was social inequalities made most visible by diverse ethnicities, and not so much by social class, that lay behind the radical mobilization. She arrived at this conclusion after systematically comparing the experiences of class and ethnicity among the revolutionary elite leaders.

Of course, these leaders have long since died, and so Riga (2008) could not interview or observe them. What she could do, however, was reconstruct their biographies. She used autobiographies, biographies, and memoirs, supplemented by police arrest records where ethnic backgrounds were often noted. She used sources predominantly constructed before the late 1920s. This latter refinement was essential when you recall that revolutionary leaders first had to mask their true identities in Tsarist Russia but even more importantly had to maintain social identities consistent with the *Soviet* revolutionary movement (especially problematic in the Stalinist era from 1922 to 1953).

The logic of Riga's (2008) analysis is not unlike that of other sociological research. Her key dependent variable is the revolutionary identity and politics of the Bolshevik elite. She wanted to know how important social class, ethnicity, and their intersection was to formation of this radical group. She therefore needed to measure social class and did so by examining such indicators as landholding, occupation, education, and relations to capital of individual members of the elite (and their parents). She also needed to measure ethnicity, and this too is complicated. In the end she used a mixture of birthplace, religion, and nationality. She concluded by noting that "ethnocultural identities were often more salient dimensions to many of their social experiences—and therefore to identities and politics—than was class."

Documentary Analysis

Sociologists have also made useful contributions to knowledge through the examination of official documents. Scott Davies (2002) examined how education reformers consciously designed their recommendations about policy change to fit with historically current political priorities and cultural settings. He showed how three successive education commissions in Ontario (1950, 1968, and 1995) each designed messages based on "progressive education," while simultaneously making policy recommendations that were diametrically opposed (e.g., some supported and some rejected standardized testing). Most change agents want to do "progressive" things. By carefully analyzing commission reports, Davies showed how the language of progressive education was reshaped by successive commissions to sell their brand of education reform.

Renisa Mawani (2003) examined archival documents, including colonial maps, to demonstrate a social process whereby geographical spaces were rendered "vacant" and therefore accessible to settlement and development. By showing how Aboriginal land use was made to vanish at some points, only to have later colonial authorities redraw the maps to show their presence, Mawani demonstrates the contested nature of landscape, both then and now. She also draws on legal documents, such as cases and statutes, to understand how the rule of law was also used to displace Aboriginal peoples and, again reflecting contestation, how it was used by Aboriginal peoples in resistance. As a third methodological strategy, she examined the ways in which an Aboriginal presence has been commemorated (e.g., via totem poles). By a careful comparison of the evidence offered through these documented sources, she argued that Vancouver's civic identity has shifted from a settler society to a postcolonial, multicultural city.

Use of Official Statistics

Governments have a long history of collecting statistical data (Box 20.4). Government bureaucracies first began to collect statistics to help rulers determine both the size of their taxation base and the number of men they could put on the battlefield. Since then, the scope of government or official statistics has expanded and now includes information on births and deaths, unemployment rates, imports and exports, and so on. Sociologists have made good use of official statistics (see especially Haggerty, 2001).

Wortley and Tanner (2003) used official arrest records from Toronto to examine the extent of racial profiling in patterns of search and arrests practices. Detecting racial profiling requires determining that law enforcement officers use race as a significant factor in their decisions. That might sound easy, but it is incredibly complex because higher search or arrest rates among certain groups might be due to reasonable assumptions based on existing crime patterns, surveillance, or neighbourhood requests

BOX 20.4 POLITICS AND RESEARCH METHODS

Governments routinely use a survey of the entire population, called a census, to monitor key indicators of a country, such as the distribution of age cohorts, marital statuses, and so on. In June 2010, the federal government decided to change a critical component of the Canadian census. It decided to make the long-form census non-mandatory, keeping only a small number of questions on a short-form census, on the grounds that in previous censuses, a few Canadians had objected to being required to answer questions about ancestry, income, or housing characteristics.

The questions previously asked on the long-form census are now included in a *voluntary* survey to which Canadians are urged, but not required, to respond. This change might seem like allowing free choice to flourish by keeping the state out of the private business of individual citizens. However, a closer look reveals that the long-form census played a pivotal role in understanding a wide array of critical issues, from housing policy, to immigrant adaptation, to unemployment. A significant proportion of Canadians chose not to answer the long-form census in 2011. This means that the validity of the voluntary responses are suspect.

The government uses a host of other surveys, such as the *Labour Force Survey* (LFS), to measure key social and economic indicators, such as the male–female wage rate differences and the unemployment rate. The validity of these other surveys was always measured in relation to the long-form census, for which the response rate was close to 100 percent because it was mandatory. Now, however, not only is the validity of the long-form census in question but so too is the validity of the LFS and every other survey that previously relied on the long-form census as a measurement standard (Green and Milligan, 2010). Furthermore, the long-form census contained questions about education, occupation, and income, along with questions about sex, ethnicity, and region. These and related questions allowed for a careful assessment of issues related to the Charter of Rights and Freedoms and other issues pertaining to social justice and fairness. Such assessments are now more difficult to achieve.

for greater police presence. Ruling out these latter factors, and other possible explanations for racial differentials in police decision making must occur before conclusions about racial bias in decision-making can be claimed.

Wortley and Tanner (2003) were following up on an investigative report published in the *Toronto Star* in October 2002. The *Star* analysis alleged that racial profiling did occur in Toronto, an accusation that police officials disputed. Wortley and Tanner, two sociologists at the University of Toronto, examined both the *Star's* original claims and the subsequent findings put forward by the Toronto Police Service. Wortley and Tanner cautiously claimed that their analyses of both official statistics and survey research were consistent with the findings of other international studies that racial profiling is a practice used by law enforcement officers (Wortley and Tanner, 2003, 2005).

The racial profiling example illustrates a central problem with official statistics. These statistics are not objective facts on which everyone agrees. The very definition of racial profiling makes it difficult to prove. Furthermore, different interest groups have much at stake over whether such practices occur (Gabor, 2004). The police are charged with the difficult task of upholding the law fairly and without prejudice. Certain groups may request more police presence than do other groups and so what might appear to be racial profiling might actually reflect community requests. Official statistics require interpretation and such interpretation can be complex.

THE ANALYSIS OF NUMERICAL DATA

Sociological evidence frequently comes in numerical form—that is, as quantifiable evidence (e.g., number of disciplinarians, arsons, or voters). Finding and interpreting patterns in numerical data is complex. To help in summarizing numerical information, social scientists routinely rely on statistical techniques. In this section, I briefly illustrate some key aspects of the process. I explore the following simple question: Do women and men earn the same income as a result of having the same levels of education? Men and women have, on average, similar levels of schooling. However, as a group, men have higher incomes than do women.

Notice the causal logic here. Education is hypothesized to affect income. However, since women and men earn different wages in the labour market, yet have similar levels of schooling, maybe the causal link between education and income differs by sex. Although I can present only an elementary analysis here, issues of a wage gap between the sexes are part of the continuing debate over pay equity, comparable worth, and employment equity, all important policy questions (Fortin, 2005).

To begin, we need to examine the link between education and income. I do this by using data from the *General Social Survey* (Statistics Canada, 2004), a survey conducted by Statistics Canada of a nationally representative sample of Canadians (24 951 randomly chosen Canadians, to be precise). Does education have a big effect on income? Table 20.1, called a contingency table or a cross-tabulation, gives us an answer. Education, the independent variable displayed across the top of the table, has three categories (low: high school or less; medium: some postsecondary education; and high: university degree or higher). For ease of presentation, annual personal income, the dependent variable, has two categories (low: personal income below $30 000 annually; and high: annual income at or above $30 000).

Notice first the table's arrangement. The title describes the two variables being related. The independent variable (education) is placed on the top of the table and its values are clearly delineated. Below each value for education is a column of numbers. The dependent variable (income) is arrayed on the side of the table, again with the value labels clearly shown. Beside each value of the dependent variable is a row of numbers. To illustrate, Table 20.1 shows that there are 333 people in the top left cell, the cell defined by a low level of education and a low income. At the intersection of each column and row is a table cell (there are six cells in Table 20.1 because row and column totals are ignored in counting the number of cells in a table).

TABLE 20.1 THE RELATIONSHIP BETWEEN LEVEL OF EDUCATION AND INDIVIDUAL INCOME FOR PEOPLE AGED 25–34

	LEVEL OF EDUCATION			
Income	Low	Medium	High	Row Totals
Low	53% (333)	45% (783)	31% (358)	42% (1473)
High	47% (296)	55% (939)	69% (814)	58% (2049)
Column Totals	100% (629)	100% (1722)	100% (1172)	100% (3522)

SOURCE: Data is adapted from Statistics Canada, "SCF Public Use Microdata File: Income of Census Family Units," Catalogue no. 13M0001XDB, 19 August 1999.

The concept of a contingency table comes from the idea that the category into which a person falls on the dependent variable may be contingent on, or depends on, the category that a person occupies on the independent variable. If the hypothesis were true in this case, we would expect that, as we move across the education categories from low to high, the number of people receiving high incomes ought to rise. Do the data reveal this pattern? For people with low education, 296 had high incomes. For people with a high level of education, 814 had high incomes. These figures seem, at first glance, to support our expectation. Notice, however, that because of how education was categorized, 629 people had what I defined as low education, while 1172 had high education. Comparing the actual number of people in each cell is therefore misleading, because there are different numbers of people in each column.

Rather than focusing on the raw numbers, a better understanding of the patterns comes when we standardize the data. We need to ask what *percentage* of people in each education category had high incomes. By expressing the numbers as percentages—that is, by standardizing the data—it is much easier to see the patterns. So, 296 of 629 people in the low-education column had high incomes, or 47 percent (296 divided by 629 and then multiplied by 100). This tells us that for every 100 people with low education, 47 had high incomes. Making the same calculation for the high education column—(814/1172) × 100—we find that 69 percent of highly educated people earned high incomes (or 69 of every 100 people).

If you examine Table 20.1, you will see that the percentages are entered in the table. The actual number of people in each cell appears in parentheses. Notice that the percentages are calculated separately for each column, summing to 100 percent at the bottom of each column.

So, do relatively more people with high education receive high income in comparison with people with low education? Yes. Of every 100 people in the high-education column, 69 receive high income (69 percent), compared with only 47 of every 100 in the low-education column (47 percent). The difference between these two percentages (22 percent) is one measure of the strength of the relationship between education and income; the higher the percentage difference, the stronger the relationship.

In studying this table, some readers may have taken exception to my definitions of high and low incomes. Why should earning more than $30 000 be considered a high income? What is defined as low and high income is arbitrary. However, when I define the lows and highs of income and education differently and produce several different tables, the basic patterns in the tables do not change. This replication gives me confidence that my decisions about how to categorize the variables do not affect the results.

The evidence in Table 20.1 corroborates the first part of the question about the relationship between education and income. But how does gender figure into the pattern? Table 20.2 contains two contingency tables separated by a dotted vertical line. Here the question is how the link between education and income varies for women in comparison with men. Table 20.2 can be usefully thought of as Table 20.1 but with women and men separated into their own subtables.

For women, the basic pattern of Table 20.1 is repeated in Table 20.2, although the relationship between income and education is stronger: 66 percent of women with a high level of education are likely to have high income, whereas only 23 percent of women with a low level of education are likely to have a high income. The difference between these two cell percentages is 43 percent.

For men, although the pattern is similar, the percentage difference is smaller (and therefore the relationship between income and education is weaker). Of men with a high level of education, 73 percent have a high income, whereas for men with a low level of education, 64 percent have a high income. The percentage difference is only 9 percent. This suggests that for men, education level is not as important as it is for women in earning a high income. Contrasting the percentage differences between the two subtables in Table 20.2 gives us a way of comparing the strength of the link between income and education for women versus men. A more complex method of investigating the causal linkages among gender, education, and income relies on multiple regression (see Box 20.5).

So what do we learn from this analysis? We learn first, from Table 20.1, that people with more education are likely to earn higher incomes. Second, from Table 20.2 we learn that this is especially true for women, in that for men education level has less of an impact on earning high incomes than is the case for women (remember only people between 25 and 34 are included in the tables).

Why is the link between education and income different for women and men? First, men without university education may still earn high pay in resource and manufacturing jobs. That could account for the difference. Second, the labour force is still at least partially differentiated into "male" and "female" jobs, and education level may be more important for finding work in traditional female jobs than in certain

TABLE 20.2 THE RELATIONSHIP BETWEEN LEVEL OF EDUCATION, INDIVIDUAL INCOME, AND GENDER FOR PEOPLE AGED 25–34

	WOMEN LEVEL OF EDUCATION				MEN LEVEL OF EDUCATION			
Income	Low	Medium	High	**Total**	Low	Medium	High	**Total**
Low	78%	60%	34%	(893)	37%	32%	27%	(580)
High	23%	40%	66%	(778)	64%	68%	73%	(1270)
Totals	100%	100%	100%			100%	100%	100%
	(252)	(822)	(599)	(1671)	(377)	(900)	(573)	(1851)

NOTE: Column and row totals are not equal for women because of rounding.

SOURCE: Data from Statistics Canada (2004), *General Social Survey*.

BOX 20.5 INTRODUCING STATISTICAL IDEAS ABOUT REGRESSION ANALYSIS

In further exploring the linkage among gender, education, and income, I would want to introduce a series of alternative explanations. Testing each of these ideas by using contingency tables would be difficult because, with so many possible confounding variables, the tables would quickly become huge and unwieldy. An alternative to contingency-table analysis is regression analysis. The basic idea of regression can be explained most easily in graphic form.

Figure 20.2 is a graph with years of schooling arrayed along the horizontal axis (*x*-axis) and annual income displayed along the vertical axis (*y*-axis). On this graph, I can plot where each person in the sample falls. In other words, I can choose someone from the sample and move along the *x*-axis until I come to the level of education attained by the selected person. I can then proceed up from there, now using the *y*-axis as a guide, until I reach the level of the same person's annual income. The point that I reach is the intersection of two perpendicular lines, one drawn vertically from the *x*-axis (at the person's level of education) and the other drawn horizontally from the *y*-axis (at that person's annual income). For each person in the sample, I can locate exactly where these two lines fall in the graph and place a mark at the appropriate spot. The result, similar to what I have depicted, is a scatter plot.

FIGURE 20.2 HYPOTHETICAL RELATIONSHIP BETWEEN EMPLOYMENT INCOME AND YEARS OF SCHOOLING

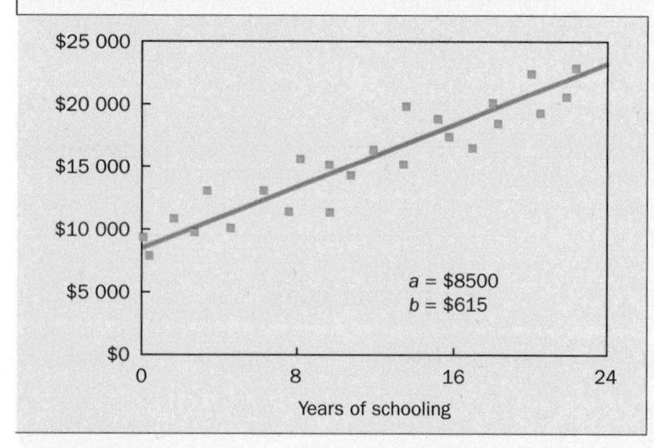

A scatter plot can be summarized statistically using regression techniques. To summarize the relationship between education and income, a straight line can be drawn through the data points in such a way that the distance from each point to the line is minimized. If all points lie exactly on the line, the fit of the line to the data will be perfect. The farther the points are from the best-fitting line, the poorer is the ability to use a straight line to summarize the information and the weaker is the association between the two variables. The strength of association between two variables in a scatter plot is given by the correlation coefficient (*r*). The value of *r* can vary from –1 (a perfectly inverse relationship or negative association) to 0 (no association) to +1 (a perfectly proportionate relationship or positive association). The farther *r* is from 0, the stronger the association. The correlation coefficient is, then, analogous to the percentage difference in tables.

With the education and income scatter plot, I can capture the central characteristics of the best-fitting line with two numbers. One number captures the slope of the line and tells how much vertical increase (or decrease) occurs in the line for every unit of horizontal change along the *x*-axis. Using my example, for every additional year of schooling, how much does annual income increase? An easy way to remember this is to think of this number as the rise (income increase) over the run (change in years of schooling). A second number tells at what point the line intersects the *y*-axis. If I have a perfectly fitting line, the equation for a straight line can be expressed as $y = a + bx$, where x and y are values on the two axes of the graph, a is the point at which the line crosses the *y*-axis, and b is the slope of the line.

What I have described here is a statistical technique known as simple linear regression, for one independent and one dependent variable. To explore the alternative interpretations for the link among gender, education, and income that I offered earlier, you would need to use multiple regression, where one dependent variable can be linked to a series of independent variables. This data analysis approach has been instrumental in shaping social policy and refining sociological knowledge.

male jobs (e.g., nursing versus oil rigging). Third, women and men could be working different numbers of hours per week, or weeks per year, and these differences could be related to both education and income. Many other possible explanations exist, and further research is essential to sort them out (Drolet, 2011; Fortin, 2005; Guppy and Davies, 1998).

THE FUTURE OF SOCIAL RESEARCH

Social research involves systematically studying the social world. The aim of such research activity is to develop explanations and understandings of social patterns beneficial to improving the human condition.

Today, it is becoming increasingly obvious that we need to find innovative ways of organizing and running human affairs. Starvation, environmental degradation, terrorism, and social injustice are among the many social problems we must confront. Solutions require adequate explanations for, and understandings of, how these problems arise and persist.

Earlier in the chapter, I outlined several sources of knowledge: common sense, religious faith, and science. Although these forms of knowledge share certain features (e.g., they are all imperfect), scientific reason encourages a set of practices, open review and critical skepticism, which together work to reduce error.

Another way of emphasizing what is distinctive about the scientific method is to compare how social research differs from the work of other professionals who concentrate on similar social issues (e.g., the environment, gender relations). For example, what differentiates the work of documentary filmmakers, novelists, or journalists from that of social researchers? I have emphasized three features of scientific research that, in combination, separate it from the work of these other professionals:

1. Research results are subjected to the critical skepticism of other scientists.
2. Social theory guides, either directly or indirectly, the evidence gathered.
3. Evidence is systematically collected and analyzed.

Although some of these features are found in the work of other professionals, such as journalists, all three features are found in good social research. Replication and reproducibility have high currency in science as ways of encouraging skepticism. Good research contributes new ideas or evidence to our common stock of social theory. Finally, good research publicly displays the careful collection and analysis of evidence.

These principles are a feature of all good research, but the methods that sociologists use to pursue their goal of explaining and understanding the social world take many forms. This diverse array of methods, including observing, questioning, and experimenting, offers sociologists many ways of inquiring responsibly and ethically about the social world. Each method has different strengths and weaknesses, which makes the choice of research strategy dependent on the sociological question being asked.

Social science research will continue to contribute to knowledge of the world around us. Research on the environment, reproductive technology, multiculturalism, violence, and social-support networks all point to practical ways in which human problems can be influenced by research findings. Effective policy solutions that benefit all people require sound social research.

SUMMARY

1. Research methods are ways of gathering evidence to test suppositions about the world. Behind the various techniques we use (e.g., experiments, interviews) lie important assumptions about facts, objectivity, and truth.
2. Science is one of several sources of knowledge. Like other kinds of knowledge, scientific knowledge can be wrong. However, unlike other ways of knowing, science incorporates explicit methods designed to reduce error in what is currently accepted as scientific knowledge. Evidence must be systematically collected, and rigorously and publicly evaluated.
3. Good science integrates strong theory and robust research. Theories are ideas about how the world works or claims about how to explain or understand the recurring, patterned nature of human activity.
4. Evidence is crucial to developing, revising, or discarding theoretical claims. In comparison with the evidence available in the natural sciences, the evidence available to social scientists presents added complexity because of the meaningful character of human social action. People, unlike molecules, assign meaning to their actions and to the actions of others.
5. Sociologists have devised many useful methods for obtaining evidence about the social world. Observing and questioning people are the two principal techniques, although each of them

is conducted by using a variety of formats, including experiments, surveys, participant observation, and interviews.

6. Good research adds to our knowledge of the world. Such knowledge expands our opportunities and options. Sociological knowledge helps either in solving social problems or, by sensitizing us to the human condition, expanding our social horizons.

QUESTIONS TO CONSIDER

1. The teaching effectiveness of faculty members in university and college departments could be evaluated in various ways. Suggest different sociological methods of doing such an evaluation and comment on the strengths and weaknesses of each approach.
2. Lenton (1990) chose to examine issues of child abuse by focusing on child discipline and surveying parents about their disciplinary techniques. Suggest alternative designs for her study, commenting on the strengths and weaknesses of the various approaches, including important ethical considerations.
3. Policymakers frequently debate raising or lowering age restrictions on activities, such as driving a car, drinking alcoholic beverages, or voting. Suggest how you might design a study that could provide evidence about the possible consequences of either raising or lowering one of these age restrictions.
4. Immigration levels remain a contentious issue in Canada. Construct a short series of interview questions designed to assess people's knowledge of current immigration practices. Ask these questions of your friends or family. Ask how many immigrants enter Canada and from which countries they originate. Compare your findings with official statistics that are available in government publications at your college or university or on the Internet. How might you explain the patterns you discovered?
5. Discuss the claim that "facts speak for themselves." What problems exist in making this claim? Conversely, what problems exist in claiming that facts do not speak for themselves? Consider especially the claim that we need firm standards against which to evaluate ideas or theoretical claims. Is it possible to establish such standards?
6. At parties, people are expected to be relaxed. Parties are times for having fun, for stepping outside the routines of school or work. However, phrases like "party pooper" or "killjoy" suggest that parties have rules and that violators of such rules can be ostracized. Others are glorified as "party animals," implying that some people take to partying better than others. How might you engage in a participant observation study to investigate these hunches systematically? Do such categories as "party animal" or "party pooper" exist, and, if so, how are they understood? Do "rules" exist at a party even though parties are in very important ways "escapist"? How might a sociologist seek to understand party life at your college or university?

GLOSSARY

A **causal relationship** (p. 499) involves a relationship between two variables in which change or variation in one variable produces change or variation in a second variable. Four criteria are essential to establishing a causal relation between two variables: association, time ordering, nonspuriousness, and theoretical rationale.

The **dependent variable** (p. 502) is a variable that is assumed to depend on or be caused by one or more other variables (independent variables); it is the variable that is the effect, or outcome, in a cause–effect relationship.

Ethnography (p. 510) is the detailed description of a particular culture or way of life, or the written results of a participant-observation study.

An **experiment** (p. 501) is a controlled test of the causal effects of a particular variable or set of variables on a dependent or outcome variable.

An **explanation** (p. 498) is an account of the causal logic that shows how and why variables influence one another.

External validity (p. 504) is the generalizability of a particular finding from the study group to a larger population; the relevance of conclusions for a larger population; or the ability to infer that the results of a study are representative of processes operating in a broader population.

In the **Hawthorne effect** (p. 504), people involved in a study may be influenced by the very process of being studied; the study has an impact on the subjects of the study.

A **hypothesis** (p. 502) is a knowledge claim or hunch about how the world works; it is a testable statement, derived from a theory, about the relationship between two variables.

The **independent variable** (p. 502) is a variable that is presumed to affect or influence other variables; it is the causal variable.

An **interview** (p. 504) is a method of collecting information by asking people questions, either in person or over the telephone. Interviews range from highly structured (preset questions in a fixed order) to loosely structured (topic guidelines, but no prescribed question wording).

In **meaningful action** (p. 497), human action, as distinct from physical behaviour, occurs with specific intentions or reasons in mind. The uncontrollable tic in a person's eye is physical behaviour, which differs from that of a person who is winking at someone, where intention or purpose is central to understanding what is happening. Most human activity is meaningful action, or social action.

Measurement (p. 505) comprises procedures for assigning numbers to observations according to preset rules; it is the act of finding data or information relevant to theoretical concepts.

Objectivity (p. 496) is the attempt to minimize the effect of personal bias on research results or the idea of impartiality, of "fair hearings." Objectivity is an ideal enhanced by the work of any single researcher being open to the critical scrutiny of others. Objectivity as complete impartiality is a myth.

In **participant observation** (p. 508), the study of social life involves the participation of the researcher, to varying degrees, in the activities of the group under investigation; it attempts to give an "insider's" account of a particular way of life or cultural system.

Randomization (p. 502) is a procedure used in experiments to assign test subjects to experimental conditions on the basis of chance.

Reliability (p. 505) is the consistency of measurements and the ability to reproduce the same measurements on repeated occasions.

Sampling (p. 505) is the process of selecting units from a larger population. Random sampling involves the selection of representative units (e.g., people, organizations) from a population (e.g., all Canadians, voluntary organizations in a city). Samples can be selected by probability (where every unit has a nonzero chance of selection) or nonprobability (where chance does not enter into the selection of sample units).

A **self-administered questionnaire** (p. 504) is a method of collecting information by having people record their own answers to preset questions.

Spurious relationships (p. 498) involve an incorrect inference about the causal relations between variables.

Understanding (p. 499) is the ability to provide a definition of a situation that members of a culture find authentic and valid.

Validity (p. 505) is the relevance or accuracy of measurement in relation to the theoretical concept that it is supposed to measure.

A **variable** (p. 502) is something that varies or an attribute or event that can take on more than one value (e.g., unemployment rates, age, sex).

SUGGESTED READING

Babbie, Earl and Lucia Benaquisto. (2009). *Fundamentals of Social Research,* 2nd ed. Toronto: Thomson Nelson. Babbie and Benaquisto provide the best general account of research methods available in sociology.

Becker, Howard. (1998). *Tricks of the Trade: How to Think about Your Research While You're Doing It.* Chicago: University of Chicago Press. Written by one of sociology's best qualitative researchers, Becker's book discusses how to think about research and is valuable to both qualitative and quantitative researchers.

Cresswell, John. (2009). *Research Design: Qualitative, Quantitative, and Mixed Methods Approaches,* 3rd ed. Thousand Oaks, CA: Sage Publications. This text offers an excellent, balanced view of the strengths and weaknesses of various research designs and is a useful guide to conducting good research by using multiple methods.

Denzin, Norman. (1997). *Interpretative Ethnography: Ethnographic Practices for the 21st Century.* Thousand Oaks, CA: Sage. Denzin provides a good general introduction to the practices and debates of qualitative research.

Guppy, Neil and George Gray. (2008). *Successful Surveys: Research Methods and Practice,* 4th ed. Toronto: Thomson Nelson. This is a practical guidebook to developing research designs and using effective survey research techniques. The authors cover questionnaires and interviews.

NOTES

1. Black swans, native to Australia, were unknown to Europeans before exploration. The idea that all swans are white is thus similar to the idea that Earth is the central body in the solar system—a claim once understood to be true but now thought to be false.
2. Please do not overinterpret this claim. As a community, we have frequently treated humans as exceptional. We have distanced ourselves from nature. Our theories and actions often evince a "control of nature" paradigm. Highlighting differences between the subject matter of the natural and the social sciences is complicated. For example, monkeys make friends with zoologists and, when studied, may react in similar ways as humans. It is important to consider in what ways the study of people by people may add complexity to research, and how this in turn may stimulate us to think differently about how people study non-humans. For example, issues of animal rights and environmental ethics raise questions about our traditionally human-centric view of the world. Perhaps bacteria do blush and we are just too ignorant to notice!

EPILOGUE

THE FUTURE OF SOCIOLOGY

Michael Burawoy
UNIVERSITY OF CALIFORNIA, BERKELEY

MARKETIZATION

A wave of marketization is sweeping the world. Entities that used to be embedded in human bodies, communities, and nature are being ripped out of their habitats, appropriated by new classes of merchants, and sold in chains of markets that stretch across the globe. This is not the first wave of marketization; it is not the first time markets have expanded their reach by turning common goods and public services into new commodities. The Industrial Revolution of the nineteenth century worked through a similar global expansion in the marketization of labour and its products. The financial revolution of the twentieth century turned money into a full-blown commodity, eventually threatening the very viability of markets. The ecological transformation that now besets us digs even deeper, making land, water, air, and genes the subject of market exchange, thereby threatening human existence.

So far, each wave of marketization has set in motion a counter-movement, erecting institutions to regulate, channel, and contain commodification. Yet each wave also swept away the ramparts erected against the previous wave. Under demolition today are rights won by Western labour movements against the marketization of the nineteenth century (such as the right to form unions) and the social rights guaranteed by states against the marketization of the twentieth century (the provision of minimum standards of economic security). In the end, nothing seems immune to the third wave of marketization. Will there be a counter-movement strong enough to contain its destructive powers?

Behind the third wave are predatory classes colluding with nation-states and sometimes also with multilateral agencies, such as the World Bank and the International Monetary Fund, imposing their will on the desperate and the destitute, on workers, students, farmers, and the middle class. The last holdout against this economic storm is society itself, or more precisely civil society, composed of *associations* with a measure of collective self-regulation, *movements* forged out of a collective will, and *publics* of mutual recognition and communication. Will society measure up to the challenge? What role can sociology play in meeting it?

SOCIOLOGY VERSUS THE MARKET

If there is a common thread to sociology's diverse traditions, it is opposition to the reduction of society to a market. Whether it is Marx's critique of capitalism, Durkheim's critique of the abnormal forms of the division of labour, Weber's critique of rationalism, or Parsons's critique of utilitarianism, each tradition opposes market reductionism, albeit from different viewpoints. Today, it is even more important for sociology to continue its tradition of opposing market reductionism as commodification actually threatens to destroy society and with it human existence. In meeting this challenge, sociologists can join one of four groups of practitioners:

1. *Policy sociologists* help to formulate policies that side with the state against the market, using what remains of state autonomy to help regulate market forces. In Northern European countries with a continuing legacy of social democratic politics or welfare provision, this approach might make sense.
2. *Professional sociologists* argue that their discipline must be based on firm scientific foundations before it can be of any practical use. From this point of view, by wading into stormy seas prematurely, we will discover only that we cannot swim. Professional sociologists may understand the dangers of rampant marketization, but they sit tight waiting for the storm to pass, hoping that it will not sweep them up with the rest of society.
3. *Critical sociologists* agitate against the first two groups, writing tracts against their moral bankruptcy, complaining about those who collude with state and market, and also about those who busy themselves writing scientific papers. Critical sociologists are a shrinking band. Like the professionals, they live in insulated communities, seeking to preserve the power of critique, acting as if their words have the power to hold the storm at bay. Yet their message is often incomprehensible and few are listening.
4. *Public sociologists* refuse to collaborate with the market and the state. They say that science without politics is blind and that critique without intervention is empty. They engage directly with communities, institutions, and social movements, listening and speaking, observing and participating, learning and writing in order to defend society against rampant marketization. Third-wave marketization calls forth the age of public sociology.

There may be a need for public sociology, but it can move forward only on the legs of policy, professional, and critical sociologies. Without the kind of sociological knowledge accumulated in our discipline and presented in this book, public sociology cannot exist. Public sociology also depends on critical knowledge that keeps professional science honest, steering it away from irrelevance and self-referentiality. At the same time, critical knowledge infuses public sociology with the values and direction that motivate its engagement with publics. Public sociology is nothing if it cannot help to bring about social change. It cannot, therefore, dismiss policy science. It can examine it from without, pushing it in appropriate directions, opposing the temptations of serving power. Public sociology must be the conscience of policy sociology.

Together, public, professional, critical, and policy sociologists form a discipline that takes civil society as its standpoint—as opposed to political scientists, who take the standpoint of the state, and economists, who take the standpoint of the market. Sociology's existence depends on the health of civil society, thereby declaring its commitment to the future of humanity that is currently threatened by the collusion of state and market. Here is the paradox: sociology has never been so important, yet its foundations have never been more precarious.

THE GREAT TRANSFORMATION

To appreciate the future of sociology, we must understand the context of third-wave marketization, within which it is forced to operate. For that, I draw on Karl Polanyi's classic, *The Great Transformation* (1944).

Polanyi (who, incidentally, lived outside Toronto from the early 1950s until his death in 1964) devoted himself to understanding the dangers and potentialities of the market. He showed that markets that advance too far cause a social counter-movement. This was the "great transformation"—not the rise of the market, but the *reaction* to its rise.

Perhaps Polanyi's most important but least developed idea was that of "fictitious commodities"—entities that lose their value when subject to unrestricted exchange, unrestricted commodification. For Polanyi, there were three fictitious commodities: labour, money, and land.

When *labour* is overly commodified, people lose their capacity to work. For example, in a perfectly free labour market, where only supply and demand determine the cost of labour, the absence of laws governing minimum wages, child labour, safety standards, and the length of the working day allows some workers to die prematurely because of accidents, ill health, or starvation. Typically, when the New Poor Law was passed in England in 1834, revoking certain forms of labour protection and poor relief, the ensuing desperation forged a spontaneous reaction in the form of social movements, such as the factory movement to restrict the length of the working day, and associations, such as burial societies, trade unions, cooperatives, and experiments in creating utopian communities. The nineteenth-century commodification of labour led to the spontaneous self-reconstitution of society.

Similarly, when *money* is overly commodified, it loses the capacity to facilitate exchange. The full commodification of money began in the early twentieth century and continues today. Thus, before the global financial crisis that began in 2008, important American laws regulating financial institutions were scrapped, encouraging banks to invest ordinary people's money in extraordinarily risky ways. In the process, the richest 1 percent of Americans multiplied their wealth many times over. However, when mortgages and other credit vehicles began to fail, millions of ordinary Americans lost their homes. Soon, the Occupy Wall Street movement emerged to protest growing economic inequality.

Finally, when *land* is overly commodified, it loses its capacity to deliver human subsistence. When land is enclosed and sold as real estate, as is happening in so many parts of the world, the livelihood of small farmers is threatened. However, it is not just land but other elements of nature that are being commodified. For instance, in Bolivia in the mid-1990s, the government decided to sell water supplies and delivery systems to a private company. The company soon set water prices higher than many poor Bolivians could afford. Water's availability—its human value as a source of life—fell as the cost of commodified water skyrocketed. Poor Bolivians naturally rebelled to protest the untenable conditions of their existence.

Polanyi (1944) wrote about the first two waves of marketization and the reactions to them—the nineteenth-century marketization of labour (and the ensuing rise of workers' rights) and the twentieth-century marketization of money (which led to the Great Depression of 1929–39 and the ensuing rise of the New Deal in the United States, Nazism in Germany, and Stalinism in the Soviet Union). Polanyi believed that, after the horrors of World War II, most people would come to understand the importance of regulating markets. He was wrong. In the mid-1970s, a third wave of marketization began, whose distinctive feature would be the commodification of nature as well as labour and money. How, more specifically, should we characterize the third wave of marketization? What societal reactions to it can we observe?

THIRD-WAVE MARKETIZATION

First-wave marketization generated a counter-movement against the commodification of labour. Second-wave marketization generated a counter-movement against the commodification of money. Third-wave marketization is generating a counter-movement against the commodification of land or, more broadly, of nature. Of course, land began to be commodified before the third wave. However, the commodification of nature as a whole did not yet threaten the devastation of the planet. Today it does. Squatters and shack dwellers now defend themselves against local governments trying to clear them out of cities. Middle-class city residents oppose high-rise developers. Indigenous peoples refuse to give up their land so large commercial plantations can take their place. Farmers battle against dams that threaten their existence. Activists struggle for clean air, against the dumping of toxic waste, and against privatization of water and electricity. The list goes on. The commodification of labour and of money, of course, continue to be important, generating their own counter-movements, but the reaction to the commodification of nature will define the reaction to third-wave marketization and, thus, the future of humanity.

A second way to characterize the third-wave marketization is by its scale, which is global in its causes and ramifications. The response to the commodification of labour under first-wave marketization was mainly local, although it eventually aspired to become national (through the creation of national trade unions and political parties, for instance). The response to the commodification of money under second-wave marketization was mainly at the level of the nation-state (through central banks) but eventually aspired to be global (through the creation of the International Monetary Fund and the World Bank, for instance). The response to the commodification of nature under third-wave marketization has to be initiated by society—first at the local level but then rising almost immediately to the global level. Because the effects of climate change, nuclear accidents, water privatization, and the spread of contagious diseases are global, so the response to third-wave marketization must ultimately assume a global scale.

A third way of characterizing successive waves of marketization is in terms of the destruction of the defences people have erected against marketization. Second-wave marketization destroyed the trenches defended by labour before it generated a counter-movement to build new trenches of state social protection (the welfare state). Third-wave marketization is rolling back labour and social rights. We see this almost everywhere as trade unions decline, the real wages of workers stagnate or fall, and budgets for social security, pensions, and welfare contract. On what foundation will the next round of defences be built—defences that will fend off the degradation of nature but also recover labour and social rights? The deeper the challenge to humanity and community, the deeper the reaction must be. In response to third-wave marketization, we will need to develop the defence of human rights—the defence of a community of mutual recognition as human beings—that will necessarily incorporate labour and social rights, too.

Of course, human rights may be appropriated and narrowed to suit particular interests. For instance, electoral democracy has become a human right that, for some people, can justify invasion, killing, and subjugation abroad. Similarly, markets have been promoted in the name of the human right to freedom of choice and the protection of private property, ignoring what this means to those who cannot choose and who lack property. Human rights that are universal, and that therefore include labour rights and social rights, must aim for the protection of the human community as a whole, which involves first recognizing and treating each other as ends rather than means. Human rights, then, is a complex terrain of struggle in which groups stake their claim on the basis of their own interests, but ultimately human rights are about the protection of humanity with the potential to galvanize struggles of global proportions against third-wave marketization. Now that I have described the major characteristics of third-wave marketization and its counter-movement, what is their significance for sociology?

THREE WAVES OF SOCIOLOGY

A distinctive sociology emerges with each wave of marketization. Sociology grew up in the nineteenth century together with civil society, itself a response to first-wave marketization. Thus, sociology began as a moral enterprise defending society against the market, especially the destruction of community, as newly proletarianized, destitute, and degraded populations made the city their home. It was foremost a critical enterprise, but it was also utopian. Sociology imagined life outside the market. For example, Marx and Engels postulated communism, which they expected to arise out of the ashes of capitalism. Comte imagined a familial order led by sociologists. Durkheim envisaged an organic solidarity built on corporatist organization. In English Canada, the religious principles of the social gospel movement influenced sociology in its early stages.

Comte, Marx, Durkheim, and other early sociologists would object to my characterization. They saw themselves as scientists, committed to what is and what could be by virtue of the laws of society. Still, from today's standpoint, for all the scientific breakthroughs they brought to the study of society, their science was partly speculative, especially regarding the future, and strongly imbued with moral concerns aimed at reversing the degradation brought about by nineteenth century capitalism. At the heart of their utopianism lay the critique of the division of labour and its transformation.

Second-wave marketization, which took off following World War I, challenged the rights that labour had won through trade unions and political parties. As Polanyi (1944) argued, the ravages of international trade and exchange threatened the conditions of capital accumulation and prompted protectionist reactions by the state. In countries that reacted to second-wave marketization with authoritarian regimes, notably Germany and the Soviet Union, sociology was eclipsed, but in countries that reacted with some form of social democracy, a new type of sociology emerged. It collaborated with the state to defend society against the market. In the United Kingdom, the United States, Sweden, Canada, and elsewhere, a policy-oriented sociology developed. Even in the colonies, there was a policy science, although there it was called anthropology. This was the golden era of state-funded research into social problems.

Where sociology remained relatively divorced from the state, as in the United States, it also developed a strong professional branch, committed to the expansion of specific research programs chiefly concerned with social stability. There, stratification studies highlighted achievement-based mobility up the occupational hierarchy. Family studies emphasized the benefits of the smoothly functioning nuclear family. Studies of crime and deviance focused on regulation and control. Industrial sociology was chiefly concerned with pacifying labour and maximizing the extraction of value from it. Political sociology underscored the social bases of electoral democracy and the containment of extremism. The overarching theoretical framework was summed up by structural functionalism—the delineation of the functional prerequisites needed to keep any social system in equilibrium and the mechanisms allowing social institutions to meet those prerequisites. During this period, sociologists gave detailed attention to empirical research, new methods of data collection and analysis, and the elaboration of "middle-range" theories that nestled in the scaffolding of structural functionalism. This approach was a reaction against the earlier, more speculative traditions that were propelled by the desire for moral reform. It wanted to expunge moral questions from sociology.

If the first wave of sociology invented utopias, the second wave of policy-oriented and professional sociology opposed utopian thinking, in effect claiming that utopia was almost within reach, or even already at hand. Indeed, in the United States and the Soviet Union, structural-functionalism and Marxism-Leninism, respectively, mistook utopia for reality. These were sociological traditions that were riveted to the present, concerned only with ironing out its small irrationalities. A critical sociology developed in reaction to these presuppositions of harmony and consensus, restoring an interest in struggle and conflict, but also in imagining a world beyond capitalism.

What sort of sociology marks the response to third-wave marketization? As we have seen, the third wave rolls back the statist defence of society, taking the offensive against labour and social rights. Unlike the second wave, which provoked an anti-market reaction from the state—variously involving protectionism, economic planning, wage guarantees, the welfare state, and public ownership of the means of production—third-wave marketization is promoted by the state. Still a regulatory state, it is nonetheless regulation *for* rather than *against* the market. It undoes all that was achieved against second-wave marketization. Society is thus under a double assault from economy and state. Unable to gain much leverage in the state or from the market, the fate of sociology rests with society. In other words, sociology's self-interest lies in the constitution of civil society where it barely exists and in its protection where it is in retreat—hence the claim we are living in the age of public sociology.

Today, sociology cannot limit its engagement to local or national publics, but must be concerned with knitting together a global civil society. Moreover, the third wave of sociology calls for a science quite different from the speculative science of the nineteenth century and the policy-oriented professional science of the mid-twentieth century—one that seeks to combine scientific rigour with the development of alternative values. We no longer strive for a single paradigmatic science but a discipline made up of multiple intersecting research programs, founded on the values of different publics, working out theoretical frameworks through engaging their anomalies and contradictions. I call this a reflexive science, a science that is not frightened of reflecting on its value foundations or of articulating them publicly, but a science nonetheless (see Table 1).

As sociology becomes more global, borrowings across national lines become more feasible and important. For example, after its 1974 anti-authoritarian revolution, Portugal drew on critical and professional traditions in American and French

TABLE 1 SOCIOLOGY VERSUS THE MARKET

	FIRST-WAVE MARKETIZATION	SECOND-WAVE MARKETIZATION	THIRD-WAVE MARKETIZATION
Dominant "fictitious commodity"	labour	money	land ("nature")
Dominant locus of response	local	national	global
Dominant rights protected	labour	social	human
Dominant orientation of sociology	utopian and critical	policy and professional	public
Dominant thrust of sociological science	speculative	positivist	reflexive

sociologies, harnessing them to a vibrant civil society. This small country is one of the leaders in public sociology, connected to policy, critical, and professional sociologies. Public sociology has flourished in other countries, such as Brazil, South Africa, and India, based on selectively imported North American or European professional sociology but reshaped in anti-authoritarian or anti-colonial struggles.

Global borrowings present dangers as well as possibilities. Notably, the domination of the United States' professional sociology can constrain the responsiveness of national sociologies to local concerns. Facing the dilemma of having the United States on its doorstep in the late 1960s and early 1970s, many Canadian sociologists led a hostile attack on the Americanization of academic life. Farther afield, the dilemma can be even deeper. Pressures to write in English for remote professional audiences not only disadvantage peripheralized sociologists, but inevitably threaten the vitality of local public sociology. Writing of the Middle East, Sari Hanafi (2011) has expressed the dilemma as follows: publish globally and perish locally or publish locally and perish globally. Are there ways to transcend this chasm, to constitute a public sociology that is not isolationist but globally connected? That remains our challenge.

CONCLUSION

I have argued that sociology is taking a public turn in response to third-wave marketization. Sociology lives and dies with society. When society is threatened, so is sociology. We can no longer rely on the state to contain the market, and so sociologists have to forge their own connections to society, that is, to develop public sociologies. We have to do more than serve society passively. We must conserve and constitute society. In this, sociology has many potential allies and partners as they too come under increasing assault from state and market. That is the broader contemporaneous context within which public sociology can be a guiding spirit and directing force.

However, we cannot think of the contemporary context outside of its past. We cannot compartmentalize the three waves of marketization and the corresponding configurations of sociology as three separate periods. Each wave deposits its legacy in the next wave. The waves of commodification deepen as they move *regressively* from labour to money to nature, each wave incorporating the commodification of the previous period, just as the counter-movement leads *progressively* from labour rights to social rights (which includes labour rights) and then aspires to human rights that include all three.

The development of sociology is different. Policy and professional sociology, with their value-neutral, scientific approach, are a reaction against utopian and critical sociology, with their speculations and moral infusions. Public sociology tries to synthesize the value commitment of the first period with the scientific advances of the second. However, even here we should be careful not to think in terms of discrete sociologies, but rather reconfigurations of the four elements of sociology, in which the weights of professional, policy, critical, and public sociologies shift over time. Indeed, a public sociology cannot really take off in a sustained manner unless it is impelled by critical sociology and grounded in professional sociology.

The rhythm and spacing of the waves of sociological development vary from country to country. For the advanced capitalist world today, the waves are more clearly separated in time, whereas for such countries as Russia, India, and China, the waves are compressed, with the commodification of labour, money, and nature occurring almost simultaneously in recent decades. National variation notwithstanding, we can still identify the present era as one in which the commodification of nature concentrates within itself the cumulative impact of the commodification of labour and money. In its subsumption of all commodification, the commodification of nature becomes the planet's most pressing problem, generating social movements that are held together by the principle of human rights.

It is unclear whether these movements can reverse third wave marketization and whether the result will be to expand or narrow the confines of human freedom. It is possible that sociology itself will succumb to commodification—the commodification of the production of knowledge in the university and elsewhere, the commodification of the distribution of knowledge by the mass media, and the commodification of the consumption of knowledge as student fees continue their upward trajectory. Conversely, there may be a place for public sociology to participate in the knitting together of organizations, movements, and publics across the globe, helping to fortify a civil society beyond the control of market and state. The world needs public sociology engaging publics across the globe: one that rests on the shoulders of a dynamic professional sociology that is inspired by a vital critical sociology, while holding policy sociology to account.

REFERENCES

CHAPTER 1

Allen, Robert C. (1999). *Education and Technological Revolutions: The Role of the Social Sciences and the Humanities in the Knowledge Based Economy.* Ottawa: Social Sciences and Humanities Research Council of Canada. On the World Wide Web at http://www.sshrc.ca/english/resnews/researchresults/allen99.pdf (retrieved 8 May 2001).

Babbie, Earl. (1992). *The Practice of Social Research*, 6th ed. Belmont, CA: Wadsworth Publishing.

Bell, Daniel. (1976). *The Coming of Post-Industrial Society: A Venture in Social Forecasting.* New York: Basic Books.

Carole, Melissa. (2011). "Mental Illness? Yes, but also Homophobia." *Globe and Mail* 7 October: A21.

Clark, S.D. (1968). *The Developing Canadian Community*, 2nd ed. Toronto: University of Toronto Press.

Coleman, James S. (1961). *The Adolescent Society.* New York: Free Press.

Douglas, Jack D. (1967). *The Social Meanings of Suicide.* Princeton, NJ: Princeton University Press.

Durkheim, Émile. (1951 [1897]). *Suicide: A Study in Sociology*, G. Simpson, ed., J. Spaulding and G. Simpson, trans. New York: Free Press.

Edel, Abraham. (1965). "Social Science and Value: A Study in Interrelations." In Irving Louis Horowitz, ed., *The New Sociology: Essays in Social Science and Social Theory in Honor of C. Wright Mills* (pp. 218–38). New York: Oxford University Press.

Eichler, Margrit. (1987). *Nonsexist Research Methods.* Boston: Allen and Unwin.

Eichler, Margrit. (1988). *Families in Canada Today*, 2nd ed. Toronto: Gage.

Fukuyama, Francis. (1992). *The End of History and the Last Man.* New York: HarperCollins.

Garfinkel, Harold. (1967). *Studies in Ethnomethodology.* Englewood Cliffs, NJ: Prentice-Hall.

Giddens, Anthony. (1982). *Sociology: A Brief but Critical Introduction.* New York: Harcourt Brace Jovanovich.

Giddens, Anthony. (1990). *The Consequences of Modernity.* Stanford, CA: Stanford University Press.

Goffman, Erving. (1959). *The Presentation of Self in Everyday Life.* Garden City, NY: Anchor.

Granovetter, Mark. (1973). "The Strength of Weak Ties." *American Sociological Review, 78* (6), 1360–80.

Guillén, Mauro F. (2001). "Is Globalization Civilizing, Destructive or Feeble? A Critique of Five Key Debates in the Social Science Literature." *Annual Review of Sociology, 27.* On the World Wide Web at http://knowledge.wharton.upenn.edu/PDFs/938 pdf (retrieved 6 February 2003).

Guppy, Neil and R. Alan Hedley. (1993). *Opportunities in Sociology.* Montreal: Canadian Sociology and Anthropology Association.

Hersch, Patricia. (1998). *A Tribe Apart: A Journey into the Heart of American Adolescence.* New York: Ballantine Books.

Hochschild, Arlie and Anne Machung. (1989). *The Second Shift: Working Parents and the Revolution at Home.* New York: Viking.

Jubilee Debt Campaign. (2010). "Getting into Debt." On the Word Wide Web at http://www.jubileedebtcapmaign.org.uk/Getting%20into%20Debt+6281.twl (retrieved 20 December 2011).

Kuhn, Thomas. (1970). *The Structure of Scientific Revolutions*, 2nd ed. Chicago: University of Chicago Press.

Marx, Karl. (1904 [1859]). *A Contribution to the Critique of Political Economy*, N. Stone, trans. Chicago: Charles H. Kerr.

Marx, Karl and Friedrich Engels. (1972 [1848]). "Manifesto of the Communist Party." In R. Tucker, ed., *The Marx-Engels Reader* (pp. 331–62). New York: Norton.

Merton, Robert K. (1968 [1949]). *Social Theory and Social Structure.* New York: Free Press.

Mills, C. Wright. (1959). *The Sociological Imagination.* New York: Oxford University Press.

Organisation for Economic Cooperation and Development. (2008). "Aid Targets Slipping Out of Reach." On the World Wide Web at http://www.oecd.org/dataoecd/47/25/41724314.pdf (retrieved 20 December 2011).

Ornstein, Michael D. (1983). "The Development of Class in Canada." In J. Paul Grayson, ed., *Introduction to Sociology: An Alternate Approach* (pp. 224–66). Toronto: Gage.

Parsons, Talcott. (1951). *The Social System.* Glencoe, IL: Free Press.

Porter, John. (1965). *The Vertical Mosaic: An Analysis of Social Class and Power in Canada.* Toronto: University of Toronto Press.

Robbins, Liz. (2005). "Nash Displays Polished Look: On the Court, of Course." *New York Times* January 19. On the World Wide Web at http://www.nytimes.com (retrieved 19 January 2005).

Russett, Cynthia Eagle. (1966). *The Concept of Equilibrium in American Social Thought.* New Haven, CT: Yale University Press.

Statistics Canada. (2004). "Suicide in Canada's Immigrant Population." *The Daily* 29 March. On the World Wide Web at http://www.statcan.ca/Daily/English/040329/d040329a.htm (retrieved 6 July 2006).

Statistics Canada. (2011a). "Deaths and Mortality Rate by Selected Grouped Causes, Age Group and Sex, Canada, Annually." CANSIM. On the World Wide Web at http://www5.statcan.gc.ca/cansim/a26?lang=eng&id=1020552&p2=46 (retrieved 20 December 2011).

Statistics Canada. (2011b). "Table 1: Labour Force Characteristics by Age and Sex, Canada— Seasonally Adjusted." On the World Wide Web at http://www.statcan.gc.ca/pub/71-001-x/2011011/t001-eng.htm (retrieved 20 December 2011).

Thompson, Kenneth, ed. (1975). *Auguste Comte: The Foundation of Sociology.* New York: Wiley.

Tierney, John. (1997). "Our Oldest Computer, Upgraded." *New York Times Magazine* 28 September: pp. 46–49, 97, 100, 104–05.

Tillyard, E. M. W. (1943). *The Elizabethan World Picture.* London, UK: Chatto and Windus.

Toffler, Alvin. (1990). *Powershift: Knowledge, Wealth, and Violence at the Edge of the 21st Century.* New York: Bantam.

Weber, Max. (1946). *From Max Weber: Essays in Sociology*. Hans Gerth and C. Wright Mills, eds. and trans. New York: Oxford University Press.

Weber, Max. (1958 [1904–05]). *The Protestant Ethnic and the Spirit of Capitalism*. New York: Scribner.

World Health Organization. (2011). "Suicide Rates per 100,000 by Country, Year and Sex (Table): Most Recent Year Available, as of 2011." On the World Wide Web at http://www.who.int/mental_health/prevention/suicide_rates/en/ (retrieved 20 December 2011).

Yates, Gayle Graham, ed. (1985). *Harriet Martineau on Women*. New Brunswick, NJ: Rutgers University Press.

CHAPTER 2

Adams, Michael. (1997). *Sex in the Snow: Canadian Social Values at the End of the Millennium*. Toronto: Penguin.

Akwagyiram, Alexis. 2009. "Hip Hop Comes of Age." *BBC News* 12 October. On the World Wide Web at http://news.bbc.co.uk/2/hi/8286310.stm (retrieved 11 January 2011).

Albas, Daniel and Cheryl Albas. (1989) "Modern Magic: The Case of Examinations." *The Sociological Quarterly*, *30*, 603–13.

Baudrillard, Jean. (1988 [1986]). *America*, Chris Turner, trans. London: Verso.

Bibby, Reginald W. (1987). *Fragmented Gods: The Poverty and Potential of Religion in Canada*. Toronto: Irwin.

Bissoondath, Neil. (2002). *Selling Illusions: The Cult of Multiculturalism in Canada*, rev. ed. Toronto: Penguin.

Boroditsky, Lera. (2010). "Lost in Translation." *Wall Street Journal* 23 July. On the World Wide Web at http://online.wsj.com/article/SB10001424052748703467304575383131592767868.html (retrieved 14 March 2012).

Brym, Robert J. (2001). "Hip Hop from Dissent to Commodity: A Note on Consumer Culture." In R. Brym, ed., *New Society: Sociology for the 21st Century*, 3rd ed. (pp. 78–81). Toronto: Harcourt Brace.

Brym, Robert J. (2009). *Canadian Society and the 2006 Census*. Toronto: Nelson.

Brym, Robert J. and Bonnie J. Fox. (1989). *From Culture to Power: The Sociology of English Canada*. Toronto: Oxford University Press.

Cardozo, Andrew and Ravi Pendakur. (n.d.). "Canada's Visible Minorities: 1967–2017." http://aix1.uottawa.ca/~pendakur/pdf%20docs/VisMin_1967–2017.pdf (retrieved 16 March 2012).

Carpenter, Dave. (2003). "McDonald's High-Tech with Kitchen, Kiosks." KioskCom. On the World Wide Web at http://www.redorbit.com/news/technology/12629/mcdonalds_hightech_with_kitchen_kiosks/ (retrieved 23 October 2003).

Citizenship and Immigration Canada. (2010). "Canada—Permanent Residents by Source Country." On the World Wide Web at http://www.cic.gc.ca/english/resources/statistics/facts2010/permanent/10.asp (retrieved 16 March 2012).

Clarke, Harold D., Jane Jenson, Lawrence LeDuc, and Jon H. Pammett. (1996). *Absent Mandate: Canadian Electoral Politics in an Era of Restructuring*, 3rd ed. Toronto: Gage.

Damisch, Lysann, Barbara Stoberock, and Thomas Mussweiler. (2010). "Keep Your Fingers Crossed! How Superstition Improves Performance." *Psychological Science*, *21*, 1014–20.

Davis, Mike. (1990). City of Quartz: Excavating the Future in Los Angeles. New York: Verso.

Delmos, Monika. (2002). "Mangled Words Divide Generations in Japan." *Globe and Mail* 24 August: A14.

Deutscher, Guy. (2010). "Does Your Language Shape How You Think?" *New York Times* 26 August. On the World Wide Web at http://www.nytimes.com/2010/08/29/magazine/29language-t.html?pagewanted=all (retrieved 14 March 2012).

Durkheim, Émile. (1976 [1915]). *The Elementary Forms of the Religious Life*, Joseph Ward Swain, trans. New York: Free Press.

Elections Canada. (2012). "Voter Turnout at Federal Elections and Referendums." On the World Wide Web at http://www.elections.ca/content.aspx?section=ele&dir=turn&document=index&lang=e (retrieved 16 March 2012).

Fleras, Augie and Jean Leonard Elliott. (2002). *Engaging Diversity: Multiculturalism in Canada*. Toronto: Nelson.

Forman, Murray. (2001). "It Ain't All About the Benjamins: Summit on Social Responsibility in the Hip-Hop Industry." *Journal of Popular Music Studies*, *13*, 117–23.

Fox, Yale and Robert Brym. 2009. "Musical Attention Deficit Disorder." On the World Wide Web at http://www.darwinversusthemachine.com/2009/10/musical-attention-deficit-disorder/ (retrieved 10 January 2011).

Frank, Thomas and Matt Weiland, eds. (1997). *Commodify Your Dissent: Salvos from the Baffler*. New York: Norton.

Gap.com. (1999). On the World Wide Web at http://www.gap.com/onlinestore/gap/advertising/khakitv.asp (retrieved 14 September 1999).

Ghosh, Bobby. (2011). "Rage, Rap, and Revolution: Inside the Arab Youth Quake." *Time.com* 17 February. On the World Wide Web at http://www.time.com/time/world/article/0,8599,2049808,00.html (retrieved 17 February 2011).

Gleick, James. (2000). *Faster: The Acceleration of Just About Everything*. New York: Vintage.

Hall, Edward. (1959). *The Silent Language*. New York: Doubleday.

Harris, Marvin. (1974). *Cows, Pigs, Wars and Witches: The Riddles of Culture*. New York, Random House.

Ignatieff, Michael. (2000). *The Rights Revolution*. Toronto: Anansi.

Kristof, Nicholas D. (1997). "With Stateside Lingo, Valley Girl Goes Japanese." *New York Times* 19 October: sections 1, 3.

Lipset, Seymour Martin. (1963) "Value Differences, Absolute or Relative: The English-Speaking Democracies." In *The First New Nation: The United States in Historical Perspective* (pp. 248–73). New York: Basic Books.

McCrum, Robert, William Cran, and Robert MacNeil. (1992). *The Story of English*, new and rev. eds. London, UK: Faber and Faber.

McLuhan, Marshall. (1964). *Understanding Media: The Extensions of Man*. New York: McGraw-Hill.

Neal, Mark Anthony. (1999). *What the Music Said: Black Popular Music and Black Public Culture*. New York: Routledge.

Nevitte, Neil. (1996). *The Decline of Deference: Canadian Value Change in Cross-National Perspective*. Peterborough, ON: Broadview Press.

Peters, Russell. (2009). "Russell Peters: Canadian East Indian Comedian." On the World Wide Web at http://thebookmarketingnetwork.com/video/russell-peter-canadian-east (retrieved 16 March 2012).

Pinker, Steven. (1994). "Apes—Lost for Words." *New Statesman and Society* 15 April: 30–31.

Piven, Frances Fox and Richard A. Cloward. (1977). *Poor People's Movements: Why They Succeed, How They Fail*. New York: Vintage.

Ritzer, George. (1993). *The McDonaldization of Society: An Investigation into the Changing Character of Contemporary Social Life*. Thousand Oaks, CA: Pine Forge Press.

Ritzer, George. (1996). "The McDonaldization Thesis: Is Expansion Inevitable?" *International Sociology, 11*, 291–308.

Schlosser, Eric. (2002). *Fast Food Nation: The Dark Side of the All-American Meal.* New York: Perennial.

Schor, Juliet B. (1992). *The Overworked American: The Unexpected Decline of Leisure.* New York: Basic Books.

Scott, James C. (1998). *Seeing Like a State: How Certain Schemes to Improve the Human Condition Have Failed.* New Haven, CT: Yale University Press.

Statistics Canada. (2012). "Labour Force Survey Estimates (LFS), Employees Working Overtime (Weekly) by National Occupational Classification for Statistics (NOC-S), Sex and Age Group Annually." CANSIM Table 2820082. On the World Wide Web at http://dc2.chass.utoronto.ca.myaccess.library.utoronto.ca/cgi-bin/cansimdim/c2_getArrayDim.pl (retrieved 16 March 2012).

Thompson, E. P. (1967). "Time, Work Discipline and Industrial Capitalism." *Past and Present, 3*, 59–67.

United Nations. (1998). "Universal Declaration of Human Rights." On the World Wide Web at http://www.un.org/Overview/rights.html (retrieved 29 August 2002).

Weber, Max. (1946 [1922]). "Bureaucracy." In *From Max Weber: Essays in Sociology*, H. Gerth and C. Mills, eds. and trans. (pp. 196–264). New York: Oxford University Press.

Whorf, Benjamin Lee. (1956). In John B. Carroll, ed., *Language, Thought, and Reality.* Cambridge, MA: MIT Press.

Wilson, William Julius. (1987). *The Truly Disadvantaged: The Inner City, the Underclass and Public Policy.* Chicago: University of Chicago Press.

Woodbury, Anthony. (2003). "Endangered Languages." Linguistic Society of America. On the World Wide Web at http://www.lsadc.org/web2/endangeredlgs.htm (retrieved 19 July 2003).

World Health Organization. (2012). "Female Genital Mutilation." On the World Wide Web at http://www.who.int/mediacentre/factsheets/fs241/en/ (retrieved 16 March 2012).

World Values Survey. (2012). "Online Data Analysis." On the World Wide Web at http://www.wvsevsdb.com/wvs/WVSAnalize.jsp (retrieved 16 March 2012).

CHAPTER 3

Adams, Natalie and Pamela Bettis. (2003). "Commanding the Room in Short Skirts: Cheering as the Embodiment of Ideal Girlhood." *Gender & Society, 17* (1), 73–91.

Adler, P. A. and P. Adler. (1998). *Peer Power: Preadolescent Culture and Identity.* New Brunswick, NJ: Rutgers University Press.

Adler, P. A. and P. Adler. (2011). *The Tender Cut: Inside the World of Self-Injury.* New York: New York University Press.

Albas, Daniel and Cheryl Albas. (1994). "Studying Students Studying: Perspectives, Identities and Activities." In Mary Lorenz Dietz, Robert Prus, and William Shaffir, eds., *Doing Everyday Life: Ethnography as Human Lived Experience* (pp. 273–89). Toronto: Copp Clark Longman Ltd.

Armstrong, Elizabeth M. (2000). "Lessons in Control: Prenatal Education in the Hospital." *Social Problems, 47* (4), 583–605.

Arnett, Jeffrey Jansen. (1995). "Adolescents' Use of Media for Self-Socialization." *Journal of Youth and Adolescence, 24*, 519–533.

Baker, Maureen. (1985). *What Will Tomorrow Bring? A Study of the Aspirations of Adolescent Women.* Ottawa: Canadian Advisory Council on the Status of Women.

Ballantine, Jeanne. (1997). *The Sociology of Education: A Systematic Analysis*, 4th ed. Englewood Cliffs, NJ: Prentice-Hall.

Barber, K. and K. Allen. (1992). *Women and Families: Feminist Reconstructions.* New York: Guilford Press.

Beckford, J. A. (1985). *Cult Controversies: The Societal Response to New Religious Movements.* London: Tavistock.

Begley, S. (1995). "Gray Matters." *Newsweek* 7 November: 48–54.

Berger, Ellie D. (2009). "Managing Age Discrimination: An Examination of the Techniques Used When Seeking Employment." *Gerontologist, 49* (3), 317–332.

Blau, F. and M. Ferber. (1992). *The Economics of Women, Men and Work.* Englewood Cliffs, NJ: Prentice Hall.

Bodine, A. (2003). "School Uniforms and Discourses on Childhood." *Childhood, 10* (1), 43–63.

Brim, Orville G., Jr. (1968). "Socialization through the Life Cycle." In Orville G. Brim, Jr. and Stanton Wheeler, eds., *Socialization after Childhood: Two Essays* (pp. 3–49). New York: John Wiley.

Brooks, B., J. Jarman, and Robert M. Blackburn. (2003). "Occupational Gender Segregation in Canada, 1981–1996: Overall, Vertical and Horizontal Segregation." *Canadian Review of Sociology and Anthropology, 40* (2), 197–213.

Brym, R. and J. Lie. (2003). *Sociology: Your Compass for a New World.* Toronto: Thomson.

Burgess, R. L. and R. A. Richardson. (1984). "Child Abuse during Adolescence." In R. M. Lerner and N. L. Galambos, eds., *Experiencing Adolescents: A Sourcebook for Parents, Teachers and Teens* (pp. 119–52). New York: Garland.

Buysse, Jo Ann M. and Melissa Sheridan Embser-Herbert. (2004). "Constructions of Gender in Sport: An Analysis of Intercollegiate Media Guide Cover Photographs." *Gender & Society, 18* (1), 66–81.

Chua, Amy. (2011). *Battle Hymn of the Tiger Mother.* New York: Penguin Press.

Clausen, John A (1986). *The Life Course.* Englewood Cliffs, NJ: Prentice Hall.

Cohen, Philip N. (2004). "The Gender Division of Labor: "'Keeping House'" and Occupational Segregation in the United States." *Gender & Society, 18* (2), 239–52.

Coleman, John C. and Leo Hendry. (1990). *The Nature of Adolescence*, 2nd ed. New York: Routledge, Chapman and Hall.

Cooley, Charles Horton. (1902). *Human Nature and the Social Order.* New York: Scribner's.

Corsaro, William A. (1992). "Interpretive Reproduction in Children's Peer Cultures." *Social Psychology Quarterly, 55*, 160–77.

Curtiss, Susan. (1977). *Genie: A Psycholinguistic Study of a Modern Day Wild Child.* New York: Academic Press.

Davies, Bronwyn. (1990). *Frogs and Snails and Feminist Tales.* New York: Pandora Press.

Devine, D. (2002). "Children's Citizenship and the Structuring of Adult-Child Relations in Primary School." *Childhood, 9* (3), 303–20.

Dyson, Lily. (2005). "The Lives of Recent Chinese Immigrant Children in Canadian Society: Values, Aspirations, and Social Experiences." *Canadian Ethnic Studies, 37* (2), 49–66.

Evans, Donald and William W. Falk. (1986). *Learning to be Deaf.* New York: Mouton de Gruyter.

Fox, Bonnie. (1998). "Motherhood, Changing Relationships, and the Reproduction of Gender Inequality." In S. Abbey and A. O'Reilly, eds., *Redefining Motherhood.* Toronto: Second Story Press.

Fox, Bonnie, ed. (2001). *Family Patterns, Gender Relations*, 2nd ed. Toronto: Oxford University Press.

"French Vogue Slammed for Sexy Photos of Preteen." (2011). *CTV News.ca*. On the World Wide Web at http://www.ctvnews.ca/french-vogue-slammed-for-sexy-photos-of-preteen-1.679285 (retrieved 15 July 2012).

Freud, Sigmund. (1962 [1930]). *Civilization and Its Discontents*, James Strachey, trans. New York: Norton.

Freud, Sigmund. (1973 [1915–17]). *Introductory Lectures on Psychoanalysis*, James Strachey, trans., James Strachey and Angela Richards, eds., Harmondsworth, UK: Penguin.

Friedenberg, Edgar Z. (1959). *The Vanishing Adolescent*. Boston: Beacon Press.

Giddens, Anthony. (1991). *Modernity and Self-Identity: Self and Society in the Late Modern Age*. Cambridge, UK: Polity Press.

Giordano, C. Peggy, Stephen A. Cernkovich, and Alfred DeMaris. (1993). "The Family and Peer Relations of Black Adolescents." *Journal of Marriage and the Family, 55* (May), 277–87.

Goffman, Erving. (1961). *Asylums: Essays on the Social Situation of Mental Patients and Other Inmates*. Garden City, NY: Anchor Books.

Gooden, Angela M. and Mark A. Gooden. (2001). "Gender Representation in Notable Children's Picture Books: 1995–1999." *Sex Roles, 45*, 89–101.

Gracey, Harry L. (1967). "Learning the Student Role: Kindergarten as Academic Boot Camp." In D.H. Wrong and H.L. Gracey, eds., *Readings in Introductory Sociology* (pp. 288–99). New York: Macmillan.

Haas, Jack and William Shaffir. (1977). "The Cloak of Competence." *Symbolic Interaction, 1*, 1 (Fall), 71–88.

Haas, Jack and William Shaffir. (1987). *Becoming Doctors: The Adoption of a Cloak of Competence*. Greenwich, CT: JAI Press.

Hamarus, Paivi and Pauli Kaikkonen. (2008). "School Bullying as a Creator of Pupil Peer Pressure." *Educational Research, 50* (4), 333–45.

Handel, Gerald. (1990). "Revising Socialization Theory." *American Sociological Review, 55*, 463–66.

Hebdige, Dick. (1979). *Subculture: The Meaning of Style*. London: Methuen.

Hogan, Dennis P. and Nan Marie Astone. (1986). "Transition to Adulthood." *Annual Review of Sociology, 12*, 109–30.

Kellehear, A. (1984). "Are We a 'Death-Denying' Society? A Sociological Review." *Social Science and Medicine 18* (9), 713–23.

Kirmayer, Laurence, Cori Simpson, and Margaret Cargo. (2003). "Healing Traditions: Culture, Community, and Mental Health Promotion with Canadian Aboriginal Peoples." *Australian Psychiatry, 11*, 15–23.

Kohn, Melvin L., Atsushi Naoi, Carmi Schooler, and Kazimiercz M. Slomczynski. (1990). "Position in the Class Structure and Psychological Functioning in the United States, Japan, and Poland." *American Journal of Sociology, 95*, 964–1008.

Kortenhaus, C. M. and J. Demarest. (1993). "Gender Role Stereotyping in Children's Literature: An Update." *Sex Roles, 28*, 219–32.

Lapidus, Steven. (2006). *To Connect or Not to Connect: The Internet Controversy among Haredi Jewry*. Paper presented at the Annual Meeting of the Canadian Society for Jewish Studies. Toronto, May.

Lareau, A. (1987). "Social Class Differences in Family-School Relationships." *Sociology of Education, 60*, 63–72.

Lawson, David. (1996). "The Brave New World of Work." *The Silhouette* 7 November.

Light, Donald L., Jr. (1980). *Becoming Psychiatrists: The Professional Transformation of Self.* New York: W.W. Norton.

Lightfoot, Cynthia. (1997). *The Culture of Adolescent Risk-Taking*. London: Guilford Press.

Mackie, Marlene. (1991). *Gender Relations in Canada: Further Explorations*. Toronto: Butterworth.

Massoni, Kelley. (2004). "Modeling Work: Occupational Messages in *Seventeen Magazine*." *Gender & Society, 18* (1), 47–65.

Mead, George H. (1934). *Mind, Self, and Society*. Chicago: University of Chicago Press.

Montemurro, Beth. (2005). "Add Men, Don't Stir. Reproducing Traditional Gender Roles in Modern Wedding Showers." *Journal of Contemporary Ethnography, 34* (1), 6–35.

National Film Board of Canada. (2007). *Sexy Inc.: Our Children Under Influence* [film]. Sophie Bissonnette (Writer & Director). Patricia Bergeron (Producer). Yves Bisaillon (Executive Producer).

Newton, Michael. (2002). *Savage Girl and Wild Boys: A History of Feral Children*. London: Faber and Faber.

Patterson, Charlotte J. and Paul D. Hastings. (2007). "Socialization in the Context of Family Diversity. In Joan E. Grusec and Paul D. Hastings, eds., *Handbook of Socialization: Theory and Research* (pp. 328–51). New York: Guilford Press.

Raby, Rebecca. (2005). "Polite, Well-Dressed and on Time: Secondary School Conduct Codes and the Production of Docile Citizens." *Canadian Review of Sociology and Anthropology, 42* (1), 71–91.

Richer, Stephen. (1988). "Equality to Benefit from Schooling: The Issue of Educational Opportunity." In D. Forcese and S. Richer, eds., *Social Issues: Sociological Views of Canada* (pp. 262–86). Toronto: Prentice Hall.

Russell, Rachel and Melissa Tyler. (2002). "Thank Heaven for Little Girls: 'Girl Haven' and the Commercial Context of Feminine Childhood." *Sociology, 36*, 619–37.

Salazar, Lilia P., Shirin M. Schludermann, Edward H. Schludermann, and Cam-Loi Huynh. (2001). "Canadian-Filipino Adolescents Report on Parental Socialization for School Involvement." *Canadian Ethnic Studies, 33* (2), 52–77.

Sebald, H. (1992). *Adolescence: A Social Psychological Analysis*. Englewood Cliffs, NJ: Prentice Hall.

Shepard, Jon M. (1993). *Sociology*, 5th ed. New York: West.

Solomon, Yvette, Jo Warin, Charlie Lewis, and Wendy Langford. (2002). "Intimate Talk between Parents and Their Teenage Children: Democratic Openness or Covert Control?" *Sociology, 36*, 965–83.

South, S. and S. Spitze. (1994). "Housework in Marital and Nonmarital Households." *American Sociological Review, 59*, 327–47.

Statistics Canada. (2011). "Study: Generational Change in Paid and Unpaid Work." *The Daily*. On the World Wide Web at http://www.statcan.gc.ca/daily-quotidien/110712/dq110712c-eng.htm (retrieved 15 July 2012).

Stebbins, Robert A. (1990). *Sociology: The Study of Society*, 2nd ed. New York: Harper and Row.

Steinberg, Stephen. (1981). *The Ethnic Myth: Race, Ethnicity and Class in America*. Boston: Beacon Press.

Stryker, Sheldon. (1980). *Symbolic Interactionism*. Menlo Park, CA: Benjamin/Cummings.

Thorne, B. (1993). *Gender Play: Girls and Boys in School.* New Brunswick, NJ: Rutgers University Press.

Turkle, Sherry. (2011). *Alone Together: Why We Expect More from Technology and Less from Each Other*. New York: Basic Books.

Willis, Paul. (1990). *Common Culture: Symbolic Work at Play in the Everyday Cultures of the Young.* Milton Keynes: Open University Press.

Wolf, Naomi. (1977). *Promiscuities: The Secret Struggles of Womanhood.* New York: Vintage.

Wuthnow, Robert. (1998). *Loose Connections.* Cambridge, MA: Harvard University Press.

Yelaja, Prithi. (2011). "U.K. Riots Reveal Social Media Double Standard." *CBC News* 10 August. On the World Wide Web at http://www.cbc.ca/news/world/story/2011/08/10/social-media-riots.html (retrieved 15 January 2012).

CHAPTER 4

Averett, Susan and Sanders Korenman. (1996). "The Economic Reality of the Beauty Myth." *The Journal of Human Resources, 31* (2), 304–30.

Bagley, Christopher and Kathleen King. (1990). *Child Sexual Abuse: The Search for Healing.* London, UK: Tavistock/Routledge.

Berch, D. B. and B. G. Bender. (1987). "Margins of Sexuality." *Psychology Today* December: 54–57.

Bergen, D. J. and J. E. Williams. (1991). "Sex Stereotypes in the United States Revisited: 1972–1988." *Sex Roles, 24*, 413–23.

Bibby, Reginald W. (1995). *The Bibby Report: Social Trends Canadian Style.* Toronto: Stoddart.

Bibby, Reginald W. (2006). *The Boomer Factor.* Toronto: Bastian Books.

Bibby, Reginald W., Sarah Russell, and Ron Rolheiser. (2009). *The Emerging Millenials.* Lethbridge, AB: Project Canada Books.

Bleier, Ruth. (1984). *Science and Gender: A Critique of Biology and Its Theories on Women.* New York: Pergamon.

Blum, Deborah. (1997). *Sex on the Brain: The Biological Differences between Men and Women.* New York: Penguin Books.

Broverman, I. K., S. R. Vogel, D. M. Broverman, F. E. Clarkson, and P. S. Rosenkratz. (1972). "Sex-Role Stereotypes: A Current Appraisal." *Journal of Social Issues, 28*, 59–78.

Buss, D. M. (1994). *The Evolution of Desire.* New York: Basic Books.

Buss, D. M. (1995a). "Evolutionary Psychology: A New Paradigm for Psychological Science." *Psychological Inquiry, 6*, 1–30.

Buss, D. M. (1995b). "Psychological Sex Differences: Origins through Sexual Selection." *American Psychologist, 50*, 164–68.

Buss, D. M. (1998). "The Psychology of Human Mate Selection: Exploring the Complexity of the Strategic Repertoire." In C. Crawford and D. L. Krebs, eds., *Handbook of Evolutionary Psychology: Ideas, Issues and Applications* (pp. 405–29). Mahwah, NJ: Erlbaum.

Buss, D. M., M. Abbott, A. Angleitner, A. Asherian, A. Biaggio, A. Blanco-Villasenor, et al. (1990). "International Perspectives in Selecting Mates: A Study of 37 Cultures." *Journal of Cross-Cultural Psychology, 21* (1), 5–47.

"Canadian Public Opinion Polls on Same-Sex Marriage: 2005-JAN-01 to the Present." (2005). On the World Wide Web at http://www religioustolerance.org/homssmpoll05.htm (retrieved 10 December 2005).

Caplan, Paula J. and Jeremy B. Caplan. (1999). *Thinking Critically about Research on Sex and Gender*, 2nd ed. New York: Longman.

Chodorow, Nancy. (1997). "The Psychodynamics of the Family." In Linda Nicholson, ed., *The Second Wave: A Reader in Feminist Theory* (pp. 181–97). New York: Routledge.

Colapinto, John. (1997). "The True Story of John/Joan." *Rolling Stone* 11 December: 54–73, 92–97.

Colapinto, John. (2001). *As Nature Made Him: The Boy Who Was Raised as a Girl.* New York: Perennial.

Condry, J. and S. Condry. (1976). "Sex Differences: A Study of the Eye of the Beholder." *Child Development, 47*, 812–19.

Coontz, Stephanie and Peta Henderson, eds. (1986). *Women's Work, Men's Property: The Origins of Gender and Class.* London: Verso.

Creighton, Sarah and Catherine Minto. (2001). "Managing Intersex." *British Medical Journal, 323* (7324), 1264–65.

Davis, Simon. (1990). "Men as Success Objects and Women as Sex Objects: A Study of Personal Advertisements." *Sex Roles, 23*, 43–50.

Davis, T., G. Peck, and J. Stormant. (1993). "Acquaintance Rape and the High School Student." *Journal of Adolescent Health, 14*, 220–24.

Dawkins, Richard. (1976). *The Selfish Gene.* London: Oxford University Press.

DeKeseredy, Walter S. and M. D. Schwartz. (1998). *Woman Abuse on Campus: Results from the Canadian National Survey.* Thousand Oaks, CA: Sage.

Duffy, Ann. (1998). "The Feminist Challenge: Knowing and Ending the Violence." In Nancy Mandell, ed., *Feminist Issues: Race, Class, and Sexuality* (pp. 132–59). Scarborough, ON: Prentice Hall Allyn & Bacon Canada.

Durex. (2005). "Give and Receive: 2005 Global Sex Survey Results." On the World Wide Web at http://www.durex.com/cm/gss2005result.pdf (retrieved 10 December 2005).

Durex. (2012). "Sexual Well-Being Global Survey, 07/08." On the World Wide Web at http://www.durex.com/en-CA/SexualWellbeingSurvey/pages/default.aspx (retrieved 20 February 2012).

Dworkin, Andrea. (1981). *Pornography: Men Possessing Women.* New York: Penguin.

Dworkin, Andrea. (1987). "Intercourse." Chapter 7 in *Occupation/Collaboration.* On the World Wide Web at http://www.nostatusquo.com/ACLU/dworkin/IntercourseI.html (retrieved 9 December 2011).

Eagley, Alice H. and Wendy Wood. (1999). "The Origins of Sex Differences in Human Behavior. Evolved Dispositions versus Social Roles." *American Psychologist, 54*, 408–23.

Eccles, J. S., J. E. Jacobs, and R. D. Harold. (1990). "Gender-Role Stereotypes, Expectancy Effects and Parents' Socialization of Gender Differences." *Journal of Social Issues, 46*, 183–201.

Eichler, Margrit. (1980). *The Double Standard.* London: Croom Helm.

Eisler, Riane. (1987). *The Chalice and the Blade.* New York: HarperCollins.

Elkin, F. and G. Handel. (1989). *The Child and Society: The Process of Socialization*, 5th ed. New York: Random House.

Ellis, Lee, Brian Robb, and Donald Burke. (2005). "Sexual Orientation in United States and Canadian College Students." *Archives of Sexual Behavior, 34*, 569–81.

Feiring, C. and M. Lewis. (1979). "Sex and Age Differences in Young Children's Reactions to Frustration: A Further Look at the Goldberg and Lewis Subjects." *Child Development, 50*, 848–53.

Fischtein, Dayna S., Edward S. Herold, and Serge Desmarais. (2007). "How Much Does Gender Explain in Sexual Attitudes and Behaviors? A Survey of Canadian Adults." *Archives of Sexual Behavior, 36*, 451–61.

Fitzgerald, Louise F. (1993). "Sexual Harassment against Women in the Workplace." *American Psychologist, 48*, 1070–76.

Freud, Sigmund. (1977 [1905]). *On Sexuality*, James Strachey, trans., Angela Richards, ed., Vol. 7, Pelican Freud Library. Harmondsworth, UK: Penguin Books.

Gadd, Jane. (1997). "More Boys Physically Abused than Girls." *Globe and Mail* 9 July: A1, A6.

Garner, David M. (1997). "The 1997 Body Image Survey Results." *Psychology Today, 30* (January/February): 30–44, 74–80, 84.

Gimbutas, Marija. (1982). *Goddesses and Gods of Old Europe: 6500–3500 B.C. Myths and Cult Images*. Berkeley and Los Angeles: University of California Press.

Goldberg, S. and M. Lewis. (1969). "Play Behavior in the Year-Old Infant: Early Sex Differences." *Child Development, 40*, 21–31.

Green, Adam Isaiah. (2007). "Queer Theory and Sociology: Locating the Subject and the Self in Sexuality Studies." *Sociological Theory 25*, 26–45.

Grescoe, P. (1996). *The Merchants of Venus: Inside Harlequin and the Empire of Romance*. Vancouver: Raincoast.

Gruber, J. E. (1997). "An Epidemiology of Sexual Harassment: Evidence from North America and Europe." In W. O'Donohue, ed., *Sexual Harassment: Theory, Research and Treatment* (pp. 84–98). Boston: Allyn and Bacon.

Gunderson, Elizabeth A., Gerardo Ramirez, Susan C. Levine, and Sian L. Beilock. (2012). "The Role of Parents and Teachers in the Development of Gender-Related Math Attitudes." *Sex Roles*, 66, 153–66.

Hamer, D. and P. F. Copeland. (1996). *The Science of Desire: The Search for the Gay Gene and the Biology of Behavior*. New York: Touchstone Books.

Hatfield, Elaine. (1995). "What Do Women and Men Want from Love and Sex?" In E.D. Nelson and B.W. Robinson, eds., *Gender in the 1990s: Images, Realities, and Issues* (pp. 257–75). Toronto: Nelson Canada.

Hesse-Biber, Sharlene. (1996). *Am I Thin Enough Yet? The Cult of Thinness and the Commercialization of Identity*. New York: Oxford University Press.

Hobart, Charles. (1996). "Intimacy and Family Life: Sexuality, Cohabitation, and Marriage." In Maureen Baker, ed., *Families: Changing Trends in Canada* (pp. 143–73). Toronto: McGraw-Hill Ryerson.

Hughes, Fergus P. (1995). *Children, Play, and Development*, 2nd ed. Boston: Allyn and Bacon.

Human Rights Watch. (1995). *The Human Rights Watch Global Report on Women's Human Rights*. New York: Human Rights Watch.

Jeffreys, Sheila. (1990). "Heterosexuality and the Desire for Gender." In Diane Richardson, ed., *Theorising Heterosexuality* (pp. 75–90). Buckingham, UK: Open University Press.

Jensen, Margaret Ann. (1984). *Love's Sweet Return: The Harlequin Story*. Toronto: Women's Press.

Kerig, Patricia K., Philip A. Cowan, and Carolyn Pape Cowan. (1993). "Marital Quality and Gender Differences in Parent-Child Interaction." *Developmental Psychology, 29*, 931–39.

Kitzinger, Celia and Sue Wilkinson. (1994). "Problematizing Pleasure: Radical Feminist Deconstructions of Sexuality and Power." In H. L. Radtke and H. J. Stam, eds., *Power/Gender: Social Relations in Theory and Practice*. London: Sage.

Koff, Elissa and Amy Benavage. (1998). "Breast Size Perception and Satisfaction, Body Image and Psychological Functioning in Caucasian and Asian American College Women." *Sex Roles, 38* (7/8), 655–73.

Koss, Mary P., L. A. Goodman, A. Browne, L.F. Fitzgerald, G. P. Keita, and N. F. Russo. (1994). *No Safe Haven: Male Violence against Women at Home, at Work, and in the Community*. Washington, DC: American Psychological Association.

Lenton, Rhonda, Michael D. Smith, John Fox, and Norman Morra. (1999). "Sexual Harassment in Public Places: Experiences of Canadian Women." *Canadian Review of Sociology and Anthropology, 36*, 517–40.

Lightfoot-Klein, Hanny, Cheryl Chase, Tim Hammond, and Ronald Goldman. (2000). "Genital Surgery on Children below the Age of Consent." In Lenore T. Szuchman and Frank Muscarella, eds., *Psychological Perspectives on Human Sexuality* (pp. 440–49). New York: John Wiley and Sons.

Lips, H. M. (1993). *Sex and Gender: An Introduction*, 2nd ed. Mountain View, CA: Mayfield.

Lisak, David. (1992). "Sexual Aggression, Masculinity, and Fathers." *Signs, 16*, 238–62.

MacDonald, K. and R. D. Parke. (1986). "Parent-Child Physical Play: The Effects of Sex and Age on Children and Parents." *Sex Roles, 15*, 367–78.

Mackay, Judith. (2000). *The Penguin Atlas of Human Sexual Behavior*. New York: Penguin.

Mackinnon, Catharine A. (1997). "Sexuality." In Linda Nicholson, ed., *The Second Wave: A Reader in Feminist Theory* (pp. 158–80). New York and London: Routledge.

Matrix, C. ed. (1996). *Tales from the Clit*. Edinburgh, UK: AK Press.

Mead, Margaret. (1935). *Sex and Temperament in Three Primitive Societies*. New York: Dell.

Michael, Robert T., John H. Gagnon, Edward O. Laumann, and Gina Kolata. (1994). *Sex in America: A Survey*. Boston: Little, Brown.

Milligan, Shelly. (2011). "Criminal Harassment in Canada, 2009." *Juristat* 3 March. On the World Wide Web at http://www.statcan.gc.ca/pub/85–005-x/2011001/article/11407-eng.pdf (retrieved 20 February 2012).

Nelson, E. D. and Barrie W. Robinson. (1999). *Gender in Canada*. Scarborough, ON: Prentice Hall Allyn & Bacon Canada.

Nolen, Stephanie. (1999). "Gender: The Third Way." *Globe and Mail* 25 September: D1, D4.

Peele, Stanton and Richard De Grandpre. (1995). "My Genes Made Me Do It." *Psychology Today*, 50–68.

Pipher, M. (1994). *Reviving Ophelia: Saving the Selves of Adolescent Girls*. New York: Ballantine.

Power, Nina. (2009). *One-Dimensional Woman*. Winchester, UK: Zero Books.

Pryor, John B., J. L. Giedd, and K. B. Williams. (1995). "A Social Psychological Model for Predicting Sexual Harassment." *Journal of Social Issues, 51*, 69–84.

Raag, Tarja and Christine L. Rackliff. (1998). "Preschoolers' Awareness of Social Expectations of Gender: Relationships to Toy Choices." *Sex Roles, 38*, 685–700.

Reiss, I. (1986). *Journey into Sexuality: An Exploratory Voyage*. Englewood Cliffs, NJ: Prentice Hall.

Rich, Adrienne. (1996). "Compulsory Heterosexuality and Lesbian Existence." In Stevi Jackson and Sue Scott, eds., *Feminism and Sexuality: A Reader* (pp. 130–43). New York: Columbia University Press.

Ropelato, Jerry. (n.d.) "Internet Pornography Statistics." On the World Wide Web at http://internet-filter-review.toptenreviews.com/internet-pornography-statistics.html (retrieved 9 December 2011).

Rosenkrantz, P., S. R. Vogel, H. Bee, I. K. Broverman, and D. M. Broverman. (1968). "Sex-Role Stereotypes and Self-Concepts in College Students." *Journal of Consulting and Clinical Psychology, 32*, 287–95.

Rotermann, Michele. (2008). "Trends in Teen Sexual Behavior and Condom Use." *Health Reports, 19* (3), 1–5.

Rubin, Gayle. (1993). "Thinking Sex: Notes for a Radical Theory of the Politics of Sexuality." In Henry Abelove, Michèle Aina Barale, and David M. Halperin, eds., *The Lesbian and Gay Studies Reader* (pp. 3–34). London: Routledge.

Rubin, J. Z., F. J. Provenzano, and Z. Lurra. (1974). "The Eye of the Beholder." *American Journal of Orthopsychiatry, 44*, 512–19.

Ryan, Kathryn M. and Jeanne Kanjorski. (1998). "The Enjoyment of Sexist Humor, Rape Attitudes and Relationship Aggression in College Students." *Sex Roles, 38*, 743–56.

"Same-Sex Marriage in Canada: Public Opinion Polls from 2006 to Now." (2008). On the World Wide Web at http://www.religioustolerance.org/homssmpoll06.htm (retrieved 6 December 2008).

Sanday, Peggy. (1981). *Female Power and Male Dominance.* Cambridge, UK: Cambridge University Press.

Saxton, Lloyd. (1990). *The Individual, Marriage, and the Family*, 7th ed. Belmont, CA: Wadsworth.

Shorter, Edward. (1997). *A History of Psychiatry.* New York: John Wiley and Sons.

Statistics Canada. (2006). "Prevalence and Severity of Violence against Women." On the World Wide Web at http://wwwstatcan.gc.ca/pub/85–570-x/2006001/findings-resultats/4144393-eng.htm (retrieved 6 December 2008).

Statistics Canada. (2011a). "Family Violence in Canada: A Statistical Profile." On the World Wide Web at http://www.statcan.gc.ca/pub/85–224-x/85–224-x2010000-eng.pdf (retrieved 20 February 2012).

Statistics Canada. (2011b). "Statistics Canada, 2006 Census of Population." Statistics Canada. Catalogue No. 97-553-XCB2006024. On the World Wide Web at http://www12.statcan.gc.ca/census-recensement/2006/dp-pd/tbt/Rp-eng.cfm?TABID=1&LANG=E&A=R&APATH=3&DETAIL=0&DIM=2&FL=A&FREE=0&GC=01&GID=614135&GK=1&GRP=1&O=D&PID=89034&PRID=0&PTYPE=88971,97154&S=0&SHOWALL=0&SUB=0&Temporal=2006&THEME=68&VID=12749&VNAMEE=&VNAMEF=&D1=0&D2=0&D3=0&D4=0&D5=0&D6=0 (retrieved 20 February 2012).

Steinem, G. (1994). *Moving beyond Words.* New York: Simon and Schuster.

Straus, Murray. (1995). "Trends in Cultural Norms and Rates of Partner Violence." In Sandra M. Stith and Murray A. Straus, eds., *Understanding Partner Violence: Prevalence, Causes, Consequences and Solutions* (pp. 30–33). Minneapolis, MN: National Council on Family Relations.

Sutfin, Erin L., Megan Fulcher, Ryan P. Bowles, and Charlotte J. Patterson. (2008). "How Lesbian and Heterosexual Parents Convey Attitudes about Gender to Their Children: The Role of Gendered Environments." *Sex Roles* 58, 501–13.

Tavris, Carol. (1992). *The Mismeasure of Woman: Why Women Are Not the Better Sex, the Inferior Sex or the Opposite Sex.* New York: Touchstone.

Thompson, Linda. (1991). "Family Work: Women's Sense of Fairness." *Journal of Family Issues, 12*, 181–96.

Twenge, Jean M. (1997). "Changes in Masculine and Feminine Traits over Time: A Meta-analysis." *Sex Roles, 36*, 305–25.

Udry, J. R. (1971). *The Social Context of Marriage*, 2nd ed. Philadelphia, PA: J. B. Lippincott.

Vrangalova, Zhana and Ritch C. Savin-Williams. (2012). "Mostly Heterosexual and Mostly Gay/Lesbian: Evidence for New Sexual Orientation Identities." *Archives of Sexual Behavior.* On the World Wide Web at http://rd.springer.com/article/10.1007/s10508-012-9921-y#page-1 (retrieved 20 February 2012).

Walters, Vivienne. (1992). "Women's Views of Their Main Health Problems." *Canadian Journal of Public Health, 83* (5), 371–74.

Weeks, Jeffrey. (1986). *Sexuality.* London: Routledge.

Welsh, Sandy and A. Nierobisz. (1997). "How Prevalent Is Sexual Harassment? A Research Note on Measuring Sexual Harassment in Canada." *Canadian Journal of Sociology, 22*, 505–22.

Welsh, Sandy. (1999). "Gender and Sexual Harassment." *Annual Review of Sociology, 25*, 169–90.

Williams, J. E. and D. L. Best. (1982). *Measuring Sex Stereotypes: A Thirty Nation Study.* Beverley Hills, CA: Sage Publications.

Williams, J. E. and S. M. Bennett. (1975). "The Definition of Sex Stereotypes via the Adjective Check List." *Sex Roles, 1*, 327–37.

Wilson, Edward O. (1975). *Sociobiology.* Cambridge, MA: Harvard University Press.

Wilson, Edward O. (1978). *On Human Nature.* Cambridge, MA: Harvard University Press.

Wilson, Margo and Martin Daly. (1998). "Lethal and Nonlethal Violence against Wives and the Evolutionary Psychology of Male Sexual Proprietariness." In R. Emerson Dobash and Russell P. Dobash, eds., *Rethinking Violence against Women* (pp. 199–230). Thousand Oaks, CA: Sage Publications.

Wolf, Naomi. (1991). *The Beauty Myth.* Toronto: Vintage Books.

CHAPTER 5

Albrechtslund, Anders. (2008). "Online Social Networking as Participatory Surveillance." *First Monday, 13* (3). On the World Wide Web at http://firstmonday.org/htbin/cgiwrap/bin/ojs/index.php/fm/article/view/2142/1949 (retrieved 22 December 2008).

Anderson, J. and L. Rainie. (2010). "The Future of the Internet IV." *Pew Internet and American Life Project.* On the World Wide Web at http://pewinternet.org/Reports/2010/Future-of-the-Internet-IV/Overview.aspx?r=1 (retrieved 21 December 2011).

Banks, S. and J. Humphreys. (2008). "The Labour of User Co-creators: Emergent Social Network Markets?" *Convergence, 14* (4), 401–18.

BCE Inc. (2010). "2010 Annual Report." On the World Wide Web at http://www.bce.ca/data/documents/BCE_annual_2010_en.pdf (retrieved 21 December 2011).

Bertelsman. (2010). "The Annual Report: App-ward Bound." On the World Wide Web at http://www.bertelsmann.com/bertelsmann_corp/wms41/customers/bmcorp/pdf/BAG_AR_2010_english.pdf (retrieved 21 December 2011).

"The Big Ten." (2002). *The Nation* 7–14 July. On the World Wide Web at http://www.thenation.com/special/bigten.html (retrieved 12 August 2006).

Boyd, D. (2007). "Why Youth (Heart) Social Network Sites: The Role of Networked Publics in Teenage Social Life." In David Buckingham, ed., *Youth, Identity and Digital Media Volume* (pp. 119–42). MacArthur Foundation Series on Digital Learning. Cambridge, MA: MIT Press. On the World Wide Web at http://www.danah.org/papers/WhyYouthHeart. pdf (retrieved 22 December 2008).

Boyd, D. and H. Jenkins. (2006). "Discussion: MySpace and Deleting Online Predators Act (DOPA)." *MIT Tech Talk* 26 May. On the World Wide Web at http://www.danah.org /papers/MySpaceDOPA.html (retrieved 22 December 2008).

Buckingham, D. (1998). "Children and Television: A Critical Overview of Research." In R. Dickinson, R. Harindranath, and O. Linné, eds., *Approaches to Audiences: A Reader* (pp. 131–45). London: Arnold.

Canadian Radio-television and Telecommunications Commission. (2011a). "Communications Monitoring Report, 2011 (Table 4.3.5)". On the World Wide Web at http://crtc.gc.ca/eng /publications/reports/PolicyMonitoring/2011/cmr4.htm#n3 (retrieved 21 December 2011).

Canadian Radio-television and Telecommunications Commission. (2011b). "Communications Monitoring Report, 2011." On the World Wide Web at http://crtc.gc.ca/eng/publications /reports/PolicyMonitoring/2011/cmr4.htm#toc (retrieved 15 December 2011).

Candussi, D. and J. Winters. (1988). "Monopoly and Content in Winnipeg." In R. Picard, J. P. Winter, M. McCombs, and S. Lacy, eds., *Press Concentration and Monopoly: New Perspectives on Newspaper Ownership and Operation* (pp. 139–45). Norwood, NJ: Ablex.

Carroll, W. and R. Ratner. (1999). "Media Strategies and Political Projects: A Comparative Study of Social Movements." *Canadian Journal of Sociology, 24* (1), 1–34.

Collins, R. (1990). *Culture, Communication, and National Identity: The Case of Canadian Television.* Toronto: University of Toronto Press.

Comcast Corporation. (2010). "2010 Annual Report on Form 10K." On the World Wide Web at http:// www.cmcsk.com/common/download/sec. cfm?companyid=CMCSA&fid=1193125-11-47243&cik=1166691 (retrieved 21 December 2011).

Dickinson, P. and J. Ellison. (2000). *Plugging In: the Increase of Household Internet Use Continues into 1999.* Ottawa: Ministry of Industry, Connectedness Series. Catalogue No. 56F0004MIE.

Ellis, D. (1992). *Split Screens: Home Entertainment and the New Technologies.* Toronto: Friends of Canadian Broadcasting.

Ericson, R., P. Baranek, and J. Chan. (1989). *Negotiating Control: A Study of News Sources.* Toronto: University of Toronto Press.

Fiske, J. (1987). *Television Culture.* London: Methuen.

Freedman, J. L. (2002). *Media Violence and its Effect on Aggression: Assessing the Scientific Evidence.* Toronto: University of Toronto Press.

Friedrich-Cofer, L. and A. Huston. (1986). "Television Violence and Aggression: The Debate Continues." *Psychological Bulletin, 100* (3), 364–71.

Geen, R. and S. Thomas. (1986). "The Immediate Effects of Media Violence on Behavior." *Journal of Social Issues, 42* (3), 7–27.

Gerbner, George, Larry Gross, Michael Morgan, and Nancy Signorielli. (1994). "Growing Up with Television: The Cultivation Perspective." In J. Bryant and D. Zillmann, eds., *Media Effects: Advances in Theory and Research* (pp. 17–41). Hillsdale, NJ: Lawrence Erlbaum Associates.

Ghosh, Shauvik. (2011). "Internet Penetration Expected to Rise with 3G Services Roll-Out." *Livemint.* On the World Wide Web at http://www.livemint.com/2011/02/23190032/Internet -penetration-expected.html?atype=tp (retrieved 30 July 2012).

Gillett, J. (2003). "The Challenges of Institutionalization for AIDS Media Activism." *Media, Culture & Society, 25* (5), 607–24.

Gitlin, T. (1980). *The Whole World Is Watching.* Berkeley, CA: University of California Press.

Gladwell, M. (2010). "Small Change: Why the Revolution Will Not Be Tweeted." *New Yorker* 4 October. On the World Wide Web at http://www.newyorker.com /reporting/2010/10/04/101004fa_fact_gladwell (retrieved 21 December 2011).

Goffman, E. (1974). *Frame Analysis.* Philadelphia, PA: University of Pennsylvania Press.

Gosselin, A, J. DeGuise, G. Pacquette, and L. Benoit. (1997). "Violence on Canadian Television and Some of Its Cognitive Effects." *Canadian Journal of Communication, 22,* 143–60.

Greenberg, J. (2006). *The Media and Mental Health: An Analysis of Local News Coverage.* Ottawa: Canadian Mental Health Association.

Greenberg, J. and H. Gilberds. (2011). "Alternative Media." In W. Straw, S. Fabriele, and I. Wagman eds., *Intersections of Media and Communications* (pp. 197–216). Toronto: Emond Montgomery.

Greenberg, J. and M. MacAuley. (2009). "NPO 2.0?: Exploring the Web Presence of Nonprofit Environmental Organizations in Canada." *Global Media Journal: Canadian Edition, 2* (1), 63–88.

Hackett, R. (1991). *News and Dissent: The Press and the Politics of Peace in Canada.* Norwood, NJ: Ablex.

Hall, S. (1980). "Encoding/Decoding." In S. Hall, D. Hobson, A. Lowe and P. Willis, eds., *Culture, Media, Language: Working Papers in Cultural Studies, 1972–79* (pp. 128–138). London: Hutchinson.

Harris, J. L., M. B. Schwartz, and K. D. Brownell. (2010). "Fast Food Facts: Evaluating Fast Food Nutrition and Marketing to Youth." Rudd Centre for Food Policy and Obesity. On the World Wide Web at http://www.fastfoodmarketing.org /media/FastFoodFACTS_Report.pdf (retrieved July 30, 2012).

Haskell, D. (2010). "SunTV News a Move in the Right Direction." *London Free Press* 28 June. On the World Wide Web at http: //www.lfpress.com/comment/columnists/2010/06/28/14551106 .html (retrieved 20 December 2011).

Hembrey, J. (2011). "Canadian Youth Increasingly Aware of Online Privacy." *CBC News Canada* 30 August. On the World Wide Web at http://www.cbc.ca/news/canada /story/2011/08/30/f-social-media-teenagers.html (retrieved 31 December 2011).

Herman, E. and N. Chomsky. (1988). *Manufacturing Consent: The Political Economy of the Mass Media.* New York: Pantheon.

Hilts, M. (2008). "Internet Dependency, Motivations for Internet Use, and Their Effect on Work Productivity: The 21st Century Addiction." ETD Thesis. On the World Wide Web at http: //hdl.handle.net/1850/6920 (retrieved 22 December 2008).

Horkheimer, M. and T. Adorno. (1972 [1947]). *Dialectic of Enlightenment,* John Cumming, trans. New York: Continuum Books.

Huesmann, L. and N. Malamuth. (1986). "Media Violence and Anti-Social Behavior: An Overview." *Journal of Social Issues, 42* (3), 1–6.

Idate. (2009). *DigiWorld Yearbook, 2009*. Montpellier, France: Idate.

Innis, H. (1951). *The Bias of Communication*. Toronto: University of Toronto Press.

International Telecommunication Union. (2011). "Fixed Broadband Subscriptions, 2010." On the World Wide Web at http://www.itu.int/ITU-D/ict/statistics/material/excel/2010/FixedBroadbandInternetSubscriptions_00–10.xls (retrieved 21 December 2011).

Internet World Stats. (2008). "Internet Usage Statistics." On the World Wide Web at http://www Internetworldstats.com/stats.htm (retrieved 22 December 2008).

Internet World Stats. (2011). "Internet Usage Statistics." On the World Wide Web at http://www.internetworldstats.com/stats.htm (retrieved 21 December 2011).

Ivory, J. D. and T. F. Waddell. (n.d.). "Do Violent Video Games Produce Violent Children?" In J. G. Greenberg and C. Elliott, eds., *Communication in Question: Competing Perspectives on Controversial Issues in Communication Studies*, 2nd ed. Toronto: Nelson.

Kahn, R. and D. Kellner. (2005). "Oppositional Politics and the Internet: A Critical/Reconstructive Approach." *Cultural Politics, 1* (1), 75–100.

Kaiser Family Foundation. (2010). "Generation M2: Media in the Lives of 8- to 18-Year-Olds." On the World Wide Web at http://www.kff.org/entmedia/upload/8010.pdf (retrieved 21 December 2011).

Kann, M., J. Berry, C. Grant, C., and P. Zager. (2007). "The Internet and Youth Political Participation." *First Monday, 12* (8). On the World Wide Web at http://firstmonday.org/htbin/cgiwrap/bin/ojs/index.php/fm/article/view/1977/1852 (retrieved 22 December 2008).

Klapper, J. (1960). *The Effects of Mass Communication*. Glencoe, Il: Free Press.

Knight, G. (1982). "News and Ideology." *Canadian Journal of Communication, 8* (4), 15–41.

Knight, G. (1998). "Hegemony, the Media, and New Right Politics: Ontario in the Late 1990s." *Critical Sociology, 24* (1/2), 105–29.

Lee, A. (2011). "Sean Power Tracks down Stolen Laptop Using Twitter, Prey from Hundreds of Miles Away." *Huffington Post* 14 May. On the World Wide Web at http://www.huffingtonpost.com/2011/05/14/sean-power-prey-stolen-laptop-twitter_n_861895.html (retrieved 21 December 2011).

Lenhart, A. and M. Madden. (2007). "Teens, Privacy and Online Social Networks: How Teens Manage Their Online Identities and Personal Information in the Age of MySpace." Pew Internet and American Life Project. On the World Wide Web at http://www.PewInternet.org/PPF/r/211/report_display.asp (retrieved 22 December 2008).

Lewis, B. (2007). "Should the Internet be Used to Promote Healthy Living?" *The Lancet, 370* (9603), 1891–92.

Livingstone, S. (2005). "Assessing the Research Base for the Policy Debate over the Effects of Food Advertising to Children." *International Journal of Advertising, 24* (3), 273–96.

Marwick, A. (2008). "To Catch a Predator? The MySpace Moral Panic." *First Monday, 13* (6). On the World Wide Web at http://firstmonday.org/htbin/cgiwrap/bin/ojs/index.php/fm/article/view/2152/1966 (retrieved 22 December 2008).

McChesney, R. (1996). "The Global Struggle for Communication." *The Monthly Review, 48* (2), 1.

McCombs, M. (1988). "Concentration, Monopoly and Content." In R. Picard, J. Winter, M. McCombs, and S. Lacy, eds., *Press Concentration and Monopoly: New Perspectives on Newspaper Ownership and Operation* (pp. 129–37). Norwood, NJ: Ablex.

McCormack, T. (1994). "Codes, Ratings and Rights." *Institute for Social Research Newsletter, 9* (1).

McLuhan, M. (1964). *Understanding Media: The Extensions of Man*. New York: Mentor Books.

Melanson, M. (2012). "What Glee Means for Twitter & Television." *ReadWriteWeb* blog 19 January. On the World Wide Web at http://www.readwriteweb.com/archives/what_glee_means_for_twitter_television.php (retrieved 20 January 2012).

Merchant, M. Raina, Stacy Elmer, and Nicole Lurie. (2011). "Integrating Social Media into Emergency Preparedness Efforts." *New England Journal of Medicine, 365*, 289–91. On the World Wide Web at http://www.nejm.org/doi/full/10.1056/NEJMp1103591 (retrieved 21 December 2011).

Miljan, L. and B. Cooper. (2003). *Hidden Agendas: How Journalists Influence the News*. Vancouver: UBC Press.

Moreno, M. A., M. R. Parks, F. J. Zimmerman, T. E. Brito, and D. A. Christakis. (2009). "Display of Health Risk Behaviors on MySpace by Adolescents." *Archives of Pediatrics & Adolescent Medicine, 163* (1), 27–34.

Morley, D. (1986). *Family Television: Cultural Power and Domestic Leisure*. London: Comedia.

Morley, D. (2000). *Home Territories: Media, Mobility and Identity*. New York: Routledge.

Morozov, E. (2011). *The Net Delusion: The Dark Side of Internet Freedom*. New York: Perseus.

National Endowment for the Arts. (2007). "To Read or Not to Read: A Question of National Consequence." Research Report No. 47. On the World Wide Web at http://www.nea.gov/research/ToRead.pdf (retrieved 22 December 2008).

National Media Archive. (1993). "Immigration 1: The Human Interest Story." *On Balance, 6* (3), 1–8. Vancouver: The Fraser Institute.

Network Wizards. (2011). "Data on Internet Activity Worldwide (Hostcount)." On the World Wide Web at http://web.mclink.it/MC8216/data/data1.htm (retrieved 21 December 2011).

News Corporation. (2010). "Annual Report 2010." On the World Wide Web at http://www.newscorp.com/Report2010/AR2010.pdf (retrieved 21 December 2011).

O'Reilly, T. (2005). "What Is Web 2.0?" *O'Reilly Network* 30 September. On the World Wide Web at http://www.oreillynet.com/pub/a/oreilly/tim/news/2005/09/30/what-is-web-20.html (retrieved 22 December 2008).

Parenti, M. (2004). "Methods of Media Manipulation." In C. Jensen, ed., *20 Years of Censored News* (pp. 27–32). New York: Seven Stories Press.

Partsinevelos, K. (2011). "Social Media Risks Desensitizing Us to Others' Tragedies." *Calgary Herald* 8 January. On the World Wide Web at http://www.calgaryherald.com/technology/Social+media+risks+desensitizing+others+tragedies/5963463/story.html?id=5963463 (retrieved 20 January 2012).

Perse, E. M. (2001). *Media Effects and Society*. Mahwah, NJ: Lawrence Erlbaum Associates, Publishers.

Press Information Bureau, Government of India. (2011). "Indian Telecom Sector Growth: an International Success Story." On the World Wide Web at http://pib.nic.in/newsite/erelease.aspx?relid=79183 (retrieved 31 December 2011).

PricewaterhouseCoopers. (2003). *Global Enterntainment and Media Outlook.* Toronto: PwC.

PricewaterhouseCoopers. (2009). *Global Enterntainment and Media Outlook.* Toronto: PwC.

Quebecor. (2010). "2010 Activity Report." On the World Wide Web at http://www.myvirtualpaper.com/doc/Edition-sur-mesure/annualreporten2010/2011052501/ (retrieved 21 December 2011).

Rogers Communications Inc. (2010). "2010 Annual Report." On the World Wide Web at http://www.rogers.com/cms/investor_relations/annual_html/2010/HTML2/default.htm (retrieved 21 December 2011).

Shaw. (2010). "Annual Report 2010." On the World Wide Web at http://www.shaw.ca/uploadedFiles/Corporate/Investors/Financial_Reports/SCIAR10.pdf (retrieved 21 December 2011).

Statistics Canada. (2008a). "Canadian Internet Use Survey—Internet Use by Location of Access, Sex and Age Group, every Two Years." CANSIM Table 358-0124. On the World Wide Web using E-STAT at http://estat.statcan.ca/cgi-win/cnsmcgi.exe?Lang=E&ESTATFile=EStat\English\CII_1_E.htm&RootDir=ESTAT/ (retrieved 22 December 2008).

Statistics Canada. (2008b). "Canadian Internet Use Survey—Internet Use at Home by Internet Activity, Urban or Rural Distribution, every Two Years." CANSIM Table 358–1030. On the World Wide Web at http://cansim2.statcan.gc.ca/cgi-win/cnsmcgi.exe?Lang=E&RootDir=CII/&ResultTemplate=CII/CII&Array_Pick=1&ArrayId=3580126 (retrieved 22 December 2008).

Statistics Canada. (2010). "Internet Use by Individuals by Selected Characteristics." On the World Wide Web at http://www40.statcan.gc.ca/l01/cst01/comm35a-eng.htm (retrieved 21 December 2011).

Statistics Canada. (2011a). "Canadian Internet Use Survey." *The Daily* 25 May. On the World Wide Web at http://www.statcan.gc.ca/daily-quotidien/110525/dq110525b-eng.htm (retrieved 20 December 2011).

Statistics Canada. (2011b). "Culture, Goods, Trade: Data Tables, 2003 to 2010." Catalogue No. 87-007-X. On the World Wide Web at http://www.statcan.gc.ca/pub/87-007-x/87-007-x2011001-eng.pdf (retrieved 21 December 2011).

Statistics Canada. (2011c). *Canada Year Book 2011.* Catalogue No. 11-402-X. On the World Wide Web at http://www.statcan.gc.ca/pub/11-402-x/2011000/pdf/information-eng.pdf (retrieved 15 July 2012).

Taras, D. (1990). *The Newsmakers: The Media's Influence on Canadian Politics.* Scarborough, ON: Nelson.

Time Warner. (2011). "10-K, Annual Report Pursuant to Sections 13 and 15(d)." On the World Wide Web at http://phx.corporate-ir.net/External.File?item=UGFyZW50SUQ9NDE5Njk3fENoaWxkSUQ9NDMzMDEwfFR5cGU9MQ==&t=1 (retrieved 21 December 2011).

Tomlinson, J. (1997). "Cultural Globalization and Cultural Imperialism." In A. Mohammadi, ed., *International Communication and Globalization* (pp. 170–90). London: Sage Publications.

Trim, K., with G. Pizante and J. Yaraskavitch. (1983). "The Effect of Monopoly on the News: A Before and After Study of Two Canadian One-Newspaper Towns." *Canadian Journal of Communication, 9* (3), 33–56.

Vivendi. (2010). "2010 Annual Report." On the World Wide Web at http://www.vivendi.com/vivendi/IMG/pdf/20110408_annual_raport_2010_2.pdf (retrieved 21 December 2011).

Walt Disney Company. (2010). "Fiscal Year 2010, Annual Financial Reports and Shareholder Letters." On the World Wide Web at http://amedia.disney.go.com/investorrelations/annual_reports/WDC-10kwrap-2010.pdf?int_cmp=corp_IR_ARview_link1__Intl (retrieved 15 December 2011).

Winseck, D. (2011a). "The Growth of the Network Media Economy- in Canada, 1984–2010." *Mediamorphis* 20 August. On the World Wide Web at http://dwmw.wordpress.com/2011/08/20/the-growth-of-the-network-media-econo-myin-canada-1984–1010/ (retrieved 20 December 2011).

Winseck, D. (2011b). "Media Concentration in Canada and the Internet." *Mediamorphis* (blog), 12 February. On the World Wide Web at https://dwmw.wordpress.com/2011/02/12/media-concentration-and-the-internet/ (retrieved 21 December 2011).

Wober, J. M. (1998). "Cultural Indicators: European Reflections on a Research Paradigm." In R. Dickinson, R. Harindranath, and O. Linné, eds., *Approaches to Audiences: A Reader* (pp. 61–73). London: Arnold.

Zimmer, Michael. (2008). "Critical Perspectives on Web 2.0." Preface. *First Monday, 13* (3). On the World Wide Web at http://firstmonday.org/htbin/cgiwrap/bin/ojs/index.php/fm/article/view/2137/1943 (retrieved 22 December 2008).

CHAPTER 6

Abma, Derek. (2012). "Gap Between Rich and Poor Growing by the Hour." *Edmonton Journal 3* January: A8.

Al-Momani, Mohammad. (2011). "The Arab 'Youth Quake': Implications for Democratization and Stability." *Middle East Law and Governance*, 3 (1–2), 159–170.

Brym, Robert J. (1979). "Political Conservatism in Atlantic Canada." In Robert J. Brym and R. James Sacouman, eds., *Underdevelopment and Social Movements in Atlantic Canada* (pp. 59–79). Toronto: New Hogtown Press.

Calliste, Agnes. (1987). "Sleeping Car Porters in Canada: An Ethnically Submerged Split Labour Market." *Canadian Ethnic Studies, 19*, 1–20.

Canadian Press. (2011). "N.S. Paper Mill Closing Marks End of an Era." *Globe and Mail* 17 September: B9.

Cavanagh, John and Chuck Collins. (2008). "The Rich and the Rest of Us." *The Nation* 30 June. On the World Wide Web at http://www.thenation.com/doc/20080630/cavanagh_collins (retrieved 12 July 2009).

Davies, Scott and Neil Guppy (2006). *The Schooled Society: An Introduction to the Sociology of Education.* Toronto: Oxford University Press.

Davis, Kingsley and Wilbert E. Moore. (1945). "Some Principles of Stratification." *American Sociological Review, 10*, 242–49.

Derreck, Tom. (2003). "In Bondage." *The Beaver, 83* (1), 14–19.

Dorling, Daniel, J. Rigby, B. Wheeler, D. Ballas, B. Thomas, E. Fahmy, D. Gordon, and R. Lupton. (2007). *Poverty, Wealth, and Place in Britain—1968 to 2005.* Bristol, UK: Policy Press.

Esping-Andersen, Gøsta. (1990). *Three Worlds of Welfare Capitalism.* Princeton, NJ: Princeton University Press.

Fitzgerald, Robin T. and Peter J. Carrington. (2008). "The Neighbourhood Context of Urban Aboriginal Crime." *Canadian Journal of Criminology and Criminal Justice, 50* (5), 523–57.

Fuller, Sylvia and Leah F. Vosko. (2008). "Temporary Employment and Social Inequality in Canada: Exploring Intersections of Gender, Race and Immigration Status." *Social Indicators Research, 88*, 31–50.

Gougeon, Philippe. (2009). "Shifting Pensions." *Perspectives on Labour and Income.* (Summer) 43–51.

Grabb, Edward G. (2007). *Theories of Social Inequality*, 5th ed. Toronto: Harcourt Canada.

Hagerty, James R. and Caroline van Hasselt. (2012). "Global Giants Play Hardball with Canadian Unions." *Globe and Mail* 3 January: B3. On the World Wide Web at http://www.rogerannis.com/181/ (retrieved 29 July 2012).

Hansen, Darah. (2011). "Immigrants Face Higher Jobless Rate, Lower Pay Despite Education: Study." *Edmonton Journal* 22 December: C1.

Human Resources and Skills Development Canada. (2012). *Indicators of Well-being in Canada: Financial Security/Low Income Incidence*. Ottawa: HRSDC. On the World Wide Web at http://www4.hrsdc.gc.ca/.3ndic.1t.4r@-eng.jsp?iid=23#M_8 (retrieved 15 January 2012).

King, Douglas E. and John A. Winterdyk. (2010). *Diversity, Inequality, and Canadian Justice*. Whitby, ON: de Sitter Publications.

Kleiss, Karen. (2011). "20,000 More Alberta Children Living in Poverty." *Edmonton Journal* 24 November: A4.

Krahn, Harvey, Graham S. Lowe, and Karen Hughes. (2011). *Work, Industry and Canadian Society*, 6th ed. Toronto: Nelson Education Ltd.

Krahn, Harvey. (2009). "Choose Your Parents Carefully: Social Class, Postsecondary Education and Occupational Outcomes." In Edward Grabb and Neil Guppy, eds., *Social Inequality in Canada: Patterns, Problems, Policies*, 5th ed. (pp. 171–87). Toronto: Pearson.

Krugman, Paul. (1994). "Long-Term Riches, Short-Term Pain." *New York Times* September: F9.

Lenski, Gerhard. (1966). *Power and Privilege: A Theory of Social Stratification.* New York: McGraw-Hill.

Li, Peter. (1982). "Chinese Immigrants on the Canadian Prairie, 1919–47." *Canadian Review of Sociology and Anthropology, 19*, 527–40.

Livingstone, David. (1999). *The Education-Jobs Gap: Underemployment or Economic Democracy.* Toronto: Garamond Press.

Luong, May. (2011). "The Wealth and Finances of Employed Low-Income Families." *Perspectives on Labour and Income, 23* (Autumn), 29–38.

Mackenzie, Hugh. (2012). "Canada's CEO Elite 100: The 0.01%." On the World Wide Web at http://www.policyalternatives.ca/sites/default/files/uploads/publications/National%20Office/2012/01/Canadas%20CEO%20Elite%20100FINAL.pdf (retrieved 18 July 2012).

Mackrael, Kim. (2011). "UN Blasts Ottawa over Attawapiskat." *Globe and Mail* 21 December: A11.

Marglin, Stephen A. and Juliet B. Schor, eds. (1990). *The Golden Age of Capitalism: Re-interpreting the Postwar Experience*. Oxford, UK: Clarendon.

Morissette, René and Xuelin Zhang. (2001). "Experiencing Low Income for Several Years." *Perspectives on Labour and Income* (Summer), 25–35.

Morissette, René and Xuelin Zhang. (2007). "Revisiting Wealth Inequality." *Perspectives on Labour and Income* (Spring), 6–17.

Myles, John and Adnan Turegun. (1994). "Comparative Studies in Class Structure." *Annual Review of Sociology, 20*, 103–24.

National Council of Welfare (2011). *Poverty Profile 2009.* Ottawa: Author. On the World Wide Web at http://www.ncw.gc.ca/c.4mm.5n.3ty@-eng.jsp?cmid=3 (retrieved 30 July 2012).

National Council of Welfare. (2008a). *Welfare Incomes, 2006 and 2007.* Ottawa. Author. Catalogue No. HS51-1/2007E.

National Council of Welfare. (2008b). *Poverty Profile, 2004.* Ottawa: Author. On the World Wide Web at http://www ncwcnbes.net/en/research/povertyprofile/webonly2004.html (retrieved 12 July 2009).

National Council of Welfare. (2010). *Welfare Incomes 2009.* Ottawa. Author. Catalogue No. HS51-1/2009E.

O'Neill, Jeff. (1991). "Changing Occupational Structure." *Canadian Social Trends* (Winter), 10.

Organisation for Economic Co-operation and Development. (2011). *Divided We Stand: Why Inequality Keeps Rising.* On the World Wide Web at http://www.oecd.org/document/51/0,3746,en_2649_33933_49147827_1_1_1_1,00.html (retrieved 14 January 2012).

Palmer, Bryan. (1986). *The Character of Class Struggle: Essays in Canadian Working Class History, 1850–1985.* Toronto: McClelland and Stewart.

Parkin, Frank. (1972). *Class Inequality and Political Order.* London: Paladin.

Parkin, Frank. (1979). *Marxism and Class Theory: A Bourgeois Critique.* London: Tavistock.

Pratt, Sheila. (2011). "Baby Boomers Living Good Life while Their Children Struggle." *Edmonton Journal* 19 December: A4.

Raphael, Dennis. (2011). *Poverty and Policy in Canada: Implications for Health and Quality of Life*, 2nd ed. Toronto: Canadian Scholars' Press.

Sauvé, Roger. (2006). *The Current State of Canadian Family Finances: 2005 Report.* Ottawa: Vanier Institute of the Family

Silverman, Bertram and Murray Yanowitch. (2000). *New Rich, New Poor, New Russia: Winners and Losers on the Russian Road to Capitalism*, 2nd ed. New York: M.E. Sharpe.

Statistics Canada. (2005). *Income in Canada.* Ottawa: Minister of Industry. Catalogue No. 75-202-XIE.

Statistics Canada. (2006). "Employment Income Statistics (4) in Constant (2005) Dollars, Work Activity in the Reference Year (3), Occupation-National Occupational Classification for Statistics 2006 (720A) and Sex (3) for the Population 15 Years and Over with Employment Income of Canada, Provinces and Territories, 2000 and 2005–20% Sample Data." *2006 Census: Data Products/Topic-based Tabulations.* Catalogue No. 97-563-XWE2006062. On the World Wide Web at http://www5.statcan.gc.ca/bsolc/olc-cel/olc-cel?catno=97-563-X2006062&%20lang=eng (retrieved 12 July 2009).

Statistics Canada. (2008a). *Earnings and Income of Canadians over the Past Quarter Century, 2006 Census.* Ottawa: Author. Catalogue No. 97-563-X.

Statistics Canada. (2008b). *Canada's Changing Labour Force, 2006 Census.* Ottawa: Author. Catalogue No. 97-559-X.

Statistics Canada. (2011). "Low-Income Lines, 2009–10." On the World Wide Web at http://www.statcan.gc.ca/pub/75f0002m/75f0002m2011002-eng.htm (retrieved 14 January 2012).

Swanson, Jean. (2001). *Poor-Bashing: The Politics of Exclusion.* Toronto: Between the Lines.

Tanner, Julian, Harvey Krahn, and Timothy F. Hartnagel. (1995). *Fractured Transitions from School to Work: Revisiting the Dropout Problem.* Toronto: Oxford University Press.

Taylor, Alison and Harvey Krahn. (2009). "Streaming in/for the New Economy." In Cynthia Levine-Raskyed ed., *Canadian Perspectives on the Sociology of Education* (pp. 103–23). Toronto: Oxford University Press.

Usalcas, Jeannine. (2010). "Labour Market Review 2009." *Perspectives on Labour and Income* (Summer), 5–15.

Wallis, Maria A. and Siuming Kwok (2008). *Daily Struggles: The Deepening Racialization and Feminization of Poverty in Canada.* Toronto: Canadian Scholars' Press.

Wanner, Richard A. (2009). "Social Mobility in Canada: Concepts, Patterns, and Trends." In Edward Grabb and Neil Guppy eds., *Social Inequality in Canada: Patterns, Problems, Policies,* 5th ed. (pp. 116–32). Toronto: Pearson.

Weber, Max. (1948 [1922]). *Max Weber: Essays in Sociology.* H.H. Gerth and C.W. Mills, eds., and trans. London: Routledge & Kegan Paul.

Westergaard, John. (1995). *Who Gets What? The Hardening of Class Inequality in the Late Twentieth Century.* Cambridge, UK: Polity Press.

Wilkinson, Richard and Kate Pickett. (2010). *The Spirit Level: Why Equality is Better for Everyone.* London: Penguin Books.

"The World's Billionaires." (2011). *Forbes Magazine.* On the World Wide Web at http://www.forbes.com/wealth/billion-aires/list (retrieved 13 January 2012).

Wolff, Edward N. (1991). "The Distribution of Household Wealth: Methodological Issues, Time Trends, and Cross-sectional Comparisons." In Lars Osberg, ed., *Economic Inequality and Poverty: International Perspectives* (pp. 92–133). Armonk, NY: Sharpe.

Wright, Erik Olin. (1985). *Classes.* London: Verso.

Wu, Xiaogang and Yu Xie. (2002) "Does the Market Pay Off? Earnings Returns to Education in Urban China." *American Sociological Review* 68 (June), 425–42.

Yalnizyan, Armine. (2010). *The Rise of Canada's Richest 1%.* Ottawa: Canadian Centre for Policy Alternatives.

Zeitlin, Irving M. and Robert J. Brym. (1991). *The Social Condition of Humanity.* Toronto: Oxford University Press.

CHAPTER 7

Agocs, Carol (2002). "Canada's Employment Equity Legislation and Policy, 1987–2000." *International Journal of Manpower, 23* (3), 256–76.

Andersen, L. Margaret. (2005). "Thinking about Women: A Quarter Century's View." *Gender and Society, 19* (4), 437–55.

Armstrong, Pat and Hugh Armstrong. (1994). *The Double Ghetto: Canadian Women and Their Segregated Work,* 3rd ed. Toronto: McClelland and Stewart.

Arscott, Jane and Linda Trimble. (1997). "Introduction—In the Presence of Women: Representation and Political Power." In Jane Arscott and Linda Trimble, eds., *In the Presence of Women: Representation in Canadian Governments* (pp. 1–17). Toronto: Harcourt Brace.

Baron, Ethan. (2010). "Equal Work Is Still Resulting in Unequal Pay." Province 17 December: A11.

Bashevkin, Sylvia B. (1993). *Toeing the Lines: Women and Party Politics in English Canada,* 2nd ed. Toronto: Oxford University Press.

Bashevkin, Sylvia B. (2009). *Women, Power, Politics: The Hidden Story of Canada's Unfinished Democracy.* Toronto: Oxford University Press.

Berdahl, Jennifer L. and Celia Moore. (2006). "Workplace Harassment: Double Jeopardy for Minority Women." *Journal of Applied Psychology, 91* (2), 426–36.

Black, Jerome H. (2008). "Ethnoracial Minorities in the 38th Parliament: Patterns of Change and Continuity." In Caroline Andrew, John Biles, Myer Siemiatycki, and Eric Tolley, eds., *Electing a Diverse Canada: the Representation of Immigrants, Minorities and Women* (pp. 229–54). Vancouver: University of British Columbia Press.

Boyd, Monica. (1990). "Sex Differences in Occupational Skills: Canada, 1961–1986." *Canadian Review of Sociology and Anthropology, 27,* 285–315.

Boyd, Monica. (1999). "Integrating Gender, Language and Visible Minority Groups." In Shiva S. Halli and Leo Driedger, eds., *Immigrant Canada: Demographic, Economic, and Social Challenges* (pp. 282–306). Toronto: University of Toronto Press.

Boyd, Monica, Brenda Hughes, and Jamie Miller. (1997). "Power at Work: Women and Men in Management, Supervision and Workplace Planning." Department of Sociology, Florida State University.

Boyd, Monica, Maryann Mulvihill, and John Myles. (1991). "Gender, Power and Post-Industrialism." *Canadian Review of Sociology and Anthropology, 28,* 407–36.

Brodie, Janine. (1991). "Women and the Electoral Process in Canada." In Kathy Megyery, ed., *Women in Canadian Politics: Toward Equity in Representation* (pp. 3–59). Toronto: Dundurn Press.

Broverman, I., S. R. Vogel, S. M. Broverman, F. E. Clarkson, and P. S. Rosenkranz. (1972). "Sex Role Stereotypes: A Current Appraisal." *Journal of Social Issues, 28* (2), 59–78.

Burt, Sandra. (1993). "The Changing Patterns of Public Policy." In Sandra Burt, Lorraine Code, and Lindsay Dorney eds., *Changing Patterns: Women in Canada,* 2nd ed. (pp. 212–37). Toronto: McClelland and Stewart.

Canada. (1995). *Laws. Statutes of Canada. Employment Equity Act.* Elizabeth II, Vol. II. Chapter 44 (pp. 43–44).

Chafetz, Janet Saltzman. (2006). "The Varieties of Gender Theory in Sociology." In Janet Saltzman Chafetz, ed., *The Handbook of the Sociology of Gender* (pp. 3–23). New York: Springer.

Chui, Tina and Hélène Maheux. (2011). "Visible Minority Women." In *Women in Canada: A Gender-Based Statistical Report, 2010–2011.* Statistics Canada. Catalogue 89-503-XWE. On the World Wide Web at http://www.statcan.gc.ca/pub/89-503-x/2010001/article/11527-eng.pdf (retrieved 30 July 2012).

Collins, Patricia Hill. (1990). *Black Feminist Thought, Knowledge, Consciousness, and the Politics of Empowerment.* Boston: Unwin Hyman.

Connelly, Patricia. (1978). *Last Hired, First Fired: Women and the Canadian Work Force.* Toronto: Women's Press.

Cooke-Reynolds, Melissa and Nancy Zukewich. (2004). "The Feminization of Work." *Canadian Social Trends, 72* (Spring), 24–29.

Cool, Julie. (2011). *Women in Parliament.* Publication No. 2011-56-E. Ottawa: Library of Parliament.

Cranford, Cynthia J., Leah F. Vosko, and Nancy Zukewich. (2003). "The Gender of Precarious Employment in Canada." *Industrial Relations, 58* (3), 454–79.

Cranswick, Kelly and Donna Dosman. 2008. "Elder Care: What We Know Today." *Canadian Social Trends, 86* (Winter), 48–56.

Das Gupta, Tania. (1996). *Racism and Paid Work.* Toronto: Garamond Press.

Duffy, Ann. (1986). "Reformulating Power for Women." *Canadian Review of Sociology and Anthropology, 23*, 22–46.

Duffy, Ann and Norene Pupo. (1992). *Part-Time Paradox: Connecting Gender, Work and Family.* Toronto: McClelland and Stewart.

England, Paula. (1993). *Comparable Worth: Theories and Evidence.* New York: Aldine de Gruyter.

Ferrao, Vincent. 2011. "Paid Work." *Women in Canada: A Gender-based Statistical Report, 2010–2011.* Statistics Canada. Catalogue No. 89-503-XWE. On the World Wide Web at http://www.statcan.gc.ca/pub/89–503-x/2010001/article/11387-eng.pdf (retrieved 30 July 2012).

Fuller, Sylvia and Leah F. Vosko. (2008). "Temporary Employment and Social Inequality in Canada: Exploring Intersections of Gender, Race and Immigration Status." *Social Indicator Research, 88*, 31–50.

Gagne, Patricia and Richard Tewksbury. (1998). "Rethinking Binary Conceptions and Social Constructions: Transgender Experiences of Gender and Sexuality." In Marcia Texler Segal and Vasilikie Demos, eds., *Advances in Gender Research*, Vol. 3 (pp. 73–102). Bingley, UK: Emerald Group.

Galloway, Gloria. (2010). "Women: Half the Population, a Fifth of the Seats in Parliament." *Globe and Mail* 12 October: A16.

Gaskell, Jane. (1986). "Conceptions of Skill and the Work of Women: Some Historical and Political Issues." In Roberta Hamilton and Michele Barrett, eds., *The Politics of Diversity: Feminism, Marxism, and Nationalism* (pp. 361–80). London: Verso.

Haq, Rana and Eddy S. W. Ng. (2010) "Employment Equity and Workplace Diversity in Canada." In Alain Klarsfeld, ed., *International Handbook on Diversity Management at Work: Country Perspectives on Diversity and Equal Treatment* (pp. 68–82). Northampton, MA : Edward Elgar.

Jackson, Chris. (1996). "Measuring and Valuing Households' Unpaid Work." *Canadian Social Trends, 42* (4), 25–29.

Kite, Mary E., Kay Deaux, and Elizabeth L. Haines. (2008). "Gender Stereotypes." In Florence Denmark and Michele Antoinette Paludi, eds., *Psychology of Women: A Handbook of Issues and Theories* (pp. 205–36). Westport, CT: Praeger.

Krahn, Harvey. (1995). "Non-standard Work on the Rise." *Perspectives on Labour and Income*, 7 (4), 35–42.

Leacy, Frank, H. (1983). *Historical Statistics of Canada*, 2nd ed. Ottawa: Statistics Canada. Catalogue No. 11-516-XIE.

Lengermann, Patricia Madoo and Jill Niebrugge-Brantley. (2001). "Classical Feminist Theory." In George Ritzer and Barry Smart eds., *Handbook of Sociological Theory* (pp. 125–135). London: Sage Publications.

Looker, E. Dianne and Victor Thiessen. (1999). "Images of Work: Women's Work, Men's Work, Housework." *Canadian Journal of Sociology, 24*, 2 (Spring), 225–54.

Lorber, Judith. (2010). *Gender Inequality: Feminist Theories and Politics*, 4th ed. New York: Oxford University Press.

Lowe, Graham. (1987). *Women in the Administrative Revolution: The Feminization of Clerical Work.* Cambridge, UK: Polity Press.

Lu, Vanessa. (2011). "Women Still Hitting Glass Ceiling," *Toronto Star* 3 March. On the World Wide Web at http://mmsearch.com/html/research/women_still_ceiling.php (retrieved 9 March 2012).

Luxton, Meg and Leah F. Vosko. (1998). "Where Women's Efforts Count: The 1996 Census Campaign and 'Family Politics' in Canada." *Studies in Political Economy, 56* (Summer), 49–81.

Martin, Y. Patricia. (2003). "'Said and Done' Versus 'Saying and Doing': Gender Practices, Practicing Gender at Work." *Gender and Society, 17* (3), 342–66.

McCormack, Thelma. (1975). "Toward a Nonsexist Perspective on Social and Political Change." In Marcia Millman and Rosabeth Moss Kanter, eds., *Another Voice: Feminist Perspectives on Social Life and Social Science* (pp. 1–33). Garden City, NY: Anchor Books.

Milan, Anne, Leslie-Anne Keown, and Covadonga Robles Urquijo. (2011). "Families, Living Arrangements and Unpaid Work." In *Women in Canada: A Gender-Based Statistical Report. 2010–2011.* Statistics Canada. Catalogue 89-503-XWE. On the World Wide Web at http://www.statcan.gc.ca/pub/89–503-x/2010001/article/11546-eng.htm#a5 (retrieved 30 July 2012).

Myles, John and Gail Fawcett. (1990). "Job Skills and the Service Economy." Working Paper No. 4. Ottawa: Economic Council of Canada.

Newman, Jacquetta and Linda A. White. (2006). *Women, Politics, and Public Policy: The Political Struggles of Canadian Women.* Toronto: Oxford University Press.

O'Neill, Brenda and Lisa Young. (2010). "Women in Canadian Politics." In John C. Courtney and David E. Smith, eds., *The Oxford Handbook of Canadian Politics* (pp. 321–38). Toronto: Oxford University Press.

Pal, Leslie. (1989). *Public Policy Analysis.* Toronto: Nelson Canada.

Parliament of Canada. (n.d.). "Representation, Party Standings." On the World Wide Web at://www.parl.gc.ca/parlinfo/lists/PartyStandings.aspx?Section=b571082f-7b2d-4d6a-b30a-b6025a9cbb98&Gender (retrieved 9 March 2012).

Pendakur, Krishna and Ravi Pendakur. (2011). "Colour by Numbers: Minority Earnings in Canada 1996–2006." Metropolis British Columbia Working Paper Series No. 5. On the World Wide Web at http://www.sfu.ca/~pendakur/Colour%20By%20Numbers%20final%20all%20tabs%20and%20figs.pdf (retrieved 30 July 2012).

Phillips, Paul and Erin Phillips. (1983). *Women and Work.* Toronto: Lorimer.

Pierson, Ruth. (1977). "Women's Emancipation and the Recruitment of Women into the Labour Force in World War II." In Susan Mann Trofimenkoff and Alison Prentice, eds., *The Neglected Majority* (pp. 125–45). Toronto: McClelland and Stewart.

Pilkington, Ed. (2011). "Slut Walking Gets Rolling after Cop's Loose Talk about Provocative Clothing." *Guardian* 6 May. On the World Wide Web at http://www.guardian.co.uk/world/2011/may/06/slutwalking-policeman-talk-clothing (retrieved 13 March 2012).

Prentice, Alison. (1977). "The Feminization of Teaching." In Susan Mann Trofimenkoff and Alison Prentice, eds., *The Neglected Majority* (pp. 49–65). Toronto: McClelland and Stewart.

Segal, Edwin S. (1998). "Male Genders: Cross Cultural Perspectives." In Marcia Texler Segal and Vasilikie Demos, eds., *Advances in Gender Research*, Volume 3 (pp. 37–77). Bingley, UK: Emerald Group.

Statistics Canada. (2008). *Canada's Changing Labour Force, Census 2006*. Ottawa: Ministry of Industry. Catalogue No. 97-559-X

Statistics Canada. (2011a). "Family Income Groups (22) in Constant (2005) Dollars, Economic Family Structure (3), Age Groups of Spouses or Partners (3), Presence and Age Groups of Children (5) and Presence of Spousal or Partner Earnings (4) for the Couple Economic Families in Private Households of Canada, Provinces, Territories, Census Metropolitan Areas and Census Agglomerations, 2000 and 2005—20% Sample Data." On the World Wide Web at http://www12.statcan.gc.ca/census-recensement/2006/dp-pd/tbt/Rp-eng.cfm?LANG=E&APATH=3&DETAIL=0&DIM=0&FL=A&FREE=0&GC=0&GID=0&GK=0&GRP=1&PID=94196&PRID=0&PTYPE=88971,97154&S=0&SHOWALL=0&SUB=813&Temporal=2006&THEME=81&VID=0&VNAMEE=&VNAMEF= (retrieved12 March 2012).

Statistics Canada. (2011b). Family Income Groups (22A) in Constant (2005) Dollars, Economic Family Structure (3A), Presence and Age Groups of Children (4) and Presence of Parental Earnings (3) for the Lone-Parent Economic Families in Private Households of Canada, Provinces, Territories, Census Metropolitan Areas and Census Agglomerations, 2000 and 2005—20% Sample Data. On the World Wide Web at http://www12.statcan.gc.ca/census-recensement/2006/dp-pd/tbt/Rp-eng.cfm?LANG=E&APATH=3&DETAIL=0&DIM=0&FL=A&FREE=0&GC=0&GID=0&GK=0&GRP=1&PID=94195&PRID=0&PTYPE=88971,97154&S=0&SHOWALL=0&SUB=813&Temporal=2006&THEME=81&VID=0&VNAMEE=&VNAMEF= (retrieved 12 March 2012).

Statistics Canada. (2011c). "Full-Time and Part-Time Employment by Sex and Age Group." CANSIM Table 282–002. On the World Wide Web at http://www40.statcan.gc.ca/l01/cst01/labor12-eng.htm (retrieved 9 March 2012).

Statistics Canada. (2011d). *General Social Survey—2010 Overview of the Time Use of Canadians*. Catalogue No. 89-647-x. On the World Wide Web at http://www.statcan.gc.ca/pub/89–647-x/89–647-x2011001-eng.pdf (retrieved 30 July 2012).

Statistics Canada. (2011e). "Occupation—National Occupational Classification for Statistics 2006 (720), Class of Worker (6) and Sex (3) for the Labour Force 15 Years and Over of Canada, Provinces, Territories, Census Metropolitan Areas and Census Agglomerations, 2006 Census—20% Sample Data" On the World Wide Web at http://www12.statcan.gc.ca/census-recensement/2006/dp-pd/tbt/Rp-eng.cfm?LANG=E&APATH=3&DETAIL=0&DIM=0&FL=A&FREE=0&GC=0&GID=0&GK=0&GRP=1&PID=92104&PRID=0&PTYPE=88971,97154&S=0&SHOWALL=0&SUB=0&Temporal=2006&THEME=74&VID=0&VNAMEE=&VNAMEF= (retrieved 12 March 2012).

Statistics Canada. (2011f). "Unpaid Work (20), Sex (3), Age Groups (9), Labour Force Activity (5), Census Family Status (6) and Presence and Age of Youngest Child (6) for the Population 15 Years and Over Living in Private Households of Canada, Provinces, Territories, Census Metropolitan Areas and Census Agglomerations, 2001 to 2006 Censuses—20% Sample Data." On the World Wide Web at http://www12.statcan.gc.ca/census-recensement/2006/dp-pd/tbt/Rp-eng.cfm?A=R&APATH=3&D1=0&D2=0&D3=0&D4=0&D5=0&D6=0&DETAIL=0&DIM=0&FL=A&FREE=0&GC=01&GID=837928&GK=1&GRP=1&LANG=E&O=D&PID=92100&PRID=0&PTYPE=88971%2C97154&S=0&SHOWALL=0&SUB=0&TABID=1&THEME=74&Temporal=2006&VID=0&VNAMEE=&VNAMEF= (retrieved 12 March 2012)

Steinberg, Ronnie J. (1990). "Social Construction of Skill." *Work and Occupations, 17*, 449–82.

Tremblay, Manon and Caroline Andrew, eds. (1998). *Women and Political Representation in Canada*. Women's Studies Series. Ottawa: University of Ottawa Press.

Trimble, Linda and Jane Arscott. (2003). *Still Counting: Women in Politics across Canada*. Peterborough, ON: Broadview Press.

Ursel, Jane. (1992). *Private Lives, Public Policy: 100 Years of State Intervention in the Family*. Toronto: Women's Press.

Vickers, Jill. (1997). "Toward a Feminist Understanding of Representation." In Jane Arscott and Linda Trimble, eds., *In the Presence of Women: Representation in Canadian Governments* (pp. 20–46). Toronto: Harcourt Brace.

Vosko, Leah, Nancy Zukewich, and Cynthia J. Cranford. (2003). "Precarious Jobs: A New Typology of Employment." *Perspectives on Labour and Income, 4* (10), 16–26.

Welsh, Sandy, Jacquie Carr, Barbara MacQuarrie, and Audrey Huntley. (2006). "'I'm Not Thinking of It as Sexual Harassment:' Understanding Harassment across Race and Citizenship." *Gender and Society, 20* (1), 87–107.

West, Candace and Sarah Fenstermaker. (1993). "Power, Inequality and the Accomplishment of Gender: An Ethnomethodological View." In Paula England, ed., *Theory on Gender/Feminism on Theory* (pp. 151–74). New York: Aldine de Gruyter.

Wharton, S. Amy. (2000). "Feminism at Work." *The Annals of the American Academy, 571*, 167–82.

Williams, Cara. (2004). "The Sandwich Generation." *Perspectives on Labour and Income, 5* (9), 5–12.

Williams, Cara. (2011). "Economic Well-Being." *Women in Canada: A Gender-based Statistical Report, 2010–2011*. Statistics Canada. Catalogue 89-503-XWE. On the World Wide Web at http://www.statcan.gc.ca/pub/89–503-x/2010001/article/11388-eng.pdf (retrieved 14 March 2012).

Yanz, Lynda, Deena Ladd, Joan Atlin, and Maquila Solidarity Network. (1999). *Policy Options to Improve Standards for Garment Workers in Canada and Internationally*. Ottawa: Status of Women Canada.

Zinn, Maxine Baca with Bonnie Thorton Dill. (1997). "Theorizing Difference from Multiracial Feminism." In Maxine Baca Zinn, Pierrette Hondagneu-Sotelo, and Michael A Messner, eds., *Through the Prism of Difference: Readings on Sex and Gender* (pp. 23–9). Boston: Allyn and Bacon.

CHAPTER 8

Abella, Irving and Harold Troper. (1982). *None is Too Many: Canada and the Jews of Europe, 1933–1948*. Toronto: Lester & Orpen Dennys.

Alfred, Taiaiake. (1999). *Peace, Power and Righteousness: An Indigenous Manifesto*. Toronto: Oxford University Press.

Anderson, Benedict. (1983). *Imagined Communities: Reflections on the Origin and Spread of Nationalism*. London: Verso.

Angus Reid Group. (1991). *Multiculturalism and Canadians: National Attitude Study, 1991*. Ottawa: Multiculturalism and Citizenship Canada.

Appleby, Timothy. (2006). "Harnick Testimony 'Shocked' Harris." *Globe and Mail* 17 February: A7.

Avery, Donald. (1995). *Reluctant Host: Canada's Response to Immigrant Workers*. Toronto: McClelland and Stewart.

Balthazar, Louis. (1993). "The Faces of Quebec Nationalism." In Alain-G. Gagnon, ed., *Quebec: State and Society*, 2nd ed. (pp. 2–17). Toronto: Nelson.

Barkan, Elazar. (1992). *The Retreat of Scientific Racism*. Cambridge, UK: Cambridge University Press.

Barker, Martin. (1981). *The New Racism: Conservatives and the Ideology of the Tribe*. London: Junction Books.

Basran, Gurcharn and Li Zong. (1998). "Devaluation of Foreign Credentials as Perceived by Non-White Professional Immigrants." *Canadian Ethnic Studies, 30*, 6–23.

Bissoondath, Neil. (1994). *Selling Illusions: The Cult of Multiculturalism*. Toronto: Stoddart.

Bolaria, B. Singh and Peter Li. (1988). *Racial Oppression in Canada*. Toronto: Garamond.

Boldt, Menno. (1993). *Surviving as Indians: The Challenge of Self-Government*. Toronto: University of Toronto Press.

Bonacich, Edna. (1972). "A Theory of Ethnic Antagonism: The Split Labor Market." *American Sociological Review, 37*, 547–59.

Bonacich, Edna. (1979). "The Past, Present, and Future of Split Labor Market Theory." *Research in Race and Ethnic Relations, 1*, 17–64.

Bonacich, Edna. (1980). "Class Approaches to Ethnicity and Race." *Insurgent Sociologist, 10*, 9–23.

Bouchard, Gérard and Charles Taylor. (2008). *Building the Future: A Time for Reconciliation*. On the World Wide Web at http://www.accommodements.qc.ca/documentation/rapports/rapport-final-integral-en.pdf (retrieved 16 July 2009).

Bourgeault, Ron. (1988). "The South African Connection." *Canadian Dimension, 21*, 6–10.

Brown, Louise and Brett Popplewell. (2008). "Board Okays Black-Focused School." *Toronto Star* 30 January. On the World Wide Web at http://www.thestar.com/News/article/298714 (retrieved 15 July 2009).

Brym, Robert and Bonnie Fox. (1989). *From Culture to Power: The Sociology of English Canada*. Toronto: Oxford University Press.

Brym, Robert and Rhonda Lenton. (1993). "The Distribution of Anti-Semitism in Canada in 1984." In Robert Brym, William Shaffir, and Morton Weinfeld, eds., *The Jews in Canada* (pp. 112–19). Toronto: Oxford University Press.

Castles, Stephen and Godula Kosack. (1984). *Immigrant Workers and Class Structure in Western Europe*. London: Oxford University Press.

Citizenship and Immigration Canada. (1996). *You Asked About ... Immigration and Citizenship*. Ottawa: Supply and Services Canada.

Citizenship and Immigration Canada. (2002). "Family Class Immigration." On the World Wide Web at http://www.cis.gc.ca/english/sponsor/index.html (retrieved 10 September 2003).

Citizenship and Immigration Canada. (2010). "Facts and Figures 2010—Immigration Overview: Permanent and Temporary Residents." On the World Wide Web at http://www.cic.gc.ca/english/resources/statistics/facts2010/permanent/10.asp (retrieved 15 July 2012).

Citizenship and Immigration Canada. (2011). "Skilled Workers and Professionals: Who Can Apply—Six Selection Factors and Pass Mark." On the World Wide Web at http://www.cic.gc.ca/english/immigrate/skilled/apply-factors.asp (retrieved 15 July 2012).

Clement, Wallace. (1975). *The Canadian Corporate Elite*. Toronto: McClelland and Stewart.

Cole, Douglas and Ira Chaikin. (1990). *An Iron Hand upon the People: The Law against the Potlatch on the Northwest Coast*. Vancouver, BC: Douglas and McIntyre.

Collins, Jock. (1988). *Migrant Hands in a Distant Land: Australia's Post-War Immigration*. Sydney: Pluto Press.

Congress of Aboriginal Peoples. (2008). "The Forgotten People and the Indian Act." On the World Wide Web at http://www abo-peoples.org/about/Indian_Act.html (retrieved 15 July 2009).

Curry, Bill. (2005). "The Government Responds: Indian Affairs Minister Announces Plan to Relocate Settlement, Improve Sanitation." *Globe and Mail* 28 October: A1.

Daenzer, Pat. (1993). *Regulating Class Privilege*. Toronto: Canadian Scholars Press.

Darroch, Gordon. (1979). "Another Look at Ethnicity Stratification and Social Mobility in Canada." *Canadian Journal of Sociology, 4*, 1–25.

Department of Indian Affairs and Northern Development. (2004). *Basic Departmental Data 2003*. Ottawa: Minister of Public Works and Government Services Canada

Doob, Christopher. (1996). *Racism: An American Cauldron*. New York: HarperCollins.

"A Dream That Does Not Fade (Quebec's Sovereignty)." (2005). *Economist* 3 (December), p. 8.

Economic Council of Canada. (1991). *Economic and Social Impacts of Immigration*. Ottawa: Supply and Services Canada.

Edwards, Peter. (2001). *One Dead Indian: The Premier, the Police and the Ipperwash Crisis*. Toronto: McClelland and Stewart.

Farmer, Nathan. (2005). "Kingston Police Chief Apologizes for Force's Systemic Racism." On the World Wide Web at http://friendsofgrassynarrows.com/item.php.?427F (retrieved 12 November 2005).

Fiske, Jo-Anne. (1996). "The Womb Is to the Nation as the Heart Is to the Body: Ethnopolitical Discourses of the Canadian Indigenous Women's Movement." *Studies in Political Economy 51*, 65–96.

Fleras, A. and J. L. Elliot.(1996). *Unequal Relations: An Introduction to Race, Ethnic, and Aborignal Dynamics in Canada*. Scarborough, ON: Prentice Hall Canada.

Fleras, Augie. (2012). *Unequal Relations: An Introduction to Race, Ethnic, and Aboriginal Dynamics in Canada*, 7th ed. Toronto: Pearson.

Fournier, Marcel, Michael Rosenberg, and Deena White. (1997). *Quebec Society: Critical Issues*. Scarborough, ON: Prentice Hall.

Frideres, James and René Gadacz. (2012). *Aboriginal Peoples in Canada*, 9th ed. Toronto: Pearson.

Gerber, Linda. (1990). "Multiple Jeopardy: A Socioeconomic Comparison of Men and Women among the Indian, Métis and Inuit Peoples of Canada." *Canadian Ethnic Studies, 22*, 69–84.

Gibbins, Roger and J. Rick Ponting. (1986). "Historical Background and Overview." In J. Rick Ponting, ed., *Arduous Journey* (pp. 18–56). Toronto: McClelland and Stewart.

Granatstein, Jack. (2007). *Whose War Is It? How Canada Can Survive in the Post 9/11 World*. Toronto: HarperCollins.

Gray, Jeff. "Officers Make Racist Remarks on Tape. Members of Ontario Provincial Police Slag Natives before Protester Killed in 1995." *Globe and Mail* 21 January: A7.

Groupe de recherche ethnicité et societé. (1997). "Immigration and Ethnic Relations in Quebec: Pluralism in the Making." In Marcel Fournier, Michael Rosenberg, and Deena White, eds., *Quebec Society: Critical Issues* (pp. 95–112). Scarborough, ON: Prentice Hall.

Ha, Tu Thanh. (1995). "The PQ's Narrow Ethnic Vision." *Globe and Mail* 11 November: D1.

Harries, Kate. (2005). "Harris Uttered Slur, Ipperwash Inquiry Told." *Globe and Mail* 29 November: A1.

Hawkins, Freda. (1989). *Critical Years in Immigration: Canada and Australia Compared.* Montreal and Kingston, ON: McGill-Queen's University Press.

Henry, Frances. (1989). "Who Gets the Work in 1989?" Background Paper. Ottawa: Economic Council of Canada.

Henry, Frances and Effie Ginsberg. (1985). *Who Gets the Work? A Test of Racial Discrimination in Employment.* Toronto: Urban Alliance on Race Relations and the Social Planning Directorate.

Henry, Frances and Carol Tator. (2006). *The Colour of Democracy: Racism in Canadian Society,* 3rd ed. Toronto: Thomson Nelson.

Herberg, Edward. (1990). "The Ethno-Racial Socioeconomic Hierarchy in Canada: Theory and Analysis in the New Vertical Mosaic." *International Journal of Comparative Sociology, 31,* 206–21.

Holton, Robert and Michael Lanphier. (1994). "Public Opinion, Immigration and Refugees." In Howard Adelman, Allan Borowski, Meyer Burstein, and Lois Foster, eds., *Immigration and Refugee Policy: Australia and Canada Compared,* Vol. 1. Toronto: University of Toronto Press.

Hou, Feng and Simon Coulombe. (2010). "Earnings Gaps for Canadian-Born Visible Minorities in the Public and Private Sectors." *Canadian Public Policy, 36* (1), 29-43.

Howard, Rhoda. (1998). "Being Canadian: Citizenship in Canada." *Citizenship Studies, 2,* 133–52.

Howard-Hassmann, Rhoda. (1999). "Canadian as an Ethnic Category: Implications for Multiculturalism and National Unity." *Canadian Public Policy, 25* (4), 523–37.

Iacovetta, Franca. (1992). *Such Hardworking People: Italian Immigrants in Postwar Toronto.* Montreal and Kingston, ON: McGill-Queen's University Press.

Immen, Wallace. (2011). "How an Ethnic Sounding Name may Affect the Job Hunt," *Globe and Mail* 18 November: B21.

Isajiw, Wsevolod. (1999). *Understanding Diversity: Ethnicity and Race in the Canadian Context.* Toronto: Thompson Educational Publishing.

Jenson, Jane. (1993). "Naming Nations: Making Nationalist Claims in Canadian Public Discourse." *Canadian Review of Sociology and Anthropology, 30,* 337–58.

Kazemipur, Abdolmohammad and Shiva Halli. (2000). *The New Poverty in Canada.* Toronto: Thompson Educational Publishers.

Krosenbrink-Gelissen, Ernestine. (1994). "The Native Women's Association of Canada." In James Frideres, ed., *Native Peoples in Canada* (pp. 335–64). Scarborough, ON: Prentice Hall.

Laforest, Guy. (2005). "Can Canada Win Back the Children of Bill 101? YES: Canada Can Woo Back Quebeckers by Admitting Past Insults and Decentralizing, Says a Former ADQ Leader, Guy Laforest."*Globe and Mail* 20 December: A25.

Latouche, Daniel. (1993). "'Quebec: See under Canada'—Quebec Nationalism in the New Global Age." In Alain-G. Gagnon, ed., *Quebec: State and Society,* 2nd ed. (pp. 40–51). Toronto: Nelson.

Léger Marketing, 2007. *Sun Media: Racial Tolerance Report.* On the World Wide Web at http://www.legermarketing.com/documents/SPCLM/070119ENG.pdf (retrieved 15 July 2009).

Lewis, Oscar. (1961). *The Children of Sanchez.* New York: Random House.

Li, Peter. (1988). *The Chinese in Canada.* Toronto: Oxford University Press.

Li, Peter. (2003). *Destination Canada: Immigration Debates and Issues.* Toronto: Oxford University Press.

Lieberson, Stanley. (1991). "A New Ethnic Group in the United States." In Norman Yetman, ed., *Majority and Minority* (pp. 444–56). New York: Allyn and Bacon.

Macmillan, David. (1985). "Scottish Enterprise and Influences in Canada, 1620–1900." In R.A. Cage, ed., *The Scots Abroad: Labour, Capital and Enterprise, 1750–1914* (pp. 46–79). London: Croom Helm.

Manpower and Immigration. (1967). *Immigration Statistics, 1966.* Ottawa: Queen's Printer.

Marger, Martin. (1997). *Race and Ethnic Relations: American and Global Perspectives,* 4th ed. New York: Wadsworth.

Marx, Karl. (1967 [1867]). *Capital,* Vol. 1. New York: International Publishers.

McMillan, Alan. (1988). *Native Peoples and Cultures of Canada.* Vancouver, BC: Douglas and McIntyre.

Métis National Council. (1983). *A Brief to the Standing Committee on Legal and Constitutional Affairs.* Ottawa: Author.

Miles, Robert and Malcolm Brown. (2003). *Racism,* 2nd ed. London: Routledge.

Miles, Robert. (1982). *Racism and Migrant Labour.* London: Routledge.

Milner, Henry and Sheilagh Hodgins Milner. (1973). *The Colonization of Quebec.* Toronto: McClelland and Stewart.

Mitchell, Marybelle. (1996). *From Talking Chiefs to a Native Corporate Elite.* Montreal and Kingston, ON: McGill-Queen's University Press.

Montagu, Ashley. (1972). *Statement on Race.* London: Oxford University Press.

Moore, Robert B. (1976). *Racism in the English Language.* New York: Council on Interracial Books for Children.

Nagler, Mark. (1972). "Minority Values and Economic Achievement: The Case of the North American Indian." In Mark Nagler, ed., *Perspectives on the North American Indian* (pp. 131–42). Toronto: McClelland and Stewart.

Nakhaie, M. Reza. (2006). "A Comparison of the Earnings of the Canadian Native Born and Immigrants, 2001," *Canadian Ethnic Studies, 38* (2), 19–46.

Nikolinakos, Marios. (1973). "Notes towards an Economic Theory of Racism." *Race, 14,* 365–81.

Omi, Michael and Howard Winant. (1986). *Racial Formation in the United States: From the 1960s to the 1980s.* New York: Routledge and Kegan Paul.

Oreopoulos, Phillip and Diane Dechief (2011). "Why Do Some Employers Prefer to Interview Matthew but not Samir? New evidence from Toronto, Montreal and Vancouver." Vancouver, BC: Metropolis British Columbia, Centre of Excellence for Research on Immigration and Diversity, Working Paper No. 11–13.

Parkin Andrew and Mattew Mendelsohn. (2003). *A New Canada: An Identity Shaped by Diversity.* Montreal: Centre for Research and Information on Canada.

Pentland, H. Clare. (1981). *Labour and Capital in Canada, 1650–1860.* Toronto: Lorimer.

Pettipas, Katherine. (1995). *Severing the Ties That Bind.* Winnipeg, MB: University of Manitoba Press.

Pineo, Peter and John Porter. (1985). "Ethnic Origin and Occupational Attainment." In Monica Boyd, John Goyder, Frank Jones, Hugh McRoberts, Peter Pineo, and John Porter, eds., *Ascription and Achievement: Studies in Mobility and Status Attainment in Canada* (pp. 357–93). Ottawa: Carleton University Press.

Porter, John. (1965). *The Vertical Mosaic.* Toronto: University of Toronto Press.

Ramirez, Bruno. (1991). *On the Move: French-Canadian and Italian Migrants in the North Atlantic Economy 1860–1914.* Toronto: McClelland and Stewart.

Rex, John and David Mason, eds. (1986). *Theories of Race and Ethnic Relations.* Cambridge, UK: Cambridge University Press.

Roy, Patricia. (1989). *A White Man's Province.* Vancouver, BC: University of British Columbia Press.

Royal Commission on Aboriginal Peoples. (1996). *Report.* Ottawa: Supply and Services Canada.

Satzewich, Vic. (1991). *Racism and the Incorporation of Foreign Labour.* London: Routledge.

Satzewich, Vic and Linda Mahood. (1994). "Indian Affairs and Band Governance: Deposing Indian Chiefs in Western Canada, 1896–1911." *Canadian Ethnic Studies, 26,* 40–58.

Satzewich, Vic and Lloyd Wong. (2003). "Immigration, Ethnicity and Race: The Transformation of Transnationalism, Localism, and Identities." In Wallace Clement and Leah Vosko, eds., *Changing Canada: Political Economy as Transformation.* Montreal and Kingston: McGill-Queen's University Press.

Satzewich, Vic and Terry Wotherspoon. (2001). *First Nations: Race, Class and Gender Relations.* Regina: Canadian Plains Research Centre.

Satzewich, Vic and William Shaffir. (2009). "Racism versus Professionalism: Claims and Counter-claims about Racial Profiling." *Canadian Journal of Criminology and Criminal Justice, 51* (2), 199–226.

Scott, George. (1990). "A Resynthesis of the Primordial and Circumstantial Approaches to Ethnic Group Solidarity: Towards an Explanatory Model." *Ethnic and Racial Studies, 13,* 147–71.

Special Committee on the Participation of Visible Minorities in Canadian Society. (1984). *Equality Now!* Ottawa: Supply and Services Canada.

Statistics Canada. (2003). *Ethnic Diversity Survey: Portrait of a Multicultural Society.* Ottawa: Minister of Industry. Catalogue No. 89-593-XIE.

Statistics Canada. (2008). "Immigration and Citizenship Highlight Tables, 2006." On the World Wide Web at http://www12.statcan.ca/english/census06/data/highlights/Immigration/index.cfm (retrieved 15 July 2009).

Statistics Canada. (2009). "Ethnocultural Portrait of Canada Highlight Tables, 2006 Census." On the World Wide Web at http://www12.statcan.ca/english/census06/data/highlights/ethnic/index.cfm?Lang=E (retrieved 16 July 2009).

Statistics Canada. (2010). 2011 "National Household Survey Questions." On the World Wide Web at http://www12.statcan.gc.ca/NHS-ENM/ref/Questionnaires/2011NHS-ENM-eng.cfm#Q17 (retrieved 28 July 2012).

Steckley John. (2003). *Aboriginal Voices and the Politics of Representation in Canadian Introductory Sociology Textbooks.* Toronto: Canadian Scholars Press.

Steinberg, Stephen. (1981). *The Ethnic Myth.* New York: Knopf.

Stoffman, Daniel. (2002). *Who Gets In: What's Wrong with Canada's Immigration Program and How to Fix It.* Toronto: Macfarlane Walter and Ross.

Thomas, W. I. and Florian Znaniecki. (1918). *The Polish Peasant in Europe and America.* New York: Knopf.

Titley, Brian. (1986). *A Narrow Vision: Duncan Campbell Scott and the Administration of Indian Affairs in Canada.* Vancouver, BC: University of British Columbia Press.

Turp, Daniel. (2005). "Can Canada Win Back the Children of Bill 101? No: Canada Isn't First in the Hearts of Young Quebeckers regardless of Their First Language, says PQ MNA Daniel Turp." *Globe and Mail* 20 December: A25.

van den Berghe, Pierre. (1986). "Ethnicity and the Sociobiology Debate." In John Rex and David Mason, eds., *Theories of Race and Ethnic Relations* (pp. 246–63). Cambridge, UK: Cambridge University Press.

Voyageur, Cora. (2008). *Firekeepers of the Twenty-First Century: First Nations Women Chiefs.* Montreal, QC, and Kingston, ON: McGill-Queen's University Press.

Walcott, William. (2003). "The Toronto Mayor and the Mombassa Natives." *Canadian Ethnic Studies, 35* (2), 100–15.

Whitaker, Reginald. (1987). *Double Standard: The Secret History of Canadian Immigration.* Toronto: Lester & Orpen Dennys.

Whitaker, Reginald. (1993). "From the Quebec Cauldron to the Canadian Cauldron." In Alain-G. Gagnon, ed., *Quebec: State and Society*, 2nd ed. (pp. 18–39). Toronto: Nelson.

White, Pamela. (1992). "Challenges in Measuring Canada's Ethnic Diversity." In Stella Hryniuk, ed., *20 Years of Multiculturalism: Success and Failure* (pp. 163–82). Winnipeg, MB: St. John's College Press.

Widdowson, Frances and Albert Howard. (2008). *Disrobing the Aboriginal Industry:* The Deception behind Indigenous Cultural Preservation. Montreal, QC: McGill-Queen's University Press.

Wiley, Norbert. (1967). "Ethnic Mobility and Stratification Theory." *Social Problems, 15,* 147–59.

Wilkes, Rima, Neil Guppy, and Lily Farris. (2008). "'No Thanks, We're Full': Individual Attitudes, National Context, and Changing Attitudes toward Immigration." *International Migration Review, 42* (2), 303–28.

Williams, Eric. (1964). *Capitalism and Slavery.* London: Andre Deutsch.

Wilson, Edward. (1978). *On Human Nature.* New York: Vintage.

Woodsworth, J. S. (1972). *Strangers within Our Gates.* Toronto: University of Toronto Press.

Wortley, Scot. (2005). *Bias Free Policing: The Kingston Data Collection Project, Preliminary Results.* Toronto: Centre of Criminology, University of Toronto, and the Centre of Excellence for Research on Immigration and Settlement (CERIS).

York, Geoffrey (1989). *The Dispossessed.* Toronto: Lester & Orpen Dennys.

Zong, Li. (1994). "Structural and Psychological Dimensions of Racism: Towards an Alternative Perspective." *Canadian Ethnic Studies, 26,* 122–34.

CHAPTER 9

Acheson, T. W. (1972). "The National Policy and the Industrialization of the Maritimes, 1880–1910." *Acadiensis, 1* (Spring), pp. 3–28.

Alexander, David. (1978). "Economic Growth in the Atlantic Region, 1880–1940." *Acadiensis, 8* (1), pp 47–76.

Antonenko, Oksana. (2001). "Russia's Military Involvement in the Middle East." *Middle East Review of International Affairs, 5* (1). On the World Wide Web at http://meria.idc.ac.il /journal/2001/issue1/jv5n1a3.html (retrieved 18 March 2009).

Arrighi, Giovanni. (1970). "Labour Supplies in Historical Perspective: A Study of the Proletarianization of the African Peasantry in Rhodesia." *Journal of Development Studies, 6* (3), 197–234.

Bairoch, Paul. (1982). "International Industrialization Levels from 1750 to 1980." *Journal of European Economic History, 11*, 269–331.

Blaut, James M. (2000). *Eight Eurocentric Historians.* New York: Guilford Press.

Bluestone, B. and B. Harrison, eds. (1982). *The De-Industrialization of America: Plant Closings, Community Abandonment and the Dismantling of Basic Industries.* New York: Basic Books.

Bluestone, B. and B. Harrison. (1988). *The Great U-Turn: Corporate Restructuring and the Polarizing of America.* New York: Basic Books.

Bornschier, Volker. (2002). "Changing Income Inequality in the 2nd Half of the 20th Century: Preliminary Findings and Propositions for Explanation." *Journal of World Systems Research, 8*, 100–127.

Borras, Saturnino. (2008). "Contemporary Land Policies and Land Struggles." In *Critical Development Studies: Readings for Change.* Zacatecas, Mexico: Global Capital and Alternative Development Unit, Doctorate in Development Studies, Universidad Autónoma de Zacatecas and CDS Network.

Braun, D. (1997). *The Rich Get Richer: The Rise of Income Inequality in the United States and the World.* Chicago: Nelson-Hall Publishers.

Brenner, Robert. (1977). "The Origins of Capitalist Development: A Critique of Neo-Smithian Marxism." *New Left Review, 104* (July/August), 25–92.

Brown, Lester. (2003). *Plan B: Rescuing a Planet under Stress and a Civilization in Trouble.* New York: Norton.

Brym, Robert J., et al. (2005). "In Faint Praise of the World Bank's Gender Development Policy." *Canadian Journal of Sociology, 30*, 95–100. On the World Wide Web at http://www.cjsonline.ca /articles/brymetal05.html (retrieved 7 March 2009).

Brym, Robert J., Lance Roberts, John Lie, and Steven Rytina. (2012). *Sociology: Your Compass for a New World*, 4th Canadian ed. Toronto: Nelson.

Cardoso, Fernando Henrique and Enzo Faletto. (1979). *Dependency and Development in Latin America.* Berkeley, CA: University of California Press.

Chappell, Bill. (2011). "Occupy Wall Street: From a Blog Post to a Movement." National Public Radio, October 20. On the World Wide Web at http://www.npr .org/2011/10/20/141530025/occupy-wall-street-from-a -blog-post-to-a-movement (retrieved 19 January 2012).

"Chavez: Venezuela Aiding Latin America." (2007). *Miami Herald* 15 March.

Chesnais, François. (2004). "Globalisation against Development: Liberalisation, Deregulation, Privatisation and the Contemporary Performance of the International Economy." On the World Wide Web at http://www.nadir.org/nadir /initiativ/agp/free/wsf/mumbai2004/0117chesnais.htm (retrieved 7 March 2009).

Diamond, Jared. (1999). *Guns, Germs and Steel: The Fates of Human Societies.* New York: Norton.

Ellis, Frank. (1983). *Las Transnacionales del Banano en Centroamérica [Banana Transnationals in Central America].* San Jose, CA: EDUCA.

Falla, Ricardo. (1994). *Massacres in the Jungle: Ixcan, Guatemala 1975–1982.* Boulder, CO: Westview.

Frank, Andre Gunder. (1966). *Capitalism and Underdevelopment in Latin America: Historical Studies of Chile and Brazil.* New York: Monthly Review Press.

Gareau, Frederick H. (2004). *State Terrorism and the United States.* Atlanta: Clarity Press.

Handy, Jim. (1985). *A Gift of the Devil: A History of Guatemala.* Toronto: Between the Lines.

Hochschild, Adam. (1999). *King Leopold's Ghost: A Story of Greed, Terror, and Heroism in Colonial Africa.* New York: Mariner Books.

Inkeles, Alex and David H. Smith. (1976). *Becoming Modern: Individual Change in Six Developing Countries.* Cambridge, MA: Harvard University Press.

La Via Campesina. (2007). "Declaration of Nyéléni." On the World Wide Web at http://viacampesina.org/en/index .php?option=com_content&view=article&id=282:declara tion-of-nyi&catid=21:food-sovereignty-and-trade&Itemid=38 (retrieved 20 March 2009).

Marchak, Patricia. (1999). *God's Assassins: State Terrorism in Argentina in the 1970s.* Montreal, QC, and Kingston, ON: McGill-Queen's University Press.

Marshall, Jonathan, Peter Dale Scott, and Jane Hunter. (1987). *The Iran-Contra Connection.* Montreal: Black Rose Books.

McClelland, David. (1961). *The Achieving Society.* Princeton, NJ: Van Nostrand.

Milanovic, Branko. (2005). "Global Income Inequality: What It Is and Why It Matters?" DESA Working Paper No. 26. On the World Wide Web at http://www.un.org/esa/desa/papers/2006 /wp26_2006.pdf (retrieved 7 March 2009).

Milanovic, Branko. (2008). "An Even Higher Global Inequality than Previously Thought: A Note on Global Inequality Calculations Using the 2005 International Comparison Program Results." *International Journal of Health Services, 38*, 421–29.

Milanovic, Branko. (2009). "Developing Countries Worse Off than Once Thought." Washington: Carnegie Endowment for International Peace. On the World Wide Web at http://www .carnegieendowment.org/publications/index .cfm?fa=view&id=19907 (retrieved 12 July 2009).

Murmis, Miguel and Juan Carlos Portantiero. (1969). *Estudios Sobre Los Orígenes del Peronismo.* Buenos Aires: Siglo XXI.

Neilsen, François. (2007). "Income Inequality in the Global Economy: The Myth of Rising World Inequality." *Harvard College Economics Review, 1* (2), 23–26.

"Occupy Protests Around the World." (2011). *Guardian* October 17. http://www.guardian.co.uk/news /datablog/2011/oct/17/occupy-protests-world-list-map (retrieved 19 January 2012).

Parpart, Jane and Henry Veltmeyer. (2003). "The Dynamics of Development Theory and Practice: A Review of Its Shifting Dynamics." *Canadian Journal of Development Studies, 25* (1).

Pickover, Clifford. (1997). "Why Did Human History Evolve Differently on Different Continents for the Last 13,000 Years?" Edge Foundation. On the World Wide Web at http: //www.edge.org/discourse/diamond_evolution.html (retrieved 7 March 2009).

Richards, Alan. (1976). "The Political Economy of Gutswirtschaft: A Comparative Analysis of East-Elbian Germany, Egypt, and Chile." *Comparative Studies in Society and History, 21* (3), 483–518.

Rodney, Walter. (1972). *How Europe Underdeveloped Africa*. London: Bogle-L'Ouverture Publications.

Rodriguez Gomez, Guadalupe, and Gabriel Torres. (1996). "El Barzón y la Comagro: La Resistencia de los Agricultores a la Politica Neoliberal." In Grammont and Tejera Gaona, eds., *La Sociedad Rural Mexicana Frente al Nuevo Milenio*. Mexico City: Plaza y Valdez Editores.

Rostow, W. W. (1960). *The Stages of Economic Growth: A Non-communist Manifesto*. Cambridge, UK: Cambridge University Press.

Shiva, Vandana. (1993). "GATT, Agriculture and Third World Women." In Maria Mies and Vandana Shiva, eds., *Ecofeminism* (pp. 241–5). Halifax: Fernwood Books.

Stiglitz, Joseph. (2003). *Globalization and Its Discontents*. New York: Norton.

Stone, Samuel. (1975). *La Dinastia de los Conquistadores*. San Jose, Costa Rica: EDUCA.

Sutcliffe, Robert. (2005). "Interview with Bob Sutcliffe: Measuring Global Inequality." Amherst: University of Massachusetts, Political Economy Research Institute, February 23. On the World Wide Web at http://www.peri.umass.edu/338/ (retrieved 12 July 2009).

United Nations. (2009). "Indicators on Income and Economic Activity." *Social Indicators*. On the World Wide Web at http://unstats.un.org/unsd/demographic/products/socind/inc-eco.htm (retrieved 12 July 2009).

Vilas, Carlos. (1986). *The Sandinista Revolution*. New York: Monthly Review Press.

Waldman, Carl. (2005). "Teotihuacán." *Microsoft Encarta* 2006 [CD]. Redmond, WA: Microsoft.

Winson, Anthony. (1983). "The Formation of Capitalist Agriculture in Latin America and Its Relationship to Political Power and the State." *Comparative Studies in Society and History, 25*, 83–104.

Winson, Anthony. (1985). "The Uneven Development of Canadian Agriculture: Farming in the Maritimes and Ontario." *The Canadian Journal of Sociology, 10* (4) pp. 411–438.

Winson, Anthony. (1989). *Coffee and Democracy in Modern Costa Rica*. London: Macmillan.

Winson, Anthony and Belinda Leach. (2002). *Contingent Work, Disrupted Lives: Labour and Community in the New Rural Economy*. Toronto: University of Toronto Press.

World Social Forum. (2009). "World Social Forum Charter of Principles." On the World Wide Web at http://www forumsocialmundial.org.br/main.php?id_menu=4&cd_language=2 (retrieved 20 March 2009).

CHAPTER 10

Abbott, Elizabeth. (2010). *A History of Marriage*. Toronto: Penguin Canada.

Adams, Mary Louise. (1997). *The Trouble with Normal: Postwar Youth and the Making of Heterosexuality*. Toronto: University of Toronto Press.

Ambert, Anne-Marie. (2012) *Changing Families: Relationships in Context*, 2nd Canadian ed. Toronto: Pearson Education Canada.

Baker, Maureen. (2009a). "Introduction to Family Sociology." In Maureen Baker, ed., *Families: Changing Trends in Canada*, 6th ed. (pp.1–25) Toronto: McGraw-Hill Ryerson.

Baker, Maureen. (2009b). "Strengthening Families? The State and Family Policies." In Maureen Baker, ed., *Families: Changing Trends in Canada*, 6th ed. (pp. 206–24) Toronto: McGraw-Hill Ryerson.

Basten, Stuart. (2009). "Voluntary Childlessness and being Childfree. The Future of Human Reproduction." Working Paper No. 5: University of Oxford. On the World Wide Web at http://www.spi.ox.ac.uk/fileadmin/documents/pdf/Childlessness_-_Number_5.pdf (retrieved 30 July 2012).

Bradbury, Bettina. (1993). *Working Families: Age, Gender, and Daily Survival in Industrializing Montreal*. Toronto: McLelland and Stewart.

Burgoyne, C. B. and V. Morison. (1997). "Money in Remarriage: Keeping Things Simple—and Separate." *The Sociological Review, 45*(3), 363–95.

Calliste, Agnes. (2001). "Black Families in Canada: Exploring the Interconnections of Race, Class, and Gender." In Bonnie Fox, ed., *Family Patterns, Gender Relations*, 2nd ed. Toronto: Oxford University Press.

Carroll, Laura. (2000). *Families of Two: Interviews with Happily Married Couples without Children by Choice*. Bloomington, IN: Xllibris.

Colavecchia, Sandra. (2009). "Moneywork: Caregiving and the Management of Family Finances." In Bonnie Fox, ed., *Family Patterns: Gender Relations*, 3rd ed. (pp.417–27). Toronto: Oxford University Press.

Coontz, Stephanie. (1992). *The Way We Never Were: American Families and the Nostalgia Trap*. New York: Basic Books.

Coontz, Stephanie. (2005). *Marriage, a History: From Obedience to Intimacy or How Love Conquered Marriage*. New York: Viking.

Cory, Jill and Karen McAndless-Davis. (2008). *When Love Hurts: A Women's Guide to Understanding Abuse in Relationships*. New Westminister, BC: WomanKind Press.

Cott, Nancy. (2009). "Domesticity." In Bonnie Fox, ed., *Family Patterns, Gender Relations*, 3rd ed. (pp. 111–17). Toronto: Oxford University Press.

DeVault, M. (1991). *Feeding the Family*. Berkeley, CA: University of California Press.

DeVault, M. (1999). *Liberating Method: Feminism and Social Research*. Philadelphia, PA: Temple University Press.

Dunne, Gillian. (1997). *Lesbian Lifestyles: Women's Work and the Politics of Sexuality*. Toronto: University of Toronto Press.

Eichler, Margrit. (1983). *Families in Canada Today: Recent Changes and Their Policy Consequences*. Toronto: Gage.

Engels, Friedrich. (1972). *The Origin of the Family, Private Property and the State*. New York: International Publishers.

Fetner, Tina. (2008). *How the Religious Right Shaped Lesbian and Gay Activism. Minneapolis*. MN: University of Minnesota Press.

Fox, Bonnie. (2009). *When Couples Become Parents: The Creation of Gender in the Transition to Parenthood*. Toronto: University of Toronto Press.

Fox, Bonnie and Meg Luxton. (2001). "Conceptualizing Family." In Bonnie Fox, ed., *Family Patterns, Gender Relations*, 2nd ed. Toronto: Oxford University Press.

Furstenberg, Frank and Andrew Cherlin. (1991). *Divided Families: What Happens to Children When Parents Part*. Cambridge, MA: Harvard University Press.

Gartner, Rosemary, M. Dawson, and M. Crawford. (2001). Women Killing: Intimate Femicide in Ontario, 1874–1994. In D.E.H. Russell and R. A.Harmes, eds., *Femicide in Global Perspective* (pp. 147–65). New York: Teachers College Press.

Gerson, Kathleen. (1985). *Hard Choices: How Women Decide about Work, Career, and Motherhood.* Berkeley and Los Angeles: University of California Press.

Green, Adam Isaiah. (2011). "The Changing Face of Matrimony: Same-Sex Civil Marriage in the Twenty-First Century." In Robert J. Brym, ed., *Society in Question*, 6th ed. Toronto: Nelson.

Hochschild, Arlie Russell. (1989). *The Second Shift: Working Parents and the Revolution at Home.* New York: Viking.

Hochschild, Arlie Russell. (1997). *The Time Bind: When Work Becomes Home and Home Becomes Work.* New York: Henry Holt and Co.

Javed, N. (2008). "GTA's Secret World of Polygamy." *Toronto Star*, 24 May 24: A10.

Juby, H., N. Marcil-Gratton, and C. Le Bourdais. (2004). *When Parents Separate: Further Findings from the National Longitudinal Survey of Children and Youth.* Ottawa: Department of Justice.

Luxton, Meg. (1980). *More than a Labour of Love.* Toronto: Women's Press.

Margolis, Nancy. (2009). "Putting Mothers on the Pedestal." In Bonnie Fox, ed., *Family Patterns, Gender Relations*, 3rd ed. (pp. 118–34) Toronto: Oxford University Press.

McGill Institute for Health and Social Policy. (2012). "Raising the Global Floor." On the World Wide Web at http://raisingtheglobalfloor.org/index.php (retrieved 30 July 2012).

Murdock, George Peter. (1949). *Social Structure.* New York: Macmillan.

Nelson, Fiona. (1996). *Lesbian Motherhood: An Exploration of Canadian Lesbian Families.* Toronto: University of Toronto Press.

Oakley, Ann. (1975). *The Sociology of Housework.* New York: Pantheon Books.

Organisation for Economic Co-operation and Development. (2011). "Key Characteristics of Parental Leave Systems." Available on the World Wide Web at http://www.oecd.org/dataoecd/45/26/37864482.pdf (retrieved 30 July 2012).

Parsons, T. 1951. *The Social System.* New York: Free Press.

Phipps, Shelley A. (2009). "Lessons from Europe: Policy Options to Enhance the Economic Security of Canadian Families." In Bonnie Fox, ed., *Family Patterns: Gender Relations*, 3rd ed. (pp. 552–73). Toronto: Oxford University Press.

Popenoe, David. (1993). "American Family Decline: 1960–1990: A Review and Appraisal." *Journal of Marriage and the Family*, *55*, 527–555.

Richards, John. (2010). "Reducing Lone-Parent Poverty: A Canadian Success Story." C.D. Howe Institute Commentary. On the World Wide Web at http://www.cdhowe.org/reducing-lone-parent-poverty-a-canadian-success-story/4425 (retrieved 30 July 2012).

Sev'er, Aysan. (1992). *Women and Divorce in Canada.* Toronto: Canadian Scholars' Press.

Stacey, Judith. (2011). *Unhitched: Love, Marriage, and Family Values from West Hollywood to Western China.* New York: New York University Press.

Stacey, Judith and Timothy Biblarz. (2001). "How Does the Sexual Orientation of Parents Matter?" American Sociological Review, *66* (2), 159–183.

Statistics Canada. (2005). "Divorces." *The Daily 9*, 2–5.

Statistics Canada. (2007). "2006 Census Dictionary: Census Family." On the World Wide Web at http://www12.statcan.ca (retrieved 30 July 2012).

Statistics Canada. (2009a). "Married-Couple Families with Children Aged 24 and Under is Largest Family Structure, but Declining." On the World Wide Web at http://www12.statcan.ca/census-recensement/2006/as-sa/97-553/figures/c1-eng.cfm (retrieved 19 August 2011).

Statistics Canada. (2009b). "Figure 8: Persons in Common-Law Couples Increasing for All Age Groups." On the World Wide Web at http://www12.statcan.ca/census-recensement/2006/as-sa/97-553/figures/c8-eng.cfm (retrieved 20 August 2011).

Statistics Canada. (2009c). "Figure 13: Proportion of Children aged 14 and Under Living with Married Parents Continues to Decrease." On the World Wide Web at http://www12.statcan.ca/census-recensement/2006/as-sa/97-553/figures/c13-eng.cfm (retrieved 18 August 2011).

Statistics Canada. (2009d). "Figure 6: One-Person Households and Households Containing Couples without Children Are Growing the Fastest." On the World Wide Web at http://www12.statcan.ca/census-recensement/2006/as-sa/97-553/figures/c6-eng.cfm (retrieved 18 August 2011).

Statistics Canada. (2009e). "Figure 15: More Young Adults in Their Twenties Live in the Parental Home in 2006." On the World Wide Web at http://www12.statcan.ca/census-recensement/2006/as-sa/97-553/figures/c15-eng.cfm (retrieved 18 August 2011).

Statistics Canada. (2011). "Births and total fertility rate, by province and territory." On the World Wide Web at http://www.statcan.gc.ca/tables-tableaux/sum-som/l01/cst01/hlth85b-eng.htm (retrieved 1 September 2012).

Sudarkasa, N. (1993). "Female-Headed African American Households: Some Neglected Dimensions." In H. P McAdoo ed., *Family Ethnicity: Strength in Diversity.* Newbury Park, CA: Sage.

Walzer, Susan. (1998). *Thinking about the Baby: Gender and Transitions into Parenthood.* Philadelphia, PA: Temple University Press.

West, Candace and Don Zimmerman. (1987). "Doing Gender." *Gender and Society*, *1* (2) 125–51.

Wilson, Sue. (2009). "Partnering, Cohabitation, and Marriage." In Maureen Baker, ed., *Families: Changing Trends in Canada*, 6th ed. (pp.68–90) Toronto: McGraw-Hill Ryerson.

Wilson, W. J. (1987). *The Truly Disadvantaged: The Inner City, the Underclass, and Public Policy.* Chicago: University of Chicago Press.

Wu, Zheng and Christoph Schimmele. (2009). "Divorce and Repartnering." In Maureen Baker, ed., *Families: Changing Trends in Canada*, 6th ed. (pp.1–25) Toronto: McGraw-Hill Ryerson.

CHAPTER 11

Adams, Tracey and Sandy Welsh. (2008). *The Organization and Experience of Work.* Toronto: Nelson.

Adams, Tracey L. (2000). *A Gentleman and a Dentist: Gender and the Rise of Dentistry in Ontario.* Toronto: University of Toronto Press.

Althauser, Robert. (1989). "Internal Labor Markets." *Annual Review of Sociology*, *15*, 143–61.

Baldwin, John R. and Desmond Beckstead. (2003). "Knowledge Workers in Canada's Economy, 1971–2001." Statistics Canada, Catalogue No. 11-624-MIE, Research Paper No. 004. Ottawa: Ministry of Industry.

Becker, Gary S. (1975). *Human Capital: A Theoretical and Empirical Analysis with Special Reference to Education*, 3rd ed. Chicago: University of Chicago Press.

Bell, Daniel. (1973). *The Coming of Post-Industrial Society*. New York: Basic Books.

Bendix, Reinhard. (1974). *Work and Authority in Industry*. Berkeley, CA: University of California Press.

Berinstein, Juana. (2004). "Temp Workers and Deadbeat Bosses." *Our Times* (October/November).

Blauner, Robert. (1964). *Alienation and Freedom*. Chicago: University of Chicago Press.

Boswell, W. R. and J. B. Olsen-Buchanan. (2007). "The Use of Communication Technologies after Hours: the Role of Work Attitudes and Work-Life Conflict." *Journal of Management 33*, 592–610.

Braverman, Harry. (1974). *Labor and Monopoly Capital: The Degradation of Work in the Twentieth Century*. New York: Monthly Review Press.

Bridges, William. (1994). *Job Shift: How to Prosper in a Workplace without Jobs*. Don Mills, ON: Addison-Wesley.

Burawoy Michael. (1979). *Manufacturing Consent: Changes in the Labour Process under Monopoly Capitalism*. Chicago: University of Chicago Press.

Burman, Patrick. (1997). "Changes in the Patterns of Unemployment: The New Realities of Joblessness." In Ann Duffy, Daniel Glenday, and Norene Pupo, eds., *Good Jobs, Bad Jobs, No Jobs: The Transformation of Work in the 21st Century* (pp. 190–216). Toronto: Harcourt Brace.

Calliste, Agnes. (1993). "Sleeping Car Porters in Canada: An Ethnically Submerged Split Labour Market." In Graham S. Lowe and Harvey Krahn, eds., *Work in Canada: Readings in the Sociology of Work and Industry* (pp. 139–53). Toronto: Nelson.

Campbell, Andrew. (1996). "From Shop Floor to Computer Room." *Globe and Mail* 30 December: A1, A8.

Canadian Policy Research Networks. (2006a). "It's More Than the Money—What Canadians Want in a Job." On the World Wide Web at http://www.jobquality.ca/indicator_e/rew001.stm (retrieved 9 March 2006).

Canadian Policy Research Networks. (2006b). "Job Satisfaction." On the World Wide Web at http://www.jobquality.ca/indicators/rewards/rew2.shtml (retrieved 9 March 2006).

Canadian Press/Leger Marketing. (2001). *How Much Importance Canadians Place on Their Work*. Montreal.

Carey, Alex. (1967). "The Hawthorne Studies: A Radical Criticism." *American Sociological Review, 32*, 403–16.

Carriére, Yves and Diane Galarneau. 2011. "Delayed Retirement: A New Trend?" *Perspectives on Labour Market and Income* (Spring), 3–16. Statistics Canada. Catalogue No. 75-001-X.

Chaykowski, Richard. (2005). *Non-Standard Work and Economic Vulnerability*, Vulnerable Workers Series, No. 3. Ottawa: CPRN.

Cranford, Cynthia, Leah Vosko, and Nancy Zukewich. (2003). "The Gender of Precarious Employment in Canada." *Relations Industrielles/Industrial Relations, 58* (3), 454–79.

Dassbach, Carl H. A. (1996). "Lean Production, Labor Control, and Post-Fordism in the Japanese Automobile Industry." In William C. Green and Ernest J. Yanarella, eds., *North American Auto Unions in Crisis: Lean Production as Contested Terrain* (pp. 19–40). Albany, NY: SUNY Press.

Economic Council of Canada. (1991). *Good Jobs, Bad Jobs: Employment in the Service Economy*. Ottawa: Supply and Services Canada.

Edwards, P. K. and Hugh Scullion. (1982). *The Social Organization of Industrial Conflict*. Oxford: Blackwell.

Edwards, Richard. (1979). *Contested Terrain: The Transformation of the Workplace in the Twentieth Century*. New York: Basic Books.

Ehrenreich, Barbara. (2005). *Bait and Switch: The (Futile) Pursuit of the American Dream*. New York: Metropolitan Books.

Epstein, Cynthia Fuchs and Arne Kalleberg. (2001). "Time and the Sociology of Work: Issues and Implications." *Work and Occupations, 28* (1), 5–16.

Erickson, Bonnie. (2001). "Good Networks and Good Jobs: The Value of Social Capital to Employers and Employees." In Nan Lin, Karen Cook, and Ronald Burt, eds., *Social Capital: Theory and Research* (pp. 127–58). New York: Aldine de Gruyter.

Flap, Henk and Ed Boxman. (2001) "Getting Started: The Influence of Social Capital on the Start of the Occupational Career." In Nan Lin, Karen Cook,and Ronald Burt, eds., *Social Capital: Theory and Research* (pp. 159–81). New York: Aldine de Gruyter.

Fountain, Christine M. (2005). "Finding a Job in the Internet Age." *Social Forces, 83* (3), 1235–62.

Friedson, Eliot. (1970). *The Profession of Medicine: A Study in the Sociology of Applied Knowledge*. New York: Harper and Row.

Fudge, J. and L. F. Vosko. (2001). "By Whose Standards? Re-Regulating the Canadian Labour Market." *Economic and Industrial Democracy, 22* (3), 327.

Gilmore, Jason. (2009). "The 2008 Canadian Immigrant Labour Market: Analysis of Quality Employment." November, 1–39. Statistics Canada. Catalogue No. 71-606-X.

Gilmore, Jason and Sébastien LaRochelle-Côté. (2011). "Inside the Labour Market Downturn." *Perspectives on Labour Market and Income* (Spring), pp. 3–14. Statistics Canada. Catalogue No. 75-001-X.

Granovetter, Mark. (1995 [1974]). *Getting a Job: A Study of Contacts and Careers*, 2nd ed. Cambridge, MA: Harvard.

Hodson, Randy. (1991). "The Active Worker: Compliance and Autonomy at the Workplace." *Contemporary Ethnography, 20* (April), 271–90.

Hodson, Randy and Teresa Sullivan. (1990). *The Social Organization of Work*. Belmont, CA: Wadsworth.

Houseman, Susan, Arne Kalleberg, and George Erickcek. (2003). "The Role of Temporary Agency Employment in Tight Labour Markets." *Industrial and Labor Relations Review, 57* (1), 105–27.

Jones, Frank E. (1996). *Understanding Organizations: A Sociological Perspective*. Cooksville, ON: Copp Clark.

Kalleberg, Arne. (2000). "Nonstandard Employment Relations: Part-time, Temporary and Contract Work." *Annual Review of Sociology, 26*, 341–65.

Kalleberg, Arne. (2003). "Flexible Firms and Labor Market Segmentation: Effects of Workplace Restructuring on Jobs and Workers." *Work & Occupations, 30* (2), 154–75.

Kalleberg, Arne (2011). *Good Jobs, Bad Jobs: The Rise of Polarized and Precarious Employment Systems in the United States, 1970s-2000s*. New York: Russell Sage Foundation, American Sociological Association Rose Series in Sociology.

Kalleberg, Arne L., Barbara F. Reskin, and Ken Hudson. (2000). "Bad Jobs in America: Standard and Nonstandard Employment Relations and Job Quality in the United States." *American Sociological Review, 65*, 256–78.

Krahn, Harvey J. (1992). *Quality of Work in the Service Economy*. General Social Survey Analysis Series 6. Ottawa: Statistics Canada. Catalogue No. 11-612E.

Krahn, Harvey J. (1995). "Nonstandard Work on the Rise." *Perspectives on Labour and Income* (Winter), 35–42.

Krahn, Harvey J. and Graham S. Lowe. (1998). *Work, Industry and Canadian Society*, 3rd ed. Toronto: ITP Nelson.

Kunda, Gideon, Stephen R. Barley, and James Evans. (2002). "Why Do Contractors Contract? The Experience of Highly Skilled Technical Professionals in a Contingent Labor Market." *Industrial and Labor Relations Review, 55* (2), 234–61.

LaRochelle-Côté., Sébastien, and Sharanjit Uppal. (2011). "The Financial Well-being of the Self-Employed." *Perspectives on Labour Market and Income.* Winter. Statistics Canada. Catalogue No. 75-001-X. pp. 3–15.

Laxer, Gordon. (1989). *Open for Business: The Roots of Foreign Ownership in Canada.* Toronto: Oxford University Press.

Livingstone, D. W (1993). "Conclusion: Aging Dinosaurs or All-Round Workers?" In June Corman, Meg Luxton, D. W Livingstone, and Wally Secombe, eds., *Recasting Steel Labour: The Stelco Story* (pp. 145–55). Halifax, NS: Fernwood.

Lowe, Graham S. (1987). *Women in the Administrative Revolution: The Feminization of Clerical Work.* Toronto: University of Toronto Press.

Marsden, Peter and J. Hurlbert. (1988). "Social Resources and Mobility Outcomes." *Social Forces, 66*, 1038–59.

Matusik, Sharon F. and Amy E. Mickel. (2011). "Embracing or Embattled by Converged Mobile Devices? Users' Experiences with a Contemporary Connectivity Technology." *Human Relations 64* (8), 1001–1030.

Mazmanian, Melissa, Wanda J. Orlikowski, and JoAnne Yates. (2005). CrackBerrys: Exploring the Social Implications of Ubiquitous Wireless Email Devices. In *Proceedings of the IFIP 8.2 Working Conference on Ubiquitous Computing*, Cleveland, OH.

McKay, Shona. (1993). "Willing and Able." In Graham S. Lowe and Harvey Krahn, eds., *Work in Canada: Readings in the Sociology of Work and Industry* (pp. 166–71). Toronto: Nelson.

McKenzie, Donald. (2001). "Poll: 90% Satisfied with Their Jobs, 70% Happy with Salary." *Financial Post* 31 December: FP3.

Morissette, René. (1991). "Are Jobs in Large Firms Better?" *Perspectives on Labour and Income* (Autumn), 40–50.

MSNBC. 2007. "Graveyard Shift Linked to Cancer Risk." On the World Wide Web at http://www.msnbc.msn.com /id/22026660/ (retrieved 26 March 2009).

Olsen, Karen M. and Arne Kalleberg. (2004). "Nonstandard Work in Two Different Employment Regimes: Norway and the United States." *Work, Employment and Society, 18* (2), 321–48.

Olson-Buchanan, J. B. and W. R. Boswell (2006). "Blurring Boundaries: Correlates of Integration and Segmentation between Work and Non-Work. *Journal of Vocational Behavior 68*, 432–45.

Osterman, Paul. (1995). "The Transformation of Work in the United States: What the Evidence Shows." In Bryan Downie and Mary Lou Coates, eds., *Managing Human Resources in the 1990s and Beyond* (pp. 71–92). Kingston, ON: Industrial Relations Centre Press.

Pescocolido, Bernice, Steven Tuch, and Jack Martin. (2001). "The Profession of Medicine and the Public: Examining Americans' Changing Confidence in Physician Authority from the Beginning of the 'Health Care Crisis' to the Era of Health Care Reform." *Journal of Health and Social Behavior, 42* (March), 1–16.

Polanyi, Karl. (1957). *The Great Transformation.* Boston: Beacon Press.

Pold, Henry. (2004). "Duration of Nonstandard Employment" *Perspectives on Labour and Income*, 5 (12).

Preisler, Marie. (2011). "EU Directive on Temporary Agency Work Could Reduce Social Dumping." *Nordic Labour Journal.* April. On the World Wide Web at http://www.nordiclabour-journal.org/i-fokus/in-focus-2011/temporary-workers /article.2011-04-01.4693831011 (retrieved 30 July 2012).

Presser, Harriet. (1999). "Toward a 24-Hour Economy." *Science, 284* (June 11), 1778–89.

Presser, Harriet. (2003). "Race, Ethnic, and Gender Differences in Nonsandard Work Shifts." *Work & Occupations, 30* (4), 412–39.

Presser, Harriet. (2004). *Employment in a 24/7 Economy: Challenges for American Families.* New York: Russell Sage.

Rifkin, Jeremy. (1995). *The End of Work: The Decline of the Global Labor Force and the Dawn of the Post-Market Era.* New York: G. P. Putnam.

Rinehart, James. (1996). *The Tyranny of Work: Alienation and the Labour Process*, 3rd ed. Toronto: Harcourt Brace.

Ritzer, George. (1993). *The McDonaldization of Society.* Newbury Park, CA: Pine Forge.

Robertson, David, James Rinehart, Christopher Huxley, Jeff Wareham, Herman Rosenfeld, Alan McGough, and Steve Benedict. (1993). *The CAMI Report: Lean Production in a Unionized Auto Plant.* North York, ON: CAW Research.

Rogers, Jackie Krasas. (1995). "Just a Temp: Experience and Structure of Alienation in Temporary Clerical Employment." *Work and Occupations, 22* (2), 137–66.

Rosenthal, Patrice, Stephen Hill, and Riccardo Peccei. (1997). "Checking out Service: Evaluating Excellence, HRM and TQM in Retailing." *Work, Employment and Society, 11* (3), 481–503.

Schieman, S. and P. Glavin. (2008) "Trouble at the Border? Gender, Flexibility at Work, and the Work-Home Interface. "*Social Problems 55* (4), 590–611.

Schmitt, R. and T. E. Moody. (1994). *Alienation and Social Criticism.* Atlantic Highlands, NJ: Humanities Press.

Shain, Alan. (1995). "Employment of People with Disabilities." *Canadian Social Trends* (Autumn), 8–13.

Shalla, Vivian. (2002). "Jettisoned by Design? The Truncated Employment Relationship of Customer Sales and Service Agents under Airline Restructuring." *Canadian Review of Sociology and Anthropology, 27* (1), 1–32.

Shields, Margot. (2002). "Shift Work and Health." *Health Reports, 13* (4), 11–33. Statistics Canada. Catalogue No. 82–003.

Shields, Margot. (2003). "The Health of Canada's Shift Workers. *Canadian Social Trends* (Summer), 21–25. Statistics Canada. Catalogue No. 11–008.

Smith, Michael. (1999). "Insecurity in the Labour Market: The Case of Canada since the Second World War." *Canadian Journal of Sociology, 24* (2), 193–224.

Smith, Vicki. (2001). *Crossing the Great Divide: Worker Risk and Opportunity in the New Economy.* Ithaca and Cornell, NY: IRL Press.

Spenner, Kenneth. (1983). "Deciphering Prometheus: Temporal Change in the Skill Level of Work." *American Sociological Review, 48* (6), 824–37.

Statistics Canada. (2003). "The Changing Profile of Canada's Labour Force." *2001 Census: Analysis Series.* Ottawa: Ministry of Industry. Catalogue No. 96F0030XIE2001009.

Statistics Canada. (2004). *Canada E-book.* On the World Wide Web at http://142.206.72.67/r000_e.htm (retrieved 22 September 2006).

Statistics Canada. (2006a). "The Canadian Labour Market at a Glance, 2005." Ottawa: Industry Canada. Catalogue No. 71-222-XIE.

Statistics Canada. (2006b). "Latest Release from the Labour Force Survey." *The Daily* August 4. On the World Wide Web at http://www.statcan.ca/english/Subjects/Labour/LFS/lfs-en.htm (retrieved 22 September 2006).

Statistics Canada. (2009). "The Canadian Labour Market at a Glance, 2007." Ottawa: Industry Canada. Catalogue No. 71-222-X.

Statistics Canada. (2011a). *Canada Year Book 2011* (pp. 302–325). Statistics Canada. Catalogue No. 11-402-X.

Statistics Canada. (2011b). *Employment, Earnings, and Hours,* December, 1–384. Statistics Canada. Catalogue No. 72–002-X.

Statistics Canada. (2012a). "Educational Attainment and Employment: Canada in an International Context." Fact Sheet No. 8, Statistics Canada. Catalogue No. 81-599-X. pp. 1–9.

Statistics Canada. (2012b). Table 282–0008 (CANSIM). "Labour Force Survey Estimates (LFS), by North American Industry Classification System (NAICS), Sex and Age Group." http://www5.statcan.gc.ca/cansim/pick-choisir?lang=eng&p2=33&id=2820008 (retrieved 15 February 2012).

Statistics Canada. (2012c). Table 282–0079 (CANSIM). "Labour Force Survey Estimates (LFS), Employees by Job Permanency, North American Industry Classification System (NAICS), Sex and Age Group, Unadjusted for Seasonality." On the World Wide Web at http://www5.statcan.gc.ca/cansim/pick-choisir?lang=eng&p2=33&id=2820079 (retrieved 1 March 2012).

Statistics Canada. (2012d). "Labour Force Survey, July 2012. *The Daily* August 10. On the World Wide Web at http://www.statcan.gc.ca/daily-quotidien/120810/dq120810a-eng.htm (retrieved 2 September 2012).

Toffler, Alvin. (1980). *The Third Wave.* New York: Bantam.

U.S. Bureau of Labor Statistics. (2010). "Occupational Outlook Handbook, 2010–11 Edition." On the World Wide Web at http://www.bls.gov/oco/ (retrieved 30 July 2012).

Uppal, Sharanjit. (2011). "Unionization 2001. Inside the Labour Market Downturn." *Perspectives on Labour Market and Income.* Winter, 3–12. Statistics Canada. Catalogue No. 75-001-X.

Usalcas, Jeannine. (2008). "Hours Polarization Revisited." In *Perspectives on Labour Market and Income* (March), 5–15. Statistics Canada. Catalogue No. 75-001X.

Vosko, Leah. (2000). *Temporary Work: The Gendered Rise of a Precarious Employment Relationship.* Toronto: University of Toronto Press.

White, Julie. (1993). "Patterns of Unionization." In Linda Briskin and Patricia McDermott, eds., *Women Challenging Unions: Feminism, Democracy, and Militancy* (pp. 191–206). Toronto: University of Toronto Press.

Williams, Cara. (2008). "Work-Life Balance of Shift Workers." *Perspectives on Labour and Income, 9* (8), 5–16. Statistics Canada. Catalogue No. 75-001-X.

Womack, J., D. Jones, and D. Roos. (1990). *The Machine That Changed the World.* New York: Rawson and Associates.

Yakubovich, Valery (2005). "Weak Ties, Information and Influence: How Workers Find Jobs in a Local Russian Labor Market." *American Sociological Review, 70* (3), 408–21.

Zuboff, Shoshana. (1988). *In the Age of the Smart Machine: The Future of Work and Power.* New York: Basic Books.

CHAPTER 12

Adler, Patricia A. and Peter Adler. (1994). "Reproduction of the Corporate Other: The Institutionalization of After-School Activities." *Sociological Quarterly, 35* (2), 309–28.

Alexander, Karl L., Doris Entwisle, and Linda Steffel Olsen. (2007). "Lasting Consequences of the Summer Learning Gap." *American Sociological Review,* 72, 167–80.

American Association of University Women Educational Foundation. (1998). *Gender Gaps: Where Schools Still Fail Our Children.* American Institutes for Research. Washington, DC: AAUW Educational Foundation.

Anglin, P. M. and R. Meng. (2000). "Evidence on Grades and Grade Inflation at Ontario's Universities." *Canadian Public Policy, 26,* 361–68.

Anisef, P. (1974). *The Critical Juncture.* Toronto: Ministry of Colleges and Universities.

Arai, A. Bruce. (2000). "Changing Motivations for Homeschooling in Canada." *Canadian Journal of Education, 25* (3), 204–17.

Arum, Richard and Josipa Roksa. (2010). *Academically Adrift: Limited Learning on College Campuses.* Chicago: University of Chicago Press.

Aurini, Janice. (2002). "Fostering the Unique Child: New Trends in Childrearing, A Case Study." Unpublished paper, McMaster University, Hamilton, Ontario.

Aurini, Janice. (2004). "Educational Entrepreneurialism in the Private Tutoring Industry: Balancing Profitability with the Humanistic Face of Schooling." *Canadian Review of Sociology and Anthropology, 41* (4), 475–91.

Aurini, Janice and Scott Davies. (2004). "The Transformation of Private Tutoring: Education in a Franchise Form." *Canadian Journal of Sociology, 29* (3), 419–38.

Aurini, Janice and Scott Davies. (2005). "Choice without Markets: Homeschooling in the Context of Private Education." *British Journal of Sociology of Education, 26* (4), 461–74.

Axelrod, Paul. (1997). *The Promise of Schooling: Education in Canada 1800–1914.* Toronto: University of Toronto Press.

Becker, Gary. (1964). *Human Capital,* 2nd ed. New York: Columbia University Press.

Bennett DeMarrais, Kathleen and Margaret D. LeCompte. (1995). *The Way Schools Work: A Sociological Analysis of Education,* 2nd ed. White Plains, NY: Longman.

Blossfeld, H. P. and Y. Shavit. (1993). "Persisting Barriers: Changes in Educational Opportunities in Thirteen Countries." In Y. Shavit and H. P. Blossfeld, eds., *Persistent Inequality: Changing Educational Attainment in Thirteen Countries.* Boulder, CO: Westview.

Borja, Rhea R. (2005). "Growing Niche for Tutoring Chains: Pre-Kindergartners' Academic Prep." *Education Week, 25* (8), 19 October: 10.

Bosetti, Lynn. (2001). "The Alberta Charter School Experience." In Claudia R. Hepburn, ed., *Can the Market Save Our Schools?* (pp. 101–20). Vancouver, BC: The Fraser Institute.

Bowles, Samuel and Herbert Gintis. (1976). *Schooling in Capitalist America: Educational Reform and the Contradictions of Economic Life.* New York: Basic Books.

Brint, Steven, M. F. Contreras, and M. T. Matthews. (2001). "Socialization Messages in Primary Schools: An Organizational Analysis." *Sociology of Education, 74,* 157–80.

Buchmann, Claudia, Thomas A. DiPrete, and Ann McDaniel. (2008). "Gender Inequalities in Education." *Annual Review of Sociology, 34,* 319–37.

Burkam, David, Douglas Ready, Valerie Lee, and Laura LoGerfo. (2004). "Social Class Differences in Summer Learning between Kindergarten and First Grade: Model Specification and Estimation" *Sociology of Education*, 77, 1–31.

Canadian Council on Learning. (2007). *2007 Survey of Canadians' Attitudes towards Learning: Results for Elementary and Secondary Learning.* Ottawa: Author.

Chubb, John E. and Terry M. Moe. (1990). *Politics, Markets and America's Schools.* Washington, DC: The Brookings Institution.

Cohen, Albert. (1955). *Delinquent Boys: The Culture of the Gang.* Glencoe, IL: Free Press.

Coleman, James. (1961). *The Adolescent Society.* New York: Free Press.

Collins, R. (1979). *The Credential Society.* New York: Academic Press.

Côté, James and Anton Allahar. (2006). *Ivory Tower Blues: A University System in Crisis.* Toronto: University of Toronto Press.

Côté, James and Anton Allahar. (2011). *Lowering Higher Education: The Rise of Corporate Universities and the Fall of Liberal Education.* Toronto: University of Toronto Press.

Daly, Kerry. (2004). *The Changing Culture of Parenting.* Ottawa: Vanier Institute of the Family.

Davies, Lynn. (1984). *Pupil Power: Deviance and Gender in School.* London: Falmer Press.

Davies, Scott. (1992). *In Search of the Culture Clash: Explaining Class Inequalities in Education.* Doctoral Dissertation, Department of Sociology: University of Toronto.

Davies, Scott. (2004). "Stubborn Disparities: Explaining Class Inequalities in Schooling." In James Curtis, Edward Grabb, and Neil Guppy, eds., *Social Inequality in Canada: Patterns, Problems and Policies*, 4th ed. (pp. 138–150). Toronto: Prentice Hall.

Davies, Scott and Neil Guppy. (1997). "Fields of Study, College Selectivity, and Student Inequalities." *Social Forces, 73* (4), 131–51.

Davies, Scott and Neil Guppy. (2006). *The Schooled Society: An Introduction to the Sociology of Education.* Toronto: Oxford University Press.

Davies, Scott and Floyd Hammack. (2005). "Channelling Competition in Higher Education: Comparing Canada and the US." *Journal of Higher Education, 76* (1), 89–106.

Davies, Scott and Linda Quirke. (2005). "Providing for the Priceless Student: Ideologies of Choice in an Emerging Educational Market" *American Journal of Education, 111* (4), 596–608.

De Broucker, Patrice and Laval Lavallée. (1998). "Getting Ahead in Life: Does Your Parents' Education Count?" *Education Quarterly Review, 5* (1), 22–28.

Dei, George. (2005). "The Case for Black Schools." *Toronto Star* 4 February.

Dennison, John D., ed. (1995). *Canada's Community Colleges at the Crossroads.* Vancouver, BC: UBC Press.

Downey, Douglas and James Ainsworth-Darnell. (2002). "The Search for Oppositional Culture among Black Students." *American Sociological Review, 67*, 156–64.

Downey, Douglas B., Paul T. von Hippel, and Beckett A. Broh. (2004). "Are Schools the Great Equalizer? Cognitive Inequality during the Summer Months and the School Year." *American Sociological Review, 69* (5), 613–35.

Dreeben, Robert. (1967). *On What Is Learned in School.* Reading, MA: Addison-Wesley.

Durkheim, Émile. (1961 [1925]). *Moral Education: A Study in the Theory and Application of the Sociology of Education.* New York: Free Press.

Fordham, Signithia and John Ogbu. (1986). "Black Students' School Success: Coping with the 'Burden' of 'Acting White.'" *The Urban Review, 18*, 176–206.

Frenette, Marc. (2005). "The Impact of Tuition Fees on University Access: Evidence from a Large-Scale Price Deregulation in Professional Programs." Ottawa: Statistics Canada. Catalogue No. 11F00119MIE.

Frenette, Marc and Klarka Zeman. (2008). "Why are the Majority of University Students Women?" *Education Matters, 5* (1). On the World Wide Web at http://www.statcan.gc.ca/pub/81-004-x/2008001/article/10561-eng.htm (retrieved 2 August 2012).

Gamoran, Adam. (2001). "American Schooling and Educational Inequality: A Forecast for the 21st Century." *Sociology of Education* (Extra Issue), 135–53.

Gardner, Howard. (1998). "A Multiplicity of Intelligences." [Special Issue]. *Scientific American 9* (4), 18–23.

Gardner, Howard. (1999). *Intelligence Reframed: Multiple Intelligences for the 21st Century.* New York: Basic Books.

Government of Ontario. (1950). *Aims of Education: Report of the Royal Commission on Education in Ontario (The Hope Report).* Toronto: The King's Printer.

Guppy, Neil and Bruce Arai. (1994). "Teaching Sociology: Comparing Undergraduate Curricula in the United States and Canada." *Teaching Sociology, 22*, 217–30.

Holland, D. C. and M. Eisenhart. (1990). *Educated in Romance: Women, Achievement, and College Culture.* Chicago: University of Chicago Press.

Hurn, C. J. (1993). *The Limits and Possibilities of Schooling: An Introduction to the Sociology of Education.* Boston: Allyn and Bacon.

Jackson, Philip W., Robert E. Boostrom, and David T. Hansen. (1998). *The Moral Life of Schools.* San Francisco: John Wiley and Sons.

Kelly, Gail and Ann Nihlen. (1982). "Schooling and the Reproduction of Patriarchy: Unequal Workloads, Unequal Rewards." In Michael Apple, ed., *Cultural and Economic Reproduction in American Education: Essays in Class, Ideology and the State* (pp. 162–80). London: Routledge.

Kerckhoff, Alan C. (2002). "The Transition from School to Work." In Jeylan Mortimer and Reed W. Larson, eds., *The Changing Adolescent Experience* (pp. 52–87). New York: Cambridge University Press.

Kingston, P. W., R. Hubbard, B. Lapp, P. Schroeder, and J. Wilson. (2003). "Why Education Matters." *Sociology of Education, 76* (1), 53–70.

Kirp, David L. (2004). *Shakespeare, Einstein and the Bottom Line: The Marketing of Higher Education.* Cambridge, MA: Harvard University Press.

Knighton, T. (2002). "Postsecondary Participation: The Effects of Parents' Education and Household Income." *Education Quarterly Review, 8* (3), 25–31.

Krahn, Harvey. (2004). "Social Class, Postsecondary Education, and Occupational Outcomes: Choose Your Parents Well." In James E. Curtis, Edward Grabb, and Neil Guppy, eds., *Social Inequality in Canada: Patterns, Problems, Policies*, 4th ed. (pp. 187–203). Scarborough, ON: Pearson Prentice-Hall.

Krahn, Harvey and Alison Taylor. (2007). "Streaming in the 10th Grade in Four Canadian Provinces in 2000." *Education*

Matters, 4 (2). On the World Wide Web at http://www.statcan.gc.ca/pub/81-004-x/2007002/9994-eng.htm (retrieved 30 July 2012).

Lewis, Amanada, ed. (2003). *Race in the Schoolyard: Negotiating the Color Line in Classrooms and Communities.* New Brunswick, NJ: Rutgers University Press.

Livingstone, David W. (1998). *The Education-Jobs Gap: Underemployment or Economic Democracy.* Boulder, CO: Westview Press.

Looker, Diane and Victor Thiessen. (1999). "Images of Work: Women's Work, Men's Work, Housework." *Canadian Journal of Sociology, 24* (2), 225–51.

Maclean's Guide to Canadian Universities, 2011 edition. (2011). Toronto: Author.

McMullen, Kathryn. 2011. "Postsecondary Education Participation among Underrepresented and Minority Groups." Statistics Canada. On the world Wide Web at http://www.statcan.gc.ca/pub/81-004-x/2011004/article/11595-eng.htm (retrieved 6 August 2012).

Milner, Murray, Jr. (2004). *Freaks, Geeks and Cool Kids: American Teenagers, Schools, and the Culture of Consumption.* London: Routledge.

Mullen, Ann. (2010). *Degrees of Inequality: Culture, Class and Gender in American Higher Education.* Baltimore: Johns Hopkins University Press.

Ontario Department of Education. (1968). *Living and Learning: The Report of the Provincial Committee on the Aims and Objectives of Education in the Schools of Ontario.* Toronto: Author.

Ontario Human Rights Commission. (2003). *The Ontario Safe Schools Act: School Discipline and Discrimination.* Ottawa: Author. On the World Wide Web at http://www.ohrc.on.ca/english/consultations/safe-schools.pdf (retrieved 20 September 2005).

Ouchi, William. (2003). *Making Schools Work: A Revolutionary Plan to Get Your Children the Education They Need.* New York: Simon and Schuster.

Pallas, A. (2000). "The Effects of Schooling on Individual Lives." In M.T. Hallinan, ed., *Handbook of the Sociology of Education* (pp. 499–525). New York: Kluwer Academic/Plenum Publishers.

Porter, J., M. Porter, and B. Blishen. (1982). *Stations and Callings: Making It through the School System.* Toronto: Methuen.

Powell, A. G., E. Farrar, and D. K. Cohen. (1985). *The Shopping Mall High School: Winners and Losers in the Educational Marketplace.* Boston: Houghton Mifflin.

Prentice, A. (1977). *The School Promoters.* Toronto: McClelland and Stewart.

Quirke, Linda. (2006). "'Keeping Young Minds Sharp': Children's Cognitive Stimulation and the Rise of Parenting Magazines, 1959–2003." *Canadian Review of Sociology, 43* (4), 387–406.

Ryan, B. A. and Adams, G. R. (1999). "How Do Families Affect Children's Success in School?" *Education Quarterly Review, 6* (1), 30–43.

Sayer, L. C., S. M. Bianchi, and J. P. Robinson. (2004). "Are Parents Investing Less in Children? Trends in Mothers' and Fathers' Time with Children." *American Journal of Sociology, 107,* 1–43.

Schleicher, Andreas. (2010). PISA 2009: Evaluating Systems to Improve Education. Paris, France: OECD.

Slaughter, Sheila and Gary Rhoades. (2004). *Academic Capitalism and the New Economy.* Baltimore: Johns Hopkins University Press.

Solomon, R. Patrick. (1992). *Black Resistance in High School: Forging a Separatist Culture.* Albany, NY: SUNY Press.

Statistics Canada. (2001). *Education in Canada, 2000.* Ottawa: Ministry of Industry.

Statistics Canada. (2002). "Survey of Approaches to Educational Planning." Public Use Microdata File.

Statistics Canada. (2011). "University tuition fees." On the World Wide Web at http://www.statcan.gc.ca/daily-quotidien/110916/dq110916b-eng.htm (retrieved 2 September 2012).

Stevens, Mitchell L., Elizabeth A. Armstrong, and Richard Arum. (2008). "Sieve, Incubator, Temple, Hub: Empirical and Theoretical Advances in the Sociology of Higher Education." *Annual Review of Sociology, 34,* 127–51.

Stinchcombe, Arthur. (1964). *Rebellion in a High School.* Chicago: Quadrangle Books.

Tanner, Julian. (2001). *Teenage Troubles: Youth and Deviance in Canada,* 2nd ed. Toronto: Nelson Thomson Learning.

Taylor, A. and L. Woollard. (2003). "The Risky Business of Choosing a High School." *Journal of Education Policy 18* (6), 617–35.

Turner, Ralph H. (1960). "Sponsored and Contest Mobility and School *System.*" *American Sociological Review, 25,* 855–67.

Tyack, David B. (1974). *The One Best System: A History of American Urban Education.* Cambridge, MA: Harvard University Press.

Tyack, David B. and Larry Cuban. (1995). *Tinkering toward Utopia: A Century of Public School Reform.* Cambridge, MA: Harvard University Press.

Tyson, Karolyn, William Darity, Jr., and Domini Castellino. (2005). "It's Not a Black Thing: Understanding the Burden of Acting White and Other Dilemmas of High Achievement." *American Sociological Review, 70* (4), 582–605.

Walters, David. (2004). "'Recycling': The Economic Implications of Obtaining Additional Postsecondary Credentials at Lower or Equivalent Levels." *Canadian Review of Sociology and Anthropology, 40* (4), 463–77.

Wanner, Richard. (2000). "Expansion and Ascription: Trends in Educational Opportunity in Canada 1920–1994." *Canadian Review of Sociology and Anthropology, 36* (3), 409–43.

Weis, L. (1990). *Working Class without Work: High School Students in a De-Industrializing Economy.* New York: Routledge.

Willis, Paul. (1977). *Learning to Labour: How Working Class Kids Get Working Class Jobs.* Farnborough: Saxon House.

Wolf, Alison. (2002). *Does Education Matter? Myths about Education and Economic Growth.* London: Penguin.

CHAPTER 13

Allen, John L., Jr. 2009. *The Future Church.* New York: Doubleday.

Bell, Daniel. (1977). "The Return of the Sacred: The Argument on the Future of Religion." *British Journal of Sociology, 28,* 419–49.

Bellah, Robert. (1967). "Civil Religion in America." *Daedalus, 96* (1), 1–21.

Berger, Peter. (1961) *The Noise of Solemn Assemblies.* New York: Doubleday.

Berger, Peter L. (1974). "Some Second Thoughts on Substantive Versus Functional Definitions of Religion. *Journal for the Scientific Study of Religion, 13,* 125–33.

Beyer, Peter. (1993). "Roman Catholicism in Contemporary Quebec." In W.E. Hewitt, ed., *The Sociology of Religion: A Canadian Focus* (pp. 133–55). Toronto: Butterworths.

Beyer, Peter. (1997). "Religious Vitality in Canada: The Complementarity of Religious Market and Secularization Perspectives." *Journal for the Scientific Study of Religion, 36*, 272–88.

Bibby, Reginald W. (1987). *Fragmented Gods: The Poverty and Potential of Religion in Canada.* Toronto: Stoddart.

Bibby, Reginald W. (1993). *Unknown Gods: The Ongoing Story of Religion in Canada.* Toronto: Stoddart.

Bibby, Reginald W. (1995). *The Bibby Report: Social Trends Canadian Style.* Toronto: Stoddart.

Bibby, Reginald. (2002). *Restless Gods: The Renaissance of Religion in Canada*. Toronto: Stoddart.

Bibby, Reginald W. (2004a). *Restless Gods: The Renaissance of Religion in Canada*, 2nd ed. Ottawa: Novalis.

Bibby, Reginald W. (2004b). *Restless Churches: How Canada's Churches Can Contribute to the Emerging Religious Renaissance.* Ottawa: Novalis.

Bibby, Reginald. 2006. *The Boomer Factor.* Lethbridge AB: Project Canada Books.

Bibby, Reginald W. (2009) *The Emerging Millennials.* Lethbridge, AB: Project Canada Books.

Bibby, Reginald W. (2011a). *Beyond the Gods & Back: Religion's Rise and Demise and Why It Matters.* Lethbridge, AB: Project Canada Books.

Bibby, Reginald W. (2011b). "Continuing the Conversation on Canada: Changing Patterns of Religious Service Attendance." *Journal for the Scientific Study of Religion, 50* (4), 831–39.

Bibby, Reginald W. (2012). "Why Bother with Organized Religion?" *Canadian Review of Sociology, 49* (1), 91–101.

Bramadat, Paul and David Seljak. (2008). "Charting the New Terrain: Christianity and Ethnicity in Canada." In Paul Bramadat and David Seljak eds., *Christianity and Ethnicity in Canada* (pp. 3–48). Toronto: University of Toronto Press.

Brannon, Robert. (1971). "Organizational Vulnerability in Modern Religious Organizations." *Journal for the Scientific Study of Religion, 10*, 27–32.

Brown, Callum. (2009). *The Death of Christian Britain*, 2nd ed. London: Routledge.

Brym, Robert and Bader Araj. (2006). "Suicide Bombing as Strategy and Interaction: The Case of the Second Intifada." *Social Forces, 84*, 1965–82.

Brym, Robert J., William Shaffir, and Morton Weinfeld, eds. (2010). *The Jews in Canada.* Toronto: Oxford University Press.

Catto, Susan. (2003). "In Search of the Spiritual." *Time* November 24: 72–80.

Clark, S. D. (1948). *Church and Sect in Canada.* Toronto: University of Toronto Press.

Cogley, John. (1968). *Religion in a Secular Age.* New York: New American Library.

Cox, Harvey. (2009). *The Future of Faith.* New York: Harper One.

Crysdale, Stewart. (1961). *The Industrial Struggle and Protestant Ethics in Canada.* Toronto: Ryerson Press.

Davies, Alan and Marilyn F. Nefsky. (1997). *How Silent Were the Churches? Canadian Protestantism and the Jewish Plight during the Nazi Era.* Waterloo, ON: Wilfrid Laurier University Press.

Dawson, Lorne L. (2006). *Comprehending Cults: The Sociology of New Religious Movements.* Toronto: Oxford University Press.

Durkheim, Émile. (1965 [1912]). *The Elementary Forms of the Religious Life.* New York: Free Press.

Eagle, David E. (2011). "Changing Patterns of Attendance at Religious Services in Canada, 1986–2008." *Journal for the Scientific Study of Religion, 50* (1), 187–200.

Fallding, Harold. (1978). "Mainline Protestantism in Canada and the United States: An Overview." *Canadian Journal of Sociology 2*, 141–60.

Finke, Roger and Rodney Stark. (1992). *The Churching of America, 1776–1990.* New Brunswick, NJ: Rutgers University Press.

Frankel, B. Gail and W. E. Hewitt. (1994). "Religion and Well-Being among Canadian University Students." *Journal for the Scientific Study of Religion, 33*, 62–73.

Freud, Sigmund. (1962 [1928]). *The Future of an Illusion.* New York: Doubleday

Gallup. (2012). *Religion.* On the World Wide Web at http://www.gallup.com/poll/1690/Religion.aspx (retrieved 25 February 2012).

Gee, Ellen M. and Jean E. Veevers. (1990). "Religious Involvement and Life Satisfaction in Canada." *Sociological Analysis, 51*, 387–94.

General Social Survey. (1985). "Health and Social Support (Cycle 1)." Statistics Canada. On the World Wide Web at http://sda.chass.utoronto.ca.myaccess.library.utoronto.ca/sdaweb/html/gss.htm (retrieved 7 August 2012).

General Social Survey. (2010). "Time-Stress and Well-being (Cycle 24)." Statistics Canada. On the World Wide Web at http://sda.chass.utoronto.ca.myaccess.library.utoronto.ca/sdaweb/html/gss.htm (retrieved 7 August 2012).

Gerth, H. and C. Wright Mills. (1958). *From Max Weber: Essays in Sociology.* New York: Oxford University Press.

Ghafour, Hamida. (2006). "Muslim Fury over Cartoons Hits Britain." *Globe and Mail* 4 February.

Glock, Charles Y., Benjamin Ringer, and Earl Babbie. (1967). *To Comfort and to Challenge.* Berkeley, CA: University of California Press.

Glock, Charles Y. and Rodney Stark. (1965). *Religion and Society in Tension.* Chicago: Rand-McNally.

Gorsuch, Richard and Daniel Aleshire. (1974). "Christian Faith and Ethnic Prejudice: A Review and Interpretation of Research." *Journal for the Scientific Study of Religion, 13*, 281–307.

Graham, Ron. (1990). *God's Dominion: A Sceptic's Quest.* Toronto: McClelland and Stewart.

Herberg, Will. (1960). *Protestant, Catholic, Jew*, rev. ed. New York: Doubleday.

Hiller, Harry H. (1976). "Alberta and the Bible Belt Stereotype." In Stewart Crysdale and Les Wheatcroft, eds., *Religion in Canadian Society* (pp. 372–83). Toronto: Macmillan.

Hobart, Charles. (1974). "Church Involvement and the Comfort Thesis." *Journal for the Scientific Study of Religion, 13*, 463–70.

Johnson, Benton. (1961). "Do Holiness Sects Socialize in Dominant Values?" *Social Forces, 39*, 309–16.

Kiefer, Heather Mason. (2004). "Divine Subjects: Canadians Believe, Britons Skeptical." On the World Wide Web at http://www.gallup.com/poll/14083/divine-subjects-canadians-believe-britons-skeptical.aspx (retrieved 30 July 2012).

Kirkpatrick, Clifford. (1949). "Religion and Humanitarianism: A Study of Institutional Implications." *Psychological Monographs 63* (9).

Lee, Gary and Robert Clyde. (1974). "Religion, Socioeconomic Status and Anomie." *Journal for the Scientific Study of Religion, 13*, 35–47.

Lewis, David L. (1993). "Canada's Native Peoples and the Churches." In W.E. Hewitt, ed., *The Sociology of Religion: A Canadian Focus* (pp. 235–51). Toronto: Butterworths.

Mann, W. E. (1962). *Sect, Cult and Church in Alberta.* Toronto: University of Toronto Press.

Marx, Karl. (1970 [1843]). *Critique of Hegel's "Philosophy of Right,"* Annette Jolin and Joseph O'Malley, trans. Cambridge, MA: Harvard University Press.

Marx, Karl and Friedrich Engels. (1964). *On Religion.* New York: Schocken Books.

Mead, Walter Russell. (2010). "Pentecostal Power." A blog in *The American Interest*, May 28.

Metz, Donald. (1967). *New Congregations: Security and Mission in Conflict.* Philadelphia, PA: Westminster Press.

Monahan, Susanne C. (1999) "Who Controls Church Work? Organizational Effects on Jurisdictional Boundaries and Disputes in Churches." *Journal for the Scientific Study of Religion, 38*, 370–85.

Nason-Clark, N. (1993). "Gender Relations in Contemporary Christian Organizations," in W.E. Hewitt, ed., *The Sociology of Religion* (pp. 215–34). Toronto: Butterworth.

Nesbitt, P. D. (1997). *The Feminization of the Clergy in America.* New York: Oxford University Press.

Newport, Frank. (2007). "Just Why Do Americans Attend Church?" April 6. On the World Wide Web at http://www.gallup.com/poll/27124/just-why-americans-attend-church.aspx (retrieved 30 July 2012).

Newport, Frank. (2010). "Americans' Church Attendance Inches Up in 2010." June 25. http://www.gallup.com/poll/141044/americans-church-attendance-inches-2010.aspx

Newport, Frank, David W. Moore, and Lydia Saad. (1999). "Long-Term Gallup Poll Trends: A Portrait of American Public Opinion through the Century." December 20. On the World Wide Web http://www.gallup.com/poll/3400/longterm-gallup-poll-trends-portrait-american-public-opinion.aspx (retrieved 30 July 2012).

Niebuhr, H. Richard. (1957 [1929]). *The Social Sources of Denominationalism.* New York: Henry Holt and Co.

O'Toole, Roger, Douglas F. Campbell, John A. Hannigan, Peter Beyer, and John H. Simpson. (1993). "The United Church in Crisis." In W.E. Hewitt, ed., *The Sociology of Religion: A Canadian Focus* (pp. 273–87). Toronto: Butterworths.

Poloma, Margaret M. (1997). "The 'Toronto Blessing': Charisma, Institutionalization and *Revival." Journal for the Scientific Study of Religion, 36*, 257–71.

Poloma, Margaret M. and Lynette F. Hoelter. (1998). "The 'Toronto Blessing': A Holistic Model of Healing." *Journal for the Scientific Study of Religion, 37*, 257–72.

Putnam, Robert. (2000). *Bowling Alone: The Collapse and Revival of American Community*. New York: Simon and Schuster.

Ray, Julie. (2003). "Worlds Apart: Religion in Canada, Britain, the U.S." On the World Wide Web at http://www.gallup.com/poll/9016/worlds-apart-religion-canada-britain-us.aspx (retrieved 30 July 2012).

Reimer, Sam. (2003). *Evangelicals and the Continental Divide.* Montreal: McGill-Queen's University Press.

Reynolds, Neil. (2011). "The Globalization of God in the 21st Century." *Globe and Mail* 10 January.

Rokeach, Milton. (1965). *Paradoxes of Religious Belief.* Information Service, National Council of Churches, 1–2.

Rokeach, Milton. (1969). "Religious Values and Social Compassion." *Review of Religious Research, 11*, 3–23.

Roof, Wade Clark and Dean R. Hoge. (1980). "Church Involvement in America: Social Factors Affecting Membership and Participation." *Review of Religious Research, 21*, 405–26.

Rouleau, Jean-Paul. (1977). "Religion in Quebec: Present and Future." *Pro Mundi Vita: Dossiers, 3* (November/December).

Smith, Tom W. (1999). "The Religious Right and Anti-Semitism." *Review of Religious Research, 99*, 244–58.

Speaker-Yuan, Margaret, ed. (2005). *Women in Islam.* Detroit: Greenhaven Press/Thomson Gale.

Stackhouse, John G., Jr. (2005). *Finally Feminist: A Pragmatic Christian Understanding of Gender.* Grand Rapids, MI: Baker Academic.

Stahl, William. (1986). "The Land That God Gave Cain: Nature and Civil Religion in Canada." Presented at the Annual Meeting of the Society for the Scientific Study of Religion, Washington, DC, November.

Stark, Rodney and Charles Y. Glock. (1968). *American Piety.* Berkeley, CA: University of California Press.

Stark, Rodney and Roger Finke. (2000). *Acts of Faith: Explaining the Human Side of Religion.* Berkeley, CA: University of California Press.

Stark, Rodney and William Sims Bainbridge. (1985). *The Future of Religion.* Berkeley, CA: University of California Press.

Statistics Canada. (2003). *2001 Census: Analysis Series—Religions in Canada.* Ottawa: Minister of Industry. Catalogue No. 96F0030XIE2002015.

Statistics Canada. (2004a). "General Social Survey: Social Engagement. *The Daily* July 6.

Statistics Canada. (2004b). National Survey of Non-Profit and Voluntary Organizations. *The Daily* September 20.

Stiller, Brian. (1997). *From the Tower of Babel to Parliament Hill.* Toronto: HarperCollins.

Thomas, Scott M. (2010). "A Globalized God." *Foreign Affairs* (November/December) *89*, 93–101.

Thomas, W. I. and Florian Znaniecki. (1918). *The Polish Peasant in Europe and America.* New York: Knopf.

Valpy, Michael and Joe Friesen. (2010). "Canada Marching from Religion to Secularization." *Globe and Mail* 11 December.

Weber, Max. (1958 [1904–05]). *The Protestant Ethic and the Spirit of Capitalism.* New York: Scribner's.

Weber, Max. (1963 [1922]). *The Sociology of Religion*, Ephraim Fischoff, trans. Boston: Beacon Press.

Whyte, Donald. (1966). "Religion and the Rural Church." In M. A. Tremblay and W. J. Anderson, eds., *Rural Canada in Transition* (pp. 79–92). Ottawa: Agricultural Economics Research Council of Canada.

Wilcox, W. Bradford. (1998). "Conservative Protestant Childrearing: Authoritarian or Authoritative?" *American Sociological Review, 63*, 796–809.

Winseman, Albert L. (2004). "Britons Lack American Cousins' Piety." November 9. On the World Wide Web at http://www.gallup.com/poll/13990/britons-lack-american-cousins-piety.aspx (retrieved 30 July 2012).

CHAPTER 14

Adler, Freda. (1975). *Sisters in Crime.* New York: McGraw-Hill.

Agnew, Robert. (1992). "Foundation for a General Theory of Crime and Delinquency." *Criminology, 30*, 47–87.

Aldridge, Judith, Fiona Measham, and Lisa Williams. (2011). *Illegal Leisure Revisited.* London: Routledge.

Beattie, Sara and Adam Cotter. (2010). "Homicide in Canada, 2009." *Juristat*, Fall. Statistics Canada. Catalogue No. 85-002-X.

Becker, Howard. (1963). *Outsiders: Studies in the Sociology of Deviance.* New York: Free Press.

Ben-Yehuda, Nachman. (1986). "The Sociology of Moral Panics: Toward a New Synthesis." *Sociological Quarterly, 4*, 495–513.

Brennan, Shannon and Mia Dauvergne. (2011). "Police-Reported Crime Statistics in Canada, 2010." *Juristat, 28* (7). Statistics Canada. Catalogue No. 85-002-X. On the World Wide Web at http://www.statcan.gc.ca/pub/85-002-x/2011001/article/11523-eng.pdf (retrieved 16 January 2012).

Brown, Ian. (2011). "Unlocking the Crime Conundrum." *Globe and Mail* April: F1, F5.

Brym, Robert J. (2009). *The 2006 Census and Canadian Society.* Toronto: Nelson

Chase, Stephen. (2011). "Weighty Tory Crime Bill Targets Drugs, Sex Offenders, 'Out-of-Control' Youth." *Globe and Mail* 20 September.

Chesney-Lind, Meda, Merry Morash, and Katherine Irwin. (2007). "Policing Girlhood? Relational Aggression and Violence Prevention." *Youth Violence and Juvenile Justice, 5* (3), 328–45.

Chibnall, Steve. (1977). *Law and Order News.* London: Tavistock.

Cloward, Richard and Lloyd Ohlin. (1960). *Delinquency and Opportunity: A Theory of Delinquent Gangs.* New York: Free Press.

Cohen, Albert. (1955). *Delinquent Boys.* Chicago: Free Press.

Cohen, Lawrence and Marcus Felson. (1979). "Social Change and Crime Rate Trends: A Routine Activity Approach." *American Sociological Review, 44* (August), 588–608.

Conrad, Peter and Joseph Schneider. (1992). *Deviance and Medicalization.* Philadelphia, PA: Temple University Press.

Cook, Shirley. (1969). "Canadian Narcotics Legislation, 1880–1923: A Conflict Model Interpretation." *Canadian Review of Sociology and Anthropology, 6, 36–46.*

Daigle, Leah, Francis Cullen, and John Paul Wright. (2007). "Gender Differences in the Predictors of Juvenile Delinquency: Assessing the Generality-Specificity Debate." *Youth Violence and Juvenile Justice, 5*, 254–86.

Dauvergne, Mia. (2008). "Crime Statistics in Canada, 2007." *Juristat, 28* (7). Statistics Canada. Catalogue No. 85-002-X.

Doob, Anthony and Carla Cesaroni. (2004). *Responding to Youth Crime in Canada.* Toronto: University of Toronto Press.

Doob, Anthony and Jane Sprott. (2004). "Changing Models of Youth Justice in Canada." In M. Tonry and A. Doob, eds., *Youth Crime and Youth Justice: Comparative and Cross-national Perspectives.* Chicago: University of Chicago Press.

Doob, Anthony and Cheryl Webster. (2003). "Sentence Severity and Crime: Accepting the Null Hypothesis." In Michael Tonry, ed., *Crime and Justice: a Review of Research. 30*, 143–95.

Dunn, Jennifer (2008). "Everyone Knows Who the Sluts Are: How Young Women Get around the Stigma." In Alex Thio, Thomas C. Calhoun, and Aadrain Conyers, eds., *Readings in Deviant Behavior*, 5th ed. (pp. 226–29). Pearson: New York.

Felson, Marcus and Rachel Boba. (2010). *Crime and Everyday Life*, 4th ed. Thousand Oaks, CA: Pine Forge Press.

Frey, James. (2003). *A Million Little Pieces.* New York: Doubleday.

Fuller, John and Wozniak, John. (2006). "Peacemaking Criminology: Part, Present and Future." In Francis Cullen, John Paul Wright, and Kristie Blevins, eds., *Taking Stock* (pp. 251–73). New Brunswick, NJ: Transaction.

Gartner, Rosemary and Sarah Thompson. (2004). "Trends in Homicide in Toronto." In Bruce Kidd and Jim Phillips, eds., *Research on Community Safety* (pp. 28–41). Toronto: The Centre of Criminology, University of Toronto.

Giddens, Anthony. (1991). *Introduction to Sociology.* New York: Norton.

Goffman, Erving. (1963). *Stigma: Notes on the Management of Spoiled Identity.* Englewood Cliffs, NJ: Prentice Hall.

Gordon, Robert. (2000). "Criminal Business Organizations, Street Gangs, and Wannabe Groups: A Vancouver Perspective." *Canadian Journal of Criminology, 42* (1), 39–60.

Gottfredson, Michael and Travis Hirschi. (1990). *A General Theory of Crime.* Palo Alto, CA: Stanford University Press.

Grekul, Jana and Patti LaBoucane-Benson. (2008). "Aboriginal Gangs and Their (Dis)placement: Contextualizing Recruitment, Membership, and Status." *Canadian Journal of Criminology and Criminal Justice, 50* (1), 59–82.

Hagan, John. (1991). *The Disreputable Pleasures: Crime and Deviance in Canada*, 3rd ed. Toronto: McGraw-Hill Ryerson.

Hagan, John, Ron Gillis, and John Simpson. (1987). "Class in the Household: A Power-Control Theory of Gender and Delinquency." *American Journal of Sociology, 92*, 788–816.

Hagan, John and Bill McCarthy (1997). *Mean Streets.* Cambridge, UK: Cambridge University Press.

Harris, John. (2011). "Big Brother Goes to School." *Guardian* 6 June: G2, pp. 5–8.

Hartnagel, Timothy. (2004). "Correlates of Criminal Behavior." In R. Linden, ed., *Criminology: A Canadian Perspective*, 5th ed. (pp. 120–63). Toronto: Harcourt Brace.

Hier, Sean. (2002). "Raves, Risks and Ecstasy Panic: A Case Study in the Subversive Nature of Moral Regulation." *Canadian Journal of Sociology*, 27 (1), 33–57.

Hirschi, Travis. (1969). *Causes of Delinquency.* Berkeley, CA: University of California Press.

Jenkins, P. (2001). *Beyond Tolerance: Child Pornography on the Internet.* New York: New York University Press.

Keane, Carl, Paul Maxim, and James Teevan. (1993). "Drinking and Driving, Self-Control and Gender: Testing the General Theory of Crime." *Journal of Research in Crime and Delinquency, 30*, 30–46.

Krahn, Harvey, Tim Hartnagel, and John Gartrell. (1986). "Income Inequality and Homicide Rates: Cross-National Data and Criminological Theories." *Criminology, 24*, 269–95.

Larsson, Stieg. (2008). *The Girl with the Dragon Tattoo.* Toronto: Viking.

Lawrence, Richard and David Mueller. (2003). "School Shootings and the Man Bites Dog Criterion of Newsworthiness." *Youth Violence and Youth Justice, 1* (4), 330–45.

Li, Geoffrey. (2008). "Homicide in Canada, 2007." *Juristat, 28* (9). Statistics Canada. Catalogue No. 85-002-X.

Link, Bruce. (1982). "Mental Patient Status, Work, and Income: An Examination of the Effects of a Psychiatric Label." *American Sociological Review, 47*, 202–15.

Liska, Allen and Steven Messner. (1999). *Perspectives on Deviance*, 3rd ed. Englewood Cliffs, NJ: Prentice-Hall.

Mahony, Tina Hotton. (2011). "Homicide in Canada, 2010." *Juristat.* Statistics Canada. Catalogue No. 85-002-X.

Merton, Robert. (1938). "Social Structure and Anomie." *American Sociological Review, 3*, 672–87.

Morgan, Rod and Alison Liebling. (2007). "Imprisonment: An Expanding Scene." In Mike Maguire, Rod Morgan, and Robert Reiner, eds., *The Oxford Handbook of Criminology*, 4th ed. (pp. 1100–38). New York: Oxford University Press.

Nakhaie, Reza, Robert Silverman, and Teresa LaGrange. (2000). "Self-Control and Resistance to School." *Canadian Review of Sociology and Anthropology, 37* (4), 444–60.

Parnaby, Patrick. (2003). "Disaster through Dirty Windshields: Law, Order and Toronto's Squeegee Kids." *Canadian Journal of Sociology, 28* (3), 281–307.

Parnaby, Patrick and Vince F. Sacco. (2004). "Fame and Strain: the Contributions of Mertonian Deviance Theory to an Understanding of the Relationship between Celebrity and Deviant Behavior. *Deviant Behavior, 25*, 1–26.

Reinarman, Craig and Harry Levine. (1989). "The Crack Attack: Politics and Media in America's Latest Drug Scare." In J. Best, ed., *Images of Issues: Typifying Contemporary Social Problems* (pp. 147–90). New York: Aldine De Gruyter.

Reiner, Robert. (2007). "Media-Made Criminality: The Representation of Crime in the Mass Media." In Mike Maguire, Rod Morgan, and Robert Reiner, eds., *Oxford Handbook of Criminology* (pp. 302–37). New York: Oxford University Press.

Roberts, Julian. (2004). "Public Opinion and the Evolution of Juvenile Justice Policy in Western Nations." In Michael Tonry and Anthony Doob, eds., *Youth Crime and Youth Justice: Comparative and Cross-National Perspectives* (pp. 495–542). Chicago: University of Chicago Press.

Robertson, Ian. (1989). *Society: A Brief Introduction.* New York: Worth.

Sacco, Vince. (2005). *When Crime Waves.* Thousand Oaks, CA: Sage.

Sacco, Vince and Les Kennedy. (2011). *The Criminal Event: An Introduction to Criminology in Canada*, 5th ed. Toronto: Nelson.

Savoie, Josée. (2006). "Youth Self-Reported Delinquency. Toronto." *Juristat, 27* (6).

Siegel, Larry and Chris McCormick. (2006). *Criminology in Canada.* Toronto: Nelson.

Simon, Ruth. (1975). *Women and Crime.* Lexington, MA: Lexington Books.

South, Nigel. (2007). "Drugs, Alcohol and Crime." In M. Maguire, R. Morgan, and R. Reiner, eds., *The Oxford Handbook of Criminology*, 4th ed. (pp. 810–4-0). New York: Oxford University Press.

Staples, William G. (2008). "Everyday Surveillance in Postmodern Society." In Alex Thio, Thomas C. Calhoun, and Aadrain Conyers, eds. *Readings in Deviant Behavior*, 5th ed. (pp. 356–61). New York: Pearson.

Sutherland, E. H. (1947). *Principles of Criminology*, 4th ed. Chicago: Lippincott.

Sykes, Gresham. (1958). *Society of Captives: A Study of a Maximum Security Institution.* Princeton: Princeton University Press.

Tanner, J. (2010). *Teenage Troubles: Youth and Deviance in Canada*, 3rd ed. Toronto: Oxford.

Tanner, Julian and Scot Wortley. (2002). *The Toronto Youth Crime and Victimization Survey.* Toronto: Centre of Criminology, University of Toronto.

Thio, Alex. (2010). *Deviant Behavior*, 10th ed. Boston: Allyn and Bacon.

Venkatesh, S. (2008). *Gang Leader for a Day: A Rogue Sociologist Takes to the Streets*. New York: Penguin.

Vold, George, Thomas Bernard, and Jeffrey Snipes. (2002). *Theoretical Criminology*, 5th ed. New York: Oxford University Press.

Von Hirsch andrew, Anthony Bottoms, Elizabeth Burney, and Per-Olöf Wikstrom. (1999). *Criminal Deterrence: An Analysis of Recent Research.* Oxford, UK: Hart Publishing

Walmsley, Roy. 2009. *World Prison Population List*, 8th ed. On the World Wide Web at http://www.kcl.ac.uk/depsta/law /research/icps/downloads/wppl-8th_41.pdf (retrieved 16 January 2012).

Wortley, Scot (2011). "Interview with." *University of Toronto Bulletin*, 11 November.

Wortley, Scot and Julian Tanner. (2004). "Social Groups or Criminal Organizations? The Extent and Nature of Youth Gang Activity in Toronto." In B. Kidd and J. Phillips, eds., *Research on Community Safety.* Toronto: Centre of Criminology, University of Toronto.

Wortley, Scot and Julian Tanner. (2005). "Inflammatory Rhetoric? Baseless Accusations? A Response to Gabor's Critique of Racial Profiling Research in Canada." *Canadian Journal of Criminology and Criminal Justice, 47* (3), 581–614.

CHAPTER 15

Abu-Lughod, Janet L. (1991). *Changing Cities: Urban Sociology.* New York: HarperCollins.

Beaujot, Roderic. (2004) "Population, Aging, and Health." In Robert J. Brym, ed., *New Society: Sociology for the 21st Century*, 4th ed. (pp. 431–64). Toronto: Nelson.

Bélanger, Alain and Éric Caron Malenfant. (2005). "Ethnocultural Diversity in Canada: Prospects for 2017." *Canadian Social Trends, 79*, 18–21.

Bell, Wendell. (1968). "The City, the Suburbs and a Theory of Social Choice." In Scott Greer, Dennis McElrath, David W. Minar, and Peter Orleans, eds., *The New Urbanization* (pp. 132–68). New York: St. Martin's Press.

Berger, Bennett. (1960). *Working Class Suburb.* Berkeley, CA: University of California Press.

Berry, Brian J. L. and Quentin Gillard. (1977). *The Changing Shape of Metropolitan America.* Cambridge, MA: Ballinger Publishing Co.

Blumenfeld, Hans. (1982). *Have the Secular Trends of Population Distribution Been Reversed?* Research paper 137. Toronto: Centre of Urban and Community Studies.

Blumenfeld, Hans. (1983). "Metropolis Extended." *Journal of the American Planning Association, 52* (3), 346–48.

Bonner, Kieran. (1997). *A Great Place to Raise Kids: Interpretation, Science, and the Urban-Rural Debate.* Montreal, QC, and Kingston, ON: McGill-Queen's University Press.

Bourne, L. S. (1996). "Reinventing the Suburbs: Old Myths and New Realities." *Progress in Planning, 46*, 163–84.

Brym, Robert J. (1986). "An Introduction to the Regional Question in Canada." In Robert J. Brym, ed., *Regionalism in Canada* (pp. 1–45). Toronto: Irwin.

Burgess, Ernest W. (1961). "The Growth of the City: An Introduction to a Research Project." In George A Theodorson, ed., *Studies in Human Ecology* (pp. 37–44). Evanston, IL: Row, Peterson and Co.

Castells, Manuel. (1989). *The Informational City: Information, Technology, Economic Restructuring and the Urban-Regional Process.* Oxford and Cambridge, MA: Blackwell.

Champion, A. G. (1993) "Urban and Regional Demographic Trends: The Developed World." In Ronan Paddison, Bill Lever, and John Money, eds., *International Perspectives in Urban Studies 1* (pp. 136–59). London and Philadelphia, PA: Jessica Kingsley.

Chandler, Tertius and Gerald Fox. (1974). *3000 Years of Urban Growth.* New York and London: Academic Press.

Clark, David. (1996). *Urban World, Global City.* London and New York: Routledge.

Davis, Judy S., Arthur C. Nelson, and Kenneth J. Dueher. (1994). "The New 'Burbs': The Exurbs and their Implications for Planning Policy." *Journal of the American Planning Association, 60,* 45–59.

Davis, Kingsley. (1955). "The Origin and Growth of Urbanization in the World," *American Journal of Sociology, 60,* 430.

Davis, Mike. (1990). *City of Quartz: Excavating the Future in Los Angeles.* London and New York: Verso.

De Oliveira, Orlandina and Bryan Roberts. (1996). "Urban Development and Social Inequality in Latin America." In J. Gugler, ed., *The Urban Transformation of the Developing World* (pp. 250–314). Oxford: Oxford University Press.

Drakakis-Smith, David. (1988). "Third World Cities: Sustainable Urban Development II—Population, Labor, and Poverty." In R. Paddison and B. Lever, eds., *International Perspectives in Urban Studies 5* (pp. 70–101). London and Bristol, UK: Jessica Kingsley.

Driedger, Leo. (1991). *The Urban Factor: Sociology of Canadian Cities.* Toronto: Oxford University Press.

ECLAC. (2008) *Panorama social de América Latina 2008.* Economic Commission for Latin America and the Caribbean. December, United Nations: Santiago.

Ehrlich, Paul R. (1968). *The Population Bomb.* New York: Ballantine Books.

Epp, Roger and Dave Whitson. (2001). "Writing Off Rural Communities." In R. Epp and D. Whitson, eds., *Writing Off the Rural West* (pp. xii–xxxv). Edmonton: The University of Alberta Press/Parkland Institute.

Fava, Sylvia Fleis. (1956). "Suburbanism as a Way of Life." *American Sociological Review, 21,* 34–37.

Filion, Pierre. (1991). "The Gentrification-Social Structure Dialectic: A Toronto Case Study." *International Journal of Urban and Regional Research, 15,* 553–74.

Firey, Walter. (1947). *Land Use in Central Boston.* Cambridge, MA: Harvard University Press.

Fishman, Robert. (1987). *Bourgeois Utopias: The Rise and Fall of Suburbia.* New York: Basic Books.

Fishman, Robert. (1990). "Megalopolis Unbound." *The Wilson Quarterly* (Winter), 25–45.

Fishman, Robert. (2005). "Longer View: The Fifth Migration." *Journal of the American Planning Association, 71,* 357–66.

Flanagan, William G. (1995). *Urban Sociology: Images and Structure.* Boston: Allyn and Bacon.

Fong, Eric. (1996). "A Comparative Perspective of Racial Residential Segregation: American and Canadian Experiences." *The Sociological Quarterly, 37,* 501–28.

Fong, Eric and Kumiko Shibuya. (2005). "Multiethnic Cities in North America." *Annual Review of Sociology, 31,* 258–304.

Fong, Eric and Rima Wilkes. (1999). "The Spatial Assimilation Model Re-examined: An Assessment by Canadian Data." *International Migration Review, 33,* 594–620.

Fowler, Edmund P. (1992). *Building Cities That Work.* Montreal and Kingston, ON: McGill-Queen's University Press.

Frieden, Bernard J. and Lynne B. Sagalyn. (1989). *Downtown, Inc.: How America Rebuilds Cities.* Cambridge, MA: MIT Press.

Garreau, Joel. (1991). *Edge City: Life on the New Frontier.* New York: Doubleday.

Ginsburg, N., B. Koppel, and T. G. McGee, eds. (1991). *The Extended Metropolis: Settlement Transition in Asia.* Honolulu: University of Hawaii Press.

Goldberger, Paul. (1996). "The Rise of the Private City." In Julia Vitullo-Martin, ed., *Breaking Away: The Future of Cities* (pp. 135–47). New York: Twentieth Century Fund Press.

Golden, Hilda H. (1981). *Urbanization and Cities.* Lexington, MA: Heath.

Gordon, Ian and Saskia Sassen. (1992). "Restructuring the Urban Labor Markets." In Susan S. Fainstein, Ian Gordon, and Michael Harloe, eds., *Divided Cities: New York and London in the Contemporary World* (pp. 105–28). Oxford and Cambridge, MA: Blackwell.

Grant, Jill. (2005). "The Function of the Gates: The Social Construction of Security in Gated Developments." *Town Planning Review, 76,* 291–313.

Gugler, Josef. (1996). "Preface." In J. Gugler, ed., *The Urban Transformation of the Developing World.* Oxford: Oxford University Press.

Hannigan, John A. (1995). "The Postmodern City: A New Urbanization?" *Current Sociology, 43* (1), 180.

Harris, Chauncey and Edward Ullman. (1945). "The Nature of Cities." *Annals of the American Academy of Political and Social Science, 242* (November), 7–17.

Hauser, Philip M. (1965). "Urbanization: An Overview." In Philip M. Hauser and Leo F. Schnore, eds., *The Study of Urbanization.* New York: Wiley.

Heisz, Andrew and Sébastien LaRochelle-Coté. (2005). "Getting to Work." *Canadian Social Trends, 79* (Winter), 16.

Hou, Feng and Garnett Picot. (2004). "Visible Minority Neighbourhoods in Toronto, Montréal and Vancouver." *Canadian Social Trends, 72,* 8–13.

Hoyt, Homer. (1939). *The Structure and Growth of Residential Neighborhoods in American Cities.* Washington, DC: Federal Housing Authority.

Jackson, Kenneth T (1985). *Crabgrass Frontier: The Suburbanization of the United States.* New York: Oxford University Press.

Kleniewski, Nancy. (1997). *Cities, Change and Conflict: A Political Economy of Urban Life.* Belmont, CA: Wadsworth.

Kremarik, Frances. (2000). "Urban Development." *Canadian Social Trends, 59,* 18–22.

Leinberger, Christopher B. and Charles Lockwood. (1986). "How Business Is Reshaping America." *The Atlantic Monthly* (October): 43–52.

Ley, David. (1991). "Gentrification." In Kent Gerecke, ed., *The Canadian City* (pp. 181–96). Montreal: Black Rose Books.

Little, Bruce. (1999). "Tale of Three Canadian Cities: What Makes Them Grow So Big." *Globe and Mail* 20 September: A20.

Lofchie, Michael F. (1997). "The Rise and Demise of Urban-Biased Developmental Policies in Africa." In Josef Gugler, ed., *Cities in the Developing World: Issues, Theory and Policy* (pp. 23–39). Oxford: Oxford University Press.

Logan, John R., Richard D. Alba, and Wenquan Zhang. (2002). "Immigrant Enclaves and Ethnic Communities in New York and Los Angeles." *American Sociological Review, 67,* 299–322.

Logan, John R. and Harvey L. Molotch. (1987). *Urban Fortunes: The Political Economy of Place.* Berkeley, CA: University of California Press.

Lorimer, James. (1978). *The Developers.* Toronto: Lorimer.

Malthus, T. R. (1798). *An Essay on the Principle of Population, as It Affects the Future Improvement of Society. With Remarks on the Speculations of Mr. Godwin, M. Condorcet and Other Writers.* London: J. Johnson.

McGahan, Peter. (1995). *Urban Sociology in Canada,* 3rd ed. Toronto: Harcourt Brace.

McGee, T. G. (1991). "The Emergence of Desakota Regions in Asia." In N. Ginsberg, B. Koppel, and T. G. McGee, eds., *The Extended Metropolis* (pp. 3–25). Honolulu: University of Hawaii Press.

McQuillan, Kevin. (1994). "Population." In Robert Hagedorn, ed., *Sociology,* 5th ed. Toronto: Harcourt Brace.

Michelson, William D. (1973). *Environmental Change.* Research Paper No. 60. Centre for Urban and Community Studies: University of Toronto.

Montgomery, Shannon. (2008). "Avalanche Survivors Devastated by 7 Deaths." *Toronto Star* 30 December: A1, A4.

Nader, George A. (1975). *Cities of Canada, Volume One: Theoretical, Historical and Planning Perspectives.* Toronto: Macmillan.

Ness, Gayl D. and Michael M. Low. (2000). *Modelling Asian Urban Population—Environment Dynamics.* Singapore: Oxford University Press.

Palen, J. John. (1995). *The Suburbs.* New York: McGraw-Hill.

Preville, Philip. (2011) "The New Suburbanites." *Toronto Life* September: 34–44.

Reid, Barton. (1991). "A Primer on the Corporate City." In Kent Gerecke, ed., *The Canadian City* (pp. 63–78). Montreal: Black Rose.

Reynolds, Malvina. (1964). *Little Boxes and Other Handmade Songs.* New York: Oak.

Rose, D. (1984). "Rethinking Gentrification: Beyond the Uneven Development of Marxist Urban Theory." *Environment and Planning D: Society and Space, 2* (1), 47–74.

Rowland, Allison and Gordon, Peter (1996) "Mexico City in the International Economy." In Alan Gilbert (ed.), *The Mega-City in Latin America* (pp. 173–202). Tokyo: United Nations University.

Sanchez, T. W., R. E. Lang, and D. M. Dhavale. (2005). "Security versus Status? A First Look at the Census's Gated Community Data." *Journal of Planning Education and Research, 24,* 281–91.

Seeley R. A. Sim and E. W. Loosley. (1956). *Crestwood Heights: A Study of the Culture of Suburban Life.* New York: Wiley.

Sewell, John. (1993). *The Shape of the City: Toronto Struggles with Modern Planning.* Toronto: University of Toronto Press.

Simmel, Georg. (1950). "The Metropolis and Mental Life." In Kurt H. Wolff, ed., and trans., *The Sociology of Georg Simmel* (pp. 409–24). Glencoe, IL: Free Press.

Simon, Julian L. and Herman Kahn. (1984) *The Resourceful Earth: A Response to Global 2000.* Oxford: Blackwell.

"Slain Man Mystery to Tenants." (2004). *Metro* (Toronto) 29 December: 4.

Smith, David A. (1996). *Third World Cities in Global Perspective: The Political Economy of Uneven Urbanization.* Boulder, CO: Westview Press.

Smith, Neil. (1979). "Towards a Theory of Gentrification." *Journal of the American Planning Association, 45,* 538–48.

Smith, Neil and Michael LeFaivre. (1984). "A Class Analysis of Gentrification." In John J. Palen and Brian London, eds., *Gentrification, Displacement and Neighborhood Revitalization* (pp. 43–64). Albany, NY: SUNY Press.

Statistics Canada. (2008). "Census Snapshot—Immigration in Canada: A Portrait of the Foreign-Born Population, 2006 Census." *Canadian Social Trends, 85* (Summer), 46–53. Statistics Canada. Catalogue No. 11-008-X.

Statistics Canada. (2009). "Population, Urban and Rural, by Province and Territory (Canada)." On the World Wide Web athttp://www.statcan.gc.ca/tables-tableaux/sum-som/l01/cst01/demo62a-eng.htm (retrieved 22 September 2010).

Statistics Canada. (2010). "Study: Projections of the Diversity of the Canadian Population: Table 1: Proportion of Foreign-Born and Visible Minority Populations by Census Metropolitan Area, 2006 and 2031." *The Daily* 9 March. On the World Wide Web at http://www.statcan.gc.ca/daily-quotidien/100309/t100309a1-eng.htm (retrieved 9 March 2011).

Statistics Canada. (2011a). "Deaths: Table 1: Life Expectancy at Birth and at Age 65 by Sex, Canada, Provinces and Territories, 2006–2008." *The Daily* 27 September. On the World Wide Web at http://www.statcan.gc.ca/daily-quotidien/110927/t110927a1-eng.htm (retrieved 30 July 2012).

Statistics Canada. (2011b). "Infant Mortality Rates by Province and Territory (Both sexes)." On the World Wide Web at http://www.statcan.gc.ca/tables-tableaux/sum-som/l01/cst01/health21a-eng.htm (ret rieved 30 July 2012).

Statistics Canada. (2012a). "The Canadian Population in 2011: Population Counts and Growth— Part 3: Portrait of Metropolitan and Non-Metropolitan Canada." On the World Wide Web at http://www.statcan.gc.ca (retrieved 8 February 2012).

Statistics Canada. (2012b). "Population and Dwelling Counts for Census Metropolitan Areas and Census Agglomerations, 2011 and 2006 Censuses." On the World Wide Web at http://www.statcan.gc.ca (retrieved 30 July 2012).

Statistics Canada. (2012c). "Canada's Rural Population since 1851." On the World Wide Web at http://www12.statcan.gc.ca/census-recensement/2011/as-sa/98-310-x/98-310-x2011003_2-eng.cfm (retrieved 30 July 2012).

Stone, Leroy O. (1967). *Urban Development in Canada.* Ottawa: Dominion Bureau of Statistics.

Stren, R. and M. Halfari. (2001). "The Cities of Sub-Saharan Africa: From Dependency to Marginality." In Ronan Paddison, ed., *Handbook of Urban Studies* (pp. 466–85). London: Sage Publications.

Thomas, William I. and Florian Znaniecki. (1918–20). *The Polish Peasant in Europe and America,* 5 Vols. Chicago: University of Chicago Press.

Tönnies, Ferdinand. (1957 [1887]). *Community and Society,* Charles Loomis, trans. East Lansing, MI: Michigan State University Press.

Van de Kaa, Dirk. (1987). "Europe's Second Demographic Transition." *Population Bulletin, 42* (1), 1–58.

Warde, Alan. (1991). "Gentrification as Consumption: Issues of Class and Gender." *Environment and Planning D: Society and Space, 9* (2), 223–32.

Weber, A. F. (1963 [1899]). *The Growth of Cities in the Nineteenth Century.* Ithaca, NY: Cornell University Press.

Whyte, William H. (1956). *The Organization Man.* New York: Simon and Schuster.

Wilson, Elizabeth. (1991). *The Sphinx in the City: Urban Life, the Control of Disorder and Women.* London: Virago Press.

Winchester, Lucy and Raquel Szalachman. (2009). "The Urban Poor's Vulnerability to the Impacts of Climate Change in Latin America and the Caribbean: A Policy Agenda." Fifth Urban Research Symposium: Cities and Climate Change. Expert Group Meeting on Population Dynamics and Climate Change. London, June 24–25.

Wirth, Louis. (1938). "Urbanism as a Way of Life." In *American Journal of Sociology, 44,* 1–24.

Wittberg, Patricia. (1992). "Perspectives on Gentrification: A Comparative Review of the Literature." *Research in Urban Sociology, 2,* 17–46.

Zorbaugh, Harvey. (1929). *The Gold Coast and the Slum.* Chicago: University of Chicago Press.

CHAPTER 16

Agyeman, Julian, Peter Cole, Randolph Haluza-DeLay, and Pat O'Riley. (2009). *Speaking for Ourselves: Environmental Justice in Canada.* Vancouver, BC: UBC Press.

Alberta Royalty Review Panel. (2007). *Our Fair Share.* Edmonton: Alberta Government. September.

Ali, S. Harris. (2002). "Dealing with Toxicity in the Risk Society: The Case of the Hamilton, Ontario, Plastics Recycling Fire." *Canadian Review of Sociology and Anthropology, 39* (1), 29.

Ali, S. Harris. (2008). "Environmental Health and Society." In B. Singh Bolaria and Harley D. Dickinson, eds., *Health, Illness, and Health Care in Canada,* 4th ed. (pp. 370–87). Toronto: Nelson.

Beck, Ulrich. (1992). *Risk Society: Towards a New Modernity,* Mark Ritter, trans. London: Sage.

Beck, Ulrich. (1995). *Ecological Enlightenment: Essays on the Politics of the Risk Society,* M. Ritter, trans. Atlantic Highlands, NJ: Humanities Press.

Blow, P. (Director) (1999). *The Village of Widows: The Story of the Sahtu Dene and the Atomic Bomb* [videorecording]. Peterborough, ON: Lindum Films.

Brown, Steven D. (2009). "The Green Vote in Canada." In Debora L. VanNijnatten and Robert Boardman, eds., *Canadian Environmental Policy and Politics,* 3rd ed. (pp. 14–28). Toronto: Oxford University Press.

Buell, Frederick. (2004). From *Apocalypse to Way of Life: Environmental Crisis in the American Century.* New York: Routledge.

Bullard, Robert. (1993). *Confronting Environmental Racism: Voices from the Grassroots.* Boston: South End Press.

Buttel, Fred. (1975). "The Environmental Movement: Consensus, Conflict and Change." *Journal of Environmental Education, 7,* 53–63.

Camcastle, Cara. (2007) "The Green Party of Canada in Political Space and the New Middle Class Thesis." *Environmental Politics, 16* (4), 625–42.

"Canada Wins Battle to Keep Asbestos off Hazardous List." (2011). *CBC.* On the World Wide Web at http://www.cbc.ca/news/canada/montreal/story/2011/06/24/pol-harper-asbestos.html (retrieved 30 July 2012).

Carson, Rachel. (1962). *Silent Spring.* Boston: Houghton Mifflin

Cato, Molly Scott. (2011). *Environment and Economy.* New York: Routledge.

Davidson, Debra J. and Scott Frickel. (2004). "Understanding Environmental Governance: A Critical Review" *Organization and Environment, 17* (4), 471–92.

Derber, Charles. (2010). *Greed to Green: Solving Climate Change and Remaking the Economy.* Boulder, CO: Paradigm Publishers.

Diamond, Jared. (2011). *Collapse: How Societies Chose to Fall or Succeed.* New York: Penguin.

Elections Canada. (2012). "2011 General Elections." On the World Wide Web at http://enr.elections.ca/National_e.aspx (retrieved 15 February 2012).

England, J. Lynn and Stan L. Albrecht. (1984). "Boomtowns and Social Disruption." *Rural Sociology, 49* (2), 230–46.

Environment Canada. (2010). "Areas of Concern in the Great Lakes-St. Lawrence River Basin." Environment Canada. On the World Wide Web at http://www.ec.gc.ca/raps-pas/(retrieved 30 July 2012).

Erikson, K. (1995). *A New Species of Trouble: The Human Experience of Modern Disaster.* New York: Norton.

Faber, Daniel. (2009). "The Unfair Trade-off: Globalization and the Export of Ecological Hazards." In Leslie King and Deborah McCarthy, eds., *Environmental Sociology: From Analysis to Action* (pp. 181–99). Toronto: Rowman & Littlefield Publishers.

Freidman, Thomas. (2006). "The First Law of Petropolitics." *Foreign Policy* (May/June).

Freudenburg, William R. (1984). "Boomtown's Youth: The Differential Impacts of Rapid Community Growth in Adolescents and Adults." *American Sociological Review, 49* (5), 697–705.

Germanwatch. (2011). "Overall Results: Climate Change Performance Index 2012." On the World Wide Web at http://www.germanwatch.org/ccpi (retrieved 16 March 2012).

Giddens, Anthony. (2009). *The Politics of Climate Change.* Cambridge, UK: Polity Press.

Girard, April L., Suzanne Day, and Laureen Snider. (2010). "Tracking Environmental Crime through CEPA: Canada's Environment Cops or Industry's Best Friend?" *Canadian Journal of Sociology, 35* (2), 219.

Gladwell, Malcom. (2002). *The Tipping Point.* New York: Back Bay Books.

Goffman, Erving. (1974). *Frame Analysis: An Essay on the Organization of Experience.* Boston: Northeastern University Press.

Gramling, Bob and Sarah Brabant. (1986). "Boomtowns and Offshore Energy Impact Assessment: The Development of a Comprehensive Model." *Sociological Perspectives, 29* (2), 177–201.

Guha, Ramachandra and Juan Martinez-Alier. (1998). *Varieties of Environmentalism: Essays North and South.* New Delhi: Oxford.

Hannigan, John. (2006) *Environmental Sociology,* 2nd ed. New York: Routledge.

Hardin, Garrett. (1968). "The Tragedy of the Commons." *Science, 162* (3859), 1243–48.

Indian and Northern Affairs Canada. (2003). *National Assessment of Water and Wastewater Systems in First Nations Communities.* Ottawa: Government of Canada.

Jerrett, Michael, R. T. Burnett, P. Kanaroglou, J. Eyles, N. Finkelstein, C. Giovis, and J. R. Brook. (2001) "A GIS-Environmental Justice Analysis of Particulate Air Pollution in Hamilton, Canada. *Environment and Planning, A 33,* 955–73.

Kriesi, H. (1989). "New Social Movements and the New Class in the Netherlands." *American Journal of Sociology, 94,* 1078–116.

"Kyoto and Beyond." (2007). *CBC.* On the World Wide Web at http://www.cbc.ca/news/background/kyoto/#s5 (retrieved 30 July 2012).

Mackenzie, Constanze A., Ada Lockridge, and Margaret Keith. (2005). "Declining Sex Ratio in a First Nation Community." *Environmental Health Perspectives, 113* (10). On the World Wide Web at http://ehp03.niehs.nih.gov/article/info:doi/10.1289/ehp.8479 (retrieved 4 August 2012).

Markoff, John. (2002). "Technology's Toxic Trash Is Sent to Poor Nations." *New York Times* 25 February: C1.

Mascarenhas, Michael. (2009). "Environmental Inequality and Environmental Justice." In Kenneth A. Gould and Tammy L. Lewis, eds., *Twenty Lessons in Environmental Sociology* (pp. 127–141). Toronto: Oxford University Press.

McCright, Aaron and Riley Dunlap. (2010). "Anti-Reflexivity: The American Conservative Movement's Success in Undermining Climate Science and Policy." *Theory, Culture & Society, 27* (2/3), 100–33.

Meadows, Donella H., Dennis L. Meadows, Jørgen Randers, and William W. Behrens III. (1972). *Limits to Growth: A Report for the Club of Rome's Project on the Predicament of Mankind.* New York: Universe Books.

Milly, Pascal and William Leiss. (1997). "Mother's Milk: Communicating the Risks of PCBs in Canada and the Far North." In Douglas Powell and William Leiss, eds., *Mad Cows and Mother's Milk: The Perils of Poor Risk Communication* (pp. 184–209). Montreal: McGill-Queen's University Press.

Mitchell, Bruce. (2010). *Resource and Environmental Management in Canada.* Toronto: Oxford.

Nikiforuk, Andrew. (2010). *Tar Sands: Dirty Oil and the Future of a Continent.* Vancouver, BC: Greystone Books.

Paehlke, Robert. (2009). "The Environmental Movement in Canada." In Debora L. VanNijnatten and Robert Boardman, eds., *Canadian Environmental Policy and Politics: Prospects for Leadership and Innovation,* 3rd ed. (pp. 1–13). Toronto: Oxford University Press.

Pearce, Fred. (2010). "Controversy behind Climate Science's 'Hockey Stick' Graph." On the World Wide Web at http://www.guardian.co.uk/environment/2010/feb/02/hockey-stick-graph-climate-change (retrieved 11 February 2012).

Raffensperger, Carolyn and Joel Tickner. (1999). *Protecting Public Health and The Environment: Implementing the Precautionary Principle.* Washington, DC: Island Press.

Rich, Bruce. (1994). *Mortgaging the Earth: The World Bank, Environmental Impoverishment, and the Crisis of Development.* Boston: Beacon Press.

Shingler, Benjamin. (2011). "Data Shows Climate Injustice." *Toronto Star* 7 March: A1.

Smith, Rick and Bruce Lourie. (2009). *Slow Death by Rubber Duck: How the Toxic Chemistry of Everyday Life Affects Our Health.* Toronto: Alfred A. Knopf.

Tarbell, Alice and Mary Arquette. (2000). "Akwesasne: A Native American Community's Resistance to Cultural and Environmental Damage." In Richard Hofrichter, ed., *Reclaiming the Environmental Debate: The Politics of Health in a Toxic Culture* (pp. 93–111). Cambridge, MA: MIT Press.

"The Toilet Paper Chase." (2012). *Marketplace.* On the World Wide Web at http://www.cbc.ca/marketplace/2012/thetoiletpaperchase/ (retrieved 30 July 2012).

United Nations World Commission on Environment and Development. (1987). *Our Common Future.* Oxford, UK: Oxford University Press

Urry, John. (2011). *Climate Change and Society.* New York: Routledge.

Wackernagel, Mathis and William E. Rees. (1996). *Our Ecological Footprint: Reducing Human Impact on the Earth.* Gabriola Island, BC: New Society Publishers.

Walpole Island First Nation. (n.d.). "Walpole Island First Nation, Canada." On the World Wide Web at http://www.iisd.org/50comm/commdb/desc/d09.htm (retrieved 17 February 2012).

Zlomislic, Diana. (2011). "Ontario Teens Doused with Agent Orange while Helping with Northern Ontario Forestry Spraying Programs." *Toronto Star.* On the World Wide Web at http://www.thestar.com/news/canada/article/940243--star-exclusive-agent-orange-soaked-ontario-teens (retrieved 18 February 2012).

CHAPTER 17

Allard, Y. E., R. Wilkins and J.-M. Berthelot. (2004). Premature Mortality in Health Regions with High Aboriginal Populations. *Health Reports, 15* (1), 51–60.

Anand, S. S., S. Yusuf, R. Jacobs, A. D. Davis, Q. Yi, H. Gerstein. P.A. Montague, and E. Lonn. (2001). "Risk Factors, Atherosclerosis, and Cardiovascular Disease among Aboriginal People in Canada: The Study of Health Assessment and Risk Evaluation in Aboriginal peoples (SHARE-AP)." *The Lancet, 358,* 1147–53.

Antonucci, T.C. (1990). "Social Supports and Social Relationships." In R. H. Binstock and L. K. George, eds., *Handbook of Aging and the Social Sciences,* 3rd ed. (pp. 205–44). New York: Academic Press.

Arber, S. and Ginn, J. (1991). *Gender and Later Life.* London: Sage Publications.

Armstrong, P., H. Armstrong, and D. Coburn. (2001). *Unhealthy Times: Political Economy Perspectives on Health and Care in Canada.* Toronto: Oxford University Press.

Brownell M. D., N. P. Roos, and L. L. Roos. (2001). "Monitoring Health Reform: A Report Card Approach." *Social Science Medicine, 52,* 657–70.

Brym, Robert J. et al. (2012). "The Social Bases of Cancer." In R. Brym, ed., *Sociology as a Life or Death Issue,* 2nd Cdn ed. (pp. 81–102). Toronto: Nelson.

Buckley, N. J., F. T Denton, A. L. Robb, and B. G. Spencer. (2005). "Healthy Aging at Older Ages: Are Income and Education Important?" *Canadian Journal on Aging, 23* (Suppl. 1), S155–S169.

Canadian Home Care Association. (2004). "Realizing the Potential of Home Care." On the World Wide Web at http://www.cdnhomecare.ca/media.php?mid=464 (retrieved 30 July 2012).

Canadian Institute for Health Information. (2005). *Select Highlights on Public Views of the Determinants of Health. Canadian Population Health Initiative.* Ottawa: Author.

Canadian Institute for Health Information. (2007). Released 10 January. *Significant 10-Year Increase in the Number of Surgeries Performed in Canadian Hospitals.*

Canadian Study on Health and Aging. (1994). "The Canadian Study of Health and Aging: Study Methods and Prevalence of Dementia." *Canadian Medical Association Journal, 150* (6), 899–913.

Carriere, K. C, L. L. Roos, and D. C. Dover. (2000). "Across Time and Space: Variations in Hospital Use during Canadian Health Reform." *Health Services Research, 35* (2), 467–87.

Chappell, N. L. (2005). "Perceived Change in Quality of Life among Chinese Canadian Seniors: The Role of Involvement in Chinese Culture." *Journal of Happiness Studies, 6* (1), 69–91.

Chappell, N. L., B. Havens, M. J. Hollander, J. Miller, and C. McWilliam. (2004). "Comparative Costs of Home Care and Residential Care." *The Gerontologist, 44* (3), 389–400.

Chappell, N. L. and M. J. Hollander. (2011). *Evidence-Based Policy Prescription for an Aging Population. Invited Essay. HealthcarePapers, 11* (1), 8–18. The volume includes 11 commentaries by diverse experts. The authors' responses, 86–91.

Chappell, N. L., L. MacDonald, and M. Stones. (2008). Aging in *Contemporary Canada*, 2nd ed. Toronto: Pearson.

Chappell, N. L. and M. J. Penning. (2012). *Health Inequalities in Later Life: Differences by Age/Stage.* Ottawa: Public Health Agency of Canada.

Chen J., E. Ng, and R. Wilkins. (1996). "The Health of Canada's Immigrants in 1994–95." *Health Reports,* 7 (4), 33–45.

Citizenship and Immigration Canada. (2011). "Facts and Figures 2010—Immigration Overview: Permanent and Temporary Residents." On the World Wide Web at http://www.cic.gc.ca/english/resources/statistics/facts2010/permanent/06.asp (retrieved 4 January 2012).

Colin, C. and Jensen, H. (2009). *A Statistical Profile of Poverty in Canada.* Ottawa: Library of Parliament.

Commission on the Future of Health Care in Canada. (2002). *Building on Values: The Future of Health Care in Canada—Final Report.* Ottawa: National Library of Canada. Catalogue No. CP32-85/2002E-IN.

Cooke, M., F. Mitrou, D. Lawrence, E. Guimond, and D. Beavon. (2007). "Indigenous Well-being in Four Countries: An Application of the UNDP's Human Development Index to Indigenous Peoples in Australia, Canada, New Zealand, and the United States." *BMC International Health and Human Rights,* 7, 9.

Cranswick, K. (2003). *General Social Survey, Cycle 16: Caring for an Aging Society.* Ottawa: Statistics Canada.

Crompton, S. (2000). "100 Years of Health." *Canadian Social Trends, 59,* 12–17.

DeNavas-Walt, C., B.D. Proctor, and Jessica C. Smith (2010). "U.S. Census Bureau—Current *Population* Reports." In *Income, Poverty, and Health Insurance Coverage in the United States: 2009* (pp. 60–238). Washington: U.S. Government Printing Office.

DesMeules, M., D. Manuel, and R. Cho. (2004). "Mortality: Life and Health Expectancy of Canadian Women." *BMC Women's Health, 4* (Suppl. 1), S1–S9.

Desmeules, M., L. Turner, and R. Cho. (2004). "Morbidity Experiences and Disability among Canadian Women." *BMC Women's Health, 4* (Suppl. 1), S10.

Dubois, M-F. and Hébert, R. (2006). "Cognitive-Impairment-Free Life Expectancy for Canadian Seniors." *Dementia and Geriatric Cognitive Disorders, 22,* 327–333.

Dunlop, S., P. C. Coyte, and W. McIsaac. (2000). "Socio-economic Status and the Utilization of Physician's Services: Results from the Canadian National Population Health Survey." *Social Science & Medicine, 51,* 123–133.

Estes, C. L. (1979). *The Aging Enterprise.* San Francisco: Jossey-Bass.

Ferrario, C. G., F. J. Freeman, G. Nellett, and J. Sheel. (2008). Changing Nursing Students' Attitudes about Aging: An Argument for the Successful Aging Paradigm. *Educational Gerontology, 34* (1), 51–66.

Fries, J. F (1983). "Compression of Morbidity." *Milbank Memorial Fund Quarterly, 61,* 397–419.

Gee, E. M. (2000). "Living Arrangements and Quality of Life among Chinese Canadian Elders." *Social Indicators Research, 51,* 304–29.

Gee, E. M., K. M. Kobayashi, and S. G. Prus. (2004). "Examining the Healthy Immigrant Effect in Mid-to-Later life: Findings from the Canadian Community Health Survey." *Canadian Journal on Aging* (Supplement), S55-S63.

Gilmour, H. and J. Park. (2005). "Dependency, Chronic Conditions and Pain in Seniors." *Health Reports, 16* (Supplement), 21–31.

Hagestad, G. and P. Uhlenberg. (2005). "The Social Separation of Old and Young: A Root of Ageism." *Journal of Social Issues, 61,* 343–60.

Helliwell, J. F. (2003). "How's Life? Combining Individual and National Variables to Explain Subjective Well-being." *Economic Modelling, 20,* 331–60.

House, J. S. (2001). "Understanding Social Factors and Inequalities in Health: 20th Century Progress and 21st Century Prospects." *Journal of Health and Social Behavior, 43* (125), 2–4.

Huisman, M., A. Kunst, D. Deeg, F. Grigoletto, W. Nusselder, and J. Mackenbach. (2005). "Educational Inequalities in the Prevalence and Incidence of Disability in Italy and the Netherlands Were Observed." *Journal of Clinical Epidemiology, 58,* 1058–65.

Human Resources and Skills Development Canada. (2009). "Indicators of Well-being in Canada." On the World Wide Web at http://www4.hrsdc.gc.ca/indicator.jsp?lang+eng&indicatorid=3 (retrieved 19 August 2009).

Ikels, C. (2002). "Constructing and Deconstructing the Self: Dementia in China." *Journal of Cross-Cultural Gerontology, 17,* 233–51.

Indian and Northern Affairs Canada. (2003). *National Assessment of Water and Wastewater Systems in First Nations Communities.* Ottawa: Author.

Kane, R. L. (1990). "Introduction." In R. L. Kane, J. G. Evans, and D. MacFadyen, eds., *Improving the Health of Older People: A World View* (pp. 15–18). New York: Oxford University Press.

Keating, N., J. Fast, J. Frederick, K. Cranswick, and C. Perrier. (1999). *Elder Care in Canada: Context, Content, and Consequences.* Ottawa: Statistics Canada, Housing, Family and Social Statistics Division. Catalogue No. 89-570-XPE.

Lewis, S., C. Donaldson, C. Mitton, and G. Currie. (2001). "The Future of Health Care in Canada." *British Medical Journal, 323,* 926–29.

Link, B. G. and J. C. Phelan. (2000). "Evaluating the Fundamental Cause Explanation for Social Disparities in Health." In C. E. Bird, P. Conrad, and A. M. Fremont, eds., *Handbook of Medical Sociology,* 5th ed. (pp. 33–46). Upper Saddle River, NJ: Prentice Hall.

Litwak, E. (1960). "Geographic Mobility and Extended Family Cohesion." *American Sociological Review, 25,* 385–94.

Lynch, J. and G. Kaplan. (2000). "Socioeconomic Position." In L.F. Berkman and I. Kawachi, eds., *Social Epidemiology* (pp. 13–35). New York: Oxford University Press.

Markides, K. S. (1983). "Minority Aging." In M.W. Riley, B. B. Hess, and K. Bond, eds., *Aging in Society: Reviews of Recent Literature*. Hillsdale, NJ: Lawrence Erlbaum Associates.

Marmor, T. R. and K. Sullivan. (2000). "Canada's Burning! Media Myths about Universal Health Coverage." *Washington Monthly* (July/August). On the World Wide Web at http://www.washingtonmonthlycom/features/2000/0007.ma rmorsul.html#byline (retrieved 21 November 2006).

Martel, L., A. Bélanger, J.-M. Berthelot, and Y. Carrière. (2005). *Health Aging*. Ottawa: Statistics Canada. Catalogue No. 82-618- MWE2005004.

Martens, A., J. L. Goldenberg, and J. Greenberg. (2005). "A Terror Management Perspective on Ageism." *Journal of Social Issues, 61*, 223–39.

McMullin, J. (2004). *Understanding Social Inequality: Intersections of Class, Age, Gender, Ethnicity and Race in Canada*. Toronto: Oxford University Press.

Milan, A. and M. Vézina. (2011). "Table 5: Characteristics of Social Networks and Senior Women's and Men's Feeling about Life as a Whole by Age Group, 2008." In *Women in Canada: A Gender-Based Statistical Report* (p. 14). Component of Statistics Canada. Catalogue No. 89-503-X.

Montgomery, R. J.V, E. F Borgatta, and M. L. Borgatta. (2000). "Societal and Family Change in the Burden of Care." In William T. Liu and Hal Kendig, eds., *Who Should Care for the Elderly?: An East-West Value Divide* (pp. 27–54). Singapore: Singapore University Press, National University of Singapore, and World Scientific Publishing.

Munroe, S. (2003). "2003 Canadian Life and Death Statistics—Life Expectancy and Statistics on Deaths in Canada." On the World Wide Web at http://canadaonline.about.com/od/statistics/a/deathstats2003.htm (retrieved 19 August 2009).

Mustard, C. A., S. Derkson, J.-M. Berthelot, M. Wolfson, and L. L. Roos. (1997). "Age-Specific Education and Income Gradients in Morbidity and Mortality in a Canadian Province." *Social Science and Medicine, 45* (3), 383–97.

Noh, S., M. Beiser, V. Kaspar, F., Hou, and J. Rummens. (1999). "Perceived Racial Discrimination, Depression, and Coping: A Study of Southeast Asian Refugees in Canada." *Journal of Health and Social Behavior, 40* (3), 193–207.

Organisation for Economic Co-Operation and Development. (2009). "Health Data 2008: Statistics and Indicators for 30 Countries." On the World Wide Web at http://www.ecosante.org/OCDEENG/111000.html (retrieved 19 August 2009).

Palmore, E. B. (1998). *Facts on Aging Quiz: A Handbook of Uses and Results*. New York: Springer.

Penning, M. J., M. Brackley, and D. E. Allen. (2006). "Home Care and Health Reform: Changes in Home Care Utilization in One Canadian Province, 1990–2000." *The Gerontologist, 46* (6), 744–58.

Pérez, C. E. (2002). "Health Status and Health Behaviour among Immigrants." *Health Reports, 13*, 1–12.

Prus, S. G. and Gee, E. (2002). *Gender Differences in the Influence of Economic, Lifestyle and Psychosocial Factors on Later-Life Health*. Hamilton. ON: Program for Research on Social and Economic Dimensions of an Aging Population, McMaster University.

Raina, P. S., C. Wolfson, S. A. Kirkland, L. E. Griffith, M. Oremus, C. Patterson, H. Tuokko, M. Penning, C. M. Balion, D. Hogan, A. Wister, H. Payette, H. Shannon, and K. Brazil. (2009). "The Canadian Longitudinal Study on Aging (CLSA)." *Canadian Journal on Aging, 28* (3), 221–29.

Raphael, D. (2005). "Introduction to the Social Determinants of Health." In D. Raphael, ed., *Social Determinants of Health: Canadian Perspectives* (pp. 1–19). Toronto: Canadian Scholars Press.

Rogers, R. G., R. A. Hummer, and C. Nam. (2000). *Living and Dying in the USA*. San Diego, CA: Academic Press.

Ross, C.E. and C. Wu. (1996). "Education, Age, and the Cumulative Advantage in Health." *Journal of Health and Social Behavior, 37*, 104–20.

Schalick, L. M., W. C. Hadden, E. Pamuk, V. Navarro, and G. Pappas. (2000). "The Widening Gap in Death Rates among Income Groups in the United States from 1967 to 1986." *International Journal of Health Services, 30*, 13–26.

Segall, A. and N. L. Chappell. (2000). *Health and Health Care in Canada*. Toronto: Pearson Education Canada.

Simon, R. (2000). "The Importance of Culture in Sociological Theory and Research on Stress and Mental Health. A Missing Link?" In C.E. Bird, P. Conrad, and A. M. Fremont, eds., *Handbook of Medical Sociology*, 5th ed. Englewood Cliffs, NJ: Prentice-Hall.

Statistics Canada. (2001). *Self-Esteem by Age Group and Sex, Household Population Aged 12 and over, Canada Excluding Territories, 1994/95*. Ottawa: Author. Catalogue No. 82-221-XIE.

Statistics Canada. (2003a). *Annual Demographic Statistics, 2003*. Ottawa: Author. Catalogue No. 91-213-XIB/XPB.

Statistics Canada. (2003b). *Aboriginal Peoples Survey 2001—Initial Findings: Well-being of the Non-Reserve Aboriginal Population*. Ottawa: Author. Catalogue No. 89-589-XIE.

Statistics Canada. (2004). *Canadian Community Health Survey, 2003*. Ottawa: Author.

Statistics Canada. (2005a). *Canadian Community Health Survey, 2004*. Ottawa: Author.

Statistics Canada. (2005b). *Projections of the Aboriginal Populations, Canada, Provinces, and Territories, 2001 to 2017*. Ottawa: Author. Catalogue No. 91-547-XIE.

Statistics Canada. (2006a). "Causes of Death, 2003." On the World Wide Web at http://www.statcan.ca/english/freepub/84-208-XIE/ 84-208-XIE2005002.htm (retrieved 10 October 2006).

Statistics Canada. (2006b). "Life Tables, Canada, Provinces and Territories, 2000 to 2002." On the World Wide Web at http://www.statcan.gc.ca/pub/ 84-537-x/4064441-eng.htm (retrieved 10 October 2006).

Statistics Canada. (2007a). "2006 Census: Immigration, Citizenship, Language, Mobility and Migration." On the World Wide Web at http://www.statcan.gc.ca/daily-quotidien/071204/dq071204a-eng.htm (retrieved 4 January 2012).

Statistics Canada. (2007b). *A Portrait of Seniors in Canada, 2006*. Ottawa: Author. Catalogue No. 89-519-XIE.

Statistics Canada. (2008). *Aboriginal Peoples in Canada in 2006: Inuit, Métis and First Nations, 2006 Census*. Ottawa: Author. Catalogue No. 97-558-XIE.

Statistics Canada. (2011a). "Life Expectancy at Birth and at Age 65 by Sex and by Province and Territory." CANSIM, Table 102–0512. On the World Wide Web at http://www.statcan.gc.ca/tables-tableaux/sum-som/l01/cst01/health72a-eng.htm (retrieved 3 August 2012).

Statistics Canada. (2011b). "Canada's Population Estimates: Age and Sex." *The Daily* 28 September. On the World Wide Web at http://www.statcan.gc.ca/daily-quotidien/110928/dq110928a-eng.htm (retrieved 30 July 2012).

Stones, M. J. and L. Stones. (1997). "Ageism: The Quiet Epidemic." *Canadian Journal of Public Health, 88* (5), 293–94.

Trottier, H, L. Martel, C. Houle, J.-M. Berthelot, and J. Légaré. (2000). "Living at Home or in an Institution: What Makes the Differences for Seniors?" *Health Reports, 11*, 49–59.

United Nations Department of Economic and Social Affairs, Population Division. (2011). *World Population Prospects: 2006 Revision*. CD-ROM Edition—Comprehensive Dataset. On the World Wide Web at http://unstats.un.org/unsd/ demographic/products/indwm/tab3a.htm (retrieved November 2008).

Williams, A. P., R. Dever, P. Baranek, and A. Gildiner. (2001). "From Medicare to Home Care: Globalization, State Retrenchment and the Profitization of Canada's Health Care System." In P. Armstrong, H. Armstrong, and D. Coburn, eds., *Unhealthy Times: Political Economy Perspectives on Health and Care in Canada* (pp. 7–30). New York: Oxford University Press.

Williamson, D. J. (2000). "Health Behaviors and Health: Evidence That the Relationship Is Not Conditional on Income Adequacy." *Social Science and Medicine, 51* (12), 1741–54.

World Health Organization. (1948). *Official records of the World Health Organization, No.* 2. New York: WHO Interim Commission, UN.

Zola, I. K. (1983). *Socio-Medical Inquiries*. Philadelphia, PA: Temple University Press.

CHAPTER 18

Adam, Barry, Jan Willem Duyvendak, and André Krouwel. (1999). *The Global Emergence of Gay and Lesbian Politics*. Philadelphia, PA: Temple University Press.

Adamson, Nancy, Linda Briskin, and Margaret McPhail. (1988). *Feminist Organizing for Change: The Contemporary Women's Movement in Canada*. Toronto: Oxford University Press.

Andersen, Robert, Robert Brym, and Bader Araj. 2012. "Citizen Inclusion in the Greater Middle East." In Dalia Mogahed, ed., *Citizen Inclusion in the Arab World*. Abu Dhabi, United Arab Emirates: Gallup.

Bashevkin, Sylvia. (1986). "Independence Versus Partisanship: Dilemmas in the Political History of Women in English Canada." In V. Strong-Boag and A. Fellman, eds., *Rethinking Canada: The Promise of Women's History* (pp. 246–75). Toronto: Copp Clark Pitman.

Blais, André, Elisabeth Gidengil, Richard Nadeau, and Neil Nevitte. (1997). *1997 Canadian Election Survey*. On the World Wide Web at http://prod.library.utoronto.ca/datalib/ codebooks/utm/elections/1997/ (retrieved 20 June 2002).

Block, Fred. (1979). "The Ruling Class Does Not Rule." In R. Quinney, ed., *Capitalist Society* (pp. 128–40). Homewood, IL: Dorsey Press.

Boyd, Monica. (2011). "Gender Inequality: Economic and Political Aspects." In Robert Brym, ed., *New Society*, 6th ed. (pp. 154–78). Toronto: Nelson.

Brint, Stephen. (1984). "'New-Class' and Cumulative Trend Explanations of the Liberal Political Attitudes of Professionals." *American Journal of Sociology, 90*, 30–71.

Brodie, Janine. (1991). "Women and the Electoral Process in Canada." In Kathy Megyery, ed., *Women in Canadian Politics: Toward Equity in Representation* (pp. 3–59). Toronto: Dundurn Press.

Brym, Robert J. (1979). "Political Conservatism in Atlantic Canada." In Robert J. Brym and R. James Sacouman, eds., *Underdevelopment and Social Movements in Atlantic Canada* (pp. 59–79). Toronto: New Hogtown Press.

Brym, Robert J. (1980). *Intellectuals and Politics*. London, UK: Allen and Unwin.

Brym, Robert J. (1989). "Canada." In Tom Bottomore and Robert J. Brym, eds., *The Capitalist Class: An International Study* (pp. 177–206). New York: New York University Press.

Brym, Robert J. (2008). "Affluence, Power and Strikes in Canada, 1973–2000." In Edward Grabb and Neil Guppy eds., *Social Inequality in Canada: Patterns, Problems, Policies*, 6th ed. (pp. 55–68) Scarborough, ON: Prentice-Hall Canada.

Bureau of Labor Statistics, US Department of Labor. (2012). "Table 1. Union Affiliation of Employed Wage and Salary Workers by Selected Characteristics." On the World Wide Web at http://www.bls.gov/webapps/legacy/cpslutab1.htm (retrieved 21 January 2012).

Canada Department of Labour. (1970). *Strikes and Lockouts in Canada, 1968*. Ottawa: Economic and Research Branch, Department of Labour. Catalogue No. L2-1-1968.

Canada Department of Labour. (1973). *Labour Organizations in Canada, 1972*. Ottawa: Economics and Research Branch, Canada Department of Labour. Catalogue No. L2-2-1972.

Canada Department of Labour. (1985). *Strikes and Lockouts in Canada, 1985*. Ottawa: Minister of Supply and Services Canada. Catalogue No. L160-2999/85"Canadian Election Panel Study, 2004–2006–2008." (2010). On the World Wide Web at http://sda.chass.utoronto.ca/cgi-bin/sdapub/hsda?harcsda+ces040608 (retrieved 27 November 2010).

Casper, L. M., S. S. McLanahan, and I. Garfinkel. (1994). "The Gender-Poverty Gap: What Can We Learn from Other Countries?" *American Sociological Review, 59*, 594–605.

Clarke, Harold D., Jane Jenson, Lawrence LeDuc, and Jon H. Pammett. (1996). *Absent Mandate: Canadian Electorial Politics in an Era of Restructuring*, 3rd ed. Toronto: Gage.

Clement, Wallace. (1975). *The Canadian Corporate Elite: An Analysis of Economic Power*. Toronto: McClelland and Stewart.

Dahl, Robert A. (1961). *Who Governs?* New Haven, CT: Yale University Press.

Davies, James C. (1969). "Toward a Theory of Revolution." In Barry McLaughlin, ed., *Studies in Social Movements: A Social Psychological Perspective* (pp. 85–108). New York: Free Press.

Evans, Peter B., Dietrich Rueschemeyer, and Theda Skocpol. (1985). *Bringing the State Back In*. Cambridge, UK: Cambridge University Press.

Frank, Jeffrey. (1994). "Voting and Contributing: Political Participation in Canada." In *Canadian Social Trends* (pp. 333–37). Toronto: Thompson Educational Publishers.

Gladwell, Malcolm. (2010). "Small Change: Why the Revolution Will Not Be Tweeted." *The New Yorker* 4 October. On the World Wide Web at http://www.newyorker.com/reporting/2010/10/04/101004fa_fact_gladwell (retrieved 21 January 2012).

Goffman, Erving. (1974). *Frame Analysis*. Cambridge, MA: Harvard University Press.

"Greenpeace Contacts Worldwide." (1999). On the World Wide Web at http://adam.greenpeace.org/information.shtml (retrieved 29 April 2004).

Hourani, Albert. (1991). *A History of the Arab Peoples.* New York: Warner Books.

Human Resources Development Canada. (1995). *1994–1995 Directory of Labour Organizations in Canada.* Ottawa: Minister of Supply and Services Canada. Catalogue No. L2-2-1995.

Human Resources Development Canada. (1998). *1998 Directory of Labour Organizations in Canada.* Ottawa: Workplace Information Directorate.

Human Resources and Skills Development Canada. (2006). "Chronological Perspective on Work Stoppages in Canada" [for 1999, 2001, 2004]. On the World Wide Web at http://srv131.services.gc.ca/wid-dimt/ pcat-cpws/tirir-sort.aspx (retrieved 27 March 2006).

Human Resources and Skills Development Canada. (2011). "Union Membership in Canada, 2010." On the World Wide Web at http://www.hrsdc.gc.ca/eng/labour/labour_relations/info_analysis/union_membership/2010/unionmembership2010.shtml (retrieved 21 January 2012).

International Labor Organization (2012). "Strikes and lockouts." On the World Wide Web at http://laborsta.ilo.org/ (retrieved 5 October 2012).

Jenkins, J. Craig. (1983). "Resource Mobilization Theory and the Study of Social Movements." *Annual Review of Sociology, 9,* 527–53.

Kelley, Jack. (2001). "Terror Groups Hide Behind Web Encryption." *USA Today* 19 June. On the World Wide Web at http://www.usatoday.com/life/cyber/tech/2001–02–05-binladen.htm (retrieved 13 September 2001).

Korpi, Walter. (1983). *The Democratic Class Struggle.* London: Routledge and Kegan Paul.

Lipset, Seymour Martin. (1971). *Agrarian Socialism: The Cooperative Commonwealth Federation in Saskatchewan,* rev. ed. Berkeley, CA: University of California Press.

Lipset, Seymour Martin. (1981). *Political Man: The Social Bases of Politics,* 2nd ed. Baltimore: Johns Hopkins University Press.

Lodhi, Abdul Qaiyum and Charles Tilly. (1973). "Urbanization, Crime and Collective Violence in 19th Century France." *American Journal of Sociology, 79,* 296–318.

Marshall, T. H. (1965). "Citizenship and Social Class." In T. H. Marshall, ed., *Class, Citizenship, and Social Development: Essays by T. H. Marshall* (pp. 71–134). Garden City, NY: Anchor.

Mayer, Gerald. (2004). "Union Membership Trends in the United States." *Federal Publications,* Paper 174. On the World Wide Web at http://digitalcommons.ilr.cornell.edu/key_workplace/174 (retrieved 21 January 2012).

McAdam, Doug. 1982. *Political Process and the Development of Black Insurgency, 1930–1970.* Chicago: University of Chicago Press.

McCarthy, John D. and Mayer N. Zald. (1977). "Resource Mobilization and Social Movements: A Partial Theory." *American Journal of Sociology, 82,* 1212–41.

McCullagh, Declan. (2000). "Bin Laden: Steganography Master?" *Wired* 7 February. On the World Wide Web at http://www.wired.com/news/print/0.1294.41658.00.html (retrieved 13 September 2001).

McDonald, Michael P. (2008a). "This May Be the Election of the Century." On the World Wide Web at http://www.politico.com/news/stories/0908/13798.html (retrieved 5 November 2008).

McDonald, Michael P. (2008b). "Voter Turnout." On the World Wide Web at http://elections.gmu.edu/voter_turnout.htm (retrieved 5 November 2008).

Melucci, Alberto. (1980). "The New Social Movements: A Theoretical Approach." *Social Science Information, 19,* 199–226.

Melucci, Alberto. (1995). "The New Social Movements Revisited: Reflections on a Sociological Misunderstanding." In Louis Maheu, ed., *Social Classes and Social Movements: The Future of Collective Action* (pp. 107–19). London: Sage.

Miliband, Ralph. (1973 [1969]). *The State in Capitalist Society.* London: Fontana.

Mills, C. Wright. (1956). *The Power Elite.* New York: Oxford University Press.

Mishler, William. (1979). *Political Participation in Canada: Prospects for Democratic Citizenship.* Toronto: Macmillan.

Moore, Barrington, Jr. (1967). *Social Origins of Dictatorship and Democracy: Lord and Peasant in the Making of the Modern World.* Boston: Beacon Press.

"Muslim Brotherhood Movement Homepage." (2002). On the World Wide Web at http://www.ummah.org.uk/ikhwan/ (retrieved 7 May 2003).

Myles, John. (1989). *Old Age in the Welfare State: The Political Economy of Public Pensions,* rev. ed. Lawrence, KS: University Press of Kansas.

O'Connor, Julia S. (1996). "From Women in the Welfare State to Gendering Welfare State Regimes." *Current Sociology, 44* (2), 1–130.

O'Connor, Julia S. and Robert J. Brym. (1988). "Public Welfare Expenditure in OECD Countries: Towards a Reconciliation of Inconsistent Findings." *British Journal of Sociology, 39,* 47–68.

O'Connor, Julia S. and Gregg M. Olsen, eds. (1998). *Power Resources Theory and the Welfare State: A Critical Approach.* Toronto: University of Toronto Press.

Oberschall, Anthony. (1973). *Social Conflict and Social Movements.* Englewood Cliffs, NJ: Prentice-Hall.

Occupy Together (2012). On the World Wide Web at http://www.occupytogether.org/downloadable-posters/ (retrieved 21 January 2012).

Olsen, Dennis. (1980). *The State Elite.* Toronto: McClelland and Stewart.

Olsen, Gregg. (2002). *The Politics of the Welfare State: Canada, Sweden and the United States.* Toronto: Oxford University Press.

Olsen, Gregg and Robert J. Brym. (1996). "Between American Exceptionalism and Swedish Social Democracy: Public and Private Pensions in Canada." In Michael Shalev, ed., *The Privatization of Social Policy? Occupational Welfare and the Welfare State in America, Scandinavia and Japan* (pp. 261–79). London: Macmillan.

Pew Research Center. 2012. "Rising Share of Americans See Conflict between Rich and Poor." On the World Wide Web at http://www.pewsocialtrends.org/files/2012/01/Rich-vs-Poor.pdf (retrieved 21 January 2012).

Piven, Frances Fox and Richard A. Cloward. (1989). *Why Americans Don't Vote.* New York: Pantheon.

Polsby, Nelson W. (1959). "Three Problems in the Analysis of Community Power." *American Sociological Review, 24,* 796–803.

Porter, John. (1965). *The Vertical Mosaic: An Analysis of Social Class and Power in Canada.* Toronto: University of Toronto Press.

Poulantzas, Nicos. (1975 [1968]). *Political Power and Social Classes.* T. O'Hagan, trans. London: New Left Books.

Roche, Maurice. (1995). "Rethinking Citizenship and Social Movements: Themes in Contemporary Sociology and

Neoconservative Ideology." In Louis Maheu, ed., *Social Classes and Social Movements: The Future of Collective Action* (pp.186–219). London: Sage.

Rootes, Chris. (1995). "A New Class? The Higher Educated and the New Politics." In Louis Maheu, ed., *Social Classes and Social Movements: The Future of Collective Action* (pp. 220–35). London: Sage.

Shahar, Yael. (2001). "Tracing bin Laden's Money: Easier Said Than Done." International Policy Institute for Counter-Terrorism. On the World Wide Web at http://www.ict.org.il/articles/articledet.cfm?articleid=387 (retrieved 30 July 2002).

Skocpol, Theda. (1979). *States and Revolutions: A Comparative Analysis of France, Russia and China.* Cambridge, UK: Cambridge University Press.

Snow, David A., E. Burke Rochford, Steven K. Worden, and Robert D. Benford. (1986). "Frame Alignment Processes, Micromobiization and Movement Participation." *American Sociological Review, 51*, 464–81.

Snyder, David and Charles Tilly. (1972). "Hardship and Collective Violence in France, 1830–1960." *American Sociological Review, 37*, 520–32.

Spilerman, Seymour. (1970). "The Causes of Racial Disturbances: A Comparison of Alternative Explanations." *American Sociological Review, 35, 627–49.*

Spilerman, Seymour. (1976). "Structural Characteristics of Cities and the Severity of Racial Disorders." *American Sociological Review, 41*, 771–93.

Statistics Canada. (2008). "Table E175–177: Union Membership in Canada, in Total and as a Percentage of Non-Agricultural Paid Workers and Union Members with International Affiliation, 1911–1975." On the World Wide Web at http://www.statcan.gc.ca/pub/11–516-x/sectione/4147438-eng.htm#6 (retrieved 23 January 2011).

Statistics Sweden. (2011). "A More Equal Election Turnout." On the World Wide Web at http://www.scb.se/Pages/PressRelease_311614.aspx (retrieved 21 January 2012).

Strong-Boag, Veronica. (1986). "Ever a Crusader: Nellie McClung, First-Wave Feminist." In V. Strong-Boag and A. Fellman, eds., *Rethinking Canada: The Promise of Women's History* (pp. 178–90). Toronto: Copp Clark Pitman.

Tilly, Charles. (1978). *From Mobilization to Revolution.* Reading, MA: Addison-Wesley,

Tilly, Charles. (1979a). "Collective Violence in European Perspective." In H. Graham and T. Gurr, eds., *Violence in America: Historical and Comparative Perspective*, 2nd ed. (pp. 83–118). Beverly Hills, CA: Sage.

Tilly, Charles. (1979b). "Repertoires of Contention in America and Britain, 1750–1830." In Mayer N. Zald and John D. McCarthy eds., *The Dynamics of Social Movements: Resource Mobilization,Social Control and Tactics* (pp. 126–55). Cambridge, MA: Winthrop.

Tilly, Charles, Louise Tilly, and Richard Tilly. (1975). *The Rebellious Century, 1830–1930.* Cambridge, MA: Harvard University Press.

Turner, Bryan S. (1986). *Citizenship and Capitalism: The Debate over Reformism.* London: Allen and Unwin.

"United States—President." (2008). *MSNBC.* On the World Wide Web at http://www.msnbc.msn.com/id/26843704 (retrieved 5 November 2008).

"Voter Turnout Inches Up to 61.4%." 2011. CBC News. On the World Wide Web at http://www.cbc.ca/news/politics/canadavotes2011/story/2011/05/03/cv-election-voter-turnout-1029.html (retrieved 21 January 2012).

Weber, Max. (1946 [1922]). "Class, Status, Party." In H.H. Gerth and C. Wright Mills, eds., and trans., *From Max Weber: Essays in Sociology* (pp. 180–95). New York: Oxford University Press.

Weber, Max. (1947). *The Theory of Social and Economic Organization*, T. Parsons, ed., A.M. Henderson and T. Parsons trans. New York: Free Press.

Wolf, Eric. (1999 [1969]). *Peasant Wars of the 20th Century.* Norman, OK: Oklahoma University Press.

"Women in National Parliaments." (2012). On the World Wide Web at http://www.ipu.org/wmn-e/world.htm (retrieved 21 January 2012).

Worth, Robert. (2001). "The Deep Intellectual Roots of Islamic Terror." On the World Wide Web at http://www.nytimes.com (retrieved 13 October 2002).

Yardley, William. 2011. "The Branding of the Occupy Movement." *New York Times* November 27. On the World Wide Web at http://www.nytimes.com (retrieved 21 January 2012).

CHAPTER 19

Adbusters. (2005). On the World Wide Web at http://www.adbusters.org/home/ (retrieved 20 March 2005).

African Centre for Biosafety. (2005). On the World Wide Web at http://www.biosafetyafrica.net/index.htm (retrieved 7 March 2005).

Agence France-Presse. (2004). "Chirac Lashes Out against US Cultural Domination." *Free Republic.* 7 October. On the World Wide Web at http://www.freerepublic.com/focus/f-news/1237687/posts (retrieved 16 August 2012).

American Apparel. (n.d). "Legalize LA." On the World Wide Web at http://www.americanapparel.net/contact/legalizela/Legalize_LA.pdf (retrieved 14 December 2011).

Anderson, Sarah and John Cavanagh with Thea Lee and the Institute for Policy Studies. (2005). *Field Guide to the Global Economy.* New York: New Press.

Babson, Steve. (2000). "Cross-Border Trade with Mexico and the Prospect for Worker Solidarity: The Case of Mexico." *Critical Sociology, 26* (1,2), 13–35.

Bales, Kevin. (1999). *Disposable People: New Slavery in the Global Economy.* Los Angeles: University of California Press.

Barlow, Maude. (2001). "The Global Monoculture: 'Free Trade' Versus Culture and Democracy." *Earth Island Journal, 16*, 3. On the World Wide Web at http://www.earthisland.org/eijournal/new_articles.cfm?articleID=270&journalID=48 (retrieved 22 November 2006).

Basok, Tanya. (2002). *Tortillas and Tomatoes: Transmigrant Mexican Harvesters in Canada.* Montreal: McGill-Queen's University Press.

Bedell, Denise. (2010). "OTC Foreign Exchange Market Turnover by Country, 1998–2010." *Global Finance.* On the World Wide Web at http://www.gfmag.com/tools/global-database/economic-data/10774-otc-foreign-exchange-market-turnover-by-country-1998–2010.html#axzz1d8ItS3YH. (retrieved 8 November 2011).

Beder, Sharon. (2000). *Selling the Work Ethic: From Puritan Pulpit to Corporate PR.* Carlton North, Victoria, Australia: Scribe.

Bello, Walden. (2002). "Drop Till We Shop?" *The Nation Online.* On the World Wide Web at http://www.thenation.com/doc.mhtml?i20021021andc51ands5bello (retrieved 3 October 2002).

Bentley Stephen. (2004). "Fighting Global Warming at the Farmers' Market. The Role of Local Food Systems in Reducing Greenhouse Gas Emissions." *A FoodShare Research in Action Report.* On the World Wide Web at http://www.foodshare.net/resource/files/ACF230.pdf (retrieved 9 January 2004).

Bird, Kate and David Hughes. (1997). "Ethical Consumerism: The Case of 'Fairly-Trade' Coffee." *Business Ethics. A European Review, 6,* 159–67.

Bivens, Lyle J. and Adam Hersh. (2003). "A Rough Row." *Global Policy Forum.* On the World Wide Web at http://wwwglobalpolicy.org/socecon/bwi-wto/wto/2003/0909rough.htm (retrieved 9 September 2003).

Borosage, Robert. (2008). "The Great Corporate Tax Heist." *Huffington Post.* On the World Wide Web at http://www.huffingtonpost.com/robert-l-borosage/the-great-corporate-tax-h_b_118479.html (retrieved 18 August 2009).

Brown, Lester. (2005). *Outgrowing the Earth: The Food Security Challenge in an Age of Falling Water Tables and Rising Temperatures.* Washington, DC: Earth Policy Institute.

Brownell, Kelly and Katherine Battle Horgen. (2004). *Food Fight. The Inside Story of the Food Industry, America's Obesity Crisis, and What We Can Do About It.* Toronto: Contemporary Books.

Brym, Robert J., et al. (2005). "In Faint Praise of the World Bank's Gender Development Policy." *Canadian Journal of Sociology, 30,* 95–111.

Bureau of Labor Statistics. (2011). "Union Members." *News Release.* USDL-11-0063 January 21. On the World Wide Web http://www.bls.gov/news.release/union2.nr0.htm (retrieved November 29, 2011).

"Canada's Corporate Income Tax Fight." (2011). *CBC News.* On the World Wide Web at http://www.cbc.ca/news/business/story/2011/04/14/f-corporate-tax-cuts-for-against.html (retrieved 18 November 2011).

"Canadians Made Little Economic Headway in Last 15 Years: TD Economists." (2005). *CBC News.* On the World Wide Web at http://www.cbc.ca/news/business/story/2005/01/18/tdeconomy-050118.html (retrieved 18 January 2005).

Cardoso, Fernando Henrique. (1993). "The Challenges of Social Democracy in Latin America." In Menno Vellinga, ed., *Social Democracy in Latin America: Prospects for Change.* Boulder, CO: Westview Press.

Castells, Manuel. (1998). *The Information Age: Economy, Society, and Culture: Vol. 3, End of the Millennium.* Malden, MA: Blackwell.

Central Intelligence Agency. (2011). "GDP (Purchasing Power Parity)." *The World Factbook.* On the World Wide Web at https://www.cia.gov/library/publications/the-world-factbook/rankorder/2001rank.html (retrieved November 24 2011).

CIA World Factbook. (2011). "Mexico: Economy." *CIA World Factbook.* On the World Wide Web at https://www.cia.gov/library/publications/the-world-factbook/geos/mx.html (retrieved 14 December 2011).

Cisco Systems Inc., 2011. *Cisco Connected World Technology Report.* On the World Wide Web at http://www.cisco.com/en/US/netsol/ns1120/index.html (retrieved November 8 2011).

Clay, Jason. (2004). *World Agriculture and the Environment: A Commodity-by-Commodity Guide to Impacts and Practices.* Washington, DC: Island Press.

"Corporate Tax: Escaping the Shakedown." (2009). *The Economist.* On the World Wide Web at http://www.economist.com/node/13962472?story_id=13962472 (retrieved 18 November 2011).

Denny, Charlotte. (2002). "The Contented Malcontent." *Guardian* July 6. On the World Wide Web at http://www.guardian.co.uk/business/2002/jul/06/globalisation (retrieved 13 December 2011).

Durning, Alan. (1992). *How Much Is Enough? The Consumer Society and the Fate of the Earth.* New York: Norton.

"Egypt Protests: Q and A." (2011). *Telegraph* 27 January. On the World Wide Web at http://www.telegraph.co.uk/news/world-news/africaandindianocean/egypt/8286864/Egypt-protests-Q-and-A.html (retrieved 13 December 2011).

"Egypt Uprising: Timeline." (2011). *Telegraph* 22 November. On the World Wide Web at http://www.telegraph.co.uk/news/worldnews/africaandindianocean/egypt/8907227/Egypt-uprising-timeline.html (retrieved 13 December 2011).

Ehrenreich, Barbara. (2001). *Nickel and Dimed. On (Not) Getting By in America.* New York: Henry Holt.

Ehrenreich, Barbara. (2005). *Bait and Switch. The (Futile) Pursuit of the American Dream.* New York: Henry Holt.

Ellwood, Wayne. (2001). *The No-Nonsense Guide to Globalization.* London, UK: Zed Books.

Evans-Pritchard, Ambrose. (2009). "There's No Quick Fix to the Global Economy's Excess Capacity." *Telegraph* 15 August. On the World Wide Web at http://www.telegraph.co.uk/finance/comment/ambroseevans_pritchard/6035300/Theres-no-quick-fix-to-the-global-economys-excess-capacity.html (retrieved 16 November 2011).

Fairtrade Foundation. (2011). *The Arabica Coffee Market, 1989–2011: Comparison of Fairtrade and New York Exchange Prices.* London: Author.

Fallows, James. (2008). "'Be Nice to the Countries that Lend You Money.' An Interview with Gao Xiqing." *Atlantic Monthly, 302* (December), 62–65.

Federoff, Nina. (2011). "Engineering Food for All," *New York Times.* On the World Wide Web at http://www.nytimes.com/2011/08/19/opinion/genetically-engineered-food-for-all.html (retrieved 30 July 2012).

Ferguson, Niall. (2004). *Colossus: The Rise and Fall of the American Empire.* New York: Penguin Books.

Forbes. (2011). "The World's Billionaires." *Forbes* March 9. On the World Wide Web at http://www.forbes.com/wealth/billionaires (retrieved 24 November 2011).

Frank, Thomas. (1997). *The Conquest of Cool.* Chicago: University of Chicago Press.

Freeland, Chrystia. (2011). "Protesters Should Get Occupied with Economic Solutions." *Globe and Mail* 4 November: B2.

Frundt, Henry. (2000). "Models of Cross-Border Organizing in the Maquila Industries." *Critical Sociology, 26* (1–2), 36–55.

Ghemawat, Pankaj. (2007). "Why the World Isn't Flat." *Foreign Policy.* (March/April 2007), 54–60.

Ghemawat, Pankaj. (2011). "Implications of a Borderless World—Interview with Pankaj Ghemawat." *Process Excellence Network.* July 20. On the World Wide Web at http://www.processexcellencenetwork.com/change-management/articles/the-temptation-of-a-borderless-world-interview-wit/ (retrieved 7 November 2011).

Grant, Tavia. (2011a). "Canada's Wage Gap at a Record High: OECD." *Globe and Mail* December 5. On the World Wide

Web at http://www.theglobeandmail.com/report-on-business/economy/canadas-wage-gap-at-record-high-oecd/article4099041/ (retrieved 13 December 2011).

Grant, Tavia. (2011b). "Rich Earn 155 Times More than Average Worker." *Globe and Mail* 3 January. On the World Wide Web at http://www.theglobeandmail.com/report-on-business/economy/rich-earn-155-times-more-than-average-worker/article1855906/ (retrieved 29 November 2011).

Grant, Tavia and Greg Keenan. (2011). "Factory Employment Hits a 35-Year Low as More Plants Close." *Globe and Mail* 5 November: B1.

Haight, Colleen. (2011). "The Problem with Fair Trade Coffee." *Stanford Social Innovation Review* Summer. On the World Wide Web at: http://www.ssireview.org/articles/entry/the_problem_with_fair_trade_coffee (retrieved 14 December 2011).

Hall, Sally. (2005). "Hungry for an Alternative." *Independent* (UK) 28 June.

Harvey, David. (1990). *The Condition of Postmodernity.* Cambridge, MA: Blackwell.

Hays, Constance. (2000). "Learning to Think Smaller at Coke." *New York Times* 6 February: Business Section.

Heath, Andrew and Joseph Potter. (2004). *The Rebel Sell: Why the Culture Can't Be Jammed.* Toronto: Harper Collins.

Hickman, Martin. (2008). "All Starbucks' Coffee to be Fairtrade." *Independent* November 26. On the World Wide Web at http://www.independent.co.uk/life-style/food-and-drink/news/all-starbucks-coffee-to-be-fairtrade-1035162.html (retrieved 14 December 2011).

Hoogvelt, Ankie. (1997). *Globalization and the Postcolonial World.* Baltimore, ML: Johns Hopkins University Press.

Hopkins, Terrence and Immanuel Wallerstein. (1986). "Commodity Chains in the World Economy Prior to 1800." *Review* (a Journal of the Fernand Braudel Center), *10* (1), 157–70.

Howlett, Karen. (2005). "Ontario Eyes Brightest Immigrants." *Globe and Mail* 11 October: A7.

Human Resources and Skills Development Canada. (2011). "Work-Unionization Rates." *Indicators of Well-being in Canada.* On the World Wide Web http://www4.hrsdc.gc.ca/.3ndic.1t.4r@-eng.jsp?iid=17 (retrieved 29 November 2011).

Institute for Global Labour and Human Rights. (2011). "Reports." On the World Wide Web at http://www.globallabourrights.org/reports (retrieved 24 November 2011).

Institute for Policy Studies and United for a Fair Economy. (2006). "Executive Excess 2006." On the World Wide Web at http://www.ips-dc.org/getfile.php?id=155 (retrieved 19 August 2009).

International Forum on Globalization. (2001). *Does Globalization Help the Poor? A Special Report by the International Forum on Globalization.* San Francisco: Author.

International Telecommunication Union. (2011a). "Fixed Telephony." *World Telecommunication/ICT Indicators Database.* On the World Wide Web at http://www.itu.int/ITU-D/ict/statistics/ (retrieved 12 December 2011).

International Telecommunication Union. (2011b). "Mobile Telephony." *World Telecommunication/ICT Indicators Database.* On the World Wide Web at http://www.itu.int/ITU-D/ict/statistics/ (retrieved 12 December 2011).

Internet World Stats. (2011). "World Internet Usage and Population Statistics." Internet World Stats. On the World Wide Web at http://www.internetworldstats.com. (retrieved 1 November 2011).

ISAAA (International Service for the Acquisition of Agri-Biotech Applications). (2010). "Crop Biotech Update Special Edition." ON the World Wide Web at http://www.isaaa.org/kc/cropbiotechupdate/specialedition/2011/default.asp (retrieved 16 August 2012).

Jackson, Andrew. (2005). *The Case Against More Corporate Tax Cuts.* Ottawa: Canadian

Jacobs, Andrew and David Barboza. (2008). "Chinese Exports Decline Sharply in November." *New York Times* December 10. On the World Wide Web at http://www.nytimes.com/2008/12/11/business/11yuan.html?em (retrieved 19 August 2009).

Jones, David and Brad Dorfman. (2010). "Kraft Snares Cadbury for $19.6 billion." *Reuters* 19 January. On the World Wide Web http://www.reuters.com/article/2010/01/19/us-cadbury-idUSTRE60H1N020100119 (retrieved 18 November 2011).

Jordan, Mary. (2003). "Workers Falling Behind in Mexico." *Washington Post* July 15. On the World Wide Web (Global Policy Forum) at http://www.globalpolicy.org/globaliz/special/2003/0716mexico.htm (retrieved 15 July 2003).

Kahn, Jeremy. (2008). "Recession Trickles to India." *New York Times* 3 December. On the World Wide Web at http://wwwnytimes.com/2008/12/04/business/worldbusiness/04rupee.html (retrieved 19 August 2009).

Kara, Siddharth. (2008). *Sex Trafficking—Inside the Business of Modern Slavery.* New York: Columbia University Press.

Kennedy, Dawn. (2004). "Nollywood Thinks Outside the Box." *Sunday Independent.* On the World Wide Web at http://www.sundayindependent.co.za/index.php?fSectionId51083andfArticleId52324573 (retrieved 28 November 2004).

Kindall, Henry and David Pimentel. (1994). "Constraints on the Expansion of the Global Food Supply," *Ambio, 23,* 3.

Klein, Naomi. (2000). *No Logo.* Toronto: Knopf Canada.

Landler, Mark. (2008). "The US Financial Crisis Is Spreading to Europe." *New York Times* September. On the World Wide Web at http://www.nytimes.com/2008/10/01/business/worldbusiness/01global.html?partner=rssnyt&emc=rss (retrieved 19 August 2009).

Lang, Tim and Jules Pretty. (2005). "Farm Costs and Food Miles: An Assessment of the Full Cost of the UK Weekly Food Basket." *Food Policy, 30* (1).

Lappé, Anna and Frances Moore Lappé. (2002). *Hope's Edge: The Next Diet for a Small Planet.* New York: Tarcher/Penguin.

Lappé, Frances Moore. (2005). "Diet for a Smaller Planet: Real Sources of Abundance." In Andrew Heintzman and Evan Solomon, eds., *Feeding the Future* (pp. 125–54). Toronto: Anansi Press.

Liao, Carol, Hubert Hsu, Youchi Kuo, Jeff Walters, and Veronique Yang. (2010). *Big Prizes in Small Places: China's Rapidly Multiplying Pockets of Growth.* Boston: Boston Consulting Group.

Lindstrom, Martin. (2003). *Brand Child. Remarkable Insights into the Minds of Today's Global Kids and Their Relationships with Brands.* Sterling, VA: Millward Brown.

Lynn, Barry. (2002). "Unmade in America. The True Cost of the Global Assembly Line." *Harper's Magazine, 304* (1825), 34–41.

Manning, Richard. (2004). "The Oil We Eat: Following the Food Chain Back To Iraq." *Harper's Magazine* (February). On the World Wide Web at http://www.harpers.org/TheOilWeEat.html (retrieved 15 October 2006).

Marx, Karl and Friedrich Engels. (1972 [1848])."Manifesto of the Communist Party." In R. Tucker, ed., *The Marx-Engels Reader* (pp. 331–62). New York: Norton.

May, Christopher, ed. (2006). *Global Corporate Power*. Boulder, CO: Lynne Rienner.

"McDonald's Apologizes for Beefy Fries." (2001). *CBC News*. On the World Wide Web at http://www.cbc.ca/news/canada/story/2001/05/24/fries_010524.html (retrieved 25 May 2001).

McDonald's Canada. (2011). "Frequently Asked Questions." On the World Wide Web at http://www.mcdonalds.ca/ca/en/contact_us/faq.html (retrieved 7 November 2011).

McKibben, Bill. (1993). *The Age of Missing Information*. New York: Plumb.

McKibben, Bill. (2005). "The Cuba Diet: What Will You Be Eating When the Revolution Comes?" *Harper's Magazine* (April). On the World Wide Web at http://www.harpers.org/TheCubaDiet.html (retrieved 15 October 2006).

"Media Giants." (2011). *Frontline*. PBS. On the World Wide Web at http://www.pbs.org/wgbh/pages/frontline/shows/cool/giants/ (12 December 2011).

Milanovic, Branko. (2005). "Global Income Inequality: What It Is and Why It Matters?" DESA Working Paper No. 26. On the World Wide Web at http://www.un.org/esa/desa/papers/2006/wp26_2006.pdf (retrieved 7 March 2009).

Milkman, Ruth. (2000). "Immigrant Organizing and the New Labor Movement in Los Angeles." *Critical Sociology*, *26* (1/2), 59–81.

National Farmers Union. (2009). "Open letter to the Competition Bureau Regarding the Proposed XL/Tyson sale." On the World Wide Web at http://nfu.ca/press_releases/press/2009/February-09/NFU%20letter%20to%20Competition%20Bureau%20re%20Tyson-XL%20sale.pdf (30 retrieved November 2011).

Navdanya. (2005). Homepage. On the World Wide Web at http://www.navdanya.org/ (retrieved 1 October 2006).

Nestle, Marion. (2011). "Coke's New Buddy: Oxfam Helps Coca-Cola Reduce Poverty." *Atlantic Monthly*. On the World Wide Web at http://www.theatlantic.com/health/archive/2011/04/cokes-new-buddy-oxfam-helps-coca-cola-reduce-poverty/237666/ (retrieved 21 April 2011).

Nicholson, Chris V. (2010). "Chinese Carmaker Geely Completes Acquisition of Volvo from Ford." *New York Times* August 2. On the World Wide Web at http://www.nytimes.com/2010/08/03/business/global/03volvo.html (retrieved 16 November 2011).

Nissen, Bruce. (2000). "Editor's Introduction: The Labor Movement in a New Globalized Environment." *Critical Sociology*, *26* (1/2), 3–8.

No Sweat. (2005). "Changing an Industry." On the World Wide Web at http://www.nosweatapparel.com/ (retrieved 1 October 2006).

Organic Consumers Association. (2005). "Prohibited Gene-Altered Corn Found in Latin American & Caribbean Food Aid Shipments. Source: Environmental News Service. On the World Wide Web at http://www.organicconsumers.org/ge/caribbean21705.cfm (retrieved 16 February 2005).

Oxfam. (2002). "Mugged: Poverty in Your Coffee Cup." (Research paper). On the World Wide Web at http://www.oxfamamerica.org/newsandpublications/publications/research_reports/mugged (retrieved September 2002).

Paarlberg, Robert. (2010). *Food Politics: What Everybody Needs to Know*. New York: Oxford University Press.

"Paid to be Poor." (2004). *The Current* series. CBC Radio One. On the World Wide Web at http://www.cbc.ca/paidtobepoor/index.html (retrieved 28 March 2004).

Peters, Enrique Dussell. (2004). "Conditions and Evolution of Wages and Employment in Mexico." Occasional Paper published by *The Jus Semper Global Alliance*. On the World Wide Web at http://www.jussemper.org/Resources/Economic%20Data/mexicowagecondit.html (retrieved 15 April 2004).

Picot, Garnett and John Myles. (2005). "Income Inequality and Low Income in Canada: An International Perspective." Statistics Canada Research Paper. On the World Wide Web at http://www.statcan.ca/english/research/11F0019MIE/11F0019MIE2005240.pdf (retrieved 10 February 2005).

Pimentel, David and Anne Wilson. (2004). "World Population, Agriculture and Nutrition." *World Watch Magazine*, September/October. *Energy Bulletin*. On the World Wide Web at http://www.energybulletin.net/3834.html (retrieved 5 January 2005).

Robbins, Richard H. (2005). *Global Problems and the Culture of Capitalism*, 3rd ed. Boston: Pearson.

Ross, Andrew, ed. (1997). *No Sweat: Fashion, Free Trade and the Rights of Garment Workers*. New York: Verso.

Ross, Robert J. S. (2004). *Slaves to Fashion: Poverty and Abuse in the New Sweatshops*. Ann Arbor, MI: University of Michigan Press.

Sachs, Jeffrey D. (2005). *The End of Poverty: Economic Possibilities for Our Time*. New York: Penguin.

Schor, J. B. (1998). *The Overspent American*. New York: Basic Books.

"Seven Countries Raising The Minimum Wage." (2011). *Financial Edge*. 21 January. On the World Wide Web http://financialedge.investopedia.com/financial-edge/0111/7-Countries-Raising-The-Minimum-Wage.aspx#axzz1f8DCs6uE. (retrieved November 29 2011).

Sheak, Bob and Melissa Morris. (2002). "The Limits of the Job Supply in U.S. Capitalism: Subemployment Measures and Trends." *Critical Sociology*, *28* (3), 389–415.

Shipler, David. (2004). *The Working Poor*. New York: Knopf.

Shrybman, Steven. (2000). *Trade, Agriculture and Climate Change: How Agricultural Trade Policies Fuel Climate Change*. Institute for Agriculture and Trade Policy. On the World Wide Web at http://www.iatp.org (retrieved 3 November 2000).

Sobal, Jeffrey. (2001). "Commentary: Globalization and the Epidemiology of Obesity." *International Journal of Epidemiology*, *30* (5), 1136–37.

Soros, George. (1998). *The Crisis of Global Capitalism: Open Society Endangered*. New York: PublicAffairs

Speidel, Joseph. (2003). "Environment and Health. Population, Consumption, and Human Health." In *Global Environmental Challenges of the 21st Century. Resources, Consumption, and Sustainable Solutions* (pp. 1–13). Wilmington, DE: Scholarly Resources Inc.

Starr, Amory. (1999). *Naming the Enemy: Anti-Corporate Movements Confront Globalization*. London: Zed Books.

Statistics Canada. (2009). "Latest Release from the Labour Force Survey." *The Daily* August 7. On the World Wide Web at http://www.statcan.gc.ca/subjects-sujets/labour-travail/ lfs-epa/lfs-epa-eng.htm (retrieved 19 August 2009).

Statistics Canada. (2011). "Foreign Direct Investment." *The Daily* April 15. On the World Wide Web at http://www.statcan.gc.ca/daily-quotidien/110415/dq110415a-eng.htm (retrieved 16 November 2011).

Stiglitz, Joseph. (2003). *Globalization and Its Discontents.* New York: W.W. Norton.

Strange, Susan. (1986). *Casino Capitalism.* London: Blackwell Books.

Sustain/Elm Farm Research Centre Report. (2001). "Eating Oil: Food in a Changing Climate." On the World Wide Web at http://www.sustainweb.org/pdf/eatoil_sumary.pdf (retrieved 15 December 2001).

"Tahrir Square's Place in Egypt's History." (2011). *BBC News,* 22 November. On the World Wide Web at http://www.bbc.co.uk/news/world-middle-east-12332601 (retrieved 13 December 2011).

"There's Rich and then There's Rich." (2010). *Economist* 2 September. On the World Wide Web at http://www.economist.com/blogs/freeexchange/2010/09/income_inequality_1 (retrieved 24 November 2011).

Tomlinson, John. (1991). *Cultural Imperialism: A Critical Introduction.* Baltimore, MD: John Hopkins University Press.

U.S. Bureau of Labor Statistics. (2009). *Labor Force Statistics from the Current Population Survey.* On the World Wide Web at http://www.bls.gov/cps/ (retrieved 19 August 2009).

United Nations. (2001). *United Nations Human Development Report, 2001.* New York: UNDP.

United Nations Conference on Trade and Development. (2010). "Exports and Imports of Merchandise and Services, 1980–2010." On the World Wide Web at http://unctadstat.unctad.org/ReportFolders/reportFolders.aspx (retrieved 8 November 2011).

Wall, Melissa. (2000). "KFC into India: A Case Study of Resistance to Globalization Discourse." In Robin Andersen and Lance Strate, eds., *Critical Studies in Media Commercialism* (pp. 291–309). Oxford: Oxford University Press.

Wallerstein, Immanuel. (2002). "The Eagle Has Crash Landed." *Foreign Policy, 131* (July/August), 60–68.

Walt, Vivienne. (2008). "The World's Growing Food-Price Crisis." *Time* 27 February. On the World Wide Web at http://www time.com/time/world/article/0,8599,1717572–2,00.html (27 February 2008).

"Warren Buffett: Read My Lips; Raise My Taxes." (2010). *ABC News.* On the World Wide Web at http://abcnews.go.com/ThisWeek/warren-buffett-read-lips-raise-taxes/story?id=12199889#.Ts6QUkqiLbF (retrieved 24 November 2011).

Waters, Malcolm. (1995). *Globalization.* New York: Routledge.

Welch, David. (2008). "Automakers' Overcapacity Problem." *Bloomberg Businessweek* December 31. On the World Wide Web at http://www.businessweek.com/magazine/content/09_02/b4115040763998.htm (retrieved 16 November 2011).

Wheeler, David and Jane Thompson. (2004). "The Brand Barons and the Business of Food," In A. Heintzman and E. Solomon, eds., *Feeding the Future* (pp. 191–236). Toronto: Anansi Press.

Whitaker, Brian. (2010). "How a Man Setting Fire to Himself Sparked an Uprising in Tunisia." *Guardian* 28 December. On the World Wide Web at http://www.guardian.co.uk/commentisfree/2010/dec/28/tunisia-ben-ali (retrieved 13 December 2011).

White, D. Steven. (2009). "The Top 175 Economic Entities, 2009." On the World Wide Web at http://dstevenwhite.com/2010/09/13/the-top-175-global-economic-entities-2009–2/ (retrieved 8 November 2011).

Woodroffe, Jessica and Mark Ellis-Jones. (2000). "States of Unrest: Resistance to IMF Policies in Poor Countries." *World Development Movement Report* (Global Policy Forum). On the World Wide Web at http://www.globalpolicy.org/ socecon/bwi-wto/imf/2000/protest.htm (retrieved 8 September 2000).

Workman, Daniel. (2006). "McDonalds' Global Sales: Big Mac's International Revenues Sizzle in 2006." *Suite 101.com.* On the World Wide Web at http://internationaltrade.suite101.com/ article.cfm/mcdonalds_global_sales (retrieved 19 August 2009).

World Bank. (2011a). "Microfinance." On the World Wide Web at http://web.worldbank.org/WBSITE/EXTERNAL/NEWS/0,,contentMDK:20433592~pagePK:64257043~piPK:437376~theSitePK:4607,00.html (retrieved 12 December 2011).

World Bank. (2011b). "Agriculture and Rural Development." On the World Wide Web at http://data.worldbank.org/indicator/SP.RUR.TOTL.ZS/countries/1W-CA-CN?display=graph (retrieved 30 July 2012).

World Health Organization. (2011). *Obesity and Overweight.* Factsheet No 311 (March). On the World Wide Web at http://www.who.int/mediacentre/factsheets/fs311/en/ (retrieved 12 December 2011).

World Wildlife Fund. (2004). "Soy Boom: Doom or Boon for South America's Forests and Savannah?" On the World Wide Web at http://www.wwf.org.uk/news/scotland/n_0000001332.asp (retrieved 2 September 2004).

Yalnizyan, Armine. (2007). *The Rich and the Rest of Us: The Changing Face of Canada's Growing Gap.* Toronto: Canadian Centre for Policy Alternatives.

CHAPTER 20

Aruni, Janice. (2004). "Educational Entrepreneurialism in the Private Tutoring Industry: Balancing Profitability with the Humanistic Face of Schooling." *Canadian Review of Anthropology and Sociology, 41* (4), 475–91.

Brym, R. (1978). *The Jewish Intelligentsia and Russian Marxism: A Sociological Study of Intellectual Radicalism and Ideological Divergence.* London: MacMillan.

Brym, R. and R. Lenton. (2001). *Love Online: A Report on Digital Dating in Canada.* Toronto: MSN.CA.

Cresswell, J. W. (1998). *Qualitative Inquiry and Research Design: Choosing among Five Traditions.* Thousand Oaks, CA: Sage.

Davies, Scott. (2002). "The Paradox of Progressive Education: A Frame Analysis." *Sociology of Education, 75* (4), 269–86.

Davies, Scott and Neil Guppy. (2010). *The Schooled Society: An Introduction to the Sociology of Education.* 2nd ed. Toronto: Oxford University Press.

DeVault, Marjorie. (1996) "Talking Back to Sociology: Distinctive Contributions of Feminist Methodology." *Annual Review of Sociology, 22,* 29–50.

Douglas, J. (1970). "Understanding Everyday Life." In J. Douglas, ed., *Understanding Everyday Life* (pp. 3–44). Chicago: Aldine.

Drolet, M. (2011). "Why Has the Gender Wage Gap Narrowed?" *Perspectives on Labor and Income* (Spring), 3–13.

Fisher, R. A. (1966 [1936]). "Has Mendel's Work Been Rediscovered?" In C. Stern and E. Sherwood, eds., *Origin of Genetics: A Mendel Sourcebook* (pp. 139–72). San Francisco: WH Freeman.

Fortin, N. (2005). "Gender Role Attitudes and the Labour-Market Outcomes of Women across OECD Countries." *Oxford Review of Economic Policy, 21* (3), 416–38.

Foshci, Martha and Jerilee Valenzuela (2008). "Selecting Job Applicants: Effects from Gender, Self-Presentation and Decision Type." *Social Science Research, 37* (3), 1022–38.

Gabor, T. (2004). "Inflammatory Rhetoric on Racial Profiling Can Undermine Police Services." *Canadian Journal of Criminology and Criminal Justice, 46* (3), 457–66.

Goffman, E. (1961). *Asylums: Essays on the Social Situations of Mental Patients and Other Inmates.* New York: Doubleday/Anchor.

Gold, A. D. (1998). "President's Report." *Criminal Lawyers' Newsletter, 19* (2). On the World Wide Web at http://www.criminallawyers.ca/newslett/19–2/gold.html (retrieved 3 November 2000).

Green, D. and K. Milligan. (2010). "The Importance of the Long Form Census to Canada" *Canadian Public Policy—Analyse de Politiques, XXXVI* (3), 383–88.

Gross, N. (2009). "A Pragmatist Theory of Social Mechanisms." *American Sociological Review, 74,* 358–79.

Guppy, N. and S. Davies. (1998). *Education in Canada.* Ottawa: Statistics Canada.

Guppy, N. and S. Davies. (2009). "School's Out for the Summer: Should It Be?" In E. Grabb and N. Guppy, eds., *Social Inequality in Canada: Patterns, Problems, and Policies* (pp. 429–31). Toronto: Pearson Prentice Hall.

Guppy, Neil and George Gray. (2008). *Successful Surveys: Research Methods and Practice,* 4th ed. Toronto: Thomson Nelson.

Haggerty, K.D. (2001). *Making Crime Count.* Toronto: University of Toronto Press.

Haggerty, K.D. (2004). "Ethics Creep: Governing Social Science Research in the Name of Ethics." *Qualitative Sociology, 24* (4), 391–414.

Houtkoop, H. (2000). *Interaction and the Standardized Survey Interview: The Living Questionnaire.* Cambridge, MA: Cambridge University Press.

Kleppner, D. and R. Jackiw. (2000). "One Hundred Years of Quantum Physics." *Science, 289* (August), 893–98. On the World Wide Web at http://vega.bac.pku.edu.cn/,rxxu/teach/qp100.htm (retrieved 21 September 2000).

Kuhn, T. S. (1962). *The Structure of Scientific Revolutions.* Chicago: University of Chicago Press.

Lauster, Nathan and Adam Easterbrook. (2011). "No Room for New Families? A Field Experiment Measuring Rental Discrimination against Same-Sex Couples and Single Parents." *Social Problems, 58* (3), 389–409.

Lenton, R. (1990). "Techniques of Child Discipline and Abuse by Parents." *Canadian Review of Sociology and Anthropology, 27,* 157–85.

Mawani, Renisa. (2003). "Imperial Legacies and Postcolonial Identities: Law, Space, and the Making of Stanley Park, 1859–2001." *Law/Text/Culture,* 7, 98–141.

Orel, Vitezslav. (1996). *Gregor Mendel: The First Geneticist,* Stephen Finn, trans. Oxford, UK: Oxford University Press.

Park, R. (2000). *Voodoo Science: The Road from Foolishness to Fraud.* New York: Oxford University Press.

Pineo, P. and J. Porter. (1967). "Occupational Prestige in Canada." *Canadian Review of Anthropology and Sociology, 4,* 24–40.

Popper, Karl. (1977 [1934]). *The Logic of Scientific Discovery,* 14th ed. New York: Harper.

Riga, L. (2008). "The Ethnic Roots of Class Universalism: Rethinking the 'Russian' Revolutionary Elite." *American Journal of Sociology, 114,* 649–705.

Roethlisberger, F. J. and D. W. Dickson. (1939). *Management and the Worker.* Cambridge, MA: Harvard University Press.

Scarce, R. (2000). *Fishy Business: Salmon, Biology, and the Social Construction of Nature.* Philadelphia, PA: Temple University Press.

Statistics Canada. (2004). *General Social Survey on Social Engagement, Cycle 17: An Overview of Findings.* Catalogue No. 89-598-XIE. Ottawa: Statistics Canada. On the World Wide Web at http://www.statcan.ca/bsolc/english/bsolc?catno589598-XIE (retrieved 14 October 2006).

Tanner, J. (2001). *Teenage Troubles: Youth and Deviance in Canada,* 2nd ed. Toronto: Nelson Thomson Learning.

Urmetzer, P., D. Blake, and N. Guppy (1999). "Individualized Solutions to Environmental Problems: The Case of Automobile Pollution." *Canadian Public Policy, 25* (3), 345–59.

Weber, M. (1949 [1904]). *The Methodology of the Social Sciences.* Glencoe, IL: Free Press.

Wilson, B. (2002). "The Canadian Rave Scene and Five Theses on Youth Resistance." *Canadian Journal of Sociology, 27,* 373–412.

Wortely, S. and J. Tanner (2003). "Data, Denials, and Confusion: The Racial Profiling Debate in Toronto." *Canadian Journal of Criminology and Criminal Justice, 45* (3), 367–89.

Wortely, S. and J. Tanner (2005). "Inflammatory Rhetoric? Baseless Accusations? A Response to Gabor's Critique of Racial Profiling Research in Canada" *Canadian Journal of Criminology and Criminal Justice, 47* (3), 581–609.

EPILOGUE

Hanafi, Sari. (2011). "University Systems in the Arab East: Publish Globally and Perish Locally vs. Publish Locally and Perish Globally." *Current Sociology, 59* (3), 291–309.

Polanyi, Karl. (1944). *The Great Transformation.* New York: Farrar & Rinehart.

INDEX

Bold numbers indicate pages where a term is defined; numbers starting with "21-" refer to Online Chapter 21.

N